WESTERN ADMIRERS *of* RAMAKRISHNA AND HIS DISCIPLES

Author

GOPAL STAVIG PH.D.

Editor

SWAMI SHUDDHIDANANDA

Advaita Ashrama

(PUBLICATION DEPARTMENT)

5 DEHI ENTALLY ROAD • KOLKATA 700 014

Published by
Swami Bodhasarananda, Adhyaksha
Advaita Ashrama
Mayavati, Champawat · 262 524
Uttarakhand, INDIA
from its Publication Department, Kolkata
www.advaitaashrama.org
mail@advaitaashrama.org

First Edition: October 2010
2M2C

ISBN 978-81-7505-334-2

Typeset in Baskerville Ten Pro 10/14

Printed in India at
Trio Process
Kolkata · 700 014

PUBLISHER'S NOTE

Sri Ramakrishna had once said, "I felt I was in a far-off country where people were of fair complexion. They were different from us and spoke a language I could not understand. As I was wondering about the vision, the Divine Mother revealed to me they too would follow my teachings. How sincere their devotion was!" By "people of fair complexion", his reference was, in all probability, to the westerners. During his lifetime some westerners had paid visit to him and expressed their admiration for his life and teachings. Since his passing away in 1886, their number has been seen to be steadily on the rise. Similar has been the case with his monastic disciples, Swami Vivekananda and others, who attracted the attention of the West with their purity of life and nobility of thought, self sacrifice and service to humanity. Throughout the last century we find a gradual increase in the number of westerners entering into the stream of Ramakrishna-Vivekananda and Vedanta thought. This development is important not only for the Ramakrishna and Vedanta Movement but also for the chroniclers of the conceptual changes witnessed in the western society in the 20th century, as has been stated by the Editor in his "Introduction". As a result, there has been an urgent need to bring these admirers together in a single volume and document information about them.

We are extremely delighted that that need has been fulfilled in the present book *Western Admirers of Ramakrishna and His Disciples*. It is a classic work of research by Mr. Gopal Stavig Ph.D. who is based in Southern California. He has been closely associated with the Vedanta Centre of Hollywood for about five decades. A disciple of the late Swami Prabhavananda, he has presented massive information in this book. Among the around 600 persons dealt with herein, there are some who had directly come in touch with Ramakrishna and his disciples, a large number of persons who had only read about them and had been impressed by their lives and ideas, many who had made literary contributions, and also many more who had only indirect associations.

We admit, therefore, that some of them arguably do not deserve to be included in the category of "admirers", in the literal sense of the term. When there are varying degrees of "association" between persons, it becomes difficult to categorize them as "admirers" and as mere "acquaintances" by drawing a strict line between them. Yet, there is no denying the fact that this book is a meticulously researched out documentation of a large number of persons, mainly westerners, associated with Ramakrishna and his disciples and their thoughts, directly or indirectly. Their background and vocation are presented in brief, and also, in most of the cases, the accolades they showered. All this makes this work unquestionably important, both for the scholars interested in studying the western mind coming in touch with these spiritual luminaries as well as for the ordinary devotee. For the former the book is a mine of information presented precisely, and for the latter, it is an inspiring account of western admiration for Ramakrishna and his disciples and Indian thought.

The book is divided into four parts. Part I deals with "Western admirers of Sri Ramakrishna", Part II with "Western admirers of Sri Sarada Devi", Part III with "Western admirers of Swami Vivekananda", and Part IV with "Western admirers of the other disciples of Sri Ramakrishna". Except in Part II, in every Part the admirers are classified in different chapters according to their vocation, e.g. biographers, translators, devotees, supporters, religious leaders, professional writers, musicians, etc. This systematic arrangement facilitates easy access to the personalities the reader wishes to know about. The work is copiously referenced, letting the scholars make further probings. At the end of the book the author has supplied seven "Appendices" which we are sure would be of much help to the scholars.

Swami Shuddhidananda of Advaita Ashrama thoroughly edited the work and also wrote an insightful "Introduction". Brahmachari Yogadachaitanya (Alok) gladly undertook the task of carefully proofreading the manuscript and helping the Editor in various ways. We are thankful to both for their labour of love.

This year the Government of India has constituted a National Committee to chart programmes and core modules to spread the life-building message of Swami Vivekananda during his 150th birth anniversary due in 2013. Bringing out books dealing with the Swami is one of the areas which will derive considerable attention. In this light we take the publication of the present book as a beginning of our efforts in furtherance of this aim.

We expect the book to be well received and chalk out for itself a place among the other scholarly works on Ramakrishna and Vivekananda.

2 October 2010 — PUBLISHER

CONTENTS

Part IV
Western Admirers of the Other Disciples of Sri Ramakrishna

AUTHOR'S NOTE

This book is dedicated to the fond memory of my guru Swami Prabhavananda.

I am extremely thankful and indebted for the excellent job Swami Shuddhidananda of Advaita Ashrama has done in undertaking the editing of this book. I also appreciate the confidence that Swami Bodhasarananda, the President of Advaita Ashrama, has shown in this manuscript, and the encouragement I received from Swami Sarvadevananda, the Assistant Minister of the Vedanta Society of Southern California. In addition, I want to thank Brahmachari Jnana Chaitanya, a monastic member of the Vedanta Society of Southern California and the diligent curator of the Vedanta Archives Research Library, for giving me access to the valuable collection of older issues of the *Prabuddha Bharata*, *Vedanta Kesari*, *Bulletin* of the Ramakrishna Mission Institute of Culture and other literature that has significantly enhanced the quality of this book. Writing a history of the Vedanta Society of Southern California for the Vedanta Archives also proved very beneficial for me, in getting a better idea on how to present the material in a way that would be appreciated by the readers. Lastly, university research librarians, particularly at U.C.L.A., guided me to databases that produced a great deal of useful information that appears in the book.

October 2010 —Gopal Stavig

LIST OF ILLUSTRATIONS

(Arranged Alphabetically)

between pages

Sri Ramakrishna

INTRODUCTION

Though a major portion of the present book deals with the western admirers of the disciples of Sri Ramakrishna, it would be fitting to start the book with a brief narrative of Ramakrishna's life, for, he is the mainspring from where his disciples emerged and later dazzled the western world with their spiritual eminence. His short lifespan of fifty years is symbolic of the story of India's spiritual culture and civilization of unknown antiquity. And India being "the cradle of human race", it is also the story that reflects the spiritual aspirations of the entire human race of all times. In the modern period his life has been the fountainhead of many of the positive trends seen in the fields of religion and thought.

LIFE OF SRI RAMAKRISHNA
A BRIEF PRESENTATION

The protagonist of this story with such global appeal was, paradoxically, born in one of the remotest obscure hamlets of Bengal in India. Ramakrishna was born in 1836 in Kamarpukur. His parents, Kshudiram and Chandramani Devi, were pious. The people of the village were deeply impressed by their exemplary lives. Due to their devotion to their family deity and kind-hearted gesture towards all those who came to them for succour, the villagers held them in high esteem. Though poor, they were unstintingly charitable.

Ramakrishna's childhood name was "Gadadhar", and people affectionately called him "Gadai". He was an unusual boy of exceptional capabilities. Even at a tender age, people saw in him combined "fine spiritual sensibility and deep humanism" to an astonishing degree. Within this trait of his was the germ of the ideology of true human well-being, which his disciples were to later develop and spread throughout the world. He was ingenuous, and, at the same time, endowed with a marked intelligence and a kind heart. The first time when he experienced spiritual ecstasy, he was hardly six or seven years old. To put it in his words:

> ...I was walking along a narrow path separating paddy fields, eating some of the puffed rice which I was carrying in a basket. Looking up at the sky, I saw a beautiful sombre thunder cloud. As it spread rapidly enveloping the whole sky, a flock of snow-white cranes flew overhead across it. It presented such a beautiful contrast that my mind wandered to far-off regions. Lost to outward sense, I fell down, and the puffed rice was scattered in all directions....That was the first time I completely lost consciousness in ecstasy.[1]

And that was also the time when the boy was unconsciously getting ready to start off on the different paths to ecstasy and enlightenment. But his path was not to be without difficulties. The untimely death of his beloved father in 1843 made his childhood particularly poignant, leaving his tender heart bruised. In and through this sad event glared the transiency of earthly life. He started frequenting a neighbouring cremation ground and used to remain there for long hours absorbed in deep thought. Even as his mind soared high in search of the eternal, he could not disregard his duty towards his dear mother and did everything possible to lessen her grief and burden. Nevertheless, the deep undercurrents of apathy for worldly pleasure often drew him towards wandering monks and seek their company.

When he was nine years old, he was invested with the sacred thread. According to the Hindu custom, the newly initiated was supposed to receive his first alms from some relative or at least from a brahmin. But Gadai had the pluck to overrule the prevalent custom and accept the first alms from a low caste woman. This woman had earlier prayed to him to allow her the privilege of giving him the first alms. Moved by her earnestness, he had agreed. And when the time came, the little boy stuck to his words and defied the citadels of orthodoxy and timeworn traditions of his village. Through this act he was inadvertently sending out signals to his surrounding world that the walls of caste-prejudice need to be razed to the ground and the dignity of every human being upheld. The boy, and his life, had already started displaying the traits of his being a teacher of humankind, come to remove the barriers between man and man.

Gadai had an aversion for school learning, and especially for mathematics. He would skip his classes and pass most of his day with his friends in various sports. They would enact scenes from the life of Krishna and often Gadai would go into deep trance. He derived pleasure listening to the epics and stories from the Indian mythology, which, in turn, spurred his spiritual aspirations. To realize God now became the one goal of his life. Torn apart between his wish to renounce the world and his duty towards his widowed mother, he bowed down in surrender to his Lord and waited in eager anticipation.

Years rolled by, and destiny brought him to Calcutta to help his elder brother Ramkumar. Gadai was entrusted with priestly duties, which he gladly discharged. But here too he displayed his gross disinterestedness for studies. Annoyed with his apathy towards academic pursuits, Ramkumar admonished him, upon which the young Gadai remarked, rather characteristically, "Brother, what shall I do with a mere bread-winning education? I would rather acquire wisdom which will illumine my heart, and getting which, one is satisfied for ever." In these words the boy had a point to make, that life was too precious and sacred to be squandered on dead-end pursuits. It was now clear to him that, unlike the multitudes, his was the pathless path towards God realization.

The turn of events now brought the young Ramakrishna to the precincts of the Dakshineswar Kali Temple, which was founded in 1855. The silent and congenial surrounding of the temple-garden was just the setting he needed for pursuing his spiritual goal. Soon he was assigned the task of decorating the image of Kali. He discharged his duty with all the devotion of his heart and spent rest of his time singing the glories of the Divine Mother, which used to leave the listeners spellbound. His ingenuous behaviour and fervent devotion soon favoured him and he was made the priest of the Radha-kanta temple, and later the chief priest of the Kali temple. But there was something ominous waiting for him. The death of his brother Ramkumar at this time came as a rude shock. The transient nature of the world now began to haunt him as never before. His soul, now on fire, began to plunge into itself in search of the Eternal. Divine Mother now became the polestar of his life whom he depended on for spiritual illumination. For him her image was not mere inert stone but one pervaded by consciousness.

Shunning the company of worldly people, he began spending his time in devotional practices. When others would be fast asleep in the dead of the night, he would repair to the nearby grove and spend the night in fervent prayer and meditation. His eyes would swell owing to continuous shedding of tears. His one absorbing passion now was to get the vision of the Divine Mother, which was driving him almost mad. At the close of each day his disconsolate heart would bewail, "Another day is spent in vain, Mother, for

I have not seen Thee! Another day of this short life has passed, and I have not realized the Truth!"

Because of this intensity of his devotional mood, he could no more conduct the formal worship of the Divine Mother regularly. His state of mind and behaviour at this time was beyond the ken of ordinary people, and many considered him mad. At the same time there were also a few who were charmed to see his God-intoxicated state and for whom he became an object of admiration and reverence. But approbation or condemnation, he was indifferent to these worldly evaluations, and all his energies remained converged on his Divine Mother. At last the day arrived when the bounds of his endurance gave way. Possessed by the all-consuming fire of spiritual longing and unable to bear his separation from the Divine Mother, he rose to put an end to his life with the sword hanging on the wall of the shrine. Just then the Mother revealed Herself to him and he fell unconscious on the floor. He didn't know how that day passed and even the next. He was inundated with undiluted bliss never experienced before, and he felt the presence of the Divine Mother.

From now on the Divine Mother became a living reality for him, just like any other living being. The formal ritualistic mode of approaching the Mother came to an end. He became the Mother's child, conversing with her, feeding her, and relying on her for everything. After having realized God in the form of the Divine Mother, now his heart yearned to see God in the form of Rama. Accordingly he commenced his spiritual disciplines and, within a short time, had the vision of Sita, Rama's consort, and also realized Rama to be an incarnation of God. With this ended the first phase of his spiritual practices and experiences.

Ramakrishna was now twenty-three years old. His indifference to worldly life caused much worry to his mother. Over and above this, when the rumour that her son had gone mad reached her, she became all the more anxious. She now set about to get him married thinking that it would rouse his interest in worldly affairs and cure his mental imbalance. And this marriage, as we shall see, was going to be of the most unusual kind. A bride was found in the village of Jayrambati. She was a five-year old girl, Saradamani. After the marriage ceremony was officiated in Jayrambati, Ramakrishna returned to Dakshineswar.

Now began his long series of experiments which was to have widespread religious ramifications for the future of humankind. This was the second phase of his spiritual practices. At a time when the nineteenth century was just seeing the rise of "comparative study of religions" in the modern sense, Ramakrishna ventured into verifying the major religions of the world with the touchstone of experience. He embarked upon experiencing God in and through the paths laid down in the different religions. From now on for more than a decade he was to pass through many a fiery ordeals. He had earlier realized Rama as an incarnation of God. Now he underwent the difficult Tantric disciplines and realized the Divine Mother; then through the path of knowledge he attained the acme of Vedantic realization, a state in which he remained absorbed for almost six months; then he realized God through the path of Islam, and also vindicated the path of Christianity by having a vision of Jesus and realizing him to be an incarnation of God. He would take up one path, remodel himself according to its needs, and see its end; and then he would take up the next, and so on; one after the other he experientially researched the different paths to God. Finally, his more-than-a-decade long trailblazing experiential researches in religion made him declare, "As many faiths, so many paths." He pronounced:

> I have practised all religions—Hinduism, Islam, Christianity, and I have also followed the paths of the different Hindu sects. I have found that it is the same God towards whom all are directing their steps, though along different paths.

In a single life he lived, as if, the religious life of an entire race of several millenniums. He had a mission to accomplish—to spread the universal message of harmony of religions, divinity of everything, and solidarity of human race. His advent, as we shall see, was to eventually speed up the emergence of the modern trends in the fields of religion and thought, and these areas were to slowly undergo a change.

The foremost among his disciples was his wife, Sarada Devi, who all these years lived in her native village with her heart yearning to be at the side of her God-intoxicated husband. The young nineteen-year-old woman now reached Dakshineswar to serve him. This was in 1872. Though having attained the acme of spiritual experience and being absorbed in God, he, like any other dutiful husband, cordially welcomed her and made arrangements for her comfortable stay. The couple stayed in the same room and shared the same bed for about eight months. But they were the most exceptional couple ever to have entered wedlock. Their marriage remained forever unconsummated on the physical plane, and they attained union in the Divine, making their relationship a monument of platonic love. The young lady in no way lagged behind her husband in purity and spiritual fervour. In fact, Ramakrishna looked upon her as the Divine Mother in human form and offered the results of his twelve-year long spiritual exercises at her holy feet in a formal worship. She was to become in future the Holy Mother of the Ramakrishna Order.

People from far and near now began to flock the saint of Dakshineswar. Many prominent members of the Calcutta elite visited him. Among them there were also some westerners. Ramakrishna's heart however eagerly looked forward to the arrival of his intimate disciples, who were to become monks and the pillars of his future spiritual organization. He would climb the roof of the building in the temple-garden and, his heart writhing in anguish, cry out, "Come, my boys! Oh! Where are you? I cannot bear to live without you!" He would later say that a mother would never have longed to see her child as he did for them at that time. As a result, some of the close householder devotees began arriving from 1879 onwards.

After this arrived the purest of the souls who would be later carrying his torch of renunciation and spiritual humanism around the world, who would be renouncing everything to become monks and spread his message. The first to come among them was Latu. Then came, one by one, Rakhal, Gopal, Naren, Tarak, Baburam, Niranjan, Yogin, Sharat, Shashi, Hari Nath, Gangadhar, Hari Prasanna, Kali, Subodh, and Sarada. He now began training these sixteen disciples and helped them attain the highest spiritual realization. But they were not supposed to remain immersed in the bliss of the Self. The Great Master had a mission, and these sixteen disciples of his were to be his associates in fulfilling it. The leader of this group was Naren, who later became the world renowned Swami Vivekananda. On him the Master entrusted the responsibility of guiding the flock. Naren received special training and instruction from him as to the form and the mode of operation of his future monastic order. Ramakrishna had predicted that "Naren will teach the world."

As days and months rolled on, the time for the curtain to fall on Ramakrishna's life was drawing near. It was late 1885 when he began to suffer from an acute pain in his throat, which was later diagnosed to be cancer. For the sake of better treatment he was first shifted to Shyampukur, and then to Cossipore. Every type of medical treatment was tried but to no avail, and, finally, on 16 August 1886 the Great Swan merged into the source from where he had come. One of the glorious lives in the spiritual history of mankind had come to an end.

SRI RAMAKRISHNA'S DISCIPLES IN THE WEST

Immersed in the ocean of grief, his disciples decided to undertake severe austerities to remain unbrokenly absorbed in spiritual bliss. Some set out on pilgrimage, some moved about on foot throughout the length and breadth of India. During his peregrination, Swami Vivekananda, the leader of this flock, came to know about the impending World Parliament of Religions to be held in Chicago. It was time for the Great Master's prediction about his dearest disciple to come true. Wading through untold obstacles and difficulties, Swami Vivekananda left the Indian shore to attend the Parliament of Religions and created a piece of history by his rousing message to the world. It was September 11, 1893, a landmark in the history of religions and philosophic thought.

Vivekananda electrified the Parliament with the age-old Vedic message of one supreme Truth, harmony of faiths, and solidarity of human race. He proved that there could be no one religion dominating the others; that all religions stood on equal footing, being different paths to the same goal; that no one race could arrogate to itself the right to rule others. He thundered, and the hollow balloon of Christian and western superiority over the other religions and races burst into thin air. Through his mouth Hinduism was reborn in its pristine form. Hinduism, which was until then considered by the westerners to be a mass of superstitions and a savage religion, was proved to be the acme of mankind's religious strivings and aspirations. The West discovered the true India, and India too re-discovered her true self. The invaluable findings of India's timeless spiritual and religious researches were placed on the world platform, with Ramakrishna as its crowning glory. The fame of Ramakrishna from then on began to spill into the western religious and intellectual corridors, evoking a sense of reverential wonder from all those who were receptive.

Overnight Swami Vivekananda became a renowned figure—in the West as well as in India. From then on until his passing away in 1902, he was engaged in a whirlwind of activities to spread the universal message of Vedanta in the West and attract the best minds of that world. From the U.S. he went also to Europe in furtherance of this aim and met with some of the brilliant minds of the time.

The other disciples of Ramakrishna who joined Vivekananda at different times to carry forward the work initiated by him in the West were Swami Saradananda, Swami Abhedananda, Swami Turiyananda, and Swami Trigunatitananda. They were followed by a band of young swamis who were the disciples of Ramakrishna's direct disciples. Their dedication for the cause, nobility, concerted effort, austere life, spiritual humanism, as well as universal love won for them the admiration of a large number of people from a wide cross-section of western society. Western admirers of Ramakrishna and his disciples, as will be seen in this book, included men of letters, artists, philosophers, religious leaders, musicians, stage artists, social reformers, spiritual aspirants, and even persons in business. They were showered with accolades during their lifetime, and the trend has continued unabated; in fact, it has gradually intensified throughout the last century even after their disappearance from the mortal gaze. This trend has a significance, because it is the external form of a subtle transformation undergoing in the western mindset.

THE PSYCHOLOGY OF ADMIRATION AND THE PROCESS OF SOCIAL TRANSFORMATION

Admiration is a type of positive emotion involving a sense of wonder and reverence. It is always focused on some person or thing other than oneself. When one admires a thing or a person, one extends oneself towards the object of admiration. There can be no admiration without mentally reaching out to the other in praise. In this it allows the energies of the human mind to flow into a wider channel. That means, to be less self-centred and, as a corollary, that also means, widening the circumference of one's self to positively encompass others into one's stream of thought and feeling. And as with other positive emotions of love and compassion, it contributes to one's psychological well being and moral health.

How far the mind expands in admiration is determined by the nature of the object admired. The expansion and the depth of mind attained while admiring someone's physical beauty is far less in comparison to that attained in admiring someone's art, or altruism, or spiritual qualities. In every one of the latter cases there is a progressive increase in the mind's reach in depth, subtlety and expanse. The admiring mind penetrates the gross limited crust of physical forms and reaches the subtle and more expansive depths. This characteristic of admiration contributes to the well-being of the admirer by throwing open the doors of his or her soul to the sublime influence of the object he or she admires. Needless to state, one attains the utmost well-being when the object of admiration is spiritual. When one admires the spiritual qualities of a saint, the admiring mind is filled with wonder and reverence for the noblest of human virtues. And when a large number of people in society take to admiring things spiritual, it slowly results in bringing about a deeper and lasting change in the social mindset. A spiritual ideal held in admiration in a society is bound to make that society more tolerant, peace-loving, and moral; for these are the gifts of that ideal which it slowly lets trickle and settle down deep in the collective mind.

Seen in this light, the western admiration for Ramakrishna and his disciples discussed in this book will help us understand in a general way the process of healthy conceptual changes that have been witnessed in the twentieth-century western world. Whether it is religion or statecraft, literature or art, philosophy or psychology, the rules of these games have been seen to be drafted and redrafted from time to time from a deeper, holistic and sublime perspective. Every nation, every race, every religious group has been progressively realizing the futility of the cult of mutual hatred and violence in the conduct of human affairs. The demands of the spirit of the age have been forcing nations and peoples to come out of their enclosed lives and throw open their doors to reach out at others in mutual admiration, trust, and creative interactions.

Deep beneath these developments has been an ideological spring, bringing about a change from within—an undercurrent silently processing and treating the surface anomalies of our social, political, and religious life. Today, in long retrospect, if we attempt to historically trace this spring, we shall land up in India.

THE SPRING OF INDIAN SPIRITUAL THOUGHT: AN OBJECT OF "PERENNIAL" ADMIRATION

According to the English essayist, poet, and dramatist Joseph Addison, "Admiration is a short-lived passion that immediately decays upon growing familiar with its object, unless it be fed with fresh discoveries and kept alive by a perpetual succession of miracles rising into view." This rule with regard to admiration, I feel, applies only to the gross objects we admire. The gross physical beauties around, which elicit our admiration at the very outset, turn out to be stale when we become fully familiar with them. They fail to continue to be objects of admiration for us unless they re-present themselves in newer forms. Every relationship based on gross physical factors is therefore bound to grow putrid with the passage of time. In this sense, admiration is certainly something "short-lived".

However, the more the object of admiration belongs to subtler realm, the more does that object defy this rule. For most people the subtler entities are difficult to grow familiar with, and therefore these retain their enigmatic character and keep throwing the human mind into a state of prolonged wonder. And when we come to spiritual verities and ideals, which belong to the subtlest realm, this rule seems to get nullified. This is one of the *raisons d'être* for man's admiration for God and spiritual verities never growing stale. It is "eternally" an object of wonder. The ordinary human mind fails to fully comprehend God, or the Supreme Reality, which is indescribable. It has been aptly stated by some European thinker that "we admire the things we really don't understand."

The Indian mind has always been preoccupied with God and spiritual verities. And, hence, among all the nations of the world, she has a perennial quality about her. Right from the beginnings of known history she has been evoking a sense of admiration from all those who have been coming in touch with her thoughts rooted in the Vedas. Even in those ancient times her strivings were as much focused on the search for the highest reality as much are the thoughts of the modern thinkers in the West busy with understanding the true nature of man and this world. As such, though most ancient, her discoveries in this area are perennially fresh and modern. In the insightful words of Raimundo Panikkar, a Roman Catholic priest and professor of religious studies:

> The Vedic experience introduces nothing alien to modern man, but helps him to realize his own life and emphasizes an often neglected aspect of his own being. In this sense the Vedas occupy a privileged position in the crystallized culture of Man. They are neither primitive nor modern. Not being primitive, they present a depth, a critical awareness, and a sophistication not shown by many other ancient cultures. Not being modern, they exhale a fragrance and present an appeal that the merely modern does not possess.[2]

And in the words of Will Durant, the renowned historian from the University of California:

> They are the oldest extant philosophy and psychology of our race; the surprisingly subtle and patient effort of man to understand the mind and the world, and their relation. The Upanishads are as old as Homer, and as modern as Kant.[3]

We may quite well say that Indian thought is "anciently modern". It is in this oxymoronic feature that lies one of the secrets of her "fascination". In the words of Swami Vivekananda, it is "silent mesmerism". And this quality of the Indian thought of imperceptibly influencing the world was stated by him in 1897 in his lecture "The Work before us". There he said:

> Our message has gone out to the world many a time, but slowly, silently, unperceived. It is on a par with everything in India. The one characteristic of Indian thought is its silence, its calmness. At the same time the tremendous power that is behind it is never expressed by violence. It is always the silent mesmerism of Indian thought.... Like the gentle dew that falls unseen and unheard, and yet brings into blossom the fairest of roses, has been the contribution of India to the thought of the world. Silent, unperceived, yet omnipotent in its effect, it has revolutionized the thought of the world, yet nobody knows when it did so.

INDIAN THOUGHT INVADES THE WEST

India has been silently influencing the thought of the world from ancient times. In the modern history, the beginning of western admiration for Indian thought can be traced back to the second half of the 18th century, more than hundred years before Swami Vivekananda's appearance at the Chicago Parliament of Religions in 1893. It was the beginning of the Romantic Era in Europe when a number of European scholars dedicated themselves wholeheartedly to the study of Oriental languages, religions, culture, as well as Sanskrit literature. Some of the most notable Orientalists of this as well as the later period were: Sir William Jones, Henry T. Colebrooke, Sir Charles Wilkins, Horace H. Wilson, Monier Monier-Williams, R. T. H. Griffith, Sir Edwin Arnold, Sir John Woodroffe, and T. W. Rhys Davids, all from Britian; from France there were Eugène Burnouf, Sylvain Lévi and Louis Renou; from Germany, Friedrich Schlegel, Georg Thibaut, Hermann Jacobi, Rudolf Otto, Heinrich Zimmer, and Helmuth von Glasenapp; from America,

Edward E. Salisbury, Charles R. Lanman, Maurice Bloomfield, Edward W. Hopkins and Franklin Edgerton; and from Italy, Giuseppe Tucci.

Their works and contribution to Indology paved the way for India's gradual recognition as a land of high culture and thought. They were the initiators of the subject of comparative philology and comparative study of religions. The 19th century saw some of the great European minds like Max Müller, Paul Deussen, and Arthur Schopenhauer paying their heart's homage to India and her thought, which further enhanced her esteem in the eyes of the western world. Then there were the great American admirers belonging to the New Thought Movement and the Transcendentalist School of the 19th century, which included Henry David Thoreau, Ralph Waldo Emerson, Theodore Parker, and Walt Whitman, to mention a few. They were all awestruck with the grandeur of what they found in Indian thought and culture.

The combined outcome of their inestimable efforts in studying the Indian thought and religion was that the world began to take note of India as the motherland of all philosophies and spiritual strivings, the cradle of civilization, and its ancient language, Sanskrit, as the mother of all languages. Nevertheless, their influence remained constricted to the elite of the western world; and their evaluations lacked spiritual power and authority which was providentially reserved for Swami Vivekananda. His appearance in the Chicago Parliament of Religions towards the end of the 19th century once and for all times clinched a permanent place for India in the federation of world religions, philosophic thoughts, and cultures. Backed by immense spiritual power and authority, he awakened the western world to the universal Vedantic thoughts which underlie all religions and cultures, and thenceforth the western mind was never to remain the same.

THE WESTERN MINDSET TODAY

Today if we are to take stock of the western mindset, the marks of Indian influence, or rather, Hindu or Vedantic influence, stand conspicuous by their presence. Ideas like karma, reincarnation, avatar, maya, yoga, and meditation have struck roots and have started bearing fruits. This subject has been seriously dealt with by a number of western scholars in their insightful books, some of them with suggestive titles like: *Hinduism Invades America* (1930), *Religion in Transition* (1937), *Vedanta for the Western World* (1945), *Oriental Religions and American Thought* (1981), *Vedanta for the West: The Ramakrishna*

Movement in the United States (1994), *A New Religious America: How a "Christian Country" has Become the World's most Religiously Diverse Nation* (2001), etc.

In the middle of nineteenth century, Schopenhauer was uttering some pregnant words when he stated, "Indian wisdom will flow back upon Europe, and produce a thorough change in our knowing and thinking." And in this context, a portion of a revealing article published in the *Newsweek* magazine of America in its August 31, 2009 issue deserves to be reproduced here. Therein Lisa Miller, the author of the article "We are all Hindus now", reflects the conceptual changes that have been seen to have occurred in the Americans' view of life, God, self, eternity, etc., which are along the lines of Indian thought. She states:

> ...The *Rig Veda*, the most ancient Hindu scripture, says this: "Truth is One, but the sages speak of it by many names." A Hindu believes there are many paths to God. Jesus is one way, the Quran is another, yoga practice is a third. None is better than any other; all are equal.....
>
> According to a 2008 Pew Forum survey, 65 percent of us [Americans] believe that "many religions can lead to eternal life"—including 37 percent of white evangelicals, the group most likely to believe that salvation is theirs alone. Also, the number of people who seek spiritual truth outside church is growing. Thirty percent of Americans call themselves "spiritual, not religious", according to a 2009 *Newsweek* poll, up from 24 percent in 2005. Stephen Prothero, religion professor at Boston University, has long framed the American propensity for "the divine-deli-cafeteria religion" as "very much in the spirit of Hinduism. You're not picking and choosing from different religions, because they're all the same," he says. "It isn't about orthodoxy. It's about whatever works. If going to yoga works, great—and if going to Catholic mass works, great. And if going to Catholic mass plus the yoga plus the Buddhist retreat works, that's great, too."
>
> Then there's the question of what happens when you die. ...24 percent of Americans say they believe in reincarnation, according to a 2008 Harris poll. ...More than a third of Americans now choose cremation, according to the Cremation Association of North America, up from 6 percent in 1975.[4]

This is the creative outcome, as well as one of the beautiful instances, of inter-racial ideological romance in history with far-reaching consequences. It is inter-racial because India too has been freely receiving from the West the ideas and techniques for her material and economic progress. And the West has been imbibing the universal and eternal ideas of spirituality emanating from her, which has been affecting a healthy transformation in their lives. It has slowly resulted in the weakening of old religious shibboleths rooted in church dogmas and creed. And India, as ever, has been affecting this change through the power of her silent "fascination" and never through "force". Also it needs to be stated here that in acceptance of these eternal values the West has shown remarkable sensitivity and courage.

And if this be the state of affairs presently in the West as far as the subjects of religion and thought are concerned, in the following pages the reader will be able to discern, in and through the western admirers of, and their admiration for, Ramakrishna and the Indian thought, the earlier stages of this development, beginning from the last quarter of the 19th century.

WESTERN ADMIRERS OF RAMAKRISHNA AND HIS DISCIPLES

For all the above reasons and much more, the present book is a colossal work by Mr. Gopal Stavig who has put in several years of hard labour in creating this monument. It is a monument because it is one of a kind in the genre of Ramakrishna-Vivekananda literature. Dealing with, as the title clearly states, the "Western Admirers" of Ramakrishna and his disciples, the book documents brief information about over 600 western admirers of these spiritual luminaries. Not just information about these admirers, it also presents the glowing tributes showered by most of them.

The admirers can be classified into two groups: 1) Those who are renowned figures, known to the world for the success they had achieved in their respective fields, and 2) Those who are known only within the circle of Ramakrishna-Vivekananda devotees. In the former class come personalities like Max Müller, Will Durant, Romain Rolland and others, and in the latter come devotees like Laura Glenn, Sister Christine, Josephine MacLeod, and Mr. and Mrs. Hale. The author has deftly included even personalities who had indirect connections with Ramakrishna and his disciples and the Indian thought.

The significance of this work, therefore, lies on more than one ground: firstly, here, in a single book, we find recorded brief data about a large number of western admirers of Ramakrishna and his disciples and their acclamation spanning over a period of more than a century—from the early 1880s up to the present time. The book is therefore indispensable for scholars researching on the westerners who were, and are, associated with Ramakrishna and his disciples and Indian thought; secondly, as discussed earlier, for a more careful reader, it lets him or her gain some understanding of the process of change that has been taking place in the western mindset owing to the presence of an universal spiritual ideology that emanated from the Indian sub-continent, rather feebly from the last quarter of the 18th century, and robustly from the end of the 19th.

2 October 2010 —The Editor

ENDNOTES

1. *A Short Life of Sri Ramakrishna*, Advaita Ashrama, 2009, pp. 15-16.
2. *The Vedic Experience: Mantramanjari* (London, 1979), p. 9.
3. Web: www.hinduwisdom.info/quotes1_20.htm.
4. http://www.newsweek.com/id/212155.

PART I

WESTERN ADMIRERS OF SRI RAMAKRISHNA

CHAPTER I

DEVOTEES, ACQUAINTANCES AND BIOGRAPHERS

On one occasion, between 1868 and 1871, at Sri Ramakrishna's request Mathurnath Biswas took him to the Wesleyan Methodist Church in Calcutta. They both witnessed the Christian mass from outside. In 1874, Sambhucharan Mallick read the Bible to him, and a desire arose in the Master to practice Christianity.[1] At Jadu Mallick's garden house located at the south side of the Dakshineswar Kali temple, Ramakrishna observed a wonderful picture hanging on the wall, depicting the child Jesus on his mother's lap. Swami Saradananda tells us:

> One day he sat in that room and intently studied that image, thinking of the wonderful life of Jesus. Just then he saw the picture become animate and luminous. Rays of light emanated from the bodies of Mother Mary and the child Jesus, entering the Master's heart and revolutionizing his mental attitudes.... He then had a vision of Christian clergymen offering incense and lights in front of the image of Jesus in a church, expressing their inner longing through prayer.
>
> After he returned to the Dakshineswar temple garden, the Master remained uninterruptedly absorbed in meditation on those experiences pertaining to Jesus. He completely forgot to visit the Divine Mother in the temple. The waves of Christian faith that swayed him lasted for three days. When the Master was walking in the Panchavati at the end of the third day, he saw a beautiful but unfamiliar godman with a fair complexion advancing towards him, gazing at him steadily. The Master immediately realized that he was a foreigner, and that he belonged to a different race. He saw that his eyes were large and beautiful, and though his nose was a little flat at the tip, it in no way marred the handsomeness of his face. The Master was charmed by the unique divine expression on his serene face and wondered who he

could be. Very soon after that the figure drew near, and a voice from within told him, "This is Jesus Christ, the great yogi, the loving Son of God who is one with his Father, who shed his heart's blood and suffered torture for the salvation of humanity." Then the godman Jesus embraced the Master and merged into him. In ecstasy, the Master lost external consciousness and his mind remained united with Saguna Brahman [Personal God with attributes] for some time. With this vision, the Master became convinced that Jesus was truly a divine incarnation.[2]

Mr. Williams, a Protestant Christian whom Akshay Kumar Sen identified as a European, lived in the northwestern section of India. He probably was employed as a schoolteacher. From Kedarnath Chatterjee, the Brahmo preacher, he learned about Ramakrishna. He made a special trip to Calcutta just to meet with the Paramahamsa. On Good Friday, probably in the year 1881, Williams, accompanied by Kedarnath Chatterjee, made a visit to Dakshineswar. Williams was a hefty middle-aged man with large eyes, wearing European dress. He stood in front of the door of Ramakrishna's room. The Paramahamsa was conversing with a small group of devotees including Ramchandra Datta, an intimate disciple of his. When he was told, "That Sahib, about whom Kedar Babu spoke, has come," Ramakrishna's mind was suddenly filled with spiritual emotion and he rushed out of the room to receive the new arrival. Swami Prabhananda adds:

> As Sri Ramakrishna stood merged in samadhi, Williams reverentially knelt before him with hands folded, and tears rolling down his face. Looking at the Saint, he kissed his feet, and his tears wetted them. Williams later said he received the blessings of a direct vision of Christ in the person of Sri Ramakrishna. On being asked by the Saint, "Well, what's your idea about me? Who am I?" Williams replied, "You are, Sir, Jesus Himself, the Son of God, the embodiment of eternal consciousness."

Williams visited Ramakrishna at least three times at Dakshineswar. Following the Master's advice he renounced secular activities, went to the Himalayas north of the Punjab, and passed away after practising demanding austerities.[3]

The *New Dispensation* was an Indian publication, put out by the Brahmo Samaj under the leadership of Keshab Sen. Concerning a meeting with Ramakrishna, the February 26, 1882 edition reported:

On the Thursday last [February 23] there was an interesting excursion by a steam launch up the river to Dakshineswar. The Rev. Joseph Cook, Miss Pigot, and the apostles of the New Dispensation together with a number of our young men embarked at about 11 o'clock. The revered Paramahamsa of Dakshineswar [Sri Ramakrishna], as soon as he heard of the arrival of the party, came to the riverside, and was taken on aboard. He successively went through all the phases of spiritual excitement which characterizes him. Passing through a long interval of unconsciousness, he prayed, sang, and discoursed on spiritual subjects. Mr. Cook represented the extreme culture of Christian theology and thought. The Paramahamsa represented the extreme culture of Indian Yoga and Bhakti, in short, the traditional piety of the East. And the apostles of the Brahmo Samaj in bringing together the two proved that they combined both in the all-inclusive harmony of the New Dispensation.[4]

Swami Saradananda's *Sri Ramakrishna and His Divine Play* describes Reverend Joseph Cook's meeting with Ramakrishna:

[The Master mentioned]: One day Keshab sent word that he would take me for a boat trip on the Ganges and bring with him a Westerner (Reverend Joseph Cook who was visiting India).... When they arrived and I got into the boat, I had the same experience that I did when the pandit came. I said many things unconsciously. Later, they said, "You gave much wonderful advice." But you see, I was completely unaware of it.[5]

According to the *Gospel of Sri Ramakrishna* (p. 79), the Master had not forgotten Joseph Cook, and in March 1882 he asked M:

Tell me, do you know of a certain Mr. Cook who has come to Calcutta? Is it true that he is giving lectures? Once Keshab took me on a steamer, and this Mr. Cook, too, was in the party.

M: Yes sir, I have heard something like that; but I have never been to his lectures. I don't know much about him.

Concerning this experience on the steamer in February, the Master later narrated:

> Something crept immediately afterwards towards the head, and fear vanished in no time. I became completely overwhelmed; the face turned upwards; and I felt a flow of words gushing out of my mouth. The more the words came out, the more were words pushed forward and supplied, as it were, by someone from within.[6]

An obituary for Ramakrishna appearing in the September 10, 1886 edition of the *Indian Mirror* mentioned:

> Mr. Cooke [Cook], the American evangelist, who came to this country a few years ago, once witnessed Ramakrishna's divine exercises and he expressed his great surprise at it and remarked that he was not aware before that a man could become so much immersed in divine spirit as to lose all perception of the external world.[7]

Reverend Joseph Cook (1838-1901) was a prominent Christian Congregational evangelist. During the year 1878, in a period of about seventy days, he delivered forty-three lectures in ten different states in the United States, speaking to fifty-thousand people. He authored over three-dozen books during his lifetime. His "Boston Monday Lectures" ran for a series of years, drawing audiences of three-thousand people at the Tremont Temple. In March of 1887, Pundita Ramabai Sarasvati (1858-1922), the social reformer from Bombay, as a guest of Reverend Cook spoke before a Boston audience on "High-Caste Hindu Widows". Cook's organization later published and sold her speech, recommending that the reader purchase her book on the same subject.[8] Six years later in a letter to Alasinga sent on August 20, 1893, Swami Vivekananda indicated he would go to Boston "to speak at a big Ladies' Club here, which is helping Ramabai".[9]

In 1882, Reverend Cook, with the accompaniment of his wife, came to India and stayed during the months of January to March. At the Town Hall in Calcutta and other locations in India and Ceylon (Sri Lanka), he made forty-two public appearances. Cook spoke before large audiences of well-educated English-speaking Indians. While sojourning in Calcutta, he held several religious discussions with Keshab Sen and other leaders of the Brahmo Samaj. Although Cook did not agree with Keshab Sen's theology describing him as a "Quaker-Unitarian", he greatly admired his spiritual nature. He provides us with some significant insights into the mystical temperament of Keshab Sen, who was very much influenced by Sri Ramakrishna at that time. Sri Ramakrishna first went to visit Keshab in March 1875, and their meeting at Keshab's house on March 11, 1882 is described in the *Gospel of Sri Ramakrishna.*[10] In his travelogue about his trip to the Orient, Cook devotes over twenty-five pages to Keshab Sen and the New Dispensation, paying him the following tribute:

> It was Mr. Burlingame, I believe, who said that in Asia there are at least ten-thousand Emersons. The characteristic type of mind in India is the intuitive and not the philosophical. Mr. Sen speaks through his lofty moral feelings. He sees religious truths through his conscience, rather than through mere reason.... He is not an Occidental; he is a thorough Oriental, and feels the touch of God within him, as the Oriental always has done at his best. He listens to the Inner Voice with the devoutness of one of the best of the Quaker mystics. He instinctively believes in Providence. He is perpetually inculcating the duty and blessedness of prayer and of self-surrender to all the loftiest impulses of conscience, which, as he teaches, are really supernatural touches of God upon the spirit of man.... He has a splendid physique, excellent quality of organization, capacity of sudden heat and of tremendous impetuosity, and lightning-like swiftness of thought and expression, combined with a most iron self-control. You cannot throw him off his balance before any audience, with manuscript or without one. He is unquestionably the most eloquent Asiatic I have ever heard. He speaks English as perfectly as any man in this assembly.... He usually fascinates every one who comes near him, and he has a strange ascendancy over his immediate followers, several of whom are men of high intellectual endowments and finished education....[11]
>
> The news from the Ganges that Keshub Chunder Sen is dead overwhelms me with a more profound sense of personal bereavement than I can now remember to have felt before at the departure of any public man. Keshab Chunder Sen was not a reformer and orator merely; he was also a religious seer. When his influence over his followers is closely analyzed, it will be found that his deep communion with the unseen world was the chief source of the authority he was allowed to exercise among his friends and disciples.[12]
>
> He depends for his knowledge of religious truth on religious exercises continued through three, four and sometimes five hours a day. I thoroughly believe him to be an honest and devout man. My feeling is not that he should pray less, but that he should study more.[13]

Nine years later Cook was a delegate at the 1893 Parliament of Religions held in Chicago.[14]

Miss Mary Henrietta Pigot (b. 1837), who accompanied Joseph Cook on the boat trip to Dakshineswar according to the *New Dispensation* report cited above, also had the privilege of seeing Ramakrishna in samadhi. Mary Pigot, a baptized Christian, was an Anglo-Indian lady, being the daughter of Julius Pigot, an indigo planter, and Desiree Casabon. She had been in charge of the Lucknow Girls' School, the Bethune School in Calcutta, as well as the Calcutta Girls' School. In 1870 she distinguished herself by becoming the lady superintendent of the Female Mission of the Scottish Ladies' Association in Calcutta. It was under the control of the Foreign Mission of the Presbyterian Church of Scotland, with headquarters in Edinburgh. She held the position until 1883. The Female Mission contained a zenana (secluded household) teaching establishment, an upper school, a lower school with two sections, and an orphanage. In March of 1883, Mary Pigot lived at No. 19 High Street in the town of Serampore, about five miles north of Dakshineswar on the Hooghly River.[15]

In 1878 William Hastie (1842-1903) [q.v.] became the principal of the General Assembly's Institution in Calcutta, later known as the Scottish Church College. He remained in the College under the operation of the Missionary Board of the Church of Scotland until 1884. It was William Hastie who recognized the potential talent of Narendranath Datta, the future Swami Vivekananda. From Hastie, Narendra first heard about Ramakrishna. On that occasion, the professor of literature was absent from his class, and Hastie, the principal of the College, replaced him. During the course of the lecture, Hastie spoke about William Wordsworth's book-length poem, the *Excursion* (1814). He mentioned that Wordsworth had an ecstatic experience when he felt the sublime beauty of nature. Hastie then explained to his students:

> The state of samadhi originates from a pure mind and its concentration on a particular object. Rarely does one find a person who has achieved that state. At present I have seen only Ramakrishna Paramahamsa of Dakshineswar in the state of samadhi. You will understand this subject if you go there and see him in that state.

Taking his advice, soon after this event, Narendra met Ramakrishna for the first time at Surendra Mitra's house in 1881.[16]

William Hastie sent a series of letters to *The Statesman* (Calcutta) in 1882, which criticized Hindu image worship. Writing under a pseudonym, Bankim Chatterji, the well-known Bengali novelist, Neo-Hindu theorist, and social reformer, replied at length. He expressed the view that in spite of their knowledge of Sanskrit and the Vedas, no European scholar adequately understands the fundamental doctrines of the Hindu religion. During his lifetime, Bankim composed the *Vande Mataram* in Sanskrit that inspired the Indian freedom fighters, and later became the National Song of India. His doctrine of the "New Dharma", as being an aspect of religion, extended beyond traditional duties to the family, caste and local community, to loyalty to the country (*svadesha-priti*) and even to the entire world (*vishva-priti*). Chapter thirty-four of *The Gospel of Sri Ramakrishna* describes the meeting of Bankim with Ramakrishna two years later.[17]

After William Hastie wrote his critique of Hindu image worship, things did not go well for him in India to say the least. Ironically, he and Miss Mary Pigot were involved in a feud that began in 1879. It culminated on March 21, 1883, when she raised an action for libel in the High Court in Calcutta against Hastie. The sensational trial is described in a 343-page book. The contention concerned Hastie, the principal of the Male College Mission, and Pigot, the head of the Female Missionary Mission in Calcutta, both of whom were connected with the Church of Scotland. Pigot asserted that when Hastie came to India he made the attempt to gain control over the Female Mission, by placing her in a subordinate role. She also made the accusation that Hastie and others had charged her with mismanagement of the school, cruelty to children, and immoral conduct, which damaged her reputation and deprived her of her livelihood. Earlier, in May of 1882, Mary Pigot travelled to Edinburgh to improve her relations with the Scottish Church authorities. The Pigot vs. Hastie case began on August 31, 1883. While the original judge decided in Hastie's favour, the Appellate Bench of the High Court reversed the decision and Hastie was found guilty of malicious libel. Hastie failed to pay Mary Pigot's damages and costs and, consequently, in February of 1885, the former principal of a premier educational institution in India spent nearly a month in the Presidency Jail. Fortunately, they permitted him to leave the jail after he paid a fine of three-hundred pounds. It took him years to save up this money by undergoing a frugal lifestyle. Some people thought Hastie received unjust treatment and there were protests, but he wisely made the decision to return to Scotland.[18]

In May of 1885, the Commissioners of the General Assembly exonerated Mary Pigot. In Edinburgh she had the support of the mother of the famous Scottish writer Robert Louis Stevenson (1850-94). After her employment was terminated, she received a small pension. For about six years from 1884 she was the headmistress of Victoria College, a girls' school. She was then paid a pension by Keshab Sen's daughter, the Maharani of Cooch Behar, and went to live in Darjeeling in a cottage called "Rook's Nest" belonging to the Cooch Behar Estate. She was still alive in 1921.[19]

In 1885, William Hastie made the decision to return to Scotland, where he became a scholar of high academic attainment. Among other things, he translated and edited seventeen books from German into the English language. At Edinburgh University, he taught courses in law, while translating a difficult two-volume jurisprudence manuscript from Italian. The versatile Mr. Hastie wrote or translated books dealing with scientific cosmology, ethics, Christian missions, mysticism, politics, and poetry. For his efforts, in 1895 he became the Doctor of Divinity at the University of Glasgow. His translations include four difficult works written by the German philosopher Immanuel Kant, as well as one by Rumi, the Sufi. Portions of two of Hastie's translations of Immanuel Kant's writings were later selected to be part of the University of Chicago's *Great Books of the Western World* in volume 42. He also authored at least six religious books on the subject of Protestant reformed theology. It is most unfortunate that this Glasgow scholar died suddenly during the peak of his career in 1903 at the age of sixty-one. After his death, Hastie became a local legend. At the University of Glasgow, the Hastie Lecturer series began in 1906, the faculty formed the Hastie Club with a membership of over fifty ministers, and in 1926 a minister put together a three-hundred-page biography of his life.[20]

Interestingly, an adaptation of one of Sir Edwin Arnold's [q.v.] hymns appears in *The Gospel of Sri Ramakrishna* (pp. 871-72). It is taken from *The Light of Asia* (1879), the life and teachings of Buddha as told in verse by an Indian Buddhist. On October 23, 1885, when Ramtaran sang the song, Sri Ramakrishna entered into samadhi upon hearing the words:

> Shine forth, O Shining One, and with Thy shafts of light
> Slay Thou the blinding dark!

Swami Vivekananda showed appreciation for *The Light of Asia*[21] and Arnold's other works.[22] During 1856-61, Edwin Arnold was the principal of the government school, Deccan College, in Bombay. At that time he gained an appreciation for Indian culture, literature, and philosophy. Arnold's poetical biography of Buddha enjoyed tremendous public and critical popularity, undergoing eighty editions in the United States. These stories proved fascinating to Western readers, for the life and teachings of Buddha were nearly unheard of in the West before the publication of Arnold's work.[23] After revisiting India, in 1886 Arnold wrote most appreciatively of her people:

> We brought our goodwill to India, and leave it with that goodwill doubled and trebled. I myself have found nothing but friendliness and courtesy among the countless millions of this land ... I have witnessed a thousand instances of simple virtues—of charity, of domestic affection, of natural courtesy, of inherent modesty, of human dignity, of devotion, of piety, of glad human life ... I wish that there were space to speak here of the Indian wives and mothers, among whom are to be counted humble saints and angels by the lakh—gentle, patient, laborious, faithful, pure, contented, cheerful, and affectionate souls.... I declare myself not so much her [India's] friend as her lover. I leave my heart behind me in leaving these Indian peoples, who have taught me, as I have wandered among them, that manners more noble and gentle, learning more modest and profound, loyalty more sincere, refinement more natural, and sweeter simplicities of life, and love, and duty exist in the length and breadth of British Asia than even I had gathered from my old experiences, before India was "revisited".[24]

On March 15, 1886, Ramchandra Datta, a householder disciple of the Master and the Chemical Examiner of the Calcutta Medical College, made arrangements for John Martin Coates M.D. (1832-95) to visit the ailing Ramakrishna. At Cossipore, he met Shashi, the future Swami Ramakrishnananda. Dr. Coates remarked, "He [Ramakrishna] is naturally a gentleman." After examining the patient, he correctly diagnosed his illness as throat cancer. Swami Prabhananda tells us more about his meeting with Ramakrishna:

> Devout Christian that he was, Dr. Coates wanted to hear religious discourses from the Saint. The latter could not oblige him as he had practically lost the power of speaking. Nonetheless, he told him by signs that God was one and that he was immanent in all beings. The topic itself threw Sri Ramakrishna into a deep ecstasy. Dr. Coates was amazed and considered

himself fortunate for he had never seen such ecstasy although he had learned from the Bible of a similar experience of Jesus Christ.[25]

John Coates, a Presbyterian born in Belfast in the northern section of Ireland on July 6, 1832, was a student at Queens University in Ireland. In 1885 he joined the British army in the Bengal Presidency as an assistant surgeon, and later went on to successively become a surgeon, surgeon major, and brigade surgeon, retiring with an extra pension in 1890. During the Indian Mutiny of 1857, Coates was a physician, and, in 1866, the superintendent of Jails in Hazaribag. As a scholar, in 1875 Coates demonstrated his interest in the Indian culture by authoring *Vocabulary of Seven Languages or Dialects of Chota Nagpore*. He was the ninth principal of the Calcutta Medical College (1880-90) during the time he came to examine Ramakrishna. The British founded the College in 1835 with an adjoining hospital built in 1838 to train Indian doctors. When Dr. Coates served as the College principal, the Eden Hospital in 1881-82 and the Ezra Hospital in 1887 became part of the facilities. On July 18, 1895, he died in Calcutta.[26]

Four days after Ramakrishna's mahasamadhi, on August 20, 1886 *The Englishman* published this report, which was reprinted in the *Indian Mirror* newspaper the following day. The Calcutta based *The Englishman* (founded in 1821) later merged with *The Statesman* in 1934. A short biography of Ramakrishna was included in the eulogy, which concluded with this tribute:

> The late Paramahamsa was held in the highest respect by all sections of the Hindu community. The educated Hindus appreciated his teachings highly and among his followers were many graduates and undergraduates of the University. The great Brahmo leader, the late Babu Keshab Chunder Sen had a profound love and respect for him. If faith, love, self-sacrifice, purity of character and entire resignation to the will of the Almighty be the chief qualifications of a religious man, they found their highest perfection in him and the veneration of the people was not misplaced.[27]

English Language Publications on Sri Ramakrishna

Pratap C. Mazumdar (Mozoomdar, 1840-1905) [q.v.], the future leader of the Brahmo Samaj, wrote the first English language biographical article about Sri Ramakrishna entitled "The Hindu Saint" published in the October 1879 issue of *Theistic Quarterly Review*. During 1879-81, this journal was put out by the Brahmo Samaj in Calcutta. Twenty pages of excerpts from this article appeared in Vivekananda's *My Master* (1901). The piece was reissued in 1907 by the Ramakrishna Mission in Calcutta as a pamphlet with the title *Paramahamsa Ramakrishna.*[28] A number of Westerners first learned about Ramakrishna while reading this biography. Some of the people previously mentioned in this chapter might have been acquainted with this article. Future writers on Ramakrishna, like Lewis Janes and S. Fletcher Williams, each refer to Mazumdar's article. Max Müller, in his article "A Real Mahatman", quoted Mazumdar at length in his description of Ramakrishna:

> His face retains a fullness, a childlike tenderness, a profound visible humbleness, an unspeakable sweetness of expression, and a smile that I have seen in no other face.... His religion meant ecstasy, his worship transcendental insight, his whole nature burnt day and night with the permanent fire and fever of a strange faith and feeling. His conversation was a ceaseless breaking forth of his inward fire and lasted for long hours. He was often merged in rapturous ecstasy and outward unconsciousness during the day, particularly when he spoke of his favourite spiritual experiences or heard any striking response to them.[29]

Written studies on Ramakrishna in the West received a powerful impetus when in 1895 the newly-founded *Brahmavadin* began publishing the teachings of Ramakrishna. On December 22, 1895, Leon Landsberg (b. 1853) [q.v.], a follower of Swami Vivekananda, produced an article in the *New York Herald* newspaper. It was a compilation with his introductory remarks on the "Sayings of Sri Ramakrishna", drawn from four issues of the *Brahmavadin*.[30]

The first Westerner to publish a journal article on Ramakrishna was Charles Henry Tawney (1837-1922), a former university professor. Tawney was the principal of Presidency College in 1880 when Narendra (later Swami Vivekananda) was a student there. When Swami Vivekananda attended the meeting of the Royal Asiatic Society in London in 1896 (and possibly in 1895), it is likely that he met Charles Tawney who was a member of the organization.[31] With the title "A Modern Hindu Saint", the article appeared in the London based *The Imperial and Asiatic Quarterly Review* in January 1896. The article later came out in the *Indian Mirror* of February 15. Tawney presented a short biography and some of the sayings and parables of Ramakrishna. They were drawn from a recent Bengali book titled *Paramahamsa Srimad Ram Krishner Upadesa* written by Sureshchandra Datta, a householder disciple of the Master. Tawney mentioned Vivekananda's "hearty reception at Chicago, and in other parts of America". He concluded:

> It is impossible to read his [Sri Ramakrishna's] sayings without conceiving a genuine respect for him. But the paramount importance of the work seems to us to consist in the fact that it contains the ideas of a teacher who has profoundly influenced his educated fellow-countrymen. It must be remembered that it is written by an Indian for Indians, and is not an article prepared for European consumption. Such books should be literally translated into English. Probably more could be learnt from them with regard to the real feelings of seriously-minded Hindus, than from the volumes of travels written by gentlemen who rush through India at railway speed, and associate only with European officials and Europeanized natives.[32]

From 1864 to 1876 Tawney worked as a history and English professor, then as the principal of Presidency College in Calcutta during 1876-92 (with some breaks), and also as the registrar of Calcutta University during the years 1877-81, 1884-86, and 1889. After returning to England, he became the librarian of the Great Britain India Office (1893-1903), where he catalogued collections of Sanskrit manuscripts. As a writer, between the years 1874-99 Charles Tawney translated into English traditional Sanskrit works written by Bhavabhuti, Bhartrhari, Somadeva, Kalidasa, and Merutunga.[33]

Swamiji's younger brother Mahendranath Datta lived with him in England during 1895-96 and later recalled:

> The former Presidency College Principal, Mr. Tawney, had written and published an article in a paper of the time about Sri Ramakrishna [January 1896]. Because of Swami Vivekananda's London speeches [beginning in October 1895 and a month earlier in Caversham] and his mixing with the "big people", there began to be some discussion of Ramakrishna in academic circles. At Kankhal in 1917, the famous Aswinikumar Datta told ... that he and Prof. Tawney wrote that the latter [Tawney] tries to read "M's" *Kathamrita* in Bengali, but cannot make it out in many places because of the village dialect. Yet he reads it daily just like the Bible. Aswini told this with great joy.[34]

The World's Advance Thought, a mental-healing New Thought publication, was edited and published by Mrs. Lucy A. Mallory (b. 1846) in far-off Portland, Oregon. Leo Tolstoy in Russia subscribed to this monthly magazine. The following appeared in her periodical during the Spring of 1896:

> We gladly welcome to the journalistic brotherhood of those engaged in disseminating the Light of the New, the True and the Good, the *Brahmavadin*. He who reads this new, enlightened Hindu publication will see that all truth is one and that the true religion of the soul is not bounded by geographical lines, nor restricted to certain creedal systems. Its editor is a ripe scholar and a spiritual man. The *Brahmavadin* will be successful beyond the expectations of its projectors.[35]

Lucy Mallory's poem on "God" appeared in the November 1913 issue of *Prabuddha Bharata*. The city of Roseburg, Oregon, was named after her father Aaron Rose who was a pioneer settler in that community in 1851. Swami Prakashananda "formed many warm friends, and created a new impetus for deeper study of the Vedanta teachings" at "advanced thought societies" in Portland when he spoke there in 1914.[36]

Also during the spring of 1896, Friedrich Max Müller (1823-1900) [q.v.], the well-known Sanskrit scholar and philologist at Oxford University, made the following wonderful statement about Ramakrishna in a letter written to Vivekananda:

> As for your beloved master of blessed memory, Bhagaban Sri Ram Krishan, how can I ever tell you what he is to me, I love and worship him with my whole heart. To think of him makes my eyes fill with tears of gladness that I was permitted to hear of him. His sayings, published in the *Brahmavadin*, are my greatest delight. How wonderful that his teachings should have been borne to this far-off land where we have never even known of his existence! If I might only have known him, while he was yet with us! My greatest desire is to one day visit the spot which [was] sanctified by his presence, while he lived, and I may be so fortunate as to fulfill the wish.[37]

Many years before this, on June 18, 1883 a devotee named Navadvip had told Ramakrishna, "Previously one hardly saw a copy of the Vedas in this country. Max Müller has translated them; so people can now read these books." He translated the *Rig Veda* from Sanskrit to English. Swami Vivekananda twice met Müller at his home in England during the month of May 1896, and he took the newly arrived Swami Abhedananda to meet him in September or October.[38] When Swamiji told Müller, "Ramakrishna is worshipped by thousands today," the professor responded, "To whom else shall worship be accorded, if not to such."[39] Max Müller came out with an article about Ramakrishna entitled "A Real Mahatman" in the prestigious English journal the *Nineteenth Century* of August 1896. In the article Müller wrote:

> He seems to have been not only a high-souled man, a real *Mahatman*, but a man of original thought.... he was certainly thoroughly imbued with the spirit of the Vedanta philosophy. His utterances which have been published breathe the spirit of that philosophy; in fact, are only intelligible as a product of Vedantic soil.[40]

Soon after "A Real Mahatman" came out, on August 15, 1896 Dr. Joseph Estlin Carpenter (1844-1927) [q.v.] of Oxford University published an article in the *Inquirer*, a Unitarian periodical of London. It read in part:

> The same indefatigable scholar [Max Müller] has sketched for us in the current number of the *Nineteenth Century* a modern figure of singular interest, the late Ramakrishna Paramahansa who so deeply influenced Keshab Chunder Sen in the last stage of his career, and died after him, near Calcutta in 1886. He did not belong to any of the orthodox Hindu sects, but came nearest, perhaps, to the teaching of the Vedanta. He represents that tendency, planted so deep in the Hindu mind, towards spiritual abstraction which enabled him to accept the doctrines and practice the usages of each religious cult in turn. His disciples have carried his teachings over India, and one of them, Vivekananda, has been recently in this country.[41]

The article went on to praise Swami Vivekananda whom he had formerly met.* Joseph Estlin Carpenter, a Unitarian Minister (1866-75), worked at Manchester College, which, after 1889, was associated with Oxford University. He became a professor of theology and religious studies (1875-85), the vice-principal (1885-99), and, after a break of seven-years, the principal (1906-15). Being a comprehensive scholar, Carpenter, the author of many works on the *Bible*, became a leader in the new discipline of comparative religion. Professor Carpenter collaborated with T. W. Rhys Davids (1843-1922)

* See Chapter VI.

in translating Pali texts of Indian Buddhism into the English language. His later publications include *Theism in Medieval India* (1921) as well as *Buddhism and Christianity, a Contrast and a Parallel* (1923).[42]

After reading "A Real Mahatman", Annie Besant (1847-1933) [q.v.], a leader in the Theosophical movement, made the following statement in *The Theosophic Review* of London (also reported in the *Prabuddha Bharata* of January 1898):

> All who work for the revival of spirituality in India must be regarded as fellow-labourers by students of the "Divine Wisdom", and we heartily wish God-speed to all the efforts made in this direction by the disciples of Paramahansa Ramakrishna. This holy man—to whom Professor Max Müller paid a well-deserved tribute in the *Nineteenth Century*, our readers may well remember—has drawn many young men to the religious life by the magic of his purity and devotion.[43]

In February and March 1898, Lewis Janes (1844-1901) [q.v.] submitted two letters to the *Outlook*, a Christian periodical, as a response to its statements about Swami Vivekananda's lack of success in America and England. In the first letter Janes mentioned the influence among Western people of the Mozoomdar's (Pratap Chandra Mazumdar) and Müller's articles on Ramakrishna:

> If, in his [Vivekananda's] statement about the master, Sri Ramakrishna, the word "reverenced" were substituted for "worshipped", the fact would hardly be greatly exaggerated. There are doubtless hundreds, if not thousands, in Europe and America who have been deeply touched by the accounts of that remarkable man which have been written by Professor Max Müller ("A Real Mahatman", *Nineteenth Century*, August 1896), and by Protap Chunder Mozoomdar, the eloquent minister of the Brahmo-Samaj, in a pamphlet [about Ramakrishna] which has been circulated in the United States. His influence over the remarkable coterie of educated young men who, as his disciples, are now spreading the doctrines of the Vedanta in India, Europe, and America, and of whom the Swamis Vivekananda, Saradananda, and Abhedananda have been teachers in this country, has eventually been notable and worth tracing to its causes.[44]

Between 1896 and 1899, Swamiji often referred to Müller's article in the *Nineteenth Century*.[45] In his own article contributed to the *Udbodhan* of March 14, 1899, Swami Vivekananda mentioned that Professor Müller discussed Ramakrishna's life in "A Real Mahatman":

> There he expressed himself to the effect that this new sage easily won his heart by the originality of his thoughts, couched in novel language and impregnate with fresh spiritual power which he infused into India when she was merely echoing the thoughts of her ancient sages for several centuries past, or, as in recent times, those of Western scholars.... The learned people of Europe and America read the article with great interest and many have been attracted towards its subject, Shri Ramakrishna Deva ... he has collected more complete information and given a fuller account of his life and utterances, so that the reading public may get a better knowledge of this great sage and his religious ideas.[46]

After reading a recent edition of the *Brahmavadin*, an unidentified writer published a number of Ramakrishna's sayings and made the following comments in the New York based *The Literary Digest*:

> There has, it appears, been a recrudesce of India's best philosophy, the Vedanta, in the life of one of her most remarkable saints and sages of modern times, Ramakrishna.... Ramakrishna was not in the ordinary sense a man of the world. He was a great spiritual yogi, teaching the highest spiritual methods of how to acquire the superconscious state of the mind... his face retained fullness and childlike tenderness, a profound visible humbleness, an unspeakable sweetness of expression, and a smile seen in no other face. He was singularly devoid of any claims to superiority over other men.... His religion ... meant ecstasy; his worship meant transcendental insight; his conversation was a ceaseless breaking forth of inward fires and lasted for hours. In these superconscious states, he would become unconscious to the outer world; but, as he communed with the inner world, a sweet smile would come over his face. Soon he would burst into a flood of tears, and break forth in prayers and songs and utterances the force and pathos of which would pierce the hardest hearts of those around him. But these utterances were no senseless hypnotic jabberings, but a spontaneous outburst of profound wisdom, clothed in beautiful, poetic language.[47]

The great Orientalist Max Müller desired that Vivekananda send him more information on Ramakrishna.[48] Vivekananda wrote to Swami Ramakrishnananda on 24 June 1896:

> Max Müller wants all the sayings of Shri Ramakrishna classified, that is, all on Karma in one place, on Vairagya in another place, so on Bhakti, Jnana, etc., etc. You must undertake to do this forthwith.... We must take care to present only the universal aspect of his teachings.[49]

Müller used the material he acquired from Swamiji in his future publication *Ramakrishna His Life and Sayings* (1898), which included 395 sayings of the Master.[50] It was this book that brought Ramakrishna to the attention of many educated Westerners. The 1898 or 1901 volume can now be found in over one-hundred university libraries in the West.[51]

Swami Saradananda relates that

> [Müller] asked Swamiji to furnish him with enough material for a book so he could write about Sri Ramakrishna in greater detail. Swamiji agreed to help. When he returned, he asked me to undertake the job forthwith. I worked hard and gathered all the incidents in the life of the Master and the teachings of the Master and showed the manuscript to Swamiji. I thought Swamiji would edit it and make extensive corrections. He didn't do that. He simply changed a few words for fear of exaggeration and sent the whole manuscript to Professor Müller. As I remember, Professor Müller incorporated the completed manuscript in his book and published it without making any alterations.[52]

Saradananda's writing about the life of Ramakrishna for Müller began in 1896, thirteen years before he first serialized in part the more complete biography of Ramakrishna, which appeared in the *Udbodhan* of 1909. In his book Müller acknowledged, "I applied therefore to one of his most eminent pupils, Vivekananda, asking him to write down for me what he could tell of his own knowledge of his venerable teacher, and I received from him a full description of his Master's life." Müller rejected some of Swamiji's narrative, which he got from Swami Saradananda, as being miraculous and not being acceptable to a Western audience. Other sources for Müller's two publications are Ramakrishna's sayings that appeared in the *Brahmavadin* and the *Prabuddha Bharata*, and the articles on Ramakrishna by Pratap

Mazumdar and Charles Tawney.[53] It is to Max Müller's credit that he was the one Western Indologist to take a keen interest in the contemporary Neo-Hindu and Neo-Vedanta movements. In addition to Ramakrishna, he also penned essays on Rammohan Roy, Dwarakanath Tagore, Debendranath Tagore, Raja Radhakanta Deva, Keshab Sen, with whom he corresponded for a long time, Ramtanu Lahiri, Dayananda Saraswati, Pavhari Baba, and other prominent nineteenth-century Indian figures.

One quotation from Müller's biography on Ramakrishna reads as follows:

> He was a wonderful mixture of God and man. In his ordinary state he would talk of himself as servant of all men and women. He looked upon them all as God. He himself would never be addressed as Guru, or teacher. Never would he claim for himself any high position. He would touch the ground reverently where his disciples had trodden. But every now and then strange fits of God-consciousness came upon him. He then became changed into a different being altogether. He then spoke of himself as being able to do and know everything. He spoke as if he had the power of giving anything to anybody. He would speak of himself as the same soul that had been born before as Rama, as Krishna, as Jesus, or as Buddha, born again as Ramakrishna. He told Mathuranatha, long before anybody knew him, that he had many disciples who would come to him shortly, and he knew all of them. He said that he was free from all eternity, and the practices and struggles after religion which he went through were only meant to show the people the way to salvation. He had done all for them alone. He would say he was a Nitya-mukta, or eternally free, and an incarnation of God Himself.[54]

Concerning Ramakrishna's teachings, Müller added:

> The fervent love of God, nay, the sense of complete absorption in Godhead, has nowhere found a stronger and more eloquent expression than in the utterances of Ramakrishna. They show the exalted nature of his faith. How deep he has seen into the mysteries of knowledge and love of God we see from his sayings.... These utterances of Ramakrishna reveal to us not only his own thoughts, but the faith and hope of millions of human beings.... This constant sense of the presence of God is indeed the common ground on which we may hope that in time not too distant, the great temple

of the future will be erected, in which the Hindus and non-Hindus may join hands and hearts in worshipping the same Supreme Spirit—who is not far from every one of us, for in Him we live and move and have our being.[55]

Two years after his passing away, his wife Georgina Müller revealed that the biography was written by Müller, "feeling that attention ought to be drawn in this country to the utterances of men like Ramakrishna, who gather large multitudes round them, and who exercise a powerful influence not only on philosophers but on large masses of the people."[56]

A respected English Unitarian missionary, Reverend S. Fletcher Williams, sent a letter dated March 4, 1899 to a disciple of Ramakrishna. Williams authored the book *Beliefs and Opinions of a Unitarian* (1885) and, for two or three years, preached in Brahmo Samaj churches in India. The letter expressed his appreciation of Ramakrishna:

> Sir,—I am much indebted to you for the copy of "Leaves from the Gospel of the Lord Sri Ram Krishna", which you kindly gave me. I have read through the little work with great interest. I already knew something of Ram Krishna from an article by P. C. Mazumdar in the *Theistic Quarterly Review*, 1879, and from the testimony there given, and from the deep devotion he inspired in a band of disciples, including "M". I have no doubt whatever that he possessed the prophetic power. I should suppose that as in the case of other great souls, his influence proceeded rather from what he was than from what he said. There must have been a strangely magnetic charm about his personality, and in this respect he, no doubt, resembled Jesus of Nazareth.
>
> What always impresses me in reading of such souls that have arisen from time to time in India is the limited area of their influence—always, excepting Buddha. One would imagine that men of such power would become the spiritual masters, not simply of a small circle of disciples, but of a race and a nation.[57]

Book Reviews of "Ramakrishna His Life and Sayings"

The book was released in November 1898 and, with a rapid sale, the third edition came out the following May. In a long appraisal of Müller's book, the reviewer for the *Brahmavadin* mentioned one limitation of this wonderful study:

> Though in many places we cannot agree with his sentiments and remarks, the entire book will amply repay perusal. The subject of the sketch is as all of us know a very interesting personality, and it is not easy for a mind nurtured in Western tradition and Western ways of thinking to appreciate all the phases of a Hindu saint's character.... This sympathetic sketch of the life and teachings of an Indian Saint from the pen of an Oriental scholar of such high repute as Prof. Max Müller will therefore be heartily welcomed by all seekers after truth both in India and elsewhere.[58]

Müller coined the term "The Dialogic Process" meaning the miraculizing tendency of devoted disciples to create legends around their religious teacher. He assumed this occurred with statements made about Ramakrishna, which he, as a Western rationalist, could not accept. In turn, the editor of the *Brahmavadin* rejected Müller's modern secularized point of view on this subject.

The fact that at that time Max Müller was a famous scholar added to the prestige of the volume. The biography of Ramakrishna received many scholarly reviews, particularly in the United States. The quickest response came however from the British Isles, *The London Times* of December 24, 1898 (p. 10) bringing out the following similarity:

> [When Ramakrishna] cried out, "Mother, oh! my mother, is this the result of calling upon thee and believing in thee?" to which a sweet voice from a sweeter smiling face replied, "My son! how could you hope to realize the highest truths if you don't give up the love of your body and of your little self," he might quite well have been a Roman Catholic praying to the Virgin Mother. Indeed, the whole record of the saint's life strongly resembles the history of an early Christian devotee or medieval friar, consumed like St. Francis with the love of holy poverty, overwhelmed like St. Augustine by a sense of man's natural weakness and sin. The "Sayings" of Ramakrishna suggest the same comparison.

Another evaluator, *The Scotsman*, a daily national newspaper, wrote to its readers:

> Many as are the books in which Professor Max Müller has enriched the literature by which the religious teaching of the Brahmans has been made familiar to the learned, he has written no work more likely than this

> to appeal with a like force to the erudite and to the simple, and the work deserves to be widely read.[59]

Under the title "A Modern Hindoo Saint", an unidentified writer for the *Literary World; a Monthly Review of Current Literature* concluded:

> The venerable and right honourable Max Müller lives in hope that in time, not too distant, the great temple of the future will be erected, in which Hindoos and non-Hindoos may join hands and heart in worshiping the same Supreme Spirit. We are indebted to him for very much of our knowledge about religious movements in modern India.... Professor Müller has gathered up from various sources several hundred of the sayings of the preacher. These give a good idea of the general cast and colour of the modern advanced Hindoo thought. They are not only surcharged with Oriental philosophy but are rich in metaphors and illustrations drawn from the teacher's environment.[60]

A literary critic for the *New York Times* criticized Müller for "writing the biography of a man so utterly uninteresting to Europeans as was Ramakrishna". A week later on June 10, 1899, seventy-five-year old Mrs. Eliza Boardman Burnz (1823-1903) responded to the *New York Times* review. She expressed her appreciation for learning about the teachings of a contemporary Indian saint and wrote in part:

> I imagine that Prof. Max Müller cares far less that this work should be sold by the million to the million, than he does to lead the truly scientific minds of Europe and America into a thorough understanding and a better appreciation of present Hindu thought.... Our knowledge of Oriental modes of thought and living has hitherto been gathered from records of their wise men who lived ages ago, or else from reports given by prejudiced travellers, who are utterly unable to comprehend what they see or to sympathize with the actors. We are apt to think of the Hindu religion, in its highest expression, as belonging only to the past. Our missionaries find nothing but gross idol worship. In this book Prof. Müller has shown us the life of a nineteenth-century Hindu teacher. He has given us a specimen of the highest philosophic and religious thought of India as it exists today. Our literary critics may protest against the writing of books which tell of things as they really exist; but the scientists and humanitarians who desire to fully

understand the workings of vital force in all races, so that the "federation of the world" may be in time accomplished, will recognize in this biography of Ramakrishna an impetus toward that end.

Eliza Burnz immigrated to the United States from Great Britain as a young girl. After the Civil War she travelled to Nashville, Tennessee, and taught English to freed ex-slaves, using textbooks printed in a phonetic alphabet. She taught simplified phonetic spelling and shorthand throughout the nation, published a number of successful textbooks on this subject, and was in charge of the Burnz School of Shorthand. For many years she also served as vice-president of the Spelling Reform Association in Philadelphia.[61]

For the *New World: A Quarterly Review of Religion, Ethics and Theology*, Reverend George William Gilmore expressed this view concerning the biography of Ramakrishna:

> Professor Müller's apparent object in writing the volume was to illustrate for the benefit of Indian statesmen, missionaries and students of philosophy and comparative religion the fact that for each of them there are elements of life and thought in the great peninsula that should inspire their respect and influence their action in their various spheres. The veteran author desired to show that ... there is often revealed in the life and utterances of religious teachers in India such a profundity of conception and exaltation of vision as evince a lofty perception and knowledge of God and his love.[62]

George W. Gilmore (1858-1933) was a professor of Biblical history and a lecturer on comparative religion at Bangor Theological Seminary in Portland, Maine, and of the Old Testament and history of religion at Meadville Theological School. He served as the associate editor (1905-14) of the multi-volume *Schaff-Herzog Encyclopedia of Religious Knowledge*, which featured short articles on Swamis Abhedananda and Vivekananda, and the Vedanta Society.[63]

Canadian born Alfred William Stratton (1866-1902), a professor of Sanskrit and Indo-European philology at the University of Chicago, was a former student at Johns Hopkins University under Maurice Bloomfield. He put together a book review of *Ramakrishna His Life and Sayings* for the prestigious *American Journal of Theology* stating that Max Müller sought to secure in the West a better appreciation of Hindu ideals. The book before us is of distinct value in this regard and deserved to be read widely. Ramakrishna's life and teachings drew to him a large number of seekers after spiritual enlightenment. The well-known reformer Keshub Chunder Sen and Mozoomdar were among those who came under his influence.[64]

In his appraisal, Stratton supplies a few sayings of Ramakrishna "to show something of the teacher's spirit and manner". In 1899 Stratton gave up his chair at the University of Chicago and became the principal of Oriental College at Lahore and the registrar of the Punjab University in India. He replaced the legendary Sir Marc Aurel Stein (1862-1943), who held the position for eleven years (1888-99), and then became principal of the Calcutta Madrasah. While vacationing at Gulmarg in 1902, Stratton fell ill and died prematurely of Malta fever. His book *Letters from India* was published posthumously in 1908.[65] Sir M. A. Stein might have heard Vivekananda when he lectured in Lahore for a week in November of 1897. As an archeologist and explorer in Northwest India, Afghanistan, Persia and Central Asia, Stein's most prominent discovery was the *Diamond Sutra*, the world's oldest dated printed text, along with 40,000 ancient Buddhist scrolls. He further discovered the remains of many Buddhist stupas and monasteries, images of Buddhist and Hindu deities, and manuscripts written in the Indian language. When he was not undertaking expeditions in Central Asia, Stein, who never married, spent most of his time writing books and living alone in a tent with his dog in Gulmarg, Kashmir. During the same month that Stratton's review came out, an evaluation in the Christian *Biblical World* considered Müller's book to be "A most interesting presentation of the power of Hinduism in our day".[66]

Three eminent Jewish thinkers paid a tribute to Müller's book: Maurice Bloomfield, Sylvain Lévi and Dr. Arthur Pfungst. No reviewer showed more appreciation for Ramakrishna's life and teachings than did Stratton's teacher and close friend Maurice Bloomfield (1855-1928). In his December 1899 assessment of Müller's book, Bloomfield mentions:

> The reader of this Review will remember Vivekananda, the Brahman ascetic and apostle of advanced Hinduism, who appeared in America at the Parliament of Religions during the summer of the exposition in 1893.

During a prolonged stay in England and America his teachings attracted no little attention.

He went on to write:

> Max Müller has added a sketch of Ramakrishna's life, and an analysis of the essentials of Vedanta philosophy, both written with his wonted charm and skill of presentation. As a whole the little book marks one of the summit points of recent scientific religious literature. Müller's penetrating insight into the broad facts of Hindu intellectual history is coupled in this instance with all the just criticism needed for a true evaluation of Ramakrishna's personality and teaching. A Hindu John Tauler or Thomas Á Kempis is what we have before us, a man consumed with the passion for God. His strenuous efforts to realize the Divine in himself lead on a strangely exact parallel line to the mysticism of the European "friends of God", but that the man is genuine, that his thoughts and teachings have searched out some of the innermost recesses of religious consciousness, no one will doubt after reading the book. "As a lamp does not burn without oil, so a man cannot live without God," this is the keynote.... Mystic that he is, Ramakrishna is at the same time a man of the people; his sayings often have a homely, almost drastic flavour.[67]

Maurice Bloomfield of Austrian birth studied Sanskrit under Charles Rockwell Lanman, a supporter at Harvard University of Vivekananda and Abhedananda. For many years beginning in 1881, Bloomfield was America's greatest Vedic scholar and a professor of Sanskrit and comparative philology at Johns Hopkins University in Baltimore, Maryland. He is best remembered for his *Atharva Veda* (1899), being the world's number one authority on the subject, the *Vedic Concordance* (1906), which is an indispensable tool for scholars, and *The Religion of the Veda* (1908) that covers the period down to the Upanishads. Bloomfield concluded that the *Rig Veda* is not only "the most ancient literary document of India" but also "the most ancient literary document of the Indo-European peoples". For his numerous publications on the sacred texts of the Vedas, he was honoured as the president of the American Oriental Society (1910-11).[68] In *The Religion of the Veda* (pp. 228-29), Bloomfield added:

> Remarkable as this may sound, we have really no record of any period of Hindu thought of which we can say definitely that it was wanting in the highest and most strenuous thought, from the time of the riddle-hymn of Dirgatamas and the creation-hymn [*Rig Veda* I:164 and X:129], to the modern Vedantins and Paramahansas of the type of Ramakrishna and Vivekananda.[69]

In his French language review of Müller's biography of Ramakrishna, the Orientalist Sylvain Lévi (1863-1935) indicated:

> Sometimes he would teach through brief aphorisms, sometimes through the form of a fable or allegory typical of Hindu preachers. But never a hateful word, or any remark that would deprecate the belief of another: the boundless sweetness of the Indian soul has left its imprint on the utterances of Ramakrishna. From time to time, out of the impersonal depths of these pious maxims, a detail of modern life bursts out that places the speaker clearly in the setting of British Calcutta. Locomotives, cooking gas, and policemen enrich his already abundant stock of similes and examples drawn from the Indian classics. Those souls endowed with broad and intelligent piety will not remain unmoved on reading this collection of Sayings of Ramakrishna—one feels a tingle of intense love which makes itself known despite the quaintness of his vocabulary. Lovers of the picturesque will find this very quaintness entertaining and will relish the sketches of daily life where the lesson often takes place. And everyone will be grateful to the celebrated editor [Max Müller] of the *Rig-Veda* for having submitted to their curiosity a uniquely vivid slice of modern India.[70]

Sylvain Lévi, the author of numerous untranslated books and articles, was a professor of Sanskrit language and literature at the College de France (1894-1935). After meeting Rabindranath Tagore in Paris, he travelled to the poet's school in India at Shantiniketan in 1921, and also delivered a series of lectures on ancient India at Calcutta and Dacca University. Lévi was one of the vice-presidents of the General Committee formed to celebrate the Sri Ramakrishna Birth Centenary, but unfortunately passed away before the celebration began in 1937. In an article he contributed to the *Grande Encyclopedie*, Lévi showed his reverence for India stating in part:

> The multiplicity of the manifestations of Indian genius as well as their fundamental unity give India the right to figure on the first rank in the history of the civilized nations. Here civilization, spontaneous and original, unrolls itself in a continuous time across at least thirty centuries without interruption and without deviation.[71]

Jawaharlal Nehru, in his book *Discovery of India*, cited the following quote from Lévi's discussion of India's role among nations that appeared in *L'Inde et le Monde* (*India and the World*):

> She has left indelible imprints on one fourth of the human race in the course of a long succession of centuries. She has the right to reclaim in universal history the rank that ignorance has refused her for a long time and to hold her place amongst the great nations summarizing and symbolizing the spirit of humanity.[72]

Dr. Arthur Pfungst (1864-1912) from Frankfurt authored the monograph about his friend titled *A German Buddhist: Theodor Schultze* (1899). In the later part of his life, Theodor Schultze (1824-98) studied the religion and philosophy of India, and firmly believed that they might supply the vital spark needed to regenerate the decaying religious spirit of the West. Pfungst owned the Frankfurt Naxos union, a prominent importer and a producer of emery. As a religious humanist and one of the leaders of the German Society for Ethical Culture, Pfungst promoted free education for labourers, libraries and community centres, and opposed aggressive German militarism.[73] Writing in English, he sent a ten-page review of Müller's book on Ramakrishna to the *Brahmavadin*, which they published. Much of the article is devoted to discussing the life and sayings of Ramakrishna. Pfungst believed that an enormous amount of money was being spent on Christian Missions in India, because most of the people in Europe and the United States did not understand the spiritual life of the Indians. He also held that the "Esoteric Buddhist" movement in the West was not properly expressing Indian religious ideas. Consequently, Pfungst endorsed the necessity of Müller's book and wrote:

> We must warmly welcome a book of Max Müller, which has recently appeared and which deals in detail with the life and opinions of Ramakrishna, an Indian saint of our day. It gives us an instructive insight into an

important modern religious tendency.... It is therefore fortunate that we are made acquainted with an Indian thinker of our times whose thoughts—as expressed in the words of the editor—are still of value to those who went to school with Plato and Aristotle, Kant and Hegel.... We must now leave the Sayings of Ramakrishna which contain many original and witty thoughts. After reading Max Müller's book we can heartily endorse the words, with which we now close the paper, "A land penetrated with thoughts such as we find in Ramakrishna cannot be in any way regarded as a land of ignorant idolaters, whom we may convert."[74]

What follows in the next two chapters are the twentieth and twenty-first century responses in the West to the teachings and life of Ramakrishna. Upon further reading, it becomes evident that the majority of people who expressed written appreciation concerning Ramakrishna, Vivekananda, and Abhedananda were highly successful people from the upper echelon of Western society.

ENDNOTES

1 Sri Ramakrishna was born on February 18, 1836 at a very auspicious time, when a number of important and highly influential people in the West were anticipating the return of Christ, and some in Islam expected the return of the Madhi. In Germany Johann Bengel (aka Bengal) (1687-1752), a Minister in the Lutheran Church, was the father of Swabian Pietism and of modern premillennianism (the belief that Christ will return at the beginning and not at the end of the millennium). From his study of the Biblical books of Daniel and Revelation, in 1742 Bengel used unusual arithmetic calculations to prove that Christ would return to earth and the millennium would commence in the year 1836 (T. W. Doane, *Bible Myths*, University Books, 1971, p. 242). The founder of the sizeable Methodist religion, John Wesley (1703-91) of England, wrote, "I know of no commentator on the *Bible* equal to Bengal" (*Letters*, June 24, 1788). In the early decades of the nineteenth century, "Many godly scholars, in many countries and of many denominations, simultaneously concluded from their study of *Bible* prophesy that the coming of Christ was near. Between 1820 and 1830, more than 300 clergymen of the Church of England, and twice that number of the Nonconformists, were advocating this belief. In America, a similar advent movement began, supported by 200 leading clergymen—including Presbyterians, Baptists, Congregationalists, Episcopalians and Methodists" (*Religions in America*, ed.

Leo Rosten, Simon and Schuster, 1963, p. 179). After spending many hours and days in meditation and prayer, eighteen-year-old Joseph Smith (1805-44) told his followers that he received a series of divine revelations concerning the second coming of Christ and the organization of a new Church to prepare for his return. He founded the Latter Day Saints (Mormons) for that purpose in 1830 (*Encyclopedia of Religion*, ed. Vergilius Ferm, Philosophical Library, 1945, p. 431). William Miller (1782-1849), the founder of the Seventh-day Adventist Religion, deduced from the Bible that Christ would return in 1843. This reckoning assumes Christ lived from AD 0-33, that Daniel's prophecy occurred in 457 BC, and that Christ would be crucified in 490 years (Daniel 9:24) and return to earth in 2300 years (Daniel 8:13-14). A crucifixion date of AD 26 would yield a revised estimate of 1836 for the advent of Christ. Miller had between 25,000 and 50,000 followers (Web: www.osv.org/ explore_learn/ document_viewer.php?DocID=937). Hasan al-Idwi al-Hamzawi (1806-85), following the Sufi tradition in Egypt, wrote in 1858-59 that the Madhi was born in 1839 (*The Encyclopedia of Islam*, E. J. Brill, 1986, v, p. 1237). Bab-ed-Din, the founder of the Baha'i movement, in 1844 claimed to be the Messiah or Iman who prepares the way for the coming of the Madhi (E. Royston Pike, *Encyclopedia of Religion and Religions*, Meridian Books, 1964, p. 42). There was a space between Ramakrishna's two upper teeth in the centre below the nose, a physical characteristic that some people consider to be a sign of the Madhi. In 1895, Swami Vivekananda wrote in a letter to Swami Brahmananda, "From the day Shri Ramakrishna was born dates the growth of modern India and of the Golden Age" (*CW*, VI:318).

2 Saradananda, sec. II.21.3, pp. 356-58; Swami Prabhananda, *More About Sri Ramakrishna* (Calcutta: Advaita Ashrama, 1993), pp. 115-22.

3 Prabhananda (1993), pp. 131-32; Swami Prabhananda, *First Meetings with Sri Ramakrishna* (Mylapore: Sri Ramakrishna Math, 1987), pp. 164-70; Saradananda, sec. V.7.28, p. 817; Akshay Kumar Sen, *A Portrait of Sri Ramakrishna*, Amrita Salm et al. ed. (Gol Park: The Ramakrishna Mission Institute of Culture, 1999), p. 505.

4 Mookerjee, p. 127; Prabhananda (1993), pp. 130-35, discusses other Christians who met or saw Sri Ramakrishna.

5 Saradananda, sec. IV.5.29, pp. 671-72.

6 Prabhananda (1993), p. 130.

7 Mookerjee, p. 135; Harold French, *The Swan's Wide Waters* (London: Kennikat Press, 1974), p. 33.

8 Steven Pointer, Joseph Cook, Boston Lecturer and Evangelical Apologist (Lewiston: Edwin Mellen Press, 1991), p. 65; Pundita Ramabai, "High-Caste Hindu

Widows", *Boston Monday Lectures* (July 15, 1887), pp. 251-66; Joseph Cook. Web: www.famousamericans.net/josephcook/.

9 *CW*, V:17-18.

10 Joseph Cook, *Orient* (Boston: Houghton, Mufflin, 1891), pp. vi-xv, 80, 283; Saradananda, sec. II., appendix.15, p. 372.

11 Cook (1891), pp. 110, 114-15.

12 Ibid., pp. 283, 285-86.

13 Manilal Parekh, *Brahmarshi Keshub Chunder Sen* (Rajkot: Oriental Christ House, 1926), pp. 177-78.

14 Hal French [q.v.] made the discovery that the "missionary Cook" referred to in Saradananda's biography of Ramakrishna was the same person who knew Keshab Sen in India, and spoke at the Parliament of Religions (French, 1974, pp. 33-34, 55-57). For more details on Reverend Cook, see G. Stavig, "Reverend Joseph Cook and Vedanta in the Nineteenth Century", *American Vedantist* (1998), pp. 21-26; G. Stavig, "Reverend Joseph Cook and India in the Nineteenth Century", *Religion and Society* (India) (1999), pp. 112-18; Pointer (1991), pp. 117-23, 130-33, 163-64, 206, 210.

15 The Pigot Case: *Report of the Case Pigot vs. Hastie* (Calcutta: Thos. S. Smith, 1884), pp. 1, 195, i at the end; Donald Macmillan, *The Life of Professor Hastie* (Paisley: Alexander Gardner, 1926), p. 94.

16 Saradananda, sec. V.5.3, p. 778; *Life*, I, pp. 46-48; Joseph Jaiboy, "Reverend William Hastie", *The Hindu* (June 23, 2002); on the Web type into Google: www.thehindu.com/thehindu/mag/.../2002062300310400.htm. The alumni of General Assembly's Institution include not only Swami Vivekananda but also the founders of Self Realization Fellowship (Paramahansa Yogananda) and Krishna Consciousness (A. C. Bhaktivedanta), along with Brahmabandhab Upadhyaya and Swami Gambhirananda.

17 Ursula King, "Bankim Chandra Chatterjee's Reinterpretation of Hinduism", *Religion* (1977), pp. 132, 140.

18 The Pigot Case (1884), pp. 1-6, 195-96, 229-30, 329-30, i-v; Macmillan (1926), pp. 94-97, 100-01, 157-59; Kenneth Ballhatchet, *Race, Sex and Class Under the Raj* (London: Weidenfeld and Nicholson, 1980), pp. 112-16; on the Web type into Google: www.thehindu.com/thehindu/mag/.../ 2002062300310400.htm.

19 Personal email correspondence with Sally Harrower, Archival Historian for the National Library of Scotland, Manuscripts Division; *Maharani of Cooch Behar, Autobiography of an Indian Princess* (New Delhi: Tarang, 1921, 1995).

20 Macmillan (1926), pp. 202, 226, 279, 284-85, 297-303; Macmillan appears to have left out Hastie's translation of Kant's *Metaphysics of Morals*; on the Web

type into Google: www.thehindu.com/thehindu/mag/.../2002062300310400.htm; for a list of Hastie's books see UCLC and type in "Hastie, W".

21 *CW*, I:86, 407; III:511; VI:97; VII:287; VIII:97.

22 Ibid., II:155.

23 CA (2003), vol. 209.

24 Edwin Arnold, *India Revisited* (Boston: Roberts Brothers, 1886), pp. 321-22, 324; M. Sivaramkrishna, ed., *Perspectives on Ramakrishna-Vivekananda Vedanta Tradition* (New Delhi; Sterling Publishers, 1991), p. 80.

25 Prabhananda (1993), pp. 133-35.

26 D. G. Crawford, *Roll of the Indian Medical Service* (London: W. Thacker, 1930), p. 151; D. G. Crawford, *A History of the Indian Medical Service* (2 vols.; London: W. Thacker, 1914), II, pp. 427-28, 435, 438; Prabhananda (1993), pp. 133-35; Web: using Google, type in, "John Martin Coates" army list 1873.

27 Mookerjee, pp. 133-34; *VFEW* (Nov-Dec. 1972), pp. 6-7.

28 Web: www.eng.vedanta.ru/library/prabuddha_bharata/sri_ramakrishna's_impact_on_contemporary_indian_society_may04.php; WorldCat.

29 Max Müller, "A Real Mahatman", *Nineteenth Century* (Aug. 1896), pp. 317-18.

30 Burke, III, p. 376.

31 *Reminiscences*, pp. 296-97; *Journal of the Royal Asiatic Society*, Jan. 1923, pp. 152-54.

32 Basu, pp. 86-88; *TLWG*, p. 233; Web: wapedia.mobi/en/ Presidency_College,_Kolkata.

33 *India Office List* (London: Harrison, 1900); Buckland, p. 415; UCLC; Web: www.wollamshram.ca/1001/Ocean/oosPreface.pdf.

34 Datta, Pt. I, ch. VI.

35 Basu, p. 491; *Brahmavadin* (May 23, 1896).

36 Frances Willard and M. Livermore, *American Women* (New York: Mast, Crowell & Kirkpatrick, 1897), p. 491; *PB* (Sept. 1914), p. 179.

37 Burke, IV, pp. 170-71; Basu, p. 96.

38 Radhakrishnan, p. 51; Swami Nikhilananda, tr., *The Gospel of Sri Ramakrishna*, pp. 253-55.

39 *CW*, IV:280.

40 Müller (1896), p. 309.

41 Burke, IV, pp. 290-91.

42 DNB 1922-30 (1953), pp. 161-62; UCLC.

43 Basu, pp. 607-08.

44 Lewis Janes, "American Vedantism", *Outlook* (Feb. 19, 1898), p. 466; "American Vedantism Once More", *Outlook* (March 19, 1898), p. 740 on APS.

45 *CW*, IV:160, 279, 411, 414-15, 417; V:109, 111, 114, 203; VI:362-63; VIII:378, 380-81.

46 Ibid., IV:411, 414-15.

47 *The Literary Digest* (April 2, 1898), pp. 408-10.

48 *CW*, IV:279; V:109:111.

49 Ibid., VI:364.

50 Ibid., IV:409-21.

51 BRMIC (May 1993), p. 164: WorldCat.

52 Aseshananda, p. 20.

53 Burke, IV, pp. 168-72, 197, 272-74, 289-99; Tathagatananda2, pp. 208-09, 285-89; *CW*, IV:411; V:111.

54 F. Max Müller, *Ramakrishna His Life and Sayings* (Calcutta: Advaita Ashrama, 2001), p. 58.

55 Tributes to Sri Ramakrishna Paramahamsa. Web: www.hinduism.fsnet.co.uk/namoma/tributes.htm.

56 *The Life and Letters of Friedrich Max Müller*, ed. Georgina Müller (London: Longmans, Green, 1902), p. 399.

57 Basu, p. 210.

58 *Brahmavadin* (Dec. 15, 1898), pp. 191, 209.

59 *New York Tribune* (Mar. 11, 1899), p. 10.

60 *The Literary World* (Apr. 29, 1899), p. 138.

61 NCAB (1896), VI, p. 46; *American Women* (New York: Mast, Crowell & Kirkpatrick, 1897), I, p. 140.

62 *New World* (Sept. 1899), pp. 563ff.

63 Schaff-Herzog Encyclopedia. Web: www.ccel.org/ccel/schaff/encyc01.ii.ii.htm.

64 *American Journal of Theology* (Oct. 1899), pp. 761-62.

65 *The American Journal of Philology* (1902), pp. 351-353; *Journal of the American Oriental Society* (1903), pp. 1-6; JSTOR; Marc Aurel Stein. Web: http://en.wikipedia.org/wiki/Marc_Aurel_Stein.

66 *Biblical World* (Oct. 1899), p. 318; Bhattacharya, p. 794; Riddick, p. 344.

67 *The American Historical Review* (Dec. 1899), pp. 347-49 on GBS; JSTOR.

68 Tathagatananda2, pp. 67, 454-55; DAB (1928-1936).

69 Tathagatananda2, p. 67; Maurice Bloomfield, *The Religion of the Veda* (New York: AMS Press, 1908), pp. 228-29; Riepe, pp. 132-34.

70 *Revue De L'Histoire Des Religions* (1899), pp. 287-88; translated by Karl Whitmarsh of the Vedanta Society of Southern California.

71 Tathagatananda2, pp. 201-04; Gambhirananda pp. 341-42.

72 Londhe, #27. Sylvain Lévi.

73 Arthur Pfungst. Web: http://hpd-online.de/node/1315. To get an English language version plug this website into the Google Translator at Web: http://translate.google.com; Luzac's Oriental List (July-Aug. 1901), p. 144.

74 *Brahmavadin* (March 1900), pp. 335-44.

CHAPTER II

TWENTIETH AND TWENTY-FIRST CENTURY EUROPEAN BIOGRAPHERS, TRANSLATORS, AND TRIBUTES

SWAMI VIVEKANANDA had a great Irish disciple named Sister Nivedita (1867-1911) [q.v.]. In *Kali the Mother* (1900), she wrote this of Ramakrishna:

So large loomed the Divine through him, that many of those who knew and loved him then, speak his name to this day with bated breath, calling him, "Our Lord". For in the case of Ramakrishna, innumerable prayers and unheard-of austerities had culminated in a realization so profound that there was scarcely a memory of selfhood left. The man who lived and moved before his disciples was a mere shell, that could not fail to act as the indwelling motherhood willed. He never used, it is said, the expression "I" and "mine", preferring "He who dwells here" (indicating His own heart), or usually "My holy Mother". That his original physique must have been extraordinary, we can infer, since it stood the strain under which his religious yearning hurried it, for fifty years. But far more wonderful was the complexity and many-sidedness of character and of development, that made him feel the perplexities of every heart as if they were his own....

An unlettered peasant, from the Brahmins of the villages, scarcely able to read and write he seemed, yet if original thought and wide reading are enough, he was a profound scholar. For he had a remarkable ear and memory that made him retain the sounds of the Sanskrit perfectly, with the translation, and as a vast quantity of literature was read and recited to him from time to time, he had acquired in this way an uncommonly large store.[1]

Nivedita also made this astute comment:

> To belong to a new sect does not often have the effect of opening a man's heart to all about him. Sects, as a rule, unite us to the few, but separate us from the many.... Sri Ramakrishna represents a synthesis in one person, of all the leaders [Shankara, Chaitanya, Nanak, Ramanuja, and Madhva]. It follows that the movement of his age will unify and organize the more provincial and fragmentary movements of the past.[2]

In his book *Prosperous India* of 1901, William Digby (1849-1904), an accomplished author of several political science texts, made the following statement:

> During the last century the finest fruit of British intellectual eminence was, probably, to be found in Robert Browning and John Ruskin. Yet they are mere gropers in the dark compared with the uncultured and illiterate Rama Krishna, of Bengal, who, knowing naught of what we term "learning", spake as no other man of his age spoke, and revealed God to weary mortals.[3]

We do not know whether Digby or Charles Tawney ever came in contact with Swami Vivekananda or his brother disciples. Digby had been a journalist in England (1868-71) and Ceylon (1871-76), and also the editor of the *Madras Times* (1877-79). The Indian government decorated him for the great humanitarian work he performed on the Famine Relief Funds in South India (Madras, Bombay and Mysore). Writing to the *London Times* in the year 1877, he created a sensation by successfully appealing for 800,000 pounds in four months, thereby saving an estimated four million lives. After returning to England, Digby became the secretary of the National Liberal Club (1882-87), a senior partner in the firm William Hutchinson & Co. East India Merchants (1887-1904), the founding director of the Indian Political Agency (1888-92), secretary of the British Committee of the Indian National Congress (1889-1902), and the editor of their journal *India* (1890-92). As the author of several texts, he was highly critical of British rule and advocated self-government for the Indians. According to William Digby's estimate, between 1757 and 1815, one billion pounds was transferred from India to the British banks, thereby contributing significantly to England's rapid industrial growth.[4]

Maurice Bloomfield

Joseph Cook

Sylvain Lévi

Max Müller

Arthur Pfungst

Georg Feuerstein

Sigmund Freud

Carl Jung

Hermann Keyserling

Hans Küng

Thomas Mann

Gustav Meyrink

Romain Rolland

Arnold Toynbee

Frithjof Schuon

Albert Schweitzer

Francis Younghusband

Heinrich Zimmer

Joseph Campbell

Ananda Coomaraswamy

Philip Glass

Gerald Heard

Lex Hixon

Aldous Huxley

Gerald Larson

Thomas Merton

Amado Nervo

B. F. Skinner

Huston Smith

Pitirim Sorokin

Eugene Wigner

Chester Bowles

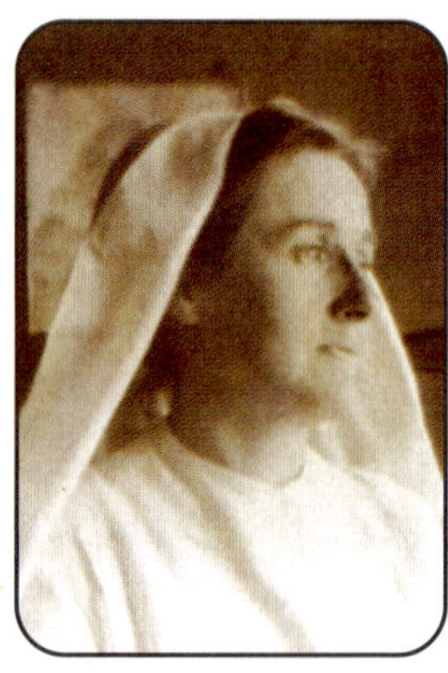
Sister Devamata

Joanne Kilgour Dowdy

Daniel Gomez-Ibanez

John Haynes Holmes

In 1902, Eric Hammond [q.v.], an admirer of Vivekananda in England, prepared an essay of over five-thousand words on Ramakrishna titled "An Eastern Saint of Today". His purpose was to acquaint the Western reader with the life and teachings of Ramakrishna. It appeared in *The Theosophical Review* and the *Brahmavadin*, and mentioned that on the 24th of February more than 30,000 people attended his birthday festival held in Calcutta.[5]

An appreciation for Ramakrishna's sayings appeared in the London based *Luzac's Oriental List* (1903) in the following book review:

> An altogether delightful little book has just been published by the Vedanta Society of New York entitled: *The Sayings of Sri Ramakrishna*. The Compiler, Swami Abhedananda, is already well known both here and in America as an exponent of Vedanta and it is not too much to say that he has given us quite the best of the great Bengali's teaching. In some respects these sayings remind us of Marcus Aurelius [AD 121-80], but there is a deeper spirituality about them, and the Oriental setting is distinctly helpful to the realization of the Divine. We would especially commend to the reader's attention the Sayings on the Ego as a servant of God.[6]

During the last decade of his life, Leo Tolstoy (1828-1910) [q.v.], the famous Russian writer, read some issues of the 1902-03 German publication *Der Theosophischer Wegweiser* (*The Theosophical Guide*), which contained several sayings and parables of Ramakrishna. Afterwards in his diary he jotted down, "There is much in common with my understanding." Tolstoy then took five of Ramakrishna's parables and entered them into his book *Wise Men for Every Day* (1903). Three years later P. A. Sergeyenko, a friend and biographer, sent him passages from Ramakrishna's teachings. Tolstoy replied to Sergeyenko stating, "Ramakrishna I know. And I have many excerpts from him.... I know Ramakrishna from theosophical journals. [But] those excellent thoughts that you have copied out are not there. Where did you take [them] from?" In this regard Tolstoy told his friend D. P. Makovitsky, "Sergeyenko has sent me excerpts from Müller's book *Ramakrishna*. He has copied out wonderful sayings. Ramakrishna died about 50 [sic] years ago. A most remarkable wise man." The following year Tolstoy told an Orthodox Christian monk, "Ramakrishna—was an Indian saint, he lived in the last century, his sayings are very good." It came as a surprise to the monk that a non-Christian could be a saint. Tolstoy explained, "Indian and Chinese religio-ethical teachings teach the same as the Christian ones." A few years later in November of 1909, Tolstoy read a copy of *The Sayings of Sri Ramakrishna Paramahamsa*, a 1905 English language book published in Madras. He selected about a hundred sayings from this book for translating and publishing in the Russian language, but he passed away before he could perform the task. Tolstoy also expressed admiration for the teachings of Swami Vivekananda and Swami Abhedananda.[7]

As a young man in 1847, Leo Tolstoy made the acquaintance of a Buddhist Lama in a Kazan hospital. From him he found out about the ethical principle of non-resistance to evil, which remained a lifelong theme for Tolstoy. He opposed the British in the Indian Sepoy Mutiny of 1857-58. After studying the works of Arthur Schopenhauer in 1869, he underwent a transformation. As a result, he felt "constant raptures over Schopenhauer and a whole series of spiritual delights ... never experienced before", and at that time he considered Schopenhauer to be "the most brilliant of men". Tolstoy hung a portrait of Schopenhauer on the wall of his study. Unfortunately, a ten-year spiritual crisis followed this revelation during 1869-79, along with an obsession with the thought of his own death. His two most insightful novels *War and Peace* (1869) and *Anna Karenina* (1877) came out at this time. During the 1870s and 1880s, he made a study of the religion, philosophy and history of India, and after 1887, he read numerous books on Buddhism. In his diaries and letters, Leo Tolstoy often enthusiastically refers to the Upanishads and the *Bhagavad Gita*. He also read the *Ramayana* as well as the *Mahabharata*, and was acquainted with the teachings of Shankara. Tolstoy greatly admired the ethical teachings of these scriptures. Because of his heterodox beliefs and actions, in 1901 the Russian Orthodox Church excommunicated him.[8]

Leo Tolstoy drew many disciples to his moral philosophy because of the force of his personality and his voluminous writings. Soon after it was published in 1894, Mahatma Gandhi was greatly inspired by his book *The Kingdom of God is Within You*. Gandhi wrote, "It left an indelible impression.... faced with the independent thinking, deep morality and truthfulness of this book." In 1928 Gandhi recalled, "When I was passing through a severe crisis of skepticism and doubt, I came across this book *The Kingdom of God is Within You*, and was deeply impressed by it. I was at that time a believer in violence. Its reading cured me of my skepticism and made me a firm believer in ahimsa." Tolstoy Farm was the name given to Gandhi's dwelling place in South Africa. Toward the end of his life, Tolstoy and Gandhi exchanged letters during 1909-10. Gandhi sought Tolstoy's consent to translate and circulate among the Indians in South Africa his "Letter to an Indian" in 1908, which advocated nonviolent resistance to British rule. Tolstoy asserted that Indians should not actively participate in the British government by refusing to take jobs as soldiers, tax collectors, and law court personnel. In the last year of his life, after he read Gandhi's book on *Indian Home Rule*, Tolstoy expressed his opposition to colonial imperialism, his support for the suppressed Indians, and the use of civil disobedience and nonviolence to bring about these ends.[9]

By 1908 Tolstoy was a firm believer in reincarnation. In a letter he stated, "As we live through thousands of dreams in our present life, so is our present life only one of many thousands of such lives which we enter from the other, more real life ... and then return after death. Our life is but one of the dreams of that more real life, and so it is endlessly, until the very last one, the very real life,—the life in God.... I wish you would understand me; I am not playing, not inventing this: I believe in it, I see it without doubt."[10]

After Tolstoy's death one of his followers, Ivan F. Nazhivin (1874-1940) [q.v.], translated and published Max Müller's *Ramakrishna His Life and Teachings* (*Shri Ramakrishna Paramagamza*, 1913) into Russian. In doing so, he purposely deleted some of Ramakrishna's sayings. Nazhivin had formerly translated some of Vivekananda's writings. The following year *The Gospel of Ramakrishna* (*Provozviestie Ramakrishny*) translated by Swami Abhedananda with a Foreword and Introduction was rendered into Russian in St. Petersburg, and reprinted in 1931 in Riga, the capital of Latvia. These volumes are now housed at Stanford University as part of the Konstantinoff and John Gladchenko Collections.[11]

Julius Baumann (1837-1916), a believer in reincarnation, was a professor of philosophy at the University of Goettingen in Germany. In his *Über Religionen und Religion: Worte zur Verständigung* (*About Religions and Religion: Words for Understanding*, 1905), he wrote a seven-page synopsis of Müller's volume on Ramakrishna. He cites many of Ramakrishna's sayings and speaks of him as a saint, a servant of all men and women who looked upon others as if they were divine, and says that he was the same soul as Rama and Krishna, that others considered his spiritual wisdom to be the result of genius and practical observation, and that he taught universal tolerance.[12]

In 1909 Lewis Sydney Steward O'Malley (1874-1941) [q.v.] of the Indian Civil Service and Monmohan Chakravarti [q.v.] of the provincial civil service in Bengal wrote up an account of the Howrah District in Bengal, with a dimension of 510 square miles and a population of 850,000. O'Malley later authored *History of Bengal, Bihar & Orissa under British Rule* (1925), and *The Indian Civil Service, 1601-1930*. The book stated in part:

> Ramakrishna went with him [Ramkumar] to Dakshineswar, and there for 12 years practised yoga (meditation on and rapt communion with God) under a big banyan tree, which is still pointed out to the visitors. His asceticism and religious fervour, his poetical and mystical view of life, combined, however, with homely common sense, began to attract attention; Keshab Chandra Sen of the Brahmo Samaj being the first to bring him to the notice of the educated classes of society in Calcutta. He found many admirers.

In addition, many nice things are said in the book about Ramakrishna, drawn from excerpts taken from Müller's *Ramakrishna His Life and Sayings*.[13]

Also relying on Müller's biography, along with Abhedananda's *Gospel of Sri Ramakrishna* and Vivekananda's *My Master*, John Nicol Farquhar (1861-1929) [q.v.], a liberal Christian Congregationalist missionary, devoted fourteen pages to Sri Ramakrishna in his *Modern Religious Movements in India* (1915). He provided photos of Ramakrishna, Vivekananda, and the famous drawing of "Ramakrishna Teaching Keshab the Harmony of All Religions", which he described. In further appreciation, Farquhar wrote:

> It was his teaching on the religions that laid hold of his disciples. He impressed all who came in contact with him as a most sincere soul, a God-intoxicated man; but what distinguished his message from the teaching of others was his defense of everything Hindu and his theory that all religions are true. This gave his teaching a universalistic turn, and provided the ordinary Hindu with a defense which he could use to meet Christian criticism and the Brahma Samaj.
>
> His personal influence over all who came within his range was very remarkable. Mozoomdar says, "My mind is still floating in the luminous atmosphere which that wonderful man diffuses around him whenever and wherever he goes. My mind is not yet disenchanted of the mysterious and indefinable pathos which he pours into it whenever he meets me." Over his personal disciples he exercised a still more wonderful power. Their love and reverence for him was boundless. They worshipped him.[14]

To overcome mutual exclusion, John Farquhar, who served the London Missionary Society at Calcutta from 1891 to 1923, sought a more satisfactory relation between Hinduism and Christianity. His goal was to bring about a new missionary evaluation of non-Christian religions. In *The Crown of Hinduism* issued in 1913, he explains his interesting "fulfillment theory". Farquhar considers higher Hinduism to be a valid and legitimate religion, but he believed it will eventually be "reproduced in perfect form, completely fulfilled, consummated in Christ". Following an evolutionary approach, he held the position that the best in Hinduism is fulfilled and perfected in Christianity. Many educated Westerners learned about the religion of India from his literary productions that include: *Permanent Lessons of the Gita* (1912), *A Primer of Hinduism* (1912), *Modern Religious Movements in India* (1915), and the scholarly *An Outline of the Religious Literature of India* (1920). After returning to England, he became a professor of comparative religion at Manchester University, succeeding after an eight-year interval the eminent Buddhist scholar T. W. Rhys Davids (1843-1922).[15]

The *Sedition Committee 1918 Report* was put out by its president, the Honourable Justice Sir Sidney Rowlatt (1862-1945) [q.v.], judge of the King's Bench Division of His Majesty's High Court of Justice, along with five others. A scholarly judge with energy and affability, he is "best remembered for his controversial presidency of the Rowlatt committee, a sedition committee appointed in 1918 by the British Indian Government to evaluate the links between political terrorism in India, especially Bengal and Punjab, and the German government and the Bolsheviks in Russia." Because of some revolutionary activity in India, the commission recommended the harsh and unpopular Rowlatt Act of 1919.[16]

While the Rowlatt Commission was highly critical of some subversive Indian organizations, conversely their view of the Ramakrishna Mission was very favourable. For example, they mention:

> In 1886 had died the Bengali ascetic Rama Krishna. He was undoubtedly a remarkable and purely religious man. He strongly defended Hinduism but taught that all religions were true, that all deities were manifestations of the impersonal Supreme, and that Brahmin disdain of low castes was wrong. To him the goddess Kali was the goddess of divine strength, although another of her attributes is destruction. She was his mother and the mother of the universe. If he worshipped through idols, it was because he

believed that these idols were filled with the presence of the Divinity. He taught social service as the service of humanity.[17]

A Christian Socialist (Unterneubrunn), Pastor Carl (Karl) Theodor Vogl (1866-1944) produced two German language biographies of Ramakrishna, one with the title *Srî Ramakrischna, der Letzte Indische Prophet* (*Sri Ramakrishna, the Last Indian Prophet*), published in Vienna, Austria, in 1921, and the other titled *Sri Ramakrischna, ein Prophet des Neuerwachenden Indien* (*Sri Ramakrishna, a Prophet of the Awakening India*) in 1927.* The 1921 edition shows a full-page picture of Ramakrishna standing with Hriday. One of his biographies of Ramakrishna was reprinted in 1991. In his writings, Vogl imparted to his reader teachings like the following. When someone asked Ramakrishna:

> "Why don't you employ your yogic powers to heal yourself?" He replied, "These powers of the soul have been consecrated to the Lord; do you expect me to take them back again and use them on the body, which is nothing more that a prison for the soul?"

A well-known German novelist Gustav Meyer Meyrink (1868-1932) penned the Foreword for Vogl's 1921 biography of Ramakrishna.[18] Meyrink mentions:

> In the book, Pastor Dr. Carl Vogl tells about the prophet Ramakrishna and his experiences with such in-depth knowledge and such a high level of detail.... Swamis Vivekananda and Abhedananda came to Europe.... Sri Ramakrishna, a prophet greater than Muhammad, lived during our lifetime.... a professor like Max Müller certainly would not have spoken and written of Ramakrishna with the extreme enthusiasm that he did, if he did not see the towering personality that Ramakrishna was.[19]

Being a popular Austro-German writer of satire, Meyrink vigorously opposed war, modern materialism, the police, military, clergy and medical profession, academia, financiers, and the German literary establishment. As a result, a writer's association considered him to be a public enemy. His most

---

* See Appendix VII for European language translations of books on Sri Ramakrishna.

acclaimed 1915 novel *The Golem* was made into movies in Germany, France, and Poland. Meyrink made an intensive study of theosophy, Christian and Jewish mysticism, and Eastern religions and philosophies, particularly Buddhism, all of which were present in his writings. As a practitioner of yoga, he claimed to have made telepathic contact with Sri Ramana Maharshi (1879-1950). Meyrink also came out with a German translation of *Nature's Finer Forces: The Science of Breath and the Philosophy of the Tattvas* (1894) by Rama Prasad.[20]

Lieutenant Colonel Sir Francis Younghusband (1863-1942) devoted eleven pages of his book, *The Gleam* (1923), to a brief sketch of Ramakrishna along with an appreciation. Among other things he wrote:

> And so wonderful was his purity of soul, his childlike innocence, his perfect unselfishness, and the simplicity of the language in which he propounded the highest truths of religion and philosophy, that he profoundly influenced not only the humbler folk, but men of the highest spiritual attainment like Keshub Chunder Sen, Vivekananda and Mazoomdar.
>
> "He who yearns for God finds Him," and "he finds God quickest whose yearning and concentration are the greatest," was one of his sayings. And those who knew Rama Krishna speak of his being deluged with Divine bliss, and of his heart being immersed in the depths of holy love and overflowing with its Divine fervour....
>
> But in any case Rama Krishna did by his life and teaching bear witness to the reality of God and the value of spiritual things at the very time when cold waves of materialism were spreading over India from the West, and when doubts were being thrown upon the value of religion and the very existence of God. And this, in Svabhava's [referring to himself] view, was the greatest service he did to India.[21]

Eight years later, in his book *Dawn in India* (1931) Younghusband emphasized other aspects of Ramakrishna's nature:

> Rama Krishna was gentle, sympathetic, and loving.... He himself was of a peculiarly religious and lovable disposition, and from his childhood, through all his life, made religion his supreme interest.... Rama Krishna believed the image of Kali in his temple to be living and breathing and taking food out of his hand. He would sit for hours singing hymns and talking and praying to her as a child to his mother and begging her to reveal

> herself more fully to him. His whole soul would melt in a flood of tears as he appealed to her.... The great idea he conceived was of the *Motherhood* of God. In his early stages, when worshipping the image of Kali, he would look upon it as his mother and the mother of the whole universe. God was not so much our Father as our Mother. And he would weep for hours when he could not see his Mother as perfectly as he would have wished.... No one could be more humble than Rama Krishna in his ordinary everyday state. He would regard himself as the servant of all men and women and would perform the most menial offices. Yet in his moments of God-consciousness he would regard himself as an actual incarnation of God.... Rama Krishna, as I have said, made no attempt to start a new religion or found a new sect. But by his intense spirituality, by his combined meekness and unlimited confidence, and by his sweet lovability, he profoundly impressed such men as Keshub Chunder Sen and Vivekananda. And since his death a Rama Krishna Mission has been founded which teaches a wider conception of spirituality, that sees the value of renunciation and sacrifice for the good of others, and fully recognizes each man's responsibility for others.[22]

At the birth centenary of Sri Ramakrishna held in India in March 1937, Sir Francis Younghusband is pictured speaking to Swami Shuddhananda (1872-1938), the then Vice-President of the Ramakrishna Math and Mission. The Swami single-handedly translated the entire eight volumes of the *Complete Works of Swami Vivekananda* from English to Bengali, using a sweet and powerful language. There Younghusband proclaimed, "For many years past I have had the profoundest admiration for the great Saint whose Centenary is being celebrated now." He addressed the subject of "Sri Ramakrishna: Apostle of Religious Harmony" stating:

> I have travelled all the way from England to attend the Celebrations of the Centenary of Sri Ramakrishna because of the very great and deep regard which I have had for many years for the great work of Sri Ramakrishna. I was first drawn to him, because he, more than any other man, expounded the great yet simple principle of not merely tolerating other religions, but deeply appreciating them and penetratingly entering into them. I speak as a Christian, and what profoundly moved me was the way in which the great Saint entered into our Christian religion, entered into the very simple life and teachings of Christ. In a way, we Christians were able to understand our own religion better by the way in which he had entered into it.... Great

> men like the Saint Sri Ramakrishna come into this world from time to time, and we humbler individuals have to make the most of this great privilege of knowing their worth, knowing their life, and we have to look to them and try to enter into their spirit.[23]

Sir Francis Younghusband was born in Muree, India. An explorer, soldier, mystic and author, Major Younghusband served as British commissioner to Tibet during 1902-04, negotiating the Anglo-Tibetan Peace Treaty at Lhasa. He was the first Westerner to enter Lhasa in over a half a century. In December of 1903, Swami Abhedananda publicly denounced the military invasion of Tibet, which led to a war. He believed the invasion was due to greed and, if it persists, will bring immorality to the country. Miraculously, in 1904 Younghusband had a mystical experience in the mountains of Tibet that convinced him that "men at heart are divine", and he regretted the invasion of the country. The experience left a lasting mark on Younghusband who devoted a portion of his future life to religious studies.

Younghusband typified the best of the old-style British patriots during the British Empire period. In 1919 he was elected president of the Royal Geographical Society. A courageous soldier and explorer, he was deeply sympathetic to the aspirations and spiritual ideals of Eastern religions. He also favoured self-government for India as a whole. His extensive explorations in the Gobi Desert, Himalayas, and Tibet are discussed in his numerous writings. A gifted extempore speaker, he authored a number of mystical works, including *Life in the Stars* (1927), *The Living Universe* (1933), and *Modern Mystics* (1935), where, using extensive quotations, he has devoted thirty-one pages to the life of Sri Ramakrishna and eleven to Swami Vivekananda. To promote religious unity, Younghusband founded the World Congress of Faiths (WCF) in 1936 and devoted the remaining years of his life to its objectives. To this day the WCF continues to promote understanding between people of different faiths through conferences, a journal, retreats, visits and group travel. Its present patrons include the Dalai Lama, Reverend Desmond Tutu, and Diana Eck at Harvard University.[24]

In the book *The Heart of Aryavarta* (1925), the former governor of Bengal Lord Ronaldshay (a.k.a. Lawrence Zetland, 1876-1961) [q.v.] devoted eleven pages to Sri Ramakrishna and told his readers:

> It was here that the famous saint of Dakshineswar spent the greater part of his life. Few men have made a deeper impress upon the mind of

> Bengal in recent years than Gadadhar Chatterji, known to history as Sri Ramakrishna Paramahamsa, and his chief disciple Narendra Nath Dutt, better known under the title of Swami Vivekananda. At a time when the craze for the ideas and ways of the West was at its height, these men stood for the ancient ideal of the East, for renunciation in an age of megalomania, for simplicity at a time when discoveries in mechanical science were making life elaborately complex.... It is clear from the testimony of his disciple that he himself constantly attained that pitch of spiritual exaltation which is called by the Hindus Samadhi, a state of trance induced by God-consciousness—that communion with the Infinite enjoyed by the Rishis of old and spoken of by Professor B. N. Sen as the bliss of Brahman, which is beyond all words and above all reason.[25]

In the book Lord Ronaldshay presents a sketch of the life and teachings of Ramakrishna drawn from the account given by "M", the recorder of the *Gospel*. He also twice quotes from Swamiji's book *Bhakti Yoga*. Ronaldshay, the president of the Royal Asiatic Society (1928-31) and the secretary of state for India (1937-40), found out about Ramakrishna when he was the governor of Bengal during the years 1917-22. As governor, on Ramakrishna's birthday he paid a visit to the Belur Math in 1919. Swami Saradananda told him about the Mission's secular activities and escorted him to the Ramakrishna Temple. Lord Ronaldshay came to the conclusion that the Ramakrishna Order stands

> for renunciation and service respectively, declared by the late Swami Vivekananda to be the two national ideals of India. The Mission undertakes service of all kinds, social, charitable, and educational. The monasteries are dedicated to the perpetuation through their spiritual culture of the great Ideal and Revelation which Sri Ramakrishna Paramahamsa embodied in his life.[26]

Ronaldshay sent a message to the Ramakrishna Centenary Parliament of Religions, which commenced on March 1, 1937 in Calcutta, telling them:

> I still carry with me vivid and happy memories of my contacts with office-bearers and members of the Ramakrishna Mission during the period of my sojourn in Bengal, and I feel sure that the fact that the gathering is

being held under the auspices of the Mission is in itself a guarantee of its success.[27]

An appreciative review of the *Life of Sri Ramakrishna* published by the Advaita Ashrama appeared in the English *Quarterly Review*, which emphasized his human nature:

> Out of these many words, the figure of Ramakrishna emerges as, with all his unaffected saintliness, helpfully human. His love of sweetstuffs, his simplicity and naive humour, his extraordinary faculty for losing himself, almost accidentally at any odd moment, in the ecstasies of trance, combine to make him a living person, a true man, with the becoming weaknesses of normal humanity; but that is not all, for in spite of his eager Hinduism and passion for Kali, the divine Mother ... he had the gift of an exalted charity and an unusual breadth of mind. Brahmin as he was, he studied Islam sympathetically, and followed the teachings of Christ. "The Lord is one," said he, "but he is called by a thousand names."[28]

Earlier, on June 15, 1914 Josephine MacLeod (Tantine) sent a letter to her sister from Los Angeles, mentioning her meeting with a young Dhan Gopal Mukherji (1890-1936). She wrote, "I have certainly found here in Mr. Mukherji a new expression of India. Brilliant, strong mind, somehow my responsibility to India is suddenly lifted to his shoulders." Two days later she added, "I've poured out all my heart of all the wealth that Swamiji poured into me—on him [Mr. Mukherji]—and now my work is done and I feel a curious lightness." As a young man Mr. Mukherji chose to forsake his ancestral occupation as a Bengali Brahmin priest, realizing that was not his right place in life. He studied at the University of Calcutta and Tokyo, and later became a graduate student and lecturer in comparative literature at Stanford University in California. During his lifetime, he became well known as a prolific author of many volumes and was highly praised for a series of books written for children. He is considered to be the first Asian Indian writer of significance in the United States. In 1922, Josephine MacLeod took Mukherji to Swami Shivananda, the second President of the Ramakrishna Order, who gave him initiation. Four years later he composed a more imaginative than factual life of Ramakrishna with the title *The Face of Silence*. Mukherji acknowledged his debt to Josephine MacLeod by dedicating the book to her and to three others as "those who pointed me the path".

The League of Nations selected the work as one of forty outstanding books of 1926, to become part of the International Library of Geneva. Two years later he came out with *A Son of Mother India Answers*, which was a rejoinder to Katherine Mayo's recently published diatribe titled *Mother India*.[29]

Concerning *The Face of Silence*, an evaluation in the magazine *The Living Age* read:

> Rama Krishna, a holy man who literally practised what he preached, lived in India during the middle of the last century. By birth a Brahman, he came, as his spiritual life blossomed, to the point where he realized that every religion leads to God, by one path or another. By the power of his example and teaching he drew followers from every walk of life, and at his death left behind him a devoted band who followed along the path which he had trod. His was no facile eclecticism, no novel teaching: it was the translation of age-old doctrine into terms of daily practice which marked Rama Krishna as a preeminent religious teacher. The Westerner finds it hard to grasp the all-pervading sense of God which is natural to the Indian. Mr. Mukherji, by his mastery of lovely English prose, is among the few who can bring some idea of his overpowering reality home to Occidental readers.[30]

Hans Kohn (1891-1971) [q.v.], the Middle East correspondent for *Frankfurter Zeitung* and *Neue Zuercher Zeitung* between 1925 and 1933, in his book *A History of Nationalism in the East* (1929)* has included chapters on "The Religious Renaissance in India", "India's Awakening", and "Indian Nationalism". He realized that these nationalistic movements in the East were not confined to a single country but to many nations stretching from Egypt to India. About Sri Ramakrishna he expressed this view:

> This rebirth of orthodox Hinduism is associated with the public appearance of Ram Krishna.... Gradually he attained the gift of utter ecstasy. He did not seek to solve the riddle of the universe by way of knowledge, but through the service of God. He burned with the ardour of his faith and the vastness of his transcendental experience.... His influence grew. His activities came at a time when the educated youth of India was looking yearningly towards the West. He preached the East to them in his words and his life. In an age which, under European influence, aimed at self-asser-

* Originally published in German in 1928.

tion and self-realization, he taught renunciation and asceticism. In contrast to a life devoted to the cult of comfort and machinery and growing more and more elaborate by reason of new discoveries, he held up the example of great simplicity. And herein precisely lay his influence over the best of India's youth. Pratap Chandra Mazumdar, the most distinguished disciple of Keshab Chandra Sen, was among Ram Krishna's devotees and experienced the miracle of his influence.

As a Jewish refugee, Kohn immigrated to America and joined the faculty at Smith College (1934-41), became a summer professor at Harvard University (1935-58), and a professor of modern European history at the City College of the City University of New York (1949-62). He authored or edited an amazing forty-nine books, and held the position of president of the American Association for Adult Education and honorary president of the International Society for the History of Ideas.[31]

Romain Rolland and After

Saddened by the horrifying effects of the First World War, Romain Rolland (1866-1944) [q.v.], the celebrated French novelist, sought the truth that would bring peace and harmony to the modern world. His belief in nonviolence led to his 1923 biography of *Mahatma Gandhi*, which Catherine D. Groth translated into English. Rolland discovered Ramakrishna when he read Mukherji's *The Face of Silence*, after which he sent Dhan Gopal Mukherji an invitation to visit his home in Switzerland. The two met on October 4, 1926, and at that time Rolland's interest in Ramakrishna and Vivekananda increased significantly. In *The Life of Ramakrishna*, first released in 1929, Rolland expresses his appreciation to Dhan Gopal Mukherji, "I can never forget that it was to the perusal of this beautiful book that I owe my first knowledge of Ramakrishna and the impetus leading me to undertake this work. I here record my gratitude."[32]

Rolland conversed about his visit to Switzerland along with Josephine MacLeod during May 13-16, 1927, and wrote that he received "a whole library of books" on Ramakrishna and Vivekananda "through the medium of Miss MacLeod". Her visit also motivated him to write biographies about Ramakrishna and Vivekananda. He received aid in this endeavour from "Swami Shivananda who", he said, "has been good enough to give me his precious personal memories of the Master", and also from Swami Ashokananda* "who", he remarked, "was never wearied of my unwearied questions, but has answered them with the most precise erudition. It was he who gave me the most complete information with regard to the actual position of the Ramakrishna Mission."[33] Ashokananda wrote a letter to Rolland "asking his opinion about the lives and teachings of Ramakrishna and Vivekananda in whom ... he was deeply interested." In reply, Rolland sent the Swami a letter dated June 26, 1927, telling him in part:

> A year ago some pages of Dhan Gopal Mukherjee [Mukherji] revealed to me the great soul of Sri Ramakrishna, and this revelation has excited me to know more of his life and thoughts. For several years my sister and myself have read books published by the Prabuddha Bharata Office or from the Ramakrishna Mission, that our Indian friends were kind enough to send us. The last month we had a visit from Miss M. [Josephine MacLeod] and during the days we passed together we often spoke of the Swami Vivekananda. I look upon the Swami Vivekananda as a dynamo of spiritual force and Sri Ramakrishna as a river of Love. Both of them reveal God and life eternal. And the most genial is Vivekananda. But Ramakrishna is above him in genius. I wish to dedicate to them a book which would make them known to the great masses of the West.[34]

In a letter of September 12 dispatched to Swami Shivananda, the President of the Ramakrishna Math and Mission, Rolland explained one of his reasons for writing the biography:

> Our epoch, too intellectualistic as it is, has a tendency to doubt the human existence of all the superhuman personalities of history.... One sees today those who deny that Jesus or Buddha had ever existed. It will not be slow in doing the same for Sri Ramakrishna, if his living witnesses do not leave in writing the proof of his life amongst them on earth.[35]

Romain Rolland, in his famous biography the *Life of Sri Ramakrishna*, paid him the following tribute:

* Later the Head of the Vedanta Society of San Francisco.

> And it is because Ramakrishna, more fully than any other man, not only conceived but realized in himself the total Unity of this river of God, open to all rivers and all streams, that I have given him my love; and I shall have drawn a little of his sacred water to slake the great thirst of the world.... I am bringing to Europe, as yet unaware of it, the fruit of a new autumn, a new message of the Soul, the symphony of India, bearing the name of Ramakrishna.... The man whose image I here evoke was the consummation of two thousand years of the spiritual life of three hundred million people. Although he has been dead forty years, his soul animates modern India. He was no hero of action like Gandhi, no genius in art or thought like Gandhi or Tagore. He was a little village Brahmin of Bengal whose outer life was set in a limited frame without striking incident, outside the political and social activities of his time. But his inner life embraced the whole multiplicity of men and Gods. It was a part of the very source of Energy, the Divine Shakti, of whom Vidyapati, the old poet of Mithila, and Ramprasad of Bengal sing.... Ramakrishna expressly maintains that it is absurd to pretend that the world is unreal so long as we form part of it, and receive from it for the maintenance of our own identity the unquenchable conviction (although hidden in our own lantern) of its reality. Even the saint who comes down from Samadhi (ecstasy) to the plane of ordinary life is forced to return to the envelope of his "differentiated" ego, however attenuated and purified. He is flung back into the world of relativity. "So far as his ego is relatively real to him, so far will this world also be real; but when his ego has been purified, he sees the whole world of phenomena as the manifold manifestation of the Absolute to the senses."[36]

It is important to realize that one of the main reasons that Romain Rolland was interested in Ramakrishna and Vivekananda is because he himself was a mystic. Louis Beirnaert tells us that at the age of 63, Rolland stressed the profound effect of his early mystical experiences on the course of his life. In a letter of 1929 written to Beirnaert, Rolland revealed:

> I had, between the ages of 15 and 20 ... several brief and staggering contacts with the Unity. These obscure illuminations were the key to the spiritual world where I lived for the next forty years. I passionately explored this world among the trials and torments of my life of flesh and blood, here and there visited by new revelations.[37]

Rolland was known to the public as a French novelist, biographer, musicologist, historian, critic, and dramatist. In 1915 he received the Nobel Prize in literature, primarily for his ten-volume novel *Jean Christophe*. He contributed the money he received for the prize entirely to charitable causes. Rolland, an outspoken internationalist, pacifist and humanist, wanted to help in unifying the nations of the world. After the First World War, he sought the aid of other prominent European intellectuals to establish an international community. As a result, he organized the International Congress against War and Fascism in 1932. Six years later Rolland, accompanied by Jean Herbert, met Swami Siddheswarananda (1897-1957) who had established a Vedanta Centre in Paris. After France was invaded in 1940, Siddheswarananda and one or two close devotees moved to Madame Verdier's apartment building near the city of Montpellier in the south of France. After the war ended, the Swami established the Ramakrishna Ashrama in Gretz, France, in 1947.[38]

Rolland was not familiar with English and the history and languages of India. Consequently his sister Madeleine, a dedicated helper, translated the English works verbally to him in French. Nevertheless, his biographies of Ramakrishna and Vivekananda were a tremendous success. Rolland mentioned that after the French author Jean Herbert travelled to India, he learned from him that "the whole Ramakrishna Order recognizes that the widespread extension of the thought and the glory of Ramakrishna and Vivekananda is due to my [Rolland's] books."[39] In 1930 Rolland's *The Life of Ramakrishna* and *The Life of Vivekananda* were rendered from the original French into the single six-hundred-page English language volume *Prophets of the New India*. This book had a great impact on Westerners and found its way into over two-hundred university and public libraries in North America. Writing from Ahmedabad, India, the translator Elizabeth Frances Malcolm-Smith (b. 1891) indicated that she came out with an Indian edition of the book for the Advaita Ashrama, Mayavati, Himalayas. She worked as a research fellow at Newnham College, Cambridge, England. Her subsequent translation published in England and the United States contains additional notes for the benefit of the Western reader. Rolland's sister and Swami Ashokananda reviewed the translation before it was cast in final form. It is sad that many of the Western translators of Ramakrishna-Vedanta books like Malcolm-Smith have received so little credit for their valuable and demanding efforts. Rolland's two biographies were translated into many languages and did much to spread the message of Ramakrishna and Vivekananda.[40]

On November 10, 1931, Dhan Gopal Mukherji sent a letter to Rolland from New York, communicating his praise of Rolland's biographies on Ramakrishna and Vivekananda by stating in part:

> Now I can say without any modification that the book equals your *Beethoven* and *Jean Christophe*. This is not a book but the epic poem of the holiness of our time. You have traced the holiness of all mankind under every sentence.... Of course, the book goes beyond the limits of India and embraces the holy and the (one word here is impossible to decipher) in all humanity. This is what an epic of holiness should do. Your Ramakrishna is as simple and as fierce as the one, they, his apostles, knew. I wish Vivekananda were alive to gaze upon the portrait that you have drawn of the Master. He alone could give you the praise that you deserve. As for Vivekananda, yours is the only one that India recognizes.[41]

On December 5, 1927, during the time Rolland worked on his biography of Ramakrishna, he sent a letter to Sigmund Freud (1856-1939), the world famous Vienna psychiatrist. Rolland mentioned the "oceanic feeling" and noted that he would like Freud to "make an analysis of spontaneous religious feelings, or more exactly, religious sensations which are entirely different from religions proper and much more enduring.... the simple and direct fact of the *sensation of the Eternal*." In the letter Rolland refers to two Indians he will write about in his next two books [Ramakrishna and Vivekananda] "who have manifested a genius for thought and action powerfully regenerative for their country and for the world." Concerning this religious feeling Rolland mentioned, "I am familiar with this feeling. All my life I have never been without this feeling. I always found in this feeling a source of vital renewal. In this way I can say that I am deeply religious."[42]

Professor J. M. Masson thought that Rolland received the inspiration to use the term "oceanic feeling" after reading about Ramakrishna's mystical experience of the Divine Mother. But Rolland had used the term "oceanic feeling" back in 1888. In Rolland's biography based on the 1920-21 Madras edition of *Sri Ramakrishna, the Great Master*, Ramakrishna tells us:

> I saw an ocean of the Spirit, boundless, dazzling. In whatever direction I turned, great luminous waves were rising.... How I passed that day and the next I know not. Round me rolled an ocean of ineffable joy. And

in the depths of my being I was conscious of the presence of the Divine Mother.

In typical Freudian fashion, in *Civilization and its Discontents* (1930) he traces the "oceanic feeling" to the earliest differentiation made by the infant between itself and the external world "as regressions to primordial states of mind". Freud disavowed ever having any "oceanic feeling". However, in 1936, on the occasion of Rolland's seventieth birthday, Freud sent him an essay describing a profound experience he had way back in 1904. It said, "On this occasion I am reminded of another, very remarkable, experience. I was already a man of mature years when I stood for the first time on the hill of the Acropolis in Athens, between the temple ruins, looking out over the blue sea. A feeling of astonishment mingled with my joy." In a 1930 letter Freud mentioned, "My warm thanks for the gift" of Rolland's biographies of Gandhi, Ramakrishna and Vivekananda, adding, "I shall now try with your guidance to penetrate into" Indian thought, but he honestly admitted, "It isn't easy to pass beyond the limits of one's nature." Though they differed considerably, Freud also wrote to Rolland, "I may confess to you that I have rarely experienced that mysterious attraction of one human being for another as vividly as I have with you."[43]

Freud had some interesting contacts with the Indian religion. For example, during 1904/05, in a private conversation, the Swiss poet, Bruno Goetz (1885-1954), then a student at the University of Vienna, spoke to Sigmund Freud about Leopold von Schroeder's (1851-1920) lectures on the *Bhagavad Gita*. Von Schroeder, a professor at Wien, later in 1912 translated the *Gita* into German. As Goetz was speaking, "Freud sprang briskly to his feet and began pacing up and down the room." Freud emphasized in part:

> The *Bhagavad Gita* is a great and profound poem with awful depths.... If, however, without the aid of a clear intellect you become immersed in the world of the *Bhagavad Gita*, where nothing seems constant and where everything melts into everything else, then you are suddenly confronted by nothingness.... And yet this very nothingness is simply a European misconception: the Hindu Nirvana is not nothingness, it is that which transcends all contradictions. It is not, as Europeans commonly take it to be, a sensual enjoyment, but the ultimate in superhuman understanding, an ice-cold, all-comprehending yet scarcely comprehensible insight.... What do these European would-be mystics know about the profundity of the East?[44]

In another example, on the occasion of Sigmund Freud's 75th birthday anniversary in 1931, his good friend, Professor Girindrasekhar Bose (1887-1953), first president of the Indian Psycho-Analytic Society in Calcutta (1922-53), sent him a statuette of Vishnu with four arms on a mahogany base, presently located in the Freud Museum, London. The cover letter, which begins with "My dear Prof. Freud", mentions sending him "one ivory statuette with stand and a roll containing two copies of a Sanskrit address ... printed on silk and three copies of the same printed on paper with the translation in type." Freud replied to Dr. Bose:

> I feel gratefully elated and accept these presents ... Please give my hearty thanks to all your members and accept it especially for yourself. The statuette is charming. I give it the place of honour on my desk. As long as I can enjoy life it will recall to my mind the progress of psycho-analysis, the proud conquest it has made in foreign countries and the kind feelings for me it has aroused in some of my contemporaries at least.[45]

Back in 1922, Freud was elated when Bose initiated the first Psycho-Analytic Society on the continent of Asia in Calcutta, since he wanted psychoanalysis to become an international discipline. Freud responded by putting G. Bose's name on the cover of the *International Journal of Psychoanalysis* as one of its editors, and they maintained a long and lasting friendship.[46]

During the 1930s, there was some interest in Ramakrishna in Germany. Paul Amann (Amschelberg) (1884-1958) translated Romain Rolland's *The Life of Ramakrishna* (*Das Leben des Ramakrishna*, 1929) and *The God-Man Ramakrishna and the Universal Gospel of the Vivekananda* (*Der Gotter-Mensch Ramakrishna und Das Universale Evangelium des Vivekananda*, 1930) into the German language. The Austrian translator, novelist and poet, moved to the United States in 1941. In his published *Diary*, Christopher Isherwood refers to his friend Paul Amann whom he associated with in Los Angeles during the years 1941-42. Amann taught in Austria and at Mohawk College and Champlain College in New York State. His correspondence with the esteemed novelist Thomas Mann between 1915 and 1952 has been put into book form.[47] Also, in 1930 Emma von Pelet came out with a volume with the title *Worte des Ramakrishna* (*Words of Ramakrishna*), published in Leipzig, Germany. The book received reviews in some German journals.

In November 1930, Rolland's book on Ramakrishna and Vivekananda was reviewed by John Carter for *The Bookman: A Review of Books and Life*. He brings out the political importance of this work stating:

> Rolland has written an account of the two great religious leaders of the Hindu awakening—Ramakrishna, who was regarded in his lifetime as the reincarnation of the Divinity, and Vivekananda, who was the Saul of Tarsus of the Hindu revival. Their lives embraced the period, roughly, from the end of the rule of the East India Company to Lord Curzon's Viceroyalty. Of the two, Ramakrishna embodies Hindu mysticism at its best and purest, Vivekananda Hinduism at its most virile. Vivekananda's two missions to the West brought out in sharp relief the conflict between Hindu mysticism and Occidental materialism, which is at the heart of the Asian conflict today; his work quickened the movement led by Tagore and Ghose, which produced Gandhi. To understand Hindu Nationalism you should read this book.[48]

Writing a review for *The Nation*, Gertrude Emerson Sen (1893-1982), the wife of Boshi Sen and the author of *Voiceless India* (1944) and *Pageant of India's History* (1948), stated in part:

> Romain Rolland's long elaborate study of certain Hindu mystics and religious leaders of the past few decades, chief among them Ramakrishna and his disciple Vivekananda, is a distinguished searching after the most profound spiritual thought of India. If one hopes to grasp what is fundamental in Indian life, one must apprehend the spiritual values that India has stressed through countless centuries.[49]

Richard Lawrence Pelly (b. 1886), the vice-principal of Anglican Bishop's College in Calcutta, translated the *Katha Upanishad* with notes in 1924. Writing for the Christian based *International Review of Missions*, he observed about Ramakrishna:

> The secret of his influence was twofold. In the first place, there was undoubtedly a certain Christ likeness of character. He loved men and entered with deep sympathy into their problems and troubles. No wonder his friends found it restful and inspiring to ... sit with the gentle-hearted priest and hear his talk. Often it was shrewdly humorous, and sometimes

clothed in parables of charming simplicity and force. The second secret of his power appeals more to the Hindu than to the Christian or western mind. He frequently fell into a state of ecstasy.[50]

Mrs. Caroline Rhys Davids (1858-1942) in her 1933 essay on "Sakyamuni and Ramakrishna" pointed out:

> Ramakrishna saw in the modes of realization known as Sadhana, a More in [the man] and for the Man. In that quest he sought to bridge the great gap in the Actual, between the That and the Thou of the Upanisadic teaching; he sought communion with this or that aspect of the Most, the Highest, the Best.... No man, not even Ramakrishna, can even conceive the Highest as yet, and Ramakrishna now knows that well enough. But we can dwell on the Highest as if knowable under this and that aspect, conceiving each in the utmost worth we are yet capable of: the Mother, the Child, the Friend, the Beloved. It is a high and noble work of will, and by it the man expands in a lovely More such as Ramakrishna's circle saw and were stirred to imitate.

Mrs. Caroline Rhys Davids, the wife of the famous Buddhist academic, was herself a front-ranking Buddhist scholar who edited and translated many Pali texts into English. She believed that the world-negating pessimism and the idea of the non-self of the Pali Canon was not the original message taught by Buddha.[51]

While on a 1935 expedition in the Mongolian desert, the Russian artist Nicholas Roerich (1874-1947) and his companions came across a large elm (karagatch) tree. It reminded them of the huge banyan trees [the Panchavati under which Ramakrishna meditated and realized God] of India. At that time Roerich's

> thoughts turned to the radiant giant of India—Sri Ramakrishna. Around this glorious name there are so many respectful definitions. Sri, Bhagavan, Paramahamsa—all best offerings, through which the people wish to express their esteem and reverence. The consciousness of a nation knows how to bestow names of honour. And after all, above all most venerable titles, there remains over the whole world the one great name—Ramakrishna. The personal name has already changed into a great all-national, universal

> concept. Who has not heard the Blessed Name! The conception of goodness and benevolence truly befits him....
>
> We recollect how in various countries has grown the understanding of the radiant Teaching of Ramakrishna. Beyond shameful words of hatred, beyond evil mutual destruction—the word of Bliss, which is close to every human heart, spreads widely like the mighty branches of the sacred banyan tree. On the paths of human searching, these calls of goodwill were shining like beacons. We ourselves witnessed and have often heard how books of Ramakrishna's Teaching were as if unexpectedly found by sincere seekers....
>
> Ramakrishna never belittled anyone. And not only in the Teaching, in parables, but even in his own deeds he never tolerated bemeaning. Let us remember his reverent attitude towards all religions. Such broad understanding will move even a stony heart. In his broad outlook, the Blessed Bhagavan of course possessed a real straight-knowledge. His power of healing he in turn gave out freely. He never hid anything useful. He exhausted his strength in innumerable blessed givings. And even his illness of course was due to such constant self-sacrificing outpouring of his spiritual energy for the healing of others. And in these generous gifts Ramakrishna manifested his greatness....
>
> The thoughts about the Good, which Ramakrishna so generously taught, should awaken the best sides of human hearts. Ramakrishna always preached against deniers and destruction. He was in all respects a builder for the Good, and his admirers should unfold on the examples of his Teachings the best-hidden treasures of their hearts.[52]

In a letter Roerich dispatched to Swami Abhedananda in 1928, he revealed, "The precious teaching of Sri Ramakrishna first attracted our thought to India."* He journeyed to the Belur Math, where one of his paintings can be found in the old monastery building. Over the years he came out with twenty-one articles for the *Prabuddha Bharata* (1930-45), and eight in the *Vedanta Kesari* (1931-37), plus an additional item posthumously.

Nicholas Roerich, an internationally known artist, drew thousands of paintings, many based on Indian themes and mythology. His paintings include Himalayan landscapes and portraits of the Buddha, Tibetan heroes and saints. Under the inspiration of Alice Bailey, Rudolph Steiner and

---

* See Chapter XVI for more on Roerich.

Helena Blavatsky, he and his wife Helena cofounded the Agni Yoga Society. In subsequent years, Roerich made a study of Buddhistic philosophy, the teachings of Ramakrishna and Vivekananda, the poetry of Rabindranath Tagore and several other Indian thinkers. In his early years in Russia, he filled the position of director of the School for Encouragement of Fine Arts, president of the Museum of Russian Arts and of Mir Iskusstva, an elected member of the Russian Imperial Academy of the Fine Arts, and a leader in the Moscow Art Theatre Diagilev Ballet. During the revolution in 1917, he left Russia to settle in the United States, where he founded the Master Institute of the United Arts. With the assistance of his wife Helena, in 1923 the Roerich Museum, which is still open today, was inaugurated in New York. After visiting India the same year, he eventually settled in the Punjab from 1929 until his death. To carry out archaeological research, he founded the Himalayan Research Institute in the Punjab. As head of an expedition, Roerich spent five years in Central Asia. Establishing an institute in Kulu, India, he sent specimens of drought-resistant plants gathered in Central Asia to botanical research agencies in the United States. According to the "Roerich Pact and Banner of Peace", the nations of the earth would agree to keep sites of educational and cultural significance inviolate during the time of war. At the White House in Washington, D.C. in 1935, this plan had the signature of twenty-two Pan-American countries. Roerich received honours from many counties including Sweden, France, Yugoslavia, Russia, and Belgium. His son Jurij (Yuri) Roerich (1902-60) resided in India from 1923 until 1957, and then went back to Russia. Jurij, a well-known Soviet Orientalist, was a specialist in Tibetan history and language. His another son, Svajoslav, remained in India as a distinguished painter.[53]

The world traveller from Germany, Count Hermann Keyserling (1880-1946), in 1936 told us about his view of Sri Ramakrishna:

> When I think back now to the years 1911-14, when Indian wisdom was my daily food, I cannot help being overcome by a feeling of particular *warmth*, when concentrating on the saint of Dakshineswar. He does indeed stand for something eternal. For Bhakti in its aspect of gentleness, of unworldly goodwill, for a kind of "charity" which is probably the most truly Christian of all but which has almost disappeared from the West.[54]

Count Hermann Keyserling, born in the Baltic area, travelled around the world in 1911, and then described his spiritual journey in his best-selling two volume *The Travel Diary of a Philosopher*. In his *Diary* he records:

> I want to [enter into] the Indian mode of consciousness, ... and then watch what will become of me.... I content myself with establishing the fact that India, and not Europe, has produced the profoundest metaphysics we know of and the most perfect religious system.

About his experience of the sacred in the holy city of Benares, he wrote:

> I feel nearer here than I have ever done to the heart of the world; here I feel everyday as if soon, perhaps even today, I would receive the grace of supreme revelation.... The atmosphere of devotion which hangs above the river is improbable in strength; stronger than in any church that I have ever visited.[55]

Keyserling met Rabindranath Tagore in India and ten years later in Germany. In 1920 in Darmstadt, Germany, he founded the "School of Wisdom" to promote a global civilization, beyond nationalism and cultural ethnocentrism. The school's political beliefs recognize the equal value and validity of non-western cultures and philosophies. Keyserling encouraged his friends like the eminent psychologist Carl Jung, Richard Wilhelm, Rabindranath Tagore, Hermann Hesse, and Paul Tillich to participate in the project. He served on the General Committee and submitted a long paper to the Ramakrishna Centenary held during March 1937 in Calcutta.[56]

Up until the mid 1930s, most of the support for Sri Ramakrishna came from professional writers, high-ranking government officials and clerics. About this time he began to attract interest in the European and American Universities. One reason for this change is that Rolland's biography of Ramakrishna was attracting attention in intellectual circles. In addition, the well-publicized Sri Ramakrishna Centenary drew the interest of some Western scholars.

Support from Leading Professors and After

A leading French Orientalist and philosopher, Paul Masson-Oursel (1882-1956), held the chair of Indian philosophy at the Sorbonne University in Paris. Two of his books were translated into English: *Comparative Philosophy* (1926) and *Ancient India and Indian Civilization* (1934). He believed that true philosophy is comparative philosophy. On March 30, 1936, at the Sorbonne in the auditorium of the "Institute of Indian Civilization", a commemoration celebration for Sri Ramakrishna was held. Accompanied by Josephine MacLeod and Swami Yatishwarananda, Professor Masson-Oursel lectured to an audience. There he provided a remarkable interpretation of Ramakrishna's spiritual experiences:

> [Ramakrishna] wanted to walk in one life the full length of each of the four paths which the *Gita* says lead to liberation. And as if it were not enough to live to their end each of the four yogas, Ramakrishna had also wanted to live each one of the various religions known in his country. By that he did not mean simply to become an adept of each but actually to re-live the life of the great prophets. He became not a Moslem, but Mohammad himself, not a Christian, but Jesus himself, just as he became Kali and Rama and Krishna and all the other forms which the Absolute has taken in the Indian world.
>
> That experience cannot possibly be judged or appreciated from our plane of life and thought. Unless Ramakrishna was only a visionary given to ecstasy, we may say of him not only what was said of Spinoza, that he was intoxicated with God, but that he was the God who was both the basis and the goal of his religious experience.

In addition, Masson-Oursel submitted a paper to the Ramakrishna Centenary Parliament of Religions, which commenced on March 1, 1937 in Calcutta.[57]

Helmuth von Glasenapp (1891-1963) was one of the most eminent German Indologists of his generation (along with Heinrich Zimmer). In 1936, the professor at Koenigsberg (1928-45), and later at Tübingen (1945-59), expressed his admiration for Ramakrishna's spiritual practices in the following words:

> The holy personage [Sri Ramakrishna] whose centenary we are celebrating this year had done a great service to humanity by exhibiting, in a new light, the deep wisdom of the Vedic Rishis and the great Acharyas in his famous sayings for the benefit of religious men and by realizing them in his own life. Being deeply conscious of the fact that by living in a definite concrete religious world of imagination and following the discipline of rigidly sketched forms of belief it is possible to realize the truth, he succeeded in penetrating into a higher consciousness. By systemically testing the experiences realized by following the different paths of salvation, he realized that the various forms of belief have equal claim for recognition and overcame their limitations. He thus obtained a standpoint which lies "on the other side" of all multiplicity and realized the harmony of religions, which can be never understood with our limited means of thought.[58]

In 1927 at Berlin University, Professor von Glasenapp invited Swami Raghavananda (1887/88-1957) of the Ramakrishna Order to speak on "Yoga and Its Relation to Indian Life". The Swami was returning to India after having stayed in New York and Philadelphia since 1923. For those professors and students who did not understand English, he translated the lecture into German. A decade later Von Glasenapp served on the General Committee for the Ramakrishna Centenary held during March 1937 in Calcutta.[59]

Inspired by Arthur Schopenhauer's high regard for Asian thought, Helmuth von Glasenapp published extensively on Indian philosophy and religion and its impact on German philosophy and literature. In his autobiography he describes his widespread journeys in India. Von Glasenapp's scholarly works are on Hinduism, Jainism and Buddhism. His publications include 692 books, articles, book reviews and chapters, etc., consisting of writings on the philosophy of Vallabhacharya, the Yogavashishtha, Adhyatma Ramayana, Shankara, and other subjects. In *Kant and the Religions of the East* (1954), he includes passages from Indian religions located in Kant's books and lectures, unknown before 1949. He concluded that Kant's ideas about the destiny of the soul after death indicate the influence of the Indian concept of transmigration.[60]

In the words of Albert Schweitzer (1875-1965), the Nobel Prize winning humanitarian and Christian missionary in Africa:

> In his childlike humility Ramakrishna is akin to Francis of Assisi. To kill the last stirrings of caste pride in himself he would undertake the most

menial tasks. This mystic, who found such delight in the experience of ecstasy, was inspired also by a spirit of warmest love for his fellows. "Oh Mother," he entreats the goddess Kali, whom he deeply reverenced to the end of his life, "let me remain in contact with mankind; let me not become a hard ascetic." For him there were no questions of dogma. He decided the question whether personality is to be ascribed to God or not by saying that men imagine Him according to their natural gifts as a personality or as non-personal. In thorough Hindu fashion Ramakrishna judged that God Himself is somehow or other present in an image and draws to Himself the worship given to it. He did not trouble about the universal religion comprising all religions within itself which Debendranath Tagore, Keshab Chandra Sen and Dayananda Sarasvati were concerned [with]. What men believe he held to be of secondary importance. Piety is all that matters. Every religion, whatever its doctrine, becomes the true religion when man dedicates himself in love to God and serves his neighbour in love.[61]

Albert Schweitzer, a noted German theologian, philosopher, musicologist, physician, missionary and author, won the 1952 Nobel Peace Prize for his humanitarian efforts. In 1914 he made a journey to Lambarene in French Equatorial Africa (now Gabon), establishing a hospital and working there in "the direct service of humanity". Renouncing a comfortable life in Europe, he chose to labour in one of the most inhospitable areas of Africa. Schweitzer came back to France in 1918, and then returned to Lambarene in 1924, remaining there the rest of his life. He financially supported his humanitarian work by giving organ recitals, lecturing around the world, and by writing many books about applied ethics, theology, music, and his experiences in Africa.

Schweitzer's ethical conception of "Reverence for Life" bears a striking resemblance to the Vedantic ideal taught by Swami Vivekananda of serving the Atman (the Divine Essence) in other beings. In 1915, on a small steamer in rural Africa, Schweitzer was trying to solve the problem of how modern culture could manifest greater moral depth and energy. He related that weary with despair, tired and discouraged at sunset, "there flashed upon my mind, unforeseen and unsought, the phrase 'Reverence for Life'." Schweitzer interpreted this maxim as an elemental and universal conception of a spiritual and humane ethics. He came to the following conclusions that are quite compatible with Vedantic ethics:

> Through reverence for life, we come into a spiritual relationship with the universe. The inner depth of feeling we experience through it gives us the will and capacity to create a spiritual and ethical set of values that enables us to act on a higher plane, because we then feel ourselves truly at home in our world.[62]
>
> [A basic principle of morality is that] good consists in maintaining, promoting, and enhancing life, and that destroying, injuring, and limiting life are evil. Affirmation of the world, which means affirmation of the will-to-live that manifests itself around me, is only possible if I devote myself to other life.... For in world and life-affirmation and in ethics I carry out the will of the universal will-to-live which reveals itself in me. I live my life in God, in the mysterious divine personality which I do not know as such in the world, but only experience as mysterious Will within myself. Rational thinking which is free from assumptions ends therefore in mysticism. To relate oneself in the spirit of reverence for life to the multiform manifestations of the will-to-live which together constitute the world is ethical mysticism.[63]
>
> Reverence for Life arising from the Will-to-Live that has become reflective therefore contains affirmation of life and ethics inseparably combined. It aims to create values, and to realize progress of different kinds which shall serve the material, spiritual, and ethical development of men and mankind.[64]
>
> Reverence for life gives the fundamental principle of morals, namely, that the good consists in the preservation, enhancement, and exaltation of life and that the destruction, injury, and retardation of life is evil. The ethic of reverence for life is the ethics of Jesus, philosophically expressed, made cosmic in scope, and conceived as intellectually necessary. The great error of earlier ethics is that it conceived itself as concerned only with the relations of man to man. The real question is, however, one concerning man's relations to the world and to all life which comes within his reach. A man is ethical only when life, as such, is holy to him.[65]

Hermann Goetz addressed the gathering for the Ramakrishna Centenary held in Calcutta in March 1937 telling his audience:

> I am proud to be with you all in this Assembly which has come together under the name of one of the greatest saints of humanity, Sri Ramakrishna,

whose teachings have brought all mankind into a homogeneous order, into one people, and this is what is expected of all religions.

German born Hermann Goetz (1898-1976) was then the conservator at the Kern Institute in Leiden (Leyden), Holland. During his lifetime he published thirty books specializing in Indian art and architecture, one of his works being translated into fourteen languages. Colonel Charles Lindbergh (1902-74), who made the first solo nonstop transatlantic air flight in 1927, and his wife also attended the Centenary.[66]

Major Francis Yeats-Brown (1886-1944) [q.v.], who spent nineteen years in India, was awarded the Distinguished Flying Cross during World War I. After two failures he succeeded on his third try, by escaping from a Turkish prison camp near Constantinople in the guise of an Austrian mechanic. He is best known for his celebrated best-selling autobiography *The Lives of a Bengal Lancer* (1930), that at times covers the spiritual side of India. It was translated into seven languages and adapted into an award-winning motion picture of the same name. Yeats-Brown also penned *Yoga Explained* (1937), a pioneer text in the field, and *Lancer at Large* (1937), where he mentioned his friendship with Rabindranath Tagore and Jagadish Bose and his yoga training at Trivandrum under Chidambaram Swami. In the latter volume he made the following observation:

> Ramakrishna (1836-86) is one of the great figures of the modern world. That "illiterate genius who knew all the pages of the book of life" was one of the first to proclaim that all the great faiths of the world are true, and that they all lead to one Centre. To attempt an appraisal of his teachings would not be fitting here, but Vivekananda and Romain Rolland have left records of him which all should read and mark who would know more of Indian philosophy. Especially should they read Vivekananda, who is a mirror of the high thought of Hinduism.[67]

An in-depth study of the famous Swiss psychologist Carl Jung (1875-1961) was undertaken by Steven F. Walker, a professor of comparative literature at Rutgers University and a longtime associate of the Vedanta Society of Boston. He discovered that when Jung visited India during the winter of 1936-37, he was very much impressed by the statue of Ramakrishna at Belur Math. Jung later commented on the statue, that whatever the word samadhi might mean exactly, every Indian would associate it with the image of Ramakrishna in that state.[68] In writing an introduction to Heinrich Zimmer's German translation of the teachings of Ramana Maharshi in 1944, Jung noted:

> The Eastern peoples are threatened with a rapid collapse of their spiritual values, and what replaces them cannot always be counted among the best that Western civilization has produced. From this point of view one could regard Ramakrishna and Sri Ramana as modern prophets, who play the same compensatory role in relation to their people as that of Old Testament prophets in relation to their "unfaithful" children of Israel. Not only do they exhort their compatriots to remember their thousand year-old spiritual culture, they actually embody it and thus serve as an impressive warning, lest the demands of the soul be forgotten amid the novelties of Western civilization with its materialistic technology and commercial acquisitiveness.[69]

Because Jung interpreted psychology from a religious standpoint, he was very popular with the Indian Swamis. He held discussions on spiritual topics with Swamis Pavitrananda (1937 or 1938, in New York), Akhilananda (before 1949, in Boston), and Ghanananda (1952, in England). Jung made comments like, "While we are overpowering the Orient from without, it may be fastening its hold upon us from within." In 1944 Jung was recuperating from the effects of amoebic dysentery that he had contracted in India. This was followed by a heart attack that left him on the verge of death. He then experienced a series of visionary experiences that lasted for about three weeks, which he called "the most tremendous things I have ever experienced". Jung wrote:

> On the whole my illness proved to be a most valuable experience, which gave me the inestimable opportunity of a glimpse behind the veil. The only difficulty is to get rid of the body, to get quite naked and void of the world and the ego-will. When you can give up the crazy will to live and when you seemingly fall into a bottomless mist, then the truly real life begins with everything which you were meant to be and never reached. It is something ineffably grand. I was free, completely free and whole, as I never felt before.[70]

Jung added, "I would never have imagined that any such experience was possible. It was not the product of the imagination. The visions and experiences were utterly real; there was nothing subjective about them; they had the quality of absolute objectivity." The first experience involved the vision of a Hindu yogi in a lotus posture outside of an Indian temple. Jung felt that inside the temple were "all those people to whom I belong in reality" and that he would find the answers to his fundamental questions about the meaning of life. The vision was interrupted and he recalled, "I was not to be allowed to enter the temple, to join the people in whose company I belonged." A year later he wrote that his visions were accompanied by "an incomparable, indescribable feeling of eternal bliss, such as I never could have imagined as being within the reach of human consciousness."[71]

Another representative of the Institute in Leiden (Leyden), Holland, Gualtherus H. Mees (b. 1903), author of *Dharma and Society* (1935), presented a paper and attended many events along with his wife at the Ramakrishna Centenary. Among other things he emphasized the point:

> It is one of the supreme achievements of Sri Ramakrishna that he opened the eyes of the 19th and 20th century world to the deep significance of religious symbolism and that he demonstrated that symbols are not mere empty forms, but partake of divine life in all its fullness. Symbols, and in particular religious symbols, are not mere objective pictures, but are highly subjective, in that they form the most sacred and intimate part of our being. In them we live and move and have our being, and in truth they hold more reality—if I may use this expression—than we do ourselves in our surface consciousness.[72]

Concerning the newly published *The Gospel of Sri Ramakrishna* (1942), Heinrich (Henry) Zimmer (1890-1943) [q.v.] affirmed:

> A new portrait of Ramakrishna, and a most fascinating one, comes to us through this first complete and authentic translation of the amazing diary by his faithful disciple "M". The famous figure of the outstanding embodiment of India's religious wisdom and message for mankind discloses his magic secret. A fervent experimentalist and devotee, Ramakrishna passes through every kind of religious tradition. Endowed with a Proteus-like vitality and voluptuousness for metamorphosis, his soul measures the celestial heights and fathoms the abyss. He achieves an unparalleled integration

of the mystic heritage of India and the West. By enacting a sequence of kāleidoscopic transformations he realizes and simultaneously transcends the tangible forms of the formless Divine.[73]

A year before his passing at the 106th birth anniversary of Ramakrishna, Heinrich Zimmer brilliantly addressed the Vedanta Society in New York City stating in part:

> The India which Sri Ramakrishna's teaching stands for, believes, instead, in the unique value of co-operative melioration, in the paramount power of the individual, of the lonely man who, through his being, sanctifies and enlightens his environment,—a solitary beacon, shining forth with a steady light ... The solitary ascetic, striving for enlightenment and freedom, the lonely Yogi, the fervent devotee, like Sri Ramakrishna takes the lead with the figures of the Jinas and Buddhas. He, conquering himself and freeing men from bondage by his example and teaching, is looked upon as the true hero, the Vira. The anonymous saint, in his own right, the mendicant beyond caste, becomes the highest type of man. The homeless messenger from the higher sphere, the "highest swan" (Parama-hamsa), the Self incarnate, assumes infallible authority, not because he has learned for years and years traditional knowledge,—he is omniscient by having pierced through and attained at the fountainhead of supra-personal existence, where wisdom wells up ever-fresh at its deepest well, where he has identified himself with life's supra-phenomenal paradoxical reality.[74]

Zimmer, a professor of Indology in Heidelberg University, came under the influence of John Woodroffe and the psychologist Carl Jung in his interpretation of Indian myths and legends. His book *Art and Yoga* (1926) impressed Jung with its discussion of mandalas along with postures, breathing exercises and the kundalini. Zimmer once made this provocative statement:

> We of the Occident are about to arrive at a crossroads that was reached by the thinkers of India some seven hundred years before Christ. This is the real reason, why we become both vexed and stimulated, uneasy and yet interested, when confronted with the concepts and images of Oriental wisdom.[75]

After migrating to the United States in 1940, followed by his death three years later, Joseph Campbell produced three books from Zimmer's notes, including the well-received *Philosophies of India* (1951).* Zimmer's last book *The Path to Self* dealing with the life and teachings of Sri Ramana Maharshi was published posthumously in German by Carl Jung.[76]

The novelist Thomas Mann (1875-1955), recipient of the 1929 Nobel Prize in literature, expressed this view about the *Gospel*:

> This highly noteworthy document ... conveys the personality of a great mystic in such an intimate, direct, and almost astounding manner that to read it must be an enriching experience for any intellect which is receptive and open to all things human.

Mann had met Rabindranath Tagore in Germany. Being one of the foremost German writers of the twentieth century, as a "novelist of ideas" Thomas Mann used fiction to conduct a lifelong exploration of philosophical topics, ranging from the role of a creative individual in society to the nature of Western society. He was a great admirer of Arthur Schopenhauer, stating, "Once he was fashionable and famous, then half-forgotten. But his philosophy may still exert a ripe and humanizing influence upon our age." Mann's writings are steeped in a German tradition that is not fully appreciated by many English-speaking readers of other cultures.[77]

About Christian organizations in Central Africa, two African historians wrote:

> Others have had a transcendental kind of air about them; for example, the universalist type of church which Peter Nyambo founded when, as an old man, he returned to Nyasaland in 1943, preaching, in the spirit of the teachings of Sri Ramakrishna, a conception of the best that is to be found in all religions.

Peter Nyambo (b. 1884), the man who taught some of Sri Ramakrishna's ideas in Central Africa, was born in Nyasaland (now Malawi), a part of British Africa. He received education in England during 1903-04, and then up to 1911 travelled through Western Europe and East Africa as a paid missionary for the Seventh-day Adventist Church. After that time he vented native

* See Chapter III.

grievances against European rule in South Africa and Nyasaland. Being secretary of the Central African Committee of the British Christian Union, he was of a non-violent disposition against the use of force.[78]

In his book of quotations titled *Man and God* (1951), Sir Victor Gollancz (1893-1967) offers six fair sized passages taken from the teachings of Sri Ramakrishna. Gollancz formed his own publishing company, and for his support of humanitarian ideals he earned many honours in the United States, England, Ireland, Germany and China.[79]

In a 1953 article on "Ramakrishna Paramahamsa", Professor Giuseppe Tucci (1894-1984) [q.v.], Italy's most outstanding Oriental scholar, explained Ramakrishna's teaching thusly:

> Therefore, like sparks of the absolute and symbols by means of which He attracts religious souls, the infinite shapes under which God has shown himself to man, are equally real, inasmuch as all that changes into spiritual values is real. No religion can claim to be above another one, because all of them are equally true inasmuch as they preach a symbolic shape, particular and personal, of the eternal; whereas from an absolute point of view, the experiences prepared by them disappear in a supreme, indiscriminate blending with the germinal essence of all things....
>
> And so Ramakrishna, through these principal phases of interior life, had also become a Siddha, a perfect man, on account of the natural development of his personality and of an intrinsic and nearly inevitable necessity that had brought him, step by step, to the highest peak of contemplative life.... A century after his birth, Ramakrishna is still—nay, today more than when he was alive—a living and operating force in the moral conscience of India. He has taught the great value of the strength of character and, with the example of his own life, has shown that coherence between thinking and acting is worth more than any preaching.[80]

From 1925 until 1930, Giuseppe Tucci settled in India teaching Chinese and Italian at the university in Shantiniketan founded by Rabindranath Tagore, and at Calcutta University. He accepted the chair in the department of religion and philosophy of India and the Far East at the University of Rome (1932-69) and was the president of the Italian Institute for the Middle and Far East. The Sri Ramakrishna Centenary Parliament of Religions Committee invited him to attend the proceedings held at Belur Math in March 1937. Tucci replied, "I can assure you that the message of Sri Ramakrishna is widely known and appreciated by the cultural circle in Italy, and our Institute shall spare no pains to contribute to the success of your Congress." Being an outstanding explorer, for many years he engaged in archaeological expeditions to Tibet, Nepal, Pakistan, Afghanistan and Iran. In 1976 he received the Jawaharlal Nehru Award for International Understanding. This award was especially dear to him because of his friendship with Nehru, and his ties with Rabindranath Tagore, Sarvepalli Radhakrishnan, and Mahatma Gandhi. His bibliography contains 360 published titles, including books, articles, encyclopedia entries, reviews, and so on.[81]

The Western thinker, Frithjof Schuon (1907-98), expressed these insights (translated from French):

> By virtue of his unalterable individual substance, Shri Ramakrishna was a bhakta. Now a bhakta is not a man who "thinks", that is, one whose individuality actively participates in supra-individual knowledge and who consequently knows how "himself" to apply his transcendent knowledge to cosmic and human contingencies. This amounts to saying that the bhakta attains and possesses knowledge, not in an intellectual, but in an ontological way....
>
> The procedure described above is quite legitimate within the framework of bhakti, since, as we have said, it is a priori not "intellectual"; bhakti plums mysteries through "being", not through "intelligence", and this ontological plasticity allows it to realize a point of view from which it appears as superior to "intellectuality" when the latter is conceived in its mental and external aspect....
>
> It must be said that he readily came to look on opinions as "forms" expressing—in what they had that was positive—an underlying basis of truth. In other words, he loved to discover at the root of opinions one single and self-same essence; therefore he did not place himself a priori at the intellectual point of view of orthodoxy, but at the ontological point of view of reality....
>
> With Ramakrishna, "argumentation" could not be intellectual as it was with Shankara, but had to be—if one can express it—existential or ontological. This it is which explains why he did not reply to the doubts of his disciple Narendra by means of a doctrinal demonstration but by an experience of "realization" of a state of consciousness, and so of "being", not of "thinking"....

> In Ramakrishna there is something which seems to defy every category: he was like the living symbol of the inner unity of religions; he was, in fact, the first Saint to wish to penetrate foreign spiritual forms, and in this consisted his exceptional and, in a sense, universal mission—that something which, without making of him a prophet in the strict sense of the word, does make him akin to the prophets. In our times of confusion, disarray and doubt, he was the saint called to "verify" forms and "reveal", if one can so express it, their single truth.[82]

Born in Switzerland, Frithjof Schuon was a writer who could be quite disparaging and who was, at times, not easy to understand. On the positive side he did teach "The Transcendent Unity of Religions", that every religion has, besides its literal meaning, an essential, primordial and universal dimension. Formal religions are superimpositions on the core-essence of the Perennial Religion. Schuon studied the ideas of Plato, Plotinus, Ibn Arabi and Meister Eckhart, made an in-depth study of Sufism in Algeria and Morocco, and was solemnly adopted by the American Sioux and Crow Indian Tribes. The Internet report in Wikipedia interprets his ideas from the standpoint of Sanatana Dharma, Nirguna Brahman, Atman, Mahashakti, Ishvara and Prakriti, but it is not clear how far Schuon pursued this line of thought.[83]

Sir John Stewart-Wallace (b. 1874) held the notable position of chief land registrar for England and Wales during the period 1923-44. He and Swami Ghanananda edited the volume *Women Saints: East and West* (1955). There Stewart-Wallace affirms:

> That Ramakrishna was the greatest Indian Prophet of the XIXth century a growing multitude in India and in Europe agree—a Prophet in the same sense as the Hebrew Prophets were, men who had been exalted in spirit to a direct revelation of God and who in ecstasy handed on that revelation to mankind.... With great discernment the actual sayings of Ramakrishna are often given and, in giving, enable us to get some grasp of the depth of Ramakrishna's spiritual insight, the soundness of his virile common sense and the greatness of his comprehension of the differing needs of men.... These high insights, visions and manifestations to Ramakrishna are unique in the history of the Great Ones who appear as the very incarnations of the Godhead itself. They elevate him to a place among the greatest of the Prophets and reveal him as the Arch-Prophet of a coming

transcendentalism, when it will be perceived that for sincere believers all religious experience is in essence the same.[84]

After the Second World War, Sir John Stewart-Wallace took over the re-organization of the World Council of Faiths, an organization initiated by Sir Francis Younghusband in 1936. He believed, "Only through a high religion, all-embracing and tolerant as the love of God, can mankind be linked in the bond of peace for which the whole world so piteously travaileth—and for which, without religion, the politicians travail in vain." "Behind and above all the World Faiths there is today, here and now, a transcendent *oneness*, a Fellowship of the Spirit ... At the heart of the synthesis lies the ever-living spring of all religion ... the mystic vision."[85]

Professor A. L. Basham (1914-86) [q.v.] held the chair of the history of South Asia at London University. In 1958 he delivered an extempore address at the Ramakrishna-Vivekananda Anniversary meeting in London, stating in part:

> With the growing evidence of the practical blessings of science, telegraph, railway trains, and so on, more and more educated Hindus began to feel that their culture was not up to scratch, and that the best thing for Indians was to accept the West, lock stock and barrel, and to make themselves as good imitations of Englishmen as possible. I believe that it was this very simple and humble man, Ramakrishna, who was more responsible than any other for altering this attitude. Probably he was one of the most saintly personalities to have lived on this planet for the last two centuries. To humble the last vestige of pride in his high-caste birth he would perform the dirty and despised tasks of the sweeper in the temple. To understand fully the religious attitude of men of other faiths he would take to living the life of Christian, Muslim and Jain in turn, repeating their prayers, studying their scriptures and sacred writings, thinking their thoughts.... The slogan "All religions are true", must be interpreted in another sense. The great mystic, in his "experiment with truth" (to take a Gandhian phrase out of its context), found that the experience of truly religious souls, whatever their sectarian background, was fundamentally the same, and that all religions ultimately led to the same goal, however much they lingered on the way—the freeing of the human spirit from the fetters of selfhood, the transcendence of fear in communion with that which is ultimate, and brotherly love. In this sense I have no doubt of the righteousness of Ramakrishna's message.[86]

While in Greece, Swami Ghanananda of the London Centre spoke in the same programme as Professor N. Louvaris of the theology department of Athens University. In a lecture on "Indian Philosophy", the professor, who published many books in the Greek language, made the following comment on the liberality of Hinduism:

> One of these prophetic personalities, according to Ramakrishna, is that of Christ. He too—Ramakrishna—is one of the revelations of God. So here we have the belief in the universal revelation of God as held by our Greek Fathers and as in Hellenistic times. Ramakrishna pleads for the harmonious concord of all religions, for he deems them all to be revelations of the same God.... We must concede the broadmindedness of Indian spiritual thought in not rejecting the creeds of the other religions just because they are foreign, and in accepting them all.[87]

An author of more than fifty volumes of theological works, Scottish clergyman Stephen Charles Neill (1900-1984) served as an Anglican missionary in South India from 1924 to 1944, and as the Bishop of Tinnevelly, India, from 1939 to 1945. In 1948 Neill rose to prominence as associate general secretary of the World Council of Churches, and in 1951 he began his twenty-year association with World Christian Books, whose directorship he assumed in 1962. A world leader of the ecumenical movement, he held the position of a professor at Cambridge, Oxford, Hamburg, Union Seminary and other universities. Following an ecumenical spirit, he wrote:

> Ramakrishna Paramahamsa, the devotee whom most Hindus constantly cite as the most notable example of a human being who attained in this life to perfect union with the divine. About 1871, Ramakrishna began to study other religions, very much in the spirit which has been commended to Christians in this book. For a certain period he would read only the Scriptures of the faith that he was studying, as far as was possible carrying out all the appointed prayers and rituals. At the end of several years of such study and experiment he reached the conclusion that all religions in their inmost content are one—they all lead back to the truth apprehended by the mystic of the unity of all things in the supreme and universal Spirit.[88]

Dr. Jacques-Albert Cuttat, a Roman Catholic and the Swiss ambassador to India, disclosed:

> It was in Argentina, twenty years ago, that I happened to read, for the first time, *The Gospel of Sri Ramakrishna*, translated by Swami Nikhilananda. I read it from the first to the last line, with growing attention, growing recollection, feeling drawn, as it were, into increasingly deeper spheres of my consciousness. How could I, a Westerner, brought up in Christianity and Western logic, living at the opposite extreme of the globe over fifty years after Ramakrishna's death, experience the biography of this humble, poor, and God-intoxicated Bengali, who "had not read books", as the encounter with somebody whom I recognized without knowing him, with somebody who was nearer to my own soul than my friends around me, and who seemed to know me better than my myself?... what Ramakrishna Paramahamsa shares with all saints is that he remains personally present to all generations, through his personal perfection, through his unique inner countenance, through his spiritual, mental, and physical transparency to God, which make him transparent to himself and to others.[89]

On February 25, 1969, John C. Travell (b. 1930), a Congregational minister from London and later the president of the Congregational Federation, spoke at the public meeting of the Ramakrishna Vedanta Centre in London. Addressing the subject "The Wisdom of Sri Ramakrishna", he mentioned the following:

> He possessed a true wisdom, an inspired common sense, which shines out in the incidents of his life and which overflows in the riches of his recorded sayings. He knew nothing of formal logic, although "M" once tried to explain it to him. He conveyed his ideas in pictures and parables, in the time-honoured form in which the traditional wisdom of the East has always been taught. He used metaphors and illustrations taken from life, describing scenes which were easily recognized and understood by simple people, as vehicles of profound thought. This was the language used by the Buddha, and the language of Jesus. It was a language which Ramakrishna had learnt in the villages and streets of his native Bengal, picked up from the wandering poets and singers, and it was a language which he was divinely gifted.... Humility was an integral part of his character, the kind of humility which belongs to the truly wise and the truly great. He never ceased to make use of every opportunity to learn, from the humblest and the poorest as well as from the greatest and most famous.... He found God in each religion because he did not merely take from them what fitted

his own ideas, he sought first to know them from the inside, to understand them for themselves. His devotion was always to God and the truth first. His belief in the underlying unity and harmony of all religions was an expression of that devotion.[90]

Born in Bombay, P. J. Saher later pursued his studies in England and Germany. Coming under the influence of the philosopher Martin Heidegger, and then Sarvepalli Radhakrishnan and Aldous Huxley, he gave up a career in law to study mysticism and yoga. Saher came out with several widely-read books in German, one on Zen-Yoga. In *Eastern Wisdom and Western Thought*, a 1969 comparative study of the modern philosophy of religion, Saher notes:

> Then Sri Ramakrishna, the greatest spiritual genius born in India since Gautama Buddha, mastered the method of bhakti and at once succeeded with that of jnana. Moreover, he was able to explain philosophically the inner workings of this oft-predicted, but seldom observed, success.[91]

1970s and After

The celebrated English historian at London University, Arnold Toynbee (1889-1975), in his Foreword to Swami Ghanananda's *Sri Ramakrishna and His Unique Message* published in 1970, made the following brilliant assessment concerning Ramakrishna's place in contemporary history:

> Sri Ramakrishna's message was unique in being expressed in action. The message itself was the perennial message of Hinduism.... In the Hindu view, each of the higher religions is a true vision and a right way, and all of them alike are indispensable to mankind, because each gives a different glimpse of the same truth, and each leads by a different route to the same goal of human endeavours. Each, therefore, has a special spiritual value of its own which is not to be found in any of the others.
>
> To know this is good, but it is not enough. Religion is not just a matter for study; it is something that has to be experienced and to be lived, and this is the field in which Sri Ramakrishna manifested his uniqueness. He practised successively almost every form of Indian religion and philosophy, and he went on to practise Islam and Christianity as well. His religious activity and experience were, in fact, comprehensive to a degree that had

perhaps never before been attained by any other religious genius, in India or elsewhere. His devotion to God in the personal form of the Great Mother did not prevent him from attaining the state of "contentless consciousness"—an absolute union with absolute spiritual Reality.

Sri Ramakrishna made his appearance and delivered his message at the time and the place at which he and his message were needed. This message could hardly have been delivered by anyone who had not been brought up in the Hindu religious tradition. Sri Ramakrishna was born in Bengal in 1836. He was born into a world that, in his lifetime, was for the first time, being united on a literally worldwide scale. Today we are still living in this transitional chapter of the world's history, but it is already becoming clear that a chapter which had a Western beginning will have to have an Indian ending if it is not to end in the self-destruction of the human race. In the present age, the world has been united on the material plane by Western technology. But this Western skill has not only "annihilated distance"; it has armed the peoples of the world with weapons of devastating power at a time when they have been brought to point blank range of each other without yet having learnt to know and love each other. At this supremely dangerous moment in human history, the only way of salvation for mankind is an Indian way. The Emperor Ashoka's and the Mahatma Gandhi's principle of non-violence and Sri Ramakrishna's testimony to the harmony of religions: here we have the attitude and the spirit that can make it possible for the human race to grow together into a single family—and, in the Atomic Age, this is the only alternative to destroying ourselves.[92]

The remarkable English historian Arnold Joseph Toynbee worked as a professor of Byzantine and Modern Greek language, literature and history at the University of London (1919-24), as a director of studies at the Royal Institute of International Affairs (1925-55), and as a professor of international history at London University. Being an author of many important works, Toynbee is best known for his massive twelve-volume series *A Study of History* published between 1934 and 1961. It is a study of twenty-eight civilizations in recorded history, analyzing their genesis, growth, breakdown and disintegration. Historians look upon this study as a major contribution to modern thought. Toynbee once mentioned, "[My classical education] has given me a mental standing ground outside the time and place into which I happen to have been born." His philosophy of history involves prophetic implications for the future of humankind. When studying prior civilizations, he utilizes theoretical concepts like challenge-and-response, withdrawal-and-return, creative minority, internal proletariat, the fossilization of societies, universal churches, and the character of universal states. In *An Historian's Approach to Religion* (1956), Toynbee concerns himself increasingly with the value of religion in bringing about world unity. In *One World and India* (1960) Toynbee emphasized that India has been a source of spiritual strength for humanity, and that today the world needs India's philosophy to bring about lasting world peace.[93]

A Jesuit missionary originally from Belgium, Father Robert Antoine, S.J. (1914-81) was a reader in comparative literature at Jadavpur University. He spent forty-two years in India, primarily in Calcutta, where he mastered Sanskrit and Bengali. The following excerpt comes from a lecture he gave at the Ramakrishna Mission Institute of Culture on "Sri Ramakrishna: A Symbol of Harmony". In the spirit of ecumenism, Father Antoine stressed that the members of the various religions are all pilgrims on this common quest to realize God:

> To all of us Sri Ramakrishna has given the call of spiritual liberation. He has never told us to shed our differences which, in their positive aspect, are nothing but the manifestation of the manifold richness of the divine call. He has never told us to make of those differences occasions to tear each other to pieces. He has told us to seek in those very differences the revelation of our limitation and of the necessity to share together, not only our abstract theologies, but chiefly our experience of God. The harmony to which he invites us is not the ready-made harmony of syncretism, but the dynamic harmony of a common quest.... it is imperative for all of us to come together, in a spirit of mutual respect and love, and with the inspiration of Sri Ramakrishna, to enter the spiritual dialogue with no other desire than to give and to receive, to enrich one another and to make our common response to God's call a little more adequate than it would have been.[94]

Karel Werner (b. 1925) [q.v.] became a lecturer in Sanskrit and Indian civilization at the University of Olomouc in Czechoslovakia. In 1951 he was dismissed "because he refused to adopt a Marxist perspective in his teaching". For thirteen years he worked as a coal miner, tram driver and gas worker. He returned to academic work in Czechoslovakia in 1964, and four years later, in the wake of the Soviet invasion of Czechoslovakia, emigrated to the United Kingdom. There he became a lecturer at the University of

Durham, England, teaching Sanskrit and Hindu and Buddhist scriptures, while being a visiting lecturer at other institutions. In tracing the life of Ramakrishna in his popular *Yoga and Indian Philosophy* (1977), he brought out this fact:

> A sincere truth-seeker finds help at the right moment. The help came in the form of a sannyasini, a homeless, female wanderer known as Bhairavi Brahmani. This remarkable woman knew both the Hindu scriptures and the practical methods of Yoga, and what Ramakrishna had achieved on his own by the force of his devotion, she helped him to go through again with full consciousness and in a disciplined way. Thus he realized consciously his oneness with God not only in the shape of Kali, his Divine Mother, but also in whatever form he chose to approach him. He reached the summit of Bhakti Yoga and became widely recognized as one in whom God himself was revealed as in previous divine incarnations, such as that of Krishna.[95]

Hans Torwesten (b. 1944) [q.v.] is a writer, lecturer, yoga teacher, and painter. He studied art in Vienna, and Indian philosophy, meditation, and yoga in England. His writings include *Vedanta: Heart of Hinduism* and the comparative study *Ramakrishna and Christ* (1981), which contains a chapter on Sarada Devi. John Phillips translated the latter book into English. It covers such topics as the idea of multiple divine incarnations, religions not as an institution but as a path to God, personal and impersonal God as two aspects of the same reality, and that God can be worshipped as a Mother or Father. Torwesten observed:

> In regard to Ramakrishna, his disciples saw in him just the embodiment of Indian spiritual wisdom accumulated over thousands of years. In him the Upanishads, the "Gita" and the Puranas were again embodied, and it was also not difficult for his worshippers to see in him a re-embodiment of Rama, Krishna and Chaitanya. He saw himself as the last link so far—and in no way the "seal"—in the chain of divine manifestations, the avatars or "descents" of God, among whom he also included Buddha and above all Christ.[96]

Four years later, in *Vedanta: Heart of Hinduism*, Torwesten added:

He criticized the one-sidedness of his guru Totapuri, who sought salvation exclusively in a rigid monism which left no room for diversity, who was incapable of accepting a more flexible Advaita that would include Shakti and her Creation. Why this one-sidedness? Why only the static, the formless, and the impersonal? Why not also the overflowing abundance of his Divine Mother? Ramakrishna often said that he did not want to play just one note on his flute but wanted to elicit from it all possible notes....

In Ramakrishna's case all aspects of the divine reality were equally valid, not because of indifference but because his intense love embraced them all—including even Christ and the God of Islam. He did not just "tolerate" them. Quite the contrary. He lived with them, became totally absorbed in them, and in turn discovered each to be a gateway to the impersonal absolute, in his eyes their common ground.

In *A Sourcebook of Modern Hinduism* (1985), Reverend Glyn Richards (1923-2003) [q.v.] devoted twelve pages to excerpts from *The Gospel of Sri Ramakrishna*. He describes Ramakrishna as "undoubtedly one of the most remarkable religious leaders of his time". Many times during his life Ramakrishna had mystical experiences. Glyn Richards states, "From his personal experience of different religions he was able to claim that they were simply different paths to the same goal even as rivers flowed into the same ocean. Kali, the Divine Mother, and Brahman were two aspects of the same reality." Welsh born Reverend Glyn Richards, an ordained Minister of the Congregational Church, became a senior lecturer (1973-90) and head of the department of religious studies (1977-90) at Stirling University in Scotland. A student of Hinduism, he authored a book on *The Philosophy of Gandhi*.[97]

Three years later, writing the chapter on "Modern Hinduism" for Routledge's *The World's Religions*, Reverend Glyn Richards added:

> His personal experiences of other religious traditions, especially Islam and Christianity, enabled him to make the claim that different religions are simply different paths to the same goal. As Kali, the Divine Mother, and Brahman are two aspects of the same reality, so the mystical experience of Christ is at one with the mystical experience of Allah. God may be called by different names but he is one and the same. There is no necessity to choose between the formless Absolute and the personal God, for God with form is as real as God without form, and the difference between them is no more than that between ice and water. The impediment to spiritual development

is worldliness which is maya. It is man's ignorance of his true self that causes him to become enmeshed in maya in the first place, and release is attained through discrimination which recognises God alone as real and eternal. Social reform, including the elimination of cast distinctions, should derive from the love and worship of God.[98]

Martin Kämpchen (b. 1948) [q.v.] produced twelve books, including *Rabindranath Tagore and Germany* (1997) and *Günter Grass in Indien und Bangladesch* (2005). He translated two volumes of the *Gospel of Sri Ramakrishna* from Bengali into German. Back in 1973, Kämpchen taught German language at the Ramakrishna Mission Institute of Culture in Calcutta and later received a Ph.D. and did post-doctoral research at Vishvabharati University in Shantiniketan. In his doctoral dissertation submitted to the University on "Sri Ramakrishna and Francis of Assisi [1182-1226] as Lovers of God", Kämpchen concluded:

> What strikes one is that their approaches were very similar. Both the saints cultivated a predominately emotional love of God. Sri Ramakrishna stressed the emotional aspects of love like singing, dancing, kirtans praising God, conversing about God and listening to stories about God. As fruits of pure bhakti, Ramakrishna mentioned "tears" and spiritual excitement to the point of horripilations. These acts require spontaneity and the capacity to rouse oneself emotionally.[99]

In a 1989 essay "Sri Ramakrishna can be Appreciated in the West", Kämpchen expressed the view:

> Sri Ramakrishna, as he appears to us in the "*Kathamrita*", is intensely lovable. His life has a radiance, an ethereal lightness about it which is very uncommon for spiritual personalities of our modern age.... that his characteristic quality was childlikeness, is a special gift of God to mankind. This childlikeness made Sri Ramakrishna serene; it is also the reason why he is so lovable. Childlikeness means direct perception of reality, be it social reality or transcendental reality. The child does not go through complicated rational processes as the adult does to arrive at a perception or a decision; he is not encumbered by psychological complexes or inhibited by emotional blemishes received in the past, or worry about the present and the future.... The childlike Ramakrishna had not a speck of pomposity, he never celebrates

himself, never consciously plays a "role". His holiness is as natural to him as breathing. His ecstasies have a flair of childlike exuberance. What a man! One who could reach that stage of spiritual elevation where all the suffering, the complications, and traumas of *sadhana* become invisible, where all the scars of "spiritual warfare" are removed by enlightenment![100]

With the publication of the trend setting book *India and Europe* (1981), Wilhelm Halbfass (1940-2000) [q.v.] established himself as the leading Western thinker on the subject of the intellectual encounter of India with the West primarily since AD 1500. Coming from a German hermeneutical tradition, Halbfass ably and comprehensively explains the ideology of the Neo-Hindu and Neo-Vedantic movements, which includes Ramakrishna and Vivekananda as their key members. He also authored popular books on the ethical and social dimensions of Mimamsa and Advaita Vedanta, and on the Vaisheshika "conceptualization of being". The German born Halbfass became a professor of Indian philosophy in 1974 at the University of Pennsylvania in the United States. About Ramakrishna he stated:

> Ramakrishna who was probably the most famous representative of "living Hinduism" and has become the very symbol of the potential of undogmatic religious experience and ecstasy contained within the Hindu tradition.... The value and richness of Hinduism ... consists in its organic totality, which Ramakrishna conceives in the sense of a non-historical inner perfection, the timeless of presence of the *santana dharma* ("eternal religion"). Even without "reform", Hinduism is prepared for the encounter with Christianity and the other religions of the world; its potential of "experience" and its inner diversity offer room enough for the inclusion and recognition of other names and forms of worship. Ramakrishna saw no problem in adding the worship of Jesus to the various cult forms of Hinduism, and he was convinced that his own meditative experiments could demonstrate that the various religions were all paths to the same goal. The metaphor of the different expressions for the *one* water which all drink, together with other parables and metaphors, illustrates the Unity of God in the diversity of forms of worship.[101]

Writing a review of Hixon's book on Ramakrishna, the renowned yoga expert Georg Feuerstein (b. 1947) offered this praise:

> Sri Ramakrishna Paramahamsa, who was made famous in the West by his chief disciple Swami Vivekananda, was an extraordinary spiritual personage. He was a master of yoga, a saint, a God-intoxicated mystic, an expert ecstatic, and a lifelong devotee of the Great Mother. Many Hindu theologians pronounced him to be a genuine embodiment of the Divine—an avatara—who had descended into the material realm out of compassion for suffering humanity. But Ramakrishna himself was indifferent to all these labels. He was a true original, a spiritual genius....
>
> Ramakrishna Paramahamsa's childlike spontaneity has fooled some into thinking of him as an unsophisticated villager who happened to have great spiritual abilities and insights. Hixon corrects this mistaken impression, presenting Sri Ramakrishna as the man of refined philosophical understanding, universal tolerance, and traditional learning that he was. "He remembered every Sanskrit scripture he heard chanted, even once, as well as every mystic hymn in Bengali and Hindi," writes Hixon. This extraordinary feat of memory he interprets as a clear sign of Ramakrishna's unobstructed mind, which was constantly eclipsed and purified by the overwhelming bliss of God-realization.[102]

German born Georg Feuerstein immigrated to England in 1966, and to the United States in 1981. He has produced a vast number of well-read texts primarily on the subject of yoga. In Feuerstein's own words, "Since the age of fourteen, I have been fascinated with India's wisdom traditions, and most of my books deal with one aspect or another of the five-thousand-year-old tradition of Yoga. From the beginning, my focus has been on making Yogic wisdom accessible to Westerners." "I did not narrow my personal quest and scholarly research to Hindu and Buddhist wisdom but always consciously endeavoured to integrate, on the levels of understanding and feeling, the two great halves of the human family—East and West." "Many of my published writings are attempts to communicate with a wider audience while fully respecting the exacting standards of sound scholarship." *Booklist* contributor Donna Seaman wrote that Feuerstein "performs a truly Yogic feat by combining commentary with translated Sanskrit teachings, history with theory, the spiritual with the practical, and the classical with the contemporary.... No more adept or comprehensive study of yoga aimed at a Western audience is to be found."[103]

A news correspondent in Moscow, Ms. Natalia Tots effectively reported on crime for the Tass News Agency. After coming across a few references on Ramakrishna written by Elena and Nikolai (Nicholas) Roerich, she left her employment to learn more about him. The result of her in-depth study is an eighty-page book that came out in 1993, with the title *The Teachings of Ramakrishna*. Ms. Tots reveals, "All that I have attempted to do is capture the essence of Ramakrishna's preachings into an easy-to-read book." The volume includes impressions of Swamis Vivekananda and Lokeswarananda. It also contains articles by prominent Indologists like Nikolai Roerich and R. B. Rybakov. Natalia Tots explained, "All the books which were available earlier on Ramakrishna were elaborate philosophical essays. Now, for the first time, a book which even the general mass[es] could understand was published. Naturally, the people took to the book well." Since then she has received letters from people asking her to tell them more about Ramakrishna.[104]

In an essay concerning "Post-Communist Russia", R. B. Rybakov [q.v.], deputy director at the Institute of Oriental Studies, Russia Academy of Sciences in Moscow, stressed:

> The teachings of Sri Ramakrishna and his closest disciple Swami Vivekananda have always constituted an issue of lively interest for the Russian readers from the beginning of this [twentieth] century. Several years before the October Revolution, or more precisely, even before the commencement of the First World War, the first volumes of the translated versions of the precepts of Sri Ramakrishna and the works of Swami Vivekananda were published and became known among the elite circles of the Russian intelligentsia.
>
> ... the prophetic teachings of Sri Ramakrishna and Swami Vivekananda are of universal import and of great moral worth for the whole of humanity. Transcending the barriers of political frontiers and time, these ideas are bound to be embraced sooner or later by all the people of the earth seeking to reach the realm of truth—irrespective of their caste, creed, colour, sex, social standing, or religion and other doctrinal beliefs.[105]

Mariasusai Dhavamony, S.J. (b. 1925), an eminent Indian theologian, was a professor of theology, Indology, and the history of religions at Gregorian University in Rome, Italy. He served as the director and editor-in-chief of *Studia Missionalia* and *Documenta Missionalia*, and as a formal consultant to the Pontifical Council for inter-religious dialogue. In a very appreciative book entitled *Hindu Spirituality* (1999), Dhavamony expounded:

We shall single out Ramakrishna, a bhakta who has by word and example shown that the Hindu ideals of holiness are realizable in the concrete way in day to day life, as witnessed by other men who came into contact with him and knew him closely. We do not deal with his biography but with the main ideals of bhakti as lived and experienced by him.... Among the different kinds of yoga Ramakrishna chose as his favourite yoga the path of love (bhakti); but this did not prevent him from practising jnana-yoga which led him to gain the supreme knowledge of God. In fact one of the striking aspects of Ramakrishna's spirituality was the plurality of his experiences and the rapidity of the results that he obtained from the spiritual point of view.... Ramakrishna has passed through various higher states of spiritual discipline (*sadhana*) that are described in the Bhakti-Shastras; he is said to have attained at this stage the state of Mahabhava, the supreme rapture that crowns all other states of love of God. Sri Chaitanya alone was known to have reached such a sublime state of exaltation in recent centuries.[106]

One of the leading Christian theologians of the twentieth century, Hans Küng (b. 1928), in pursuing an ecumenical viewpoint, made these statements:

The Hindu Renaissance led in the nineteenth century to modern Reform Hinduism. In it appeared an uncouth, barely educated, childlike peasant boy from a poor village Brahmin family who finally, after some resistance, became a priest in a quite new temple in Calcutta. In time he began to show even the intelligentsia with a modern English upbringing that Hinduism was not dying out, that it was by no means finished. Rather, once again it could become an inexhaustible source of spiritual renewal. From his youth Ramakrishna, as his name now was, had had trance-like experiences and visions, the expression of an excessive longing and love of God....

For Ramakrishna and his disciples, who became increasingly numerous, meditation, praise of the name of God and emotional love of a personal God (whether Kali or whoever) were decisive: this was bhakti-marga, the "way of dedication".

Thus Ramakrishna became convinced that all religions were true, even if they are not free from errors. Whether it is a primitive veneration of images which does not in fact venerate the image but the deity, or the contemplation of Brahman without images, which certainly represents a higher form of religion, they are all different ways to the one all-embracing deity....

> It should not be difficult even for Christians to recognize this extraordinary man as a saint of Hinduism and as an embodiment of a being mystically filled with the deity.[107]

Swiss-born Hans Küng, who in 1954 became an ordained Roman Catholic priest, was appointed professor of theology at the University of Tübingen in Germany (1960-96). He sought reunion with other Christian churches, indicating that contemporary differences stem from different ways of talking rather than from substantive disagreement. Being antagonistic to authoritarian institutional church structures, he emphasized freedom of thought. He also stressed the need for a global ethic to which all nations and peoples would subscribe. Küng's views on the divinity of Christ, papal infallibility, and the dogma of the Virgin Mary led to his censorship by the Vatican in 1979. He continued teaching at Tübingen under secular rather than Catholic auspices.[108]

In an essay on "Hindus and Muslims in Bengal", Victor van Bijlert mentioned among other things that Ramakrishna

> was a seeker for and realizer of the mystical vision. During his lifetime Sri Ramakrishna had followed the many Hindu paths to God and found always in the end the ultimate experience of his chosen Deity, the Goddess Kali. After having practised the ways of Tantrism and Vaishnavism and realized their supreme goals, Sri Ramakrishna was initiated into non-dual Vedanta by an itinerate monk, Tota Puri, who had come to Dakshineswar sometime in 1864. After his initiation, Sri Ramakrishna began to practise Vedantic meditation and quickly experienced the ultimate state of consciousness called *nirvikalpa samadhi* (the deepest concentration without conceptualizations).

Victor van Bijlert devoted several years to teaching Bengali language and Indian philosophy in the Netherlands. He then assumed a research and teaching position at the Indian Institute of Management, Calcutta. In 1996 he completed a volume on Tagore that was translated into Dutch. Creating the Bengal Studies Page of the IIAS Newsletter, van Bijlert hopes to promote the study of Bengal in Europe in terms of its modern cultural aspects: literary, political, social, religious, films, songs, and visual arts.[109]

Born in Sri Lanka, Christopher Pinney, a professor of anthropology and visual culture at University College, London, was a visiting professor at

Jawaharlal Nehru University in New Delhi (2006). He is now in the department of art history at Northwestern University in Illinois (2007-09). His research specially covers the art and visual culture of South Asia, with a focus on the history of photography and chromolithography in India. Pinney's *Photo's of the Gods* is a history of Hindu chromolithography covering the time period from 1878 to 2000, demonstrating the inappropriateness of applying Western aesthetic standards for an Indian History of Art. There he displays a full-page religious picture of Kali inducing samadhi in Ramakrishna, and, using two quotations, describes some aspects of his samadhi:

> "In religious ecstasy he would pass into that form of trance which is called in Hinduism samadhi. When this came on him, he became unconscious. When he was in this condition, the best doctors could find no trace of pulse or heart action." Most often, Ramakrishna fell into samadhi before the image of the goddess Kali in the Dakshineswar temple, where he had become assistant priest shortly after its construction in 1855. This state of samadhi became a testament—almost a guarantee—of the immanence of Kali's presence within the Dakshineswar murti: he expounded the potency of the idols—"he believed it to be living and breathing and taking food out of his hand." Ramakrishna's devotional ecstasy is a hugely popular subject in current Bengali chromolithograph production. His deity-like qualities are also very clear in many of these images.[110]

An ordained Minister of the Reformed Church, Jan (Johan) Peter Schouten [q.v.] served as the chairman of the committee on Hinduism for the council of religions in the Netherlands. In *Jesus as Guru: The Image of Christ among Hindus and Christians in India* (2008), Reverend Schouten has done the admirable job of explaining to Christians that

> Hindus have given Jesus a place among the teachers and gods of their own religion, seeing in his life something of the wisdom and mysticism that is so central to Hinduism.... Thus, in any case, Jesus is for Hindus and Christians a guru, a teacher of wisdom who speaks with divine authority. But for many Hindu philosophers and Christian theologians there is much more that can be said about him within the Indian framework. He can be described as an avatara, a divine descent, or linked to the Brahman, the all-encompassing Reality.

In the section on the Master he mentions among other things:

> Ramakrishna had the same trance experience regularly in the cultus of Kali and in tantric practice. To eyewitnesses, it seemed that he was not at all a part of the world: his body became rigid and contact with his surroundings stopped and he merged entirely with his internal life. Sometimes his followers had to intervene after hours so that he could return to ordinary life. One time, the samadhi was so deep and intense that it was six months before he could function normally again.[111]

The number of tributes presented here are divided almost evenly among three national groups: the English, the Germans, and the rest of the Europeans. Before 1930, the tributes were shared by professional writers, high-level government workers and clerics. After that time, about half of the accolades have come from university professors. Since the end of World War II, there have been a large number of translations of Ramakrishna-Vedanta books, including those of Ramakrishna into European languages, which this chapter does not discuss.

ENDNOTES

1 Sister Nivedita, *Kali the Mother* (Advaita Ashrama, 1900, 1953), pp. 53-54, 56.

2 Swami Chetanananda, *How to Live with God* (St. Louis: Vedanta Society of St. Louis, 2008), p. 548.

3 William Digby, *Prosperous India* (New Delhi: Sagar Publications, 1969), p. 99; Prabhananda (1993), p. 131.

4 Stavig, pp. 469-70; WWIE (1905), p. 489; Buckland, pp. 119-20; NDB (1901-11), pp. 501-02; UCLC; Leading Men of London (1895) as part of the World Biographical Index; Indian Ethos. Web: www.indianethos.com/history/ pageant.htm.

5 Basu, pp. 564-69; *Brahmavadin* (March 1902), pp. 243-57.

6 Luzac's Oriental List (1903), p. 248; Marcus Aurelius, a Roman Emperor and Stoic philosopher of merit, produced the book *The Meditations*. There he makes statements like, "One should continually think of the universe as one living being, with one substance and one soul—how all it contains falls under one unitary perception; how all its actions derive from one impulse, how all things together cause all that happens."

7 Sergei Serebriany, "Leo Tolstoy and Sri Ramakrishna", *BRMIC* (1987), pp. 164-67, 198; Stavig3, pp, 476-81.

8 Bryan Magee, *The Philosophy of Schopenhauer* (Oxford: University Press, 1983), pp. 379-80; Mircea Eliade, ed., *The Encyclopedia of Religion* (New York: Macmillan Publishing Co., 1987), XIV, p. 546; Shifman, pp. 9, 11-12, 16, 24, 27-28, 45-48; Stavig3, pp, 476-81.

9 Shifman, pp. 93-108; P. M. Shastitko, *Russia and India* (Calcutta: Votok, 1986), pp. 274-77; V. V. Murti, Ramana Murty, "Influence of Western Tradition on Gandhian Doctrine", *Philosophy East and West* (1968), p. 60; Stavig3, pp, 476-81.

10 Head, p. 226.

11 Serebriany (1987), pp. 198-99.

12 *Über Religionen und Religion* (1905), pp. 74-80; WorldCat. The Google Translator produced ambiguous text and so direct quoting of his text is not possible.

13 L. O'Malley and M. Chakravarti, *Howrah* (Calcutta: Bengal Secretariat Book Depot, 1909), p. 48 on GBS.

14 J. N. Farquhar, *Modern Religious Movements in India* (New York: Macmillan, 1915), pp. 198-99 on GBS.

15 Robin Boyd, *Indian Christian Theology* (New Delhi: ISPCK, 1994), pp. 89-90, 280, 283-86; *DNB*, 1922-30 (1961), p. 296; UCLC.

16 Wikipedia. Web: en.wikipedia.org/wiki/Sidney_Rowlatt; Web: en.wikipedia.org/wiki/Rowlatt_Act.

17 *Sedition Committee 1918 Report* (Calcutta: Superintendent Government Printing, India, 1918), pp. 16-17 on GBS.

18 World Library Catalogue. Web: www.ubka.uni-karlsruhe.de/hylib/en/kvk.html; Web: Google under "Carl Theodor Vogl".

19 The German language material from Meyrink's introduction was translated by Gerda Wissar and the computer programme at Web: www.freetranslation.com.

20 *EOP* (1991), p. 1094; *Twentieth Century Literary Criticism* (Detroit: Gale Research Co., 1986), XXI, pp. 215-17.

21 Sir Francis Younghusband, *The Gleam* (London: John Murray, 1923), pp. 221-21, 225 on GBS.

22 Francis Younghusband, *Dawn in India* (London: John Murray, 1931), pp. 237-41.

23 Ramakrishna, pp. 22-23; *PB* (April 1937), p. 252; also in Centenary, I, pp. xvi, 44, 73-74, 134-38; II, pp. 871-84; Web: www.vivekananda.net/PPlHeKnew/.../Shuddhananda.htm.

24 *CA* (1985), vol. 113; *EOP* (1991); Swami Abhedananda, *New York Tribune* (Dec. 7, 1903), p. 5; Riddick, p. 402; World Congress of Faiths. Web: www.worldfaith.org; Wikipedia. Web: en.wikipedia.org/wiki/ Francis_Younghusband.

25 Lord Ronaldshay, *The Heart of Aryavarta* (Boston: Houghton Mifflin, 1925), pp. 204, 208; *PB* (Feb. 1936), pp. 130-33.

26 Swami Aseshananda, *Glimpses of a Great Soul* (Hollywood: Vedanta Press, 1982), pp. 58-60; Riddick, p. 110; *Who Was Who Among English and European Authors 1931-1949* (Detroit: Gale Research, 1978), pp. 1561-62.

27 Centenary, I, p. 79.

28 *Quarterly Review* (Oct. 1925), pp. 416-17.

29 Prabuddhaprana1, p. 202; Tathagatananda2, p. 211; Swami Tathagatananda, "Dhan Gopal Mukerji and the Face Of Silence", *PB*, Jan. 2006, pp. 109-13; *CA* (2000), New Rev. Ser., vol. 90; *EWB*.

30 *The Living Age* (Oct. 1, 1926), p. 93 on APS.

31 Hans Kohn, *A History of Nationalism in the East* (London: George Routledge, 1929), pp. 69-70 on GBS; *CA* (1981), vol. 4.

32 Rolland, p. 302; Tathagatananda2, pp. 211-12.

33 Tathagatananda2, pp. 212-13; Rolland, p. ix; for the content of what Swami Shivananda sent Rolland on Sri Ramakrishna, see Swami Lokeswarananda, tr., *Letters for Spiritual Seekers* (Calcutta: Advaita Ashrama, 1896), pp. 288-95. In his book on Sri Ramakrishna, Rolland quoted from Saradananda's two volume, *Sri Ramakrishna, The Great Master* (1920-21) published by Ramakrishna Math, Mylapore, Madras, with the preface by Swami Sharvananda.

34 *PB* (March 1928), pp. 122-23; also in *BRMIC* (Jan. 1992), p. 19.

35 Sankari Basu, "Romain Rolland's Biography of Ramakrishna", *BRMIC* (Nov. 1991), p. 336.

36 Rolland, pp. 2-3, 12-13, 65.

37 William Parsons, "The Oceanic Feeling Revisited", *The Journal of Religion* (Oct. 1998), p. 505.

38 *CA* (2002), vol. 197, pp. 348-53; Web: www.vedanta-atlanta.org/provisions/ProVisionsAug07.pdf; Web: en.wikipedia.org/wiki/ Swami_Siddheshwarananda.

39 Tathagatananda2, pp. 212, 218.

40 *Prophets of New India*, p. v; UCLC; Jean Herbert, "Ramakrishna in Continental Europe", Centenary, II, pp. 551-53.

41 Tathagatananda2, p. 222.

42 Irving Harrison, "Oceanic Feeling", *American Psychoanalytic Association Journal* (1979), pp. 409-10; *VK* (Sept. 2005), p. 355. The letter is translated a bit differently in varying sources.

43 Rolland, pp. 33-35; Saradananda, II:6.13, p. 212; Harrison (1979), pp. 409-13, 416-18; Ernst Freud, *Letters of Sigmund Freud* (New York: Basic Books, 1960), p. 392; Parsons (1998), pp. 502-04, 512-14; David Werman, "Sigmund Freud and Romain Rolland", *International Review of Psycho-Analysis* (1977), pp. 225, 227; William Harrison in *Vishnu on Freud's Desk* (Oxford University Press, 2003), pp. 67-70.

44 Bruno Goetz, "Reminiscences of Sigmund Freud", *International Review of Psycho-Analysis* (1975), p. 141.

45 T. C. Sinha, "Development of Psycho-Analysis in India", *International Journal of Psych-Analysis* (1966), pp. 430-31.

46 Christiane Hartnack, "Vishnu on Freud's Desk", *Social Research* (Winter 1990), pp. 921-49.

47 *Biographisches Handbuch der Deutschsprachigen Emigration Nach* (München 1980-1983); *Christopher Isherwood Diaries: 1939-1960* (New York: HarperCollins, 1996), pp. 189, 200, 207, 227.

48 *The Bookman* (Nov. 1930), p. 331 on APS.

49 *The Nation* (Dec. 3. 1930), pp. 619-20.

50 *International Review of Missions* (Oct. 1931), pp. 602-03; UCLC; Bishop's College Calcutta. Web: http://anglicanhistory.org/india/ bishops1970.

51 *PB* (July 1933), p. 327; Guy Welbon, *The Buddhist Nirvana and its Western Interpreters* (Chicago: University of Chicago Press, 1968), pp. 240-42; UCLC.

52 *PB* (Feb. 1936), pp. 121-24; Mookerjee, pp. 80-83.

53 *RLOA* (1991), p. 398; *EOP* (1991), II, pp. 1423-24; Tathagatananda2, p. 545; G. Stavig, "India in Russian Thought", *Bulletin of the Ramakrishna Mission Institute of Culture* (Oct. 1999), pp. 476-81. Nikolai Rerikh. Web: www.vor.ru/culture/cultarch90_eng.html#1; Roerich Himalayan Museum of Folk and Tribal Art. Web: http://ignca.nic.in/nl_01202.htm.

54 *PB* (Feb. 1936), p. 125; Mookerjee, p. 91.

55 Londhe, #18. Hermann Keyserling.

56 Count Hermann Keyserling. Web: www.schoolofwisdom.com/count.html; Tathagatananda2, p. 308; Centenary, I, p. 10; II, pp. xii, 942-56.

57 *PB* (July 1936), pp. 349-52; UCLC; Centenary, II, pp. xi, 824-25.

58 *PB* (April 1936), p. 343; Mookerjee, p. 90.

59 *PB* (Oct. 1927), pp. 479-80; Centenary, I, p. 1.

60 Stache-Weiske, pp. 219-20; Lindsay Jones, ed., *Encyclopedia of Religion* (Detroit: Thomson Gale, 2005), V, pp. 3496-97; Tathagatananda2, p. 251.

61 Albert Schweitzer, *Indian Thought and Its Development* (Boston: Beacon Press, 1936), p. 217.

62 Albert Schweitzer, *A Treasury of Albert Schweitzer*, ed. Thomas Kiernan (New York: Citadel Press, 1966), pp. 74-75.

63 Albert Schweitzer, *The Philosophy of Civilization*, tr. C. T. Campion (New York: Macmillan, 1949), p. 79.

64 Schweitzer (1966), pp. 92-93.

65 Schweitzer (1966), p. 214.

66 Centenary I, pp. xvii, 42, 74, 256-61; *PB* (April 1937), pp. 252-56; Stache-Weiske, pp. 229-30.

67 Francis Yeats-Brown, *Lancer at Large* (New York: Viking Press, 1937), pp. 129-30 on GBS; *CA* (1987), vol. 119; *Time Magazine* (Jan. 18, 1937); *New York Times* (Dec. 21, 1944), p. 21.

68 Steven Walker, "Jung on Yoga and Realization", *BRMIC* (July 1995), p. 263; *Mission* (Vrajaprana), p. 1111.

69 Carl Jung, *Psychology and Religion: West and East*, tr. R. F. C. Hull (Princeton, NJ: Princeton University Press, 1973), p. 584; *Mission* (Vrajaprana, "World Thinkers on Ramakrishna Movement"), p. 1112.

70 Walker (1995), p. 326; Londhe, #79. Carl Jung.

71 Walker (1995), pp. 326-27; *Mission* (Vrajaprana), p. 1112.

72 Centenary I, pp. 43; II, pp. viii, 560-75.

73 Barnes and Noble. Web: http://search.barnesandnoble.com/booksearch/isbninquiry.asp?ean=9780911206012&z=y.

74 Henry Zimmer, "Sri Ramakrishna and Our Modern Tortured World", *PB* (Nov. 1942), p. 514.

75 Londhe, #102. Heinrich Zimmer.

76 Stache-Weiske, pp. 216-18.

77 amazon.com. Web: http://www.amazon.com/Gospel-Sri-Ramakrishna-Swami-Nikhilananda/dp/0911206019; *CA* (1990), vol. 128; Bryan Magee, *The Philosophy of Schopenhauer* (New York: Oxford University Press, 1983), p. 388.

78 George Shepperson and Thomas Price, *Independent African* (Edinburgh: University Press, 1987), pp. 203-09, 413.

79 Victor Gollancz, *Man and God* (Boston: Houghton Mifflin, 1951), pp. 13, 95, 129, 140, 313, 470; CA (1986), vol. 116.

80 *PB* (Feb. 1953), pp. 83-85.

81 Lindsay Jones, *Encyclopedia of Religion* (Detroit: Thomson Gale, 2005), XIV, pp. 9391-92; Wikipedia. Web: http://en.wikipedia.org/wiki/Giuseppe_Tucci; Centenary, I, p. 95; WorldCat.

82 Frithjof Schuon, *Spiritual Perspective and Human Facts*, tr. M. Matheson (London: Faber and Faber Limited, 1954, 2007), pp. 113-15 on GBS.

83 Web: en.wikipedia.org/Frithjof_Schuon; *CA* (2002), New Rev. Ser. vol. 108.

84 *VFEW* (May-June 1954), pp. 150-51; (Jan-Feb. 1955), p. 100.

85 A History of the World Congress of Faiths. Web: www.religion-online.org/showchapter.asp?title=3378&C=2775.

86 *VFEW* (May-June 1958), pp. 142-47.

87 *VFEW* (Jan-Feb. 1961), pp. 67-71.

88 Stephen Neill, *Christian Faith and Other Faiths* (London: Oxford University, 1961), p. 76; *CA* (1982), New Rev. Ser., VII.

89 *PB* (June 1962), pp. 262-63.

90 *VFEW* (May-June 1969), pp. 25, 28, 30-31; *Marquis Who's Who* (2008).

91 P. J. Saher, *Eastern Wisdom and Western Thought*, p. 231; On Sri Ramakrishna. Web: www.vedanta-newyork.org/articles/on_sri_ramakrishna.htm#wigner; Zen-Yoga. Web: www.bagchee.com/BookDisplay.aspx?Bkid=B10383.

92 Swami Ghanananda, *Sri Ramakrishna and His Unique Message* (London, 1970), pp. vii-ix; Tathagatananda2, pp. 49-51.

93 *CA* (1976), vol. 61; *EWB* (1998); Book review of "*One World and India*", *BRMIC* (Jan. 1961), pp. 29-30.

94 *BRMIC* (April 1974), p. 86; Robert Antoine. Web: www.goethals.org/ robert.htm.

95 Karel Werner, *Yoga and Indian Philosophy* (Motilal Banarsidass, 1977, 1998), p. 154 on GBS; *Perspectives on Indian Religion: Papers in Honour of Karel Werner*, ed. Peter Connolly (Delhi: Sri Satguru, 1986), p. Preface; Web: www.soas.ac.uk/staff36441.php.

96 Hans Torwesten, *Ramakrishna and Christ* (Calcutta: The Ramakrishna Mission Institute of Culture, 1981), pp. 26-27; Londhe, #128. Hans Torwesten.

97 Glyn Richards, *A Sourcebook of Modern Hinduism* (London: Curzon Press, 1985), pp. 63-76 on GBS; Glyn Richards. Web: www.independent.co.uk/news/obituaries/the-rev-glyn-richards-.

98 Stewart Sutherland et al., ed., *The World's Religions* (Routledge, 1988), p. 708.

99 *PB* (March, May 1986), p. 127.

100 *VFEW* (July-Aug. 1989), pp. 26-28, 33-35; (Jan-Feb. 1991), p. 21; Web: www.martin-kaempchen.com; WorldCat.

101 Wilhelm Halbfass, *India and Europe* (Delhi: Motilal Banarsidass, 1990), pp. 226-27; "In Memoriam", *Journal of Indian Philosophy* (2000), pp. 425-27.

102 *Yoga Journal* (Sept-Oct. 1992), pp. 76-77.

103 *CA* (2008), New Rev. Ser., vol. 174.

104 Tathagatananda2, pp. 551-52; *BRMIC* (Jan. 1998), p. 40.

105 Vivekananda, pp. 746, 750; also in Swami Tathagatananda, "Dhan Gopal Mukherji and the Face of Silence", *PB*, Feb. 2006, pp. 167-68.

106 Mariasusai Dhavamony, *Hindu Spirituality* (Roma: Editrice Pontificia Universita' Gregoriana, 1999), pp. 121-22; *CA*, 1st Rev. (Detroit: Gale Research, 1978), vols. 33-36.

107 Hans Küng, *Tracing the Way: Spiritual Dimensions of the World Religions*, tr. John Bowden (Continuum International, 2001, 2006), pp. 73-74 on GBS.

108 *EWB; CA* (2005), New Rev. Ser., vol. 134.

109 Jerald Gort et al., *Religion, Conflict, Reconciliation* (Rodopi, 2002), pp. 46-47 on GBS; Victor van Bijlert. Web: www.iias.nl/iiasn/23/regions/23B1.htm.

110 Christopher Pinney, *Photos of the Gods* (Reaktion Books, 2004), p. 40 on GBS: Web: www.wcas.northwestern.edu/arthistory/faculty/pinney.htm.

111 Jan Peter Schouten, *Jesus as Guru* (Rodopi, 2008), p. 83; *WWIA* (2008).

CHAPTER III

TWENTIETH AND TWENTY-FIRST CENTURY AMERICAN BIOGRAPHERS, TRANSLATORS, AND TRIBUTES

EXCERPTS FROM seven 1901 journal and newspaper reviews of Vivekananda's eighty-nine-page book *My Master*[1] dealing with Sri Ramakrishna appear in Chapter XIII. Through the influence of Max Müller's biography, Richard Bucke (1837-1902), the Canadian author of the highly influential *Cosmic Consciousness* (1901), gained the following insight into Sri Ramakrishna's nature:

> His face retained a fullness, a childlike tenderness, a profound visible humbleness, an unspeakable sweetness of expression, and a smile such as Mozoomdar says he never saw on any other face. A Hindu saint is always particular about his externals.... But the man Ramakrishna was singularly devoid of any such claims. His dress and diet did not differ from those of other men, except in the general negligence he showed towards both, and as to caste, he openly broke it every day. He repudiated the title of a teacher, showed displeasure at any exceptional honour which people tried to pay him, and he emphatically disclaimed the knowledge of secrets and mysteries. He worshipped no particular Hindu deity, neither Siva, Vishnu, nor the Saktis, and yet he accepted all the doctrines, the embodiments, the usages and devotional practices of every religious cult. Each in turn was infallible to him. His religion meant ecstasy, his worship transcendental insight, his whole nature burnt day and night with the permanent fire and fever of a strange faith and feeling. His conversation was a ceaseless breaking forth of his inward fire and lasted for long hours. He was often merged in rapturous ecstasy and outward unconsciousness during the day, particularly when he spoke of his favourite spiritual experiences or heard any striking response

to them. Krishna became to him the incarnation of loving devotion, and we are told that, while meditating on him, his heart full of the burning love of God, his features would suddenly become stiff and motionless, his eyes lose their sight, and while completely unconscious himself, tears would run down his rigid, pale, yet smiling face; and while in that state he would sometimes break out into prayers, songs and utterances, the force and pathos of which would pierce through the hardest heart and bring tears to eyes that never wept before through the influence of religion.

Bucke then provided a few characteristic passages from Ramakrishna's teachings. Born in Methwold, Norfolk, England, Bucke immigrated to Canada the following year. In 1868 he was greatly inspired by *Leaves of Grass* written by the renowned poet Walt Whitman (1819-92), who became a close friend. Bucke described a life-changing mystical experience which he called an "intellectual illumination" that he experienced in 1872:

> I saw and knew that the Cosmos is not dead matter but a living Presence, that the soul of man is immortal, that the universe is so built and ordered that without any peradventure all things work together for the good of each and all, that the foundation principle of the world is what we call love and that the happiness of every one is in the long run absolutely certain.

It was Bucke's opinion that Walt Whitman was the ultimate example of "cosmic consciousness". He spent the next thirty years in reading about other people who had a similar mystical experience that he documents in his work *Cosmic Consciousness*. Bucke believed that cosmic consciousness was an emerging faculty of humanity and the next stage of human development.[2] Being an M.D., he held the challenging post of superintendent of an insane asylum in London, Ontario, Canada (1876-1902).

One of Americas leading Episcopalians, Reverend R. Heber Newton* (1840-1914) [q.v.] was the Rector of All Souls' Church in New York City for over thirty years. Being the resident preacher at Stanford University in California, he delivered an appreciative address on Ramakrishna that was published in *Unity*, and also appeared in the *Prabuddha Bharata* of June 1906.

* See Chapter XVIII for more details on Newton's involvement with Vedanta.

Newton was a good friend of Swami Abhedananda, Pratap Mazumdar and Reverend Hugh Haweis. At the end of his talk Newton stressed:

> One whom we knew in this land well and honoured deeply [P. C. Mazumdar] said of this saint: "In the midst of his emaciation his face retains its fullness and childlike tenderness, a profound humbleness and unspeakable sweetness of expression, and a smile that I have seen on no other face that I can remember." This saint of God was known in his land as Paramahamsa Srimat Ramakrishna. He is regarded by thousands of his fellow countrymen in India today as a divine incarnation. Even in our Western world he is recognized as perhaps the greatest saint of God in the modern world. The men whose testimony I have quoted are no less eminent than Swami Vivekananda and Protap Chunder Mazumdar.
>
> Did this Hindu saint not embody "pure religion and undefiled"? Was not his the one essential, pure, vital religion?... If we draw the limits of religious fellowship short of this Hindu saint, then those limits shut out religion itself.[3]

In 1907 James Creelman (1859-1915) [q.v.], a renowned international journalist, paid a visit to the Vedanta Society of New York, after which he wrote an article for *Pearson's Magazine* describing Ramakrishna as a "great Saint, Yogi and Mahatma". After paying a tribute to Vivekananda,* he added:

> The most wonderful and impressive figure in the movement was Ramakrishna, teacher of the Swami Vivekananda. Ramakrishna is today revered by half of India as a divine incarnation. Up to the very hour of his death, twenty-one years ago, he was regarded as the ancient God Vishnu reappearing in human form. Professor Max Müller, of Oxford University, the greatest European authority on Indian religions and literature, wrote a notable book on the life and teachings of Ramakrishna. As this most inspiring and thrilling romantic personality of spiritual India, which today challenges America through her dusky Brahmin missionaries, actually taught the men who began the Vedanta crusade in New York, it is worthwhile knowing who and what he was.[4]

* See Chapter XIII.

Creelman then followed with a condensed biography of Ramakrishna of over a thousand words. His article contains excellent pictures of Ramakrishna, Vivekananda and Abhedananda, and the Dakshineswar Temple gardens.

James Creelman was a journalist on the staff of six New York newspapers from 1878 until his death, and associate editor of *Pearson's Magazine* (1906-10). Being a lifelong adventurer, he worked as a top-level in-the-field foreign war correspondent during the Sino-Japanese War (1894) and the Greco-Turkish War (1896-97). As an on-the-scene participant in world events, during the Hatfield-McCoy feud in Kentucky, Creelman received gunshot wounds. In 1898 he was wounded in the shoulder after suggesting tactics that resulted in the seizure of Fort El Caney during the Spanish-American War. His high profile interviews of historical individuals include those with Leo Tolstoy in Russia, Pope Leo XIII in Italy, President Diaz in Mexico, and Sitting Bull, Thomas Edison, Theodore Roosevelt, and William Howard Taft in America.[5]

Concerning the practitioners of Tantra, in 1907 Ernest P. Horrwitz (b. 1866) wrote:

> Many a noble soul may be found among them worshipping the Impersonal under the personality of Kali. Such a one was Ramakrishna Paramahamsa, a fervent Hindu saint and Tantrist.... Ramakrishna looked on Kali as his Divine Mother, and the charm which he found in holy communion with her proved more potent than all the spells of mystery mongers... The saint died near Calcutta in 1886, and so broad and universal were his religious views that they have been largely accepted not only in India, but also in England and America.

Twenty-nine years later, in 1936, Professor Horrwitz of Hunter College, the City University of New York, added:

> Neo-Vedanta, worldwide in its sympathies, points to the one divine and dynamic life which is profuse in all of God's messengers, Moses and Mohammed, Buddha and Jesus. Ramakrishna fulfilled the same charitable mission reclaiming erring mortals from gloom to light. Like a ship furrowing the seven seas, the Bengal God-man left behind him a long and luminous trail which the restless waves of Maya or cosmic nescience threaten to efface and obliterate.

Horrowitz's book *Veda and Vedanta* (1937) was published by the Advaita Ashrama.[6]

An article appeared in the *Prabuddha Bharata* of 1912 entitled "Sri Ramakrishna: An Interpretation", written by a young Frank J. Alexander (1887/88-1917) [q.v.], a Vedanta devotee who lived in India.* It stated:

> To have come to understand Sri Ramakrishna is to have understood and grasped the whole meaning of life. It is to have come into direct and real touch with spirituality in its dynamic and powerful relations. It is verily to have seen the soul become conscious of itself,—as the soul. It is to have entered the realm of understanding as to the opportunities and factors for the making of true spirituality. And why? Because in Sri Ramakrishna one perceives humanity becoming divinity; verily, it sees divinity incarnate. And why, again? Because all the longing that man has ever known to perceive reality was made incarnate. One sees in him, living and breathing before one's very eyes, the desire of man to see God,—yes, and the triumphant realization of that desire. One witnesses in him a tremendous sincerity and a tremendous sanity.[7]

Annie Rix Militz (1856-1924) [q.v.] founded the Home of Truth, a New Thought religious organization in the United States, Canada, and Great Britain, and in three cities in California where Vivekananda stayed and lectured. As the editor of *Master Mind Magazine*, she published the following favourable evaluation of *The Gospel of Sri Ramakrishna* according to "M", a reprint of the Madras edition brought out by the San Francisco Vedanta Society in 1912.† The book review reads:

> This is an account of the life, works, and conversations with his disciples, of a great soul who was the spiritual Father of Vivekananda of World's Parliament of Religion fame and Abhedananda, Turiyananda, Trigunatita and many other spiritual Hindus whose ministrations have helped students of Truth. Sri Ramakrishna's words are full of life and light and pearls of wisdom fell from his lips continually. He was large enough to bless all aspirations towards God, and to understand the various methods. One

* Frank Alexander's involvement with the Vedanta movement is presented in more detail in Chapter XIII.

† See Chapter VI for a discussion on Militz's relationship with Vivekananda.

ardently wishes he might have received the healing gift from God, instead of humbly renouncing it, for then he might be with us still.

The book is indirectly an excellent description of the way the Hindus live and act as devotees of the spiritual life. There is a wholesome, happy tone in all the communings of the Master and his disciples that is charming—one is impressed with how often they laughed and were the object of Sri Ramakrishna's loving play of wit and sympathy. The book is a good contribution to our libraries of spiritual literature, and well worthy of deep study.[8]

English born Alexander J. McIvor-Tyndall (d. 1940) was the editor of the *Swastika Magazine* (1906-11), and the president of the International New Thought Fellowship. In 1913, writing under the pseudonym of Ali Nomad in the book *Cosmic Consciousness: The Man-God Whom We Await* (a book still being published), he affirmed:

> Sri Ramakrishna Paramahamsa, the latest incarnation of God in India, and the master to whom the late Swami Vivekananda gives such high praise and devotion, lived almost wholly in that exalted state of consciousness which would appear to be more essentially spiritual than cosmic in the strict sense of the latter word, since cosmic should certainly imply all-inclusiveness, rather than wholly spiritual (spiritual being used here as an extremely high vibration of the cosmos).
>
> We learn that Sri Ramakrishna was a man comparatively unlettered, and yet his insight was so marvellous, his consciousness so exalted that the most learned pundits honoured and respected him as one who had attained unto the goal of all effort—liberation, mukti, while to many persons throughout India today, and indeed throughout the whole world, he is looked upon as an incarnation of Krishna....
>
> This wonderful insight he displayed in all the after years of his earthly mission, and he not only attained glimpses of the cosmic consciousness state, but he also retained the Illumination, and the power to impart to a great degree, the realization of that state of being which he himself possessed.[9]

James Bassett Pratt (1875-1944), an outstanding professor of philosophy and comparative religion at Williams College in Williamstown, Massachusetts (1905-43), made three trips to India, was a visiting professor at Rabindranath Tagore's school in Shantiniketan (1931-32), and in 1934 became the national president of the prestigious American Philosophical Association. Early in his career, under the tutelage of the great William James at Harvard, he pursued research in the field of the psychology of religious consciousness, following which he published *The Psychology of Religious Belief* (1907).[10] Pratt made his first trip to India in 1913-14, and in his "Traveller's Record" titled *India and Its Faiths* (1915), he enthusiastically declared:

> Ramakrishna was a man in whom the Indian type of spirituality expressed itself to an unusual degree. Brought up as a servitor in a temple of Kali, he became possessed while still a boy with extreme devotion to the Great Mother, and with a longing for perfect purity and for an immediate realization of the Divine. Early in life he turned sannyasi and for a period of years put himself through trying ordeals with the aim of overcoming every weakness of the flesh and all attachment to this world. In order to understand better the nature of the Divine,—not by theological discourses, but through immediate experience,—he joined in the worship of the various Hindus sects...
>
> Ramakrishna seems to have been a man of remarkable personal magnetism. Though with no knowledge of the English language nor of European culture, and with no wide reading in Indian literature, he made a deep impression upon the many hundreds who came to talk with him. And he seems to have left on nearly all who knew him the conviction that here was a man who had communed face to face with God....
>
> The culture of the soul has been, and is still, the one great ideal of India. Conquest, government, moneymaking, pleasure, the things that have occupied the chief attention in the West, have been for India of very secondary importance.[11]

On his way to India for the first time, Pratt made the acquaintance of a successful German businessman who lived for many years in Bengal. Several years before the businessman made contact with an Indian teacher and saint. At first, being sceptical, he "went to scoff", but "remained to pray". The life and personality of the Indian had a profound affect on him, which he had never experienced before or after. Following several months of contact with the holy man, he realized he would have to choose between the new life of spirituality and his business ventures. With much regret, he turned away from the higher life and broke completely with his teacher.

With little evidence, Pratt thought the German might have been referring to Ramakrishna.[12]

Concerning Ramakrishna's spiritual awakening, Pratt ascertained in *The Religious Consciousness: A Psychological Study* (1920):

> At length the victory was won,—not by any sudden insight or reformation, but by a gradual process, in which both increased self-control, intellectual illumination, and (most important of all) an absolute unification of values played important and mutually helpful parts. The moral and intellectual and emotional unification thus attained, together with the peace and joy that flowed from it, were now permanent. The flesh no longer felt any incitements to insurrection, love of things and Brahmin pride were gone forever. He lived to the end of his days in complete poverty, and in never failing intuition of the presence of God in low and high, in himself and in everything. "I have now come to a stage of realization," he said toward the close of his life, "in which I see that God is walking in every human form and manifesting Himself alike through the saint and sinner, the virtuous and the vicious."[13]

In a 1935 letter to the editor of *Vedanta Kesari*, James Pratt revealed, "Ramakrishna and Vivekananda have been almost household words with my wife and myself for more than 22 years. We have read books by and about them and have visited the Ramakrishna Centres in both India and America." Another insightful statement made by Pratt shortly before his passing was:

> For most Westerners "histories of philosophy" begin with the Greeks and end with the Americans, and convey not the least suggestion that anyone outside of the West ever had a philosophical idea.... To one who has had a taste of the riches which Indian thought and Indian literature can contribute to our intellectual life and our spiritual experience, this deprivation which we Westerners inflict upon ourselves and upon our young people seems pitiful in the extreme.[14]

Concerning the late Professor J. B. Pratt, the *Vedanta Kesari* noted:

> In him India loses a sincere and understanding friend of Indian aspirations and a good devotee of Indian Religion and philosophy. Professor

> Pratt was an intimate friend of the Mission and has been for many years a distinguished contributor to the columns of the Mission's English journals, the *Vedanta Kesari* and the *Prabuddha Bharata*.[15]

The Sociedad Vedanta of Buenos Aires in Argentina was formed under the direction of the Vedanta Society of New York. In 1912, Swami Abhedananda's English language translation of the *Ramakrishna Kathamrita* (*The Gospel of Sri Ramakrishna*) was rendered into Spanish with the title *El Evangelio de Ramakrishna* by the Sociedad Vedanta of Buenos Aires. The book is now published by "Sarada Ma Publishing" in Southern California. Ricardo Vivie of the Buenos Aires Centre dispatched seven books to Amado (Ruiz de) Nervo (1870-1919), a renowned Mexican poet, novelist, short story writer, dramatist, and essayist. In reply, Nervo sent the following July 30, 1916 letter to Vivie from Madrid, Spain:

> You have made me a very valuable present by sending seven books. All of them are really nice; but I must say the admirable *Gospel of Sri Ramakrishna*—which has been a revelation for me—excels them all. What a profundity under its crystalline innocence! How beautiful are the parables! (For example, of the wall behind which there is the Absolute!) I had read long ago with deep emotional interest the *Gospel of Buddha*, classified and arranged methodically by Paul Carus. It impressed me much, but less than this delightful *Gospel of Sri Ramakrishna*, so profoundly familiar, so familiarly profound. From today it will be one of the books at my bedside, one of those which I carry with me everywhere. It is a small mystic lamp for searching God, outside this spider-net of philosophies, of rituals, and of metaphysical disputes. It is impregnated with very pure love and no threat casts its shadow over those pages of mysterious whiteness.[16]

Amado (Ruiz de) Nervo served as secretary of the Mexican legation in Madrid, Spain (1905-18), and as minister to Argentina and Uruguay (1919). He is widely regarded as one of the two foremost Mexican writers of the modernist period. Religion, philosophy, and mysticism are the central themes of his literary productions. Amado Nervo desired to solve, both theoretically and practically, the problem of God and the struggle for spiritual wholeness. His writings involve the search for truth and the meaning of existence. Twenty-eight volumes of Nervo's works were published posthumously. Writing on Vedantic themes, Nervo supported reincarnation, the law of karma, maya, pantheism, renunciation, meditation, and the identity of the human soul with the Supreme Being. He actively practised renunciation and detachment from worldly desires, and believed that meditation is the only method for discovering spiritual truths and becoming one with the Divine Spirit.[17]

When Hereward Carrington (1880-1958) [q.v.] wrote his well-received text *Higher Psychical Development: Yoga Philosophy* (1920), he wisely utilized several long quotes from Vivekananda's *Raja Yoga* and from the works of Abhedananda. He also covers the subjects of the kundalini, prana, asana, pranayama, mantra, dhyana, sushumna, pingala, mudra, tattvas, samadhi, pratyahara, yogi and sahasrara. Hereward Carrington, the author of numerous books, was born on the Isle of Jersey in the United Kingdom. He became a member of the American Society for Psychical Research assisting James H. Hyslop of Columbia University until 1908, founded and directed the American Psychical Institute, and authored books on spiritualism and astral projection.[18]

In 1921, Irish born Brian Brown (b. 1881) [q.v.] produced a very successful anthology titled *The Wisdom of the Hindus: Philosophies and Wisdom from their Ancient and Modern Literature*. It was his intention to edit a non-technical book that could be understood by an educated person outside of the field of Indian studies. Jagadish Chandra Chatterji, head of the department of Sanskrit research for the Maharaja of Baroda, wrote the Foreword. In the Introduction, Brown emphasizes, "All of the spiritual sages mentioned in this anthology are among the foremost men the Indian nation has produced." What is unique about Brown's presentation is that modern Indian thought is represented entirely by verbatim writings of four Ramakrishna-Vedantists, which he was obviously familiar with. They are "Ramakrishna on Yoga Philosophy" and "Sayings of Ramakrishna", "Vivekananda on Yoga Philosophy" and the "Wisdom of Vivekananda", "Wisdom of Abhedananda", and "Wisdom of Paramananda". In addition, during the 1920s Brian Brown educated Western audiences concerning the spiritual writings of the Orient with *The Wisdom of the Chinese*, *The Wisdom of the Hebrews*, *The Story of Buddha and Buddhism*, and *The Story of Confucius*.[19]

During the first quarter of the twentieth century, we find people interested in psychical phenomena and/or spiritualism, and making appreciative statements about the founders of the Vedanta Society. One example is Walter Winston Kenilworth [q.v.], an author of books on the "psychic". In *Practical Occultism* (1921), which deals with Brahman, raja yoga and karma yoga, along with occult subjects, he made the following two favourable references to Ramakrishna:

> Another great teacher [after mentioning Buddha], Bhagavan Sri Ramakrishna, instructed his disciples that psychological phenomena, in themselves, had a tendency to lead the seeker after Truth in vaingloriousness from the noble path leading to the goal. It is related that, on a certain occasion, when a disciple said: "Master, I have acquired the power to read the human heart," he replied: "Shame on thee, boy, for following such practices."
>
> The first and indispensable requisite for realization is a sincere desire. This desire should not be the haphazard result of a passing emotion. It should be real. Sri Ramakrishna, India's latest incarnation of the Supreme, telling his followers of this desire, likened it to the desire of the drowning man to be rescued from immanent death. When the desire is that sincere, then you will see the Lord; you will know, "I and My Father are One"; you will attain realization.[20]

In 1923 Ernest C. Brown (Sajjana, 1871-1960/61) [q.v.], an old-time Vedanta Society devotee who had met Swami Vivekananda, delivered a lecture titled "Sri Ramakrishna: Divine Incarnation of this Age" at the Hindu Temple in San Francisco. He stated:

> What a wonderful thing that a Divine Incarnation should have attained to the highest realization of God as Divine Mother at a time when women all over the world were struggling for emancipation! Is it difficult to believe that the incarnation on earth of this great advocate of womanhood should have given their cause a powerful impetus?... The great outstanding purpose of Sri Ramakrishna's advent as the Divine Incarnation of this age was that he came to show that the paths of all men lead to the same goal and that the same Divine Self dwells within the heart of all. Who can measure the glory and greatness of that life? He came to India, but he came for all, and no one county can claim him for its own. Let us give him our heart's adoration, and generations yet unborn shall call him blessed and find liberation through his name.

Ernest C. Brown attended the lectures of Swami Vivekananda in Northern California. As an early disciple of Swami Trigunatita, he was part of the month-long gatherings at Shanti Ashrama, and became a member of the monastery in San Francisco. Using the pseudonym "His Western Disciples", he published every month in the *Prabuddha Bharata* for the entire year of 1928 his reminiscences, "The Work of Swami Trigunatita in the West".[21]

In March of 1922, Sister Devamata (1867-1942) [q.v.], who worked with Swami Paramananda for many years, suffered a severe illness. Partially paralysed, she remained a semi-invalid for the rest of her life. Unable to make public speaking appearances, she devoted most of her creative talents to literary pursuits. Devamata's outstanding *Days in an Indian Monastery*, first issued in 1927, tells of her two-year stay in India during 1907-09. A year later she followed it with *Sri Ramakrishna and His Disciples*, which has been reissued. A principle source of these two books is her lengthy conversations with Swami Ramakrishnananda in Madras. In the latter book, she writes of the Swami's intimate experiences of living with Ramakrishna and his brother disciples. Two examples are:

> "He [Sri Ramakrishna] never condemned any man. He was ready to excuse everything," the disciple Shashi [Swami Ramakrishnananda] declared. He used to tell us that the difference between man and God was this: "If a man failed to serve God ninety-nine times, but the hundredth time served him with even a little love, God forgot the ninety-nine times he had failed and would say: 'Oh! My devotee served me well today.'"... So Sri Ramakrishna, if there is the least spark of good in any one, sees only that and overlooks all the rest.
>
> [Ramakrishna] used to tell us: "The people whose Karma I have taken think that they are attaining salvation through their own strength. They do not understand that it is because I have taken their Karma on me." We do not know how much we owe to him; but some day we shall realize what he has done for us and then we shall know how to be grateful to him.[22]

Her other literary works include the two-volume *Swami Paramananda and His Work* (1926, 1941), and the comparative study *Sri Ramakrishna and St. Francis of Assisi* (1935).[23] Chapters IV and XXI in this book discuss Devamata's relationship with Holy Mother and some of Ramakrishna's disciples.

In *The Way of Power* (1928) Lily Adams Beck (1862-1931) [q.v.] expressed her admiration for Sri Ramakrishna in the following words:

> His life is a wonderful record of realization and powers that follow upon it, powers which in themselves did not particularly interest him, drowned

as they were in the knowledge of the higher vision, but allied with the purpose of this book and therefore to be noted. Realization came to him in the typical way—devotion, longing for liberation from the bondage of the senses, and then one day, suddenly, a flood of light and the temporary loss of self-consciousness.

I will mention some of the powers it brought with it. They are described as "characteristics distinctive of the highest degree of concentrations."... He had his own nervous force so completely under control that during his last illness he could remove all consciousness from the cancer in his throat and allow it to be operated upon as if under a local anesthetic.... Above all he could by his touch (and this power is strangely related to the central Figure of our own Scriptures) exercise a compelling power over other lives. Through this touch they also received flashes of the higher consciousness which moulded their futures.

An example is given of his placing his hand on the heads of a row of persons with a different phrase for each, and each receiving a different gift. With one, overwhelming joy; to another a great light which never left him.[24]

The daughter of a British Admiral, Lily Adams Beck lived and travelled widely in India, Ceylon, Tibet, China, Burma, Japan and Egypt studying native customs and religions, particularly transcendentalism, reincarnation and yoga. In 1919 she made her permanent home in Victoria, British Columbia, Canada, and at the age of sixty began a very successful writing career in 1922, publishing thirty books in less than ten years. Being a staunch Buddhist, a strict vegetarian, she was highly critical of the "arid scepticism and the curse of a cruel materialism" found in the West. She claimed that due to the practice of yoga she knew no weariness of mind or body. As L. Adams Beck, she wrote stories set in Asia that were influenced by Oriental philosophy and religion. As E. Barrington, she composed historical novels, and as Louis Moresby, she penned works of nonfiction, and consequently was assumed by many of her readers to be a man. One of her goals was to bring the message of Eastern philosophy to thousands of people who would otherwise never know of it. *The Story of Oriental Philosophy* and *The Splendour of Asia* deal with the life and teachings of Buddha. Her book entitled *The House of Fulfillment: The Romance of a Soul* incorporates some of the Indian philosophy found in the Upanishads to explain supernatural phenomena. Other novels incorporate mystical ideas from the East.[25]

1930s and After

For over 100 years the Chicago based *The Christian Century* has informed and shaped progressive, mainline Christianity. The magazine has published articles by the most respected Protestant theologians and church leaders. Writing for *The Christian Century* under the title "India's Men of Vision", Grace D. Phillips composed a very favourable review of Rolland's biography of Ramakrishna and Vivekananda. She particularly appreciated the respect they both showed for Jesus Christ and concluded:

> Ramakrishna was an idealist who identified himself with all sorts and conditions of men and recognized that "all religions lead by different paths to God". But, more than that, he was a thinker who developed a deep, broad religion and gathered together disciples who have had such a profound effect upon their country that it is being spoken of in terms of the "New India". His religion was not one of creed or ritual; it was a vital belief that God is in everything and that he is everything. It required a severe discipline to keep body, senses and spirit pure and it called for work "without attachment", that is, work done without the hope of reward or the fear of punishment. His religion was made up of the best from all the great religions; he had practised each for a long time to have entered into the heart of it.[26]

Ricardo Güiraldes (1886-1927), the son of a rich landowner who became the mayor of Buenos Aires, was an important figure in Argentine literature. In 1910, on a world tour, he visited Europe, India and other Asiatic countries. As a novelist, poet, essayist, and short story writer, he was awarded Argentina's Gran Premio Nacional de Literatura for his epic novel *Don Segundo Sombra* (1926), which was translated into several languages. According to one evaluator, this work made him "the most famous Argentine novelist of the first half of the century". The following year he attempted to make a pilgrimage to India because of his interest in Vedanta, but his journey ended in Paris, where he passed away. A few years later, in the preface to his insightful *El Sendero* (*The Path: Notes on My Spiritual Evolution in Light of the Future*, 1932), his wife Adelina Güiraldes (1889-1967) wrote:

> Güiraldes longed for the real sources of oriental spiritual wisdom. The *Aphorisms of Patanjali*, commented on by Swami Vivekananda made a well-aimed impact on his feelings and understanding, and he was fascinated by

them. The same deep impression was created by the abridged *Gospel of Sri Ramakrishna*. The unity of God and His creation is the great message for this age.[27]

Ricardo's widow Adelina spoke at the Ramakrishna Centenary Parliament of Religions in Calcutta, which was held during March 1937. She mentioned that in Buenos Aires a Centenary Celebration had been conducted for Sri Ramakrishna on September 16, 1936, in which India was represented by Sophia Wadia and Kalidas Nag. She also made reference to

> our beloved Swami Vijayananda of the Ramakrishna Mission, who at our request came over there [Buenos Aires, Argentina] to bring us the marvellous gift of Vedanta embodying the truth of all times, which had been actually seen by the great Rishis who taught it, and which, with its perfect logic, satisfies the mind and the heart of those who have the good fortune to become acquainted with it.

Adelina Güiraldes remained in India for fourteen years until 1951, living in a bungalow near the Ramakrishna Ashrama in Bangalore. There she translated into Spanish Nikhilananda's rendering of the *Gospel of Sri Ramakrishna*. About this translation Graciela Devita commented:

> She applied in this translation the literary style she had amply imbued from her husband, where the colloquial blends with the erudite—surprisingly enough the same style in which the original *Sri Sri Ramakrishna Kathamrita* in Bengali is written, as far as I have been informed. Unconsciously mirroring the original, Adelina's translation presents Sri Ramakrishna's words in an appealing idiomatic style, while other descriptions are framed in a refined, cultured Spanish, making of the whole an exquisitely accomplished literary and spiritual piece of art.

Adelina Güiraldes continued to be an active member of the Buenos Aires Ashrama, becoming its first president in 1957.[28]

A U.C.L.A. professor, Will Durant (1885-1981) [q.v.], in July of 1935, came out with the first volume of *The Story of Civilization* entitled *Our Oriental Heritage*. The book contains a large segment on the history of Indian thought, which helped to communicate these ideas to the educated reading public. It was during the 1935-37 period that Ramakrishna and Vivekananda began receiving attention from university professors in the West. Before this time Sri Ramakrishna's main support (with the exception of Max Müller) came from professional Western writers outside of the university system. Regarding Ramakrishna's attitude toward other religions, Durant affirmed:

> All religions are good, he taught his followers; each is a way to God, or a stage on the way, adapted to the mind and heart of the seeker.... "All rivers flow to the ocean. Flow, and let others flow, too!" He tolerated sympathetically the polytheism of the people, and accepted humbly the monism of the philosophers; but in his own living faith, God was a spirit incarnated in all men, and the only true worship of God was the loving service of mankind. Many fine souls, rich and poor, Brahman and Pariah, chose him as *Guru*, and formed an order and mission in his name.

After his visit to India, Durant authored *The Case for India* (1930), a volume that endorsed the independence of India from the British Empire. When Durant gave a copy of *The Case for India* to Rabindranath Tagore, he inscribed on it, "You alone are sufficient reason why India should be free." Tagore thought highly of the book stating among other things, "Will Durant treated us with the respect due to human beings.... I am especially thankful to him for the service he has rendered to the English nation by largely quoting from its own members the condemnation of British policy."[29]

On the occasion of Rabindranath Tagore's 70th birthday, Will Durant sent a message to him stating:

> Gurudeva, Revered Master: If we may call you by this name so dear to your pupils, who express through it their consciousness that you are not only a poet and a teacher, but one of the voices of divinity itself, we thank you for coming to us.... We see in you not merely the poet who, many years ago, won the highest recognition of all nations, but the noblest symbol and representative of a people whose language was the mother of our languages.[30]

Other American supporters of Gandhi and/or Indian Independence included: Jane Addams, Roger Baldwin, Senator John Blaine, Pearl Buck, Prof. John Dewey, Gertrude Emerson, Louis Fisher, William Lloyd Garrison, Samuel Gompers, John and Frances Gunther, Rev. John H. Holmes, Robert Hutchins, Senator Robert LaFollette, Prof. Robert Lovett, Clara and Henry Luce, Myron Phelps, Rev. Jabez Sunderland, Norman Thomas, and Rabbi Stephen Wise.[31]

The eldest daughter of former President of the United States Woodrow Wilson (1856-1924), Miss Margaret Wilson (1886-1944) is credited in the Preface of the *Gospel of Sri Ramakrishna* for helping Swami Nikhilananda in editing his translation. In 1936 she sent a letter to Franklin D. Roosevelt, who was then the President of the United States. She suggested during the Centenary of the Indian saint Ramakrishna Paramahamsa's birthday that he address a message to India. Roosevelt liked the idea and wrote to his press secretary Stephen Early, "Take this up with the State Department. Because he was a very great saint, this would have a very great effect all through the East." Unfortunately, the State Department rejected the idea because it might lead to problems with the British, and some Americans at that time would not want their President celebrating the birthday of a Hindu saint. Margaret Wilson spent the last five years of her life in Pondicherry, India, pursuing a path of understanding under the saint Sri Aurobindo.[32]

It should be mentioned that Holy Mother referred to Aurobindo as "my heroic son". She told his wife Mrinalini Devi that he was protected under the shelter of God and that with Thakur's (Ramakrishna's) blessings he would be exonerated and set free from jail after the 1909 Alipore bomb trial. Aurobindo later wrote that Ramakrishna "was certainly quite as much an Avatar as Christ or Chaitanya".[33] He also realized:

> Of all these souls [avatars] Sri Ramakrishna was the last and greatest, for while others felt God in a single or limited aspect, he felt Him in His illimitable unity of an illimitable variety. In him the spiritual experiences of the millions of saints who had gone before were renewed and united. Sri Ramakrishna gave to India the final message of Hinduism to the world. A new era dates from his birth, an era in which the peoples of the earth will be lifted for a while into communion with God and spirituality becomes the dominant role of human life.[34]

In 1936, Dr. Frederick B. Robinson joined in the fellowship to pay tribute to Ramakrishna. He contrasted his thinking with that of ordinary people:

> Ramakrishna clearly lived an inner life so abundant and far reaching, so ethereal and serenely abstract that few men, concerned mostly with con-

fusing duties in a narrow world of concrete and petty incidents, can even dimly appreciate its free and spacious calm. We hear people today taking pride in the fact that they are realists. They shape their conduct according to opportunity and do what is expedient in practical affairs, with little or no control by permanent principles.... Ramakrishna was just the opposite of these. To him realization was a process of discovering his own essential self and of identifying it with the source of life, thought and action.... Ramakrishna and the divines of all religions render the great service to mankind of stressing the abiding joy that can be had only from a life in harmony with ultimate truth.[35]

At the Ramakrishna Centenary Parliament of Religions which commenced on March 1, 1937 in Calcutta, papers of at least three pages in length were submitted by university professors and presidents from European countries like Belgium, Czechoslovakia, England, France, Germany, Holland, Italy, Poland, Rumania, Switzerland, and Yugoslavia, along with Afghanistan, China, Egypt, Iran, Japan and the United States. The list of distinguished scholars included Hermann Goetz, Jean Herbert, A. Berriedale Keith, Gualtherus Mees, Leopold von Wiese, and Moriz Winternitz.[36] Frederick Robinson submitted a paper to the Ramakrishna Centenary indicating in part:

> The essential teaching of Ramakrishna has been that:
>
> 1. To find God man must look within and the goal is attained when there is a realization of oneness with God.
>
> 2. There is good in all religious systems, they are but different languages or modes of expression suitable to people of different countries, speech and circumstances. Properly pursued, all lead to the one realization. Therefore creeds and rituals are but incidents; the essential helps to realization are love and sincerity.
>
> 3. But realization for self, or self-salvation is not enough: there is need to bring others to this realization.[37]

Frederick Bertrand Robinson (1883-1941) [q.v.], a professor of economics (1915-27), developed the largest evening programme of instruction in the world. As the fifth president of the College of the City of New York during the years 1927-39, he founded a School of Business that more than doubled the student enrolment, making it one of the largest colleges in the

United States. He was also the president of the Association of Colleges and Universities of the State of New York in 1930.[38]

Polish-born Reform, Rabbi Samuel H. Goldenson (1873-1962) served the Congregation Rodef Shalom in Pittsburgh from 1918 to 1934 and Temple Emanu-El in New York from 1934, remaining in that capacity until 1947. Known "as the spiritual leader of American Reform Judaism", he encouraged other Rabbis to practise social justice through individual righteousness. He belonged to an interfaith group of clergymen who in 1940 urged the U.S. government to supply England with food and weapons to maintain Judaic-Christian values in the Western world.[38] At the Ramakrishna Birth Centenary meeting held in the New York Town Hall during March 1936, Rabbi Goldenson affirmed:

> I feel it a privilege to participate in recalling the life and teaching of a great Hindu Saint and Prophet, Ramakrishna. For, in human life, the spirit is nourished by philosophy and religion more than by any other discipline, and this man, Ramakrishna, in his own life, achieved the highest and noblest reaches of both of these departments of human thought and sentiment.
>
> ...the important thing is that a contemporary of ours was able to demonstrate in an extreme fashion that one can find joy, real joy and great satisfaction in life, without forever looking for the things that will give us bodily comforts and bodily conveniences.
>
> The second great lesson that we may draw from Ramakrishna's teaching is his affirmation of the spiritual unity that underlies the universe. This affirmation is related to the negation. Once we discipline our minds to transcend the divisions that have to do with material things, then we are in a position to see nothing but over-arching unity.[40]

Rabbi Goldenson attended the unveiling of the statue of Vivekananda in 1950, and of the bust of Ramakrishna in 1952, both dedications being held at Nikhilananda's Ramakrishna-Vivekananda Centre in New York City.[41]

At the Ramakrishna Centenary held in New York during March 1936, Ananda Coomaraswamy (1877-1947) told his audience what impressed him was that Sri Ramakrishna, in

> about 1866, completely surrendered himself to the Islamic way, repeated the name of Allah, wore the costume, and ate the food of a Muslim. This self-surrender to what we should call in India the waters of another

current of the single river of truth resulted only in a direct experience of the beatific vision, not less authentic than before. Seven years later, Ramakrishna in the same way proved experimentally the truth of Christianity. He was now for a time completely absorbed in the idea of Christ, and had no room for any other thought.... no one can finally pronounce upon the truth of a given religion who has not lived it, as Ramakrishna lived both Christianity and Islam, as well as Hinduism.

Ananda Coomaraswamy, the son of a Ceylonese lawyer and a British mother, joined the Boston Museum of Fine Arts in 1917 as the Keeper of Indian and Mohammedan Art. There he devoted his life to re-educating the Western intellectuals, establishing new standards in the field by employing a scholarly interpretation of the philosophy of Indian art. In his writings he also took an intense interest in Indian religion, philosophy, psychology, myth and folklore.[42]

Born in Bloxwich, England, Alban Widgery (1887-1968) [q.v.] in 1914 assisted the great Western Absolute Idealist (resembling Qualified Non-dualism) philosopher Alfred E. Taylor (1869-1945) at St. Andrews. He became a professor of philosophy at Baroda College, University of Bombay, in India (1915-22), where he edited the speeches and addresses of H. H. Sayaji Rao III, Maharaja of Baroda. Widgery served as head of the new department of philosophy at Duke University in the United States during 1930-52, as president of the prestigious American Theological Society in 1940, and as editor of *The Indian Philosophical Review*. In *Living Religions and Modern Thought* in 1936, he quoted some of Ramakrishna's sayings and explained the difference between him and the leaders of the Brahmo Samajes:

> The leaders of the Brahmo Samajes and the Prarthana Samaj have been serious-minded men with a Western form of education, but not religious saints in the Hindu sense. They have been of the type of the comfortable Protestant Christian pastor. Their appeal has been in no small degree cold and ineffective. Ramakrishna Paramahamsa, a saint born in Bengal about the year 1834 [sic], was quite different: a man of religious ecstasy and devotion, who adopted the traditional life of the Hindu ascetic and teacher. From him has sprung the widespread Ramakrishna movement. Its well-trained teachers travel over India expounding a doctrine of the unity of the purified soul with God. With the spirit of Hindu devotion they arouse interest in the social welfare of mankind and in its religious peace and blessedness. Rama-

krishna was a striking personality. One of the leaders of the Brahmo Samaj [P. C. Mazumdar] thus wrote of him: "a childlike tenderness, a profound visible humbleness, an unspeakable sweetness of expression, and a smile that I have seen on no other face that I can remember."[43]

Accompanied by her husband Ted and Josephine MacLeod, in January 1926 Ruth St. Denis (1879-1968) left Calcutta by ferryboat and proceeded to Belur Math. Ruth had previously read Vivekananda's *My Master*, the brief biography of Ramakrishna, which she alluded to in her 1939 autobiography:

> My soul had fed on that picture of this God-intoxicated man, whose spirit has penetrated to the far ends of the earth! And now, after all these years, I was coming to the tomb of Ramakrishna, and to the place where his monks meditate and send forth their spiritual beauty to the rest of the world.[44]

As an outstanding American dancer and choreographer, Ruth St. Denis became one of the founders of modern dance, which crossed over many cultural boundaries. She assembled a company of East Indians and choreographed a dance production, "Radha", which was performed in New York at the Hudson Theatre between 1906 and 1909. Throughout her career she danced in over fifteen-hundred performances of Radha, which brought about a greater appreciation of Indian Culture in the West. In Los Angeles, she and her husband formed the Ruth St. Denis School of Dancing, later called the Denishawn School and Dance Company in 1915. During the summer of 1925, the company embarked on a fifteen-month tour of the Far East, including many cities in India, where its Oriental dances were enthusiastically received.[45]

In 1939, Robert Ballou (1892-1977) and Friedrich (Frederic) Spiegelberg (1897-1994) [q.v.] edited the anthology *The Bible of the World*. The volume included sacred scripture from all of the major religions of the world. Eighteen pages were devoted to a verbatim presentation of the teachings and parables of Ramakrishna, drawn from *The Sayings of Sri Ramakrishna* (1903) compiled by Swami Abhedananda and Laura Glenn. This book, which underwent at least nine printings, made Ramakrishna's message known to a wide intellectual audience. The editors described Ramakrishna's teachings as, "The engaging and wise philosophy of a great nineteenth century sage, illustrated by parables." Spiegelberg, an outstanding lecturer, was a professor of Indian religion and philosophy at Stanford University from 1941 to 1962. In Germany he studied under Rudolph Otto, Paul Tillich, Rudolph Steiner and Martin Heidegger. Spiegelberg later visited spiritual teachers at ashramas and monasteries in India, Tibet, Siam, Ceylon, China and Japan, meeting with both Ramana Maharshi and Sri Aurobindo. He helped found the American Academy of Asian Studies in San Francisco in 1951, which was the first accredited graduate school in the United States devoted exclusively to the study of Asiatic lands and people.[46]

Reverend Dr. Allen E. Claxton (1901-66) of the Broadway Methodist Temple in the city of New York was widely known as an ecumenical leader and a national radio and television preacher for the National Council of the Churches of Christ in the United States. He proved instrumental in introducing Swami Akhilananda to several prominent church organizations, religious groups, and distinguished educators like Edgar Brightman and Dean Earle Marlatt of Boston University. In a 1939 article on "Sri Ramakrishna's Contribution to the Christian World", he brought out this point:

> In the personality of Sri Ramakrishna we come face to face with that which is truly India. For if we can lay hold of him, I feel that we shall be able to lay our fingers upon the pulse of the heart of India.... To receive from Sri Ramakrishna requires a certain spiritual tempo, a prepared ground, what Jesus called "good soil", without which the teachings and the life of Sri Ramakrishna will fall either upon barren land or thorny ground.[47]

The Swamis living in the United States have made many important literary contributions in support of the Ramakrishna Movement. In 1942 Swami Nikhilananda (1895-1973), the founder and leader of the Ramakrishna-Vivekananda Centre in New York City, brought out *The Gospel of Sri Ramakrishna*—a full-length translation of Mahendranath Gupta's classic book in Bengali *Sri Ramakrishna Kathamrita*. Thirty-five years before this, in 1907 Abhedananda and Mahendranath Gupta (M) translated *Sri Ramakrishna Kathamrita* into English. Unlike the new 1942 edition, their 436-page version concentrated on the teachings of Ramakrishna, with the devotees asking him questions and playing a smaller role. This volume was later translated into many languages. The San Francisco Vedanta Society came out with a reprint of the Madras edition in 1912, but in the West it did not achieve the popularity of Abhedananda's edition. In Nikhilananda's translation, the words and stories of Ramakrishna are recorded with an almost stenographic precision. Described as "The first full English translation of one of the world's most extraordinary religious documents", the book received a four-page review in the prestigious *Time Magazine* together with photos of Mother Kali and Sri Ramakrishna. This well-publicized version of the *Gospel* attracted more attention in the United States than the previous ones and brought about a great deal of interest in Sri Ramakrishna. Next, Nikhilananda followed this work with an excellent volume entitled *Ramakrishna: A Biography* in 1953. Aldous Huxley (1894-1963), the world famous British-American author born in Godalming, Survey, England, wrote in the Foreword to the *Gospel*:

> "M" produced a book unique, so far as my knowledge goes, in the literature of hagiography. No other saint has had so able and indefatigable a Boswell. Never have the small events of a contemplative's daily life been described with such a wealth of intimate detail. Never have the casual and unstudied utterances of a great religious teacher been set down with so minute a fidelity.... [Ramakrishna's life] was intensely mystical and therefore universal. To read through these conversations in which mystical doctrine alternates with an unfamiliar kind of humour, and where discussions of the oddest aspects of Hindu mythology give place to the most profound and subtle utterances about the nature of Ultimate Reality, is in itself a liberal education in humility, tolerance and suspense of judgment. We must be grateful to the translator for his excellent version of a book so curious and delightful as a biographical document, so precious, at the same time, for what it teaches us of the life of the spirit.[48]

In the Introduction to Swami Prabhavananda and Christopher Isherwood's rendering of the *Bhagavad Gita* (1944), Aldous Huxley outlined four doctrines that constitute his prestigious "Perennial Philosophy". Here Huxley expresses Vedantic and Upanishadic ideas using the vocabulary of Western philosophy, mysticism, and theology. Sanskrit terms are added in parenthesis, which Huxley did not use, in order to emphasize the Vedantic concepts that pervade his thinking. His four fundamental tenets are:

> First: the phenomenal world [*vyavaharika-satya*] ... is the manifestation [*nirmana shakti*] of a Divine Ground [Brahman] within which all partial realities have their being [*sat*], and apart from which they would be non-existent [*asat*]. Second: human beings are capable not merely of knowing

> [*vritti-jnana*] about the Divine Ground [Brahman] by inference [*anumana*]; they can also realize its existence by a direct intuition [*anubhava*], superior to discursive reasoning [*tarka*]. This immediate knowledge [*para vidya*] unites the knower [*jnata*] with that which is known [*jneya*]. Third: man possesses a double nature, a phenomenal ego [*ahamkara*] and an eternal Self [*Atman*], which is the inner man, the spirit, the spark of divinity within the soul. It is possible for a man, if he so desires, to identify himself with the spirit and therefore with the Divine Ground [Brahman], which is of the same or like nature with the spirit. Fourth: man's life on earth has only one end and purpose: to identify himself with his eternal Self [*Atman*] and so to come to unitive knowledge [*anubhava*] of the Divine Ground [Brahman].[49]

Aldous Huxley was a renowned and productive writer of both fiction and nonfiction articles, essays, short stories, plays, poetry and films. His novels display a remarkable breadth of style and vision. Modern Library rated two of his novels (*Brave New World*, and *Point Counter Point*) in the top hundred for the twentieth century. In England around 1934, Gerald Heard taught yogic breathing exercises to Huxley to help him with his vision problems. Five years later Heard encouraged Aldous Huxley to visit Swami Prabhavananda (1893-1976) at the Vedanta Society of Los Angeles. Huxley became a church member and an initiated devotee of Prabhavananda. During the 1940s and 1950s, Aldous submitted over fifty essays to *Vedanta and the West*, the *Vedanta Kesari* and the *Prabuddha Bharata*.[50]

From his association with Swami Prabhavananda and the Vedanta Society, Huxley learned a great deal about mystical philosophy and theology. It was this training that provided him with the background knowledge he needed to formulate a universal ideology of mysticism in *The Perennial Philosophy* (1945). Both this work and *The Gospel of Sri Ramakrishna* were judged to be two of the "100 Most Important Spiritual Books of the 20th Century" by a panel of writers for the magazine *Spirituality & Health* convened by Philip Zaleski and HarperCollins publishers.[51] According to a 1956 booklet on "Vedanta in Southern California" that appeared in *Vedanta and the West*, Huxley wrote *The Perennial Philosophy* while at Trabuco College, which later became the Ramakrishna Monastery. Professor Huston Smith, an old friend of Huxley and Heard, supports this idea stating that:

> Huxley had spent six months there [at Trabuco College], dividing his time between meditating and writing *The Perennial Philosophy*. Vedanta (the

philosophical expression of Hinduism as taught in America by monks of the Ramakrishna Order) had sparked Heard's project [Trabuco College], for he and Huxley had found those monks to be the most serious and knowledgeable mystics around.[52]

The library at Trabuco provided a wealth of volumes on religious mysticism that Huxley could use to write his book.[53] This masterpiece is an anthology of religious and mystical writings, combined with Huxley's profound commentary. It contains excerpts from the following Indian sources: Ashvaghosha, Shankara, and Sri Aurobindo; the *Bhagavad Gita*, *Srimad Bhagavatam*, Upanishads and the *Yogavashishtha*.

An enthusiastic response to the *Gospel* was made by Stark Young (1881-1963) for *The New Republic* in the following appraisal:

> Certainly this is one of the notable books of our time, one of the marvellous books in all time. It is a book where gentle, deathless goodness softens whatever humiliation I might feel for any inadvertent glibness of comment; and where the piety—in the deepest Latin sense of the word—and the brilliant, easy scholarship of the translation into English is enough to knock us down....
>
> "The Gospel of Sri Ramakrishna" may be said to be a very nearly unique instance of biography, or record, in the famous, rare Boswell vein, but infinitely more lucent and inspired, of a remarkable man whose genius most appeared in direct communication, which is to say in talk with disciples and friends. M., the disciple and note-taker, remains a shadow. The picture of Ramakrishna (1836-86) is amazing, and, sometimes disconcertingly for the Western mind, complete. Sri Ramakrishna is not only one of the complete cases of mysticism and hagiography that we possess for laboratory purposes, so to speak; he is also one of the animating spirits of the national consciousness of India today. It might be easily possible that "The Gospel of Ramakrishna" should be the most important book of the year for Western readers, if only for practical reason that our understanding of the Indian mind is destined to be a more and more pressing matter.

When reviewing *The Bhagavad Gita* translated by Swami Nikhilananda, Stark Young added, "This new translation and commentary of the great Indian classic has the same brilliant ease and almost incredible sense of rightness and, as it were, natural clarity that characterized Swami Nikhilananda's volume, 'The Gospel of Sri Ramakrishna', which was reviewed in these columns two years ago."[54]

During his early years, Stark Young worked as a professor of English literature at the Universities of Mississippi and Texas, and then at Amherst College (1904-21). Young resigned from Amherst to enjoy a variety of careers as a playwright, drama critic, novelist, translator and magazine editor. He was regarded in theatre circles as the leading drama critic of his time. The *New Republic* credited Young with initiating, "almost single-handedly, a tradition of serious American theatre journalism which set the highest standards of style, sensibility and judgment for contemporaries and for those who were to follow." His novel *So Red the Rose* (1934), focusing on the Civil War South, sold over 400,000 copies in one month, undergoing twenty printings.[55]

Canadian born A. Eustace Haydon (1880-1975), a Baptist and Unitarian minister, was a professor and head of the department of comparative religion at the eminent University of Chicago Divinity School, a post he filled during 1919-45. At the Vivekananda Society of Chicago, under the direction of Swami Vishwananda, Haydon delivered a lecture on "The West Needs Vedanta" that appeared in the October 1940 edition of the *Prabuddha Bharata*. About Vivekananda he declared in his speech, "He really was able, by his dynamic personality, to present his idealism to our audience. He was real—he gave them the straight stuff and America listened and America has not forgotten." He also made the interesting statement, "I wish I could be a Vedantist or an absolute idealist. I cannot, but I wish I could." In 1956 he was the recipient of the American Humanist Association's "Humanist of the Year" award. Haydon edited *Modern Trends in World Religions* (1968) along with his other publications. In his affirmative assessment in *The Christian Century* of *The Gospel of Sri Ramakrishna* translated by Nikhilananda, he articulated:

> Here is not only a vivid life-size picture of a modern Hindu saint but also a valuable source book for the transition period when classical Indian culture was beginning to feel the impact of the forces of modernization.... Ramakrishna was a late flowering of three thousand years of India's quest for salvation. In him were embodied the findings of the long search for truth—the exaltation of the reality of the spiritual realm, the depreciation of this world and its enjoyments, the ideal of the saintly life detached from the world, emphasis upon bhakti (devoted love) as the easiest and best way of emancipation, and acceptance of mystical insight as proof of

the reality of God.... its presentation of the teaching of one of the world's great saints.[56]

Before he was confined to a wheelchair in 1937, Thomas Sugrue (1907-53) was a reporter for the *New York Herald Tribune*. He then wrote his first novel, doing most of his editing mentally, since he could type only one hour per day. Next, he wrote a biography of his intimate friend Edgar Cayce, whom he considered to be a saint and a prophet. About the *Gospel*, Sugrue expressed this insight for the *New York Times Book Review*:

> East and West agree that he was the most radiant religious personality of the nineteenth century. The record of his life and teachings is a mine of inspiration, wisdom, theology, and metaphysics. It is also a tremendous adventure story, the odyssey of a man who set out on the mystical way and journeyed to its end. The English version is a triumph of creative translation.[57]
>
> Ramakrishna is the only saint of whom I know who has climbed up the ladder of the soul and found God and come down again and said, "Well, I can do it another way, if you like, or I can do it your way or I can do it some other person's way," and went up the ladder of the soul according to his own tradition, and according to our Western Christian tradition, and according to the Islamic tradition.[58]

In response to Swami Nikhilananda, John Haynes Holmes (1879-1964), minister of the Community Church in New York City, indicated:

> I have examined the proofs of your new volume, *The Gospel of Sri Ramakrishna*, and send you herewith my praises for a work of noble scholarship and utter devotion. You have added to the scriptures of our English tongue a new Bible. When the volume appears, I shall add it proudly and reverently to my Bible of Humanity. I feel inexpressibly grateful to you for your labours thus crowned with this great achievement.[59]

Originally a Unitarian minister, John Haynes Holmes devoted his life to a ministry of social activism. In 1909 he was one of the founders of the National Association for the Advancement of Coloured People (NAACP) and served as that organization's national vice-president for more than fifty years. Holmes also helped organize the American Civil Liberties Union.

In an April 1921 sermon, he proclaimed Mahatma Gandhi as the "greatest man in the world". When he met Mahatma Gandhi in England in 1931, his pacifist tendencies were reinforced, and he subsequently became the leading American proponent of Gandhi's nonviolent philosophy. Holmes, along with Roger Baldwin and Rabbi Stephen Wise, established an American League for India's Independence. He was a member of the General Committee for the Ramakrishna Centenary held in Calcutta in March 1937. His last major trip abroad was to India in 1947, to meet Gandhi again. Holmes' book *My Gandhi* (1953) is a tribute from an American disciple to his admired Indian teacher.[60] In his praise of Rabindranath Tagore, he pointed out:

> He has expounded in prose as noble as his poetry, and in thought as clear as it is beautiful, the seer idealism of the East. In an age when this type of speculation and belief has all but disappeared here in the West, Tagore's philosophical and religious writings have come like the pouring of a pure spring of living water into the past area of a desert land.[61]

About the *Gospel of Sri Ramakrishna*, the distinguished Harvard philosophy Professor William Ernest Hocking (1873-1966) [q.v.] designated:

> The Gospel ... is a work of absorbing interest. Your biographical introduction sets the reader at once into the atmosphere of India, its customs and its ways of thinking about the unseen world and about deity. I take it to be a high merit of the book that you have not omitted the details which will seem most strange to the Western reader; you have allowed them to bear their own message and to offer themselves intact for judgment. As you tell the life of Sri Ramakrishna, it engages with so much of the spiritual history of India during the last century that one gains a living sense of the forward movement of that history. The whole promises to be a document of importance for every one who wishes to gain a personal impression of Indian religious aspiration and to realize how naturally it spans the wide gamut from the particular and local symbols to the most universal conceptions.[62]

Irwin Edman (1896-1954) [q.v.] spent his entire teaching career in the department of philosophy at Columbia University in New York City. He described himself as "an empiricist homesick for Platonism". Edman had a persistent interest in the contribution of mysticism to human thought, and its relation to rational philosophy. Concerning the *Gospel* he stressed:

> The spirit of Ramakrishna, as given in his reported conversations, and his life, as rendered in the admirable Introduction by Swami Nikhilananda, constitute a unique and absorbing document for any serious student of the philosophy of religion. Ramakrishna is revealed as that rarity, the real thing in metaphysical mysticism and saintliness. He belongs in the great tradition of classic religious leaders. His teachings and his spirit here come wonderfully alive, and Western readers will have a new dimension added to their conception of the religious life.[63]

After World War II

Two professors from Northwestern University, Charles Braden (1887-1970) and Edward Schaub (1881-1953), along with Swamis Vishwananda and Akhilananda, spoke at the Ramakrishna Anniversary Banquet held on 24 April 1946 at the Hotel Maryland in Chicago. According to the paraphrasing report in the *Prabuddha Bharata*, Braden stated:

> In all probability the young Ramakrishna would have been confined in an institution, his intense spiritual response to beauty and religion regarded as a mental disease. How different from this was the tender understanding which the Master received as a child from his family, and from all the people of his village.... [Compare the noisy machine-oriented West with] the quiet introspective India, where in a temple garden Ramakrishna sat quietly invoking divine realization.... If Americans wish to save themselves from the doom of their own machines, then they should listen to *The Gospel of Ramakrishna* and try to learn some part of that truth ... it is time that we stop all our useless activities and listen to this quiet, inspired voice.[64]

Charles Braden, an ordained Methodist minister, was a professor of the history and literature of religions at Northwestern University (1926-54), and sometimes chairman of the department. His numerous works include *Modern Tendencies in World Religions* (1933), *The World's Religions* (1939), and *Scriptures of Mankind* (1952). Braden considered the Ramakrishna movement to be the most dynamic phase of Hinduism in existence in India today.... It has succeeded in combining the mystical and practical in a way that makes it a real force in modern India. Throughout the world it is interpreting Hinduism in a broad way and making a real contribution to a better understanding between peoples of different races and religious faiths."[65]

The Vedanta Society received a half-page discussion in his book, *These also Believe*, in the section on "Minority Religious Movements", which mentions "the Ramakrishna Movement in India, one of the most vigorous modern reform movements in Hinduism". Braden penned favourable reviews of two books written by Akhilananda, who, he said, "has become well known for his ability to interpret Hinduism and Hindu culture to the West". Concerning Akhilananda's *Hindu View of Christ*, Braden remarked, "In this book the Christian has an opportunity to acquaint himself with what Hinduism at its best thinks about Christ, the centre of his own faith. To the reviewer it is a challenging book."[66]

Edward Schaub, a professor of philosophy at Northwestern University (1913-46), served as the 1923 president of the Western division of the American Philosophical Association, and was the president of the American Theological Society. In 1929 he held a lecturing fellowship in Calcutta. He is best remembered for his 1928 book *Philosophy Today*, and he also issued an affirmative book review of Surendranath Dasgupta's *Yoga Philosophy* back in 1931. In a paraphrased version in the *Prabuddha Bharata* of 1946, Schaub's admiration for Ramakrishna was expressed:

> He was grateful for many acts of kindness and assistance on his behalf by professors, teachers and students down through the years. But his greatest gratitude, he said, went out to one man [Ramakrishna] who had, actually, done nothing tangible, yet by reason of what that man was in himself, he had conferred more benefit than came from all the external gifts and benefits of lesser men.
>
> The quality of "being", the professor said, was the outstanding legacy left to the world by Ramakrishna. He dwelt upon various occasions when the Master himself had explained to his followers that the first necessity is to purify one's own soul and become acquainted with God....
>
> The strength and power and "sweetness" of the message of Ramakrishna, the professor said, arises from the quality of divine realization of the

Master's own life and personality. Ramakrishna did not "do" anything, nor did he need to "do" anything. His gift to the world lay in what he was.

For all the crowding ills, which afflict America and the other Western nations, Dr. Schaub said he could see no cure except the inward, direct understanding of that quality of "being" which Ramakrishna possessed in such abundant measure. As Ramakrishna always said, the professor concluded, you may call that inner illumination by whatever name you will, it does not matter. All that does matter is that you should seek and if possible find it. Ramakrishna knew this truth and it made him what he was. It is for us to learn it, if we can.[67]

John Cage (1912-92) is recognized as "the most influential composer, worldwide, of his generation". The controversial avant-garde composer is considered by musical experts to have "pioneered the development of the percussion orchestra, experimented with the use of noise, invented the prepared piano, acted as the earliest American proponent of electronic and taped music, originated the multi-discipline, multi-media "happening", initiated the use of chance and indeterminate methods in composition, and pursued, almost alone, the notion of extended silence as musical material." In 1946 he received a copy of *The Gospel of Sri Ramakrishna* from Geeta Sarabhai, a student of music from India. Cage devoted the next year to reading this material, describing it as "a gift from India, which took the place of psychoanalysis". He would often quote from the *Gospel* such parables of a man nearly being killed by an elephant, because he did not realize that God was speaking to him through the elephant driver's voice. Cage's music was influenced by the *Gospel*, along with the writings of Ananda Coomaraswamy and D. T. Suzuki, under whom he studied at Columbia University.[68]

The London born author Gerald Heard (1889-1971) once discerned, "Ramakrishna is an apostle to the world and not merely to India, because he was able to say that 'all roads lead to God', and that devotion to Him in whatever form will lead the devotee to enlightenment." Heard, an initiated disciple of Swami Prabhavananda, penned thirty-eight books of nonfiction and fiction. His four major contributions to the Vedanta Society were: bringing prominent figures like Aldous Huxley and Christopher Isherwood to the Centre; his eighteen religious essays appearing in *Vedanta for the Western World* (1945) and *Vedanta for Modern Man* (1951); delivering over eighty scheduled public lectures at the Vedanta Society Temple in Hollywood, primarily during the 1950s; and, most important, donating the land and buildings for the Trabuco Monastery.[69]

The anthology *Religion in the Twentieth Century* (1948), edited by Vergilius Ferm (1896-1974), informs the reader about twenty-seven different religions. Ferm selected Swami Nikhilananda of the Vedanta Society in New York City to write the sixteen-page essay on "Hinduism", and Swami Satprakashananda (1888-1979), founder of the St. Louis Centre in 1938, to author the twenty-one-page report on "The Ramakrishna Movement" that includes material on Ramakrishna. It is significant that Ferm selected the Ramakrishna Movement for special study. Ferm, an ordained Lutheran minister, and for over forty years a professor at the College of Wooster in Ohio, was the president of the Eastern division of the American Theological Society. Few people did more than Vergilius Ferm, writing in an ecumenical spirit, to acquaint the American public with the various religions in the United States and the world. A list of thirty-one books that he wrote or edited includes *Religion in Transition* (1937), and the one volume masterpiece *An Encyclopedia of Religion* (1945), with contributions from over 190 outstanding North American theologians and philosophers.[70]

Joseph Campbell (1904-87) brought out the point that what makes *The Gospel of Sri Ramakrishna* so interesting is not only the teachings, but also the accompanying events. Concerning Ramakrishna, Campbell noted the appeal of his "personality and the rich texture of the life around him", and that "the playfulness and quick virtuosity of Sri Ramakrishna's always amazing spirit appeared in precisely those twists and turns". He stated:

> [We] experience the force of a doctrine so filled with the blissful knowledge of God that the normal difficulties, queries, judgments, and ideals of virtuous, thoughtful men lose weight before it. The universally tolerant and compassionate view of mind suffused with transcendent understanding dissolves the barriers of creeds, caste, race, and culture-style. A divine joy pervades the dialogues, and throughout resounds echoes of those other devotional idylls of the Buddha and his monks, Krishna and his Gopis, Chaitanya and his devotees, and Jesus and his company.[71]

Many long quotations from Nikhilananda's *The Gospel of Sri Ramakrishna* appear in the popular book *Philosophies of India* (1951) edited by Joseph Campbell. There Ramakrishna is described as "the perfect embodiment of the orthodox religious philosophy of India". The book contains frequent and extensive passages of many pages dealing with Ramakrishna's statements on bhakti vs. jnana yoga, bondage, Brahman and Shakti, God with and without form, Goddesses, the kundalini, Mahamaya, samadhi, sin, transformation, and vijnana. *Philosophies of India* is based primarily on notes for courses of lectures on Indian art and philosophy delivered at Columbia University during 1942 by the German Indologist Heinrich Zimmer (1890-1943) [q.v.]. Campbell also used Zimmer's (whom he met in 1940) notes to edit *Myths and Symbols in Indian Art and Civilization* (1946) and *The Art of Indian Asia, Its Mythology and Transformation* (1955).[72]

On the subject of Yoga, Campbell came to this conclusion:

> This popular form of yoga, no less than the very much sterner and more difficult discipline of Patanjali's Yoga Sutras, to which I first alluded, is a technique to link consciousness to the ultimate truth: the mystery of being. The sense of the whole universe as a manifestation of the radiance of God and of yourself as likewise of that radiance, and the assurance that this is so, no matter what things may look like round about, is the key to the wisdom of India.[73]

Joseph Campbell first learned of Hinduism and Buddhism in 1923 when he came across Jiddu Krishnamurti on an ocean liner sailing to Europe. Fifteen years later he met Swami Nikhilananda through a student's introduction. For some years Campbell was the president of Nikhilananda's Ramakrishna-Vivekananda Centre in New York City. He devoted much of his time to aiding Nikhilananda with his translation of the Bengali work *Sri Ramakrishna Kathamrita*, and with his four-volume translation of the *Upanishads*. Teaching literature at Sarah Lawrence College in Bronxville, New York (1934-72), he was known as one of the world's foremost authorities on mythology and folklore. As a result he produced a massive body of literature in the fields of comparative mythology, folklore, and religion, including *Oriental Mythology*, which deals in part with the mythology of India. After his retirement he enjoyed growing popularity in both intellectual and popular culture, especially after being interviewed by Bill Moyer on a highly successful six-part public television series, "The Power of Myth", that appeared posthumously in 1988.[74]

A disciple of Swami Brahmananda, Swami Akhilananda (1894-1962) was the founder and head of the Vedanta Society in Providence (1928) and in Boston (1941). He established a lasting friendship with many nationally prominent theologians, philosophers, psychologists, and sociologists, some of whom spoke at his Centre. He himself gave regular classes at Brown University and other educational institutions. Scholars were drawn towards him for several reasons: his "warm personality and spiritual acumen", according to Dean Walter Houston Clark (Hartford Seminary); because, says Harold Ehrensperger (Boston University school of theology), he "touched the lives of at least three groups of students who have come into the school here, and that means a whole generation of the students, and I can assure you that this is a tremendous influence"; owing to his "radiant, loving spirit, and his profound depth of religious experience and understanding", says Paul E. Johnson (Boston University school of theology); and, according to John Lavely (Boston University, department of philosophy), because of "the number of great minds he knew, in a personal way. For many of these he performed a pastoral function which no local clergyman could have." The extremely impressive list of his companions also includes: Edgar Brightman, Dean Earle Marlatt and Dean Richard Millard at Boston University; Gordon Allport, Harlow Shapley, Pitirim Sorokin and George H. Williams at Harvard University; Dean Arthur H. Chandler, George Burches, Albin Gilbert, F. S. S. Northrop, and Joachim Wach at other universities; and Rabbi William Braude and Reverend Allen Claxton, Ralph Harpole and Frederick Wilmot.[75] In addition to Reverend Claxton previously mentioned, at least five people from this list expressed their affirmative beliefs about Ramakrishna in writing.

First is Joachim Wach (1898-1955), a student of Rudolph Otto in Germany, who became a professor of religion at Brown University and at the University of Chicago. In Boston, Wach spoke at the 100th anniversary celebration of Ramakrishna, along with Arthur Chandler, the dean of Providence College, and two noted ministers and a rabbi mentioned above. Wach is well known for his penetrating work on comparative mysticism entitled *Types of Religious Experience Christian and Non-Christian* (1951).[76] Wach, in his book review of Nikhilananda's abridged *Gospel of Sri Ramakrishna*, commented:

> There is no doubt that Ramakrishna's influence upon modern India has been exceedingly strong; hence an acquaintance with his life and teachings is essential for anyone interested in modern India and the religious trends shaping it. Moreover, this Hindu saint, the pupils of whose disciples are still among us, represents in this age a long tradition of spiritual culture

which has produced a galaxy of religious leaders in India. Any student of the history of religions or of the psychology and sociology of religious life will find the abbreviated version of the *Gospel of Sri Ramakrishna*, which was originally written by Mahendranath Gupta, a mine of interesting information.... There is great wisdom and insight in these sayings of the "Paramahamsa". They pertain to the quest for ultimate truth and the way to attain it. They include beautiful metaphors and images and reveal him as a keen observer of the motivations of the human heart. The setting is that of Hindustan, but the validity of much that is said transcends geographical, ethnic, and cultural frontiers.[77]

Second, in 1952 Professor Gordon Allport (1897-1967), a Harvard psychologist, provided the following positive assessment of Ramakrishna:

> It is to the East, especially to India, and to holy personalities like Ramakrishna, that we have to look for example and guidance in this matter. The West is almost totally lacking in knowledge of the techniques of silence, of meditation, of concentration, and orison prayer. There is much we can learn from Hinduism about these matters.... A second lesson for me lies in Ramakrishna's catholicity of mind and sympathy. He is well known for his study and practise of all the great religions. He entered understandingly into the Christian frame of mind, into the Mohammedan, into the Buddhist. He utilized their techniques of worship and thought their thoughts. By all roads he found he could attain inner peace and God-consciousness.... We learn from the life and example of Ramakrishna the sensitivity that we may develop, if we will, for each other's mode of living. We can, with goodwill, gain new compassion, not only for other races and nations, but for our neighbour who sits next to us.[78]

Gordon Allport penned the Introduction for Swami Akhilananda's *Hindu Psychology*. There he states, "I am convinced, American psychology would improve in richness and wisdom if it accommodated in some way the wise things that the author says about meditation and the necessity for an adequate philosophy of life." From 1930 until the year of his death, Allport, a long-term professor of psychology at Harvard University, became the president of the eminent American Psychological Association in 1939, and director of the National Opinion Research Centre. As a social psychologist, he specialized in personality theory describing fifty-two different methods for studying the human personality.[79]

Third, a psychology professor, Albin R. Gilbert (1897-1990), in 1954 spoke on "Sri Ramakrishna's Significance for Western Thought" at the Vedanta Society in Providence, Rhode Island, during the birthday celebration held for Ramakrishna. He told his audience:

> It seems to me that very few spiritual leaders have soared so far beyond the culture into which they had been born as Sri Ramakrishna did. He is like a singular mountain peak towering over smaller summits, and overlooking reaches which are beyond the horizon from lesser heights.... While Western psychology has been exploring extensively the sub-conscious and conscious strata of personality, Hindu psychology has specialized on the superconsious. Sri Ramakrishna, whose life was devoted to an insatiable pursuit of religious experience, spectacularly demonstrated by his own personality to his disciples and to the world how human nature can be turned toward superconsious communion. To me he was a living verification of the theory that there is in man a hidden source of superconsious experience. This source can be tapped and kept flowing, if only an indomitable yearning can shift our psychic energy away from vital and self-centred motivation toward superconsious experience.

Albin Gilbert, a professor of psychology at Prague University in Czechoslovakia (1931-39), moved to Wheaton College in Norton, Massachusetts (1949-63), and to West Virginia Wesleyan College (1963-68). Personality theory was his main area of study, and in 1969 he authored *From Buddha to Pavlov: the Technique of Mysticism*.[80]

Fourth, after quoting a description of a profound spiritual experience had by Ramakrishna, Pitirim Sorokin (1889-1968), an eminent socio-cultural thinker born in Touria, Russia, who would meet and talk with Akhilananda, indicated in 1954:

> After this first vision of the Divine, "the darkest night" of his self-identification was essentially over. Though subsequently there were some dark periods, they progressively decreased and the God-intoxicated state of samadhi became more frequent. Ramakrishna arrived at his goal. His reintegration of egos, values, and activities around the supreme value of God was fully achieved. With it, a profound peace of mind, interrupted

frequently by the ecstatic state of blissful samadhi (union with God), became the normal state of Ramakrishna.[81]

Earlier, being unable to attend the Ramakrishna Centenary Parliament of Religions held in Calcutta during March 1937, Sorokin replied:

> If my academic duties would permit me, I would be glad to come to Calcutta and participate in the Congress. Since I am deeply interested in Hindu culture and, with my limited knowledge, have a profound respect for Ramakrishna, such a desire on my part is comprehensible.[82]

In another context, Sorokin expressed his appreciation for contemporary Indian thought indicating, "Aurobindo treatises are among the most important works of our time in philosophy, ethics and humanities. Sri Aurobindo himself is one of the greatest living sages of our time, and a most eminent moral leader." Sorokin was in full agreement with Aurobindo's criticism of modern psychoanalysis. Concerning the Ramakrishna Order, Sorokin, at a 1957 banquet held in Boston to observe the Birth Anniversary of Ramakrishna, affirmed:

> A successful growth of Sri Ramakrishna and of the Vedanta movements in the West is one of many symptoms of two basic processes which are going on at the present time in the human universe. One of these changes is the epochal shift of the creative centre of mankind from Europe to the larger area of the Pacific-Atlantic, while the other consists in a double process of continued decay of sensate [sensual, secular] culture and society and of the emergence and growth of the new—Integral [creatively integrating sensate and Ideational] or Ideational [supersenuous, sacred]—socio-cultural order.[83]

Hopefully, modern civilization is working toward integrating the higher creative and humanistic secular culture with the higher spiritual ideational culture. Pitirim A. Sorokin was arrested three times by the Tsarist government, and again three times by the Russian Communists (as A. Kerensky's secretary, 1881-1970) for opposing their regime. Exiled to the United States, he founded the department of sociology at Harvard University where he remained until his retirement in 1959. He also established the Harvard Research Centre in Creative Altruism, of which Swami Akhilananda of Boston was a member. Sorokin's provocative ideas made him an internationally known sociologist and a dominant philosopher of history.[84]

And fifth, George Huntston Williams (1914–2000), who came from a Unitarian background and was a lecturer and professor in the Harvard Divinity School from 1947 until 1980. He specialized in ecclesiastical history and served as president of the American Society of Church History during 1957-58.[85] Being a good friend of Swami Akhilananda, he gave an address on "Harvard and Hinduism" at the Vedanta Society in Boston on the occasion of the birthday celebration for Ramakrishna. Professor Williams asserted:

> On the philosophical level, it is perhaps sufficient to make clear that, while the Swamis of the Ramakrishna Order look back to their founder as one more than a Saint, the philosophical significance of their enterprise is that they have found in Ramakrishna a formula for adapting the philosophy of India, Vedanta, for expansion beyond the borders of India, and for serious scrutiny in the centres of philosophy and psychology around the world. Without the impulse of Ramakrishna, the great treasures of the Indian philosophical speculation might not have become so available, in the present flexible and constructive form, to the Western world.[86]

The birthday celebrations for Ramakrishna attracted a great deal of attention at the Vedanta Centres in America. For example, the speakers at the public banquet celebrating Ramakrishna's birthday in 1955 at Swami Akhilananda's Ramakrishna Vedanta Society of Boston included the following dignitaries: Harlow Shaply, George Williams, dean of the School of Theology at Harvard, George Burches of Tuft University, and also a Harvard astronomer who gave an address at that time. Also, taking an active part in the celebration were deans of Harvard, Boston University, and Massachusetts Institute of Technology, the president of Andover-Newton Theological Seminary, and other prominent scientists, philosophers, ministers and professional men.[87]

Stephen N. Hay (1925-2002) [q.v.] compiled the section on "The Renascence of Hinduism" for the definitive anthology *Sources of Indian Tradition* (1958). He selected Debendranath Tagore, Keshab Chandra Sen, Dayananda Saraswati, Ramakrishna, and Vivekananda as the five most representative sources. Ten pages are devoted to the teachings and life of Ramakrishna conveying this:

> Amid the hubbub of these self-conscious efforts to check the advance of Christian influence, Hindu society suddenly discovered in its midst a genuine saint and mystic. In the end, Sri Ramakrishna's simple devotion to the traditional concepts and deities of his faith proved a more effective force than all the oratory of his predecessors.... Like Dayananda, he personified the rebirth of an ancient tradition in the midst of an era of increasing Westernization and modernization. But unlike the militant Gujarati, he practised and preached a gentle faith of selfless devotion to God and of ultimate absorption in Him.
>
> Ramakrishna imbibed from his boyhood days as the son of a village priest the spirit of devotion to Kali, the Divine Mother, which the songs of Ramprasad had made popular in rural Bengal in the eighteenth century. Ecstatic communion with the Divine, an aspect of this tradition, came naturally to the attractive young brahman, and at the age of seven he experienced his first mystical trance.[88]

As a young man Stephen Hay conversed with Sri Aurobindo in India, became a research associate in East Asian study at Harvard University, and then a professor of history at the University of California, Santa Barbara (1966-90). He penned a book on Rabindranath Tagore and another on the youth of the man he most admired, Mahatma Gandhi. His associates wrote, "No one could know Stephen without deeply profiting from his deep spirituality and his original thought."[89]

The lead essay in John Yale's *What Does Vedanta Mean to Me* (1961) was written by Gerald Sykes who disclosed that:

> My first real contact with Indian thought ... came when by chance I picked up an abridgement of M's biography of Sri Ramakrishna. Within a few minutes it became clear that I should have to read it carefully, and that night I found myself waking, after only two hours' sleep, to go on with it. It spoke to me more directly than any book I had read since the *New Testament*. I no longer regarded myself as a Christian, but I had been hit hard. I soon arranged for a termination of my job, withdrew from my friends, lived in a lonely place, drew upon my savings, and devoted myself to the study of many volumes of Eastern literature.[90]

Concerning the Swami Prabhavananda-Christopher Isherwood translation of the *Bhagavad Gita* (1944), Sykes wrote for the *New York Times Book Review*:

> Democracy would have been impossible without the dissemination of knowledge and its continuance will be impossible without the dissemination of wisdom. For that reason alone this paperback edition of one of the most profound books ever written, often compared to the Sermon on the Mount, is a publishing event of major importance ... We are finding that we cannot hope to know Indians without knowing their ideals. Meanwhile, perhaps, a few of us without political roles will be enjoying this classic for itself. It is presented in one of the outstanding translations of the day.[91]

Gerald Sykes (1903-1984) established a reputation with both his novels and his socio-philosophical writings. He came out with three novels in the 1950s characterized by "cultivated dialogue and intelligent reflection". From then on Sykes specialized in insightful nonfiction with works such as *The Cool Millennium* describing materialistic society as dehumanizing, alienated, and socially fragmented. He lectured at many universities, including New York and Columbia University, and produced influential literary reviews for a number of sophisticated periodicals.[92]

In his 1965 biographical *Ramakrishna and His Disciples*, novelist and playwright Christopher Isherwood (1904-86) [q.v.], who was born in High Lane, Cheshire, England, reached the conclusion that

> Ramakrishna's life, being comparatively recent history, is well documented. In this respect, it has the advantage over the lives of other, earlier phenomena of a like nature. We do not have to rely, here, on fragmentary or glossed manuscripts, dubious witnesses, pious legends. What Ramakrishna was or was not the reader must decide for himself; but at least his decision can be based on words and deeds Ramakrishna indubitably spoke and did.... I myself am a devotee of Ramakrishna; I believe, or am at least strongly inclined to believe, that he was what his disciples declared that he was: an incarnation of God upon earth.[93]

Swami Vidyatmananda (1913-2000), formerly of the Vedanta Society of Southern California before transferring to the Centre in Paris, informs us:

> Swami Prabhavananda had always hoped to inspire Chris [Isherwood] to write the life of Sri Ramakrishna. Swami said that realizing this project was to be the culminating accomplishment of his life.... The entire text was submitted chapter by chapter to the then General Secretary in India, Swami Madhavananda [later the 9th President of the Ramakrishna Order, 1962-65], who often made corrections of fact and even of language.

Undergoing this process, the biography constitutes an important contribution to the Vedanta literature. During the winter months of 1963-64 Isherwood accompanied Swami Prabhavananda on his trip to India. He researched his upcoming biography of Ramakrishna by visiting his birthplace at Kamarpukur, and the Kali Temple at Dakshineswar where he spent most of his adult life. In India they treated Isherwood with great respect, as a literary personality who worked with Prabhavananda.[94]

The result was Isherwood's thoroughly absorbing and profound *Ramakrishna and His Disciples* (1965), which, to some extent, is a selective editing, rewriting, and chronologicalizing of Swami Saradananda's *Sri Ramakrishna, the Great Master* (1952), and to a lesser extent of M's *The Gospel of Sri Ramakrishna* (1942). These two first-hand accounts, written by two disciples of Ramakrishna, are the most important sources of this book. This impressive work strives to present the life of Ramakrishna to the Western reader in a clear and restrained manner. Working with plenty of reliable source materials, Isherwood convincingly presents this absorbing story. Also contained in the narrative are abbreviated life stories of Holy Mother, Vivekananda and other disciples of Ramakrishna. Isherwood donated all of the financial returns from this book to the Vedanta Society of Southern California, as he had done with his other Vedanta writings in the past.[95]

The Belur Math appreciated Isherwood's book. According to the evaluation of Swami Gambhirananda (1899-1988), who was initiated into sannyasa by Swami Shivananda in 1928, became the editor of the *Prabuddha Bharata* and the president of Advaita Ashrama, Mayavati, and in time the 11th President of the Ramakrishna Order during 1985-88:

> This magnificent biography of Sri Ramakrishna ... faithfully recounts in his own charming, lucid, and succinct style the absorbing story of God-realization lived by Sri Ramakrishna. All the important details of Sri Ramakrishna's life have been stringed together beautifully so as to give us a vivid picture of the different facets of his wonderful life, and the total effect is

> marvellous. He approaches the subject with devotion, candour, objectivity, and a scientific spirit.... The book is a must to all seekers of Truth, and the author has laid them under a deep debt of gratitude by this monumental work.[96]

The *New York Herald Tribune* rated the book as one of the five most outstanding "Philosophy and Religion" volumes of the year. *Ramakrishna and His Disciples* has been translated into French, Italian, Russian and other languages.

In the Foreword for Swami Gambhirananda's *History of the Ramakrishna Math and Mission*, Isherwood discerned:

> The Ramakrishna Movement is unique because its Founder was unique.... And who, in the world's recent history, can stand beside Ramakrishna's disciples, Vivekananda and Brahmananda? Spiritual truth is eternal, but it has to be restated and redemonstrated in a human life in order that it may solve the varying problems of each succeeding epoch. Ramakrishna's teaching is our modern gospel. He lived and taught for us, not for the men of two thousand years ago; and the Ramakrishna Movement is responsible for the spreading of his gospel among us, here and now. For this reason alone, the Movement must be regarded as the most important of all existing religious movements.[97]

A novelist and authority on Eastern religions, Nancy Wilson Ross (1910-86) produced a number of books in that field of study, including *Three Ways of Asian Wisdom: Hinduism, Buddhism, Zen, and their Significance for the West* (1974). She made her first trip to India in 1939, and lectured on Zen Buddhism in 1964 at the Carl Jung Institute in Zurich, Switzerland.[98] Ross considered *Ramakrishna and His Disciples* to be an "absorbing study", "a fresh and important contribution to the history of religious mysticism", and concluded that Isherwood

> points out that there is a singular amount of reliable contemporary documentation on this spiritual genius, this "theocentric saint" as Aldous Huxley once described him. Since Isherwood is a gifted writer, he unfolds a fantastic story with a calm finesse.... in his [Ramakrishna's] personal relations he was capable of the simplicity, joy, compelling charm and total unselfconsciousness of a fun-loving child. The indescribable sweetness of

his smile, the magic potency of his touch, the homely and often humorous wisdom of his speech, his profound knowledge and bewildering, irresistible waywardness have been attested to by many people.[99]

Harry Oldmeadow [q.v.], the coordinator of philosophy and religious studies at La Trobe University in Australia, adds that Isherwood's book, "Whilst clearly written by an adherent, is informative, judicious and sensible as well as being finely attuned to the spiritual modalities in which Ramakrishna's religious genius expressed itself."[100]

Max Müller, Romain Rolland, and Isherwood are the three most prominent Western authors who established a reputation outside of the Ramakrishna Order, and devoted their writing skills in authoring books in service of the Ramakrishna Movement. Isherwood was Swami Prabhananda's co-author in the English translation of the *Gita,* entitled *The Song of God: Bhagavad Gita* (1944), of *Vivekachudamani*, with the title *Shankara's Crest Jewel of Discrimination* (1947), and of the translation and commentary of *Yoga-sutras*, entitled *How to Know God: The Yoga Aphorisms of Patanjali* (1953). By 1992 their translation of the *Gita*, a unique combination of verse and prose, had sold over one million copies. Isherwood's clear and lucid writing style made him an ideal working partner on these projects. Prabhavananda would first translate the Sanskrit terms into the English language, and then Chris would render the words into his masterful prose.[101] Isherwood also edited the anthology *Vedanta for the Western World* (1945), and then followed-up with *Vedanta for Modern Man* (1951). These volumes are made up of selected articles drawn from the bimonthly magazine *Vedanta and the West.* India's spiritual message is presented as a modern way of life, focusing on inner religious experience rather than on theological dogmas. The contributions are thought provoking, while providing practical directions for the spiritual aspirant. These two volumes are not systematic textbooks but are insightful and stimulating presentations of the Vedantic way of thinking.

In addition, Isherwood's comprehensive autobiographical *My Guru and His Disciple* was published in 1980, four years after Prabhavananda's passing away. Isherwood summarizes his relationship with Prabhavananda this way: The guru "is the one reality of which I am never in doubt, the one guarantee that I shall ultimately surmount my own weakness and find knowledge of eternal peace and joy. If, having known this relationship, I could in some terrible way be deprived of it again, then my life would become a nightmare of guilt, boredom and self-disgust." "I do believe it—that it is a tremendous privilege to set eyes on Swami [Prabhavananda] even once and that a single meeting might have incalculable effects upon an individual throughout the rest of his life."[102] Outside of the Vedantic world, Christopher Isherwood, a British-American novelist and playwright, is best known for his semi-autobiographical *The Berlin Stories* (1946), which is set in Germany in the early 1930s. This book later inspired the hit Broadway musical and motion picture *Cabaret*. Nearly all of Isherwood's literary productions are to a large extent autobiographical, presented in an insightful and entertaining manner.[103]

No doubt, the foremost artist of the American Vedanta movement is Swami Tadatmananda (1932-2008), whom Swami Prabhavananda described as an "artistic genius". The Trabuco, California based Swami devoted nearly fifty years to creating inspired works of religious art, which are enthusiastically sought by devotees throughout the world. In the 1960s he painted a large portrait of Ramakrishna, which the devotees placed on the top altar in the Santa Barbara Temple. To support the principle of universality, he was requested to produce paintings of Jesus Christ and Gautama the Buddha for the side niches. His work is known for its exceptional purity of style and intuitive grasp of its subjects. Tadatmananda's oil paintings of Ramakrishna, Holy Mother, Jesus Christ, and Lord Buddha are located in the shrine area of the Seattle Temple. On the wall at the Trabuco Canyon monastery hangs his two feet by three feet original oil painting on canvas of the upper body of Ramakrishna. Over the years he has also painted coloured portraits of great spiritual figures like Swamis Vivekananda and Brahmananda, all sixteen direct monastic disciples of Ramakrishna in a group, and Sri Ramana Maharshi. Tadatmananda humbly and sincerely stated, "I just feel fortunate that I was able to do these religious paintings and I was encouraged by Swami Prabhavananda to do so."*[104]

1970s and After

Thomas Berry (b. 1914) [q.v.], an ordained Roman Catholic priest, revealed his appreciation for the spirituality of Sri Ramakrishna in the following words:

---

* To view his classic artwork on the Internet, consult Web: www.vedanta.org/photos/pages/tadat or www.vedantawest.org/eyesToSee.htm.

> He showed from his earliest years an extremely sensitive religious soul. At nineteen he became priest at a temple dedicated to Kali near Calcutta. There he lived an ecstatic life, performing extraordinary visionary penances and in almost constant prayer to God. With extraordinary visionary capacity, he saw divine reality shining forth everywhere in a great splendour. Any beautiful sight was sufficient to evoke in him the overwhelming awareness of the divine presence. During his later years he was the spiritual guide for many people who came to consult him. The guidance that he offered was noted down by one of his followers and later published as *The Gospel of Sri Ramakrishna*; he, himself, could neither read nor write. His spiritual teachings were simple, pure, and noble; and he was all his life a devout, ecstatic, yet simple, prayerful person.... Often he pointed to the need for a more confident relationship with God to the forgetfulness of a person's self. He taught especially that God dwells in all things and can be found everywhere if only one responds to the divine presence that is there. Vividly aware of the needs for divine grace, he insisted that all one's strength is from God.[105]

Thomas Berry taught Asian history at Seton Hall and St. John's University, and chaired the history of religions programme at Fordham University. Influenced by Teilhard de Chardin's philosophy of evolutionary history, Berry, as an eco-theologian, reflected on the means by which humankind might regain the sense of reverence for nature that has been lost in an industrialized society. He has a long-standing appreciation for the spirituality of indigenous traditions in both Asia and the Americas. His philosophy is, "Diversity is no longer something that we tolerate. It is something that we esteem as a necessary condition for a livable universe, as the source of earth's highest perfection.... To demand an undifferentiated unity would bring human thought and history itself to an end. The splendour of our multicultural world would be destroyed."[106]

One of Ramakrishna's teachings was explained by Dr. Walter H. Maurer, a professor of Sanskrit at the University of Hawaii and chairman of the department of Indo-Pacific languages:

> To the individual with deep metaphysical insight (jnanin) who has thus withdrawn from the material world of objects, the only reality is Brahman, formless and indeterminate; but to the ordinary devotee (bhakta) of Brahman as God (Ishvara), He has manifold shape and form, though it is one and the same Brahman throughout. Just as, says Ramakrishna, the same

water may in severe cold take the form of ice, but melt away in the heat of the sun, so to the devotee (bhakta) the same Brahman takes the form of the world, but to the jnanin it is formless.[107]

The controversial B. F. Skinner (1904-90) of Harvard University, the leader of the behaviourist school of psychology, when writing about compassion, cited the following example:

> It is said that Ramakrishna, walking with a wealthy friend [Mathur], was shocked by the poverty of some villagers. He exclaimed to his friend, "Give those people one piece of cloth and one good meal each, and some oil for their heads." When his friend at first refused, Ramakrishna shed tears. "You wretch", he cried, "... I'm staying with these people. They have no one to care for them. I won't leave them." We note that Ramakrishna was concerned not with the spiritual condition of the villagers but with clothing, food, and protection against the sun. But his feelings were not a by-product of effective action; with all the power of his samadhi he had nothing to offer but compassion.

Skinner believed that human behaviour is due solely to external factors in the environment, that rewarded behaviour is encouraged and unrewarded behaviour is discouraged. People's acts are determined by rewards and punishment, positive and negative reinforcement, which in turn determine mental processes and feelings. These principles have been widely applied to behaviour modification procedures in society.[108]

According to Professor Norman Adams of the department of religion and philosophy at Westminster College:

> Sri Ramakrishna himself (1836-86) was an extraordinary mystic who is acknowledged by many Indians to have been an avatar, a divine incarnation.... Another characteristic of Ramakrishna according to his biographers was his uncanny wisdom and profound understanding of human nature and its problems. Without theological training he was able to offer remarkably apt solutions to knotty problems like the relation between freedom and grace and he was able to express his answers in vivid and memorable language. He could also physically touch one of his disciples at just the right psychological moment and in so doing throw him into samadhi (a trance state of absorption in God). He often lifted a whole group of people

into an exalted mood of ecstasy, the main ingredient of which were usually kirtans (religious songs of adoration of the deity).[109]

French born Claude Alan Stark (1935-1980) [q.v.] authored the 1974 religious biography *God of All: Sri Ramakrishna's Approach to Religious Plurality*. The volume includes a chapter written by Swami Akhilananda on "Practical Application of Sri Ramakrishna's Approach". Stark desired to present the life and teachings of Ramakrishna "in a systematic and thorough going manner". In the "Conclusion" section of the book, Stark expresses the affirmative view:

> Sri Ramakrishna's approach to the dilemma of religious plurality has been documented as an exposition of his experiences of God-consciousness in different religious traditions. It is hoped that this exposition, in and of itself, represents a contribution to inter-religious understanding....
>
> Sri Ramakrishna's life and teachings form an approach to the dilemma of religious plurality, an approach based on the experience of God, which is worthy of closer examination by sincere adherents of all religious traditions. One may conclude, by the details of his life, that this approach is a significant one.
>
> The fact that Sri Ramakrishna experienced God in different religions is a matter of historical record. The fact also that God or ultimate Reality had been realized directly and immediately by many persons of diverse religious backgrounds cannot be ignored. Whole civilizations have been based on the strength of their testimony.
>
> Sri Ramakrishna taught that any person who wishes to verify the authenticity of the experience of God may do so by raising his or her level of consciousness to a higher plane through prayer and spiritual practices. Then he or she can affirm with Sri Ramakrishna, "I actually see God, more clearly than I see you," or declare with Swami Vivekananda, "I have touched the feet of God."[110]

After 1969 Claude Alan Stark became the president of Sodesmir Development Company, a business involved in the social, industrial, mining, energy, and rural development of Zaire (Congo), Africa. He worked as an economic counsellor for the U.S. Senate and as an ordained minister. The Claude Stark & Company came out with the biographical *God of All*, and a volume by and about Swami Akhilananda of which he and his wife were the editors, *Spiritual Practices: Memorial Edition with Reminiscences by His Friends*. Stark describes himself as a disciple of Swami Akhilananda and of Mama Ndona Santu of Zaire. He disclosed, "Knowing these two great souls, and experiencing their intense love, has motivated and guided my life and activities."[111]

In the Foreword to Stark's book, *God of All*, Reverend Leroy Rouner mentioned:

> Sri Ramakrishna, a nineteenth-century Indian saint and mystic, experienced God directly and immediately in the context of Hinduism, Buddhism, Christianity and Islam.... [In] Sri Ramakrishna's story ... [our] fellow Christians may find the authentic Spirit of the one true God at work in their inner dialogue with this Hindu neighbour/stranger. In the midst of this meeting and knowing, that Spirit may lead us into some as yet undiscovered new truth.[112]

Reverend Leroy Rouner, an ordained minister of the United Church of Christ, became a professor of philosophy and theology at the United Theological College in Bangalore, India (1961-66), missionary at large (1967-69), and then a professor of philosophical theology at Boston University since 1970. As the editor of the fourteen-volume *Boston University Studies in Philosophy and Religion*, he contributed to six of the volumes. His frequent trips to India along with his study of William Hocking's view of the relationship between Christianity and other world religions provided him with a background for the study of religious pluralism and the prospect of a global community.[113]

In Stark's book *God of All* (p. 188), Professor Jane I. Smith made a distinction between the unity of God and the unity of religions:

> In Ramakrishna one sees that not only was the experience of a personal God, in his case as Mother Kali, of utmost importance, but that the question of the unity of religions gave way to a clear and overriding concern for the unity of God and of the approaches to God, for an understanding of the oneness of Being, both personal and absolute, and the oneness of the ways in which God has chosen to reveal him/her-self. The emphasis on the unity of God over the unity of religions seems especially important to consider in this age of ecumenicity.

Jane Smith worked as a professor of the history of religions and comparative religion at Harvard University (1973-86), Illif School of Theology (1987-95), and then as a professor of Islamic studies and co-director at the Hartford Seminary since 1997. She has written many books about Islam and its practical application in the modern world, especially in the United States. Two of her goals are to explain the contributions of Islam to the American society, and to counter anti-Muslim prejudices, as well as misinformation put out by the media.[114]

The Islamic scholar Muhammad Daud Rahbar, a professor of world religions at Boston University, perceived Ramakrishna this way:

> Like a magnet, Sri Ramakrishna attracted ardent disciples. More than thirty of them maintained intimate association with him. Hundreds of them derived solace and blessing by beholding him and talking to him.
>
> I have read some of the delightful portions of the one-thousand-page *Gospel of Sri Ramakrishna*. This marvellous volume has extraordinary revelations. Immediately one recognizes a cherishable friend in Sri Ramakrishna. His open, passionate, and transparent devotion humbles and chastens us. He is no common mortal. He is a man of phenomenal gifts. His presence is a haven. His conversations, recorded abundantly in the *Gospel of Sri Ramakrishna* by his disciple M., are charming, inspired. Their literary merit is due to the inspired goodness of Sri Ramakrishna.... The list of his virtues is magnificent: wisdom (as distinct from journalistic encyclopaedism), inspired intellect, devotion, renunciation, concerned detachment, sublimation, genuine gregariousness, brilliant conversationalism, friendliness, gracious wit, variety and vastness of life experience.[115]

Thomas Merton (1915-68), the famous Catholic monk, paid a visit to Narendrapur Ramakrishna Mission composed of a college, agricultural school, poultry farm, school for the blind, and orphanage. He recalled, "The warmth of the Ramakrishna monks, alert and quiet. Especially Swami Lokeswarananda [1909-98], whom I liked very much. They invited me back." In his *Asian Journal*, Merton made this brief statement:

> Shri Ramakrishna (1836-86) was a Bengali visionary saint, and teacher who founded the Ramakrishna movement, in which God is worshipped as the Mother of the Universe. Combining the scriptures and disciplines of Hinduism, Christianity, and Islam, Shri Ramakrishna reached the realiza-

tion of a single God-Consciousness. The world centre of the movement is the Ramakrishna Mission at Belur Math, near Calcutta. The teachings of Shri Ramakrishna were popularized in the West by his leading disciple, Swami Vivekananda (1863-1902), who founded the Vedanta Societies of Europe and America.

Thomas Merton was brought up in France, the United States and England. He became a Roman Catholic Trappist monk who lived in isolation for several years, and then a prolific writer. Merton's literary output was enormous, more than forty books in all. Two of Merton's works *New Seeds of Contemplation* and *The Seven Storey Mountain* were judged to be two of the "100 Best Spiritual Books of the Twentieth Century". One of the most well-known Catholic writers of the twentieth century, Merton is credited with introducing the mysticism of Eastern spirituality to Western Christians. He wrote, "If the West continues to underestimate and to neglect the spiritual heritage of the East, it may well hasten the tragedy that threatens man and his civilization." *Mystics and Zen Masters* (1967) revealed his interest in inter-religious dialogue, the underlying commonality of religious experience, Eastern mysticism, and meditation practices.[116]

Inspired as a young man by his meeting with Mahatma Gandhi, Eknath Easwaran (1910-99), a professor of English literature in India, came to the United States in 1959, and two years later set up the Blue Mountain Centre of Meditation in Northern California. As the originator of "passage meditation" during four decades of active spiritual teaching, Easwaran brought the universal ideals of timeless wisdom into the daily life of many people. He denoted:

> Earlier I mentioned *The Gospel of Sri Ramakrishna*, the one volume I brought with me when I came to this country. It was written by a retired schoolmaster totally devoted to Sri Ramakrishna, the tremendous mystic of nineteenth-century Bengal. This schoolmaster, who modestly signed himself "M", loved his teacher so deeply that he would sit in his little room after the sunset and write down from memory everything that had been said by the Master and his disciples and guests, sometimes from morning till evening. The result is an extraordinary achievement which Aldous Huxley called the greatest piece of hagiographic literature in the world, full of lively parables, lucid explanations of difficult spiritual matters, and dazzling ac-

counts of mystical union. If you take this book up, I don't think you will want to part from it.[117]

The author of *Coming Home* (1978), Lex Hixon (1941-95) [q.v.] explained Ramakrishna's attitude toward religious pluralism:

> Ramakrishna was completely at home in all the moods of spiritual expression he encountered, from Christianity and Islam to widely contrasting strands of Hinduism. Born in 1836 in a rural village of Bengal untouched by European influence, Ramakrishna expressed a universal spiritual vision rare in any culture. He experienced all religions as a single spectrum of wisdom and devotion, as a communion of the Divine with the Divine in which both worshipper and worshipped emerge from the same Ultimate Consciousness. Ramakrishna never preached. For him, each individual's spiritual development is unique: to one person he would suggest a certain approach and to another perhaps the contrary approach. His utterances were ecstatic. His parables are songs for meditation, not rational explanations that constitute any system of theology.[118]

In 1992, Lex Hixon came out with his most influential work, the highly imaginative and somewhat fictionalized *Great Swan—Meetings with Ramakrishna*. The volume was intended to provide a bridge between East and West, a bridge that many people will be able to cross comfortably, maintaining their intellectual, cultural and spiritual integrity. Hixon introduces his work stating:

> By meeting Ramakrishna, which is possible here and now, we enter a unique realm of experience where the Wisdom Goddess reigns—the one Ramakrishna calls my blissful Mother. The wonderful nature of this realm cannot be analyzed, yet it describes itself. The present volume contains that mysterious description—not only in words, which are merely instruments, but as the living presence of Ramakrishna Paramahamsa, the Great Swan, the God-intoxicated sage of Bengal.[119]

Lex Hixon, a talented spiritual practitioner and teacher, comprehensively explored many enlightening religious traditions. He documented these investigations in nine books and many articles and teachings given to various groups. Most of his writings concentrate on his conviction that in their higher aspects all of the great religions are true. During his lifetime, for many years Lex Hixon was actively involved in the following spiritual traditions: the Hindu-Vedantist Ramakrishna Order, Sufi lineage, Native American heritage of vision-quest, Japanese Zen Buddhism and Tibetan Tantric Buddhism, and the Eastern Orthodox Church. He also hosted a weekly radio programme "In the Spirit" (1971-84), interviewing representatives of the world's religions like the Dalai Lama and Mother Teresa.[120]

An ordained minister of the United Methodist Church, Donald H. Bishop served as a professor of philosophy at Washington State University since 1961. His books include: *Indian Thought: An Introduction* (1975), editor of *Thinkers of the Indian Renaissance* (1981), and editor of *Mysticism and the Mystical Experience: East and West* (1995). Bishop revealed, "I have travelled extensively in the Far East—India, Thailand, Japan, Taiwan, Mainland China. My vital concern is bringing about understanding and better relations between the United States and the rest of the world. I am interested in the basic philosophies, religions, and motivations of people. I look upon the world as one and all people as brothers and sisters."[121] Concerning Ramakrishna he signified:

> The two other beliefs which Ramakrishna turned to the past for and declared to be true and useful for the present are the definition of religion as realization and the truth of all religions. The first belief in religion as realization he found in the ancient Vedas and elsewhere. These early scriptures declare God is a being to be realized internally. He is the spiritual essence latent in the individual, which the individual perceives in the inner self and brings to the surface when the Divine becomes part of or infuses all our thoughts and outer activities. Ramakrishna believed that each person is divine and the task of religion is to help each individual to recognize or realize that he or she is divine and to make that inner divinity or spirituality the centre or driving force of all we think, say, and do.... [Secondly,] religion is universal and that there is truth in all religions because each is a particular manifestation in time and place of that universal religion and the universal and eternal Brahman. God has revealed or incarnated himself in numerous times and places and the various religions are a result of those incarnations. Each religion is a particular path or way to God.[122]

The 1963 Nobel Prize winning physicist Eugene Wigner (1902-1995) explained:

> The waves of religious thought rise and fall, and on the topmost one stands the prophet of the period. Ramakrishna came to teach the religion of today, constructive, not destructive. He had to go afresh to nature to ask for facts, and he got scientific religion which never says "believe", but "see". "I see and you too, can see"—said Vivekananda.

Born in Budapest, Hungary, Eugene Paul Wigner was a Princeton University professor of mathematical physics (1931-71, except for one year). He received a Nobel Prize for his discovery and application of fundamental principles of symmetry together with group theory, applying them in atomic, nuclear, and elementary particle physics. Wigner formulated many of the laws relating to this scientific theory.[123]

Katherine Whitmarsh (Prasanna, 1897-1992) [q.v.], a Vedanta devotee from Santa Barbara, California, and her assistants devoted fifteen years to compiling the in-depth *Concordance to the Gospel of Sri Ramakrishna*, first released in 1985. This magnificent easy-to-use reference manual of over five-hundred pages is a comprehensive index, which lists thousands of key words drawn from the *Gospel*. Words and phrases of the *Concordance* are arranged alphabetically and cross-referenced in sub-categories. This invaluable guide helps the reader to find out what Ramakrishna said on different subjects, to locate specific stories, and to identify the people he met on various occasions. In his review of the book Swami Vidyatmananda concluded:

> This must be one of the best and most complete scriptural indexes ever devised. Its publication is a major event in the Ramakrishna chronicle. The Concordance is a tool capable of making the serious study of Ramakrishna's life and teaching very much easier and infinitely more profound. Untold thousands of future Ramakrishna enthusiasts will reverently thank its compiler.... Every word Sri Ramakrishna uttered, every teaching he gave, every example he used, every song he sang or listened to, every person he addressed his remarks to may quickly be found by page number and position.[124]

During his stay at Ridgely Manor in 1899, Swami Vivekananda would play with the three Whitmarsh children who lived there and give them pennies. Swamiji held the youngest child, almost two-year-old Katherine Whitmarsh (Prasanna), on his lap. He entrusted the publication of his four yoga volumes to her father Theodore Whitmarsh. Prasanna dearly loved her great-aunt Josephine MacLeod, who proved to be an important and positive influence in her life, particularly in generating enthusiasm for Swami Vivekananda. In 1949, she lived in Santa Barbara, California, as a devotee of Swami Prabhavananda. The house Prasanna had built across from the Temple in Santa Barbara now belongs to the Vedanta Society. In 1986 she also wrote for the *Prabuddha Bharata* on "Swami Vivekananda at Camp Percy". Prasanna had the unique distinction of being the last known living devotee in the world who met Swami Vivekananda.[125]

Father Francis X. Clooney, S.J. [q.v.], a Catholic Jesuit Priest and a professor of comparative theology formerly at Boston College and now at Harvard University Divinity School, was the first president of the International Society for Hindu-Christian Studies. His books include *Theology after Vedanta* (1993), *Hindu Wisdom for All God's Children* (1998), *Hindu God, Christian God* (2001), *Divine Mother, Blessed Mother: Hindu Goddesses and the Virgin Mary* (2005), and other texts on India. He is currently finishing a book on surrender to God, comparing the writings of the fourteenth-century Indian Vedanta Desika with the seventeenth-century Catholic Francis de Sales.[126] In an essay on "Ramakrishna and World Religions" that first appeared in the March 29, 1986 issue of *America*, Clooney expressed the insight:

> His second method relied on the idea that the ways human beings relate to each other are the ways in which they relate to God. He practised five modes of relationship: the quiet reverence and worship one shows to a great potentate; faithful service towards a master and the master's family; friendship and relaxed companionship; "parenting", being mother or father to one's child; marriage and the consummation of intimacy. He related to God according to each mode—my ruler, my master, my friend, my child, my beloved—and enjoyed the special graces appropriate to each.[127]

The following year Clooney wrote on "Ramakrishna and Christ", making this knowledgeable statement:

> Ramakrishna's experience of Christ asks us to realize that the set of religious experiences available to believers within various traditions is much more extensive, more astonishing, than we usually think: we can have religious experiences which go beyond what, by any normal, orthodox standard, is available within one's own tradition. For if this Hindu seems indeed to have had an authentic experience outside his own tradition, an

> experience he could talk about in terms meaningful to himself while yet recognizing it as "foreign"(i.e., as truly "Christian", not "Hindu"), then it must also be true that a Christian, in likewise graced, supernatural circumstances, can experience some of the profound mysteries of Hinduism (such as those of Tantra and Vedanta) without becoming less a Christian or more a Hindu—and without imagining oneself to be disclosing, through some added Christian insight, the true meaning of the Hindu mystery (as if it were previously unknown to the Hindus).... Ramakrishna can tell us a great deal about the future of world religion, if we listen to him—and, even better, do as he did; I for one, have learned much from him—about Hinduism, but also about Christ and being a Christian.[128]

Bhavamukha is a high state of spiritual awareness where the sage experiences both divine and human existence concurrently. At the invitation of Swami Sarvagatananda, Francis X. Clooney gave a talk at the Vedanta Society of Boston on 1 March 1987 emphasizing this point:

> "Remain in bhavamukha:" thus the Divine Mother commanded Ramakrishna several times in his life, telling him that he must not spend his life entirely in ecstasy, as if beyond the world and turned away from it, and that neither should he forget the divine by being too fully immersed in material reality. Rather he was to remain in something of an in-between state, on the "edge" between the finite and the infinite, aware of how the former is always flowing from the latter.... His "mission" was to dwell at that crucial meeting point of the divine and human where all experiences begin, and to make known in this world—using the concrete resources of his own life—what it means to be religious and conformed to the divine. He also learned that even when he finally would pass away and be taken back to his Mother, the "waves" of his inner spiritual experience would radiate throughout the world.[129]

Born in Bucharest, Romania, Mircea Eliade (1907-86) earned a degree studying Indian philosophy under Surendranath Dasgupta at the University of Calcutta from 1928 to 1932. While spending six months in an ashrama in Rishikesh in the Himalayas, he learned Sanskrit. Eliade met Josephine MacLeod at Belur Math during the winter of 1929 and she later sent him some of Vivekananda's volumes. He went on to establish an international reputation in the area of the history of religions, and composed three excellent books on yoga. Shortly before he died, he was the editor-in-chief of the fifteen-volume *The Encyclopedia of Religion* (1987). This was the first large-scale encyclopedia to devote a large number of pages to Indian religions including Sri Ramakrishna and Swami Vivekananda, thereby reflecting the present day understanding of religion in a universal and ecumenical manner.[130]

A professor at the University of Wisconsin at Milwaukee, Walter G. Neevel was assigned to write about Ramakrishna for *The Encyclopedia of Religion*. Asian religions, Hindu and Buddhist religious thought, and the theory and method in the comparative study of religion are his main areas of interest. Neevel published *Yamuna's Vedanta and Pancaratra* (1977). In the encyclopedia he expounded:

> Crucial to Ramakrishna's lasting impact was the articulation of a widely inclusive worldview that integrated the many diverse and often conflicting aspects of Hindu religion and that offered to many the basis for a more harmonious relationship among the religions of the world.... he maintained that reality is one and that everything that exists is to be affirmed as a manifestation or form of that One. The formless Brahman is real, but so is the Divine Mother, or Shakti, at play in the changing world of form. Brahman and Shakti are thus two sides of the same reality, "like fire and its power to burn".[131]

Italian born Eli Raphael Marozzi (1913-99), the president of the Vedanta Society of Hawaii from its inception, was a professional sculptor and instructor, commissioned by the Hawaii State Foundation on Culture and the Arts. He won first prize in sculpturing from the Honolulu Association of Artists. His friends say he led an exemplary life devoted to the study and teaching of Vedantic principles. Marozzi contributed essays to *Swami Vivekananda in East and West* (1968) and other Vedantic publications. The following unique teaching of Ramakrishna appealed to Marozzi:

> Love for man, relatives, children, etc. need not be given up but is to be spiritualized, understood and sublimated with the knowledge that all the bonds of love are due to the presence of God or Self that exists in the object of love, and that it is God or Self that we really love, and not the person or thing.[132]

Leonard A. Gordon, a professor of history at Columbia University and then Brooklyn College, held a Fulbright-Hays senior faculty research grant to India (1972-73). He penned a biography of the Indian Nationalists Sarat and Subhas Chandra Bose. Writing on "Ramakrishna" for the *Encyclopedia of Asian History*, he indicated:

> Ramakrishna (1836-86), or Sri Ramakrishna as he is more commonly known, was an Indian religious teacher of great magnetism. Though a temple priest at Dakshineswar north of Calcutta and devoted to the goddess Kali, he experimented with other religions and proved to his satisfaction that there were several equally viable paths to God. Using earthy wisdom and parables, Ramakrishna persuaded westernized Bengalis that there was much of value in their own traditions. He did not engage in social reform work, but encouraged his disciples to undertake God's work in the world through social service.[133]

Another serious study is Richard Schiffman's *Ramakrishna: A Prophet for a New Age* (1989). The volume was first put out by Paragon House and then by the Ramakrishna Mission Institute of Culture, Calcutta. Mr. Schiffman spent many years in India and studied under Jillellamudi Mother, of whom he wrote a biography, and Sri Sathya Sai Baba. He stressed:

> Over a century since his passing, the great prophet Sri Ramakrishna Paramahamsa remains one of the most profoundly beloved figures in India. Of all the nations of the world, India alone seems to possess the ripened wisdom to honour him above all other men. And what exactly did India see in this unformed son of a peasant and heedless madman of God? In our efforts to understand Sri Ramakrishna, we must first try to understand India....[134]
>
> During his life he would go on to be acknowledged as a great spiritual Master and his teachings and techniques would earn him a following of devoted disciples. Today, slightly more than a century since his death, those teachings have spread far from his home, inspiring countless others, and his message of mankind's deep spiritual unity remains one of critical importance to the well-being of our world.[135]
>
> A song, a word, or a touch from Ramakrishna could awaken their dormant spiritual consciousness of his devotees. In those who were poised to receive it, even a casual glance from the Master during one of his ec-

stasies might release a veritable flood tide of bliss.... No one could have been simpler, less authoritarian, or more self-effacing than Ramakrishna. Nevertheless, without intending it—without for the most part even being aware of it—Ramakrishna exerted a tremendous sway on those who came within his orbit.[136]

Schiffman described the Upanishads thusly:

> These sparse treatises of great beauty, intensity, and revelatory power are set for the most part in the form of dialogues of spiritual guidance between youthful seekers and their enlightened masters, the immortal rishis. The approaches pioneered by the rishis remain to this day the mainstays of Hindu mystical practices.[137]

1990s and After

Since 1979, Swami Chetanananda has been in charge of the Vedanta Society of St. Louis, Missouri. He created a video entitled *Ramakrishna: A Documentary* (1988), which covers the life and teachings of Ramakrishna, using old photographs, paintings, and videos of the places and deities he saw. His *They Lived with God* (1989) provides thirty-one biographies of the principal lay disciples who interacted with Ramakrishna. The volume includes new material about Ramakrishna previously unavailable in English. *Ramakrishna as We Saw Him* (1990), edited by Chetanananda, is a collection of forty reminiscences of disciples, friends, and relatives who describe their association with Ramakrishna in detail.[138]

In his book review, Francis X. Clooney, S.J. affirmed that

> *Ramakrishna as We Saw Him* is a rich addition to the literature available on Sri Ramakrishna. These extensive, detailed and interesting reminiscences of those who knew him document an important moment in India's modern spiritual history. They provide the modern reader with a vivid sense of how Sri Ramakrishna lived daily the spiritual message he taught, and how he excelled in opening a path for God into the human heart. Readers of every culture and religion will profit from reflection on these accounts and the spiritual and human truths they communicate.[139]

Concerning the same book, Gerald Larson concluded:

> The present collection is a masterful achievement. Not only does Ramakrishna Paramahamsa come forth in these pages, but more than that, the larger spiritual life of which his own pilgrimage formed but a part, also comes forth.[140]

Gerald Larson carried out post-doctoral research (1968-69) and worked as a visiting professor at Benares Hindu University (1976-77), became a professor of religious studies at the University of California in Santa Barbara (1970-95), and then the director of the India Studies Programme at Indiana University. He is the foremost Sankhya expert in the West, having authored *Classical Sankhya* (1969), and having been specially selected to be the first of two author-editors of the prestigious *Encyclopedia of Indian Philosophies* Vol. IV: *Sankhya* (1987). In addition, he served as the Western division president of the American Oriental Society (1973-74), and the president of the Society for Asian and Comparative Philosophy (1982-85),[141] after which he became extensively involved with the Ramakrishna movement in India, addressing audiences at the Ramakrishna Mission Institute of Culture in Calcutta on many occasions in 1989, 1995-96, 1998-2001 and 2003. He came out with thirteen articles for the *Bulletin* of the Ramakrishna Mission Institute of Culture.[142]

A lecturer on psychiatry at the Harvard Medical School, Eugene I. Taylor is the founder and director of the Cambridge Institute of Psychology and Religion. He has authored three books on William James with an emphasis on higher levels of consciousness and spiritual healing.[143] Taylor described the biography *Ramakrishna as We Saw Him* as:

> An important contribution to the oral history tradition of 19th century Hindu spiritual life; a work that is invaluable not only for details about the life of Sri Ramakrishna ... but also a useful guide to the identity of his many disciples, several of whom were responsible for the spread of Vedanta to the West.[144]

Concerning the volume, Philip Glass [q.v.], the world famous musical writer and composer of the "Passion of Ramakrishna", acknowledged:

> It happened that I had just been re-reading Swami Nikhilananda's *Gospel of Sri Ramakrishna* (something I've done from time to time over the last twenty years) when I came across Lex Hixon's *Great Swan* [1992], and

found it to be an unexpected and delightful surprise. In it the now familiar words of Sri Ramakrishna are newly presented. Hixon's thorough research has made available to him (and so to us) a wealth of new descriptive material that has made it possible to present Ramakrishna's encounters with his disciples in a fresh and vivid setting. It seems to me that Hixon's *Great Swan* is giving us a new interpretation of a great classic—much as a modern interpreter/performer might rediscover Schubert or Chopin for a contemporary audience. I don't think Hixon's work will replace Nikhilananda's "*Gospel*" nor do I suspect it is meant to. But it will surely bring the words and something of the presence of Ramakrishna to a new generation, perhaps both larger and more receptive than any in the past. This is a work of devotion, beautifully accomplished.[145]

The five-volume biographical encyclopedia *Historic World Leaders* (1994) devoted over twenty-five hundred words in respectfully describing the life and teachings of the Indian religious leader Ramakrishna. A few of its comments include:

> For Ramakrishna, religion was neither religious knowledge of God nor philosophical speculation about God; it was, rather, the direct experience or realization of God. A man might be very learned in the scriptures and still might be irreligious. Without sadhana or spiritual discipline, the meaning of scriptures could not be grasped. In an effort to know and experience God directly, he made his whole life a single-pointed thrust toward the Divine, eschewing even natural human needs, such as sleep....
>
> Ramakrishna's spiritual views of himself and of religion in general took several aspects. First, he considered himself a specially commissioned person whose spiritual experiences were for the benefit of humanity; second, he was convinced that all religions were true, that every doctrinal system represented a path to God. For Ramakrishna, Allah, Hari, Christ, and Krishna were but different names under which the same great God was worshipped....
>
> Sri Ramakrishna became a household name in India. Among the savants of the West, Max Müller of Germany and Romain Rolland had written about him. Both in India and in places around the world there are those who recognize him as belonging in the line of such religious prophets as Lord Krishna, Buddha, and Christ. He represented the very core of the spiritual

wisdom of India and brought to humanity a direct report from the realm of the Spirit in an age of reason and scepticism.[146]

God Lived with Them (1997), written by Swami Chetanananda, presents the life stories of the sixteen monastic disciples of Ramakrishna. Assessments of three professors concerning these biographies follow. About the volume, Francis X. Clooney, S.J. affirmed:

> *God Lived with Them* shows how Sri Ramakrishna affected those who knew him best, and how he inspired them to dedicate their whole lives to his message and mission. We learn how these fascinating figures grew as individual persons, each finding his own way to be true to Sri Ramakrishna's heritage, doing their work in India and the West.
>
> *God Lived with Them* may be read as the inner account of a religious community and its founding fathers, as the story of the early expansion of a powerful religious movement that affects the world even today.
>
> *God Lived with Them* can also be an immediate resource for prayerful reading and contemplation, as the reader savours and takes personally to the heart the encounters and words of practical wisdom which fill its pages.[147]

Professor Gerald Larson's evaluation of *God Lived with Them* states:

> Swami Chetanananda continues his usual critical pattern of meticulous research, careful documentation, engaging presentation and critical reflection. Devout followers of Ramakrishna and curious outsiders will find in this new book a wealth of fascinating material about the Master, as well as intriguing anecdotes about the Master's immediate monastic disciples.[148]

Carl Thomas Jackson [q.v.], a professor of history at the University of Texas at El Paso, emphasized:*

> Western students of the history of the Ramakrishna movement have come to recognize the critical role this important movement has played in spreading knowledge of Hinduism and the Vedanta philosophy in the West. Swami Chetanananda's new book offers revealing sketches of sixteen of

* See Chapter XIII for more on Jackson.

> Ramakrishna's monastic disciples that testify to their Master's great powers as a religious teacher.[149]

Amrita Salm, Satchidananda Dhar, and Prasun Kumar De are the editors of *A Portrait of Sri Ramakrishna* (1998), a book with many translators. Dr. Amrita Salm, the lead editor, has been a member of the Vedanta Society of Southern California for over twenty-five years. This work is a translation of the four-volume Bengali biography by Akshay Kumar Sen (1854-1923) written in verse form during 1894-1901. Sen was an intimate householder disciple of Ramakrishna, who witnessed many episodes in the Master's life. This biography offers new information and insights about Ramakrishna previously unknown to English language readers. Swami Vivekananda indicated, "Just now I read Akshay's book. Give him a hundred thousand hearty embraces from me. Through his pen Shri Ramakrishna is manifesting himself.... Well, I do not find a single irrelevant word in it. I cannot tell in words the joy I have experienced by reading his book."[150] Swami Ranganathananda, the 13th President of the Ramakrishna Order, commented, "This book makes Ramakrishna come alive."[151]

An article in the *Encyclopedia of World Biography* (which is composed of an editorial staff largely of women) made the following comment concerning his position as a spiritual leader:

> Ramakrishna had a wide following from all classes and groups. He was not merely a great teacher; he was regarded as an embodiment of the sacred source of Indian religious tradition and of the universal ideals toward which all men strive. His spiritual vitality and magnetism were combined with a sharp sense of humour—often aimed at himself or his disciples when the hazards of pride and self-satisfaction seemed imminent.
>
> Ramakrishna's teachings do not appear in systematic form. He wrote nothing. His disciples recorded his words only in the context of the spiritual force of his personality, and consequently in collected form these sayings have the character of a gospel—a message of salvation centred in the spiritual paradigm of his own life.... Above all, Ramakrishna had a "grass-roots" appeal equalled by few others in any religious tradition, marked by his love of all men and his enthusiasm for all forms of spirituality.[152]

Judyth Reichenberg-Ullman (b. 1948) intensively studied homeopathy with many experts from Bombay. Centring in the state of Washington, she is the past president of The International Foundation for Homeopathy. Her *Mystics, Masters, Saints, and Sages* (2001), beginning with Buddha focuses on the enlightenment of saints and masters that led to their witnessing divine reality. Eight pages are devoted to Ramakrishna, opening with a short sketch of his life, followed by selections from the *Sayings of Ramakrishna*. She wrote in part:

> It was there, amidst an image of the blissful Mother Kali, that Ramakrishna worshipped. More important, it was in this temple that the boy was seized, to the point of obsession, with a single question: Does Kali (the Divine Mother) truly exist? Kali's dark colour, necklace of skulls, and belt of human limbs, symbolizing the death inherent in every birth, is fearsome to many. But to Ramakrishna, she was the gentlest, most loving of mothers....
>
> Vision upon vision was bestowed on Ramakrishna by his Divine Mother, Kali. Convinced of her existence, he set out to learn the truth about the world religions. A practitioner of Vedanta (a non-dualistic approach to Hinduism), in which the belief is that there is only one in the universe, not two, and that one is consciousness, manifesting itself in and as all beings and things, Ramakrishna also undertook practices of Islam, Christianity, and various other sects under the guidance of knowledgeable teachers. He concluded that the goal of all religions is the same: to embody the Divine.[153]

More recently Chetanananda, working with a team of editors, devoted five years to translating the Bengali work *Sri Ramakrishna Lila Prasanga* to English, titled *Ramakrishna and His Divine Play* (2003). It is the definitive well-documented life of Ramakrishna written by Swami Saradananda, from which many other accounts have been drawn. It provides a great inspiration for his followers. This biography was described by Huston Smith as a

> detailed eyewitness accounts of spiritual geniuses—whose impact on history far surpasses that of kings and potentates—are second only to sacred scriptures in the place they occupy in the library of humanity. Now at last, we have a splendid translation of the source biography from which all previous accounts of Sri Ramakrishna have drawn. Swami Chetanananda's long-awaited translation of *Sri Ramakrishna and His Divine Play* is an epic in the unfolding saga of world spirituality.[154]

Huston Smith served as a professor of philosophy and religion at many universities. He authored *The Religions of Man* (1958) (renamed as *The World's Religions*, 1991), which has been a standard textbook in college-level comparative religion classes for a half century. The volume has sold over two million copies since it was first released. He was the guest of a five-hour 1996 Public Broadcasting System series hosted by Bill Moyer on "The Wisdom of Faith". There he mentioned his indebtedness to the Vedanta movement in general, and Swami Satprakashananda (1888-1979) of the St. Louis Centre in particular. At the dedication of the new home and chapel of the Vedanta Society of St. Louis on December 10, 1952, Smith "declared that the marked increase of interest in Eastern philosophy here in St. Louis is due to the presence of Swami Satprakashananda in the city". Professors from Washington University in St. Louis, Iowa State University and the Unitarian Church gave addresses at the dedication ceremony.[155] In his writings Smith makes such insightful statements as:

> Hinduism's cosmology was prodigious in scope and depth, but India did not stop there. She went on to advance what was probably the most daring hypothesis man has ever conceived. We ourselves are the infinite, the very infinite from which the Universe proceeds. Everything in Hinduism works to drive the point home.[156]

Concerning *Ramakrishna and His Divine Play*, William Page, an American devotee and a retired teacher of English from Thammasat University in Bangkok, Thailand, pointed out:

> In a labour of love lasting five years, the swami and his team of editors have produced a stunningly beautiful translation of this Vedantic classic.... As a source book on the details of Sri Ramakrishna's life, the *Lilaprasanga* has always been unparalleled. Every biographer of Sri Ramakrishna who has had access to the earlier translation has drawn heavily from it. Devotees, and future biographers, will find this new translation indispensable.[157]

Garnette Arledge, who holds a divinity degree from Drew Theological School, is the president of the Kingston, New York branch of the American Association of University Women (AAUW). As a hospice chaplain and a spiritual mentor, she wrote a book to help people face death, which she refers to as "Angel's Eve". Her section on "The Inspiring Death Story of Sri Ramakrishna Paramahamsa" states in part:

> When Ramakrishna died, the people attending him at his bedside did not know if he actually had died. For prior to his terminal illness and continuing through it, he could stiffen and stop breathing at any given moment in what the philosopher Spinoza called God-intoxicated Bliss. His hair would stand on end, and his flesh became covered with goose bumps. These physical signs indicate both the deep ecstatic state of union with the Unmanifest, called samadhi, and the physical death of a holy person, called maha-samadhi. The followers knew that when Ramakrishna thought of Devi, he merged with Devi instantly. For years, his students witnessed, in awe, how he would regain everyday consciousness after being in the altered state of complete ecstasy. Therefore, in hopes it was the divine mood of samadhi, attendants at Ramakrishna's death kept chanting holy sounds—mantras—to lure him back to waking consciousness. Yet, as the great teacher was severely wracked with cancer and failing extremely, they also knew death was coming for his body. It did, and his last words were the sacred mantra, Om Tat Sat.[158]

In *Holy People of the World: A Cross Cultural Encyclopedia* (2004), a cross-cultural encyclopedia of the most significant holy people in history, June McDaniel [q.v.], an admirer of Holy Mother and a member of the department of philosophy and religious studies at the College of Charleston in South Carolina, makes this important point:

> Ramakrishna came to be recognized as a siddha, or perfected being, during his lifetime, and disciples came to learn from him and follow him as a teacher (guru).... During his lifetime, Ramakrishna was understood to be a saint by many of his followers. After his death, and until the present day, there have been followers who claimed to sense his presence, and they say that he comes to them in dreams and visions as a spiritual guide.[159]

A landmark book *Prayer: A History* by Philip and Carol Zaleski "explores the spiritual, artistic, literary and social history of prayer around the world". They focus on the people whose lives were changed by prayer. The authors did an excellent job in devoting fourteen pages to describing the many religious experiences of Sri Ramakrishna. A sample of their portrayal includes:

> At least during long stretches of his life, ecstasy was Ramakrishna's regular state of consciousness, during rapture he would dance, sing, chant the divine name, pray, drink, eat, and even carry on conversation; what we experience as normal waking consciousness was for him the exception rather than the rule.
>
> Given this, the abundance of bewildering revelations is perhaps to be expected. We may note, then, that Ramakrishna enjoyed visions of Shiva, the Divine Mother, and God ("I used to see God directly with these very eyes, just as I see you now.")....
>
> For Ramakrishna, prayer meant rapture. There was no other way. "The slightest thing," he observes, "awakens God-Consciousness in me." Meditating, chanting hymns, listening to sacred music or scripture readings, reciting the divine name, walking by the sacred Ganges, worshipping statues, even observing the religious practices of others were enough to ignite his mind...
>
> During rapture, he would sing, dance, eat, drink, converse. Sometimes he would engage in erratic behaviour—slapping devotees on the cheek if they seemed far from God—or even forbidden acts, such as accepting food from a prostitute. Once he broke his teeth during rapture, another time his arm. He would stagger like a drunk or tremble uncontrollably. He would talk like a child. His hair would stand on end. At times he became speechless and motionless.... His flesh would turn red; his disciples reported a divine glow emanating from his body. Sometimes he would fall unconscious.

Philip Zaleski headed a group of writers for the magazine *Spirituality & Health* that selected the "100 Most Important Spiritual Books of the 20th Century" for HarperCollins publishers, which included *The Gospel of Sri Ramakrishna*. A Roman Catholic, he was a lecturer in religion at Smith College, and a longtime senior editor of the erudite magazine *Parabola*. His wife Carol is a professor of the philosophy of religion, world religions and Christian thought at Smith College.[160]

One of America's most celebrated neo-classical composers, Philip Glass [q.v.] received a commission to compose the music for the "Passion of Ramakrishna". Its world premiere took place on September 16, 2006 at the Segerstrom Concert Hall in Costa Mesa, California. It was performed by

Orange County's Pacific Symphony Orchestra conducted by Carl St. Clair, with the Pacific Chorale directed by John Alexander. The cast of individuals for the opera includes Ramakrishna, Sarada Devi, Mahendranath Gupta, Dr. Mahendralal Sarkar, Narendra and two devotees. In Christianity "Passion" refers to the suffering of Jesus from the Last Supper until his crucifixion. Glass' musical "The Passion of Ramakrishna" is meant to describe, in an abbreviated fashion, the last few months of the Master's life. In this musical, the words of Ramakrishna are sung by the chorus. Solo parts are sung by Sarada Devi, Mahendranath Gupta the narrator, Dr. Mahendralal Sarkar, Narendra, and two devotees.

After the performance, Timothy Mangan, a music critic for the *Orange County Register*, expressed the view:

> The 45-minute "Ramakrishna" is a winner. It is direct, interesting, moving. The subject matter—the life, teachings and death of a 19th-century Indian holy man, told largely in his own words—seems to have genuinely inspired and revived the composer out of his old formulas to write something fresh. Some of it doesn't even sound like Glass (though much does). The Ramakrishna speaks via the choir (the Pacific Chorale), giving his words and wisdom an extra-human quality. The words of his wife and devotees are given to solo singers, thus creating a fascinating dialogue between the terrestrial and celestial. With its crisp word-setting (usually one note per syllable) and short sentence phrases, the narrative and drama remain front and centre. The orchestra provides drive and mood—the latter quickly changing or ruminative, as need be—and introduces spicy harmonies and jagged rhythms, not just the usual Glassian thrum.[161]

In the programme for his musical presentation "The Passion of Ramakrishna", there are excellent pictures of Ramakrishna, Holy Mother and Vivekananda. Philip Glass expressed his appreciation for Ramakrishna by writing in the programme:

> As a young man, he was largely self-taught, having absorbed knowledge of the ancient tradition of India through reading and hearing the religious stories in the Puranas as well as his association with the holy men, pilgrims and wandering monks who would stop at Kamarpukur on their way to Puri and other holy places. In time he became famous throughout India for his ability to expound and elucidate the most subtle aspects of that profound

> and vast tradition. It was not uncommon in the years of his maturity for pundits from all over India to come and "test" his knowledge. Invariably, they were astonished by the ease and eloquence with which he addressed their questions. It appeared that his first-hand spiritual experiences were more than adequate when it came to explaining the scriptures of ancient India. In this way he was able to remove all doubt about their meaning and, indeed, his own authority.... The genius of Ramakrishna was to restore and reaffirm the ancient Hindu culture from its spiritual source. It would be hard to overestimate the impact that the life, presence and teaching of Sri Ramakrishna had on the formation of the modern India we know today. It was as if the sleeping giant of Indian culture and spirituality—certainly one of the foremost cultures of the ancient world—had been re-awakened and empowered to take its rightful place in modern times.

Philip Glass studied with Indian performers Ravi Shankar and Alla Rakha, which very much influenced his own perception of rhythm in Indian music. For his innovative symphonies, operas, and film scores he has won Obie, Golden Globe, and Cannes International Film Festival Awards, and received an Academy Award nomination. During 1980, Glass came out with his second opera, "Satyagraha". There the composer "examined the life of Hindu leader Mohandas Gandhi, focusing on his early experiences. The opera's words, sung in Sanskrit, are taken from the sacred Hindu text the *Bhagavad-Gita*; most audience members, therefore, must depend upon the visual tableaux presented for meaning". Leo Tolstoy, Rabindranath Tagore and Martin Luther King are also featured in the opera. Glass considers Sanskrit to be a beautiful vocal language, far exceeding German or English.[162]

In regards to Swami Chetanananda's *How to Live with God: In the Company of Ramakrishna* (2008), Huston Smith expounded:

> In my study of the world's religions I have been fortunate in coming upon inspiring firsthand accounts of the world's great spiritual geniuses, including Sri Ramakrishna, India's greatest 19th century saint. During the summer of the 1950s while I was writing the chapter on Hinduism in what was to become my book, *The World's Religions*, I read and meditated on ten pages of *The Gospel of Sri Ramakrishna* each day, and I credit those meditations for the acclaim that has greeted that chapter.

Concerning the volume, Francis X. Clooney, S.J. of the Harvard divinity school ascertained:

> For over thirty years Swami Chetanananda has researched the details of the life of Sri Ramakrishna and performed for us the great service of making available in attractive form many valuable archival and historical resources that had long been inaccessible. It is appropriate—and wonderful—to see that in *How to Live with God* Swami not only continues that research, but also provides us with his own wide-ranging and deep reflections on the meaning of Sri Ramakrishna for the world today.

In the words of Gerald Larson, professor emeritus of Indiana University:

> As one moves through the thirty chapters of this book, one begins to get a sense of what it means to live with God through every aspect of one's personal and professional life. In this book we are very much in the presence of a "god-intoxicated" person.[163]

In summary, one must take note of the fact that from the above-quoted authors, Richard Bucke, Alexander McIvor-Tyndall, Ernest Brown, Lily Adams Beck, Alban Widgery, Aldous Huxley, Gerald Heard, and Christopher Isherwood were born in England; and Rabbi Samuel Goldenson, Frederich Spiegelberg, Heinrich Zimmer, Joachim Wach, Albin Gilbert, Pitirim Sorokin, Claude Stark, Eugene Wigner, Mircea Eliade, and Eli Marozzi on the rest of the European continent; indicating the cordiality of the dignified Old World culture with the ideals of Ramakrishna-Vedanta. While the largest number of combined European and American tributes occurred in the decade of the 1930s, the number of combined tributes for each decade from the 1890s until the present time has not varied to a large extent.

Concerning the literature on Ramakrishna, see Appendix V for the publication dates of his teachings, Appendix VI for a selected list of books and articles about him; and Appendix VII for European language translations of his books up to 1930.

ENDNOTES

1 *CW*, IV:154-87.

2 Richard Bucke, *Cosmic Consciousness* (New York: E. P. Dutton, 1905), pp. 258 ff on GBS; *CA* (2000), vol. 178; *EOP;* Web: en.wikipedia.org/ wiki/Richard_Bucke.

3 *PB* (June 1906), pp. 115-17.

4 "The Ramakrishna Movement in the West", *PB* (Jan. 1908), pp. 10-12; reproduced from *Pearson's Magazine* (Oct. 1907).

5 *DAB* (1958), II, p. 533, *CA* (2000), vol. 178, pp. 110-12.

6 E. Horrwitz, *A Short History of Indian Literature* (London: T. Fisher Unwin, 1907), pp. 104-06; *PB* (Feb. 1936), p. 127.

7 *PB* (1912), p. 69.

8 *Master Mind Magazine* (1913), p. 74. Web: In Google type "Master Mind Magazine" Ramakrishna.

9 Ali Nomad, *Cosmic Consciousness* (Chicago: Advance Thought Publishing Company, 1913), pp. 30-32; *WWWA* (1962), I, p. 815.

10 *DAB* (1941-45), Sup. III; Riepe, pp. 129-32.

11 James Pratt, *India and Its Faith* (Boston: Houghton Mifflin, 1915), pp. 177-79, 471 on GBS; Riepe, p. 131.

12 *VK* (Feb-March 1936), pp. 392-93.

13 James Pratt, *The Religious Consciousness: A Psychological Study* (New York: Macmillan, 1920), pp. 132-33.

14 *VK* (Feb-March 1936), p. 392; Londhe, #206. James Bissett Pratt; Christopher Isherwood, *Vedanta for Modern Man*, pp. 41-43; *VW* (1945).

15 *VK* (June 1944), p. 72.

16 Swami Pareshananda, "Sri Ramakrishna and the Vedanta Movement in Argentina", *PB* (Jan. 1991), p. 47; Spanish language books on Ramakrishna Vedanta can be purchased for a low price from Web: www.saradmapublishing.org.

17 *CA* (1991), vol. 131, pp. 338-40; G. W. Umphrey, "Amado Nervo and Hinduism", Hispanic Review (1949), pp. 133-45.

18 Hereward Carrington, *Higher Psychical Development: Yoga Philosophy* (San Bernardino, CA: Borgo Press, 1920), pp. Index; *EOP*; *WWWA* (1976), VI, p. 70.

19 *The Wisdom of the Hindus*, ed. Brian Brown (New York: Brentano's 1921), pp. v-vi, xxi, 273-75 on GBS; *WWWA* (1976), VI, pp. 55-56.

20 Walter Kenilworth, *Practical Occultism* (Boston: Badger, 1921), pp. 8, 308 on GBS.

21 *PB* (May 1923), pp. 183-84; Lokeswarananda, p. 13; Gargi, pp. 88, 151, 211, 267.

22 Sister Devamata, *Sri Ramakrishna and His Disciples* (La Crescenta; Advaita Ashrama, 1928), pp. 104, 181.

23 Levinsky, pp. 265-68; *RLOA* (1991), p. 260.

24 L. Adams Beck, *The Way of Power* (New York: Cosmopolitan Book Corporation, 1928), pp. 241-44 on GBS.

25 Wikipedia. Web: en.wikipedia.org/wiki/Elizabeth_Louisa_Moresby; Lily Adams Beck. Web: www.maltwood.uvic.ca/k_maltwood/maltwoods/lilyadamsbeck.html; *World Authors 1900-1950*, ed. M. Seymour-Smith and A. Kimmens (New York: H. W. Wilson, 1996), pp. 168-69.

26 *The Christian Century* (April 1, 1931), p. 450.

27 *PB* (Jan. 1991), pp. 47-48; *CA* (1991), vol. 131, pp. 223-24; Wikipedia. Web: en.wikipedia.org/wiki/Ricardo_Güiraldes.

28 Centenary, I, p. 155; Graciela Devita, *PB* (Nov. 2009), pp. 625-28.

29 *CA* (1998), vol. 61, pp. 196-98; Will Durant, *Our Oriental Heritage* (New York: Simon and Schuster, 1954), pp. 616-18; Will and Ariel Durant, *A Dual Autobiography* (New York: Simon and Schuster, 1977), pp. 152-53.

30 Saha, p. 148.

31 N. Gerald Barrier, *India and America* (New Delhi: American Institute of Indian Studies, 1986), pp. 9, 14-26.

32 Kamath, pp. 108, 141.

33 *BRMIC* (Aug. 2003), pp. 371-73.

34 Lokeswarananda, pp. 16-19.

35 *PB* (July 1936), pp. 326-27.

36 Centenary, I, pp. xv-xx; II, pp. vii-xiii.

37 Centenary, II, pp. 599-600.

38 *WWWA*, I, p. 1045; John Ohles, *Biographical Dictionary of American Educators* (London: Greenwood Press, 1978), p. 1111; *Time Magazine*. Web: www.time.com/time/magazine/article/0,9171,772195,00.htmlRobinson.

39 *NCAB* (1966), vol. 49, p. 378.

40 *PB* (Sept. 1936), pp. 599-600, 634; Mookerjee, pp. 99-103.

41 *VK* (Sept. 1950), p. 198; (March 1952), p. 437.

42 Harry Oldmeadow, *Light from the East* (World Wisdom, 2007), pp. 229, 234; *DAB* (1946-50), Sup. 4; *CA* (1985), vol. 115.

43 *CA* (1969), Rev. Ser., vol. 5-8; Alban Widgery, *Living Religions and Modern Thought* (New York: Round Table, 1936), pp. 42-43; Stuart Brown ed., *The Dictionary of Twentieth-Century British Philosophers* (Thoemmes, 2005), II, pp. 122-23.

44 Ruth St. Denis, *An Unfinished Life* (New York: Harper & Brothers, 1939), pp. 287-90.

45 *DAB*, Sup. VIII, pp. 620-21; *EWB* (1998), XIII, pp. 430-31.

46 Robert Ballou and Friedrich Spiegelberg, *The Bible of the World* (New York: Viking Press, 1984); Stanford News Service. Web: www.stanford.edu/dept/news/pr/94/941115Arc4042.htm.

47 *PB* (Dec. 1939), p. 601; *New York Times* (Sept. 28, 1966), p. 50; *WWWA* (1974-76), VI, p. 179; Nelson, pp. 120, 127-28.

48 Swami Nikhilananda, tr., *The Gospel of Sri Ramakrishna* (New York: Ramakrishna-Vivekananda Centre, 1952), pp. v-vi; *Time Magazine* (Nov. 2, 1942), pp. 48-52; WorldCat.

49 Swami Prabhavananda and C. Isherwood, *The Song of God: Bhagavad-Gita* (Hollywood: Vedanta Press, 1951), p. 7.

50 Pravrajika Varadaprana, *Vedanta in Southern California: A Brief History* (Santa Barbara: Vedanta Society of Southern California, 1993), pp. 5-7; "Gerald Heard and Vedanta", *Vedanta* (July-Aug. 2008), p. 151.

51 Web: www.spiritualityhealth.com/spirit/node/60.

52 Huston Smith, *Cleansing the Doors of Perception* (New York: Jeremy P. Tarcher/Putnam, 2000), p. 6.

53 *VW* (July-Aug. 1956), p. 49; "World of Religion", Garden Grove *Daily News* (July 29, 1956); *The Journal of Transpersonal Psychology* (2000), p. 182.

54 *The New Republic* (Feb. 1, 1943), pp. 154-55; (Aug. 21, 1944), p. 224.

55 *CA* (1998), New Rev. Ser., vol. 60.

56 *The Christian Century* (Feb. 3, 1943), pp. 135-36; *PB* (Oct. 1940), p. 453; Eustace Haydon. Web: www25.uua.org/uuhs/duub/articles/eustacehaydon.htm.

57 Web: http://www.amazon.com/Gospel-Sri-Ramakrishna-Swami-Nikhilananda/dp/0911206019; *New York Times* (Jan. 7, 1953), p. 31.

58 *VK* (March 1954), pp. 453-54.

59 amazon.com. Web: http://www.amazon.com/Gospel-Sri-Ramakrishna-Swami-Nikhilananda/dp/0911206019.

60 *DAB* (1981), Sup. VII; *RLA*; Spencer Lavan, *Unitarians and India* (Boston: Beacon Press, 1977), pp. 181-96; Raucher, pp. 101-02.

61 Saha, p. 153.

62 amazon.com. Web: http://www.amazon.com/Gospel-Sri-Ramakrishna-Swami-Nikhilananda/dp/0911206019.

63 amazon.com. Web: http://www.amazon.com/Gospel-Sri-Ramakrishna-Swami-Nikhilananda/dp/0911206019; *DAB* (1977), Sup. V.

64 *PB* (Dec. 1946), pp. 486-87.

65 *CA* (1969), 1st Rev., vol. 5-8; Charles Braden, *The World's Religions* (New York: Abingdon Press, 1954), pp. 114-15.

66 *Journal of Bible and Religion* (Apr. 1950), pp. 135-36; (Oct. 1952), pp. 294-96; Charles Braden, *These Also Believe* (New York: Macmillan, 1949), p. 473.

67 *PB* (Dec. 1946), pp. 486-87; *NCAB* (1958), XLII, pp. 284-85.

68 David Nicholls, *The Cambridge Companion to John Cage* (Cambridge University Press, 2002), pp. 48-50 on GBS; *CA* (1983), New Rev. Ser., vol. 9.

69 *PB* (March 1948), p. 108; Stavig2; "Gerald Heard and Vedanta", *Vedanta* (July-Aug. 2008), pp. 149-55.

70 Vergilius Ferm, *Religion in the Twentieth Century* (New York: Philosophical Library, 1948), xvii-xviii; *CA* (1975), vol. 49.

71 Review of "Ramakrishna: Prophet of New India" in *The Review of Religion* (Nov. 1949), p. 94.

72 *Philosophies of India* (Princeton, NJ: Princeton University Press, 1969), pp. v-vii, 5-8, 21-22, 560-69, 589-90, 593-94, 614, 618, 630, 671.

73 Londhe, #15. Joseph Campbell.

74 *CA* (2002), vol. 107; *Mission* (Vrajaprana), pp. 1108-10; Riepe, p. 227.

75 Nelson, pp. 120, 125, 127-31, 133, 135.

76 *Merriam-Webster's Biographical Dictionary* (Merriam-Webster Incorporated, 1995).

77 *Journal of Religion* (Oct. 1948), p. 304.

78 *PB* (Aug. 1952), pp. 325-26.

79 Carl Jackson, *Vedanta for the West* (Bloomington, IN; Indiana University Press, 1994), p. 112; *DAB*, Sup. VIII.

80 *PB* (Oct. 1954), pp. 497-98; (Aug. 1958), p. 340; *American Men and Women of Science* (1979), p. 799.

81 Pitirim Sorokin, *The Way and Power of Love* (Chicago: Henry Regnery, 1954, 1967), pp. 259-60; Nelson, p. 135.

82 Centenary, I, p. 93.

83 *PB* (Sept. 1957), p. 377; Lokeswarananda, p. 10.

84 *CA* (1977), 1st Rev., vol. 25-28; *EWB*, Nelson, p. 135.

85 *CA* (1986), New Rev. Ser., XVI.

86 *PB* (Jan. 1956), pp. 57, 59, 62; Lokeswarananda, p. 12.

87 *PB* (Jan. 1956), p. 76.

88 *Sources of Indian Tradition*, comp. William de Bary, et al. (New York: Columbia University, 1958), pp. xxiii-xxv, 603, 637-38.

89 Web: www.universityofcalifornia.edu/senate/inmemoriam/StephenNorthrupHay.htm; *CA* (1969), 1st Rev., V-VIII.

90 Yale, p. 27.
91 *New York Times Book Review* (March 28, 1954).
92 *CA* (1992), vol. 134.
93 Christopher Isherwood, *Ramakrishna and His Disciples* (New York: Simon and Schuster, 1965), pp. 1-2.
94 Swami Vidyatmananda, *Making of a Devotee*. Web: http://theworld.com/~elayj/Chapter5.htm.
95 Swami Vidyatmananda, *Making of a Devotee*. Web: http://theworld.com/~elayj/Chapter5.htm.
96 *PB* (Aug. 1965), p. 359; (1989).
97 Gambhirananda, p. ix.
98 *CA* (1981), vol. 97.
99 *New York Times Book Review* (Nov. 14, 1965), pp. 22, 24.
100 Harry Oldmeadow, *Journeys East* (World Wisdom, 2004), p. 82.
101 Christopher Isherwood, *My Guru and His Disciple* (New York: Farrar, Straus, Giroux, 1980), pp. 149-53; *Hinduism Today*. Web: www.hinduismtoday.com/archives/1999/9/1999-9-12.shtml.
102 Yale, p. 58; Isherwood (1980), p. 309.
103 *CA* (1992), New Rev. Ser., vol. 35, pp. 238-42.
104 Pravrajika Varadaprana, *Vedanta in Southern California: A Brief* History (Santa Barbara: VSSC, 1993), pp. 13-14; "History of the Vedanta Society of Western Washington", p. 9, VSSC Archives; photographs of Swami Tadatmananda's paintings can be purchased through Web: www.vedanta.com.
105 Thomas Berry. *Religions of India: Hinduism, Yoga, Buddhism*, Bruce (New York: Bruce, 1971), pp. 68-69 on GBS.
106 *CA* (1977), 1st Rev., vols. 21-24; Web: www.thomasberry.org.
107 *PB* (March 1972), p. 105; *WWIA* (1990-91), p. 2153.
108 B. F. Skinner, *Beyond Freedom and Dignity* (New York: Alfred A. Knopf, 1972), pp. 170-71; *CA* (1994), New Rev. Ser., vol. 42.
109 Norman Adams, "Background of Some Hindu Influences in America—The Ramakrishna Movement", *Journal of Ecumenical Studies* (1972), pp. 320-21.
110 Claude Alan Stark, *God of All* (Cape Cod, MA: Claude Stark, 1974), pp. 178, 186 on GBS; Lokeswarananda, p. 31.
111 *CA*, New Rev. Ser., vol. 85.
112 Stark (1974), pp. xv-xvii; Lokeswarananda, pp. 30-31.
113 *CA* (1978), vol. 73; Boston University Philosophy Department. Web: www.bu.edu/philo/faculty/rouner.htm.
114 *CA* (2003), vol. 181.

115 Stark, pp. 190-91.

116 Thomas Merton, et al., *Asian Journal of Thomas Merton* (New Direction Publishing, 1975), pp. 33-34, 48 on GBS; *CA* (1997), vol. 53; *DAB* (1966-1970), Sup. VIII, *RLOA*; *100 Best Spiritual Books of the Twentieth Century*. Web: www.spiritualityhealth.com/spirit/node/60.

117 Eknath Easwaran, *Passage Meditation* (Nilgiri Press, 1978, 2008), pp. 212-13; Web: en.Wikipedia.org/wiki/Eknath_Easwaran.

118 Lex Hixon, *Coming Home* (Garden City, NY: Anchor Books, 1978), p. 42.

119 Swami Ranganathananda, "Sri Ramakrishna and Our Stranded Freudian Writers", *VK* (March 2001), p. 108.

120 Wikipedia. Web: en.wikipedia.org/wiki/Lex_Hixon; Nationmaster. Web: www.nationmaster.com/encyclopedia/Lex-Hixon; *New York Times* (Nov. 9, 1995), p. B17.

121 *CA* (1982), vol. 105.

122 *BRMIC* (Jan. 1979), pp. 29-30; also in Ramakrishna, pp. 158-59.

123 Web: www.vedanta-newyork.org/articles/ on_sri_ramakrishna.htm#wigner; *EWB* (1998).

124 Swami Vidyatmananda, *Making of a Devotee*. Web: http://theworld.com/~elayj/Chapter12.htm.

125 *VK* (1992), p. 319; Burke, V, p. 123; *WWWA*, V, p. 777; "Katherine Whitmarsh Interviewed by Swami Chetanananda" (Aug. 6, 1979), p. 6, VSSC Archives.

126 Francis X. Clooney, S.J. Web: www.hds.harvard.edu/faculty/clooney.htm.

127 *PB* (Dec. 1986), p. 534; also in *VFEW* (May-June 1987), p. 6.

128 Ramakrishna, pp. 95-96, 98.

129 *PB* (July 1988), pp. 255-57.

130 G. Stavig, "India in Russian Thought", *BRMIC* (Oct. 1999), pp. 476-81; Prabudhapranai, p. 221; Stavig, pp. 476-81.

131 *Encyclopedia of Religion*, Mircea Eliade ed. (New York: Macmillan Publishing, 1987), XII, p. 210; University of Wisconsin at Milwaukee. Web: http://cfprod.imt.uwm.edu/dept/news/speakers/details.cfm?id=256.

132 *VK* (Sept. 1987), p. 379; *Honolulu Star-Bulletin* (Sept. 8, 1999); *Who's Who in American Art 1993-94* (New Providence, NJ: R. R. Bowker, 1993), p. 774.

133 "Ramakrishna." *Encyclopedia of Asian History* (Charles Scribner's Sons, 1988); *CA* (1979), 1st Rev., vol. 37-40.

134 Swami Ranganathananda, "Sri Ramakrishna and Our Stranded Freudian Writers", *VK* (March 2001), p. 108.

135 Richard Schiffman, *Ramakrishna: A Prophet for a New Age* (New York, Paragon House, 1989), back cover.

136 *BRMIC* (Feb. 2003), p. 51.
137 Londhe, #435. Richard Schiffman.
138 Vedanta Press and Catalog. Web: www.vedanta.org.
139 Swami Chetanananda, *Ramakrishna as We Saw Him* (St. Louis: Vedanta Society of St. Louis, 1990), back cover.
140 *Ramakrishna as We Saw Him*, back cover.
141 Web: www.indiana.edu/~isp/gjl/larson_cv.doc; *CA* (1980), vol. 93-96.
142 Gerald Larson. Web: www.indiana.edu/~isp/gjl/larson_cv.doc; *CA* (1980), vol. 93-96.
143 *WWIA* (2008); Eugene Taylor. Web: http://barzuncentennial.murphywong.net/EugeneTaylor.htm.
144 Chetanananda (1990), back cover.
145 "Passion of Ramakrishna." Philip Glass. Web: www.philipglass.com/html/compositions/passion-of-ramakrishna.html; "Great Swan", Lex Hixon. Web: www.lexhixon.org/simplesite/bookfrms/ greatsrevs.htm.
146 *Historic World Leaders* (Detroit: Gale Research, 1994).
147 Chetanananda (1997), back cover.
148 Chetanananda (1997), back cover.
149 Chetanananda, back cover.
150 *CW*, VI: 334.
151 UCLC; WorldCat.
152 *Encyclopedia of World Biography* (Detroit: Gale Research, 1998).
153 Judyth Reichenberg-Ullman, *Mystics, Masters, Saints, and Sages* (Conari, 2001), pp. 91-92 on GBS; Homeopathy. Web: www.wholehealthnow.com/homeopathy_pro/judyth_reichenberg_ullman.htm.
154 Saradananda, back cover.
155 *CA* (2002), vol. 106, pp. 395-97; *VK* (March 1953), p. 485.
156 Londhe, #55. Huston Smith.
157 *Global Vedanta* (Summer 2004), p. 16.
158 Garnette Arledge, *On Angel's Eve* (Square One Publishers, 2004), p. 96 on GBS; Garnette Arledge. Web: garnettearledge.com.
159 *Holy People of the World*, ed. Phyllis Jestice (ABC-CLIO, 2004), p. 723 on GBS.
160 Philip and Carol Zaleski, *Prayer: A History* (Houghton, Mifflin, Harcourt, 2005), pp. 161-74 on GBS; *CA* (2007), New Rev. Ser., vol. 159; Smith College. Web: www.smith.edu/religion/fac_czaleski.html; *100 Spiritual Books*. Web: www.spiritualityhealth.com/spirit/node/60.

161 From Joanne Euler, director of the Vedanta Archives, Vedanta Society of Southern California.

162 *CA* (1999), vol. 171.

163 All three book reviews are from Swami Chetanananda, *How to Live with God* (St. Louis: Vedanta Society of St. Louis, 2008), back cover.

PART II

WESTERN ADMIRERS OF SRI SARADA DEVI THE HOLY MOTHER

Sri Sarada Devi

CHAPTER IV

SRI SARADA DEVI
THE HOLY MOTHER

HOLY MOTHER (1853-1920)[1] received visits from Western devotees like Sister Christine, Laura Glenn (Sister Devamata) and, years later, from Betty Leggett, Alberta Sturges and George Montagu (the future Earl of Sandwich). On March 17, 1898, Sister Nivedita, Sara Bull, and Josephine MacLeod (Tantine) first met Holy Mother in Calcutta, and they ate a meal together. Speaking in Bengali, Holy Mother greeted each of them affectionately as "my daughter".[2] During two Sunday lectures on Holy Mother, Swami Prabhavananda (1893-1976), the founder in 1929 and leader of the Vedanta Society of Southern California, mentioned:

> How she received the Western disciples of Swamiji is something [interesting]. I remember one thing how when Swamiji went back from this country, he took some women disciples, Nivedita, Tantine and Mrs. Ole Bull. They were introduced to Holy Mother. And so Holy Mother was seated by them and there was a seat for them and they were all sitting on the floor. They were given sweets on a plate and, of course, there was no talk because Mother didn't know their language. Swamiji was standing and these disciples were taking their food. Suddenly, Holy Mother stooped down and took one of the sweets. That even shocked Swamiji. He knew that she accepted his Western disciples.[3]

When Holy Mother met with Sara Bull (1850-1911) [q.v.], she had a recollection of Sri Ramakrishna speaking of a spiritual vision and saying:

> I felt I was in a far-off country where people were of fair complexion. They were different from us and spoke a language I could not understand. As I was wondering about the vision, the Divine Mother revealed to me they too would follow my teachings. How sincere their devotion was!

Holy Mother said he was referring to devotees in the West. It was Sara who in November of 1898 arranged for Holy Mother to have three pictures taken by the English photographer Harrington. She was reluctant, but Sara told her, "I shall take the picture to America and worship it." One of these pictures is now the most widely known and universally worshipped photograph of the Mother. The third photo was of Mother and Nivedita together. Later, as long as Sara was alive, she sent Holy Mother a donation of sixty rupees a month, which was a substantial addition to her financial resources.[4]

On July 11, 1898, Sara Bull wrote a letter from Srinagar in Kashmir informing Max Müller, the famous Western Indologist, about Holy Mother:

> We were the first foreigners who were allowed to see Sarada Devi, the widow of Ramakrishna. She called us her children, and saying that our visit to her was of the Lord, she felt no strangeness in being with us.... When she gladly gave her husband, to whom she had been united by child-marriage, her assent that he should lead a Sannyasin's life, she gained his intimate friendship, and became his disciple, receiving daily instruction. During the years of her life with him she was his adviser, praying earnestly for such purity of motive that she might never fail him. She had also taken the vow of poverty and chastity, and in renouncing the natural joys of a mother, she became with him the spiritual parent of many children.[5]

Two months after Sister Nivedita (1867-1911) [q.v.] first met Holy Mother on May 22, 1898, she wrote about her to Mrs. Nell Hammond in London saying:

> Sri Ramakrishna always consulted her before undertaking anything and her advice is always acted upon by his disciples. She is the very soul of sweetness—so gentle and loving and as merry as a girl.... She has always been terribly orthodox, but all this melted away the instant she saw the first two Westerners—Mrs. Bull and Miss MacLeod, and she tasted food with them! Fruit is always presented to us immediately, and this was naturally offered to her, and she, to the surprise of everyone, accepted it. This gave us all a dignity and made my future work possible in a way nothing else could possibly have done.[6]

During the summer, Nivedita moved into a room in Holy Mother's house for a period of a week to ten days. She wanted to learn more about the behaviour of women in Indian society. Swami Yogananda, Yogin Ma, Golap Ma, Lakshmi and Gopal-Ma also lived in the house. Holy Mother would ask Nivedita to sit near her when she meditated. For Nivedita this was an "hour of peace" and she wrote, "A tremendous dynamic power emanated from Sarada Devi while she remained completely absorbed within herself. She touched upon the very heart of life." One evening Nivedita laid her head at Holy Mother's feet. The Mother placed her own hand on Nivedita's head and stroked it for a long time as she blessed her saying, "Now your work is about to begin." On November 12 or 13, 1898, Holy Mother attended the dedication of Nivedita's Girls' School. She gave the blessing, "May the Divine Mother of the Universe bless the school. May the girls trained here be ideals for society." Swamis Brahmananda and Saradananda attended the ceremony. Nivedita mentioned that Holy Mother spent much time reading the *Ramayana*.[7]

In his lectures, Swami Prabhavananda explained:

> One time in Sister Nivedita's house, she invited Holy Mother to listen to Easter music. You know she did not understand the words, but she caught the spirit of the resurrection of Christ and went into samadhi listening to the music. At one time Sister Nivedita was explaining to her the Western ceremony of marriage, and she was repeating the vows that they take. As she listened to those words, she said these are righteous words. You see how appreciative she was for everything. She was conscious all the time that she was the Mother of the Universe. At the same time you could see that she was just like your own mother, a simple little woman. You know Josephine MacLeod, Tantine, said, "I never saw anything in her except that she was a very simple good woman."[8]

Years later in 1910, Nivedita made the following observation about Holy Mother:

> One of her most striking traits is the absolute detachment with which she speaks of the husband she worships. She stands like a rock, through cloud and shine, as those about her tell, for the fulfillment of every word of his. But "Guru Deb!" "Divine Master", is the name she calls him by, and not one word of her uttering ever conveys the slightest trace of self-assertion with

regard to him. One who did not know who she was, would never suspect, from speech of hers, that her right was stronger, or her place closer, than that of any other of those about her. It would seem as if the wife had been long ago forgotten, save for her faithfulness in the disciple. Yet so deeply is she reverenced by all about her, that there is not one of them who would, for instance, occupy a railway berth above her, when travelling with her. Her very presence is to them a consecration.

To me it has always appeared that she is Sri Ramakrishna's final word as to the ideal of Indian womanhood. But is she the last of an older order, or the beginning of a new? In her one sees realized that wisdom and sweetness to which the simplest of women may attain. And yet, to myself the stateliness of her courtesy and her great open mind are almost as wonderful as her sainthood. I have never known her hesitate in giving utterance to large and generous judgment, however new or complex might be the question put before her. Her life is one long stillness of prayer.[9]

In a letter of December 11, 1910 from Boston addressed to Holy Mother, Sister Nivedita wrote in part:

I thought I had been very foolish to sit in your room, at the evening service to Sri Ramakrishna, trying to meditate. Why did I not understand that it was quite enough to be a little child at your dear feet? Dear Mother! You are full of love! And it is not a flushed and violent love, like ours, and like the world's, but a gentle peace that brings good to everyone and wishes ill to none. It is a golden radiance, full of play. What a blessed Sunday that was, a few months ago, when I ran in to you, the last thing before I went on the Ganges, and ran back to you for a moment, as soon as I came back! I felt such a wonderful freedom in the blessing you gave me, and in your welcome home! Dearest Mother, I wish we could send you a wonderful hymn, or a prayer. But somehow even that would seem too loud, to full of noise! Surely you are the most wonderful thing of God—Sri Ramakrishna's own chalice of His Love for the world—a token left with His children, in these lonely days, and we should be very still and quiet before you—except indeed for a little fun! Surely the "wonderful things of God" are all quiet—stealing unnoticed into our lives—the air and sunlight and the sweetness of gardens and of the Ganges. These are the silent things that are like you![10]

Holy Mother preserved a scarf given to her by Nivedita. When it was old and worn out, Holy Mother told an acquaintance, "Don't throw it away. Let it be. Nivedita lovingly gave it to me. I am reminded of her whenever I see it. What a wonderful person she was! In the beginning she could not talk with me but later she learnt Bengali."[11]

Josephine MacLeod (1858-1949) [q.v.] came to see Holy Mother on many occasions stretching from 1898 to at least 1916. One day she paid her respects to Holy Mother at the Udbodhan Office and then went back to Belur Math. After meditating in the chapel, she proceeded to the Guest House with the accompaniment of a brahmachari holding a lantern. He heard her repeating to herself, "I've seen her. I've seen her." Then she whispered to him, "The Holy Mother! I've seen her." She walked the furlong in an elated mood muttering the word "Mother" and some other words he did not understand.[12] In his personal journal dated May 13, 1927, Romain Rolland recorded that Josephine MacLeod told him the following:

> The Holy Mother had a natural affinity with Western women, able to speak with them on any subject, and had a simplicity, a fineness, a delightful disposition. Just as pure as Ramakrishna or Vivekananda, she was all the while living a holy life and at the same time capable of being interested, with the joy of a child, in the attire of her European friends. Her great valour, however, was not recognized in her own village, where she did not show that she was any different from other women.[13]

In some early English language biographies of Sri Ramakrishna, there was some mention of Holy Mother. In his 1898 book *Ramakrishna, His Life and Sayings*, Max Müller [q.v.] wrote:

> Vivekananda told us that when at the age of seventeen his [Ramakrishna's] wife went to find him, he received her with real kindness, and that she was quite satisfied to live with him on his own terms, if he would only enlighten her mind and make her to see and serve God.[14]

That same year a description of Ramakrishna appeared in *The Literary Digest* of New York, penned by an unknown writer based on an earlier account in the *Brahmavadin*. It mentioned:

> Ramakrishna had a wife, but he never associated with her. She is now living. She is so simple, pure, and highly advanced in spirituality that people regard her as the personified divine Motherhood and the embodiment of chastity, purity, and spirituality.[15]

A devotee of Swami Vivekananda in England, named Eric Hammond, [q.v.] wrote an article on Sri Ramakrishna for *The Theosophical Review* in 1902. After describing a picture of Holy Mother, he stated:

> Her photograph, sent to us from herself with loving greetings, occupies an honourable place in our home. It is the portrait of Sarada Devi, of whom Swami Abhedananda recently said in a lecture on "Women's Place in Hindu Religion", she "has become a living example of the great honour and reverence that are paid by Hindus to a woman of pure, spotless, spiritual life". Yet it is not only her life, pure, spotless, spiritual, that places her on the pedestal of worship. It is also—and perhaps primarily—because she is the widow and disciple of Ramakrishna—designated in the lecture referred to "the great Hindu saint of the nineteenth century."[16]

Describing a spiritual vision that she had in Philadelphia, Pennsylvania, in 1902, before having any knowledge of the Vedanta Movement, Gertrude Topham (Suniti) wrote:

> I wakened one morning with a great peace surrounding me, and there before my eyes was a holy vision of Sri Ramakrishna and Holy Mother sitting together on what seemed to be a high platform. Now, I never heard of Sri Ramakrishna or Holy Mother. But I lay there with a quiet mind looking at them. They were both in yogic posture, although at the time I did not know the posture by name.[17]

Soon after Miss Gertrude Topham and her sister moved from Philadelphia, where she worked as a bookkeeper in a business firm, to Pasadena, California. There Gertrude met Mrs. Taylor, a friend of the Mead sisters who had lived with Swami Vivekananda for four weeks. She became a disciple of Swami Trigunatita when he journeyed to Los Angeles during 1903 or 1904, and he made her one of the eleven Mothers (and Fathers) of the reorganized Los Angeles Vedanta in 1911. Most important, in 1922 Gertrude Topham gave Swami Prakashananda a thousand dollars to travel to India and bring a Swami to Los Angeles. As a result, the following year he brought Swami Prabhavananda back from India. He became Prakashananda's assistant in San Francisco, since Swami Paramananda had just opened a new centre near Los Angeles. Until her death around 1970, the elderly Gertrude Topham kept in touch with the Hollywood Vedanta Society. The more youthful nuns would drive her around Los Angeles on her errands.[18]

At the end of 1907, Laura Glenn (1867-1942) [q.v.], who later became Sister Devamata, journeyed to India, remaining there until September 1909. She recorded her two-year experience in the book *Days in an Indian Monastery* (1927). While living in Calcutta, she spent a considerable time at Holy Mother's living quarters. When Devamata met Holy Mother, she laid herself and her offerings at the Mother's feet. Devamata tells us, "She repeated my name twice with tender surprise. Then she placed her hand in blessing on my head. At her touch a spring of new life seemed to bubble up from my innermost heart and flood my being." Sister Devamata had the blessed good fortune of taking care of Holy Mother's room and massaging her rheumatic legs. The Mother addressed her as "my sweet daughter". Before leaving India Holy Mother told her, "Devamata, be careful. If you get even the hem of your garment caught in the American work, you will not get back." Planning to return to India, she came to the United States for a short visit in 1909, and ended up remaining there for the rest of her life. After returning to the U.S., she received a letter from Sister Nivedita dated September 8, 1909 telling her, "The Holy Mother speaks of you often. The first night, she pointed to your empty place, with great pathos!" In 1910 and 1911, Swami Paramananda had Devamata running the newly founded Vedanta Centre in Washington, D.C. After that she was centred in Boston, but made seasonal trips to Washington, D.C. up to 1917 and then to the Los Angeles area.[19]

The Mother would dictate her letters to a scribe. One letter from Holy Mother to Devamata read in part:

> My sweet daughter: Your loving letters are duly to hand. Excuse me please not to answer you in time. I always remember you. Whenever I see the place you used to sit and meditate your loving form comes to my mind. All the inmates of this house speak of you....
>
> With my blessings,
>
> Your most affectionate Mother

In another letter Holy Mother wrote to Devamata:

> I am very glad to hear of your so much devotion to my Lord. You are my daughter. May infinite devotion rise up in your heart—this is my blessing to you. For this I pray to my Lord. May you live long and along with all my other children may you remain merged in bliss eternal.... I am doing well.
>
> Your affectionate Mother[20]

Concerning Holy Mother, Devamata expressed her admiration this way:

> By her outward manner she was the most obscure of all the household, yet beneath the veil of simplicity which enveloped her, there was a lofty majesty of bearing which caught the heart and bowed it in prayerful homage at her feet. The human covering was too thin to hide the radiance of divine consciousness beneath....
>
> Those who had the rare blessing of living with Holy Mother learned that religion was a sweet, natural, joyous thing; that purity and holiness were tangible realities; that the odour of sanctity was literally a sweet perfume overlaying and destroying the foulness of material selfishness. Compassion, devotion, God-union were her very nature; one scarcely knew that she possessed them. It was through the soothing benediction of a word or touch that one sensed their presence.[21]

Three years after her husband's death, in 1912 Betty Leggett (1852-1931), the wife of Francis Leggett, came to India. Her companions were Alberta Sturges (1877-1951), a daughter by her first marriage, and the latter's husband George Montagu (1874-1962, the future Earl of Sandwich). There they met Swamis Turiyananda, Shivananda, and Premananda. Much to his surprise and embarrassment, Swami Premananda embraced George at Belur Math. George took the dust of the feet of Holy Mother and later said, he will "always remember the calm and somewhat detached expression of the eyes set in that noble countenance". Alberta had a "vast and intense experience with Sarada Devi". Betty wrote to her sister Josephine MacLeod that Holy Mother

> was very gentle and halting and full of reverence for him [Sri Ramakrishna] as she talked, and made many gestures of adoration and little

prayers during her stories.... She took my face in her hands several times, and I kissed her hands, and we parted several times with much emotion.... I visited all her rooms and objects, images and pictures, and thought of the similar simplicity and almost poverty of our Madonna, who must have been so like [her] at fifty. When I had gone all over the house, I found her at the head of the stairs, fairly radiant, again taking my face in her hands and blessing me. I had tears, and I thought she had, but I couldn't quite see for my own.[22]

Yogin Ma (1851-1924), a personal attendant and close companion of Holy Mother, experienced many high spiritual states. Sister Devamata expressed the following positive assessment of her:

Yogin Ma always seemed to me one of the noblest of Sri Ramakrishna's disciples. She possessed an uplifted, heroic quality ... Yogin Ma was most loving to me always. It troubled her apparently that I was born in America instead of India. Often she would say to me: "Devamata, I wonder why Thakur sent you so far away to be born. You belong here. You are one of us."... By look and gesture and primer-like sentences we exchanged our thought. Her manner told me more vividly than words could that she felt a deep affection for me. Occasionally she brought me a gift. Once she sent the Brahmacharin who did the buying for the Holy Mother's household to purchase for me a Benares incense burner and an image holding the tiny cups for the five lights and the camphor.... As I look across the years at this noble figure, clear-cut against the skyline of a past that is ever present, and remember her steadfastness, her loyal devotion, the spiritual continuity of her life, these words of the Spanish mystic, Alonzo de Orozco, rise in my mind as aptly descriptive of the way she met the turn of circumstances: "If dryness is as sweet to thee as devotion because the Lord wills, if in sickness thou dost find the joy of health, if poverty is as sweet as thee as riches, if in dishonour thou does find the saviour of honour, thou has profited greatly."[23]

Holy Mother also gave spiritual encouragement to some of the young Swamis who later took charge of the operation in America. For example, Swami Prabhavananda, the future leader of the Vedanta Society of Southern California, had the blessed fortune to see her on many occasions. He described one of those experiences:

One time another friend of mine [who became Swami Amriteswarananda] and I came together to Vishnupur.... In our home we stayed, and then we hired a bullock cart and travelled, sleeping in the bullock cart, all night. First, we went to Koalpara [about three miles from near Jayrambati], where Holy Mother used to come and stay occasionally. In Koalpara there is an adobe house where there is a picture of Holy Mother and Sri Ramakrishna. We saw a picture of Holy Mother, which she installed and worshipped herself. And so we had the blessed fortune to see that picture and bow down to it. As we went to Mother's house, we were late to arrive. She had told her attendant Rashbehari, a swami [Swami Arupananda] who later recorded the teachings of Holy Mother [during 1909-13, 1918], "Two of Rakhal's sons are coming. Save some food for them." We did not write to her nor was there any telephone, but she knew we were coming.

When we would go to her village, she didn't have a veil or anything like that. Then like a mother she served us food on leaf plates. One very interesting thing: she looked like one's own Mother to whoever saw her. So she appeared to me as my own mother. I saw no difference. It was not only like that with me, but also with many others I have known. When we would see her, she would act and behave just like our own mother. She sat by us and asked us if we liked the food, just as our own mother does. If we liked something, then she would give us more. So in that way she fed us. I have never eaten such food in my life. It was like nectar, I still remember that.

After finishing the leaf plates, we were going to throw them out. Then Mother said, "What are you doing?" [We replied], "We cannot leave these leaf plates here. We ate in those." Then she said, "What would you have done if your mother had been present?" So we left them there. Both of us stayed there for three days and three nights. When we left Holy Mother, she stood by the door and kissed us, by placing her fingers on the chin and then putting them to her lips. And as far as she could see, she kept looking at us. This was the custom she had with everybody that used to go to her. These were wonderful times. We did not have any teaching or anything; she did not teach us anything. Just to see her and to touch her feet was enough.[24]

Later Accounts of the Holy Mother

The French Nobel Prize recipient and author of a biography of Sri Ramakrishna, Romain Rolland [q.v.] made the important point that the Master made Holy Mother part of his Divine mission:

> She irradiated peace and serenity throughout her life on all who came in contact with her. Moreover there is a fact, which has never before been revealed except by Vivekananda, that Sri Ramakrishna himself was gravely aware of his responsibility and offered his wife the greatest sacrifice of which he was capable if she demanded it—his mission.... One night in May, when everything had been prepared for worship, he made Sarada Devi sit in the seat of Kali, and as priest he accomplished the ritual ceremonies, the Shodashi Puja, the adoration of womanhood. Both of them were in a condition of semi-consciousness or super-conscious ecstasy. When he came to himself he hailed his companion as the Divine Mother. In his eyes she was incarnate in the living symbol of immaculate humanity.[25]

In 1940 Swami Tapasyananda brought out a biography of Holy Mother entitled *Sri Sarada Devi the Holy Mother*. He was the later President of the Ramakrishna Math, Madras (1971-91), and a Vice-President of the Ramakrishna Order (1985-91). This volume initially contained a section "Conversations of Holy Mother", which is Swami Nikhilananda's translation of the Bengali *Sri Sri Mayer Katha*. It was removed in the book's later editions and brought out as an independent work *The Gospel of the Holy Mother*. Swami Pavitrananda, the long-time leader of the Vedanta Society of New York (1951-77), originally founded by Swami Vivekananda, came out with *A Short Life of the Holy Mother* in 1942. Swami Nikhilananda [q.v.], the founder and leader of the Ramakrishna-Vivekananda Centre in New York City, published his biography of Holy Mother in 1962 titled *Holy Mother—Being the Life of Sri Sarada Devi Wife of Sri Ramakrishna and Helpmate in His Mission*. He penned this biography basing it on all the then extant materials both in English as well as Bengali.[26]

Winifred Iles (1905-42) wrote a lucid and compact forty-eight-page biography *A Holy Mother of India Sarada Devi*, which was released posthumously in 1944. In Bath and Bristol, England, she was well known as a talented actress, elocutionist and lecturer. Only three years after joining the Vedanta movement, Winifred died at a relatively young age. Among other things she wrote this about Sarada Devi:

> The Mother's loving service to Ramakrishna was a component part of her intense spiritual practice. She used to say to the disciples, "To me Ramakrishna is the symbol of the Highest. He is the Impersonal in the personal. He is my all in all. He is the Teacher: he is the Chosen Ideal. He is the Supreme Man."... Ramakrishna saw the Divine Mother in Sarada Devi and had a great reverence for her. One day as he was taking a nap in his cot, someone came to give him some food. He thought it was his young niece and asked her to close the door, using the word "Tui" (Thou), a familiar term for one much younger. Just then he saw that it was the Mother and not his niece. "I am so sorry for uttering 'Tui'," he said to her, "I thought it was my niece Lakshmi. Please do not mind." The memory of this incident disturbed him several times and he went to the Mother's room and asked her to forget what had happened.... At Belur the Mother practised a hard penance known as *Pancha-Tapa*. On the sides of an open square, four fires were made five cubits apart, while the fierce rays of the sun beat down from above. The Mother sat down between these fires for five days from early morning till sundown, practising prayer, meditation and repetition of the *mantrams*. When she was asked about this penance she said, "It was just to show people that discipline is necessary."... One day he [Sri Ramakrishna] had said to her, "I have a spiritual mission to fulfill, it is a great trust. But remember it is also yours." He anticipated that the Mother might wish to pass away after his death, and so he said to her, "People are like worms groping in darkness. You will have to look after them. What have I done? You have to do greater things." The Mother really wanted to forsake her body after his death. But she was told in a vision, "No, you must stay. Much work remains still to be done."... Once to a dejected devotee, who felt that the Mother would soon leave the world, she had said, "Do you think that I can have any rest after leaving the body until all my disciples are out of bondage? I must constantly be with them, as I have taken complete charge of everything, good or bad, regarding them. Is it a trifle to give initiation?" Soon after the Mother's passing away, a lady disciple dreamt that the Mother came and told her, "My daughter, my body is gone, but I am always behind you and am always looking after you." Another disciple dreamt that the Mother appeared to him and said, "The body you have seen me forsaking is an illusion-body, but just see, I am still existing."[27]

The writer Jean Herbert (1897-1980) [q.v.] is discussed in Chapter XII, because of his translations of Swamiji's books into the French language. During the Holy Mother Birth Centenary, Mr. Herbert drew the following insights concerning her compassion for humanity:

> Although she admitted that "to initiate is no fun; it is a tremendous burden to bear", she would readily give initiation to practically anybody who asked for it, and even to some who did not. That wide-open generosity, which so few—if any—of the real great gurus ever dared assume, is the greatest proof of love that can possibly be given. She actually took upon herself the "burden" of people whom in many cases she hardly knew, and for those later mistakes and faults she gladly accepted to suffer. Her long and close connection with Sri Ramakrishna cannot possibly have left her in any doubts as to the "tremendous" weight she was taking on her own shoulders....
>
> About the cult of images, which already raised so much doubt in the minds of the young generation, particularly under the iconoclastic influence of Christian missionaries, she boldly affirmed: "Stoned-symbols of Shiva are true. Many great sinners who visit Benares are redeemed of their sins by touching the symbol of Vishwanath. He is graciously accepting everybody's sins." She quite naturally asked visitors to salute her image of Raghuvir, and even went so far as to suggest that they should make money-offerings to it, and she pointed out that "from time immemorial men have been realizing spiritual freedom through image-worship."...
>
> To mention just one more point on which her behaviour seems totally inconsistent to the modern Western mind, she certainly had the cosmic vision, and yet she "cried bitterly" on being apprised of the death of a child. We must be content to note that such a combination of the impersonal and equal vision, which neither desire nor aversion, neither pleasure nor pain can ever affect, with the deep heartfelt sympathy for the sufferings of others can exist in fact, as was explained by Jagadguru Sri Krishna and as was so strikingly illustrated in our own times by Sri Ramakrishna and other sages of India.[28]

In 1954, a Centenary Celebration was held honouring the 100th anniversary of Holy Mother's birth. Among others, the following seven inspirational messages were mailed to the Vedanta Society in England:[29] From Chester Bowles, former U. S. Ambassador to India, came the following words:

> May I join with you in honouring the memory of Sri Sarada Devi, whose life of devotion and service is an inspiration to all. The activities to be carried on during the Centenary Celebration will help to bring her closer to many people, and all of us sorely need the spiritual strength and peace which her memory brings.

After being the governor of the state of Connecticut and a U.S. congressman, Chester Bowles (1901-86) became the U.S. Ambassador to India in 1951-53 and again in 1963-69. He was impressed by Gandhi and Nehru's ability to achieve democratic independence through nonviolence. While ambassador, Bowles and his family learned Hindi, lived outside the official U.S. residence in a modest bungalow, and he rode a bicycle to his office. His efforts facilitated substantial long run increases in American economic aid to India, and he backed major agricultural reforms that brought about the "Green Revolution", which ultimately made India self-sufficient in food grains.[30]

Kurt Friedrichs from Hamburg translated from English into the German language Indian classics such as the *Katha Upanishads*, *Panchadasi*, and Shankara's *Viveka-Chudamani* (*Crest Jewel of Discrimination*). He wrote:

> We all revere the Holy Mother as the ideal of spiritual womanhood, sent to our age, and are convinced that every striving student must first meet Sri Sarada Devi on his way to the Jagad-Guru Sri Ramakrishna. The Holy Mother seems to us the personification of the *Lalita-Sahasranama*. By listening to the Sanskrit chant of the Thousand Names of the Mother Beautiful, it is her picture which arises before our spiritual eyes. In our age she gets more and more importance as a symbol of selflessness and benediction.

For Reverend John Haynes Holmes [q.v.], Minister emeritus of the Community Church of New York:

> Sri Sarada (the Holy Mother) represents the true genius of India, and at the same time the inward spirit of a world struggling for light and life. In the Holy Mother there befell the full flowering of the mysteries which make up the wonder of the soul. In her own perfection she forecast the vision of what all men yet shall be. It is fitting that this commemoration should mark the one hundredth anniversary of the Holy Mother's birth. In this miracle of time, we approach eternity, and "in light see Light".

Joan Pope, the general secretary of the London Buddhist Society, noted:

> The life of Sri Sarada Devi was truly a great one, and it is inspiring to think that those who lead such lives can in truth raise up others by their splendid example.

According to Baroness Ravensdale, the chairman of the World Congress of Faiths in London:

> Such an example as she (Sri Sarada Devi) gave to distracted unhappy souls in this materialistic world, in loving them, caring for them and ministering to their spiritual needs, is something we all should copy. Only by seeking God and holding on to spiritual values as the background of our daily lives can we rebuild a shattered world that is losing hold of all the priceless truths that Sri Sarada Devi and Sri Ramakrishna preached to their fellowmen.

Mary Irene Curzon, Baroness Ravensdale (1896-1966), was the eldest child of Lord George Curzon (1859-1925), the governor-general and viceroy of India (1899-1905).* While Curzon did many good things for the country, his highly unpopular partition of Bengal in 1905 and other acts stimulated Indian nationalism and support for the Indian National Congress, which eventually brought about the end of the British Empire. He later became chancellor of Oxford University, and during World War I a member of Lloyd George's war cabinet (1916-19). Along with its founder Sir Francis Younghusband [q.v.], Baroness Ravensdale was involved in the World Congress of Faiths from 1936 onwards, and continued to work for what she called a "spiritual design for living in a greater universalism". Throughout her life she continued to be a generous and loyal supporter of the Congress. She had a considerable knowledge of Eastern religions and wrote movingly of a pilgrimage to Benares.[31]

Otto Ritschl of Wiesbaden, Germany, added:

> We have heard and read about other women-saints. We can scarcely judge what aims they reached, for saintliness has a wide margin. The Holy

* *CW*, V:170, 366-67.

> Mother's life leaves us no doubt. She reached the aim. And herewith we are definitely convinced that all the prejudices against women, hundreds and thousands of years old, are unjustifiable. There exists no more limitation for her to gain perfection.

Ritschl led the German Vedantins during World War II. The works of the award-winning professional artist Otto Ritschl (1885-1976) went through many stages: from an Expressionist phase to representations that were critical of his times and thus approached New Objectivity, to Late Cubist and Surrealist-inspired abstract symbolic forms of the 1930s, to a strong Picasso influence, and finally in 1960 to independent elements of monochrome pictures for meditation. His compositions dealt from then on with the themes of being and becoming, active forces and energies, creation and meditation.[32]

Dr. Günter Zühlsdorf (b. 1912) of Frankfurt-am-Main, an author of a number of religious books in the German language, made this statement:

> Born one hundred years ago, Sri Sarada Devi, consort of Sri Ramakrishna Paramahamsa, lived deep into this century of ours, the very embodiment of purity and peace.... She was not only the timeless noble ideal of womanhood, but that of the spiritual being as well.

Swami Nikhilananda [q.v.], the head of the Ramakrishna-Vivekananda Centre in New York City, experienced three profound dreams. In each case his guru Sarada Devi appeared before him, urging him to write her life story for the West. As a result of her divine command, in 1962 he penned the definitive biography *Holy Mother*.[33] Nikhilananda not only was blessed by initiation from Holy Mother, but he intimately associated with seven of Sri Ramakrishna's monastic disciples. Concerning this work Filmer S. C. Northrop (1893-1992) [q.v.], the Sterling professor of philosophy and law at Yale University, commented:

> This is a well-nigh incredible book. It is the story of the wife of a recent Hindu saint who herself became a saint. Only India could have produced her.... Because however of the Hindu's quest for the timeless factor in human nature, she speaks also for all women everywhere and for all mankind. Today there is a Hindu religious and political reaction against the secular surface of India's politics. Thus Holy Mother typifies at once both the cause

and the meaning of this reaction. To understand why, one must realize that two-thirds of all Indians are Hindus and most of the Hindu's life is never seen by the tourist or visiting social scientist since it occurs in the privacy of the Hindu family and in silent meditative attempts, frequently before dawn, to experience the timeless Brahman. It is because this book takes its readers into this unseen India that it must be read by all who want to know these remarkable people.[34]

Filmer S.C. Northrop attended church events such as the unveiling of the statue of Swami Vivekananda held in 1950 at Swami Nikhilananda's Ramakrishna-Vivekananda Centre in New York. The professor was affiliated with Yale University for nearly forty years (1923-62), chairing Yale's department of philosophy. He was the president of the Association for the History and Philosophy of Science (1947), and the distinguished American Philosophical Association (1952). Among his better-known works is *The Meeting of East and West* (1946) in which he proposes the theme that cultural discord between East and West originated from differing value systems. He believed that a traditional Indian and Buddhist philosopher,

> even when he develops logically formulated systems containing most subtle distinctions and technical concepts, his aim tends to be to direct the reader away from the persisting, postulated, determinate theoretical components in the nature of things in which the West believes, toward the indeterminate, indescribable, ineffable, and immediately apprehendable aesthetic factor, which neither logical methods nor philosophical or scientific theory can convey.... The Orient has restricted its knowledge to that factor in the nature of things which is given wholly and with immediacy, and as a consequence, has been enabled to gain basic premises which are verifiable immediately and completely, rather than indirectly and only partially.[35]

Donald S. Harrington (1914-2005) [q.v.], the minister of the Unitarian Community Church in New York City (1944-82), expressed the view, "I have read with great pleasure your new biography of Sarada Devi. It is an extraordinary story, of a rare human being, and how beautifully you have told it! Sarada Devi, humble and unpretentious, takes her place among the world's great souls." Harrington was also an instructor in human relations at the New School for Social Research in New York City, and president of the United World Federalists.[36]

Another appreciation came from Lex Hixon in *Coming Home* (1978), affirming that Sri Ramakrishna's

> wife and first disciple, Sarada Devi, is regarded as his spiritual equal, a twin emanation of Kali. They were a single feminine current of Divine Energy expressed through two bodies. Sarada always regarded her divinely intoxicated husband as the blissful Goddess Herself, not only as a human being. And once, Sarada asked Ramakrishna, "What do you think of me?" Ramakrishna replied, "She who gave me physical birth also appears as the Divine Mother Kali, and you too, are the same Mother." Sarada became the spiritual successor of Ramakrishna, guiding his disciples and transmitting visionary power to thousands of seekers after his death.[37]

1980s and After

Hans Torwesten (b. 1944) [q.v.], a native of Germany who lives in Austria, authored the comparative study *Ramakrishna and Christ* (1981), which includes a chapter on Sarada Devi. There he describes an important event that took place:

> The divinity which Ramakrishna worshipped in Sarada was revealed one spring day in the year 1872, the 25th May—a day on which a special service was held in honour of Kali. On this day Ramakrishna "enthroned" Sarada, prayed to her as the Divine Mother and made all the offerings to her that were usually made to Kali. When he gave her some of the offered food to eat, her soul passed into samadhi. Ramakrishna's soul at once followed hers, and the two remained for several hours in a condition of the highest union. More than half the night had passed before Ramakrishna returned to consciousness of the outside world. He then presented the last offering, himself. He laid at the feet of the Divine Mother, who sat before him in the form of Sarada, the fruits of all of his religious practices, together with a garland of roses. He now possessed nothing more.[38]

Holy Mother initiated the young Swami Aseshananda (1899-1996), the future leader of the Vedanta Society of Portland, Oregon, in 1917, at the Udbodhan before he became a monastic. He added:

> I was attracted to Vedanta when I first met Swami Turiyananda, a disciple of Sri Ramakrishna in Benares.... His words gave me courage. His personality gave me assurance. My hesitant steps became steady. I made up my mind not to falter. That day I made the final decision to renounce, and embrace the monastic order of Sri Ramakrishna.[39]

So he joined the Ramakrishna Order in 1921, receiving his final vows of sannyasa from Swami Saradananda two years later. Being a passionate and dynamic speaker, his lectures uplifted many devotees during his lifetime.[40] Aseshananda began his biography, *Glimpses of a Great Soul: A Portrait of Swami Saradananda* (1982), with the statement, "Dedicated to Sri Sarada Devi (My teacher) Whom the devotees of Sri Ramakrishna lovingly called Holy Mother. I have seen her face, I have heard her words; now I seek her grace with all the longing of my heart." He often told his disciples:

> I bow down in reverence to Holy Mother because what she has done for me, I cannot express.... She has become the source of strength, the source of knowledge, and the source of my infinite realization. Through her grace I have seen Her face, I have touched her feet. I long for release so that I can realize the highest truth in this very life.

Nancy Pope Mayorga (1904-83), a professional author and devotee at the Vedanta Society of Southern California, made the following statement found in *Sri Sarada Devi the Great Wonder* (1984):

> Holy Mother, with thousands of children, made each one feel that he was specially her own. One disciple, wondering at her loving interest in his welfare, asked her, "Shall I always have this affection?" And she answered, "Yes. In my love there is no ebb tide or flood tide." Many times she was asked, "Are you our real mother?" There was never any hesitation in her answer, "I am your real mother." How many times in how many first-hand accounts we read these same touching words, "When I was leaving, she followed me part of the way and stood watching me with tears in her eyes." She never allowed anyone to say "Goodbye". She always said, in the Indian way, "Come again"....
>
> From beginning to the end of her life was a complete giving of herself. She felt that through her efforts people could be helped to achieve liberation, and she was constantly performing japa for the good of the world.

In spite of all her outer activity, her life was, as Sister Nivedita said, "one long stillness of prayers". This could be true only because she knew God in the depth of her soul.

She knew her divinity, and as she grew older, she was more outspoken about it. It was not only that she could give extraordinary intuitive and right advice, as Sister Nivedita noted, no matter what the unfamiliar problem was, she always went right to the heart of the matter and "set the questioner in the true attitude to the difficulty". No, it was more than that. She accepted the fact that the power of God was working through her.[41]

Nancy Pope Mayorga, a Vedanta devotee from Santa Barbara, California, in 1936 authored *We Three*, an account of her life with her parents, and *The Sentence of Youth*, both of which made the *New York Times* best seller list. Married to the eminent Nicaraguan poet Aristides Mayorga (1888-1964), she contributed articles and short stories to *The Saturday Evening Post*, *Colliers*, *Redbook Family Circle*, and other popular magazines. Her 1981 autobiographical work, *The Hunger of the Soul*, drawn from her diary, describes her spiritual life and acquaintance with Swami Prabhavananda in Southern California.[42]

Leta Jane Lewis, a professor emeritus at California State University, Fresno, where she taught the German language and its literature, has been a Vedantist for over fifty years. Concerning Holy Mother she discerned:

> She did, however, experience their spiritual union on the occasion of the Shodashi Puja when he [Sri Ramakrishna] enshrined her and worshipped the Divine Mother in her form. Then both Sri Ramakrishna and she went into samadhi, realizing their oneness with Brahman and their oneness with each other in Brahman. At the close of the ritual, Sri Ramakrishna offered the Divine Mother within Sarada everything he possessed, the fruit of all his spiritual practices, his rosary, and finally himself....
>
> Like the great God Shiva, she assumed responsibility for ill-favoured persons who were rejected by society. Thus, she initiated everyone who asked for it, including extremely wicked persons whom Sri Ramakrishna's direct monastic disciples could not bring themselves to accept. She refused to find fault with anyone, for she saw the Lord's presence so vividly in even the worst human beings that their weaknesses faded into insignificance for her. She lovingly served all who came to her just as she served Sri Ramakrishna, cooking for good and bad alike, inviting them to stay in her home,

and doing what their mothers might have done to make them comfortable and happy.[43]

A few additional statements made in *Sri Sarada Devi the Great Wonder* (1984) follow:

> What inspires me most in Holy Mother's life, besides her utter humility, her patience, and her life of service, is her great, compassionate Mother-heart. Those of us who know of the Holy Mother are indeed blessed to have before us always the picture of a supremely endowed spiritual woman who lived among us and showed by her example how our lives should be lived. More important, however, Mother showed us a side of the Godhead that is little known, and that is the great, compassionate Mother-heart of the lord that is ever ready to shower us with unconditional love (Sarah N. David, a California devotee).
>
> What are the qualities which so endear her to us? On the one hand we find in her the perfect example of gentleness, humility, purity, patience, and self-dedication, while on the other hand there is great liberal-mindedness, common sense, boldness, fearlessness, and strength. The quiet aspect of her personality is more apparent, while the bold side remains more hidden. Perhaps for this reason her modesty and self-effacement are emphasized, whereas her fearlessness and strength are passed over more lightly (Pravrajika Bhaktiprana, a nun at the Hollywood, California Convent).
>
> As we meditate on the Holy Mother, the endless waves of desire and attachments are stilled; through her the clashing fragments of experience fall into their proper places and perspective. Feeling her pure and loving presence in our hearts, a new tranquility is born, and we are assured that through constant striving our human will must ultimately become united with the will of God (Elizabeth Davidson, a devotee from New York City).[44]

An interesting statement made in 1989 by Susan Walters of the Vedanta Society of St. Louis at the Ramakrishna Mission Institute of Culture reads:

> Sri Sarada Devi was always full of bliss because she was always conscious of the blissful Self within. This bliss was utterly unaffected by her

surroundings. Even while she was confined to one small, cramped room at Dakshineswar, she said she always felt as if a pitcher of bliss had been placed in her heart.[45]

Inspired by the life and teachings of Holy Mother, the Sri Sarada Society of Albany, New York, was formed in 1992. Taking Sri Sarada Devi as their role model, the members try to apply the principles of Vedanta in their daily lives. The devotee organization is "dedicated to promoting the study of the life and teachings of Sri Sarada Devi, viewing her example as an inspiration through which the principles of Vedanta may find full and practical application in Western life." Their first project was to collect American subscriptions to *Samvit*, an English language journal that is published by the Sri Sarada Math women's monastic order in India. After its inception, Sri Sarada Society sponsored three Pravrajikas of the Sri Sarada Math in India as participants in the 1993 second Parliament of the World's Religions held in Chicago. They worked to raise funds to purchase and preserve the Ridgely estate as a spiritual residence from 1994 through 1997. Together with other devotee groups, they continue to facilitate visits and public tours by the Pravrajikas in America. In addition, Sri Sarada Society encourages informal retreats by small devotee groups, which may be held in one's own home.[46]

The author of *Kali: The Black Goddess of Dakshineswar* (1993), Elizabeth (Usha) Harding, wrote of Sarada Devi's true nature:

> The Holy Mother had visions of Kali throughout her life, and it is safe to infer that she was aware of her own divinity at all times. Although she lived like any other Indian woman—taking care of cooking, cleaning, and family affairs—yet whoever came in contact with her felt something special. People felt her extraordinary sweet love—she gave more than their mother at home could give them. It was a subtle divinity people felt, and it was truly rare that Sri Sarada Devi was provoked enough to reveal her true nature. Once she showed herself as Kali to a robber and his wife.[47]

A nun from the Vedanta Society of Northern California, Pravrajika Madhavaprana wrote a delightful portrait of Holy Mother in which she said:

> In her lifetime she was the spiritual head of the Order of monks which Sri Ramakrishna started; she was, in fact, the Mother of the entire worldwide organization which bears his name. Hundreds and hundreds of men and

women became her disciples, and all of Sri Ramakrishna's disciples, giants of spirituality themselves, revered her as their guru. Many who knew her in life and many of her own disciples came to this country as ministers of Vedanta. All of them spoke of her, as one swami put it, with bated breath. She is sometimes called an Incarnation of the Divine Mother, the Goddess Kali, and the same Divine Being as her husband. Sri Ramakrishna himself made the statement to the effect that she was even greater in power than he was. Such stories of her greatness have been told to us by people who actually knew her....

Swami Ashokananda [q.v.], another swami who taught in San Francisco and who had known her, ... said that in his opinion she was the greatest human being ever born on earth.... He often used to say that we should study the life and teachings of Holy Mother to learn how to live on the highest plane of spiritual consciousness in this ordinary world, taking part in human affairs as she did, from that high vantage point.[48]

Women in Religion, edited by Jean Holm, an author of many volumes, and John Bowker, a professor of religious studies at the Universities of Cambridge and Lancaster, has a chapter on each of the major religions of the world. In that volume Sharada Sugirtharajah, a senior lecturer in Hinduism at the University of Birmingham in England, makes this appreciative statement about Holy Mother:

Modern Hinduism also has examples of such saintly figures. One of them is Sarada Devi, who was married at an early age to Sri Ramakrishna, a well-known saint of nineteenth-century Bengal. He recognized the spiritual eminence of his wife and looked upon her as an equal partner in his spiritual mission and journey. She became his disciple, helpmate and spiritual partner, and combined the roles of wife, ascetic, mother and guru. Sri Ramakrishna taught her not only the sacred mantras for the worship of the Divine Mother, but also how to initiate people into them. After the death of Ramakrishna she became the spiritual guide to all disciples—monks as well as lay people—of the Ramakrishna Order.[49]

Joanne Kilgour Dowdy is a professor at Kent State University in the department of teaching, leadership, and curriculum studies. An expert on the education of African American women, she is the author of *GED Stories:*

Black Women and their Struggle for Social Equity. Emphasizing the practical aspects of Holy Mother's life, she explained:

> It is clear from these quotes that Mother lived a life that inspired her children to reach for their highest potential in manifesting their divine essence. Her life was a living symbol of active spirituality.... The Mother's life was clearly created to ensure that we would always have a model of the ideal spiritual life on earth. When she lay down her earthly burden, she was sure that she had set enough examples by her actions for her talented students to lead enlightened spiritual lives.[50]

A nun of the Vedanta Society in Northern California, Pravrajika Virajaprana [q.v.] reflected on Holy Mother's teachings and concluded:

> "I tell you one thing, if you want peace, do not find fault with others. Rather learn to see your own faults. Learn to make the world your own. No one is a stranger, my child; the whole world is your own." This was Mother's last message to a woman devotee and through that devotee to all of us. This message contains the whole of Vedanta philosophy—universalism, oneness of all beings, global outlook, all-embracing compassion, and practical advice for its realization, service, the worship of God in man. This is the way Mother lived throughout her life.... This is one of the most touching and elevating aspects of Mother's character, her all-inclusive love. Everyone who came to her felt full to the brim. Her love was boundless, without borders or conditions.[51]

In 2004 Swami Adiswarananda (1925-2007), leader of the Ramakrishna-Vivekananda Centre of New York since 1973, brought out an edited version of Nikhilananda's translation entitled *Sri Sarada Devi, The Holy Mother: Her Teachings and Conversations*. It includes excerpts from diaries of several of the monastic and lay disciples offering unique insight into Holy Mother's life and conversations with her devotees. Adiswarananda's "Introduction" imparts the inspiring message:

> To the Master, Sri Ramakrishna, she was the goddess of wisdom in human form. To her disciples she was the Divine Mother herself. To her devotees she was a more real mother than their own earthly mother. To

the seekers of truth she was the final word, and to sinners she was the last refuge.[52]

When reviewing this book, Jerome J. Pollitt, professor emeritus and former dean of the Yale University graduate school (1986-91), affirmed:

> The conversations of Sarada Devi, the Holy Mother—full of practical, kindly, down-to-earth advice, and yet punctuated by sudden and quite stunning revelations of her cosmic awareness—are a unique document in the world's devotional and mystical literature. This is not only a perfect introduction to her teachings but also an enduring spiritual testament that many readers will want to return to again and again.

Jerome Pollitt, the president of the Ramakrishna-Vivekananda Centre of New York, was a professor of classical archaeology and history of art at Yale University from 1964. He also served as the editor-in-chief of the *American Journal of Archeology* (1973-77). Much of his career and book writing was devoted to exploring how ancient Greek art is an expression of the same cultural currents, which can be found in Greek literature and philosophy.[53]

Concerning the volume, Daniel Gomez-Ibanez expounded:

> What a gift it is to have reliable, first-person accounts of the life of a great saint and spiritual teacher. It is a special blessing when, as in these pages, we get to know someone who—like most of us—spent most of her life with the daily demands of family and household, while at the same time remaining completely faithful to the highest spiritual calling. Sarada Devi is an inspiration for all of us who struggle to bring the sacred into our everyday lives.[54]

Daniel A. Gomez-Ibanez, a former university professor, organized the 1993 Parliament of the World's Religions, which attracted eight-thousand representatives from the faiths of the world for a nine-day conference in Chicago. He is the executive director of the International Committee for the Peace Council, an organization that brings together highly respected leaders of many religions in the pursuit of world peace.[55]

Professor June McDaniel [q.v.] is a member of the department of philosophy and religious studies at the College of Charleston in South Carolina.

Writing for *Holy People of the World: A Cross-Cultural Encyclopedia* (2004), she informed her readers that

> Sarada Devi is best known as the devoted wife of the Bengali saint Ramakrishna Paramahamsa of Dakshineswar, India. However, she was also considered to be a holy woman in her own right and was worshipped as the Mother of the universe by Ramakrishna's disciples after his death in 1886. She is respected today as a guiding force and inspiration in the development of the Ramakrishna Math, a devotional and social service order based on the teachings of Ramakrishna and his disciple Vivekananda.... at one point he stated that she was really an incarnation of a form of the goddess Kali, and he ritually worshipped her as a goddess. He gave her gifts and mantras and offered her the fruits of his austerities as well as everything that was his. He told his disciples to worship her also, and they called her "Divine Mother".... They continued to call her mother, and she cooked and cared for them and began to initiate people in Ramakrishna's name. His disciples offered flowers at her feet, calling her goddess, and they wrote hymns of praise to her.[56]

Formerly in her book *The Madness of the Saints: Ecstatic Religion in Bengal* (1989), Professor McDaniel offered many quotations from the works of Swamis Gambhirananda and Tapasyananda to demonstrate that Holy Mother was a divine incarnation according to Sri Ramakrishna, initiated many devotees, took on the karma of other people, often experienced spiritual bliss in samadhi, and lived in a state of great humility.[57]

Neelima Shukla-Bhatt earned her Ph.D. in 2003 in religious studies from Harvard University. She became a professor at Wellesley College for women in Massachusetts, teaching courses within the South Asia Studies programme. Writing a short biography of Holy Mother for the prestigious fifteen-volume *Encyclopedia of Religion* (2005), she stressed:

> Sarada Devi became the chief source of spiritual and emotional support for his disciples after his [Sri Ramakrishna's] death, when they began to establish a spiritual order in his name. Up to this point she had led her life in accordance with the Indian cultural ideal of a quiet and dutiful wife; however, she played a pivotal role in the burgeoning order with her piety, pragmatism, and motherly qualities. In the early twenty-first century Sarada Devi receives the highest degree of honour in the order's many centres

throughout the world, along with Ramakrishna himself ... Ramakrishna then declared that Sarada was the Mother of the Universe and performed an elaborate ritual of worship for her. He also asked his disciples to address her as the Holy Mother.... Moving back and forth between Jayrambati and Calcutta, she initiated disciples with mantras, advised them in spiritual and practical matters, and provided the community with motherly warmth. Her ministry was markedly different from that of Ramakrishna. While the latter instructed his disciples in the intricacies of meditation and mystical experiences, she taught them devotion to the master, simplicity in living, and loving service to others through her own example. Following Vivekananda's visit to America, his Western followers also came to regard her as the Holy Mother.... Sarada Devi's life demonstrated the strength of simplicity and motherly affection—a quality that was considered a distinctive characteristic of Mother India in the nationalist discourse of the early twentieth century. In Devi's ability to combine traditional values with a liberal outlook and to transform mundane work into spiritual practice through selfless service, she provided a model of inspiration for modern Indian women.[58]

The editor-in-chief of the *Journal of Vaishnava Studies*, Steven J. Rosen [q.v.], is also associate editor of *Back to Godhead*, the magazine of the Hare Krishna movement. His recent books include *Essential Hinduism*, *Krishna's Song: A New look at the Bhagavad Gita*, and *The Hidden Glory of India*. In his six-volume *Introduction to the World's Major Religions* (2006), Rosen insightfully wrote:

Sarada Devi was a spiritual luminary in her own way, and yet she served Ramakrishna and his disciples as a humble servant for many years. After Ramakrishna died, she carried on the religious ministry, serving as guide and inspiration for the fledgling spiritual movement.

The example set by Sarada Devi for Ramakrishna's followers, as an ideal disciple, nun, wife, teacher, and especially mother, who took great care of her many spiritual children—his other followers—will be remembered for centuries to come. Those who associated with her were overwhelmed by her spirit of love and selfless service. She accepted them all as her children, irrespective of nationality, religious affiliation, or social position. She turned no one away. Her love seemed all-encompassing.[59]

In 2008 the Vedanta Society of Southern California came out with a 43 minute DVD titled "Unsolicited Grace: Accounts of Holy Mother Sri Sarada Devi". It gives inspiring and charming first hand accounts of Holy Mother narrated by four Swamis who knew her, viz. Aseshananda, Gauriswarananda, Nikhilananda, and Prabhavananda. Gauriswarananda, a disciple of Holy Mother (as were Aseshananda and Nikhilananda), was well known throughout the Ramakrishna Order for his musical compositions and for his gardening talents. Drawn from videos of their lectures, the Swamis tell us about their personal experiences with Holy Mother.[60]

In 2009, Advaita Ashrama came out with a new and revised translation of Holy Mother's Bengali biography *Sri Sri Sarada Devi* entitled *The Compassionate Mother*. Swami Shuddhidananda, the editor of the book, mentions:

> It is the English rendering of Holy Mother's "oldest biography" in Bengali penned by Brahmachari Akshaychaitanya. For this very reason the book assumes singular importance, being her first complete life story published in Bengali in 1937. All her subsequent biographers have, directly or indirectly, drawn from this source, among the others.

William Page, a retired teacher of English from Thammasat University in Bangkok, Thailand, adds:

> This new translation of the "oldest biography of Holy Mother" is an invaluable addition to the growing canon of English-language works about her. It was one of the sources that Swami Tapasyananda and Swami Gambhirananda drew from in compiling their own biographies of the Mother. Over the years Holy Mother's significance has become increasingly recognized.... Her preeminent quality is her motherliness. We have hundreds of anecdotes testifying to her motherly compassion.... She is the ideal vehicle for the Spirit which lived in Sri Ramakrishna, and she can function as an ideal mother-figure for the whole world. In her, the Mother-worship which gave birth to the Ramakrishna movement has come full circle.[61]

Concerning the literature on Holy Mother, see Appendix V for the publication dates of her teachings, and Appendix VI for a selected list of books about her.

ENDNOTES

1 Holy Mother took birth on December 22, 1853, and one year following on December 8, 1854, Pope Pius IX's proclamation of the Immaculate Conception was issued by the Catholic Church. According to one source, "It is no exaggeration that the hundred years from 1854 to the close of the Second Vatican Council [1965] were the most prolific in doctrinal development in Mariology. Nothing like it was seen in any comparable period of Catholic history." According to the doctrine of the Immaculate Conception, Mary, from the moment of her conception, was free from original sin. (John Hardon, S.J., *The Catholic Catechism*, Garden City, NY: Doubleday, 1975, pp. 155-60.)

2 Nikhilananda, pp. 280-86.

3 "Swami Prabhavananda lectures on Holy Mother" (Sept. 16, 1973), cassette; (Jan. 7, 1962), p. 4.

4 Nikhilananda, pp. 114, 280, 285; Swami Purnatmananda, ed., *Reminiscences of Sri Sarada Devi* (Kolkata: Advaita Ashrama, 2004), pp. 125-26, 149.

5 Max Müller, *Ramakrishna His Life and Sayings* (Calcutta: Advaita Ashrama, 1898), pp. 64-65.

6 Purnatmananda (2004), p. 107.

7 Nikhilananda, p. 284; Atmaprana, pp. 63-66, 69; Purnatmananda (2004), p. 112.

8 "Swami Prabhavananda lectures on Holy Mother" (Dec. 31, 1950), p. 4; (Dec. 9, 1962), p. 3.

9 Sister Nivedita, *The Master as I Saw Him* (Calcutta: Udbodhan Office, 1910), pp. 142-43; *PB* (March 1954), p. 100.

10 Nikhilananda, pp. 285-86; Nivedita, II, pp. 1168-69; Atmaprana, pp. 256-57; Purnatmananda (2004), p. 119.

11 Atmaprana, p. 257.

12 Nikhilananda, p. 280; Prugh, pp. 352-53.

13 Prugh, p. 347.

14 F. Max Müller, *Ramakrishna His Life and Sayings* (Calcutta: Advaita Ashrama, 2001), pp. 64-65.

15 *The Literary Digest* (April 2, 1898), p. 409.

16 Basu, p. 564; *Brahmavadin* (March 1902), p. 244.

17 Gargi, p. 233.

18 Gargi, pp. 107-08, 113, 233-34; Christopher Isherwood, *An Interview with Swami Prabhavananda* (Unpublished Manuscript, 1972), III, p. 7.

19 Devamata, pp. 213-14; *Nivedita*, II, pp. 1003-04; Levinsky, pp. 140-41.

20 Devamata, pp. 211, 215; Purnatmananda (2004), pp. 129, 132.

21 Devamata, pp. 226, 228; Nikhilananda, p. 282; *Sarada Devi*, p. 290.

22 "From Besse MacLeod Leggett to her sister, Josephine MacLeod", *VK* (May 1973), pp. 33-35; The Earl of Sandwich, "A Journey in India", *VW* (March-April 1957), pp. 29-33; Purnatmananda (2004), pp. 147-48; Prugh, pp. 335-36.

23 *PB* (Sept. 1932), pp. 456, 458-59; *Disciples*, pp. 470-77.

24 See Swami Prabhavananda, "Holy Mother", *BRMIC* (Dec. 2007), pp. 532-42 for more on Sarada Devi.

25 *Sarada Devi*, pp. 257-58.

26 Vedanta Press and Catalogue. Web: www.vedanta.org; Swami Yogeshananda, *Six Lighted Windows* (United States: Swami Yogeshananda, 1995), pp. 207-08; Web: en.wikipedia.org/wike/Swami_Tapasyananda_(Ramakrishna_Mission).

27 Winifred Iles, *Holy Mother of India Sarada Devi* (London: The Vedanta Movement, 1994), pp. inside front cover, 17, 19, 24-26, 56-57.

28 *Sarada Devi*, pp. 281, 284-85; *VK* (1954), pp. 63-64.

29 *VFEW* (Sept-Oct. 1954), pp. 54-58.

30 *The Scribner Encyclopedia of American Lives* (New York: Charles Scribner's Sons, 1999, 2003).

31 World Congress of Faiths. Web: www.religion-online.org/showchapter.asp?title=3378&C=2775; Surjit Mansingh, *Historical Dictionary of India* (Oxford: Scarecrow Press, 2006), pp. 169-70; Riddick, p. 95.

32 Otto Ritschl. Web: www.otto-ritschl.com; *PB* (1983), p. 37.

33 Vedanta Press and Catalogue. Web: www.vedanta.org; Swami Yogeshananda, *Six Lighted Windows* (United States: Swami Yogeshananda, 1995), pp. 207-08.

34 Swami Nikhilananda, *Holy Mother* (New York: Ramakrishna-Vedanta-Centre, 1997), back cover.

35 Filmer S.C. Northrop, *The Meeting of East and West* (New York: Collier Books, 1966), pp. 364, 400-01; *CA* (1986), *New Rev. Ser.*, XVII; *VK* (Sept. 1950), p. 198.

36 Nikhilananda (1997), back cover; *CA* (1977), 1st Rev., XXI.

37 Lex Hixon, *Coming Home* (Garden City, NY: Anchor Books, 1978), pp. 55-56.

38 Torwesten (1981), pp. 119-20.

39 Aseshananda, Swami, "What Vedanta Means to Me", *PB* (Oct. 1951), p. 400.

40 Vedanta Society of Portland. Web: www.srv.org.

41 Sarada Devi, pp. 363-64; also in *PB* (June 1969), pp. 280-81.

42 "Spiritual Hunger". High Beam Research. Web: http://static.highbeam.com/i/indiacurrents/november301996/ spiritualhungernancypopemayorgasdiary-documentsawri/; Vedanta Online Catalog. Web: www.vedanta.com.

43 *Sarada Devi*, pp. 391-94; also in *PB* (Dec. 1970), pp. 546-47.

44 *Sarada Devi*, pp. 300, 315-16, 345.

45 *BRMIC* (Dec. 1990), p. 304.

46 Sri Sarada Society. Web: www.srisarada.org/society1.htm.

47 Elizabeth Harding, *Kali: The Black Goddess of Dakshineswar* (York Beach, ME: Nicholas-Hays, 1993), p. 284.

48 *VK* (1994), pp. 18-19.

49 J. Holm and J. Bowker, *Women in Religion* (London: Pinters, 2000), p. 69 on GBS; University of Birmingham. Web: www.theology.bham.ac.uk/staff/sharada.htm.

50 *VK* (Jan. 2003), p. 29; Kent State University. Web: www.educ.kent.edu/tlcs/faculty/melillo.htm.

51 "Mothers Prescription for Peace", *VK* (Dec. 2003), pp. 486-89.

52 Sarada Devi. Web: www.skylightpaths.com/Merchant2/ merchant.mvc?Screen=PROD&Store_Code=SP&Product_Code=1-59473-070-9.

53 *WWIA* (2003), p. 4185; *CA* (1977) 1st Rev., vol. 21, Jerome J. Pollitt. Web: www.yale.edu/ arthistory/faculty/page/pollittpage.htm.

54 Vedanta Press and Catalog. Web: www.vedanta.com/showbook.cfm?booknum=10000965.

55 Daniel A. Gomez-Ibanez. Web: www.millenniuminstitute.net/boardstaff/gomez.htm.

56 *Holy People of the World: A Cross-Cultural Encyclopedia*, ed. Phyllis Jestice (Santa Barbara, CA: ABC CLIO, 2004), pp. xix, 767-68. Phyllis Jestice teaches in the department of history, University of Southern Mississippi.

57 June McDaniel, *The Madness of the Saints* (Chicago: University of Chicago Press, 1989), pp. 202-09 on GBS.

58 *Encyclopedia of Religion*, ed. Lindsay Jones (Detroit: Macmillan Reference USA, 2005), XII, pp. 8111-12; Neelima Shukla-Bhatt. Web: www.lokvani.com/lokvani/article.php?article_id=3571.

59 Steven J. Rosen, *Introduction to the World's Major Religions* (Westport, CT: Greenwood Press, 2006), VI, pp. 124-25.

60 The DVD is available from the Vedanta Online Catalogue in Hollywood, California. Web: www.vedanta.com and selected video clips are accessible online at Web: www.youtube.com/thakurma. Web: www.vedanta.org/reading/monthly/.../ 9.reminis_hm.htm.

61 Email from Mr. William Page to Swami Shuddhidananda at Advaita Ashrama (Nov. 2009); *American Vedantist* (Fall 2007).

PART III

WESTERN ADMIRERS OF SWAMI VIVEKANANDA

Swami Vivekananda

CHAPTER V

DEVOTEES AND SUPPORTERS

SWAMI VIVEKANANDA (1863-1902) lectured to tens of thousands of people in the United States and Europe. From that large group, a select number of individuals have been specially selected for study in Chapters V through XI. These are the people who made personal contact with Swamiji, and/or aided him in his mission by making a positive contribution to the Vedanta movement. His supporters include those people who were present at numerous lectures, introduced him to significant individuals, provided lodging for him in their home, made financial contributions to the Ramakrishna movement or to his welfare, transcribed his lectures and classes, accompanied him to India to work for the good of the people, wrote reminiscences or positive statements about him, and/or helped him with his work in various ways. After his mahasamadhi, some Western devotees became long-time active members of the local Vedanta Societies and were extensively involved with aiding the progress of the movement. They gave assistance to the new Swamis that came to America, and/or wrote on Vedantic themes. An ample number of endnote references are provided throughout the book for devotees and scholars who want to do additional research on the subject.

A number of Vivekananda's inner circle of devotees made a major contribution to his work in the West. Since detailed accounts of their activities have been described in a number of books and articles, their contributions will be briefly covered in this chapter. When Swamiji came to Chicago in September of 1893, Mrs. George (Belle) Hale (1836-1930) found him sitting in front of her house one day without funds. He had misplaced the address of the office of the World's Parliament of Religions. She took him in, fed him breakfast and then made sure he got to the Parliament office. Her husband, the retired George W. Hale (1829-1900), had been a senior partner in a Chicago iron firm. Mary Hale (1865-1933) and her younger sister Harriet (1871/72-1929), and their cousins Isabelle and Harriet McKindley, lived in the house with George and Belle Hale. Swamiji often stayed with the Hales in their home where he was treated as a member of their family, and they conscientiously took care of his daily needs. They were his good friends, but not his religious disciples. On at least five occasions during his stay in the West, he came back to live at the Hale household for a period totalling over two months. For years he maintained a correspondence with Belle Hale and her daughter Mary. We have the content of over one hundred personal letters that Swamiji sent to the Hale family, which provide insight into his views on various subjects. On 26th June 1894, Swamiji wrote to the Hale sisters, "It is impossible to express my pain, my anguish at being separated from you, noble and sweet and generous and holy ones."[1] In a letter dated 10 February 1896 to Mary Hale, Swamiji states, "I am ever grateful to you four sisters; to you I owe everything I have in this country. May you be ever blessed and happy. Wherever I be, you will always be remembered with the deepest gratitude and sincerest love."[2] He wrote to Mary Hale in September of 1899, "Your family ... have made more impression on me than any family I know of."[3] Mary Hale described Swamiji as

> the great and glorious soul that came to the Parliament of Religions, so full of love of God, that his face shone with the Divine light, whose words were fire, whose very presence created an atmosphere of harmony and purity, thereby drawing all souls to himself.

When Mary Hale passed away on New Year's Day of 1933, she bequeathed the then sizable sum of $18,500 (equivalent to $303,000 in 2008) to Belur Math.[4]

Miss Grace Thatcher Howe (1837/38-1920) was a close friend of the Hale and the McKindley family in Chicago. Vivekananda wrote in correspondences to his Chicago friends between August 1894 and September 1899: "Kindly tender my heartfelt love and gratitude to Miss Howe. She has been so, so kind to me." "Kindly convey my best regards and love to Miss Howe and Mr. Frank Howe." "Kindly give my love to Miss Howe." "Where is Miss Howe? She is such a noble soul, such a friend."[5] While residing in Washington, D.C. in October-November 1894, the Swami lived with a niece of Miss Howe named Mrs. Enoch Totten. Grace Howe sent a letter to the Unitarian minister Jenkin Lloyd Jones (1843-1918), probably in late November or early December 1893. In this correspondence, she writes of the insights she received through her associations with Swamiji:

I have had the chance of becoming well acquainted with him. He is living with the Hales and they have invited me several times to visit there. So I have had long day—long talks with him and have got that inner sense of him that comes from just such association and in no other way. I believe thoroughly in his purity, sincerity, and a certain kind of simplicity. It is the simplicity that is natural to a person of high breeding who has nothing to conceal. I mean nothing in his deeds, but much in his nature that shrinks from too strong light. You know what I mean.

He has a finely trained mind, draws easily on his resources, has had a refined bringing up, has a long line of scholarly ancestors behind him, has a most religious nature, has naturally [underscored by the writer of the letter] dominion over his senses, and with it all, a nature so sympathetic that as a child he had a passion for humanity. By nature [underscored by the writer again] understands the sufferings of those beneath him in advantages. He has a rich nature full of mirth, the soul of gayety, when he is not most serious and uplifted.

The kind of boy I have tried to describe came under the influence of a monk, a half insane mystic as I gather, who so influenced him as to throw the whole force of his nature into religion. His love of God is a revelation to me—and his love of humanity just as dominating. These are the foundations of his spiritual life and on that has been reared a curious admixture of the monk the mystic and the free thinker. It all together makes him the most interesting person I ever met.

I write this to you because you ought to know him. It's too bad to lose such a chance because he is so unlike any one I ever knew.[6]

Grace Howe's obituary in the *Kenosha* [*Wisconsin*] *Evening News* of July 29, 1920 described her as

> ...a brilliant conversationalist, widely known as a reader of the best literature and she had a close personal grasp on the inside political life in Washington.... Her home in New York for years was a literary shrine for men and women who knew the best things in literature and she was the most gracious of entertainers.[7]

Mrs. John (Frances Elizabeth) J. Bagley (1833-98) proved to be a caring hostess and a faithful friend of Swami Vivekananda. Her husband, the former two-term governor of the state of Michigan (1873-77), died in 1887.

She first made contact with Swamiji at the Parliament of Religions in Chicago where she served as one of the lady managers of the World's Fair. During part of February and March of 1894, Mrs. Bagley hosted Vivekananda at her residence in Detroit, Michigan. Swamiji mentioned that the Bagley family is "very rich, kind and hospitable. Mrs. Bagley is especially interested in India.... Mrs. Bagley is a very nice and kind lady".[8] She held a gala reception at her home, inviting three-hundred members of the social elite of Detroit to come and meet with Vivekananda. Invitations were sent to the mayor and his wife, and to representatives of the major religious faiths. The *Detroit Journal* of February 14 pointed out, "There has not gathered in a home in Detroit in many a day and perhaps never such a distinguished assemblage of Detroiters as were present last evening to meet the polished Hindoo monk." Vivekananda spoke for two hours on "The Ancient Hindu Philosophers". In his correspondence he mentions, "Next summer, if I do not go away, which Mrs. Bagley insists I should not, I may go to Annisquam [Massachusetts] where Mrs. Bagley has engaged a nice house. Mrs. Bagley is a very spiritual lady."[9] From Annisquam Swamiji jotted down, "I am with the Bagleys once more. They are kind as usual."[10] In the spring of 1895, Mrs. Bagley also attended several of his New York classes.[11] The next August she sent a letter to Swamiji in England with the message:

> We all unite in wishing you a pleasant journey to England but with it the hope that you will come back again to America to Detroit and to us. When you come to Detroit we shall be glad to have you make our house your home.... I am sure your own mother would be glad to know that her son has done so much good in this far-away country. I should be very glad to send to her cordial and kindly greetings.[12]

In a letter dated June 22, 1894, Mrs. Bagley sent a friend this wonderful tribute to Vivekananda:

> I am glad of an opportunity to express my admiration of his character, and it makes me most indignant that anyone should call him in question. He has given us in America higher ideas of life than we have ever had before.... all who say one word against him are jealous of his greatness and his fine spiritual perceptions; and yet how can they be? He does nothing to make them so.

> He has been a revelation to Christians ... He has made possible for us a diviner and more noble practical life. As a religious teacher and an example to all I do not know his equal.... All who have been brought in contact with him day by day, speak enthusiastically of his sterling qualities of character, and men in Detroit who judge most critically, and who are unsparing, admire and respect him.... He has been a guest in my house more than three weeks, and my sons as well as my son-in-law and my entire family found Swami Vivekananda a gentleman always, most courteous and polite, a charming companion and an ever-welcome guest.... He is a strong, noble human being, one who walks with God. He is as simple and trustful as a child.... Whenever he spoke, people listened gladly and said, "I have never heard man speak like that." He does not antagonize, but lifts people up to a higher level—they see something beyond man-made creeds and denominational names, and they feel one with him in their religious beliefs.
>
> Every human being would be made better by knowing him and living in the same house with him.... I want everyone in America to know Vivekananda, and if India has more such, let her send them to us.[13]

On August 27, 1895, Kripananda (Leon Landsberg), who was teaching Vedanta in Detroit, wrote to Sara Bull:

> I had the pleasure of making the acquaintance of Mrs. [John J.] Bagley who regularly attends my classes. She is a very lovely woman. She practises meditation under my directions and though I cannot expect to make of her a Sanyasyna [sic], I am sure that she will turn out a good Karma Yogi if not a sincere Bhakti Yogi.[14]

After hearing Vivekananda give an oral presentation in Detroit in February of 1894, Christina Greenstidel, then a public school teacher at Duffield School and who later became Sister Christine (1866-1930), recalled:

> The power that emanated from this mysterious being was so great that one all but shrank from it. It was overwhelming. It threatened to sweep everything before it. This one sensed even in those first unforgettable moments.... It was the mind that made the first great appeal, that amazing mind! What can one say that will give even a faint idea of its majesty, its glory, its splendour? It was a mind so far transcending other minds, even of those who rank as geniuses, that it seemed different in its very nature. Its

ideas were so clear, so powerful, so transcendental that it seemed incredible that they could have emanated from the intellect of a limited human being. Yet marvellous as the ideas were and wonderful as was that intangible something that flowed out from the mind, it was strangely familiar. I found myself saying, "I have known that mind before."...

He stood on the platform of the Unitarian Church pouring forth glorious truths in a voice unlike any voice one had ever heard before, a voice full of cadences, expressing every emotion, now with a pathos that stirred hitherto unknown depths of tragedy, and then just as the pain was becoming unbearable, that same voice would move to mirth only to check it in a mid-course with the thunder of an earnestness so intense that it left one awed, a trumpet call to awake. One felt that one never knew what music was until one heard that marvellous voice....

He had power of attraction so great that those who came near him, men and women alike, even children, fell under the magic spell he cast.... I had come to one in whom I had seen such spirituality as I had never even dreamed of. From his lips I had heard truths unthought of before. He knew the way to attainment. He would show me the way.[15]

After Swamiji's second visit to Detroit in March of 1896, Sister Christine recorded in her memoirs:

He told us that usually before a lecture he heard a voice saying it all. The next day he repeated what he had heard. He did not say whose voice he heard. Whatever it was, it came as the expression of some great spiritual power, greater than his own normal power, released by the intensity of his concentration.... The spiritual force generated at such times was so great that some in the audience were lifted above the normal state of consciousness, so that it was possible to remember only the beginning of a lecture. After a certain point, there seemed a blank. The normal mind was no longer functioning; a higher state of consciousness, beyond reason and memory, had taken its place. Long after, perhaps, it would be found that during that period when the mind seemed blank, a specially deep impression had been made.[16]

Describing his stimulating first lecture in Detroit, Mrs. Mary C. Funke, a good friend of Sister Christine, recollected:

> I can see him yet as he stepped upon the platform, a regal, majestic figure, vital, forceful, dominant, and at the first sound of the wonderful voice, a voice all music—now like the plaintive minor strain of an Eolian harp, again deep, vibrant, resonant—there was a hush, a stillness that could almost be felt.[17]

The next year Sister Christine and Mary Funke went to Thousand Island Park to hear Swamiji speak. When they greeted him, Sister Christine said, "We have come, just as we would go to Jesus if he were still on earth and ask him to teach us." The Swami replied, "If only I possessed the power of Christ to set you free now!" There, she and four others were chosen to receive brahmacharya vows. On Wednesday, August 7, 1895, the last day of Swamiji's departure from Thousand Island Park, he went out for a walk with Mary Funke and Sister Christine:

> The Swami suddenly said to them, "Now we shall meditate. We shall be like Buddha under the Bo-tree." He then became still as a bronze statue. A thunderstorm came up and it poured; but the Swami did not notice anything. Mrs. Funke raised her umbrella and protected him as much as possible. When it was time to return, the Swami opened his eyes and said, "I feel once more I am in Calcutta in the rains." It is reported that one day at Thousand Island Park he experienced nirvakalpa samadhi.[18]

After Swamiji left India to return to the West in 1899, Christine and Mary Funke were waiting for him at the dock in England. Together they set sail on a steamer back to New York along with Swami Turiyananda. In July 1900, Swamiji was with the Greenstidel family in Detroit for six days, and she met him again at the New York Vedanta Society. The Swami sent at least seventy letters to her telling her things like, "God bless you at each step, my dear Christine, such is my constant prayer! Your letter, so beautiful and so calm, has given me that fresh energy which I am often losing."[19] She made contact with Swamiji again at Belur Math in India in the year of his passing. For most of the next twelve years, she devoted her life to educating Indian women. Sister Christine was a manager and teacher at the Nivedita Girls' School, allowing Sister Nivedita the opportunity to write and lecture. There she became friends with Holy Mother. Nivedita wrote, "It was to Sister Christine and her faithfulness that the school owes its success up to the present."[20] Sister Devamata explains that Christine possessed "an exceptionally unselfish character with a rare spirit of service.... There was an appealing sweetness about [Christine] which endeared to the heart." Consequently, the school was a tremendous success. Due to ill health in 1914, Sister Christine had to return to Detroit where she lectured extensively on India and the Vedanta philosophy. She later returned to India in 1924 for four years and then came back to the U.S. While in very poor health, she told others, "Would I have it different? No, a thousand times no. It is seldom that Vivekananda comes to this earth. If I am to be born again, gladly will I endure a thousand times the hardships of this life for the privilege that has been mine."[21]

Incidentally, Sister Christine had a sister named Fredericka Greenstidel who was employed as a dressmaker in Detroit. An unmarried woman by the same name (whom we might assume is the same person or a relative) later lived in Los Angeles and was selected by Swami Trigunatita in 1911 to be one of the eleven Mothers (and Fathers) of the newly formed "Vedanta Centre" in that city.[22]

Swamiji first came to New York City in April of 1894. It was in this city that over the next couple of years he was to come across many of his most outstanding Western devotees. The list includes: Mr. and Mrs. Egbert Guernsey, Mary Phillips, Leon Landsberg, Emma Thursby, Lewis Janes, Myron Phelps, Charles Higgins, Ella Wheeler Wilcox, Josephine MacLeod, Sarah Ellen Waldo, Laura Glenn (Sister Devamata), Francis and Betty Leggett, Mary Elizabeth Dutcher, Walter and Frances Goodyear, Marie Louise, Malvina Hoffman, Josiah Goodwin, Henry Van Haagen, John P. Fox, Cornelius Heijblom (Swami Atulananda), Herschel Parker, Lillian Montgomery, and others. Vivekananda conversed on various subjects at Miss Mary A. Phillips' (b. 1843/44) residence in New York City.[23] She was prominent in women's charitable and intellectual work in the city. Phillips at one time had been wealthy, but then gave away a portion of her inheritance. At her home Swamiji met Emma Thursby, Leon Landsberg, and the young Malvina Hoffman. He stayed in her house for eleven or more days in 1894 and 1895, after which he wrote, "Miss Phillips was very kind to me. She is an old lady, about 50 or more."[24] In a number of correspondences, he asked the Swamis in India and devotees in America to kindly send his letters, books and clothing in care of Mary Phillips at 19 W. 38th Street.[25] For years she proved to be an eager worker, helping arrange his New York classes in 1895,[26] and as secretary of the New York Vedanta Society. She held an informal reception for Swami Saradananda in her home, inviting many prominent men and women, and took care of his meals while he addressed audiences in New York in the winter of 1897. In the year 1900, Vivekananda and Abhedananda were guests at her quiet and friendly boardinghouse.[27]

Three days after receiving a letter from Swami Ramakrishnananda on May 3rd, 1896, the New York students of Vivekananda sent a reply to the Swamis in India. Mary Phillips' name appeared first on the long list of senders. It said:

> We believe with you that a strong bond of union now exists between your land and ours, established by the Swami Vivekananda. The grand truths of the Vedanta, as presented by him, interested thinking minds of all classes, and met with a ready acceptance by many of those, who had the privilege of hearing them.... We did not realize until now, that the Hindus, so distant and so ancient, held so much wisdom and knowledge in trust for us, the youngest among nations.[28]

After Swamiji came back to India in 1897, he received a letter sent to "Our Indian Brethren", signed by Mary Phillips, the secretary of the New York Vedanta Society. The letter said in part:

> He came, a stranger, unheralded, but, by the force of his magnetic eloquence, and the purity of his personal character, he commanded the attention and interest of thousands, and attracted their minds to the study of a subject almost entirely unknown to them. Here, in New York, where he taught and lectured for two seasons, the impression he produced is so deep that we hope and trust it will extend until the Vedanta Philosophy shall take permanent root among us, and its comprehensive and tolerant teachings shall find lodgment in hearts, and expression in the lives of large numbers of our people. We who came into more immediate contact with him are deeply grateful for the noble work he did among us, for the unselfish and self-sacrificing efforts he made in our behalf; and we will try to the best of our ability to establish on a lasting basis the study of the Vedanta Philosophy and to promote the growth of knowledge concerning it.[29]

Before meeting Vivekananda, Sara Chapman Bull (1850-1911) [q.v.] translated two full-length Norwegian novels written by Jonas Lie (1833-1908) into the English language, which were published in 1876 and 1879. Also in 1882, she came out with a four-hundred page plus biography about her deceased husband, an internationally renowned Norwegian violinist, entitled *Ole Bull: a Memoir*, which a leading Boston publisher distributed. During 1886-87 Sara attended many classes given by the Bengali Mohini Mohan Chatterji (Chatterjee), whom she very much admired. She studied Mohini's translation of the *Bhagavad Gita*, and from him learned about the Vedanta and Sankhya philosophy. All this proved a wonderful preparation for her future meeting with Swamiji. Mohini, originally a member of the Brahmo Samaj, became Madam Blavatsky's (1831-91) secretary, but eventually separated from the Theosophical movement. In 1885 Mohini introduced the *Gita* to the future Nobel Prize winning Irish poet William Butler Yeats (1865-1939). Yeats, a Dublin Theosophist, also had a positive encounter with Rabindranath Tagore in 1910, wrote a poem about his friend Mohini, and associated with Gerald Heard before the latter became a member of the Vedanta Society in Southern California. In 1937, Shree Purohit Swami (1882-1941) and Yeats translated *The Ten Principal Upanishads*. For a year, Mohini held discussions on Indian thought in the Boston area with distinguished people like Sara Bull, Julia Ward Howe and Clara Rogers. Mohini would visit the salon of the well-known poetess Celia Thaxter (1835-1894), and she kept a portrait of Mohini in her drawing room that Swami Abhedananda saw.[30]

Swami Vivekananda might have met Sara Bull in Boston in May of 1894, and certainly did during the months of July-August at Greenacre, Maine.[31] Concerning Swamiji's public lecture given at Greenacre on August 3, 1894, she submitted a report to the *Boston Evening Transcript* published on August 11, saying in part:

> The speaker, Swami Vivekananda, gave what only a great soul is capable of giving. It was an hour never to be forgotten. This man brought those present into the light of truth, whatever their prejudice and training, as Phillips Brooks united Unitarian and Episcopalianism, and all who love the good and true came to hold him for their bishop. So this Hindu, in his constructive thought, when he will give it, can make the power of the prophets known to us by his own presence.[32]

Phillips Brooks (1835-93), who wrote the words for the popular Christmas carol "O Little Town of Bethlehem", was an Episcopal Bishop, who, like Vedantists, believed in the pre-existence of the soul before earthly life.

Sara organized the Cambridge Conferences, which attracted many well-known and scholarly people. Her many contributions to the Vedanta movement include: requesting Swamiji to speak at the Cambridge Conferences at her home in October 1894[33] where he met the famous Harvard professor William James; inviting Swamiji to live in her house in December;[34] arranging classes for Swamiji to lecture in Cambridge, and later in New York City during the spring of 1895, and in Cambridge-Boston in March 1896;[35] preserving the notes of Swamiji's "Six Lessons on Raja Yoga";[36] aiding in the publication of *Raja Yoga* and some of his other writings;[37] requesting Holy Mother to be photographed, creating the picture that is most often worshipped today; and donating generous sums of money to construct and maintain the Belur Math[38] and the J. C. Bose Institute in Calcutta. Vivekananda refers to Sara Bull as "a very spiritual lady", "my guardian angel", "a saint, a real saint", and as "a great, great woman".[39] Seventy-nine letters sent by Swamiji to Sara have been preserved.[40] Swami Vivekananda was very appreciative of those devotees who aided him in his Western mission.[41]

Swami Saradananda lived at Sara Bull's home, and gave a sequence of classes on "The Vedanta Philosophy" at the Cambridge Conferences. At Cambridge on December 10, 1899, Turiyananda read a paper on "Shankaracharya", which some Harvard professors spoke highly of. In 1904 she prepared a report entitled "Misguided Pilgrims to India", which appeared in newspapers. Sara Bull advised American devotees not to go to India since the life conditions there are not suitable for most Westerners.[42] In 1909, she invited Paramananda to Boston to establish a new Vedanta Centre in the city.

Sara Bull passed away in 1911, leaving a half million-dollar (equivalent to over 11 million in 2008) estate, largely inherited from her wealthy father, bequeathing $30,000 to Sister Nivedita, $20,000 to J. C. Bose and $5,000 to Swami Saradananda in India. She had been giving Nivedita $1500 a year since 1899. Her daughter Olea Bull Vaughan (1871-1911) contested the will and eventually became the sole heir of the estate. During the trial, Olea contracted tuberculosis and died on July 18, 1911, the day the judge awarded her the money. To win the case her lawyers discredited the Swamis and the Vedanta Society and paid off the household servants to lie, in an attempt to prove that Sara Bull was mentally unbalanced. They tried to show that Mrs. Bull was under the continual influence of the Indian Swamis, though she bequeathed only one percent of her funds to the Swamis of the Ramakrishna Order. An article with the subtitle, "Mrs. Bull a Believer in Malicious Animal Magnetism under another Name—The Eight Stages of Raja Yoga", appeared in the *Boston Daily Globe* of May 28, 1911 and concluded:

> Invested with elements of mysticism and psychological problems involving, in a way, an inquiry as to what the Raja Yogi or Vendanta [sic] philosophy originating in India, really is, the contest now in progress in the probate court here over the will of Mrs. Ole Bull is, in many respects, the most remarkable litigation in the legal history of New England.

Since Indian religious practices were negatively misrepresented and sensationalized during the trial, some upper class people did not want their name publicly associated with the Vedanta Society. In far off Miami, Florida, a newspaper article added, "So fearful are many prominent men and women that their names will be brought into the proceedings that private detectives and lawyers are attending the court sessions in secret."[43] The case attracted a great deal of media attention. Unfortunately, the lies perpetrated during the trial led to some highly critical articles and a book concerning yoga and the Swamis in the United States.

The *Brahmavadin* of October 1911 (reprinted in Trigunatita's *Voice of Freedom* in December) related the statements made by Ella Wheeler Wilcox [q.v.] concerning the trial dealing with Sara Bull's will:

> The sensational statements made in the Will contest case of Mrs. Ole Bull regarding the teachings of Vedanta are most misleading and unjust to that great philosophy. It was my privilege to be a pupil of Swami Vivekananda during his tour in New York. This I regard as the greatest intellectual and spiritual opportunity of my life. Neither in the lectures of Vivekananda, his books or the Vedanta philosophy are to be found any of "weird" "uncanny" or unwholesome teachings related by the witnesses as a part of Mrs. Bulls "lessons".

Miss Siri Swanander, a Scandinavian woman and a Brooklyn schoolteacher, was a friend of Sarah Waldo. During the winter of 1896 she met Sara Bull at a lecture given by Vivekananda in New York City. The following October she and her mother Edith again came across Sara Bull at a lecture delivered by Swami Saradananda at the Brooklyn Ethical Society. Swami Abhedananda mentions meeting Siri in September 1897. Beginning on October 15, 1910, during a portion of the last three months of her life on earth, Sara Bull stayed at the Brooklyn residence of Edith and Siri Swanander. They were visited by Sara's daughter Olea. Because of this association, Siri

Swanander was called to be a key witness during the 1911 trial concerning Sara Bull's will.[44]

In July 1911 (and possibly longer), Bhupendranath Datta (1880-1961), the youngest brother of Swami Vivekananda, was living as a guest of Mrs. Edith Swanander in Brooklyn when he attended New York University. A political radical in India, in 1907 Bhupendranath had been sentenced to one year's rigorous imprisonment for editing *Yugantar*, a revolutionary publication in Bengal. He spent six years in America and long afterwards authored the interesting and popular *Swami Vivekananda, Patriot-Prophet* (1955). Previously Swami Vivekananda, whom the Swananders adored, addressed Edith as "mother". While living at their residence, Bhupendranath dreamt that his mother in India had died. Edith pooh-poohed the idea, but a month later he found out his dream was correct. He had some association with Abhedananda when he lived in the United States.[45]

1895 in New York

Swamiji wrote, "There is a cottage belonging to Miss Dutcher, one of my students, and a few of us will be there in rest and peace and seclusion. I want to manufacture a few 'Yogis' out of the materials of the classes."[46] Mary Elizabeth Dutcher (b. 1832) owned a cottage at Thousand Island Park in the St. Lawrence River. She had been an art teacher in Rochester, New York, who now attended the Swami's New York classes. Sister Christine later revealed:

> Miss Dutcher, our hostess was a conscientious little woman, a devout Methodist. How she ever came to be associated with such a group as gathered in her house that summer would have been a mystery to anyone who did not know the power of Swami Vivekananda to attract and hold sincere souls. But having once seen and heard him, what could one do but follow?[47]

At Thousand Island Park between June 18 and August 6, 1895, for varying intervals of time twelve students were present at Swamiji's series of classes, now referred to as "Inspired Talks".[48] Mary Dutcher had to leave for days at a time. Swamiji explained, "It is a reaction of the body against the chaos that is going on in her mind. She cannot bear it." Vivekananda went to the sermon at the local Methodist Tabernacle on the Island. At the conclusion of the sermon, he placed several silver dollars into the collection plate, which was a sizable donation in those days. Mary Dutcher asked, "Why did you give so much?" He looked at her with surprise and replied, "The man said to give all we had with us. That is what I had."[49]

As a member of the Brooklyn Ethical Association, Miss Sarah Ellen Waldo (Haridasi, Sister Yatimata, 1845-1926), a relative of Ralph Waldo Emerson, heard Swamiji lecture near the end of 1894. After that she became a leading member of the Vedanta Society of New York, and received brahmacharya vows. She has left us with a wonderful account of her seven-week pilgrimage at Thousand Island Park along with Vivekananda and eleven other disciples:

> To those who were fortunate enough to be there with the Swami, those were weeks of ever-hallowed memory, so fraught were they with unusual opportunity for spiritual growth. No words can describe what that blissful period meant (and still means) to the devoted little band who followed the Swami from New York to the Island in the St. Lawrence, who daily served him with joy and listened to him with heartfelt thankfulness. His whole heart was in his work, and he taught like one inspired. Every morning he could hardly wait for the household duties to be attended to, so eager was he to begin his work of teaching. As early as it could be managed, we gathered around him, and for two and sometimes three hours he would steadily expound the teachings of his Master Shri Ramakrishna. These ideas were new and strange to us, and we were slow in assimilating them; but the Swami's patients never flagged, his enthusiasm never waned.... The Swami did not appear to address us directly, but rather seemed to be speaking to himself in words of fire, as it were, so intense were they, so eloquent and convincing, burning into the very hearts of his listeners never to be forgotten. We listened in utter silence, almost holding our breath for fear of disturbing the current of his thoughts, or losing one of those inspired words....[50]
>
> None of us can ever forget the sense of uplift, the intense spiritual life of those hallowed hours. The Swami poured out all his heart at those times, his own struggles were enacted again before us; the very spirit of his Master seemed to speak through his lips, to satisfy all doubts, to answer all questioning, to sooth every fear. Many times the Swami seemed hardly conscious of our presence, and then we almost held our breath for fear of disturbing him and checking the flow of his thoughts. He would rise from his seat and pace up and down the narrow limits of the piazza, pouring forth a perfect torrent of eloquence....

> It was a perpetual inspiration to live with a man like Swami Vivekananda. From morning till night it was ever the same, we lived in a constant atmosphere of intense spirituality. Often playful and fun-loving, full of merry jest and quick repartee.[51]

Sarah Ellen Waldo's, who in 1897 became Brahmacharini Yatimata, most outstanding contribution proved to be her wonderful accuracy in preserving the notes of Swamiji's forty-three classes delivered for seven weeks during the summer of 1895 at Thousand Island Park under the title "Inspired Talks".[52] Writing in longhand, she could transcribe only a portion of what Swamiji uttered. Marie Louise Burke denoted, "Aphoristic, often startling in their clarity, beauty, and depth, they seem like scripture itself. Indeed one can find on almost any page of *Inspired Talks* a wealth of Vedantic thoughts as concentrated and sharply focused as in an Upanishad. Swamiji was himself amazed at the faithfulness with which she captured his thoughts, and one day he expressed his delight." He asked her, "How could you have caught my thoughts and words so perfectly? It was as if I heard myself speaking."[53]

In the preface of the first edition of *Inspired Talks*, Sister Devamata informs us, "It was she [Sarah Waldo] also who prepared all his American publications for the press. And so great was Vivekananda's confidence in her ability, that he would pass the typewritten transcriptions of his lectures over to her with the instruction to do with them what she thought best." Quite likely she recorded in longhand most of the "Discourses on Jnana Yoga". While living in America, Saradananda made copies of the discourses from her notebook.[54]

Swamiji dictated portions of his translation of "Patanjali's Yoga Aphorisms" to Sarah Waldo, along with some of the profoundly thought-out ideas contained in his commentaries and his appendix to *Raja Yoga*, which she took down in longhand.[55] The work is also based on Goodwin's transcripts. She revealed:

> It was inspiring to see the Swami as he dictated to me the contents of the work. In delivering his commentaries on the Sutras, he would leave me waiting while he entered deep states of meditation or self-contemplation, to emerge therefrom with some luminous interpretation. I had always to keep the pen dipped in the ink. He might be absorbed for long periods of time, and then suddenly his silence would be broken by some eager expression or some long deliberate teaching.[56]

A book review of Swamiji's *Raja Yoga* was written by Sarah Waldo for the March 1897 edition of *The Arena* journal. After explaining what the book is all about, she added:

> The whole spirit of the book is candid in the extreme. It appeals to what is best and noblest in man. It makes no foolish mysteries, and demands no blind belief. It puts forth its system in a plain and simple manner. It is able to present its own method without in any way attacking the methods of others. It manifests a charity that it is usual to call "Christian", but which Vivekananda proves is equally the property of the Hindu. If this little book had nothing to teach but the beautiful toleration it advocates, it would be well worth reading; but many will find in it valuable suggestions to aid in reaching the higher life.

Along these lines, the following book review appeared in the Columbus, Georgia *The Sunday Herald* on October 24, 1897 (p. 7):

> Vedanta Philosophy: Lectures by the Swami Vivekananda on Raja Yoga and Other Subjects, is a volume that eminently deserves the attention that it is receiving. Vivekananda came from Bombay to the Columbian Exposition as the representative of the most ancient order of monks in the world. At the Parliament of Religions he was enthusiastically received, and in his little speeches he commended himself for his modest and his genial liberality. With a perfect mastery of English, and an apparent knowledge of all the difficulties that the system presents to the Western mind, it is explained in these lectures by one of its ablest exponents.

Sarah Waldo also edited *Karma Yoga* and the London lectures of Vivekananda that were put into book form.[57] In addition, the fragmentary notes on "The Worship of the Divine Mother" delivered in June 1900 are also attributed to her.[58] With Swamiji's encouragement after his departure for England, she gave classes in New York in 1896. Due to acute eye trouble, in 1901 she had to relinquish her position as the head of the New York Vedanta Society Publication Committee under Abhedananda.[59] After his departure she described Swamiji thusly:

> He was a man who would shine in any environment, by virtue of his splendid presence, his brilliant conversational powers, his magnetic elo-

quence and above all by his unworldly simplicity and purity of character.... Under his clear eyes, shams, and frauds were quickly unveiled, and for religious hypocrisy he had nothing but contempt. He demanded truth and sincerity before all else.... in nearly all quarters of the globe are to be found groups of men and women whose lives have been broadened and whose inspirations have been elevated through the ministrations of the noble soul whose departure from the tenement of flesh is a source of deep sorrow to the many who loved him. A great man has left the earth and all the world is the poorer in consequence. He lived a noble life and left behind him many mourning hearts [February 1903].[60]

His many Western friends saw him no more, but his memory will never die in our hearts and our gratitude for his loving service to us can never fail. It is a priceless privilege to have known such a man. He was truly a *mahatman* and did a great work, work that will long be an influence in the lives of his own countrymen as well as in those of his European and American friends. May he be forever blessed [January 1906]![61]

He travelled on foot all over India, walking barefooted thousands of miles, during many years, teaching and helping the people. In the snowy Himalayas, in the marshy plains of Bengal, amidst pestilence and famine, undergoing privation of every kind, he persevered in his loving ministry, bringing hope and comfort to thousands of disconsolate hearts...To know Vivekananda was to love him, and to know him well was to revere him.[62]

In 1923 Sarah Waldo was still listed on the cover of the *Prabuddha Bharata* as their American representative.

On January 29, 1895, thirty-six year old Josephine MacLeod (Tantine, 1858-1949) [q.v.] heard Swamiji speak for the first time. In her reminiscence she later wrote:

He said something, the particular words of which I do not remember, but instantly to me that was truth, and the second sentence he spoke was truth, and the third sentence was truth. And I listened to him for seven years and whatever he uttered was truth to me. From that moment life had a different import. It was as if he made you realize that you were in eternity.[63]

Josephine MacLeod had the rare distinction of attending Vivekananda's classes in New York City, Ridgely Manor, Camp Percy, New Hampshire, and Paris in 1895; London and Ridgely Manor in 1896; India in 1898; Ridgely

Manor and Los Angeles in 1899; and Los Angeles in 1900. She had the good fortune to meet Holy Mother and Gopaler Ma in India during the year 1898. Among Josephine MacLeod's many accomplishments during her long association with the Vedanta movement are: making monetary contributions to the Belur Math during the early years; buying a press to start the *Udbodhan*, the Bengali magazine published by the Ramakrishna Mission that is still in print; being the municipal commissioner for West Bengal and head of the anti-malaria board dealing with irrigation work; inspiring Nobel Prize winning author Romain Rolland to write biographies of Sri Ramakrishna and Swamiji (1927-28); encouraging Maud Stumm to write up her reminiscences of Vivekananda; motivating Jean Herbert to translate Swamiji's four yogas and *Inspired Talks* into the French language (1935); and aiding in the formation of the Paris Vedanta Society (1937). In addition, shortly before her death she wrote down her experiences of Swamiji, which were featured in the *Prabuddha Bharata* of December 1949, and in the volume *Reminiscences of Swami Vivekananda*. Ten articles attributed to her appeared posthumously in the *Vedanta Kesari* (1972-75). Pravrajika Prabuddhaprana in 1990 and Linda Prugh in 1999 wrote two full-length books about her lifelong adventures.[64]

Concerning her experiences in India, Tantine revealed:

> I found myself laughing to think that a man called Ramakrishna, whom I had never seen, should be the magnet that has brought me to India, where I loved being! Why? Sometimes Eternity seems to enfold one! There being no why or that, or anything else—just Isness!
>
> Being here [Belur Math] on this beloved Ganges is a constant joy. Odd people turn up, some interesting, some not. Days go past without my going to the Math, or hardly seeing any of them, but I know one long prayer and worship service goes on to Ramakrishna as if he were the most beloved of living gurus. Day and night thinking of him! His tastes, his likes, his predilections—absorbing all the love and devotion of these thirty or forty monks. It's the youth and enthusiasm of it all that amazes me. It never grows stale to them.[65]

She also informed the Indian Swami Abhayananda that after receiving a mantra from Vivekananda, she told him:

"Swamiji, I can't do this." And he said, "All right; don't worry." Then many years later when she was staying at the Belur Math, that mantra began to well up within her without any effort on her part. Every day she would meditate in the early morning and it would come automatically.[66]

In regards to Swami Vivekananda, Tantine told her friends:

The thing that held me in Swamiji was his unlimitedness. I never could touch the bottom—or top—or sides. The amazing size of him!... It is the Truth I saw in Swamiji that has set me free! It was to set me free that Swamiji came, that was as much a part of his mission as it was to give renunciation to Nivedita.[67]

... that prepared us for the recognition of this tremendous life force which he was. His power lay, perhaps, in the courage he gave others. He did not ever seem to be conscious of himself at all. It was the other man who interested him.... He used to make us realize there was nothing secular in life; it was all holy. "Always remember, you are incidentally an American, and a woman, but always a child of God. Tell yourself day and night who you are. Never forget it." That is what he used to tell us. His presence, you see, was dynamic.[68]

Vivekananda was everything to everyone. Each one could take what suited him best. From him I took mainly energy and manifested this most. Because this was what did me good and I know that it was best for me. But when I used to tell Sister Nivedita, "He is all energy," she used to answer, "He is all tenderness." I would argue, "But I never felt it." The answer was, "That was not meant for you." Because he could give to each according to his or her nature and according to the way that would lead him to the divine.[69]

One day in New York I heard him preaching in his deep, melodious voice. He was explaining how human beings can cleanse themselves of their passions and feel that they are all brothers and so be saved. He believed that all the religions worship the same God, except that there are different faces, according to the times and the peoples. That was his message, and I listened to him carefully, weighing his every word. And when he'd finished, I got up and said, "I agree. I'll go with him!"[70]

And Swamiji was such fun and such joy. He knew he was divine and because of that he could pass it on. If you have money you can give money.

If you have spirituality you can give that. You can only give what you yourself have earned.[71]

In Josephine MacLeod's obituary, the *Vedanta Kesari* wrote in part:

> Her great love for Swamiji cannot be described in words. She lived, moved and had her being in Swamiji, as it were, always talking—and that with unabating enthusiasm—of her Master. And how much vigour and strength were in those talks! Anyone who even casually listened to her words would catch through them a glimpse of the Fire that was Swami Vivekananda.[72]

Josephine MacLeod tried to persuade Nikos Kazantzakis (1883-1957) to translate some of Vivekananda's works into the Greek language. Kazantzakis is regarded as the most important writer in twentieth-century Greek literature. He received several nominations for a Nobel Prize in literature. Two of his novels became well-known motion pictures, *Zorba the Greek* and the highly controversial *The Last Temptation of Christ*. While in England during 1939, Kazantzakis described his good friend Josephine MacLeod this way:

> This marvellous woman was over eighty years old, finely made, slender, supple, with bright blue eyes, a powerful jawbone, a smile all severity and thoughtfulness. I had never seen such vitality, such an insatiable urge to see and hear, such a triumph of the human being in conquering time.

She often spoke to Kazantzakis about Vivekananda, and told him of a story that she had heard from Swamiji that had a decisive influence on her life:

> Once upon a time a bird catcher caught a number of doves and shut them up in a big net. The doves immediately began trying to squeeze through the holes and get free, but they were too big. So they submitted to their fate. Every day the bird catcher came and fed them. He threw them food in abundance so they would get fat quickly, and he could slaughter and sell them. All the doves ate with a great appetite, not realizing that the more they ate the fatter they got and the fatter they got the closer they came to death. Only one dove refrained from eating. It got thinner and thinner, and finally one day it was able to get out of the net and fly away.[73]

Mrs. John J. Bagley

Sara Bull

George W. Hale

Mrs. George (Belle) Hale

Josephine MacLeod

Sister Nivedita

Frank Rhodehamel

Edward T. Sturdy

William Butler Yeats

John Henry Barrows

Annie Besant

Anagarika Dharmapala

Charles Fillmore

Pere Hyacinthe

Bishop John Joseph Keane

Annie Rix Militz

Ralph Waldo Trine

Canon Basil Wilberforce

Halide Edib Adivar

George Cable

Edward Carpenter

Stanton Coit

Moncure Conway

Mary Mapes Dodge

Ralph Waldo Emerson

John Galsworthy

Sir William Wilson Hunter

Archer Huntington

Augustus Le Plongeon

Harriet Monroe

Franklin Sanborn

Ella Wheeler Wilcox

Paul Deussen

Elisha Gray

G. Stanley Hall

Hermann von Helmholtz

Off to England

An active member of the Theosophy Society in England named Edward T. Sturdy (1860-1957) came across Swami Shivananda in Almora, India, in 1893. Sturdy visited India to study and practise Indian Yoga and philosophy. Shivananda wrote to a friend about Mr. Sturdy:

> I am charmed by his manner, behaviour and steadfastness in the way of Yoga. They are all like those of a Hindu Sannyasin, and he is a good companion. He lives quite close to the ashrama where I am staying. Therefore, very often we have a discussion on religious topics.

Two years later, for six weeks during the months of September-October 1895, Swamiji stayed with him in Caversham, England, tutoring him in Sanskrit. Sturdy's 1896 commentary on the sixty-eight page *Narada Sutra an Inquiry into Love* begins with the acknowledgement, "To Swami Vivekananda this work, undertaken with his assistance, is affectionately dedicated by the author." Unfortunately, we do not know precisely what Swamiji contributed to this literary production. In the first edition of the commentary, Sturdy included an Appendix giving an account of Vivekananda entitled "An Indian Yogi in London" from *The Westminster Gazette* of 23 October 1895.[74] Concerning this well-received commentary, *India* (an English monthly) wrote in part, "No Christian could study 'Narada Sutra' without gaining a new sympathy, a new and strange sense of kinship, with those who through many generations have regarded these maxims as divine." He played a prominent role in Swamiji's life in England. While Vivekananda lived in New York, Sturdy published transcripts of the karma yoga and bhakti yoga classes in two books, plus a pamphlet on raja yoga, without consulting Swamiji. This brought the ire of the New York Society, to whom Vivekananda had given the rights of publication. Later Sturdy put out a book consisting of twelve of Vivekananda lectures given in London. In addition, Sturdy held his own weekly classes on Vedanta. He made a donation of five-hundred pounds to help establish a Math in Calcutta as a training ground for Vedanta teachers. Swamiji also spent eleven days in April 1896 and two weeks in August 1899 with him in England. In order to get the Indian work going, Swamiji left England at the end of 1896. Without the presence of the dynamic personality of Vivekananda, there was a major decline in attendance and a collapse of the London work. Sturdy was despondent and angry with Swamiji because he did not return to England in the summer of 1897. He wanted the Swami to tend to a small number of people in London rather than appear before large gatherings in India. Also, he did not think Vivekananda was ascetic enough and in a long letter of November 1899 from New York, the Swami answered his charges.[75]

Concerning Swamiji, Sturdy wrote to Miss MacLeod at the end of the nineteenth century, "I realized at once on meeting him that he was far above most of the men I had met in India in many directions and his contact with the West had furnished his mind with many new examples and illustrations and he had heart and head equally developed. I still look up to Swami as a very great man-teacher." In a 1937 *Vedanta Kesari* article, Sturdy gave his impression of Vivekananda:

> He had a magnetic personality, associated with great tranquility. Whether he was walking in the street or standing in a room, there was always the same dignity.
>
> He had a great sense of humour and as a natural correlative, much pathos and pity for affliction. He was a charming companion and entered with ease into any environment he found. And I found that all classes of educated persons that he was brought in contact with looked up to and admired the innate nobility that was in the man. One felt at all times that he was, to use a modern expression, "conscious of the presence of God". In walking, travelling, and leisure times, there constantly came from him some hardly formulated invocation or expression of devotion.
>
> As a teacher he had a great capacity for perceiving the difficulty of an inquirer, and would elucidate it with great simplicity and point to its solution. At the same time he could enter into great intricacies of thought.[76]

In the preface to his 1935 book *Tibetan Yoga and Secret Doctrines*, the famous Buddhist writer W. Y. Evans-Wentz mentions that his "good friend and helper, Mr. E. T. Sturdy", went over his book, particularly reviewing the Sanskrit terms and the exposition of Vedantic doctrines contained in the volume. Sturdy gave Madam Blavatsky's diagram of meditation to Christmas Humphreys in around 1940, and it appeared in a Buddhist magazine. Following an austere regimen, Sturdy lived to a ripe old age. In New Delhi in 1976, they republished the commentary on the *Narada Sutra* that Swamiji and Saradananda helped him with.

Margaret Noble (the future Sister Nivedita, 1867-1911) [q.v.] first heard Swamiji speak at the home of Lady Isabel Margesson in London in November of 1895 and described the event this way:

> A majestic personage, clad in saffron gown and wearing a red-waist band, sat there on the floor, cross-legged. As he spoke to the company he recited Sanskrit verses in his deep, sonorous voice. His serene face, his dignified bearing and his divine voice cast a spell upon the listeners, who felt electrified by his frequent utterances of the name of "Shiva, Shiva!"[77]

Thereafter she attended many of his public addresses in England during 1895-96 and 1899. Her good friend Eric Hammond later in 1927 recalled, "Everywhere she went she hailed him as the Prophet of the age.... she spoke of him and about him unceasingly.... There is no one like him, no one to equal him, no one at all!" In March of 1898 she received initiation into brahmacharya and received the name Nivedita, which means "the dedicated one". That year Nivedita travelled with Swamiji, Sara Bull and Josephine MacLeod in Northern India, and the following year she accompanied Vivekananda and Turiyananda on a ship during his return visit to the West. During September 1900, Nivedita visited the Swami in France,[78] and she later met with him in India.[79] Nivedita submitted about sixty articles to the *Prabuddha Bharata* and many more have been printed since her death.[80]

Concerning Swami Vivekananda, she stressed:

> He stands merely as the Revealer, the Interpreter to India of the treasures that she herself possesses in herself. The truths he preaches would have been as true, had he never been born. Nay more, they would have been equally authentic. The difference would have lain in their difficulty of access, in their want of modern clearness and incisiveness of statement, and in their loss of mutual coherence and unity. Had he not lived, texts that today will carry the bread of life to thousands might have remained the obscure disputes of scholars. He taught with authority, and not as one of the Pundits. For he himself had plunged to the depths of the realization which he preached, and he came back like Ramanuja only to tell its secrets to the pariah, the outcast, and the foreigner.[81]
>
> [In a letter to Josephine MacLeod] You see, when we who understood Swamiji and remembered him are dead, there will come a long period of obscurity and silence, for the work that he did. It will seem to be forgotten,

until, suddenly, in 150 or 200 years, it will be found to have transformed the West.[82]

The last statement echoes what Swamiji wrote to Alasinga in September 1894, "It will take a long time for the Westerners to understand the higher spirituality. Everything is £.s.d. to them. If a religion brings them money or health or beauty or long life, they will all flock to it, otherwise not."[83]

A number of biographies have described the many achievements of this outstanding spiritual personality, the Irish born Sister Nivedita, the daughter of a Congregationalist minister. Most important are the two volumes she composed that record the first-hand teachings of Vivekananda, which give us new insights into his nature and interests. While working on the volume *The Master as I Saw Him*, she wrote to Josephine MacLeod, "I am trusting, trusting that He will guide my hand line by line, that I might write down more aspects of Him that are eternal, and be able to discard remorselessly all the rest." The *Complete Works* (IX:333-96) contains excerpts from her *Notes of Some of the Wanderings with the Swami Vivekananda*. In addition, she was a great admirer of Holy Mother and some of her intimate disciples with the blessings of Holy Mother, who performed the opening ceremon on the auspicious day of the Kali Puja in November 1898, she founded and managed the Nivedita Girls' School in Calcutta that extended educatio to Indians; she selflessly helped to combat a 1899 plague in Calcutta b cleaning the streets and nursing the victims; as a patriot she gave active sup port to the Indian nationalist movement in numerous ways, such as goin on a lecture tour throughout India to rouse the national consciousness o the people during 1902-04; she established friendship with Rabindranat Tagore, whom she spoke to about Swami Vivekananda, Mahatma Gandh Sri Aurobindo, Bal Gangadhar Tilak and others; and through her powerf pen she authored a number of books that are widely read even today. At th end, Nivedita chanted from the Upanishads, "Lead us from the unreal to th Real. Lead us from darkness to Light. Lead us from death to Immortality and breathed her last.[84]

The daughter of the famous American poet Henry Wadsworth Longf low (1807-82), Miss Alice Mary Longfellow (1850-1928) sent letters Nivedita, whom she met in 1899 at the Free Religious Association meetin in Boston. When Nivedita passed away, she contributed a eulogy to t *Boston Evening Transcript* of June 29, 1911 praising her. She stated in pa "Her bright, intelligent face, her earnest manner and attractive personali enhanced by the simple white habit of her order, made a strong impression on the audience." In a 1911 letter to Josephine MacLeod, Longfellow indicated, "I love to think of Margot's [Nivedita's] alert, alive face, and the way she grappled with conversation. It made all of the rest of us seem only half alive—and now she must be more alive than then." Alice Longfellow probably attended the talks of Swamiji at the Cambridge Conferences in October 1894. They were held at Sara Bull's residence, near the Craigie House where Alice Longfellow lived her entire life. Sara and her husband were friends of Henry Longfellow, and Alice's younger sister married Sara Bull's brother Joseph. Alice was one of the founders of Radcliffe College, where on May 8, 1894 Vivekananda spoke on "Hinduism". At the College, she held the position of manager, treasurer and a member of the Executive Committee. She also came to at least one of Abhedananda's 1898 addresses, and again to his discourse sponsored by the Channing Club of Boston in 1900.[85]

Josiah John Goodwin (1870-98), a handsome young Englishman, quickly answered a newspaper advertisement of December 12, 1895 for "A rapid short-hand writer to take down lectures for several hours a week" to be employed by the Vedanta Society in New York. The position required intellectual and spiritual understanding in order to write down the profound ideas that Vivekananda presented to his audiences. Working as a stenographer, Goodwin no doubt recorded a large share of Vivekananda's lectures and classes given between December 13, 1895 and December 6, 1896. A best estimate is that these lectures and classes fill over one-thousand pages, comprising about 75% of the first two volumes of the *Complete Works*,[86] with additional newspaper accounts given in the ninth volume for this time period,[87] but with one qualification, that the portions of Swamiji's *Raja Yoga* were taken down in longhand by Sarah Waldo. This was Vivekananda's most productive period as a public speaker in the West. At that time talks on *Karma Yoga*, *Raja Yoga*,[88] *Jnana Yoga*, *Practical Vedanta*,[89] *Para-Bhakti or Supreme Devotion*,[90] and *Addresses on Bhakti Yoga*[91] were given and recorded, along with a number of Swamiji's finest lectures. Only two months later Goodwin received brahmacharya vows from Swamiji.[92]

Sarah Waldo, in her reminiscences of 1906, paid this tribute to Goodwin:

> We were fortunate enough to secure the services of a good stenographer, who, to unusual abilities, later added the service of a devoted adherent. He became strongly attached to the Swami and his teachings and never

spared himself in his work for the cause. He subsequently accompanied the Swami to England and to India, and it is entirely due to his efforts that the Swami's utterances in those countries have been preserved. The fruits of his labours in New York are known to us in the books, *Raja-Yoga*, *Bhakti-Yoga*, *Karma-Yoga*, besides several pamphlets of the Sunday lectures.[93]

Goodwin earlier worked as an editor on three newspapers and as a court reporter. Swamiji wrote earlier in the year to E. T. Sturdy, "I have intense faith in Truth. The Lord will send help and hands to work with me."[94] Goodwin proved to be well qualified in faithfully taking down in excellent shorthand Swami's class talks and lectures, and then transcribing them. In addition, he aided in Swamiji's business dealings and personal affairs. "The Swami told him many incidents of his past, and this created such a moral revolution in him that his whole life was changed." Later he told Saradananda:

> Being poor from childhood, I have gone many places trying to make a living. I have hobnobbed with all kinds of people; they gave me work and a salary, but no one gave me his heart's love. Then in America I met Swami Vivekananda; then alone could I understand what love was. So, income or no income, I am caught! Never have I found such a noble being as Swami Vivekananda. One is drawn to him as if to one's very own.[95]

Goodwin was Swamiji's companion in New York, Detroit, Boston, London and Greenacre, Maine. Two months before going to India he wrote in a letter to Josephine MacLeod, "Shall I shock you very much if I tell you that the Swami takes the place of Christ to me? I think not, for you will understand what I mean." Swamiji, and Captain and Charlotte Sevier, set sail for India in December 1896. In India, Goodwin aided the *Brahmavadin* journal and the Madras Math, which had then come into being (in April 1897) under the supervision of Swami Ramakrishnananda, and made written records of Swamiji's lectures. He suddenly passed away in 1898 after attending a cricket match in the pouring rain.[96]

After hearing of his passing, Sara Bull wrote the following letter to Alasinga, which he published in the *Brahmavadin* of June 16, 1898:

> I have never received a sadder message than the words from you announcing the death of dear Goodwin. It causes all of us who know him a

> great sorrow.... Such a life calls for reverent recognition, so utterly generous, silent and untiring has he been in the service of his beloved guru Swami Vivekananda and others... His entire devotion to the Swami as his servant and friend was the fruit of his new hope and belief and the Swami's published lectures as recorded by Mr. Goodwin are his permanent contribution to us. This young man embodied the integrity and honour of the gentleman to enemy and friend alike, in brief, he was a true Englishman with the spirit of sympathy, responsive to the noble and divine wherever he found it, at home or abroad.[97]

Swami Vivekananda sent the following tribute to Goodwin's mother, which appeared in the *Prabuddha Bharata* of August 1898:

> The debt of gratitude I owe him can never be repaid, and those who think they have been helped by any thought of mine ought to know that almost every word of it was published through the untiring and most unselfish exertions of Mr. Goodwin. In him I have lost a friend true as steel, a disciple of never-failing devotion, a worker who knew not what tiring was, and the world is less rich by one of those few who are born, as it were, to live only for others.[98]

That same month the Swami composed a poem in memoriam to J. J. Goodwin.[99]

A young unmarried draftsman and printer from Holland named Henry Van Haagen became a brahmachari along with J. J. Goodwin and Sarah Waldo in February 1896. The following year Van Haggen undertook the publishing work for a book of over three-hundred pages on Swamiji's Raja yoga lectures, along with his commentaries on Patanjali's yoga. After Abhedananda came to America, Van Haagen was at times his companion and guide for the next few years. Miss Anna Josephine Ingersoll's article on "The Swamis in America" in *The Arena* journal of 1899 includes pictures of Swamis Vivekananda, Abhedananda and Saradananda, copyrighted by H. J. Van Haagen.[100]

Sister Devamata in "Memories of India and Indians" related an interesting story, which occurred after Swamiji returned to the New York Centre in the summer of 1900:

> Mrs. Crane, the housekeeper [at the Vedanta Society], told me that Swami was sitting at the breakfast table one morning when the printer arrived. He said he was making a circular for the Society and wished to have an emblem to go on it; could the Swami suggest something? Swamiji took the envelope from a letter he had just received, tore it open and on the clean inner surface drew the waves, the swan, the lotus, and the sun circled by a serpent.... He threw the bit of paper with the design on it across the table and said, "Draw it to scale." Henry van Haagen, the printer, was an able draftsman as well as printer. He converted the rough sketch into a finished drawing.[101]

Eleven years later Van Haagen described a wonderful characteristic of Vivekananda:

> The strong impression which this lovable teacher always gave to his students was that of causing them to feel that they alone, while with him, had his whole attention and sympathy. Always willing to devote his entire attention to heeding his students' most humble wants and queries, he, by this most pleasing attitude, made them most enthusiastic and faithful disciples. This created that enduring bond of love between teacher and disciple which is so necessary for any teacher's real success. And how glorious was his success![102]

During Vivekananda's second visit to London in May of 1896, he had his first meeting with Captain James Henry Sevier (c. 1846-1900) and his wife Charlotte Sevier (1846/47-1930). Sevier, a retired army officer, had served in India for five years. Within a period of only two months they were Swamiji's host in France, the Swiss Alps, Germany and Holland, and on a later occasion in Italy.[103] As his disciples, the Seviers always desired to be of service to Vivekananda, and to take him wherever he wanted to go. Charlotte Sevier later wrote, "Every phase of human activity, and every department of knowledge had interest for Swamiji, and his mental attitude of cheerfulness and kindness, combined with his fine intelligence and personal charm, made him the most delightful of travelling companions." After the Seviers moved to India, the death of the editor of *Prabuddha Bharata* in May 1898 in Madras brought the journal's publication to an unanticipated halt. Vivekananda asked Captain Sevier to take up the management of the journal. Sevier agreed and offered to meet the initial costs associated with reviving it, which included purchasing and bringing up a hand-press, types, paper, ink and other supplies required for the purpose from Calcutta. The *Prabuddha Bharata* resumed publication in August 1898 from Almora with Swami Swarupananda (1871-1906), one of Vivekananda's monastic disciples, as the new editor, and Captain Sevier as the manager and publisher. At first, they published the journal from Sevier's rented house in Almora. The following year the Seviers bought the land at Mayavati in the Himalayas 7,000 feet above sea level, where the Advaita Ashrama was to be located, and they transferred the *Prabuddha Bharata* to that location.[104]

Swamiji wrote the following, "Mrs. Sevier is a jewel of a lady—so good, so kind!" "In England Capt. and Mrs. Sevier, who have clad me when I was cold, nursed me better than my own mother would have, borne with me in my weakness, my trials; and they have nothing but blessings for me. And that Mrs. Sevier, because she did not care for honours, has the worship of thousands today; and when she is dead, millions will remember her as one of the great benefactresses of the poor Indians." "Cap. Sevier gave me 8,000 Rs. with the express desire of helping my mother." In addition, Charlotte Sevier gave Swamiji 6,000 rupees for the use of his family. At Mayavati, Captain Sevier "led a very austere life. He used to wear simple clothes, and work very hard for the Ashrama. He practises austerity and poverty on principle; so much so that the people were astonished." In the winter of 1900 the Swami wrote, "Poor Captain Sevier passed away, a few days ago—thus two great Englishmen gave up their lives for us—us the Hindus. This is martyrdom if anything is."[105] After the passing of her husband, for many years Charlotte Sevier functioned as an assistant editor for the *Prabuddha Bharata*, and also worked on some of Swamiji's lectures. She helped to start a charitable dispensary for the ashrama servants and local hill people. Swami Atulananda wrote in a letter, "It was Mrs. Charlotte Sevier who established Mayavati. Through her efforts we now have the Complete Works of Sw. Vivekananda, and it was she who paid Frank Alexander to write the Life of Sw. Vivekananda. She worked hard in India" and then she returned to England in 1916.[106]

In the December 1899 issue of the *Brahmavadin* (pp. 126-27), the Seviers and Swami Swarupananda, the first president of the Ashrama, outlined the main principle behind the Advaita Ashrama in the Himalayas at Mayavati near Almora. They stated in part:

> Wherever there has been expansion in love or progress in well-being, of individuals or numbers, it has been through the perception, realisation and the practicalisation of the Eternal Truth,—THE ONENESS OF ALL BEINGS.... To give this ONE TRUTH a freer and fuller scope in elevating the lives of individuals and leavening the mass of mankind, we found the Advaita Ashrama on the Himalayan heights, the land of its first expiration, with the fullest approval and under the guidance of the Swami Vivekananda. Here it is hoped to keep the Advaita free from all superstitions and weakening contaminations. Here will be taught and practised nothing but the Doctrine of Unity, pure and simple, and though with entire sympathy with all other systems, this Ashrama is dedicated to Advaita and Advaita alone.

Miss Emmeline Souter was a member of Reverend Hugh Haweis' Anglican congregation, who often attended Vivekananda's London lectures during May-July 1896. On October 22 she hosted a luncheon at her home with Vivekananda and Abhedananda, and Haweis and Bishop Thornton of Ballarat in attendance. She repeatedly invited the two Swamis to her house in Marylebone, where they had the opportunity to meet many of London's most prominent citizens. In December she had Alfred Ellis, a president of the Professional Photographers' Association, take a dozen photographs of Vivekananda. Ellis had a studio at 20 Upper Baker Street in London during 1884-98, specializing in theatrical photography of many famous actors. They met again in August 1899, when Swamiji arrived in England during the commencement of his second voyage to the West. She had great admiration for the Swami and proved her loyalty to him. In a letter of September 14, 1899, Swamiji mentions that she contributed Rs. 15,000 (equivalent to $1,000 Pounds) to help buy the land at Belur for his Indian monastery.[107]

Second Voyage to the West

Josephine MacLeod resided at Ridgely Manor with Vivekananda during the autumn of 1899. On October 9, 1899 she received a letter from an unknown lady named Mrs. S. K. (Roxie) Blodgett (1832-1915). The letter made it clear that Taylor MacLeod (1849-99), the elder brother of Josephine and her sister Betty Leggett, was lying seriously ill with tuberculosis in the house of Mrs. Blodgett in Los Angeles. Taylor owned a silver mine and the "Free Gold" mines in Yuma County, Arizona. He became ill with tuberculosis and then moved to the rented house of Roxie Blodgett, whose deceased husband

S. K. Blodgett had been his business partner. When Josephine MacLeod left the Manor, Vivekananda blessed her, and as she got into the carriage, called out, "Get up some classes and I will come." Josephine journeyed to Los Angeles and found her dying brother lying in bed. Much to her surprise, above the bed hung a large coloured poster of Vivekananda dressed in a robe and turban. On November 3 Josephine wrote to Sara Bull, "My brother died peacefully ... plucky and witty to the end." Roxie Blodgett told Josephine that in 1893 she heard the Swami, whom she greatly admired, speak many times at the Parliament of Religions in Chicago.[108] Roxie added:

> When that young man got up and said, "Sisters and Brothers of America", seven thousand people rose to their feet as a tribute to something they knew not what; and when it was over and I saw scores of women walking over the benches to get near him, I said to myself, "Well, my lad, if you can resist that onslaught, you are indeed a god."

In reply, Josephine told her that she had just left Vivekananda in New York State, and that if Roxie sent him an invitation, he would come to her house. Concerning a trip to California, Swamiji wrote to Sister Christine on November 21, 1899, "It is for my physical benefit too; as the doctor says, I had better be off where the severe winter of the North cannot reach."[109]

Seven weeks later Swamiji made the journey from the cold weather conditions of New York State to the mild climate of Los Angeles. On December 3rd he became the house-guest first of Miss Mary E. Spencer (1843-1920), and then, from December 8/10 to January 3, 1900, of the elderly widowed Roxie Blodgett. He gave informal talks at Mrs. Blodgett's rented three-bedroom white cottage, which was covered with roses and unfortunately no longer exists.[110] In a letter dated September 2, 1902 to Josephine MacLeod, Roxie Blodgett recalled:

> I am ever recalling those swift, bright days in that never to be forgotten winter, lived in simple freedom and kindness. We could not choose but to be happy and good.... I knew him personally but a short time, yet in that time I could but see in a hundred ways the child side of Swamiji's character which was a constant appeal to the Mother quality in all good women. He depended on those near him in a way which brought him very near one's heart. Possessing as he did an almost inexhaustible knowledge of things old as the world, a sage and philosopher, he yet appeared to me

> utterly to lack the commercial knowledge which so distinguish men of the Western world.... Ah, those pleasant "tea party" days, as you used to call them. How we used to laugh.[111]

Years later, Charlotte Sevier wrote to Josephine MacLeod, "I remember perfectly the delight of Swamiji during his stay with (good old) Mrs. Blodgett, he often spoke of it." Roxie Blodgett continued to correspond with her friend Josephine, and in 1915, the year of her death (on December 16), she informed her about Swami Abhedananda's visit to Los Angeles.[112]

During his two-and-a-half month stay in Southern California, the Swami spoke at Blanchard Hall with a capacity of about eight-hundred,[113] the Unity Church that could hold over a thousand people,[114] the Los Angeles Home of Truth,[115] Payne's Hall,[116] the Shakespeare Club,[117] the Universalist Church,[118] and at an unspecified location.[119]

On December 8, 1899, Alice Mead Hansbrough (later Shanti, 1864-1955) [q.v.] and her two sisters Carrie Mead Wyckoff (later Sister Lalita, 1859-1949) and Miss Helen Mead (1866-1907), a secretary in a Los Angeles insurance firm, first heard Swamiji speak at Blanchard Hall in Los Angeles.[120] Already Hansbrough had thoroughly read the Swami's books *Raja Yoga* and *Karma Yoga*. For the rest of their lives the three sisters were to remain his enthusiastic supporters. Mrs. Hansbrough later added:

> He was a most impressive personality. You know, you have told me that it is not possible to get an impression of a personality from the individual's writings; but that I had sensed Swamiji's personality from his books, and the impression was verified when I heard him speak. His voice I should say was baritone—certainly nearer to bass than tenor; and it was the most musical voice I have ever heard.... Once later on he apologized for quoting in Sanskrit, and explained that he still thought in that language and then had to translate his thoughts into English.... I can only describe myself as enchanted by him. As I mentioned, this was my feeling from his books before I ever saw him, and the feeling has stayed with me throughout my life.[121]

The three Mead sisters visited Vivekananda on December the 13th, and subsequently arranged to have three classes for him held in Blanchard Hall during December 19-22. Probably on Christmas Eve, he and Josephine MacLeod took an electric train ride of about one hour and arrived for Sunday dinner at the Mead residence. One morning a month later on January the

25th Swamiji drove up in a horse carriage to their residence and announced, "I have come to stay with you." For four weeks (January 25-February 20/21) during the winter of 1900, Vivekananda stayed with the Mead family in their rented house in South Pasadena. The atmosphere of their home provided a sattvic environment that was most beneficial for him.[122] During his stay Sister Lalita received a spiritual transmission from Swamiji. Sister Sudhira (Helen Hall), a well-respected devotee who lived at the Vedanta Society in Hollywood, heard the following from her intimate friend Sister Lalita:

> At the house in Pasadena, the bedrooms were on the second floor. Steep, narrow steps connected the first and second floors. One morning they were all coming down to breakfast, and Sister [Lalita] was right behind Swamiji. Suddenly, she got a little unsteady on those steep stairs, and she reached out in front of her using Swamiji's shoulder to brace herself. According to Sister, the whole world just went away. She was in another place, in another consciousness, and she never remembered getting down the rest of the steps. But somehow he got her into the dining room and seated her, and then he took over. And he was so charming, and so entertaining, and so much fun that nobody noticed that Sister was all blanked out; that she was in another place. Just touching his shoulder had taken her there. From that moment on, Swamiji was God to Sister.[123]

Sister Lalita proclaimed it is "as if Christ himself were in their midst". Years later the devotees asked her, how it was to live with Swamiji? Her reply was, "You know, he was just like a brother. He raised our consciousness up, so we didn't feel while we were with him anything but love and joy. And he was so much fun!"[124]

Swamiji enjoyed his restful stay with the Mead family. In a February 15 letter from Los Angeles to Mrs. Bull he wrote, "My heart is growing stronger every day, physically and mentally. Some days I feel I can bear anything and suffer everything."[125] On the same day he corresponded with Nivedita stating, "I am strong now, Margo, stronger than ever I was mentally. I was mentally getting a sort of ironing over my heart. I am getting nearer a Sannyasin's life now."[126]

When Swamiji lived in the house in South Pasadena, Ralph Wyckoff (1882-1925), the seventeen-year-old son of Carrie Wyckoff, was one of the boarders along with Dorothy Hansbrough, the four-year-old daughter of

Alice Hansbrough. Concerning Swami Vivekananda, Mrs. Hansbrough later recalled:

> It must have been one morning in our home in [South Pasadena] that Swamiji gave what I call a "baptism" to Dorothy and Ralph. I remember that he laid his pipe aside and called Dorothy to him, and he only smoked after breakfast and dinner. Dorothy was four years old at the time. She went and stood between his knees with her hands on his thighs. Swamiji put his hands at the back of her head where the hairline joins the neck, and tapped up over the top of her head to the eyebrows. Then he called Ralph and did the same thing. Ralph must have knelt, because I remember that Swamiji did not leave his seat. My two sisters may have been there too; I am not sure.[127]

In her reminiscences, Alice Hansbrough tells us:

> Sometime before he [Swami Vivekananda] left for San Francisco, he said one day, "I always leave something wherever I go. I am going to leave this pipe when I go to San Francisco." He left it on the mantelpiece in the living room, and we kept it there for a long time as an ornament. Then one day Mrs. Carrie Wyckoff saw it. For some time she had been suffering a good deal from some nervous ailment. For some days the pain of her illness had been almost unbearable, and this, added to her other troubles, made her feel extremely depressed. She went to the mantelpiece and picked up Swamiji's pipe. No sooner did she have it in her hands than she heard Swamiji's voice, saying, "Is it so hard Madam?" For some reason she rubbed the pipe across her forehead, and instantly the suffering left her and a feeling of well-being came over her. After that we felt the pipe should belong to her; and she still has it today.[128]

When Swamiji travelled to Northern California, for a few months Hansbrough became his personal attendant, secretary, and housekeeper. In a letter, Swamiji wrote in March, "Lord bless their hearts. The three sisters are angels—are not they? Seeing such souls here and there repays for all the nonsense of this life."[129] Near the end of June 1900, Swamiji sent a letter to Hansbrough informing her of the recent events. He added, "After all you three sisters have become part of my mind forever."[130]

Swamis Turiyananda, Abhedananda, and Trigunatita also were guests at the Mead sisters' home in South Pasadena between 1900 and 1903. The interactions of Mrs. Hansbrough and Mrs. Wyckoff with these three Swamis from 1900 to 1921 are briefly mentioned in Chapters XV, XIX and XX.

Alice Hansbrough (Sister Shanti) and Carrie Wyckoff (Sister Lalita) were in attendance at Swami Prabhavananda's three Los Angeles lectures of 1928, held in the Blanchard Building where they had first heard Vivekananda speak in 1899. As a result, both sisters soon moved to Portland, Oregon, to be near the Swami. Sister Lalita offered her house in Hollywood as the home of the new Vedanta Society of Los Angeles, and was with Swami Prabhavananda for two decades (1929-49). Shanti and her daughter Dorothy lived in the house next door to the Vivekananda Home at the Vedanta Society of Southern California in Hollywood for two years during 1932-33. When Lalita travelled to India with the Swami in August 1935, Percy Houston "read the following address on behalf of the members of the Society":

> She has become for us the symbol of what Vedanta may do for Western women. Under its benign influence her life has been a fitting ideal towards which other women may strive, and in her egolessness, her humility, her sweet simplicity, and her love, she has been a shining example for all.

In 1938 Lalita made a contribution of eight-thousand dollars (equivalent to 121 thousand in 2008) to build the Vedanta Temple that now stands in Hollywood.[131]

While living in San Francisco, in 1941 Swami Ashokananda asked Shanti to tell of her reminiscences of the Vivekananda period. He informally interviewed Shanti, resulting in her priceless "Reminiscences". They were recorded by Alfred T. Clifton (later Swami Chidrupananda) who was present for the interviews. Marie Louise Burke cites Alice Hansbrough's "Reminiscences" nearly fifty times in writing up the California chapters of Swami Vivekananda in the West. From these "Reminiscences", we learn a great deal about Swamiji's activities while he resided in Southern California. Fortunately, the "Reminiscences" were published in their entirety in six issues of the *Prabuddha Bharata* during February-July 2007 covering thirty-five pages. We learn of things previously unknown such as, in San Francisco "he often went to Chinatown. For some reason, incidentally, he had a fascination for the Chinese. They would just flock after him, 'Shaking themselves by the hand' as the saying went, to express their pleasure at his presence."[132]

There was a fourth Mead sister who was the eldest named Mrs. Ida Herman (b. 1857). In 1900 she was married, living with her husband in the Los Angeles area and not with her three sisters in South Pasadena. Little is known of her, but she was a personal friend of Swami Prabhavananda. One day she handed the Swami a notebook that contained an unpublished lecture delivered by Vivekananda at the Shakespeare Club in Pasadena, California, on January 27, 1900. The speech "My Life and Mission" appeared in a 1944 edition of *Vedanta and the West*, and now occupies nineteen pages in the *Complete Works of Swami Vivekananda*.[133]

William Mead (1862-1927), the wealthy brother of the four sisters, owned a large real estate business in Los Angeles. He also served as a member of the California State Legislature and the Board of Water Commissioners, president of Los Angeles' first City Planning Commission and of the Municipal Housing Commission, and director of the Chamber of Commerce for six years. Mr. Mead was always very generous toward his sisters, and the Vedanta Society in Hollywood now stands on the land that he purchased in 1901.[134]

In the year 1900 when Swamiji made his journey to Northern California for a little over three months, he came across a number of outstanding devotees. Under the guidance of Swamis Turiyananda and Trigunatita, many of them were to remain active Vedantists throughout their lifetime. Most promising were Christina Albers, Thomas and Edith Allan, Ida Ansell, Ernest Brown, Sarah and Rebecca Fox, Cara French, Louis Juhl, Milburn Logan, Carl and Bertha Petersen, Frank and Agnes Rhodehamel, George and Eloise Roorbach, and Albert and Claudina Wollberg. In Northern California, Sarah Fox (1862-1948) and her sister Rebecca belonged to a small religious group in Oakland headed by Paul Militz. As their leader, he spoke highly of Vivekananda who was soon coming to the city. Being "bound and determined to hear him", they attended his first oral presentation at the Unitarian Church in Oakland. In her "Memoirs" Sarah related that Swamiji

> walked down the aisle nearest the wall to the front of the church in long, slow, measured steps. This wonderful man, clad in an ochre robe, and wearing a turban, looked as if he feared nothing and cared for nothing. He seemed like an immense wave going along; his back was straight as a rod, yet his entire bearing was a perfect blending of dignity and grace. He reached the pulpit and stood there for a long time just looking out over the

congregation. Then after what seemed like an hour, he said, "Ladies and gentlemen ..." We were seated too far away to see his face closely, but how we enjoyed his discourse! He did not seem old, as indeed he was not, but tremendously wise and experienced.

At the age of sixty Miss Sarah Fox (Premika) and her sister Miss Rebecca Fox (Radhika) visited India in 1922. They remained in India for three years teaching at the Nivedita School, until they were overcome by health problems and left in January 1926. They received spiritual initiation from Swami Saradananda in Varanasi in 1923. After she returned to the U.S., the Indian Swamis at the San Francisco Vedanta Centre considered Sarah to be far along the spiritual path. She served as the president of the Vedanta Society in Berkeley from 1939 until her passing away.[135]

A youthful married man from Oakland, Franklin (Frank) Sprague Rhodehamel [q.v.] recorded notes of some of Swamiji's lectures in Oakland, San Francisco, and Alameda, California. They later found his notebook in the archives of the Vedanta Society of Northern California. At the time the discovery was made, without personal identification his notes were part of the *Complete Works* in volume six. Rhodehamel's notes are incomplete and sometimes not verbatim. Nevertheless, Marie Louise Burke points out that these notes are "clear and in places supply a word or phrase that Miss Ida Ansell missed or could not make out". It is not easy to determine exactly what Frank Rhodehamel contributed to the *Complete Works*. For one thing, he sometimes altered the name of a lecture. Reading volumes five and six of Burke's biography of Swamiji, he appears (though it is not entirely clear) to have taken partial notes on fifteen of Swamiji's lectures plus two short excerpts, totalling thirty-six (not full) pages in the *Complete Works*, plus adding a part of a page in the "Sayings and Utterances" section.[136] He later took initiation from Swami Turiyananda. A number of years after Swamiji's passing away, Frank and his wife Agnes were part of an informal study and discussion group under the leadership of Gurudasa (the future Swami Atulananda).[137] Frank left us with an account in the *Prabuddha Bharata* regarding Swami Turiyananda who, for seven weeks, spoke twice weekly at his home in Oakland, and of his experience at Shanti Ashrama.[138]

In his reminiscences, Frank Rhodehamel wrote this about Swamiji's lectures:

> There were a few who would have resisted if they could, but whose power of resistance were neutralized by the irresistible logic, acumen, and childlike simplicity of the Great Teacher. Indeed, there were a few who arose to demur, but who resumed their seats either in smiling acquiescence or in bewildered impotency.
>
> The Swami's personality impressed itself on the mind with visual intensity. The speaking eyes, the wealth of facial expression, and gesticulation; the wondrous Sanskrit chanting, sonorous, melodious, impressing one with the sense of mystic potency; the translations following in smiling confidence—all these, set off by the spectacular apparel of the Hindu sannyasin—who can forget them?...
>
> "Ask all the questions you like—the more the better," was the Swami's good-natured reply. "That is what I am here for, and I won't leave you till you understand."[139]

When Swami Vivekananda came to San Francisco, twenty-two year old Ida Ansell (Ujjvala, 1877-1955) made his acquaintance at a ship launching ceremony, a dinner at the Home of Truth, at Camp Taylor where the devotees lived in tents for two-weeks, and she attended many of his speaking engagements. As a member of a small band of students, she lived at the Shanti Ashrama with Turiyananda, and from him received the Sanskrit name of Ujjvala (the shining one).[140]

Concerning Swamiji's oral presentations, her observations were:

> He was phenomenally prolific. How he could speak so often and yet always with such originality is something no one has ever been able to explain. He himself confessed that time after time on his lecture tours he felt exhausted intellectually and incapable of appearing the next day. Then, as his authorized *Life* explains, he would be aided in various ways: "For instance, at dead of night he would hear a voice shouting at him the very thoughts he was to speak on the morrow.... Or again it would be like someone delivering a lecture alongside of him, as he lay on his bed listening. At other times two voices would argue before him, discussing at great length subjects that he would find himself repeating on the following day upon the platform or in the pulpit. Sometimes these discussions involved ideas that he had never heard or thought of previously... To his disciples he would explain that these incidents betrayed the powers and potentialities of the Self."

Swamiji's lectures attracted all levels of people, drawn by various incentives such as curiosity, interest, a desire for information, and a real yearning for truth. There was something in every one of Swamiji's discourses for each.[141]

> All the superlatives in the language couldn't convey one's impression of Swami Vivekananda when he introduced us, early in 1900, to a completely new conception of life and religion.... He was surely a Mahatma or a divine being, more than human. No one had ever been so sublimely eloquent or so deliciously humorous, such an enchanting storyteller, or such a perfect mimic.[142]

During the 1930s, Ujjvala lived in Los Angeles and often came to the Vedanta Society. In 1949, at the insistence of Swami Prabhavananda, she became a permanent resident of the Vedanta Society in Hollywood. Swami Yogeshananda, now in Atlanta, Georgia, who knew her, mentions, "Ujjvala was almost sacred to some of us as a last link with the age of Swamiji.... Lively, game, alert, intelligent and sometimes pathetic, Ujjvala added much to the life of the Centre."[143]

Ujjvala made shorthand transcriptions of Swamiji's lectures, with no thought of their ever being published. She revealed:

> [I] was long hesitant about transcribing and releasing these lectures because of the imperfections of my notes.... Since his death in 1902, Swami Vivekananda has become an international figure. The religious ideas he taught are being considered and accepted by people all over the world. Now we see that Swamiji was a special messenger of God and that every word he said was full of significance. So even though my notes were somewhat fragmentary, I have yielded to the opinion that their contents are precious and must be given for publication.[144]

Ujjvala contributed transcripts of twenty lectures delivered by Swamiji in Northern California, totalling an amazing 220 pages in the *Complete Works*.[145] Four of her transcriptions in Volume VIII of the *Complete Works* previously appeared in the *Voice of India* (1946) and were edited by Swami Ashokananda. The remaining sixteen transcriptions came out in *Vedanta and the West* (1955-59). Ujjvala made no alterations or additions to her shorthand transcriptions. Omissions in the text due to missing phrases are indicated in the *Complete Works* by ellipses. Words added for the purpose of clarifications are placed in square brackets.[146]

Turiyananda's translation of Shankara's *Vivekachudamani* published in 1991 edited by Pravrajika Brahmaprana is drawn from a shorthand rendering taken by Ujjvala when she attended his classes in Northern California at the turn of the twentieth century. In addition, Ujjvala came out with published reminiscences of Swamis Vivekananda and Turiyananda. Her legacy also includes fifteen formerly unpublished letters from Swami Turiyananda to her and to Dhira (Mrs. Bertha Petersen) during the 1900-1919 period. In January 1955, after living at the Hollywood Vedanta Centre for over five years, Ujjvala passed away. Swami Vidyatmananda relates on January 31, 1955, "I was present during her final hours, and I know that Ujjvala was in contact with something or someone divine in her last moments.... Swami Prabhavananda had waited gravely in his room. When I brought him the news, he said, 'Her guru came for her.'" After her death they discovered in her personal belongings two-hundred and fifty letters sent to her from Swami Atulananda. Excerpts of the correspondences covering a period of over fifty years from 1901 to 1954 form a large part of *With the Swamis in America and India* (1988). The book editor Pravrajika Brahmaprana disclosed that, "His letters, which are full of reminiscences, reflections, and observations, provide us with an eye-witness account of this early period."[147]

After hearing Swamiji speak for the first time, Thomas Allan (1863/64-1953) relates:

> The impression he made on me was, "Here is a man who *knows* what he is talking about. He is not repeating what some other person told him. He is not relating what he thinks, he is telling what he knows." Going home from the lecture I was walking on air. When I got home I was still acting like a crazy man. When I was asked what sort of man he was, I replied, "He is not a man, he is a god." I can never forget the impression he produced on me.[148]

Many years after his wife Edith Allan (Viraja Devi) went to have her first interview with Swamiji, she recounted:

> I could not speak, but began to weep and kept on weeping as though the floodgates had been opened.... as I went from his presence, my problems were solved and my questions were answered, though he had not asked

me anything. It is now over twenty-four years since that interview with the Swami, yet it stands out in memory as the greatest blessing of my life. I had the wonderful privilege of seeing Swamiji every day for a month.[149]

Also, the Allans have left us with a few of Swamiji's statements.[150]

Another Northern California devotee Ernest C. Brown (Sajjana, 1871-1960/61) [q.v.] was a lifelong associate of the Vedanta Society in Northern California. A native of England, Brown came to San Francisco in his youth. He attended Vivekananda's lectures, and many years later became the president of the Vedanta Society in Northern California. Brown, a monastic under Swami Trigunatita, later came out with a series of articles in the *Prabuddha Bharata* about his experiences with the Swamis. Past the age of eighty, he made a trip to India, where he passed away after two or three years. He describes Swamiji's arrival at a lecture in Northern California this way:

> His walk was that of a god, a man accustomed to ruling. When he sat down the audience burst into tumultuous applause. But he sat there unmoved, his face reflecting the perfect calm within. Then he rose and just held up his hands with palms facing the audience, and at once there was a silence that you could feel, it was so tense, so palpable. I said to my companion, "Who is this person who can make a large audience like this yield and in a moment give silence?".... Other people were lining up so I went along too. Then he said a few words which were not of significance to me then, because I did not know his greatness. I did not appreciate them until years afterwards.[151]

Upon Swamiji's mahasamadhi, the San Francisco Class of Vedanta Philosophy published a tribute in the *Pacific Vedantin*, which also appeared in *The Hindu* newspaper of September 26, 1902 and the *Indian Mirror* of October 17. It was signed and reverently submitted by President Milburn Logan, Vice-President Carl Petersen, and Secretary Albert Wollberg. The eulogy read in part:

> As he loved and revered his Master, so we will love and cherish his sacred memory. He was one of the greatest souls that has visited the earth for many centuries.... Coming to this country as he did, a young man, a stranger in foreign land, and meeting with the modern world's choicest divines, and holding those great and critical audiences of the Worlds Con-

> gress of Religion in reverential awe, with his high spiritual philosophy and sublime oratory, was an unusual strain for one so young. No other person stood out with such magnificent individuality; no creed or dogma could so stand. No other one had a message of such magnitude. Professors of our great universities listened with profound respect. "Compared to whose gigantic intellect these were as mere children." ... We consider that we were exceedingly fortunate to have known him in the flesh, to have communed with him in person and to have felt the sweet influence of his Divine presence.... In the death of the Swamiji, our cause at large has suffered the loss of a great and beloved leader, whose genial smile, pleasant words, and affable address made his presence ever welcome. He was a pronounced personality with the noblest of attributes, both human and divine; he gave himself to the world. He lived up to the highest standard of spirituality, so that his name, character and memory are an inspiration and benediction to his followers.[152]

After leaving San Francisco, Swamiji travelled to Chicago and then on to New York City. Mrs. Lillian Montgomery [q.v.], who was not an inner circle devotee, attended Vivekananda's public speeches when he came to the New York Centre during June-July of 1900. A few excerpts from her reminiscences given at the New York Vedanta Society on April 27, 1955 include:

> Swami Vivekananda was so entirely different from anything that we had known in America. I had heard all my life, it seemed to me, of power and repose, and the first time I had seen it was in the presence of Swami Vivekananda. And it all came as such a surprise, because I wasn't prepared for it ... Power seemed to emanate from him. I was fascinated; he looked like a living Buddha; he looked entirely different from any personality I had ever seen.... It seemed to me that there was an ocean of consciousness back of Swami Vivekananda, and in some way it focused and flowed through his words.... there was a purity, and an intense power, such a power as I think we have never seen—that I had never seen, and I don't expect I will ever see it again. It seemed to pour from an infinite source, and it was perfectly calm, perfectly reposed.

Additional excerpts from her letter to Swami Pavitrananda of June 22, 1954 are:

> He had the most perfect head I had ever seen. Perfectly poised.... Then came the voice in the chant of a Sanskrit invocation—but a voice of what exceptional quality! It was mellow, but full—resonant—in tone, bell-like—but, above all, it rang so true.[153]

Concerning Swami Vivekananda's mahasamadhi, Frank Parlato mentions on the Internet that it occurred a few hours after the aphelion in 1902.* It most often takes place each year during the first week of July. Also on July 4, 1776, the U.S. Independence Day, the earth had experienced its aphelion. It has been said in Vivekananda's biographies that some days prior to his passing away, he studied the almanac to determine what time and date would be best for his mahasamadhi. Frank Parlato estimates that the aphelion occurred about 6:30 p.m. Calcutta time and, according to Swami Nikhilananda, he left the body at 9:10 p.m. As the earth began its return toward its source, the sun, the enlightened Swami returned to his Spiritual Source.[154]

An anonymous "A Western Disciple", who personally knew Swamiji, sent this erudite and glowing tribute to the *Prabuddha Bharata* stating in part:

> By the death of Swami Vivekananda, we have lost a dear friend, and suffered an irreparable loss. He is best remembered by us as having been "the greatest figure in the Parliament of Religions" held at Chicago in 1893, where he addressed crowded audiences, the quality of his teaching and his unaffected eloquence winning a most sympathetic hearing. He had a vivid, eager personality, singularly magnetic, persuasive and enthusiastic. He was no mere visionary anchorite of the Himalayas, giving the truths of Indian philosophy. On the contrary, he was a man born with perfectly developed spiritual sense, discerning spiritual truths without effort: calm and steadfast, giving forth power from the spiritual centre within, and living for the advancement of his race: a true lover of his fellow-men, devoting his energies in trying to rouse them to their true selves, content to use up his gifts and talents for their benefit. Clad in his habit of red or ochre did this Indian Sannyasin, standing upon all sorts of platforms, in all manners of places, with a strong beautiful voice, expound the philosophy of Vedanta. Again and again in his lectures did he recur to the central idea of Advaita,

* An aphelion is the point in the orbit of the earth, or any other celestial body, that is farthest from the sun.

the One in everything, the potential divinity in all. Gifted with an original outlook upon life, he displayed that fervour and vigour that one associated with monks, who have for centuries held to their spirituality with a power and staunchness unrivalled in worldly affairs.[155]

ENDNOTES

1 *CW*, VI:257.

2 Ibid., V:100.

3 Ibid., VIII:474.

4 *WWSV*, pp. 15-27; *PB* (March 1985),p. 139; Cost of Living.

5 *CW*, V:39, 49; VIII: 319, 376, 463, 474; IX:22-23.

6 Chaudhuri1, pp. 148-49.

7 Chaudhuri1, pp. 154-55.

8 *CW*, IX:9-10.

9 Ibid., VIII:305.

10 Ibid., V:38.

11 Ibid., IX:57.

12 *WWSV*, pp. 28-35; Burke, I, pp. 290-96, 452-53; III, pp. 191-92.

13 *Life*, I, pp. 491-92.

14 Burke, III, pp. 319-20.

15 *Reminiscences*, pp. 148-50, 197; *PB* (Mar. 1978).

16 Burke, IV, pp. 43-44.

17 *Life*, I, p. 466.

18 Swami Vivekananda, *Inspired Talks, My Master, and Other Writings* (New York: Ramakrishna-Vivekananda Center, 1976), pp. 14-15; *WWSV*, pp. 36-40; Hohner, pp. 16, 50, 52, 62; Chaudhuri2, p. 218.

19 *CW*, VIII:537.

20 *VK* (May 1930), p. 40.

21 *WWSV*, pp. 40-46; Pravrajika Vrajaprana, *A Portrait of Sister Christine* (Calcutta: The Ramakrishna Mission Institute of Culture, 1996), pp. 39-41, 77, 83-87, 91-107; Hohner, pp. 86, 88, 90, 109-10.

22 Chaudhuri2, p. 552; Gargi, p. 113.

23 *CW*, IX:463.

24 Ibid., IX:24, 26, 69.

25 Ibid., VI:322, 339; VIII:340; IX:44, 56.

26 Ibid., V:63.

27 Burke, II, pp. 45-46; III, pp. 183-85; IV, p. 339; VI, pp. 284; *Life*, II, p. 71.

28 Basu, pp. 101-02; Burke, IV, pp. 560-61.
29 *Life*, II, p. 211.
30 Frances Willard, *American Women* (New York: Mast, Crowell & Kirkpatrick, 1897), p. 135; Prabuddhaprana2, pp. 61-63, 66-67, 154; R. F. Foster, *W. B. Yeats: A Life* (New York: Oxford University Press, 1998), I, pp. 16-17, 48, 85, 469-70; II, pp. 384, 516-17, 536-38; *Brahmavadin* (March 15, 1899), p. 396; Prabuddhaprana2, p. 62.
31 *CW*, IX:28-29.
32 Ibid., IX:470.
33 Ibid., IX:43-44.
34 Ibid., IX:49.
35 Ibid., IX:494.
36 Ibid., VIII:36-52.
37 Ibid., VIII:372-73; IX:154-55.
38 Ibid., VI:434; VIII:430, 468, 482, 495-98.
39 Ibid., V:39; VIII:474; IX:125, 132.
40 Ibid., IX:572.
41 Prabuddhaprana2, pp. 91-92, 100, 105, 108, 118, 124-25, 131-32, 269-70, 320, 391.
42 *San Francisco Call* (Mar. 27, 1904).
43 *Boston Daily Globe* (Feb. 9, 1911), p. 1; (May 19, 1911), p. 2; (May 28, 1911), p. 25; (June 4, 1911), p. 8; (June 9, 1911), p. 18; (June 16, 1911), p. 4; (July 19, 1911), p. 8; *Miami Herald* (Florida) (June 14, 1911), p. 8; *New York Times* (May 27, 1911), p. 3; (June 28, 1911), p. 1; (July 19, 1911), p. 2; Prabuddhaprana2, pp. 496-97; *Life*, II, p. 485; Jackson, p. 92; *Lewis G. Janes: Philosopher, Patriot, Lover of Man* (Boston: James H. West, 1902), p. 53; Cost of Living.
44 Prabuddhaprana2, pp. 487, 490-92; *CWSV*, X, p. 13; *Boston Daily Globe* (June 9, 1911), p. 18; (June 16, 1911), p. 4; *Miami Herald* (Florida) (June 14, 1911), p. 8. According to this newspaper article, the people that Siri Swanander named attended the lectures of Vivekananda. The list was composed of friends of Abhedananda, and one distinguished person on the list, Heber Newton, never met Vivekananda according to Abhedananda.
45 Datta, B., pp. 112-14, 190; *Eminent Indians: Who Was Who 1900-80* (1985).
46 *CW*, VI:306, 308; VIII:339.
47 *Reminiscences*, pp. 164-65; Chaudhuri2, p. 204; *PB* (Mar. 1978).
48 *CW*, VII:3-104.
49 Burke, III, pp. 93, 119-21 157-59, 180; Hohner, pp. 46-51.
50 *Reminiscences*, p. 117; *PB* (Jan. 1906).

51 *Life*, II, pp. 24-25.
52 *CW*, VII:3-104.
53 Burke, III, pp. 131-32, 540.
54 *WWSV*, pp. 48-49; Web: www. vivekananda.net/PDFBooks/InspiredTalks/InspiredTalks.pdf; Burke, III, p. 520; *CW*, VIII:3-35.
55 *CW*, I:195-313.
56 *Life*, II, pp. 60-61; *WWSV*, p. 53; Burke, III, p. 366; IV, p. 117.
57 *CW*, VIII:507; IX:142-43.
58 Ibid., VIII: 252-53.
59 *WWSV*, pp. 47-59.
60 Basu, pp. 597-99; *Brahmavadin* (Feb. 1903).
61 *Reminiscences*, p. 120; *PB* (Jan. 1906).
62 Swami Vivekananda's Impact. Web: www.davedeluca.com/ VivekanandaTestimonials.htm.
63 *Reminiscences*, p. 228; Chaudhuri2, p. 165; *PB*, (Dec. 1949); *VW*, (Nov-Dec. 1962).
64 Prugh, pp. 113-15, 381-82, 406-08, 412, 438, 538-39; *Vedanta in Southern California* (Hollywood, Vedanta Press, 1960), pp. 45-46; *WWSV*, pp. 99-110.
65 Swami Chetanananda, *How to Live with God* (St. Louis: Vedanta Society of St. Louis, 2008), p. 549.
66 Burke, III, p. 97; Prugh, pp. 362-63.
67 Jyotirmayananda, p. 184.
68 *Reminiscences*, p. 229; *PB*, (Dec. 1949); *VW*, (Nov-Dec. 1962).
69 Prabuddhaprana1, p. 209.
70 Vivekananda, pp. 678-79.
71 Swami Chetanananda, "Vivekananda as We Saw Him" (video).
72 *VK* (Nov. 1949), p. 356.
73 Prabuddhaprana1, pp. 246-47, 272-77; Nikos Kazantzakis, *England* (New York: Simon and Schuster, 1965), pp. 249-50, 253-54; *CA* (1991), vol. 132.
74 *CW*, V:185-88.
75 Burke, III, pp. 216-17, 221, 232-34, 349; IV, pp. 105-21, 484-85, 527; V, pp. 57-61; Hohner, pp. 54-56, 67, 72, 80, 82, 87-88; Vividishananda, pp. 32-33. See GBS for Sturdy's Appendix in the "Narada Sutras"; *CW*, VII:515-19.
76 Burke, IV, p. 177; *Reminiscences*, p. 294; *VK* (Feb. 1937).
77 Sister Nivedita. Web: www.balagokulam.org/teach/biographies/ sister.php.
78 *CW*, VI:436-37.
79 Ibid., V:172-73, VII:243; IX:172-73.

80 Sri Sarada Math. Sister Nivedita. Web: www.srisaradamath.org/ sisternivedita. htm; Burke, III, pp. 257, 283, 289; IV, pp. 512-13, V:140-42.

81 Web: rkmissionashrama.wordpress.com/swami-vivekananda-in-belgaum/.

82 Nivedita, II, p. 800.

83 *CW*, V:44-45.

84 Sister Nivedita. Web: www.srisaradamath.org/sisternivedita.htm; Atmaprana, passim.

85 Burke, II, pp. 186-87; Shivani, p. 98; Nivedita, II, pp. 1247-48, 1254; Satyananda, p. 90; A Walking Tour of Cambridge. Web: http://cox-marylee.tripod.com/cambridgecrowd.htm.

86 *CW*, I:25-313, 344-436; II:38-358, 375-96, 406-62; III:1-28, 70-100; IV:1-60, 154-87, 192-95, 203-17; V:277-79, 297-311; VI:3-17, 128-45; IX:223-64.

87 Ibid., IX:484-89, 491-98, 519-21.

88 Ibid., I:25-313.

89 Ibid., II:55-358.

90 Ibid., III:70-100.

91 Ibid., IV:1-60.

92 Stavig5; Stavig6; Burke, III, pp. 335, 366.

93 *Reminiscences*, p. 118; Chaudhuri2, pp. 224-25; *PB*, (Jan. 1906).

94 *CW*, VIII:336.

95 *Life*, II, p. 59; Burke, III, pp. 335-38, 520; Pravrajika Vrajaprana, *My Faithful Goodwin* (Calcutta: Advaita Ashrama, 1994).

96 Basu, pp. 611-12; Burke; IV, 486-88, 491, 495-96; V, p. 92; Vrajaprana (1994).

97 Burke, IV, pp. 564-65; Pravrajika Vrajaprana, *My Faithful Goodwin* (Calcutta; Advaita Ashrama, 1994), pp. 106-07.

98 *CW*, IX, pp. 106-07.

99 Ibid., IV:389.

100 Burke, III, p. 520; VI, pp. 306-07; *CWSA*, X, pp. 4, 6, 63, 71, 80, 84; *The Arena* 22 (1899), pp. 429, 482-88; WorldCat.

101 Prugh, pp. 236-37; Chaudhuri2, p. 332.

102 *Reminiscences*, p. 144; *Brahmavadin* (May 1911), pp. 193-96.

103 *CW*, V:225.

104 Web: en.wikipedia.org/wiki/Prabuddha_Bharata; *WWSV*, pp. 140-45; *Life*, II, p. 570; Burke, IV, pp. 165, 247-48, 280, 439-40, 537; V, p. 55: Web: en.wikipedia.org/wiki/Swami_Swarupananda.

105 *CW*, VII:512, 517; IX:119; VI:439.

106 *WWSV*, pp. 144-48; "A Letter from Swami Atulananda to Haridasa" (April 4, 1925), VSSC Archives.

107 Burke, III, p. 277; IV, pp. 165, 386-87, 400, 485, 521; V, pp. 75, 83- 86, 88. $1,000 Pounds = $4,870 (= $124,000 in 2007); Alfred Ellis. Web: www.npg.org.uk/live/search/person.asp?LinkID=mp67419&role=art.

108 *WWSV*, pp. 149-51; *PB* (Feb. 2007), p. 173; Chaudhuri2, p. 702.

109 Burke, V, pp. 198-99; Stavig2, ch. I; *CW*, IX:127.

110 Chaudhuri2, pp. 684-87.

111 *Reminiscences*, pp. 358-59; *PB* (July 1963).

112 *WWSV*, pp. 150-53, 156; Hohner, pp. 95, 97; Chaudhuri2, p. 702.

113 *CW*, IX:499-501, 505-06.

114 Ibid., IX:501-04.

115 Ibid., II:24-37; IX:509.

116 Ibid., II:1-23, 397-405; IV:138-53.

117 Ibid., III:511-37; IV:63-101,120-34; VIII:53-91; IX:506-07.

118 Ibid., II:359-74.

119 Stavig5; Stavig6; Chaudhuri2, p. 698; *CW*, IV:111-19.

120 *CW*, IX:499-501.

121 Alice Hansbrough, "Reminiscences of Swami Vivekananda", *PB* (Feb. 2007), pp. 175, 177.

122 Hansbrough, *PB* (Feb. 2007), p. 177; (March 2007), p. 242; *WWSV*, pp. 157-62; Hohner, pp. 99-106; Chaudhuri2, p. 699. Hohner writes he left Pasadena on February 20 and Hansbrough says on February 21.

123 Linda Prugh, "Sister Lalita", *PB* (Jan. 1985), pp. 18-19; Pravrajika Prabhaprana, "Sister Lalita", *VK* (May 1988), p. 179.

124 Burke, V, p. 258; Prugh (1985), pp. 18-19.

125 *CW*, VIII:491.

126 Ibid., VI:424.

127 Hansbrough, *PB* (May 2007), p. 348; Burke, V, pp. 253-54 gives a slightly different version.

128 Hansbrough, *PB* (April 2007), p. 295.

129 *CW*, VII:522.

130 Ibid., IX:144.

131 Anandaprana, pp. 93-94, 100; *PB* (Nov. 1935), p. 570; (Feb. 2007), pp. 172-77; *Los Angeles Directory* (1932-33); Cost of Living.

132 *PB* (July 2007), p. 439; Burke, V, p. 190.

133 *CW*, VIII:73-91; *VW* (July-August 1944), pp. 104-16; *Los Angeles Times* (Nov. 25, 1927), p. A3.

134 *Los Angeles Times* (Nov. 25, 1927), p. A3; (Nov. 26, 1927), p. A5; (Nov. 29, 1927), p. A1; (June 27, 1987), Part View.

135 Burke, V, pp. 326-27; *WWSV*, pp. 183-205; Atulananda, pp. 318, 343.

136 *CW*, VI:28-40, 46-48, 93-97, 101-02, 125-27; IX:271, 274-82, 405.

137 Burke, V, pp. 339-40, 369, 371, 378-79, 407; VI, pp. 1-3, 20, 47-48, 108-09, 203-05; Burke points out that Rhodehamel's notes on "The Power of the Mind" consist of two of Swamiji's lectures.

138 Rhodehamel writing under the pseudonym of "A Western Disciple", *PB* (1918), pp. 107-12, 131-35, 156-60; (1923), pp. 223-26.

139 *Life*, II, pp. 516-17.

140 Burke, VI, pp. 36-37, 97, 149- 50; *WWSV*, pp. 170-71.

141 *VW* (Jan-Feb. 1955), pp. 7-8; Vidyatmananda12

142 *Reminiscences*, pp. 362-63; *VW* (May-June 1954).

143 Swami Yogeshananda, *Six Lighted Windows* (United States: Swami Yogeshananda, 1995), p. 85; *WWSV*, pp. 170-72.

144 *VW* (Jan-Feb. 1955), pp. 8-9; Vidyatmananda6.

145 *CW*, I:437-84, 489-521; II:463-74; IV:218-49; VI: 49-78; VII:430-37; VIII:92-141, 244-49; IX: 272-73.

146 *VW* (Jan-Feb. 1955) p. 7; (Nov-Dec. 1958), p. 64; (Jan-Feb. 1959), p. 63; Burke V, pp. 375-76, 384; VI, pp. 47, 59, 67-68, 82-83, 93, 109, 123, 204, 207, 216. Ansell's excerpts in the ninth volume are from Burke, V, pp. 401-03.

147 *WWSV*, pp. 181-82; Atulananda, p. xxiii; "Unpublished Letters of Swami Turiyananda", *VK* (1989, pp. 22-27, 68-72, 102-06, 151-55, 177-80, 221-25.

148 Burke, V, p. 342.

149 *Reminiscences*, p. 383; *VK* (Sept. 1924), p. 170.

150 *CW*, IX:330-31, 406-07.

151 *VFEW* (July-Aug. 1959), p. 187; Swami Atulananda, *The Atman Alone Abides* (Madras: Sri Ramakrishna Math), p. 40.

152 Basu, pp. 239-40; *PB* (Dec. 1902), pp. 222-23.

153 Burke, VI, pp. 277-82, 423.

154 Frank Parlato. Web: www.vivekananda.net/NewDiscoveries/Vivekanandas-Death.htm.

155 Basu, p. 638; also in *PB* (July 1902); (July 2002), pp. 348-49.

CHAPTER VI

RELIGIOUS LEADERS

New biographical information is supplied in this book concerning the supporters of Swamiji who were prominent figures at that time in American and British society. Emphasis is placed on the affirmative statements made about him by his admirers. During his lifetime, Vivekananda received the benefit of helpful support from the liberal members of the Western clergy. He enjoyed considerable popularity with many creative and well-educated Ministers. The first cleric to be mentioned is William Hastie (1842-1903) [q.v.], an ordained missionary who in 1878 became the principal (equivalent to president) of the General Assembly's Institution in Calcutta, later known as the Scottish Church College. Until 1884 he remained in the College under the control of the Missionary Board of the Church of Scotland. Hastie, an intelligent man, lived an austere life style, and had a loving rapport with his students. Narendranath Datta, the future Swami Vivekananda, expressed his fondness for Hastie saying, he "lived on nothing and regarded his room as his boys' home as much as his own.... Towards the end of his stay in India he used to say, 'Yes, my boy, you were right, you were right!—It is true that all is God.' I am proud of him!"[1] It was the insightful William Hastie who uttered the prophetic statement, "Narendranath is really a genius. I have travelled far and wide, but I have never yet come across a lad of his talents and possibilities, even in the German Universities, amongst philosophical students. He is bound to make his mark in life!" Narendra first found out about Sri Ramakrishna from Hastie, and made contact with him for the first time at Surendra's house. Chapter I discusses Hastie's many intellectual accomplishments as a university professor in Scotland.[2]

In 1899, Swamiji translated into Bengali the first six of the 114 chapters of the *Imitation of Christ* with quotations of parallel passages from the Hindu scriptures. He submitted it to a Bengali monthly *Sahitya Kalpadruma* and, in the beginning of the Preface, wrote:

> The *Imitation of Christ* is a cherished treasure of the Christian world. This great book was written by a Roman Catholic monk. "Written", perhaps, is not the proper word. It would be more appropriate to say that each letter of the book is marked deep with the heart's blood of the great soul who had renounced all for his love of Christ.[3]

This Christian classic was written in 1418, probably by Thomas Á Kempis (1380-1471), a medieval Catholic monastic and priest. Born on the western border of Germany, he joined the Brothers of the Common Life monastery in the Netherlands. With emphasis on mystical spirituality, he devoted his life to "prayer, study, copying manuscripts, teaching novices, offering Mass, and hearing the confessions of people who came to the monastery church.... He wrote a number of sermons, letters, hymns, and lives of the saints." After the *Bible*, it is the most widely translated of all Christian books.[4]

After coming to the West, at the request and invitation of the presiding Ministers, Vivekananda delivered multiple lectures at the Unitarian Churches in Salem, Massachusetts, Chicago and Hinsdale, Illinois, and Minneapolis, Minnesota, all in 1893; Detroit, Michigan, and Lawrence, Massachusetts, in 1894; Hartford, Connecticut, in 1895-96; West Croyden, London, in 1896; Los Angeles, California, in 1899; and Oakland, California, in 1900.

He also spoke at the Universalist Church in Annisquam, Massachusetts, and Chicago, Illinois; Methodist, Wesley Church in Salem, Massachusetts; Congregational Church in Evanston, Illinois, and Madison, Wisconsin; and the Disciples of Christ, Central Church of Christ in Des Moines, Iowa, all in 1893; Nondenominational, People's Church in Washington, D.C., in 1894; South Place Chapel in London, in 1895; Nondenominational, People's Church in New York; Temple Beth El Synagogue in Detroit, Michigan; Theosophical Society of London, in 1896; New Thought, Home of Truth in Los Angeles, California, in 1899; Universalist Church in Pasadena, California, in 1900; and the New Thought, Home of Truth in San Francisco and in Alameda, California, in 1900. As far as we know, after 1893 he did not speak in a mainstream Christian church, but was the guest at Unitarian, New Thought and other religious organizations. His greatest support came from the Unitarians, yet according to the census of 1906, in the United States only 0.2% of the religious population were Unitarians, approximately one church member in every five-hundred.[5]

During the fifteen days preceding the World's Parliament of Religions, invited by Reverend George Penniman (d. 1943), Vivekananda spoke to the congregation at the Universalist Church in Annisquam, Massachusetts. He conversed on "Customs and Life in India". Penniman's daughter, who was born in 1903, said her father spoke of Vivekananda when she was a child. Next Swamiji made the journey to the Wesley Church in Salem, Massachusetts, to deliver a lecture that was covered in the *Salem Evening News*.[6] Prior to his talk the newspaper mentioned, "He is extremely generous to all persons of other faiths, and has only kind words for those who differ from him."[7] It is now known as the Wesley United Methodist Church, since John Wesley (1703-91) of England was the founder of the Methodist denomination. It is significant that Vivekananda's final oral presentation in the city took place at the East Church. The First Church in Salem being the first Congregational Church to be organized in America, is the oldest continuing Protestant Society there. It dates back to the Puritan settlers in 1629. Roger Williams (c. 1603-83), the third Pastor of the Church, founded the colony of Rhode Island in 1836, and Nathaniel Hawthorne (1804-64), the famous American writer, became a member of the laity. The First Church of Salem subdivided into five branches, including the East Church (1719-1899), which Reverend Edward D. Towle directed from 1892 to 1897 when Vivekananda spoke there. By the time Swamiji conversed there, the church had changed its allegiance from Congregational to Unitarian. Because of a merger, the East Church is now again a part of the First Church in Salem.[8]

John Henry Barrows (1847-1902), the sixth Pastor of the Chicago First Presbyterian Church (1881-96), held the position of president of the 1893 World's Parliament of Religions. This was the first time in the history of the world that delegates representing religions from all over the globe came together to discuss their similarities and differences. This remarkable gathering brought respect for non-Christian religions from many intelligent people. Later Barrows preserved the history of the Parliament by editing a two-volume 1600 page book *The World's Parliament of Religions: An Illustrative and Popular Story of the World's First Parliament of Religions, Held in Chicago in Connection with the Columbian Exposition of 1893*. Concerning Reverend Barrows, Swami Vivekananda wrote to the *Indian Mirror* of October 28, 1896, "It was the great courage, untiring industry, unruffled patience, and never-failing courtesy of Dr. Barrows that made the Parliament a grand success."

In 1896, over a three-month period, Barrows delivered over a hundred addresses to tens of thousands of educated Hindus in India, representing the Haskell Foundation associated with the University of Chicago. He became the president of Oberlin College in Ohio from 1899 until his premature death from pneumonia.[9]

Dr. Barrows must be credited for the magnificent job he did in spreading the news of the upcoming Parliament of Religions throughout a large portion of the world. He wrote to Reverend William Miller (1838-1923), the principal of Madras Christian College, about the forthcoming Parliament in America. Miller, a missionary of the Free Church of Scotland, arrived in Madras in 1862; through negotiations in 1877, he extended the school he taught at to create Madras Christian College, the largest in India, and he later became the vice-chancellor of Madras University (1901-04), returning to Scotland in 1907. Being a liberal thinker, Miller, a bachelor, did not believe that education should be used to induce conversion. He believed India should be allowed to make its own unique contribution to world culture. Sarvepalli Radhakrishnan later praised the college for successfully training new Indian leadership for the country. According to the *Indian Mirror*, though the missionary Miller "despaired for a time of securing any Hindu representative at Chicago", there were many who represented the different thought systems of Hinduism, Vivekananda being one of them. Later Miller joined Vivekananda "in declaring that Hinduism has a mission in the world, and that it has to teach great lessons to the Christian nations of the world."[10] Miller's wish was granted since he became a link in the chain that brought Vivekananda to America. He told the news of the upcoming parliament to Yogi Parthasarathi Ayyangar of Triplicane, who in turn informed his sister's son, the young Alasinga Perumal (1865-1909) [q.v.]. Alasinga worked as the head master of Pachiappa's High School in Madras, and a year before his death taught in the physics department at Pachiappa's College. Alasinga approached Swamiji and enthusiastically requested him to attend the event. Swamiji prayed for guidance. Many days later,

> ...as he lay half-asleep one night, the command did come, in a symbolic dream. He saw the figure of his Master, Shri Ramakrishna, walking from the seashore into the waters of the ocean, and beckoning him to follow. Peace and joy filled his whole being as he became fully awake: the order "go" had been impressed on his mind, as it were. The vision convinced him. He knew it to be a divine command.[11]

Next he wrote to Holy Mother for permission, which she granted. After he concurred, Alasinga became the leader in collecting funds to send the Swami to Chicago. He collected 3,000 rupees, which he personally deposited at Thomas Cook and Sons in Bombay in the Swami's name. After Swamiji came to America, Alasinga raised an additional 1,000 rupees, which he sent him.[12]

Cornelia Conger (1887-1973) informs us that:

> My grandmother [Mrs. John (Emily Wright) Lyon] and my mother [Mrs. Emily Lyon Conger, 1861-1937] belonged to the First Presbyterian Church and our Minister Dr. Barrows had charge of looking after all the delegates to the Parliament of Religions. And so on one Sunday he asked his congregation if they would offer to take a delegate in their house as a guest for two reasons. One was that the delegates didn't have much money, and the other was especially for the foreign ones for whom, he said, it would be very interesting to live in an American home and see how we all lived. Well my grandmother had a rather dry sense of humour and she said to Dr. Barrows, "I'd be willing to take a delegate if you could find me one who isn't bigoted." She said, "My husband is interested in philosophy but he doesn't like narrow minded people." So Dr. Barrows laughed and remarked, "Well I will do my best for you." And my grandmother said, "I would really like somebody who does not live in this country."

In time, it was arranged through the efforts of Dr. Barrows and others that Swamiji would stay with the family of John B. Lyon (1829-1904) for about seventeen days while the Parliament was in session.[13]

On September 20, 1893, Vivekananda gave the talk "Religion not the Crying Need of India".[14] He criticized the negative statements made at the Parliament by a missionary to China. At that time, the Swami "stepped back on the platform and whispered to Bishop Keane", who responded by telling him, "Americans would not be offended at honest criticism [of the missionaries]".[15] Bishop John Joseph Keane (1839-1918) was born in Ireland, and because of a potato famine, his family came to the United States in 1848. He became the Bishop of Richmond, Virginia (1878-88), the first Rector of the Catholic University of America in Washington, D.C. (1887-97), the Archbishop of Damascus, Syria (1897-99), and the Archbishop of Dubuque, Iowa (1900-11). His associates describe Archbishop Keane as a man of erudition, oratorical skills, constant industry and broad sympathies, gifted with a charming personality.[16]

In his two-volume *The World's Parliament of Religions*, Reverend John Henry Barrows included a section entitled "Introduction to the Parliament Papers". There he quotes a statement made by Bishop John Keane in response to impromptu remarks made the previous day by Vivekananda. Bishop Keane emphasized:

> I endorse the denunciation that was hurled forth last night against the system of pretended charity that offered food to the hungry Hindus at the cost of their conscience and faith. It is a shame and a disgrace to those who call themselves Christians.... we do not hear half enough of such criticisms, and that if by these criticisms Vivekananda can only stir us and sting us into better teachings and better doings in the great work of Christ in the world, he [Bishop Keane] for one would only be grateful to our friend the Hindu monk.[17]

In his report to the Parliament of Religions, Bishop Keane revealed:

> My heart was glad when I listened last night and heard our good friend, the Hindu [Swamiji], confess that for years he did not know where he was going to get his next meal. That was the way with these poor Franciscan monks. They were reduced to poverty in order that they might better concentrate themselves to the service of God everywhere.[18]

At the Parliament of Religions on September 15, Vivekananda delivered a short speech with the title "Why we Disagree", analogously relating the "Frog in a Well" fable to the subject of religious intolerance.[19] Dr. Eliza Sunderland (1839-1910) represented the Unitarian women of America at the Parliament. In her oration she explained that the study of all religions was necessary for "the intelligent comprehension of any one religion".[20] Eliza's husband Jabez Sunderland (1842-1936) [q.v.], a Civil War veteran, served as a Unitarian Minister. In his written commentary on the Parliament, Sunderland refers to Swamiji as "a learned Hindu" and a "distinguished Hindu". The reverend very much appreciated the "Frog in the Well" narrative, which advocates universal tolerance. He devoted over five-hundred words of his published manuscript to the transcript of this speech.[21]

The thoughtful and serene Reverend Jabez Sunderland met Pratap C. Mazumdar (1840-1905), the Brahmo Samaj leader at the Parliament of Religions in 1893. He came to India in 1895-96 and again in 1913-14, being the first American to speak at a meeting of the Indian National Congress in Poona. Sunderland, a Unitarian Pastor in Oakland, California (1898-99), missed Vivekananda who spoke from the pulpit of the First Unitarian Church in Oakland in February 1900. A long quotation from Jabez Sunderland appears in Abhedananda's 1906 book *India and Her People* on the subject of Indian education. As a Minister in Hartford, Connecticut (1907-11), Sunderland met with Abhedananda in 1908, and Sister Nivedita in 1911 during her visit to the United States. For decades Sunderland was the leading American spokesman who supported the freedom of India. He worked with nationalist leaders in exile like Lala Lajpat Rai, and fulfilled the duties of president of the Indian Home Rule League, and of the Indian Society of America (1924-28) (whose officers included Jane Addams, Ruth St. Denis, Professor John Dewey, Reverend John Haynes Holmes, and other dignitaries). Beginning with an article published in the *Atlantic Monthly* of October 1908, Sunderland came out with many manuscripts advocating India's political freedom. The British government in India banned his 529-page *India in Bondage, Her Right to Freedom and a Place among Nations* issued in 1928, which the patriots referred to as the "Bible of Indian Struggle for Freedom". In the volume he affirmed:

> India has produced great literature, great arts, great philosophical systems, great religions, and great men in every department of life—rulers, statesmen, financiers, scholars, poets, generals, colonizers, ship-builders, skilled artisans and craftsmen of every kind, agriculturists, industrial organizers and leaders in far-reaching trade and commerce by land and sea.[22]

Reverend Sunderland acknowledged that Abhedananda's statements on India inspired him to write this book. He also submitted ten articles to the *Prabuddha Bharata* between 1932 and 1936, and served on the General Committee for the upcoming Ramakrishna Centenary in Calcutta, but passed away before it commenced in March 1937. At his Memorial Service, Swami Bodhananda of the New York Vedanta Society spoke on the immortality of the soul.[23]

Annie Besant (1847-1933) [q.v.], the English leader of the Theosophy Movement, wrote a glowing tribute to Swamiji:

> A striking figure, clad in yellow and orange, shining like the sun of India in the midst of the heavy atmosphere of Chicago, a lion head, piercing eyes, mobile lips, movements swift and abrupt—such was my first impression of Swami Vivekananda, as I met him in one of the rooms set apart for the use of the delegates to the Parliament of Religions. Monk, they called him, not unwarrantably, but warrior-monk was he ... Purposeful, virile, strong, he stood out, a man among men, able to hold his own.
>
> On the platform another side came out. The dignity and inborn sense of worth and power still were there, but all was subdued to the exquisite beauty of the spiritual message which he had brought, to the sublimity of the matchless evangel of the East which is the heart, the life of India, the wondrous teaching of the Self. Enraptured, the huge multitudes hung upon his words; not a syllable must be lost, not a cadence missed![24]

At the request of Annie Besant, the Swami graciously accepted her invitation to discuss "Bhakti Yoga" at the Theosophical Society of London on July 9, 1896. He said he did this "to show my sympathy for all sects". Colonel Henry Steel Olcott (1832-1907), the president and cofounder of the religion of Theosophy in 1875, attended the address.[25] At the Star Theatre in Calcutta during March of 1898, Vivekananda offered praise for the "noble and distinguished" Annie Besant for giving "her whole life to work for the good of India and India's regeneration". He also refers to her as "a sincere well-wisher of this motherland of ours, and that she is doing the best in her power to raise our country", "a very good woman" possessing "exceptional powers".[26] In 1898 the Swami went to visit G. N. Chakravarti, who five years before represented Theosophy at the Parliament of Religions. At that time, says Swamiji, "Annie Besant told me entreatingly that there should be friendship between her organisation and mine all over the world."[27] She once wrote, "After a study of some forty years and more of the great religions of the world, I find none so perfect, none so scientific, none so philosophical and none so spiritual than the great religion known by the name of Hinduism."[28]

Annie Besant founded Central Hindu College that evolved into Benares Hindu University, and in 1907 was elected president of the Theosophical Society. For political reasons, in 1914 she brought into being the weekly newspaper *The Commonweal*, and bought the *Madras Standard*, renaming it *New India*, established the Home Rule League in 1916, and in 1917 became the president of the Calcutta Session of the Indian National Congress. At that time, it was rare for a woman in any country of the world to hold such an important non-hereditary political position. In 1917 the British authorities in Madras interned her. During the same year, she initiated and gave her influential support to the Women's Indian Association, which grew to have fifty-one branches by 1924. Besant's popularity waned after 1919 because of her lack of support for Mahatma Gandhi, and she died in India in 1933.[29]

In 1889 Charles Fillmore (1854-1948) and Myrtle Fillmore (1845-1931) began publishing the highly successful magazine *Modern Thought*, later renamed *Unity*. During the Parliament of Religions, the Fillmores became interested in Indian religious ideas as taught by Vivekananda, whom they admired. Consequently, they quoted him, and advertised and sold his works. To give two examples, on December 14, 1893 their periodical named *Unity* published the only extant six-page report of Swami Vivekananda's speech on "The Divinity of Man" delivered that month in Chicago. Six years later they published the tribute given to Swamiji by J. Ransome Bransby of the Los Angeles Home of Truth. The Fillmores incorporated reincarnation, vegetarianism, and the idea that everyone is a Son of God into the theology of the emerging Unity School of Christianity. In 1903, and possibly other years, *Unity* listed the books of Vivekananda and Abhedananda along with their selling price, and included affirmative reviews of the latter's books. Suresh Chandler Varma, a Christian missionary, came out with a 1984 booklet concerning Charles Fillmore's sect with the title the *Unity School of Christianity: Christianized Hinduism*. In 1903 the Unity movement was officially formed, and in 1922 they withdrew from the New Thought Alliance. Since that time they have grown larger in membership than New Thought and Christian Science. After existing for sixty years, the Unity School of Christianity claimed to have reached one million homes.[30]

When the Parliament of Religions was in progress, on September the 24th Vivekananda delivered an oration at the Third Unitarian Church in Chicago. The *Chicago Herald* tells us:

> The Pastor, Rev. Mr. Blake, said that he was glad to invite Mr. Vivekananda into his pulpit and to introduce him, believing still in the faith of his fathers. Rev. Mr. Blake said he would turn his hand neither one way or the other to make such a man a Christian. He would do all he could to make such a man think for himself along the lines of the exalted spiritual conceptions which he had acquired.

Swamiji spoke on “The Love of God”.[31] James Vila Blake (1842-1925) was the Pastor of the Third Unitarian Church in Chicago (1883-97), and the All Souls Unitarian Church in Evanston (1892-1916). He became one of the six leaders of the liberal Western Unitarian Conference during 1878-94. For many years in Chicago, he conducted a class on the study of the world’s great religions. Blake is best remembered for the large number of religious hymns, chorales, sonnets and poems he composed and published.[32]

In his book *Review of the World’s Religious Congress* (1893), Reverend L. P. Mercer wrote:

> Swami Vivekananda of Bombay, India, arose, a magnificent figure of manly beauty, in his orange robe and turban, with striking, strong, and reposeful countenance, and said: “Sisters and Brothers of America”, whereupon there arose a peal of applause in acknowledgement of the originality of the salutation, and perhaps not less as testifying interest in the personality of the speaker.

The author of the volume Lewis Pyle Mercer (1847-1906) was a leading Swedenborgian clergyman in the Chicago area, possessing considerable literary talent. He became the presiding Minister of the Illinois Association of the New Church in 1884, and the general Pastor in 1895. In the volume, he also quoted verbatim two of Swamiji’s speeches at the Parliament.[33]

Swami Vivekananda received an invitation from Reverend Jean Frederick Loba, the Pastor of the First Congregational Church in Evanston, Illinois, to speak on September 30 on “Hindu Altruism” and on October 3, 1893 on “Monism”. The family of the Swiss born Jean Loba (b. 1846) immigrated to Utah to join the Mormons in 1854. Unhappy with the Mormon religion, the family went back to Kansas in 1857. Loba was called to be the Pastor of the First Congregational Church in 1892, where he served until 1907. During that time, he composed a religious text for young men in 1899.[34] For his three engagements at the Congregational Church in Evanston, Swamiji shared the platform with his friend Professor Carl Friedrich von Bergen (1838-97), a Unitarian Swedish representative from Stockholm at the Parliament of Religions, who had earlier played an important role in introducing Theosophy into Sweden and had founded in 1890 the Swedish Society for Psychical Research. The newspaper account tells us this about Vivekananda:

> He has attracted a great deal of attention on account of his unique attire in Mandarin colours, by his magnetic presence and by his brilliant oratory and wonderful exposition of Hindu philosophy. His stay in Chicago has been a continual ovation.[35]

About four months later Carl von Bergen attended a small intimate luncheon with Swamiji in Chicago.[36]

Charles Frederick Bradley (1852-1932), a doctor of divinity, held the position of professor of New Testament exegesis at the Garrett Biblical Institute of Northwestern University (1883-1901). He compiled two volumes of an English-Greek word list for the New Testament, which came out in 1889 and 1893. His colleagues described Bradley as "the soul of a courtesy, the pattern of chivalry". Writing to Professor John Henry Wright on the 2nd day of October 1893, Vivekananda stated concerning the Parliament of Religions, "Your friend Prof. Bradley was very kind to me and he always cheered me on.... I am going to Evanston tomorrow and hope to see Prof. Bradley there."[37] The Swami conversed again in Evanston, Illinois, on the 5th day of October on the subject of "Reincarnation".[38] In an August 20, 1894 letter to Isabelle McKindley, Swamiji relates that "Mr. Bradley of Evanston, whom you have met at Evanston, was here [Annisquam, MA]. His sister-in-law had me sit for a picture several days and had painted me."[39] Eight days later Vivekananda wrote to Mrs. G. W. (Belle) Hale, "Prof. Bradley of Evanston has gone home. If you ever meet him at Evanston, give him my best love and regards. He is really a spiritual man."[40]

In October, Vivekananda received an invitation to deliver a series of talks at the Unitarian Unity Church in Hinsdale, Illinois, from its leader Reverend Allen Walton Gould (1847-1901). Two other speakers from the Parliament of Religions were also part of the lecture programme. They were B. B. Nagarkar (b. 1860) of the Brahmo Samaj from Bombay, and Kinza Riuge M. Hirai, a Buddhist layman from Japan with loyalty to Theosophy. Reverend Gould worked as an instructor in French at Harvard, and a professor of Latin at Olivet College (1883-88). In 1888 he became a Unitarian Pastor and the presiding Minister at Hinsdale (1891-93). Gould, the secretary of the Western Unitarian Conference (1893-1901), became the president of the Western Sunday-School Association in 1894, after being a Minister for only six years. He published a book in Chicago for the Western Sunday-School Association (1893), and another text in Boston for youthful Unitarians (1895).[41]

An admirer of Swamiji, Reverend Hiram Washington Thomas (1832-1909), the head of the People's Church of Chicago in 1893, mentioned in July 1902 after Swamiji's mahasamadhi that:

> Vivekananda was a frequent visitor at my house. He came frequently and freely. Whenever he desired he would make his appearance and stay as long as he desired. We enjoyed him, and came to know him well. He told me that his name, Vivekananda, which he took after the completion of his studies, meant "living conscience" [consciousness?]. At the time he took this name he was consecrated, or as he considered it, created anew.
>
> Many of our customs were surprising to him. He could not understand the reason for keeping time. He never bound himself to engagements or dates of any kind, nor would he consult a calendar. He was a Brahmin, not a priest, and as such he preached whenever the fancy took him. We had not heard from him in a long time.[42]

Reverend Thomas wrote a letter to Henry L. Slayton, the president of the Slayton-Lyceum Bureau of Chicago. The letter appeared as an advertisement on November 18, 1893 in the *Wisconsin State Journal* and the *Daily Cardinal*, a student newspaper of the University of Wisconsin at Madison. Slayton published it to promote Swamiji's upcoming speech at the Congregational Church in Madison, Wisconsin, on the 20th. It read as follows:

> Dear Mr. Slayton: Of the many learned men in the East who took part in the great World's Parliament of Religions, Vivekananda was the most popular favourite, and when it was known that he was to speak, thousands were turned away for want of room. Nor was it curiosity that drew the masses; but those who heard him once were so impressed by the magnetism of his fine presence, the charm and power of his eloquence, his perfect command of the English language and the deep interest in what he had to say, that they desired all the more to hear him again. It will be opportunity of a lifetime for the cities of our land to see and hear this noble, earnest, loving Brahmin, dressed in the costume of his order, telling the true story of the religion and customs of his far-off country.
>
> Affectionately,
>
> W. H. Thomas[43]

The Slayton-Lyceum Bureau mentioned above was located at #36 in the Central Music Hall. The upper floors of the building housed the Chicago Musical College founded by Dr. Florenz Ziegfeld, whose son of the same name became the well-known producer of Broadway musicals. The latter and Eugen Sandow, the famous muscleman, appeared at the sideshow at the 1893 Chicago World's Fair. Mrs. Florence Milward Adams, a friend of Swamiji, also had a studio (#60) in that building. It is not generally known that, when Vivekananda was working in conjunction with the Slayton-Lyceum Bureau, he spoke on "The Divinity of Man" at the Central Music Hall on December 4, 1893. Due to the Swami's popularity, a sophisticated and sizable crowd attended the lecture, paying from 35 cents to $6 for a box seat ticket (equivalent to $8.32 and $142 respectively in 2007). Reverend Thomas introduced Swamiji to the audience saying:

> The speaker of the evening comes from a land of ancient scholarship, in whose philosophy are found the roots of the philosophy of England, Germany, France, and all Europe, whose religion is the most ancient in the world, whose bible antedates the Hebrew Bible—and he speaks to us in our own language.[44]

Asim Chaudhuri discovered a six-page account of the speech in the magazine *Unity*, and Ray Ellis of St. Louis, Missouri, in the *Chicago Daily Inter-Ocean* of December 5, which should be added to the *Complete Works*. The *Unity* presentation can now be read and printed or downloaded on the Internet using Google Book Search.[45]

For reasons of heresy, in 1879-80 they expelled Hiram Washington Thomas from both the Methodist Episcopal clergy and the laity, because of the liberality of his sermons. In the same year he accepted the invitation to be the Pastor of the People's Church of Chicago, receiving support from a loyal group of followers. His popular sermons held at various locations focused on the religion of humanity, brotherly love and the love of God. Beginning in 1894, Hiram Thomas became the president of the Liberal Congress of Religion, a nonsectarian Christian organization. Swami Saradananda, along with Lewis Janes and many others, spoke at their convention in Nashville, Tennessee, on October 22, 1897 when Thomas served as president of the organization.[46]

Under the direction of Pastor R. A. White, on November 12, at 8 p.m. Swamiji spoke at the Universalist Church located at the corner of the Sixty-fifth Street and Stewart in Chicago. The title of his presentation is presently unknown.[47] Eight days later, he gave a talk before the congregation at the Congregational Church in Madison, Wisconsin. The newspaper of the University of Wisconsin at Madison, the *Daily Cardinal*, recognized that:

> The "Religions of India", was an inspiration to all who heard him. He has a pleasant, clear-cut, dusky face, and a decidedly impressive manner and bearing. His voice is low and pleasant, with a secret something which rivets your attention at the start.[48]

The *Wisconsin State Journal* (November 21) noted, "The lecture at the Congregational Church [Madison] last night by the celebrated Hindoo monk, Vivekananda, was an extremely interesting one, and contained much of sound philosophy and good religion."[49] In a letter written that day to Mrs. G. W. (Belle) Hale, Swamiji mentions that he

> went to a hotel, and sent a message to Mr. Updike. He came to see me. He is a Congregational and so, of course, was not very friendly at first; but in the course of an hour or so became very kind to me, and took me over the whole place and the University. I had a fine audience and $100. Immediately after the lecture I took the night train to Minneapolis.[50]

Reverend Eugene Grover Updike (b. 1850) held the position of Pastor of the Methodist Episcopal Church in five different cities in Wisconsin, and in a suburb of Chicago during 1878-90. After transferring his denominational allegiance, he became the very popular Minister of the Congregational Church in Madison, Wisconsin, from 1890 to 1917. Updike is described as an earnest, efficient and respected leader of the largest congregation of any Protestant denomination in the state of Wisconsin with over a thousand members. Six days after Swamiji's public speech, Reverend Updike preached on "Vivekananda and the Christian Policy of Foreign Missions".[51]

Swami Vivekananda gave a talk at the First Unitarian Church in Minneapolis, Minnesota, on November 24 (on "Hindu Religion") and 26 (on "Oriental View of Religion"), and on December 14 (on "Manners and Customs in India"). H. M. Simmons, the presiding Minister, introduced him to the audience.[52] The *Minneapolis Star* expressed the view that, "He presented his faith in all sincerity, speaking slowly and clearly, convincing his hearers by quietness of speech rather than by rapid action. His words were carefully weighed, and each carried its meaning direct."[53] Following his third engagement, the *Minneapolis Tribune* discerned, "Vive Kananda is a bright, quick-witted talker, ready at all points to attack or defend, and inserts a humour into his speeches that is not lost upon his auditors."[54]

Reverend Henry Martyn Simmons (1841-1905), the Pastor of the Unitarian Church in Kenosha, Wisconsin, and concurrently the superintendent of schools (1871-79), became the Minister in the state capital Madison, Wisconsin (1879-81). Along with James Vila Blake, he was one of the six leaders of the Western Unitarian Conference (1878-94). Being a powerful and provocative public speaker, Simmons founded and directed the First Unitarian Society of Minneapolis from 1881 until 1905. Due to deafness, he lived a life of solitude, extensively studying literature written in the Greek, Latin, French and German languages, along with many of the modern sciences. Three years later in December of 1896, the Buddhist Anagarika Dharmapala from Ceylon (Sri Lanka) addressed the congregation twice in the same Unitarian Church. In his diary Dharmapala jotted down, "In the study Mr. Simmons. A noble, unselfish, persevering soul. Mr. Simmons is one of the best men I have ever met."[55]

Swamiji's first speech was so well received that prior to his second engagement on December 14, a student magazine at the University of Minnesota in Minneapolis paid him this glowing tribute:

> The most impressive figure at the World's Parliament of Religions was the Hindu monk Swami Vivekananda. He was sent to that body as a representative of the Brahmin faith. The convincing sincerity of his words and the magnetic power of his personality fascinate all who hear him and have given him the title of "an orator of divine right".... His strongly intellectual face, in its picturesque setting of yellow and orange, is hardly less interesting than his earnest words. It is sensitive to every thought in the shifting humour of the speaker. One is reminded in seeing him of the elder [Tommaso] Salvini [an Italian actor, 1829-1915]. There is the same repose, yet glow of feeling and fiery burst of passionate power. Vive Kananda has something to say, something new, refreshing and important for thinking persons to learn. He seeks to enlighten us in regards to his religion and the words of its philosophers to give a true account of the lives of his people in their far away eastern home.[56]

Asim Chaudhuri discovered a church newspaper called the *Christian Worker*, edited by Reverend Harvey O. Breeden. Concerning Vivekananda's upcoming talks at the Central Church of Christ in Des Moines, Iowa, he wrote in part:

> The second lecture in the course will be by SWAMI VIVEKANANDA a Hindoo monk. Vivekananda is one of the most remarkable men of the world. He came to the world's parliament of religions to represent the Hindoo faith, the mother religion of India. He is, to begin with, a profound philosopher, a trained thinker and a scholar with few superiors in the world. He is proficient in the use of the English language as any American, and as eloquent as any lecturer today on the American platform.
>
> Those who attended the parliament of religions will recall the fact that every appearance of Vivekananda on the platform was a signal for a demonstration of applause. The reporter witnessed a scene in the science department of the parliament so striking that he can never forget it. After delivering a discourse on the "Theory of the Incarnation", Vivekananda turned to his auditors, who were bright and critical scholars, teachers, preachers, and literary women, with the statement: "If you have any questions concerning my religion or philosophy I will be glad to answer you." It was a hazardous thing for an American scholar to do, but he was equal to the emergency. Though questions were poured upon him, bearing almost an avalanche of thought, he caught them all and turned them back in such lucid and logical answers as to astound everyone present.[57]

On November 27 Vivekananda received an invitation to deliver a two or three-hour talk at the home of Reverend and Mrs. Harvey O. Breeden in Des Moines, Iowa. That night the Swami gave a discourse on "Hindu Religion" before a full house at the Central Church of Christ, where Breeden served as the Pastor. The *Iowa State Register* mentioned:

> The people of Des Moines had a glimpse of Oriental life and thought at its best yesterday, from the lips of the famous Hindoo monk, Swami Vive Kananda. A central figure in the great Parliament of Religions at Chicago this summer, where he coped with some of the greatest minds of the country with honour to himself and his people, he gave those who heard him, and especially those who met him at Dr. Breeden's, something new to think about.[58]

Another local newspaper noted that, "The lecturer is an able, dignified and forcible speaker. His mastery of English is perfect."[59]

On November 28, before a large audience Swamiji addressed the subject of "Reincarnation" at the Central Church of Christ. The front page of the *Des Moines Leader* described the people's reaction to him this way:

> The lecturer whose fame has preceded him to the city and whose address Monday night resulted in increasing the interest felt in him by Des Moines people is a pleasing speaker and has a rare command of the English language. He is a man of little more than 30 years, with dark brown skin, coal black hair and jetty eyes. He is of medium height, compactly built, and with a highly intelligent cast of countenance from which beams kindness and interest when speaking or answering questions....
>
> Vivekananda has rather the best of the ordinary questioner who tries to trip him. He is highly educated in philosophy, his mind acts quickly, and in addition he uses the English language with that fine discrimination as to the meaning of terms which, while absolutely necessary in philosophical discussions, is ordinarily neglected. That is why the audience found so many occasions to applaud the visiting lecturer last night, as his quick answers silenced, if they did not convince his questioners.

In addition, Vivekananda spoke at Drake University at the Old Main Auditorium in Des Moines on the morning of November the 29th.[60]

Soon after Vivekananda left Des Moines on December 3, 1893, the *Iowa State Register* wrote in a long article:

> It is to the credit of Dr. Breeden that, knowing what Vivekananda would say, he brought him here to address the members of his congregation. He did not look at it as one woman did, who tried to get Dr. Breeden to suppress the monk's address wherein he criticized some features of Christianity because it would prevent Christians from going to hear him. Dr. Breeden thinks that a religion that cannot stand discussion, or being looked at from the other side, is not of much account.[61]

Harvey Oscar Breeden (1857-1933) was described by his contemporaries as having a commanding appearance, strength of character, self-poised, with an easy and winning manner, possessing an unusual degree of magnetic power, a born leader and organizer, a tireless worker with undaunted courage and energy, with sympathetic kindliness and generosity diffused through his whole life, a loving, warm hearted and devoted friend. Dr. Breeden held the position of president of the International Convention of the Disciples of Christ in 1904, and for twenty years functioned as a trustee of Drake University in Des Moines. Breeden showed interest in Christian missions and, in 1904, his church supported Dr. Ada McNeil, a missionary in India. After he moved to Oakland, California, he became a member of the board of the United Christian Missionary Society.[62]

The Year 1894

In mid-January of 1894, Swamiji paid a visit to Memphis, Tennessee. He was a guest of the Nineteenth Century Club, the largest and most influential women's club in the city. At the home of Colonel R. B. Snowden he met Assistant Bishop Thomas F. Gailor, Reverend George Patterson, and other clergymen. The writer for the *Appeal-Avalanche* newspaper described the Hindu monk in glowing terms as:

> ...one of the most eloquent men who has ever appeared on the religious or lecture platform in this country. His matchless oratory, deep penetration into things occult, his cleverness in debate, and great earnestness captured the closest attention of the world's thinking men at the World's Fair Parliament of Religion, and the admiration of thousands of people who have since heard him during his lecture tour through many of the states of the Union.
>
> In conversation he is a most pleasant gentleman; his choice of words are the gems of the English language, and his general bearing ranks him with the most cultured people of Western etiquette and custom. As a companion he is a most charming man, and as a conversationalist he is, perhaps, not surpassed in the drawing-rooms of any city in the Western World. He speaks English not only distinctly, but fluently, and his ideas, as new as sparkling, drop from his tongue in a perfectly bewildering overflow of ornamental language....
>
> His wonderful first address before the members of the World's Fair Parliament stamped him at once as a leader in that great body of religious thinkers. During the session he was frequently heard in defence of his religion, and some of the most beautiful and philosophical gems that grace the English language rolled from his lips there in picturing the higher duties

> that man owed to man and to his Creator. He is an artist in thought, an idealist in belief and a dramatist on the platform.[63]

In addition, the *Memphis Commercial* commented that, "His delivery is very good, his use of English being perfect as regards choice of words and correctness of grammar and construction."[64] Thomas Gailor (1856-1935), professor of ecclesiastical history at the University of the South in Sewanee, Tennessee, became the vice-chancellor of the University in 1891, and the chancellor from 1908 to 1935. He was consecrated Bishop coadjutor in 1893, and five years later he became the Episcopal Bishop of the state of Tennessee. Theologically he was a high-churchman with wide sympathies, who came out with many religious writings.[65] Reverend George Patterson (1828-1901), whose original name was Papathakes, worked with Bishop Gailor. Previously, he served as a Civil War chaplain (1861-65), and the Pastor of the Episcopal Grace Church in Memphis, Tennessee (1886-1901).[66]

On February 14 Swamiji appeared before Reed Stuart's Unitarian Church in Detroit, Michigan, addressing the subject "Manners and Customs of India". The *Detroit Free Press* described the event this way:

> An audience that filled the Unitarian Church heard the renowned monk, Swami Vivekananda, deliver a lecture last night on the manners and customs of his country. His eloquent and graceful manner pleased his listeners, who followed him from beginning to end with the closest attention, showing approval from time to time by outbursts of applause.... It is upon matters religious and philosophic (and necessarily spiritual) that the Eastern brother is most impressive, and, while outlining the duties that follow the conscientious consideration of the great moral law of nature, his softly modulated tones, a peculiarity of his people, and his thrilling manner are almost prophetic. He speaks with marked deliberation, except when placing before his listeners some moral truth, and then his eloquence is of the highest kind.[67]

On that occasion, Methodist Bishop William Xavier Ninde (1832-1901) introduced Vivekananda's address at the Unitarian Church. Previously, Bishop Ninde travelled to Europe and the East in 1868-69, became a professor and the president of the prestigious Garrett Biblical Institute on the campus of Northwestern University in 1879, and then a Methodist Bishop in 1884. He had been in British India visiting the Methodist's missions, and planned to depart for the Orient where he was the president of the Methodist missionary conference in China, Japan, and Korea in 1894-95. His peers described him as "a man of attractive presence and great personal magnetism, and excelled as a presiding officer".[68] According to the *Detroit Free Press* of February 15, 1894, during the talk Swamiji said:

> Such a country [India] has no need of Christian missionaries to "preach ideas", for theirs is a religion that makes men gentle, sweet, considerate, and affectionate towards all God's creatures, whether man or beast. Morally, said the speaker, India is head and shoulders above the United States or any other country on the globe. Missionaries would do well to come there and drink of the pure waters, and see what a beautiful influence upon a great community have the lives of the multitude of holy men.[69]

The *Detroit Free Press* was critical of Ninde for introducing Swami Vivekananda before his public speech. In response, the following day Ninde wrote to the editor of the *Detroit Free Press*, "I felt no hesitation under the circumstances in rendering so simple a courtesy to a gentleman of such acknowledged ability and learning as Mr. Kananda." Considering Swamiji to be a "distinguished speaker", Bishop Ninde continued:

> The lecture, though able and interesting, instead of weakening my faith in the value of Christian missions in India, has strongly confirmed my conviction of their importance and ultimate triumph.... while I differ very widely from him in my conception of the religious idea and religious duty, yet I long and pray for the day when, in the clearer light which God's spirit may vouchsafe to each one of us, the people of all lands and all races may see eye to eye and be perfectly joined together in the service of a common divine Redeemer.[70]

In February and March, Swamiji conversed on five occasions before large audiences at Reed Stuart's Unitarian Church in Detroit.[71] The writer for the *Detroit Journal* observed:

> If Vive Kananda, the Brahmin monk, who is delivering a lecture course in this city, could be induced to remain for a week longer, the largest hall in Detroit would not hold the crowds which would be anxious to hear him. He has become a veritable fad, as last evening every seat in the Unitarian

church was occupied, and many were compelled to stand throughout the entire lecture.[72]

Reed Stuart (1845-1910), a Civil War veteran who very much opposed war, was in charge of the Congregational-Presbyterian Church during 1877-86. Possessing somewhat of a radical nature, he became dissatisfied with traditional Christian theology, and made the switch to the more liberal Unitarian Church in Detroit in 1886. Being a learned and widely read man, Stuart produced a couple of books containing the sermons he delivered between 1887 and 1904. He used the language of everyday life, and his sermons were vivid and pictorial.[73] On Sunday February 18, Vivekananda sat in his audience and often nodded his head in approval during Stuart's sermon on "The Gates Opening toward the East". Among other things the Reverend said:

> The eastern mind deals with the larger aspect of things; the western with the minute and measurable. The one believes in the All; the other also believes in the All, but separates it into the many. The one unites, the other divides. The one believes in infinity; the other in boundaries. The one meditates; the other acts.[74]

Rabbi Louis Grossmann (1863-1926), a lifelong bachelor, was born in Vienna, Austria, and attended high school and university in the United States. He served as the Rabbi at the Temple Beth El in Detroit (1884-98), and the Congregation B'nai Yeshurun in Cincinnati (1898-1922). Beginning in 1898, he worked under Rabbi Isaac M. Wise (1819-1900), who was a speaker at the Parliament of Religions. Rabbi Wise, a pioneer of American Reform Judaism, founded and became the president of Hebrew Union College. At the College from 1898 until 1922, Grossmann, a professor of ethics, pedagogy and theology, was the Institute's principal during 1909-18. Being a prolific lecturer and popular with his students, he authored ten or more books. Grossmann founded and became the principal of Teacher's College (1909-26), which trained Jewish instructors. Being a very active person, Grossmann carried out the duties of president of the Central Conference of American Rabbis and some other religious organizations, and in 1924 became the founder and honorary president of the Western Association of Jewish Ministers.[75]

On February 18, 1894, Rabbi Grossmann of Detroit expressed his convictions on "What Vive Kananda Has Taught Us".[76] He praised Vivekananda's teaching of universal brotherhood and made reference to a speech the Swami gave the night before at the Unitarian Church. Two days later in a letter to Mrs. G. W. (Belle) Hale, Swamiji mentions that Reed Stuart and Rabbi Grossmann "take great interest in me and eulogize me".[77] Two years later on March 9, 1896 in a Detroit newspaper *Evening News*, Grossmann defended Vivekananda and Hinduism against a missionary accuser. In a letter of April 26, 1896 to Christina Greenstidel (later Sister Christine), the Swami sent his love to the Rabbi.[78]

In this regard, Mary Caroline Funke clarified that:

> His [Swamiji's] last public appearance in Detroit [March 15, 1896] was at the Temple Beth-El of which the Rabbi Louis Grossman[n], an ardent admirer of the Swami, was the Pastor.... Vivekananda held the large audience spellbound ... He gave us a most brilliant and masterly discourse. Never had I seen the Master look as he looked that night. There was something in his beauty not of earth. It was as if the spirit had almost burst the bonds of flesh, and it was then that I first saw a foreshadowing of the end.[79]

Dr. Egbert Guernsey proved to be influential in introducing Vivekananda to New York society. At the home of the doctor and his wife, they held a Sunday afternoon dinner party in April 1894. According to the plan, each of the fourteen participants at the dinner table would represent a different religious creed. Constance Towne, the representative of Catholicism, wrote:

> The Swami would make from time to time a little speech apparently in explanation of his native land and the customs of its people so different from our own, but always to gain his point in philosophy and religion. A more broadminded and tolerant man surely could not have been found anywhere in India to carry out the mission of founding Vedanta Centres in America.[80]

Towne and Vivekananda became good friends, "a purity of the spirit, absolutely apart from the material love and hates". With other people, they attended the presentation of "Faust" at the Metropolitan Opera. Constance Towne continued:

> He taught me much of the philosophy he preached and wrote about, how to meditate, and what power it would be against the hurts of life; what force of purpose it would attain for the preservation of the body, for logical thought, for self-control, for ecstasy, for the attraction of others; its power for good, its knowing how to read others and their needs; not to dull the edge of your sword, to be moderate in one's consumption of food, to know what one's own body needs to make it live well; of chastity, tolerance, purity of thought, and love for the world—not of one person but of everyone and of all created things.[81]

Charles Henry Parkhurst (1842-1933) attended Guernsey's dinner party, but we do not know how he and Swamiji got along. In 1880 Reverend Parkhurst, originally a Congregational Minister, took charge of the Madison Square Presbyterian Church in New York City. Early in life in 1870, Parkhurst taught Greek and Latin and wrote the book *Analysis of the Latin Verb Illustrated by the Forms of the Sanskrit*. He was elected to be the president of the Society for the Prevention of Crime in New York City. In a sermon from the pulpit preached in February 1892, he denounced the mayor, district attorney and the police for their support of vice in New York City, and the public indifference to this situation. As a result the voters elected a new mayor; a sweeping reform movement took place in the city government accompanied by a reduction in vice.[82]

On May 1, the Swami wrote in a letter to Isabelle McKindley that Lyman Abbott invited him for a luncheon engagement.[83] Reverend Abbott (1835-1922), a delegate to the Parliament of Religions, directed the prestigious Plymouth Congregational Church in Brooklyn (1888-98) and was an author of several religious books. For many years he worked as the editor-in-chief of the *Outlook*, a widely read Protestant periodical that was not favourable to Swamiji. It proved to be advantageous for the circulation of the *Outlook*, to stand firmly behind the ideas of the mainline Christian clergy. Abbott also served as a member of the first Board of Officers of the Ramabai Association of the United States.[84]

Two weeks later, on the 15th, Vivekananda discussed the subject of the "Manners and Customs of India" at the Lawrence Women's Club. Among other things the *Lawrence American and Andover Advertiser* wrote on May 18:

> His beauty is undoubtedly remarkable. An erect, fine form, a face strong and yet refined, most intelligent eyes and perfect expressive mouth, a voice rich and musical,—a voice capable of electrifying an audience and also, when combined with the flash of his eye and the curve of his lip, expressive of the utmost scorn.[85]

After the event Swamiji went to the residence of Reverend and Mrs. Young, "where he has been entertained and has proven himself to be a most delightful guest".[86] At that time or more likely in December of 1894, Vivekananda spoke at the Vesper service at the Unitarian Church of George Henry Young. In 1901, for the Unitarian Sunday-School Society, Young came out with a manual in Boston with the title *Character Lessons*.[87]

In her writings Marie Louise Burke clarified that the following article which appeared in the *Boston Evening Transcript* of July 28 "was almost certainly written by Ralph Waldo Trine" (1866-1958), a special correspondent for the newspaper at Greenacre. The statement reads:

> Friday an extra lecture will be given by Swami Vivekananda of India, who is spending a few weeks at Greenacre. He is deeply interested in this unitary work which has been inaugurated, and each morning may be seen, attired in his flowing red robes and yellow turban, sitting cross-legged on the ground near a wide-spreading pine, and surrounded by a group of eager listeners, men and women, to whom he pours out freely his treasures of knowledge and experience. It is a rich opportunity to us who are privileged to enjoy it, and our only regret is that so many hungry souls are missing it.

There is a well-known group picture of Swamiji seated at Greenacre, and the tall lean man wearing a hat in the front row is a young R. W. Trine.[88]

On January 3, 1896, Vivekananda sent a correspondence to Sara Bull saying, "I have had a letter from Mr. Trine asking me to have some classes at the Procopeia [in Boston] in February. I do not see my way to go to Boston in February, however I may like it."[89] Swami Saradananda, R. W. Trine and Rabbi Fleischer spoke to a New Thought group in Boston. During one season, R. W. Trine and his wife were present at Abhedananda's discourses at the Greenacre Conference. In 1900, from October 23 to 26, R. W. Trine lectured in New York City at the Second Convention of the New Thought International Metaphysical League held at Madison Square Garden. On that occasion Abhedananda spoke about Vedanta philosophy, sharing the platform with Lewis Janes, Reverend R. Heber Newton, Annie Rix Militz, Horatio W. Dresser, and others. Trine produced three short articles that appeared in the *Prabuddha Bharata* of 1905. For many years Trine and his wife lived in the Hollywood Hills in Los Angeles. They attended some events at Swami Paramananda's Ananda Ashram in La Crescenta during 1938 and 1939. There R. W. Trine spoke of some incidents in his relation with Vivekananda whom he greatly admired.[90]

R. W. Trine authored many best-selling books on New Thought philosophy. His greatest success, *In Tune with the Infinite* (1897), sold over two-million copies and was translated into twenty languages including Gujarati in 1918. He successfully presents the religious ideal that the goal of human existence is to attain harmony with the divine realm. This book was published three years after Trine attended Vivekananda's classes at Greenacre. The writings of Ralph Waldo Emerson influenced him, and he held a number of ideas cordial to those of the Vedanta philosophy, possibly picked up from Swamiji and to a lesser extent from Saradananda.[91] Trine presents ideas like:

> The central fact in human life, in your life and mine, is the coming into a conscious, vital realization of our oneness with the Infinite Life, and the opening of ourselves fully to this divine inflow. The more we realize this oneness, the more we become godly.
>
> When we realize that we are all one with this Infinite Spirit, then we realize that in a sense we are all one with each other.... We can do no harm to anyone, to anything.
>
> All is law, all is cause and effect. As we sow, so shall we also reap, not only in this life but in all lives.[92]
>
> We are partakers of the life of God; and though we differ from Him in that we are individualized spirits, while He is the Spirit including us as well as all else beside, yet in essence the life of God and the life of man are identically the same, and so are one. They differ not in essence, in quality; they differ in degree.[93]
>
> We are all living, so to speak, in a vast ocean of thought, and the very atmosphere around us is continually filled with the thought forces that are being continually sent or that are continually going out in the form of thought waves.
>
> Everything exists in the unseen before it is manifested or realized in the seen, and in this sense it is true that the unseen things are the real,

while the things that are seen are the unreal. The unseen things are *cause*; the seen things are *effect*.[94]

The automobile manufacturer Henry Ford (1863-1947) credited *In Tune with the Infinite* with some of the financial success he later achieved. After he read the book, Ford freely distributed a large number of copies to high-ranking industrialists. In 1916 the poet Rabindranath Tagore referred to Ford as "a friend of mine". In a 1938 interview, Henry Ford, a firm believer in reincarnation, expressed his belief that:

> When I was a young man, I, like so many others, was bewildered. I found myself asking the question ... "What are we here for?" I found no answer.... One day a friend handed me a book.... That little book gave me the answer I was seeking. It changed my whole life. From emptiness and uselessness, it changed my outlook upon life to purpose and meaning. I believe we are here now and will come back again.... Of this I am sure ... that we are here for a purpose. And that we go on. Mind and memory—they are the eternals.[95]

In a letter of 5 August 1894 to Mrs. G. W. (Belle) Hale, Swamiji mentions he had the "very nice company" of Everett Hale of Boston.[96] A photograph taken at the Greenacre Conference on August 2nd shows the Swami and Hale pictured together along with Sarah Farmer and an Armenian guest. A highly esteemed Unitarian Pastor of a church in Boston from 1856 until 1903, Edward Everett Hale (1822-1909) also was a popular speaker at the Parliament of Religions in 1893. Hale wrote many volumes, including the classic short novel *A Man without a Country* (1863). Into his revised edition of Thomas Bullfinch's *The Age of Fable* (1881) he added part of James Clarke's chapter on Hinduism in the textbook *Ten Great Religions* (1871). For decades this very well-read book taught many Americans about the Hindu Trinity of Brahma, Vishnu and Shiva. Hale was a member of the first Board of Officers of the Ramabai Association in the United States. After his eightieth birthday, he received the national honour of being the sole chaplain of the United States Senate from 1903 until his death. There he took every opportunity to promote international peace.[97]

Pratap Mazumdar (Mazoomdar, 1840-1905) [q.v.] gave a talk before a small group at the home of Mrs. Ralph Waldo Emerson in Concord, Massachusetts, in 1883, the year after the remarkable philosopher died.

The American Unitarians appreciated his two speeches at the Parliament of Religions. They very much approved of his emphasis on social reform in India. Afterwards they invited Mazumdar to tour the country and to present four Lowell lectures at Harvard University in October and November of 1893. Consequently, a committee headed by Edward Everett Hale of the American Unitarian Association raised the money to endow Mazumdar with a life-long annual stipend. Mazumdar also received an all-expense paid trip to the American Unitarian Association's 75th anniversary celebration held in 1900.[98]

Swamiji mentions in a letter to Anagarika Dharmapala that he spoke with Dr. Joseph Estlin Carpenter (1844-1927) [q.v.] of Oxford University at the annual meeting of the Free Religious Association at Plymouth, Massachusetts, on August 12, 1894. At that time the professor discussed the "Ethics of Buddhism". During the Cambridge Conferences at Sara Bull's residence in December, Vivekananda conversed with Carpenter.[99] Two years later in the *Inquirer*, a Unitarian paper of London, Carpenter discerned:

> The philosophical and religious addresses of this remarkable personality [Swami Vivekananda], who produced a great effect at the Chicago Parliament of Religions, have been issued in three little volumes, well worth the study of all who are interested in the present developments of religion in India.... The Swami speaks, as I had the good fortune to hear at the annual meeting of the Free Religious Association ... in perfect English, with that mastery over both matter and form which comes of long meditation and possession of his subject.... The essence of religion for him lies in *yoga*,—union between God and man,—which must be based on the harmonious activity of all man's powers. How to achieve it, what discipline of reason and will, of unselfish labour, of spiritual affection, is needed for the soul that would know itself in God,—this is set forth with much earnestness in these discourses. Whatever message we may have to send to India, we must not ignore the insight of its own seers.[100]

The Unitarians in Boston created the world's first permanent international interfaith organization in May 1900. They called it the International Association for Religious Freedom, and Professor Carpenter functioned as its first president. One of its founders helped organize the 1893 Parliament of Religions, and this Association was considered to be its logical extension. By 1901 religious groups from fifteen different countries were members of the Council. They held the Congress every two years, lasting for three days in 1901, attracting two-thousand people in London. Over the years, this organization received the active support of the Ramakrishna Mission, the Brahmo Samaj and Arya Samaj, and other Asian religious groups.[101]

Swami Vivekananda came to Baltimore at the invitation of the youthful Vrooman brothers.[102] For racial reasons, at first he was denied admittance to at least one hotel.[103] This story was "big news" that went out on the wire around the country. An African-American newspaper from Philadelphia, the *Christian Recorder* (October 18, 1894), took Swamiji's side and reacted with this insightful statement, "Should Christ appear in Baltimore as he did in Palestine he would probably not only be refused at hotels but be rejected from the leading churches of that caste-bound city." Swamiji ended up lodging at the refined Hotel Rennert. The *Baltimore American* of October 14 informs us:

> He was accepted there [Hotel Rennert] as a guest without the slightest hesitancy—indeed, the management was glad to have under its roof a hostelry of men renowned in art, in letters, in business—this man of the Orient who is known the world over.[104]

Twice during that time on the 14th and 21st of October 1894, he, along with three young brothers, Walter, Hiram and Carl Vrooman, expressed their views on the subject of "Dynamic Religion". Following the "Social Gospel", their idea of a civic humanitarian religion soon faded, and their series of sermons ended in February 1895. They spoke at the Lyceum Theatre before an audience of three-thousand people.[105] According to a newspaper report, Reverend Hiram Vrooman made the remark that "Mr. Vivekananda is one of the most intelligent men I have ever met. He came to this city at our invitation."[106] Concerning his second speech, the *Morning Herald* of October 22 reported:

> The speakers of the evening were seated on the stage, the Rev. Vivekananda being an object of particular interest to all. He wore a yellow turban and a red robe tied in at the waste [sic] with a sash of the same colour, which added to the Oriental cast of his features and invested him with a peculiar interest. His personality seemed to be the feature of the evening. His address was delivered in an easy, unembarrassed manner, his

diction being perfect and his accent similar to that of a cultured member of the Latin race familiar with the English language.[107]

Hiram Vrooman attended a meeting of the New Church of Maryland, a Swedenborgian organization, on the 16th, lecturing on "The New Church in Relation to Oriental Beliefs". The report in the *Washington Post* of October 17 continued:

> A very interesting account was given in this of Dr. Vrooman's interview with Swami Violkanananda [sic], who belongs to the oldest order of Hindoo Monks. He represented the Hindoo religion of India at the world's congress of religions at Chicago during the Fair. Dr. Vrooman said that the humane ideals in the New Church [Swedenborgian] doctrine were especially pleasing to the famous priest.

Eventually the three brothers went their separate ways. Most successful of them was Carl Vrooman (1872-1966), a farmer who owned four-thousand acres in the Midwest. As President Woodrow Wilson's wartime assistant secretary of agriculture (1914-19), he pushed for "war gardens", later known as "victory gardens" during the Second World War. He urged city residents to create their own food-supplying gardens during the First World War. A second major accomplishment of his was working for postwar agricultural relief legislation for the Europeans. After the war, on an eight-month mission in Europe, Carl Vrooman directed the shipment of more than a million bushels of corn to the continent to restore their shattered economy. Reverend Hiram Vrooman (1871-1954) became the Pastor of the New Jerusalem (Swedenborgian) Church in Baltimore in 1893, and later in Sheridan Park, Illinois, and Toronto, Canada. During his lifetime as a productive religious scholar, he came out with at least fifteen books, including three volumes dealing directly with the theology of Emanuel Swedenborg that were issued in 1911, 1943, and 1948 respectively. In 1894 Walter Vrooman (1869-1909) worked as a member of *The Arena* magazine staff. Swami Abhedananda wrote articles for this journal in December 1899 and in February 1900. Proclaiming a new ideal for society, in 1899 Walter Vrooman initiated the Ruskin Hall socialist movement in Oxford, England. Returning to the United States in 1900, he created (John) Ruskin College in Trenton, Missouri, later moving it to Ruskin, Florida. Within an academic setting, the male and female students of this vocational college received instructions on subjects such as the dignity of labour.[108]

On October 28 Vivekananda spoke from the pulpit of the nondenominational People's Church in Washington, D.C.[109] The presiding Pastor, Dr. Alexander Kent (1837-1908) [q.v.], a former Universalist Minister in four churches from 1865 until 1889, invited the Swami to speak there. When Dr. Kent introduced Swamiji to the podium, he said, among other things:

> The World's Parliament of Religions had given the people so generally misrepresented an opportunity to tell the truth about themselves. But we must not expect too much. Many denominations, like the turtle, have withdrawn themselves into their shells and refused to hear.[110]

After being the Pastor for twelve years in the Universalist Church in Washington, D.C., Reverend Kent became an independent clergyman in 1889 and organized the People's Church in 1891 for the purpose of serving humanity. He later came out with a book on *Cooperative Communities in the United States* in 1902.[111]

The *Complete Works*[112] gives the report in the *Washington Times* of two of Vivekananda's speeches in the city. In addition, the *Washington Post* of October 29, 1894 provided this account:

> ONLY A HINDU MONK
>
> Vive Kananda Believes not in the Tricks of the Yogis
>
> A Hindoo who is a member of no religious sect, who claims no knowledge or powers of occultism, who is not a believer in the miracles of the yogis ... but who simply announces himself as a religious student and a teacher to the world at large, is certainly something of a rarity.
>
> This Hindoo monk, of "swami", is Mr. Vive Kananda, now the guest of Col. Enoch Totten, of this city. Mr. Kananda is booked to lecture twice in Washington within the next week and a half, but he spoke twice yesterday without special announcement, before the congregation of the People's Church in Typographical Temple. He attended the parliament of religions in Chicago during the World's Fair, and is now touring the country, lecturing and preaching in various cities. Though a member of the parliament of religions, Mr. Kananda claims no sect, calls himself simply a Hindoo, which term he uses to indicate both race and religion. His position regarding the

religion of this country would be about that of a Unitarian in this country but for the fact that the Brahma Samaj claim the title of Hindoo Unitarians, leaving Mr. Kananda a free lance, outside the very outer wall.

All Religions are Good

Mr. Kananda spoke yesterday at the People's Church on the invitation of Dr. Kent, Pastor of the church. His talk in the morning was a regular sermon, dealing entirely with the spiritual side of religion, and presenting the, to orthodox sects, rather original proposition that there is good in the foundation of every religion, that all religions like languages, are descended from a common stock, and that each is good in its corporal and spiritual aspects so long as it is kept free from dogma and fossilism. The address in the afternoon was more in the form of a lecture on the Aryan race, and traced the descent of the various allied nationalities by their language, religion and customs from the common Sanskrit stock.

After the meeting, to a *Post* reporter Mr. Kananda said: "I claim no affiliation with any religious sect, but occupy the position of an observer, and so far as I may, of a teacher to mankind. All religion to me is good. About the higher mysteries of life and existence, I can do no more than speculate as others do....

When asked whether he knew anything of the alleged miraculous performances of the yogis and adepts Mr. Kananda replied that he was not interested in miracles, and that while there were of course a great many clever jugglers in the country, their performances were tricks. Mr. Kananda said that he had seen the mango trick but once, and then by a fakir on a small scale. He held the same view about the alleged attainments of the lamas. "There is a great lack of trained, scientific, and unprejudiced observers in all accounts of these phenomena," said he, "so that it is hard to detect the false from the true."

Mr. Kananda will remain in Washington until Thursday [November 1], when he lectures at Metzerott Hall on "Reincarnation" and after a short visit to New York will return to speak on "Gods of all Nations" on the following Tuesday [November 6].[113]

An advertisement in the *Washington Post* of October 28 also mentions his upcoming lecture on November 6.

When Abhedananda made a visit to Washington, D.C. three and one-half years later during the period May 9-25, 1898, he also addressed Kent's People's Church congregation. Before a large audience, on May 15 he spoke about "The Religion of the Hindus". A third person to speak at the People's Church in Washington, D.C. was Sister Devamata. On April 18, 1915 she was the guest speaker at their Sunday morning service, her subject being the "Evolution of Spiritual Consciousness". By that time, the People's Church had relocated to a new location at 1012 9th NW.[114]

1895 and After

Prior to meeting Vivekananda, Miss Laura Glenn (the future Sister Devamata, 1867-1942) [q.v.], one of the most outstanding of the American Vedantists, spent time as a lay sister in an Episcopal convent. During the winter of 1895, she attended the classes of Vivekananda in New York City. Thirty-seven years later, she described the sublime event this way:

> Swami Vivekananda passed in stately erectness up the aisle to the platform. He began to speak; and memory, time, place, people, all melted away. Nothing was left but a voice ringing through the void. It was as if a gate had swung open and I had passed out on a road leading to a limitless attainment. The end of it was not visible; but the promise of what it would be shone through the thought and flashed through the personality of the one who gave it. He stood there—prophet of infinitude.... Our real loyalty belonged to the Swami. We recognized in him a power that no other teacher possessed. It was he alone who was shaping our thought and conviction.[115]

Laura regularly attended all of Vivekananda's talks in the city of New York for two seasons during the years 1895 and 1896. There was an unseen "intangible barrier" between her and the Swami, so she never came "in close personal touch with him". She left her written personal memories of these events, which Marie Louise Burke used in her biography of Swamiji in the West. In 1901 they placed Laura in charge of the Publishing Department for the Vedanta Society of New York replacing Sarah Waldo. One of her assignments was to edit the Swami's two-volumes on *Jnana Yoga* for publication. Another was the compiling of *The Sayings of Sri Ramakrishna* (1903) for Abhedananda. After exhausting every possible source, she thought there were 694 sayings, but the 1985 volume lists only 554. The three chief sources were the *Brahmavadin*, *Prabuddha Bharata* and Max Müller's book on Ramakrishna. This book underwent at least nine printings, and for many decades was one of only a few books available on Sri Ramakrishna in the West. Miss Sara E. Waldo took notes of Vivekananda's conversations at Thousand Island Park during the summer of 1895. Laura told her, "It is criminal for you to keep these note to yourself. They belong to the world." She said to Laura:

> They have always seemed to me too fragmentary, too inadequate, to publish. They would give a false idea of the wonderful teachings Swamiji gave us during those six weeks at Thousand Island Park. If you are willing to take them and work on them and bring them out, I am glad to pass them over to you.

So in 1907 Laura Glenn edited the notes with Waldo's approval, and they were published as the *Inspired Talks* in 1908. She was in India at that time and Swami Brahmananda took an active part in their publication. He insisted that Laura write a Foreword for the book. She added:

> The Swami [Brahmananda] also had the determining word in all matters pertaining to the form the book was to take,—size, binding, paper, type. He supervised every detail. Swami Ramakrishnananda read every page of the manuscript with enthusiasm. He added a number of footnotes. For the second edition he wrote a supplementary Foreword. Also he shared with me the labour of correcting the proof.[116]

At the Vivekananda birthday celebration held on January 14, 1907, at the Vedanta Society House in New York, she told her audience:

> The most fitting commentary on Swami Vivekananda's teaching was in silent strenuous activity. She pointed to the significance of the fact that his life was nearly over before he gave his message; that every word he uttered he had first lived in silence, in meditation, and in action; and it was because thus weighted with experience that his word had so much effect. We must learn to be disciples, to understand the truths we hear, to live them, and then we will never have to speak them. It is after all Swami Vivekananda's life which speaks strongest for him.[117]

In March 1907 Laura Glenn became Swami Paramananda's first initiated disciple, receiving the name Devamata (Mother of the Deities). She was born seventeen years before Paramananda, and he always thought of her as his mother. Less than a year after Paramananda came to the United States, Devamata edited the instructive portions of his letters into the book *Path of Devotion* in 1907. Near the end of 1907 she journeyed to India, remaining there until September 1909, working with Swami Ramakrishnananda in Madras and also living in Calcutta. She assisted the Swami in publishing his first book, *The Soul of Man*, which marked the beginning of the Madras Math Publishing House. Devamata had the blessed good fortune of taking care of Holy Mother's room and massaging her rheumatic legs. The Mother addressed her as "my sweet daughter". After returning to the U.S. in 1909, for the next thirteen years she worked at Paramananda's Centres as an administrator, lecturer, secretary, editor of their journal *The Message of the East*, author, and a domestic labourer. She quickly became one of the most notable American Vedantists. Paramananda created a community of nuns under the supervision of Sister Devamata, whom he ordained to teach Vedanta from the platform. Being an ideal disciple, she had unwavering faith and confidence in her guru. One of her students, Sister Shivani, later wrote, "She was as a hen taking care of her brood. She also had the gift to impart spirituality." Devamata became the first Western monastic to be placed in charge of a Vedanta Centre, though, of course, she worked to some extent under Paramananda's direction. In 1910 and 1911 for about nine months each year, she managed and carried on the work at the Centre in Washington, D.C. For the remainder of the year, Devamata took control of the Boston Centre while Paramananda taught in Washington, D.C. During the 1912-17 period she visited the nation's capital for only one season every year. After 1917 she devoted much of her attention to the work in the Los Angeles area.[118]

Possibly because of over work, in 1922 Devamata suffered a severe illness. Partially paralyzed, she remained a semi-invalid for the rest of her life. Unable to make public speaking appearances or to be heavily involved in the administrative work, she devoted most of her creative talents to literary pursuits. She recorded her two-year experience in India from 1907 through 1909 in *Days in an Indian Monastery* (1927), which includes a twenty-page tribute to Ramakrishnananda and insights into some of the other Swamis.*

* See Chapter XXI.

Her other literary works include the two-volume *Swami Paramananda and His Work* (1926, 1941), *Sri Ramakrishna and His Disciples* (1928), and *Sri Ramakrishna and St. Francis of Assisi* (1935).[119] She also published her writings fifteen times in the *Prabuddha Bharata* (1918-33), fourteen times in the *Vedanta Kesari* (1927-37), and an additional five posthumously in either journals (1978-2000).

A Universalist clergyman in New York City (1881-1902), Reverend Charles H. Eaton (1852-1902) attended Swamiji's discourse on "The Vedanta Philosophy: Soul" at Amzi Barber's home on February 28, 1895. The arrangements were made by Sara Bull.[120] At Unity Hall in Hartford, Connecticut, on March 8, 1895 Swamiji's topic was "God and the Soul". At the same location on January 31, 1896 he addressed the subject of "The Ideal of a Universal Religion".[121] Unity Hall was part of the Unitarian Church of Hartford. The presiding Minister was Reverend Joseph Waite (d. 1905) who took over the Church in 1892 and held the position until his death. Originally a Methodist, then a Congregationalist, and finally a Unitarian, Waite was an outspoken champion of liberal causes such as women's suffrage, civil rights and labour reform. Under the leadership of this very popular Minister, the Church entered a period of prosperity, though there were some who did not care for his progressive political views.[122]

Later in the summer, Vivekananda received an invitation to speak on July 27, 1895 at the prestigious four-day Oak Island Christian Unity Conference. The purpose of the conference was to bring various Protestant denominations closer together by creating some form of organic Christian unity. A portion of his speech that appeared in the *New York Tribune* of July 28 is also in the *Complete Works*,[123] though this newspaper is not mentioned there. Held at a pleasant resort on the Atlantic Coast, a large crowd attended the event. The Conference came to a close on Saturday with addresses by Vivekananda and Dr. Paul Carus (1852-1919) on worldwide religious unity. From the accounts given in the *New York Tribune*, *Brooklyn Daily Eagle*, and *Outlook* magazine, one would think that Swamiji attended the event. Yet, Marie Louise Burke points out that according to the *Inspired Talks* he was giving a class at Thousand Island Park, and would not have had time to travel to the conference. She thinks that he may have written a paper on the subject that someone else read at the conference.[124] A couple of months before the conference, Paul Carus, the Buddhist scholar who spoke at the 1893 Parliament of Religions, advised the leaders of the Pan-American Congress of Religion and Education to invite Vivekananda to their meetings to be held from 18 to 25 July 1895 in Toronto, Canada. The clergy of Toronto objected to Swamiji's presence, and instead he taught classes at Thousand Island Park at that time.[125]

On August 4, 1895, the following complementary statement about Swamiji written by Hamilton DeGraw appeared in *The Manifesto*, a journal of the Shaker religion:

> We notice Prof. Edgar Beall has given us, in the Phrenological Journal for August, a very interesting account of Swami Vivekananda, a young Hindoo monk who was a delegate to the "World's Parliament of Religions", and who is now travelling in this country, as a religious teacher. One of the most favourable signs of the times is that the demon of religious intolerance and bigotry is retiring into the shades of night, whence it emerged in the past, causing so much suffering to the advocates of advanced thought. The unfolding of the truths of the Divine life is not confined to sects or parties; and the different manifestations of it all move harmoniously together. This young Hindoo monk is teaching celibacy and maintains that for attaining to the highest unfoldment of the spiritual life, the perfect and complete renunciation of the emotions and passions of the lower life is imperative. To all such the hand of fellowship is extended of whatever race, colour or creed.[126]

Founded in England in 1747, the Shakers originally broke off from the Quaker Church. Their governing principles included strict celibacy for everyone, communal living, and seeking personal communion through the Inner Light with a God who is both the Eternal Father and the Eternal Mother. As a religious minority the Shakers came to the United States to avoid religious intolerance.[127]

The ecumenical anthology, *Rays of Light from all Lands* (1895), was edited by Reverend Edward Cornelius Towne (1834-1911), the Pastor of the Church of the Fraternity in New Haven, Connecticut, Reverend A. J. Canfield, a member of the executive committee of the 1893 Parliament of Religions, and George Jotham Hagar (1847-1921) who devoted his life to editing many Encyclopedias, including Harper's and Appleton's. The volume dedicated to presenting "Notable Utterances by Foremost Representatives of all Faiths" has nearly a full-page photograph of Swamiji with the caption reading:

> SWAMI VIVEKANANDA: a Brahman of India; a man of fine genius and great learning in the Sanskrit Veda; one of an order of monks on whom caste distinctions are not binding; a reformer devoting his life to the education and elevation of his countrymen.

Eleven pages of the volume under the title "Parliament Utterances" are devoted to a verbatim report of "Brahminism: Eloquent Words of Swami Vivekananda, 'the great Hindu Monk:' His exposition of Brahminical Beliefs", with three additional pages by the Brahmin scholar Manilal N. Dvivedi.[128]

In 1895, during the time when Swamiji went to Europe, the French-American woman, Marie Louise Davitt (or David), who became Swami Abhayananda, and Swami Kripananda worked hard to spread the teachings of Vedanta in the United States. She later mentioned in an 1896 newspaper article that she went by the name Marie Louise, and never found it necessary to reveal her last name. In an 1899 newspaper article her last name was given as "Davitt" and in a 1915 report as "David".[129] They and Swami Yogananda (Mr. Street) were each employed as teachers possessing public speaking talent before coming to Vedanta. At a relatively young age, she originally came from Paris to the United States to teach foreign languages. Vivekananda at one time took French lessons from her. In Vivekananda's absence, Abhayananda and Kripananda continued on as teachers of Vedanta, attracting only a few people. Unlike the Swamis in India, they were not financially supported by the Order. When they ran into financial difficulty combined with having poor relations with other members of the Vedanta Society, they became disgruntled. In an 1896 newspaper article she was described as "an attractive woman of about fifty, with a large head, broad, masculine face, and rough, short, gray hair". After leaving the New York Vedanta Society, Abhayananda did some good by preaching the tenets of Vedanta to the general public. Beginning in 1897, she led her own Advaita Society group with hundreds of followers in Chicago, Illinois. Abhayananda also made two trips to India.[130] In a letter sent to Miss Mary Hale dated 16 March 1899 from Belur Math, Swamiji wrote, "Here is Abhayananda, Marie Louise you know, and she has been very well received in Bombay and Madras. She will be in Calcutta tomorrow, and we are going to give her a good reception too."[131] After returning from India, she placed more emphasis on Vaishnava principles and Bhakti Yoga. She attracted much attention, receiving large newspaper spreads along with her photograph in Boston,

Chicago, Los Angeles, and other locations. Then things changed. In 1913 Abhayananda lost all she had in a fire that burned down her house on the Midway in Chicago. By 1915 the white haired woman of about seventy years of age lived at 2807 Calumet Avenue in Chicago. According to the newspaper report at that time, "She was cold, hungry, and penniless." She stoically and sadly concluded, "My poverty is karma—the ethical consequences of all my acts. I have lived unwisely. I must learn my lesson, no matter how bitter. I must work out my karma here and hereafter. Have I some bright hopes? I cannot say I have."[132]

During late October of 1895, Vivekananda met English Anglican Reverend Hugh Reginald Haweis (1838-1901), head of the Anglican St. James Church in London, and his wife Mary Eliza Haweis (d. 1898). She asked Swamiji to be the speaker-of-honour at the Reverend's home in the Chelsea section of London. There he described "The Religion of Love".[133] Being an artist, Mary Haweis drew illustrations for her husband's books as well as her own. She wrote popular magazine articles on the domestic art of decoration and housekeeping, and on proper dress. Mary Haweis was also a strong supporter of the women's franchise movement. Both Hugh Haweis and Canon Basil Wilberforce (1841-1916) of Westminster "made interesting speeches in reply to the Swami".[134] Swami Vivekananda quickly became friends with Wilberforce, and on the 17th visited his home in Westminster. According to Professor John Henry Wright, Wilberforce told Vivekananda, "They were trying to teach in substance the Vedanta philosophy in the Church at the present time, and that he [Swamiji] was really a missionary to the Church of England."[135]

In a section on the 1893 Parliament of Religions in his two-volume *Travel and Talk* (1896), Hugh Haweis expresses his admiration for Swamiji:

> Vivekananda, the popular Hindu monk, whose physiognomy bore the most striking resemblance to the classic face of the Buddha, denounced our commercial prosperity, our bloody wars ... I consider that Vivekananda's personality was one of the most impressive, and his speech one of the most elegant speeches which dignified the great congress. This remarkable person appeared in England in the autumn of 1895, and although he led a very retired life, attracted numbers of people to his lodgings, and created everywhere a very deep impression. He seemed completely indifferent to money, and lived only for thought. He took quite simply anything that was given to him, and when nothing came, he went without, yet he never seemed to

lack anything; he lived by faith from day to day, and taught Yogi science to all who would listen, without money and without price. His bright orange flowing robe and white turban recalled forcibly the princely Magians who visited the birthplace of the Divine Babe.[136]

Reverend Hugh Haweis served under Giuseppe Garibaldi (1807-82) in the Italian War of Independence in 1860. His diminutive size, lively manner and unconventional methods brought large numbers of people to his church. Haweis of the St. James Church in London showed interest in the welfare of the lower classes and designated special evening services for them. In 1885 he received an invitation to be the Lowell lecturer in Boston. During the 1885-95 period Haweis travelled one-hundred thousand miles across the globe and gave addresses in Britain, America, Canada, Australia and New Zealand, and went to Ceylon (Sri Lanka). As an unofficial Anglican delegate, he spoke at the Parliament of Religions in 1893. Haweis wrote at least a dozen books, including a popular five-volume history of the church entitled *Christ and Christianity* (1886-87). In addition, he was a gifted violinist, author, journalist, lecturer and preacher.[137] Haweis' friend, the Venerable Albert Basil Orme Wilberforce, received appointment as canon residentiary of Westminster and in 1894 as Rector of St. Johns Church. Wilberforce held the distinguished position of chaplain of the British House of Commons (1896-1916) and archdeacon of Westminster (1900-16). He also published several volumes of the sermons he delivered to his congregation.[138]

Swami Vivekananda left England in November 1895 and returned in April 1896. In May 1896 he met Haweis and Wilberforce in London, and the former attended many of his classes. Swami Saradananda sent a letter to the editor of the *Brahmavadin* from London stating, "Canon Haweis, one of the leaders of the Anglican Church, came the other day, and was much interested. He saw the Swami before, in the Chicago fairs, and loved him from that time."[139] On June 21, 1896, Hugh Haweis gave a morning and evening sermon on "Swami Vivekananda" at his Anglican Church in London. He spoke of how the Swami's teachings support those of Jesus Christ. The following month Haweis sent Swamiji a booklet made up of parts of his sermons with the written inscription, "To the Master Vivekananda from one who both reverences and admires his teachings, H. R. Haweis." In an accompanying note Haweis added, "Your teaching is of a kind peculiarly adapted to the Western mind & you are doing inestimable good."[140]

During the month of October, Swami Vivekananda and Swami Abhedananda, along with Hugh Haweis, the Bishop of Ballarat in Australia, and others, ate lunch at the house of Emmeline Souter. Miss Souter later made the contribution of Rs. 15,000 (1,000 pounds), and Henrietta Müller of Rs. 30,000 (2,000 pounds), for the construction of a "Monastery in Calcutta [Belur Math] as a training ground for Vedanta teachers". A letter from Vivekananda to Sara Bull of October 22, 1900 mentions that Haweis "keeps track of my work in England".[141] The Right Samuel Travers Thornton (1835-1917), the first Anglican Bishop of Ballarat (1875-1900), was a charming friend of Haweis, whom he came across during a visit to Australia. Thornton returned permanently to England in the year 1900, and brought out a book of poems in 1904. He worked as the assistant Bishop to the Bishop of Manchester (1901-10), and the assistant Bishop at the diocese of London (1911-17).[142] Vivekananda later mentioned in 1897:

> Many of the best English Church clergymen became my firm friends, and without asking I got much help for my work ... The English Church people are all gentlemen born ... They greatly sympathized with me. I think that about thirty English Church clergymen agree entirely with me on all points of religious discussion.[143]

After returning to the United States, in January 1896 Swamiji gave an address before the congregation at the People's Church in New York City. Thomas Dixon (1864-1946) founded this non-denominational church in 1895, and after 1902 became a popular novelist.[144]

On March 25, Vivekananda gave an address on "The Vedanta Philosophy" before the Graduate Philosophical Society of Harvard University.[145] A long question and answer discussion session took place after the lecture came to an end.[146] Charles Carroll Everett (1829-1900), dean of the Harvard Divinity School, attended the discussion. The speech was transcribed into a book, and in the Introduction, Everett made the following appreciative statement about Swami Vivekananda:

> Everywhere he has made warm personal friends; and his expositions of Hindu philosophy have been listened to with delight. It is very pleasant to observe the eager interest with which his own people in India follow his course, and the joy that they take in his success. I have seen a pamphlet filled with speeches made at a large and influential meeting in Calcutta, which

> was called together to express enthusiastic approval of the manner in which he has fulfilled his mission ... Vivekananda has created a high degree of interest in himself and his work. There are indeed few departments of study more attractive than the Hindu thought. It is a rare pleasure to see a form of belief that to most seems so far away and unreal as the Vedanta system, represented by an actually living and extremely intelligent believer.... The reality of the One is the truth which the East may well teach us; and we owe a debt of gratitude to Vivekananda that he has taught this lesson so effectively.[147]

The Unitarian theologian Charles Carroll Everett became a professor of theology in 1869 at Harvard, and the dean of the Harvard Divinity School in 1878, holding the position until his death. As early as 1872, and throughout the remainder of his life, he taught a course in East Asian Religions. This might have been the first university course in comparative religions given in the United States. Being a man of modesty and dignity, many Ministers of different denominations considered Everett to be the spiritual inspiration of their life. He produced many books and journal articles. "Inspired by Swami Vivekananda's delineation of "The Vedanta Philosophy", in 1899 Everett came out with an article "The Psychology of the Vedanta and the Sankhya Philosophies" in the *Journal of the American Oriental Society*.[148]

After returning to England, Vivekananda made contact with Reverend Charles Voysey (1828-1912). Previously, due to his unorthodox religious views, he had been expelled from the Anglican Church. In 1885 Voysey established his own Theistic Church, which rejected the ideas of eternal punishment, Biblical inspiration, the sacramental system, the divinity of Christ and his miracles, and favoured cremation.[149] The Reverend John Page Hopps (1834-1911) invited Vivekananda to present a series of five talks in November and December of 1896 at his Unitarian and Free Christian Church in West Croyden, a residential suburb south of London. Hopps, the respected Pastor of the Church (1892-1903), was formerly the editor of the monthly *Truth Seeker* (1863-87), a hymnal writer, and the author of over twenty-five books. In a 1907 article in *The Modern Review*, Hopps maintained:

> Who says the people of India are not fit for home rule? We, Englishmen, who profit by ruling them; we, who do not want to surrender power; we, who in our egotism think we are the best and ablest rulers in the world. But it is an old cry. It was raised against the middle class in our own Eng-

land; it was raised against the mechanics of our great towns; it was raised against the country farmers, it had been raised against our women.[150]

Returning to the Orient, Vivekananda arrived at Colombo, Ceylon (Sri Lanka) on January 15, 1897. He was greeted by the presence of a steam launch with Swami Niranjanananda and T. G. Harrison aboard. Harrison, an English Buddhist from Ceylon, travelled with Swamis Vivekananda and Niranjanananda, the Seviers, and Goodwin to Pamban. The *Madras Times* mentions their coming together again in February in Madras.[151] Later in the month Harrison is pictured in an extant photo sitting on the lawn at Gopal Lal Seal's house at Cossipore in Calcutta along with Swamiji, some of his brother disciples, and others. Harrison attended a public address of Swamiji at the Star Theatre in Calcutta on March 4, and accompanied him to the Temple of Kali at Dakshineswar on the 27th. Little is known of Mr. Harrison except that in early 1913 he presented a lecture during the fifty-first birthday celebration of Swami Vivekananda held at the Vivekananda Society of Colombo. There he affirmed his admiration for Swamiji's character and teachings stating in part:

> We have met today to honour a great, good, religious and spiritual devotee, a saint whose highest ideal was to raise humanity above their sensual tendencies and attributes into the knowledge of a virtuous, moral and spiritual life.... Swami Vivekananda combined the heart of an innocent child with the imagination of a poet and the magnanimity of a divine spirit. His soul was large, benignant and sincere, and within his bosom throbbed a heart of Infinite Love. He preached and was favourably received, and lectured and discoursed in various parts of America. His silvery eloquence was irresistible in its charm and awakened in every heart a feeling for the knowledge of that Inward Search for the Divine.... Swami Vivekananda's sermons, lectures and discourses have fulfilled the expectations of those who appreciate the highest class of religious literature. Many have expressed their conviction that they deserve to be ranked among the very noblest productions of spiritual eloquence which have reached them for many years. They are full of thought and vigour and surpass anything yet known in their simplicity for the illustration of spiritual truth, which is the greatest boon conferred on the Western student. The Swami's works are unutterably precious and a combination of the richest and priceless gems. How many troubled hearts have they comforted!... Swami Vivekananda's

character was manly, and godly, and affords an admirable study for those who wish to see true religion developed in contemplative exercise. His life was full of earnest, devoted labour and offers a model for every true Sannyasin and householder.[152]

In February 1897, Lucy Guinness (1865-1906), who belonged to the Woman's Foreign Missionary Society of the Methodist Episcopal Church, attended his lecture on "My Plan of Campaign"[153] held at Victoria Hall in Madras. She wrote, "I had the most interesting experience I have had since coming to India," and quoted the last paragraph of his talk. The next morning before breakfast, she attended the "discussion meeting held in a tent by the seashore, at a place called Ice-house". Among five or six-hundred men, she was the only woman present. She related, "They gave me a chair near the door, where I sat and listened to the various interesting questions put by the crowd to the teacher." Miss Guinness described Vivekananda as "a large, strong man, with a powerful voice, a very calm way of speaking." Coming from a missionary standpoint, she added, "I asked about three points especially—child-marriage, widowhood, and idolatry. The Swami answered them fully, and the result was that the rest of the meeting became a sort of public conversation between him and me."[154]

Reverend E. Sherman Oakley (d. 1934) of the London Missionary Society served in the Almora region, India, from 1888 to 1934. He was a teacher at Ramsay College and a hymn writer who "gave steadfast service to the people of the town and district". Against George Grierson, in a 1907 article Oakley quoted Swami Vivekananda and others to prove that the idea and practice of bhakti in India was not derived from Christianity. Grierson later realized that Hindu bhakti preceded the origin of Christianity. Oakley's book *Holy Himalaya: The Religion, Traditions and Scenery of a Himalayan Province* (1905) describes the sacred places of pilgrimage in Kumaun and Garhwal. In this volume he pointed out:

> Along with the return of the old Puranic ritual, there has gone in recent years a marked revival of Vedantist philosophy, especially under the leadership of the late Swami Vivekananda, who was the means of introducing it to the English-speaking public at the Chicago Parliament of Religions. The Swami, with whom I had some acquaintance, was a man of remarkable ability, and full of ideas, which he expounded in various public lectures.[155]

Second Voyage to the West

The Improvement Era periodical, initiated in 1897 and published until 1970, was an official organ of a large section of the Mormon Church. In 1899, under the title "Oriental Religious Faiths, III. Hinduism", the Mormons showed their respect for Swamiji by using his teachings to represent the Hindu faith. In their journal they published an eleven-page article, containing over ninety percent of Vivekananda's presentation of "Paper on Hinduism" read at the Parliament of Religions on 19 September 1893.[156] The Mormons, like Vedantists, advocate universal salvation.[157]

Originally from Amsterdam, Holland, Cornelius J. Heijblom (Heyblom; the future Swami Atulananda, 1870-1966) came across Vivekananda at the New York Vedanta Society in November of 1899. He later discerned:

> He walked about the room, sat on the floor, laughed, joked, chatted—nothing formal. Of course, I had noticed his magnificent, brilliant eyes, his beautiful features and majestic bearing, for these were parts of him that no circumstances could hide. But when I saw him for a few minutes standing on a platform surrounded by others, it flashed into my mind: "What a giant, what strength, what manliness, what a personality! Every one near him looks so insignificant in comparison." It came to me almost as a shock and seemed to startle me. What was it that gave Swamiji this distinction?... It seemed to be more in the expression of the face than anything else is. Was it his purity? What was it? I could not analyze it. I remembered what had been said of Lord Buddha—"a lion among men". I felt that Swamiji had unlimited power, that he could move heaven and earth if he willed it. This was my strongest and lasting impression of him.[158]

Taking the vows of brahmacharya from Abhedananda in New York, Heijblom received the name Gurudasa (servant of the guru) on Easter Sunday, April 2, 1899. He was a student in close association with Turiyananda during the years 1900-02. He came and stayed in the Shanti Ashrama in Northern California during 1900-06 and 1912-14, and the United States during 1918-22. He resided in India during the years 1906-12, 1914-18, and 1922-66. Holy Mother initiated him at the Udbodhan Office, and he received the monastic name Swami Atulananda from Abhedananda at Belur Math in 1923. In his book *With the Swamis in America*, he describes his monastic experiences, and his spiritual conversations are recorded by Swami Dhireshananda in *Atman alone Abides*. In the *Prabuddha Bharata* Atulananda published an amazing fifty-one articles between 1907-54, and five posthumously; and he contributed twenty-one articles to the *Vedanta Kesari* between 1926-67, and therein five of his articles were posthumously published. Swamis Vivekananda and Turiyananda in the West, and Jesus the Christ were his favourite writing topics.

Pravrajika Brahmaprana, a nun at the Vedanta Society of Southern California, wrote:

> Especially in his later life, Gurudasa Maharaj's saintly characteristics inspired many American and Indian devotees, and he received recognition from his fellow monastics as a *sadhu* of deeper realization. With this reputation, Gurudasa Maharaj attracted many devotees, who travelled sometimes great distances just for his *darshan*.[159]

In addition, Swami Vidyatmananda, who knew him personally, explained:

> As the years went by, other historical figures died, and Gurudasa Maharaj himself became a celebrity. Indians, both monastic and lay, planned for years to go on a pilgrimage to the Himalayan foothills, in order to see him. And devotees from the West, hearing of him and feeling for him a kind of patriotic pride, as was my case, made a point to journey up to Kankhal when visiting India.

He himself told the future Swami Vidyatmananda in 1953, "It is nice to be elderly in India. In the good old U.S.A. you're not wanted when you are aged. But here elderly people are respected. Look at the way they love and spoil me! In India old age is really an advantage."[160]

After returning from India to the West, Vivekananda spoke before a "large and appreciative" audience at the Southern California Academy of Sciences on "The Cosmos, or the Veda Conception of the Universe". The event took place on December 12, 1899, at Unity Church, corner of Third and Hill Streets in Los Angeles.[161] Reverend C. J. K. Jones came from Kentucky in September 1898 to become the Pastor of this church, and left six years later to attend to his Florida orange grove property.[162]

Swami Vivekananda received an invitation from J. Ransome Bransby to be the guest speaker at the New Thought Home of Truth in Los Angeles.

Bransby and his wife were the directors of the Los Angeles Home of Truth. In 1899 he lectured there on eight occasions between December 21 and 30.[163] In the *Unity* magazine of February 1900, Bransby wrote:

> Of all the Vedantist missionaries who have visited this country, probably Vivekananda is the most widely known, he has done the most public works here and was such a notable figure at the World's Parliament of Religions at Chicago.... There is combined in the Swami Vivekananda the learning of a university president, the dignity of an Archbishop, with the grace and winsomeness of a free natural child. Getting on the platform without a moment's preparation he would soon be in the midst of his subject ... We had a lecture on Christmas day from the Swami entitled, "Christ's Mission to the World", and a better one on this subject I never heard. No Christian Minister could have presented Jesus as a character worthy of the greatest reverence more eloquently or more powerfully than did this learned Hindoo.[164]

Many years later in a letter of January 17, 1936, Bransby recalled the eminence of Vivekananda and told Thomas Allan that his talks at the Home of Truth

> were attended by large appreciative audiences. The Swami spoke with great charm and spirit. He spoke as one having authority; as one who had an inexhaustible reservoir of knowledge to draw from. Speaking in a language not native to him he manifested a fluency seldom, if ever, attained by those whose natural speech is English.[165]

On January 28, 1900, the Swami spoke at the Universalist Church in Pasadena on "The Universal Religion".[166] Ralph E. Connor, a young man of about thirty years of age, held the position of presiding Minister. During the preceding November or December, he transferred from a Universalist congregation in Waltham, Massachusetts, a city where Swamis Saradananda and Abhedananda had previously lectured before the Psychomath Society.[167]

A charismatic Christian evangelist, Reverend Benjamin Fay Mills (1857-1916) delivered an address before the World's Parliament of Religions at Chicago in 1893. Concerning Vivekananda's appearance at the Parliament, Mills later told Alice Hansbrough, "This man altered my life," which he did in the following way. By the year 1897, Mills withdrew from the evangelical ministry, sacrificing a highly successful career where he was credited with making a half-million converts in ten years. One reason for his action was, he said, "Because of the universal viewpoint which came to me through my study of the great books of all ages and nations, through which the Bible ceased to be to me the exclusively inspired Word of God." Possibly Mills had memories of Swamiji, when he and Swami Abhedananda and Colonel Robert Ingersoll were the three-featured speakers at the Free Religious Association meetings held at the Hollis Street Theatre in Boston in July 1899.[168] Mills was responsible for Swamiji's coming to Northern California. Writing to Josephine MacLeod on March 2 of 1900, Swamiji stated, "Rev. Benjamin Fay Mills, a very popular Unitarian preacher in Oakland, invited me from here and paid the fare to San Francisco. I have spoken twice in Oakland to 1500 people each time."[169] Two days later in a letter to Sara Bull, Vivekananda indicates that, "The people here have been prepared by my writings beforehand and they come in big crowds.... Rev. Benjamin Fay Mills invited me to Oakland and gave me big crowds to preach to. He and his wife have been reading my works and keeping track of my movements all the time."[170] Mills wrote to Vivekananda that he wanted to manage his Northern California speaking engagements, but Swamiji turned down the offer. In late February and in March Swamiji presented seven lectures at Mills' First Unitarian Church.[171] The *Oakland Enquirer* of February 25, 1900 emphasized that:

> The announcement that Swami Vivekananda, a distinguished savant of the East, would expound the philosophy of Vedanta in the Parliament of Religions at the Unitarian Church last evening, attracted an immense throng. The main auditorium and ante-rooms were packed, the annexed auditorium of Wendte Hall was thrown open, and this was also filled to overflowing, and it is estimated that fully 500 persons, who could not obtain seats or standing room where they could hear conveniently, were turned away.
>
> The Swami created a marked impression. Frequently he received applause during the lecture, and upon concluding, held a levee of enthusiastic admirers.[172]

According to Edith Allan, a longtime Northern California devotee:

When Swamiji was lecturing in Oakland, he stayed with B. Fay Mills overnight. Next morning he was walking slowly for the train and B. F. Mills was with him. B.F.M. said, "I'm afraid we will have to hurry Swami or we will miss the train." Swamiji calmly said, "Is there not another train?" No one could make him hurry.

At that time Judge John W. Stetson, a prominent member of the Unitarian Church in Oakland, emphasized:

> I challenge any one to go and listen to the Swami and then show where there is anything in his teachings that is not for the good of humanity.... any one who heard the Swami will admit that his teachings regarding morality are good.

Two years later when lecturing on "The Hindu Way of Salvation", Mills referred to Swamiji as, "A man of gigantic intellect, indeed, one to whom our greatest university professors were as mere children."[173]

Being a truth seeker, Mills' religious life went through many contradictory phases. He became a Congregational Minister (1878-86), a highly successful inter-denominational revival evangelist (1886-97), a liberal advocate of the new social gospel with some association with the Unitarian Minister Edward Everett Hale (1897-03), and a Minister of the First Unitarian Church of Oakland, California (1899-1903). After leaving the Unitarian Church, Mills became an itinerant evangelistic Pastor in Los Angeles (1904-11). Another effect that Swami Vivekananda had on Mills was a respectful attitude toward Indian religion. In August 1905, Mills brought the Bengali Vaishnava religious teacher Baba Premananda Bharati (1858-1914) [q.v.] from Boston to Los Angeles. For the next two years he continued to support Baba Bharati's ministry in Los Angeles and Venice, California. In New York City Bharati made some contact with Abhedananda during 1902-03. Bharati's students and followers included Ella Wheeler Wilcox, Christina Albers, Rose Reinhardt Anthon, and other people who were the supporters of Vivekananda a few years before. He spoke on "The Love of God" and "The Golden Age" at the Greenacre Conference in 1904. In May of 1907, Mills presented a series of five discourses on the *Bhagavad Gita* in Chicago, Denver, Portland, and during a ten-day period in Los Angeles at Blanchard Hall. Near the end of his life in 1915-16, he was readmitted back into the mainstream Christian ministry as a Presbyterian evangelist in Chicago. His publications reflect the various phases of his religious life.[174]

In a tribute on November 12, 1977, the First Unitarian Church in Oakland "commemorated Swamiji's lectures in the church by installing with due ceremony a bronze plaque on the pulpit from which he had spoken and also by placing a large photograph of him in the church foyer." The plaque reads, "Swami Vivekananda (1863-1902), Foremost Disciple of Sri Ramakrishna (Great Saint of Modern India) and Representative of Hinduism at the World's Parliament of Religions Chicago, September 1893, Delivered Two Lectures on Vedanta from this Pulpit February 1900."[175]

Annie Rix Militz (1856-1924) [q.v.] was the founder and leader of the Home of Truth movement. According to the present Home of Truth website:

> In 1893, Sister Annie met Swami Vivekananda of the Vedanta tradition at the Parliament of Religions (sometimes known as the First World Conference on Religion) in Chicago. Later she brought him to Alameda and the San Francisco Bay Area where he stayed for a month and spoke to thousands.

To date there is no proof that Mrs. Militz made contact with Swamiji while he was in California. According to the U.S. Census, she was living in Chicago during the year 1900. Meeting Vivekananda and hearing his teachings in 1893 caused her to broaden out her strictly Christian view of New Thought, to adopt an interfaith approach. Annie's husband, Paul Militz, who emigrated from Germany, attended some of the Swami's addresses and classes in New York and thought highly of him. Annie Rix Militz introduced Alice Hansbrough (Shanti) and many others to Vivekananda's book on *Raja Yoga*. When Swamiji came to Northern California, Paul Militz persuaded devotees like Sarah Fox to come and listen to him in Oakland. Militz told his followers:

> Now, you folks have been waiting for me to show you a real renouncer such as I have been telling you about—one who has renounced everything for the Truth. Very well, a great teacher has recently come from India. His name is Swami Vivekananda. I advise you all to go and hear him. He is one of the greatest teachers and greatest ascetics India has ever produced.[176]

While in Northern California, Vivekananda accepted an invitation to live at the Home of Truth on Pine Street in San Francisco for ten days, and in Alameda for over three weeks from April 11 to May 1, 1900. Swami Vivekananda told Mrs. Edith Allan "that he thought the work of the Home of Truth was the best then available in the West, and he appreciated the fact that the workers there did not charge for spiritual assistance, as some others did." Most of the devotees who studied under Turiyananda at the Shanti Ashrama came from the Home of Truth in Alameda or San Francisco.[177]

In 1893 Annie Rix Militz, an ordained Christian Science Minister, and her sister Harriet Rix (b. 1863) founded the Home of Truth in Alameda and later in San Francisco, California. She and her sister Harriet Rix established the Home of Truth in Los Angeles in 1896, becoming the leading New Thought teachers in California. They both received their training from Mrs. Emma Curtis Hopkins (1849-1925), the founder and teacher of the New Thought Movement. Annie Rix Militz maintained a celibate marriage with Paul Militz during 1892-95, and then they lived apart for the rest of their lives. During the 1890s she worked as a feature writer for the journal *Unity* founded by Charles and Myrtle Fillmore, the two admirers of Vivekananda, whom she had some influence on. In time the organization grew to embrace dozens of Home of Truth churches from Victoria, Canada, down the west coast to Los Angeles. There were also six Home of Truth churches in the central part of the United States, four on the east coast and one in England. The leaders of most of the congregations and their members were primarily women. This organization was actively involved in the New Thought movement along with two other groups influenced by Emma Hopkins: the Unity Church and the Church of Religious Science. Annie Rix Militz brought out many volumes stressing mental-healing, celibacy and other topics. She later spent four months living in India teaching and healing. At the turn of the twentieth century, some people considered the idea of a patriarchal God to be inappropriate, especially women who sensed an internal, impartial and universal God. Annie believed that, "Those who take the stand that the Real Self is God give the most perfect liberty to each individual to carry out his idea of God, and do not dictate his method." After the death of Militz in 1924, the Home of Truth movement underwent a rapid decline.[178]

The only extant Home of Truth built in 1905 to replace the original building in Alameda, is used today for religious services. Annie Rix Militz, Swami Abhedananda, and Ralph Waldo Trine delivered addresses at the Second Convention of the International Metaphysical League held at Madison

Square Garden in New York from 23rd to 26th October, 1900. Concerning Militz's book *Spiritual Housekeeping*, Swami Trigunatita's journal the *Voice of Freedom* of 1913 states, "The book is ably written and we recommend it to all spiritual aspirants." In May of 1919 Swami Paramananda of the Vedanta Society, Harriet Rix and others gave orations at a New Thought Festival held in Los Angeles. In 1925 Swami Paramananda sold his Vedanta Society home in Boston to the Home of Truth. Years later in April 1931 Paramananda and Harriet Rix were both guest speakers at the dedication of the Christian Unity Church in Los Angeles.[179]

Swamiji's first lecture in San Francisco after leaving Oakland was on March 9, 1900. The *San Francisco Chronicle* reported:

> Swami Vivekananda gave the third of his series of lectures last evening in Washington Hall, taking for his subject "Indian Ideals". He dwelt on the homes of the East and the home influences surrounding the baby. He told of the great epics which mothers recited for their little ones and which grandmothers told to their grandchildren, instilling in their minds principles of heroic virtue. He spoke of love, purity, peace and dominating devotion prevailing and gave as one of the precepts of his country "He who looks on every being as he does upon himself is learned." After illustrating these characteristics he asked: "What will you give us for these truths of ours? I find nothing in your Old or New Testament to replace them." Then giving special attention to the subject of purity and the marriage state, which he considered an invention of man's brute nature, he extolled the blessedness of that conception of life where there is neither giving nor taking in marriage.

The same newspaper gave a much longer account of Swamiji's speech on "Buddha's Message to the World" before "a crowded house", the full text of which we are not reproducing here as it is found in the *Complete Works* (VIII:92-105).[180]

There are a number of sublime photographs of Swamiji taken while he sojourned in Northern California. His then spiritual state is indicated in a letter dated 28 March 1900 to Mary Hale:

> I am attaining peace that passeth understanding, which is neither joy nor sorrow, but something above them both. Tell Mother that.... Now I

am nearing that *Peace*, the eternal silence. Now I mean to see things as they are, everything in that peace, perfect in its way.[181]

After returning to Europe, in Paris Vivekananda met Father Pere Hyacinthe (aka Charles Loyson, 1827-1912) in August 1900.[182] In October, Swamiji travelled from Paris to Constantinople with Pere and his wife. According to Swamiji:

> His scholarship, extraordinary eloquence, and great austerities won for him a high reputation in France and in the whole Catholic Order.... The very aged Loyson is going to Jerusalem to try to establish cordial relations among the Christians and Mussulmans.... Old Loyson is very affable in speech, modest, and of a distinctly devotional turn of mind. Whenever he meets me, he holds pretty long talks about various religions and creeds.... Old Pere Hyacinthe is a really sweet-natured and peaceful man, he is happy with his wife and family.[183]

In 1851 Charles Loyson became an ordained Priest of the Catholic Church and received the new name of Father Pere Hyacinthe. He taught philosophy and theology, and became perhaps the best-known preacher in France. Because Hyacinthe opposed the new doctrine of the infallibility of the Pope, the Church excommunicated him for heterodoxy. During the year 1871, he left the Catholic Church and a year later married an American widow. Pere Hyacinthe became the Pastor of the Liberal Catholic Church in Geneva, Switzerland (1873-74), and the founder of the Gallican Catholic Church in Paris (1879), which later merged with the Jansenists of Utrecht in the Netherlands (1893). He produced a number of books in the French language dealing with religious subjects like Catholic reform. During his eighty-fifth year, Pere Hyacinthe, a man of spiritual depth and charm, became weak and feeble. When dying he had a vision and was radiant. He triumphantly called out "He is there!" Pere seized the hand of his daughter-in-law and said, "I am overflowing with joy. You understand me, my dear girl?"[184]

Harvey Reeves Calkins (1866-1941), an American missionary, became acquainted with Vivekananda on a ship sailing to India in late November and early December of the year 1900. They met after the ship left Suez during their first meal on the Red Sea, and were together until they arrived in Bombay. About Vivekananda, Calkins made this statement in 1923:

> His answers were ready and usually sufficient; but, more than that, they were brilliant. They sparkled with epigram and apt quotation.... During the last day or two of the voyage our understanding of each other increased greatly, and, as I believe, our mutual respect. The mysticism of Vivekananda was a fascination and wonder. For it was not affected. When our conservation touched, as it was bound to, on the hidden things of the spirit, his heavy eyelids would droop slowly and he wandered, even in my presence, into some mystic realm where I was not invited.

Calkins graduated from Garrett Bible Institute in 1890, where Swamiji's friend, professor Charles Bradley, was an instructor. Reverend Calkins became a missionary in India during the years 1900-10, and again in 1922-29. He held the stewardship position between 1912 and 1920, and was the director of stewardship for the schools of religion of the Methodist Episcopal Church during 1932-36. As an author he wrote at least eight books, including *Ganga Dass, a Tale of Hindustan* (1916), and *Ten Weeks, the Journal of a Missionary* (1920).[185]

Swami Vivekananda arrived at the Advaita Ashrama at Mayavati on January 3, 1901 and stayed there for a fortnight. There is a picture of Brahmachari Amritananda (Charles Johnston) from New York along with Swamis Swarupananda and Prakashananda, Mrs. Sevier and others at the Ashrama. Little is known of Charles Johnston, except that he is not the book-producing Irish Orientalist of the same name.[186]

In summary, one cannot help but be impressed by the notable achievements of the clerics who were friends of Swami Vivekananda and who aided him in his Western mission. It is quite evident that his greatest admirers represented the more intelligent and dynamic members of the Christian clergy.

ENDNOTES

1 *CW*, IX:350.

2 *Life*, I, pp. 46-48; Jaiboy Joseph, "Reverend William Hastie", *The Hindu* (June 23, 2002) on the Internet as Web: www.hinduonnet.com/thehindu/mag/2002/06/23/stories/2002062300310400.htm.

3 *CW*, VIII:159-61; IX:292-99.

4 Web: www.answer.com/topic/thomas-kempis.

5 Hohner. The newspaper account in the *Salem Evening News* (Sept. 1, 1893) reported that Swami Vivekananda "preached in the Episcopal church at Annisquam" (*CW*, III, p. 469), but M. L Burke researched the matter and says it was a Universalist Church (Burke, I, pp. 40, 51; Schaff, XII, p. 90).

6 *CW*, III:465-69.

7 Ibid., III:469.

8 Nelson, pp. 253-54; Hohner, pp. 3-5; Wesley United Methodist Church. Web: www.salemwesley.org/history.htm; The First Church in Salem, Unitarian. Web: www.firstchurchinsalem.org/history.htm.

9 *Life*, II, pp. 260-61; John Henry Barrows. Web: www.oberlin.edu/archive/holdings/finding/RG2/SG5/biography.htm.

10 Basu, pp. 62, 72-73; *Biographical Dictionary of Christian Missions*, ed. Gerald Anderson (New York: Macmillan, 1998), p. 459; Buckland, pp. 289-90; Riddick, p. 254; Sherwood Eddy, *Pathfinders of the World Missionary Crusade* (New York: Abingdon-Cokesbury, 1945), pp. 95-104.

11 *Life*, I, p. 380; According to one report this dream occurred on the Shivaratri night during February-March 1893, *VK* (Dec. 1941), p. 302.

12 "Alasinga Perumal", *VK* (Dec. 1941), pp. 300-02; *PB* (Aug. 1947), pp. 321-24; (April 1990), p. 182.

13 Swami Chetanananda, *Vivekananda as We Saw Him* (Video, 1988). Cornelia's parents' names being William Perez Conger (1851-87), a lawyer, and Emily Lyon Conger, are found in a section on Cornelia Conger in *Who's Who of American Women* (Marquis-Who's Who, 1961-62), II, p. 206; Using Google, type in "William Perez Conger".

14 *CW*, I:20; IX:431-34.

15 Ibid., IX:431-32.

16 There are a few minor inconsistencies among the sources, concerning the years of the key events in Keane's life. *DAB* (1933), X, pp. 267-68; John Joseph Keane. Web: http://students.cua.edu/38alderfer/keane.htm.

17 John Barrows, ed., *The World's Parliament of Religions* (Chicago: Parliament Publishing Co., 1893), I, pp. 228-29; Burke, I, pp. 124, 126-27.

18 Barrows (1893), p. 1036; Burke, I, p. 127.

19 *CW*, I:4-5.

20 Jabez T. Sunderland. Web: www.uua.org/uuhs/duub/articles/ jabezsunderland.htm.

21 Chaudhurii, pp. 90-92.

22 Londhe, #221. Rev. Jabez T. Sunderland.

23 "Homage to Rev. Dr. J. T. Sunderland", *Modern Review* (1936), pp. 367-71; *IHP*, pp. 210-11; Bagchi, pp. 350-51; *ANB*, XXI, pp. 1152-53; Thomas, pp. 198-201; Atmaprana, p. 213; Centenary, I, p. 10; Jabez T. Sunderland. Web: www.mkgandhi.org/letters/chrchmisn/sunderland.htm; Jabez T. Sunderland. Web: www.uua.org/uuhs/duub/articles/jabezsunderland.htm.

24 *Life*, I, p. 429.

25 *CW*, V:111.

26 Ibid., III:208, 442; V:224; VI:407.

27 Ibid., V:20; VIII:453.

28 Londhe, #8. Annie Besant.

29 Bhattacharya, p. 128; Riddick, p. 31; Indian National Congress. Web: www.aicc.org.in/dr_annie_besant.htm.

30 Walter Martin, *The Kingdom of the Cults* (Minneapolis, MN: Bethany Fellowship, 1968), p. 277; *DAB* (1974), Sup. IV, pp. 270-72; J. Gordon Melton, *Religious Leaders of America* (Detroit: Gale Group, 1991), pp. 149-50. Swamiji's speech on "The Divinity of Man" can be found in Chaudhuri1 pp. 159-64 and on GBS; *Unity* (1899), p. 379; (1903) on GBS.

31 *CW*, VIII:200.

32 *Chicago Herald* (Sept. 25, 1893); Burke, I, p. 95; *ANB*, II, pp. 923-24; *NCAB*, XX, pp. 283-84; UCLC.

33 L. P. Mercer, *Review of the World's Religious Congress* (Chicago, Rand McNally, 1893), p. 44; *DAB*, *NCAB*, XII, p. 82; Chaudhuri1, p. 89.

34 Chaudhuri1, p. 128; Kansas Heritage Group. Web: www.kansasheritage.org/werner/mormroad.html; a letter from Thomas E. S. Miller, the present Pastor of the Church; UCLC; Hohner, pp. 5-7.

35 *CW*, III:478-79.

36 Burke, I, pp. 165-69, 225; www.teosofiskakompaniet.net/CarlVonBergen_Biografi.htm.

37 *CW*, VII:453-54.

38 Ibid., III:478-79.

39 Ibid., V:38-39.

40 Chaudhuri1, pp. 130-31; UCLC; *CW*, IX:36.

41 Chaudhuri1, pp. 88, 141-42, 157; Samuel Eliot, *Heralds of a Liberal Faith* (Boston: Beacon Press, 1952), p. 17; UCLC.

42 *Chicago Daily Tribune* (July 25, 1902), p. 2. The article featured a rare picture of Swami Vivekananda.

43 Burke, I, p. 180; Chaudhuri2, p. 365.

44 *Unity* (Dec. 14, 1893), pp. 232-33; Chaudhuri1, pp. 159-64, 166 on GBS.

45 Ray Ellis, "Swami Vivekananda in Chicago", *VK* (Aug. 1995), pp. 310-13; *Chicago Daily Inter-Ocean* (Dec. 5, 1893); *Chicago Daily Tribune* (Nov. 26, 1893), p. 27; Cost of Living.

46 *NCAB* (1899), IX, pp. 316-17; *WWWA* (1962), I. p. 1229; Stavig4, p. 407-08; *Outlook* (Oct. 9, 1897), p. 387.

47 Ray Ellis, "Swami Vivekananda in Chicago", *VK* (Aug. 1995), p. 313; *Chicago Daily Inter-Ocean* and *Chicago Sunday Times* (Nov. 12, 1893).

48 *CW*, IX:436-37; III:481.

49 Ibid., III:481.

50 Ibid., IX:7.

51 Stavig4, p. 408; *WWWA* (1968), IV, p. 961; Chaudhuri2, p. 372; Eugene Grover Updike. Web: www.rockvillemama.com/dane/updikeeugenegrover.txt.

52 *CW*, VII:416-19.

53 Ibid., III:481-82.

54 Ibid., IX:443.

55 Stavig4, p. 408; *ANB*, XIX, pp. 951-52; Eliot (1952), pp. 214-16; Hohner, pp. 9-11; A History of the Church. Web: www.bradforduu.org/history.asp; First Unitarian Society of Minneapolis. Web: www.firstunitariansociety.org/greeting/main.html; "Personal Diary of Anagarika Dhammapala". www.geocities.com/anagarikadhammapala/adiary.htm.

56 Chaudhuri2, pp. 386-88.

57 Chaudhuri2, pp. 398-99.

58 *CW*, IX:439.

59 Ibid., IX:437-40; III:482-84.

60 Chaudhuri2, pp. 402-04 (gives the newspaper report in full), 410-15.

61 Burke, I, p. 211.

62 Stavig4, p. 408; *WWIA* (1928), XV, p. 352; Harvey Oscar Breeden. Web: www.mun.ca/rels/restmov/texts/jtbrown/coc/COC1356.htm.

63 *CW*, III:484-85.

64 Ibid., III:486.

65 *DAB* (1944), XXI, Sup. 1, p. 329; The New Schaff-Herzog Encyclopedia. Web: www.ccel.org/s/schaff/encyc/encyc04/htm/0434=418.htm; UCLC.

66 Rossiter Johnson, ed., *The Biographical Dictionary of America* (Boston: American Biographical Society, 1906), VIII.

67 *CW*, VIII:204-05.

68 *NCAB* (1906), XIII, p. 17; R. Johnson, *The Biographical Dictionary of America* (Boston: American Biographical Society, 1906).

69 *CW*, VIII:207.

70 Burke, I, pp. 294, 307, 311-13.
71 *CW*, III:490-510.
72 Ibid., III:504.
73 Eliot (1952), pp. 233-34; UCLC.
74 Chaudhuri2, pp. 494-95.
75 The Louis Grossmann original manuscript collection, which he donated, covering the years 1897-1925, is available at the American Jewish Archives in Cincinnati, Ohio. Lewis Grossmann Papers. Web: www.americanjewisharchives.org/aja/FindingAids/Grossmann.htm; "Louis Grossmann", *DAB* (1960), IV, pp. 23-24; UCLC; *WWIA* (1926) p. 847.
76 *CW*, IX:447.
77 Ibid., IX:11.
78 Ibid., IX:84. For a condensed version of Rabbi Grossmann's speech see Burke, I, pp. 346-49; IV, pp. 26-28.
79 *Life*, II, p. 74.
80 *Reminiscences*, p. 247; *PB* (Feb. 1927).
81 *Reminiscences*, pp. 249-50.
82 *Reminiscences*, p. 247; *DAB* (1928-1936).
83 *CW*, VII:464.
84 Burke, II, pp. 46-47; *Encyclopedia Britannica* (Cambridge, England: University Press, 1910-11), X, p. 26-27; Lyman Abbott. Web: www.sacklunch.net/biography/A/LymanAbbott.html; UCLC; Burke, II, p. 277.
85 Burke, II, pp. 68-69; also in Nelson, p. 40.
86 *CW*, IX:466-69.
87 Editor, "Autograph of Swami Vivekananda", *VK* 48 (1962), pp. 396-97; Burke, II, pp. 71, 73; UCLC.
88 Burke, II, pp. 141-42; Nelson, p. 50.
89 *CW*, IX:77.
90 New Thought. Web: http://website.lineone.net/~newthought/ahotntm9.htm; *New York Times* (Feb. 1, 1903), p. SM10; Satyananda, p. 85; *MOTE* (1938), p. 253; (1939), pp. 55, 57; *PB* (1905), pp. 29-30, 135-37, 150-53.
91 Melton (1991), pp. 479-80; Ralph Waldo Trine. Web: http://website.lineone.net/~ralphtrine/; UCLC.
92 Tripura Sen, "Ralph Waldo Trine and Indian Culture", *PB* (Sept. 1967), pp. 297-303.
93 Excerpts from *In Tune with the Infinite*. Web: ralphwaldotrine.wwwhubs.com.
94 Ralph Waldo Trine, *In Tune with the Infinite* (Indianapolis: Bobbs-Merrill, 1942), pp. 25-26.

95 Head, p. 270; Saha, p. 50.
96 *CW*, IX:28.
97 Burke, II, pp. 138-39, 142, opposite 150, 154, 277; *DAB* (1960), IV, pp. 99-100; UCLC; Thomas Reid, *Indian Influence in American Literature and Thought* (Bombay: Bhatkal Books International, 1965), p. 66.
98 Unitarians like Jabez Sunderland thought that Swami Vivekananda's support of traditional Hinduism would slow down the reform movement in India. Spencer Lavan, *Unitarians and India* (Boston: Beacon Press, 1977), pp. 140, 155-56.
99 *CW*, V:59; IX:49.
100 Burke, IV, pp. 290-91.
101 International Association for Religious Freedom. Web: www.geocities.com/~iarf/shorthistory.htm.
102 *CW*, IX:45, 472.
103 *Chicago Daily Tribune* (Oct. 15, 1894), p. 4.
104 Chaudhuri2, pp. 604-05.
105 *CW*, II:492-97.
106 Ibid., IX:475-76.
107 *CW*, II:494.
108 Burke, II, pp. 193-95, 205; Ross Paulson, *Radicalism & Reform: The Vrooman Family* (Lexington: University of Kentucky, 1968), pp. 100, 182-85, 258-61; Ruskin College, Trenton Missouri. Web: www.umsystem.edu/whmc/invent/3803.html; UCLC; *WWIA*, IV, p. 973; *New York Times* (April 10, 1966), p. 76.
109 *CW*, II:497-99; IX:476-79.
110 *VK* (Sept. 1991), p. 371; Chaudhuri2, p. 634.
111 Stavig4, p. 409; *WWWA*, I, p. 668; *WWIA* (1908), p. 1043; UCLC.
112 *CW*, IX:476-79.
113 *The Washington Post* (Oct. 29, 1894), p. 6; (Oct. 28, 1894), p. 14.
114 *CWSA*, X, p. 38; *The Message of the East* (1915), pp. 115-16; *Washington, D.C. Directory* (1915).
115 *Reminiscences*, 122-24; *PB* (Apr-May, 1932).
116 *PB* (May 1932), p. 244; (June 1932), pp. 302-03; Burke, III, pp. 46-47, 102, 132-33, 347-48, 463-64.
117 *VMB* (Feb. 1907), p. 224.
118 Levinsky, pp. 94, 103-07, 139-48, 159, 172, 211; Shivani, p. 234; *RLOA*, p. 260.
119 Levinsky, pp. 265-68; Devamata, p. 16; *RLOA*, p. 260.
120 Stavig1, p. 467; *WWWA* (1962), I, p. 355; "The Social World", *New York Times* (Mar. 1, 1895), p. 8.
121 *CW*, I:317-28; IX:484-87.

122 Chaudhuri2, pp. 655-59; Horner, pp. 41, 61; Unitarian Society of Hartford. Web: www.ushartford.com/timeline.htm.

123 Ibid., V:292-93.

124 Burke, III, pp. 169-72; *New York Tribune* (July 28, 1895); *Outlook* (Aug. 3, 1895); *Open Court* (July 25, 1895), p. 413.

125 S. Sengupta and M. Paranjape, ed., *The Cyclonic Swami* (New Delhi: Samvad India Foundation, 2005), pp. 75, 81-85; *CW*, IX:59-61, 64.

126 *Manifesto* (Sept. 1895), p. 213; in GBS.

127 The Shakers. Web: www.pbs.org/shakers/.

128 *Rays of Light from all Lands* (New York: Gay Brothers, 1895), pp. cover, xxviii, photographs, 701-11; *Allibone's Critical Dictionary of English Literature*, ed. John Kirk (Philadelphia: J. B. Lippincott, 1908), Sup (Towne); *WWWA*, I, p. 499 (Hagar).

129 *New York Times* (March 20, 1896), p. 9; *New York Tribune* (June 18, 1899) on CAM; *Chicago Daily Tribune* (Dec. 20, 1915), p. 15.

130 Burke, III, pp. 322-25, 328, 379-80, 466-67, 521-22; *Atlanta Constitution* (April 1, 1896), p. 8; *Brahmavadin* (March 16, 1898), pp. 535-37; *Los Angeles Times* (Aug. 7, 1898), p. 2; *Chicago Daily Tribune* (April 16, 1899), p. 46.

131 *CW*, VIII:463.

132 *Boston Daily Globe* (July 19, 1901), p. 8; *Chicago Daily Tribune* (Dec. 20, 1915), p. 15.

133 *CW*, VIII:220-24.

134 Ibid., IX:518-19.

135 Burke, III, pp. 273, 278; *DNB* (1901-11), Sup. I, p. 227.

136 H. R. Haweis, *Travel and Talk* (New York: Dodd, Mead, & Co., 1896), I, pp. 198-200; Burke, III, pp. 257, 270-71.

137 *Encyclopedia Britannica* (1910-11), XIII, p. 93; Hugh Reginald Haweis. Web: www.whistler.arts.gla.ac.uk/biog/hawe_rev.htm; Swami Yogeshwarananda, "A British View of the Parliament of Religions", *Vedanta for East and West* (1970), pp. 6-13; Haweis (1896), I, pp. iii, v; *DNB* (1963), Sup. I, pp. 225-27; UCLC.

138 *WWIE* (1916), p. 2368; *Encyclopedia Britannica* (1910-11), XXVIII, p. 630.

139 *CW*, IX:535.

140 Burke IV, pp. 192-94.

141 Burke, IV, 165, 386, 400, 485; V. p. 84; *CW*, IX:149.

142 *WWIE* (1917), p. 2296; Haweis (1896), II, pp. 100-01, 154-55; UCLC.

143 *CW*, V:135, 221.

144 Burke, III, pp. 467-69.

145 *CW*, I:357-65.

146 Ibid., V:297-310.

147 Swami Vivekananda, *The Vedanta Philosophy* (Cambridge: Harvard University Press, 1896); Basu, pp. 601-02; *Life*, II, p. 76.

148 *DAB* (1959), III, pp. 221-22; *Journal of the American Oriental Society* (1899), pp. 310-16; UCLC; Charles Carroll Everett. Web: www.hds.harvard.edu/library/exhibits/online/hdsturncentury/everett.htm.

149 *Life*, II, p. 132; *DNB 1912-21* (1961), pp. 545-46.

150 Sunderland, pp. 319-20; Burke, IV, p. 476; *Modern Review* (June 1907); John Page Hopps. Web: www.cyberhymnal.org/bio/h/o/p/hopps_jp.htm; UCLC.

151 *CW*, V:218, 225.

152 *PB* (May 1913), pp. 94-95; Basu, pp. 132-33, 177-78, 187-88, 191; *Life*, II, pp. 169, 179, 188, 190.

153 *CW*, III:207-27.

154 *Woman's Missionary Friend* (July 1897), pp. 15-16.

155 *Holy Himalaya*, pp. 14-15; *East and the West* (April 1907); *Expository Times* (1905), p. 323 on GBS; Norman Goodall, *A History of the London Missionary Society 1895-1945* (London: Oxford University Press, 1954), pp. 32-33.

156 *CW*, I:6-20.

157 *The Improvement Era* (1899), pp 176-86 in GBS.

158 Atulananda, pp. 59-60.

159 Atulananda, pp. 3-16, 59-60, 339-41; *PB* (Sept. 1966), p. 400; *VK* (Sept. 1966), pp. 254-55; *CWSA*, X, p. 91; UCLC; "A letter from Swami Atulananda to John Yale" (May 13, 1958), VSSC Archives. According to letters in the Atulananda's book, he was in India in 1909-10 and 1917-18, and thus the dates given in *PB* (Oct. 1989), p. 430 are incorrect.

160 Vidyatmananda12.

161 *CW*, IX:501-04.

162 *Los Angeles Times* (Sept. 24, 1898), p. 14; (Sept. 1, 1904), p. 12.

163 *CW*, II:24-37; IX:507-09.

164 Burke, V, pp. 218-20; *Brahmavadin* (June 1900), p. 565.

165 Burke, V, pp. 212; Hohner, pp. 95-96.

166 *CW*, II:359-74.

167 Stavig2; *Los Angeles Times* (Oct. 30, 1899), p. 9; (Dec. 12, 1899), p. 15.

168 *San Francisco Chronicle* (July 30, 1899), p. 19.

169 *CW*, IX:133-34.

170 Ibid., VIII:494-95.

171 Ibid., IV:196-97; VI:46-48; VIII:231-43; IX:510-11.

172 Ibid., VIII:231.

173 Stavig4, p. 411; *Life*, II, p. 508; Burke, V, pp. 310, 318-25, 337-38; "A letter from Edythe Allan to Ida Ansell" (June 7, 1950), VSSC Archives; *DAB* (1934), pp. 2-3; Hansbrough, *PB* (May 2007), p. 346.

174 Stavig4, p. 411; Stavig2; *DAB* (1934), pp. 2-3; Melton (1991); *Los Angeles Times* (Aug. 23, 1905), p. II9; (May 18, 1907), p. II6; (June 22, 1907), p. II6; UCLC; Carney Gerald, "Baba Premananda Bharati", *Journal of Vaisnava Studies* (Spring 1998); *New York Herald* (Dec. 23, 1902); Cameron, pp. 162, 165; The New Thought Web Directory. Web: http://website.lineone.net/~newthought/ahotntm11.htm.

175 Burke, V, p. 370; Chaudhuri2, pp. 789-90.

176 Burke, V, p. 383; *Vedanta for East and West* (July-Aug. 1959).

177 Stavig4, p. 411; Home of Truth. Web: http://thehomeoftruth.org/id4.html; Wikipedia. Web: http://en.wikipedia.org/wiki/Annie_Rix_Militz; Hohner, pp. 103-06; Burke, V, pp. 310, 326, 372; VI, pp. 96-98, 110-12; *PB* (Feb. 2007), p. 173; Chaudhuri2, p. 817.

178 Stavig4, p. 411; Stavig2; Beryl Satter, *Each Mind a Kingdom* (Berkeley: University of California Press, 1999), pp. 80, 103-05, 108, 228; Annie Rix Militz. Web: http://cornerstone.wwwhubs.com/militz.htm; UCLC.

179 *Los Angeles Times* (April 11, 1931), p. A8; *Voice of Freedom* (July 1913), p. 78; Horatio Dresser. Web: http://horatiodresser.wwwhubs.com/ ahotntm9.htm.

180 *San Francisco Chronicle* (March 10, 1900), p. 8; (March 19, 1900), p. 7.

181 *CW*, VIII:504.

182 *CW*, IX:147.

183 Ibid., VII:376-78, 398-99.

184 *Schaff*, VIII, p. 52; Web: www.ccel.org/php/ disp.php3?a=schaff&b=encyc07&p=52; William Justice, *Outposts of the Spirit; Columbia Encyclopedia* (2001). Web: www.bartleby.com/65/lo/Loyson-C.htm.

185 *Reminiscences*, pp. 386-90; *PB* (March 1923); *WWWA*, I, p. 184.

186 *Life*, II, pp. 567, 570.

CHAPTER VII

PROFESSIONAL WRITERS

According to the author Romain Rolland, somewhere between the years 1881 and 1884, Swami Vivekananda, as the young Narendranath Datta, exchanged correspondence with the world famous English philosopher-sociologist Herbert Spencer (1820-1903). Narendranath wrote to Spencer for permission to translate his book on *Education* into Bengali for his publisher Gurudas Chattopadhyaya. Spencer's system of thought focuses on an Unknowable God who exists as an unconditioned unitary Being. He manifests in phenomena—both in physical nature, and in human society and its institutions—in accordance with the laws of evolutionary growth. The young Naren challenged one of his ideas and "Spencer was astonished, so it was said, by his daring criticisms, and admired the precociousness of his philosophical intellect." On more than ten occasions, in his writings Vivekananda refers to the ideas of Spencer. For one thing, Spencer taught a doctrine of unilinear evolutionary progress of human societies that Swamiji did not accept. At that time many European social thinkers believed in the "Doctrine of Progress", that modern education and technology would eventually bring about a heaven on earth. As a critic of the British government's colonial policies, Spencer believed that the Indians were capable of making economic progress as they had in the past, provided they become politically independent. He did not consider polytheistic religious beliefs to be an obstacle to social progress.[1] While in India Swami Abhedananda indicated, "The modern theory which is so beautifully explained by Herbert Spencer is not very dissimilar to that ideal theory of evolution which was started by Kapila at least seven centuries before the Christian Era. He may be called the Herbert Spencer of ancient India."[2]

Swami Vivekananda wasn't in North America but for a few days before Miss Kate Sanborn (1839-1917), a popular American writer of rural literature, recognized his uniqueness. While travelling on the Canadian Pacific Railway from Vancouver en route to Winnipeg, Canada, she noticed that of all the beautiful and interesting sights:

> Most of all was I impressed by the monk, a magnificent specimen of manhood—six feet two [i.e., a man of tall appearance], as handsome as Salvini at his best, with a lordly, imposing stride, as if he ruled the universe, and soft, dark eyes that could flash fire if roused or dance with merriment if the conversation amused him.... He spoke better English than I did, was conversant with ancient and modern literature, would quote easily and naturally from Shakespeare or Longfellow or Tennyson, Darwin, Müller, Tyndall; could repeat pages of our Bible, was familiar with and tolerant of all creeds. He was an education, an illumination, a revelation![3]

She is referring either to the Italian stage actor Tommaso Salvini (1829-1915), or to his handsome son Alessandro (Alexander) Salvini (1860-96) of the same profession. The former "had a majestic figure and a mobile face with a large forehead, dark striking eyes, and an aquiline nose" combined with a mellifluous voice.[4]

Kate Sanborn told Vivekananda that she would "be most pleased to present him to some men and women of learning and general culture, if by any chance he should come to Boston." They parted company and Swamiji lived for about twelve days in Chicago. He then proceeded to Boston with Chabildas Lalubhai and soon telegraphed her.* Her response was:

> Just risen from a sick bed, I received a telegram of forty-five words announcing that my revered friend of the observation car was at the Quincy House, Boston, and awaiting my orders.
>
> Then I remembered vividly, I had urged him to accept my hospitalities if he felt lonely and needed help. I had promised those introductions to Harvard professors, Concord philosophers, New York capitalists, women of fame, position and means, with brilliant gifts in writing and conversation. It was mid-August. Not a soul was in town, and how could I entertain my gayly apparelled pundit? I was aghast, but telegraphed bravely; "Yours received. Come today: 4.20 train, Boston and Albany."[5]

* See Chapter XI for more details.

Fortunately, she lived up to her word and Swamiji associated with many distinguished people during his stay of less than four weeks in the East, prior to journeying to the World's Parliament of Religions. At Kate Sanborn's invitation he spent about a week up until August 24, 1893 at "Breezy Meadows", her countryside home about twenty-five miles west of Boston.[6] Living with this amiable and gregarious woman gave the Swami some idea of the American social environment, which he was now a part of.[7] The following year Kate Sanborn wrote that she "had the honour of entertaining a Hindoo monk last summer, a man of wondrous learning, eloquence, and philanthropy." She went on to explain her reaction to one of Swamiji's informal talks at Breezy Meadows:

> One evening.... fully a dozen ladies were gathered around my honoured guest, looking at him admiringly and at each other with approving words as he explained at length his creed and philosophy ... My overstrained mind began to wobble, and I found I was sitting on the edge of my chair, with eyes aching from a prolonged stare of wonder, my mouth positively ajar, like a rustic at a muster; and as he talked on and on in glowing rhapsody, I suddenly saw myself as an extremely mature American Desdemona, listening intently to the marvellous eloquence of my Bengalese Othello.[8]

Because of his commanding presence, by August 31 the news of Vivekananda's stay with Kate Sanborn had already gone out over the wire and appeared in newspapers in far off places like Correctionville, Iowa, stating:

> The Swami Vivekananda of India, a Brahmin monk, on his way to the parliament of religions to be held in Chicago next month, is a guest of Miss Kate Sanborn at her abandoned farm in Metcalf, Mass. He is said to be a gentleman of much learning and ability.[9]

Katherine "Kate" Abbott Sanborn formerly taught women at the Mary Institute, which was connected with Washington University in St. Louis (1859-63). She became an instructor of elocution at Packer Collegiate Institute in Brooklyn, and of English literature at Smith College for women (1880-83). In 1880 she attended Mrs. Sara Bull's birthday party. She left Smith College and spent some time travelling on lecture tours in the Western section of the United States and in Alaska. After 1881 she enjoyed a very successful career as a writer, publishing over fifteen books. Her writings on her rural life experiences and travels are delightfully humorous, and represent an early contribution to the "back to the land" literature. She was a New England Yankee product, being a stimulating, witty and a suggestive teacher and conversationalist, with an extensive knowledge of literature. In her archives are found personal letters of correspondence with Vivekananda's friends like Julia Ward Howe, Frances Willard, and Mary Mapes Dodge.[10]

Kate Sanborn introduced Swamiji to John Henry Wright (1852-1908) [q.v.], a professor of Greek at Harvard University* who invited him to spend three days at the seaside resort village of Annisquam, Massachusetts. It is Professor Wright's wife Mary who provides us with a portrayal of Vivekananda at that time:

> So astonishing a sight did Swamiji present in this quiet little New England village that speculations set in at once as to who this majestic and colourful figure might be. From where had he come? At first they decided that he was a Brahmin from India, but his manners did not fully conform to their ideas.[11]

Mary Wright described Swamiji as "a most gorgeous vision. He had a superb carriage of the head, was very handsome," and "was one of the most interesting people I have yet come across.... The town was in a fume to see him; the boarders at Miss Lane's in wild excitement." In turn, Vivekananda praised the professor's wife as being "nonpareil" and as "strong and pure".[12] A woman of culture, Mary Tappan Wright (1851-1916) worked as a professional novelist and writer of many short stories in the fashionable Harper's Magazine and other periodicals. She came out with at least five books of fiction between 1895 and 1912.[13]

Another member of the household was Austin Tappan Wright (1883-1931), the ten year old son of John and Mary. Swamiji presented him with a copy of Edwin Arnold's *The Light of Asia* (1879), with the inscription, "Presented to Austin Wright with love and blessings of Vivekananda". Austin's name appears in three of Vivekananda's letters.[14] In later life Austin worked as a member of the Boston law firm of Louis Brandeis† (1908-16), the law school faculty at the University of California at Berkeley (1916-24), and the University of Pennsylvania (1924-31), before his life was cut short in an au-

* See Chapter VIII.

† A U.S. Supreme Court judge after 1916.

tomobile accident. He is best remembered as the author of the posthumous *Islandia* (1942), which experts consider to be a classic in utopian literature. It deals with a fictional community in the South Pacific. The God of Islandia is called "Om" who cannot be seen with the eyes or ears, felt by the hand, nor understood by man. One excerpt reads, "But it is well for men to sit in the halls of Om/ And, so sitting, to be lost in his darkness/ Or so sitting, to be dazzled by his brightness/ And to know that Om is."[15]

Austin's younger brother John Kirtland Wright (1891-1969) later became an instructor in history at Harvard University (1916-17), worked for the American Geographical Society as a librarian (1920-36), research editor (1936-37), the director (1938-49), and a research associate (1949-56). He served as the president of the distinguished Association of American Geographers in 1946, producing several textbooks and numerous articles on the subject of geography that exerted a considerable influence on the field. He gave the Vedanta Society some letters, now in the *Complete Works*, written by Vivekananda to his father Professor Wright.[16]

Mrs. Kate Tannant Woods (1838-1910), author of over twenty books written for children, invited Swamiji to stay at her house for seven days in Salem, Massachusetts. There the Swami spoke at the Methodist Wesley Church, the Unitarian East Church, and to a group of young people in Kate Woods' garden. Upon leaving her house, Swamiji gave his staff, trunk and blanket to Kate Woods and her son named Prince. Swamiji then said, "Only my most precious possessions should I give to my friends who have made me at home in this great country."[17] During October and November they exchanged friendly letters.[18] Speaking of Vivekananda in 1950, the wife of her son Prince Woods signified, "I have heard that he and Mahatma Gandhi were more Christ like than any the world has known." Kate Woods also published articles in many leading magazines and three Boston newspapers. In addition, she was one of the original officers of the presently existing General Federation of Women's Clubs, and a cofounder of the Massachusetts Chapter. As the vice-president of the Women's National Press Association and a leader in other groups, she endeavoured to raise the status of women in the nation.[19]

Kate Sanborn wanted her cousin Franklin to meet the Swami. In reply Mr. Franklin Sanborn wrote to her, "A real Hindu devotee is an interesting study but I am too old to be cheated by the esoteric Buddhists!" After they got together, Vivekananda so impressed Franklin Sanborn (1831-1917), "the last of the great Transcendalists", that he asked him to be his guest for six days in Saratoga, New York.[20] There he encouraged the Swami to deliver several discourses before the prestigious American Social Science Association founded by Sanborn himself. Pratap Mazumdar, the leader of the Brahmo Samaj, had spoken at the meeting a decade earlier in 1883. They held the General Meeting at the new Town Hall in Saratoga, New York, during September 4-8.[21]

It was formerly thought that Swamiji left Saratoga for Chicago on September 6, but on the final day of the meetings held on September 8, upon the request of Franklin Sanborn, Swamiji gave a talk to the social scientists on the present social and economic conditions of India. *The Journal of Social Science* of January 1894 informs us, "Vive Kananda had previously spoken in the debate on the Silver Question, in the Finance Department, and was heard on both occasions with great attention, contributing much to the interest of the two meetings which he attended." Over five-hundred words in the journal, probably written by Franklin Sanborn, were devoted to discussing the content of Swamiji's speech.[22]

Swamiji wrote, "One of the objects of my going to the West to preach religion was to see if I could find any means for feeding the people of this country,"[23] and in 1897 he wrote, "Travelling through many cities of Europe and observing in them the comforts and education of even the poor people, there was brought to my mind the state of our own poor people, and I used to shed tears."[24] Consequently, he addressed the subject of India's poverty at the Wesley Methodist Church on August 28, at the East Church in Salem on September 3,[25] and again on September 8, 1893 at the meetings of the American Social Science Association. He quickly realized this approach was not bringing the desired results, and having a very flexible mind he turned his attention to other subjects. Swami Paramananda once mentioned Swamiji's "great, loving heart.... I have seen him weeping. I have seen this great soul weeping, when he thought no one saw him, for the suffering poor of India."[26] Liberation theology is a movement that came into being in around 1968 in Latin America and other third world countries, focusing on liberating people from poverty and oppression. This radically new approach to theology recognizes God and the Church's presence in the struggle to throw off political and economic subjugation. It has been shown that Vivekananda conceived of many of the ideas and put them into practice through the Ramakrishna Math and Mission, which resemble those of the modern liberation theologists.[27]

Even before the World's Parliament of Religions began, Vivekananda's presence was attracting attention. The *New York Times* (September 10, 1893, p. 10) noted:

> Saratoga, N.Y., Sept. 9—A most picturesque figure at these meetings has been the Hindu priest (Swami Vive Kananda,) who has spoken at several of them ... He speaks most fluent and musical English, and is a master of a natural and dramatic oratory that is most persuasive. On Thursday [September 7] afternoon in the drawing room of the United States Hotel he gave an informal talk, and in his habit of orange cloth which, girded about the waist, is monkish only in cut, and his turban of orange stuff wound about his fine head with a grace that would be the despair of a coiffeur, his dark, chiselled face, with the expression of sadness that is usually seen in the Oriental, he made a marked personality in striking contrast to the conventional Westerns who surrounded him. He left to-day [September 9] for Chicago to attend the Congress of Religions.

The following year Swamiji and Franklin Sanborn were guest speakers at the Greenacre Conference, and then in August of 1894 they travelled together to Plymouth, Massachusetts, for the meeting of the Free Religious Association.[28]

In 1854 Sanborn married a young lady who was on her deathbed and succumbed eight days later. Franklin Sanborn, a member of the "secret six", knew in advance about John Brown's raid on Harpers Ferry, Virginia.* When the federal deputies came to get Sanborn, Ralph Waldo Emerson led a group of citizens that drove the deputies out of town. Sanborn was the editor of the *Boston Commonwealth* (1863-67) and the *Springfield Republican* (1868-72) newspapers. He worked hard and successfully in his humanitarian endeavours as the founder and an officer of the American Social Science Association, National Prison Association (1863-68), National Conference of Charities, Clarke School for the Deaf, Massachusetts Infant Asylum, and also as a cofounder of the Concord School of Philosophy. The Governor appointed him to be the chairman of the State Board of Charities in 1874-76 and 1879-88. He lectured as a guest speaker at Cornell University, Smith College, and Wellesley College.

* Harpers Ferry raid was one of the major incidents that precipitated the U.S. Civil War. John Brown was a militant American Abolitionist.

A number of friends of Swami Vivekananda were intensely inspired by Ralph Waldo Emerson (1803-82). Two Harvard students, Franklin Sanborn and Moncure Conway (1832-1907), made his acquaintance as early as 1853. Thomas Higginson and Edward Carpenter met Emerson and were influenced by him, as were Ralph Waldo Trine and Pratap C. Mazumdar, who was a guest of Emerson's widow. Sarah Waldo was a relative of his. Franklin Sanborn, the "Last of the Great Transcendalists", was the world's leading expert on both Emerson, the famous American essayist, philosopher and poet, and Henry David Thoreau (1817-62), the profound mystic. Sanborn wrote biographies of his intimate friends, particularly Transcendentalists of whom he had first-hand knowledge. After 1878 he produced highly original books on Emerson, Thoreau (the first extensive biography on him), John Brown, Samuel G. Howe (husband of Julia Ward Howe), Amos Bronson Alcott, Pliny Earle, as well as Nathaniel Hawthorne. He also edited works on the writings of William Ellery Channing and Theodore Parker.[29] Transcendentalists like Sanborn, Channing and Alcott authored highly favourable reviews of Edwin Arnold's life of the Buddha, *The Light of Asia* (1879), which enhanced the American sale of the volume. Sanborn edited the volume *The Genius and Character of Emerson* (1885), which contains an essay written by Pratap Mazumdar with the title "Emerson as Seen from India". After studying the subject Mazumdar came to the conclusion that:

> Amidst all this soul-absorbing philosophy of things, it is a true happiness to find that Emerson so deeply felt the reality and earnestness of life,—the reality of the inner and outer world as well.... Emerson has all the wisdom and spirituality of the Brahmans.

Swami Abhedananda considered Emerson to be the first person to reveal the principles of the Vedanta philosophy to the American mind. A few months after meeting Vivekananda, in December Sanborn published an article in *The Atlantic Monthly*. It told of how Thoreau's English friend, Thomas Cholmondeley, had sent him a gift of forty-four books dealing with India and its scriptures back in 1855. Sanborn himself was present as a young man when Thoreau enshrined these treasured volumes in his homemade bookcase.[30]

Emerson and Thoreau had a great admiration for Indian knowledge, which is exemplified in their numerous praises of Hindu religious literature and culture. They learned of Indian thought primarily from reading early

English language versions of the *Bhagavad Gita*, *Law of Manu*, *Vishnu Purana*, *Bhagavata* and a few other translations. For example, Emerson wrote, "The subtle Hindoo, who carried religion to ecstasy and philosophy to idealism, produced the wonderful epics of which, in the present century, the translations have added new regions to thought." He once made this remarkable prophesy:

> By the law of contraries, I look for an irresistible taste for Orientalism in Britain. For a self-conceited modish life, made up of trifles, clinging to a corporeal civilization, hating ideas, there is no remedy like the Oriental largeness. That astonishes and disconcerts English decorum. For once, there is thunder it never heard, light it never saw, and power which trifles with time and space. I am not surprised to find an Englishman like Warren Hastings, who had been struck with the grand style of thinking in the Indian writings, depreciating the prejudices of his countrymen while offering them a translation of the *Bhagvat* [*Gita*].[31]

The mystic Henry David Thoreau enlightened his reader with such statements as:

> In the morning I bathe my intellect in the stupendous and cosmogonal philosophy of the *Bhagavat-Geeta*, since whose composition years of the gods have elapsed, and in comparison with which our modern world and its literature seem puny and trivial; and I doubt if that philosophy is not to be referred to a previous state of existence, so remote is its sublimity from our conceptions.
>
> The contemplations of those Indian sages have influenced, and still influence, the intellectual development of mankind,—whose works even yet survive in wonderful completeness, are, for the most part, not recognized as ever having existed.... In comparison with the philosophers of the East, we may say that modern Europe has yet given birth to none. Beside the vast and cosmological philosophy of the *Bhagvat-Geeta*, even Shakespeare seems sometimes youthfully green and practical merely.[32]

The three well-known litterateurs who most influenced Mahatma Gandhi were Thoreau, Tolstoy and John Ruskin. After reading Thoreau's essay on "Civil Disobedience" during his second stay in jail, Gandhi described it as a "masterly treatise" that "left a deep impression on me".[33]

A third Transcendentalist, Amos Bronson Alcott (1799-1888), a good friend of Emerson, was the father of the renowned author Louisa May Alcott. He apprehended:

> I read more of the *Bhagavad Gita* and felt how surpassingly fine were the sentiments. These, or selections from this book, should be included in a Bible for Mankind. I think them superior to any of the other Oriental scriptures, the best of all reading for wise men.[34]

Upon leaving Saratoga, Swamiji boarded a train for Chicago on the 9th of September to attend the Parliament of Religions. The speakers at the Parliament met in a special room to talk to each other or to President Charles Bonney. Francis Albert Doughty gained entrance to this room and sent an article to the *Boston Evening Transcript* of September 30 that included the following character sketch. Little is known of the author except that during the 1890s he published pieces on various subjects in *Metaphysical Magazine*, *The Forum*, *Lippincott's Magazine* and in *Appleton's Popular Science Monthly*.

> The most striking figure one meets in this anteroom is Swami Vivekananda, the Brahmin monk. He is a large, well-built man, with the superb carriage of the Hindustanis, his face clean shaven, squarely moulded regular features, white teeth, and with well-chiselled lips that are usually parted in a benevolent smile while he is conversing. His finely poised head is crowned with either a lemon coloured or a red turban, and his cassock (not the technical name for this garment), belted in at the waist and falling below the knees, alternates in a bright orange and rich crimson. He speaks excellent English and replies readily to any questions asked in sincerity.
>
> Along with his simplicity of manner there is a touch of personal reserve when speaking to ladies, which suggests his chosen vocation....
>
> Vivekananda's address before the parliament was broad as the heavens above us, embracing the best in all religions, as the ultimate universal religion—charity to all mankind, good works for the love of God, not for fear of punishment or hope of reward. He is a great favourite at the parliament, from the grandeur of his sentiments and his appearance as well. If he merely crosses the platform he is applauded, and this marked approval of thousands he accepts in a childlike spirit of gratification, without a trace of conceit. It must be a strange experience too for this humble young Brahmin

monk, this sudden transition from poverty and self-effacement to affluence and aggrandizement.[35]

After the Parliament of Religions came to a close, Lucy Monroe (1865-1950), the first Chicago correspondent for *The Critic*, a New York based magazine of literature and art, composed two articles that mention Vivekananda. On October 7 she pointed out:

> But the most impressive figures of the Parliament were the Buddhist priest, H. Dharmapala of Ceylon, and the Hindoo monk, Suami Vivekananda.... no one expressed so well the spirit of the Parliament, its limitations and its finest influence, as did the Hindoo monk. I copy his address in full, but I can only suggest its effect upon the audience, for he is an orator by divine right, and his strong intelligent face in its picturesque setting of yellow and orange was hardly less interesting than these earnest words and the rich, rhythmical utterance he gave them.[36]

On November 11, 1893 Lucy followed with:

> His [Vivekananda's] culture, his eloquence, and his fascinating personality have given us a new idea of Hindoo civilization. He is an interesting figure, his fine, intelligent, mobile face in its setting of yellows, and his deep, musical voice prepossessing one at once in his favour.... He speaks without notes, presenting his facts and his conclusions with the greatest art, the most convincing sincerity; and rising at times to a rich, inspiring eloquence. As learned and cultivated, apparently, as the most accomplished Jesuit.[37]

Swami Vivekananda appreciated this statement so much that he quoted it in a letter written to Diwanji Saheb four days later.[38]

Lucy Monroe Calhoun is best known for her one-hundred and thirty-four installments of the "Chicago Letter" (1893-96) that appeared in *The Critic*. These articles helped to establish Chicago as a leading cultural centre. Monroe worked as an editorial reader for the Herbert S. Stone publishing company (1898-1905), and as a little-theatre actress. She married William Calhoun who became United States President William Howard Taft's foreign minister to China (1909-13). After his death she was deemed to be the unofficial "first lady" of the diplomatic corps in Peking. Because of the war in Asia, she left China in 1941 and returned to the United States.[39]

Miss Harriet Monroe (1860-1936), the sister of Lucy Monroe, worked as an editor, poet, essayist, critic, autobiographer, biographer, journalist, and dramatist. She mentions in a "Chicago Letter" written for *The Critic* magazine that a pamphlet containing a speech by Swamiji

> has penetrated to the office of *The Spectator*, whose editor receives it "with some surprise as well as much interest", and gives it a three-column review. He deplores Asiatic reticence to explain its creed, and declares that this pamphlet is the first indication of a change. The Swami, according to the reviewer, "understands at least part of what is wanted of him, and succeeds in telling any Englishman who will read him patiently what the essential thought of Hindooism is." But if the Englishman had attended the Parliament, he would have found little trace of Asiatic reticence; on the contrary, a frank readiness to explain itself in response to the first invitation ever extended from the Occidental races. And if these unique explanations are interesting in cold print, what adjectives would the English student have applied to them, if he heard them presented by men with whom oratory is an instinct, inherited from generations of fervid ancestors, and trained to fine accomplishment even in the alien English tongue?[40]

In her autobiography completed near the time of her death, Harriet Monroe describes her impression of Swamiji at the Parliament of Religions:

> Swami Vivekananda, the magnificent, who stole the whole show and captured the town.... the handsome monk in the orange robe gave us in perfect English a masterpiece. His personality, dominant, majestic; his voice, rich as a bronze bell; the controlled fervour of his feelings; the beauty of his message to the Western world he was facing for the first time—these combined to give us a rare and perfect moment of supreme emotion. It was human eloquence at its highest pitch.
>
> One cannot repeat a perfect moment—the futility of trying to has been almost a superstition with me. Thus I made no effort to hear Vivekananda speak again ... Later I knew him quite well, and always I shall remember an encounter and talk years after in Fifth Avenue, when his eyes soared up to the tip of a skyscraper, and he said something which made me realize that all this newness was as romantic to him as old things are to us, and

that his vision entrusted to our fresh energies his hope of a more united and glorious world.[41]

Earlier, Harriet Monroe received a commission to compose "The Columbian Ode", the well-received official poem of the Chicago World's Fair of 1893, celebrating the 400th anniversary of Christopher Columbus' discovery of America. Between 1891 and 1911, Miss Monroe brought out five volumes of poetry and drama. Her greatest achievement was being the founder and editor of *Poetry: A Magazine of Verse* from 1912 until her death. Due to her competence and open-mindedness as an editor, this journal became the main vehicle and representative showplace for the new renaissance in twentieth-century poetry. Many world-renowned poets like Robert Frost, T. S. Eliot, James Joyce, Carl Sandburg, and Rabindranath Tagore published in her journal, Tagore having contributed six poems. She described Tagore's works as "beautiful devotional poems, and the religious feelings they expressed was a tribute to the universal God of all races and creeds." Harriet Monroe invited Tagore to Chicago and was happy when he won the Nobel Prize for Literature in 1913. She wrote, "We used to spend evenings around Mrs. Moody's fire listening to the chanting of poems in Bengali, or the recitation of their English equivalents, and feeling as if we were seated at the feet of some ancient wise man of the East." While visiting the ruins of the Incas, she passed away and was buried in the Andes.[42]

Rabindranath Tagore made five trips to the West, totalling about seventeen months between the years 1912 and 1930. A new generation of highly select Indian religious leaders born between 1854 and 1873 who came to the West before 1912 were: Vivekananda and his four brother disciples, Sri Aurobindo, Baba Bharati, Mohini Chatterji, Mahatma Gandhi, Rabindranath Tagore and Swami Rama Tirtha. In addition to the former president of the United States Calvin Coolidge, Henry Ford, the then president Herbert Hoover, Henry Morgenthau, the future president Franklin D. Roosevelt, William Rothenstein, Ruth St. Denis, and Emma Thursby, as an "ambassador of good will", Tagore, with his spiritual insights, knowledgeable and likable personality, made friends with professors Will Durant, Albert Einstein, William Hocking, James Pratt, Josiah Royce, Rufus von Klein Schmidt, Giuseppe Tucci, and J. H. Woods; writers Jane Addams, Rev. C. F. Andrews, Jules Bois, James Cousins, Theodore Dreiser, T. S. Eliot, Rev. John H. Holmes, Helen Keller, Hermann Keyserling, Sinclair Lewis, Thomas Mann, Harriet Monroe, Myron Phelps, Ezra Pound, Gertrude E. Sen,

Rev. Jabez Sunderland, William Yeats and Francis Yeats-Brown.[43] While in England in 1913, Tagore combined talents with Evelyn Underhill (1875-1941) who authored the first great book on comparative mysticism two years earlier. She assisted Tagore in compiling and translating *One Hundred Poems of Kabir* (1914, later called *Songs of Kabir*), to some extent mistakenly attributed to the fifteenth-century mystical poet, in which she wrote a scholarly eighteen-page introduction. She also composed the introduction for *The Autobiography of Devendranath Tagore* in the same year.[44]

Myron Henry Phelps (1856-1916), a member of the prestigious Union League Club and the Anti-Imperialist League, was a successful patent attorney in New York during 1887-98 and 1907. In a 1910 address delivered at the Hindu College Hall in India, he told his audience about Vivekananda:

> I first saw him at the Chicago Parliament of Religions in 1893. I shall never forget his handsome and brilliant face and his fine form, most impressively set out by his orange robe and turban. When he first spoke, before many thousands of people in the great auditorium, he took that vast audience by storm. I saw him frequently in New York between 1893 and 1896. For a while he was a guest at my house. The education of his people was very near his heart. We had many talks about it.[45]

Five years earlier in an article on P. Ramanathan, Phelps briefly mentioned:

> Then came the Parliament of Religions at Chicago in 1893, which did much to bring Eastern thought home to us; and there the striking figure and the fervid and elegant eloquence of Swami Vivekananda secured for him a respectful and interested attention which later followed him in his journeying to many other parts of this country.[46]

Due largely to his association with Swamiji, between 1898 and 1907 Myron Phelps decided to alter his lifestyle and engage himself in literary pursuits and travels. Though he was not a member of the Baha'i faith, he stayed in Akka, Palestine, for a month as a guest of Abdu'l Baha (1844-1921), the Baha'i leader. Phelps wrote the first full-length book in English about Abdu'l Baha, a classic of Baha'i literature called the *Life and Teachings of Abbas Effendi*, renamed *The Master in Akka* (1903). For about a year he studied under P. Ramanathan (aka Sri Parananda) [q.v.], the Solicitor General of

Ceylon (Sri Lanka), later wrote two articles about him, and invited him to come to the United States, which he did. In 1904 Phelps returned from India and became the director of The Monsalvat School for the Comparative Study of Religion at Greenacre, a position formerly held by Lewis Janes. His lecturers included Swami Rama Tirtha and Baba Bharati, both of India, in 1904, and P. Ramanathan in 1905. In New York, Phelps served as president of the Society for the Advancement of India, accompanied by Jabez Sunderland, the vice-president. He organized the Indo-American National Association, and in March 1908 the India House (cofounded by Jabez Sunderland), which was used as a lodging residence and meeting place for Indian students in New York. Swami Bodhananda visited the India House when Myron Phelps was its director. In one of his speeches in London, the American President Theodore Roosevelt vehemently praised British rule in India. Upon hearing this, Myron Phelps immediately protested. He took the initiative to collect signatures of many eminent Americans who opposed this rule, and then published the list in newspapers.[47] Because of his opposition to British rule in India, in 1909 he was placed on a list of twenty-one undesirables, maintained by the Government of India in the United States. A London newspaper opposed his projected tour of India.[48]

By April 1910 Myron Phelps was living in India as a vegetarian, wearing Indian garb, and calling himself an "American Hindu". In India, Phelps was greatly interested in making a first-hand study of the prevailing educational and social movements. In June he arrived in Ceylon (Sri Lanka) and spent some time with P. Ramanathan, and then moved to Madras to live with Dr. Nanjunda Rao. He paid a visit to Rabindranath Tagore's farm in India, where the two conversed on political-social issues. Annie Besant did not allow Phelps to join the Theosophical Society because he held an anti-British political position, was connected with the India House in New York, and supposedly supported the Krishnavarma political extremists. After visiting schools in South India, he submitted articles about them to *The Hindu* newspaper in Madras. In a written account he praised the Gurukul school near Haridwar founded by Munshi Ram, which Phelps wrote, is "saturated with the Vedas and Upanishads". Phelps was popular with the Indians because of his support of their struggle for freedom. He published two articles in the *Prabuddha Bharata* (July 1910, February-March 1911). The latter piece, "Swami Vivekananda's Work and Mission in India", mentions that Phelps gave an exposition in Madras on Vivekananda's idea of education. In the article he wrote, "Swami Vivekananda had drunk deep at the fountainhead of your religion—of all religions—he knew the greatness of Hinduism, he knew that it was the root of all that is great in India, and that it was the only sure foundation for his work." At locations like the Vivekananda Reading Hall at Kuala Lumpur and the Law College Association at Trivandrum, Myron Phelps gave many long lectures on the Hindu educational system based on the principles laid down by Vivekananda. These and other discourses were published in the *Brahmavadin* during 1910-12 covering over eighty pages. He also authored the book *R. S. Notes of Discourses on Radhasoami Faith/Delivered by Babuji Maharaj 1913-14*, published by the Radhasoami Satsang in Agra, India. Myron Phelps died of tuberculosis in Bombay in 1916.[49]

The following letter appeared on the Internet:

> To Lydia Coonley Ward
> Chicago, IL,
> 2nd Nov '93,
>
> Dear Madam
>
> I will be very glad to pay you a visit on Sunday [Nov. 5]. You may come any time in the afternoon Saturday when I will be very glad to accompany you. Only if I have to go out of town on Saturday or Sunday, I hope to be excused, but of which there is almost no chance. Mrs. and Mr. Mills express their regrets in not being able to take advantage of your kind invitation.
>
> Sincerely,
> Vivekananda[50]

Since Lydia Coonley Ward (1845-1924) did not marry the scientist Henry Ward until March 18, 1897, the letter would have been addressed to Lydia Coonley. Sister Nivedita later wrote to Josephine MacLeod in 1900, "Mrs. Ward had Swami in her house once—but he did not like it—and fled to the Hales [November 15, 1893]. She remembers him as 'the most interesting human being she ever met.'" Sister Nivedita stayed with her for nearly a week, and she wished to donate one-hundred dollars to support Nivedita's work in India. During her lifetime, Lydia Coonley composed several popular and charming books of poetry, including a three-volume collection edition in 1921, and was president of the Chicago Women's Club (1895-96). She certainly would have welcomed Vivekananda as a guest in her house, which served as a social and cultural gathering place. Her biographer noted, "For nearly a quarter-century her home was a centre of 'light and leading' for all who were in any way identified with Chicago's higher interests, and for many distinguished visitors to the city as well." Jane Addams made clear, "In that home I first unfolded plans for founding a settlement in Chicago, and met with that ready sympathy and understanding which her adventuring and facile mind was always ready to extend to a new cause she believed to be righteous."[51]

On December 3, 1893, a few days after Swamiji's departure from Des Moines, Iowa, the *Iowa State Register* commented on his visit to the city. It wrote in part:

> Probably the most practical thing that Vivekananda has done is to give us a truer idea of India and to correct some of the mistaken ideas that we have obtained from reading what he calls the 10 cent books about India, written by Americans and Englishmen who have spent a few weeks in India talking with their servants and in sport and then come home and written five volumes about the customs and religion of the higher classes. Vivekananda recommends Sir W. Wilson Hunter's "Short History of the People of India" as being official and perfectly reliable, and almost the only book published in English about India and the religion and customs of the Hindoo people that can be depended upon.[52]

In other lectures Vivekananda referred to Hunter's books as verification of ancient India's contribution to modern medical science and the education of Indian women in the Middle Ages.[53] In Madras, Swamiji was the guest of Manmathanath Bhattacharya for three and one half months beginning on December 22, 1892. It is quite possible that Vivekananda read the Bengali edition of the above-mentioned history book by Sir William Wilson Hunter (1840-1900), which Bhattacharya had translated. During his stay as a guest in his house, Bhattacharya might have stimulated his interest in history that served as preparation for his mission in the West.[54]

Hunter's book, originally published in 1880, was an authentic and unbiased history of India, which helped counter many of the false notions about the country's history and culture that were prevalent at that time in the West. His informative, objective, and pleasant reading books made India better known to the English-speaking world. He was very appreciative of ancient Indian mathematic, astronomy, physics and grammar. Born in

Glasgow, Scotland, Hunter acquired a knowledge of Sanskrit and joined the Indian Civil Service in 1862, remaining in India for twenty-five years and travelling from one end of the country to the other. Posted in the remote district of Birbhum in the lower province of Bengal, he compiled *A Comparative Dictionary of the Non-Aryan Languages of India*, and organized and directed a twenty-volume statistical survey of Bengal (1875-1877) and a two-volume survey of Assam (1879). Hunter's 260 page *A Brief History of the Indian Peoples* (1880) was widely translated and utilized in Indian schools. In 1886 he was elected vice-chancellor of the University of Calcutta. After retiring in 1887 he returned to England and authored a number of history books covering British rule in India.[55]

The Year 1894

When Swamiji spoke to the women students at Smith College, "George W. Cable, the novelist, introduced the Brahmin as a lover of truth, a member of a divine order, and a representative of the mother of European nations." After the speech, George W. Cable (1844-1925) was present for the symposium where Vivekananda held a discussion with the College president, the head of the philosophy department and other professors, and leading Ministers of the Northampton churches who believed that Christianity is the only true religion. Coming from a Southern background, Cable was an important regional writer whose best-received books were set in New Orleans and the Louisiana plantation country. In 1879 his volume *Old Creole Days* was recognized as an American classic in its field. Northern readers were especially fond of his uniquely graceful and delicate evocations. He engaged in a joint reading tour with Mark Twain in 1884-85. Cable was also an early Southern advocate of civil rights for African Americans and prison reform.[56]

In two letters addressed to the Hale sisters in Chicago from Greenacre during July-August 1894, Swamiji mentioned, "Miss Stockham, and several other ladies and gentlemen live in tents which they have pitched on the open ground by the river.... Cora Stockham has made a bathing dress for me,"[57] and "Herewith I send a photograph Cora Stockham took of the group under the tree."[58] It was Cora L. Stockham (b. c. 1858) who photographed Vivekananda with the famous author Edward Everett Hale, Sarah Farmer and M. (Moses) H. Gulesian at Greenacre in 1894. Gulesian (c. 1863-1951), an Armenian immigrant, entered the United States penniless in 1882, and then amassed a million-dollar fortune through real estate investments in the Boston area, only to lose most of his funds in the 1929 stock market crash. As president of the Old Ironsides Foundation, he is best known for his efforts in saving the historic vessel "The U.S.S Constitution" from destruction in 1905. This vessel was built in 1797 and was commonly known as "Old Ironsides". It was the oldest commissioned ship in the U.S. Navy and the champion of the War of 1812.[59] Five years later Cora attended a party for Swamiji held at the Hale house during November 1899. She was the editor of a monthly magazine, *The Kindergarten: For Teachers and Parents*, and wrote a book called *Mothers' Portfolio: A Book for Every Mother Containing Messages from the Froebel and the Kindergarten for the Benefit of Little Folks* (1889) that was reprinted in 2001 by the Froebel Foundation.[60]

Cora lived with her mother Dr. Alice Bunker Stockham (1833-1912) in Evanston, Illinois. Dr. Carl von Bergen, a good friend of Swamiji, was the Swedish delegate to the Parliament of Religions. As a co-lecturer with Vivekananda at the First Congregational Church in Evanston (September 30-October 3, 1893), he was staying with Alice Stockham.[61] In a letter addressed to Mrs. G. W. Hale, in April 1894 Swamiji wrote, "There was a certain Mrs. Smith in Chicago. I met her at Mrs. [Alice] Stockham's. She has introduced me to the Guernseys."[62] An interesting chain of events, Mrs. Stockham being indirectly responsible for Swamiji being introduced to Mr. Guernsey, one of his key supporters in New York City. Dr. Alice Stockham, an obstetrician and gynaecologist, was the fifth woman in the United States to become a doctor. Before making contact with Swamiji, she met Count Leo Tolstoy in Russia in 1889 and he had her book on maternity, *Tokology* (1883), translated into Russian (with a foreword by Leo Tolstoy). The book sold over half a million copies. Alice Stockham also visited India and other Asian countries in 1891, being the guest of Colonel Olcott at a Theosophical Convention held in Madras. Her interests were in education and the condition of women in East Asian countries. She considered Tolstoy to be "truly a great soul, but his greatness as simple as a child." She came out with a short book entitled *Tolstoi: A Man of Peace* (1900), telling about her visit to Russia to meet him. Over the years Alice supported many causes for the benefit of women. Her daughter Cora later married a man named Skaife, and she and her mother in 1911 moved to Alhambra, California, near Los Angeles, where Alice passed away.[63]

One of Ramakrishna Vedanta's staunchest supporters in the West, Lewis George Janes (1844-1901) [q.v.], to some extent a self-educated man, became the first president of the Brooklyn Ethical Association (1885-96), a lecturer on sociology and civics at the school of political science of the Brooklyn Institute of Arts and Sciences (1893-96), instructor in history at Adelphi College in Brooklyn (1894-95), director of Sara Bull's winter Cambridge Conferences for the study of ethics, philosophy, sociology, and religion (1896-1901), cofounder and director of the Monsalvat (Mount of Peace) School for the Comparative Study of Religion at Greenacre during the summer of 1896-99, and, in addition, president of the Free Religious Association beginning in June 1899, fostering religion free of theological dogma and ecclesiastical control. The retiring president of the Free Religious Association, Thomas Higginson, affirmed that Janes was "capable of great labour, and possessing the greatest facility in bringing together amicably persons of the most opposing opinions."[64]

It is possible that Vivekananda first met Lewis Janes in New York City in late June or early July 1894. Janes was the president of the Brooklyn Ethical Association, and in July his assistant, Charles Higgins, was already lining up future New York speaking engagements for Swamiji.[65] They made contact at Greenacre and travelled together to the Free Religious Association in Plymouth, Massachusetts, in August. On December 28 Janes attended Charles Higgins' reception for Vivekananda in New York. In a letter Swamiji mentioned, "Dr. Janes was as usual very kind and good."[66] Swamiji gave a series of six talks (December 30-April 7, 1895) sponsored by the Brooklyn Ethical Association, and made a single appearance the following year in February.[67] After his first lecture, a number of questions were put to him by Robert G. Eccles, M.D. (1848-1934), who, during his lifetime, held the position of vice-president of the Brooklyn Ethical Society, president of the New York Pharmaceutical Association, and the first dean of the Brooklyn College of Pharmacy. Questions also came form Asa W. Tenney (1833-97), a leading lawyer of the city who previously had been appointed by three U. S. presidents to be U. S. distinct attorney for the eastern district of New York. On the 3rd of January 1895 Swamiji wrote to Mrs. Bull:

> Some of them thought that such Oriental religious subjects will not interest the Brooklyn public. But the lecture, through the blessings of the Lord, proved a tremendous success. About 800 of the elite of Brooklyn were present, and the very gentlemen who thought it would not prove a success are trying for organising a series in Brooklyn.[68]

Janes was a strong supporter of the Vedanta Movement and a loyal defender of the faith. In two 1895 publications, he sent long letters to the *Brooklyn Eagle* (published March 6, 17) defending Vivekananda against the allegations of the Ramabai Circle.[69] Swamiji very much appreciated Janes' letters in the *Eagle* and wrote to him on the 25th of April:

> It was so scholarly, truthful and noble and withal so permeated with your natural universal love for the good and true everywhere. It is a great work to bring this world into a spirit of sympathy with each other but it should be done no doubt when such brave souls as you still hold your own. Lord help you ever and ever my brother and may you live long to carry on the mighty work you and your society has undertaken.[70]

In November 1896 the Swami noted in a letter to Sara Bull, "Dr. Janes is doing splendid work indeed. I can hardly express my gratitude for the many kindnesses and the help he has given me and my work."[71] After Vivekananda returned to India, Janes, along with other people, mailed a letter to the Swami in 1897, asking him to come again to the United States. Z. Sidney Sampson, the president, and Janes, the ex-president of the Brooklyn Ethical Association, sent another letter to the *Indian Mirror* stating in part:

> We wish also to testify to our high appreciation of the value of the work of the Swami Vivekananda in this country. His lectures before the Brooklyn Ethical Association opened up a new world of thought to many of his hearers and renewed the interest of others in the comparative study of religions and philosophy systems, which gives breadth to the mind and an uplifted stimulus to the moral nature.[72]

Swami Saradananda visited Janes' wife and son in January 1897, and mailed him a copy of N. N. Ghose's critique of Reverend John Henry Barrows' first lecture in Calcutta. The next month and in March of 1898, Janes sent two letters to the *Outlook*, a Protestant periodical, as a rejoinder to a criticism they made about Swamiji. In the first letter he praised Sri Ramakrishna.*[73] Janes wrote to the editor of the *Brahmavadin* in June:

---

* See Chapter I.

> In Cambridge, the classes in the Vedanta philosophy, constituting a single feature in the broad field of comparative study outlined for the Cambridge Conferences, attracted large and intelligent audiences, in part made up of Professors and Students in Harvard University. The Swami's exposition of the principles of the Advaita doctrine, in just comparison with other views which are held in India, was admirably lucid and clear. His replies to questions were always ready and satisfactory. His great fairness of mind and soundness of judgment enabled him to present the doctrine in a manner which at once convinced all of his sincerity and earnestness, while it disarmed the factious opposition which is sometimes stirred up by a more dogmatic and assertive manner.[74]

At the invitation of Lewis Janes, Abhedananda spoke before the Free Religious Association in May, then at Greenacre in August 1898, and at the Cambridge Conference the following April. A year or two before that time, Saradananda gave talks before these and other groups, no doubt largely as a result of Janes' influence.*

In an article that appeared in the journal *Mind* (January 1899) and in the *Brahmavadin* (January 1, 1899), Janes defended Oriental Philosophy, particularly "the profound metaphysics of the Vedanta, the noble ethics and psychology of Buddhism". He cites German thinkers like Schopenhauer, Müller, Deussen and the American Emerson to defend his point of view. In 1900 Janes wrote a letter of over fifteen-hundred words to the editor of the *Herald* attacking anti-Hindu addresses given before the Ramabai Association in Brooklyn, New York, and published in part in the newspaper. Having read the *Law of Manu* in its entirety, he defended its teachings against its critics. In the article Janes provided evidence to show that most Hindus are "gentle, humane, and truthful", and show a reverence for women. He cited four Westerners, viz. Max Müller (1823-1900), Horace Wilson (1786-1860), translator of the *Vishnu Purana* with extensive notes, Sir William H. Sleeman (1788-1856), a major-general in the British Indian Service, and Sir Thomas Munro (1761-1827), a brigadier-general and the governor of Madras, all of whom spoke well of the Indian moral character. Swamiji and Janes probably met again in Paris in 1900. Janes wrote a letter to the editor of the Protestant journal *Outlook* in October 1900, showing the errors in their article "Indian Famine Notes". He pointed out how Saradananda and the Ramakrishna

---

* See Chapter XIV for more details.

Mission took an active part in famine relief, and that the famines were due largely to the inadequacies of the government. Before his sudden death from a heart attack at Greenacre, Maine, Janes published four articles in the *Prabuddha Bharata* between 1899 and 1901, including "In Defense of the Swami Vivekananda". His last words before his passing were, "It is a beautiful world."[75]

After his departure from this life, Saradananda wrote to Sara Bull, "I thought of him [Janes] as an Indian Rishi of old born in the West to fight the growing materialistic tendency of the age."[76] A year later a book of tributes from Swamis Saradananda and Abhedananda, and many other eminent people, was published about him. In the book, Thomas Higginson adeptly described Janes as "the most wholly stainless man I knew".[77]

Swami Abhedananda wrote the following tribute:

> He was a soul adorned with those noble qualities that make one just, honest, and self-sacrificing. Doctor Janes was an indefatigable worker for the good of humanity, and he sacrificed his health in his ardent efforts to help mankind.... He carried with him the courage of his convictions wherever he went, and succeeded in commanding the respect of his hearers and friends. He was a true lover of peace and justice, and was always surrounded by a peaceful atmosphere. That such a gentle, noble, and peace-loving soul may rest in the eternal abode of Peace forever and ever is the constant prayer of his friend, Swami Abhedananda, of India.[78] .

On July 19, 1894, Swamiji wrote to Mrs. George Hale from Fishkill Landing (now a part of the city of Beacon), New York:

> I have seen Mr. Page, the writer of the Forum here, he was so sorry not to get the article on the missionaries. But I have promised to write on other interesting subjects. Hope I have the patience to do so.

Walter Hines Page (1855-1918) became the editor of the *Forum* in 1891, turning a moribund monthly review into one of the most entertaining and influential reviews in America. After being the editor of the *Atlantic Monthly* and other magazines, in 1913 his old friend, President of the United States Woodrow Wilson, appointed him the ambassador to Great Britain. Vigourously seeking American involvement in the First World War and extensive aid for the allies, he was very popular with the British people during the five years he held the position.[79]

In a letter from Greenacre dated July 31, 1894, Vivekananda mentioned, "One Mr. Colville from Boston is here; he speaks every day, it is said, under spirit control."[80] In her "Reminiscences" Alice Hansbrough added:

> While he was under contract with that lecture bureau [Slayton-Lyceum Bureau of Chicago] during his first visit to the West, he travelled with a very well-known spiritualist named Colville, who apparently was also under contract to the same bureau. Swamiji used to say, "If you think X is hard to live with, you should have travelled with Colville." The man seems to have had a nurse to look after him all the time.[81]

Sarah Farmer wrote that she received the inspiration for the Greenacre Religious Conference while listening to a lecture by W. J. Colville in Boston in 1892.[82] English born Wilberforce J. Colville (1859-1917), an inspirational speaker and author of little formal education, from the age of fourteen would enter into a trance and an entity would appear to speak through him. While apparently unconscious, he answered questions on a variety of subjects suggested by the audience, demonstrating knowledge he did not normally possess. Under the pressure of some foreign influence, his lips moved mechanically. At the audience's request, he frequently composed impromptu poems. Colville toured England and the United States where he settled down permanently, and authored many books on the occult.[83]

The main accomplishments of Leon Landsberg (b. 1853) [q.v.], a correspondent for the *New York Tribune* newspaper whom Swamiji met in May 1894, were: taking care of the practical details of Vivekananda's New York activities during the winter of 1894-95, which the Swami sincerely appreciated;[84] being Vivekananda's host for two months in the city of New York during the winter of 1896 and at other times; sending news of his activities in America to the editors of the *Brahmavadin*; recording Jnana-Yoga class on "The First Step towards Jnana",[85] prior to the hiring of Goodwin; typing transcripts of some of the bhakti, jnana, karma, and raja yoga classes; and publishing three affirmative articles in the *New York Herald* that reached a wide audience. The newspaper articles dealt with "The Sayings of Sri Ramakrishna" taken from four issues of the *Brahmavadin* (December 22, 1895), extended quotations from Swamiji's karma yoga (December 29) and from the bhakti yoga classes (January 19, 1896).[86]

Landsberg became Swami Kripananda who noted in a long letter to the *Brahmavadin* published on February 15, 1896:

> The wonderful success which the Swami Vivekananda achieved in spreading the religious and philosophical ideas of the Hindus in our country, may lead one to the erroneous conclusion that his happy result is due to a coincidence of favourable circumstances, rather than to the extraordinary ability of the agent chosen by destiny to carry out this difficult task.... considering the numerous difficulties to be overcome in this attempt, that we come to fully appreciate the grandeur of the work accomplished, and to realize that the great success accompanying it is solely due to the personality of the agent, to his extraordinary moral, intellectual and spiritual endowments, and to his exceptional energy and willpower and to no other cause whatever.[87]

During December or early January 1896, Swamiji spoke before "a society of so-called Free-thinkers" in New York City. In the same newsletter of February 15, Landsberg informed the *Brahmavadin*:

> I shall never forget that memorable evening when the Swami, accepting the challenge, appeared single-handed to face the matador's of materialism, all arrayed with their heaviest armour of law, and reason, and logic, and common sense, of matter, and force, and heredity, and all the stock phrases calculated to awe and terrify the ignorant mass. Imagine their surprise and consternation when they found that, far from being intimidated by these big words, he proved himself a master in wielding their own weapons, and as familiar with the arguments of materialism as with those of Advaita philosophy.[88]

In a letter of February 26, 1896 dispatched from the Alambazar Math in Baranagore to the students of Swami Vivekananda, Swami Ramakrishnananda expressed his appreciation of Landsberg who was now Swami Kripananda:

> P.S. The Sanyasin disciple of the Swami sends very interesting letters to the *Brahmavadin*. We cannot adequately thank him for them. We look with eagerness in every fresh issue of the paper for the letter of K [Kri-

> pananda]. We would be very glad if he (K) condescends to communicate with us directly.[89]

Unfortunately, in the newsletter of February 15 Landsberg was quite critical of Theosophy and some other religious groups. The following month Vivekananda wrote to Alasinga, the editor of the *Brahmavadin*:

> A letter you published from Kripananda in the *Brahmavadin* was rather unfortunate. Kripananda is smarting under the blows the Christians have given him and that sort of letter is vulgar, pitching into everybody. It is not in accord with the tone of the *Brahmavadin*. So in future when Kripananda writes, tone down everything that is an attack upon any sect, however cranky or crude. Nothing which is against any sect, good or bad, should get into the *Brahmavadin*. Of course, we must not show active sympathy with frauds.[90]

By the end of the winter of 1896, the volatile Landsberg had made many false accusations against people like Josiah Goodwin and officers of the New York Vedanta Society, and consequently fell into disrepute with the other members of the Society. Having left the Vedanta movement, in 1898 Landsberg wrote a full-page article with illustrations for the *New York Herald* ridiculing the practice of yoga, for which Abhedananda and Francis Leggett reproved him.[91]

Leon Landsberg received his formal education in Leipzig, Germany. Before coming to New York, he taught modern languages in the Southern part of the United States, which included Birmingham, Alabama, and Nashville, Tennessee. In 1890 Landsberg was a co-author, along with James Connelly, of the first of two translations from the French language of the Russian Nicholas Notovitch's widely-read *Unknown Life of Christ*. Swami Vivekananda considered this report of Jesus' life in India to be a fraud, a view that he expressed in a March 2, 1896 letter to Saradananda, and the following year in India.[92] Landsberg became a member of the New York Theosophical Society and spoke on Islamic morality at the Moslem Temple of Alexander Webb in 1893. Landsberg contributed articles to English, French and Spanish newspapers, and in 1904 he was listed to have been a departmental editor of the *New York Tribune* since 1889. During the First World War in 1915, the city officials granted him a substitute license to teach German language in New York City high schools.[93]

A 1920 newspaper article went out on the wire, showing a photograph of the elderly Leon Landsberg that appeared in the *Ogden Standard-Examiner* in the state of Utah. He was again referring to himself as Swami Kripananda, a disciple of Swami Vivekananda recommending the practice of raja yoga, and not always showing the best of judgment. The piece tells us that he published weekly articles on Sunday in the *New York World* concerning the practice of yoga. Kripananda, a resident of Brooklyn, New York, told a newspaper reporter the following: Through the practice of yoga, "Death can be abolished. It is within man's power to fix the limit of his own life, or to abolish that limit entirely, if he desires. There are men living today in India, who have been alive for several hundred years and who can continue their lives indefinitely." According to Landsberg, breathing controls our heartbeat, and the heartbeat controls the brain which determines longevity. To reach the superconscious state the eight-fold path of yoga should be followed. "In practising one of the asanas it is helpful to repeat slowly and softly some word, as it aids you in fixing your attention. The word usually chosen is 'Om', which is the Hindoo word to express divinity."[94]

When Swamiji lectured in a hired hall in New York, Miss Elizabeth L. Hamlen took tickets at the door while Landsberg seated people. She lived as a guest at Sara Bull's house in Cambridge when Landsberg lodged there for three or four weeks.[95] Concerning Miss Hamlen, Swamiji made this revealing statement in a letter to Sara Bull:

> She wants me to be introduced to the "right kind of people". This is the second edition of the "Hold yourself steady" business, I am afraid. The only "right sort of people" are those whom the Lord sends—that is what I understand in my life's experience. They alone can and will help me. As for the rest, Lord help them in a mass and save me from them.[96]

During his lifetime, Civil War Colonel Thomas Wentworth Higginson (1823-1911) wrote a number of important essays, biographies, historical works, novels, poems, translations and an autobiography. Originally a Unitarian Minister, he invited Ralph Waldo Emerson to speak at his church. Higginson reportedly gave a new translation of the *Vishnu Purana* to Henry David Thoreau, and later wrote two essays on Buddhism (1871-72). Samuel Johnson's book *Oriental Religions and their Relation to Universal Religion—India*, received the praise of Higginson in 1872. He lauded its treatment of Indian and Buddhist religion, and considered it to be a "really good book in the religious faiths of mankind". Being a liberal-minded Unitarian, Higginson delivered a lecture as a delegate to the Parliament of Religions in 1893 on "The Sympathy of Religions", stressing that in fundamentals all religions are alike. As early as 1871 he wrote, "Every year brings new knowledge of the religions of the world, and every step in knowledge brings out the sympathy between them." The result is "one religion under many forms", the "essential creed" the "Fatherhood of God, and the Brotherhood of Man". At the Parliament, Swamiji described Colonel Higginson as "a very broad man" who "was very sympathetic to me".[97] In August 1894 Higginson, the president of the Free Religious Association during 1878-99, invited Swamiji to speak before the group in Plymouth, Massachusetts.[98] After giving his presentation, the *Old Colony Memorial*, a Plymouth weekly, wrote, "His ideas were well expressed, conveying broad sentiments with regard to religious unity on the foundation of the absolute truth in all, and his hearers were deeply interested in the presentation." Ralph Waldo Emerson was one of the founders of the Association. They made contact again the following December at the Cambridge Conferences, where Higginson spoke in support of "Women's Suffrage".[99]

At the invitation of Lewis Janes, Swami Abhedananda spoke before the Free Religious Association on May 27, 1898. Abhedananda wrote, "Col. Higginson was the president who introduced me to the audience as the accredited teacher from India, on whom had fallen the mantle of the illustrious Swami Vivekananda." Sister Nivedita spoke before the same Association the following year in Boston. Thomas Higginson served as one of the honorary vice-presidents of a group formed by Nivedita called "The Ramakrishna Guild of Help in America".[100]

As a social reformer and Unitarian pastor strongly under the influence of Transcendentalism, Colonel Thomas Higginson campaigned for anti-slavery, women's suffrage and rights, religious pluralism, labour reform, and temperance. In 1854 he made an attempt to free a fugitive slave from the Boston Court House by battering a passage through a door. As a result, he received a life-long scar on his chin from a saber cut administered by a policeman. Being a member of the "secret six", he supported John Brown's raid at Harpers Ferry. During the Civil War, Colonel Higginson commanded the First South Carolina Volunteers, the first regiment of former slaves organized by the Union Army. He held the position from 1862 to 1864 until he was wounded in battle. From his wartime experience, he wrote his magnum opus *Army Life in a Black Regiment* (1870), which is now a classic text in African

American history. In his later years, he held the position of vice-president of the Anti-Imperialist League from 1899 to 1908, which opposed the U.S. takeover of the Philippine Islands. A biographer tells us, "Higginson is a memorable example of what an American man of letters in the nineteenth century could be."[101]

The Year 1895

Twice when Swamiji travelled north from New York City to Hartford, Connecticut, for an oral presentation at Unity Hall (March 8, 1895; and January 31, 1896), "he was introduced by Mr. C. B. Patterson, in some fitting remarks".[102] The *Hartford Post* of March 8, which Asim Chaudhuri came across, wrote:

> It is by the merest good fortune due to the personality of Charles B. Patterson of this city that he was induced to come to Hartford. The celebrated Hindoo monk was met by Mr. Patterson who has an office in New York, and after some persuasion consented to lecture here.

Charles Brodie Patterson (1854-1917), a prominent pioneer leader in the New Thought Movement, was an editor of three periodicals, viz. *Mind*, a leading New Thought publication, the Boston based *Arena* (1900-04), and of the widely circulated *Library of Health*. During that time his journals produced very favourable reviews of books authored by Swami Abhedananda. He also served as president of the International Metaphysical League and the New Thought Federation. Patterson produced many books on New Thought, most of which were written after he made the acquaintance of Swamiji. On the Internet, there is an inspiring and joyous picture of Patterson preserved by the Maine Historical Society. In it he is along with Ralph Waldo Trine, Abhedananda, and Charles Malloy at Greenacre during the 1898-1900 period.[103]

The famous American poetess and New Thought writer, Ella Wheeler Wilcox (1850-1919), and her husband were present at many of the day and evening discussions of Swami Vivekananda during the winter of 1895 in the city of New York. Twelve years later in the *New York American* of May 26, 1907, she described the first Swamiji lecture she and her husband attended:

> We went out of curiosity (the Man whose name I bear and I) and before we had been ten minutes in the audience, we felt ourselves lifted up into an atmosphere so rarefied, so vital, so wonderful, that we sat spellbound and almost breathless, to the end of the lecture. When it was over we went out with new courage, new hope, new strength, new faith, to meet life's daily vicissitudes. "This is the philosophy, this is the idea of God, the religion which I have been seeking," said the Man [her husband]. And for months afterwards he went with me to hear Swami Vivekananda explain the old religion and to gather from his wonderful mind jewels of truth and thoughts of helpfulness and strength.[104]

Her husband Robert was undergoing severe business worries at that time. He told Ella, "This man makes me rise above every business worry; he makes me feel how trivial is the whole material view of life and how limitless is the life beyond. I can go back to my troubles at the office now with new strength." They continued to come to the Swami's New York classes later in 1895, in November 1899 and possibly in the summer of 1900. After receiving lessons in concentration from Vivekananda, she wrote:

> I made a practice of sitting quite alone for a quarter or a half hour, seeking to bring my too active mind under the check rein of my will. I endeavoured to drive out every thought save that of God—the one supreme, omnipotent creator of all the worlds which exist or ever have existed.[105]

In May of 1895, Ella Wheeler Wilcox sent a letter to a fellow writer, Kate Tannant Woods, telling her:

> I was listening to Vivekananda this morning an hour. How honoured by fate you must feel to have been allowed to be of service to this Great Soul. I believe him to be the reincarnation of some great Spirit—perhaps Buddha—perhaps Christ. He is so simple—so sincere, so pure, so unselfish. To have listened to him all winter is the greatest privilege life has ever offered me.... His discourse this morning was most uplifting—his mere *presence* is that.... "To do good for good's sake"—with no expectation or desire of reward, and never to speak of what we have done—but to keep on working for the love of doing God's work—is Vivekananda's grand philosophy of life.[106]

Being inspired by one of Swamiji's classes, she later recited a poem she composed with the title "Illusion". Wilcox continued her interest in Vedanta, publishing fourteen articles, primarily poems, in the *Prabuddha Bharata* between 1901 and 1917, and one posthumously in 1994. She produced a short article in the year 1910 or 1911 in Baba Bharati's American journal *Light of India* stating:

> The passing of Vivekananda was like the flashing of a mighty star upon our wondering eyes, for, in truth, no greater, wiser, truer, holier soul ever dwelt among us than this marvellous man who has gone into the spirit life.[107]

In 1911 Wilcox made a trip to India visiting Calcutta, Benares, Bombay and other locations. Her autobiography shows her riding on an elephant. Wilcox came to the conclusion, "I do not think a missionary was needed to convert these deeply religious women to a different creed: or to make them accept a life of fashionable dissipation, bridge, dancing, and extravagant dressing, motor riding and travelling about from resort to resort to find distraction." In addition, she wrote how the Vedanta movement and philosophy were distorted in the 1911 court case involving Sara Bull's will,* and also a long newspaper article praising the Arya Samaj.[108]

At that time Wilcox wrote to a Calcutta newspaper:

> India has been to me, since my earliest recollection, a word of lure and charm. Its five letters spelled wisdom, mystery, and magic, as well as India. Its literature has ever held a potent power over my mind, and from India's greatest modern teacher, Swami Vivekananda, I received incalculable and lasting benefit.[109]

By the time Ella Wheeler Wilcox was eighteen years of age, her poems were contributing substantively to the family income. In her twenties she brought out three popular volumes of poetry. At the turn of the century Wilcox became one of the most popular poets in America, often publishing in mass circulation magazines. For several years she composed a daily poem for a syndicated newspaper column that brought comfort to many people. They adapted her poems into four silent big screen movies during 1914-19.

---

* See Chapter V.

She recited her poems to the soldiers in France during World War I, and came out with her autobiography in 1918. Back in 1887, Wilcox enrolled in the class of Emma Curtis Hopkins (1849-1925), a Christian Science practitioner who founded the New Thought Movement. Emma Hopkins' students included five other future supporters of Vivekananda: Annie Rix Militz and Harriet Rix (founders of the Home of Truth), Paul Militz, and Charles and Myrtle Fillmore (founders of the Unity School of Christianity). Between 1902 and 1914 Wilcox put out three books emphasizing the themes of the New Thought philosophy. In her writings she made mention of raja yoga, prana, and other ideas she learned from Swamiji.[110]

After Swamiji came to New York City in 1895, Mary (Elizabeth) Mapes Dodge (1831-1905) took an active interest in his classes. The *New York Times* (March 3, 1895, p. 8) mentions that she attended Vivekananda's class on the "Vedanta Philosophy", held at the residence of the wealthy Amzi Barber. As a premier author of juvenile literature, during her lifetime she yielded a wide influence on the reading of children. Widowed in 1858, Dodge is best remembered as the writer of the classic best-selling children's tale, *Hans Brinker, or the Silver Skates* (1865), which Walt Disney and other companies produced for television in the 1960s. A leading reviewer pointed out that "The influence of Mary Mapes Dodge on literature for children was unequalled in the nineteenth century.... Dodge was loved and appreciated in her own time." She worked as the editor of *St. Nicholas*, the foremost illustrated monthly magazine for children during 1873-1905. Famous writers like Louisa May Alcott, Henry Wadsworth Longfellow, John Greenleaf Whittier, Alfred Lord Tennyson and Rudyard Kipling contributed poems and stories to the journal.[111]

A friend of Mary Mapes Dodge named Kate Douglas Wiggin (1856-1923) attended Swamiji's New York lecture series. Earlier she had helped to found the first free kindergarten in California in 1878 when teaching at Santa Barbara College, and established a training school for kindergarten teachers in 1880. The prolific Kate Wiggin came out with many books of fiction for children and plays, edited anthologies of juvenile tales, rhymes, and songs, wrote on childhood education, authored novels for adults, and published an autobiography in 1923. Five of her literary productions were made into nine motion pictures between 1917 and 1963. They include the popular *Rebecca of Sunnybrook Farm* in 1917, 1932, and in 1938 staring Shirley Temple.[112]

Augustus Le Plongeon (1826-1908) and his wife attended the annual meeting of the Sorosis Woman's Club dinner in New York City on January 24, 1895. At that time Swamiji sat at the President's table facing the other prominent guests along with the ex-governor of the state of New York, Elihu Root, the future U. S. Secretary of State and Nobel Peace Prize winner, and others. But in his statement given below, Le Plongeon is referring to a later date when Swamiji was lecturing on Yoga. He was born on the island of Jersey, and attended and graduated from Ecole Polytechnique in Paris. His main contribution was the earliest thorough and systematic photographic documentation of archaeological sites of the pre-Columbian Mayan civilization in northern Yucatan. Le Plongeon is widely known for his imaginative history of the Mayan sites in Yucatan as being the cradle of world civilization. According to him, Mayan travellers journeyed to Southeast Asia, then to the lost continent of Atlantis, and later founded the civilization of Ancient Egypt. An elderly Le Plongeon sought Swamiji's support for one of his ideas stating:

> The Swami Vive Kananda, a learned Hindoo monk, when lecturing in New York on Yogi [sic], the Vedanta, and the religious doctrines of India, in speaking with the author on the origin of the *Nagas*, assured him that it was the received opinion of the learned pundits of that country that they originally came from *Patala*, the antipodes, that is, Central America. Patala was the name given by the inhabitants of India to America in those remote times.

It was Le Plongeon's contention that the Nagas were highly civilized Mayans from Central America who migrated to Burma, and then created an empire that ruled all of Hindustan. They then travelled "all over Western Asia to the shores of the Mediterranean, introducing their civilization in every ancient country, leaving traces of their worship in almost every system of religion." Though his primary idea has been discredited by the scientific community, since the Egyptian civilization is considered to be of greater antiquity than the Mayan, the possibility of some form of cultural diffusion, linking the ancient civilizations of the world, has not been disproven.[113]

Edgar Charles Beall M.D. (b. 1853) carried out in detail a personal statistical phrenological examination on the physiognomy of Swami Vivekananda. As the lead article in the *Phrenological Journal* of New York in August 1895, Beall published his description and interpretation. His analysis, which contains two well-known photographs of Vivekananda, is positive and complimentary. Two years before Thomas Harrison had photographed the Swami in Chicago. The article reappeared in an 1897 edition of the *Indian Mirror* newspaper. In a letter to the Indian newspaper, Beall describes Swamiji's "charming appearance" and the "attractiveness of his feature". While other people mention the manliness of Swamiji's nature, Beall noticed his "femininity indicated in nearly every contour of the figure, face, head and hands". Beall previously authored *The Brain and the Bible* (1881), with the preface written by his supporter the agnostic Robert Green Ingersoll. Four years later the *Phrenological Journal* came out with a book review of Swamiji's *Vedanta Philosophy*. They concluded, "The whole book breathes with the sincerity of the writer, who is highly cultured and profound in the doctrines of this particular philosophy."[114]

After Swamiji began the work in America, Alasinga Perumal (1865-1909) [q.v.] strongly felt the need for initiating an English language periodical that would tell of the life and teachings of Sri Ramakrishna (that significantly inspired Max Müller), publish the lectures of Swamiji, and write of his various activities in the West. In 1895 he started the *Brahmavadin*, remaining its editor until his passing. His son carried on the editorialship until 1914 when the *Brahmavadin* was discontinued and the *Vedanta Kesari* came into existence. Alasinga also recommended the establishment of the *Prabuddha Bharata*, but it was too difficult for him to be the editor of two journals. We are very fortunate that the *Brahmavadin* preserved a great deal of material on Vivekananda in the West that cannot be found in any other source. Alasinga's contribution to Vivekananda's studies was enormous. In the book *Vivekananda in Indian Newspapers*, Sankari Basu and Sunil Ghosh have produced over 90,000 words that appeared in the *Brahmavadin* from 1895 to 1902 dealing with Vivekananda's activities primarily in the West. In addition, the *Brahmavadin* printed many of Swamiji's lectures that are now in the *Complete Works*. The journal also adds new information, particularly about the activities of Swamis Saradananda and Abhedananda in the West, which did not appear in any other publication. Swamiji very much encouraged Alasinga by sending him forty-three letters. In August 1896 Swamiji gave him this unique and inspiring advice concerning karma yoga, indicating that an "Ishtadevata" (Chosen Ideal) need not be a person. Swamiji wrote, "Secondly, entire devotion to the cause, knowing that your SALVATION depends upon making the *Brahmavadin* a success. Let this paper be your Ishtadevata, and then you will see how success comes."[115] In his "Memoirs of

European Travel", Swamiji indicated, "However, one rarely finds men like our Alasinga in this world—one so unselfish, so hard-working and devoted to his Guru, and such an obedient disciple is indeed very rare on earth."[116]

In a letter from England to Josephine MacLeod, Swamiji mentions, "I shall be only too glad to come to lunch on Friday and see Mr. [Stanton] Coit at the Albemarle," and "I have been also invited to Moncure Conway's Ethical Society where I speak on the 10th [November 1895]."[117] They held the public presentation at the South Place Chapel, the church with "the largest congregation in London". Hindu and Buddhist scriptures were often read at their Sunday services. On that occasion, Vivekananda explained "The Basis of Vedantic Morality".[118] The *Christian Commonwealth* perceived, "Observing his calm and easy bearing, his perfect command of English, his unbounded confidence in the finality of his statements, one can understand the stir he made at the Parliament of Religions."[119]

As a student at Harvard Divinity School in 1853, the Unitarian Moncure Conway (1832-1907) made contact with both Emerson, his "spiritual father", and Thoreau, two events that changed his life. In Emerson's house he read Charles Wilkins' translation of the *Bhagavad Gita*, which introduced him to Indian thought. Conway, the regular Minister of the non-denominational South Place Chapel in London (1864-84), later was partially connected with the Chapel (1892-97). Keshab Chandra Sen and Pratap Mazumdar in 1874 spoke at the South Place Chapel where Swamiji lectured, and Conway later invited Max Müller to give an address there. Conway, probably the only Transcendentalist to make a pilgrimage to India, attended the meeting of the social conference of the London Hindu Association on July 18, 1896. He advised against rash action of radical reform in India. An article by Moncure Conway on "China and the Missionaries" appeared in the September 1901 issue of the *Prabuddha Bharata*. Being a prolific writer he brought out the 1906 volume *My Pilgrimage to the Wise Men of the East*, covering his 1884 visit with many religious leaders in India. In Calcutta he met Pratap Mazumdar after Keshab Sen's recent death, and went to the Star Theatre to watch a play about Sri Rama.[120]

In 1886 the American born Stanton Coit (1857-1944) worked with Felix Adler in New York City. At that time Coit created the first social settlement for the working classes in America for the purpose of regenerating the slums. Succeeding Moncure Conway, he became the Minister of the South Place Chapel (1888-92), which he referred to as the South Place Ethical Society. He later established some Neighborhood Guilds and Ethical Societies in

London and other areas of England. Coit authored many books on social ethics, and one on the sociology of religion in 1914.[121]

Concerning Swamiji's lecture on "Self-Knowledge" in London on October 22, three days later the *Evening Star* correspondent wrote:

> It has been your correspondent's good fortune to see many strange entertainers and lecturers on the platform of Princes Hall, Piccadilly. I do not think, however, the public have often seen a quainter figure or enjoyed a more remarkable discourse than that of the Indian Yogi, who for an hour and a quarter discoursed in fluent English to a large audience on Tuesday evening. His name is Swa [sic] Vivekananda, and he is a light-brown being, with a beautiful face, a gentle manner, and lustrous yet piercing eyes. The lecture was a most fearless and eloquent exposition of the Pantheistic philosophy of the Vedanta school.

Professor John Henry Wright sent a letter to his wife stating that Vivekananda "succeeded in winning Sir F. Arbuthnot", and that "they became fast friends", probably in London during November 1895. Born in Bombay, Sir Forster Fitzgerald Arbuthnot (1833-1901) received his education in Continental Europe. He returned to India in 1853 as a member of the Bombay Civil Service, where until 1878 he held an important position as a high-ranking tax collector. As mentioned in the next chapter, Vivekananda, accompanied by Romesh Chunder Dutt, attended at least one of the meetings of the Royal Asiatic Society. They might have met at these meetings since Arbuthnot was a trustee and a member of the council and the Oriental translation fund committee of the Royal Asiatic Society. He is remembered for writing manuscripts on Arabic and Persian history and literature particularly in 1887 and 1890.[122]

1896 and After

Miss Caroline Duer (1865-1956) attended Austin Corbin's party in February 1896 along with Nikola Tesla, Sarah Bernhardt and others according to the *New York Times* newspaper.* She later edited the widely distributed

---

* Miss Caroline was one of the twelve persons mentioned in the newspaper who attended the party where Swamiji was the guest of honour.

Vogue national magazine and wrote poetry books and numerous magazine articles.[123]

In a correspondence to the *Washington Post*, the future authoress Esther Singleton (1865-1930) wrote her impression of Vivekananda:

> Serious people in New York have been very much impressed with the lectures and talks that have been given here by Swami Vivekananda during the past two seasons. The Hindu philosopher made a great impression at the Parliament of Religions at the World's Fair and has remained here to continue his work of instructing those who desire it in the mystical and philosophical religion of India. Addressing small audiences, his circle grew, until this year he gave talks on Sunday afternoon at Hardman Hall, and, outgrowing this, he has just finished a course of lectures at the Madison Square Concert Hall packed to overflowing. These lectures have been free to all; for the Hindu monk, if he may so be termed, lives entirely upon charity. He is about thirty-two or thirty-three years of age, nearly six feet tall, and intensely handsome. Although he was born in one of the highest caste families in Bengal, he took voluntarily the vows of celibacy and poverty, yet he is a graduate of the University of Calcutta, and culture and intellect of unusual order are revealed, not only in the substance of his addresses and essays, but in the oratory that he displays. His name Swami means master or rabbi, and is pronounced swarmee [sic].
>
> What he does is to preach the gospel of universal peace and love, of kindness, contentment, and charity, and even those who would not care to accept Eastern philosophy in its entirety may certainly gain profit and aid for daily life. To tell us that we waste our energy and thought on many unworthy objects is perfectly true, and no theories that wish to develop nobility of nature and spirituality can help but have good for their issue. Very impressive is Swami Vivekananda, very majestic, and very noble in appearance and manner, and he realizes not only in his words, but in his costume—a cerise coloured habit tightly girded and a snowy turban folded with infinite grace around his splendid brow, all that the magic word India implies.[124]

She then added a few excerpts from his New York lectures. Esther Singleton, an author, editor, and music critic, was originally a proficient violinist. Music remained one of the chief enthusiasms during her life, and she penned books such as *A Guide to Modern Opera* (1909) and *The Orchestra and its Instruments* (1917). Her popular nonfiction books written for the general public deal with interesting cities and countries of the world; noteworthy pictures, statues, cathedrals, and natural wonders; well-known women, the world's great events, and translations from the French language. Singleton's accurate research, historical insight, and artistic selection make her writings both interesting and authentic. She enjoyed the society of gifted people and was herself a talented conversationalist. Her interest in music, art, literature, and history was keen, and her memory extraordinary.[125]

Helen Huntington (d. 1950), a devotee from Brooklyn, New York, and a future poetess, novelist and playwright, put into writing two glowing accounts concerning "Swami Vivekananda in America". She wrote in part to the *Brahmavadin* of May 7, 1896:

> Next to Swami Vivekananda's presence the *Brahmavadin* is the most excellent and comforting thing we could desire.... It has pleased God to send to us out of India a spiritual guide, a teacher whose sublime philosophy is slowly and surely permeating the ethical atmosphere of our country; a man of extraordinary power and purity who has demonstrated to us a very high plane of spiritual being, a religion of universal unfailing charity, self-renunciation, and the purest sentiments conceivable by the human intellect. The Swami Vivekananda has preached to us a religion that knows no bounds of creed or dogmas, is uplifting, purifying, infinitely comforting, and altogether without blemish; based on the love of God and man and on absolute chastity.... If we could have the Swami with us always, the nature of our progress would be different, it would be easier, for while we believe in him implicitly and are his devoted followers, we are also woefully human ... Swami Vivekananda has made many friends outside the circle of his followers; he has met all phases of society on equal terms of friendship and brotherhood; his classes and lectures have been attended by the most intellectual people and advanced thinkers of our cities; and his influence has already grown into a deep strong under-current of spiritual awakening. No praise or blame has moved him to either—approbation or expostulation; neither money nor position has influenced or prejudiced him.

In addition, in the *Brahmavadin* of November 21, 1896 Helen Huntington added in part:

> It is impossible not to wish for Swami Vivekananda's return to our midst, because he has endeared himself so deeply to all of us. As he said of the *Guru*, Ramakrishna Paramahamsa, "His presence was a blessing to everyone, saint and sinner." So was his own life among us; for he influenced us to a better living and brotherly-kindness to all men.[126]

The wealthy Helen Gates Huntington's first volume *The Solitary Path* appeared in 1892. A poet and novelist of some distinction, her second marriage in 1918 was to the highly successful English playwright Harley Granville-Barker (1877-1946). She then wrote under the name Helen Granville-Barker, receiving praise for her translations of Spanish language literature, four of which became Broadway plays between 1926 and 1929.[127]

Earlier, in 1895, Helen Huntington married Archer Milton Huntington (1870-1955), the son of Arabella Huntington, the San Francisco woman who admired Swami Vivekananda and in 1900 gave Sister Nivedita five-thousand dollars for her girls' school in India. Archer joined the India House organization in New York founded by Myron Phelps, the New York Chamber of Commerce, and became president of the American Geographical Society. As the founder and president of the Hispanic Society of America, which included a free library, museum and educational institution, he did a great deal to promote Hispanic studies in the United States. Archer's second wife Anna Hyatt Huntington, the daughter of professor Alpheus Hyatt, met Vivekananda in Annisquam, Massachusetts, in 1893 and during the following year. We do not know if Archer was involved in the Vedanta movement, yet strangely he had the karma of having his mother and two wives each meet Vivekananda independently in three different cities in three different years.[128]

A man with a love for India, Will Levington Comfort (1878-1932) met Swamiji when he was a young man. Sister Christine reveals in a 1924 letter to Josephine MacLeod that Will Comfort told her, "Everyone connected with Swamiji whom he had ever known had a glow." Will Levington Comfort worked as a foreign war correspondent in the Philippines, China and the Russo-Japanese War. He wrote several novels including one called *Samadhi*, each characterized by range and vividness of imagination, with an emphasis on passivism, mysticism, and other subjects.[129]

An article with illustrations appeared in the *New Thought* magazine around 1909 with the title "The Teachings of Swami Vive Kananda". Without giving any dates, its author Uriel Buchanan mentioned he was "in close personal relation to the Swami [Vivekananda] during his period of teaching in the United States". Uriel's book, *The Mind's Attainment* (1902), contains chapters covering the divinity of man, the science of breath, self-mastery, mental control, mental influences, the higher life, human progress, Divine guidance and the highest goals. These subjects suggest an influence of Vivekananda, expressed in the ideology and terminology of New Thought.[130]

In England John Galsworthy was "very much interested" in the Vedanta classes offered by Edward Sturdy in January of 1896. During the following July in London, the Galsworthys were "very very kind" to Swamiji and they continued to attend his classes.[131] In November, Galsworthy attended one of Swamiji's discussions and they had lunch together. It is not known whether the references are to the father John, to his son John who then worked as a lawyer before becoming a writer, or to both of them. The younger John Galsworthy (1867-1933), the last major Victorian writer, being a highly productive author wrote about eighty volumes of novels, short stories and plays published from 1897 to 1935. As a novelist and a playwright Galsworthy was regarded as one of England's leading writers and, consequently, he was awarded the Nobel Prize for Literature in 1932. Though his writings were commercially successful and critically esteemed during his day, his popularity has declined considerably since that time. A twenty-six-hour serial adaptation for television of a series of his novels, *The Forsyte Saga*, in 1967 and 2002 brought some renewed interest in his literary productions.[132]

During May of 1896, Sister Nivedita urged her two friends in their mid-forties, Eric Hammond [q.v.] and his wife Nell Hammond, to come to Swamiji's speaking engagements in London. Eric worked as a journalist and poet in Wimbledon, England. The Hammonds were devoted admirers of Swamiji, attending many of his discussions, including Abhedananda's first speech in the West in October 1896. In a letter from India Swamiji informed Sister Nivedita that, "Mr. and Mrs. Hammond wrote two very kind and nice letters and Mr. Hammond a beautiful poem in the *Brahmavadin*, although I did not deserve it a bit."[133] When Vivekananda returned to the West, during August 2-15, 1899 he met the Hammonds in England. Sister Nivedita then sent a letter to Sara Bull describing Nell Hammond's spiritual vision of Mother Kali (August 24). Nell Hammond received ten letters from Nivedita during 1898-1902. In 1901 Swami Vivekananda wrote in a letter from Belur Math to Sara Bull, "I had a beautiful letter also from Mrs. Hammond. She is a great soul."[134]

Eric Hammond described Swamiji this way in the *Brahmavadin* of 1907:

> Carrying himself with dignity and grace, he showed not only perfect acquaintance with the English grammatical style but a marvellous intimacy with British and Continental Schools. The purity of his phrasing, the sweet flexibility of his voice, the force of his eloquence were instantly realised. He compelled and retained attention. His courage equalled his ability.[135]

In the *Prabuddha Bharata* of February-March 1910, Eric Hammond depicted Swamiji as:

> Dignified in bearing, fine of feature, eloquent to a degree, with consummate mastery of English; steeped in Sanskrit text and tradition; more than well-versed in the Vedas; he knew, too, much of the various schools of theology in West and East.

Again four years later in the same journal he stated:

> The "Life of the Swami Vivekananda" is a revelation. Those among us in the West whose privilege it was to know him, to esteem and revere him, to cherish a warm personal affection for him, may have imagined themselves possessed of something akin to a complete comprehension of this wonderful Seer.[136]

In a 1922 *Vedanta Kesari* article Hammond made the following statements about his first meeting with Vivekananda:

> No more fitting or outstanding person could have arrived at the centre of British thought. Fortified by his intimate acquaintance of, and his infinite belief in, Shri Ramakrishna, he brought the full force of that great soul to bear upon the minds of his hearers.... Above all eloquence acclaimed him, the eloquence of inspiration. Again, his surprising command of the English language delighted and held his audience.... Such then was our first meeting with him; a meeting which resulted in reverent friendship, in genuine admiration and in most grateful remembrance.[137]

Hammond kept up his interest in Vedanta by publishing in the *Brahmavadin*, contributing thirty articles in the *Prabuddha Bharata* between 1902 and 1938, and three in the *Vedanta Kesari* during the period 1915-21, and two more posthumously. In these articles he narrated stories about Vivekananda and Nivedita, and composed poems and hymns. Eric Hammond was still listed on the cover of the 1923 edition of the *Prabuddha Bharata* as their British representative.[138]

In 1907 Eric Hammond joined the Baha'i group in London. Inspired by their doctrine of universal brotherhood, he wrote the text *Splendour of God*, being extracts from the sacred writings of the Baha'i. In September 1911, Hammond and others spoke at the large farewell reception for Abdu'l Baha (1844-1921), the leader of the Baha'i faith, who spent four weeks in London. At that time, Eric compiled the book *Abdul Baha in London; Addresses, & Notes of Conversations* issued in 1912. Sarah Farmer, Myron Phelps, Phoebe Hirsch, T. K. Cheyne, and Dhan Gopal Mukherji were other Vivekananda supporters who showed varying degrees of interest in Abdu'l-Baha and the Baha'i faith.[139] Vivekananda created an interest in Asian holy men, but it is difficult to assess his importance in influencing any of these people in taking an interest in the Baha'i leader.

Swami Vivekananda also received many complimentary evaluations from the newspapers. For example, the *London Daily Chronicle* of June 10, 1896 reported:

> The gentleman known as the Swami Vivekananda was one of the most striking figures at the Chicago Parliament of Religions, and who went there to expound the ancient teachings of India to the newest of Western nations, is at present in England, returning to his own land in September. The Swami is one of the greatest living exponents of the Vedantic philosophy; his calm manner, distinguished appearance, the ease with which he expounds a profound philosophy, his mastery of the English tongue, explain the great cordiality with which Americans received him, and the fact that they almost compelled him to remain a year or two among them. The Swami had taken the vow of complete renunciation of worldly position, property, and name. He cannot be said to belong to any religion, since his life is one of independent thought which draws from all religions. Those who desire that his teaching may be made known, arrange the entire business part of the work, and the lectures are, so far, made free.[140]

Swamiji remarked in a letter of July 18, 1896 that in London Edward Carpenter (1844-1929) "used to call on me on many occasions and sit near me. Many other socialists and democrats also used to visit me. Finding in the religion of Vedanta a strong support for their ideals, they felt much attracted towards its teachings." Carpenter's elder brother joined the Indian Civil service in 1857 and informed Edward about life in India. Being an ordained Anglican priest (1870-74), Carpenter left the Church to become a writer of nonfiction, specializing in utopian socialism, women's rights, vegetarianism, simplification of life, and environmental matters. During Carpenter's trip to America, Ralph Waldo Emerson showed him his translations of the Upanishads. There he paid a visit to Walt Whitman (1819-92) in 1877, and they exchanged letters until the poet's death. Under the influence of Whitman, Carpenter brought out several volumes of his own poetry and indicated parallels between Whitman's *Leaves of Grass* and the Upanishads. A friend from Ceylon (Sri Lanka), Sir Ponnambalam Arunachalam (1853-1924), added to Carpenter's knowledge of the Indian religion and gave him a translation of the *Bhagavad Gita* during 1880-81. At a market farm near Sheffield, England, Carpenter founded a socialist society in 1885. In his travelogue *From Adam's Peak to Elephanta* (1892), Carpenter describes his excursion to Ceylon and India two years earlier, his meeting with a Jnani or Wise Man, and the attainment of consciousness without thought. In *Pagan and Christian Creeds* (1920), he includes his essay on the "Teachings of the Upanishads". P. Arunachalam wrote the book *Light from the East: Being Letters on Gnanam, the Divine Knowledge*, which Edward Carpenter edited in 1927.[141]

Swamiji published articles on "Metaphysics in India: Reincarnation" and the "Song of the Sannyasin" in the *Metaphysical Magazine* during 1895-96. The literary editor of the periodical was J. Elizabeth Hotchkiss, Ph.D., a teacher of metaphysics and psychology in New York City. In *Who's Who in America* (1901), she is mentioned taking "special studies in metaphysics and psychology under Leander Edmund Whipple, Swami Vivekananda and Charles Brodie Patterson," the New Thought expert and friend of Vivekananda and Abhedananda.

During Swamiji's absence from the country, his book *Raja Yoga*[142] published in 1896 received this review from *The Arena* in March 1897:

> The whole spirit of the book is candid in the extreme. It appeals to what is best and noblest in man. It makes no foolish mysteries and demands, no blind belief. It puts forth its system in a plain and simple manner. It is

> able to present its own method without in any way attacking the method of others. It manifests a charity that it is usual to call Christian, but which Vivekananda proves is equally the property of the Hindu. If this little book had nothing to teach but the beautiful toleration it advocates, it would be well worth reading; but many will find in it valuable suggestions to aid in reaching the higher life.[143]

A review of Swamiji's *From Colombo to Almora* (1897) appeared in the *San Francisco Call* in September with the title "By a Hindu Sage", stating in part:

> He is regarded by his people with all the reverence due to a divine messenger. In the enthusiastic addresses to him upon his arrival in his old home in Calcutta he was told that he had a world to conquer, that it was for him to interpret and vindicate the religion of the Hindus to the ignorant, the skeptical and the willfully blind.[144]

A favourable assessment of *From Colombo to Almora* appeared in the English *Manchester Guardian* of August 31, 1897, stating in part:

> This is a book full of interest for the student of Indian affairs and Indian thought. Vivekananda was selected to represent Hindoo religion at the so-called Parliament of Religions held at the Chicago World's Fair of 1893. His powerful addresses there produced a deep impression, and he has since lectured in other parts of America and in this country. On his return to India he was hailed as the champion of the national faith, and this volume records the addresses presented to him, addresses couched in very enthusiastic and reverential language, together with his replies and some more formal lectures on the Vedanta philosophy. He has a remarkable command of English and much spontaneous eloquence.

After selecting out and quoting appealing ideas from the book, the newspaper columnist concluded, "It is interesting to watch the efforts of a man who in the eyes of a large part of the population of India combines learning and holiness for the purification of the religion he professes and the elevation of its followers."

A "Student in Vedanta" published a journal article in the London based *Fortnightly Review* with the title "A Vindication of Vedanta" in December 1898.

His article is replete with Swamiji's ideas and reappeared verbatim in the *Brahmavadin*. There is no doubt that the intelligent "Student in Vedanta", who remained anonymous, was very much under the influence of the sublime, rational, and original ideas of Vivekananda, whom he did not cite. There is a noticeable difference between the presentation of Vedanta by Vivekananda and that of the Western Indologist like Deussen and Müller. By contrast, Rabbi Maurice Fluegel's (1832-1911) *Philosophy, Qabbala and Vedanta* (1902) presented Vedantic ideas employing the dry scholastic intellectual approach of Max Müller's *Three Lectures on the Vedanta Philosophy* (1901) and other Indologists. Forged in this academic framework, these difficult to understand ideas appealed to only a small number of elite Western scholars. The "Student in Vedanta" wrote the article as a reaction against John B. Crozier (1849-1921), a Canadian born English academic, who severely criticized the Hindu religion in a chapter of his 1897 book on the *History of Intellectual Development*. The *Brahmavadin* followed with a nine-page article showing the baselessness of the charges that Dr. Crozier levelled against the Vedanta and its system of ethics.[145]

Second Visit to the West

Though Horatio Dresser (1866-1954) [q.v.] was a critic of the Advaita Vedanta philosophy,* he admired the Swamis, which is evident from the following statement that appeared in an 1899 book of his:

> The Swami Vivekananda, one of the most striking figures in that parliament, soon became a popular lecturer, and was followed by other exponents of the great Oriental system. Regular societies for the study of the Vedanta have been founded, books and papers devoted to the subject have been issued, and the Vedanta has held a prominent place on the programmes of summer schools founded in the interests of universal thought.... "No one," says the Swami Saradananda, "can rise to the highest state of spirituality without being perfectly and absolutely pure and high in morals." No one can dispute this. I would not for a moment doubt the high purpose which inspires the Swamis. One of the gentlest, sweetest, most broadly sympathetic and spiritual men of my acquaintance is a Swami (master), who once

---

* See Chapter XVIII.

declared to me that if he ever found a larger system than the Vedanta he would accept it.[146]

Dresser often quotes Vivekananda in his "An Interpretation of the Vedanta". He enjoyed success as a leading writer and lecturer in the New Thought movement. In addition, he was one of the founders of the New Thought, the Metaphysical Club of Boston in 1895, where Swami Saradananda spoke on December 15, 1896. The following year he became the founder and editor of the *Journal of Practical Metaphysics*, which in November 1897 included an article by Saradananda entitled "The Literary Beauties of the Vedas and Upanishads". The journal merged with the influential *The Arena* in 1898, where Dresser became the associate editor. This journal published articles by Swami Abhedananda. After the turn of the century Dresser worked as an assistant in the philosophy department at Harvard University (1903-11), being friends with William James and Josiah Royce. In 1919 he became an ordained minister of the Swedenborgian Church, and in later years a member of a Unitarian Church in Brooklyn.[147]

In 1899 an enlarged edition entitled *Lectures by the Swami Vivekananda on Raja Yoga and other Subjects* was released that drew attention from the American press. It included lectures on Raja Yoga, Patanjali's Yoga Aphorisms with commentary, a Sanskrit glossary, and a lecture on "Immortality" and on "Bhakti Yoga". Like *My Master* (1901), the fact of being published by [James] Baker & [Nelson] Taylor in New York helped create, among the readers, a lot of interest in the book. The reports read as follows:

> The methods of practical realization of the divine within the human are applicable to all religions, and all peoples, and only vary in their details to suit the idiosyncrasy of race and individuals (*Washington, D.C. Post*, June 12, 1899).
>
> A valuable portion of the volume to students is the glossary of Sanskrit technical terms. This includes not only such terms as are employed in the book, but also those frequently employed in works on the Vedanta philosophy in general (*New York Times*, July 22, 1899).
>
> His [Vivekananda's] successor at present in New York is the Swami Abhedananda. Both these men, as well as others like them, are thoroughly earnest in their desire to teach the great truths of Vedantism to all who care to hear. It is unfortunate that their work is too often confounded with the deplorable excesses of the fanatical devotees of theosophy. In reality, it is

possible for anyone to believe in the Vedanta philosophy and still belong to any religion. Although there are things in the system which are difficult to receive, still the great doctrines are the same which pervade our own religion. It teaches a pure morality, charity, and kindness to all and it aims to install into its followers a desire for perfection, without which they can never enjoy eternal happiness.

This perfection is to be attained in various ways, and one of the most important of these is by Raja Yoga, or conquering the internal nature (*New York Times*, July 29, 1899).[148]

That he [Swami Vivekananda] is master of the science of Raja Yoga, that contains so much that is mysterious to the Western world, there can be no doubt. These lectures give a thorough and lucid explanation of it, and contain much that Christians must accept as sound and wise (*Bestseller, Newsdealer, and Stationer*, August 1, 1899).

A large part of the book is occupied with that method of attaining perfection known as Raja Yoga, and there are also translations of a number of aphorisms and an excellent glossary (*Living Age*, August 5, 1899).

As a study of Vedanta Philosophy and Raja Yoga it is, perhaps, unequalled by any other book in the English language (*The Progressive Thinker*, September 26, 1899).

A new edition with enlarged glossary, which will be welcomed by students of comparative religion, who are already familiar with the author's lectures in this country (*Review of Reviews*, October 1899).[149]

This work embraces a series of lectures that fully explain the doctrines and principles of the philosophy of the Indian monks, who have aroused such a widespread interest in this country. To the reader who is seeking after the truth and light, this volume will be indeed welcome. It is written in an unusually clear style that all readers can understand (*Bookseller and Newsman*).

How to get at the soul and put the reins of the mind and the body into its hands, is the problem that Raja Yoga attempts to solve, and all those persons who practise Yoga are known as Yogis. Then—how to become a Yogi, how to rise to a high state of psychic control is what Vivekananda endeavours to point out in these lectures (*Literary Digest*).[150]

The book *Raja Yoga* was also reviewed by *Light of Truth*, *Los Angeles Times*, *Occult Truths*, *Public Opinion*, and *The Truth Seeker*.

Rollin Daggett (1831-1901) was an early California and Nevada literary journalist, publisher and newspaper editor (1852-78). He served in the U.S. House of Representatives (1878-81), and was the U.S. Minister to Hawaii (1882-85). He obviously took an interest in Swamiji's book on *Raja Yoga*, since in his later years he authored a long review of the book for the *San Francisco Chronicle* in August 1899. While he offers few value judgments, using many quotations Daggett did his best to explain the contents of the volume. He made statements like, "The mental and physical process are described through which man may be brought back to full knowledge in life of the secrets of his being."[151]

Miss Anna Josephine Ingersoll (1852-1940) [q.v.] of New York City published an article "The Swamis in America" in *The Arena* journal of 1899. The text includes pictures of Swamis Vivekananda, Abhedananda and Saradananda, copyrighted by H. J. Van Haagen. Her article discusses the Vedantic activities of Sri Ramakrishna, the three Indian Swamis, Sarah Farmer, Lewis Janes, Sister Nivedita, and Max Müller, all in a favourable light. In the following year she came out with a twenty-two-page booklet about the Greenacre Conferences with the title *Greenacre on the Piscataqua* (1900), including a photograph of "Swami's Pine" under which Swamiji spoke to a class, and one of Abhedananda. She died in Switzerland or Italy.[152]

An article "The Vedanta Philosophy" was written for *The Arena* journal (1900) by Edward Clarence Farnsworth, which explains this philosophical system in a favourable light. Farnsworth lived in Portland, Maine, about forty miles north of Greenacre. He mentions that at Greenacre:

> When the Swami Vivekananda, standing beneath the evergreen pine—emblem of constancy and stability—uttered these words: "I am neither body nor changes in the body; neither am I senses nor object of the senses; I am Existence Absolute, Bliss Absolute, Knowledge Absolute; I am It; I am It," he spoke in the language of prophecy, for at the base of his being was the Atma of the universe (his higher Self), awaiting, as it had awaited throughout the ages, his self-conscious recognition.

Farnsworth published volumes of poetry and prose dealing with Christian Science, the *Bible*, Theosophy, and modern art and music from 1909 until 1928. He quotes from Swami Abhedananda's works in one of his books.[153]

The American playwright Henry A. Du Souchet (1852-1922), a former actor and newspaperman, wrote many plays, of which *My Friend from In-*

dia in 1894 is his most successful production. To some extent it is a satire concerning the lionizing of Swamiji by New York Society. It deals with a barber dressed in a yellow silk bedspread who is presented as one who "has been studying mysticism of the East and has learned all there is to know of Theosophy and attained that most exalted state, Nirvana." A nouveau riche widower from Kansas City introduced the barber as "my friend from India", whose desire is to break into New York High Society. After returning to the West in 1899, Swamiji travelled to Southern California where he attended the three-act comedy *My Friend from India* on December 23, 1899 at the Los Angeles Theatre. Swamiji thoroughly enjoyed the play and Bernhard Baumgardt observed, "He had never seen anyone laugh so hard or so much." The play later became a six-reel silent motion picture in 1927.[154]

An imaginative young lady, Blanche Partington (d. 1951) was at the turn of the century a reporter for the *San Francisco Chronicle*. Subsequently she served for many years as a theatre reviewer and music editor of the *San Francisco Call* newspaper, and was also a Christian Science practitioner. She wrote newspaper articles for the *Chronicle* about Swamiji's activities in Northern California, and about her visit in August to the Shanti Ashrama under the guidance of Turiyananda. In June 1900 the *Prabuddha Bharata* published her correspondence to the editor which read in part:

> The impression made by the Swami's teaching has been most profound, the impress of his brilliant and distinguished personality,—what he is,—not less, but even deeper than his spoken word, strange and electrifying to us to see, the face of the warrior-thinker leap like a sword from its scabbard as the childlikeness of the master's countenance falls away under the power of the spirit! Dear and beautiful to see his absolute kindness to all with whom he comes in contact, his admirable simplicity of manner, his charming humility, and strange and lovely to our unaccustomed ears the music of his words, his wonderful eloquence in a foreign tongue, for the Swami Vivekananda is more than the teacher, master, philosopher, he is a poet from the land of poetry!

In a letter to the *Brahmavadin* that appeared the following month, Blanche Partington wrote:

> All hail the Light of Asia! Thus, poet, sage, and devotee in speaking of the advent of the Swami Vivekananda upon the Western shores! It were

> not difficult to you who know him, to understand the vivid and profound impression made by this brilliant and charming personality upon all those with whom he comes in contact, and the temptation to extravagance in speaking of him and his work. But we will attempt such sweet reasonableness as is possible to us, in this little appreciation of one of the deepest thinkers and finest spirits who has yet visited among us for our blessing and delight....
>
> The interest in his doctrine has been steadily increasing,—even reaching the hopeful limit of a mild martyrdom of pulpit denunciation!—and, though it is yet early to prophesy results, it seems safe to say that the enthusiasm thus awakened is of a permanent character.[155]

The following November 25 she wrote an article for the "Music World" section of the *San Francisco Call* on Madame Calve, describing Vivekananda in this manner:

> The Swami himself is well known and well loved in America. He came first to this country to the World's Fair of Religions, where his magnetic and lovable personality, his brilliant contributions to the Congress, his keen and polished intellect and, not least, his picturesque and majestic figure in its robe of wonderful red, made all sorts of favourable impressions upon his audiences.

Born in Germany and educated in America, during the period from March to May 1900, Miss A. Christina Albers (1866-1948) heard Swamiji speak on many occasions in Northern California. About him she wrote many years later in the *Prabuddha Bharata* of August 1938:

> He began to speak, and there was a transformation. The soul-force of the great man became visible. I felt the tremendous force of his speech—words that were felt more than they were heard. I was drawn into a sea of being, of feelings of a higher existence, from which it seemed almost like pain to emerge when the lecture was finished. And then those eyes, how wonderful! They were like shooting stars—lights shooting forth from them in constant flashes.

Albers also produced the poem "A Tribute to Vivekananda", which appeared in the *Indian Mirror* of July 10, 1902 and in the *Prabuddha Bharata* and *Brahmavadin*. The poem ends with the phrase, "His noble work will live throughout all time; His monument, washed in a nation's tears, Will be a holy shrine in future years." On September the 19th of that year, Albers and Sister Nivedita attended the Vivekananda memorial meeting held at the Town Hall in Calcutta. Five of her articles appeared in the *Prabuddha Bharata* during 1902-41, including the 1938 reminiscence of Vivekananda.[156]

Swamiji significantly affected the life of Christina Albers. Like Myron Phelps, she took a great deal of interest in India, but worked independently of the Ramakrishna Order. Two years after Vivekananda left the country, Baba Premananda Bharati (1858-1914) [q.v.], a Bengali Vaishnava monastic and religious teacher, came to New York City. After attending the "Chaitanya Lila" at Girish Ghosh's Star Theatre in Calcutta, Bharati formerly converted to Bengal Vaishnavism. Swamiji's success in the U.S. and England motivated other Indian teachers to come to the West and obtain a following. It is possible that Bharati met Vivekananda in India and might have received the names of some contacts from him. He later left New York and transferred his base of operation to Los Angeles. In 1907 a small group of people including Bharati and Christina Albers returned to India. On their way to India, they received a warm reception from Swamis Trigunatita and Prakashananda in San Francisco in July. Bharati describes Trigunatita as "amiability itself", and "His old-world goodwill, the merry twinkle of his eye are still twinkling in our memory." He also alludes to the "ascetic heart and soul" of Prakashananda. The *Prabuddha Bharata* mentioned, "The party has been enthusiastically welcomed along their route from Colombo to Calcutta." In Calcutta, Bharati founded the Indo-American Zenana Mission for the purpose of educating Indian women. Albers established a school for teaching English and the vernacular languages to young Indians. After Bharati's passing away the organization came to an end.[157]

On February 26, 1915 the *Indian Mirror* of Calcutta noted in part:

> There are few Europeans who can say of India with greater enthusiasm "This is my own native land" than Miss Christina Albers, the author of the book of poems, *Palms and Temple Bells*. No European lady living in India has observed with greater closeness the manners and customs of its people and evinced her sympathy with its women-fold with greater sincerity than she. The title of the book is eminently suggestive of its contents. The physical aspects of the country and the spirituality of its peoples form the principle themes of the collection of poems which this volume embodies.

The volume includes a poem in tribute to Swami Vivekananda. For many years Albers continued to publish a number of books from Calcutta such as *Ancient Tales of Hindustan; Yogmaya, and other Dramatic Poems* (1927), and the *Ram-Sita, the Ramayana in Verse* (1927). The Maha Bodhi Society in Calcutta reprinted one of her books in 1949.[158]

When Sister Avabamia (or Avavamia, May Elizabeth Stevenson) [q.v.] heard Swami Vivekananda lecture, she considered him to be a superior public orator than Colonel Robert Ingersoll "because of the wonderful calmness and childlike meekness through which at times the great philosopher burst forth in a magnificent blending of silver and gold." She informs us that:

> As a man Swamiji was very attractive, both in figure and deportment. His wonderful eyes were sometimes terrible, and again mild, gentle and loving. When sympathy moved him, his eyes became the expressers of his great soul: when he spoke in real earnest they were like blazing fires in which one saw evil being consumed. His voice was gentle, round and full; and whether in conversation, or as teacher, or upon the platform, the "mellowness with which he spoke brought forth an unusual amount of magnetism, so much so that he at once captivated all who heard him."…. In conversation he spoke slowly and with great forethought; he moderated his voice in a manner which gave indisputable proof of soul-refinement. He could be very jolly and would laugh heartily when he told of some amusing experience which he had had…. his voice, which he knew how to moderate and increase like an artist, electrified his audience. No matter how long he spoke, he was fresh after two hours of speaking as he was at the commencement of his lecture. To lose sight of the self and let God have the vocality at His merciful disposal is another secret which none knows but he who had experience and has been taught by the Lord Himself. Swamiji showed such superior knowledge. He spoke with such magnetism that it was impossible not to give your whole attention to him.[159]

It is not known when Sister Avabamia heard Swamiji speak. But she did live in Seattle, Washington, and took classes in San Francisco at "The Hindoo Breathing School" beginning in 1903 or an earlier date. Under the influence of the New Thought Movement, she authored metaphysical books on thought communication, Hindu internal breathing, and soul travel during 1903-08. After making contact with Swami Abhedananda, she organized some Vedanta groups in Australia, New Zealand, and India.*[160]

On July 26, 1900 Swami Vivekananda left the U.S. for France. There he met the writer Jules Bois (1868/69-1943) who informs us:

> When the Congress [Parliament] of Religions was in progress in Chicago, I, in Paris, eagerly followed its debates. One declaration which arrested by attention was that of the young Hindu prophet promulgating a "universal religion". Though profound, his address was beautifully incisive,—a refreshing contrast to the usual pronouncements of that kind, which are apt to be gelatinous. These sentences bore the stamp of genius, and they dwelt in my mind until the day when I received an invitation to meet the Swami himself at the home of a rich American friend in Paris.[161]

In time Swamiji moved into the Paris flat of Jules Bois. He lived with Bois, who spoke little English, for several weeks during September-October of 1900. Bois, being "a student and admirer" of Swamiji's works, had already translated some of Swamiji's pamphlets into the French language.[162] At that time Bois described the Swami as "my best friend". They travelled together with other devotees to Perros-Guirec on the Brittany coast, and on the Orient Express to Constantinople, Turkey, Greece and Egypt.[163] Bois contacted Swamiji at Belur Math in February 1901.[164] After returning from India where in 1903 he met Rabindranath Tagore (1861-1943), Jules Bois wrote in French the travelogue *Visions of India*. The *Prabuddha Bharata* in March of 1918 printed an English translation of the eighth chapter of the book, which dealt with Swamiji at Belur Math.[165]

Jules Bois emigrated to the United States in 1915. A poem on Swamiji by Bois appears in the March 1925 number of *Prabuddha Bharata*, with the title "To a Sage (To the memory of Swami Vivekananda)". In a 1927 article entitled "The New Religions of America", Bois wrote of what Swamiji had told him many years before. "The Swami's emotion was profound when he told me of his first meeting with the last great saint of his race [Sri Ramakrishna]:"

> As a boy I went to hear him. "Do you believe in God, sir?" I asked. "Yes," he replied. "Can you prove it?" "Yes." "But how?" With a transfigured

* See Chapter XVIII.

smile he murmured: "Because I see Him, just as I see you there, only in a much more intense sense." Oh, the unforgettable moment! I realized that one glance, one touch can change a whole life. I understood the apostolic succession. Putting aside everything, I consecrated my youth to sitting at his feet, to question and listen.

Ramakrishna gradually exhausted his strength in instructing whoever came. "While I can speak I must teach them," he would say, and he kept his word. One day he told us he would lay down his body that very day, and, with the most sacred word of the Vedas on his lips he entered into samadhi, and so passed away.

"After a long silence, and in a voice that had fallen to a whisper, my companion continued:"

He had called me Vivekananda, but after his death I was as though mad. I felt as if I had lost my soul. I became a sannyasin, throwing aside everything, even clothing. I traversed India on foot, covered with ashes, taking meals now with rajahs, now with the humblest peasants, sleeping on porches or in trees, bewailing the loss of my guru and vowing to render immortal the gospel I had received from him. When I felt morally strengthened by this sacrificial wandering, I set out for America. There my lectures permitted me to amass a certain sum which does not belong to me. It is in the hands of an American friend and will be devoted to the monastery of Ramakrishna near the Ganges, and then I too shall die.[166]

Bois made an appearance at the Sri Ramakrishna Birth Centenary held at the Vedanta Society of New York on March 15, 1936. He spoke about his relationship with Swamiji at their banquet, with Swamis Bodhananda and Akhilananda in attendance. Swami Pavitrananda reports that he heard that Bois was very close to Bodhananda. Outside of Vedanta, Bois received recognition for his dramatic plays, novels, essays, poetry, opera, and his works on psychology and the supernatural. His novels supported Catholic humanism, the superconscious and women's emancipation, placing emphasis on the ideal marriage as a means to regenerate society. Jules Bois served as the president of the Society for Psychological Research, and as the head professor of the superconscious at the School of Psychology in Paris. In France he was an officer of the Legion of Honour and he received honours from Greece, Belgium, Tunisia, and the United States, being awarded an honorary LL.D. degree from Providence College in Rhode Island.[167]

Before leaving for India on November 2, 1900, Swamiji gave a talk in French or English at the American College for Girls at Scutari (now Usküdar) in Constantinople (now Istanbul), Turkey. In the audience was a young Halide Edib who remembered the Swami and later wrote in her memoirs:

> Swami Vivicananda [sic], a celebrated Brahmanist, also visited the college and gave one of his famous speeches ... The dark slender man was clad in a loose robe, the thin hands moving with a life which seemed distinct from the rest of his body; the expressiveness of his graceful physique, and the mystic charm of Asia's voice, these were evident in him.
>
> I was captivated by his artistic manner, but even at that age I could feel that he had a certain quality of make-up and that he appealed to one's senses rather than to one's head and heart.[168]

Vivekananda's powerful spiritual presence was no doubt very appealing to the sense of sight, and his voice to the sense of hearing. Years later many people did not recall what he said when they first heard him speak, but they remembered his uplifting appearance. In 1901 Halide Edib Adivar (1884-1964) was the first Muslim Turkish woman to graduate from American College for Girls (aka American Girls' College). Focusing on the subject of modern nationalism, by 1912 she became one of the most gifted and influential Turkish novelists and nonfiction writers. As a woman of action she was commissioned a sergeant major, fighting along side Kemal Ataturk (1881-1938) in the Turkish war of independence (1921-22). Later opposing Ataturk's dictatorship, she and her husband fled to France, and returned to Turkey after his death. She also penned *Inside India* in 1937 after lecturing at major universities in the country, devoting four chapters to support the efforts of Mahatma Gandhi. During 1950-54 she served in the Turkish parliament, as did her husband who was also the editor-in-chief of the Turkish edition of the *Encyclopedia of Islam*.[169] She was a friend of Arnold Toynbee.

Yakov A. K. Popov[a] (1844-1918), a Russian military man and philanthropist, donated money for the construction of a hospital and school on his family estate of Shabalinovo in the Chernigov region. He was grief stricken over the accidental death of his wife, a chemist, who perished while performing an experiment in the laboratory. Hoping to make contact with his departed wife, Popov sought help from spiritualists and Theosophists in many centres throughout Europe. In Italy he was told to go to India in search of an Indian yogi. By good fortune, he met Vivekananda either in Bombay when the Swami returned from America, or in Calcutta. Swamiji brought peace to Popov's agitated mind and inspired him to live a religious life in service of humanity. Between 1906 and 1914 Popov translated into the Russian language Vivekananda's writings on *Karma Yoga*, *Bhakti Yoga*, *Jnana Yoga*, *Raja Yoga*, *Yoga Philosophy* and also his *Philosophy of Vedanta*. Vivekananda's popular book on *Raja Yoga* underwent three Russian editions. These translations were read by Leo Tolstoy, Boris Lenidovich Smirnov(a), who translated the *Mahabharata* and the *Bhagavad Gita* into Russian, Nicholas Roerich and others. Though Popov made a major contribution to Russian Indology, like many Western translators of Ramakrishna-Vedanta literature, he was soon forgotten.[170]

ENDNOTES

1 Rolland, p. 225; Mazumder, p. 386; G. R. Madan, *Western Sociologists on Indian Society* (London: Routledge & Kegan Paul, 1979), pp. 60-61; *VK* (July 2006), p. 262; Datta, B., pp. 154, 220.

2 AII, p. 77.

3 Kate Sanborn, *Abandoning an Adopted Farm* (New York: D. Appleton, 1894), pp. 8-9.

4 Web: www.answer.com/topic/tommaso-salvini; Chaudhuri1, p. 49; *New York Times* (Dec. 16, 1896).

5 Sanborn (1894), pp. 9-10.

6 *CW*, VII:450, 458.

7 Burke, I, pp. 22-25.

8 Sanborn (1894), pp. 13-14; Joseph Peidle, *Global Vedantist* (Spring 2007), p. 6.

9 *Sioux Valley News* (Aug. 31, 1893), p. 5; ANA.

10 *DAB* (1963), VIII, pp. 327-28; UCLC; Kate Sanborn Archives. Web: http://asteria.fivecolleges.edu/findaids/smitharchives/manosca113_bioghist.htm.

11 *CW*, VII:278-82.

12 Ibid., VII:449, 500; IX:53; Burke, I, pp. 27-28.

13 Burke I, pp. 28, 30; John Leonard, ed., *Woman's Who's Who of America* (1914-15), p. 907; UCLC.

14 *CW*, VII, pp. 449, 455, 469.

15 Austin Tappan Wright. Web: www2.sjsu.edu/faculty/wooda/wright.html; Burke, I, pp. 36-39; UCLC.

16 WWWA (1969-73), V, p. 800, UCLC; Burke, I, pp. 52-53.

17 *CW*, III:466-67; IX:399.

18 Ibid., VII:456, 458.

19 Burke, I, pp. 41-43; *WWIA* (1908-09), p. 2107; Home of Kate Tannant Woods. Web: www.swht.org/site50.htm; *New York Times* (July 13, 1910), p. 7.

20 *CW*, VII, 449-50.

21 G. Stavig, "Swami Vivekananda on the Economic Plight of India", *PB* (Feb. 2007), pp. 183-85; Burke, I, pp. 26-27, 52-53, 55-58.

22 See Stavig (2007), pp. 183-86 for the full speech; Hohner, p. 5.

23 *CW*, VII:245.

24 Ibid., IV:483.

25 Ibid., III:465-70.

26 Nelson, p. 111; I submitted the article "Swami Vivekananda on the Economic Plight of India" to the *Prabuddha Bharata* (Feb. 2007), pp. 183-85, concerning a second hand account of Swamiji's speech at the American Social Science Association that appeared in the *Journal of Social Science* (Jan. 1894), pp. 69-70. Only after it was published did I realize that Swamiji discussed the poverty of India before an American audience, because, out of deep compassion, he wanted to bring back funds to India to help his people.

27 G. Stavig, *BRMIC* (Nov-Dec. 2009).

28 Burke, II, pp. 138, 160, 162.

29 *DAB* (1935), XVI, pp. 326-27; *ANB*, XIX, pp. 237-38; *WWWA*, I, pp. 1075-76; *CA* (2002), vol. 201, pp. 378-80; Franklin B. Sanborn Papers. Web: www.library.georgetown.edu/dept/speccoll/cl229.htm.

30 Dale Riepe, *The Philosophy of India and its Impact on American Thought* (Springfield, IL: Charles C Thomas, 1970), pp. 37-38, 51-52; *PB* (Jan. 1995), p. 348; Cameron, p. 224.

31 G. Stavig, "Ralph Waldo Emerson's Appreciation of India in His Own Words", *PB* (May 2001), pp. 269-72.

32 G. Stavig, "Henry David Thoreau's Appreciation of India in His Own Words", Unpublished Essay.

33 Louis Fischer, *Gandhi* (New York: Mentor Book, 1962), p. 38.

34 Londhe, #303. Amos Bronson Alcott.

35 *CW*, III:472-73; Basu, pp. 1-2.

36 Ibid., III:475.

37 Lucy Monroe, "Chicago Letters", *The Critic* (Oct. 7, 1893), pp. 232-33, 612; (Nov. 11, 1893), pp. 309-10; *CW*, III:477.

38 *CW*, VIII:327.

39 Lina Mainiero, ed., *American Women Writers* (New York: Frederick Ungar Publishing Co., 1981), pp. 208-09.

40 *The Critic* (Feb. 16, 1895), p. 133.

41 Harriet Monroe, *A Poet's Life* (New York: Macmillan, 1938), p. 137; Burke, I, pp. 85-86; II, p. 53.

42 *DAB* (1964), IX, pp. 466-67; *ANB*, XV, pp. 679-80; Saha, pp. 23-24, 118-19; Hay (1962), pp. 442-44. Regenstein Library at the University of Chicago. Web: www.lib.uchicago.edu/e/spcl/mopo.htm.

43 Saha, passim; Stephen Hay, "Rabindranath Tagore in America", *American Quarterly* (1962), pp. 439-63.

44 *CA* (2003), vol. 206; Margaret Cropper, *Evelyn Underhill* (London: Longsmans, Green and Co., 1958), p. 52.

45 *Brahmavadin* (April 1910), p. 185.

46 *Open Court* (July 1905), p. 438.

47 Saha, p. 7.

48 Burke, III, pp. 343; *WWNY* (1907), p. 1039; Spencer Lavan, *Unitarians and India* (Boston: Beacon Press, 1977), pp. 163-64, 172; UCLC; Cameron, pp. 162-63, 173; *The Open Court* (Sept. 1904; July 1905); *San Francisco Call* (June 24, 1909), p. 3; The Master in Akka. Web: www.kalimat.com/book_list.html; *VMB* (Aug-Sept. 1908), p. 72.

49 *PB* (1911), pp. 50-52; *Brahmavadin* (April 1910), p. 218; (Sept. 1910), p. 378; (Feb. 1911), p. 78; Raucher, pp. 86-87. Arthur Nethercot, *The Last Four Lives of Annie Besant* (Chicago: University of Chicago Press, 1963), pp. 156-58, 322; *Selected Letters of Rabindranath Tagore* (Cambridge: University Press, 1997), pp. 73-77.

50 Frank Parlato. Web: www.vivekananda.net/KnownLetters/1893America.html#Lydia.

51 Nivedita, I, pp. 333, 340, 342; *DAB* (1928-1936); *NCAB* (1951), XXXVII, pp. 260-61; Chaudhuri1, p, 143; Nelson.

52 Burke, I, pp. 211-12; Chaudhuri2, pp. 421-22.

53 *CW*, II:511, 513; V:203; IX:202.

54 *Vivekananda: A Mental and Spiritual Biography*, ed. Rajagopal Chattopadhyaya (Barrackpore: Vivekananda Math, 2006), pp. 221-23.

55 *1911 Encyclopedia Britannica*. Web: www.1911encyclopedia.org/ Sir_William_Wilson_Hunter; Bhattacharya, p. 432; Londhe, # 307, Sir William Hunter.

56 *Reminiscences*, pp. 139-40; Chaudhuri2, p. 36; *EWB*; *DAB* (1928-36).

57 *CW*, VI:259-60.
58 Ibid., VIII:318.
59 *New York Times* (Dec. 31, 1951), p. 13; Chaudhuri1, p. 178.
60 WorldCat; Burke, V, pp. 168-69.
61 Chaudhuri1, pp. 128-29, 157, 177-78.
62 *CW*, IX:18.
63 Frances Willard and Mary Livermore ed., *A Woman of the Century* (New York: Gordon Press, 1975), pp. 690-91; Web: http://homeopathy.wildfalcon.com/archives/2007/12/22/alice-bunker-stockham-and-homeopathy; *The Phonological Journal and Science of Health* (Nov. 1895), p. 243; Chaudhuri1, pp. 177-78.
64 *DAB* (1932), IX, pp. 606-07; *NCAB* (1904), p. 114; Prabuddhaprana, pp. 113-14, 184.
65 *CW*, VIII:319; IX:26.
66 Ibid., VI:295-96.
67 *CW*, I:329-32; II:238-53, 499-517; IV, pp, 188-91; V:63; IX:79; Horner, pp. 28, 36, 38, 40.
68 *CW*, V:63.
69 Burke, II, pp. 284-88, 300-02; Asim Chaudhuri, "Dr. Lewis G. Janes: Swami Vivekananda's Friend", *VK* (March 2008), p. 112; *CW*, V:86.
70 *CW*, VII:488.
71 Ibid., VI:382.
72 Basu, pp. 176-77.
73 *Outlook* (Feb. 19, 1898), p. 466; (March 19, 1898), p. 740; *VK* (June 2008), p. 235.
74 *Brahmavadin* (June 16, 1898); Basu, p. 531 (591); Tathagatananda2, p. 414.
75 *Brahmavadin* (Jan. 1, 1899), pp. 234-40; Lewis Janes, "To the Editor of the *Herald*", *Brahmavadin* (June 1900), pp. 560-64; *Outlook* (Oct. 27, 1900), pp. 521-22; Horner, pp. 112, 114; Burke, V, pp. 333-34, 407; VI, p. 344.
76 Prabuddhaprana2, p. 404.
77 *Lewis G. Janes* (Boston: J. H. West, 1902), p. 182.
78 Lewis G. Janes (1902), pp. 187-88; Frank Parlato. Web: www.vivekananda.net/PDFBooks/HTML/LewisJanesAbheda.htm.
79 Burke, II, p. 130; *CA* (2000), vol. 183; *DAB* (1928-1936); *EWB*.
80 *CW*, VI:259.
81 Hansbrough (May 2007), p. 343.
82 Chaudhuri2, pp, 574-75.
83 *EOP*; *RLOA*.
84 *CW*, V:73; VI:309-10; IX:23-24.

85 Ibid., IX:208-22.
86 Burke, III, pp. 16, 45-46, 366, 376, 381; Horner, pp. 38-39, 61, 63, 65.
87 Basu, p. 479.
88 Basu, p. 481; Chaudhuri2, p. 234.
89 Burke, IV, pp. 558-60.
90 *CW*, VII:490.
91 Burke IV, pp. 21, 32-38; V, pp. 152, 155; Chaudhuri2, p. 547.
92 *CW*, III:264; VI:359-60.
93 C. Adler, ed., *American Jewish Year Book* (Philadelphia: Jewish Publication Society of America, 1904-05); Jackson, p. 90; *The Path* (July 1894), pp. 131-32; *New York Times* (Oct. 8, 1893), p. 21; (Mar. 18, 1915), p. 12.
94 *The Ogden Standard-Examiner* (Utah) (May 24, 1920); *Billings Gazette* (Montana) (March 28, 1920), p. 35; Frank Parlato. Web: www.vivekananda.net/NewDiscoveries/KripanandaNewsArticles.htm.
95 Burke III, pp. 73-75, 81-84.
96 Burke, III, pp. 71, 82; *CW*, VI:302-03.
97 *CW*, VII:454.
98 Ibid., V:59; VII:465; VIII:318; IX:30.
99 Jackson, pp. 113-15, 133, 278; Burke, II, pp. 56, 156-57, 160-63, 227, 229, 235; Chaudhuri2, p, 69; *CW*, IX:49.
100 *CWSA*, X, pp. 40-41; Nivedita, II, p. 1247.
101 *DAB* (1932), IX, pp. 16-18; *CA* (1998), vol. 162, pp. 164-68; Thomas Wentworth Higginson. Web: www.prism.net/user/fcarpenter/twhigg.htm.
102 *CW*, I:317-28; IX:484-87.
103 Chaudhuri2, pp. 651, 653, 658, 662; *WWWA*, I, p. 942; Web: http://charlesbrodiepatterson.wwwhubs.com. This source gives Patterson's death date as 1936, which is at odds with the consensus view of 1917 and with the *New York Times* Obituary column (June 24, 1917), p. 19; Maine Historical Society. Web: www.vintagemaineimages.com/bin/ Detail?ln=16594.
104 *Life*, II, pp. 10-11; also in *PB* (Sept. 1907), p. 167.
105 Ella Wheeler Wilcox, *The Worlds and I* (New York: George H. Doran, 1918), p. 111; Jenny Ballou, *Period Piece: Ella Wheeler Wilcox and Her Times* (Boston: Houghton Mifflin, 1940), p. 156; Chaudhuri2, p. 169.
106 Burke, III, p. 29.
107 *PB* (Feb-March 1911), p. 58.
108 Wilcox (1918), pp. 110-12. 300-07; *Brahmavadin* (Oct. 1911), pp. 514-16; Fort Worth, Texas, *Star Telegram* (April 10, 1911); Burke, III, pp. 28-30, 97-98, 345-46; V, pp. 158, 172-73.

109 *PB* (June 1911), p. 119.

110 *RLOA*, pp. 503-04; *DAB* (1936), XX, pp. 203-04. Ella Wheeler Wilcox. Web: http://womenshistory.about.com/library/weekly/aa122900a.htm. Emma Curtis Hopkins was both a student and associate of Mary Baker Eddy (1821-1910), being the editor of the *Christian Science Journal*. In this manner, the Christian Science movement working through Curtis and her students had a positive influence on Swami Vivekananda's stay in the West.

111 Burke, III, pp. 345-46; *DAB* (1930), V, p. 351; "Mary Mapes Dodge". *Major Authors and Illustrators for Children and Young Adults* (Gale Group, 2002); The Internet Movie Database. Web: http://imdb.com/name/nm0973061.

112 Burke, III, pp. 345-46; *DAB* (1936), XX, pp. 190-91; *CA* (1984), vol. 111, pp. 509-10; The Internet Movie Database. Web: http://imdb.com/name/nm0927752. Her archives are located at Bowdoin College in Brunswick, Maine. Web: http://library.bowdoin.edu/arch/mss/kdwg.shtml.

113 *New York Tribune* (Jan. 25, 1895), p. 7 on CAM; Augustus Le Plongeon, *Maya/Atlantis: Queen Moo and the Egyptian Sphinx* (Blauvelt, NY: Steinerbooks, 1896, 1992), pp. 19, 193-95, 271 on GBS; Wikipedia. Web: en.wikipedia.org/wiki/Augustus_Le_Plongeon; Augustus Le Plongeon. Web: maya.csuhayward.edu/archaeoplanet/LgdPage/LepKehoe.htm. Vivekananda taught that one branch of the Tamilian Dravidians gave rise to the Egyptian and another to the Sumerian civilization, which provided the foundation for the Babylonian culture and some stories in the Biblical Book of Genesis (*CW*, IV:301-02; VII:52, 331, 365-67); See: Stavig7 for "Historical Contacts between Ancient India and Babylon".

114 Basu, pp. 76-78; Life, II, pp. 4-5; UCLC; *Phrenological Journal* (Sept. 1899), p. 296; Stavig1, p. 467.

115 *CW*, V:111.

116 "Alasinga Perumal", *PB* (Dec. 1941), p. 303; (Aug. 1947), pp. 324-25; (April 1990), pp. 186-87; Basu, pp. 469-599; *CW*, VII:334.

117 *CW*, VIII:355.

118 Ibid., IX:518.

119 Burke, III, p. 268.

120 Carl Jackson, *The Oriental Religions and American Thought* (London: Greenwood Press, 1981), pp. 134-37; Moncure Conway. Web: www.uua.org/uuhs/duub/articles /moncureconway.html; Moncure Conway, *My Pilgrimage to the Wise Men of the East* (Boston: Houghton, Mifflin and Co., 1906), pp. 214-27, 333-35; Basu, pp. 104-05; Burke, III, p. 287.

121 *DAB* (1973), Sup. III, pp. 175-76; History of the South Place Ethical Society. Web: www.ethicalsoc.org.uk/history.htm; Burke, III, pp. 259-61.
122 Burke, III, pp. 281-82; *DNB* (1951), Sup. I, pp. 47-48; *Journal of the Royal Asiatic Society of Great Britain and Ireland* (1896); UCLC.
123 *WWWA* (1960), III, p. 240; UCLC.
124 *Washington Post* (March 1, 1896), p. 20.
125 *DAB* (1928-1936).
126 Basu, pp. 93, 500-01; *Life*, II, pp. 66-67.
127 Internet Broadway Database. Web: www.idbd.com/person.asp?id=6191; UCLC.
128 *WWWA* (1960) III, p. 431.
129 Burke, III, pp. 123-24; *DAB* (1944), Sup. I.
130 *The Phrenological Journal and Science of Health* (Dec. 1909), p. 12; The Mind's Attainment. Web: http://cornerstone.wwwhubs.com/tma.htm.
131 *CW*, VI:365, 374; VIII:370.
132 Burke, IV, pp. 163-64, 196-97, 473; *CA* (1994), vol. 141, pp. 144-51; *Concise Dictionary of British Literary Biography* (Gale, 1991); John Galsworthy. Web: www.britannica.com/nobel/micro/225_65.htm.
133 *CW*, VIII:400.
134 Burke, IV, pp. 158-59, 387-88, 499-500, 512-14, 517-18, 523-24, 527; V, p. 75; Nivedita, I, pp. 9-10, 15; *CW*, V:153.
135 *Brahmavadin* (Feb. 1907), p. 75.
136 *PB* (Feb-Mar. 1914), p. 31.
137 *Reminiscences*, pp. 291-93.
138 Basu, pp. 507-08, 520, 531, 564-69, 571-72.
139 UCLC; Abdu'l-Baha in London. Web: www.sacred- bhi/abdulbaha/abl.txt; Thomas K. Cheyne. Web: texts.com/www.hurqalya.pwp.blueyonder.co.uk/baha'i%20encyclopedia/thomas_kelly_cheyne.htm.
140 *Brahmavadin* (July 4, 1896), pp. 266-67.
141 Burke, IV, pp. 383-84; *CA* (1998), vol. 163, pp. 62-65; Tony Brown, *Edward Carpenter and Late Victorian Radicalism* (London: Frank Cass, 1990), pp. 156-61; Londhe, #80. Walt Whitman; UCLC; Edward Carpenter. Web: http://homepage.ntlworld.com/ frank.sierowski/ecc/ec.htm.
142 *CW*, I:119-313.
143 *GSW* (1911) p. 184 on GBS.
144 *San Francisco Call* (Sept. 12, 1897), p. 23.
145 "A Vindication of Vedanta", *Fortnightly Review* (1898), pp. 901-10; (1899), pp. 358-62; *Brahmavadin* 1895-1914 (Bangalore: Swami Vivekananda Seva Samithi,

1981), I, pp. 114-24; (Nov. 15, 1899), pp. 46-54; Maurice Fluegel, *Philosophy, Qabbala and Vedanta* (Baltimore: H. Fluegel, 1902), p. 220. One New York reporter to the *Brahmavadin* (Aug. 1900, p. 688) signed their correspondence as "A Student of Vedanta".

146 Horatio Dresser, "An Interpretation of the Vedanta", in *Voice of Freedom* and *Studies in the Philosophy of Individuality* (New York: G. P. Putnam, 1899), pp. 99, 118 on GBS.

147 *RLOA*; Horatio Dresser. Web: horatiodresser.wwwhubs.com; *WWWA*, III, p. 237.

148 Chaudhuri2, pp. 356-58 gives the review in full.

149 Five of the nine reviews are in *GSW* (1911) p. 184 on GBS.

150 The last two undated reviews are in Swami Abhedananda, *Vedanta Philosophy: Three Lectures* (1908) p. 364 on GBS.

151 San Francisco Chronicle (Aug. 6, 1899), p. 4 on PQHN and GBS.

152 Stavig1, p. 49; *The Arena* (1899), pp. 429, 482-88; *Greenacre on the Piscataqua* (New York: Alliance Pub. Co., 1900); GeoCities. Web: www.geocities.com/hilmanowski_gen/dusenberry/pafn08.htm#18571.

153 Stavig1, p. 469; "The Vedanta Philosophy", *The Arena* (1900), pp. 212-18 on GBS; Stavig1, p. 469; UCLC.

154 Stavig2; Burke, V, pp. 205-07; Gerald Bordman, *The Oxford Companion to American Theatre* (New York: Oxford University Press, 1984), p. 219.

155 Basu, pp. 549-50, 630-31; *Brahmavadin* (July 1900), pp. 620-22; Burke, V, p. 389, VI, pp. 221-24.

156 *Reminiscences*, p. 378; *PB* (Aug. 1938); Basu, pp. 224, 232-35, 572.

157 *Los Angeles Times* (Nov. 20, 1910), p. IM612; Gerald Carney "Baba Premananda Bharati", *Journal of Vaisnava Studies* (Spring 1998); *Light of India* (Jan. 1908), p. 22; *PB* (Dec. 1907), p. 235.

158 *Open Court* (1917), p. 253 on GBS; Library of Congress Online Catalogue.

159 *VFEW* (Nov-Dec. 1978), pp. 27-32.

160 Jackson, pp. 93-94.

161 Jules Bois, "The New Religions of America", *The Forum* (1927), p. 416.

162 *CW*, VIII:536-37; IX:148.

163 Ibid., VII:373, 375-76, 381, 398; VIII:537.

164 Ibid., V:155, 161-62.

165 Bois (1927), pp. 413-22; *Life*, II, pp. 583-85; Horner, pp. 113-16, 118; Burke, VI, pp. 317-18, 335-41, 376, 383.

166 Bois (1927), pp. 418-19.

167 Tathagatananda1, pp. 204-05. Matthew Hoehn, ed., *Catholic Authors* (Newark: St. Mary's Abbey, 1948), pp. 367-68; Pravrajika Prabuddhaprana, *Tantine* (Calcutta: Sri Sarada Math, 1990), pp. 116-19; Henri Antoine Jules-Bois Collection. Web: http://library.lib.binghamton.edu/special/ findingaids/hajulesb_m3.html; UCLC.

168 *Memoirs of Halide Edib* (New York: Century Co., 1928), p. 202; Burke, VI, pp. 389-91.

169 *New York Times* (July 31, 1955), p. 69; (Jan. 11, 1964), p. 23; Anne Commire, ed. *Women in World History* (Detroit: Gale Group, 1999), I, pp. 82-85.

170 There are some minor discrepancies between one source and another. The writings refer to his first name as "Yakov" and the libraries as "A" or "A. K." Tathagatananda2, pp. 204-05; P. M. Shastitko, *Russia and India* (Calcutta: Vostok, 1986), p. 196; *Vedanta Kesari*. Web: www.sriramakrishnamath.org/ magazine/vk/2003/9-3-4.asp; G. Stavig, "India in Russian Thought", *BRMIC* (Oct. 1999), pp. 476-81; WorldCat.

CHAPTER VIII

PROFESSORS AND EDUCATORS

NARENDRA, WHO later became Swami Vivekananda, entered Presidency College in January 1880, remaining there for one year. Under the directions of the Scottish General Missionary Board, he then transferred over to the General Assembly's Institution (later known as Scottish Church College). His association with William Hastie, the principal (equivalent to president) of the college, is covered in Chapters I and VI. In Chicago, in 1893, when John Lyon joked with Swamiji about his slight Irish brogue, "Swami said it was probably because his favourite professor was an Irish gentleman, a graduate of Trinity College, Dublin."[1]

Attending college Narendra studied the philosophical, social and scientific ideas of Western thinkers like Jeremy Bentham, Charles Darwin, David Hume, William S. Jevons, John Stuart Mill, and Herbert Spencer (all English); Auguste Comte and Rene Descartes (both French); Johann Fichte, Georg Hegel, Immanuel Kant, and Arthur Schopenhauer (all German); Baruch Spinoza (Dutch); Aristotle (Greek); and many others. His feelings were stirred by the English poets William Wordsworth and Percy Shelley. As a student, he "had a passion for History" and had read Mountstuart Elphinstone's *The History of India*, John Clark Marshman's *Abridgement of the History of India*, John Richard Green's *Short History of the English People*, Charles Macfarlane's *History of British India from the Earliest English Intercourse*, Thomas Carlyle's *The French Revolution*, Sir Archibald Alison's *History of Europe: From the Commencement of the French Revolution*, and Edward Gibbon's *Decline and Fall of the Roman Empire*.[2] In the *Complete Works* Swamiji often mentions the Utilitarians and their doctrine founded by Jeremy Bentham (1748-1832) mentioned above.[3] They taught an ethical doctrine that equated happiness with pleasure and the absence of pain, and that social institutions should pursue "the greatest happiness for the greatest number of people".

In an interesting study, a researcher found that the ideas presented in *The History of India* (1841, 1889) by Sir Mountstuart Elphinstone (1779-1859) and the first ten pages of Vivekananda's March 1899 essay on "Modern India"[4] corresponded on eighteen topics. He also discovered seven similarities between Elphinstone's book and Swamiji's January 18, 1900 lecture on "Women of India" delivered in Pasadena, California.[5] Elphinstone wrote that the Hindus had always lived in India and did not migrate from a foreign land, had greatly surpassed the Greeks in trigonometry and algebra, and discovered geometrical theorems not known to the Europeans until the 17th century.[6]

In another example, both Vivekananda and Henry Buckle (1821-62), the British historian and proponent of the "geographical theory of history", made a comparison of the civilizations of ancient India and Greece. Both considered the differences between climate and geographical conditions of the two countries as the causal variable, but their conclusions concerning the effects of these two variables differ considerably.[7]

Narendra attended the Presidency College from January 1880. The College principal at that time was Charles H. Tawney, who in 1896 was the first Westerner to write a journal article about Sri Ramakrishna.* There Narendra might have had the opportunity to study Indian philosophy under the productive professor Archibald Edward Gough (b. 1845). His most important work was *The Philosophy of the Upanishads and Ancient Indian Metaphysics*, in addition to *Sanskrit Manual* (with the Sanskritist Sir Monier Monier-Williams), *Ancient Sanskrit Literature*, and *Theosophy of the Upanishads*. What's more, Gough translated *Vaishesika Aphorisms of Kanada*, and *Review of Different System of Hindu Philosophy* (with E. B. Cowell) by Madhva, and later became the principal of Calcutta Madrasa College. Other Westerners at Presidency College included the professor of history, Ebenezer Lethbridge, who penned *An Easy Introduction to the History and Geography of Bengal* and *An Easy Introduction to the History of India* (later attributed to his son Sir Roper Lethbridge), which the students read. William Trego Webb (b. 1847), the professor of English literature, history and political economy at Presidency College, authored *Indian Lyrics*, *Enoch Arden* (along with the notable Alfred Lord Tennyson), and *Selections from Wordsworth*. Another professor, Hugh Melville Percival, edited volumes by Edmund Spenser and Alfred Tennyson, and was later the acting principal of the Presidency College in 1909. After

---

* See Chapter I.

contracting malaria, Narendra shifted to General Assembly Institution (later Scottish Church College) in 1881 and studied there until January 1884. The list of professors there included: Suryga Kumar Agasti (b. 1857), Reverend William Hastie and Reverend A. B. Wann (philosophy); Reverend James Edwards and W. Fish (English); Reverend J. Mackinson (Biblical literature); and Reverend James Wilson (1825-1902), the author of *Female Education in Bengal.* There were also a number of Indian professors who taught mathematics, physics, chemistry, botany and physiology at the Institution. Narendra then proceeded to the three-year Law course at the Metropolitan Institution (later Vidyasagar College) in Calcutta (1883-86), where he served as a teacher for a few months. Earlier Swamiji had extended his education in 1878 by becoming a member of the Sadharan Brahmo Samaj under Pandit Shivanath Shastri and Vijaykrishna Goswami, and in 1884 he became a Freemason and later a Master Mason in the Masonic Lodge in Calcutta.[8]

After coming to America, during the latter part of August 1893, the amiable Kate Sanborn introduced Swami Vivekananda to Professor John Henry Wright (1852-1908) of Harvard University. As a guest Swamiji spent three days in his summer home in Annisquam, Massachusetts.[9] Because of the invitation of the local pastor and John Henry Wright, Swamiji spoke at the local Universalist Church on "Customs and Life in India".[10] On November 2, Vivekananda wrote to Alasinga in India that Wright

> sympathized with me very much and urged upon me the necessity of going to the Parliament of Religions, which he thought would give me an introduction to the nation. As I was not acquainted with anybody, the Professor undertook to arrange everything for me, and eventually I came back to Chicago.[11]

When Swamiji told him he had no credentials to speak at the upcoming Parliament of Religions in Chicago, Wright replied, "To ask you Swami, for your credentials is like asking the sun to state its right to shine!" Wright wrote to the chairman of the committee for selection of delegates, "Here is a man who is more learned than all our learned professors put together." He gave Swamiji a letter of introduction to present to the committee in charge of housing and providing for the Asian delegates, and paid for his train ticket.[12]

A year before this, in India Swamiji was known to a limited number of people, and now, a year later, he was famous and recognized as a great exponent of Hinduism. He and Professor Wright met again in Lynn, Massachusetts, in April of 1894, and in the following August in Annisquam.[13] Professor Wright introduced Swamiji when he spoke at the town hall in Annisquam on September 4, 1894. On the evening of March 24, 1896 they came in contact at Sara Bull's house in Cambridge, and Wright quickly wrote to his wife, "He looks good and happy and is making a great success at lecturing." The next day the Swami spoke on "The Vedanta Philosophy" before the Harvard Graduate Philosophical Club. The talk became a book, and Wright assisted in preparing its final revision. Two days later they had lunch together, and Wright wrote to his wife that Swamiji has "become so much gentler, and wiser, and sweeter. Indeed he is most charming. He says his stay in America has taught him a great deal." Through the medium of personal letters, Swamiji enjoyed a long amiable relationship with "my kind friend" John Henry Wright. When he sent him numerous letters between August 1893 and May 1896, he often referred to the professor as Adhyapakji.*[14]

John Henry Wright's parents were missionaries to the Christian Nestorians in Persia (Iran). At a college later known as Ohio State University, he taught ancient languages and literature between 1873 and 1876, and then spent two years in Leipzig, Germany, studying Sanskrit and classical philology. At Dartmouth, Wright was an associate professor of Greek, and a full professor of classical philology at Johns Hopkins University. In 1887 he became the professor of Greek at Harvard, and from 1895 until his death he held the post of dean of the Harvard Graduate School. In addition, he served as president of the American Philological Association in 1894. Wright coedited the *Classical Review* (1888-1906), and worked as editor-in-chief of the *American Journal of Archaeology* (1897-1906), *Twentieth Century Textbooks* (1900), as well as the *Classical Quarterly* (1907-08). In 1902 he became the supervisor of the twenty-four volume *A History of all Nations*, written by a group of distinguished scholars. Volume two covers the history of India and other Central and East Asian countries. He also published volumes on Greek philology, literature, history and archaeology. According to his contemporaries, Wright was gracious in his contact with his fellow educators and students. Being a witty speaker and writer with an appealing personality, he possessed an encyclopaedic range of knowledge.[15]

Before the Parliament of Religions began, Swamiji resided for a time in the town of Annisquam, Massachusetts. There, at the home of Eugene

* The word in Hindi for teacher.

Wambaugh (1856-1940), he gave an inspired historical talk, speaking prophetically of the terrible destructive aspects of future world wars.[16] Wambaugh's son Miles was four years old at the time, and many years later reported:

> Faintly I remember seeing the Swami, but I recall clearly that his name came up often in family conversation both then and later. Especially in talk between my father and my sister Sarah who was then eleven and clearly much interested.

Wambaugh was a relatively new professor at the Harvard Law School and remained there from 1892 until 1925. During the First World War, he held a number of government legal positions and attained the rank of Colonel. Being a fellow of the American Academy of Arts and Sciences, he authored several volumes dealing with constitutional law. To preserve world peace he specialized in international law. Seen in the light of Swamiji's dramatic 1893 speech on the destructiveness of future wars, it is most interesting to note that his daughter, Miss Sarah Wambaugh (1882-1955), devoted her life to bringing about world peace. She established a worldwide reputation with her 1920 monograph that examined plebiscites back to the time of the French Revolution. Sarah worked as an advisor and on commissions for the League of Nations and the United Nations, and periodically taught in Colleges. Working with plebiscites, she and her associates successfully resolved conflicting territorial claims in the Saar Basin and the Free City of Danzig, and she helped device procedures for plebiscites in Jammu and Kashmir in 1949. She and her father Eugene worked for the Peruvian government in administering a plebiscite, which resolved the conflicting territorial claims of Peru and Chile. In her later years, she became convinced that a world state with a police force was necessary to prevent conflicts between nations.[17]

On August 26, 1893, Swamiji conversed at the home of Alpheus Hyatt (1838-1902), a professor from Boston University. A year later in August 1894 when the Swami came back to Annisquam, he came in contact with Mr. Hyatt at a clambake. Mrs. John Bagley rented the Hyatt House, and Swamiji stayed there as her guest from August 17 until September 5 with a four-day break in between. His grandson A. Hyatt Mayor later reported:

> I remember my mother [Harriet] telling me that Swami Vivekananda stayed at this home in the time of my grandfather, Alpheus Hyatt ... all I

gathered was that he charmed everybody with his urbanity and his willingness to enter into the mood of the moment.[18]

Alpheus Hyatt, a Civil War captain, cofounded and became the curator of the Peabody Academy of Sciences and the custodian and curator of the Boston Society of Natural History (1870-1902). He was a fellow of the American Academy of Arts and Sciences in 1869, and in 1875 a member of the National Academy of Science. Hyatt worked as a professor of zoology and paleontology at Massachusetts Institute of Technology (1870-88) and at Boston University (1877-1902). Devoting his life to studying the lower forms of life, his primary objective was to discover the laws that govern the development of the individual and the evolution of life.[19]

As mentioned in Chapter VII, the eminent Transcendentalist Franklin Sanborn encouraged Swamiji to deliver multiple speeches before the prominent American Social Science Association founded by Sanborn himself. During September 4-8, 1893, the General Meeting was held in Saratoga, New York. At the conference, Swamiji got involved in a discussion concerning a paper on "The Silver Question in India" presented by Elisha Benjamin Andrews (1844-1917), the dynamic and successful president of Brown University located in Providence, Rhode Island.[20] In this regard, Vivekananda indicated in an 1896 letter to Mary Hale that William Jennings "Bryan was right when he said, 'We refuse to be crucified on a cross of gold.' The silver standard will give the poor a better chance in this unequal fight."[21] It is interesting that of all the American politicians to mention in the nine volumes, Swamiji selected W. J. Bryan, who, in 1899, became India's number one supporter in the West among the leading American political thinkers.* Another link with Brown University was supplied by Saradananda, who lectured as a guest of the Philosophical Club at the University when he lived in the United States.

Two years later Swamiji had another connection with Elisha Andrews. In 1895, several newspapers in the United States carried a long article on the question, "Is Man Immortal?" with the subtitle "Logic of the Belief in a Future Life", "Views of Eminent Thinkers". The answers to this profound question were supplied by Swamiji,[22] Elisha Andrews, who was originally a Baptist minister, Reverend Charles A. Briggs (1841-1913), a distinguished Biblical professor at Union Theological Seminary in New York, and Elizabeth

* See Chapter XVI.

Stuart Phelps (1844-1911), a popular fiction writer. The complete full-page article appeared in such widely-read newspapers as *The New York Morning Advertiser*, *The Independent* in Massillon, Ohio (July 11), and the Boise *Idaho Daily Statesman* (July 14).

As a young man William Ernest Hocking (1873-1966) [q.v.] was profoundly moved by Vivekananda's opening address at the World's Parliament of Religions. He later stated:

> The speaker came forward with a calm authority but also with a fraternal at home-ness: "Sisters and Brothers of America ..." In an instant the immense audience was responding with a thunderous physical wave of greeting and recognition of the accent of inner assurance. He spoke not as arguing from a tradition, or from a book, but as from an experience and certitude of his own.... For me, this doctrine was a startling departure from anything which my scientific psychology could then recognize. One must live with these ideas and consider how one's inner experience could entertain them. But what I could feel and understand was that this man was speaking from what he knew, not from what he had been told.[23]

A few years later Hocking attended two of Swamiji's informal classes in Cambridge, one at the residence of Sara Bull. He acknowledged, "It was in these informal gatherings that the quality of the man most directly spoke, and I was confirmed in my regard and my purpose to rethink my philosophical foundations." Beginning in 1899 Hocking studied under James and Royce at Harvard, and Edmund Husserl in Germany. He read Deussen's works on Vedanta, listened to James Woods' account of his years in India, and conversed with Woods about his translations of Patanajali's *Yoga Aphorisms* and its traditional commentaries. During 1931-32, Hocking visited Mahatma Gandhi in London and then had the honour of making a pilgrimage to Belur Math. In India he became acquainted with Sarvepalli Radhakrishnan, Jawaharlal Nehru, Rabindranath Tagore, Kshiti Mohan Sen, Surendranath Dasgupta, and Josephine MacLeod, "a warm and personal friend". Hocking praised Nikhilananda's translation of the *Gospel of Sri Ramakrishna* (1942).* In the Foreword to Nikhilananda's *Bhagavad Gita* (1944), Hocking articulated, "There can be no doubt about the profundity

* See Chapter III.

of Shankara's work, its great philosophical importance, and its permanent message to a world tempted to the distractions of pluralism."[24]

William Hocking taught at the University of California at Berkeley (1906-07) and Yale University (1907-13). At Harvard University (1914-43) he served as the chairman of the philosophy department (1937-43), and was honoured to be the president of the American Philosophical Association (1925-26). Being the leading exponent of philosophical idealism as championed by Josiah Royce, Hocking published over twenty texts stressing a philosophical interpretation of the human awareness of God, and the importance of interfaith dialogue, mutual appreciation and religious diversity.[25]

Merwin-Marie Snell (b. 1863), a teacher at the Catholic University of America in Washington, D.C., published the article "Was Christ a Buddhist?" in 1891, translated a book from French in 1894 written by the psychologist Theodule Ribot (1839-1916), and by the turn of the century seems to have left the public scene. At the Parliament of Religions, he presided over the prestigious Scientific Section, and Swamiji and Snell conducted a "Conference on the Modern Religions of India". Snell sent a long letter dated January 30, 1894 to the editor of the *Pioneer*, an Anglo-Indian newspaper. The *Pioneer* printed it on March 8 and the *Indian Mirror* the next day. Snell emphatically stated:

> By far the most important and typical representative of Hinduism was Swami Vivekananda, who, in fact, was beyond question the most popular and influential man in the Parliament.... on all occasions he was received with greater enthusiasm than any other speaker, Christian or "Pagan". The people thronged him wherever he went and hung with eagerness on his every word. Since the Parliament, he has been lecturing before large audiences in the principal cities of the United States and has received an ovation wherever he went.... Never before has so authoritative a representative of genuine Hinduism—as opposed to the emasculated and Anglicized versions of it so common in these days—been accessible to American inquirers; and it is certain, beyond peradventure, that the American people at large will, when he is gone, look forward with eagerness to his return... America thanks India for sending him, and begs her to send many more like him.[26]

After the parliament, Mr. Snell took up the study of the religion of India, and in 1894 published three scholarly articles in *The Biblical World* on "Hinduism's Points of Contact with Christianity". The following year, in *The Biblical*

World he came out with two articles on "Modern Theosophy in its Relation to Hinduism and Buddhism" and one on "Evangelical Hinduism".

In 1933 Henrietta Holmes Earl wrote a reminiscence of Swamiji for the *Prabuddha Bharata*. She thought back forty years to when she was a small child and a pupil at the Cook County Normal School in Chicago in 1893 and recalled:

> Each morning the entire school assembled for Chapel, and often a brief talk by some distinguished visitor was heard. On one of these occasions we were all fascinated by the spectacle of our tall Col. Parker ushering in another stately man who was dressed in flowing robes and turban. We sang, and Col. Parker read a prayer. Then the Swami [Vivekananda] spoke to us. I was too little to remember what he said, but I do remember how quiet the big room was, and how brilliant his eyes and vibrant his voice. When his talk was over he too said a prayer, and then he and Col. Parker walked down together from the platform through the assembly hall. The Hindu boy next to me sat in an aisle seat, and as the Swami passed him, bent and kissed his robe. I was so surprised at such a thing that I whispered to the boy, "Why did you do that? Who is he?" "The man is Swami Vivekananda, a great saint from my country," he said. "But," said I, "there are no more saints any more." "Not here in your country," he replied, "but we still have them in India."

Three years later in 1936 she contributed "A Litany to Ramakrishna" to the *Prabuddha Bharata*.[27]

In a letter of January 28, 1900, Sister Nivedita told Josephine MacLeod, "Dear Col. Parker ... takes so much glory to himself for 'liking Swami'. 'I did like him'—he says boastfully." Colonel Francis Wayland Parker (1837-1902), a Civil War veteran, experimented with new and radical methods of teaching that later became a model for twentieth-century educational practices. As superintendent of schools at Quincy, Massachusetts, from 1875 onward he brought science into the curriculum and did away with drill-rote memory methods. Being a lover of children, he cultivated freedom and informality in the classroom replacing rigid discipline. In 1883 he became the principal of the Cook County Normal School in Engelwood, Illinois. There he made use of vigorous liberal ideas in elementary education. Parker became the first director of the School of Education at the University of Chicago in 1901. He had the support of the famous pragmatic philosopher and educator

John Dewey who was his friend and admirer. Dewey later in 1919 met Soyen Shaku (1859-1919), the leader of the Zen Buddhists in Japan, and in 1924 was a sponsor of the India Society of America founded by Hari Govil. Seven years later Dewey joined Jane Addams and Robert Hutchins, the president of the University of Chicago, in inviting Mahatma Gandhi to the United States. Dewey was also one of many members of the General Committee for the Ramakrishna Centenary held in Calcutta in March 1937.[28]

After the Parliament of Religions came to a close in late September 1893, Vivekananda was the guest of honour at a vegetarian dinner party held at the house of the inventor Elisha Gray [q.v.]* in Chicago. Also, in attendance at the dinner were three European delegates to the Electrical Congress, viz. Lord Kelvin, Hermann von Helmholtz and probably Edouard Hospitalier.[29] The Irish born Lord Kelvin (formerly William Thomson, 1824-1907) worked as a professor of natural philosophy at the University of Glasgow in Scotland. In 1848 he came up with the absolute scale of temperature, was one of the founders of thermodynamics, wrote papers on telegraphic signalling by wire during 1855-65, which aided in the laying of the first Atlantic cable, and patented many new electric devices.[30] Hermann von Helmholtz (1821-94), the director of the Institute of Physics in Berlin, Germany, developed the first mathematical analysis of the principle of the conservation of energy, invented the ophthalmoscope to examine the inside of the eye, and investigated the physics of tone and colour perception.[31] Edouard Hospitalier (1852-1902) authored a number of texts in the French language on the subject of electricity, some of which were translated into English.[32]

On January 25, 1894, Swami Vivekananda sat next to the toastmaster Thomas B. Bryan† at the eleventh annual banquet of the Chicago Real Estate Board. The gala event was held at the auditorium managed by Milward Adams, the husband of Florence Adams, a supporter of Swamiji. Nineteen judges and many prominent citizens attended the gala front-page event. The list of many speakers included William R. Harper (1856-1906), a Biblical expert and the first president of the University of Chicago. With the funding of his close friend John D. Rockefeller, the owner of the Standard Oil Company, Harper created the University of Chicago, which opened its doors in 1892. He quickly attracted a group of world-class professors to

* See Chapter XI.

† 1828-1906; vice-president of the 1893 Chicago World's Fair.

teach at this outstanding educational institution. The *Chicago Daily Tribune* of January 26, 1894 wrote the following:[33]

SWAMI VIVE KANANDA'S STORY.

He Tells it in Response to the Toast "A Voice from the Far East."

Swami Vive Kananda, the Hindoo priest, was given a warm welcome as he arose to respond to the last toast of the evening: "A Voice from the Far East." He said in part:

I will tell you an Oriental story. A miller's son was in the habit of lying outside the mill on a board, singing all the day long. He was a sweet singer and his fame spread all over the land until at last it reached the ears of the King. He sent for the boy to sing before him. When the boy came in the presence of his ruler he could not utter a single note, try as hard as he could. His father, in urging him, gave him a push which threw him prostrate on the floor, and then his song burst forth in all its sweetness. So you could not expect me, to whom is allocated by my religion not even the meanest square inch of earth, to speak before a body of real estate men, for in your presence I am like the miller's boy. We creatures of religion think more of another estate, that of the spiritual. One of the speakers this evening, with all his admiration for the dead in the past, has referred to the "effete" East. I would remind him that from that East came all the ideas of a spiritual nature, and even the religion of which he is a minister. I admire You Americans for your practical and sympathetic principles, but unless you combine with them the spiritual, to which we in the East are so much attached, your nation will never reach the perfection to which you wish to attain.

It is possible that Swamiji met John D. Rockefeller during the early part of 1894 according to *Life*. Swamiji spoke at the University Chapel in Cobb Hall at the University of Chicago on March 1 on the subject of "Modern Schools of Hinduism". Chapel services were opened to the faculty and students daily at 12:30 p.m.[34]

On April 7, 1894, the *New York Tribune* told its readers:

Suami Vive Kanauda [sic] will soon visit Boston, and that city is in a delightful flutter of excitement over the event. "Brother Vive Kanauda," [sic] as likes to be called, is a Brahmin from India, and was among the most noteworthy delegates to the World's Parliament of Religions in Chicago.

> He is a man of vast learning and charming manners. He speaks English without an accent, and is very handsome. He is in sympathy with many of the teachings of Christ.[35]

On April 14, 1894 Vivekananda lectured at the City Hall in Northampton, Massachusetts, on "Indian Customs and Manners", and the *Daily Herald* of the 16th affirmed:

> But to see and hear Swami Vive Kananda is an opportunity which no intelligent fair-minded American ought to miss if one cares to see a shining light of the very finest product of the mental, moral and spiritual culture of a race which reckons its age by thousands where we count ours by hundreds and is richly worth the study of every mind.[36]

The following day he was present at the distinguished Smith College for women. While there, he boarded in a small guest-room in a square brown house, with four freshmen women near the campus. After Vivekananda arrived, Martha Brown Fincke (b. 1874/75), one of the freshmen women, described him as having "a finely shaped head. But the face with its inscrutable expression, the eyes so full of flashing light, and the whole emanation of power, are beyond description. We were awed and silent." Many years later in 1936, Mrs. Fincke wrote:

> I find in the universal Gospel that Swamiji preached the satisfaction of my longing. To believe that the Divine is within us, that we are from the very first a part of God, and that this is true of every man, what more can I ask? In receiving this, as I have on the soil of India, I feel that I have come Home.

On the 15th Swamiji addressed the student body of Smith College on the "Brotherhood of Man and the Fatherhood of God". "President Seelye, in a few well-chosen words, gave a cordial welcome to the speaker of the occasion, Swami Vive Kananda." Credit must be given to Laurenus Clark Seelye (1837-1924) for inviting Swamiji to speak at his prestigious college. Seelye was at first a Congregational Minister, but then became a professor of rhetoric, oratory, and English literature at Amherst College. He took a big step in 1873 in becoming the president of the newly formed Smith College. During his administration, the student body rose from only 14 to 1635 in 1910.[37]

Apparently, Vivekananda's lecture attracted a great deal of attention in the community. A symposium followed the public address for the purpose of challenging the Swami. Martha Brown Fincke tells us:

> To our house came the College president [Laurenus Seelye], the head of the philosophy department, and several other professors, the ministers of the Northampton churches, and a well-known author [George Cable].... I have a strong impression that it [the conversation] dealt mainly with Christianity and why it is the only true religion.... As his imposing presence faced the row of black-coated and somewhat austere gentlemen, one felt that he was being challenged.... How could one expect a Hindu from far-off India to hold his own with these masters ... To texts from the Bible, the Swami replied by other and more apposite ones from the same book. In upholding his side of the argument he quoted English philosophers and writers on religious subjects. Even the poets he seemed to know thoroughly, quoting Wordsworth and Thomas Gray.... I only know that I felt triumphant with him.[38]

Swamiji had made contact with Harvard University Professors John Henry Wright and Eugene Wambaugh before the Parliament of Religions in 1893. A second contact with Harvard occurred at Sanders Theatre in Cambridge, when the university student body presented the Latin play, Terence's "Phormio". The gala event was attended by the governor of the state and several university presidents and professors, particularly from Harvard. The *Boston Daily Globe* of April 20, 1894 reported, "One of the most noticeable persons in the audience was Swami Vivekanauda [sic] from Calcutta, India. He is a monk, and he attended in his native dress." Present for the event were many people whom Swamiji knew or came to know like Presidents Eliot of Harvard, Hall of Clark University, and Seelye of Smith College; John Henry Wright of Harvard and his wife; Mrs. Jack Gardner, Colonel Thomas Higginson, and Alice Longfellow. On May 8th he lectured at Radcliffe College, the coordinate college for Harvard University, and on the 16th Swamiji presented a discourse on the "Aspects of Religious Life in India" before the Harvard Religious Union, Sever Hall, at Harvard University.[39]

At the Cambridge Conferences held at Sara Bull's residence, Vivekananda made the acquaintance of the renowned Harvard professor William James

(1842-1910) [q.v.], probably in October and definitely in December 1894. With the remarkably successful two-volume work *The Principles of Psychology* (1890), and *Briefer Course* (1892), James had established himself as America's foremost psychologist. Possibly at that time Swamiji demonstrated the nature of divine communion to James by entering into samadhi in his presence. At that time Vivekananda and James met "at dinner at the residence of Mrs. Ole Bull. After dinner the Swami and the professor drew together in earnest and subdued conversation. It was midnight when they rose from their long discourse." Swamiji told Sara Bull, who made inquiries about their long conversation, that James is "A very nice man, a very nice man!"[40]

We will never know the names of many prominent and intelligent people who heard Swamiji lecture, some multiple times. "Mrs. Edith Swanander, who was called by Swamiji as 'mother', used to say that doctors, lawyers and professors used to attend the classes of Swami Vivekananda. They wanted to understand the Indian view of life." Bhupendranath Datta, the youngest brother of Swami Vivekananda, happened to be present when

> Professor Lester F. Ward, the noted scientist and sociologist, told the post-graduate class at the Brown University in 1913 that he attended the whole course of lectures of Swami Vivekananda. But his opinion was that "the Oriental view of life is pessimistic, kill the flesh is the Oriental motto."

Many people appreciated Vivekananda's brilliant ideas, but when he started to talk about renunciation, some of them did not care for it. Emily Cape, the secretary of the Vedanta Society of New York under Swami Abhedananda, worked with Lester F. Ward (1841-1913), and later produced a biography of him.* While being the chief paleontologist for the United States Geographical Survey, in 1883 he became the father of American sociology, being the first American to come out with a systematic study of sociology. For his achievements in the field he was honoured as the first president of both the International Institute of Sociology (1903) and of the American Sociological Association (then called Society) in 1906. Ward's fundamental belief was that scientific knowledge of social laws gained in pure sociology should be used to improve human society through rational social planning and education.[41]

---

* See Chapter XV.

While living in England during the fall of October 1895, Swamiji came in contact with Professor Robert Watson Frazer (1854-1921) who, it is stated, "has lived so much in ancient thought and wisdom that he does not care a fig for anything out of India!"[42] Between 1877 and 1886 he worked as a member of the Madras Civil Service in India. Later Frazer served as the principal librarian and secretary at the London Institution, and a lecturer in Tamil and Telugu at the School of Oriental Studies, University College. His scholarly writings include *British India* (1897), *A Literary History of India* (1898), and *A Text-Book in Indian History* (1907). In *Indian Thought Past and Present* (1915), he made the revealing statement that Vivekananda "attracted large audiences to his lectures in England and America. In private conversation he always maintained a quiet confidence that 'Indian thought, philosophical and spiritual, must once more go over and conquer the world.'"[43]

T. J. Desai was a member of the Royal Asiatic Society of Great Britain and Ireland. He wrote that Vivekananda, accompanied by Romesh Chunder Dutt, attended at least one of their meetings. T. W. Rhys Davids, the secretary of the Society, spoke at that time. At these gatherings it might have been possible for Swamiji to meet with Sir F. F. Arbuthnot, J. E. Carpenter, R. W. Frazer, W. Hunter, Max Müller, C. Tawney and other prominent Orientalists.[44] About Vivekananda, T. W. Rhys Davids* (1843-1922) later wrote in 1910, "He was a remarkable personality full of enthusiasm, speaking English almost like an Englishman, and gifted with an unshaken confidence in his own solution to the problems of life." An expert in the study of Pali and early Buddhism, Davids was a professor at University College, London (1882-1912), and Manchester College (1904-15).[45]

In the book *Swami Vivekananda in London*, Mahendranath Datta, who lived with Swamiji in London during 1895-96, indicated that:

> Miss [Henrietta] Müller had studied at Cambridge University with a Dr. John Venn (author of *Logic of Chance*). One day she took Swamiji to meet him. They talked about philosophy in various forms in different countries. Swamiji impressed the professor very much and he was most pleased with the encounter.

John Venn (1834-1923), originally a priest of the Anglican Church, became an expert on symbolic and inductive logic, and probability theory. He

* Who was not drawn to Swamiji's ideas.

is best known for his development of Venn Diagrams around 1880, which are used today in symbolic logic, probability statistics and computer science. A Venn diagram is a pictorial representation of the relationships among sets. There is an outer rectangle that stands for the universal set, within which are overlapping circles and their intersections representing subsets of the universal set. With his son he wrote a two-volume history of Cambridge University appearing in 1922.[46]

In England, the Swami came in contact with a friend of William James, the very interesting and unusual Frederic(k) Myers (1843-1901). It is sad that we do not have a record of their exchange of ideas. Myers, a professor of the classics at Cambridge University in England, "wanted to know if human beings survived bodily death. If they did, then life in a body must have a discoverable purpose" worth knowing. Rather than studying theological and philosophical writings, he undertook a scientific and empirical investigation of afterlife using the records of the spiritualist mediums. For this reason, he and his Cambridge colleagues founded the Society for Psychical Research in 1882. His most important work *Human Personality and its Survival of Bodily Death* was at one time a textbook in psychology at the University of Madras. In the book he attributes psychic phenomena not to external spirits but to the subliminal self. For the subliminal self which is not bound by the physical body, the so-called supernormal faculties are the ordinary channels of perception. After his death in 1901, Myers communicated what amounted to a massive twelve-thousand pages of material to a dozen spiritualist mediums in England, the United States, and India. He sent messages to many individuals up until 1932, so that people would not think his transmissions were the subjective experience of a single medium. Swami Abhedananda said that he himself received messages from the spirit of Myers. After his death, Myers sent messages stating that the soul reincarnates progressively from a rudimentary mineral form through the plant, animal and human levels over a series of lives until it reaches its true divine nature. He describes seven stages, which are levels of consciousness, or realms of existence from the earth plane to the highest formless and timeless spiritual realm. "The soul who enters that seventh state passes into the Beyond and becomes one with God." Since Myers was able to progress only to the third heaven, "at the time of his communication his reports of the higher levels of consciousness beyond this are less detailed and more speculative." He got information about the higher heavens from souls more highly evolved than himself.[47]

In the first volume of *The Classic and the Beautiful from the Literature of Three Thousand Years* (1895), Henry Coppee (1821-95), the president of Lehigh University, devoted twenty-four hundred words to giving his reader large verbatim sections of Swamiji's "Paper on Hinduism" (which he calls "The Hindu Faith") delivered on 19 September 1893 at the Parliament of Religions in Chicago.[48] In the third volume he writes this about the "distinguished Oriental scholar":

> Having left the law as a profession and taken the vows of chastity and poverty, he assumed with his new religious life the name of Swami Vivekananda. The title Swami is in the Hindu tongue somewhat similar to that of Master or Rabbi in our language. Unlike some of his countrymen, he is highly spiritual in his religious views. He believes in the Sacred Books of India, the "Vedas", in the immortality of the soul, and in a Supreme Intelligence. He has a high veneration for the founders of all the great religions of the world, and has no wish, he says, to make proselytes for his own faith, but thinks that all religions should develop according to their own mode of thought. He hails mankind as "children of immortal bliss". Addressing his audience at the World's Parliament of Religions, to which he was a delegate, "Let me call you brethren," said he, "by that sweet name, heirs of immortal bliss."

Henry Coppee was promoted to the rank of Captain "for gallant and meritorious conduct" in the war with Mexico in 1845. He then worked as a professor of English literature and history at the University of Pennsylvania, and later accepted the presidency of the newly founded Lehigh University in Pennsylvania (1866-75, 1893-95), while remaining a professor of history and literature. With a breadth of knowledge and wideness of intellectual interest, he wrote a number of history books on the Civil War in England that ran into nine volumes, and the Arab Moor's conquest of Spain.[49]

1896 and After

Not much is known of J. B. Street, a Brooklyn schoolteacher who in February 1896 was initiated by Vivekananda and christened as Swami Yogananda. He had some psychic powers and, through the gift of clairvoyance, accurately perceived the Spanish attack on the battleship Maine in Cuba that led to the Spanish-American war in 1897. At that time he attended

Abhedananda's classes and public lectures. Apparently, he did little to promote the Vedantic teachings. In a May 22, 1901 article that appeared in the *Davenport Daily Leader*, he continued to use his pre-monastic name. The article deals with Street's infatuation with crystal reading as a method of discerning future events. One of his crystals came from the top of the head of an image of Buddha in Japan, and the other from an image of Vishnu in India. Mr. Street spoke well of Swamiji at his memorial service held on October 26, 1902 at the New York Centre.[50]

Swamiji spoke before the Harvard students at the residence of Sara Bull on March 22 and 24, 1896.[51] It is quite likely that William James (1842-1910) [q.v.] listened to Vivekananda's illustrious talk on "The Vedanta Philosophy" presented before the Harvard Graduate Philosophical Club on the 25th.[52] They had held a long discussion back in the fall of 1894 at Sara Bull's residence. Before Swamiji gave the presentation, "Mr. Lough said that Vivekananda's addresses [his published pamphlets] interested not only the philosophical students, but also Prof. James and Prof. Royce, who hope to be at his Harvard talk." A long question and answer session followed the event.[53] Three days later James sent a letter to Swami addressing him as "Dear Master", inviting him to lunch at his residence. Everett, James, Royce, Lanman, and other Harvard professors admired Swamiji greatly, so he might have been offered the chair of Eastern philosophy at the University, which, as a sannyasin, he could not accept. Lewis Janes scheduled Swamiji to speak at the Cambridge Conferences in December of 1899, an event attended by some Harvard professors. He decided to travel to Los Angeles and was replaced by Swami Turiyananda who lectured on "Shankaracharya". James and the Swami met again at the Paris Exposition in 1900.[54]

Though William James was a pluralist who rejected the philosophy of monism, in a letter to Sara Bull dated August 2, 1900 he explained, "I have just been reading some of Vivekananda's addresses in England, which I had not seen. This man is simply a wonder for oratorical power.... The Swami is an honour to humanity." In a letter to Josephine MacLeod, James wrote that he "might get hold of the first 3 parts of Practical Vedanta". He felt bad that he did not present Swamiji with a copy of his book on "Psychology". In *The Varieties of Religious Experience* first released in 1902, James cites two long references taken from Swamiji's "Practical Vedanta", "The Real and the Apparent Man", and his book *Raja Yoga*.[55] Before quoting Swamiji, James wrote:

> In India, training in mystical insight has been known from time immemorial under the name of Yoga. Yoga means the experimental union of the individual with the divine. It is based on persevering exercise; and the diet, posture, breathing, intellectual concentration, and moral discipline vary slightly in the different systems which teach it. The yogi, or disciple, who has by these means overcome the obscurations of his lower nature sufficiently, enters into the condition termed *samadhi*, "and comes face to face with facts which no instinct or reason can ever know."[56]

In his volume *Pragmatism* (1907), he supplied lengthy quotes of some of the Swami's statements on monism. There he writes, "The paragon of all monastic systems is the Vedanta philosophy of Hindostan, and the paragon of Vedantic missionaries was the late Swami Vivekananda who visited our land some years ago." James described Sister Nivedita as possessing "an extraordinary fine character and mind", to be "a most deliberate and balanced person", "who has Hinduized herself (converted by Vivekananda to his philosophy) and now lives for the Hindu people". After James' death, they found volumes of the works of Vivekananda and Abhedananda in his personal library. Abhedananda said that he received messages from the spirit of James after the latter's death.[57]

Dr. Eugene I. Taylor, an associate in psychiatry at the Harvard Medical School, explained what James considered to be of value in Vivekananda's teachings:

> [William James] saw in Vivekananda's inner science a vast unexplored dimension for the understanding of personality and character formation. We know from subsequent references he made to Vivekananda's system that James saw great value in the Hindu practice of systematic, daily periods of concentrated relaxation. These, James felt, could be of great use in preparing American children for learning in the classroom. James also observed in the methods of Vivekananda's yoga, a form of spiritual discipline that could be used by anyone to penetrate into untapped reservoirs of energy and power for physical as well as mental tasks, and also in the treatment of certain neurasthenic conditions ... A language of inner experience, a rigorous psychology of character formation, and practical application to real-life problems were but a few of the advantages that James saw in Vivekananda that were being ignored by the German-trained brass

instrument psychologists then taking control of the academic psychology departments in America.[58]

Taylor also wrote that, "No doubt present at Vivekananda's talk was Crawford Howell Toy (1836-1919), professor of oriental languages and also a founder of the History of Religions Club at Harvard." Toy, a Baptist and a biblical scholar, was an expert on the subject of the history of religions, with a particular interest in Judaism and Christianity. On March 21, 1897, Crawford Toy spoke at the Cambridge Conferences when Saradananda was staying at Mrs. Bull's residence.[59]

Under the title of "Wonders of the Yoga System", in 1907 William James paid the technique the following tribute:

> The most venerable ascetic system, and the one whose results have the most voluminous experimental corroboration is undoubtedly the Yoga system in Hindustan. From time immemorial, by Hatha Yoga, Raja Yoga, Karma Yoga, or whatever code of practice it might be, Hindu aspirants to perfection have trained themselves, month in and out, for years. The result claimed, and certainly in many cases accorded by impartial judges, is strength of character, personal power, unshakability of soul.

James then goes on to praise the effects that the practice of yoga had on his Polish friend Wincenty Lutoslawski.*[60]

At Harvard University, William James, an instructor in physiology and anatomy (1872-80), switched departments to become a professor of philosophy (1880-1907). He held the position of president of the Society for Psychical Research (1894-95). His most profound philosophical writings came out after he became acquainted with Swami Vivekananda. They are *The Will to Believe* (1897, based on essays going back to 1879), *Pragmatism* (1907), *A Pluralistic Universe* (1909), and also *Essays in Radical Empiricism* (1912). James' great work in the psychology of religion is his masterpiece *Varieties of Religious Experience* (1902). The Edinburgh lectures that became this book were to some degree motivated by a spiritual experience that James had "in the Adirondacks one night" in 1898. James described it as "the most memorable of all my memorable experiences. I got into a state of spiritual alertness of the most vital description." He was profoundly impressed by

---

* See Chapter XII.

"its intense appeal and everlasting freshness."[61] In this volume, he twice quotes maxims from Müller's *Ramakrishna His Life and Sayings*. This work emphasizes that for an empiricist, religious experience is a major source of religious knowledge. Religious experience is a mystical state that claims to know God. Through the subliminal self, an individual may become aware of a sphere and power beyond the normal range of consciousness. According to the "pragmatic principle", religious beliefs should be fruitful and compatible with our moral demands. He also acknowledges that he agrees in principle with the Buddhist doctrine of karma.[62]

Another supporter of Swamiji at Harvard, Josiah Royce (1855-1916) studied for a doctorate at Johns Hopkins University during the years 1876-78. Charles Lanman taught him how to read Sanskrit fluently and they became close lifelong friends and neighbours. Royce went on to teach literature at the University of California in Berkeley (1878-82), and philosophy at Harvard (1882-1916). Royce might have associated with Swamiji at the Cambridge Conferences, where they both lectured in October and/or December of 1894. It is quite likely that Royce was very much influenced by Vivekananda's lecture on the "Vedanta Philosophy" given before the Graduate Philosophical Club at Harvard in March 1896, and by Abhedananda's debate with William James on "the unity vs. the plurality of the universe", which he attended in May 1898.[*][63]

Josiah Royce is America's most profound philosopher of Absolute Idealism (Qualified Nondualism in India), whose ideas to some extent resemble Ramanuja's system of thought. He delivered the Gifford Lectures, which in their published form became his most important philosophical work *The World and the Individual* (1900-02). In the first volume of the manuscript, Royce extensively discusses the realism of the Sankhya philosophy,[†] the Unity of Being of the *Chandogya Upanishad*,[‡] along with occasional references to the "neti neti" and the "aham brahmasmi" of the *Brihadaranyaka Upanishad*. He cites Richard Garbe's (1857-1927) book on Sankhya, and Lanman's translation of the *Chandogya Upanishad*. This presentation aided in turning the attention of Western philosophers to the Indian world of thought and its profound significance. In 1913 Royce, J. H. Woods and

---

* See Chapter XVII.
† On pp. 100-04, 109-10.
‡ On pp. 156-75.

other Harvard professors spent an evening with Rabindranath Tagore, the brilliant worldwide spokesman for the Vedanta philosophy.[64]

In lecture IV on "The Unity of Being, and the Mystical Interpretation" in *The World and the Individual*, Josiah Royce makes the following statements, which are very much in accord with the teachings of Vivekananda:

> In the Upanishads, an immediate sense of the unity of all things runs parallel with an equally strong sense that this unity is wholly in myself who knows the truth,—in my heart, just because what for me is, is precisely what I know.... The Self [Atman] is precisely the very Knower, not as a thing that first is real and then knows, but as the very act of seeing, hearing, thinking, in so far as the mediating presence of some other, of some object that is known, seen, heard, thought, is simply removed, and in so far as the very diversity of the acts of knowing, seeing, hearing, thinking, is also removed.... All our relative satisfactions take the form of finite ideas. The Absolute must be ineffable, indescribable, *and yet not outside of the circle within which we at present are conscious*. It is no other than we are.... The Absolute is the very Opposite of a mere Nothing. For it is fulfillment, attainment, peace, the goal of life, the object of desire, the end of knowledge.... The truth cannot then be independent of the Knower. But if not independent of the Knower, and yet if not given to him by his finite experience and thought, what can the truth be except what one approaches, within one's own very heart, when one gradually casts off finitude, and wins unity and peace.... I have dwelt so long upon the Upanishads, because, as I have said, they contain already the entire story of the mystic faith, so far as it had a philosophical basis. The rest of its story is not any part of philosophy. Endlessly repeated in history, perhaps often independently rediscovered elsewhere, the dialectic of Mysticism has nowhere any essentially different tale to tell, nor any other outcome to record.[65]

The chairman of the Sanskrit department at Harvard University, Charles Rockwell Lanman (1850-1941) [q.v.] most probably heard Swamiji lecture during March 1896 at the Harvard Graduate Philosophical Club. He aided in producing the final revision of the address, which became the book *The Vedanta Philosophy*.[66] A couple of years later Lanman met Abhedananda, and he became an honorary member of the New York Vedanta Society. In 1913 Charles Lanman spoke at Paramananda's Boston Centre. Lanman studied Sanskrit at Yale University under William Dwight Whitney, and in Germany with Albrecht Weber and Rudolf Roth. He converted to the Unitarian religion, and became a professor of Sanskrit at Johns Hopkins (1876-80), and then at Harvard (1880-1926). Eighty years later university courses were still using his two-volume *Sanskrit Reader* published in 1884-88. While in India for a year, he gathered five-hundred valuable Sanskrit and Prakrit manuscripts, which in 1889 became the property of the Harvard College Library. Lanman's most important contribution involved planning and extensive editing of forty-one volumes of the Harvard Oriental Series between 1891 and 1925. Applying the methods of modern scholarship Lanman edited the volumes, which for him meant rewriting, rearranging, adding, and deleting material. Included in the series were Vedic, Yogic and Buddhist texts. Lanman also wrote a number of articles on yoga. He held the distinguished position of president of the American Philological Association (1889-90), and was also twice the president of the American Oriental Society (1907-08, 1919-20). Lanman had many outstanding pupils who translated Sanskrit and Buddhist works, including James Haughton Woods, Arthur Ryder, an admirer of Swami Trigunatita at the University of California in Berkeley, Irving Babbitt, Henry Clarke Warren and Walter Eugene Clark.[67]

Granville Stanley Hall (1844-1924) wrote he met Swami Vivekananda (at an unknown date), and that "his lectures here have attracted considerable attention in some quarters." As president of Clark University in Worcester, Massachusetts, G. S. Hall invited both Saradananda and Abhedananda (on two occasions) to address the student body. In the areas of educational and adolescent psychology, Hall was a leading figure. He taught at Johns Hopkins University, founded and edited the prestigious *American Journal of Psychology*, became the first president of Clark University (1889-1919), which offered only graduate study, and founded and became the first president of the esteemed American Psychological Association. At the 1893 Columbian Exposition, he presided over an "experimental psychology in education" conference. The new field of the "Psychology of Religion" originated with two of Hall's students. This branch of learning began with a religious article in 1896 by J. H. Leuba (1868-1946), then a fellow at Clark University, and an 1897 article and a book *Psychology of Religion* (1899) by Edwin D. Starbuck (1866-1947), a doctoral student at Clark University when Saradananda spoke there.[68]

When Vivekananda went to Europe in May 1896, the famous Oxford Indologist Friedrich Max Müller (1823-1900) [q.v.] treated him and Edward Sturdy with great cordiality. In his essay "On Max Müller" Swamiji relates:

> The Professor was kindness itself, and asked Mr. Sturdy and myself to lunch with him. He showed us several colleges in Oxford and the Bodleian library. He also accompanied us to the railway station; and all this he did because, as he said, "It is not every day one meets a disciple of Ramakrishna Paramahamsa."... [Swamiji asked him], "When are you coming to India?"... The face of the aged sage brightened up—there was almost a tear in his eyes, a gentle nodding of the head, and slowly the words came out: "I would not return then; you would have to cremate me there."[69]

The Swami met Müller again at Oxford University in September or October accompanied by Captain and Charlotte Sevier, and Paul Deussen.[70] Vivekananda often praised Müller who, he said, was a reincarnation of a distinguished Indian Vedic pundit. He had stated, "Sayana [1320-87] who is born again as Max Müller to revive his commentary on the Vedas."[71] Swamiji informs us:

> I have seen professors of Sanskrit in America and in Europe. Some of them are very sympathetic towards Vedantic thought. I admire their intellectual acumen and their lives of unselfish labour. But Paul Deussen—or, as he prefers to be called in Sanskrit, Deva-Sena—and the veteran Max Müller have impressed me as being the truest friends of India and Indian thought..... We Hindus certainly owe more to him [Max Müller] than to any other Sanskrit scholar in the West.[72]

Vivekananda appreciated Müller's admiration of India, which the latter clearly brought out in such statements as:

> If I were asked under what sky the human mind has most fully developed some of its choicest gifts, has most deeply pondered over the greatest problems of life, and has found solutions of some of them which well deserve the attention even of those who have studied Plato and Kant, I should point to India.[73]

In 1896, Swamiji sent a letter to Alasinga Perumal, the editor of the *Brahmavadin*, stating, "Max Müller is getting very friendly. I am soon going to deliver two lectures at Oxford."[74] In a November 1896 letter Müller wrote to Sturdy, "During the 50 years I have spent at Oxford, I have never taken the chair and I could not have done so without giving offence. The head of each College is the right person to take the Chair in his own College."[75] If Vivekananda could have made contact with Oxford and Cambridge philosophers like F. H. Bradley, John McTaggart, G. E. Moore, Bertrand Russell, and Alfred North Whitehead, he could have had some influence on the future of British philosophy.

At Oxford University Müller was a professor of European languages (1854-68) and comparative philology (1868-1900). The extremely hard working Anglo-German Oxford Indologist translated the six-volume *Rig Veda* with Sayana's Commentary (1849-73), edited the fifty-one volume *Sacred Books of the East* (1879-1900), and also authored numerous works on comparative philology and mythology, Sanskrit literature and grammar, Indian philosophy, and the nineteenth century neo-Hindu movement. His writings stimulated widespread interest in the study of Indian linguistics, mythology, and religion. Müller wrote to England's Prime Minister William Gladstone, "The discovery of that real India, of that new intellectual hemisphere, is to my mind a far greater discovery than that of Vasco da Gama's."[76] Another interesting statement made by Müller was, "I cannot help thinking that the souls towards whom we feel drawn in this life are the very souls whom we knew and loved in the former life, and the souls who repel us here we do not know why, are the souls that earned our disapproval, the souls from whom we kept aloof in a former life."[77]

Max Müller's love for Sanskrit literature began with the Upanishads, which he first became acquainted with in 1844 while attending the lectures of the famous German philosopher Friedrich Schelling (1775-1854). He translated several Upanishads for Schelling, who, he said, "was a great admirer of the ancient Indian literature, and was quite delighted with the Upanishads." Müller tells us:

> That Schelling and his school should use rapturous language about the Upanishads, might carry little weight with the large class of philosophers by whom everything beyond the clouds of their own horizon is labelled mysticism. But that [Arthur] Schopenhauer should have spoken of the Upanishads as "products of highest wisdom", that he should have placed the pantheism taught there high above the pantheism of Bruno, Malebranche, Spinoza and Scotus Erigena, as brought to light again at Oxford in 1681,

may perhaps secure a more considerate reception for these relics of ancient wisdom than anything that I could say in their favour.[78]

In his book *Philosophy of Mythology* (1842), Schelling devoted more than one-hundred pages to Indian writings. While generally holding a philosophical position similar to qualified nondualism, he also wrote such things as:

> In all of us there dwells a secret marvellous power of freeing ourselves from the changes of time, of withdrawing to our secret selves away from external things, and of so discovering to ourselves the eternal in us in the form of unchangability. This presentation of ourselves to ourselves is the most truly personal experience upon which depends everything that we know of the supersensual world. This presentation shows for the first time what real existence is, whilst all else only appears to be. It differs from every presentation of the sense in its perfect freedom, whilst all other presentations are bound, being over-weighted by the burden of the object. This intellectual presentation occurs when we cease to be our own object, when, withdrawing into ourselves, the perceiving image merges in the self-perceived.[79]

Müller discussed a meeting he had with Arthur Schopenhauer (1788-1860) as a young man:

> I remember having a most interesting discussion on the relative importance of the Vedic hymns and the Upanishads with Schopenhauer at Frankfort. He considered that the Upanishads were the only portion of the Veda which deserved our study, and that all the rest was priestly rubbish. His own philosophy, he declared, was founded on the Upanishads, which, as he says in one of his books, "have been the solace of my life, and will be the solace of my death." To me it seemed an historical study of the Vedic religion ought to begin with the hymns of the *Rigveda*, as containing in thought and language the antecedents of the Upanishads.... I felt convinced that all mythological and religious theories would remain without a solid foundation till the whole of the *Rigveda* had been published. This idea took complete possession of me.[80]

Müller decided to prove Schopenhauer wrong and devoted twenty-five years to the study and publication of the *Rig Veda*. His translation was an important contribution to the intellectual community because formerly the Vedas were the property of a small number of elite people only.[81]

In London in 1896, and in his first public speech after returning to the East on January 16, 1897, Swamiji had this to say about the philosopher:

> I should like to remind you how Schopenhauer predicted that the influence of Indian philosophy upon Europe would be as momentous when it became well known as was the revival of Greek and Latin learning at the close of the Dark Ages. Oriental research is making great progress; a new world of ideas is opening to the seeker after truth.[82] At the beginning of this century, Schopenhauer, the great German philosopher, studying from a not very clear translation of the Vedas made from an old translation into Persian and thence by a young Frenchman into Latin, says, "In the whole world there is no study so beneficial and so elevating as that of the Upanishads. It has been the solace of my life, it will be the solace of my death."[83]

Müller quotes Schopenhauer, "Indian wisdom will flow back upon Europe, and produce a thorough change in our knowing and thinking."[84] In his magnum opus *The World as Will and Representation* (1819, 1844), Schopenhauer wrote on such topics as Asia, avatar, Bhagavad Gita, Brahma, Brahman, Brahmanism, Buddhism, Hindus, India, Krishna, maya, metempsychosis, Max Müller, nirvana, Oupnekhat (Upanishads), rebirth, sannyasis, Sanskrit, Shiva, Tat tvam asi, Upanishads, Vedanta, and Vishnu.[85]

Paul Deussen (1845-1919) was a lecturer and professor at Berlin University during 1880-88, and a professor of philosophy at Kiel University in Germany between 1889 and 1919. He and his wife spent four or five months in India in 1892-93. There he visited centres of Sanskrit learning and gave some oral presentations. In his address before the Bombay Branch of the Royal Asiatic Society in India, on February 25, 1893 Deussen remarked:

> The system of Vedanta, as founded on the Upanishads and *Vedanta Sutras* and accompanied by Shankara's commentary on them—equal in rank to Plato and Kant—is one of the most valuable products of the genius of mankind in his researches of the eternal truth.

His most important writings before meeting Vivekananda were the *System of the Vedanta* (1883) and a translation of the Badarayana's *Brahma Sutras* with the commentary of Shankara (1887).[86]

The professor sent a letter to Vivekananda in London, inviting him to visit his home in Germany. On September 9-10, 1896, with the accompaniment by Captain and Charlotte Sevier, Swamiji met with Deussen and his wife at their residence in Kiel, Germany. They travelled together to Hamburg, Bremen, Amsterdam, and then to Wimbledon, England, holding long and enthusiastic conversations in English and Sanskrit. In Wimbledon, Swamiji and Deussen moved to separate residences, but met on a daily basis for two weeks discussing Indian philosophy and related subjects. Swamiji very much enjoyed the wonderful time he had with Paul Deussen.[87] According to Charlotte Sevier's account of the meeting between Swamiji and Deussen, the professor said, "It seems that a movement is being made back towards the fountain-head of spirituality, a movement that will in the future, probably, make India the spiritual leader of the nations, the highest and greatest spiritual influence on earth." On the subject of Deussen's translations, Swamiji told him "that clearness of definition was of primary, and elegance of diction of very secondary importance." After his meeting and discussions with Vivekananda, Deussen produced a translation of the *Sixty Upanishads of the Veda* (1897), and *Outlines of Indian Philosophy* (1908).[88]

In the *Philosophy of the Upanishads* (1899), he wrote:

> The fundamental thought of the entire Upanishad philosophy may be expressed by the simple equation: Brahman = Atman. That is to say—the Brahman, the power which presents itself to us materialized in all existing things, which creates, sustains, preserves and receives back into itself again all worlds, this eternal, infinite divine power is identical with the Atman, with that which, after stripping off everything external, we discover in ourselves as our real most essential being, our individual self, the soul.

As Helmuth von Glasenapp (1891-1963) later discerned, Deussen "was the great pioneer who, like no other man in his time, contributed towards securing for Indian philosophy its due place in the entire field of philosophy."[89]

Paul Deussen and the famous German philosopher Friedrich Nietzsche (1844-1900) established a lifelong friendship beginning as students at Bonn University in 1864. Deussen's life was radically altered when Nietzsche informed him about the writings of Arthur Schopenhauer (1788-1860), who became the original source of Deussen's knowledge of Indian thought. After being a supporter of Schopenhauer for approximately nine years, Nietzsche worked out his secular philosophy in conscious opposition to Schopenhauer's life-negating pessimism. Nietzsche regarded Deussen as the foremost Western Indologist because of his deep understanding of Kant and Schopenhauer's ideas, which enabled him to grasp the depths of Indian philosophy. Soon after it was published, Deussen sent Nietzsche his *System of the Vedanta* (1883), and Nietzsche thanked him heartily, realizing that it was completely alien to his way of thinking. Nietzsche wrote in a letter to Deussen, "Everything that I already suspected in regard to this type of thinking comes to light in it in the most naive manner. I read page for page with complete 'malice', you cannot wish for yourself a more thankful reader, dear friend." When Nietzsche received Deussen's translation of the *Brahma Sutras with the Commentary of Shankara* (1887), he insightfully realized its affinity with Kant's philosophy stating, "There are pages which sound like the *Critique of Pure Reason*, and not only sound so." Nietzsche considered the *Law of Manu* to be "an incomparably intellectual and superior work. It is replete with noble values, it is filled with a feeling of perfection, with a saying of yea to life, and a triumphant sense of well-being in regard to itself and to life; the sun shines upon the whole book.... I know of no book in which so many delicate things are said of woman as in the Law Book of Manu."[90]

In 1897 when Vivekananda lived in India, Lewis Janes, Charles Everett, William James, John Henry Wright, Josiah Royce, James Lough, Arthur Lovejoy, Rachel K. Taylor (president of the Radcliffe Philosophical Club, 1896-97), Sara Bull, and John Fox sent him a letter. In three different sentences, this group specifically made a request that their "Dear Friend and Brother" return to the United States as a teacher. Among other things they stated:

> It gives us great pleasure to recognize the value of your able exposition of the Philosophy and Religion of Vedanta in America, and the interest created thereby among thinking people. We believe such expositions as have been given by yourself and your co-labourer, the Swami Saradananda, have more than a more speculative interest and utility—that they are of great ethical value in cementing the ties of friendship and brotherhood between distant peoples, and in helping us to realize that solidarity of human relationships, and interests which has been affirmed by all the great religions of the world.[91]

James Edwin Lough (1871-1952), who is mentioned above, knew of the pamphlets of Vivekananda's prior addresses, helped set up Swamiji's lecture at Harvard on the "Vedanta Philosophy" and was instrumental in the dissemination of the published version of the address. He served as the president of the Harvard Graduate Philosophical Society and taught at the university while studying for his doctorate during 1896-98. From 1901 until 1927 he worked as a professor of experimental psychology at New York University (NYU). Promoting an internationalist viewpoint, Lough originated and organized the first floating university, which brought about his dismissal from NYU in 1927. A total of five-hundred and four students and sixty-three administrators from America undertook a seven and one-half month worldwide cruise in 1926. The floating coeducational campus included classrooms, dormitories, laboratories as well as a gymnasium, cafeteria, and a library. After his dismissal from NYU, Lough became the educational director and the president of the "American Floating University". The "Semester at Sea" programme that Lough commenced in 1926 presently takes about four-hundred college students around the world twice a year.[92]

Another signer of the letter sent to Vivekananda was Arthur Oncken Lovejoy (1873-1962), the secretary of the Harvard Graduate Philosophical Society. A lifetime bachelor, he became a student in the Harvard Graduate School (1895-97), a professor of philosophy at four universities (1899-1910), and then a permanent member of the staff at Johns Hopkins University (1910-38). He held the illustrious positions of president of the American Philosophical Association (1916) and the American Association of University Professors (1919). Lovejoy's first article in 1898 dealt with the subject of Buddhism, coming out in the *Journal of the American Oriental Society*, but then he turned his attention to western philosophy. Lovejoy is well known for the "Principle of Plentitude", that anything which is possible comes into existence. The universe contains as many different kinds of things as it possibly could contain. Following "The Great Chain of Being", they exist in continuous hierarchical order of every possible grade from the meagerest form of existence up to God. He helped establish the *Journal of the History of Ideas* in 1939-40 for the purpose of fostering the study of the development of ideas in their historical context.[93] In 1907, Lovejoy expressed an interest in Indian philosophy denoting:

> There is, in both Shankara and Ramanuja, not to mention other [Indian] systems, a great mass of interesting and instructive reasoning about

questions which still engage the attention of philosophers—about the nature and meaning of consciousness, about the relation of subject and object, about the paradoxical subtleties of self-consciousness. These reasonings are entirely capable of statement in intelligible occidental terms, and of profitable comparison with modern and even contemporary reflection upon the same subjects. Such a statement and such a comparison would be a noteworthy contribution to philosophy itself, as well as to the mutual understanding of East and West.[94]

After Swamiji's return to India, Sister Nivedita mentions him discussing the following at Almora in May 1898:

With this man [Vidyasagar], as one of the educators of Bengal, the Swami coupled the name of David Hare, the old Scotsman and atheist to whom the clergy of Calcutta refused Christian burial. He had died of nursing an old pupil through cholera. So his own boys carried his dead body and buried it in a swamp and made the grave a place of pilgrimage. That place has now become College Square, the educational centre, and his school is now within the university. And to this day Calcutta students make pilgrimage to the tomb.[95]

David Hare (1775-1842) came to Calcutta in 1800, becoming a successful watchmaker. Beginning in 1816, he devoted himself fulltime to philanthropic work. It was largely through his efforts that Hindu College was opened in 1817. It was the first respectable English seminary in Bengal, and was founded by many Hindus. The following year he founded the School Book Society for printing and publishing English and Bengali books. He also helped to bring about the repeal of regulations against the Press, and to introduce the trial by jury system. After his death, a life-size marble statue of him was erected in Calcutta by the people of the city.[96]

After returning to the U.S. in 1899, Swamiji spent several months in California. There he often associated with the loyal devotees and seldom with people of renown. After returning to Europe in March of 1900, Sister Nivedita wrote a letter to Swamiji about Professor Patrick Geddes (1854-1932), which he enjoyed reading.[97] According to his biographer Philip Boardman, Geddes and Vivekananda had formerly met in Chicago. The two men became acquainted in August 1900, and each morning Swamiji would walk and converse with Geddes on their way to the Paris Exposition. In September, they came together again at a party thrown by the Leggetts in Paris. Boardman mentions that as a result of his encounter with Vivekananda, "the eastern discipline of body and mind made such a lasting impression on both Anna (Geddes' wife) and Patrick that they later handed on to their young children the simple Raja Yoga exercises for control of the inner nature." These experiences deepened Geddes' interest in the land and soul of India. Sister Nivedita worked with Geddes for many weeks in Paris. The knowledge she gained through this experience helped her to write *The Web of Indian Life* (1904), which she dedicated to him. Geddes wrote a Preface to a French translation of Swamiji's *Raja Yoga* (1910).[98]

Sir Patrick Geddes, a Scottish sociologist, biologist, educator and town planner became a lecturer in botany and zoology at Edinburgh University (1880-88), a summer professor in botany at University College, Dundee (1888-1919), and the first professor of sociology and civics at the University of Bombay (1919-24). Among other things, in 1886 Geddes founded the Edinburgh Social Union for the purpose of cleaning up slum areas, became an organizer of the first summer schools in Europe at Edinburgh (1887-1898), initiator of rural industries in Cyprus (1897), designer of the new Hebrew University in Jerusalem (1919), establisher of Scots College (1924), and conceiver of a master plan for the city of Tel Aviv in Palestine. Geddes, whose first direct contact with Hinduism began with Swami Vivekananda, made a visit to India first in 1914. There he undertook a diagnosis-and-treatment survey of fifty Indian urban areas. He concluded that the traditional strategy of British planners in slum clearance disrupted community neighbourhood life and destroyed indigenous customs. In cooperation with his lasting friend Rabindranath Tagore, he worked on plans for an international university in India "to bring East and West together for the benefit of humanity". He wrote *The Life and Work of Sir Jagadis C. Bose* (1920), the famous physicist, and also made contact with Mahatma Gandhi and Annie Besant.[99]

At the Darjeeling Summer Meetings of 1917, Geddes and others gave a series of lectures and demonstrations on social and biological sciences in relation to Indian villages and towns and the surrounding forms of life. The *Prabuddha Bharata* praised Geddes' efforts by stating, "He has distinguished himself not only by his expert knowledge in town-planning, but also by his profound learning in all subjects connected with the betterment of human life on earth, and his selfless devotion to that cause." Swami Saradananda and Mrs. Geddes were members of the Executive Committee, and Turiyananda, Rabindranath Tagore, and Sir John Woodroffe served on the general committee for the meetings.[100]

Swamiji and others journeyed to Constantinople between October 30 and November 9, 1900. There he spoke on "Hinduism" at the American College for Girls at Scutari (now Usküdar). In her travel diary, Madame Calve noted down, "Departure for Scutari. Visit to Miss Patrick, the directress of the American College." In her own memoirs Mary Patrick mentions Swami Vivekananda and states that "We had a very enthusiastic audience" for the lecture, and that "The government officials of the city also paid great honour to our distinguished visitors," which included Pere Hyacinthe and his wife. The woman they met, Miss Mary Mills Patrick Ph.D. (1850-1940), an Irish-American Protestant, was the pioneer of education for women in the Near East. Being a magnanimous and sympathetic missionary and educator, she oversaw the evolution of a girls' high school into American College for Girls, a leading centre of higher education for women in Turkey. Earlier in the 1870s, she had ridden fully three-thousand miles on horseback to the villages in the Ararat region to open schools and encourage people to read. Knowing the Armenian, Greek and Turkish languages, she became principal of the school in 1889 that eventually took on the name Constantinople (later Istanbul) Woman's College. Until her retirement in 1924, she kept the College open, even during a major fire that caused the institution to be relocated, and during the Balkan Wars, World War I, and the Turkish revolution.[101]

In addition, Chapter VI discusses a number of university presidents and professors of theology and religious studies who were supportive of Vivekananda's efforts in the West. They include William Hastie, principal of the General Assembly's Institution in Calcutta and professor of Divinity at Glasgow University, John Henry Barrows, president of Oberlin College, Bishop John Keane, rector of the Catholic University of America, Charles Bradley, professor at the Garrett Biblical Institute of Northwestern University, Bishop Thomas Gailor, chancellor of the University of the South, Bishop William Xavier Ninde, past-president and professor of the Garrett Biblical Institute of Northwestern University, Rabbi Louis Grossmann, principal and professor at Hebrew Union College, Joseph Estlin Carpenter, principal and professor at Manchester College of Oxford University, and Charles Carroll Everett, dean of the Harvard Divinity School.

ENDNOTES

1 *Life*, I, pp. 46, 102, 107-08; *Reminiscences*, p. 134.

2 *Life*, I, pp. 45, 48, 52, 105, 107-08; Saradananda, V:3.17, p. 761; V:8.4, p. 831; "Life of the Swami Vivekananda (1912-13)" in *Swami Vivekananda: A Mental and Spiritual Biography*, ed. Rajagopal Chattopadhyaya (Barrackpore: Vivekananda Math, 2006), pp. 41-43, 48-49, 51-52, 148, 192, 206; WorldCat.

3 *CW*, I:182, 515; II:63-67, 170-71; IV:39, 200, 209; VI:101; VIII:206; IX:546.

4 Ibid., IV:438-47.

5 Ibid., VIII:54-55, 57, 62-63.

6 Chattopadhyaya (2006), pp. 239-40; Londhe, # 237, Sir Mountstuart Elphinstone.

7 Henry Buckle, *Introduction to the History of Civilization in England* (London: George Routledge, 1904); *CW*, III:269-70.

8 Chattopadhyaya (2006), pp. 191-92, 231; Life, I, pp. 46-48, 56, 117-18, 122.

9 *CW*, VII:278.

10 *CW*, III:469. According to M. L. Burke the "Episcopal church" referred to in the *Salem Evening News* was actually a Universalist Church (Burke, I, p. 51).

11 *CW*, V:20.

12 *Life*, I, pp. 405-06; Burke, I, pp. 19-20, 27, 51, 87.

13 *CW*, V:38-39; VIII:322.

14 Burke, II, pp. 41, 163, 171-72; IV, pp. 69-75, 95; Horner, pp. 20, 30, 66; *CW*, VII:449-57, 461, 465-70, 500; IX:52-53

15 *DAB* (1936), XX, pp. 556-57; *WWIA* (1908-09), p. 2117.

16 *CW*, VII:278-82.

17 Burke, I, pp. 29, 31-33; Elva Nelson, "Footnotes on Swami Vivekananda in Annisquam", *PB* (1979), pp. 251-52; *WWIA* (1940-41), p. 2672; *DAB* (1977), Sup. V, pp. 723-24; UCLC.

18 Nelson (1979), p. 252; Burke, I, p. 39; II, pp. 163-65.

19 *DAB* (1932), IX, pp. 446-47.

20 *Journal of Social Science* (Jan. 1894), pp. v-vi; Elisha Andrews, *DAB* (1928-1936).

21 *CW*, VI:381.

22 Ibid., IV:253-56.

23 William Hocking, "Recollections of Swami Vivekananda", *Vedanta and the West* 163 (1962), pp. 58-62.

24 Hocking (1962), pp. 58-62; Leroy Rouner, "Hocking and India", *Philosophy East and West* (1966), pp. 59-66; Tathagatananda2, p. 413; Centenary, I, p. 82.

25 *DAB* (1988), Sup. VIII, 1966-1970, pp. 265-66; *EWB*, VII, pp. 428-29.

26 Basu, pp. 12-14; Burke, I, pp. 85, 93; Testimonials to Swami Vivekananda. Web: www.namastebooks.com/testimonials.htm.

27 Burke, I, pp. 160-61; *PB* (Sept. 1933); (June 1936), p. 281. This event occurred sometime between 1893 and 1899 in Chicago.

28 *DAB* (1934), XIV, p. 221; *American Eras* (Detroit, Gale Research 1997), VIII; Nivedita, I, p. 312; Chaudhuri, pp. 164-65; Thomas, p. 199; Centenary, I, p. 10.

29 Burke, I, pp. 158, 185.

30 *EWB*, VIII, pp. 488-89.

31 *EWB*, VII, pp. 268-69.

32 UCLC.

33 *Chicago Daily Tribune* (Jan. 26, 1894), pp. 1, 8; (Jan. 21, 1894), p. 15; *EWB*, *DAB* (Bryan, Harper).

34 Chaudhuri1, pp. 171-72; *Life*, I, p. 451.

35 *New York Tribune* (April 7, 1894), p. 6 on CAM.

36 *CW*, II:488.

37 *DAB* (1928-36); Chaudhuri2, pp. 36-38.

38 *Reminiscences* pp. 139-42, *PB* (Sept. 1936).

39 *Boston Daily Globe* (April 20, 1894), p. 6; Hohner, pp. 21-22; *CW*, II:491-92.

40 Burke, II, p. 187; IV, pp. 76-77; *Life* (1965), I, p. 405; *DAB* (1928-1936) (James).

41 Datta, B., pp. 203-04; N. Timasheff, *Sociological Theory* (New York: Random House, 1967), pp. 74-82; *EWB*.

42 *CW*, VI:344.

43 Burke, III, pp. 222-23; Buckland, p. 156; *WWIE* (1922), p. 971; UCLC.

44 *Reminiscences*, pp. 296-97.

45 *Reminiscences*, pp. 296-98; *The Manchester Guardian* (June 10, 1910), p. 5; *Merriam-Webster's Biographical Dictionary* (Merriam-Webster, 1995) *Journal of the Royal Asiatic Society of Great Britain and Ireland* (1891, 1896).

46 Datta, Pt. I, Ch. III; *World of Mathematics* (Online) (Detroit: Thomson Gale, 2006).

47 *Life*, II, p. 132; Frederick Myers. Web: www.trans4mind.com/spiritual/myers1.html; The Frederick Myers Communication. Web: www.near-death.com/experiences/paranormal05.html; *EOP* (1984), II, pp. 917-19; *LBD*, p. 205.

48 *CW*, I:6-20.

49 Henry Coppee, *The Classic and the Beautiful from the Literature of Three Thousand Years* (Carson & Simpson, 1895, 1900), I, pp. 215-17; III, p. 489; *DAB* (1928-36).

50 Frank Parlato. Web: www.vivekananda.net/NewDiscoveries/ JB%20Street%20NewsArticles.html; Tathagatananda1, pp. 142, 158-59; Burke, III, pp. 518-20; *CWSA*, X, p. 26.

51 *CW*, V:277-79.

52 Ibid., I:357-65; IX:497-98.

53 Ibid., V:297-310.

54 Burke, IV, pp. 92, 551; *Life*, II, p. 76; *CW*, VI:436-37.

55 Burke, IV, pp. 554-56; Henry James, ed., *The Letters of William James* (Boston: Atlantic Monthly Press, 1920), II, p. 144.

56 William James, *Varieties of Religious Experience* (New York: Modern Library, 1929), p. 391; also in Swami Yatiswarananda, *Adventures in Religious Life* (Mylapore: Sri Ramakrishna Math, 1962), p. 120.

57 William James, *Pragmatism* (New York: Longmans, Green, 1940), pp. 151-54; "A letter from William James to Josephine MacLeod" (Aug. 8, 1900), VSSC Archives; *LBD*, p. 205.

58 Tathagatananda2, p. 416; E. Taylor, "Swami Vivekananda and William James", *PB* (Sept. 1986), pp. 383-84.

59 *PB* (Sept. 1986), p. 380; *DAB* (1928-36); *RLOA*; *Outlook* (Aug. 7, 1897), pp. 844-49.

60 William James, *The Energies of Men* (New York: Moffat, Yard, and Co., 1907, 1914), pp. 27-30; *VMB* (Nov. 1907), pp. 146-47.

61 Yatiswarananda (1962), pp. 288-89.

62 *DAB* (1932), IX, pp. 590-600; *EWB*, VIII, pp. 215-17; *CA* (2002), vol. 193. The Vivekananda-James relationship is also discussed in *Annals of the Bhandarkar Oriental Research* (1986), pp. 117-24; and *Vedanta and the West* (July-Aug. 1970), pp. 7-17.

63 Burke, II, pp. 187, 236; Bhagwan Singh, *The Self and the World in the Philosophy of Josiah Royce* (Springfield IL: Charles C Thomas, 1973), p. 147; *ERB*, pp. 334-35; *CWSA*, X, pp. 41-44; *Journal of the American Oriental Society* (1899), pp. 310-16.

64 Kurt Leidecker, *Josiah Royce and Indian Thought* (New York: Kailas Press, 1931), pp. 5-32; Stephen Hay, "Rabindranath Tagore in America", *American Quarterly* (1962), p. 456; Singh (1973), pp. 147-59.

65 Royce, I, pp. 159, 167, 170-71, 174-75.

66 Burke, IV, pp. 92, 95, 97.

67 *DAB* (1973), Sup. III, 1941-45, pp. 444-45; *ANB*, XIII, pp. 176-77; Prabuddhaprana, p. 110; 1911 Encyclopedia Britannica. Web: http://24.1911encyclopedia.org/L/LA/LANMAN_CHARLES_ROCKWELL.htm.

68 Basu, p. 531; *Swami Vivekananda and His Guru* (London: Christian Literature Society for India, 1897), p. 21; *Brahmavadin* (June 16, 1898); *DAB* (1932), VIII, pp. 127-30; Benjamin Beit-Hallahmi, "Psychology of Religion 1880-1930", *Journal of the History of Behavioural Sciences* (1974), pp. 85-86; Satyananda, p. 82.

69 *CW*, IV:280-82; VI:362; VIII:378.

70 Tathagatananda2, pp. 283-84.

71 *CW*, IV:409, 414-15; V:222; VI:362, 495.

72 Ibid., IV:274-75.

73 Londhe, #17. Max Müller.

74 *CW*, V:117; VIII:376.

75 Burke, IV, pp. 289-90.

76 Tathagatananda2, pp. 276, 279-80; Johannes Voigt, *Max Müller* (Calcutta: Firma K. L. Mukhopadhay, 1967), pp. 51, 95-97; Jean Sedlar, *India in the Mind of Germany* (University Press of America, 1982), p. 44.

77 Head, p. 160.

78 F. Max Müller, tr., *The Upanishads* (Delhi: Motilal Banarsidass, 1879, 1969), p. lxii; The Upanishads. Web: www.blackmask.com/ books27c/1upanishads.htm#4_0_1.

79 Radhakrishnan, II, p. 360; Londhe, #148. F. W. J. Schelling.

80 F. Max Müller, *Natural Religion* (London: Longmans, Green, (1889), pp. 17-18.

81 Voigt (1967), pp. 3-4.

82 *CW*, V:195.

83 Ibid., III:109.

84 Müller (1879, 1969), pp. lxiv-lxv.

85 For Schopenhauer's relation to Indian thought see: G. Stavig, "Shankara, Kant and Schopenhauer", *Darshana International* (Oct. 1999), pp. 17-35; G. Stavig, "Shankara, Kant and Schopenhauer on Reality and Phenomenality", *Vedanta Kesari* (Feb. 2003), pp. 62-67.

86 Londhe, #50. Paul Deussen; Valentina Stache-Rosen, *German Indologists* (New Delhi: Max Müller Bhavan, 1990), pp. 104-05.

87 *CW*, IV:272-77; V:114; VI:374, 376-77, VIII:388, 391-92.

88 *Life*, II, pp. 123-27; Burke, IV, pp. 281-85, 304, 390.

89 Tathagatananda2, pp. 289-90; Stache-Rosen (1990), pp. 104-05.

90 Hans Rollmann, "Deussen, Nietzsche, and Vedanta", *Journal of the History of Ideas*, (1978), pp. 125-32; Wilhelm Halbfass, *India and Europe* (Delhi: Motilal Banarsidass, 1988), pp. 128-29; Tathagatananda2, pp. 298-300.

91 Basu, pp. 176-77; *Life*, II, pp. 209-10.

92 *WWWA* (1960), III, p. 531; Burke, IV, pp. 91-92, 97; James Edwin Lough Web: www.clements.umich.edu/Webguides/L/Lough.html; Semester at Sea. Web: www.semesteratsea.com/aboutus/historyofship_begin.htm.

93 *DAB* (1981), Sup. VII, pp. 480-83.

94 *The Journal of Philosophy, Psychology and Scientific Methods* (Jan. 3, 1907), pp. 23-24.

95 *CW*, IX:350.

96 Bhattacharya, pp. 407-08; *IHP*, p. 192.

97 *CW*, VI:430.

98 Burke, VI, pp. 286-87, 325, 327-28, 331-32, 346-47, 366; Atmaprana (1961), pp. 110-11, 113; *PB* (Mar. 1986), pp. 129-35.

99 *EWB*, VI, pp. 246-47; Patrick Geddes in India. Web: www.patrickgeddes.co.uk; Jacqueline Tyrwhitt, ed., *Patrick Geddes in India* (London: L. Humphries, 1947). The Patrick Geddes archives are located at Strathclyde University in Glasgow.

100 *PB* (May 1917), pp. 90-91.

101 *PB* (April 1977), p. 192; Hohner, pp. 115-17; *DAB*, Sup. 1-2; Web: www.britannica.com/EBchecked/topic/.../Mary-Mills Patrick; Mary Patrick, *A Bosporus Adventure* (Stanford University Press, 1934), p. 105.

CHAPTER IX

MUSICIANS, ACTRESSES AND ARTISTS

BEFORE ATTENDING the Parliament of Religions in September of 1893, Swami Vivekananda spoke at the home of Alpheus Hyatt [q.v.], a zoology and paleontology professor at Boston University living in Annisquam, Massachusetts. The following year Swamiji returned to Annisquam in August, taking part in a clambake and boating with the Hyatt family. Many years later, Hyatt's daughter Anna Hyatt Huntington (1876-1973) spoke of these events. She was a teenager at the time and described Swamiji as "a very colourful figure". From an early age Anna Hyatt acquired her father's knowledge of anatomy and behaviour of animals, and her mother's enthusiasm for drawing. Being active for a period of seventy years, Huntington is recognized today as one of America's foremost animal sculptors, and is particularly remembered for her equestrian statues. With three and half tons of clay, Huntington produced a life-sized award-winning statue of Joan of Arc on horseback. Along with her wealthy husband, she helped to found nearly twenty museums and wildlife preserves, as well as America's first modern sculpture garden, the Brookgreen Gardens in South Carolina. Huntington's originality in technique and display as revealed in her aluminium statues at Brookgreen Gardens assures her a place in the annals of art history. In 1923 she married Archer Milton Huntington, the son of Arabella Huntington, a wealthy San Francisco admirer of Vivekananda, who gave five-thousand dollars to Sister Nivedita for her Girls' School in India. Anna Hyatt Huntington's mother Ardella Hyatt (1839-1932) painted landscapes, and painted and sketched diagrams for the books on paleontology written by her husband Alpheus Hyatt. Anna's elder sister Harriet Hyatt Mayor (1868-1960), a proficient sculptor of portrait busts, reliefs, and commemorative metals, often worked with her sister in such places as Brookgreen Gardens.[1]

In 1893 Miss Emma Thursby (1845-1931) was a member of the "Advisory Council of the World's Congress of Representative Women" at the World's

Columbian Exposition in Chicago, and there she, the soprano soloist, was employed as a professional singer. Her biographer Richard Gibson adds:

> There at the "Parliament of Religions" she met the Hindu monk, Swami Vivekananda, whose teachings henceforth became a very real and active influence in her life, since they appeared to her to approach more nearly the ideal of spiritual conduct than any other teachings she had known.

Over the years Thursby made many contacts with Swamiji, attending his New York lectures in early May of 1894. At Greenacre, Maine, in July and August she kept miscellaneous notes of Swamiji's daily morning classes, which fortunately have been preserved.[2] During the Cambridge Conferences held in December, Thursby sang a series of inspiring songs at the opening and closing of each class, with the accompaniment of Wulf Fries, a noted violoncellist. In early 1895, Vivekananda held a discussion class in the parlour of Thursby's residence in New York, and they met later in the year.[3] When Swamiji returned to the U.S. in 1899, she visited Ridgely Manor. During the upcoming winter, Swamiji "sent the letter of introduction from Miss Thursby to Mrs. [Phoebe Apperson] Hearst", a wealthy Northern California admirer of Swami Vivekananda.[4] They were together again in Paris in August of 1900. On at least four occasions Swami Abhedananda spoke with Thursby during 1898 and 1899, whom he described as being an admirer of Vivekananda. In 1908 she spent some days with Sister Nivedita in New York.[5]

Emma Thursby's soprano voice had a remarkable range—from middle C to F above the staff. Beginning in 1865, she was a soprano soloist appearing in concerts and oratorios at many prominent churches. With her appearance at the London Philharmonic in France, and also before many political rulers, she attained international reputation. She had however turned down an offer to sing at the Paris Opera (1878-79). It is reported that Kaiser Wilhelm (1859-1941) always considered the German National Anthem to be the most beautiful until he heard Emma Thursby sing "The Star Spangled Banner". She performed with the Norwegian violinist Ole Bull (1810-80) during his last American tour in 1879. The husband of Sara Bull, Ole Bull became a good friend of hers. Thursby was the principal concert soloist for the German conductor Theodore Thomas (1835-1905), who later became the first director of the Chicago Symphony Orchestra in 1883. After 1898 she became a successful voice teacher, and a professor at the Institute of Musical Art in New York City (1905-11). Until her death she associated with many of the most talented figures in the musical world, along with foreign dignitaries like Rabindranath Tagore.[6]

Vivekananda came across Prince Serge Wolkonsky (Volkonsky, 1860-1937), the unofficial representative of the Russian Church at the Parliament of Religions. They became friends, and for some time maintained an active correspondence. Wolkonsky made this statement on October 30, 1893 concerning his impressions of America, which appeared in the *St. Louis (Missouri) Republic* the following day:

> The great value of the religious congress was that these people learned to know a man. There was one man there the embodiment of spirituality! I do not know what church he belonged to. He thinks and acts and speaks as a Christian. But you say he is not a Christian. So much the better. You say he is a Buddhist. Better still. If you belong to a higher religion you should try to be better still than he.

Marie Louise Burke remarked, "There can be no doubt that Wolkonsky was referring to Swamiji, who was often called a Buddhist."[7]

Years later the Prince told Albert Spalding that Swamiji "Made a—what do you call it?—a sensational 'hit' in your country." They made contact again in Chicago in 1896 at the opera "Il Trovatore". Volkonsky had earlier learned of India as a student of the eminent Russian Indologist I. P. Minaev (1840-90), and consequently maintained an ardent interest in the spiritual life of Asian societies. Years later he delivered lectures in American universities on the history of Russian culture. Volkonsky introduced the Dalcroze rhythmic into Russian ballet. In St. Petersburg he set up the Rhythmic Gymnastics courses and put out a journal. After 1917 Volkonsky became one of the organizers of the Rhythmic Institute in Moscow and taught in many schools and studios. After leaving Russia in 1921, he settled in Paris. For years he made contributions to a Russian newspaper, worked as the principal of the Russian Conservatoire and as a popular teacher in many ballet schools.[8]

An afternoon dinner party was held at the home of Dr. Egbert Guernsey during April 1894, probably on the 29th. According to the plan each of the fourteen participants at the dinner table represented a different religious creed. A lively discussion followed. One of the fourteen participants was the then famous American actress Minnie Maddern Fiske (1865-1932), who was staying with the Guernseys at that time. It is said she made her first stage appearance at the age of three under the name of "Little Minnie Maddern", and as a child actress the critics described her as "a wonder". As an adult stage actress, she had no peers in comedy and was also quite successful in drama. She was devoted to a number of humane causes throughout her life, particularly opposing cruelty to animals.[9]

Clara Kathleen Rogers (1844-1931) was an English born singer, author and composer. Using the stage-name Clara Doria, she sang soprano roles in operas in Italy, London, New York, Boston and Philadelphia from 1863 to 1873. In addition, she was the composer of many songs, author of numerous educational books on the art of singing, and producer of a three-volume autobiography during 1893-1927. In 1902 she became the professor of singing at the New England Conservatory of Music.[10]

She attended at least one of Vivekananda's lectures in Boston at the residence of Mrs. Charles Fairchild during October and December 1894. Rogers tells us that Swamiji "was a good speaker, with a fine command of our language, and a host of women of all ages and dimensions sat at his feet and hung on his words." Prior to that time, Mrs. Edwin Waters wrote to the Theosophical Society in London asking whether they would send Mohini Chatterji (Chatterjee), a young Brahmin, originally a barrister from Calcutta, to their city. They complied, and for a year Mohini lived as a guest at the house of Mr. and Mrs. Edwin Waters in the Boston area. During 1886-87 Mohini taught Hindu philosophy in the New England area to prominent people like Sara Bull, Clara Rogers, Celia Thaxter, and Julia Ward Howe, later a member of the National Women's Hall of Fame for great Americans. Celia Thaxter (1835-1894) was a frequent contributor of poems, sketches, and children's stories to various magazines. Her appreciation of poetry, painting and music, and her childlike joy for nature endeared her to many friends. After she was deceased, Swami Abhedananda saw a picture of Mohini in her house.[11] Clara Rogers wrote:

> I have never met anybody who impressed me as such a pure and selfless creature as Mohini Chatterji.... One felt at once that all mundane desires were remote from him, that the only interest or sympathy he felt for others was where they touched him in his higher vision.... He was both kind, sympathetic, and helpful.[12]

In a letter to Sara Bull dated March 26, 1897, Swamiji stated, "Mr. [Mohini] Chatterji came to see me in Calcutta, and he was very friendly. I gave him your message. He is quite willing to work with me."[13] When introducing Sister Nivedita at the Star Theatre in Calcutta on March 11, 1898, Vivekananda mentioned:

> I take this opportunity of reminding you of the name of one of our countrymen—one who has seen England and America, one in whom I have great confidence, and whom I respect and love, and who would have been present here but for an engagement elsewhere—a man working steadily and silently for the good of our country, a man of great spirituality—I mean Mr. Mohini Mohan Chatterji.[14]

Josephine MacLeod wrote to Mohini about Swamiji. His reply to her in a letter dated September 29, 1898 was:

> I am very glad to have your letter. What you say about the Swami as a public teacher is highly interesting. I am sure his published thoughts so far as I know, give a very inadequate notion of his life and mission. So far I have only seen him as a gifted interpreter of the scriptures, a popularizer of abstruse theological ideas. Surely such a personage can scarcely be imagined to be the vehicle for the pouring out of such vitalizing influences as you describe.[15]

A few years later, Clara Rogers and Phoebe Hearst, the mother of newspaper tycoon William Randolph Hearst who met Vivekananda in San Francisco, made a trip to India. They began their tour in South India and, after visiting several cities, separated in Benares. During January 1904, Rogers then met with her old friend Mohini Chatterji in Calcutta. Because of Mohini's desire and initiative, he took Rogers to the "monastery founded by Swami Vivekananda" on the Hooghly River. "Out of deference to so distinguished a personage as Mohini, we were well received and entertained by the priests and brotherhood." Clara Rogers tells us of her visit:

> [Mohini] showed us the place on the riverbank within the monastery grounds where his [Vivekananda's] body was cremated, and the enclosure where his ashes were buried in Ganges mud.... We were received with great courtesy by the Brahmins, all of whom came to greet us before we left.... One of the Brahmins, a pupil or chela of Vivekananda, spoke English quite well, and we had a good talk on serious matters.... They took me into Vivekananda's room, where everything had been left just as it was when he

> occupied it, even to his yellow robe hanging over the clotheshorse. It was touching to see with what reverence they approached it. They offered us tea, and, on our declining it, brought us Indian fruits, sweets, and a cup of water. Before leaving they gathered for me a bunch of wonderful roses, rare specimens, and, as we went down the steps to the boat, these yellow-robed brothers all came out on the *loggia* to wave us farewell. It was a goodly sight, and I went away with a sense of sweetness and repose which these refined, courteous Brahmins had left with me.

In a 1912 letter from Mohini Chatterji to Josephine MacLeod, the former revealed, "The Swamiji is gone, Mrs. Bull our Saint and lastly the radiant Nivedita.... I feel the loss of Nivedita greatly not only personally but for the cause of enlightenment."[16]

In his autobiography *Rise to Follow*, the famous violinist Albert Spalding (1888-1953) wrote:

> Once an Indian Swami came to dinner. He was none other than the renowned Vivekananda. Aunt Sally found him fascinating, though she could never quite see the exalted spirituality that his fleet of admirers claim for him.... My family had been acquainted with the Swami and had often talked about him.

Swamiji mentions going to the Spalding residence in New York City on more than one occasion in the latter part of 1894. Mrs. Marie Spalding was kind to him.[17] Albert's mother Marie Boardman Spalding, who was closest to Swamiji, was a gifted musician. Her husband James Walter Spalding (1856-1931) was a wealthy business executive. He and his brother, who was a professional baseball hall of famer, cofounded A. G. Spalding & Brothers, the most successful and affluent manufacturer and seller of sporting goods in the world. Their son Albert Spalding was unquestionably the first American violinist to gain a major international reputation. He taught classes at the Julliard School of Music in New York City, Boston University College of Music, and at the University of Florida. As a composer, he is rated as the third most productive violinist among his contemporaries. During World War II, Colonel Albert Spalding worked as a director of psychological warfare operations in North Africa and Italy, and is credited with saving thousands of lives.[18]

A young Harry Franklin Waltman (1871-1951) lodged at Miss Mary Phillips' boarding house at 19 W. 38th Street. According to his diary during his first day in New York City on November 18, 1894, he became acquainted with "Swami Vivekananda, the Indian Prince, the representative of the religion of the Hindus." Two days later Waltman did a portrait of Vivekananda. He noted, "Quite a wonderful model, in fact, never saw a finer one. Like him very much. Took a rather bold pose, head back and one hand in belt with right hand in robe near the right shoulder." The next day he went to Guernsey's house at 528 5th Avenue, but could not locate the Swami. On the 23rd and the 27th Swamiji posed for the picture, which he then completed. Waltman met Emma Thursby, Miss Haydock, Dr. Guernsey and others when Vivekananda gave talks on the 25th and December 2nd. Waltman later became a successful lifetime professional artist winning several prestigious awards, among them the Isido Prize. He worked as a portrait painter in England and the United States, and his sitters included the highly regarded musician John Philip Sousa and Senator Joseph Cannon.[19]

Swamiji mentioned Mrs. Milward (Florence James) Adams (1860/61-1910) in nineteen letters in the *Complete Works* written from December 1894 to May 1900 to members of the Hale family, Emma Thursby, Sara Bull, Mrs. Leggett, and Sister Nivedita. He often sent his love to her and the rest of his friends in Chicago. Swamiji became acquainted with her at the Cambridge Conferences and wrote to Mrs. G. W. Hale in December 1894, "Mrs. M. Adams of Chicago, who lectures on voice building and walking etc., has been lecturing here all this time. She is a very great lady in every respect and so intelligent. She knows all of you and likes the 'Hale girls' very much." Less than one month later he wrote to Emma Thursby from Chicago, "I have been lecturing every day to a class in Mrs. Adams' rooms at the Auditorium.... Mrs. Adams invited me to an organ concert in the Auditorium. She is so good and kind to me. Lord bless her."[20] Her husband Milward Adams (1857-1923) was the theatrical manager of the Chicago Auditorium, the grandest private building for public use in the country. Eight days in a row, Vivekananda lectured in her studio in the Fine Arts building during April 1896. She was a well-known teacher of charm, glamour, calisthenics and gymnastics to the debutantes of society. Her biographer Joseph Milburn described her as a "priestess of the cult of beauty". In her studio, "the dowagers and debutantes of society, rich in all the externalities that wealth commands, but sometimes deficient in the fine inheritance of the amenities, have been invested with the department that compels admiration and taught the treasured secrets of the ways that charm." Her clientele included actresses like Ethel Barrymore (who later met Swami Prabhavananda) and singers like Antoinette Sterling, an admirer of Swamiji.[21]

Miss Josephine C. Locke (1851-1920) of Chicago attended the Greenacre Conference in July-August 1894, where Swamiji came into prominence. Her name would occasionally show up in the letters of Swamiji over the 1895-96 period. Like Florence Adams, she arranged classes for the Swami in Chicago. In a correspondence addressed from Chicago to Emma Thursby in January 1895, he wrote, "Today I also lecture there and in the evening to a class of Miss Josephine Locke's at the Plaza Hotel.... Miss Locke is as kind as usual."[22] To members of the Hale family in Chicago, Swamiji mentioned, "Sister Locke writes me a long letter and perhaps wondering at my delay in reply. She is apt to be carried away by enthusiasm; so I am waiting, and again I do not know what to answer. Kindly tell her from me that it is impossible for me to fix any place just now," "Give my love to Sam and sister Locke," "Please tell Miss Locke that I was mistaken when I told her that sculpturing of the human figure was not developed in India as among the Greeks."[23] In correspondences addressed to Sara Bull from New York City, Swamiji asked, "Have you seen Josephine Locke?" "If you think after consultation with Mrs. Adams and Miss Locke that it would be practicable for me to come to Chicago for a course of lectures, write to me," "Miss Locke will see to my having classes in Chicago."[24] She attended a party for Swamiji in the last week of November 1899 before he embarked for Southern California. Born in Ireland, Miss Josephine C. Locke became a supervisor of art in the public schools of Chicago (1891-1900). As a teacher and a supervisor of other art teachers, she developed a free expression method by encouraging school children to draw what they felt like portraying. She was honoured posthumously in 1967, when they named the Locke school (kindergarten through the eighth grade) in Chicago after her.[25]

1895 and After

At the residence of the wealthy Amzi L. Barber, Miss Rose Anthon sang on the occasion of Vivekananda's talk on "Vedanta Philosophy" before a high-class New York audience on February 28, 1895. This is probably the singing actress Rose Reinhardt Anthon. She later became a disciple of Baba Premananda Bharati (1858-1914) [q.v.], a Bengali Vaishnava monastic and religious teacher. He came to teach Indian religion in New York City in

1902, and made some contact with Abhedananda. Bharati claimed to have over five-thousand followers in the U.S. His supporters included some of Swamiji's admirers like Ella Wheeler Wilcox, Benjamin Fay Mills, Christina Albers, and Count Leo Tolstoy in Russia. After Anthon became a follower of Bharati, a previously unknown writing talent emerged from within her. In New Delhi in 2001, *Stories of India*, a book she wrote in 1906, was reprinted. Anthon came with Bharati to India to work for his organization. On the way to India they received a warm reception from Swamis Trigunatita and Prakashananda in San Francisco in July of 1907. Anthon described Bharati as "a good friend to me, and a man of bigger heart, broader sympathies and greater soul it has never been my fortune to meet." After his death in 1914, his organization died out due to lack of a capable successor.[26]

Also in attendance at Amzi Barber's house for Swamiji's talk was Baxter Upham (1820-1902), the president of the Boston Music Hall Association (1854-84), the chairman of the committee on music in the Boston Public Schools (1857-72), and the chairman of the Handel and Haydn Society (1860-70). Upham also wrote books on fever epidemics and sanitary conditions in the state of Massachusetts (1862-74).[27]

A young ten-year old Malvina Hoffman (1885-1966), who eventually became an internationally acclaimed sculptor, met Vivekananda in August 1895. The incident took place when her mother brought her to meet Mary Phillips, a relative of her father. Mary lived in a modest boardinghouse at 19 West 38th Street in New York City. In 1943 Malvina described the unforgettable event this way:

> His dark eyes hardly glanced up to notice his neighbours, but there was a sense of tranquility and power about him [Swamiji] that made an imperishable impression upon me. He seemed to personify the mystery and religious "aloofness" of all true teachers of Brahma, and combined with this a kindly and gentle attitude of simplicity towards his fellowmen.

Malvina visited Swamiji's temple at Belur Math in 1931. Twelve years later she described the event this way:

> When I offered the garland of jasmine to be laid on the altar, I recalled, with emotion, that the only time I had seen this holy man, he had revealed to me more of the true spirit of India, without even uttering a word, than I

had ever sensed in the many lectures on India, or by Indians, which I had attended since.[28]

One of America's foremost sculptors, Malvina Cornell Hoffman is best known for her monumental bronze series, "The Races of Mankind". It was commissioned in 1929 by the Field Museum of Natural History in Chicago. Over a three-year period, she formed over one-hundred inspiring bronze ethnographic sculptures of people representing the various sub-races of the world. Her works can be found in many leading galleries and museum of fine arts. The prestigious American Association of University Women chose her as the 1957 Woman of the Year.[29]

In 1950, Swami Nikhilananda (1895-1973), Minister of the Ramakrishna-Vivekananda Centre of New York, asked Malvina Hoffman to create a bronze sculpture of Vivekananda. She added:

> I still recall his dark handsome face framed in a saffron turban and his spirit that radiated power through his luminous eyes. I sensed a rare privilege to be speaking with him and to hear the compassionate voice of a holy man from faraway India. This impression of his appearance never faded, and helped me to achieve an authentic likeness, which is now placed at the Vedanta Centre in East Ninety-fourth Street.[30]

The next year she formed an alabaster bust of Sri Ramakrishna, which "is the central figure on the altar of the Centre's chapel", and a bronze sculpture of Holy Mother in 1953. All three are found in the chapel of the New York Centre. Hoffman explained, "I felt both appreciative and dedicated and I did the best I could for them." Swami Prabhavananda thought so highly of the Vivekananda statue at the Ramakrishna-Vivekananda Centre in New York that he commissioned a copy of it to be made for the monastery in Trabuco, California. They installed the 420-pound bronze cast statue of Swamiji in the courtyard, with a lily pond in front of it and a sweeping view of the valley and hills behind. In November 1951 at the Vedanta Society in Portland, Oregon, they dedicated a life-size bronze sculpture of Vivekananda designed by Hoffman. At that centre there is also a bronze statue of Sri Ramakrishna created by Malvina Hoffman.[31]

Mrs. Antoinette Sterling (1843-1904) attended Vivekananda's classes in New York in December 1895, and she was "very much interested in the work".[32] Swami Vivekananda was the honoured guest at the Procopeia

(Progress) Club in Boston on March 19, 1896. The programme included illustrious special musical guests like Antoinette Sterling, Emma Thursby, Wulf Fries and John Orth. When announcing the event, the *Boston Daily Globe* (March 20) disclosed:

> The Swami is not unknown in Boston, having many friends whom he gained while fulfilling his previous engagements in the city. His powerful presentation of Hindoo religion as the Hindoo delegate to the Parliament of Religions also brought him prominently before the American public.... The idea which has made his teaching unique, and given it its great power in this and any other country in which he has worked, is that to make religion universal we must not get to work to reduce the number of sects, but rather to increase them.[33]

The day following Vivekananda's famous speech on "The Vedanta Philosophy" at Harvard University delivered on the 25th of March, a late afternoon tea reception was held at Sara Bull's house with Sterling being present along with Emma Thursby, the Leggetts and others. They met on the street in London in October 1896, and the following month after a period of absence she was present for his lecture in London.[34]

The American born Antoinette Sterling was an acclaimed contralto ballad-singer particularly in the 1870s and 1880s. Her voice had exceptional strength, volume and purity of tone. Sterling sang before Queen Victoria, and the Emperor and Empress of Germany. She lived in London, but also made musical tours of the U.S. Musicians like Arthur Sullivan (of Gilbert and Sullivan fame) composed many songs for her. Being a deeply religious woman, she associated with many philanthropic activities. Her son, Malcolm Sterling MacKinlay (1876-1952), wrote her biography. He was involved in many aspects of the musical world, and his daughter became a very popular novelist.[35]

An expert pianist, organist and composer, John Orth (1850-1932) is mentioned above as being a musician at the Vivekananda lecture in March 1896. In Germany he studied under Franz Liszt (1811-86), the Hungarian composer and pianist. John Orth published a number of teaching pieces for the piano. He regularly attended Paramananda's lectures in Boston. In a 1916 speech given at the seventh anniversary meeting of the Vedanta Society, Orth described Paramananda's lectures stating:

> We hear the fundamentals of life, the foundations of all real attainment explained and set forth in a simple yet masterful manner. It has always seemed to me the greater the Master, the simpler his language. Our leader here is only another exemplification of this fact. We also learn breadth of view.

Four years later at the annual dinner, Orth "spoke with deep appreciation of his debt to the Boston Centre and of the inspiration it had given him in his humanitarian work."[36]

Frank Parlato on the Internet has reproduced a sketch of Vivekananda drawn by a young Bertha Corbett. He informs us that it was drawn in December 1895 and appeared in the first edition of Sister Nivedita's *Notes of Some Wanderings with Swami Vivekananda* (1913). Bertha Corbett Melcher (1872-1950) is credited as being the creator of the Sunbonnet design, which depicted young girls with their face hidden by their bonnets. In the early 1900s, she illustrated school primers written by Eulalie Grover. Their books were widely read by children across the nation. Her designs were very popular and could be found on postcards, china and other items of the times. She also lectured and worked for the better treatment of both the homeless and children who lived in homes.*[37]

According to the *New York Herald* account, Sarah Bernhardt (1844-1923)

> has added "Izeyl" [based on a legend of Buddha] to her repertoire, has taken a profound interest in Hindoo mythology and the occult sciences of the East, and she was extremely anxious to converse with the well-known expounder of the religion of the Far East [Swami Vivekananda].

While in New York City, Swamiji went to see the French play "Izeyl" and related, "Madame [Bernhardt] spying me in the audience wanted to have an interview with me."[38] On February 5, 1896, the wealthy Austin Corbin family arranged a special party where the two would meet, along with Nikola Tesla, Victor Maurel, and other prominent guests. With the aid of an interpreter, Bernhardt, the Swami and others conversed in a lengthy discussion on Hindu philosophy. The event went on for several hours, and they became friends.

---

* Prints of her works can be purchased through the Internet.

In August 1900 when Swamiji went to Paris, he saw Bernhardt in the play "l'Aiglon". He wrote at that time in his memoirs:

> Madame Bernhardt has a special regard for India; she tells me again and again that our country is "*tres ancien, tres civilise*"—very ancient and very civilized.... Madame Bernhardt has a very strong desire to visit India.—"C est mon rave!—It is the dream of my life," she says.[39]

The career of "The Divine Sarah" Bernhardt, the most acclaimed stage actress of her time, spanned a period of over sixty years (1861-1923). Elite writers like Racine, Moliere, Sand, Dumas pere, Hugo, Zola and Rostand were the authors of Bernhardt's plays. In his play *Alexander the Great*, Jean Baptiste Racine (1639-99) portrays the Indian King Porus as equal to Alexander, and Alexandre Dumas (1802-70) praised India and the Indian people in *Les Mohicans de Paris*. Victor Hugo (1802-85) read with enthusiasm the *Asiatic Researches* of the Royal Asiatic Society of Bengal, and the works of its founder, the early English Indologist Sir William Jones (1746-94). In "Supremate", a poem in his *Legend of the Ages*, Hugo versified the narrative portion of the *Kena Upanishad*.[40] Bernhardt also excelled in playing male roles like Hamlet. Due to her eccentric and extravagant lifestyle, the public took great interest in her off-stage activities. Bernhardt being a cultured lady, wrote a number of plays in which she appeared, her memoirs, two novels, and essays on the theatre, set up her own theatre in Paris in 1899, and displayed talent as a painter and sculptress. During the Franco-Prussian War in 1870, she established a military hospital for wounded soldiers, and during World War I, gave money and took part in fund-raising activities to support the war effort. When she passed away, tens of thousands of people followed her funeral procession.[41]

Swamiji tells us concerning the party arranged by the Corbin family, "There were besides Madame [Bernhardt], M. Maurel, the celebrated singer, also the great electrician Tesla. Madame is a very scholarly lady and has studied up the metaphysics a good deal. M. Maurel was being interested."[42] The *New York Herald* of February 9, 1896 also mentions M. Victor Maurel as being a guest at the party. Maurel (1848-1923), the French baritone, was at that time singing at the Metropolitan Opera House. Over his lifetime he enjoyed a long international career as the lead singer in operas, appearing in St. Petersburg, Cairo, Naples, Venice, Paris, London and New York. Maurel wrote books on singing and staging operas. A critic intuited, "His art was intellectual, reflective, analytical, subtle, even hypnotically masterful at times. But it was the art of a mind ceaselessly active, enquiring, unsatisfied."[43]

For eight days in a row in April 1896 Vivekananda probably gave morning classes in the studio of Mrs. Florence Adams, and evening classes in the house of H. S. Perkins in Chicago. Vivekananda might have lived at Perkins' residence, since at that time the Swami dispatched two letters from Perkins' address at 1628 Indiana Avenue.[44] Henry Southwick Perkins (1833-1914) held the joint positions of professor of music at the University of Iowa (1867-69) and director of the National Academy of Music in Iowa City (1867-72). He became the president of the Illinois Music Teachers Association (1886-96) and held many positions with the Music Teachers National Association (1887-97). After founding the Chicago National College of Music, he became its director (1891-1914) and a noted music critic for the newspapers. In addition, he actively directed music festivals and conventions across the country. Perkins edited about thirty songbooks and composed a great deal of vocal music for choirs, public schools and Sunday schools.[45]

Second Visit to the West

A young artist with a highly entertaining and amusing personality, Miss Maud Stumm (1870-1935) came across Swamiji in Paris in September 1895 when Francis and Betty Leggett were getting married. They met again at a party given by Betty Leggett at the Metropolitan Club in New York a year later. But it was after he had returned to the United States and lodged at Ridgely Manor during August-September 1899 that she really got to know Swamiji. According to her later recollections:

> Nearly every day Swami was wonderful in a new way; and now it would be music he dwelt upon, now art.... With his flame-coloured robes draped about him, what a figure he was as he strode the lawns of Ridgely! His stride came nearer to the poet's description of a 'step that spurned the earth' than anything I ever expect to see again; and there was a compelling majesty in his presence and carriage that could not be imitated or described.

Stumm did a pastel of Swamiji and gave him some drawing lessons. After four lessons, Vivekananda drew portraits of Turiyananda and Nivedita that no longer exist.[46]

Maud Stumm studied art under Oliver Merson in Paris. Her figure paintings were quite popular at the Paris Salon, and were approved by the famous artist James Whistler (1834-1903). Some of her calendars sold nearly half a million copies. As an illustrator, Stumm depicts a kind of elegant but active young American beauty, a popular subject of illustrated magazine covers and prints during the first quarter of the twentieth century. Her paintings are in oil, watercolour and pastel. Stumm specialized in female portraits that include women engaged in outdoor activities. She did a series of portraits called "Eminent Actresses of Our Times" for Sarah Bernhardt, Lily Langtry, Julia Marlowe, and other prominent people of her day. The Society of American Artists and the American Water-Colour Society exhibited her works. Along with Anne Congdon, she cofounded the Nantucket (MA) Sidewalk Art Show.*[47]

The world famous French opera singer Madam Emma Calve (1858-1942) [q.v.] made contact with Vivekananda in Chicago on 28 November 1899 (and possibly at an earlier date) when she made a tour with the Metropolitan Opera Company. In a travel diary Madame Calve noted (on an unknown date) that Swami Vivekananda "is at the moment in New York, at the home of my friend Mrs. Leggett. I would like to know him." The Leggetts were married in September 1895 and Swamiji did not return to New York until the following December, which is the earliest date on which this entry could have been written. Swamiji wrote on 30 November 1899, "She is a great woman. I wish I saw more of her."[48] Swami Saradananda had the pleasure of making her acquaintance in Boston during the summer of 1897. She and Vivekananda met again in Paris in 1900 and travelled with Josephine MacLeod and Jules Bois on the Orient Express to Constantinople, Turkey, and then by ship to Cairo, Egypt.[49] Calve wrote in her diary of 1900:

> To live close to the Swami is a perpetual source of inspiration; we live in an intense spiritual atmosphere. For him every occasion inspires parables, quotations, ranging from Hindu mythology to the profoundest philosophy. Sometimes he is gay, full of fun, ready with rapid repartee, joking and laughing like a child. He is inexhaustible in telling us interesting stories. He possesses a voice like a cello, with low vibration that one cannot forget, and which fills both lecture halls and hearts.[50]

* Her chromolithograph prints can be purchased today through the Internet.

In her autobiography she later stressed:

> It has been my good fortune and my joy to know a man who truly "walked with God", a noble being, a saint, a philosopher, and a true friend. His influence upon my spiritual life was profound. He opened up new horizons before me, enlarging and vivifying my religious ideas and ideals, teaching me a broader understanding of truth. My soul will bear him an eternal gratitude.[51]

At one time Swamiji casually requested her to visit India. In 1910 she underwent a long singing tour in India, covering Madras, Calcutta, Darjeeling, Delhi, Agra and Bombay. She visited the Vivekananda Society of Calcutta headed by Purnachandra Ghosh (1871-1913), an *ishvarakoti*.* As a group they received her at the Grand Hotel, presented her with pictures of Ramakrishna and Vivekananda, and arranged for her journey to Belur Math. Madame Calve wrote about her visit to Belur Math on December 2, 1910:

> Years later, when I was travelling in India, I wished to visit the convent where the Swami had spent his last days. His mother [Bhuvaneswari Devi, 1841-1911] took me there. I saw the beautiful marble tomb that one of his American friends, Mrs. Leggett, had erected over his grave [where he was cremated].... The monks of the Swami's brotherhood received us with simple, kindly hospitality. They offered us flowers and fruits, spreading a table for us on the lawn beneath a welcomed shade.... The afternoon passed in a peaceful, contemplative calm. The hours that I spent with these gentle philosophers have remained in my memory as a time apart. These beings, pure, beautiful, and remote, seemed to belong to another universe, a better and wiser world.

Swami Saradananda escorted her around Belur Math. One of Swamiji's disciples asked her if she would sing a song as an offering to Sri Ramakrishna. Her marvellous voice charged the atmosphere with splendour. She also sang a delightful song to please Holy Mother who was not present at that time.[52]

---

* Unlike the ordinary individual soul who takes birth in bondage, an *ishvarakoti* is one who is eternally free and accompanies the Incarnation to be a helpmate in His spiritual mission.

Twenty years later, after reading Rolland's biography of Vivekananda, Madame Calve wrote to the author, "Vivekananda was to me the Saviour." Rolland replied on 4 April 1930, "How happy I am that my book did not in any way disappoint the eyes which had the good fortune to see the great Swami [Vivekananda] and to retain devotedly his image."[53]

The great French Soprano (with a Spanish father), Madam Emma Calve was among the most talented singers of her generation, a dramatic actress, and a notable personality. Her portrayals of Santuzza and Carmen at Covent Garden and the Metropolitan Opera were thought to be incomparable. She also enjoyed great success in the standard repertory of Mozart, Bellini, and Donizetti. During the 1930s she ran short of money and was forced to sell her house, but did receive $50 a month from the Maurice Bagby Musical Foundation. During the Second World War, Madame Calve died in Millau, France, in 1942.[54]

When Swamiji visited Paris in August 1900, he associated with artists and cultured people of the city like Auguste Rodin. For the internationally famous French sculptor Rodin (1840-1917), his lifelong preoccupation was to portray the human figure in a variety of poses, indicative of various inner emotional states. Among other things, he received commissions to create portrait busts for monuments commemorating prominent celebrities such as Victor Hugo, James McNeill Whistler, Napoleon Bonaparte, George Bernard Shaw, Henri Rochefort, Georges Clemenceau, and also Charles Baudelaire.[55]

Combing the literature, Sushama Londhe came up with the following statements by Auguste Rodin, a great admirer of ancient Indian art. Concerning the Mallipuram Temple in India, Rodin mentioned, "The descendents of those who built the magnificent temples of Bhojpur and Thanjavur, Konark and Kailas, invented mathematics and urban surgery, created mind-body disciplines (yoga) of astonishing power, and built mighty empires, would almost certainly have attained technological superiority over Europe." In a brilliant poetic outburst about the Maheshamurti (Trimurti) of the Elephanta Caves (in Bombay), he stated, "This full, pouting mouth, rich in sensuous expressions, these lips like a lake of pleasure, fringed by the noble, palpitating nostrils." He considered the statue of Nataraja or King of Dance to be the flawless embodiment of rhythmic movement. When he observed the Chola sculptures in 1913, Rodin was overwhelmed and revealed, "There are things that other people do not see: unknown depths, the wellsprings of life.... There is grace in elegance; above grace, there is modelling; everything is exaggerated; we call it soft but it is most powerfully soft! Words fail me then."[56]

ENDNOTES

1 Burke, I, p. 39; II, pp. 164-65, 178-79; *EWB* (2003), Sup. XXIII; *WWWA* (1960) III, p. 431; Chris Petteys, *Dictionary of Women Artists* (Boston: G. K. Hall, 1982), p. 361. Burke issued a caveat that there is a possibility that the clambake occurred in 1893 and not in 1894.

2 *CW*, IX:267-71.

3 Ibid., V:63, 70; VI:300, 308; IX:55, 69.

4 Ibid., VIII:495, 509.

5 Richard Gipson, *The Life of Emma Thursby* (New York: New-York Historical Society, 1940), pp. 366-71, 378; Burke, II, pp. 45-46, 138, 145-49, 227-28, 233; III, pp. 14-15, 27, 30-31; V, p. 113; VI, pp. 318, 328-30, 350-51; *CWSA*, X, pp. 18, 47, 74, 87.

6 *DAB* (1936), XVIII, pp. 516-17; H. Wiley Hitchcock and Stanley Sadie, *The New Grove Dictionary of American Music* (New York: Grove's Dictionaries of Music, 1986), IV, pp. 393-94; *New York Times* (July 5, 1931), p. 26; Emma Thursby Papers. Web: http://dlib.nyu.edu:8083/nyhsead/servlet/ SaxonServlet?source=/thursby.xml&style=/saxon01n2002.xsl&part=body.

7 Burke, I, pp. 99-100, 120, 231.

8 Albert Spalding, *Rise to Follow* (New York: Henry Holt, 1943), pp. 130-31; *Soviet Union*, pp. 3, 5; Burke, IV, pp. 125-26, 505; Ballet Magazine. Web: www.russianballet.ru/eng/archives/aug- sept/covers2.htm.

9 Burke, II, pp. 48-49; *DAB* (1940), Sup. 1-2; *EWB*.

10 Stavig1, pp. 465-66; *DAB* (1963), VIII, p. 92; UCLC.

11 *DAB* (1928-1936).

12 Clara Rogers, *The Story of Two Lives* (Norwood, MA: Plimpton Press, 1932), pp. 94, 154-58, 218-19; Stavig1, pp. 465-66.

13 *CW*, IX:93-94.

14 Ibid., III:442.

15 "A letter from M. Chatterji to J. MacLeod" (Sept. 29, 1898), VSSC Archives.

16 Clara Rogers, *Journal-Letters From the Orient* (Norwood, MA: Plimpton Press, 1934), pp. 241-43; Rogers (1932), pp. 219-20, 303; "A letter from M. Chatterji to J. MacLeod" (Oct. 3, 1912), VSSC Archives.

17 *CW*, VIII, pp. 331-32; IX, pp. 48-49.

18 Spalding (1943), pp. 23, 131; *DAB* (1977), Sup. V; *NCAB* (1893), III, p. 327; Burke, II, pp. 54-55; Albert Spalding. Web: www.netway.com/~martis/Albert_Spalding.htm.

19 Swami Vivekananda. Web: www.vivekananda.net/NewDiscoveries.html (14. H. Franklin Waltman).

20 *CW*, IX:51-52.

21 Chaudhuri1, pp. 181-83, 186-87; Joseph Milburn, *Florence James Adams—A Sketch of Her Life and Work* (Chicago: Lakeside Press, 1912), p. 15; Hohner, p. 67; Milward Adams, *NCAB* (1896), VI, p. 232; Burke, II, pp. 234-35.

22 *CW*, IX:52.

23 Ibid., V:76; VIII:377, 395-96.

24 Ibid., VI:301, 353; IX:77.

25 Burke, III, p. 95; V, pp. 168-69; *Chicago Daily Tribune* (April 23, 1920), p. 19; (March 16, 1967), p. J1.

26 *New York Times* (March 1, 1895); Gerald Carney "Baba Premananda Bharati", *Journal of Vaisnava Studies* (Spring 1998); *Los Angeles Times* (Aug. 4, 1905), p. II9; (Aug. 23, 1905), p. II9; (May 13, 1906), p. VI18; (Nov. 20, 1910), p. IM612; (March 2, 1914), p. II5; *New York Herald* (Dec. 23, 1902); *Light of India* (Jan. 1908), p. 22.

27 *New York Times* (Mar. 1, 1895), p. 8; L. J. De Bekker, *Black's Dictionary of Music and Musicians* (London: A & C Black, 1924), p. 704; UCLC.

28 Malvina Hoffman, *Heads and Tales* (Garden City, NY; Garden City Publishing Co., 1943), pp. 306-07; Burke, III, p. 184.

29 Laurie and Kevin Hillstrom, eds., *Contemporary Women Artists* (Detroit: St. James Press, 1999), pp. 289-91.

30 Malvina Hoffman, *Yesterday is Tomorrow* (New York: Crown Publishers, 1965), p. 323.

31 Malvina Hoffman Sculptures. Web: www.ramakrishna.org/ hoffman.htm; Vedanta Society of Portland. Web: www.vedantasociety.org/ history_p5.html; Hoffman (1965), pp. 323-25; *Hillstrom and Hillstrom* (1999), pp. 289-90. In their archives covering the years from 1897 to 1984, the Getty Research Library in Los Angeles has sixty pages of correspondences mostly to Malvina Hoffman from the Southern California, New York and Portland Vedanta Centers (1949-66). The Getty. Web: www.getty.edu/research/ conducting_research/finding_aids/ hoffman_m7.htm.

32 *CW*, VIII:361.

33 Chaudhuri2, pp. 92-93.

34 Burke, III, p. 345; IV, pp. 51-52, 66, 98-99, 473; *CW*, VI:375.

35 "Antoinette Sterling." Nicolas Slonimsky, *Baker's Biographical Dictionary of Musicians* (New York: Schirmer Books, 1992); Willard (1897), II, p. 684; *Encyclopedia*

Britannica. Web: http://17.1911encyclopedia.org/S /ST/STERLING_ANTOINETTE.htm.

36 *MOTE* (1916), pp. 47-48, 166; (1920), p. 167; Burke, IV, pp. 51-52; *Baker's Biographical Dictionary of Musicians* (1984), p. 1690.

37 Swami Vivekananda. Web: http://www.vivekananda.net/ NotNewButLongForgotten.html; Web: http://www.sunbonnetsue.com/ suehistory.html; John Leonard, *Woman's Who's Who of America* (New York, American Commonwealth, 1914), p. 554.

38 *CW*, V, p. 101.

39 Burke, III, pp. 493-500, 508; VI, pp. 318, 326; CW, VII:374.

40 B. Bissoondoyal, India in French Literature (London: Luzac, 1967), pp. 9, 31-32, 45, 62-68; Londhe, #394. Victor Hugo.

41 *CA* (1998), vol. 157, pp. 27-30; *EWB*, II, pp. 212-14.

42 *CW*, V:101.

43 *International Dictionary of the Opera* (Detroit: St. Peters Press, 1993); Burke, III, pp. 493-95, 498.

44 *CW*, VI:360; IX:83.

45 Burke, IV, pp. 126-27; Hitchcock and Sadie (1986), III, p. 535; Slonimsky (1992), p. 1389; Henry Southwick Perkins. Web: www.cyberhymnal.org/bio/p/e/perkins_hs.htm; UCLC.

46 Burke, III, pp. 206, 208, 492-93; V, pp. 122-27, 138-39; Prabuddhapranaı, p. 75.

47 Clara Clement, *Women in the Fine Arts* (Boston: Houghton Mifflin, 1904); Female Portraits by Maud Stumm. Web: www.printspast.com/female-prints-stumm.htm.

48 *CW*, VII:520; IX:127-28, 321-22.

49 Ibid., VII:373-75, 398; VIII:537.

50 *PB* (April 1977), pp. 191, 195; (Jan. 1911), p. 20; Burke, V, pp. 170-71; VI, pp. 318, 376-77, 394.

51 Emma Calve, *My Life* (New York: D. Appleton, 1922), p. 185.

52 Calve (1922), pp. 192-93, 201-03; Aseshananda, pp. 57-58; *PB* (Jan. 1911), p. 20; *TLWG*, p. 395; *Reminiscences*, p. 262; *PB* (Nov. 1922).

53 *BRMIC* (Dec. 1991), p. 375.

54 C. Steven Larue, ed., *International Dictionary of Opera* (Detroit; St. James Press, 1990), I, pp. 206-07; *PB* (April 1977), p. 196; Madame Calve's musical sound recordings are available at some university libraries.

55 Burke, VI, p. 322; *EWB*.

56 Londhe, #189. François-Auguste-René Rodin.

CHAPTER X

SOCIAL REFORMERS, HUMANITARIANS, & PHILANTHROPISTS

IN A LETTER to Alasinga dated August 20, 1893, from Breezy Meadows in the state of Massachusetts Swamiji wrote:

> Yesterday [Aug. 19] Mrs. Johnson, the lady superintendent of the women's prison, was here. They don't call it prison but reformatory here. It is the grandest thing I have seen in America. How the inmates are benevolently treated, how they are reformed and sent back as useful members of society; how grand, how beautiful, you must see to believe! And, oh, how my heart ached to think of what we think of the poor, the low, in India.[1]

According to the *Boston Evening Transcript* of August 23, 1893, "Last evening he addressed the inmates of the Sherborn Reformatory for Women upon the manners, customs and mode of living in his country." The Phoenix *Arizona Republican* of August 30, 1893 added that the speech occurred in the chapel of the reformatory and that "The gentleman who is of rare intellectual ability and learning was much interested in the workings of the reformatory, and expressed himself as highly pleased with what he saw."[2]

Mrs. Ellen Cheney Johnson (1829-99) succeeded the famous Clara Barton* as the superintendent of the Reformatory for Women at Sherborn, Massachusetts, near Framingham, from 1884 until her death. Swami Saradananda later spoke at the State Normal School for women located in Framingham. She acted as the spokeswoman for women's prison reform throughout the nation. As a social reformer, she worked to make women's prisons more humane than the male variety. The elderly and widowed Mrs.

---

* The founder of the American Red Cross, and a believer in the Vedantic idea that all people will eventually be liberated.

Johnson combined sympathy of feminine reform with traditional penal discipline. During her administration, she developed industries within the reformatory doors and on the farm, and a system of indenture for house services in families outside of the area. She utilized "softening" influences like flowers, farm animals, music, and visits to the infant nursery. Her philosophy was that a prisoner "must learn to do right without compulsion or she will cease to do right when the compelling force is gone". Each woman retains "the germ of goodness in the heart", which she hoped to "seek out and develop and establish". At the World's Columbian Exposition, she was awarded a bronze medal and diploma "for evidence of a model management in every detail". In her will she left money for erecting "a drinking fountain for man and beasts" in the city of Boston.[3]

When Swami Vivekananda visited Saratoga, New York, he gave an informal talk in the drawing room of the United States Hotel on the 7th of September according to the *New York Times* of September 10, 1893 (p. 10).[*] It tells us that Mr. and Mrs. Andrew Carnegie (1835-1919) were staying at the United States Hotel at that time, but not whether they attended Swamiji's talk. Incidentally, seven years later in Paris Vivekananda dined with a partner of Mr. Carnegie, Hiram Maxim, and others. Andrew Carnegie, the wealthy American industrialist and philanthropist, had some interest in Eastern thought. After visiting India and meeting many Indian and British officials, he came to the conclusion that India should gradually be moved toward independence. He said, "I do not believe God ever made any man or any nation good enough to rule another man or another nation." In his autobiography Carnegie wrote, "*The Light of Asia* [1879] by Sir Edwin Arnold came out at this time and gave me greater delight than any similar poetical work I had recently read. I had just been in India and the book took me there again." Arnold gave him the original manuscript of *The Light of Asia* on the life of Buddha, which Carnegie considered to be "one of my most precious treasures". In 1891, when the health of Edwin Arnold (1832-1904) [q.v.], a great lover of India, broke down, Carnegie sent his personal physician to oversee his recovery. Carnegie, who was born in poverty, gave away approximately 365 million dollars (equivalent to over $8 billion in 2008) to charity. His philosophy was, "It is a disgrace to die rich," and "Surplus

---

[*] This newspaper article is quoted in the Franklin Sanborn section of Chapter VII.

wealth should be considered as a sacred trust to be administered by those into whose hands it falls, during their lives, for the good of the community."[4]

Swami Vivekananda sent a letter to the Maharaja of Khetri in 1894 stating:

> What a wonderful achievement was that World's Fair at Chicago! And that wonderful Parliament of Religions where voices from every corner of the earth expressed their religious ideas! I was also allowed to present my own ideas through the kindness of Dr. Barrows and Mr. Bonney. Mr. Bonney is such a wonderful man! Think of that mind that planned and carried out with great success that gigantic undertaking, and he, no clergyman, a lawyer, presiding over the dignitaries of all the churches—the sweet, learned, patient Mr. Bonney with all his soul speaking through his bright eyes.[5]

In a June 1895 letter to Dr. Paul Carus, concerning an up coming engagement at the Oak Island Conference, Vivekananda wrote:

> I also hope Mr. [Charles] Bonney will come. He is a noble, noble soul—one who sincerely wishes the fellowship of all humanity.
>
> Is it not true, Dr., that Mr. Bonney, as I have every reason to think, originated the plan of the parliament of religions?[6]

During his lifetime, the nearly self-educated Charles Carroll Bonney (1831-1903), whom Swamiji refers to, occupied such positions as vice-president of the Illinois Teachers Association, vice-president of the American Bar Association and president of the Illinois branch (1882), president of the International Law and Order League (1885-93), and was a candidate for appointment as an associate justice in the United States Supreme Court (1887). It was his idea to hold auxiliary congresses in conjunction with the Columbian Exposition at Chicago in 1893. Bonney was the originator, manager and president of the Auxiliary of the World's Congresses, which included twenty departments such as the Parliament of Religions. The success of the venture was largely due "to his genius, industry, executive ability, tact and courtesy". Unfortunately his untiring energy, exerted on the over two-hundred congresses, undermined his health leading to paralysis.[7]

Bonney expressed his reasons for establishing the Parliament of Religions:

> I became acquainted with the great religious systems of the world in my youth, and have enjoyed an intimate association with leaders of many churches during my maturer years. I was thus led to believe that if the great religious faiths could be brought into relations of friendly intercourse, many points of sympathy and union would be found, and the coming unity of mankind in the love of God and the service of man be greatly facilitated and advanced.[8]

Bonney added, "During the organization and conduct of the World's Congresses of 1893, I was led to feel that all my life had been a preparation for this work; and that in a thousand ways provisions had been made for its extraordinary needs." Belonging to the Swedenborgian faith, Bonney believed that the religious doctrines of Emanuel Swedenborg (1688-1772) were

> the fundamental truths which made a World's Parliament of Religions possible; upon which rested the whole plan of the religious congresses of 1893, and which guided the execution of that plan to a success so great and far-reaching that only the coming generations can fully comprehend and estimate its influence.[9]

Reviewing Swamiji's lecture on "The Divinity of Man" presented at the Unitarian Church during February 1894, the *Detroit Free Press* newspaper commented:

> In this connection the lecturer delved deeply into the water of Swedenborgian philosophy, or religion, and the connection between the conviction of the Hindoo and the spiritual expressions of faith on the part of the more modern holy man was fully apparent. Swedenborg seemed like a European successor of an early Hindoo priest, clothing in modern garb an ancient conviction; a line of thought that the greatest of French philosophers and novelists [Balzac?] saw fit to embody in his elevating tale of the perfect soul. Every individual has in himself perfection. It lies within the dark recesses of his physical being.[10]

When in America in 1896, Virchand Gandhi (1864-1901) [q.v.], the Jain representative at the Parliament of Religions, heard of a severe drought in India. He formed a Relief Committee, with Charles Bonney serving as its president (following his religious convictions), and, as a result, they sent a shipload of food grains and Rs. 40,000 cash for the drought relief in India.[11]

The wealthy Mrs. Bertha Potter Palmer (1849-1918), a prominent social leader in Chicago, held a high social position in other cities as well. At the 1893 World's Columbian Exposition, she filled the position of president of the Board of Lady Managers consisting of 175 women from all over the country. When Bertha Palmer entertained the members of the Parliament at the Woman's Building on the Exposition grounds, she asked her guests to speak about the condition of women in their countries. Consequently, Vivekananda gave a brief talk on women in India. A repeat performance was held on September 22 at the Art Institute where Swamiji stated in part:

> The Hindu women are very spiritual and very religious, perhaps more so than any other women in the world. If we can preserve these beautiful characteristics and at the same time develop the intellects of our women, the Hindu woman of the future will be the ideal woman of the world.[12]

In order to increase opportunities for the education of women, Bertha Palmer was a trustee of co-education at Northwestern University. She spent a great deal of her time on philanthropic endeavours, and donated fifty-thousand dollars a year (equivalent to over a million dollars in 2008) to charities. Her husband Potter Palmer (1826-1902), a Chicago merchant, in partnership with Marshall Field and a wealthy real estate promoter, built the internationally famous Palmer House Hotel.[13]

On May 14, 1894 Vivekananda wrote to Mrs. G. W. Hale, "I have received a letter from Mrs. Potter Palmer asking me to write to some of my country women about their society etc. I will see her personally when I come to Chicago; in the meanwhile I will write her all I know."[14] The following month Swamiji dispatched a letter to Rao Bahadur Narasimhachariar of Mysore telling him:

> She was the lady president of the World's Fair. She is much interested in raising the women of the world and is at the head of a big organization for women.... She has been very kind to me in this country. Now she is going to make a tour in China, Japan, Siam, and India.... I hope she will find a warm reception at your hands and be helped to see a little of our women as they are.[15]

Swamiji wrote, "I had a letter from Mrs. Potter Palmer asking me to see her in August [1894]. She is a very gracious and kind lady."[16] The following month he noted, "The two volumes of Tod's history of Rajasthan have been presented to me by Mrs. Potter Palmer."[17] Bertha Palmer edited a book *Stories from the Classic Literature of Many Nations* (1898) containing ten legends from the *Rig Veda*, *Ramayana*, *Mahabharata*, and other Indian sources.

Swami Vivekananda once mentioned:

> At the Parliament of Religions in America, there came among others a young man, a born Negro, a real African Negro, and he made a beautiful speech. I became interested in the young man and now and then talked to him, but could learn nothing about him.[18]

The impressive young Momolu Massaquoi (1870-1938), appearing in the robes of an African chieftain, represented Liberia at the Parliament. Previously in Africa, he had the choice of being a Mohammedan like his father or accepting his mother's faith of Voodooism. Attracted by a lady missionary of the Church of England, he decided to leave Liberia at the age of twelve. Aided by an American sea captain he came to the United States and attended the Gammon School in Nashville, Tennessee, a Methodist institution for Negro students. After the Parliament, Massaquoi returned to his Val tribe in Liberia where he became their king. Later in Monrovia he was the second man in the Department of the Interior, devoting his life to helping his people. During the 1922-29 period, he became the first indigenous African diplomat in Europe, being the Minister Consul-General in Hamburg, Germany. Contesting for the presidentship of Liberia in 1931, Massaquoi was loved by the masses, but betrayed by his only opponent who deceitfully won the election.[19]

Somewhere between September 10 and November 19, 1893, Vivekananda (listed as Vivehanande) spoke at "The Working People's Social Science Club" located at Jane Addams' (1860-1935) Hull-House residence in Chicago. His lecture, "The Economic and Social Conditions of India", lasted for about forty-five minutes, followed by an hour of discussion. Swami Vivekananda's photograph is presently on the wall of the Hull-House Museum along with some of the other famous speakers. During the years 1893 and 1894, Addams wrote of fifteen other prominent people who gave lectures before the Social Science Club. They include four future friends of Vedanta, viz. William T.

Stead (1849-1912), Seth Low (1850-1916), Professor Charles Bradley (1852-1932) and Stanton Coit (1857-1944).[20]

Swami Vivekananda might have met Addams, a future Nobel Prize winning humanitarian, at the Cambridge Conferences in October 1894 and/or in Paris in August 1900. While living in Chicago, in an April 6, 1896 letter to Sara Bull, Swamiji mentions "the kindness of Miss Adams. She is so, so good and kind".[21] But we cannot be sure if he is referring to Jane Addams. "Adams" is certainly a far more common spelling of the name than "Addams". In a November 26, 1899 correspondence from Chicago, the Swami describes her "as ever is an angel".[22] Addams spoke at the Cambridge Conferences in Sara Bull's house on February 19, 1899. She and Sara Bull exchanged at least six letters during 1900-01. In 1906 Nivedita sent a letter to Addams who responded by writing to her friend Sara Bull in reply.[23]

At that time Sister Nivedita temporarily resided in Hull-House, of which Jane Addams and Ellen Gates Starr (1859-1940) were the founders. In her letters written between November 9 and 25, Nivedita mentions her association with Miss Jane Addams, who, she states, "is doing a great deal for me". Though Vivekananda criticized Miss Starr, she wished to attend his informal discussion at the Hale residence on November 27. Nivedita sought to bring her to Hale residence where she was held in disrepute, possibly because she was a well-known labour activist. Nivedita wrote to Mrs. Belle Hale, "I love her so much. She is full of the true something, and a new face is often as stimulating to Swami as to others." Ellen Starr, a physically small and somewhat frail woman, possessed eloquent manners and speech. For two decades she received newspaper attention for vigorously supporting trade unions and for being an active member of many picket lines.[24]

During the First World War, Jane Addams became a major figure in the quest for world peace. She and other women from aggressive and neutral nations met at the International Congress of Women at The Hague in 1915, attempting to stop the World War. In 1896 she had made contact with Leo Tolstoy in Russia, and in 1921 with Rabindranath Tagore in Chicago, and said about him that he "has made all these requirements of genius combined in a man who is at once a poet, a philosopher, a humanitarian, an educator", and saluted him "with gratitude, with admiration, with fellowship and affection".[25] From 1924 she served as a member of the advisory council of the India Society under president Jabez Sunderland, and sponsored other pro-India organizations. Because Mahatma Gandhi was in jail, she was not able to see him when she toured India in 1923. Addams did correspond with the fellow peacemaker Gandhi, and they told stories about each other's benevolent activities. She felt that through his spiritual practices he achieved a practical solution to war and excessive nationalism. Jane Addams' four-page article "Tolstoy and Gandhi" appeared in the *Christian Century* of November 25, 1931. She also sent a letter to Gandhi inviting him to attend the Congress of the Women's International League for Peace and Freedom (of which she was the president) to be held in Geneva in February 1932. In the letter she mentions that some women in almost every country in the world have united against the act of war.[26]

Beginning in 1889, Hull-House provided housing, child-care, vocational training and education for poor immigrants and labouring people in Chicago, along with organizing groups for young people. Jane Addams spoke widely in public for the purpose of increasing the number of social settlements in the United States. She cofounded and/or led numerous socio-political organizations such as the National American Women's Suffrage Association, the National Conference of Charities, and the Women's International League for Peace and Freedom. Addams devoted her life to aiding poor immigrants, children, workingwomen, and war victims. For her efforts she became the first American woman recipient of the Nobel Peace Prize, and is now a member of the illustrious National Women's Hall of Fame, and The Hall of Fame for Great Americans at New York University.[27]

Madame Emma Calve, who made the acquaintance of Vivekananda in Chicago, related that Swamiji met the immensely wealthy John D. Rockefeller (1839-1937) in Chicago at an unspecified date between 1893 and 1899. She told her friend Madame Drinette Verdier:

> Mr. X, in whose home Swamiji was staying in Chicago, was a partner or an associate in some business with John D. Rockefeller. Many times John D. heard his friends talking about this extraordinary and wonderful Hindu monk who was staying with them, and many times he had been invited to meet Swamiji but, for one reason or another, always refused.... But one day, although he did not want to meet Swamiji, he was pushed to it by an impulse and went directly to the house of his friend, brushing aside the butler who opened the door and saying that he wanted to see the Hindu monk.... Swamiji told Rockefeller much of his past that was not known to any but himself, and made him understand that the money he had already accumulated was not his, that he was only a channel and that his duty was to do good to the world—that God had given him all his wealth in order that

he might have an opportunity to help and do good to people. Rockefeller was annoyed that anyone dared to talk to him that way and tell him what to do. He left the room in irritation, not even saying goodbye. But about a week after, again without being announced, he entered Swamiji's study and, finding him the same as before, threw on his desk a paper which told of his plans to donate an enormous sum of money toward the financing of a public institution. "Well, there you are", he said. "You must be satisfied now, and you can thank me for it." Swamiji didn't even lift his eyes, did not move. Then taking the paper, he quietly read it, saying, "It is for you to thank me." That was all.[28]

When Rockefeller paid a visit to the University of Chicago, he said, "The good Lord gave me the money, and how could I withhold it from Chicago?"[29] As the founder of the Standard Oil Company, Rockefeller and his partners gained control of ninety percent of the oil industry in the United States. Throughout his lifetime he proved himself to be one of the greatest philanthropists who ever lived. In May 1889 he founded the University of Chicago with a large gift. By the end of 1892 he had already given away over three million dollars (equivalent to over $73 million in 2008) to colleges, hospitals, libraries, asylums, and other institutions. Though Rockefeller lived a relatively simple and frugal personal life, the total of his lifetime philanthropy is estimated at about $550 million (roughly equivalent to $8 billion in 2008), more than any person up to that time. Over the years his philanthropic activities grew, and he created the Rockefeller Institute for Medical Research (now Rockefeller University) in 1901, and the General Education Board in 1902. The Rockefeller Foundation received a charter in 1913 "to promote the well-being of mankind throughout the world".[30]

1894 and After

Vivekananda travelled to Detroit to stay as a guest for ten days in the house of Mrs. John J. (Frances) Bagley.* He mentioned in a letter of 14 February 1894, "Here I met Mr. Bagley, the youngest [Paul F. Bagley], waiting for me at the station; and, it being very late in the night, Mrs. Bagley had retired, but the daughters sat up for me."[31] In 1892 the unmarried Paul Frederick Bagley (1869-1931) joined John J. Bagley & Co., the family tobacco business,

* See Chapter V.

and subsequently became its treasurer and remained so until it was sold in 1922. Among other things he was also president of the board of the Bagley Land Co. and the Woodmere Cemetery Association. Having a humanitarian nature he worked for the improvement of Michigan industrial schools for boys and girls, was a member of the Detroit Board of Health, served in the navy during the Spanish-American War, and joined the American Red Cross living overseas for more than a year during the First World War.[32] His elder brother John N. Bagley (1860-1929), a tobacco manufacturer, was president of the Detroit board of health, a director in the Security Trust. Co., and was very active in state and local politics. At that time Swamiji also contacted their sister, the divorced Mrs. Roger (Florence) Sherman (1855-1908), who presented him with an address book.[33] Her sisters were Frances (b. 1863), Olive (1867-1909), and Helen Bagley (1872-1932), who, with her mother, wrote letters defending Swamiji against his accusers in Detroit.[34]

On 10 April 1894, Swamiji wrote to Mrs. G. W. Hale:

> For the last few days I was the guest of Miss Helen Gould—daughter of the rich Gould—at her palatial country residence, an hour's ride from the city. She has one of the most beautiful and large greenhouses in the world, full of all sorts of curious plants and flowers. They are Presbyterians, and she is a very religious lady. I had a very nice time there.[35]

At that time for three days Vivekananda was the houseguest of the young and wealthy Helen Miller Gould (1868-1938) at her estate of Lyndhurst at Irvington-on-Hudson, New York. The forty-room Gothic house was situated on "500 acres of meticulously landscaped grounds with lawns, rare shrubbery, carefully tended drives, and ornamental waters, all approached through massive gateways manned night and day by an army of private security guards."[36]

In 1892 Helen Gould fell heir to a large fortune upon the death of her father, Jay Gould, the famous financier. She contributed large sums of money to relieving distress and making the world a better place. For example, she gave away a total of over $700,000 to the New York University Library and a "Hall of Fame for Great Americans", a home for crippled children, the St. Louis cyclone sufferers in 1896, for relief of the soldiers during the Spanish-American War, and to the Young Men's Christian Association. In 1918 Helen Gould and another woman became the first female vice-presidents of the American Bible Society. Helen's sister-in-law, the wife of her brother

Harold Gould, attended the lectures of Abhedananda in New York City, which is mentioned in a couple of newspaper articles.[37]

We cannot be sure whom Vivekananda was referring to (though Helen Gould is a definite possibility) in the following reminiscences written down by Debendra Kumar Roy:

> [Roy] one day asked Swamiji to recount some of his unique experiences in America and Europe. Swamiji said that while in America, a heiress being attracted by his personality and great eloquence, once offered her vast fortune and herself to Swami "to help him in his mission of life". Swamiji thanked her heartily for this kind offer. But he said he was unable to accept it, being as he was a monk who had already dedicated his all, body, mind, and soul to the one Lord of his life, Sri Ramakrishna.[38]

Though Swamiji would accept financial gifts from a sincere devotee, there were many instances of his being reluctant to do so from other people. In the same letter written to Mrs. G. W. Hale, in which Swamiji mentioned staying with Helen Gould, he also disclosed:

> As for lecturing, I have given up raising money. I cannot degenerate myself any more.... I have not tried to earn a penny here, and have refused some presents which friends here wanted to make to me. Especially [William Joseph] Flagg—I have refused his money. I had in Detroit tried to refund the money back to the donors, and told them that, there being almost no chance of my succeeding in my enterprise, I had no right to keep their money; but they refused and told me to throw that into the waters if I liked. But I cannot take any more conscientiously.[39]

Another example is that he did not treat the extremely generous John D. Rockefeller and some other wealthy people with the admiration they were accustomed to receiving. In 1900, he did not go to a musical put on by the wealthy philanthropist Phoebe Hearst in Northern California. Swamiji told Edith Allan, "All Mrs. Hearst wants is to lionize me. Why should I go?" While he encouraged the immensely rich Arabella Collis Huntington to donate five-thousand dollars (equivalent to $132,000 in 2008) to Sister Nivedita's Girls' School, he accepted only small gifts from her.[40] Although the Baha'is acquired Greenacre, Vivekananda made no attempt to do so.[41]

Swamiji's indifference to money was brought out in a piece in the New York based *Leslie's Weekly* magazine of December 9, 1897 (and in other articles), which also contains a picture of the Swami. At the top of the "People Talked About" column they noted that Vivekananda was a

> delegate to the World's Congress of Religions held at Chicago in 1893, where he delivered a learned address which attracted much attention. Mr. Vivekananda came without money, and something which astonished Americans [was that he] refused to accept money from his numerous and enthusiastic admirers while here. He lived in the simplest manner and preached his severe Buddhist [sic] doctrines wherever he came. In New York he was detained for months by enthusiastic disciples.... Swami Vivekananda is an impressive orator and a deep thinker.

Miss Sarah Jane Farmer (1847-1916) conceived of the idea of the Greenacre Religious Conferences (1894-1915) in Boston in 1892 while "listening to a lecture by W. J. Colville on 'The Abundant Life' through the forming of the Christ within." She received further inspiration when she attended the World's Parliament of Religions in Chicago in 1893. Each year they held the Conference at her country resort on the bank of the Piscataqua River, serving as a meeting place for the representatives of the various religious faiths. The officials proclaimed:

> The Greenacre Lectures were established in 1894 with the express purpose of bringing together all who are looking earnestly forward toward the new day which is surely breaking over the entire world, and, by the recognition of truths held in common, to bring peace and unity throughout the world.

Miss Farmer saw Swamiji at the Parliament and again in New York, and invited him to speak at Greenacre in the summer of 1894. Other guest speakers included Sara Bull, W. J. Colville, Edward Everett Hale, Lewis Janes, Franklin Sanborn, Henry Wood, and Ralph Waldo Trine. While these people were successful writers, none of them was a regular university professor, indicating that the Greenacre Conference at that time was not of a strictly academic character. Concerning Swamiji's morning discourses, the reporter for the *Portsmouth Daily Chronicle* wrote on July 31:

> Vivekananda, the Hindoo monk from India, is ... a centre of much interest. Each morning he meets a company of men and women under a large pine in the woods, and sitting cross-legged, discourses to them of the things of the soul. This gentle, loving-hearted son of the east, by his simplicity and earnest devotion has won to himself some very warm friends. He is generous in the extreme, giving freely to any one from his stores of wisdom.

The large pine tree under which Swamiji sat and gave his inspired lecture at Greenacre became permanently known as "The Swami's Pine". Marie Louise Burke made this important point:

> To judge from these scraps [newspaper accounts] from Miss Thursby's more substantial notes, and from Swamiji's own letters, it was at Greenacre that he taught for the first time in America the philosophy of Advaita Vedanta (though, as far as I know, not naming it as such) to a group of eager listeners.[42]

According to the programme for "The Monsalvat School for the Comparative Study of Religion" held in 1904:

> The initial steps toward the founding of the Monsalvat School were taken in 1894 when the late Swami Vivekananda of India was invited to conduct a class in Vedanta Philosophy under the pines at Greenacre, Eliot, Maine. His exposition of the Gospel of Jesus Christ from the stand-point of an Oriental will never be forgotten by any one privileged to be a member of his class.[43]

The School had been officially inaugurated in 1896 under the direction of Lewis Janes, and was later under the leadership of Dr. Fillmore Moore (1900-03) and Myron Phelps (1904-05).

Sarah Farmer was a houseguest along with Swami Vivekananda at the Cambridge Conferences in December 1894. She asked Swamiji to be on the programme at Greenacre in the summer of 1895, but instead, he made the decision to conduct classes at Thousand Island Park.[44] Swami Saradananda gave classes at Greenacre in 1896 and the following year, Abhedananda during 1898-1900, and Paramananda during 1909-11. Swami Bodhananda was one of the main speakers in 1910, addressing the audience eleven times from July 7 to August 28, and returning in 1911.[45]

Upon the passing away of Vivekananda, Sarah Farmer made known the following in a letter to the *Brahmavadin*:

> To know him was a renewed consecration; to have him under one's roof was to feel empowered to go forth to the children of men and to help them all to a realization of their birthright as Sons of God. What Greenacre owes to him cannot be put into words.... This great soul came into our midst and did more than any other to give the work its true tone, for he *lived* every day the truths which his lips proclaimed.... When the news of the transition of this beloved servant of God reached us, we assembled in the grove consecrated by him and his brothers, and under "the Prophet's Pine", gave thanks to God for what he had been to us, for what he is now and ever will be. It was a blessed hour.[46]

Greenacre got its name in 1890 from a family acquaintance, the famous Quaker poet John Greenleaf Whittier (1807-92). Sitting before the fireplace he reportedly said, "Some people have called this God's acres, but I call it Green Acre." Previously, Whittier received a copy of the *Bhagavad Gita* from his friend Ralph Waldo Emerson (1803-82) and made the comment, "It is a wonderful book, and has greatly excited my curiosity to know more of the religious literature of the East." Whittier carefully and sympathetically studied many manuscripts on India written by Western authors. His poetry includes paraphrases from the *Law of Manu* and the *Mahabharata*. As fate would have it, he unfortunately passed away before Swamiji arrived at Greenacre. Also, the poet Walt Whitman (1819-92) departed the year before Vivekananda came to the country. In 1900, Sarah Farmer travelled to Akka, Palestine, where she met Abdu'l Baha (1844-1921), the son of Baha'u'llah, the founder of the Baha'i faith, who was imprisoned there. She considered him to be "the fulfillment of the hopes of all the religions she had worked with". After returning to the United States, she became a supporter of the Baha'i movement. In 1912, Abdu'l Baha visited Greenacre during a tour of North America and, a year later, the Baha'is took over Greenacre. Consequently, rather than being put to commercial use, Greenacre has remained to this day a centre for religious discussion and activity. Today the Greenacre Baha'i School is the oldest permanent Baha'i School in the world. Visitors lodge at the Sarah Farmer Inn, which is a part of the two-hundred and fifty acre campus. On a year-round basis they teach short courses on the Baha'i Faith and its philosophy.[47]

Mrs. Julia Ward Howe (1819-1910) was the president of the New England Woman's Club in Boston. She sent an invitation to Swami Vivekananda to speak before the Club on May 7, 1894.[48] As a representative of the Unitarians, she had spoken at the Parliament of Religions in Chicago. The Swami saw the widowed* Mrs. Howe again in December 1894 during a multiple lecture series held at Sara Bull's residence in Cambridge.[49] Five years later, she spoke well of Abhedananda after hearing his talk at the Cambridge Conferences. Howe had gained some prior familiarity with Indian thought in 1887 while attending the discourses of Mohini Mohan Chatterji in Boston.[50] A member of the National Women's Hall of Fame for great Americans, Julia Ward Howe distinguished herself as an author of lyrics, poems, prose, essays, biographies, travel sketches and plays. While listening to the song "John Brown's Body", she composed the poem "The Battle Hymn of the Republic" in 1861, for which she is best remembered. It became the best known Civil War hymn of the Union Army. As a reaction against the Civil War (1861-65) and the Franco-Prussian War (1870-71), in 1870 she issued an "Appeal to Womanhood throughout the World", to come together across national lines and to rise up and oppose war in all of its forms. Howe spoke at the Unitarian Church, served as the president of the Women's International Peace Association, cofounded the Association of Advancement of Women, and was an active leader in the anti-slavery movement, women's suffrage, prison reform, temperance, and in the support of the oppressed Greeks, Armenians and Russians.[51]

Back on October 18, 1893, the Annual Convention of the National Woman's Christian Temperance Union was held in the Hall of Washington in Chicago. Frances Willard was the president of the organization. According to the *Chicago Daily Tribune* of October 19, 1893 (page 10):

> When Lady Henry [Somerset] had finished, Dionysius Latus Archbishop of Zante was introduced and made a brief address upon temperance in his native land. He was followed by two Hindus, Vivekananda and Virchand A. Gandhi who told of strict temperance practised by every true Brahmin. The noontide hour of prayer closed the morning session.

We do not know if Vivekananda made the acquaintance of Lady Somerset in 1893, but he definitely did in December of 1894 when he spoke at

* After 1876.

the Cambridge Conferences. At that time Lady Henry Somerset (1851-1921) and Colonel Thomas Higginson discussed the subject of women's suffrage. The Swami "made friends of Lady Somerset".[52] In his speech Swamiji stated, "Lady Henry Somerset has been a revelation to me."[53] Back in October, Vivekananda told a Baltimore newspaper reporter, "I see no reason why American women should not vote."[54] At one time Lady Henry Somerset thought of becoming a nun, but instead experienced a short-lived marriage. She became the president of the British Women's Temperance Association in 1890 and an advocate of Women's Suffrage. In England she devoted much of her time and income to aiding children, the poor and needy, and alcoholic women. When she came to America to attend the World's Woman's Christian Temperance Union, she made contact with Frances Willard, who became her good friend. Lady Somerset wrote the books *Our Village Life* (1884) and *Under the Arch* (1906).[55]

Miss Frances Elizabeth Willard (1839-98) spoke in conjunction with Lady Somerset at the Cambridge Conferences in December 1894. She and Swamiji quickly became friends. On December 17 her stenographer recorded Vivekananda's long talk on "The Women of India", which now occupies seventeen pages in the *Complete Works*. There he states, "I have found such noble souls in this nation as Mrs. [Ole] Bull and Miss [Sarah] Farmer and Miss [Frances] Willard."[56] Frances Willard is a member of the prestigious National Women's Hall of Fame, and The Hall of Fame for Great Americans at New York University. Among other things, she became a college professor in 1863, and the first American woman to be the head of a college, being the president of Evanston College for Ladies (1871-73), which became part of Northwestern University where she was the dean of Women (1873-74). She was also the president of the National Woman's Christian Temperance Union (1879-98), which, under her direction, became the largest women's rights organization in the country supporting women's suffrage and enhancing the status of women. Furthermore, she was the president of the World's Woman's Christian Temperance Union in 1891, a Methodist delegate to the Parliament of Religions in 1893, and, in addition, an author of many books. When she died in 1898, more than twenty-thousand people paid their last respects at her memorial services in New York City and Chicago.[57]

In February 1895, the Swami spoke before an elite group of high society people at the mansion of multi-millionaire Austin Corbin (1827-96) in New York City. At that time Austin's daughter, Anna, offered her conservatory in the mansion for his classes. The Swami gave Upanishad classes in the conservatory later in the month and twice in March. In a letter to Sara Bull, Swamiji disclosed:

> I went to Miss Corbin's last Saturday [March 16] and told her that I should not be able to come to hold classes any more. Was it ever in the history of the world that any great work was done by the rich? It is the heart and the brain that do it ever and ever and not the purse.

Swamiji also mentions giving six lectures at the Corbin's residence in January and February of 1896.[58] According to the *New York Herald* and the *New York World*, a year later, on February 5, 1896, Mr. and Mrs. Austin Corbin and their daughter Anna were the hosts of a party at their house. Attending the party were the Corbins, Vivekananda, Nikola Tesla, Sarah Bernhardt, Peter Hewitt and other celebrities.[59]

In 1863 Austin Corbin organized the first National Bank to go into business in the United States. He held the position of president of the Long Island Railroad (1881-96), the Philadelphia & Reading Railroad (1886-90), and some other railroads, and of real estate, and coal and iron companies, and director of the Western Union Telegraph Co. in New York. Corbin's last public endeavour was to spend a million dollars on a forty-four square mile animal preservation park in Newport, New Hampshire.[60]

Miss Henrietta Müller's (1850s-1906) father was a German businessman engaged in the shipping industry, and subsequently she became a member of the wealthy rentier class. In England she won the election to be the head of the London School Board from 1879 until 1885. As a leader in the Women's Movement, in 1888 she initiated the *Women's Herald*, a weekly newspaper supporting causes like suffrage and temperance. At the World's Parliament of Religions of 1893, Henrietta was a member of the Theosophical Conference. Akshay Kumar Ghose, a student at the University of Calcutta, was a friend of Vivekananda, who sought financial aid for the young man.[61] While in India in 1893 at the annual Theosophists convention held in Adyar, Madras, Henrietta Müller adopted Akshay.[62] She felt that Akshay had considerable promise and thus sent him to England to be a student at the Cambridge University Law School. In a letter, Swamiji wrote that Akshay "sent a beautiful invitation from London to come to Miss Müller's".[63] As a consequence, during September of 1895 Vivekananda went to her house in the village of Pinkney's Green, England, and lodged there for four days the following May. Henrietta wanted Swamiji to get involved in the Temperance Union. His reply to her was, "My object is to preach religion. I cannot identify myself with other movements." For over a month during July-August 1896, Swamiji travelled with Henrietta and the Seviers in their tour of France and Switzerland.[64] She generously offered the funds so that Alasinga could devote his full time to the *Brahmavadin*. Vivekananda later spent about three weeks in her rented house, Airlie Lodge, in the city of Wimbledon, England. Henrietta's most outstanding financial contribution was a donation of Rs. 40,000 that was used to purchase the land for Belur Math in 1898. It is a very auspicious sign that Vivekananda accepted her donation.[65]

An interesting incident took place while Swamiji was walking across a field with Henrietta Müller and an English friend, when they were confronted by an angry bull. Sister Nivedita tells us:

> The Englishman frankly ran, and reached the other side of the hill in safety. The woman ran as far as she could, and then sank to the ground, incapable of further effort. Seeing this, and unable to aid her, the Swami—thinking "So this is the end after all"—took up his stand in front of her, with folded arms. He told afterwards how his mind was occupied with a mathematical calculation, as to how far the bull would be able to throw. But the animal suddenly stopped, a few paces off, and then raising his head, retreated sullenly.[66]

Henrietta Müller followed Swamiji to Almora while living in India from March 1897 until December 1898.[67] On March 11, 1897, Vivekananda, Margaret Noble (later Sister Nivedita), and Miss Müller spoke at the Star Theatre in Calcutta. Amid cheers and loud applause Miss Müller told the audience in part:

> Swami Vivekananda has told you little about the work that he has done in the West; he himself can measure in a very small degree how great is the reformation, how tremendous is the change and modification, which he has instituted in public and social life in the West. And he has also carried that great change of ideas, that great change of spirituality and religion right into the very homes and hearts of those people who have been fortunate enough to hear him. It is not only that we have heard his voice, it is not only that we have learned those noble doctrines which till now were unknown to us, it is also that we received them into our hearts, we have carried them into our homes, to our fathers, mothers, daughters and children who are

trying to put the great spiritual wisdom of India into practice—the wisdom that has been yours since time immemorial.[68]

Reports of seventeen of Swamiji's lectures delivered in India in 1897 were published under the title *From Colombo to Almora* by Vyjayanti Press. A writer for the *Indian Mirror* (August 22, 1897) felt bad that the edition

> gives quite an inadequate idea of the enthusiasm with which the Swami was greeted during his progress through this country. Full descriptions of the reception, which was accorded to him in different parts of India, would, we venture to think, have given the volume a better air of completeness.

In a prefatory note to the book, Miss Henrietta Müller stated:

> All Eastern students, and still more, perhaps, those of England and America will welcome this book, containing as it does, the latest utterances of their much loved teacher, for the lectures exhibit to the Hindu the fervid patriotism of the "Calcutta boy", and to the American and the English that larger patriotism, which counts the world as its home, and all the people in it, as fellow-countrymen.[69]

After returning to the West, Henrietta Müller caused some trouble and withdrew from the Vedanta Society.[70] In spite of her irrational behaviour, in 1901 Swamiji wrote to Sara Bull, "Kindly convey my undying love to Miss Müller the next time you see her."[71] Henrietta Müller passed away in Washington, D.C. in January of 1906.[72]

While Swamiji was in England for the second time and preparing to leave for India, the *Boston Daily Globe* of December 2, 1896 in the United States mentioned:

> Mrs. Jack Gardner has for years been noted as the most successful lion hunter in Boston. Almost every great celebrity visiting the hub has felt the attraction of her social charms—[Jan] Paderewski, Paul Bourget, Swami Vivekananda ... have all been her willing social captives.

It is difficult to determine when Swamiji and Mrs. Jack Gardner met. Back on April 20, 1894, both attended a play put on by the Harvard University student body. But the audience was sizable, so they may not have made contact at that time. The eccentric philanthropist Isabella Gardner (1840-1924) was a multi-millionaire who amassed over 2,500 works of precious art. Her will established "a museum for the education and enjoyment of the public forever". The artworks are now part of the Isabella Stewart Gardner Museum of fine art in Boston, which is open to the public.[73]

Second Visit to the West

On August 28, 1893, the elderly Caroline Severance (1820-1914) came to hear Vivekananda's presentation at the Thought and Work Club for cultured women in Salem, Massachusetts. Six years later on December 23, 1899, after Swamiji had returned to the United States, she invited him for an informal reception at her residence called "El Nido" located at 806 West Adams Street in Los Angeles. Her guests asked Swamiji to talk to them about the condition of women in India and the educational needs of the Indian people. Because Severance was a prominent socialite, the event received coverage in the *Los Angeles Herald* newspaper. The article stated in part, "The Swami answered many questions asked by the guests concerning the condition of women in India, and the educational needs of his people.... His talk was highly interesting to the guests."[74]

Known as the "Mother of Clubs", Caroline Maria Seymour Severance spent her life promoting women's suffrage and rights, social reform, and world peace. Before the Civil War, she and her husband formed an Independent Christian Church that opposed slavery. Caroline cofounded the New England Women's Club in Boston in 1868, and became its first president. Julia Ward Howe succeeded her as the president of the Club in 1872, and many years later on May 7, 1894, she invited Vivekananda to give a presentation before this organization. Caroline Severance also co-founded the American Woman Suffrage Association in 1869, and helped organize with other people the Free Religious Association in Boston where Vivekananda in 1894, Abhedananda in 1898, and Nivedita in 1899 later spoke. In 1875 her family moved to Los Angeles where she soon established the Woman's Club of Los Angeles, the first Unitarian congregation in the city, and the Orphan's Home Society. She served as president of the Los Angeles Free Kindergarten Association, the Friday Morning Club, and the Los Angeles County Women's Suffrage League. In addition, she helped to form the Los Angeles Philharmonic Orchestra, the Ebell Club, a city public library system, and a local branch of the University of California now known as U.C.L.A.[75]

After Swamiji travelled to Northern California, the *Oakland Enquirer* of February 24 and March 9, 1900 noted:

> Those who heard Vivekananda at Chicago have been enthusiastic in praise of his power as an orator. He is a large, fine looking man who has an excellent command of English and is a master of elocutionary effects.... He is a perfect master of idiomatic English so far as grammatical construction goes. He is an orator, a scholar, a wit and a man of various gifts.[76]

In March, Swamiji met the wealthy Mrs. Arabella Collis Huntington (1851-1924). As stated in Chapter VII, four years before this her daughter-in-law, Helen Huntington, was an avid fan of Vivekananda in New York. On April 20, 1900 Swamiji informed Josephine MacLeod, "A kind lady has given me a pass up to New York to be used within three months. The Mother will take care of me. She is not going to strand me now after guarding me all my life."[77] Marie Louise Burke wrote that "almost certainly" it was Mrs. Huntington who gave Swamiji the train pass from San Francisco to New York. Her husband was in the train business. Arabella heard of Nivedita's work from Swamiji. On the 18th of May Swamiji wrote to Nivedita, "Enclosed find the letter of introduction to Mrs. Huntington. She can, if she likes, make your school a fact with one stroke of her pen. May Mother make her do it!"[78] Inspired by Swamiji, Arabella met Nivedita in New York City and presented her with a gift of five-thousand dollars (equivalent to $132,000 in 2008) for her Girls' School in India.[79] The Swami heard from her in the summer when he lived in New York.[80] Her first husband, Collis Huntington, who died in 1900, was the president of the Southern Pacific Railroad, and also controlled the Chesapeake and Ohio Railroad. Thirteen years later Arabella married the wealthy Henry Huntington (1850-1927). She aided her husband in creating the renowned Huntington Library, Art Collections and Botanical Gardens in San Marino, which, upon his death, he deeded to the State of California. This extensive collection, now open to the public, focuses on a multitude of rare plant specimens covering 150 acres of gardens, as well as British and American history books, literature, and precious art objects. Henry Huntington also owned the Los Angeles Railway Company, judged to be the best urban rail system in the world.[81]

Before Swamiji visited Washington, D.C. in October of 1894, the famous singer Emma Thursby gave Swamiji letters of introduction to many people, including the wealthy Phoebe Apperson Hearst (1842-1919). On October 23, writing from the nation's capital, Mrs. Hearst wrote to Miss Thursby, "I should indeed be most happy to meet Swami Vive Kananda—and, in fact, any one in whom you are especially interested." Soon after arriving in Washington, D.C., on at least two occasions Swamiji visited the house of Mrs. Hearst, and probably met her there. Six years later in the year 1900, she invited Vivekananda to one of her Sunday musicals at Hearst Hall in Berkeley, California. He had a bad cold at that time.[82] When Mrs. Edith Allan asked him why he did not go, Swamiji replied, "All Mrs. Hearst wants is to lionize me. Why should I go?" According to Alice Hansbrough's "Reminiscences", Phoebe Hearst offered him a thousand dollars to accomplish his work in India.[83] Hearst's deceased husband was a mining magnet and a U.S. Senator. Her only child, William Randolph Hearst (1863-1951) owned many large city newspapers including the *San Francisco Examiner*. She devoted a great deal of her time to philanthropic activities, donating money to hospitals, orphanages, kindergartens and schools. The energetic Phoebe Hearst generously gave large sums of money to the University of California in Berkeley, and she became the university's first woman regent (1897-1919). An organization she founded became the forerunner of the National Council of Parents and Teachers (PTA). She visited the Baha'i leader in Akka, Palestine, in 1898, and at that time her butler became the first African American to adopt their faith. In 1912 Phoebe Hearst hosted Abdu'l Baha at her Pleasanton home during his travels in the United States. Accompanied by Clara Rogers, during the year 1903 Phoebe journeyed to South India, Bombay, Agra, Delhi, Jaipur, Amritsar, Lahore, Lucknow, and then to Benares. She collected various handcrafted objects from India for her museum in Berkeley. Due to business complications, she, with Clara Rogers, left the country before visiting Calcutta.[84]

Sister Nivedita corresponded with the Russian anarchist Peter Kropotkin (1842-1921), and associated with him in London in two different years. He also mentions his friendship with Josephine MacLeod and Sara Bull in a letter of July 1907. According to Swamiji's brother Bhupendranath, "During the Paris Exhibition in August in 1900, his American friends, Mrs. Ole Bull and others, introduced Peter Kropotkin to him." After escaping from Russia, Kropotkin was expelled from Switzerland, jailed in France, and finally settled in England in 1886. He fully supported the utopian idea of anarchism, the doctrine that any form of politically organized government is unnecessary and undesirable, that social organization and control can rest on voluntary cooperation alone. More substantially Kropotkin believed that cooperation, both within and between species, was a more fundamental evolutionary factor than competition.[85] After meeting Swamiji, he wrote in the conclusion of *Mutual Aid: A Factor of Evolution* (1902):

> The animal species, in which individual struggle has been reduced to its narrowest limits, and the practice of mutual aid has attained the greatest development, are invariably the most numerous, the most prosperous, and the most open to further progress.... The unsociable species, on the contrary, are doomed to decay.[86]

In addition to the people discussed above, a number of individuals, discussed in Chapter VII dealing with the writers, were actively involved in various types of social betterment. They were the likes of Kate Woods, Franklin Sanborn, Myron Phelps, Colonel Thomas Higginson, Edward Carpenter, A. Christina Albers, and Patrick Geddes, as well as Yakov A. K. J Popov.

ENDNOTES

1 *CW*, V:13-14.

2 Burke, I, p. 25; Chaudhuri2, p. 15; *ANA*.

3 Estelle Freedman, *Their Sisters' Keepers* (Ann Arbor: University of Michigan, 1984), pp. 54-55, 75-77, 91-92, 98, opposite 118, 164-65; *DAB*, V, pp. 98-99; *Annual Report* of Massachusetts Department of Education (1898), pp. 30-31 on GBS.

4 Sunderland, pp. 51-32; Carl Jackson, *The Oriental Religions and American Thought* (London: Greenwood Press, 1981), pp. 145, 151; Dale Carnegie, *Five Minute Biographies* (New York: Greenberg Publishers, 1937), p. 162; Mead, p. 383; Raucher, pp. 84-85.

5 *CW*, V:249-50.

6 Ibid., IX:61.

7 *DAB*, I, pp. 439-40; *NCAB*, XXVIII, p. 251; *WWIA*, I, p. 115.

8 Burke, I, p.68; *The World's Parliament of Religions*, ed. John Henry Barrows, p. 185.

9 George Dole, *With Absolute Respect: The Swedenborgian Theology of Charles Carroll Bonney* (West Chester, Penn: Swedenborg Foundation, 1993), pp. 1-4, 21.

10 *CW*, III:499.

11 *PB* (Oct. 1994), p. 379.

12 *CW*, VIII:198.

13 *DAB* (1962), VII, pp. 176-77, 190-91; *ANB*, XVI, pp. 942-43; Burke, I, pp. 77, 96-98; Chaudhuri1, pp. 42, 57, 107, 110.

14 *CW*, IX:21.

15 Ibid., VI:256-57.

16 Ibid., VIII:319.

17 Ibid., IX:41.

18 Ibid., III:192.

19 *Open Court* 27 (1913), pp. 162-68; Raymond Smyke, *The First African Diplomat* (Philadelphia: Xlibris, 2004); Web: www.smykeonafrica.ch/massaquoi.htm.

20 Jane Addams, *Hull-House Maps and Papers* (New York: Arno Press, 1895, 1970), pp. Appendix, 216-17; Chaudhuri1, pp. 136-38, 209; Web: Google: "Swami Vivehanande". We can assume the talk was not given in July or August, since he said his first public discourse was given in August in Annisquam, MA. Nelson, p. 253.

21 *CW*, VI:360.

22 Ibid., VII:519.

23 Burke, II, p. 187; V, p. 174; VI, p. 318; Chaudhuri1, p. 138.

24 Burke, V, pp. 169-70, 174; Nivedita, I, pp. 228-31, 248-51; II, pp. 787-88, 841; Chaudhuri1, p. 138; Ellen Gates Starr, *Biography Resource Center Online* (Gale Group, 1999), on the Internet through some libraries.

25 Stephen Hay, "Rabindranath Tagore in America", *American Quarterly* 14 (1962), p. 460; Saha, p. 142.

26 University of Iowa. Web: www.uiowa.edu/~socialwk/bills/newsletters/vol3_8.htm; Riepe (1970), pp. 127-28; *The Jane Addams Papers* (microfiche), reel 22-735; Raucher, p. 102.

27 *CA* (2002), vol. 194, pp. 5-8; Jane Addams, *Hull House Museum*. Web: www.uic.edu/jaddams/hull/ja_bio.htm.

28 *Life*, I, pp. 451-52; *CW*, IX:322-23.

29 Chaudhuri1, p. 170.

30 *EWB*, XIII, pp. 226-28; Allan Nevins, *Study in Power: John D. Rockefeller* (New York: Charles Scribner's Sons, 1953), II, pp. 179-80, 183-84, 187, 191, 479.

31 *CW*, IX:9.

32 *NCAB* (1948), XXXIV, pp. 136-37; Hohner, p. 15.

33 *CW*, VIII:305; IX:17.

34 *NCAB* (1933), XXII, p. 266; Bagley Family. Google: "Tales that have the Rime of Age"; Burke, I, pp. 451, 454.

35 *CW*, IX:18.

36 Burke, II, p. 22.

37 Helen Miller Gould. Web: www.historyswomen.com/moregreatwomen/HellenMillerGould.html; *NCAB* (1906), XIII, pp. 523-24: Web: http://en.wikipedia.org/wiki/Helen_Miller_Gould; *Hamilton Evening Journal* (Ohio) (April 4, 1925), p. 15; *New York Times* (Dec. 21, 1938) on PQHN.

38 *PB* (Sept. 1926), p. 424; Burke, II, p. 23.

39 *CW*, IX:18.

40 Ibid., VIII:521.

41 Burke I, p. 432; V, pp. 381-82.

42 Burke, II, pp. 135-37, 143, 150, 158-59; Chaudhuri2, pp. 574-75, 587; *WWSV*, pp. 96-97; Prabuddhaprana2, p. 88.

43 Cameron, pp. 161-62.

44 *CW*, VI:309.

45 Anna Ingersoll, "The Swamis in America", *The Arena* (1899), pp. 483-84; Prabuddhaprana2, p. 488; Bagchi, pp. 306-07; "At Greenacre", *Outlook* (Oct. 3, 1896); Burke, II, pp. 231, 233, 235, 242; Cameron, pp. 194-203.

46 *Brahmavadin* (Jan. 1903), pp. 56-57; Basu, pp. 595-96.

47 Cameron, pp. 260-62; History of the Green Acre Baha'i School. Web: http://bahai-library.org/essays/greenacre.html; Benowitz (1998), pp. 110-11; Jackson, p. 50; Arthur Christy, "Orientalism in New England: Whittier", (1930) *American Literature*, pp. 372-92.

48 *CW*, VII:465; IX:20.

49 Ibid., IX:49.

50 Burke, II, pp. 56-57, 187, 229; Prabuddhaprana2, p. 62.

51 *DAB* (1932), IX, pp. 200-03; *RLA* (1991), pp. 212-13; *EWB* (1998), VII, pp. 535-36; June Benowitz, *Encyclopedia of American Women and Religion* (Oxford: ABC-CLIO, 1998), pp. 156-37.

52 *CW*, VIII:331; IX:49, 51.

53 *CW*, IX:191.

54 Ibid., IX:474.

55 Lady Henry Somerset. Web: www.redhill-reigate-history.co.uk/lady%20somerset.htm; UCLC.

56 *CW*, IX:49, 51, 191-207.

57 *RLA* (1991), p. 504; Vincent Tompkins, *American Eras* (Detroit: Gale, 1997), pp. 323-24; *DAB* (1936), XX, pp. 233-34; Burke, II, p. 238.

58 *CW*, VI:299-302; IX:54, 81.

59 Burke, III, pp. 30-31, 48-49, 467, 493-94, 508-09; Hohner, pp. 39-41, 64.

60 *NCAB* (1903), VI, pp. 278-79; *DAB* (1930), IV, pp. 426-27.

61 *CW*, VIII:288.

62 Ibid., V:122; VIII:379.

63 Ibid., V:51; VIII:350.

64 Ibid., V:121; VI:365.

65 Burke, II, p. 215; III, pp. 223-30, 305; IV, pp. 306, 444, 485-86; V, p. 84; For more on Müller's activities see Beckerlegge, pp. 180-201. Rs. 40,000 = 2,667 Pounds = $12,987 = $347,000 in 2008; Cost of Living.

66 *Life*, I (1965), p. 443; Sister Nivedita, *Notes of Some Wanderings* (Calcutta: Udbodhan Office, 1957), pp. 97-98.

67 *CW*, VI:402; VIII:400, 404, 408.

68 *Brahmavadin* (April 1, 1898), pp. 555, 562-63.

69 Basu, p. 201.

70 *CW*, VIII:471.

71 Ibid., V:151.

72 Burke, V, p. 63.

73 *Boston Daily Globe* (April 20, 1894), p. 6 on PQHN; (Dec. 2, 1896), p. 8; *EWB* Sup. XXI; *DAB*.

74 Burke, I, pp. 49-50; V, pp. 214-16; *Los Angeles Herald* (Dec. 24, 1899).

75 *ANB*, XIX, pp. 661-62; *DAB* (1963), VIII, pp. 599-600; Caroline Severance. Web: www.uua.org/uuhs/duub/articles/carolineseverance.htm.

76 Chaudhuri2, pp. 759, 778.

77 *CW*, VIII:519.

78 Ibid., IX:136-37.

79 Ibid., VIII:521.

80 Ibid., VIII:528.

81 Burke, VI, pp. 42, 138, 287-88; *Times* (Oct. 9, 1924), p. A1; *American Decades 1900-09* (Detroit: Gale Research, 1996), pp. 327-29.

82 *CW*, VIII:495, 509.

83 Burke, II, pp. 212-13; V, pp. 346, 381-82; Chaudhuri2, pp. 629-30, 767.

84 *DAB* (1960), IV, pp. 488-89; Phoebe Apperson Hearst. Web: www.hearstcastle.org/history/phoebe_hearst.asp; The Baha'i. Web: www.pleasantonweekly.com/morgue/2001/2001_11_09.bahai9.html; Clara Rogers, *The Story of Two Lives* (Norwood, MA: Plimpton Press, 1932), pp. 302-03.

85 Datta, pp. 118-19, 320, 339; R. C. Majumdar, ed., *Swami Vivekananda Centenary Memorial Volume* (Calcutta: Swami Vivekananda Centenary, 1963), p. 514; *CA* (1987), vol. 119; Atmaprana, pp. 126, 216; Burke, IV, p. 383; Nivedita, II, p. 893.

86 Web: en.wikipedia.org/wiki/Peter_Kropotkin.

CHAPTER XI

PROFESSIONALS AND BUSINESS PERSONNEL

IN THE YEAR 1881, in a small town in Nebraska, five-year-old E. E. Dickinson (1875/76-1969) was drowning. He later recounted:

As I was about to sink for the second time under the water, a dazzling multi-coloured light appeared, filling all space. In the midst was the figure of a man with tranquil eyes and a reassuring smile. My body was sinking for the third time when one of my brother's companions bent a tall slender willow tree in such a low dip that I could grasp it with my desperate fingers. The boys lifted me to the bank and successfully gave me first-aid treatment.

Twelve years later ... the great World's Parliament of Religions was in session. Mother and I were walking down a main street, when again I saw the mighty flash of light. A few paces away, strolling leisurely along was the same man I had seen years before in vision. He approached a large auditorium and vanished within the door.

"Mother," I cried, "that was the man who appeared at the time I was drowning!" She and I hastened into the building; the man was seated on a lecture platform. We soon learned that he was Swami Vivekananda of India. After he had given a soul-striking talk, I went forward to meet him. When I went up to the lecture platform in Chicago to speak to Swami Vivekananda, before I could greet him he said: "Young man, I want you to stay out of the water!" He smiled on me graciously, as though we were old friends. I was so young that I did not know how to give expression to my feelings, but in my heart I was hoping that he would offer to be my teacher. He read my thoughts. "No my son, I am not your guru." Vivekananda gazed with his beautiful, piercing eyes deep into my own. "Your teacher will come later. He will give you a silver cup." After a little pause, he added smiling, "He will pour out to you more blessings than you are now able to hold." I left

Chicago in a few days and never saw the great Vivekananda again. But every word he had uttered was indelibly written on my inmost consciousness.

Years passed until 1925 in Los Angeles when E. E. Dickinson met his guru Paramahansa Yogananda (1893-1952) of Bengal. Dickinson added that on Christmas night of 1936 at the Mt. Washington Centre, "I saw, for the third time in my life, the same dazzling flash of light. In another minute I was gazing on my guru's gift that Vivekananda had foreseen for me forty-three years earlier—a silver cup" Yogananda had purchased in Calcutta. For many years Dickinson practised kriya-yoga meditation three times daily, and in 1965 received the title of Yogacharya, a teacher of yoga.[1]

Three years before the Parliament of Religions commenced in Chicago, Swamiji was already attracting attention from prominent Westerners. In Ghazipur, India, his friend Gaganbabu introduced him to Mr. Ross, a government official. After a long discussion on Hindu festivals and social customs, he asked Swamiji to write a paper on the Holi festival, which he did. Through Mr. Ross he met Mr. Pennington, the district judge at Ghazipur. Swamiji spoke to him about the revival of Hinduism in modern times, the scientific basis of yoga, ascetic disciplines and many other subjects. "Mr. Pennington was so impressed by the Swami's exposition of Hindu religion and social customs that he asked him to go to England to preach the ideas there." Swamiji also held an extensive discussion on Vedantic ideals and their application in daily life with Colonel John Henry Rivett-Carnac (1838-1923). According to *Life*, "His spirit of renunciation, his insight, his power and personality, became radiant. He was, as it were, Vedanta incarnate to the astonished Westerner." In 1885 Rivett-Carnac, who was known for his generosity, raised and commanded the Ghazipur volunteer horse and rifles regiment while serving in the Bengal Civil Service (1859-94). He was also a scholar who wrote a number of books on commerce and archeology in India, along with *Many Memories of Life in India, at Home and Abroad* (1910).[2]

Swami Vivekananda departed from Yokohama, Japan, on July 14, 1893 on the S. S. Empress of India, docking in Vancouver, Canada, on the 25th. He boarded the Canadian Pacific Railway and, after a two-and-a-half day ride, arrived in Winnipeg. The late Rainer Kossmann, a founding member of the Vedanta Society of Winnipeg, Canada, uncovered a clipping from the *Winnipeg Free Press* of July 31, 1893, stating, "Swami Vevekananda [sic], a Hindoo priest, arrived from the west last night on his way to Chicago, where he will attend the world's congress of religions as a delegate from

India." This being the case, Vivekananda arrived in Winnipeg two days later than previously thought, and he thus had some time to explore the city of Vancouver B.C. He reached Vancouver at 7 p.m., July 25, and, according to Rainer Kossmann, "If he stayed on the Canadian Pacific Railway Express all the way from Vancouver, he would have left Vancouver at 10:45 a.m. on Friday, 28 July", and arrived in Winnipeg at 10:30 p.m. on Sunday the 30th. At Winnipeg he switched to the Great Western Railway and journeyed via St. Paul, Minnesota, to Chicago, travelling for less than one-and-a-half days. Swamiji wrote that he "remained about twelve days in Chicago",[3] indicating that he was there from the night of August 1 or 2 (if he stayed overnight in Winnipeg) until the 13th, the date Asim Chaudhuri says he left Chicago for Boston.[4] Interestingly, in the year 1893 Mahatma Gandhi travelled to South Africa, and Sri Aurobindo and Annie Besant went separately to India, each to begin their memorable careers.

When Swamiji made his first visit to Chicago, he lived with the wealthy Erskine Mason Phelps (1839-1910), one of the directors of the World's Columbian Exposition. He was introduced to him by Varada Rao, a friend of his from Madras.[5] Phelps, the founder of one of the largest shoe manufacturing business in the Midwest, was also the president of Hahnemann Hospital, and for twenty years the president of the National Business League, vice-president of Central Church, and a director of the Merchants Loan & Trust Company and the Commonwealth Edison Company. He was an intimate friend of Grover Cleveland, the president of the United States who offered him the position of an Ambassador, which he turned down. Phelps was a generous man who left over one-hundred thousand dollars to the Hahnemann Hospital in his will, which included the Phelps-Dodge Nurses' Home of Chicago. While living in Chicago, almost every day Swamiji would go to the fair. Miss Grace Howe, a friend of the Hale family, wrote what Vivekananda had told her about the Phelps family. She wrote:

> He happened to speak of them [Phelps] the other day and said, "They are very kind friendly people—were very kind to me, but I could not live there." When we asked "Why", he said in a perplexed way—"I do not know—I think they are fashionable. They took me to the club, off on a yacht, they drank all the time—when I said I do not drink they ordered it for me just the same. They swore too, all the time. (He meant the men he met). I had seen no Americans. I did not understand it—but I could not live so—I had to go away."

While residing in the West, Swamiji always wanted to live with the right people in the right environment. Saddened and short on funds, after twelve days in Chicago he decided to leave the city and visit Kate Sanborn, the women he had previously met on the Northern Pacific train who invited him to her house near Metcalf, Massachusetts. Swamiji was accompanied by a Mr. Lalubhai as far as Boston, who "was very kind" to him.[6]

Mr. Chabildas Lalubhai (1839–1914) was a wealthy merchant who owned his own steamship, imported English cloth and amassed huge sums of wealth by selling the merchandise to wholesale traders in Bombay, owned a factory where decorative goods were made from ivory, and in Bombay he constructed a number of buildings. He and his son Ramdas Chabildas, an Indian barrister and Sanskrit scholar, had been two of Swamiji's hosts in Bombay. Vivekananda admired his rise from rags to riches, his enterprising nature. Lalubhai travelled on the same ship with him to Japan and then went to Winnipeg, Canada, and Chicago. In the *Winnipeg Free Press* of July 29 or 30, it stated, "Five Bombay merchants en route to Chicago, where they will spend two months at the World's Fair, arrived from the west last night and are at the Manor."[7] If Lalubhai was part of this group, he would have arrived in Winnipeg a day or two before Swamiji. After Swamiji spent about twelve days in Chicago, they travelled together to Boston. When they were about to separate from one another, Lalubhai discovered that Swamiji had very little money with him, so he requested him to telegraph his London firm whenever he needed financial assistance. Lalubhai told him that when he would reach London, he would advise his agent to respond to him. There is no indication that Swamiji took up his financial offer. From London Lalubhai inquired if he would like to return to India with him. Swamiji sent back the reply, "Don't wait, will go back a long period hence." In his last will Lalubhai benevolently provided funds for the construction of a hospital, sanatorium, poor lodge, industrial and technical schools and colleges, and scholarships for deserving students.[8]

During September, while the Parliament of Religions was in progress, Swamiji stayed at the house of John Bacon Lyon (1829-1904), a successful grain dealer, real-estate investor, and for forty-six years a prominent member of the Chicago Board of Trade. Also living in the household were Mr. Lyon's wife Emily, his two sons John B. and William C. (d. 1900), his widowed daughter Mrs. Emily Conger (1861-1937) and her young daughter Cornelia. From Cornelia Conger we learn that soon after John Lyon first met Vivekananda in the family library, he told his wife:

"This Indian is the most brilliant and interesting man who has ever been in our home, and he shall stay as long as he wishes...." Swami Vivekananda and my grandfather [John Lyon] got on very well. My grandfather used to take him to the Chicago Club.... My grandmother said he was deeply interested in philosophy. He and Swami would have long long talks and got on very well.

At one time John Lyon was on the Executive Committee of the Chicago Club, a private business and social club founded in 1869 where Swamiji would have encountered prominent businessmen, professionals and politicians. Swamiji wrote in a letter, "When I come to Chicago, I always go to see Mr. and Mrs. Lyons, one of the noblest couples I have seen here."[9] It is stated in a book that Mr. Lyon "was widely known in the commercial world, a man of great business sagacity and one whose name stood for the highest ideals of integrity and fair dealing."[10]

Cornelia Conger mentioned:

> My grandmother [Emily Lyon] was president of Women's Hospital in Chicago. In those days it was on 33rd and Rose Avenue. And he [Swamiji] asked her to take him there. And he spoke not only to patients and doctors and nurses but to the cooks and laundresses. He asked a thousand questions, everything about the hospital and was so interested in it.

During the mid-1950s at Belur Math, Cornelia visited Swami Shankarananda, the then President of the Ramakrishna Order. She states, "I told him about my grandmother taking him through her hospital. He said, 'Well, don't you know he founded the best maternity hospital in India.'"[11]

For six years Emily Conger had been the widow of the lawyer William Perez Conger (1851-87). In 1893 she took Swamiji to hear his first Symphony Concert. Cornelia added:

> My grandmother and my mother [Emily Conger] attended most of the meetings of the Congress of Religions and heard Swamiji speak there and later at lectures he gave. I know he helped my sad young mother who missed her young husband so much. Mother read and studied Swamiji's books later and tried to follow his teachings.[12]

In two letters written to the Hale sisters in April and July 1896, Swamiji sent his "best love and kindest remembrances" to Mrs. [Emily] Conger.[13]

Swamiji maintained a cordial relationship with Mr. Lyon's granddaughter, the six-year-old Cornelia Conger (1887-1973). When Swamiji returned to Chicago during January 1895, he stayed with their family. Cornelia Conger explained that Swamiji remained there for only a short time during his second visit because "He knew he could teach better if he lived in his own regime of food and of many hours for meditation. It also left him free to receive many who came to him for help." As stated before, in the mid-1950s Cornelia visited Swami Shankarananda at Belur Math and told him of her reminiscences of Swamiji, which he encouraged her to publish. The day before proceeding to Belur Math, Cornelia Conger received a profound preparation for her upcoming meeting. She was in a charming shop in Calcutta with her lady friend. She told a very intelligent young man in the shop:

> "I think we're going to have an interesting day tomorrow, we are going to Belur Math." "And madam", he said, "What takes you to Belur Math?" "Oh", I said quite casually, "You know when I was a little girl, Swami Vivekananda lived at our house when he was in Chicago for the Parliament of Religions." And the colour drained out of his face, and he dropped on his knees in front of me and took my hands in his long slender hands and he said, "You looked into his eyes and you heard his voice, you are deeply blessed. Will you take an hour from your life and tell me every little thing that you can remember about him and I will treasure every word until the day of my death?" You see I have always just thought of him as a darling person I loved. I didn't realize that he felt just the way a Christian would feel if you told them that Christ had lived in their house and that they had talked to Christ. Well it made a deep and, I must confess, a shattering effect on me, and for an hour he knelt before me and I held his hands, and in the most strange way everything I remembered and everything that my mother and my grandmother had told me came back to me.[14]

Her reminiscences came out in the May 1956 edition of the *Prabuddha Bharata* where she recalled:

> My memories are simply of him as a guest in our home—of a great personality who is still vivid to me! His brilliant eyes, his charming voice with the lilt of a slight well-bred Irish brogue, his warm smile!... So here is

> my very tiny "facet" offered in memory of someone I have loved for all these 62 years—not as a teacher, nor a great religious leader—but as a wonderful and vivid friend who lived in our home.[15]

Fifteen years later, during her 1971 reminiscence speech at the Vedanta Society in Chicago, she added:

> He had a keen sense of humour and was very easy for all of us to get on with. And everybody in the house loved him.... It is a memory I've never forgotten. He had the most extraordinary and magnetic personality. I was 84 years old on Thursday and his picture in my mind is just as clear. I've never known anybody like him. I still think of him as somebody I loved and who I think loved me."[16]

Cornelia Conger revealed that when Swami Vivekananda first arrived at their house, "We owned a sugar plantation on the Bayou Teche in Louisiana and we had as our guests a man and a wife who had a nearby plantation." She mentioned they would all eat breakfast together. Cornelia later added, "Tabasco sauce ... it was made by friends of ours, the McIlhennys, whose plantation was near ours in Louisiana." Inferring from this, it is a good chance that the McIlhennys were the guests that Swamiji met at their home. Swamiji very much liked the tabasco sauce they had given them. She [Cornelia] is referring to a relative of Edmund McIlhenny (1815-90), who owned a plantation on Avery Island on the Bayou Teche in Louisiana where he invented what he called Tabasco brand pepper sauce in 1868, which was sold through the McIlhenny Company that is still in business today. In 1893 the company was headed by John Avery McIlhenny (1867-1942), who, as a member of the Rough Riders during the Spanish American War, was promoted by Theodore Roosevelt for "gallantry in action" and later was appointed president of the U.S. Civil Service Commission in 1913 by U.S. President Woodrow Wilson.[17]

One Sunday evening, Cornelia's Aunt (who was John B. Lyon's daughter) Katharine (Mrs. Robert Lyon Hamill) was informing some young professors and newspapermen how remarkable Vivekananda was. Their response was, "Modern scientists and psychologists could 'show up' his religious beliefs in no time!" The "young intellectuals" agreed to meet with him the next Sunday evening at an informal supper party. "The entire evening was a lively and interesting debate on all sorts of ideas." Aunt Katharine (or Katherine) related:

> Swamiji's great knowledge of the Bible and the Koran as well as the various Oriental religions, his grasp of science and of psychology were astounding. Before the evening was over, the "doubting Thomases" threw up their hands and admitted that Swamiji had held his own on every point and that they parted from him with warmest admiration and affection.

One of the newspapermen at the party was Finley Peter Dunne (1867-1936), who, at that time, was an editorial page supervisor and columnist for the *Chicago Evening Post*. Though he finished last in his high school class, he became an exceptional political humourist authoring eight books expressing the satirical views of a fictional "Mr. Dooley". His witty observations and insights have been appreciated by American and European readers up to this day.[18]

Years later Cornelia Conger, who remained unmarried, held the position of vice-president of the National Board, and president of the Illinois branch of the American Institute of Interior Designers. For more than fifteen years she headed the furnishing committee of the Presbyterian St. Luke's Hospital. A skilled public speaker, she lectured frequently about interior decorating. During January 1971, at the Vedanta Society of Chicago she left us with a long, sublime and informative verbal reminiscence of Swamiji preserved on cassette, a portion of which can be heard on Swami Chetanananda's video, "Vivekananda as We Saw Him".[19]

Swami Vivekananda met the famous agnostic Robert Ingersoll (1833-1899) near the end of September 1893, when the World's Parliament of Religions was drawing to a close. He described Ingersoll as "a great agnostic, a very noble man, a very good man, and a very fine speaker".[20] In later years on at least five occasions Swamiji made comments on some of the things Ingersoll had told him.[21] A little before his death, Ingersoll was one of the primary attractions, along with Swami Abhedananda and Benjamin Fay Mills, at the Free Religious Association meetings held at the Hollis Street Theatre in Boston.[22] Robert Green Ingersoll, the son of a Congregationalist and Presbyterian minister, rose to the rank of Colonel in the Union Army during the Civil War, and then became the Attorney General of the State of Illinois (1867-69). Throughout the rest of his life, he proved himself to be a successful lawyer and a public orator of immense talent. Possessing a great deal of personal charm and debating skill, Ingersoll, known as "the great agnostic", attacked Bible literalism before large audiences. He lived an exemplary life and generously gave large sums of money to charity.[23]

The following reminiscence illustrates, by inference, that Swamiji's message made a distinct impression on far more people than we know about. Donald S. Harrington (1914-2005) [q.v.], the long-time minister of the Community Church of New York (1944-82), spoke at the United Nations Dag Hammarskjold Auditorium on 6 November 1993 as part of a celebration commemorating Swamiji's participation in the World's Parliament of Religions in 1893. He mentioned that his father Charles Elliot Marshall Harrington (1869-1964), a druggist by profession from Waltham and Newton, Massachusetts, attended the Parliament of Religions in 1893. Over a quarter of a century later he told his children about his experience. Donald Harrington relates:

> I will never forget his description of the august procession that came into the "court of honour" (as it was called); of the great religious figures of the world—128 pairs of men and women walking together, representing the brotherhood of religions. He said it was a moment that he could never forget, and that no one should ever forget.
>
> Among his reminiscences was a remembrance of how the gathering was electrified by the words that were spoken by Swami Vivekananda when he was first introduced, when he explained something which was a little difficult for American religionists to believe—that belief was not the central business of religion. He said, religion is not a way of believing, it is a way of being and becoming. Religion is being real yourself, and becoming part of what is real in the universe.
>
> This was a revelation and it was a very striking and important one. My father spoke of it very often....
>
> My father spoke especially of his saying that in the sacred language of his religion, Sanskrit, the word "exclusion" cannot be translated. In other words it is a uniting experience that we human beings have, and need to have, and that was the message that electrified the World Parliament of Religions a hundred years ago. Swami Vivekananda was the giver, and we are all the better for it.[24]

Swami Vivekananda spoke at the Scientific Section of the Parliament of Religions. When the assembly came to a close, the Swami was the guest of honour at a vegetarian dinner party held at the home of Elisha Gray (1835-1901) in Highland Park, a suburb of Chicago. The scientists, which included Lord Kelvin, Hermann von Helmholtz and probably Edouard Hospitalier, were impressed with Swamiji's knowledge of the subject. In conjunction with the Columbian Exposition, Gray served as the chairman of the first International Electrical Congress.[25] He cofounded Gray and Barton in 1869, an electric-equipment shop in Cleveland, Ohio, which eventually became the Western Electric Company. Elisha Gray invented an automatic self-adjusting telegraphic relay, a telegraph switch and an annunciator for hotels and large business offices, a telegraphic repeater, and a telegraph line printer. He filed his harmonic telegraph patent in 1875, two days before Alexander Graham Bell (1847-1922). In one of the most unusual events in the history of inventions the next year, only two hours after Bell filed his patent, Elisha Gray filed a caveat for a telephone at the same office. Western Union Telegraph bought the rights to Gray's telephone, but Bell Telephone objected and after a long court battle in 1888, the Supreme Court decided in their favour. Gray demonstrated his telautograph machine at the Chicago World's Fair. It electrically transmitted handwriting and drawings over long distances.[26]

During the first month of January 1894, Swamiji gave six lectures in Memphis, Tennessee. The *Appeal-Avalanche* of January 16 informed its readers:

> Swami Vive Kananda, the Hindoo monk, who is to lecture at the Auditorium [in Memphis] tonight, is one of the most eloquent men who has ever appeared on the religious or lecture platform in this country. His matchless oratory, deep penetration into things occult, his cleverness in debate, and great earnestness captured the closest attention of the world's thinking men at the World's Fair Parliament of Religion, and the admiration of thousands of people who have since heard him during his lecture tour through many of the states of the Union.[27]

In Memphis, Vivekananda had the pleasure of meeting General Robert Franklin Patterson (1836-1907) and his wife Marion. Enlisting as a Second Lieutenant in the Civil War, "for gallant and meritorious service" Patterson was later promoted to a frontline Brigadier General in the Union Army. He became the postmaster of Memphis (1889-93) and received appointment as the American Consul General in Calcutta in 1897. Josephine MacLeod believed that Marion persuaded U.S. President William McKinley to give her husband the appointment, so they could be closer to Vivekananda in India. In May of 1898, Marion went with Swamis Vivekananda, Niranjanananda, Turiyananda, Sadananda and Swarupananda, Sister Nivedita, Sara Bull and Josephine MacLeod to Almora, and later to Anantnag in Kashmir. In August the Swami was the guest of the Pattersons at Dal Lake for a couple of days. On 13 May 1901 Swamiji wrote, "Mrs. Patterson and children are off to Europe. General [R. F. Patterson] is alone and very desirous that I would call. I will the next time I go to town." In the following month he again mentioned the General in a letter.[28]

According to the Memphis, Tennessee *Appeal-Avalanche* newspaper dated 16 January 1894, "Col. R. B. Snowden gave a dinner at his home at Annesdale in honour of the distinguished visitor [Swami Vivekananda] on Sunday, where he met Assistant Bishop Thomas F. Gailor, Rev. George Patterson and a number of other clergymen." During the Civil War, Colonel Robert Bogardus Snowden served with the Tennessee regiment in the Confederate Army fighting in many battles. After the war he owned large property holdings managed through the Peabody Land Co., of which he was the president, and worked as a director of the Bank of Commerce, and an officer or director of numerous manufacturing concerns, banks, railroads and insurance and land companies. For over a week while lodging in Memphis, Swamiji was the guest of Snowden's brother-in law, Colonel Hu L. Brinkley, at a high-class boarding house. Brinkley organized one of Swamiji's lectures.[29]

In Memphis, on January 22, 1894, the Freemason, Past Grand Master George Cooper Connor, whom Swamiji met, wrote a letter of introduction to Gilbert Wordsworth Barnard (1834-1908) at the Masonic Temple in Chicago, stating in part:

> My dear Brother:—I take very great pleasure in introducing to you personally, and as a Freemason, our East India Brother SWAMI VIVEKANANDA, whom I examined in the English Work, in which he was made a Master Mason [in 1884], in Anchor and Hope, 236, E.C. He was educated in India, and is a Monk of the oldest, and most humane of the Religions of the world,—and because of my own family relations to the city of Calcutta I am anxious that this amiable representative of that wonderful land receive as cordial consideration in my country as I received in his.

George Cooper Connor, an Irishman originally from Dublin, authored a book published in Nashville, Tennessee, in 1894 entitled *The Shibboleth: A Templar Monitor*. Vivekananda had previously lectured at the Masonic Temple in Chicago the previous year on November 7 and 10.[30]

On February 16 Vivekananda went to a reception in his honour at the home of the wealthy Charles L. Freer (1856-1919) in Detroit, Michigan, which was attended by members of the Witenagamote club. The next day Freer gave a small reception and supper in honour of Swami Vivekananda. The newspaper referred to him as "the social lion of the day" and added, "All these entertainments were very elaborate affairs." Mr. Freer also contributed two-hundred dollars toward Vivekananda's work. Before the end of March, Swamiji tried to refund the money of his Detroit donors, but they would not accept it.[31] Charles Lang Freer, a self-made man, became one of the managing directors of the Michigan-Peninsular Car Company, the largest railway car building enterprise in the country. As an art collector, he acquired the largest series of pictorial works of his friend James McNeill Whistler (1834-1903), the most aesthetically valuable collection of ancient glazed pottery (including East Indian) in the world, and the greatest private collection of Chinese and Japanese masterpieces that existed outside of Japan, with the possible exception of those in the Boston Art Museum, all of which in 1906 he donated to the government as part of the Freer Gallery of Art in Washington, D.C., which is presently open to the public.[32]

During his first stay in Detroit during February 1894, Vivekananda gave a series of discourses, and the *Tribune* on the 18th noted:

> There has seldom been such a sensation in cultured circles in Detroit as that created by the advent of Swami Vive Kananda, the learned Hindu monk, whose exceptional command of our own language has enabled us to receive impressions concerning ourselves from an oriental standpoint and to acquire knowledge of a people of whose peculiar civilization and philosophy we have heard so much. Both in public and private the Hindu brother has talked freely and frankly.[33]

In 1883 Thomas Witherell Palmer (1830-1913) became a United States senator from the state of Michigan, supporting women's suffrage and government regulation of the railroads. He became one of the most popular orators in Michigan. For two years beginning in 1889, he was the U.S. minister to Spain, and shortly after was chosen by United States President Harrison to become the commissioner for the World's Columbian Exposition in Chicago. The board elected him president. Palmer devoted much of his time to philanthropy and was one of the founders of the Detroit Museum of Art.[34] On March 10, 1894, he introduced Swamiji before his speech at the Detroit Opera House. At that time Palmer told a parable about a shield that was copper on one side and silver on the other. Two knights, each seeing the shield from only one side, argued whether it was made of copper or silver. Then he said, Vivekananda

> belongs to a religion which was old long before ours was thought of by men. I am sure that it will be pleasant to hear from the copper side of the shield. We have looked at it only from the silver side. Ladies and Gentlemen, Swami Vive Kananda.[35]

Palmer very much appreciated the lecture. While Swamiji lodged at his house as a guest for a week, he reported, "I am now living with Mr. Palmer. He is a very nice gentleman." "Mr. Palmer is a very hearty, jolly, good old man and very rich. He has been uniformly kind to me." "In Palmer's house there was real 'good time'. He is a real jovial heartwhole fellow, and likes 'good time' a little too much and his 'hot Scotch'. But he is right along innocent and childlike in his simplicity."[36] Largely through the influence of Palmer, Swamiji was freed from a three-year contract with the Slayton Lyceum Bureau that swindled him out of the money he earned from lectures.[37]

After leaving Detroit, Swamiji had a one-night engagement at the Opera House in Bay City, Michigan, on March 20, 1894. "Hinduism, the Religion of India" was his topic. Dr. Charles T. Newkirk (d. 1909), the local physician, introduced his lecture.[38] To give an idea of Newkirk's background, while working in Paraguay he lived through several epidemics during which his brother died of small pox. Moving on to Buenos Aires in Argentina

> he learned that the yellow fever had broken out there in the most malignant form..... he again devoted himself to the work of saving life and alleviating suffering. He was in constant communication with the authorities for the prevention of the spread of the disease; and, by his advice, many sanitary precautions were taken which doubtless cut short one of the most frightful epidemics ever known. An idea may be formed of the danger which Dr. Newkirk was compelled to face from the fact that 26,000 persons died

in twenty-five days of this disease alone. He was engaged four months in Buenos Aires during this plague.[39]

Swamiji refers to his elderly friend William Joseph Flagg (1818-98) in letters of March, April and October of 1894, who offered him money, which he did not accept.[40] On March 23, 1896, Flagg correctly pointed out in a letter to Vivekananda the absurdity of Kripananda (Leon Landsberg) sending a correspondence to the *Brahmavadin* condemning the Theosophists, Spiritualists and other religious groups in the United States. The following fall, he made an offer to pay for Saradananda's passage to America, which other people paid for. William Flagg made a living first as a lawyer, then as an author, a member of the Ohio state legislature, and as an Ohio grape grower and viticulturist. He owned ten-thousand acres of vine land on the banks of the Ohio River, plus some other real estate interests. The fact that he grew grapes for making wine could be the reason for Swamiji refusing his money. Flagg died the day the book he had been working on for fifteen years, *Yoga or Transformation: Drawn from Many Ancient Religious Traditions*, was published. In the volume he wrote:

> In its essential nature Hinduism is beyond question the best, greatest and most admirable religious and philosophical system in the world.... And there can be no better proof that Hinduism is in full life to-day than the fact that the pious Hindus are actually turning the tables on us, by sending hither learned and eloquent teachers to convert the would-be converters, teachers whom many of our learned men listen to with attention and profit, because they have indeed something to tell.

His "Hindu Yoga" section relies partly on the English language theosophical publication from Bombay entitled *Hatha Yoga Pradipika* (1893) of Swatmaram Swami, and the Lahore publication *The Philosophy and Science of Vedanta and Raja Yoga* (1880) by Sabhapaty Swami (b. 1840). This indicates that there was some English language yogic material available during this early period.[41]

During part of April 1894, the Swami stayed in the house of the prominent Dr. Egbert Guernsey (1823-1903) and spoke at the Union League Club in New York City. In two letters addressed to Mrs. G. W. Hale, he describes Guernsey as "a very nice and learned and well-to-do man.... They are trying to help me as much as they can and they will do a good deal, I have no doubt." "Dr. Guernsey is one of the chief physicians of this city and is a very good old gentleman. They are very fond of me and are very nice people."[42] Swamiji moved to Guernsey family's summer home in Beacon, New York, for part of July and August of the same year. He notes, "The Guernseys love me very much." "Mrs. Guernsey was so kind to me, and she is ever willing to help me."[43] Dr. Guernsey's son had recently died, and he thought that Vivekananda's features resembled his deceased son. In mid-January of 1895, Swamiji returned to Guernsey's New York home, and again for thirteen days in November of 1899.[44] In February 1895, the article "The Ether" written by Swamiji appeared in the New York *Medical Times*, a journal that Guernsey founded and edited.[45]

The multi-talented Egbert Guernsey, one of New York's most affluent physicians, was a charitable, compassionate and kindly doctor. He cofounded and edited the *Brooklyn Daily Times* (1848-50), authored two nationally used elementary school textbooks concerning the history of the United States, wrote *Homeopathic Domestic Practice* (1853), which was later translated into four languages, cofounded and functioned as a professor in the New York Homeopathic Medical College during 1861-67, founded the Guernsey Maternity Hospital in 1870, created and edited the New York *Medical Times* journal (1873-1903) that accelerated the decline of organized homeopathy, presided over the medical staff of the Metropolitan Hospital from 1877 to 1903, and co-founded the Union League Club of New York and some other organizations.[46]

Vivekananda visited Washington, D.C. for eleven days (October 22-November 1, 1894) as a guest of the wife of Colonel Enoch Totten (1836-98), who treated him "very kindly". Mrs. Totten was the daughter of Postmaster-General Timothy Howe. She was also the niece of Miss Grace Howe, one of Swamiji's Chicago friends.[47] At the beginning of the Civil War, Colonel Totten enlisted as a First Lieutenant in a regiment from the state of Wisconsin. The often-wounded war hero was eventually promoted to the rank of Colonel. After the war, he was a successful lawyer in the nation's capital, frequently appearing before committees of the U.S. Congress.[48]

Charles Higgins (1854-1929), a successful business executive, was a member of the Committee of Comparative Religions at the Brooklyn Ethical Association in Brooklyn, New York, under the direction of Lewis Janes. Back in July 1894, Swamiji knew that Mr. Higgins had arranged a future series of lectures for him.[49] In November he printed a ten-page pamphlet on Vivekananda as an advanced notice of his upcoming oral presentation before the Brooklyn Ethical Society. The pamphlet consisted articles about Swamiji drawn from American and Indian newspapers.[50] On November the 30th, in a correspondence to Alasinga, Swamiji indicated that he had started a Vedanta organization in New York City:

> Now go to work for the organization. I have started one already in New York and the Vice-President will soon write to you. Keep correspondence with them. Soon I hope to get up a few in other places. We must organize our forces not to make a sect—not on religious matters, but on the secular business part of it.[51]

It is possible that Charles Higgins was its president. By late December, the Swami attended an informal reception at Higgins' residence. "Some of them thought that such Oriental religious subjects will not interest the Brooklyn public. But the lecture, through the blessings of the Lord, proved a tremendous success. About 800 of the elite of Brooklyn were present."[52] The *Brooklyn Standard Union* of December 31 made this glowing report:

> It was the voice of the ancient Rishis of the Vedas speaking sweet words of love and toleration through the Hindoo monk Paramahamsa Swami Vivekananda, that held spellbound last evening every one of those many hundreds who had accepted the invitation of the Brooklyn Ethical Society.... they had heard of his culture and his learning, of his wit and his eloquence, of his purity and sincerity and holiness, and hence they expected great things. And they were not disappointed.... his swarthy face reflecting the brilliancy of his thoughts, his large, expressive eyes, bright with the enthusiasm of a prophet and his mobile mouth uttering, in deep melodious tones and in almost perfect English, only words of love and sympathy and toleration, he was a splendid type of the famous sages of Himalayas, a prophet of a new religion, combining the morality of the Christians with the philosophy of the Buddhists.[53]

A couple of months later, Swamiji relates in a letter that Higgins was "full of joy. It was he who planned all this for me, and he is so glad that everything succeeded so well".[54] In March 1898, Higgins attended the discourses of Swami Abhedananda. The self-educated Irish born Charles Michael Higgins made many improvements in the formula for producing drawing ink, American India ink and carbon writing ink. The ink and adhesive products that he invented and manufactured bear his name. He wrote a volume *The Greek Philosophers* (1903) and co-founded the Kings County Historical Society.[55]

According to the *Brooklyn Daily Eagle*, Abram Hoagland Dailey (1831-1907) attended the reception for Vivekananda in late December of 1894 at the residence of Charles Higgins. In Brooklyn (1863-67), and in Kings County (1875-78), he carried out the duties of an elected judge. Mr. Dailey spent many years as a trial lawyer and successfully defended many prominent murder suspects. Dailey also wrote an authoritative book in 1894 on a well-known Brooklyn woman spiritualist. Another attendee at the party was Dr. Charles H. Shepard (1825-1910) who in 1863 established the first Turkish bath in America.[56]

Miss Mary Parker Follett (1868-1933) was one of the twelve women who undersigned a Christmas letter dated December 25, 1894. They sent it to Swamiji's mother Bhuvaneshwari Devi (1841-1911), praising both her and her son, stating in part:

> We, who have your son in our midst, send you greeting. His generous service to men, women and children in our midst was laid at your feet by him the other day in an address he gave us on the ideals of "Motherhood in India". The worship of his mother will be to all who heard him an inspiration and uplift. Accept dear Madame, our grateful recognition of your life and work in and through your son.

A picture of the Child Jesus on the lap of the Virgin Mary accompanied the letter. In the fall of 1896 Sara Bull sent the following message to Swamiji, "Miss Briggs and Miss Follett who used to come out mornings to meet you are here and have arranged a class [for Swami Saradananda] of exceptionally able students to begin at once."[57] It is quite possible that these meetings positively influenced her future life. Mary Follett attended Radcliffe College in Cambridge during 1892-98 where Swamiji conversed on May 8, 1894. She later belonged to many Boston school committees concerned with vocational guidance, use of public school buildings, and the creation of social centres (1900-11), and served as the vice-president of the National Community Centre Association (1917-21). Her most important books coming out in 1918 and 1924 marked her as a visionary and pioneering individual in the field of human relations, democratic organization, and business management. A deeply religious woman, her interests were in synthesizing and integrating differences between groups. Follett's writings on leadership, conflict resolution, worker empowerment, corporate social responsibility, crowd psychology, and organizational networks were far ahead of her time. Many management authors emphasize the importance and relevance of her ideas. Mary Follett associations exist today in Japan and in the state of Idaho.[58]

1895 and After

While staying with the Guernseys in New York City, on January 24, 1895 Swami Vivekananda was invited to attend the annual dinner meeting of the Sorosis Woman's Club. No record of his conversations there has been preserved. He sat at the President's Table facing the other prominent guests along with Alonzo Cornell (1832-1904), the ex-governor of the state of New York, Elihu Root (1845-1937), and others. Mr. Root went on to become the secretary of war (now secretary of defense) under United States President William McKinley, secretary of state under his good friend President Theodore Roosevelt, and a senator from New York. He was awarded the Nobel Peace Prize in 1912 for negotiating 24 bilateral arbitration treaties.[59]

In the middle of February 1895, Swamiji sat at the table of honour along with the other notable speakers at the second annual dinner of the Manufacturers' Association of Kings and Queens Counties. It was held at the Pouch Mansion in Brooklyn. His subject was "The Industrial Condition of India and Its [or India's] Relation to the United States as a Possible Market". A key speech was delivered by Joseph C. Hendrix (1853-1904), a Democratic member of the United States Congress (1893-95) who defended the gold standard. Previously he had been defeated by Seth Low as mayor of Brooklyn. He later became president of the prestigious National Bank of Commerce and the American Bankers' Association.[60]

Swamiji twice gave a talk as the guest speaker at the residence of Amzi Barber (1843-1909) on Fifth Avenue at Sixty-eighth Street in New York City. Sara Bull sponsored the event for February-March 1895. Amzi Lorenzo Barber, a man of a kindly disposition and indomitable energy, had been a professor of natural philosophy at the African American Howard University in Washington, D.C. for four years (1868-72). He later left that to enter into the business world. By 1896 Barber's Asphalt Company had laid one-half of the asphalt pavement in the United States. According to the *New York Times*, Emma Thursby, Mary Mapes Dodge, Florence Adams, and Miss Anna Corbin

William Hocking

Arthur Schopenhauer

Laurenus Clark Seelye

John Venn

Malvina Hoffman

Jane Addams

Austin Corbin

Helen Miller Gould

Julia Ward Howe

Peter Kropotkin

Bertha Palmer

John D. Rockefeller

Caroline Severance

Dr. Egbert Guernsey

Peter Cooper Hewitt

Robert G. Ingersoll

Dr. Milburn Logan

Mrs. John (Emily) Lyon

John B. Lyon

Hiram Maxim

Elihu Root

Mark Twain

Sri Aurobindo

Gwilym Beckerlegge

Henri Bergson

Dietmar Rothermund

U Thant

Alan Arkin

Sister Gargi

Will Durant

Diana Eck

Hal W. French

David D. Gilmore

Father Thomas Keating

Raimundo Panikkar

J. D. Salinger

were present for the occasion at the wealthy Amzi Barber's house in New York City. Swami Vivekananda spoke on "The Vedanta Philosophy: Soul" before a sizeable group of select people from various backgrounds.[61]

Also, in attendance at the Barber residence for Swamiji's talk were, according to the *New York Times*, the following people: Dr. Fillmore Moore (1856-1928), William Henry Lawton (b. 1853), and Peter Marie (1825-1903). Dr. Moore was a physician from New York who replaced Lewis Janes as the director of Monsalvat School of Comparative Religions during 1900-03. Before 1904 Moore was a lecturer at the Concord School of Philosophy and at Professor Davidson's School in Farmington, Connecticut, a trustee of the Greenacre Fellowship in Eliot, Maine, in 1911, and director of the Edgewood School in Greenwich, Connecticut (1919-25).[62] William Henry Lawton was the four times publicly elected street commissioner and city engineer for the city of Newport, Rhode Island.[63] Peter Marie was a wealthy New York art collector. When he died, two-hundred and eighty-six of Marie's miniature paintings (two-inch round of ivory), many of upper class women, became the property of the New York Historical Society.[64]

One of Vivekananda's foremost supporters, Francis H. Leggett (1840-1909) asked the Swami to stay as his guest at his 130-acre Ridgely estate on three occasions (April 1895, December-January 1896, August-November 1899), and in Paris (August-September 1900). Leggett owned one of the largest wholesale grocery firms in the United States. In addition, he was a member of the New York Chamber of Commerce, the Union League Club, and director of the Washington Trust Co. Shortly after Swamiji's first visit, Leggett affirmed, "Vivekananda is the greatest man I ever saw." When asked why, Leggett replied, "He has more common sense than anyone I've ever known." After his second visit to Ridgely, in a letter to Josephine MacLeod dated January 6, 1896, Leggett recalled:

> One night at Ridgely we were all spellbound by his eloquence—such thoughts I have never heard expressed by mortal man such as he uttered for two and a half hours. We were all deeply affected. Swami was inspired to a degree that I have never heard before. He leaves us soon and perhaps we shall never see him again, but he will leave an ineffaceable impression on our hearts that will comfort us to the end of our earthly careers.[65]

Francis' wife Betty "Besse" Leggett (1852-1931) was the sister of Josephine MacLeod. When Swamiji resided at Ridgely for a long period of time in 1899, she took every effort to make sure his stay was comfortable so that he could regain his health. Her interests were primarily in his Indian work and not in his Western activities. In 1900 when Francis Leggett planned to resign from the Vedanta Society of New York, she told her husband, "You can resign from the Vedanta when you choose. I care nothing for the work outside the personality of Vivekananda." She made a contribution of a thousand dollars to Sister Nivedita's Girls' School, and served as the president of "The Ramakrishna Guild of Help" in America formed by Nivedita. The purpose of the organization was to raise funds for Nivedita's proposed Widows' and Girls' Home and School in India. Alberta Sturges (1877-1951), the daughter of Betty Leggett by her first marriage, associated with Swamiji in Rome, Ridgely, Chicago, and Paris. They exchanged letters, and he mentioned her affectionately in other correspondences.[66] She once asked Swamiji, "Is there no happiness in marriage?" And he replied, "Yes, Alberta, if marriage is entered into as a great austerity—and everything is given up—even principle."[67] In 1912 Betty Leggett went to India accompanied by Alberta Sturges and her husband, the future Earl of Sandwich. Their meeting with Holy Mother is described in Chapter IV.[68]

One morning in 1899 at Ridgely, Frances (France) Leggett (1896-1977), who was under three years of age, received a special blessing from Swamiji. Alberta Sturges and Vivekananda

> were sitting in the Hall and the child [France Leggett] came in with some flowers in her hand and gave them to the Swami. "In India," he said gravely, "we give flowers to our teachers ..." and [then] he pronounced over her some Sanskrit words.[69]

In 1902 Swamiji wrote to Josephine MacLeod, "Give my infinite love to Lady Betty and Mr. Leggett, to Alberta and Holly [Hollister]—the baby [France Leggett] has my blessings from before birth and will have forever."[70] After 1910, many of Swamiji's friends lived at Ridgely for some time, including Sister Christine, Karl Whitmarsh, Hollister Sturges, France Leggett, her husband David Margesson, and Josephine MacLeod. When Betty Leggett passed away in 1931, the Ridgely estate became the property of her daughter France Leggett, the only child of Francis and Betty. She played a pivotal role in preserving Ridgely. Swamis Satprakashananda and Nikhilananda stayed in the Swamiji Cottage at Ridgely for two summers, and Swami Prabhavananda was a good friend of hers. France Leggett left us with a history of her family in *Late and Soon* (1968), which adds to our knowledge of Vivekananda's visit to Ridgely. Upon France's death in 1977, she willed her estate to her son Francis (Frank) Margesson and his wife, who eventually sold the property to a nonprofit religious organization affiliated with the Vedanta Society of Southern California.[71]

During the year 1895, the couple Walter and Frances Goodyear were ardent disciples of Vivekananda in New York City and at Thousand Island Park. Walter aided in numerous ways in the distribution and accounting of Swamiji's books such as *Karma Yoga*, *Bhakti Yoga*, and pamphlets, in getting copyright certificates for Swamiji's pamphlets, and in advertising.[72] In addition, he became the New York agent for the *Brahmavadin*. He served as treasurer of the New York Vedanta Society probably from 1894 until 1904. At the birthday celebration for Swamiji in 1904, Goodyear mentioned about

> ...the great happiness of the days passed under the same roof with the Swami during the summer holidays on the St. Lawrence River [Thousand Island Park], ... none who had shared in that daily communion with the great teacher could help but carry its inspiring influence in his heart for all time.[73]

Goodyear was the president of the New York Vedanta Society in 1918, the vice-president in 1924, and probably other years. During April 1924, Swami Raghavananda (1887/88-1957) of the New York Centre gave more than one public speech in the meeting room of the Goodyear Metropolitan Book Shop.[74]

Walter Goodyear's (1866-1939) grandfather Charles Goodyear (1800-60) became a member of the National Inventors Hall of Fame for his discovery of vulcanization, which is still the basis of the rubber-manufacturing industry. Charles Goodyear made other people wealthy, while he died in poverty. Walter Goodyear, the treasurer of the Canadian branch of the Goodyear Shoe Machinery Company (1892-96), also worked for a number of other companies. For many years he owned the Goodyear Metropolitan Book Shop, downstairs in the George M. Cohan Theatre located at Broadway and 42nd Street. Goodyear served as an officer in the New Thought organization, "The League for the Larger Life", with Orison Swett Marden as its president. This organization offered classes emphasizing mental healing and positive thought.[75]

After Vivekananda's first public presentation in London, the *Standard* on October 23, 1895 wrote:

> Since the days of Ramahoun [Ram Mohan] Roy, with the single exception of Keshub Chunder [Keshab Chandra] Sen, there has not appeared on an English platform a more interesting Indian figure than the Brahman who lectured in Princes' Hall last night.[76]

After having heard of the "Indian Yogi" at Princes' Hall, David Margesson's (1890-1965) mother Lady Isabel invited Swamiji to speak at her residence in London. He gave a class there on November 10, 1895, and that is where he first met Margaret Noble (later Sister Nivedita). Isabel had David and his two sisters brought from their beds so that Swamiji could bless them. Swami Vivekananda lived in David's parent's house for over two months in 1896 when they were gone on vacation. In 1916 David Margesson married France Leggett, the daughter of Francis Leggett. They both received special blessings from Swamiji when they were children. Josephine MacLeod thought that Swamiji had a hand in their future marriage since he knew both of them, and they were brought up on two different continents. Being a high-ranking conservative politician in England, David Margesson acted as the chief government whip in the British parliament from 1931 to 1940. Margesson succeeded Anthony Eden as Winston Churchill's secretary of State for war (1940-42). He was instrumental in developing the Women's Armed Services, the Auxiliary Territorial Service, and the Women's Auxiliary Air Force. After Britain suffered severe military setbacks, including the loss of Singapore, Churchill found a replacement for Margesson and he became the first Viscount. It was his son Frank Margesson and wife Helena who sold Ridgely in 1997 to the Vedantists.[77]

Swamiji arrived in Caversham on September 10 and in London on October 25, 1895. John Henry Wright told his wife that Swamiji "succeeded in winning" "the chief secretary for India, Sir F. Arbuthnot", and that "they became fast friends". Arbuthnot, an Orientalist, did not hold this position, so Wright may be unknowingly referring to Arbuthnot plus a second person. The three leading candidates for the second person are: two secretaries of state for India: Henry Hartley Fowler (March 10, 1894-June 21, 1895) and Lord George Hamilton (July 4, 1895-October 9, 1903); and the secretary of state for the Colonies: Lord George Robinson Ripon (August 18, 1892-June 21, 1895). Marie Louise Burke presents a strong case that since Lady Ripon probably conversed with Swamiji, her choice is Lord Ripon (1827-1909) whom Swamiji certainly would want to meet. During his distinguished career, Prime Minister Gladstone (1809-98) appointed him viceroy and governor-general of India (1880-84). At that time Lord Ripon endeared himself to the Indian people by his liberal policies that included: bringing an end to the costly second Afghan War, introducing free trade with only light duties on a few items, lowering the salt tax, establishing a local government of elected officials, supporting the establishment of the Indian National Congress where Indians could discuss social, educational and cultural reforms, allowing Indian language newspapers to have equal freedom with those of the English, improving primary and secondary schools, surrendering Mysore to the Raja subject to the conditions of an efficient administration, enacting child labour laws, and passing a bill allowing Indian judges to have equal rights with European judges that was later amended. A devout Catholic convert, he engaged in charitable work.[78]

At the beginning of this chapter, E. E. Dickinson's visitation of Swamiji in 1881 was described. There are other examples of devotees having a dream or visitation of Vivekananda without knowing his name, prior to their meeting him. Mahendranath Datta, the younger brother of Swamiji, lived with him in England during 1895-96, and later reported the following remarkable dream:

> A lady of about forty-two or three named Johnson, who was English but born in Moscow, came around. With much devotion and animation she told her dream: A luminous man came to her and said, "Come along." Without a doubt or objection she began to follow him. Going a long way across a field they came to seashore. It was a very dark night, yet a wooden ship was seen to be at hand. A voice came out of the darkness, "Board this ship." The ship spread its sail, caught the wind and moved swiftly. All around, a boundless sea. All black sky, not even stars to be seen. Gradually fear came over her; darkness all around, who this pilot was, or her fellow-passengers—nothing could she understand. Then she saw a rope stretched between the mast and the prow, and on it a lantern hanging. Small as this light was, it gave her hope. Then she saw, standing by the light, someone who was the Captain or other officer of the ship. She could see him clearly. At the sight of his face, clear as a photo, her heart rose. Looking at her and seeing her fear, he said, "There is no fear; even in the dark the ship will go to its destination; you need not be afraid." Suddenly she woke up.

Miss Johnson [stated]: "I couldn't say of what country was the man whom I saw but it affected me so much and looking in many places in Russia I could never find that face. I have been living for several years in London and decided my dream was my delusion. Several weeks ago, I heard that a preacher of Hinduism had come and was giving lectures. As soon as I saw Swami Vivekananda and heard him speak, I knew it was the same person." Then she said that she hadn't gone up to speak to him, as she was a woman and would not know what to say.[79]

After Vivekananda returned to the United States, Nikola Tesla (1856-1943), the internationally acclaimed inventor, attended many of his talks at the Vedanta Society and other locations in the New York-Brooklyn area during December 1895 and in the following month. In February 1896 they met at Austin Corbin's party, and according to the *New York Herald* report, Swamiji delighted in his conversation with Tesla. Swami Vivekananda explained his cosmological theory of akasha (cosmic matter), prana (energy) and kalpas (cosmic cycles) to Tesla, the famous Croatian-born American electrical engineer and inventor. Soon after the party, Vivekananda wrote to Edward Sturdy:

> Mr. Tesla was charmed to hear about the Vedantic Prana and Akasha and the Kalpas, which according to him are the only theories modern science can entertain. Now both Akasha and Prana again are produced from the Cosmic Mahat, the Universal Mind, the Brahma or Ishvara. Mr. Tesla thinks he can demonstrate mathematically that force and matter are reducible to potential energy. I am to go and see him next week, to get this new mathematical demonstration.[80]

Unfortunately, the assignment was never completed. Swamiji points out that Tesla considered his discourses to be "so scientific; they so exactly harmonize with the aspirations of the age and with the conclusions to which modern science is coming at the present time."[81] Later in a discourse given in London on the 21st of June 1896, Vivekananda stated:

> It is possible to demonstrate that what we call matter does not exist at all. It is only a certain state of force. Solidity, hardness, or any other state of matter can be proved to be the result of motion.... A thread of a spider's

web, if it could be moved at almost infinite velocity, would be as strong as an iron chain and would cut through an oak tree.[82]

Years later Tesla wrote that he rejects "all attempts to explain the workings of the universe without recognizing the existence of ether [akasha] and the indispensable function it plays in the phenomena." In his unpublished and undated manuscript, "Man's Greatest Achievement", Tesla affirmed:

> Long ago he recognized that all perceptible matter comes from a primary substance, or a tenuity beyond conception, filling all space, the Akasha or luminiferous ether, which is acted upon by the life-giving Prana or creative force, calling into existence, in never ending cycles, all things and phenomena. The primary substance, thrown into infinitesimal whirls of prodigious velocity, becomes gross matter; the force subsiding, the motion ceases and matter disappears, reverting to the primary substance.

In 1934-35 Tesla proposed the idea that radioactive material is a kind of conduit by which the ever-present primary akashic substance is being absorbed, causing the emission of the radioactive material. Akasha is continually supplying mass to physical bodies. The scientific community has not accepted this idea.[83]

For almost a year during 1884-85, the lifelong bachelor Nikola Tesla worked for Thomas Edison (1847-1931). While Edison relied on practical experiments involving time-consuming trial-and-error procedures,* Tesla, a visionary, would solve problems with a flash of insight. Without using models, drawings, or experiments he would visualize a future invention in his mind. Tesla revealed, "In my mind I change the construction, make improvements, and even operate the device. Without ever having drawn a sketch I can give the measurements of all parts to workmen, and when completed all these parts will fit." Ideas flashed into his mind, complete to the final details of component design and size. Of his many discoveries Tesla's greatest achievement is "the induction motor with rotating magnetic field that made unit drives for machines feasible and made AC power transmission an economic necessity." George Westinghouse paid him a million dollars for the invention in 1888, and used it to illuminate the buildings and grounds of the 1893 Chicago World's Fair. They also used it at the world's first hy-

* "Genius is one percent inspiration and ninety-nine percent perspiration."

droelectric generating plant at Niagara Falls in 1895. The Tesla coil that he invented in 1891 is used in radio and television sets, and other electronic equipments. According to some sources, in 1912 Tesla refused the Nobel Prize in physics because the committee would award it jointly to himself and Thomas Edison, with whom he had a serious dispute. Because of his important inventions, his peers inducted Tesla into the National Inventors Hall of Fame in 1975.[84]

Along with Nikola Tesla, Sarah Bernhardt and others, the following also attended Austin Corbin's party where Vivekananda was the central figure: Peter Cooper Hewitt (1861-1921), Charles Thompson Mathews (1863-1934), and Colonel George Creighton Webb (1854-1948). Peter Cooper Hewitt was an imaginative scientist who invented the mercury vapour lamp bearing his name in 1903 to replace the incandescent lamps, the static converter/mercury arc rectifier, an electrical interrupter, a wireless receiver, and an aerial torpedo for the Navy. He also directed a number of corporations in partnership with important people like George Westinghouse.[85] Charles Thompson Mathews, a fellow of the American Institute of Architects, remodelled the Church of the Holy Trinity in 1891 and the east end of New York's St. Patrick's Cathedral in 1901, and exhibited drawings at the World's Columbian Exposition in Chicago in 1893. He cofounded the American Society for the Relief of French Orphans during the First World War.[86] Colonel George Creighton Webb, a New York lawyer, founded and became the president of the Intercollegiate Amateur Athletic Association, represented the United States at the coronation of Czar Nicholas III of Russia in 1896, served as a Major in the Spanish-American War in 1898 and as the first secretary of the American Legation in St. Petersburg, Russia.[87]

The young John Pierce Fox (1872-1960) [q.v.] took an active part in setting up the March 25, 1896 date for Vivekananda's address before the Harvard Graduate Philosophical Club. In April and May Fox worked with the Swami in getting his Harvard lecture "The Vedanta Philosophy" ready for publication. Fox also came out with a Note for the booklet. Next, he corresponded with Sara Bull concerning the sale of *The Vedanta Philosophy* manuscript. On the steamer on his way to London, Fox corrected some false ideas concerning Mohini Chatterji and Vivekananda held by three Boston ladies. In June Fox lived in the same house in London with Swamiji, and after moving out, continued to see him and attend his public lectures covering a six week period. While living in London he often spoke with Saradananda whom he very much admired. An enthusiastic letter dated July 24, 1896 from John Fox to Sara Bull reads:

> If Swami [Vivekananda] returns to India and speaks as he did last Saturday to the London Hindu Association, he ought to take the country by storm. I never heard him so eloquent, so earnest—in appealing to the young Hindus to give up European dress and airs on returning home, and mingling with the people and trying to help them. He denounced the caste system in the strongest terms, and spoke finely on the position of women. I wish you had been there.

Swami Vivekananda continued to correspond with John Fox in August of 1900.[88] In 1961, the year after his death, his wife wrote to Marie Louise Burke that John "often spoke of his friend Swami Vivekananda whom he knew at Harvard and in London.... He loved and admired the Swami very much."[89]

John Pierce Fox studied transit conditions in American and European cities between 1899 and 1908. After 1908, he worked as an investigator of transit conditions and hospital buildings, consulter on city planning and zoning, a sanitary expert, and after 1914 as an executive secretary for the Murray Hill Association. His field of operation included New York City and a large number of other cities in the northeastern sector of the United States.[90]

In a letter to Mary Hale, Swamiji asked, "Do you know one Colston Turnbull of Chicago? He was here a few weeks before I reached India. He seems to have had a great liking for me, with the result that Hindu people all liked him very much."[91] At the Parliament of Religions held in Chicago, Turnbull became an admirer of Vivekananda. In January 1897, Dr. Turnbull delivered a lecture at the Emerald Theatre in India on the "Hindoo Mission in the West". Among other things, according to *The Statesman*, he told the audience:

> He wished to thank India for inaugurating a work among the thinking and educated portion of the American community, and a work of love, for he would refer particularly to one bright mind, whose brave yet tender words had aroused them out of a spiritual lethargy, and awakened a deep interest in the solution of the great problem of the universal and the nature and destiny of man. He referred to that prince of men—one of the world's

great teachers, teaching others to become men, of whom India could feel justly proud, as well as America, who claimed him as a friend—Swami Vivekananda, who appeared at the great Parliament of Religions, held in Chicago, during the World's Fair, like a star of the first magnitude, in the midst of a galaxy of stars, beaming with light and truth, and presented a new ideal. The highest ideal must be a universal ideal, one and the same to all, attainable by all.

There is a group picture taken in March at Gopal Lal Seal's garden house in Cossipore. In that Colston Turnbull is standing along with Swamis Vivekananda, Premananda, Adbhutananda, Ramakrishnananda, Shivananda, Turiyananda, and Prakashananda, the Sevier's and others. That month he attended Swamiji's address on "Vedantism" at the Star Theatre in Calcutta.[92]

Dr. John C. Wyman of Brooklyn, New York, published two poems which were tributes in commemoration of Swami Vivekananda. One appeared in the *Brahmavadin* of July 15, 1899, and the other in the *Prabuddha Bharata* of January 1903 and the *Brahmavadin* of February 1903. Back in January 1894, Wyman was the president of the Brooklyn Psychical Research Society. His name appears in a long list of senders of a May 3, 1896 letter sent to the Swamis in India praising Vivekananda. When submitting the earlier poem to the *Brahmavadin* on 23rd June 1899, Dr. Wyman wrote, "I still love him and want him to know that my heart is filled with brotherly affection for him." The poem reads:

A TRIBUTE OF AFFECTION

Brother Swami Vivekananda,
Bright pearl of the Orient sea,
Came here with his soul all illumined
By Light, Love, and Liberty.

He came here with greetings fraternal
From the mystical East to our West;
And from those wise Vedas inspired
He taught us the purest and best.

He brought us a message most gracious
From the long past ages of time;
He came as the Priest and the Prophet,
Enthused with a faith all sublime.

Right soon to our hearts he found entrance,
So loveable, so gentle was he,
And as *teacher* or *friend* was so winning,
None could other than lover be.

He proclaimed ancient truths with wisdom,
And his eloquence quickly did win
Many earnest and faithful disciples,
Whom he taught of their God-powers within.

God bless our dear brother Swami,
May his path grow ever more bright;
And when his earth journey is finished
He is clothed in God's garments of light.[93]

Second Voyage to the West

After Swamiji's return to America in 1899, Theodore Whitmarsh (1869-1936), the son of Francis Leggett's sister, Caroline (1839-1926), also visited Ridgely Manor during the "Great Summer". In conjunction with Sarah Waldo, he aided in the publication of Swamiji's four yoga books.[94] Whitmarsh became the future chairman of the board of the wholesale grocery company F. H. Leggett & Co., and president of the National Wholesale Grocers' Association. In 1917, working with United States President Herbert Hoover, he held the position of chief of the Food Administration Distribution Division, being actively involved in food relief for the people of Europe. Theodore's wife, Lillian, indicated, "Swamiji was the most delightful dinner companion she ever had imagined." Theodore Whitmarsh's three children were with Swamiji at Ridgely. They were Francis Leggett Whitmarsh (1893-1969), the future president of F. H. Leggett & Co. for the years 1936-59, director of the Irving Trust Company (1938-66), and a trustee of New York University (1947-66), Karl (1896-1926), and their sister Katherine (Prasanna, 1897-1992) [q.v.], who was later at Santa Barbara, California (discussed in

Chapter III). Prasanna later mentioned that her father Theodore "loved Swamiji and he said that when everything went wrong, he would sit down and think of Swamiji and then everything became all right again. He used to read Swamiji to me when I was growing up and talked to me about him."[95]

Prasanna mentioned that when she went to see Swami Nikhilananda, he told me about her father Theodore. She learned from the Swami that before Vivekananda went back to India, her father told him:

> "We hope to see you before long." And he said, "No, I am not coming back." Father said, "Aren't you coming back?" He said, "No, I am going to India to die." Father did not really take him seriously, because Swamiji often joked. He made some polite remarks about it, but Swami insisted that he was going to die. Father said, "If you are going to die, you should leave a will." He said, "I have nothing to will." Father said. "Yes, you've got your books." Miss Waldo was getting them together, and they mentioned my father's name with Miss Waldo. So he said, "If you make up the will, I'll sign it." So then father got busy and I do not know the details of how he arranged it, but that's how they set up the trust fund. And then many years later when the trust fund ran out and everybody had died on the trust fund, Tantine bought it and gave it to Swami Nikhilananda.[96]

Linda Prugh mentioned that Theodore Whitmarsh discussed this matter "when Swami Vivekananda went to say goodbye to Francis Leggett".[97] This event might have occurred shortly before November 7, 1899, when Swamiji left Ridgely for Los Angeles, though he did not leave the U.S.A. until July the 26th of the following year. On January 17, 1900, Swamiji wrote to Sara Bull, "I want to make out a trust-deed of the Math in the names of Saradananda, Brahmananda, and yourself. I will do it as soon as I get the papers from Saradananda. Then I am quits."[98] Consequently, on July 6, 1900 (according to the newspaper account), Vivekananda's Will was witnessed in New York City by Sarah Waldo and the lawyer Edwin Clinton Harvey. Swamiji made out a Will with his estate being divided among five executors: Swamis Brahmananda and Saradananda, the president and general secretary of the Ramakrishna Math and Mission respectively, Margaret Noble (Sister Nivedita), Sara Bull and Francis Leggett.[99]

After Swamiji's mahasamadhi, due to legal complications the Will was not admitted for probate until early 1906. According to New York law, a blood relation must be notified of the Will. Concerning the Will, Sister Nivedita wrote to Sara Bull from Calcutta:

> I beg to empower you to act on my behalf. The Swamis Brahmananda and Saradananda have also written to you in this sense, and if power of attorney be necessary, have expressed their entire willingness to obtain it. Swami Vivekananda's disciples of whom Swami Saradananda is eldest, constitute in Hindu law, as you know, his next of kin, and it is held unlawful even to mention the name or family of a Sannyasin when in the world.

It was decided "that a Swami's only heirs are his fellow monks, or Gurubhais". On July 7, 1910, in a letter to Josephine MacLeod, Sister Nivedita added, "The monks say that Swamiji's Will cannot now be probated. It is too late. This is a legal opinion. That is why all business had better be put into their own hands as it stands." At that time, Theodore Whitmarsh was still involved in the publication of Swamiji's books.[100]

Helena Zimmerman (1876-1971) was the only child of Eugene Zimmerman (1843-1914), a wealthy Cincinnati, Ohio, railroad executive. She attended Swamiji's lectures, had long talks with him, practised meditation, and looked upon his book on Raja Yoga as a Bible. Helena had the window panes of her bedroom removed, replaced by stained glass ones, so that the sun rays would filter through the excerpts of Indian script in bold relief. She had four sayings of Swamiji's philosophy painted in her room. Not knowing that Swamiji had returned to the United States and was living at Ridgely Manor, in September 1899 she decided to travel to India to become his disciple. Apparently, not all of Swamiji's followers knew he had returned to the United States. She proceeded on to England where she received a false report from two Indian noblemen that Vivekananda had died. As fate would have it, that fallacious news ended her pilgrimage to attempt to visit the Swami in India. As a traumatic reaction she entered into temporary seclusion in her London hotel seeing no one. Everything was done to tempt her out again, and she soon met England's biggest playboy, the Duke of Manchester. In November 1900 she married the Duke and, according to one report, paid off a million-dollar worth of his debts. This whole affair was a front-page story in many newspapers. Years later in 1914 her father left her with a ten million dollar (equivalent to $213 million in 2008) trust fund. After her divorce from the Duke, in 1937 she remarried and became the Countess of Kintore in Scotland.[101]

The two Indian noblemen just mentioned might have been talking not about Vivekananda but Swami Bhaskarananda, the famous ascetic of Benares who died in 1899. A few years before in Benares, Bhaskarananda gave Mark Twain (1835-1910), the celebrated American author, an autographed copy of one of his books on the Hindu scriptures, and Twain reciprocated by handing him a copy of *Huckleberry Finn*. Ironically, when Vivekananda journeyed to Mark Twain's hometown of Hartford, Connecticut, to lecture (March 8, 1895 and January 31, 1896), the gifted sixty-year-old writer was on an extended world tour. On January 31 he was in Baroda, India, visiting the sites and some of the holy men of India. In India he met Swamiji's friend Virchand Gandhi at a Jain Temple.[102] After travelling to India, Mark Twain's published observations include:

> Land of religions, cradle of human race, birthplace of human speech, grandmother of legend, great grandmother of tradition. The land that all men desire to see and having seen once even by a glimpse, would not give that glimpse for the shows of the rest of the globe combined.
>
> India had the start of the whole world in the beginning of things. She had the first civilization; she had the first accumulation of material wealth; she was populous with deep thinkers and subtle intellects; she had mines, and woods, and a fruitful soul.[103]

Swamiji remained in Chicago for eight days (November 22-29, 1899) before he proceeded on to Los Angeles. In two letters sent to Mrs. G. W. Hale during the first week of December, he mentioned, "With all love for the sisters and Mr. [Clarence] Woolley and Bud and Father Pope," and "Harriet has scored a triumph really. I am charmed with Mr. Woolley—only hope Mary will be equally fortunate. It gives me a new lease of life to see people happy. May they all be happy."[104] In Chicago, Harriet Hale (1871/72-1929) had married Clarence Mott Woolley (1863-1956), the manager and later president of the American Radiator and Standard Sanitary Corporation (1902-24), and then the board chairman until 1938. One of the pioneers in central heating, he had factories built in seven European countries and many cities in the U.S. During World War I, he was vice chairman of the War Trade Board and was decorated as a member of the French Legion of Honour.[105]

Josephine MacLeod (Tantine) possessed an amazing special talent for quickly making contact with prominent people. After being in Los Angeles for a very short time, she befriended William Atwell Cheney (1848-1925) who had been a Los Angeles City Superior Court Judge during 1885-91. In December of 1899, soon after Swamiji's arrival in Los Angeles, a city with a population of 102,500, Tantine introduced him to William Cheney. He was then a prominent attorney at law in Los Angeles, living at 1046 S. Hill Street. A member of the Unitarian faith, William Cheney later lectured on constitutional law at the University of Southern California from 1904 to 1912. His popular metaphysical book *Can we Be Sure of Mortality?* (1910) was reprinted in 1998. Years later in June 1916, while in Los Angeles Swami Paramananda wrote, "Then I had to go to speak at the residence of Judge C. in the evening. It proved most gratifying. Judge C. spoke at the close of the talk with great appreciation. He entertained Swami Vivekananda when Swamiji was here. Much was accomplished by the meeting through the Lord's Will." By that time, Judge Cheney had moved to 1913 Ocean View Avenue.[106]

Bernhard R. Baumgardt (1862-1935) learned about Swamiji from Josephine MacLeod at Judge Cheney's residence, and quickly became an ardent supporter of his. In December 1899 he arranged lectures for the Swami at Blanchard Hall, "the best in town", and introduced Swamiji when he spoke at the Church of the Unity in Los Angeles. Baumgardt's wife showed genuine interest in the Swami's teachings. They were with Swamiji on his tour of Mt. Lowe and the observatory on January 13, and on other occasions. Alice Hansbrough tells us that at the Green Hotel in Pasadena,

> Professor Baumgardt was talking with some other gentlemen before the lecture began. One of them asked him, "He is a Christianized Hindu, I suppose?" With considerable pride in Swamiji, Professor Baumgardt replied, "No, he is an unconverted Hindu. You are going to hear about Hinduism from a real Hindu."[107]

On the 14th the *Los Angeles Times* described Swamiji this way, "He is without doubt one of the greatest oriental scholars to ever visit these shores, and has aroused the enthusiasm of the cultured people of the city." Born in England, Bernhard R. Baumgardt graduated from Strengnas College in Sweden. Originally a sailor, he became a printer, an astronomer, and a linguist. At first Baumgardt worked as the secretary of the Southern California Academy of Sciences until 1901, and then as its president from 1901 to 1905, specializing in astronomy. At a later date, he was a staff lecturer at the Brooklyn Institute of Arts and Sciences, the National Geographic Society in Washington, D.C., the Academy of Science and Art in Pittsburgh, and at other similar institutions. Swami Abhedananda was also a lecturer and committee member at the Brooklyn Institute of Arts and Sciences, but we do not know whether they ever met. Many years later he died in Los Angeles, living at 626 West 30th Street.[108]

After moving on to Northern California, Vivekananda lodged for at least two days at the San Francisco residence of Dr. Albert Hiller. The German born surgeon and homeopathic physician collected a valuable library with some rare Oriental volumes. Mrs. Cara French tells us, "It was Dr. Hiller's concern for Swami Vivekananda's health under the heavy strain of constant lectures and classes that prompted him to take Swamiji away to his cabin in the Mt. Shasta region for a few days of complete rest." The Swami probably spent about five or six days in the cabin.[109]

Upon coming to San Francisco in 1902, Swami Rama Tirtha (1873-1906) had no baggage or money. When he wasn't travelling, he lived for a year and a half in the cabin of Dr. Albert Hiller in Shasta Springs, where Swamiji had stayed in May of 1900. Due to his loving and cheerful nature, the doctor wished that he should remain there longer. Born in poverty, Tirtha Rama became a professor of mathematics at the government university in Punjab. In 1897 Vivekananda spoke three times before a large outdoor gathering at Lahore, since no building could hold the sizable crowd. Swamiji ate a meal at Tirtha Rama's residence. In Lahore he convinced him to renounce the world and become a monk. In return he gave Swamiji, whom he admired, a copy of Walt Whitman's *Leaves of Grass*. Concerning Swamiji's lecture on "Vedanta" in Lahore, Tirtha Rama wrote in a letter of November 16, 1897:

> It lasted for full two and a half hours. The listeners were so deeply engrossed, and it created such an atmosphere, that all idea of time and space was lost. At times, one required absolute realization of oneness between oneself and the cosmic Atman. It struck at the roots of ego and pride in self. In short, it was such a grand success as is seldom seen.... I listened to his talks with leaders of Arya Samaj and Brahmo Samaj in private. He answered their questions in such a devastating manner, and presented before them such a picture of their principles, that they returned completely downfaced. And the beauty lies in the fact that he never uttered a single word which could offend their feelings. In a very short time, he got them to admit the baselessness of their own principles.[110]

It is written that:

> During his meeting with Swamiji, Tirtha Rama asked Swamiji to keep his gold watch as a memento of his gratitude, saying "Every time you see that watch, you'll remember me." Swamiji accepted the watch, thanked Tirtha Rama, and then handed it back, saying, "I will use it in your pocket." Tirtha Rama then asked, "Swamiji can you give me a message?" Whereupon, Swamiji countered, "What time is it?" Tirtha Rama pulled out his watch and said, "It is one." Swamiji said, "Remember that."[111]

Swami Rama also established rapport with a number of other Swamis of the Ramakrishna Order. After coming to America, as a result of his appearance in Portland, Oregon, in 1903, two groups were formed: The Swami Rama Society, and the Oregon Society for the Emancipation of India from Caste Slavery. Portland Judge Charles B. Bellinger served as the president of the latter group and Judge L. R. Webster as its 1st vice-president. In May of 1903, Theodore Roosevelt (1858-1919), the dynamic president of the United States, stopped for a short time at Shasta Springs:

> He accepted from Rama most gracefully, lovingly and cheerfully [his book] the *Appeal on Behalf of India*. He kept the book in his right hand all the time and while responding with his right hand to the salutations of the crowd, the book naturally and spontaneously rose up to his forehead at least a hundred times. When the train started, he was seen reading it attentively in his carriage, and once more he waved thanks to Rama from the leaving train.

After speaking in many cities of the United States, including the Greenacre Conference, Swami Rama returned to India in December of 1904, where up to this day he is revered as a holy man. He accidentally drowned in the Ganges River at a relatively young age.[112]

Dr. Milburn H. Logan (1855-1905), a successful physician and surgeon, had been a professor of chemistry and toxicology in the California Medical College for ten years, and the president of the State Eclectic Medical Society. He wrote *Organic Chemistry* (1893) and *System of Urinology* (1894). During the last week of May 1900, Swamiji conversed on the *Bhagavad Gita* in the downtown office suite of Dr. Milburn Logan in order to save the expense of renting a hall.[113] Swami Vivekananda stayed in Logan's San Francisco house receiving medical attention from him.[114] At other times, Turiyananda, Abhedananda, and Trigunatita resided at Logan's residence. In March-April 1902, Vivekananda and Saradananda both sent a letter to Logan, the latter asking him "to make arrangements to send Turiyananda back to India" because of ill health.[115]

Milburn indicated his loving affection for Swamiji in a letter to Swami Abhedananda:

> Many are the moments of sadness since the Swamiji has gone away. It seems that all the gods had left us, for his Divine presence spread peace and tranquility wherever he went; the tumult of uncertainty departed from my soul at the sound of his magic voice. His very form and every mood were those of tender compassion and sympathy. None knew him but to love him; those of us who have had the royal good fortune to meet him in the flesh will some day realize that we have met the true Incarnation of the divine One.... At first I attended him through a severe spell of sickness, then he sat with me partly through a paralytic stroke; he would charm me to sleep and enchant me awake. So passed the sublimest part of my life, and now that sweet memory lingers and sustains me ever and always.[116]

In addition, Milburn wrote:

> No being lived so low, be he a man or a beast, that Vivekananda would not salute. His was not only an appeal to the poor and lowly, but also to kings and princes and mighty rulers of the earth. Vivekananda shook the world of thought in all its higher lines. Great teachers bowed reverently at his feet, the humble followed reverently to kiss the hem of his garments; no other single human being was revered more during his life than was Vivekananda.[117]

A youthful George A. Applegarth (1875-1972) sang in the choir of Benjamin Fay Mills' Unitarian church in Oakland and attended a number of Swamiji's lectures in Northern California. In a 1962 interview, the octogenarian recalled:

> He was so outstanding in the portrayal of his religion that none of the other speakers could compare with him.... The other addresses had all been more or less complex and obscure. The Swami, on the other hand, presented

> a philosophy that was so simple and was presented from such a beautiful viewpoint that people were eager to hear more. He had a remarkable command of English and his lectures were full of colourful metaphors.... I was present after some of the lectures when others spoke to him. He was very approachable. He would be surrounded by many people who wanted to speak to him, so we younger people did not get very close to him.... I talked to many of the people who had attended his lectures. All were deeply impressed by the simplicity of his philosophy and by the richness and beauty of his English.

George Adrian Applegarth spent his life as an architect designing many wonderful homes, apartments, commercial and public buildings in San Francisco along with the city's biggest mansion. In 1916 he was commissioned to design a European Arts museum called the California Palace of the Legion of Honour in Lincoln Park. He served as president of the San Francisco chapter of the American Institute of Architects during 1921-22. French Beaux-Arts' influences of rigid symmetry, perfect proportions, columned entries, and coffered ceilings are seen in many of Applegarth's residential designs in the Bay area.[118]

At the 1907 celebration of the Birthday of Swamiji held at the Vedanta Society of New York, Nelson Smith told the devotees:

> Swami Vivekananda, of all the men I have ever met or known, is one of the greatest and grandest. He saw the whole universe standing up before him directed by an infinite intelligence. He had the greatest realization of that Infinite Spirit which we call God. A prodigy from his youth, a great soul, he came to us, a strange country, without invitation, without money. Everything we have we owe to him. This is an expression of but a small part of the gratitude I feel toward Swami Vivekananda.[119]

Possibly Smith met Vivekananda during the summer of 1900, when he visited the city of New York. This might be the Nelson Smith (1832-1916) who was a prominent New York lawyer. He served as the chairman of the general committee of Tammany Hall (1890-94), and of the central branch of the Irish Land League of America.[120]

The inventor Sir Hiram Maxim (1840-1916) heard Swamiji speak at the 1893 Parliament of Religions, and they met later in London and again in Paris in 1900. In his "Memoirs of European Travel" Swamiji wrote, "From Paris our friend Maxim has supplied me with letters of introduction to various places, so that the countries may be properly seen.... Having read my works long since, he holds me in great—I should say, excessive—admiration."[121] "Mr. Maxim of the gun fame is very much interested in me, and he wants to put in his book on China and the Chinese something about my work in America."[122] Concerning Swamiji's presentation at the 1893 Parliament of Religions, Maxim mentions at the beginning of his book *Li Hung Chang's Scrap-Book* (1913):

> This monk was of commanding presence and vast learning, speaking English like a Webster.... His first speech was no less than a revelation. Every word was eagerly taken down by the reporters, and telegraphed all over the country, when it appeared in thousands of papers. Vivekananda became the lion of the day. He soon had an immense following.... here was a specimen of the unsaved who knew more of philosophy and religion than all the persons and missionaries in the whole country.

Maxim's writings on Vivekananda appear in a short article in the December 1919 issue of the *Prabuddha Bharata*.[123]

Because of his contributions to the British military effort, in 1901 the American born Sir Hiram Maxim was conferred with the title of knighthood by Queen Victoria after he became a British subject. The automatic Maxim gun that he invented in 1883 fired eleven shots a second from a single barrel. This innovation in weaponry gave the British forces a major advantage during the Boer War of 1899-1902 and the Chinese Boxer Rebellion of 1900. Maxim became wealthy through the manufacturing and supplying of military weapons to several European and other armies. His remarkable range of inventions included a curling iron, locomotive headlight, graphite-rod incandescent light bulb, automatic fire extinguisher, automatic gas generator, automatic steam pumping-engine for supplying houses with water, automatic spindle, engine governor, inhaler for medicating the throat, a better mouse trap, feed-water heater, gas motor, aerial torpedo gun, and an electrical pressure regulator, for which he won the French Legion of Honour.[124]

During the Paris Exposition in 1900, the Duke of Richelieu (1875-1952) first came in contact with Swamiji at the residence of Mr. and Mrs. Francis Leggett, and then visited him regularly for several weeks. The Duke described Vivekananda as "a singularly handsome man". The *Life* tells us:

When the Swami was about to leave France, he asked the Duke why he did not renounce the world and become his disciple. The young man wanted to know what he would gain from such renunciation, and the Swami said, "I shall give you the desire for death." When asked to explain so dubious a blessing, he replied that he would give the Duke such knowledge and insight that when confronted by death he would laugh at it. But the Duke preferred to remain in the world.[125]

Thirty years later a crisis occurred in the Duke's life, and every word Vivekananda had said to him came back to his mind. He wanted to know where the Swami was and what had become of him. Later the Duke and his wife became very fond of Swami Nikhilananda and visited the Ramakrishna-Vivekananda Centre in New York City many times, the last being for the unveiling of the alabaster bust of Sri Ramakrishna created by Malvina Hoffman on January 10, 1952. Swami Nikhilananda wrote that he was a "great admirer of Swami Vivekananda, whom he had known rather intimately. He cherished his admiration for the Swamiji till the end of his life.... The Duke was full of respect for Swami Vivekananda and bore toward him sincere affection."[126]

While in Paris, Swamiji attended a small candlelit dinner hosted by Alberta Sturges on September 10, 1900. She wrote to her mother Mrs. Leggett:

> Last night we had a lovely time. The dinner went off most successfully. I put Princess Doria on my right, then Swami, Lady Anglesey at the foot of the table and between us on my left the Duke of Newcastle. Swami was in a gala mood and I could see the Princess was radiant at her brother's sympathy. The Duke asked Swami at dinner quite a number of interesting questions and immediately made Swami promise to call.

Henry Pelham-Clinton, the 7th Duke of Newcastle (1864-1928), was a staunch Anglo-Catholic, who spoke on ecclesiastical issues in the House of Lords. His sister, Lady Emily Pelham-Clinton (1863-1919), married Prince Doria Pamphilj the Duc d'Avigliano in 1882.[127]

After returning to India, while staying in Shillong, Swamiji came to see Sir Henry Cotton (1845-1915), the chief commissioner of Assam who wanted to meet him during April-May 1901. Cotton made a request that the Swami speak before a gathering of local English officials and a large number of Indians. The two of them held a discussion on India and the country's national problems. Swami Vivekananda concludes, "Such a good and kind-hearted man as Sir Henry Cotton is rarely found. Hearing of my illness, he sent the Civil Surgeon and inquired after my health mornings and evenings."[128] "The Swami spoke of him as a man who understood India's needs and aspirations, was working nobly for her cause, and deserved the love of the Indian people."[129] Cotton became a friend of Sister Nivedita. Sir Henry John Stedman Cotton held secretarial positions in the Bengal Government (1867-96), and later advanced to become chief secretary (1891-96), acting home secretary to the Government of India (1896), and then the chief commissioner of Assam (1896-1902). As the elected president of the Indian National Congress in Bombay during 1904, he envisioned "a Federation of free and separate states, the United States of India". Being a champion of Indian nationalism, he authored *New India, or India in Transition* (1885), and *Indian and Home Memories* (1911). After reading William Jennings Bryan's assessment of *British Rule in India* (1906), he wrote, "My views coincide with those of Mr. Bryan."[130]

In close, a memorial tribute written by an unidentified "A Western Disciple" reads:

> By the death of Swami Vivekananda, we have lost a dear friend, and suffered an irreparable loss. He is best remembered by us, as having been "the greatest figure in the Parliament of Religions" held in Chicago in 1893, where he addressed crowded audiences, the quality of his teaching and his unaffected eloquence winning a most sympathetic hearing. He had a vivid, eager personality, singularly magnetic, persuasive and enthusiastic. He was no mere visionary anchorite of the Himalayas, giving out the truths of Indian philosophy. On the contrary, he was a man born with perfectly developed spiritual sense, discerning spiritual truths without effort: calm and steadfast, giving forth power from the spiritual centre within, and living for the advancement of his race: a true lover of his fellow-men, devoting his energies in trying to rouse them to their true selves, content to use up his gifts and talents for their benefit. Clad in his habit of red or ochre did this Indian Sannyasin standing upon all sorts of platforms, in all manners of places, with a strong beautiful voice expound the philosophy of Vedanta. Again and again in his lectures did he recur to the central idea of Advaita, the One in everything, the potential divinity in all. Gifted with an original outlook upon life, he displayed that fervour and viguor that one associated

with monks, who have for centuries held to their spirituality with power and staunchness unrivalled in worldly affairs.[131]

In review of Swami Vivekananda's stay in the West, he spent more time in the New York-Brooklyn area than in any other, approximately 345 days. Next in length of time is: 2) London and vicinity, followed by 3) Chicago and vicinity, 4) Northern California, 5) Ridgely Manor, 6) Los Angeles-Pasadena, 7) Boston-Cambridge, 8) Paris, 9) Thousand Island Park, and 10) Detroit. Of his total stay in the United States according to Asim Chaudhuri, he lived in New York State (approximately 42% of the time), Illinois (19%), California (15%), and the Other States (24%).[132]

It is hoped that the information about some of the many talented people whom Swamiji made contact with in the West will be of benefit to the Vedanta Societies in the future. For those interested in when and where Swamiji presented his talks, Appendix III gives the dates, and city and state locations, of lectures and classes recorded in *The Complete Works of Swami Vivekananda*. Appendix IV provides a list of two or more reports of the same talk that appear in different volumes of the *Complete Works*.

ENDNOTES

1 Paramahansa Yogananda, *Autobiography of a Yogi* (Los Angeles: Self-Realization Fellowship, 1971), pp. 475-77.

2 *Life*, I, pp. 230-31; Buckland, p. 359; Riddick, p. 308; UCLC. Are they referring to Henry Francis Dumaresq Pennington (1854-1932) who arrived in India in 1875 and retired in 1901? During his stay he served in Oudh as the joint magistrate from 1887, and the district and sessions judge from 1890. *The India List and India office List* (Harrison and Sons, 1902), p. 529 on GBS.

3 *CW*, V:11.

4 R. Kossmann, *PB* (Aug. 2006), pp. 471-72; Chaudhuri1, pp. 48, 67.

5 *CW*, V:11-12, 18.

6 Chaudhuri1, pp. 149-52, *WWIA*, I, p. 967; *NCAB*, XIV, pp. 396-97; *Chicago Daily Tribune* (June 2, 1910), p. 3; *CW*, V:11-12, 19.

7 *PB* (Aug. 2006), p. 472.

8 *PB* (Jan. 2005), pp. 72-81; Swami Shuddharupananda. Web: www.eng.vedanta.ru/library/prabuddha_bharata/Jan2005_swami_vivekananda_s_first_hosts_in_Bombay.php.

9 *CW*, VII:455.

10 *Reminiscences*, p. 131; Swami Chetanananda, *Vivekananda as We Saw Him* (Video, 1988); Conger; Samuel Winans, Lyon Memorial (W. Graham, 1907), p. 200 on GBS; Josiah Currey, *Chicago Its History* (S. J. Clarke, 1912), p. 97 on GBS; Web: en.wikipedia.org/wiki/Chicago_Club.

11 Conger.

12 *Reminiscences*, p. 131; Using Google type in "William Perez Conger".

13 *CW*, VIII:377, 380.

14 Conger.

15 *Reminiscences*, pp. 131, 134, 136.

16 Conger; Chetanananda (Video, 1988). Concerning Swamiji, Cornelia Conger also mentioned, "One day he said to my grandmother [Mrs. John Lyon], 'You know, I had one of the greatest temptations of my life here... It's organization.' He then said, 'We have never had organization in the Vedanta Society. We have gone off alone and made a pilgrimage and done the best we could. I do not think Indians are particularly adapted to organization.' And yet he said, 'I am over here and I see what a tremendous lot it accomplishes, and I will have to think out how much organization could be put into our Vedanta Society that would be helpful to it and still acceptable to the people.'"

17 Chetanananda (Video, 1988); Conger; Web: en.wikipedia.org/ wiki/Edmund_McIlhenny; Web: www.spanamwar.com/rrmcilhenny.htm.

18 *Reminiscences*, pp. 135-36; Conger; Currey (1912), p. 97 on GBS; F. P. Dunne, *CA* (2000), vol. 178.

19 Albert Marquis, ed., *Who's Who of American Women* (Chicago: A. N. Marquis Co., 1961-62), II, p. 206; Burke, I, p. 496; Helen Leonard, *The Conger Family of America* (1992), II, p. 698.

20 *CW*, II:186.

21 Ibid., II:27, 186; V:25; VII:77, 520.

22 Hohner and Kenny (2000), p. 6; *Life*, I, pp. 448-49; *San Francisco Chronicle* (July 30, 1899), p. 19.

23 Stanley Kunitz and Howard Haycraft, *American Authors* 1600-1900 (New York: H. H. Wilson, 1964), pp. 401-02; *RLOA*, p. 222; *EWB* (1998), VIII, pp. 120-21.

24 *PB* (Oct. 1994), pp. 414-15; *CA* (1977), 1st Rev., XXI.

25 *Life*, I, p. 448; Burke, I, pp. 158, 185.

26 *DAB* (1931), VII, p. 514; *WOI*, p. 293.

27 *CW*, III:484-85.

28 Burke I, pp. 241, 285; *Life*, II, pp. 330, 374, 377, 384, 620; Prabuddhaprana1, pp. 44, 53, 62, 209, 213; Prabuddhaprana2, pp. 266, 279-80, 288, 406; *WWWA* (1962), I, p. 943; Almora, *PB* (May 1963) p. 276; *CW*, IX:157; V:161.

29 Burke, I, pp. 243, 246, 268; Chaudhuri2, p. 434; *NCAB* (1945), XXXII, p. 46.
30 Burke, I, p. 272; WorldCat; Chaudhuri1, pp. 143-44; Web: www.phoenixmasonry.org/goulds_history_volume_6.htm.
31 *Detroit Journal* (Feb. 19, 1894); Burke, I, pp. 362-64, 381, 432-33; *CW*, IX:18.
32 *DAB* (1928-36).
33 *CW*, IX:445.
34 *DAB* (1962), VII, pp. 192-93.
35 *CW*, IX:451.
36 Ibid., VIII:300; IX:14; VII:459.
37 Burke, I, pp. 409-11, 416, 427, 430-31.
38 *CW*, II:479-81; IX:458-59.
39 Bay City, Michigan History. Web: http://baycityhistory.blogspot.com/2003_09_01_archive.html; Chaudhuri2, p. 522.
40 *CW*, VIII:300, 303; IX:18, 46.
41 William J. Flagg, *Yoga or Transformation* (New York: J. W. Bouton, 1898), pp. 8, 163, 187; *New York Times* (April 16, 1898), p. 7; Burke IV, pp. 34-35, 313; UCLC.
42 *CW*, IX:16-19.
43 Ibid., IX:25-27; VI:267-68.
44 Ibid., IX:126-27.
45 Horner, pp. 19-20, 25-27, 37-38, 40, 52, 60, 93-94; Abhedananda (1970), X, p. 23; *CW*, IX:285-89.
46 *ANB*, IX, pp. 696-98; *DAB* (1932), VIII, p. 35; *NCAB* (1921), II, pp. 484-85.
47 *CW*, V:49; VI:279; IX:46.
48 *New York Times* (Jan. 14, 1883); (Nov. 13, 1898), p. 7; *Washington Law Reporter* (1898), p. 739 on GBS; Wooster, *Ohio Daily Record* (June 27, 2008).
49 *CW*, IX:26.
50 Ibid., VI:295-96.
51 Ibid., V:52.
52 Ibid., V:63.
53 Burke, II, pp. 247, 252-54. Additional newspaper reviews of his talks at the Brooklyn Ethical Society can be found in *CW*, II:501-03, 513-14; IX:481 and Chaudhuri2.
54 Burke, II, pp. 129-30, 138-40, 246-50; *CW*, IX:54.
55 *NCAB*, XXXV, pp. 533-34; Chaudhuri2, p. 915.
56 Burke, II, pp. 247-48; *NCAB* (1937), XXVI, p. 162; UCLC; Shepard, *WWWA*, I, p. 1114.
57 Basu, p. 67; Prabuddhaprana2, pp. 118, 222.

58 *Women in World History* (New York: Yorkin Publications, 2000), V, pp. 646-50; Mary Parker Follett. Web: http://sunsite.utk.edu/FINS/Mary_Parker_Follett/Fins-MPF-02.txt.

59 *New York Times* (Jan. 25, 1895), p. 8; *EWB*.

60 *Brooklyn Daily Eagle* (Feb. 19, 1895); *New York Times* (Feb. 19, 1895), p. 5; *New York Tribune* (Feb. 19, 1895), p. 5; Chaudhuri2, pp. 176-78; *DAB* (1928-36).

61 Burke, III, pp. 49-50; *DAB* (1964), I, pp. 586-87; *New York Times* (Mar. 1, 1895), p. 8.

62 *WWWA*, IV, p. 673; *New York Times* (Mar. 1, 1895), p. 8; (Apr. 8, 1928), p. 25; *Lexington Herald* (Kentucky) (Aug. 10, 1913); Cameron, pp. 130, 162-63.

63 *WWWA* (1961-68), IV, p. 560.

64 Carol Wallace, "A Passion in Miniature", *American Heritage* (Oct-Nov. 1984), pp. 90-93.

65 Frances Leggett, *Late and Soon* (London: John Murray, 1968), pp. 101-02; Burke, III, p. 81; *NCAB* (1921), II, p. 114; *WWNY* (1909), p. 821; Horner, pp. 43-44, 59-62, 87-94, 111-14.

66 *CW*, IX:569.

67 Ibid., IX:328.

68 Burke, V, p. 241; *WWSV*, pp. 111-21; Hohner, pp. 84, 90, 94, 112, 114.

69 Leggett (1968), p. 115.

70 *CW*, V:178.

71 Leggett (1968), pp. xiii, 235, 246, 248; Sri Sarada Society Notes 8 (Winter 2002), pp. 4-5. Web: www.srisarada.org/notes/1102.pdf; Prugh (1999), pp. 424-25.

72 *CW*, V:108; VII:490.

73 *Brahmavadin* (Feb. 1904), p. 117; Burke, III, pp. 14, 46-47, 124-25, 156-57, 525, 528; IV, pp. 97, 105-06, 324-26; Tathagatananda1, pp. 98, 136, 156, 170.

74 *Yearbook of American Churches* (1918, 1922); *New York Times* (April 12, 1924), p. 19.

75 *WWNY* (1929), p. 673; *New York Times* (July 31, 1939), p. 17; Horatio Dresser, *A History of the New Thought Movement* (New York: Thomas Y. Crowell Co., 1919), pp. 243-44.

76 *CW*, IX:515.

77 Burke, III, pp. 258-59, 282-83; V, p. 54; David Margesson. Web: www.reference.com/browse/wiki/David_Margesson,_1st_Viscount_Margesson.

78 Burke, III, pp. 281-82, 284-85, 308; Bhattacharya, pp. 729-30; Web: http://en.wikipedia.or/wiki/ George_Robinson_1st_Marquess_of_Ripon.

79 Datta, Pt. I, Ch. IV.

80 *CW*, V:101.

81 Burke, III, pp. 346, 494, 500, 507-08; *New York Herald* (Feb. 9, 1896); *CW*, III:185

82 *CW*, II:76.

83 John O'Neill, *Prodigal Genius* (New York: Ives Washburn, 1944), pp. 251-52.

84 *EOP*, pp. 1685-87; *DAB* (1973), Sup. III, pp. 767-70; Nikola Tesla. Web: http://inventors.about.com/library/inventors/bltesla.htm; Nikola Tesla. Web: www.invent.org/hall_of_fame/143.htm.

85 *New York Herald* (Feb. 9, 1896); Burke, III, p. 494; *DAB* (1932), VIII, pp. 607-08; "Peter Cooper Hewitt". Web: www.ringwoodmanor.com/peo/ch/pch/pch.htm.

86 *WWNY* (1924), pp. 863-64.

87 *New York Times* (Mar. 20, 1948), p. 13; *NCAB* (1904), XII, p. 118.

88 *CW*, V:113; VI:374; VIII:393, 531-32.

89 Burke, IV, pp. 90-91, 94-95, 97, 172, 178-79, 197-98, 233-34, 314-15; Secretary's Report by Harvard College, pp. 42-42 in GBS.

90 *WWWA* (1969-73), p. 245.

91 *CW*, VI:391.

92 Basu, pp. 124, 178, 650-51.

93 Basu, pp. 92, 102, 540 (600), 596-97; *Oswego Daily Times* (Jan. 19, 1894); *PB* (Jan. 1903), p. 12.

94 *CW*, VIII:527-28.

95 Burke, V, pp. 113, 123; "Katherine Whitmarsh Interviewed by Swami Chetanananda" (Aug. 6, 1979), pp. 2, 6, VSSC Archives; *WWWA*, V, p. 777.

96 Swami Chetanananda, "Vivekananda as We Saw Him", Video.

97 Prugh, pp. 237-38; Chaudhuri2, pp. 334-35.

98 *CW*, VIII:490.

99 *New York Times* (Jan. 17, 1906), p. 11; *Kansas City Star* (Jan. 20, 1906), p. 8; *Washington (D.C.) Times* (Feb. 16, 1906), p. 11. According to Hohner p. 109, Swamiji was in Detroit on July 6, 1900.

100 Nivedita, II, pp. 1111-12; *New York Times* (Jan. 17, 1906), p. 11; *Kansas City Star* (Jan. 20, 1906), p. 8; *Washington (D.C.) Times* (Feb. 16, 1906), p. 11.

101 *Boston Globe* (Nov. 19, 1900), p. 1; *Chicago Tribune* (Nov. 19, 1900), p. 1; *Salt Lake (City) Herald* (Nov. 29, 1900), p. 4; *San Jose Evening News* (Dec. 6, 1900), p. 2; *New York Times* (Nov. 25, 1937), p. 35; (Dec. 16, 1971), p. 38; *Los Angeles Times* (Feb. 10, 1947), p. 5.

102 Mark Twain, *Following the Equator* (Hartford, CT: American Publishing Co., 1898), pp. 379, 406-07, 507-08, 511-12; Chaudhuri2, pp. 654-55, 663.

103 Londhe, #6. Mark Twain.

104 *CW*, IX:128-29.

105 *New York Times* (July 20, 1956), p. 17; *WWWA* (1973), V, p. 798.

106 Stavig2; Burke, V, p. 178; *WWIA* (1924-25), p. 702; Directory (1899, 1916); Devamata, I, p. 247; UCLC.

107 Burke, V, pp. 178, 195-96, 244, 268, 279.

108 Stavig2; *WWIA* (1934-35), p. 268; Shivani, pp. 307-08; UCLC; Burke, V, pp. 178, 234, 244-45, 268. There was a Los Angeles based B. R. Baumgardt Publishing Company that published his works, but he did not own or manage the organization. *Los Angeles Times* (July 13, 1920, p. II5; June 20, 1935, p. A1).

109 Burke, VI, pp. 38-41, 168; Hohner, pp. 101-02, 105.

110 *Life*, II, pp. 292-93; *PB* (May 1963), p. 235; *VK* (April 2006), p. 155.

111 Pravrajika Brahmaprana, "Unpublished Letters of Swami Turiyananda", *VK* (Feb. 1989), p. 71.

112 P. B. Sharga, *Swami Rama* (Lucknow: Rama Tirtha Publication League, 1936), pp. 83-84, 278-81, 302-07; Puran Singh, *The Story of Swami Rama* (Madras: Ganesh, 1924), pp. 1, 138-39, 154, 160-61, 295; Prem Lata, *Life, Teachings & Writings of Swami Rama Tirtha* (New Delhi: Sumit Publications, 1993), pp. 4-5, 46-47, 87-88, 94-95; Cameron, pp. 162.

113 *CW*, I:446-80; IX:274-82.

114 Ibid., IX:136-38.

115 *NCAB* (1924), VIII, p. 201; Burke, VI, pp. 103-05, 122, 169-73, 297-98.

116 *Swami Abhedananda, Swami Vivekananda and His Work* (Calcutta: Ramakrishna Vedanta Math, 1924, 1982), pp. 23-24.

117 Testimonials to Swami Vivekananda. Web: www.namastebooks.com/ testimonials.htm.

118 Burke, V, pp. 343-44; Web: www.sfhistoryencyclopedia.com/under "A".

119 *VMB* (Feb. 1907), pp. 223-24; Tathagatananda1, p. 163.

120 *NCAB* (1896), VI, p. 498.

121 *CW*, VII:378.

122 Ibid., IX:149.

123 Burke, VI, pp. 319-21, 378. Using Western military weapons, Hiram Maxim's friend Li Hung-Chang (1823-1901) commanded the most formidable army in China. Being a nationalist, he encouraged a policy of military and economic development along Western lines. This would give China the strength to forcefully suppress internal rebellions, rid the country of Westerners, and preserve its traditional culture. He was responsible for, or involved in, all of China's negotiations with foreign powers from 1871 until his death. *EWB*.

124 *WOI* (1994), pp. 410-11; *DAB* (1961), VI, pp. 436-37. In a letter dated Oct. 22, 1900, Mrs. Marian Briggs wrote to Sara Bull: "Yesterday Mr. Maxim, who is wild over Swami—and who can be most useful to him—took us all to meet a Russian—Zarahoff his name was—and he is giving Miss MacLeod many letters in Constantinople. From there we all went to Mr. Achingleus [?] to a lovely lunch. We sat down to the table about one o'clock and did not rise again till after four—Swami and Mr. Maxim talking all the time" (Burke, VI, p. 378). It is of interest if Swamiji met Sir Basil Zaharoff (aka Zarahoff, 1849-1936), originally from Constantinople, who amassed a fortune as the world's most successful private armament salesman, and was financially involved in the manufacture of military weapons. Known as the "mystery man of Europe", he was not well thought of.

125 *Life*, II, p. 550.

126 *VK* (April 2005), pp. 137-39.

127 Swami Vidyatmananda, *PB* (1967), p. 133; Burke, VI, pp. 344-45; Web: en.wikipedia.org/wiki/Duke_of_Newcastle.

128 *CW*, VII:209.

129 *Life*, II, pp. 589-90.

130 Bhattacharya, p. 258; Sunderland, p. 51; UCLC.

131 *PB* (July 1902); also in (July 2002).

132 Hohner, Chaudhuri2, p. 335.

CHAPTER XII

TWENTIETH & TWENTY-FIRST CENTURY EUROPEAN BIOGRAPHERS, TRANSLATORS, & TRIBUTES

During Vivekananda's lifetime, some continental Europeans he had not met were showing interest in his ideas. In Chapter II on Sri Ramakrishna, there is a discussion regarding the Russian novelist Leo Tolstoy's (1828-1910) [q.v.][1] relation to India. Anendra Kumar Datta sent Leo Tolstoy an English language edition of Vivekananda's *Lectures on Raja Yoga*, first released in 1896. In a letter of reply dated September 13, 1896, Tolstoy jotted down:

> The book is most remarkable and I have received much instruction from it. The metaphysical side of the doctrine, the precept as to what the true 'I' of man is, is excellent. So far humanity has frequently gone backwards from the true and lofty and clear conception of the principle of life, but never surpassed it.

Concerning the volume, Tolstoy noted in his diary that he received "a charming book of Indian wisdom". A. K. Datta, the Indian scholar, wrote to Tolstoy, "You will be pleased to know that your doctrines are in complete agreement with the Indian philosophy at the period of its highest achievement." On October 14 in a letter to P. V. Verigin, Tolstoy describes Vivekananda's work as "expounding the doctrine of the Brahmins, having semblance with the essence of the teaching of Christ." Tolstoy's later contacts with Vivekananda's writings follow in the Ivan Nazhivin section.[2]

Katherine Tingley (1847-1929), a woman from the San Diego area, raised a good sum of money to take herself and two other Americans, E. T. Hargrove and C. F. Wright, on an eight-month World Crusade for Theosophy. In Europe they were instrumental in creating the new German Theological

Society. Established in August 1896, it was a branch of the International Theosophical Brotherhood that was under the leadership of William Q. Judge (1851-96) and later Katherine Tingley. Soon the German Theosophists proved to be the greatest supporters of Ramakrishna, Vivekananda and Abhedananda in the country. The German born spiritual seeker Franz Hartmann M.D. (1838-1912) lived in the United States from 1865 until late 1883, and then, under the influence of Theosophy, travelled to India in search of religious and philosophical truths. For nine months Hartmann resided at the Theosophical Society's headquarters at Adyar (Madras), serving as its temporary acting president. In April 1885 he returned to Europe accompanied by Madam Blavatsky, and four years later he cofounded a Theosophical lay-monastery at Ascona, Switzerland. His important German language writings include: a English-German translation of the *Bhagavad Gita* (by Edwin Arnold, 1892), *Three lectures on the Bhagavad Gita* given by T. Subba Row at the Theosophical Society in Madras (1893), *Katha Upanishad* (1893, by Charles Johnston), as well as the *Atma Bodha of Shankara* (1895) and books on karma, reincarnation and Buddhism. In 1896 he became the president of the new German Theosophical Society in Berlin. Most important, he rendered Vivekananda's *Karma Yoga* into a 193-page German language book in 1901 that was republished in 1921. On both occasions it was published by Theosophisches Verlags-Haus [Theosophical Publishing House] in Leipzig, Germany. Beginning in January 1900, the translation originally came out monthly in the *Lotusblüten* (*Lotus Blossoms*) periodical.[3]

Paul Zillmann (1872-1940), who lived near Berlin, was an executive committee member of the new German Theological Society. In 1896 he founded and edited the well-thought-of monthly publication *Neue Metaphysische Rundschau* [*New Metaphysical Review*], which dealt with philosophical, psychological, and occult research in science, art and religion. More specifically, the eclectic magazine covered yoga and medieval German mystics, along with occult and parapsychological subjects. In 1899 German language excerpts from Swamiji's *Raja Yoga* appeared in five editions of the *Neue Metaphysische Rundschau,* totalling about thirty pages. They concentrated primarily on prana, pratyahara, dharana, dhyana and samadhi. The following year Zillmann translated *Yoga Sutras of Patanjali* into German.[4]

In a 1902 edition of *Neue Metaphysische Rundschau*, Zillmann wrote a glowing eulogy to Swamiji:

> From India comes to us the surprising and sad news of the death of Swami Vivekananda in the Math at Belur, India. On Friday night on the 4th July, the Swami, at the age of 39 years, experienced Maha Samadhi. The next day, his earthly remains were burnt under a Bel tree on the banks of the Ganges. His death was due to dyspepsia and diabetes. We lose one of the most outstanding representatives of modern Hinduism, the faithful student of his master Ramakrishna. We are one in the feelings of deep sadness with our Indian brothers, one in the feelings of love. He taught not only in his home country the light of ancient wisdom, but to Western nations he showed them the truth of his fathers. He was a man of the highest spiritual insight and clarity. His valuable work, some of which we already published, will remain as the pearls of philosophy.[5]

Six years later Paul Zillmann offered annual subscriptions to the *Prabuddha Bharata* or *Awakened India* for 4.50 marks, mentioning that it is "produced by the brotherhood of which the Swami Vivekananda was the head".[6]

According to the Index of the *London Times*, the newspaper did not make mention of Vivekananda during his three visits to England. But after his mahasamadhi they prepared this inspiring eulogy:

> Swami Vivekananda, who died at Howrah on the 4th ult. at the age of 36 [sic], was well known in the New as well as the Old World as a religious teacher. He first came into prominence 15 [sic] years ago as an uncompromising and eloquent exponent of orthodox Hinduism, and the lectures he delivered in its support and defence in all parts of Upper India drew enormous assemblages of hearers. The unceasing controversy in which he was engaged, unsettled his convictions, and, after a year spent in close retirement, he came forward as the prophet of Vedantaism, purged of priestly ceremonials, and denounced the caste system as being responsible for much of the degradation of the Hindus. In 1893 he attended the World's Parliament of Religions in Chicago, and his speeches attracted so much attention that he was induced to remain in America for three years lecturing on Hindu philosophy, and, with the help of wealthy sympathizers, organizing a Vedanta movement, which is still being carried on there by Hindu disciples. His lectures in English fill several volumes and form a substantial contribution to modern Hindu religious literature. On his return to India he toured the country, being everywhere enthusiastically received, and continued zealously to espouse the reformed faith, in the interests of

which he established two monthly magazines. The chief formative influence in his remarkable career was afforded by his association in early days with Ramakrishna Paramahamsa, the Hindu ascetic whose "Life and Sayings" was published with Longmans by the late Professor Max Müller in 1898.[7]

News of Vivekananda's passing away also reached far away Rome. The Jesuit journal *La Civilta' Cattolica* (*The Catholic Civilization*) told its readers (in Italian) in a mixed review in 1902:

> Because of his unique gifts, the deceased Hindu monk will be remembered for years to come. He was an extraordinary man, who deserves a place in history.... His teacher was a man by the name of Ramakrishna Paramahamsa—who is deceased as well, and whose disciples venerate [him] as a saint. Under his careful guidance, Swami Vivekananda became zealous and full of fervour and, as a consequence, he turned out to be an apostle of Hinduism, both from the philosophical and religious point of view. When in 1893 the first World Conference on Religions was opened in Chicago, the Hindus sent Swami Vivekananda there to support Hinduism. The Americans liked the Hindu monk.[8]

Two years later *La Civilta' Cattolica* published an article written in Italian* by Clara Hood who, along with a Miss Danford, met Swamiji. Miss Danford was very much impressed by what he said at the Parliament of Religions. The article mentions a newspaper report about a speech the Swami gave in Milwaukee, Wisconsin, after leaving Detroit during the winter of 1894.[9]

Vivekananda's book on *Raja Yoga* had a big impact on Eustace Miles' (1868-1948) work *Avenues to Health* (1902). He mentions the "Yogi Vivekananda" on about twenty different pages, repeatedly quoting from his *Raja Yoga* volume, the "well-known work on Indian Yoga-practice". As stated later, Miles' references to the yogic teachings of Vivekananda brought about a transformation in the life of Cyril Scott, the famous composer. Eustace Miles kept himself in excellent shape, finishing second in the 1908 Olympic Games as a British Real tennis (Jeu de paume) player.† He wrote a multitude

* Found in Google Book Search on the Internet.

† In French Jeu de paume means "game of palm". It later became known as real tennis or lawn tennis. Jeu de paume was a medal event in the 1908 Summer Olympics.

of self-help books on health, diet, vegetarianism, proper breathing, memory, concentration, reincarnation, and philology.[10]

The following letter of apology appeared in March 1903:

To the Editor of the "*Hindustan Review*"

Dear Sir,

I write to acknowledge the force of the rejoinder which Swami Swarupananda* makes in your February number to my article on Swami Vivekananda. It is clear that I did not do him justice. The biography on which my article was based was not a short one (81 pp.), and was written by a professed admirer of the Swami. It was perhaps not unnatural that I should trust it; but I seem to have been mistaken. I might make this letter longer by dealing with various points in which I ought to correct myself. But the reader would probably find it tedious and no doubt Swami Swarupananda will be satisfied with what I have said.

Yours etc.,
J. Nelson Fraser

This letter demonstrates that, at least in some cases, if one explains to a writer that they are ill informed on the subject, they might realize their mistake. James Nelson Fraser (1869-1918) authored books like *The Poems of Tukarama* (1909) for the Christian Literature Society, which was reprinted in 1981.[11]

Ernst Arthur Weber was associated with the Theological Centre located at Leipzig, Germany. He founded and edited his own periodical *Der Theosophischer Wegweiser* (*The Theosophical Guide*) (1898-1907). The famous Russian writer Leo Tolstoy read some issues of the 1902-03 *Theosophischer Wegweiser*, which contained several sayings and parables of Ramakrishna. In 1905 Weber, under the name of E. A. Kernwart [q.v.], translated a 139 page German language edition of Vivekananda's writings entitled *Practical Vedanta*. It was published in Leipzig by Vedânta-Verlag. That same year the New York Vedanta Society, as the selling agent, sold two German language volumes rendered by Kernwart. The first contained five lectures by Vivekananda: "Practical Vedanta", "The Atman", "Is There a Personal God?",

* The editor of the *Prabuddha Bharata*.

"Jnana Yoga", and "The Real and Apparent Man". The second volume was composed of eight lectures by Abhedananda which, in 1909, the Orientalist N. O. Einhorn brought to Leo Tolstoy, who greatly appreciated them. A year earlier in 1908 Kernwart came out with a translation of Abhedananda's *Philosophy of Work* (*Karma*) (1902).[12]

A professor of philosophy at the University of Wilno in Poland, Wincenty Lutoslawski (1863-1954) attended the 1893 Parliament of Religions. In 1906 he dispatched a letter to his friend William James at Harvard, telling him that he had taken up the practice of hatha yoga for four months. For seven years Lutoslawski suffered from an unstable nervous system resulting in successive periods of extreme over and under activity. Lutoslawski declared, "Thus I decided to follow Vivekananda's advice: 'Practise hard: whether you live or die by it doesn't matter.'" He took up the practice of extreme dieting, yogic postures and breathing exercises. After a period of increasing lethargy he was healed, "and came to know a peace never known before, an inner rhythm of unison with a deeper rhythm above or beyond. Personal wishes ceased, and the consciousness of being the instrument of a superior power arose." Six months later, in a letter to James he mentioned, "The improvement holds good."[13] Lutoslawski wrote on the logic of Plato in 1897 and also authored two studies in support of rebirth, *The World of Souls* (1924), with a preface by William James, and *Pre-Existence and Reincarnation* (1928). He indicated that all of the great poets of nineteenth century Poland, along with a famous philosopher and a mystic, believe they have lived prior lives on earth.[14]

Léon Sorg (1862-1906), an expert on modern Hindu law, was a member of the Advisory Committee on Indian Jurisprudence in Pondicherry, India. As a result, he wrote a book *Opinion of the Indian Council of Jurisprudence*. While living in India he became interested in Indian philosophy and, with the permission of Max Müller, rendered his *Three lectures on the Vedanta Philosophy* into the French language in 1899. Shortly before his death he authored an article on yoga for the *Mercure de France* (1906), where he stated:

> The teaching of this ancient rishi [Patanjali] was summarized in a number of Sanskrit aphorisms, concise enough to be almost incomprehensible without the explanation of the commentator. We will emphasize the most recent of them by Swami Vivekananda, an outstanding philosopher and orator, a disciple of one of the most famous Sannyasi of modern India, and a representative of Hinduism at the Parliament of Religions in Chicago.

We cannot choose a better qualified guide to the mysteries of yoga, which he unveiled in a series of lectures in America and recently in the volume *Yoga Philosophy* (1897). While Patanjali's doctrine is purely deistic, Vivekananda is a follower of Vedanta, pantheistic and monistic. Despite this difference in principles, the practice of Yoga is the same in either system.

The epigraph of his book indicates the dominant ideas: "Every soul is potentially divine. The goal is to manifest this innate divinity, while controlling nature external and internal. Do this by action, worship, psychic control, or philosophy, by one or more of these means and be free. That is the whole of religion. Doctrines, dogmas, rituals, books, temples, and forms are only secondary details."

Our author then develops these aphorisms. It is generally accepted, he said, that religion, unlike science, is not based on experience, but on faith, belief, dogma. However, going back to the origin of religions, we see that they are based on the direct experience of their founders. Each of them claimed to have seen God, to have received from him the truth, to be discovered by a higher intuition. Can this possibly be repeated today? Yes, says Vivekananda, "Uniformity is the absolute law of nature, what happened once can always happen." Indeed, that experience is not only possible, it is essential to acquire a rational faith.[15]

Ivan Fedorovich Nazhivin (1874-1940) [q.v.] sent Leo Tolstoy [q.v.] his anthology *Golosa Narodov* (*The Voices of the People*) (1908), which contains a Russian translation of Vivekananda's "God and Man". Tolstoy affirmed in a letter of March 12, 1908 sent to Nazhivin, "The Hindu article [God and Man] left a great impression on me ... This is unusually good." In his diary he wrote, "Yesterday read the Hindu's wonderful article [God and Man], translated into Russian by Nazhivin. Here are my thoughts, obscurely expressed." That year Tolstoy read two volumes written by Swamiji and concluded, "Wonderfully profound: about God, soul, man, unity of religions.... He is Ramakrishna's pupil, and died in 1902." In June he told D. P. Makovitsky, "Since six in the morning I have been thinking of Vivekananda. Yesterday, read Vivekananda whole day. There is a chapter on justification of violent means of resisting evil. Very talentedly written." Concerning a writing by Swamiji, Tolstoy told Makovitsky, "Excellent book, so many thoughts are here for circle of reading." He noted in his diary of July 4, 1908, "Read Vivekananda's article on God—an excellent one. Should be translated. I myself thought of this itself. His criticism of Schopenhauer's will is quite true." Tolstoy added, "What English has Vivekananda! He has learnt all its subtleties." In March 1909, Tolstoy planned to publish in Russian a book of the sayings of Ramakrishna and Vivekananda, but it did not come about. In May he spoke with the editor of the Posrednik publishing house, telling him, "The most eminent of modern Indian thinkers is Vivekananda, and he should be published." He also wrote to a friend, "I love Indian philosophy." During January 1910, the year of his death, he told a friend, "She [Annie Besant] rests on what is weak, what is erroneous, and Vivekananda on what is true." Tolstoy conveyed to Jan Massaryk, a famous Czech thinker, that Vivekananda is the greatest philosopher of modern India. A. P. Gnatyuk-Danil'chuk, a Russian scholar, concluded, "For Tolstoy, Vivekananda had indeed become, and remained unto the last, a living personification of the spiritual richness of modern India.... Tolstoy had an exceptionally high overall assessment about him right up to the end of his life." In 1909 Tolstoy praised a German language translation of Abhedananda's writings, which he wanted to have translated into Russian.[16]

Ivan Nazhivin, a follower of Leo Tolstoy, came out with an anthology entitled *V Doline Skorbi* (*In the Valley of Grief*, 1907), which contains a Russian translation of Vivekananda's lecture "My Master". The following year his second anthology, *Golosa Narodov* (*The Voices of the People*, 1908), included a translation of Vivekananda's "God and Man" mentioned above and "Hymn of Creation". Nazhivin noted in the latter book:

> There have been rising deep and wide currents amongst the peoples of India, aimed at purifying the great centuries-old teachings of Buddhism and Brahmanism from all sorts of interpolations and superstitions. Swami Vivekananda, a pupil of Sri Ramakrishna, is one of the brilliant representatives of these great religious currents.

In 1912, after Tolstoy's death, Nazhivin rendered Max Müller's *Three Lectures on the Vedanta Philosophy* (*Filosof i~I a Vedanty*) into the Russian language. Next, he translated Müller's *Sri Ramakrishna Paramahamsa, His Life and Teachings* (*Shri Ramakrishna Paramagamza*, 1913). The following year Abhedananda's translation of *The Gospel of Ramakrishna* was rendered into Russian. These two latter volumes are presently housed at Stanford University as part of the Konstantinoff Collection.[17] Leo Tolstoy's ethical teachings and his techniques as a novelist very much influenced Nazhivin, a prolific Russian writer. He brought out a book on Tolstoy in 1911. After the Russian revolution in 1920, he and his family moved to France. Most of his thirty novels have remained untranslated from the Russian language. In France he produced historical novels as a "bitter invective hurled by a disgruntled émigré at his native land."[18]

When Abhedananda stayed in London, Cyril Scott (1879-1970) [q.v.], a prominent British composer, came to see him on many occasions during the winter of 1908. With his companion, the skilled dancer Ruth St. Denis, Scott also went to see the young Swami Paramananda in Surrey, England. Earlier he had come across copious quotations from Vivekananda's *Raja Yoga* while reading Eustace Miles' *Avenues to Health* (1902). He points out, "These struck me as so replete with wisdom that I immediately ordered a copy." Scott, like Wincenty Lutoslawski, experienced remarkable results from the private practise of yoga. Concerning Swamiji's *Raja Yoga*, Scott later disclosed in 1924:

> I read that remarkable exposition of the Science of Yoga. It was the book for which I seemed to have been seeking all my life; it showed me how a man might transform his own consciousness and become *unconditionally* happy. There was no fanaticism, no sentimentality, no hysteria about this book; it was sane, scientific, logical, and tolerant; it was also essentially poetic.... I also commenced the practices advocated, namely, breath control and mind control; and soon, to my intense delight, found that I began to experience those exalted states of consciousness promised by the author to all faithful practitioners. In fact, the change in me was so marked that I remember Holland Smith, who came to stay with me at Easter that year, observing with considerable surprise: "What on earth's happened to you? You are quite a different person. You're not only far more vivacious, but—although it sounds a paradox—far calmer than I've ever known you." I told him my vivacity was due to an alternation in diet, and my calmness to a very ancient science which I had just discovered.... from the day that book *Raja Yoga* came into my hands, the study of all forms of mysticism and transcendental philosophy became for me a passion; and not only that, but I found in their study a new and great source of musical inspiration.

During the First World War, Scott met Mrs. Milligan-Fox, an Irish woman who communicated with the spirits of the deceased. During one session, an Indian came into view "with a very benign countenance". Through the power of clairaudience, Mrs. Milligan-Fox repeated the spirit's remarks.

Scott discloses, "They were too metaphysically technical for her to understand, and I was obliged to explain them. Before the 'apparition' disappeared, I requested her to ask his name. 'Vivekananda', was the reply."[19]

Cyril Meir Scott, an English composer, poet, and writer, produced music for the piano, orchestral works, chamber and choral pieces, and violin studies. He composed an opera, a ballet and a cantata, but is best known for his piano pieces and songs. Under the influence of Annie Besant, he became a member of the Theosophical Society. Indian philosophy, yoga and meditation profoundly influenced his music. His piano pieces include "Lotus Land", a favourite of Fritz Kreisler (1875-1962), the famed Austrian violinists and composer in the U.S., the nineteen-page Hindu-style "Impressions from the Jungle Book", the fourteen-page "Indian Suite" which deals with the Juggernaut and other aspects of Indian culture, and also "Karma" composed in 1926. Scott wrote on the mystical aspects of musical inspiration and other sublime subjects.[20]

In a 1909 book written by L. S. S. O'Malley (1874-1941) [q.v.] and Monmohan Chakravarti [q.v.], which describes the Howrah District in Bengal, a brief sketch of Swamiji is followed by the statement:

> Probably, however, it was not Vivekananda's advocacy of a universal religion that appealed to Indians so much as his forceful character and the impression he made on the patriotic spirit of young Hindus. To quote from an article in a recent number of *The International Review*: "He returned to India in triumph to be hailed as the prophet of new India, as one who had dared to assert the spiritual wealth of ancient India in face of the western world. He at once became the hero of the young generation.... The spirit of Vivekananda may stand for the spirit of the new era in India. We find his name repeatedly quoted to-day as the representative of Indian national aspirations. His is the religion of the nationalists—the cult of India—the bold assertion of India's right to stand among the nations as the mother of illumination and light. At the same time he is broadly tolerant, nay, universal in his acceptance of the other world-religions. All, he claims, are contained in Vedanta."[21]

The English cleric, Thomas Kelly Cheyne (1841-1915) held the position of the Oriel Professor of the interpretation of scripture at Oxford University from 1885 to 1908. Being the initiator of the "higher criticism" of the *Bible* theological movement in England, he authored over twenty books dealing with his interpretation of the Biblical Old Testament. T. K. Cheyne and J. Sutherland Black edited the prestigious four volume, 2800-plus-page *Encyclopaedia Biblica* (1899-1903). Abdu'l Baha (1844-1921), the leader of the Baha'i faith, met Cheyne in 1912 and addressed him as "my spiritual philosopher".[22] Twenty-two letters that Sister Nivedita sent to her good friend T. K. Cheyne, from 1907 up until the time of her passing away in 1911, have been published. During her visit to England in 1908 and in 1911, she conversed with Cheyne and her other friends. He very much appreciated Nivedita's book *The Web of Indian Life*. Responding to his letter, Nivedita recommended the *Bhagavad Gita* and the writings of Vivekananda as the best sources for learning about the Hindu religion. Cheyne reveals that these books

> produced a revolution in my view of the capacity of Hindu religion for adapting itself progressively to the spiritual needs of Indians, and for contributing elements of enormous value to the purification, enrichment, and reinterpretation of Christianity.... Sister Nivedita was well aware that I looked for help to the Aryan East, and especially to her and her Master [Vivekananda], and this may have been the chief reason why she paid me in the dazzling coin of affection, reverence, and gratitude for the sympathy which I delighted to express to her.[23]

In January 1911, in the *Hibbert Journal*, the distinguished Oxford scholar Professor T. K. Cheyne came out with a review of Nivedita's book on Vivekananda, *The Master as I Saw Him* (1910).[24] This 1911 article might have been the first attempt by a Western scholar to interpret and explain the teachings of Vivekananda. The review gives an idea of which aspects of Swamiji's teachings most appealed to Western scholars. According to Cheyne's analysis:

> His later life was a fusion of two ideals, that of the apostle of Hinduism and that of the practical worker for India. Those who simply listened to him in the West only knew him as the former; it was the prize of a more intimate acquaintance to learn that he was also a fervent lover of India, and that he had elastic and far-reaching plans for its benefit.... the regeneration of India was prominent in his thoughts and aspirations. And the motive on which he rested all service was derived from the most startling of all Vedantic doctrines—the divinity of man. "Compassion," he said, "was that which served others with the idea that they were jivas, souls; love, on the

contrary, regarded them as the Atman; the very Self-Love, therefore, was worship, and this worship the vision of God."... It is claimed for Ramakrishna that he could by his touch give spiritual insight; and Vivekananda says, "Spirituality can be communicated just as really as I give you a flower." All can at any rate grant that the company one keeps has a subtle influence on the mind, and that it would certainly be good for any of us to be in the presence of an extraordinary man like the Swami Vivekananda.[25]

During the 1902-07 period, Samuel Kerkham Ratcliffe (1868-1958), a journalist and lecturer, was at first the assistant and then the acting editor of the *Statesman*, the leading English newspaper in Calcutta. He edited the *Sociological Review* during the period 1910-17, and, in 1915, received appointment to be a lecturer at the South Place Ethical Society in London, later writing a history of that organization. A prolific lecturer on both sides of the Atlantic, he favoured the cause of Indian self-government. Ratcliffe held a great admiration for the work Sister Nivedita was doing when he lived in Calcutta, and they later met again in England. He wrote a prefatory memoir for Nivedita's *Studies from an Eastern Home* (1913), and the preface for her *Religion and Dharma* (1915).[26] In a tribute to Sister Nivedita, Ratcliffe expressed his admiration for Swamiji, which he gained to some extent from his association with her. It is significant that Ratcliffe, like Nivedita's friend Cheyne, also focuses on Swamiji's plan for a regenerated India:

> He appeared before the Parliament of Religions, held during the Chicago Exhibition of 1893, as the first of the modern missionaries of Hinduism to the Western world. He was unknown and had come unheralded; but his discourse—the one incident of that curious assembly that is remembered today—was epoch making. From it must be dated the widespread interest in Indian thought and religion, and especially in the philosophy of Vedanta, which has been so unmistakable a feature of educated America during the past two decades.
>
> You will hear from those who came within the scope of this masterful teacher's influence many differing estimates of the effect created by his personality and speech.... Vivekananda was a man of action. Not only did he carry westward the message of Vedantism, but he had dreams of a renewal of the life of India through the infusion of fresh knowledge and renascent ideals. He stood entirely aloof from politics, yet it is hardly surprising that his younger followers should have claimed him as something more than

> a teacher of Vedantism—as, in truth, the prophet of New India in a sense which, it seems quite certain, he never for moment intended....
>
> Although himself obeying the impulse and fulfilling the purpose of his master Ramakrishna, he dealt always impersonally with the body of truth common to all religions, and dwelt upon the necessity, especially in the present stage of world's history, for the exchange of ideals between peoples, and especially between the East and West. He was, too, much more than a preacher. While glorifying the Indian past and the ancient contribution of his people to the intellectual wealth of the world, he was a man of modern outlook, incessantly framing concrete schemes for the social regeneration of India. He was bent upon the firm establishment of the Order of Ramakrishna, of which he was the head—an order which he designed not for contemplation alone, but for social service; he would, if he could, have commanded vast resources for educational enterprise; and he was resolved to initiate some definite agency for the education of Indian women.[27]

Concerning Swamiji's spiritual work in America and India, John Nicol Farquhar (1861-1929) [q.v.], a liberal Christian Congregationalist missionary who showed appreciation for Sri Ramakrishna, concluded in 1915:

> The gathering was held in September 1893; and Vivekananda made a great impression, partly by his eloquence, partly by his striking figure and picturesque dress; but mainly by his new, unheard-of-presentation of Hinduism.... He exercised a fine influence on young India in one direction. He summoned his fellow-countrymen to stand on their own feet, to trust themselves and to play the man; and his words were not without fruit.... He summoned his countrymen to practical service, to self-sacrificing work for India.... Vivekananda's influence still lives in America. There are societies that teach Hinduism in various ways in New York, Boston, Washington, D.C., Pittsburgh and San Francisco. His influence seems to be far stronger in San Francisco than anywhere else. There is a picturesque Hindu temple there, in which classes are held and addresses given, and the literature of the mission sold.[28]

Three years later William Edward Sladen Holland (1873-1951), the principal of St. Paul's Cathedral College, Calcutta, and fellow of Calcutta University, reemphasized the important point made by Farquhar that Vivekananda made "a great impression" at the Parliament of Religions, "mainly by his unheard of and entirely original presentation of Hinduism".[29]

The *Sedition Committee 1918 Report* led by Justice Sir Sidney Rowlatt (1862-1945) [q.v.] sought out terrorist activity in Bengal and Punjab, and yet was very approving of the Ramakrishna Mission and made such statements as:

> Subsequently famous as Swami Vivekananda, Narendranath Datta became an ascetic and attended the Parliament of Religions in Chicago as the representative of Hinduism. There he made a great impression and founded Vedanta societies for spreading the teaching of the Hindu scriptures (*Vedas*). He returned to India in 1897 with a small band of followers, and was acclaimed by many educated Hindus as a saviour and prophet of their faith. He organized centres of philanthropic and religious effort under the supervision of a Rama Krishna Mission, and carrying much further the teachings of his master.[30]

1920s and After

While Karl Jellinek (b. 1882), a professor at the Technical Institute of Danzig, specialized in writing books on chemistry, he also penned works like the German language *Das Weltengeheimnis* (*The Secret World: Lectures on the Harmonious Reunion of Natural and Spiritual Science, Philosophy, Art and Religion,* 1921). There he draws inspiration from the writings of the Theosophist Franz Hartmann, Vivekananda and Meister Eckhart. He believes in the "Brotherhood of the Human Races" and the "World Mission of the Indian spirit". For Jellinek, Vivekananda is a "titanic Thinker" who "stood among thinkers as the Himalaya stands among mountains." Jellinek taught, "If the Occident desired to know anything about the Soul, Spirit, and God, about the meaning and mysteries of the Cosmos, then, indeed, must the Occident sit at the feet of the Orient."[31]

On February 26, 1924, Lord Lytton II (Victor Bulwer-Lytton, 1876–1947) [q.v.] wrote to Josephine MacLeod:

> We were delighted with our visit to Belur [Math], and I shall long cherish grateful recollections of that haven of peace. The little Lalique statue of Vivekananda now stands upon my writing table and every afternoon as

it catches the rays of the setting sun, it shines as if lit up by a sacred flame from within.[32]

He and his wife were friendly with Abhedananda and invited him to dinner. Following his request, in 1926 they also paid a visit to Abhedananda's Ashram in Darjeeling. Born in Simla in India, his father was the Viceroy of the country. As a political conservative, Lytton held a variety of political posts, largely dealing with the arts, and he advocated women's suffrage. In 1922 he became the governor of Bengal, remaining in that position until 1927. For four months during Lord Reading's absence, he took on the duties of the viceroy of India. Being just and of a dignified nature, he was sympathetic to the Indian people, won their respect and affection, and had many Indian friends of all castes and classes. During 1927 and 1928, he led the Indian delegation at the eighth and ninth Assemblies of the League of Nations.[33]

The Tantric expert Sir John George Woodroffe (1865-1936) indicated:

> The qualities I most admire in Vivekananda are his activity, manliness and courage.... His was the attitude of a man. He spoke up and acted. For this, all must honour him, who, whatever be their own religious beliefs, value sincerity, truth and courage, which are the badges of every noble character.[34]

Sir John Woodroffe (sometimes writing under the pseudonym of Arthur Avalon) brought out nine articles in the *Prabuddha Bharata* between 1915 and 1928, and an additional thirty-six in the *Vedanta Kesari* between 1916 and 1929. Nine essays discuss the Tantra philosophy and seven deal with Shakti, relating to his work *Shakti, or the World as Power* (1920). Twenty-two of the articles that deal with the Mantra Shastra were incorporated into *The Garland of Letters* (1922).[35] For a time Woodroffe was the president of the Vivekananda Society of Calcutta, where he delivered a series of lectures during the years 1917-18.[36]

After making contacts with some outstanding pundits of Bengal, Woodroffe became the leading Western authority on the beliefs and practices of Tantra and Kundalini yoga. Shivkali Bhattacharya, the Tantric teacher, initiated Woodroffe into the discipline. Woodroffe translated from Sanskrit important Tantric texts, adding his own profound commentaries and introductions. In addition, he brought out several scholarly manuscripts explaining the philosophy underlying the Indian Tantric texts with emphasis on the kundalini, chakras and other yogic subjects. Before Woodroffe came out with his revealing books, the Tantras were often falsely interpreted and practised. He worked as an advocate of the Calcutta High Court (1890), a fellow and Tagore law professor at the University of Calcutta, standing counsel to the Government of India (1902-03), a High Court judge of Calcutta (1904-22), and the chief justice of Bengal's High Court after 1915. After returning to England, he became a reader in Indian law at Oxford University (1923-30).[37]

Born in Prague, Czechoslovakia, Hans Kohn (1891-1971) [q.v.] was the Middle East correspondent for two German newspapers. In his book *In a History of Nationalism in the East* (1929), he included some long quotations from a Madras publication of Swamiji's talks titled *From Colombo to Almora, Seventeen Lectures* (1897). Kohn added:

> Vivekananda had enjoyed a good English education and knew the world. In his new Vedanta System he taught that all religions were fundamentally the same, and that the varying customs and ritual of the peoples were only allegories and symbols of the one truth. In addition to this allegorical form for the multitude, there is esoteric wisdom for the initiated. So also in the New Testament there were three degrees of understanding. In the first it was said: "Our Father which art in Heaven;" in the second: "The Kingdom of God is within you;" and in the third: "I and my Father are one." But Vivekananda was not only a Gnostic. The spirit of the age and of the new India lived in him and he helped to create it. He taught that man can become one with God not only through meditation but by ceaseless self-sacrifice for the common good. The chief aim of his Rama Krishna Mission was social service. He was animated by a burning love of his country.[38]

A major European interest in Vivekananda's teachings deals with the translation of his books on *Karma Yoga*, *Raja Yoga*, *Bhakti Yoga*, and *Jnana Yoga*. During the period 1901-30, one or more of these four volumes were translated in Germany (by Franz Hartmann, 1838-1912; Fritz Otto Rose, b. 1876), Russia (by Yakov A. K. Popov(a), 1844-1918), France (by W. S.),

Finland (by Ilmari Saari), Czechoslovakia (by Karel Weinfurter, 1867-1942), Italy (by Giovanni Battista Penne, b. 1859), and Latvia.*

Frederico Climent Terrer produced over fifty Spanish translations of English books, primarily in Barcelona, Spain, and occasionally in Buenos Aires. The Library of Congress lists nine of his Vivekananda translations, including *Raja Yoga*, *Bhakti Yoga*, and *Jnana Yoga*, but their exact dates are unknown.† In addition, he rendered into Spanish twenty-seven New Thought works written by Orison Swett Marden (1850-1924), who knew Abhedananda. He translated ten New Thought volumes written by Ralph Waldo Trine (1866-1958), a friend of Vivekananda and Abhedananda. Also, he translated four books of Yogi Kharishnanda, three of the New Thought writer William Walker Atkinson (aka Yogi Ramachakra, 1862-1932), including the *Bhagavad Gita*, and produced a few of his own manuscripts. Many of his translations are without dates, 1913 being the earliest year given. While vacationing in Mexico in the summer of 1905, Abhedananda heard "that Swami Vivekananda's *Raja Yoga* had been translated into Spanish by a scholar in Barcelona, Spain". As this predates Terrer's work, the identity of the translator needs to be probed into.[39]

The publication of Romain Rolland's (1866-1944) [q.v.] *The Life of Vivekananda and the Universal Gospel* (1930), first in French and then in German and English, proved to be a major event in Vivekananda studies in the West. In Chapter II there is a discussion of Rolland's relationship with Sri Ramakrishna and Vedanta. The 1915 Nobel Laureate in Literature emphasizes in his biography of Vivekananda:

> His words are great music, phrases in the style of Beethoven, stirring rhythms like the march of Handel choruses. I cannot touch these sayings of his, scattered as they are through the pages of this book at thirty years' distance, without receiving a thrill through my body like an electric shock. And what shocks, what transports, must have been produced when in burning words they issued from the lips of the hero!
>
> Nothing escaped the magic of his glance, which was capable equally of enveloping with irresistible charm, sparkling with wit, with irony, with kindness, losing itself in ecstasy, or plunging imperiously to the deeps of conscience and withering with its fury. But above all nobody ever drew near

* See Appendix VII.
† See Appendix VII.

> him in India or America without being struck by his majesty. He was born a king.... His power and his beauty, the grace and dignity of his bearing, the dark light of his eyes, his imposing appearance, and from the moment he began to speak, the splendid music of his warm deep voice enthralled the crowd of American Anglo-Saxons, prejudiced against him on account of his colour. And the thought of the warrior-prophet of India left the mark of its claws on the sides of the United States. He could never be imagined in a secondary position. Wherever he was, he was first.[40]
>
> To bring Vedanta out of its obscurity and present it in a rationally acceptable manner; to arouse among his countrymen an awareness of their own spiritual heritage and restore their self-confidence; to show that the deepest truths of Vedanta are universally valid, and that India's mission is to communicate these truths to the whole world—these were the goals he set before himself.[41]

In 1927 the eminent French philosopher Henri Bergson (1859-1941) received the Nobel Prize for literature. He had some acquaintance with Rolland's biographies of Ramakrishna and Vivekananda. In regards to active ethical mysticism, an elderly Bergson made this statement in 1932:

> Perhaps such a form of complete mysticism may have existed in India also, but at a much later date. Confining our attention to people of the most recent times, what we find in men like Ramakrishna and Vivekananda is a passionate Charity and a mysticism which is comparable with Christian mysticism.[42]

Bergson also made this interesting statement about the law of karma:

> Karma has quite a karma. Long after India's seers immortalized it in the Vedas, it suffered bad press under European missionaries who belittled it as "fate" and "fatalism", and today finds itself again in the ascendancy as the subtle and all-encompassing principle which governs man's experiential universe in a way likened to gravity's governance over the physical plane. Like gravity, karma was always there in its fullest potency, even when people did not comprehend it.[43]

Clifford Bax (1886-1962) was a British playwright who often wrote in a poetic form. Some of his poems deal with reincarnation, while his most successful plays focused on historical figures. Bax's remarkable literary production of nearly ninety plays and books include a radio play on the *Life and Ideas of Buddha*, a book on the German mystic Jacob Boehme edited by him, and a translation of a volume by Rudolph Steiner. In 1933, while reviewing *The Life of Swami Vivekananda, By His Eastern and Western Disciples*, he expressed his great admiration for the vitality and intellect of the Hindu saint:

> Vivekananda, however, was probably the finest representative of any Eastern religion or philosophy who ever visited the West. His sincerity is beyond question.... his intellect must have been exceptionally powerful.... Indeed, whenever the authors quote from his letters, his conversation or his discourses, we recognize at once that we are listening to a man of intense aspiration, great beauty of life, tremendous energy and high mental voltage. The vitality of these *ipsissima verba*, even on the printed page, is astonishing. They come to us, across thirty years, with a stronger sense of his personality than any gramophone record could have captured.... no unprejudiced reader could finish these volumes without feeling that he had been in touch with a really great man—great, no matter whether or not the world should soon forget him,—without a sense of that spiritual quickening which comes from physical nearness to such a personality, or without wondering whether it is not very much as though St. John or St. Paul, or a combination of both, had been living in the world between 1863 and 1902. Many Western readers will be startled to find that the virtue which this Hindu saint extolled above all others was energy.[44]

A close friend of Romain Rolland was Jean Herbert (1897-1980), a prodigious French writer, editor, and translator, primarily of Indian texts. He served on active duty in both World Wars, and received the Croix de Guerre medal for bravery in war. Around 1935 he and his wife Lizelle Reymond met Josephine MacLeod, who encouraged him to translate Vivekananda's writings on yoga. Herbert and his wife made a trip to India where he received the blessings of Sri Ramana Maharshi, and met Mahatma Gandhi and Sri Aurobindo. They attended many events at the Ramakrishna Centenary Parliament of Religions held during March 1937 in Calcutta, where he presented a paper. He was friendly with Swami Siddheswarananda in France, and his wife completed a biography of Sister Nivedita. From 1954 to 1964 he held the chair of Oriental Mythology at Geneva University in Switzerland. Herbert was the president of the International Association of Conference

Interpreters. Since his writings are in the French language, most Americans are unfamiliar with his enormous literary contribution. Herbert's Indian studies began with the translation of ten of Vivekananda's works into French, some in collaboration with his wife. His remarkable output includes: *Mon Maitre*, *Jnana-Yoga*, *Le Yoga de la connaissance*, *Karma-Yoga*, *Entretiens inspires*, *Bhakti-Yoga* (with Reymond), *Commentaires sur les aphorismes de Patanjali*, *Conferences sur Bhakti-Yoga* (with Reymond), and *Au coeur des choses*, all between 1935 and 1940, and *Les Yogas pratiques* (with others) in 1950. In addition, he wrote *Bibliographie de l'oeuvre de Swami Vivekananda dans les langues europeennes*, *L'Enseignement de Ramakrishna* and *Lexique Ramakrishna-Vivekananda* between 1939 and 1945. Between 1937 and 1952 Jean Herbert also translated *Shri Rama-krishna, Les Paroles du maitre* (with others), Swami Yatishwarananda's *Commentaries sur la discipline monastique de Swami Brahmananda* (with Odette de Saussure), and Sister Nivedita's *Vivekananda tel que je l'ai vu* (with Rose Rigaud). He also wrote and/or translated numerous works on Sri Aurobindo, Mahatma Gandhi, Swami Ramdas, Shankara, Ramana Maharshi, Rabindranath Tagore, yoga, the Upanishads, *Bhagavad-Gita*, meditation, Hinduism, Indian mythology, hymns of Shiva, and Vedanta up until his passing away in 1980.[45]

It should be mentioned that Sri Aurobindo, who is mentioned above, has left the information about the following very interesting fact. When he was locked up in a solitary cell in Alipore jail in the first decade of the twentieth century, he states:

> I was hearing constantly the voice of Vivekananda speaking to me for a fortnight in the jail in my solitary meditation and felt his presence. The voice spoke only on a special and limited but very important field of spiritual experience and it ceased as soon as it had finished saying all that it had to say on that subject.... It was the spirit of Vivekananda which first gave me a clue in the direction of the supermind. This clue led me to see how Truth-Consciousness works in everything.... Vivekananda came and gave me the knowledge of the intuitive mentality. I had not the least idea about it at that time. He too did not have it when he was in the body. He gave me detailed knowledge illustrating each point. The contact lasted about three weeks and then he withdrew.... The going forth of Vivekananda, marked out by the Master as the heroic soul destined to take the world between his two hands and change it, was the first visible sign to the world that India was awake not only to survive but to conquer.[46]

Aurobindo's statement that Vivekananda gained new knowledge after his passing, which he did not have while living on earth, is an interesting comment.

Another connection between them is that Barindra Ghose, a brother of Aurobindo, and Bhupendranath Datta, a brother of Vivekananda, founded the *Yugantar* or "New Era" newspaper in 1906. It attained a circulation unparalleled for an Indian newspaper because of its opposition to foreign rule, and consequently it was terminated in June 1908.[47]

Major Francis Yeats-Brown (1886-1944) [q.v.], the author of the best-selling autobiography *The Lives of a Bengal Lancer* (1930), in the sequel *Lancer at Large* (1937) made the following observation:

> At the Belur Math, the headquarters of the Ramakrishna Mission, I saw the room where Vivekananda died—Vivekananda who electrified the United States with his eloquence, and, later, England. Almost his last words were: "India is immortal if she persists in her search for God. But if she goes in for politics and social conflict, she will die."…. Especially should they read Vivekananda, who is a mirror of the high thought of Hinduism.[48]

Hugh George Rawlinson (1880-1957) authored many books on India such as *Indian Historical Studies* (1913), *The Intercourse between India and the Western World, from Earliest Times to the Fall of Rome* (1916) and *The British Achievement in India* (1948). In 1941 he mentioned that Vivekananda's

> lofty and commanding personality and his striking eloquence won him a ready hearing in the United States, and he started the Ramakrishna Mission, the object of which was to wean its followers from the greed, sensuality, and materialism of the West by means of the ancient truths of Hinduism—the identity of the World Soul and the individual, the illusory nature of objects of the senses, and the theory of Karma, or the inevitable retribution following upon our deeds in former lives. Christianity teaches us to love one's neighbour as one's self. "Your neighbour is yourself," is Vivekananda's retort.[49]

After the Second World War there have been many translations of Ramakrishna-Vedanta books into European languages by different persons. One such person, Franz Frank Dispeker (d. 1955), a wealthy German banker from Berlin, as a Jewish refugee emigrated with his wife from Switzerland to

California. He became a disciple of Swami Prabhavananda and good friend of Christopher Isherwood during the early 1940s. After the war Dispeker returned to Switzerland and translated many Vedanta books from English to German, including Vivekananda's *Jnana Yoga*, *Karma Yoga*, and *Bhakti Yoga*; Nikhilananda's *Prophet of New India: Abridged from the Gospel of Sri Ramakrishna*; and Prabhavananda's *The Eternal Companion*, and others.[50]

As a university professor Ernst Wilhelm Meyer (b. 1892) authored books on political science. In 1956, as the ambassador of the Federal Republic of West Germany to India, he delivered an appreciative lecture at the Ramakrishna Mission in New Delhi, stating among other things:

> Vivekananda, moreover, left for Indian youth a sense of exemplary *enthusiasm*. Who can study his life without becoming overwhelmed by his burning enthusiasm, by giving every particle of his body and soul to the great mission which he felt he was called upon to perform! It is, as if, he himself had been nothing but spiritual fire in human shape. And in every hour of his existence this fire gave itself unsparingly to the benefit of others. What could youth be without such and similar examples in the history of mankind?... The youth of all countries in the world should read and learn and make their own the works of Vivekananda, which should be assigned the first place in the bookshelves of those who want to know what true greatness is.... I know, my friends, how impossible it is for an average man like me to try to come to a full realization of a paramount genius like Vivekananda. But let me humbly repeat what I thought he gave to youth and to all of us: The sense of religion, the sense of the true relationship between religion and politics, the sense of the unity of mankind, the sense of creative internationalism, the sense of creative patriotism, the sense of exemplary enthusiasm, the sense of the part played by great men in human history, the sense of the most important alliance, namely that of both meditation and action.[51]

The very distinguished professor of South Asiatic history from the University of London, A. L. Basham (1914-86) [q.v.] summarized Vivekananda's important contribution to the Vedanta movement:

> The most important of Ramakrishna's followers was Narendranath Datta, a well educated young Bengali who on the master's death became a *sannyasi* and devoted himself to the propagation of Ramakrishna's teachings,

> taking the religious name of Vivekananda. Vivekananda was a man of strong personality and great moral earnestness, and was a very forceful speaker and writer with a good command of English. In 1893 he visited the United States to attend a parliament of religions at Chicago. America, already ready to accept new ideas, and prepared for Hinduism by the sympathetic interest of a number of her literary men, took Vivekananda to her heart. Wherever he lectured he made a very great impression on large audiences, and several Vedanta Societies were founded in the larger cities to continue his work.... the neo-Hinduism of Vivekananda, in its many developments, is the most potent religious influence in modern India, and, adapted by the genius of Mahatma Gandhi, has provided the ideology of the Indian independence movement.[52]

Nine years later, after giving the matter more thought, Basham explained Vivekananda's significant place in world history:

> The passing of the years and the many stupendous and unexpected events which have occurred since then suggest that in centuries to come he will be remembered as one of the main moulders of the modern world, especially as far as Asia is concerned, and as one of the most significant figures in the whole history of Indian religion, comparable in importance to such great teachers as Shankara and Ramanuja.... I believe also that Vivekananda will always be remembered in the world's history because he virtually initiated what the late Dr. C. E. M. Joad once called "the counter-attack from the East". Since the days of the Indian missionaries who travelled in South East Asia and China preaching Buddhism and Hinduism more than a thousand years earlier, he was the first Indian religious teacher to make an impression outside India.[53]

Arthur L. Basham authored the 1954 classic cultural-historical textbook *The Wonder that was India*. The volume is an all-inclusive survey of the culture of the Indian subcontinent before the coming of the Muslim Mughals in the sixteenth century. Its range of subject matter covers prehistory, historical events, government, the family, economic life, religion, the arts, language, literature and science in historical India. One evaluator correctly asserted, "This is absolutely the best book on Hindu India the reviewer has seen in more than a decade. The style is lucid and makes for easy reading. Altogether a most informative and highly enjoyable book." Basham was the president of the Committee for Comprehensive Study of the Ramakrishna-Vivekananda Movement. In 1985 Basham held the post of the Swami Vivekananda Professor in Oriental Studies at the Asiatic Society of Calcutta. He died in Calcutta the following year.[54]

After devoting years to studying ancient Indian society, Basham concluded:

> Our over-all impression is that in no other part of the ancient world were the relations of man and man, and of man and the state, so fair and humane. In no other early civilization were slaves so few in number, and in no other ancient law book are their rights so well protected as in the *Arthashastra*.... In all her history of warfare, Hindu India has few tales to tell of cities put to the sword or of the massacre of noncombatants.... India was a cheerful land, whose people, each finding a niche in a complex and slowly evolving social system, reached a higher level of kindliness and gentleness in their mutual relations than any other nation of antiquity. For this, as well as for her great achievements in religion, literature, art, science and mathematics, one European student at least would record his admiration of her ancient culture.[55]

1960s and After

Robert Charles Zaehner (1913-1974) was for many years the Spalding Professor of Eastern religions and ethics at Oxford University in England. His books included *Mysticism Sacred and Profane* (1957), where he differentiates between monistic (nondualistic) and theistic (dualistic) mysticism, and *Hindu and Muslim Mysticism* (1960), in which he shows Shankarian influences on Iranian Sufism. In his 1962 volume titled *Hinduism*, he made the following important point concerning Vivekananda at the World's Parliament of Religions in 1893:

> Here for the first time he was able to present Hinduism to the world as a universal faith; and Hinduism, so long on the defensive against Muslim and Christian attack, for the first time went over to the offensive.... Vivekananda performed the extraordinary feat of breathing life into the purely static monism of Shankara. In Europe and America he proclaimed from the housetops the absolute divinity of man ... Man is by nature free (*mukta*), his liberation is permanently with him, and it is he, no other,

> who binds himself in illusion: he has within himself the power to cast off his chains ... He still believed that Hindu spirituality was supreme—for it alone proclaimed the great Advaitin Truth and the means by which it could be realized, but since the revelation he had received at Cape Comorin he realized that this must be allied to practical service to the needy and to the Western scientific techniques which make that service possible. Thus in India the Ramakrishna mission concentrated on the performance of good works.[56]

Though Burmese born U Thant (1909-74) was not a European, he will be covered here. He was elected as the first non-European president of the United Nation General Assembly from 1961 to 1971, following Dag Hammarskjold's death. During that period, in his efforts to mediate international disputes, U Thant devised a plan that brought an end to the Congolese civil war, led a UN mission in 1962 in an effort to settle the Cuban Missile Crisis, successfully mediated a cease-fire to end the Indo-Pakistani War of 1965, was involved in multilateral attempts to stop the 1967 Arab-Israeli War, and made a major effort to end the fighting in Vietnam, leading up to the halting of bombing by the U.S. and to the subsequent start of the Paris peace talks. Speaking at a dinner in honour of Vivekananda's birth centenary under the auspices of the Ramakrishna-Vivekananda Centre of New York, U Thant expounded:

> Swami Vivekananda, as most of you are aware, was the greatest spiritual ambassador of India, if I may say so, in the history of India. And for that matter, the history of Asia. The main purpose of his historic visit to the United States of America, over sixty years ago, was to find a synthesis, if I can interpret and assess his activities in this country. He was very keen to bring about a synthesis between India and the United States, between Asia and the West. To understand Swami Vivekananda, it is very important to understand the cultural and spiritual background of India, and for that matter, the cultural and spiritual background of Asia....
>
> Another aspect of Swami Vivekananda's mission, to my knowledge, is the need of tolerance in human relations. Not only religious tolerance but also tolerance in all spheres of activity. I think this message is also very necessary in these tense times; much more, if I may say so, much more than sixty years ago....

I think Swami Vivekananda attempted to present a very simple exposition of these methods of contemplation and meditation so that the Westerners may not be lopsided in their development—only exclusively in the intellectual field. Because he felt rightly, that mere intellectual development will lead only to the discovery of what is outside of us. In America, in Europe, in Russia, in these countries, what is outside of us is very clearly defined while at the same time what is inside of us remains a deep, dark, jungle tract.[57]

During the 1963 Vivekananda Centenary held at the Vedanta Society in London, England, the following six messages were received among others. Formerly a professor of mechanical engineering at the University of Leeds, and of applied science with reference to engineering at the Imperial College of Science and Technology (1949-60), Sir Derman Christopherson (b. 1915) became the vice-chancellor at Durham University (1960-78) and was at Magdalene College in Cambridge (1979-85).[58] About Vivekananda he expressed these ideas:

The Swami is rightly recognized and honoured as one of the greatest Indian leaders of recent times. The way in which he revitalized the dormant spirit of India has been and will ever be an inspiration to the citizens of that ancient land. Vivekananda combined in him the best in Indian culture with a modern and progressive outlook. He made Vedanta relevant to our times, and his message and personal example of service of God in man and of the essence of true religion.

A prophet who was admired and honoured by such diverse persons as William James, Tolstoy, Max Müller, Deussen, Tagore, Romain Rolland and Sri Aurobindo was indeed a citizen of the world. The Swami's catholicity of spirit and his comprehensive viewpoint mark him out as one of the great builders of the unity of East and West.

I am glad to say that in Durham Colleges we have made some of his wonderful works required reading for the students of the Civilization of India.[59]

A renowned Christian theologian, Friedrich Heiler (1892-1967) was a professor of the history of religions at Marburg University and president of the Protestant Ecumenical Movement. His comparative studies of Hinduism and Christianity such as *Mysticism of the Upanishads* (1925) and *Christian*

Faith and Indian Thought (1926) were published to create an understanding and a synthesis. He also wrote on Buddhist meditation.[60] His statement on Vivekananda reads:

> We honour in him one of the greatest pioneers of the religious unity of mankind. His message to the World Parliament of Religions in Chicago in 1893 was a milestone on the way to mutual understanding, tolerance, and acceptance of the great religions of the world. His appeal to serve God in the poor and suffering brother has been realized in a wonderful way by the Ramakrishna Mission founded by him. We hope that the celebration of this centenary year in the whole world will help many people of all nations to do their best in order to promote the spiritual and practical unity of the whole family of God on the earth.[61]

According to Wilhelm von Pochhammer from Bremen, West Germany, the author of *India's Road to Nationhood: A Political History of the Subcontinent* (1981) and other works on India and Tibet:[62]

> I beg to offer heartiest greetings on behalf of the Swami Vivekananda Centenary Committee in the Federal Republic of Germany. The historical significance of this great man, in my opinion, seems to lie in his double role; on the one hand he is the representative of the great religious movement of reawakening led by his Master Ramakrishna, owing to which the Indian people and their leader Mahatma Gandhi were given the religious and moral strength to stand the difficult test of the movement of independence. It would have been impossible for Gandhi to rouse up the mass of his people, asking for their standing the test in times of need, but for a revival of the faith. On the other hand, he was the first Hindu applying to the world-publicity and thus changing Hinduism from an isolated religion within India's borders into a message meant for all human beings. Before him we had known only three world-religions, i.e. Christianity, Islam and Buddhism. Vivekananda, however has shown that Hinduism is to be equally considered a world-religion, and it is in this sense that we praise the works of his life in all the countries of the world interested in spiritual things.[63]

A well-known figure in the world of New Testament studies, Hugh J. Schonfield (1901-88) gained attention for his controversial book *The Passover Plot* (1965). He believed that Christ viewed himself as the Messiah, but not as the Divine Son of God. Schonfield received a nomination for the Nobel Peace Prize, being the president of the International Arbitration League (1955-60), founder and first president of the Commonwealth of World Citizens (1959-63), and a trustee of the World Service Trust.[64] He taught:

> As we direct our thoughts to the life and work of saints and sages who have gone from us, we are inspired and strengthened by their vision and example. This is certainly true of this centenary occasion when we recall the teaching and activities of Swami Vivekananda. To be concerned for the service and welfare of mankind, as he was. To overcome all prejudices and barriers of race, colour and creed, as he did. These are surely achievements which should create in us the desire to make them our own.[65]

Reverend Sidney Spencer (b. 1888) stressed the spiritual aspects of Swamiji's message:

> Vivekananda's approach was that of the mystic, the man who knows himself as one with the Infinite and Eternal Spirit, and that for him was not a mere intellectual abstraction. It was an actual living experience; it was the culmination of his inner life.... it is an essential part of the Ramakrishna Mission's work to promote the growth of spiritual consciousness. The Mission stands, at the same time, as Vivekananda stood, for the unity of religions. "The end of all religions," he said, "is the realizing of God in the soul." That, I believe, is indeed the vital fact, to realize God in the soul, to enter into the consciousness of the Divine Presence, however we may express it so that that Supreme and Eternal reality becomes the ruling and guiding and inspiring power in our whole life.[66]

Five years later Reverend Spencer emphasized Vivekananda's concept of religious pluralism:

> The thing for which Vivekananda is most widely known is the work which he did on behalf of religious unity. At the Parliament of Religions held at Chicago in 1893 he made an impassioned plea for the recognition of this principle, and it forms the keynote of his teaching. Religious unity was for him at once an ideal and an existing fact. "In essence," he said, "all religions are one." ... "There is only one infinite religion," he says. This re-

ligion expresses itself in various ways in different countries, but "the same God is the inspirer of all."[67]

Reverend Sidney Spencer was the principal of Manchester College at Oxford University, a lecturer in religion (1951-56), and minister of the Unitarian Church at Bath and Trowbridge, England. In addition, he brought out *Mysticism in World Religions* in 1963 and served as president of the Vivekananda Centenary Committee during 1963-64.[68]

In 1963 the illustrious Italian Orientalist Giuseppe Tucci (1894-1984) [q.v.] intuited:

> I feel this [Vivekananda] Centenary is of essential significance in this moment. In fact, our troubled world needs now, more than ever, to be informed with the teachings of such Masters as Swami Vivekananda, who have brought a message of peace and goodwill to all men, irrespective of the country of their birth; the aims you are pursuing, and the efforts you are doing for spreading his words as far wide as possible, deserve the support and encouragement of all who have not surrendered to the sways of materialism and technology.[69]

The following year an Inter-Religious Conference held at the Sri Ramakrishna Math in Madras was attended by many dignitaries. There Mrs. Maria Burgi-Kyriazi of Switzerland made the following statement:

> With the appearance of Swami Vivekananda, Europe began to be more and more aware of the fact that although India could teach neither social reform nor mechanical improvements, she had the authority to teach something infinitely more important viz. the highest truth of the mind, of the heart and of the soul of man, which no time, no place and no cause can contradict.

Being a great admirer of Ramana Maharshi, in 1975 Maria Burgi-Kyriazi came out with the insightful volume *Ramana Maharshi et l'experience de l'Etre* (*Ramana Maharshi and the Experience of Being*) in French.[70]

Gustav Mensching (1901-78), head of the department of comparative religion at the University of Bonn (1936-72), was a student of Rudolph Otto (1869-1937) and Friedrich Heiler (1892-1967) in Germany. He devoted his scholarly life to promoting universal religious tolerance based on inter-religious dialogue with the hope of bringing about international peace. Professor Mensching made many appreciative statements concerning Vivekananda, including:

> Swami Vivekananda is one of the great personalities in the history of religions, and that in a twofold reference. He was not only a creative religious figure in the footsteps of his Master, Sri Ramakrishna, but he was also a man of the science of religions.... The words that we hear from Vivekananda are the everlasting words of the mystic, and because, since the days of the Upanishads, this language is in being in India, the speeches of Vivekananda contain many familiar tones. He refers continuously to the ancient scriptures. Even then, we receive those age-old truths in a new form.[71]

In another essay Mensching mentioned:

> Vivekananda also recognizes manifestations of God as "Avataras" as a path towards the unity of God: As long as we are human beings we cannot see God in any higher stage than that of the human being. The time will come when we shall pass over our human nature and see Him as He is. As long as we shall remain as human beings we are compelled to search after God amongst human beings and to worship him as man....
>
> The topic of the religious situation of the world today is, as we pointed out, understanding of different religions with one another and the tendency of this discussion must be towards bringing the struggle among the religions to a close contact, and realizing the unity with the idea of cooperation amongst the religions maintaining thereby their own specialties. The existing World Federation of Religions and other similar institutions serve such aims. Vivekananda, however, was the first preacher of such tendencies. Now-a-days a good amount of knowledge with regard to the science of religion has been gained, which does not contradict the ideas of Vivekananda, but on the other hand, establishes them.[72]

The book *Swami Vivekananda in East and West* edited by Swami Ghanananda and Geoffrey Parrinder in 1968 contains chapters by British author's F. R. Allchin, A. L. Basham, Ninian Smart, Reverend Sidney Spencer, and others. Swami Ghanananda (1898-1969) founded the Vedanta Centre in London in 1948, where he enjoyed much success until his passing away. In addition, he initiated and edited the magazine *Vedanta for East and West* from 1951. Geoffrey Parrinder (1910-2005), the editorial adviser on the project, read the book in manuscript form and offered valuable suggestions. An English Methodist clergyman, he taught at the University of London, King's College, in the department of religion (1958-77). Parrinder lectured at the University of Delhi (1973) and held the position of president of the British branch of the International Association for the History of Religions (1972-77), and co-president of the London Society of Jews and Christians from 1981. His numerous books include *Asian Religions* (1957), *Upanishads, Gita and Bible* (1962), *Avatar and Incarnation* (1970), as well as *The Bhagavad Gita: A Verse Translation* (1974).[73]

In *Swami Vivekananda in East and West* the archeologist F. R. Allchin made the following assessment:

> Although it was from the wonderful spiritual power of Ramakrishna that he took his inspiration, it was left to Vivekananda himself to remould that power in visible, practical form. This he did mainly in two ways. First, by his years of work in America and Europe, following upon the astonishing success of his participation in the Parliament of Religions in Chicago in 1893, he drew attention outside India to her civilization and to that theme of religion which was its special glory. This in turn changed the relations of Indians to the rest of the world and gave them fresh grounds for self-confidence and self-reliance. The second great step was in the organization of the Mission itself, and of the many social works which it undertook.... I do not think that it is too much to claim that Swami Vivekananda, more than any other Indian of his time, gave to his countrymen a new ideology. The ideology was a synthesis of many threads.[74]

As an archeologist, Frank Raymond Allchin, along with his wife, spent his career studying the prehistoric, Neolithic, early historic archaeology and rise of civilization in India, Pakistan and Sri Lanka. After visiting India in 1944, while serving in the military, he developed a fascination for the country's history. He taught South Asian archaeology in the School of Oriental and African Studies in London (1954-59). Later Allchin functioned as a lecturer and reader in Indian studies at the University of Cambridge (1959-90). His writings include *The Birth of Indian Civilization* (1968) and *The Rise of Civilization in India and Pakistan* (1982).[75]

English-born Professor Ninian Smart (1927-2001) emphasized the role of Advaita Vedanta in the thought of Vivekananda:

> The Universalist message of Swami Vivekananda, and of his master Ramakrishna, genuinely represents a new departure in world religions—the attempt to make the highest form of Hinduism a world faith. In doing so, the Vedanta would cease to be the highest form of Hinduism as such: but it would become the highest form of religion in general. Whether or not this faith will emerge as the unifying factor in the global manifestation of religion is something which will be settled by a process of social dialogue.... Swami Vivekananda, by giving such an incisive expression to a revitalized Hinduism ready to break beyond the bounds of India, can clarify men's insights into the choice before them. As we have seen, some of the problems tackled by Swami Vivekananda, and his solutions thereto, remain, despite changes in the intellectual and scientific climate since he wrote, highly relevant to the contemporary situation. It must be recalled too that not only did he interpret Hinduism to the West so eloquently, but he also interpreted it to India itself.[76]

Concerning Vivekananda's message, Smart later wrote in another context:

> This ideology presented Hinduism not as a backward religion but at the forefront. It was the rather benighted Christians who tended to ascribe absolute truth to their own faith and complete error to alternatives. It was the forward-looking Hindu who saw his own pluralistic faith as a foreshadowing of the emerging World Religion. Vivekananda's Neo-Vedanta also made sense of Hinduism for perhaps the first time. Now Hindus could explain the unity of their own baffling, diverse religion or religions. It could be said that now Hinduism truly came into existence, or at least into self-conscious integrity. This was why Vivekananda's message became so immediately popular with the English-speaking elite.[77]

In the next decade Smart added an additional insight concerning Swamiji's teachings:

> In reaching back into the Hindu heritage, Vivekananda picked on Advaita Vedanta, which he modified into a modern form. This argued that

the eternal Self in each being is identical with the Divine Being, Brahman. While in its classical form it argued that the universe as perceived by us as consisting of separate beings is in the higher truth illusory, made of maya, Vivekananda was more realist and world-affirming. Truths about the world would remain true, though at a lower level. The higher truth signifies the identity of Brahman and Atman, the Divine Being and the Self.

Smart also considers Vivekananda to be "the most effective in framing a nationalist ideology" that "enabled India to modernize and to retain her customs and traditions. Of all the major cultures, India did best in balancing modern effectiveness and older values."[78]

A year later in 1999 Smart wrote:

> Taking on the name of Vivekananda, he became a highly influential teacher, in part because he attended the World Parliament of Religions in Chicago in 1893, where his speech caused a sensation; in it he expounded his view of the nature of the deeper Hindu beliefs, consonant with the (at that meeting) popular idea of a truly universal or world religion.... This [the Ramakrishna Math and Mission] was strongly devoted both to educational and social enterprises, including medical work. Because the new philosophy was pan-religious in scope the Math and Mission is to be found established in many Western and other countries as well as in the Republic of India itself.
>
> Vivekananda's ideology began from the point that Hinduism had since early days a pluralistic aspect. This was evident already in the Vedas, where reality is at one point seen as One, even if the sages name it variously. Hence the many gods all really stand for the One Brahman or Holy Power. This motif was used to explain the essential unity of all religions. Differing ways of symbolizing and conceiving God conceal the essential unity of religions, and of levels of religion.[79]

As a member of the British Army Intelligence Corps, Captain Ninian Smart served in Ceylon during 1945-48. He became a professor of religious studies at the University College of Wales, at the Universities of London, Birmingham and Lancaster in England (1952-82), and at the University of California, Santa Barbara, until 1998. He was also a visiting lecturer at the Benares Hindu University (1960) and Teape lecturer at the University of Delhi (1964). Being a specialist in comparative religion, his many books include *Doctrine and Argument in Indian Philosophy* (1964) and *The Yogi and the Devotee: The Interplay between the Upanishads and Catholic Theology* (1968). A leading expert in the comparative study of religion, Smart analyzed many substantial similarities and contrasts between Hinduism and Christianity.[80]

Concerning Vivekananda, on 12 February 1969 Fenner Brockway (1888-1988) informed "Dear Swami Ghanananda":

> What has impressed me most about him is his tolerance, strength and dedication to the service of all. He was a master of the Hindu scriptures, but recognized that there was truth in all religions. He was strong because he had certainty in eternal values. His mysticism was not just self-fulfillment. It identified him with others and led to the remarkable work of Ramakrishna Order, which treats many thousands of patients and teaches many thousands of children.[81]

Born in Calcutta of missionary parents, Fenner Brockway was elected to the British Parliament's House of Commons in 1929 as a member of the Labour party. The next year he wore a Gandhi cap in the House of Commons and was suspended therefrom while protesting against the arrest of Gandhi, Nehru and others. A political activist and author, he fought all his life for the causes of socialism, peace, Indian and African independence, and campaigned for nuclear disarmament, taking part in many protest marches. As a result he served five prison terms, one for hard labour. He was a joint secretary of the British Committee of Indian National Congress (1919), wrote on the government of India, and "had the very great honour of the friendship of some of the great personalities of India including Gandhiji and Jawaharlal Nehru."[82]

During the Spanish Civil War of 1939, Dr. Felix Marti-Ibanez (1911-72) was forced to trudge across the ice and snow of the Pyrenees Mountains into France to escape the fascist armies of Francisco Franco. At that time, the only volume he took with him from his treasured collection was Rolland's biography of Vivekananda. During the last year of his life in 1972, Marti-Ibanez wrote, "That uniquely magnificent, mystical book inspired me through the years to dedicate my life to the services of others." In the United States for nearly two decades he was the founder and editor-in-chief of *MD*, a medical news magazine, chairman of the department of the history of medicine at New York Medical College, and a novelist, essayist, and short story writer.[83]

In *Yoga and Indian Philosophy* (1977), Czechoslovakian born Karel Werner (b. 1925) [q.v.], a professor of Indian religion at the University of Durham in England, emphasized:

> Vivekananda is the second great name [after Ramakrishna] connected with the spreading of knowledge about Yoga in modern times. His intelligence and intellectual capacity made him an able apostle of Ramakrishna's teaching in the West.... Vivekananda was a great Advaita Vedantist and Jnana Yogi and it was owing to him that Indian philosophy and Yoga began to fire the imagination of many people in Western countries as early as the end of the last century. Prompted by the urging of his master Ramakrishna and helped by the historical situation of India, which was responsible for his English education, Vivekananda started a trend for popularity of Yoga, which, with inevitable ups and downs, has stayed with us ever since.[84]

1980s and After

In *Modern India: The Origins of Asian Democracy* (1985), Judith M. Brown informed her readers:

> His followers, especially Vivekananda, who organized the Ramakrishna Mission to perpetuate the Master's work and teachings, and the monastic members of the Mission, almost certainly emphasized their master's commitment to Advaita Vedanta in order to make his teachings into a far more systematic and coherent "faith" than he had ever espoused or preached. It was a faith which could be presented, as Vivekananda did at the World Parliament of Religions in 1893 in America, as an equal to the world's great monotheisms, as a viable religious option for modern man, whatever his culture or race. Vivekananda also stressed the religious duty of social service, and this became one of the hallmarks of the Ramakrishna Mission. Here was a compassionate religion with a clearly defined and intellectually defensible doctrinal heart.

Judith M. Brown, who was born in India, was a professor of history at the University of Manchester (1971-90), and then at Oxford University since 1990. An author of many volumes, she came out with three books on

Mahatma Gandhi, and edited two more works. Concerning her work *Gandhi and Civil Disobedience*, an evaluator wrote that the result is "a work that will enhance Brown's reputation as one of the most interesting of the scholars now interpreting recent Indian history." In a review regarding her *Gandhi: Prisoner of Hope*, Bhikhu Parekh expressed the view that "this is the best biography of Gandhi so far and deserves to be read by everyone interested in him and in modern India."[85]

Reverend Glyn Richards (1923-2003) [q.v.] of the Congregational Church in Wales edited *A Source-Book of Modern Hinduism* (1985) in which he devoted eleven full pages to verbatim recordings from the *Complete Works*, along with an introduction that said in part:

> In pursuit of his spiritual mission he travelled the length and breadth of India visiting all the important centres of learning, acquainting himself with the diverse religious traditions of the country and the many different patterns of social life. He devolved a sympathy for the suffering and poverty of the under-privileged and resolved to arouse the nation from its lethargy and inertia. The divinity of man became a significant tenet in his teachings and he saw the service of the poor and deprived as synonymous with the service of God.[86]

Writing the chapter on "Modern Hinduism" for Routledge's *The World's Religions* (1988), Reverend Glyn Richards added:

> The Vedantic doctrine of the divinity of man is a significant tenet in Vivekananda's teaching and one aspect of the message he proclaimed at the World Parliament of Religions in Chicago. Another aspect of his message is the essential unity of all religions and the basic oneness of existence. For Vivekananda there is but one life, and one world and one existence. God permeates all that exists from stones and plants to human beings, so the difference between one life and another is one of degree and not of kind. It would be contrary to Vedantic teaching to claim that the animals were created in order to provide man with food. Similarly, he upholds the ideal of a universal religion not in the sense of a single ritual, mythology or philosophy, but in the sense that every religion proclaims an aspect of the universal truth according to its insights. Each religion is a pearl on a string and no one form of religion will do for everyone. Religion is in essence one

but diverse in application, and toleration teaches us not to look for defects in religions other than our own.[87]

In his manuscript *Vedanta: Heart of Hinduism* (1985), Hans Torwesten (b. 1944) [q.v.], a native of Germany who lives in Austria, made clear:

> [There was] a wave of spiritual expansion in India that suddenly began to inundate the West. This new expansion manifested itself ... at the end of the nineteenth century in the figure of Swami Vivekananda, the great disciple of Ramakrishna. It was Vivekananda who, on the occasion of the Parliament of Religions at the Chicago World's Fair in 1893, appeared like an Eastern comet in the Western spiritual sky and brought the word Vedanta into circulation. It seemed to him most aptly to reflect the heart of the Hindu view of religion. Hindus themselves referred to their religion as *sanatana dharma* (eternal religion). Vivekananda was facing the task of familiarizing Westerners with his master Ramakrishna's universal message and the quintessence of the sanatana dharma....
>
> His discourses do not, after all, come from the lips of a scribe who enjoys grappling with finicky scholastic detail, nor from the lips of an oversimplifier who merely seeks to appeal to the pigeonhole thinking of the masses, but from the lips of a realized yogi, someone enlightened who, like all great mystics, is at all times really only concerned with the *One*. Meister Eckhart, too, was often reproached for having spread the profoundest mystical truths among the common folk in simple (and lively) language; but anyone who reads the sermons of this master—who in so many ways resembles the combative Vivekananda—will be hard put to conclude that he watered down truth.[88]

After living in India for sometime, Dietmar Rothermund became a professor of South Asian history at the University of Heidelberg in Germany during 1968-2001. His writings include books on India's relation with the Soviet Union, Mahatma Gandhi, and an economic history of India. He coauthored the text *A History of India* (1986) where he expressed the idea:

> Active self-realization rather than passive contemplation could be propagated as the true message of Vedanta philosophy. Swami Vivekananda was the prophet of this new thought. He impressed the Western world when he propounded this message at the World Parliament of Religions

in Chicago in 1893; on his return to India in 1897 following his spiritual conquest of the West, he greatly stimulated Indian nationalism. The British rulers had usually looked down upon Hinduism as a ragbag of superstition; Vivekananda's rehabilitation of Hindu thought in the West was therefore considered to be a major national achievement. Even contemporary liberal nationalists (e.g. Gopal Krishna Gokhale) or socialists of the next generation (e.g. Jawaharlal Nehru) admired Vivekananda and found his ideas attractive.[89]

Twenty years later, for the *Encyclopedia of India* (2006), Dietmar Rothermund signified:

> In 1893 Vivekananda was invited to attend the World Parliament of Religions, convened in Chicago, as a representative of Hinduism. In his opening speech on 11 September he expressed the hope that the bell which rang at the welcome ceremony had sounded the death knell of all fanaticism. He addressed the parliament several times. In one of his speeches he praised Buddhism as the fulfillment of Hinduism. He advocated a synthesis of the intellect of Hinduism's Brahman with the heartfelt message of the Buddha. Though a Hindu monk, Vivekananda did not stress the renunciation of this world or the quest for individual salvation. He instead made a plea for active social work, seeing God in the poor (*daridra narayan*). As a philosophical justification for this approach, he emphasized Karmayoga, that is, the path to salvation by active work in this world in selfless devotion, without looking to the fruits of one's actions.[90]

Concerning Vivekananda, Julius Lipner expressed these views:

> He was a sensation at the Parliament of Religions in Chicago in 1893. This launched him as a religious teacher of repute in the West, especially in the United States which he visited more than once. It also helped him to establish the Ramakrishna Mission in India, run by an Order of monks. The aim of the Mission was to perpetuate Ramakrishna's teaching.... By the time Vivekananda died in 1902, he and his teaching had become well known among the educated in India for whom his international standing acted as a counterbalance to the humiliation of colonial rule. Vivekananda and his message played an inspiring role in the early stages of the Indian nationalist movement.[91]

Julius Lipner (b. 1946) was born in Patna, India, received his education in that country and then emigrated to England in 1971. He became a lecturer and reader in Indian religion and the comparative study of religion at the University of Cambridge, and chairman of the faculty board of divinity. He was also a visiting professor in India, Canada and the United States. His book *The Face of Truth: A Study of Meaning and Metaphysics in the Vedantic Theology of Ramanuja* (1986) examined Ramanuja's theory of sacred language and divine predication, his idea of the nature of the self and God, and the relationship between infinite and finite being.[92]

Accompanying the decline of Communism, there has been a considerable interest in Vivekananda's teachings in Russia. E. P. Chelishev (Chelyshev, b. 1921), a noted Soviet academician, first learned of Vivekananda from the biography written by Romain Rolland. Swami Ranganathananda, who later became the 13th president of the Ramakrishna Order, met Chelishev when he visited New Delhi. The Swami encouraged him to organize a series of lectures at Moscow University in honour of the 1963 Vivekananda Centenary. Twenty years later Chelishev spent some time at the Ramakrishna Mission Institute of Culture in Calcutta. There he asked for a statuette of Vivekananda to be put in his room. When asked why, he responded with intense feeling:

> I have profound emotion for this great man. Whenever I see his photograph, I see his eyes, I feel inspired, I feel a great power working within me. I become bolder, I become stronger. He is a full man, a born rebel, a valiant warrior, a real hero. And when I go through his works, his speeches, his letters, I get charged and recharged.[93]

Chelishev, a leading Indologist of Russia, became a vice-president of the Committee for the Comprehensive Study of Ramakrishna-Vivekananda Movement. The professor worked as a researcher and director of the Institute of Oriental Studies in Moscow, and as head of the department of Indian literature. Chelishev authored books on Hindi poetry and literature. In addition, he participated in numerous international conferences, including the World Conferences of Orientalists, World Sanskrit Conferences, co-chairman of Indo-Russian Joint Commission on Cooperation in Social Sciences, and chairman of the Russian Society of Friendship with India. In a November 28, 1983 letter, Chelishev informed Swami Lokeswarananda (1909-98) of the Ramakrishna Order that:

The name of Swami Vivekananda is very popular in Soviet Russia and he is held in high esteem by our countrymen. Soviet people respect him as a great democrat, humanist and patriot who contributed immensely in the development of national consciousness and the anti-colonial liberation movement in India. They also consider that his message and the message of Sri Ramakrishna, which are really one, are absolutely necessary for the survival of the human civilization which is now in great danger due to the menace of the devastating nuclear war.[94]

In 1987 Chelishev expressed his admiration for Vivekananda's humanism:

Reading and re-reading the works of Vivekananda each time I find in them something new that helps deeper to understand India, her philosophy, the way of the life and customs of the people in the past and the present, their dreams of the future.... I think that Vivekananda's greatest service is the development in his teaching of the lofty ideals of humanism which incorporate the finest features of Indian culture.... In my studies of contemporary Indian literature I have more than once had the opportunity to see what great influence the humanistic ideals of Vivekananda have exercised on the works of many writers.... Vivekananda's humanism, we recognize that it possesses many features of active humanism manifested above all in a fervent desire to elevate man, to instill in him a sense of his own dignity, sense of responsibility for his own destiny and the destiny of all people, to make him strive for the ideals of good, truth and justice, to foster in man abhorrence for any suffering.... Together with the Indian people, Soviet people, who already know some of the works of Vivekananda published in the USSR, highly revere the memory of the great Indian patriot, humanist and democrat, impassioned fighter for a better future for his people and all mankind.[95]

Chelishev added in a more recent writing:

His words sound today surprisingly modern and, what is very important, they correspond to our own thoughts and reflections. We sympathize with his search for the rebirth of the ancient spiritual greatness of India because we ourselves are now trying to clean our historic conscience and to find in popular knowledge the vital sources which could help us find the road to a better future.[96]

The founder of the Soviet School of Research in Modern Indian Thought and Ideas, A. D. Litman (1923-92) [q.v.] was the senior research associate of the Institute of Oriental Studies of the USSR Academy of Sciences. His collection of essays cover the social and political implications of Indian religions, focusing on Gandhi, Nehru and Radhakrishnan. Like many Russians, Litman admired Swamiji as an Indian patriot and social reformer stressing:

> Characterizing Swami Vivekananda's ideas of enlightenment, it must be specially stressed here that their decisive features are a steadfast faith in people, in their constructive powers, and the ardent love for the working masses, sympathy for their wants and sufferings, and a fervent urge to free them from colonial and social oppression.... His social-political and specially enlightening ideas objectively helped in the awakening of the wide masses of India, and prepared them for the subsequent growth of the national-liberation movement, which, as a result of heroic efforts of the Indian people, culminated in the historic victory, in the creation of the independent Republic of India. This is just why we, along with the friendly Indian people, greatly respect the name of her glorious son, the ardent patriot, humanist-thinker and enlightener, Swami Vivekananda.[97]

The articulate writer on the subject of Neo-Hinduism, Professor Wilhelm Halbfass (1940-2000) [q.v.] is mentioned in Chapter II. Concerning Swamiji's message to India and the West, he made the following observations in 1990:

> Vivekananda became one of the leading figures of modern Hindu thought and self-awareness and an exemplary exponent of Hindu self-representation vis-à-vis the West. His appearance in the West, his self-understanding, and his activities within India are all interwoven in a peculiar way: During his first visit to the West, Vivekananda became the man who made history; the most influential shaper and protagonist of the Neo-Hindu spirit.... he is committed to propagating Hindu principles beyond the borders of India and to utilizing their international recognition in his efforts to regenerate Hindu self-awareness and self-confidence.... However, science

is not the central issue in Vivekananda's rediscovery and reinterpretation of the Indian tradition. It is ethics, social commitment, and national identity itself, which he tries to draw from the sources of Hindu religious and metaphysical thought. The sense of identity and social initiative which he tries to awaken in his fellow Indians must not be a borrowed or derivative one. It must coincide with a sense of rediscovery and reacquisition of their own heritage—and this means, above all, the heritage of Advaita Vedanta, the tradition of Shankara.[98]

Martin Kämpchen (b. 1948) [q.v.], who has produced a dozen books, many on Indian religion, says:

> Swami Vivekananda's writing has had a decisive influence on my life. Had I not read him, I would not have come to India and stayed as long as I have for over fifteen years so far.... by strange and wonderful internal processes, my appreciation of Christ received greater depth and fervour while reading Swami Vivekananda. Had the great Swami observed me then, I think he would not have been dissatisfied with me. Had he not again and again insisted that no changes from one faith to another are necessary? Rather that his spirituality was meant to enrich every other faith and to teach us to believe more genuinely. As a consequence, within myself began the complex and strenuous process of integrating Vivekananda's ideas into the framework of Christianity or, rather, into my concept of Christianity.[99]

Federico Mayor (Zaragoza), formerly a professor of biochemistry at the University of Granada in Spain (1963-73), became the director-general of the United Nations Educational Scientific and Cultural Organization (UNESCO) (1987-99). During his twelve years as head of UNESCO, Mayor gave new life to the organization's mission. A Culture of Peace Programme was created, whose objectives revolve around four major themes: conflict prevention and education for peace; human rights and democracy; the fight against poverty; and the defense of cultural diversity and intercultural dialogue. Within the framework of this strategy, numerous international meetings and conferences were held.[100] On October 8, 1993, Dr. Mayor held a meeting before a large congregation of diplomats and dignitaries of the world in the UNESCO building. The meeting included an exhibition, lectures and a musical presentation, commemorating the 1893 Parliament of World Religions and Vivekananda's contribution to it. Mayor mentioned three remarkable similarities between the message of Vivekananda and the goals of the Ramakrishna Mission and the objectives of UNESCO:

> First, his commitment towards universalism and tolerance.... Second, his concern for the poor and destitute. The mission that he established in India and which has now spread all over the world is working to reduce poverty and eliminate discrimination among the different segments of society. He said: "The uplift of the women, the awakening of the masses must come first and only then can any real good come about." Third, his preoccupation for human development with education, science and culture as instruments for such development....[101]
>
> I am indeed struck by the similarity of the constitution of the Ramakrishna Mission which Vivekananda established as early as 1897 with that of UNESCO drawn up in 1945. Both place the human being at the centre of their efforts aimed at development. Both place tolerance at the top of the agenda for building peace and democracy. Both recognize the variety of human cultures and societies as an essential aspect of the common heritage.[102]

A researcher and director of the Institute of Oriental Studies at the USSR Academy of Sciences in Moscow, R. B. Rybakov [q.v.], participated in the World Parliament of Religions held in Calcutta 1993. He expressed his admiration for Swamiji as a social reformer:

> The people of the Soviet Union observed the 120th anniversary [1983] of the birth of the great thinker and public figure Swami Vivekananda whose fame has twice outlived his short and dramatic life, entirely devoted to the noble cause of awakening India.... Vivekananda's ideas were dear not only to [Leo] Tolstoy. They are just as dear to the Soviet people today, primarily because his life was filled with ardent love for India. Vivekananda had always desired to change the situation in India... He had not spared efforts to awaken his countrymen's feeling of national identity, the wish to work for the national benefit and the faith in India's bright future.[103]

The following year Rybakov added:

> Swamiji wanted to build men of sound moral strength, free from medieval dogmatism and inspired by the spirit of self-respect and selfless service

towards the more unfortunate children of God. For Swamiji, man is God; thus, service to mankind is the best and most elevated form of worship. He wanted man to realize and recognize this truth. Here we should bear in mind that only a person with a highly developed personality can realize the truth that there is unity in this diversity. So Swamiji's main focus is on the development of personality.

> Does Russia hear the voice of Swamiji, the universal awakener of human souls? A Preacher of an eternal philosophy, Swamiji is the most suitable person to help our country today. What is required by a tormented land is moral rejuvenation.... The philosophy of Vivekananda is a perfect blend of religion and science, and it contains ample flexibility. It is definitely not bound by an imposed rigidity, as most ideologies are.[104]

Born in Igatpuri, India, Archbishop Henry Sebastian D'Souza became the bishop, coadjutor archbishop, and from 1986 until 2002 the archbishop of Calcutta. He worked on the process for the beatification of Mother Teresa who was a longtime friend of his. Representing his church, he made the following ecumenical statement in support of Swamiji's religious pluralism:

> The Catholic Church has a deep esteem for all that is good and noble in the religious traditions and cultural life of people. Swami Vivekananda's call for an attitude of positive respect, sympathy and understanding for each others' religious traditions assumes special importance at this juncture of India's history. Its inspiration could help powerfully for peace and harmony among the different races and religions of our country.[105]

In *Female Ascetics: Hierarchy and Purity in an Indian Religious Movement*, Wendy Sinclair-Brull devotes over one-hundred pages to a discussion of the Ramakrishna Order. In reviewing the early history of the Order, she informs her reader:

> Vivekananda was a resounding success at the Parliament, stressing at the opening session the Hindu view that all paths to God are valid, and that there was no place for bigotry or dissent among fellow seekers. His striking appearance and excellent command of English soon made him the most popular religious figure, and the Chairman made him the final speaker of his sessions, thereby ensuring a packed hall until closing time.[106]

An English writer, Gwilym Beckerlegge is a senior lecturer in the department of religious studies at Open University in the United Kingdom. The author of *The Ramakrishna Mission: The Making of a Modern Hindu Movement* (2000) and *Swami Vivekananda's Legacy of Service* (2006), he has specialized in the role of social service performed by the Ramakrishna Mission. He informed his readers:

> Utilizing selected insights from Ramakrishna's teachings, Vivekananda developed a philosophy that revitalized the historical religious traditions; differences between the religions were of less significance than what was believed to be their common core or goal. This allowed a distinction to be drawn between religious truth and social custom and so made it possible for Vivekananda to speak of preserving the former intact while purifying the latter. This distinction enabled Vivekananda, unlike earlier religious teachers, to establish a stable organization with a high degree of single mindedness in its efforts to change social conditions. The organization culled the benefits of the greater cultural interaction taking place at that time and of Vivekananda's extensive travels. The strategic role given to education was one consequence of Vivekananda's realization of its importance in British India as a mechanism to facilitate social change.[107]

Beckerlegge divides those people who are undertaking Ramakrishna-Vedanta studies into two groups: the "insiders" composed primarily of monastics and loyal devotees, and the "outsiders" who are most often Western university professors interested in Indology. While the early "outsiders" like Max Müller and Romain Rolland were sympathetic with the ideals of the Ramakrishna Movement, some of the present-day "outsiders" are more critical and a few are even belligerent. "Outsiders" make an important contribution when they positively relate the ideas and ideals of Ramakrishna-Vedanta with those of the external intellectual and religious world. In his anthology *World Religions Reader*, Beckerlegge devotes a page and a half to a verbatim quote from the *Gospel of Sri Ramakrishna* on the subject "Each religion as a path to God", and two pages to Swamiji's opening "Address to the Parliament of Religions, and his modern interpretation of Vedanta."

Three writers, viz. Diane Collinson, Kathryn Plant, and Robert Wilkinson are each lecturers in philosophy at Open University, the largest academic institution in the United Kingdom. In their work entitled *Fifty Eastern Think-*

ers, before discussing Vivekananda's religious philosophy, they paid him this glowing tribute:

> In 1893, the distinguished representatives of the world's leading religions met at the World's Parliament of Religions in Chicago. A young Swami named Vivekananda, only 30 years of age, electrified this audience by his direct, forceful and moving oratory, and almost single-handedly began a movement to make the world aware of modern Hinduism, a movement which has lasted to this day. Vivekananda combined in one personality an unusual range of qualities: the intense spirituality which has attracted him to the path of the Hindu *sannyasin* or renunciant, counterbalanced by real concern for social reform in his native India; great philosophical competence, especially with regard to the ideas of Shankara, combined with insights gained from yogic, religious experience; and added to these enormous energy, powers of persuasion and oratorical skill. Vivekananda believed with absolute sincerity that the Hindu's outlook had much to offer the world, and devoted much of his short life to a brilliantly successful attempt to make these ideas known to the West.[108]

Writing about Vivekananda, one of the foremost theologians of the twentieth century, Swiss-born Hans Küng (b. 1928) [q.v.], a professor of theology at the University of Tübingen in Germany (1960-96), asserted:

> He quickly decided to travel to Chicago, an obscure and unknown Hindu monk who had some difficulties in gaining admission as a delegate. But on the very first day of the congress he put all the other speakers in the shade with an inspiring speech, given without notes and in perfect English. And he remained the most powerful figure in this Parliament, which was the first formal meeting between Christianity and the Eastern religions. It was far ahead of its time in calling for harmony between the religions of East and West instead of the previous conflicts and confrontation.
>
> According to Vivekananda, the presupposition for ethics is an orientation on the divine.... Vivekananda as a good Hindu not only opposed the over-estimation of doctrine, dogma and rites but at the same time argued that the three or four practical Hindu ways to salvation could supplement one another (in compatibility and complementarity): the way of meditation (yoga), the way of knowledge (jnana), the way of works (karma) and the way of the love of good (bhakti) all lead to the one goal, to the one God.[109]

The author of *Imperial Encounters: Religion and Modernity in India and Britain*, Peter van der Veer is a professor of comparative religion and director of the research centre on religion and society at the University of Amsterdam in the Netherlands. His text explores mutual influence between Britain and India and makes statements like:

> Perhaps the most important expounder of the doctrine of "Hindu spirituality" has been the founder of the Ramakrishna Mission, Vivekananda (1863-1902). Vivekananda was an extremely talented student who had been thoroughly educated in contemporary Western thought. He joined the Brahmo Samaj briefly before he met Ramakrishna. The encounter with Ramakrishna had a transformative impact on the young Narendranath Datta who adopted the name Vivekananda when he took his ascetic vows. As Tapan Raychaudhuri emphasizes, Vivekananda was "more than anything else a mystic in quest of the Ultimate Reality within a specific Indian tradition." It is this tradition that was vividly presented to Vivekananda not by learned discourse in which he himself was a master but by the charismatic presence of a guru, Ramakrishna.[110]

Torkel Brekke, a professor in the history of religions at the University of Oslo in Norway, studied the political consequences of religious identities during the colonial era in South Asia. In a chapter on "Swami Vivekananda and the Politics of Religion", he credits Swamiji this way:

> One of the main goals of Vivekananda was to break open the treasure-box of Sanskrit culture and spread it to everybody irrespective of caste, age, and gender.
>
> Vivekananda's view of language and the relationship between the extremes of high Sanskrit culture and village culture is particularly revealing. His most important task as a nationalist leader was to give all strata of society a share in the glorious past of India and thus make them identify with an emerging nation. T. Raychaudhuri has argued that the point where Vivekananda stood radically apart from all other Hindu reformers of the era was in his emphasis on the underprivileged masses; the centre point for his Indian agenda was an effort to create mass consciousness, he says. Vivekananda was not a revolutionary in the sense that he wished to denounce the authority of the Brahmins for its own sake. However, he was a nationalist and the cultural and religious exclusivism of Brahminical society

was not compatible with his political goals. Vivekananda said of cultural and social segregation in India: "The solution is not by bringing down the higher, but by raising the lower up to the level of the higher."[111]

An Australian, Harry Oldmeadow [q.v.] lived nine years in India as the son of Christian missionaries, developing an early interest in Asian religions. He is currently the coordinator of philosophy and religious studies at La Trobe University. In his *Journeys East: 20th Century Western Encounters with Eastern Religious Traditions* (2004) he showed his appreciation for Swamiji's forceful personality:

> At university Narendra had shown prodigious talents—intellectual, musical, theatrical, athletic—exhibiting all the vigour and vitality appropriate to the Kshatriya caste to which he belonged. He had an exceptionally intelligent, lively mind and an engaging personality, and seemed poised for a glittering career in law. Instead, answering an inner call which he had felt since childhood, Narendra turned his back on all worldly enticements and ambitions, and became one of the principle disciples of Ramakrishna at Dakshineswar, eventually becoming Swami Vivekananda....
>
> His charismatic personality, his spiritual teachings, and his nerve-tingling oratory generated a good deal of fervour and it was at this time that he attracted several Westerners who were to be amongst his most devoted and energetic disciples ... Vivekananda returned to India in a blaze of triumphant publicity and soon turned his considerable energies to the founding of the Ramakrishna Order, Mission and Math.[112]

Jan (Johan) Peter Schouten [q.v.], an ordained Minister of the Reformed Church in the Netherlands, in *Jesus as Guru: The Image of Christ among Hindus and Christians in India* explained one of Vivekananda's contributions to Hinduism:

> Swami Vivekananda (1863-1902) was a dynamic, eloquent man with great charisma. If there was anyone who could be entrusted with presenting an entirely unknown religion to the Western world, it was he. His performance in Chicago made a deep impression on many Americans. At that time Hinduism was generally considered to be a backward religion that could not hold its own against Christianity. Many church leaders also expected Christianity to triumph as a matter of course over all other religions. But

this Hinduism now had a representative who won the public over largely through his actions and his words. The young man—he had just turned thirty—cut an exotic figure in his long cloak and turban. But he convinced his listeners primarily by his self-assured presentation of Hinduism as the mother of all religions. After the conference Swami Vivekananda received various invitations to speak. Through his lecture tour Hinduism became a permanent fixture on the religious landscape of the United States.[113]

In summary, briefly over 40% of the European tributes have come from the British Isles, followed by German speaking countries. Up until the mid-1950s, professional writers led the way, but since that time two-thirds of the tributes are from university professors.

ENDNOTES

1 In the chapter, where the [q.v.] symbol is used, the short biography of the person making the tribute is often found in Chapter II and not in this chapter.

2 A. P. Gnatyuk-Danil'chuk, "Tolstoy and Vivekananda", *Soviet Union*, p. 163; also in *BRMIC* (Feb. 1986), pp. 51-53; Tathagatananda2, pp. 523-24.

3 *EOP* (1991), p. 728; *CA*, vol. 115, p. 197; Nicholas Goodrick-Clarke, *The Occult Roots of Nazism* (Tauris Parke Paperbacks, 2004), pp. 24-25 on GBS; VirtualCat; WorldCat; Union-Index to Theosophical Periodicals. Web: www.austheos.org.au/indices/LOTBLGHU.HTM; *DAB* (Tingley).

4 *Neue Metaphysische Rundschau* (1899) on GBS; Goodrick-Clarke (2004), pp. 25-26 on GBS.

5 *Neue Metaphysische Rundschau* (1902) on GBS; Google Translator. Web: http://translate.google.com/translate_t; Free Translation. Web: www.freetranslation.com.

6 *Neue Metaphysische Rundschau* (1908) on GBS.

7 *London Times* (Aug. 4, 1902), p. 8.

8 *La Civilta' Cattolica* (1902), p. 630, translated by Claudia Cosenza and Anna Gladstone in Los Angeles.

9 *La Civilta' Cattolica* (1904), pp., 64-68, 70, 74, 77-78, 555, 559 on GBS.

10 Eustace Miles, *Avenues to Health* (New York: E. P. Dutton, 1902) on GBS: Eustace Miles. Web: en.wikipedia.org/wiki/Eustace_Miles.

11 *PB* (Nov. 1903), p. 89; WorldCat.

12 *SK* (1905), p. 191 on GBS; Shifman, pp. 40-41; Nicholas Goodrick-Clarke, *The Occult Roots of Nazism* (Tauris Parke Paperbacks, 2004), p. 26 on GBS.

13 William James, "The Energies of Men", *The Philosophical Review* (Jan. 1907), pp. 9-14.

14 Head, pp. 52, 222; UCLC.

15 *Mercure de France* (1906), pp. 209 ff. on GBS; WorldCat.

16 *Soviet Union*, pp. 165-71; also in *BRMIC* (April 1986), pp. 75-79; Tathagatananda2, pp. 525-29, 531; Alexander Shifman, *Tolstoy and India* (New Delhi: Sahitya Akademi, 1969), pp. 36-41; S. D. Serebriany, "Leo Tolstoy and Sri Ramakrishna", *BRMIC* (1987), p. 197.

17 Tathagatananda2, pp. 525, 531-33; Serebriany (1987), pp. 198-99; WorldCat.

18 *World Authors 1900-1950* (New York: H. W. Wilson, 1996), III, pp. 1894-95; *Soviet Union*, pp. 7-9; *Handbook of Russian Literature* (New Haven: Yale University Press, 1985), p. 295; VirtualCat.

19 Cyril Scott, *My Years of Indiscretion* (London: Mills & Boon, 1924), pp. 110-13, 268-69; Bagchi, p. 351.

20 Nicholas Slonimsky, *Baker's Biographical Dictionary of Musicians* (New York: Schirmer Books, 1971), p. 1671; *CA* (1984), vol. 111, p. 435; Cyril Scott: The Father of British Modern Music. Web: www.alpheus.org/ html/source_materials/scott_anrias/tame.htm.

21 L. O'Malley and M. Chakravarti, *Howrah* (Calcutta: Bengal Secretariat Book Depot, 1909), pp. 50-51 on GBS.

22 *Schaff*; Cheyne. Web: www.ccel.org/php/ disp.php3?a=schaff&b=encyc03&p=27; *Encyclopaedia Britannica*. Web: http://53.1911encyclopedia.org/C/CH/CHEYNE_THOMAS_KELLY.htm; UCLC.

23 Atmaprana, pp. 210, 249-50, 264, 279; *Nivedita*, II.

24 G. Stavig, "Cheyne's Interpretation of Vivekananda's Message", *BRMIC* (Jan. 2005), pp. 13-18.

25 T. K. Cheyne, "Review of The Master As I Saw Him", *Hibbert Journal* (1910-11), pp. 431-35, reproduced fully by Stavig (2005), pp. 13-18.

26 *New York Times* (Sept. 2, 1958); S. K. Radcliffe. Web: www.philosopedia.org/index.php/Samuel_Kerkham_Ratcliffe; Atmaprana (1999), pp. 164-65 238, 254, 268.

27 *The Sociological Review* (1913), pp. 243-44.

28 J. N. Farquhar, *Modern Religious Movements in India* (New York: Macmillan, 1915), pp. 201, 204-07 on GBS.

29 W. E. S. Holland, *The Goal of India* (London: United Council for Missionary Education, 1918), p. 190.

30 *Sedition Committee 1918 Report* (Calcutta: Superintendent Government Printing, India, 1918), p. 17 on GBS.

31 Ernst Boldt, *From Luther to Steiner*, tr. Agnes Blake (New York: E. P. Dutton, 1921), pp. 147-49.

32 Prabuddhaprana1, p. 183; *Reminiscences*, p. 447; *PB* (Jan. 1979).

33 Satyananda, p. 132; *DNB* (1941-50), Sup. VI, pp. 118-21; Riddick, p. 53; Lord Lytton. Web: www.logosquotes.org/pls/vvolant/ seng.ma?lm=EN&lang=FU&autore=LORD%20LYTTON&code_author=14913.

34 Jyotirmayananda, p. 201.

35 VSSC. Web: www.vedanta.org/rko/vivekananda/sv_others.htm.

36 Taylor (2001), pp. 71, 175, 183.

37 *EOP* (1991), pp. 136, 1828; *CA* (1998), vol. 121, p. 458; Sir John Woodroffe. Web: http://users.telenet.be/ananda/jwdrf.htm; UCLC; Tathagatananda2, pp. 381-82; Kathleen Taylor, *Sir John Woodroffe, Tantra and Bengal* (Richmond Surrey: Curzon Press, 2001).

38 Hans Kohn, *A History of Nationalism in the East* (London: George Routledge, 1929), pp. 70-72 on GBS; *CA* (1981), vol. IV.

39 VirtualCat under "Library of Congress"; Shivani, pp. 123-24.

40 Lokeswarananda, p. 50; *PB* (1930), p. 56.

41 Londhe, #21. Swami Vivekananda.

42 Japanese National Commission for Unesco, *Philosophical Studies of Japan* (Tokyo: Japan Society for the Promotion of Science, 1969), pp. 97-98; Head, pp. 143-44.

43 Londhe, #424. Henri Bergson.

44 *Aryan Path* (Oct. 1933), pp. 693-95; *CA* (1985), vol. 113; Head, pp. 143-44.

45 *CA*, New Rev. Ser., IX; Prugh, pp. 407-08, 411-12; Centenary I, pp. 42; II, pp. vii, 551-53, 1028-29; *VK* (1994), p. 146.

46 *BRMIC* (Aug. 2004), p. 369; Lokeswarananda, p. 36.

47 *Fortnightly Review* (Sept. 1910), p. 393.

48 Francis Yeats-Brown, *Lancer at Large* (New York: Viking Press, 1937), pp. 129-30.

49 *Modern India and the West*, ed. L. S. S. O'Malley (London: Oxford University Press, 1941), p. 560.

50 European Online Library Catalog. Web: www.ubka.uni-karlsruhe.de/hylib/en/kvk.html; *Christopher Isherwood Diaries: 1939-1960* (New York: Harper Collins, 1996), pp. 297, 331, 362, 566, 938.

51 *VFEW* (May-June 1956), pp. 147-48; *PB* (July 1956), pp. 289-90.

52 A. L. Basham, "Hinduism" in *The Concise Encyclopedia of Living Faiths*, (later called *Encyclopedia of the World's Religions*) ed. R. C. Zaehner (London: Hutchison, 1959), pp. 257-58 on GBS.

53 Ghanananda, pp. xii, 210, 214.
54 *VFEW* (Sept-Oct. 1963), pp. 223, 226; Arthur Llewellyn Basham. Web: www.anu.edu.au/asianstudies/publications/ bash_index.html; Tathagathananda2, p. 549.
55 Londhe, #120. A. L. Basham.
56 R. C. Zaehner, *Hinduism* (London: Oxford University Press, 1971), pp. 167-69, back cover; *Bulletin of the School of Oriental and African Studies* (1975), pp. 623-24.
57 *VW* (July-Aug. 1963), pp. 11-16; Benjamin Frankel, ed. *The Cold War, 1945-1991* (Detroit: Gale Research, 1992); *EWB*.
58 *International Who's Who* (2000), p. 294.
59 *VFEW* (Sept-Oct. 1963), pp. 211-12.
60 Stache-Weiske, pp. 221-22.
61 *VFEW* (Sept-Oct. 1963), p. 213.
62 WorldCat.
63 *VFEW* (Sept-Oct. 1963), pp. 215-16.
64 *CA* (1995), New Rev. Ser., vol. 46.
65 *VFEW* (Sept-Oct. 1963), pp. 214-15.
66 *VFEW* (Sept-Oct. 1963), pp. 205-06.
67 Ghanananda, pp. 164, 172.
68 Ghanananda, p. xi.
69 *VFEW* (Sept-Oct. 1963), p. 214.
70 *VK* (Feb. 1964), p. 589; Web: www.maisonneuve-adrien.com/description/bouddhisme_hindouisme/burgi_ramana.htm.
71 *BRMIC* (March 1963), pp. 129, 133.
72 *Parliament of Religions* (Calcutta: Sri Vivekananda Centenary, 1965), pp. 360, 364; Gustav Mensching. Web: http://www.mensching.uni-trier.de; To get an English language version plug this website into the Google Translator at Web: http://translate.google.com.
73 *CA* (1983), New Rev. Ser., X.
74 Ghanananda, pp. x, 86, 103.
75 Allchin Files. Web: http://allchin.net/archaeologists.htm. *The International Who's Who 1995-96*, pp. 30-31.
76 Ghanananda, pp. 71, 82.
77 Ninian Smart, *The World's Religions* (Englewood Cliffs, NJ: Prentice Hall, 1989), p. 395 on GBS.
78 Paul Heelas, et al., *Religion, Modernity, and Postmodernity* (Wiley-Blackwell, 1998), pp. 81-82 on GBS.

79 Ninian Smart, *World Philosophies* (Routledge, 1999), p. 317 on GBS.

80 *CA* (1990), vol. 30; Ghanananda, p. x; Roderick Ninian Smart. Web: www.universityofcalifornia.edu/senate/inmemoriam/rodernickniniansmart.htm.

81 *VFEW* (May-June 1969), p. 24.

82 *CA*, New Rev. Ser., vol. 83; *New York Times* (April 30, 1988), p. 11; *BRMIC* (Oct. 2007), p. 449; Fenner Brockway, *98 Not Out* (London: Quartet Books, 1986), pp. 137-43.

83 Felix Marti-Ibanez, *The Mirror of Souls* (New York: Crown Publishers, 1972), pp. 407-08; H. A. Bogdan, "Felix Marti-Ibanez". *Jr. Royal Society Medicine* (Oct. 1993), pp. 593-96; Swami Tathagatananda, "Dhan Gopal Mukerji and The Face of Silence". *PB* (Feb. 2006), p. 166.

84 Karel Werner [q.v.], *Yoga and Indian Philosophy* (Motilal Banarsidass, 1977, 1998), pp. 157-58 on GBS; SOAS. Web: www.soas.ac.uk/staff36441.php.

85 Judith Brown, *Modern India* (Delhi: Oxford University Press, 1895), pp. 155-56; *CA* (1999) New Rev. Ser., vol. 72.

86 Glyn Richards, *A Source-Book of Modern Hinduism* (London: Curzon Press, 1985), pp. 77-89 on GBS; Glyn Richards. Web: www.independent.co.uk/news/obituaries/the-rev-glyn-richards-.

87 Stewart Sutherland et al., ed., *The World's Religions* (Routledge, 1988), pp. 709-10.

88 Hans Torwesten, *Vedanta: Heart of Hinduism*, tr. John Phillips (New York: Grove Weidenfeld, 1985, 1991), pp. 7-8 on GBS.

89 Hermann Kulke and Dietmar Rothermund, *A History of India* (London: Routledge, 1986), pp. ix-x, 261.

90 *Encyclopedia of India*, ed. Stanley Wolpert (Detroit: Charles Scribner's Sons, 2006), IV, pp. 222-23.

91 Julius Lipner, *Hindus their Religious Beliefs and Practices* (London: Routledge, 1994), p. 67.

92 *Debrett's People of Today* (Debrett's Peerage, 2008).

93 Archie and Eleanor Stark, "Vivekananda's Impact on England and Europe", *VK* (1994), p. 148.

94 Tathagatananda2, p. 549; Russian Indology. Web: www.russian-centre-mumbai.org/russianindology/personalities.htm.

95 *Soviet Union*, pp. 206-09, 220.

96 *Mission* (Chelishev), p. 471.

97 *Soviet Union*, pp. xiv, 155, 157-58; Russian Indology. Web: www.russian-centre-mumbai.org/russianindology/personalities.htm.

98 Halbfass (1990), pp. 228-29, 234.

99 *VFEW* (Jan-Feb. 1991), pp. 21-23.

100 *CA* (1997), vol. 154; Web: http://en.wikipedia.org/wiki/ Federico_Mayor_Zaragoza.

101 Tathagatananda2, pp. 228-29.

102 Swami Prabhananda, Swami Vivekananda, the Educationist Par Excellence. Web: http://sriramakrishnamath.org/magazine/vk/2006/07-3-2.asp.

103 Jyotirmayananda, p. 192; Russian Indology. Web: www.russian-centre-mumbai.com/en/ri_personalities.htm.

104 Vivekananda, p. 755. Similar to the Russians, Huang Xin Chuan, a professor of history at Beijing University and deputy director of the Institute of South Asian Studies, admired Vivekananda more as a social reformer than as a religious leader. Chuan wrote a book on Vivekananda in Chinese. He declared in 1980, "Vivekananda stands out as the most renowned philosopher and social figure of India in modern China. His philosophical and social thought and epic patriotism not only inspired the growth of nationalist movement in India, but also made a great impact abroad." Lokeswarananda, pp. 55-57, 68.

105 Vivekananda, p. 869; Bishop Henry D'Souza. Web: www.catholic-hierarchy.org/bishop/bdsouzahs.htm.

106 Wendy Sinclair-Brull, *Female Ascetics* (Richmond, UK: Curzon, 1997), p. 28 on GBS.

107 Gwilym Beckerlegge, *The Ramakrishna Mission* (New Delhi: Oxford University Press, 2000), p. 111.

108 *Fifty Eastern Thinkers* (London: Routledge, 2000), pp. 140-41 on GBS.

109 Hans Küng, *Tracing the Way: Spiritual Dimensions of the World Religions*, tr. John Bowden (Continuum International, 2001, 2006), pp. 75-76 on GBS.

110 Peter van der Veer, *Imperial Encounters* (Princeton University, 2001), pp. 46-47 on GBS; *CA* (2004), vol. 221.

111 Torkel Brekke, *Makers of Modern Indian Religion* (Oxford University Press, 2002), pp. 42-43; For biographical information on Torkel Brekke, do a Google Search using his name and then use the Google Translator.

112 Harry Oldmeadow, *Journeys East* (World Wisdom, 2004), pp. 38-39; Web: en.wikipedia.org/wiki/Harry_Oldmeadow.

113 Jan Peter Schouten, *Jesus as Guru* (Rodopi, 2008), p. 81; *WWIA* (2008).

CHAPTER XIII

TWENTIETH AND TWENTY-FIRST CENTURY AMERICAN BIOGRAPHERS AND TRIBUTES

IN 1901, THE eighty-nine-page book *My Master*[1] contained Swamiji's lecture, along with twenty pages from Pratap Chandra Mazumdar's 1879 article on Sri Ramakrishna. Published by Baker & Taylor in New York, the book received considerable attention from reviewers. What follows are portions of ten admiring evaluations from American journals and newspapers.

> This little book gives an account of the character and career of the remarkable man known in India as Paramahamsa Srimat Ramakrishna, who is regarded by a great number of his countrymen as a divine incarnation. It is not more remarkable for the story it tells of a holy man, than for the clear English in which it is told, and the expressions of elevated thought in its pages. (*Indianapolis Journal*)[2]
>
> The book, besides telling the life of Sri Ramakrishna, gives an insight into some of the religious ideas of the Hindus and sets forth the more important ideals that vitally influence India's teeming millions. If we are willing to sympathetically study the religious views of our Aryan brethren of the Orient, we shall find them governed by spiritual concepts in no way inferior to the highest known to ourselves, concepts which were thought out and practically applied by those ancient philosophers in ages so remote as to antedate history. (*Washington Post*)[3]
>
> [The book] gives an interesting account of the spiritual instructor of the author. The type of oriental spirituality here portrayed is characteristic and well worth the consideration of every mind sufficiently broad to recognize the elemental qualities of religious thought, whether they appear in an Eastern or a more familiar guise. (*New York Observer and Chronicle*)[4]

The contrast drawn by the author between the dominant ideas of the Occident and the Orient is a most instructive and interesting one, and will prove a great aid to a correct understanding of that which causes such a wide difference in their respective ideals. (*Pittsburgh Times*)[5]

Anyone at all interested in Oriental philosophy must read his last book "My Master" with a sense of its merit as a vivid biographical sketch. The "Master", Ramakrishna is considered by thousands of Hindus to have been the latest incarnation of God. The story of his life as a boy in the Brahmin temple, of his religious ecstasy and renunciation and of his influence on all the differing Hindu sects is an exposition of the religion which is "realization". Some of Vivekananda's characteristics of India are striking.... The later half of the book is a reprint of Mazoomdar's impressions of this wonderful Hindu. Though a Christian, Mazoomdar calls Ramakrishna his teacher, and bears out Vivekananda's testimony of his greatness.* (*Chicago Daily Tribune*)[6]

The book marks another short step in the long way to our comprehension of the spirit that sways the mysterious East. That they have understood more of us than we of them is shown by the Swami's comparisons.

Those who remember the forceful appearance of Vivekananda when he was here will not be astonished at the strong expressions which he gives. (*San Francisco Call*)[7]

An admiring biography of one of the remarkable "holy men" of India, who had his home in a temple near Calcutta. Paramahamsa Srimat Ramakrishna was his name.... his mind concentrated itself on religion and he set himself apart to a life of holiness; he became a teacher, and his influence went out into all India. "The essence of existence in each man," he said, "is spirituality, the more this is developed in a man the more powerful he is for good. Show by your life that religion does not mean words, and names, and sects, but spiritual realization." Thus he spoke for the religion which is universal and eternal. (*The Literary World*)[8]

An account by the Swami Vivekananda of a latter day Hindu saint, Paramahamsa Srimat Ramakrishna, who exerted a wide influence in India, and whose life and teachings attracted the attention of the late Professor Max Müller and other students of Oriental religions. Saint, ascetic and

* Written by Oscar Lovell Triggs (1865-1930), a professor of English literature at the University of Chicago who brought out two books on Walt Whitman.

philosopher, all in one, he was a representative of all that is best in the mystic faiths of the east. (*The Living Age*)[9]

The author became conspicuous in connection with the "Parliament of Religions" at Chicago. He there set forth, with great acuteness and persuasiveness, the tenets of the Vedanta Philosophy, of which he is an adherent and representative. Since that time he has been heard in various cities as an exponent and advocate of Vedantism. He will doubtless win, through curiosity of already elicited admiration, a large circle of readers who thirst to know what the sages of India have to disclose concerning the deeper problems of religion and life. They will find themselves rewarded. (*The Watchman*)[10]

The life of this Hindu saint is as romantic as the experience of many of the Christian hermits and teachers. Apart from his religious devotion he must have one of those gentle, unselfish natures who have no trouble to enter the kingdom of heaven because they are as innocent and honest as little children. Those familiar with the claims of the Theosophists understand the charm of its appeal to the higher nature of man. The Swami is a winsome pleader, as all America knows.... When he adds that far from seeking revenge India wishes to teach Occidental civilization that which it has been too busy and too dense to learn, the happiness which comes from the conquest of self and the service of others, he commands our respectful attention. It was inevitable that in writing of his teacher he should explain the tenets to which that teacher held, so this loving tribute serves a double purpose. It is an exposition as well as a eulogy. (*Brooklyn Daily Eagle*)[11]

For the *New York Saturday Review of Books* of July 12, 1902, Louis Herbert Gray (1875-1955) [q.v.][12] penned a review of Vivekananda's *Lectures on Jnana Yoga*, entitled "The Philosophy of the Vedanta". He affirmed that:

Swami Vivekananda, one of the ablest of these preachers from the East, needs no introduction.... Students of religion will find much of interest in it; those who care for India in any way will be glad to receive an indication of the high Hindu thought in one of the most striking religious movement of the day, while orthodox Christians should derive some information from the work regarding the attitude of the cultured Hindu toward Christianity and its Founder.... we find the principal tenets of the Vedanta detailed minutely and exhaustively. After reading this book one is inexcusable if his ideas concerning Vedanta are hazy.... A special feature of value is the

Swami's exceedingly clear statement of the Indian doctrine of maya.... The English of the book is excellent.

In 1901 and 1903 at Columbia University, the young Louis Herbert Gray temporarily replaced A. V. Williams Jackson as professor of Indo-Iranian languages. At that time Jackson, a friend of Abhedananda, went to India and Persia (Iran). From 1900 to 1918 Louis Gray held the position of instructor in Indo-Iranian studies at Princeton University, departmental editor of "etymology and the history of modern India" for the *New International Encyclopedia*, assistant editor for the multi-volume *Hastings' Encyclopedia of Religion and Ethics* in Edinburgh, Scotland, and also editor of *Mythology of all Races*, which includes a volume on India by A. B. Keith. For many years Gray was a professor of Oriental languages and of comparative linguistics at Columbia University (1926-44). His writings include *Indo-Iranian Phonology* (1902), and translations *Vasavadatta—A Sanskrit Romance* by Subandhu (1913) and *The Narrative of Bhoja* by Ballala of Benares. Over the years he authored many studies on the language and religion of ancient India and Iran.[13]

In addition, Swamiji's *Lectures on Jnana Yoga* received the following seven very appreciative reviews from the American press:

> Of all the Hindoo missionaries who have endeavoured to inculcate the dogmas and doctrines of the ancient Hindoo philosophy and religion throughout the Western world, the Swami Vivekananda was at once the ablest orator and most profuse writer. His energy was sufficient to put an end to the belief that the Hindoos are but an indolent and exhausted people, for he travelled as extensively, lectured as incessantly and wrote about as voluminously as any American or European of our time.... The series are connected by a central thought running through them all so that they form a genuine book and not a mere compilation of papers, having no logical relation to one another.
>
> The purpose of the lectures is to explain Vedanta philosophy to persons of strongly analytical minds, who must have the sanction of logic and reason for every belief. That method of attaining truth is known as "Jnana Yoga", and it is the elucidation of that yoga, or method, that the Swami directs himself from first to last in the series of lectures that make up the London course. (*San Francisco Call*)[14]
>
> The lectures show a wonderful insight into great truths which underlie all religious aspiration. (*Louisville Courier Journal*)[15]

It is a book which appeals to the intellectual, and no one could be the worse for reading it, since it contains much of truth even as Christians measure truth. (*Milwaukee Sentinel*)[16]

The altruism with which his preaching is permeated attracts and inspires. The love of humanity which he inculcates harmonizes with the spirit of the age. His English is good, his style easy to read, his sincerity unquestionable. Merely as an intelligent presentation of what is best in the ancient Hindu Scriptures, the Swami Vivekananda's book is deserving of attention at the hands of religious students. (*Chicago Record Herald*)[17]

One of the great thought challengers of the day is this work by the Swami Vivekananda. The book goes deep and treats of startling things, but when analyzed and viewed from the author's standpoint, they are found to be links in the great chain of truth. He alone will deny who is out of sympathy or limited in vision. (*Boston Transcript*)[18]

The Vedanta Philosophy as explained by Vivekananda is interesting.... As given by him and his followers, no more lofty teachings can be found. The work is a valuable addition to the literature of religions. (*Toledo Blade*)[19]

The lectures are all extremely interesting, the style brilliant, the reasoning often subtle. Whether the philosophy advanced is satisfactory or not to those whose theories are the outgrowth of a different system of thought, his method of presenting it affords an intellectual pleasure. (*Indianapolis Journal*)[20]

Upon hearing of Swamiji's passing, the *Chicago Daily Tribune* wrote:

Swami Vivekananda, whose death in a monastery near Calcutta was announced yesterday, was known in Chicago. His expositions of Hindu philosophy made him a unique figure during the World's Fair congress of religions. He came to America as a delegate to the congress, and was one of its most prominent figures. Long after it had closed he remained in the country preaching and writing. He went to New York, where his Indian costume and new ideas created a furore. He returned to Chicago the year after the congress to be again welcomed, this time as a "fad".

The Swami drew great crowds to his meetings, and religious leaders were of the belief that he would create a cult with a large following if he continued. His teachings were deeply philosophical and his method of expressing them clear and concise. He was a man of great personal magnetism, and with his succinct thought and language succeeded in making his influence felt.

He dressed in the garb of an Indian Brahmin. This took the form of a long white robe, with the turban headdress. He was a strikingly tall man, erect in carriage, and of light complexion for a Hindu. On the streets he was followed by crowds, and would stop and deliver lectures. When tired he would deliberately stop, even in the middle of an address, and, jumping into a cab, drive away.

The Swami remained in America until western ideas and customs palled, and then suddenly disappeared. While here he was invited to the best of homes, and the women flocked to hear him. He wrote several books while travelling about the country, and these for a time had a considerable vogue.[21]

An obituary for Swami Vivekananda that went out on the wire and appeared in newspapers like the *Kansas City Star* (July 24, 1902) and the *Des Moines Capital* (July 25, 1902) read, "Vivekananda came to America without money, and refused to accept money from his numerous and enthusiastic admirers while here. He lived in the simplest manner."

After Swamiji's passing, Dr. Edward F. Eldridge (1856-1916), a physician and poet from Colorado, came out with a not-very-successful novel entitled *California Girl: A Tale of Hinduism and Woman Suffrage* (1902). The fictionalized account concerns a young man named Penloe who teaches the ideas of Swami Vivekananda to Stella, a California girl. Together they successfully proselytize the whole country and eventually the world.[22]

An obituary account of the Swami appeared in the *Cyclopedic Review of Current History* (1903, p. 592) giving a brief account of his life in the United States and mentioning, "He had a very large following in this country, his attractive personality and charm of manner being recognized on every hand."

In 1904 Florence de v. Miller wrote an article about her "Personal Observations and Experiences in India" for the *Liberal Review: An Organ of the Independent Thinkers of America*. In it she mentioned that the New Thought Conventions, Christian Science Churches, and Theosophic Centres embody directly or indirectly the teachings of India. She suggests that not only Vivekananda but the entire list of South Asian delegates, which included Dharmapala, Dvivedi, Gandhi, Modi, Mazumdar, Nagarkar and others, made a very good impression at the Parliament:

It became a matter of much embarrassment and enlightenment, during the Parliament of Religions, to hear and meet such men as Vivekananda, Mozoomdar, Dharmapala, etc., whose remarks created such interest every time they spoke from the platform of the Art Institute. To many it was a matter of wonder that the "heathen" could say such bright, such modern, such universal things, when they were not supposed to know much in their own language, to say nothing of English....

In passing along the street one day, on the way to a meeting at the Art Institute, during the progress of the Parliament, a little girl picked up a bee which had been injured so that it could not fly. At the meeting she sat holding it on her hand, when Vivekananda, coming up behind her chair, whispered in her ear, "Don't kill it!" Her prompt reply, that she would not kill anything, led to a number of remarks, and eventually to instructions, which helped to free the mother from the burden of superstition which had depressed her life. The *Old Testament* stories of anger, war, murder, bloodshed, vengeance (a veritable chamber of horrors in her childhood) were replaced by tales of compassion, not only for human, but for all life, dethroned a God of vengeance for the principle of Justice! Dear Vivekananda! A sweet spirit, full of tender sympathy, which endeared him to all who knew him, and created a desire to know the beliefs of one so gentle and so kind, so full of human sympathy, one who placed himself in touch with all the world.[23]

A complementary book review of Vivekananda's *A Collection of his Speeches and Writings* (1902) was written by Charles Davis (1840-1917) for *The American Antiquarian and Oriental Journal* of September-October 1906. There he affirms in positive terms:

This is the first attempt to put together in a single volume a representative collection of the works of Swami Vivekananda, one of the most remarkable men India has produced in recent times. The Swami came to public notice at the Parliament of Religions held in Chicago. He travelled through various cities in this country, in England and in India, delivering addresses, and sometimes courses of lectures, and everywhere he had many friends and admirers. This book covers the whole field of Hindu religion and philosophy, and presents in a lucid and attractive form the abstruse doctrines of Eastern religious philosophy. The Swami was an eloquent teacher and preacher. He was full of the consciousness of a great mission, and to his countrymen his speeches were ever a trumpet call to duty. This book has five portraits of the Swami.

The versatile Charles Henry Stanley Davis, a physician and author of medical books, held various political positions such as the mayor and president of the board of education in Meriden, Connecticut. As a philologist and Orientalist he published *Grammar of the Old Persian Language* (1878), and took over the editorship of *Biblia, a Journal of Oriental Archeology*, which, in 1906, merged with the *American Antiquarian and Oriental Journal*. He also put out two volumes on the history of Egypt.[24]

Occasionally a book author would offer his or her reader a long quote from one of Swamiji's lectures. For example, Robert John Thompson (1865-1931) in *The Proofs of Life after Death* (1906) gives a verbatim report of over four pages drawn from Vivekananda's writings, and Helen Philbrook Patten (b. 1865) in her compilation *Intimations of Immortality* (1906) quotes over two pages from Vivekananda's books and over a page from Abhedananda's texts.[25]

In 1907, James Creelman (1859-1915) [q.v.], an outstanding international journalist, visited the Vedanta Society of New York and produced an article on the subject. About Swamiji he enthusiastically disclosed:

> The Vedantic invasion of America really began when the gentle and cultivated Swami Vivekananda, a disciple who had studied at the feet of the great Saint, Yogi and Mahatma, Ramakrishna, came to attend the international Parliament of Religions in Chicago at the time of the Columbian Exposition. This noble and courtly Hindu, a man of great learning and eloquence, impressed all whom he met in America by the depth of his spirit and the breadth of his views, as well as by his sweet forbearance, modest dignity and courtesy.
>
> To the representatives of many religions assembled in Chicago—supreme type of noisy material progress and conceit—he presented the venerable philosophy of Brahman in such lofty word pictures of unselfishness, and the unutterable calm to be achieved by freeing the soul from all earthly ties or affections, as to attract widespread attention to his teachings and to make clear the way for a Brahmin crusade in America.
>
> The Swami Vivekananda, who became the founder and leader of the Ramakrishna mission in this country, was the product of a great spiritual

upheaval in India. The most wonderful and impressive figure in the movement was Ramakrishna, teacher of the Swami Vivekananda.

This excerpt is reproduced from James Creelman's article in *Pearson's Magazine*, which contains admirable photos of Sri Ramakrishna, Swamis Vivekananda and Abhedananda, and the Dakshineswar temple gardens. It includes a biography of Sri Ramakrishna.* By contrast, in the same article Creelman severely criticizes Agumya Guru Paramahamsa, a Mahatma from India then in New York City. When Ella Wheeler Wilcox told the latter, "I wanted to see you because I have read and studied the beautiful old religion of India and because I was two years a student of your great Vivekananda. He was a great soul. He left a beautiful influence in America," the Mahatma responded with criticism. Nevertheless, the president of the Mahatma's Vedanta Society was Paul Morton (1857-1911,) who was also president of the affluent Equitable Life Assurance Society, and formerly the secretary of the navy in the cabinet of United States President Theodore Roosevelt. Officers of this short-lived society included William G. Lane, the director of many railroads.[26]

In an erudite article with the title "Intellectual Leadership in Contemporary India" written in 1910 for the widely-read *Atlantic Monthly* magazine, Paul Reinsch (1869-1923) emphasized the more traditional aspects of the teachings of Vivekananda:

> More representative of the older religious spirit of India are the followers of Ramakrishna, among whom the recently deceased Vivekananda was the most engaging figure. He received an English education, and had early in life been attracted by Brahmoism [Brahmo Samaj], though he became estranged from that movement through what he called its lack in spiritual depth. In these men the older traditions of Indian religious life were dominant. They withdrew from the world for meditation, they clung to the Vedas as revealed, they rested satisfied with the old philosophy of India. But they saw it with new eyes, they called for a stronger expression of personality, a more active devotion; to use a current word, they were more pragmatic than the older religious teachers of India had been. In this practical tendency the contact with Western civilization made itself felt rather than in the philosophic form of their thought.... Vivekananda and

* See Chapter III.

his associates, dwelling on the spiritual side of religion, and conservative in temper, do not expect much from mechanical reform. But Vivekananda himself specifically insisted upon freedom of travel and diet, and condemned the spirit of all trammelling conventions.[27]

At the University of Wisconsin, Paul Samuel Reinsch first worked as a professor of political science (1901-13), and then became the American minister to China (1913-19). In his writings he presented an inspired analysis of the risks inherent in excessive nationalism and imperialism. Always a humanitarian, he developed a keen interest in the economic, political, and social problems of the so-called "backward peoples". In *Intellectual and Political Currents in the Far East* (1911), he proclaimed himself an opponent of the imperialist aggressor and a supporter of the subject peoples. Unfailing in his sympathy for the Chinese people, Reinsch advocated representative government and a public administration under the guidance of foreign experts. Reinsch was unsuccessful in obtaining financial assistance from the United States for China after the latter entered the World War. He prematurely died from an illness contracted in China.[28]

On September 16, 1910, the New York based *The Dial*, in a review of Nivedita's book, expressed the view:

> Some there are, perhaps many, who can recall the presence among us of the Swami Vivekananda, who was an impressive figure at the Parliament of Religions in Chicago in 1893.... "The Master as I saw Him, being Pages from the Life of the Swami Vivekananda" contains characteristic passages from the Swami's teachings as noted by a devout hearer and subsequent follower, the Sister Nivedita (Margaret Noble). The volume contains much that belongs to all true religion, of whatever clime or country.

At an address given at the public celebration of the birth anniversary of Vivekananda held at the Belur Math in 1911, a young Frank J. Alexander (1887/88-1917) [q.v.] described Swamiji in this manner:

> He was the embodiment, the personification, the very incarnation of the philosophy He taught. It was the life of Him, His soul, and all His thought.... Apart from the purely religious aspect of the Swami's influence in America, this great land of yours owes to Him a particular tribute, for He was the first Oriental who patriotically and comprehensively interpreted

> India to the Occident. He swept aside the wholesale, prevailing superstitions concerning Indian life and customs that had crept into the mind of the West.... Swamiji's influence in America is imperishable, for it is founded on the invincible strength of eternal truth,—that truth for which the Swami lived and which He realized in fullest consciousness. We, in America, are grateful to your Great Teacher, for He is reckoned by thousands of my countrymen as the Genius Incarnate of India and also and especially as a Divine Teacher who came to redeem in our life that same "dharma" which Sri Krishna and the other Great Avataras came to revive and strengthen in this Eastern land.[29]

Frank J. Alexander, brought up in Omaha, Nebraska, later became a newspaper writer in the Midwest. For about five years he held interviews with United States senators and other newsworthy personalities. In 1908, at Grand Central Station in New York City, he met Sister Nivedita. Alexander noticed that Nivedita was "possessed of such a synthetic mind and cyclonic personal energy". Sister Christine, whom he met in the fall of 1910 when he was twenty-two years of age, persuaded Josephine MacLeod to render him some financial assistance. Inspired by the writing of Vivekananda, Alexander set sail for India and came to the Belur Math in 1911. With Sister Christine he travelled from Calcutta to the Advaita Ashrama at Mayavati. Along with Swamis Swarupananda and Virajananda, and Sister Nivedita he offered an invaluable service in bringing out the three-volume* *The Life of Swami Vivekananda* by His Eastern and Western Disciples (1912-18). Future writers like Marie Louise Burke used later editions of this work as the foundation for their study and historical research. In a letter Swami Atulananda mentions that Charlotte Sevier paid Alexander money to write *The Life of Swami Vivekananda*. Unfortunately, the extent of Alexander's contribution to this work, which might have been quite sizable, is unknown. Concerning Vivekananda in the West, comparing the content of early editions of this work with Sankari Basu and Sunil Ghosh's *Vivekananda in Indian Newspapers 1893-1902* would give us some idea of the added material. Often writing under pseudonyms, Alexander came out with at least twenty-seven articles in the *Prabuddha Bharata* during 1911-13. Six articles had the title "In the Hours of Meditation", which is the name of the presently selling short volume of his writings. Alexander then went to Almora where he resided for two years.

---

* Later four.

Because of ill health, he had to return to the United States in early 1916 and died of tuberculosis the following year. Sister Christine, who was with Alexander when he passed away, revealed, "Three days before [his death] he told me that Swamiji was calling him, gave me some directions ... In speaking of his Indian experience, he always said, 'I have lived. What does it matter whether the body goes now or later.'" Due to some character shortcomings, Frank Alexander received criticism from Atulananda, Josephine MacLeod, and Boshi Sen.[30]

The most popular American singer of her day was Lillian Russell (1861-1922) who, for over thirty years, enjoyed a highly successful musical and acting career on the stage. A newspaper columnist noted in 1912 that she "is to a certain extent a student of occultism, which has become the subject of such general interest since the Swamis, those masters of the Vedanta philosophy, came among us." During the day, she repeatedly practised a deep breathing technique filling her chest and abdomen fully. Rising on her toes, she would breathe in, inhaling slowly "qualities of love, health, wisdom, usefulness, power for good, and cheerfulness," and exhale "all the opposite qualities, which would do me injury, such as prejudice, weakness, folly." She might have learned this technique from Swami Abhedananda who taught, "Breathe slowly and rhythmically. Imagine that you breathe out all that is evil and weak and undesirable and that with every breath you draw in, the divine nature is flowing through you." Her life story came out in a big Hollywood movie production of 1940 titled "Lillian Russell".[31]

When Hereward Carrington (1880-1958) [q.v.] wrote his well received text *Higher Psychical Development: Yoga Philosophy* (1920), he wisely utilized several long quotes from Vivekananda's *Raja Yoga* and from the works of Abhedananda. He also covers the subjects of kundalini, prana, asana, pranayama, mantra, dhyana, sushumna, pingala, mudra, tattvas, samadhi, pratyahara, yogi and sahasrara. Hereward Carrington, the author of numerous books, was born on the Isle of Jersey in the United Kingdom. He became a member of the American Society for Psychical Research assisting James H. Hyslop of Columbia University until 1908, founded and directed the American Psychical Institute, and authored books on spiritualism and astral projection.[32]

In his popular anthology *The Wisdom of the Hindus* (1921), editor Brian Brown (b. 1881) [q.v.] wrote in the introduction:

All of the spiritual sages mentioned in this anthology are among the foremost men the Indian nation has produced. Like Swami Vivekananda, from whose "Inspired Talks" and "Raja Yoga" I have quoted, they marked eras in their respective religions although one and all taught the "Fatherhood of God and the Brotherhood of Man".

Brian Brown devoted eight pages to excerpts from Swamiji's writings along with selections from Sri Ramakrishna, and Swamis Abhedananda and Paramananda's works. His anthology successfully conveyed the ideas of the Hindu religion to a wide assortment of people.[33]

In 1921 Walter Kenilworth [q.v.] in *Practical Occultism* alluded to an interesting episode in Swamiji's life:

> The learned Swami Vivekananda, who so ably taught the philosophy of the Vedanta in this country and Europe, and was a disciple of Bhagavan Sri Ramakrishna, explained in a simple manner in his "Raja Yoga" those truths of psychology known to India for countless generations. His book was the result of the abnormal curiosity concerning the occult he found rampant in this land. Personally he never countenanced its practices. His religious aim was higher. Yet, it is said of him, when a Chicago millionaire ridiculingly insisted that he display occult powers, he simply looked in the man's eyes. Later the man declared: "In that look, I felt as if my entire life lay like an open book before the swami."[34]

Yes, Lady Saheb: A Woman's Adventurings with Mysterious India (1925) was judged the best book of the year by the League of American Pen Women. Its author Grace Thompson Seton (1872-1959) showed interest not only in travel and exploration but also in the role of women in various societies, Hinduism, metaphysics, theosophy, and Oriental mysticism. Seton visited the Math of Ramakrishna in Belur, which she very much enjoyed. Her comments were:

> Swami Vivekananda, the last Vedantian saint and seer, who, when his appointed hour came, just went out of his body quietly and left it sitting there in meditation. His disciples, seeing him in the familiar attitude, did not disturb him until they realized that this time he was not coming back, that he had joined his great predecessor, Ramakrishna.

The chapter ends with the sentence, "Also with the Western disciple [Josephine MacLeod?] of Vivekananda I shall ever do reverence before the shrine of her Vedantic Teacher." Grace Seton lived a highly active life as a successful author and lecturer, world traveller and adventurer, president of Pen and Brush, the Connecticut Woman Suffrage Association, and of the National League of American Pen Women, a cofounder of the Camp Fire Girls, recipient of three French decorations for her services in World War I, and a songwriter among other things.[35]

James Vincent Nash (b. 1886) penned a highly appreciative article "The Message and Influence of Vivekananda", which appeared in a 1925 edition of *The Open Court* monthly magazine. The author quotes Swamiji, covering some of his life events, and states in part:

> Descriptions of Vivekananda and interviews with him filled columns upon columns in the newspapers. Here was a man, the product of a religion popularly supposed to set as its goal the utter negation of personality, who by the very force of an extraordinarily distinctive, attractive, and winsome personality, had brought America to its feet. What a paradox!... The influence which he thus exercised upon the religious thought of the country can hardly be overemphasized. From that period dates the widespread interest in Oriental religion, which is today one of the marked characteristics of American life. Vivekananda was the first great missionary in modern times from Asia, the homeland of religion, to the peoples of the West.... The influence of Vivekananda, however, lived on. Vedanta Societies which sprang up as a result of this American mission, notably in New York and San Francisco, have perpetuated Vivekananda's teachings in this country.[36]

The very popular authoress Lily Adams Beck (1862-1931) [q.v.], who had so many nice things to say about Sri Ramakrishna, also made this statement:

> Of this disciple, Ramakrishna eagerly asked when he first saw him, "Tell me, do you see a light when you are going to sleep?" "Doesn't everyone?" asked the boy, in wonder. He had indeed a consciousness of light so great that he took it for granted that someone had placed a bright lamp behind his head. When he was to speak in public, which he did frequently and with power, he would hear at night in his room a voice shouting at him

the words he would say next day. It was given to him. This man was the well-known Vivekananda.

In the same book, when writing on yoga, she draws material "largely from studies of their faith written by great Indians ancient and modern." It is obvious that Swamiji's book on *Raja Yoga* was her source when she covers topics like akasha and prana, yogic breathing and other subjects. Without mentioning Vivekananda by name, she directly quotes from his "Sayings and Utterances" that is listed as number 41 in the *Complete Works* (VIII:276).[37] In *The Story of Oriental Philosophy* (1928), Lily Beck recommended the biography *Sri Ramakrishna*[*] by Swami Saradananda and four of Swamiji's volumes on yoga as five of the fourteen best books written by Indians on the subject of Indian religion and philosophy.[38]

1930s and After

In the 1930s, Vivekananda, like Ramakrishna, began getting acknowledgment from top-level professors in the United States. In an evaluation of Rolland's biography of Vivekananda written in French, Arnold Rowbotham (1888-1970) indicated:

> After the usual training of a Hindu mystic during which he became a "sannyasi" and renounced all earthly bonds, Vivekananda developed a doctrine at the heart of which was a kind of religious universalism. This conviction that all religions are true was deepened by extensive travels not only in India but also in America and the West. He attended the Parliament of Religions held in Chicago in 1893 and made a profound impression on his audiences.

Originally from Birmingham, England, Rowbotham, for nearly three decades, was a professor of the French language at the University of California, Berkeley, serving some years as the departmental chairman. His experiences in Peking led to a deep and abiding love for China and its culture.[39]

In July of 1935, Will Durant (1885-1981) [q.v.], a professor of philosophy at the University of California at Los Angeles, came out with the first of eleven volumes of *The Story of Civilization* entitled *Our Oriental Heritage*. The

---

* *Sri Ramakrishna the Great Master*.

volume contains a book length section on the history of Indian thought, which did much to convey these ideas to a large number of educated people. Will and his wife Ariel Durant's purpose was to make a large and varied amount of historical information accessible and comprehensible to a wider audience. They shared the Pulitzer Prize in 1968. Durant mentions about Vivekananda:

> In 1893 he found himself lost and penniless in Chicago. A day later he appeared in the Parliament of Religions at the World's Fair, addressed the meeting as a representative of Hinduism, and captured everyone by his magnificent presence, his gospel of the unity of all religions, and his simple ethics of human service as the best worship of God.... Returning to India, he preached to his countrymen a more virile creed than any Hindu had offered them since Vedic days.[40]

Concerning the Upanishads and how they had begun to stir Western thought, Durant wrote, "They are the oldest extant philosophy and psychology of our race; the surprisingly subtle and patient effort of man to understand the mind and the world, and their relation. The Upanishads are as old as Homer, and as modern as Kant."[41]

A year later, an admirer of Sri Ramakrishna,* Professor Alban Widgery (1887-1968) [q.v.] also quoted from some of Vivekananda's teachings. He expressed his respect for his ideas writing:

> A current of religious fervour was started by Ramakrishna. His chief disciple, Swami Vivekananda, the actual founder of the Ramakrishna Mission as it exists today, came to America to the Parliament of Religions in Chicago. Vivekananda had a keen perception for the essentials of the Advaitist form of Hinduism which formed the root of his master's teachings. He expounded its principles not in relation with Hinduism as a practical ritualistic religion of the people but as found in intellectual presentation in the Upanishads, in the *Bhagavad Gita*, and in the *Yogasutras*.... In opposition to all selfishness and superficiality he preached redemption through the recognition of the essential unity of all life, endeavouring to break down all those personal prejudices dividing men from their fellows and from God. Religion for him was essentially mystical. He was too wise to diverge much

* See Chapter III.

> from the ideas and practices with which the mystic life of his people had become associated. For this Dr. Farquhar classified him as a defender of the old faith and not as a reformer. That implies a complete misapprehension, a lack of inner understanding of the nature of reform, which consists not chiefly in rejection but in a new appreciation, a new enthusiasm for spiritual truth. This Vivekananda undoubtedly had, and has indubitably transmitted to the Ramakrishna movement.[42]

In addition to writing two essays on Sri Ramakrishna,* Frederick Robinson (1883-1941) [q.v.], the president of the College of the City of New York (1927-39), also showed appreciation for Vivekananda. In a paper written for the Ramakrishna Centenary in Calcutta in 1937 he mentioned:

> It was Vivekananda, at Chicago, who gave widespread publicity to the doctrine of the divinity in man as preached by Ramakrishna, and the idea of the fundamental oneness of all religions. He popularized and publicized among the many of average intelligence the concepts that had been clearly understood by a smaller group of intellectuals.
>
> So attractive was his personality and so clear and direct were his teachings that he won many adherents who joined the Vedanta groups he established and reaped also the profound respect of others who, while adhering to the doctrines of their own churches, recognized a common ground as described by Vivekananda where all men of goodwill could meet.[43]

Canadian born A. Eustace Haydon (1880-1975) [q.v.], a Baptist and Unitarian minister and head of the department of comparative religion at the prestigious University of Chicago Divinity School, emphasized Vivekananda's social message:

> Ramakrishna's brilliant pupil, Swami Vivekananda made the adjustment of the unknowable, impersonal, quiescent Brahman of philosophy to the pathetic need of the people for alleviation of their social ills. Like all his predecessors, he knew that the unknown God was one, eternal absolute, perfect, the only true reality, concealed in the superficial world of change, but because of that he is the soul of all souls and all men are divine. He is

* See Chapter III.

not the quiescent eternal but the true humanity of man. Consequently true worship of God means service of man.[44]

While sightseeing in France, the American novelist Henry Miller (1891-1980) experienced the strong emotions one can feel when reading about Vivekananda:

> I had just been reading Rolland's book on Vivekananda; I had put it down because I couldn't read any more, my emotions were so powerful. The passage which roused me to a state of exaltation was the one in which Rolland describes Vivekananda's triumphal return to India from America. No monarch ever received such a reception at the hands of his countrymen: it stands unique in the annals of history. And what had he done, Vivekananda, to merit such a welcome? He had made India known to America; he had spread the light. And in doing so he had opened the eyes of his countrymen to their own weakness. All India greeted him with open arms; millions of people prostrated themselves before him, saluting him as a saint and saviour, which he was. It was the moment when India stood nearer to being unified than at any time in her long history. It was a triumph of love, of gratitude, of devotion.[45]

In his biography *Path of Mahatma Gandhi*, George Catlin (1896-1979) alluded to Vivekananda,

> who had the gift of fervour, a strong sense of mission and the ability to convince others, not only in India but also in America, about his mission. To him Gandhi referred at Kottayam. The keynote of his gospel was that religion is one. But when one sought what might be in turn the keynotes of this one religion, one found, not only the injunction to join with meditation social activity, but also to join to love a certain belief in the righteousness of vitality and power, and indeed of Indian vitality and power. This positive teaching stirred the minds of young Indians who felt that their country and their religion had too long played a passive role.

Born in Liverpool, England, George Catlin, a Catholic, was an educator, political scientist, and editor, who authored about twenty books on political theory and philosophy. He was a drafter of the "International Declaration in Support of the Independence of India" in 1943. Catlin served as a special advisor to British political leaders Arthur Greenwood and Harold Wilson, and the American presidential candidate Wendell Wilkie. His teaching assignments included being a professor of politics at Cornell University (1924-35), of quantitative political science at Yale University (1935-56), and a lecturer at the University of Calcutta (1947).[46]

In her ecumenical *World Faith: The Story of the Religions of the United Nations* (1949), Ruth Cranston (d. 1956), the author of *The Story of Woodrow Wilson** and *Miracle of Lourdes*, brought out this point:

> Most dynamic of all modern [Hindu] movements has been the Ramakrishna-Vivekananda Mission, founded by the Swami Vivekananda after his visit to the Parliament of Religions in Chicago in 1893 and as a result of the strong interest and support he awakened for Hinduism at that time. Vivekananda was the scientific-minded, modern-educated disciple of a great Hindu saint of modern times, Paramahamsa Ramakrishna. Combining in himself the best of the old and the new in Hindu ideals, and admiring greatly the Western ideal of practical service to mankind, he took as the watchword for his monastic order: *Siva-Seva:* God and Service.[47]

It was at this time that a new and rising interest in the life and teachings of Vivekananda took place in America. The main catalysts were the Ramakrishna Swamis in the West, particularly the writings and influence of Swami Nikhilananda. Sister Amiya (Ella Corbin) was present when the famous playwright John van Druten (1901-57) gave an impressive talk at the dedication of Malvina Hoffman's bust of Vivekananda at the Trabuco Monastery in Southern California on July 4, 1951. His comments were:

> Swami Vivekananda was a very special person, particularly so for all of us in America. He was our especial messenger, our own personal link—and designed as just that—with the eternal religion of Sri Ramakrishna.... there came from him [Sri Ramakrishna] our own interpreter, the human messenger designed for us. This was Swami Vivekananda, with his amazing gift for the English language, and his great understanding of the needs of the people of this country. If we look at his own background, his own upbringing, we can see why he should have had them. He was a young man,

* She had a close association with the Wilson family.

literate and studious: far more studious, I would imagine than most of us present here today, and in far more subjects.

At one period during his talk, Mr. van Druten inadvertently used the name of Ramakrishna instead of Vivekananda. He corrected himself and then said: "Well, Ramakrishna or Vivekananda, what does it matter? They are one and the same." His remark was lost in the burst of applause which followed.[48]

London born John van Druten joined the Vedanta Society of Southern California in the early 1940s, and was an active member during the 1950s. His writings appeared in *Vedanta for the Western World* (1945), *Vedanta for Modern Man* (1951), and *What Vedanta Means to Me* (1961). As a Broadway playwright he is best remembered for the comedy *The Voice of the Turtle* (1943), one of the longest-running non-musical plays in Broadway history. As a writer, he also received an Academy Award nomination for *Gaslight* in 1944, and in 1951-52 he won the prestigious New York Drama Critics' Circle Award for the best Broadway play of the year.[49]

The head of the department of religion and a professor of comparative religion at the University of Southern California during 1940-56, Floyd H. Ross (1910-98) signified:

> Under the leadership of men trained in the spirit of Vivekananda and Ramakrishna, the Ramakrishna Centres are living examples of how timeless truths of the past have value when they are continuously relived and reinterpreted in the present.... In 1893, Swami Vivekananda went to America with his message of Vedanta. He received an excellent hearing not only at the World Parliament of Religions in Chicago but also in many other Centres. Many in the United States were stirred by the profound presentation of a religious way of life that transcended sectarian differences and dogmatic brittleness.... The Ramakrishna Centres in the West are playing their own part quietly in helping to prepare the way for the united pilgrimage of mankind toward self-understanding and peace.[50]

In the early 1950s Floyd Ross, an ordained Unitarian-Universalist minister, lectured at the Vedanta Society of Southern California, contributed articles to their magazine *Vedanta and the West*, received a Fulbright grant for India (1952-53), paid a visit to a Ramakrishna Mission College in India, and authored books like *The Meaning of Life in Hinduism and Buddhism*

(1952). When reviewing *The Cultural Heritage of India*, Ross concluded, "The Ramakrishna Mission Institute of Culture deserves commendation for its leadership in the project in making available in the English language so many excellent volumes bearing upon the life and thought of India."[51]

In 1953 Swami Nikhilananda came out with *Vivekananda: The Yogas and other Works*, which included a biography of Swamiji. Commenting on this work, Filmer S. C. Northrop (1893-1992) [q.v.], a professor of philosophy and law at Yale University, pointed out a difficulty in attempting to explain ancient Indian ideas to the modern Westerner:

> To convey Hindu meanings in English words is exceedingly difficult. The difficulty arises from the fact that the reader inevitably reads modern western, rather than ancient Hindu, meanings into the English words. The problem of any expositor or translator, therefore, is that of so wording the English translation of the Hindu doctrines that the Western philosophical or psychological meaning of the English words will not be introduced to the reader. Especially in his exposition of Jnana-Yoga, Vivekananda showed himself to be expert in this.... It is important also for an understanding of Vivekananda's insistence upon developing Hinduism in ways that will permit its incorporation of Western science that Swami Nikhilananda has provided us with a biography of Vivekananda which shows his intellectual development.[52]

Vivekananda: The Yogas and other Works was very much appreciated by Professor Nelson S. Bushnell, an expert on English literature from Williams College in Williamstown, Massachusetts, who stated:

> The impact of the Indian monk's personality is tremendous. Through addresses, poems, and letters—and indirectly through the introductory biography—through a thousand pages the Swami besieges us with incessant blows; we feel ourselves at the mercy of a religious genius of a very high order, and of a human being whose vitality, learning, eloquence, and scope are all—to state it baldly—enormous.... What emerges as most impressive in a re-reading of them is the unity of purpose, in keeping with the non-dualistic position that the author maintains ... because of the author's liveliness, charm, and comic spirit. These qualities are re-enforced by personal letters and biographical anecdotes.... But the chief ornament of Vivekananda's teaching is his use of the illustrative parable.... He did not

> hesitate to commit himself utterly to the simple—and staggering—proposition that the quest for the realization of God is the only occupation really worthy of a human being.[53]

Concerning this volume, Irwin Edman [q.v.] of the Columbia University philosophy department pointed out:

> This is a learned and illuminating selection from the works of a religious prophet of modern India. Swami Nikhilananda's introduction is an extremely helpful interpretation to the West of the life and wisdom of a key figure in the religious culture of the East by a responsible scholar thoroughly at home in both cultures.[54]

In 1953 Nikhilananda also brought out *Vivekananda—A Biography*. George W. Briggs of Drew University in Madison, New Jersey, concluded that:

> This is a full-length Indian portrait of one of the most distinguished religious figures of sixty years ago. Having access to all the documentary materials, speeches, letters, and reports of the press at his command, Swami Nikhilananda has given a thoroughly intimate and comprehensive study of the man. It is restrained, but enthusiastic and straightforward, which makes the volume of special value to students and scholars.[55]

Regarding the book, D. Mackenzie Brown (b. 1908) of the University of California at Santa Barbara added:

> What the author has done is to take a complex and infinitely ramified personality and life story and spell out the meaning and the major themes in an engaging narrative that the Western reader can readily grasp—without burdening the account with a mass of subsidiary detail or losing sight of the basic essence.... The American reader is fortunate in having the benefit of Nikhilananda's scholarship and lucid expression in this new and highly readable account of one of the most arresting figures of modern India.

Professor Brown authored writings that include: *The White Umbrella: Indian Political Thought from Manu to Gandhi* (1953), *Indian and Western Realism* (1954), *Traditional Concepts of Indian Leadership* (1959), and *The Nationalist Movement, Indian Political Thought from Ranade to Bhave* (1961).[56]

A disciple of Swami Trigunatita, Dorothy Mercer (1901-62) [q.v.], who became an instructor of English at the City College of San Francisco and a lifetime Vedantist, offered this summary:

> Vivekananda lived what he preached. Full of compassion for the physical debility of his people, he felt that India could learn a great deal from America's scientific and technological knowledge, social organization, and comparatively poverty-free people. He believed in turn, that America could profit from the teachings of the Vedanta, and he visualized a synthesis of science and religion which would lift the poverty of both body and spirit.[57]

A professor of Indian religion and philosophy at Stanford University, Frederich Spiegelberg (1897-1994) [q.v.] is mentioned in Chapter III. About Swamiji he disclosed in *Living Religions of the World* (1956):

> Vivekananda was an exceptionally brilliant man, and he wrote in English. He thereby created single-handed the spiritual vocabulary by means of which Indian traditions have found expression in the West, either in direct translation, or by means of discussions and commentaries upon them. He was a prolific writer, and in the sense that he did create this vocabulary, his contribution towards our knowledge of India was far greater than that of the 19th century Indologists who were his contemporaries.[58]

Sterling M. McMurrin (1914-96) became a professor of philosophy in 1948 and of history in 1970, and dean of the graduate school in 1966 at the University of Utah in Salt Lake City. A leading expert on Mormonism, he penned *The Theological Foundations of the Mormon Religion* (1965). As a United States Commissioner of Education under John F. Kennedy, McMurrin was active in promoting school desegregation and equal opportunities for women and minorities during the 1960s. In his 1957 review of *Vivekananda: The Yogas and other Works* by Nikhilananda, he emphatically asserted:

> Swami Nikhilananda and the Ramakrishna-Vivekananda Centre have made a major contribution to philosophical and religious scholarship in the publication of this massive compendium of writings of Vivekananda (Narendranath Datta) together with an extensive life of the philosopher-saint. The biography, done by Nikhilananda, is a vivid and moving account of the youth, education, dedication, and ministry of a great-souled teacher

who was a close disciple of Ramakrishna and who did more perhaps than any other person to bring attention to his master's work as well as to introduce America to Vedantic thought and Yoga discipline. The story of Vivekananda's life is simply, and one might say lovingly, recounted by Nikhilananda with such effectiveness ... it inducts the reader quite sympathetically into the mental and moral framework of the India of a few decades ago and reveals much of the character of Hinduism together with the old culture's appreciation and criticism.[59]

In the definitive anthology *Sources of Indian Tradition*, Stephen N. Hay (1925-2002) [q.v.] devoted fourteen pages to Vivekananda's writings expressing the view:

> As Jesus was followed by Saint Paul, Ramakrishna had dynamic Swami Vivekananda to preach his "Gospel" to India and to the world.... When he first visited Ramakrishna he was planning to study law in England and then follow the profession which was the high road to success in British India. Within a year's time his interviews with the master mystic had changed the course of his life. He resolved to give up worldly pursuits and adopt the life of a sannyasi. After twelve years of ascetic discipline he became famous as Swami Vivekananda, the apostle to the world of his master's philosophy of God-realization....
>
> Although he died at thirty-nine, Vivekananda's example had a powerful impact on the thinking of his own and later generations. Despite his scorn for politics, his success in preaching to the world the greatness of Hinduism gave his countrymen an added sense of dignity and pride in their own culture. His zeal to serve the downtrodden masses opened a new dimension of activity to Indian nationalist leaders, whose Western outlook had heretofore isolated them from the vast majority of their countrymen. Gandhi, the greatest to work for this new field, acknowledged his debt to the Swami in this respect.
>
> Vivekananda called India to become great by realizing her own possibilities and by living up to her own highest ideals. The heart and soul of his teaching was the message of his beloved maser, Ramakrishna: that each man was potentially divine, and so should both work to unleash the infinite power within himself, and should help other men to do the same.[60]

Marie Louise Burke (Sister Gargi, 1912-2004) is well known in Vedantic circles for her classic six-volume masterpiece *Swami Vivekananda in the West: New Discoveries*. Her monumental three-thousand-pages-plus magnum opus took fifteen years (1958-73) to research, compile and write down. Undertaking an innovative line of detailed empirical in-the-field research, she travelled around the country and found a vast amount of new material in nineteenth-century newspaper reports, old books and journals housed in libraries, Vedanta Society archives, personal archives, and through the use of private interviews. In the course of her research, she uncovered a wealth of well-documented new material about Swamiji's visit to the West that has become a substantial part of the Vedanta literature. She also located previously unknown newspaper accounts of Swamiji's speeches in the West. The late Bharat Maharaj, a revered senior monk of the Ramakrishna Order, wrote, "You have become immortal, Gargi, for your colossal and pioneering work on Swamiji." Moreover, her brilliant studies have inspired a number of scholars to undertake historical studies of Vivekananda's life events in the West and in India, which have continued up to this day. Sankari Basu and Sunil Ghosh dedicated their classic volume *Vivekananda in Indian Newspapers* (1969) "To Marie Louise Burke whose '*Swami Vivekananda in America: New Discoveries*' inspired the editors to undertake this work." Asim Chaudhuri's *Swami Vivekananda in America: New Findings* (2008) begins with "This book is fondly dedicated to Late Sister Gargi (Marie Louise Burke) who had inspired me to follow Swami Vivekananda's footprints around the world." Other notable examples of her inspiration are the volume by Terrance Hohner and Carolyn Kenny, and a host of other researchers such as Swami Vidyatmananda. Burke's six volumes also have stimulated the writing of new works on Swamiji's intimate disciples like Sara Bull, Sister Christine, Josiah Goodwin, Josephine MacLeod and Sister Nivedita.[61]

Initially her guru Swami Ashokananda encouraged her to write about Vivekananda, and he gave her permission to write about himself only when she had completed all of her other works. In 1974 she took her first vows in India from the Ramakrishna Order and received the monastic name of Gargi after the renowned Vedic woman sage. For her accomplishments, in 1983 Sister Gargi became the recipient of the first "Vivekananda Award" given by the Ramakrishna Mission Institute of Culture in Calcutta. In her later years she brought out an authentic well-written biography of Swami Trigunatita and of her own spiritual teacher Swami Ashokananda. In addition, she contributed hundreds of thousands of dollars to the purchase and upkeep of the Vivekananda Retreat at Ridgely and became its first president.[62]

About Swamiji, Sister Gargi emphasized:

> The Swami had deep feeling for the American people. He spoke to them in their own cultural language, he understood their needs, he scolded them for their faults, he admired them for the greatness of their ideals and character, for their vitality and initiative, and he felt they were worth giving the best years of his life to. "They loved me, and I love them a great deal," he once said. "I felt I was one of them." Surely a country that has been loved and blessed by so great a prophet can never really decline: surely the spiritual energy that he charged it with will suddenly surge forth. In fact, I believe this is beginning to happen—and none too soon![63]
>
> He manifested divinity to an extraordinary degree such as in our present state of existence we cannot even begin to comprehend. We are stunned when we learn that he could enter into samadhi at a moment's notice, that sometimes he had to make an effort not to enter into samadhi; we are awed by his power, by his ability to alter the thought currents of an entire nation, to bless people and to profoundly transform them; we are deeply moved by his same-sightedness, his vastness of heart, his unconditional compassion. Such characteristics as these, which spring directly from his knowledge of Brahman, are, to be sure, the most important things about Swamiji, if he did not possess them, we would not be thinking about him at all.[64]
>
> Reading of how much he accomplished in so short a time, one sometimes thinks of him as the "cyclonic" monk, forgetting that he worked with his mind always in a state bordering on profound meditation. His was the power to act with hurricane intensity from a level of intense stillness—a power (and an agony, as well) given only to World Teachers and Modern Movers. And such he was.[65]
>
> America also has been greatly blessed. If a seed of spirituality has been planted in the heart of a nation, then times of inner erosion can act as awakeners of that seed; it will surely stir and sprout. Such a seed was planted in the heart of America some eighty years ago by the towering prophet of this age—Swami Vivekananda. That is the wonderful hope.[66]

1960s and After

Swami Vivekananda can be viewed from many different perspectives. For example, the novelist and playwright Christopher Isherwood (1904-86) [q.v.] tells us what attracted him to Swamiji:

> I loved him at once, for his bracing self-reliance, his humour, and his courage. He appealed to me as the perfect anti-Puritan hero: the enemy of Sunday religion, the destroyer of Sunday gloom, the shocker of prudes, the breaker of traditions, the outrager of conventions.... That humour had its place in religion, that it could actually be a mode of spiritual self-expression, was a revelation to me.[67]
>
> Vivekananda is one of the very greatest historical figures that India has ever produced.... When one sees the full range of his mind, one is astounded. Vivekananda looked toward the West, not simply as a mass of tyrants exploiting various parts of Asia and other underdeveloped areas, but as future partners, people who had very, very much to offer.[68]

In 1962 Brahmachari Prema, who later became Swami Vidyatmananda (1913-2000), edited the book *What Religion Is: In the Words of Swami Vivekananda*, which is now being published by the Advaita Ashrama. He came up with the idea of reducing the eight volumes of the *Complete Works of Swami Vivekananda* down to a condensed 224-page edition. His compilation came out in anticipation of the Vivekananda Centenary. The work is skillfully organized in order to enable the reader to grasp the essence of the Swami's teachings. While Swamiji's words remain unaltered, the editor applied modern paragraphing, spelling and punctuation. This compact one-volume Vivekananda book was designed to be "of agreeable size and modest price". This seven-chapter manuscript, with an enlightening biographical Introduction by Christopher Isherwood, consists of a specially selected and representative collection of Swamiji's writings, specifically edited for the Western reader. Deleted are the letters, poems, repetition, and writings on reforms in India. Emphasis is on the topics of a universal religion, the principles and practice of Vedanta, the four Yogas, and four avatars as inspired World Teachers.[69] In addition, Vidyatmananda came out with a number of articles on Swamiji. Most notable are his ten pieces in the *Prabuddha Bharata* during 1967-77, discussing Swamiji's stay in France, Brittany, Normandy, Paris, Switzerland, Germany, Holland and the Near East.

In 1955, John Yale (the future Swami Vidyatmananda) dined with a Vedanta devotee named Virabhadra (Don Montague). John Yale surprised Virabhadra by informing him that in 1900 Vivekananda lived for weeks in a house not far from his residence in South Pasadena. To Virabhadra he said, "We have often wished the [Vedanta] Society might acquire it as a permanent memorial to Swamiji; but there is the problem of the purchase price and also we would need someone to look after the house should it become the Society's responsibility." Vidyatmananda recollects, "We drove over and looked at Sister's [Sister Lalita's] former residence at 309 Monterey Road. One could see that it had never been much changed, much rebuilt. You could tell by its style that the front door was the original front door by which Swamiji had entered and left the house.... Soon a sale was consummated. Virabhadra helped buy the house for the Society and made his home there as caretaker" until his death. The upstairs room that Swamiji occupied was consecrated as a shrine room. A hard worker, prior to receiving sannyasa in 1964 Vidyatmananda was instrumental in the building of the Santa Barbara Temple; he initiated the Vedanta bookshop and catalogue, and managed the publication of the Society's journal *Vedanta and the West*. In 1966 Vidyatmananda became the assistant Swami at the Centre Védantique Ramakrishna in Gretz, France. He served for many years under Swami Ritajananda, remaining there the rest of his life.[70]

At a speech delivered at the 1963 Vivekananda Centenary Dinner in New York, the foreign war correspondent Vincent Sheean (1899-1975) ascertained that Sri Ramakrishna

> needed a St. Paul, somebody who could get it going, who could organize the desirable, earthly part of his mission, and that is what Vivekananda did by means of the monastic order which has done so wonderfully well in this century. Everybody who had travelled in the East, especially in India in times of riot, famine, death, or violence, knows what the Ramakrishna Mission has meant to the poor, to the suffering. This is the third part of Vivekananda's mission, which has nothing to do with philosophy but, nevertheless, to him, it was equal.[71]

Sheean, in a five-page Foreword to John Yale's (Swami Vidyatmananda) *What Vedanta Means to Me* (1961), asserts, "In India itself the Ramakrishna Mission has evolved into an organized monasticism of far more liberal character than any known in the West. It teaches and heals; its hospitals, schools, shelters and free kitchens are models ... Amongst them are men of luminous intellect and an inner serenity which sheds peace like a benediction."

Before this, Sheean went to India to conduct an interview with Mahatma Gandhi on life's meaning, purpose, and significance. Just three days after his first interview with Gandhi, Sheean witnessed his 1948 assassination. Due to Gandhi's strong personality and influence, Sheean quickly transformed from a sceptic and materialist to a sincere believer in God. This experience led him to write a biography of Gandhi *Lead, Kindly Light* in 1949, which has a forty-six-page segment on Ramakrishna and Vivekananda, the patriotic-monk. He mentions that Gandhi came to Belur Math to see Vivekananda, but the Swami was lying ill in a house in Calcutta. Sheean also became a friend of Vedantists like Boshi and Gertrude Emerson Sen. During the 1950s, he was an occasional guest speaker at the Vedanta Society of New York.[72]

Vincent Sheean, a foreign correspondent, journalist, biographer and novelist, produced eloquent eyewitness accounts of some of the twentieth century's most significant historical events that he experienced: Mussolini's march on Rome (1922), the Chinese revolution (1927), communism in Russia, Arab-Jewish riots in Palestine (1929), Italian invasion of Ethiopia (1935), Spanish Civil War (1936-39), German conquests of Czechoslovakia, the Low Countries, and France, bombings in London (1939-41), San Francisco Conference that led to the founding of the United Nations (1945), the assassination of Mahatma Gandhi (1948), as well as the Korean War during the early 1950s. During World War II, on active duty in the intelligence division in North Africa and Italy, he attained the rank of lieutenant colonel.[73]

A professor of mathematics at the University of Washington (1956-65), Canadian born James M. G. Fell was closely connected with the Ramakrishna Vedanta Centre in Seattle. He later taught in the Ivy League at the University of Pennsylvania (1965-91). Fell summarized:

> Swami Vivekananda's philosophy of the spiritual life is so broad and potent that every spiritual ideal and every humanistic ideal finds a place within the scope of its transforming power. For example, the devotion to God as the Mother was unsurpassed in its depth; yet he was able at will to transcend the limitations of form and personality, even Divine Personality. He was a past master in the art of meditation; and at the same time his heart was open to all the sufferings of humanity.[74]

An author of four books on India, Beatrice P. Lamb (1904-97) was a lecturer at the New School for Social Research in New York and at New York University. She made this interesting point:

> It was Ramakrishna's chief disciple, Vivekananda, who brought modern Hinduism to America and laid the foundation for the Vedanta Societies ... In 1893, he went to the United States to attend a World Parliament of Religions in Chicago, where he made an impassioned defense of Hinduism, stressing its tolerance and the basic oneness of all religions. After touring the United States and England for three years, lecturing constantly, he received a hero's welcome on his return to India. The fact that he had so successfully preached Hinduism in the very lands from which the Christian missionaries came seemed to prove that political subjection need not involve religious subjection. Hindus could at least be proud of the essential truths of their religion. This reaffirmation of Hinduism served as an emotional counterbalance to the damage to Hindu self-respect caused by British political domination.[75]

Miss Alice H. Cook (1903-98) joined the faculty of the New York State School of Industrial and Labour Relations at Cornell University (1952-72). Through her numerous articles and several books she gained prominence in the field of labour relations and was a champion of equal pay and equal rights for working women. At the annual 1963 dinner of the Vedanta Society of New York, Alice Cook spoke on "Swami Vivekananda and the Spirit of America", affirming:

> The gift he brought from India to America was the religious tradition of centuries, the wisdom of the Eastern sages, and he brought himself, the product of ancestry of great devotion, of his training as a monk, of the background of his brother-monks in the Ramakrishna Order, of the benevolence and the struggle for serenity and understanding of the people of India.[76]

A committee of local Washington, D.C. devotees, with the support of the Indian Embassy in the city, arranged for a centenary celebration of Swami Vivekananda's birth held on October 4, 1963. The event was held at the auditorium of the Smithsonian Institute and attracted several dignitaries. They included Swami Nikhilananda, Grayson Kirk, Indian ambassador B. K. Nehru, and Kurt Leidecker, a professor of philosophy at the University of

Virginia. In attendance were some senior officials of the U.S. Government, presidents and professors of universities, and representatives of various foreign embassies.[77] In a well thought out analysis, Grayson Kirk (1903-97), the president of Columbia University in New York City, remarked:

> I have read of his lectures in America about India, and of his comments in India about America, and I have read some of his letters and essays on these two subjects.... Vivekananda's travels, lectures and observations in the United States were to serve such a useful purpose in both countries. In this country, his great personal charm, his intellectual brilliance and his spiritual profundity made such a great impression that he was listened to with respect when he sought to dispel some of the strange notions hitherto held by Americans about his people and their customs. They began to glimpse a view of a rich, complicated and ancient civilization quite unlike the India they had read about in Kipling or Henty.... Such a historian could not fail to be mindful of Vivekananda's service to his people in this respect. They listened to him, not only as a spiritual leader, but as a man who gave them a dream of what the India of the future might be.... Again and again he inveighed, by speech and action, against the excesses of the caste system and its debilitating effect upon the achievement either of social or material progress. He warned again and again that India's opportunities for progress were scanty until or unless the great masses were redeemed from their poverty and illiteracy. He decried the notion that progress in spirituality could be divorced from social consciousness and social progress. "It is a mockery," he said, "to offer religion to a starving man."[78]

With the publication of three books in the 1940s, Grayson Kirk cemented his reputation as an astute scholar of international relations. Participating in the United States staff at the Dumbarton Oaks Conference in 1944 and the San Francisco Conference in 1945, he assisted in writing the charter of the United Nations. Succeeding General Dwight Eisenhower, the future president of the United States, he became the president of Columbia University from 1953 to 1968. During his tenure, the dynamic Grayson Kirk quadrupled the university's endowments, established six new academic institutes, cultivated a science faculty that garnered four Nobel Prizes, had more than a dozen buildings constructed, and doubled the number of volumes in the library. A victim of the radicalism of the late 1960s, he resigned from the presidency after calling police to quell a massive student uprising at Columbia University in which 600 students were arrested.[79] Swami Nikhilananda was well known at Columbia University where he taught a special course on Indian thought, and was a member of the Seminar on Inter-religious Relations at the school.

Beginning in 1959, Charles Heimsath held the post of professor of South Asian Studies at American University in Washington, D.C. With his wife Surjit Mansingh, he coauthored *A Diplomatic History of Modern India*. In another volume titled *Indian Nationalism and Hindu Social Reform* (1964), he emphasized:

> The outstanding impression that Vivekananda made on his followers was not his adherence to a classical Hindu school of thought but his re-interpretation of ancient wisdom in order to meet actively the needs of contemporary Indian life. He argued that "Advaita alone is morality," because it postulated the oneness of God and man; "Know through Advaita that whomever you hurt you hurt yourself" was for him an ethical imperative of prime importance in the mundane world. But he acknowledged that such a command and its positive counterpart, to immerse oneself in altruistic and socially constructive work, had not produced a society which could solve its basic social and material needs. Instead, "Advaita has only been worked on the spiritual plane, and that was all; now the time has come when you have to make it practical," he told a Lahore audience in 1897.[80]

J. D. Salinger (b. 1919), the author of the classic novel *The Catcher in the Rye* (1951), appeared on a list of the century's most influential writers created by the *New York Times Book Review* in 1996. He is recognized "as one of the most popular and influential authors of American fiction to emerge after World War II." After practising Zen Buddhism and meeting Swami Nikhilananda, reading *The Gospel of Sri Ramakrishna* had a momentous effect on his life. In 1952 he urged Hamish Hamilton to consider publishing a British edition of *The Gospel of Sri Ramakrishna*, which never took place. In one of his short stories "Hapworth 16, 1924" that came out in 1965, J. D. Salinger had the fictional character Seymour Glass describe Swami Vivekananda as

> one of the most exciting, original, and best-equipped giants of this century. [Seymour later stated]: My personal sympathy for him will never be outgrown or exhausted as long as I live, mark my words, I would easily give ten years of my life, possibly more, if I could have shaken his hand or

at least said a brisk, respectful hello to him on some busy street in Calcutta or elsewhere.[81]

Italian born Eli R. Marozzi (1913-99) in 1953 initiated the new Honolulu, Hawaii, branch of the Vedanta Society, serving as the president from its inception, and attracting a loyal following of devotees. He taught art at the Honolulu Academy of Arts, and his art was commissioned by a number of agencies, including a 7-foot, 3,000-pound sculpture work. In 1968 he pointed out:

> In comparing Swami Vivekananda with other spiritual luminaries of his time Ramakrishna said of him: that if Keshab Chandra Sen had one power which made him famous, Vivekananda had eighteen such powers in the fullest measure; that though the hearts of Keshab and Vijaya Krishna Goswami were brightened by the light of knowledge like the flame of a lamp, the very sun of knowledge had risen in the heart of Swamiji and removed from there even the slightest trace of *maya* and delusion ... Sarada Devi, the spiritual consort of Ramakrishna, said about the Swami: "Naren is an instrument of Thakur (Master) who makes him write these words for inspiring his children and devotees for doing his work, for doing good to all the world. What Naren writes is true and must be fulfilled hereafter."[82]

Hal Bridges (b. 1918), a major in the U.S. Army during World War II, became a professor at the University of Colorado during 1953-64, and University of California at Riverside during 1964-79 in the history department. In his popular work *American Mysticism: From William James to Zen* (1970), he showed his appreciation for Swamiji by indicating:

> In the *Varieties*, William James illustrated his comments on Vedanta with quotations from the published addresses of Swami Vivekananda. This was appropriate, for Vivekananda had gained international fame in the nineties as India's Vedanta emissary to the West. The dynamic monk, a member of the Ramakrishna Order, combined in his magnetic personality the poise of the contemplative with the drive of the man of action. He first came to the United States as a delegate to the Parliament of Religions at the World's Columbia[n] Exposition in Chicago, where his bold oratory electrified large audiences and launched him upon national lecture tours....

Vivekananda has exerted a lasting influence upon mystical thought in America. From his lectures and organizational work of the nineties stems the present-day Vedanta movement in the United States.[83]

The popular writer Jacob Needleman articulated in his book *The New Religions*:

When considering the Indian influence in America, a special place must be reserved to the Vedanta Societies throughout the country. Historically, the Vedanta Society was the first Eastern religious tradition that took roots on our soil, having been brought here late in the nineteenth century by Swami Vivekananda, the chief disciple of the great Indian Master, Sri Ramakrishna. Intellectually, the influence of this form of Vedanta has been enormous. It was because of the American Vedantists—numbering some of the best minds of our time—that the East was first taken seriously here.

Jacob Needleman, from 1962 a professor of philosophy at San Francisco State University, focuses his writings on various manifestations of religion. His many books have been well received, and his skill for clearly conveying his beliefs has made him a popular guest on television and radio programmes.[84]

What follows is an assessment of Swamiji by Thomas Berry (b. 1914) [q.v.], an ordained Roman Catholic priest, and professor of religion at Seton Hall, St. John's University and Fordham University:

It was through his follower, Swami Vivekananda (1863-1902), that Ramakrishna became known to the West. A fervent disciple of Ramakrishna, Vivekananda dedicated his entire life to spreading the simple teaching of his Master, much as Plato sought to spread the teachings of Socrates. Vivekananda was the first Indian to teach Hinduism in any extensive way outside of India. At the first Parliament of Religions that was held at the Columbian Exposition in Chicago in 1893, he made a sensational impact on his audience by the spiritual vision he presented. Since Western religious movements had turned toward humanitarian preoccupations, the pure spiritual vision of the divine offered by Vivekananda provided something that was otherwise missing at this meeting of representative of the religions of mankind. Through Vivekananda, the world became aware that India was profoundly alive and spiritually creative and its religious heritage was capable of meeting and dealing with the intellectual and social challenges of the modern world.

Swami Vivekananda was well educated, read much of the Western thinkers, and appreciated much of the Western achievements, especially in the social order, but he found the West grown too materialistic and in need of spirituality which India could offer and was offering to the world.[85]

In his article "Background of Some Hindu Influences in America—The Ramakrishna Movement", Professor Norman Adams of the department of religion and philosophy at Westminster College indicated:

Swami Vivekananda, he was brilliant, charming, and possessed considerable organizational skills. His remarkable and lasting influence on many people in both the Eastern and Western world is the actual reason for the success of the Ramakrishna movement, especially in India and the United States today. Without him the movement would probably have died out or remained a minor order in no significant way different from the orthodox group of sannyasins (ascetic holy men). With him and because of him, the Order became a body of monks dedicated to education and a practical life of service to humanity.[86]

One of Swamiji's many virtues was mentioned by Claude Alan Stark (1935-1980) [q.v.], a biographer of Sri Ramakrishna:

Through all the personal adulation he received he remained loyal to his teacher and humble to the core. His renunciation was unsullied despite the temptations set in his path by sudden fame, by the large amounts of money that passed through his hands from lecture tours and Western contributors, and by the personal power he had to assume as founder of the Ramakrishna Order of monks. In fact, so complete was his renunciation that toward the end of his life he had to beg two annas from Swami Brahmananda, the president of the Order, for the price of the fare to cross the Ganges in a ferryboat.[87]

The 1981 edition of the prestigious *The Encyclopedia Americana International Edition* made this statement:

Desiring to further India's material advancement, he visited the United States in 1893 and made a deep impression at the Parliament of Religions which was held in Chicago. During a three-year stay in America and Europe that followed, he founded the Vedanta movement and adopted the name Vivekananda.

The Ramakrishna Mission, which became a worldwide organization embodying a cultural synthesis of East and West, was established by him in 1897. Although he was an ardent patriot, he dreamed of One World through the integration of science and Vedanta.

Ann Myren, co-editor (along with Dorothy Madison) of *Living at the Source: Yoga Teachings of Vivekananda* (1993), and the head of the Vivekananda Foundation in Northern California, discerned in 1984:

By the time Swamiji returned to India the first time, he was continuously in a superconscious state. He had reached this high state where he remained. We should remember these facts about the Swami's spiritual state for three reasons. First, he spoke from these high states and his teachings proceed from the direct consciousness of Truth. Second, he was able to affect those around him by the condition of his mind. When he was in samadhi in that New York class, one of his disciples called "...[it] the best lesson he ever gave her!" And third, he was able to give power when he initiated people, which greatly helped them to undertake spiritual practices such as meditation.[88]

In an article on Vivekananda in the *Encyclopaedia Britannica* (1985), an unidentified author apprehended:

He later became the most notable disciple of Ramakrishna, who demonstrated the essential unity of all religions. Always stressing the universal and humanistic side of the Vedas as well as belief in service rather than dogma, Vivekananda attempted to infuse vigour into Hindu thought, placing less emphasis on the prevailing pacifism and presenting Hindu spirituality to the West. He was an activating force behind the Vedanta (interpretation of the Upanishads) movement in the United States and England.[89]

Swami Chetanananda's *Vedanta: Voice of Freedom* (1986) is a condensed one-volume selection of the writings of Vivekananda. Concerning the work,

Raimundo Panikkar (b. 1918) of the department of religious studies at the University of California at Santa Barbara commented:

> Vivekananda's message is as timely and refreshing today as it was when he preached it. We have here not a scholarly and dry book, but a living Vedanta put forth by an extraordinary mind.

Raimundo Panikkar, a Spanish born Indian Christian, authored *The Vedic Experience* (1977) and *The Unknown Christ of Hinduism* (1981). His view is that one universal Christ has always been present in all of the major religions of the world, even before the birth of Jesus. The universal Christ, who differs from historical Jesus, is not limited to one particular religion. He is the inspirer and goal of all religions and is present in the Hindu sacrament.[90]

Concerning *Vedanta: Voice of Freedom*, Father Thomas Keating (b. 1923) made the statement:

> A significant contribution to the understanding of Vedanta in the Western world ... The powerful style of this great master [Swami Vivekananda] of Vedanta and pioneer of East-West dialogue is preserved in this succinct compilation.

Father Thomas Keating, a Trappist monk, lives at St. Benedict's Monastery in Snowmass, Colorado. Through a method called "Centering Prayer", he has made it possible for ordinary people to experience the essence of the Christian contemplative tradition, once thought to be available only for monks and nuns. There are now some 28,000 practitioners across the country and in several foreign countries practising "Centering Prayer", which is a modern application of an ancient spiritual discipline. The process of interior purification leads, if properly practised, to divine union.[91]

Dr. Eugene Irvine Taylor, an associate in psychiatry at the Harvard Medical School, is an expert on the religious psychology of William James. The author of *A Psychology of Spiritual Healing* (1997), Taylor earlier in 1986 made the following statement:

> Of particular interest was Vivekananda's definition of psychology. By it, he meant the spiritual evolution of consciousness, not simply the description of sense data and its analysis by the mind.... internal science, concentration of mind means drawing consciousness back towards one's

self—a process of involution, where consciousness is systematically detached from the various objects in the external world until the mind itself becomes the object of conscious absorption. Awareness is thereby cleansed or purified, so that consciousness, and hence personality, is transformed. This, he said, was yoga.[92]

More recently in *Shadow Culture: Psychology and Spirituality in America* (2000), Taylor emphasized the religious pluralism of Vivekananda at the 1893 Parliament of Religions:

> Dressed in a yellow turban and red mendicant's robe, erect in stature, radiating poise and confidence, and with great eloquence of speech, he immediately captured everyone's attention. "Sisters and brothers of America," he began—only to be interrupted by peals of applause that lasted for several minutes.
>
> In his message, he emphasized first that the religions of India were not new, but actually quiet ancient. Moreover, the greatest gift India had to offer the world was the twofold teaching of its intensive spirituality and its widespread toleration of all faiths. In India, he said, persecuted religions from around the world have been welcomed, just as the most extreme forms of religiosity have been permitted. All religions are accepted as true and universal.[93]

Robert N. Minor, a professor and chairman of the department of religious studies at the University of Kansas, penned books on Sri Aurobindo and the *Bhagavad Gita*. In his *Radhakrishnan: A Religious Biography* (1987) he gives many examples of the influence of Vivekananda on the ideas of this renowned Indian philosopher:

> Accepting "Hinduism" or "the Hindu religion" as a reified entity as did the critics, Radhakrishnan's attitude was reversed by the work of Swami Vivekananda (1963-1902), whose definition of this reified "Hinduism" would have a lasting impact in India and abroad. Radhakrishnan's own understanding can be almost directly credited to Vivekananda. In 1963 he spoke to fellow Indians about the hope Vivekananda's work gave him: "It is that kind of humanistic, man-making religion which gave us courage in the days when we were young." ... Radhakrishnan believed, he later said, that Vivekananda and the Swami's guru, Ramakrishna (1838-86), were in touch

with the essence of "Hinduism" and, not surprisingly, Radhakrishnan's definition of "Hinduism" is almost identical with that of Vivekananda.

Vivekananda's definition of "Hinduism" was as the "eternal religion", sanatana dharma, behind all religions, that recognizes the Absolute as a state of pure consciousness identical with one's true Self and this true Self as an ineffable One without a second. The basis of the eternal religion is experience, however, not doctrines and creeds.... Not only could Radhakrishnan be proud of his fellow countryman as a defender of India, but he found in Vivekananda's definition a definition of his own which agreed with the values he had absorbed from his education ...

But the Advaita he affirmed was mediated most positively to him through the work of Swami Vivekananda. Almost fifty years later he remembered that it was Vivekananda's works that provided an existential salvation, an appreciated solution to the "depressing feeling of defeat" which resulted from taking the criticisms seriously in his student days.

Vivekananda's position placed emphasis upon a second presumption accepted from his education: the value of social ethics. Vivekananda spoke of karma-yoga, as a path of selfless service to others.... Social action had become such a basic value that they knew that it must be affirmed in their own tradition, for both social action and their tradition, "Hinduism", were true.[94]

American born Swami Atmarupananda, now of the Trabuco Monastery in Southern California, composed a series of two-dozen manuscripts for the *Prabuddha Bharata* and the *Vedanta Kesari* between 1979-98, dealing with the Christian mystics St. Francis, Brother Giles, St. Teresa and Richard Rolle, and various aspects of Buddhism. In one essay he emphasized the pragmatic aspects of Swamiji's teachings:

Associated with man's divinity is the Swami's emphasis on the worship of God in man. If it is true that man is God, our only attitude towards others can be one of worship. Ideas as taught by Swami Vivekananda are not mere abstraction, for intellectual amusement, but they are living, vital. So as one internalizes the Swami's thoughts, they become centres of power which change one's behaviour and even perception of the world. To think of man as God is to approach him with a worshipful spirit.[95]

Swami Atmajnanananda [q.v.], now the resident monk-in-charge of the Vedanta Centre of Greater Washington, D.C., translated the 16th century Vaishnava classic, Jiva Gosvamin's *Tattvasandarbha* (1986). In his review of *Vedanta: Voice of Freedom* for the *Journal of the American Oriental Society*, he added the following insight:

> Vivekananda's mind was both brilliant and original. Like all great teachers, he spoke and wrote spontaneously, in a manner suited to the need of his audience ... What we find when we read Vivekananda topic by topic is a unity of thought which transcends the various ideas which he sets forth, a unity which is perhaps best explained by Vivekananda's own personality and his desire, on the one hand, to awaken and uplift his fellow countrymen, and, on the other, to spread the ancient teachings of Vedanta to a Western civilization which he felt was uniquely qualified to assimilate them.[96]

About a decade later, in his essay on "Religious Plurality and Swami Vivekananda", Atmajnanananda made the following important distinction:

> We can clearly see that for Sri Ramakrishna, and equally so for Swami Vivekananda, not only is there a clear distinction between Hinduism and the *sanatana dharma*, but that Hinduism, being one of the many different manifestations of the universal religion, is seen by them to be on an equal footing with other religions. In this sense, Hinduism, along with Buddhism, Islam, Christianity, Judaism, and other world religions are all sects within the one universal religion, termed by the Hindus *sanatana dharma*.... Vivekananda felt that each religion had its own original contribution to make, a "soul" of its own without which it could not live. Each religion thus represented a single tile in the mosaic of the universal religion without which it would be incomplete. Each was not only true but necessary.[97]

In 1988 Swami Chetanananda created the video "Vivekananda as We Saw Him", an enchanting documentary of the life of Swamiji. The story is told through ninety-one classic photographs taken of Vivekananda, and a well-done narrative, along with personal oral reminiscences from original recordings of devotees who met the Swami like Cornelia Conger, Katherine Whitmarsh, Lillian Montgomery, and Swami Satprakashananda.[98]

1990s and After

Beginning around 1990 there has been an acceleration of studies on Vivekananda and his disciples by devotees born in the United States. An American born nun, Pravrajika Prabuddhaprana, has added greatly to our knowledge of Swamiji with the publications of *The Life of Josephine MacLeod* (1990) and *Saint Sara: The Life of Sara Chapman Bull* (2002). The first volume utilizes reminiscences, conversations, letters, autobiographical notes and charming anecdotes to map out the life of this friend and life-long supporter of Swamiji. The second volume also tells us much about Saradananda in America. A great deal of original research was undertaken in these two studies.

David D. Gilmore, a professor of anthropology and head of the department at the State University of New York at Stony Brook, described

> the charismatic figure of the sage Vivekananda, a turn-of-the-century holy man activist. The founder of the Ramakrishna Order of monks, the Swami attracted a mass following in British India, foreshadowing Gandhi as a national leader.... On the one hand, Vivekananda was a confirmed yogi and spiritual advisor in the ancient sage-guru tradition. As such, he exhorted his fellows to adhere to the otherworldly preoccupations prescribed by their dharma. Yet, dismayed at India's decline into helpless colonial status, he was also a convinced believer in the efficacy of practical action, a devotee of social change, and a dedicated advocate of scientific and technological enlightenment. He and his monks were among the first holy men to go out into the Indian countryside and engage in mundane improvement activities such as building schools, wells, and hospitals and assisting relief operations during famines and epidemics.[99]

In 1992 Elva Nelson came out with *Vivekananda and his Swamis in Boston and Vicinity*. The volume also featured sections on Saradananda, Abhedananda, Paramananda and Akhilananda, and a number of pictures that were not previously published. She began coming to the Boston Centre in 1949 and has been coming ever since. Now over eighty-five years of age, the retired librarian for nine years worked on her biography of Swami Akhilananda, *A Monk for all Seasons*, that was completed in 2007.[100]

A volume came out in 1993 titled *Living at the Source: Yoga Teachings of Vivekananda* edited by Ann Myren and Dorothy Madison. After reading it Alan Arkin commented:

> The power of Vivekananda's spirit and the force of his intellect are awesome. One is tempted to be humbled by his many gifts, but his constant message in these wonderful quotations is that what he has attained is available to every one of us. It is impossible to read Vivekananda's words and not be changed.[101]

In his autobiography *Halfway through the Door* (1979), Alan relates that after 1969 the practice of meditative yoga and detachment made him more peaceful, hopeful, and he found more pleasure in life. That peacefulness is possible only in proportion to one's detachment from things. He narrated six Vivekananda lectures as video recordings, which the Vedanta Society sells to the public. During his long and varied acting career, Alan received the Golden Globe Award for best actor in a musical or comedy, the New York Film Critics Award for best supporting actor, a Tony Award, and recently a best supporting actor Academy Award for "Little Miss Sunshine" (2006).[102]

As an author of multiple writings on consciousness and transcendental meditation such as *Consciousness: East and West* (1976) and the best seller *Mind as Healer, Mind as Slayer* (1977), Kenneth R. Pelletier has made several appearances on national television. He is a clinical professor of medicine at both the department of medicine, University of Arizona, and at the department of psychiatry, University of California, San Francisco. In addition, he is chairman of the American Health Association. Dr. Pelletier expressed the view:

> For decades the wisdom of Swami Vivekananda has inspired millions of people worldwide with his spiritual teachings free of dogma and sectarianism. Now *Living at the Source* provides ready access to that inspiring wisdom for individuals seeking self-knowledge in specific areas as well as for those who are seeking a comprehensive philosophy of the highest order.[103]

In the reader *A Museum of Faiths* (1993), which is devoted to a discussion of the 1893 World Parliament of Religions, Joseph M. Kitagawa (1915-92), an expert on Japanese religions and the former dean of the Divinity School at the University of Chicago, made the following assessment concerning Swamiji:

> Under Ramakrishna, he endeavoured to translate his master's teachings into concrete measures for the reformation of Hinduism and of Hindu society. Vivekananda's neo-Vedantic belief is based on the eternalness of human soul, which is capable of becoming divine. His message to the world, as presented at the Parliament, concerned the supremacy of the eternal principle (*sanatana dharma*) of Hindu tradition as separated from its metaphysico-social principle and as exemplified by the caste dharma (*svadharma*), which is above all creeds and religions, Eastern or Western.... Understandably, his message at the Parliament for religious toleration, although reflecting his neo-Hindu perspective, was well received.

A team of about a dozen people composed of Santa Barbara nuns and devotees worked on the vast project of meticulously typing all the eight volumes of the *Complete Works of Swami Vivekananda* into a computer. The deadline set for the transcribing to be completed was 1993, the hundredth anniversary date of Swamiji's arrival in the West. This made it possible to quickly locate any word or phase in the text.[104] It was this transcription that was later used to bring out the CD "Swami Vivekananda, Life, Works, and Research" in 2001 by Advaita Ashrama.

An ordained Christian minister, Hal W. French became a professor in the department of religious studies at the University of South Carolina in 1972, and the departmental chairman during 1989-95. In *The Swan's Wide Waters: Ramakrishna and Western Culture* published in 1974, he devoted over sixty pages to Vivekananda. Later in a 1994 Commemorative Volume, French clarified:

> Vivekananda, then, appeared to have given immeasurable gifts of lasting proportions to those whom he knew in the West. Some chose the path of accepting him as guru, and this could be demanding, as with Nivedita, yet by their own testimony, richly rewarding. Others, such as Josephine MacLeod, claimed friendship, not discipleship, treasuring the independence which seemed most true to their own natures.... He communicated the wealth of its [India's] wisdom to them most authentically, through the force of his own personality, as teacher and friend.[105]

Professor French continued his interest in the Ramakrishna Order writing essays and articles on Vivekananda in relation to his use of the *Bhagavad Gita*, interpretation of Christianity, and his involvement in the Parliament of Religions.* With Arvind Sharma he coauthored *Religious Ferment in Modern India* (1981). In his book *Zen and the Art of Anything* (1999), he draws from a wide spiritual legacy, including work in the ministry and studies in Eastern spirituality. As a member of the Board of Editors, French is presently involved in the multi-volume production of the *Encyclopedia of Hinduism*.[106]

Carl Thomas Jackson, a professor of history at the University of Texas at El Paso since 1962, also held the position of dean of the college of liberal arts (1989-96). In his book *Vedanta for the West: The Ramakrishna Movement in the United States* (1994), he explains Vivekananda's importance in the Western Mission:

> The swami almost single-handedly created the Ramakrishna movement in America. He brought the movement west and gave it the direction and organizational form it has followed ever since. He founded the first Vedanta societies based on a division of functions between Indian authorities and the local followers, with the swami and Ramakrishna Math in India exercising spiritual control and American devotees responsible for financial and administrative matters. He also pioneered the method of presenting Vedanta to Americans, which combined Western-style public lectures with a traditional Hindu emphasis on individualized instruction by a guru. He initiated the first American swamis and conducted the first spiritual retreat (ashrama) at Thousand Island Park. He also moulded the message to be presented in the United States. His decision not to emphasize Ramakrishna but to dwell on philosophic Hinduism as embodied in the Vedanta has largely dominated down to the present.... The very fact that he placed such high priority on the Ramakrishna movement's American work persuaded his successors in India to commit personnel to the West that would normally have been reserved for Indian needs.[107]
>
> Swami Vivekananda revealed unusual talents. Demonstrating a fluent command of English, impressive stage manner, and gift for the memorable phrase, the Hindu spokesman was a sensation from his first address. Together with Dharmapala and Mazoomdar, he became one of the Parliament's celebrities. His blunt rejection of the stereotypical view of Hindu-

* *Prabuddha Bharata*, September 1992.

ism raised the hackles of missionary-minded Christians but attracted wide public attention.[108]

Carl Jackson's lucid and fascinating study *The Oriental Religions and American Thought: Nineteenth-Century Explorations* (1981) vividly discusses the reaction of Emerson, Thoreau and many other nineteenth-century Americans to Eastern religions and philosophy, and the influence of Asian thought on American culture. The volume received the Ralph Henry Gabriel Prize of the American Studies Association. Currently Professor Jackson is at work on a twentieth-century sequel to the earlier nineteenth-century volume, in which he will further explore American intellectual and literary interests in Asian religious and philosophical conceptions. When Jackson spoke before the Vedanta Society of Southern California in 1987, he emphasized the growing impact of Asian spirituality on Western culture and society. He said, the Ramakrishna Movement has stressed social upliftment in India, and the spiritual programme of self-realization in the West. It has produced a high quality of leadership for many decades, and offers an authentic Hinduism with emphasis on Vedanta.[109]

In review, Thomas Tweed of the University of North Carolina describes Jackson's well-written book *Vedanta for the West*, which contains an excellent bibliographic essay, this way:

> It traces the history of the Ramakrishna movement in the United States, beginning with its founding in 1894 by Vivekananda ... With admirable clarity and remarkable brevity, Jackson surveys the history of the movement and raises the most important issues in seven short chapters that consider the historical background, Indian founders, leaders and institutions, primary teachings, appeals of the movement, and its past, present and future.... This very good book should be of interest to those who study American religious history.[110]

In 1994 Swami Atmavidyananda of the Hollywood Monastery came out with a highly successful musical, the "Vivekananda Oratorio". He selected passages from the writings of Vivekananda and put them to music, utilizing six soloists and a men's chorus. It was presented as a classical Western oratorio, which is a musical composition for voices and instruments with a religious theme, without the use of costumes, scenery, or much interactive dramatic staging. In the oratorio, the spiritual journey begins by asking the question: How can we find peace, love and freedom in this world? The aspirant goes through a series of nineteen ascending stages until at last the realization of our true divine nature brings us to God and to eternal peace. At each stage Vivekananda's teachings give us the answer to the problem. Fifteen years later, this was followed by "Ramakrishna and His Teachings", with the libretto and music composed by Atmavidyananda. The acclaimed oratorio is written in the Western classical style for a mixed chorus with seven or more soloists. The oratorio presents many different facets of Ramakrishna's teachings, including three parables, using devotional songs and musical dramatizations.[111]

Vivekananda studies have been enhanced by Pravrajika Vrajaprana [q.v.] of the Santa Barbara Convent in California who published five essays in the *Vedanta Kesari* dealing with Josiah John Goodwin (1870-98), which were incorporated into the volume *My Faithful Goodwin* (1994). Goodwin took down in shorthand and transcribed many of Vivekananda's speeches that enabled his books to be published, and served as his personal secretary. Vrajaprana also came out with ten *Vedanta Kesari* articles on Sister Christine (1866-1930), which became the hundred-page biography *A Portrait of Sister Christine* (1996). The manuscript explains the life events and characteristics of Sister Christine, based on the many letters that Vivekananda sent her. This is the first biography of Sister Christine who devoted two decades to organizing the girls' school founded by Sister Nivedita. Vrajaprana also edited the anthology *Living Wisdom: Vedanta in the West* (1994), which is a collection of many finely crafted essays on Vedanta written during the Swami Prabhavananda era. It presents the essence of Vedanta in a lucid manner.

Sister Gayatriprana published a series of sixteen articles in the *Vedanta Kesari* during 1995-98, providing an interesting and detailed explanation of "How Swami Vivekananda Learned the Message of Sri Ramakrishna". She attempts to explain the logical sequence through which Ramakrishna conveyed his spiritual ideas to Vivekananda, the embodiment of Western style rationality. Currently her *Swami Vivekananda on the Vedas and Upanishads* can be downloaded free of charge on the Internet. The manuscript is composed of over 150,000 words drawn verbatim from the *Complete Works of Swami Vivekananda*. Swamiji's ideas are arranged in a complex categorical system, comprising nineteen chapters and over two-hundred topics. In this way, the reader can discover what Swamiji had to say about any of these topics. It is Gayatriprana's contention that systematizing Swamiji's ideas (which he wanted to do) makes it more evident that he was a coherent and encyclopedic thinker.[112]

Western Women in the Footsteps of Swami Vivekananda (1995) contains fifteen informative essays about the American and English women who aided Vivekananda in his work in the West. In a book review, Pravrajika Vijnanaprana provides us with a useful classification system of three "Ideal Types", whereby these women fall roughly into three groups allowing for some overlap:

> Those who introduced him to society and helped him with the immediate needs of his work—Kate Sanborn, Mrs. John J. Bagley and Sarah Farmer; those whose homes were opened to him as one of the family—Ellen Hale, Betty Leggett and Roxie Blodgett; those who dedicated themselves to his work—Sister Christine, Sarah Ellen Waldo, Sara Bull, Josephine MacLeod, Sister Nivedita, Charlotte Sevier, Alice Mead Hansbrough, Ida Ansell, and Sarah Fox.[113]

In the Preface to the ninth volume of the *Complete Works of Swami Vivekananda* completed in 1997, the publisher Swami Mumukshananda writes:

> We would like to express our gratitude to Pravrajika Brahmaprana [q.v.], under the guidance of Swami Swahananda, and the monastics and devotees at the Vedanta Society of Southern California and other American Vedanta centres, who have rendered us immense help in collecting material, editing, composing, proof-reading, indexing and in fact in everything at each stage of the project over a period of the last few long years.

Swahananda, the leader of the Vedanta Society of Southern California since 1976, has been instrumental in manifesting the creative talents of many monastics and devotees at his Centre. One example is Pravrajika Brahmaprana, a nun of over thirty-years, who worked as the editor on the ninth volume of the *Complete Works* under the supervision of the Advaita Ashrama. She utilized the talents, hard work, and generosity of about fifty monastics and devotees, many in Southern California.

Richard H. Davis formerly taught at Yale University (1987-97) and is now at Bard College as a professor of Religion and Asian Studies in New

York State. His book *Lives of Indian Images* (1997) won the A. K. Coomaraswamy Prize. In a brief summary he wrote:

> Perhaps the most renowned nineteenth-century Hindu reformer was Swami Vivekananda. He was a young member of the Brahmo Samaj when he first met Ramakrishna, a charismatic ascetic and devotee of the goddess Kali. Eventually Vivekananda became Ramakrishna's disciple, and sought to integrate within a single religious outlook the experimental devotionalism of Ramakrishna, the social agenda of the Brahma Samaj, and the nondualist philosophy of Shankara and the Advaita Vedanta. As a spokesman for Hinduism in 1893 at the World's Parliament of Religions in Chicago, he created a sensation. Building on this success, he toured the United States for three years, attracted many Western followers, and set up the Vedanta Society. Returning to India, Vivekananda founded the Ramakrishna Mission, an organization dedicated to education and social service much like Christian missions in India. Vivekananda is still celebrated as a teacher of "practical Vedanta", which scholars sometimes label "neo-Vedanta", a significant version of modern Hindu ideology. He was also the prototype of a new breed of cosmopolitan Hindu gurus who would bring their teachings to Western audiences.[114]

A lecturer in the history of religions and administrator at the centre for the study of world religions at Harvard University, Thomas L. Bryson, writing for the distinguished *Routledge Encyclopedia of Philosophy*, mentioned, "The Ramakrishna Movement, a highly successful Hindu religious and missionary order.... its understanding of Hinduism has become the standard for modern educated Indians." He summarized Swamiji's approach:

> Vivekananda convinced his contemporaries that his synthesis was fully rooted in Hinduism, that he "spoke nothing but the Upanishads". Vivekananda followed Orientalists in presenting the classic Hindu systems in Western terms. His ultimate intention, however, was to universalize key Vedantic concepts such as Brahman, Atman and moksha into a controlling framework of norms and values for the entire world.

Bryson then discusses some philosophical concepts of Vivekananda while often supplying quotations. He covers Vivekananda's ideas such as "each culture represents a unique national spirit which complemented that of other nations," "the viability of metaphysical non-dualism as a framework for cross-cultural apologetics and assimilation," and says that Vivekananda "attempted to reconcile religion and science," "linked Vedanta cosmology with Western evolutionism," taught "that religions and nations evolve and progress in history, though not without cyclical periods of decay and regression," and advocated the "Great Man theory" of history. Bryson is a lecturer in the history of religions, and administrator of the centre for the Study of World Religions at Harvard University.[115]

From 1970 until retirement in 1998, Professor David M. Miller taught courses in comparative religion, Hindu studies and Buddhist studies at Concordia University in Montreal, Canada. His principal work is *Hindu Monastic Life: The Monks and Monasteries of Bhubaneswar* (1976), co-authored with Dorothy Wertz. In a 1999 article dealing with Vivekananda's role in the modernity of Hindu monasticism, Miller emphasized:

> Swami Vivekananda was heralded by many of his followers as a Second Shankara, who, through the synthesis of the old and the new, created a New Hinduism, which was not just a "full defence of the Old Religions", as claimed by [John] Farquhar. Vivekananda's presentation of Neo-Vedantic thought and action at the World's Parliament of Religions was an attempt, like the *Bhagavad Gita* and like Shankara before him, at a creative synthesis of the old and the new, in which, traditional and modern elements were in dynamic interaction. His return to India and his attempt to institutionalize his Neo-Vedantic thought brought about a new direction in Hindu monasticism. The Ramakrishna Math and Mission became the vanguard of modernity within Hindu monasticism that sought reform compromised by revival, that demanded of its monastics a life of selfless service to others as well as spiritual enrichment of one's religious convictions and practices.[116]

Motivated by the work of Marie Louise Burke, Asim Chaudhuri, a retired engineer who has lived in the United States for forty years, put together the clear and crispy written *Swami Vivekananda in Chicago—New Findings* (2000). With meticulous attention given to details, the volume provides several new discoveries about Swamiji's activities in the states of Illinois and Indiana. For example, Asim was the first Vedantist to discover that in 1893 Vivekananda addressed a group at Jane Addams' Hull House in Chicago, and at the Unitarian Church in Hinsdale, Illinois. He also unearthed

Swamiji's lecture on the "Divinity of Man" given in Chicago on December 1893. In the Foreword of the book Sister Gargi noted:

> Outstanding among these dedicated sleuths is Asim Chaudhuri, who has supplied Swamiji's fellow devotees not only with many details, but has as well uncovered material and information that adds substantially to our knowledge. Indeed, he has unravelled a mystery that has puzzled devotees for many years and has discovered many other fascinating facts, hidden until now.... There cannot be enough books that dwell with painstaking accuracy, as does this excellent book by Asim Chaudhuri, on the details of so unique a life as Swamiji's.[117]

Asim Chaudhuri's current volume *Swami Vivekananda in America—New Findings* (2008) lucidly presents the details of Swamiji's visit to the United States. Through rigorous field research, the author does a remarkable job in uncovering many new findings, especially from previously unknown newspaper accounts of Vivekananda's lectures, and describing new facets of his encounters with the devotees, always presenting the material in an interesting way.

In the year 2000, Terrance Hohner and Carolyn Amala Kenny (d. 2007) compiled a unique volume, *Chronology of Swami Vivekananda in the West*. It is literally a day-by-day account of the life of Vivekananda in the West. From July 1893 until December 1900, the chronology records for each day: the address and city where the Swami resided, the name of his host, the location and title of the lectures he delivered, whom he corresponded with, his social engagements with the people he met, and his other key activities. Burke's six volume *Swami Vivekananda in the West: New Discoveries* is the primary source for their data. For each day's events, the page and volume number in Burke's six books are given. This book is exceptionally useful for quickly looking up factual data on Swamiji's stay in the West. Amala Kenny is the mother of Swami Vedarupananda who oversees the Vivekananda House in South Pasadena, California, and of Pravrajika Bhavaprana, a resident nun at the Sarada Convent in Santa Barbara who is in charge of the outstanding website of over one-hundred and fifty pages: www.vedanta.org.[118]

Writing for the three-volume *World Philosophers and their Works*, English born Bryan Aubrey, an independent scholar (and an author of a book on the mystic Jacob Boehme), stressed Swamiji's relation to a universal religion based on the principles of Advaita Vedanta:

As an expositor of Advaita Vedanta, the truth of which Vivekananda believed could be established by logical reasoning, Vivekananda laid out the philosophical basis for his dream of a universal religion. He envisioned a faith that would uphold differences in religious expression while honouring the underlying unity that gave rise to them. This idea, which Vivekananda developed from his master, Ramakrishna, has proved to be a powerful force in twentieth century Indian philosophical thought. It has found expression in figures such as the poet Rabindranath Tagore and the philosopher Sarvepalli Radhakrishnan. Radhakrishnan in particular was saturated in Vivekananda's thought as early as his school days, and this was not uncommon in Indian schools at his time. According to Radhakrishnan, collections of letters of Vivekananda were eagerly passed around by students in classrooms.[119]

In her book *A New Religious America: How a "Christian Country" has Become the World's Most Religiously Diverse Nation* (2001), Diana Eck expounded:

> During this time, Swami Vivekananda sowed and tended the seeds of what would become America's first Hindu organization, the Vedanta Society. Vivekananda not only was fluent in English, he also became fluent in the distinctive American idiom necessary to translate Vedanta for the West.... Vivekananda brought more than ideas; he brought a path of realization. Spiritual growth comes from inside out, he explained, like the growth of a plant. A teacher can help remove the obstructions, but spiritual growth is the flowering of one's innate oneness with God.... Not only did Vivekananda launch the Vedanta Society in America to bring Hindu spirituality to the West, he also launched the Ramakrishna Mission in India, complete with an order of monks dedicated to religious service.

Diana L. Eck, a professor of comparative religion at Harvard University, is a foremost scholar on the subject of religious diversity. She is an outspoken advocate for dialogue between religious traditions. In *Encountering God: A Spiritual Journey from Bozeman to Banaras* (1993), she makes clear, how her spirituality was enhanced by studies and travels in India. In the immensely readable *A New Religious America*, Eck explains that religious pluralism is essential to maintain stability in a country with so many diverse cultures in co-existence.[120] For Diana Eck:

> Hinduism is an imaginative, an image-making, religious tradition in which the sacred is seen as present in the visible world—the world we see in multiple images and deities, in sacred places, and in people.... Furthermore, the divine is visible not only in temple and shrine, but also in the whole continuum of life—in nature, in people, in birth and growth and death.[121]

Eugene P. Heideman (b. 1929) was a Pastor of the Reformed Church and a missionary to India (1960-70), who later became in 1977 the academic dean of Western Theological Seminary in Holland, Michigan. In *From Mission to Church: The Reformed Church in America Mission to India* (2001), the Pastor had these nice things to say about Swamiji:

> At the World Parliament of Religions, Vivekananda gave a brilliant address that affirmed the superiority of the spirituality of the East over the materialism of the West. He preached the unity of all existence, the divinity of the soul, the nonduality of the Godhead, and the harmony of religions. He called upon the followers of other religions to accept the Hindu spirit of tolerance in place of their religious exclusivisms. His evident intellectual brilliance together with his impressive manner and exotic dress gained the admiration of his hearers. No longer could India be understood as a land of ignorance and superstition. It was the place from which true spirituality and tolerance emanated. The admiration that he had earned in the West gained for Vivekananda a new respect in India. His compatriots there accepted his admonitions that they cultivate faith in themselves and accept a life of renunciation and service for the sake of national ideals.[122]

Linda Prugh (Uma), the secretary of the Vedanta Society of Kansas City, Missouri, is known in Vedanta circles for her five-hundred-page biography *Josephine MacLeod and Vivekananda's Mission* (1999). The author worked hard to research and document in detail the early history of the Ramakrishna movement in the West as well as in the East. Twice Uma went to India and met some of the old monks of the Ramakrishna Order. Many did not speak English, but she could "feel something genuine just sitting in their presence". Uma felt great admiration for them because their conversation was almost solely about God.[123] In an article in the *Prabuddha Bharata*, she mentioned Swamiji's present day influence:

> Swami Vivekananda was a true hero whose life continues today to draw devotees to the teachings of Ramakrishna and Vedanta. Swamiji was a true hero because he was a knower of Brahman, which is Reality and Truth.... As he said, he would continue to inspire the world, and today we find that the world is permeated with his message in many forms. Still, we must remember that he himself declared that it would take a long time for the world to understand the contribution he had made.[124]

In Chapter III of the present book, we had presented the interpretation of Ramakrishna's spiritual experience of Christ given by Francis X. Clooney, S.J. [q.v.], a Catholic Jesuit Priest and a professor at Harvard University Divinity School. Here we present his view of how a Catholic priest evaluates Vivekananda:

> He was eloquent and prolific. His collected works, comprised primarily of lectures recorded by followers, fill at least eight volumes. He was one of the very first Hindu teachers to travel to the West, surely the first to make a major impact on Western consciousness. In important ways he has shaped how Indians think of other religions and how Westerners think of India.
>
> Vivekananda's teachings overlap with Gandhi's, although his ideas are more philosophical and more confrontative. In his travels to the West (the contexts for most of his published writings), Vivekananda connected select Western values to important Indian concepts and values. More importantly, he noted the Western appreciation of the individual and connected this to the Upanisadic view that the Self is the ultimate reality, prized over all lesser realities. To know oneself is to be free.... There are multiple true prophets of humankind such as the Buddha, Jesus, Muhammad, and, in modern times, Ramakrishna. At a deep level they all offer the same message. Worshipping familiar deities may be helpful to some. But there is no reason either to criticize or to require such worship. Religions are rather to be judged in terms of their contribution to the self-realization of their members. The Self is simple and non-sectarian, distinctions and differences being superficial, and all efficacious religions head toward the same goal.[125]

Brian A. Hatcher is a professor in the department of religion at Illinois Wesleyan University. Specializing in the study of Indian pundits in colonial Bengal, he authored *Idioms of Improvement: Vidyasagar and Cultural Encounter in Bengal* (1996) and *Eclecticism and Modern Hindu Discourse* (1999). Hatcher teaches courses on Asian religious literature and practice, the Hindu religious tradition, Hindu-Christian encounter, Buddhism in India and Tibet, and the interpretation of religious experience.[126] According to his analysis given in the prestigious multivolume *The Encyclopedia of Religion*:

> Vivekananda's teaching of the universal truths of Hinduism and his example of a selfless love for the Indian people had an immense impact on modern Hindu discourse and apologetics in the early twentieth century, gaining appreciation and reinforcement from figures like Mohandas Gandhi (1869-1948) and Sarvepalli Radhakrishnan (1888-1975). One of his greatest legacies may be seen in the place accorded to religious experience (*anubhava*) within modern Hindu thought. As we have seen, to Vivekananda, experience was the source of truth, not books or dogma.[127]

In a section on "New Hindu Movements" in the *Encylopaedia of Women and Religion in North America*, Kathleen Erndl from Florida State University mentions American interaction with Hindu ideas and practices being divided into three historical periods:

> The second period (1893-1965) was ushered in by Swami Vivekananda, disciple of the charismatic Bengali mystic Sri Ramakrishna. Vivekananda's dramatic appearance at the World Parliament of Religions in Chicago in 1893 put a face on Hinduism and led to the establishment of the first and most influential Hindu groups in North America, the Ramakrishna Mission and Vedanta Society. Other Hindu leaders such as Paramahansa Yogananda followed Vivekananda, establishing their own centres and organizations, and multiple varieties of Hindu movements grew slowly but steadily....
>
> His speech at the Parliament made him a celebrity. His powerful personality, oratorical skills, and exotic turban and saffron robes made him a sought-after lecturer throughout the United States in the years following the Parliament. His organizational skills, and ability to synthesize the many-faceted tradition of Hinduism, led to the founding of the New York Vedanta Society in 1896, followed by others in cities across the continent. A dynamic synthesis of social service and Vedantic philosophy, his message was appealing to European Americans looking for religious alternatives.[128]

Among other things, Kathleen Erndl, a professor of South Asian religions, particularly Hinduism, as well as gender and religion, comparative studies, and Sanskrit, penned *Victory to the Mother: The Hindu Goddess of Northwest India in Myth, Ritual and Symbol* (1993).

In his six volume *Introduction to the World's Major Religions* (2006), Steven J. Rosen [q.v.], the editor-in-chief of the *Journal of Vaishnava Studies* and an author of multiple books, had this to say:

> Although virtually unknown before 1893's American Parliament of Religions Conference, at which he represented Hinduism, Vivekananda is the Hindu most responsible for the modern West's perception of the religion. A disciple of Ramakrishna, he sought to convey the rational and humanistic side of Hindu philosophy. He was chiefly concerned with creating a synthesis of East and West, of religion and science.
>
> A philanthropist with a Hindu bent, he emphasized service to humanity as among the best approaches to realizing one's unity with the Supreme. He is said to have had, like his master, direct, intuitive experience of ultimate reality. In the course of a short life of 39 years, of which only one decade was devoted to his public ministry, he contributed a number of now-classic treatises on Hindu philosophy.[129]

The same year Erik Davis, a professional writer, in his work *The Visionary State: A Journey through California's Spiritual Landscape*, in a section with large photos of Trigunatita's Hindu Temple and Prabhavananda's Hollywood Temple, writes:

> Vivekananda wowed the crowds at Chicago's epochal Parliament of Religions in 1893 with an eminently reasonable and modern brand of Vedic mind science that emphasized the nondualistic unity of spirit and the world. A handsome, lively, and fiercely intelligent man, Vivekananda travelled across the United States ... planting seeds of Vedanta, including the society in San Francisco.[130]

An English language translation of relevant portions of the Bengali book *Londone Swami Vivekananda* (*Swami Vivekananda in London*, 1937) written by Mahendranath Datta, the younger brother of Vivekananda, has been produced by Swami Yogeshananda [q.v.], the founder and head of the Vedanta Centre of Atlanta, Georgia. The manuscript of over forty-thousand words can be downloaded on the computer free of charge. Mahendra's account covers the two years 1895-96 when he lived in London with Vivekananda.

In India, some people doubt the authenticity and accuracy of parts of the book. Yogeshananda is best known as the author of *Six Lighted Windows* (1995), an extremely informative firsthand account of his personal memories of Swamis Yatishwarananda, Prabhavananda, Ashokananda, Nikhilananda, Madhavananda and Ghanananda. Being an expert storyteller, he brings out the warmth and profundity of these extraordinary souls. Yogeshananda revealed, "Whatever spirituality is, or whatever could be comprehended by me, has been revealed continually as I lived with these men."[131]

A CD put out by Vedantic Arts Recordings, *Days on Earth: A Musical Trilogy on the Life of Swami Vivekananda* (2009), affords a unique opportunity to contemplate the life and mission of Swami Vivekananda in an engaging musical setting. Composer John Schlenck, director of music for the Vedanta Society of New York, tells the story of Vivekananda with narrators, tenor soloist, chorus, and small instrumental ensemble. The libretto which draws on *The Life of Swami Vivekananda by his Eastern and Western Disciples* was created by Erik Johns (1927-2001). The universal themes that inform the libretto are paralleled by a synthesis of Western classical and world music styles into a unified musical language. The composition opens with the theme of a mother's longing for a child using a pentatonic scale.

The inspiring and uplifting musical continues through the childhood, youth, and manhood of Swami Vivekananda and closes with his directive to "Arise, awake and stop not till the goal is reached." For chorus, soloists and instrumental ensemble, John also came out with the oratorio on CD, *Ramakrishna: A Prophet for Our Time*, based on the life and teachings of Sri Ramakrishna.[132]

Of the above-quoted prominent thinkers, Hereward Carrington, Lily Adams Beck, Arnold Rowbotham, Alban Widgery, George Catlin, John van Druten, Christopher Isherwood, and Bryan Aubrey were born in England; and Frederich Spiegelberg, Eli R. Marozzi and Raimundo Panikkar on continental Europe. In summary, professional writers showed the most interest until about 1930 and then the university professors came on. Since the 1950s, over two-thirds of the tributes are from the professors, with the Vedanta devotees running second.

Concerning the literature on Vivekananda, see Appendix V for the publication dates of his writings, Appendix VI for a selected list of books and articles about him, and Appendix VII for European language translations of his books up to 1930.

In conclusion, it is evident at this time, both in India and the West, that we are undergoing a remarkable period of intellectual and cultural creativity in the study of Sri Ramakrishna and his disciples.

ENDNOTES

1 *CW*, IV:154-87.

2 *Indianapolis Journal*, May 13, 1901 on GBS.

3 *Washington Post*, May 13, 1901, p. 9 on GBS.

4 *New York Observer and Chronicle*, May 23, 1901.

5 *Pittsburgh Times*, May 24, 1901.

6 *Chicago Daily Tribune*, May 25, 1901 p. 10 on PQHN.

7 *San Francisco Call*, May 26, 1901, p. 4.

8 *The Literary World*, June 1, 1901.

9 *The Living Age*, June 8, 1901 on APS.

10 *The Watchman*, September 12, 1901, p. 18 on APS.

11 *Brooklyn Daily Eagle*, August 26, 1901. Chaudhuri2 also produced another review of *My Master* that appeared in the *Cedar Rapids* (*Iowa*) *Republican* on June 16, 1901. Chaudhuri2 pp. 333-34, 361-63.

12 In this chapter, where the [q.v.] symbol is used, the short biography of the person making the tribute is often found in Chapter III and not in this chapter.

13 *WWWA* (1960), III, pp. 341-42; *NCAB* (1916), XV, p. 194; UCLC.

14 *San Francisco Call*, December 28, 1902, p. 12.

15 *Louisville Courier Journal*, July 5, 1902.

16 *Milwaukee Sentinel*, August 15, 1902.

17 *Chicago Record Herald*, August 19, 1902.

18 *Boston Transcript*, September 24, 1902.

19 *Toledo Blade*, October 11, 1902.

20 *Indianapolis Journal*, October 13, 1902. All the six reviews are found in *GSW* (1911) p. 183 on GBS.

21 *Chicago Daily Tribune* (July 25, 1902), p. 2. The article featured a seldom seen sketch of Swamiji.

22 *Chicago Daily Tribune* (Sept. 11, 1902), p. 13; *EOAB*.

23 *Liberal Review* (1904), pp. 225-26 on GBS.

24 *DAB* (1928-1936).

25 *The Proofs of Life after Death*, pp. 253-57; *Intimations of Immortality*, pp. 85-90 on GBS.

26 *PB* (Sept. 1907), p. 168; "The Ramakrishna Movement in the West", (Jan. 1908), pp. 10-12; reproduced from *Pearson's Magazine* (Oct. 1907); *New York Times* (June 19, 1908), p. 5 on PQHN.

27 *Atlantic Monthly* (1910), pp. 220-21 on GBS.

28 *DAB* (1928-1936).

29 *PB* (Feb-Mar. 1911), pp. 48-49.

30 Hal French, *The Swan's Wide Waters: Ramakrishna and Western Culture* (1974), pp. 103, 116; F. J. Alexander, *In the Hours of Meditation* (Mayavati: Advaita Ashrama, 1925), pp. i-iii; Atmaprana, pp. 212-13, 264, 282; Prugh, pp. 343-44; Prabuddhapranaı, pp. 154-55; "A Letter from Swami Atulananda to Haridasa" (April 4, 1925), VSSC Archives; Mission, p. 773.

31 *Chicago Daily Tribune* (Nov. 17, 1912), p. 5F on PQHN; Atulananda (1988), p. 31; *DAB*.

32 Hereward Carrington, *Higher Psychical Development: Yoga Philosophy* (San Bernardino, CA: Borgo Press, 1920), pp. Index; *EOP*; *WWWA* (1976), VI, p. 70.

33 *The Wisdom of the Hindus*, ed. Brian Brown (New York: Brentano's 1921), pp. v-vi, xxi, 273-75 on GBS.

34 Walter Kenilworth, *Practical Occultism* (Boston: Badger, 1921), p. 8 on GBS.

35 Grace Seton, *Yes, Lady Saheb* (New York: Harper Brothers, 1925), pp. 307-10 on GBS; *DAB* (1956-60), Sup. VI; *ANB* (1999): *WWWA* (1960), III, p. 774.

36 *The Open Court* (1925), pp. 744-45, 754.

37 L. Adams Beck, *The Way of Power* (New York: Cosmopolitan Book Corporation, 1928), pp. 141, 178-80, 244 on GBS.

38 L. Adams Beck, *The Story of Oriental Philosophy* (New York: Farrar & Rinehart, 1928), p. 427.

39 *Books Abroad* (April 1933), p. 165; University of California. Web: texts.cdlib.org/xtf/view?docId=hb6h4nb3q7&doc.view=frames&chunk.id= div00037&toc.depth=1&toc.id=.

40 *CA* (1998), New Rev. Ser., vol. 61; Will Durant, *Our Oriental Heritage* (New York: Simon and Schuster, 1954), p. 618.

41 Londhe, #12. Will Durant.

42 Widgery (1936), pp. 43-45.

43 Centenary, II, p. 601.

44 A. Eustace Haydon, *Biography of the Gods* (New York: Macmillan, 1941), p. 123; Eustace Haydon. Web: www25.uua.org/uuhs/duub/articles/ eustacehaydon.htm.

45 Philip Rahv, *Discovery of Europe* (Boston: Houghton Mifflin, 1947), pp. 706-07 on GBS.

46 George Catlin, *Path of Mahatma Gandhi* (London: Macdonald, 1948), p. 74; *CA* (1980), vol. 85-88 on GBS.

47 Ruth Cranston, *World Faith* (New York: Harper, 1949), pp. 29-30 on GBS; *New York Times* (April 4, 1956), p. 29.

48 Sister Amiya, "Ramakrishna Monastery in America", *PB* (Jan. 1952), pp. 64-65; Sister Amiya, "Vivekananda Statue in California", *Hindustan Standard: Puja Annual* (1951), p. 125.

49 *CA* (1998), vol. 161; John William van Druten. Web: http://www.answers.com/topic/john-william-van-druten.

50 Swami Tathagatananda, *Meditation on Swami Vivekananda* (New York: Vedanta Society of New York, 1978), pre-Foreword.

51 *CA* (2004), vol. 73; *CA* (1978), vol. 73-76; *Philosophy East and West* (Jan. 1957), p. 358.

52 Swami Nikhilananda, *Vivekananda: The Yogas and other Works* (New York: Ramakrishna-Vivekananda Centre, 1953, 1996), back cover.

53 *The Review of Religion* (Nov. 1954), pp. 49-51.

54 Nikhilananda (1996), back cover.

55 *The Review of Religions* (March 1954), pp. 180-84.

56 *Philosophy East and West* (July 1955), pp. 169-70; UCLC.

57 Mercer, p. 41.

58 Frederic Spiegelberg, *Living Religions of the World* (Englewood Cliffs, N.J.; Prentice-Hall, 1956), p. 204.

59 *Philosophy East and West* (Jan. 1957), pp. 361-64; *CA* (1997), vol. 152.

60 *Sources of Indian Tradition*, comp. William de Bary, et al. (New York: Columbia University, 1958), pp. xxiii-xxv, 603, 647.

61 Kalpa Tree Press. Web: www.kalpatree.com/mlb.htm.

62 Web: www.kalpatree.com/mlb.html; *VK* (March 2004), p. 124; *CA* (2006), vol. 246.

63 *Samvit* (March 1982) pp. 34-35.

64 *Vivekananda the Great Spiritual Teacher* (Calcutta: Advaita Ashrama, 1995), pp. 194-95; *PB* (Dec. 1986), pp. 612-19.

65 Burke, V, p. 304.

66 Swami Tathagatananda, *Meditation on Swami Vivekananda* (New York: The Vedanta Society of New York, 2004), pre-Foreword.

67 Yale, p. 55.

68 Eleanor Stark, *The Gift Unopened* (Portsmouth, NH: Peter E. Randall, 1988), back cover.

69 Vidyatmananda6-1.

70 Vidyatmananda6-3; *Global Vedanta* (Summer 2000), p. 16.

71 *Swami Vivekananda Centenary Memorial Volume* (Calcutta: Swami Vivekananda Centenary, 1963), p. 529.

72 *DAB* (1994), Sup. IX, pp. 717-19; Vincent Sheean, *Lead, Kindly Light* (New York: Random House, 1949), pp. 96, 227, 308-54; *VK* (July 1969), p. 159; (Feb. 1970), pp. 433-34; *PB* (May 1955), p. 232.

73 *DAB* (1994), Sup. IX, pp. 717-19.

74 *BRMIC* (March 1963), p. 101; *WWIA* (1996), p. 1276.

75 Beatrice Lamb, *India a World in Transition* (New York: Frederick A. Praeger, 1963), p.119; *CA* (1969), 1st Rev., vols. 5-8.

76 *PB* (Sept. 1963), pp. 476-77; *CA* (2001) New Rev. Ser., vol. 94.

77 *PB* (Dec. 1963), p. 600.

78 *PB* (May 1964), pp. 42-43.

79 William O'Neill and Kenneth Jackson, eds., *The Scribner Encyclopedia of American Lives Thematic Series: The 1960s* (New York: Charles Scribner's Sons, 2003); *New York Times* (Nov. 22, 1997), p. D16.

80 Charles Heimsath, *Indian Nationalism and Hindu Social Reform* (Princeton, NJ: Princeton University Press, 1964), pp. 28-29; *CA* (1976), 1st Rev., vols. 17-20.

81 *The New Yorker* (June 12, 1965), p. 6; Ian Hamilton, *In Search of J. D. Salinger* (New York: Random House, 1988), pp. 127-29, 134; Pravrajika Vrajaprana, *PB* (Feb. 2000), pp. 109-15; *EWB*.

82 Ghanananda, pp. ix-x, 11-12; Eli R. Marozzi. Web:http://starbulletin.com/1999/09/08/news/obits.htm.

83 Hal Bridges, *American Mysticism* (New York: Harper & Row, 1970), p. 73; Tathagatananda2, p. 417; *WWIA* (2006).

84 Tathagatananda (2004), pre-Forward; Jacob Needleman, *New Religions* (Garden City, NY: Doubleday, 1970), p. 213; *CA* (2003), New Rev. Ser., vol. 115.

85 Thomas Berry. *Religions of India: Hinduism, Yoga, Buddhism*, Bruce (New York: Bruce, 1971), pp. 69-70 on GBS.

86 Norman Adams, "Background of Some Hindu Influences in America—The Ramakrishna Movement", *Jr. of Ecumenical Studies* (1972), pp. 321-22.

87 Stark, p. 139.

88 *PB* (Feb. 1984), p. 55.

89 *The New Encyclopaedia Britannica* (Chicago: Encyclopedia Britannica, 1985), XII, p. 409.

90 Swami Chetanananda, *Vedanta: Voice of Freedom* (St. Louis: Vedanta Society of St. Louis, 1986), back cover; *CA* (1996), New Rev. Ser., vol. 51; Raimundo Panikkar, *The Unknown Christ of Hinduism* (Maryknoll, N.Y: Orbis Books, 1981), pp. 2-3, 18-20, 24-26, 29-30, 49, 169.

91 Chetanananda (1986) back cover; Father Thomas Keating. Web: http://www.thecentering.org/therapy.htm.

92 *PB* (Sept. 1986), p. 383; *WWIA* (2008).

93 Eugene Taylor, *Shadow Culture* (Basic Books, 2000), pp. 185-86 on GBS.

94 Robert Minor, *Radhakrishnan: A Religious Biography* (SUNY, 1987), pp. 13-14, 133 on GBS.

95 *VK* (Nov-Dec. 1987), p. 516.

96 *Journal of the American Oriental Society* (1989), p. 171.

97 S. Elkman, "Religious Plurality and Swami Vivekananda", in Franco and K. Preisendanz, *Beyond Orientalism* (Atlanta, GA; Rodopi, 1997), pp. 509-10.

98 Vedanta Catalog. Web: http://www.vedanta.com.

99 David Gilmore, *Manhood in the Making* (Yale University Press, 1990), p. 184 on GBS; *CA* (1991), vol. 133.

100 Web: www.wickedlocal.com/ipswich/archive/x43068916/BOOK-REVIEW-A-Monk-for-all-Seasons.

101 Ann Myren and Dorothy Madison, *Living at the Source: Yoga Teachings of Vivekananda* (Boston: Shambhala, 1993), back cover.

102 CA, vol. 112, pp. 30-32; *International Dictionary of Films and Filmmakers* (Detroit: St. James Press, 2000), III, pp. 33-35.

103 Myren and Madison (1993), back cover; *CA* (1990), New Rev. Ser., vol. 29; Web: www.bigspeak.com/kenneth-pelletier.htm.

104 Email from the Santa Barbara Convent to the Vedanta Archives (Aug. 17, 2005).

105 Vivekananda, pp. 731-32.

106 University of South Carolina Department of Religious Studies. Web: http://people.cas.sc.edu/frenchh/frenchcv.html; University of South Carolina. Web: www.cas.sc.edu/RELG/facbios/french.htm.

107 Jackson, pp. 35-36.

108 Carl Jackson, *The Oriental Religions and American Thought* (London; Greenwood Press, 1981), p. 249.

109 UTEP, Department of History Faculty. Web: http://academics.utep.edu/Default.aspx?tabid=4649; Brahmacharini Vidya, "A Loving Tribute", *VK* (Oct. 1987), pp. 409-10; Letter from Carl Jackson to the Vedanta Archives (July 27, 2005).

110 *The Journal of American History* (June 1995), pp. 286-87.

111 "Vivekananda Oratorio" (Oct. 8, 1994), VSSC Archives; Email from Swami Atmavidyananda to the Vedanta Archives (July 29, 2005); *Vedanta Voices* (Jan. 2009); (Sept. 2009).

112 Hindu Academy Vivekananda Centre London. Web: www.vivekananda.btinternet.co.uk/veda.htm.

113 *VK* (June 1997), pp. 237-39.

114 *Religions of India in Practice*, ed. Donald Lopez (Princeton, NJ: Princeton University Press, 1995), pp. 47-48.

115 *Routledge Encyclopedia of Philosophy* (New York: Routledge, 1998), pp. 39-41 on GBS.

116 David M. Miller, "Modernity in Hindu Monasticism: Swami Vivekananda and the Ramakrishna Movement", *Journal of Asian and African Studies* (Feb. 1999), pp. 111ff; UCLC.

117 Chaudhuri1, pp. 14-15.

118 Hohner; Stavig2, ch. IX. An updated version of Hohner and Kenny's study can be found on the Web: www.vedanta.org.

119 *World Philosophers and their Works*, John Roth ed. (Pasadena, CA: Salem Press, 2000), III, pp. 1935-36.

120 Diana Eck, *A New Religious America* (San Francisco: Harper San Francisco, 2001), pp. 98-100; *CA* (2006), New Rev. Ser., vol. 143.

121 Londhe, #325. Diana Eck.

122 Eugene Heideman, *From Mission to Church* (Grand Rapids, MI; Wm. B. Eerdmans, 2001), pp. 383-84 on GBS; *CA* (1978), vol. 69-72.

123 Kansas City Interfaith Council Members' Biographies. Web: www.cres.org/oldifc/biography.htm.

124 L. Prugh, "Vivekananda: Conqueror of Death!" *PB* (Aug. 2002), p. 405.

125 Francis X. Clooney, "Hindu Views of Religious Others: Implications for Christian Theology", *Theological Studies* (2003), pp. 320-21.

126 Illinois Wesleyan University. Web: www.iwu.edu/~religion/hatcher.htm.

127 *The Encyclopedia of Religion*, ed. Lindsay Jones (Detroit: Thomson Gale, 2005), XIV, pp. 9630-31.

128 *Encylopaedia of Women and Religion in North America* (Bloomington: Indiana University Press, 2006), II, pp. 667-68.

129 Steven J. Rosen, *Introduction to the World's Major Religions* (Westport, CT: Greenwood Press, 2006), VI, p. 126.

130 Erik Davis, *The Visionary State* (Chronicle Books, 2006), p. 83 on GBS.

131 Hindu Academy Vivekananda Centre London. Web: www.vivekananda.btinternet.co.uk/veda.htm.

132 *American Vedantist* (Fall 2009), pp. 34-36; It can be purchased online from amazon.com. Inquiries can be sent to VedWestCom@gmail.com.

PART IV

WESTERN ADMIRERS OF THE OTHER DISCIPLES OF SRI RAMAKRISHNA

Swami Saradananda

CHAPTER XIV

SWAMI SARADANANDA

Swami Vivekananda made a request for Swami Saradananda (1865-1927) to come to the West to carry on the activities that he had initiated. Saradananda felt he was not competent to lecture before Western audiences and sought out Holy Mother's advice in Jayrambati. She told him, "My child, be not afraid. You should go to the West. Sri Ramakrishna will protect you. Sri Ramakrishna will be with you wherever you go. He will always look after you and shield you from all dangers and difficulties."[1]

For the occasion of the celebration of Sri Ramakrishna's birthday, the New York students of Vivekananda sent a telegram to the Swamis at Alambazar Math on February 22, 1896. In the reply letter written by Swami Ramakrishnananda from the Alambazar Math in Baranagore, he provided the students with the following introduction to Saradananda who was then still in India:

> This new Swami, if it be the desire of his leader at a future date to transfer him to your quarters, is sure to gain your hearts in no time, not of course by those dazzling faculties which especially mark out Vivekananda as a power among nations, but by his sweet & amiable character, diffusing peace & love wherever he goes. In him you will find a man who is void of all the vanities of the world. He is sure to carry out the onerous duty laid upon him with great credit.[2]

In March 1896 the Swami set sail for England. While in the Mediterranean Sea, a hurricane pounded the ship. Saradananda recalled:

> Some were crying; some were running here and there in fear; some were shaking with nervous excitement. The whole scene was frightening, but I

was not afraid in the least. My mind was steady and calm as the needle of a compass.[3]

It is not entirely clear if the following event occurred in 1896, or during his return trip to India when he visited Rome in the last week of January 1898:

> When the ship stopped in Rome, he went to visit Saint Peter's Cathedral. Standing in front of the sanctuary, his mind became absorbed in his previous incarnation, and he lost outer consciousness for some time (Ramakrishna had said that he and Shashi [Ramakrishnananda] had previously been companions of Christ).[4]

On April 1, the thirty-year-old Swami Saradananda arrived in London and stayed at the residence of Edward Sturdy. He aided Sturdy in his translation of some Sanskrit works into English, including the book *Narada's Bhakti Sutras*, which was eventually published. Swami Vivekananda came to London from America on April 20th, remaining in England for about three months. Saradananda informed Swamiji about all the news concerning their brother disciples in India. As stated in Chapter I, Saradananda made a major contribution by supplying a great deal of biographical material for Max Müller's *Ramakrishna His Life and Sayings*. This was thirteen years before he first serialized in part the more complete biography of Ramakrishna, which appeared in the *Udbodhan* of 1909. Saradananda also sent a letter to the *Brahmavadin* of June 6, 1896 describing Vivekananda's activities in England, which also appeared in the *Indian Mirror* of June 19.[5]

Though Saradananda remained in the West for less than two years, he received many tributes. His courteous nature drew people to him, since he was incapable of hurting other people's feelings in any way. On May 18, the young Josiah John Goodwin (1870-98) [q.v.] wrote to Sara Bull that Saradananda is

> of a retiring, modest nature ... but has evidently given his whole energies toward realization, & I should say had made enviable progress on the way. He is an able Sanskrit scholar, speaks quite as good English as Swami V., & has a very intimate knowledge of the Vedanta as our Swami, although in a combative sense probably he is not so strong. Raja Yoga however he is thoroughly competent to teach. He was with Swami V. for six years, & says

he owes the greater part of his knowledge to him. He has been a Sannyasin about ten years.... To sum up, he is a good man, in the best sense of the word, & I find his presence & association with him, almost, if not quite, as helpful as I do that of the Swami Vivekananda. He will, I have not the least doubt, succeed in endearing himself to his class.[6]

Sara Bull suggested that Saradananda come to America from London during the summer and participate in the Greenacre Conference. On May 18th Josiah Goodwin informed Mrs. Bull:

> Most undoubtedly the only plan is that the Swami Saradananda should be entirely under the care of Dr. Janes. The Swami Viv. has the highest opinion of Dr. Janes, both as regards his ability to make Swami Sar. comfortable, & as to his wisdom in the conduct of the work.

The saintly Lewis Janes (1844-1901) [q.v.], a major supporter of the Vedanta movement in America, no doubt fulfilled Swamiji's expectations. He played a crucial role in finding speaking engagements before large audiences of well-educated people for Swamis Saradananda, Abhedananda, and Turiyananda. For years he was the president of the Brooklyn Ethical Association, director of the Cambridge Conferences, cofounder and director of the Monsalvat School of Comparative Religion at Greenacre, and in 1899 became the president of the Free Religious Association.[7]

During the month of June 1896, the youthful John Fox (1872-1960) [q.v.] often spoke with Saradananda while they were living in London. John Fox wrote to Sara Bull, giving her these two impressions of the Swami (the first on June 21):

> I like Saradananda very much. He is exceedingly kind and thoughtful of other people, very quiet and reserved usually, though not without humour. From his clearness in answering questions and readiness to help, I think he will succeed as a teacher.[8]
>
> I had a long conversation with him the other evening and found him very clear in his answers and explanations. Being fresh from his practice, he ought to be able to explain Raja Yoga well. He speaks English well, is very quiet in disposition, seldom speaking unless spoken to.[9]

Swamiji wanted Saradananda to go to the United States to carry on the American work he initiated. Saradananda was reluctant, but Swamiji encouraged him by telling him, "Look, I have already lectured there. You just teach them a little *Gita* and Upanishad, and answer their questions. That is all." After living in London for less than three months, at Swamiji's request, Saradananda and Josiah Goodwin, a stenographer, arrived in New York on July 2 or 3, 1896. Soon after his arrival, on the 7th Saradananda lectured at the Monsalvat Conference of Comparative Religions held at Greenacre near Eliot, Maine. Because of rain he spoke in a large tent. Other noted guest speakers on the roster at Greenacre were Lewis Janes, Virchand Gandhi, a representative of Jainism, Horatio Dresser, Paul Carus, Sara Bull, Rabbi Charles Fleischer, and the Episcopal clergyman William Guthrie. Saradananda also taught a morning class and held a sunset service under the revered pine tree where Swamiji appeared two years earlier.[10]

Concerning his initial lecture at Greenacre, the *Boston Evening Transcript* of July 8 reported:

> The first lecture of the Swami Saradananda was listened to with great interest. In spite of the severe storm, about seventy persons were present. The Hindu teacher has the impassive fascination of his race and, although this was his first public lecture in the English tongue, he made himself heard and understood with great clearness and force. His theme, "The Philosophy of the Vedanta", though at first thought remote from common interest, was developed with practical and pertinent application to popular thinking. The philosophy of the Vedanta aims to answer the great question, "What is that thing by learning which we learn the whole truth?"...
>
> [There was then] an interesting discussion in which the profound principles were brought out with still more telling force.

The bulk of the newspaper report dealt with the content of the Swami's speech.[11]

His second address on the subject of "Raja Yoga" was presented under a large pine tree with Saradananda sitting at its base. It was followed by a question and answer session. Another American newspaper expressed its appreciation of the Swami in the following words:

> To hear a native teacher speak of far-off ideas and theories is in itself a stimulus and refreshment to the mind. It is like reading in the original what

one first became familiar with through a translation. The familiar has a new vitality, a power of meaning inexpressibly potent, and an essential force when it comes direct from the spring. We see one who has been through the severe course of speculative discipline required of Hindoo teachers, is himself his best exponent of its significance, one who, with the confidence and assurance of the adept, not so much argues as declares his faith.[12]

In covering Saradananda's question and answer session, the *Standard Union* of Brooklyn, New York, went into detail. The article begins by stating:

> Among the notable attractions of Greenacre are the philosophical conferences of Swami Saradananda of India ... He is a young man, somewhat darker in complexion than Vivekananda, with a good command of the English language, and a thorough understanding of the subtleties of Hindu thought. His features are classical in outline. His gentleness of disposition and purity and devotion of character have endeared him to all who have come within the circle of his influence.[13]

From Greenacre, Josiah Goodwin informed the *Brahmavadin* concerning these lectures and classes in a letter dated July 23, 1896:

> Swami Saradananda is proving wonderfully successful in seconding those efforts, and in confirming in this religious philosophy large numbers who were attracted to the Vedanta by the other Swami's [Vivekananda's] eloquence and example, but who had not had sufficient opportunity for personal contact to become what I would call, *established in it*.... The Swami Saradananda began his work on July 7th, with a lecture in which he gave a general presentation of the Vedanta, with the particulars of which I need not deal, excepting to add that he not only received a thoroughly sympathetic hearing for this, his first lecture in the West, but impressed people with the feeling that both from his manner, and the matter of his address, he had much to give them. The following day he began a series of classes on alternate weekdays in *Raja Yoga*. On the intervening days he holds a devotional, or meditation class, which is sincerely appreciated, and in the hours which are not occupied in this way much of his time is taken up with private instruction in practical Yoga, to many who are systematically and earnestly pursuing this method.... He has one objective at heart, to

assist and to develop the work of his *Guru Bhai*, and the unassuming and yet energetic manner in which he is doing his work is creating a profound impression.[14]

On August 8 Vivekananda, writing from Switzerland, informed Josiah Goodwin, "I am very glad at the reception the Swami has met with, also at the good work he is doing. Great work requires great and persistent effort for a long time. Neither need we trouble ourselves if a few fail."[15]

The Swami gave his final talk on September 2 with the *Boston Evening Transcript* telling its readers:

> This morning was the Swami's last talk, and as the privileges of the pine tree were not to be had, the group of disciples gathered by the roadside under the trees, presenting a unique picture to the passers-by who, on foot or in carriages, paused in unsurprised silence to hear the words of the teacher. The topic, which was the love of God and the steps in the ascent to that perfect love which is without greed or fear, the scene, and the whole atmosphere of the occasion made one understand as never before how the Master in Galilee went about teaching and preaching the kingdom of God, and how the people heard him gladly.[16]

The owner of the Greenacre property, Sarah Farmer (1847-1916) [q.v.] told Sara Bull, "I think this summer is to see a wonderful work. The coming of the Swami Saradananda is the token of it, and I feel that it is to you we owe this great privilege, under God." After two months, on September 2 the Greenacre Conference came to a close. In a correspondence sent to India on October 1, Sarah Farmer related to Vivekananda that Saradananda

> has fulfilled all the high words you spoke of him, and has been a great inspiration to us. His dignity of bearing and gentle courtesy won friends on all sides, and did not hear criticism of any kind. As it was with you, the Vedanta philosophy seemed to meet all needs. The Swami Saradananda seemed ready to meet questions of all kinds, and his patience knew no bounds. As he gained confidence, and understood our people better, he became quite fluent in speech.[17]

As a sign of appreciation, the following was written in a pamphlet published by E. T. Sturdy:

Swami Saradananda, of the same brotherhood of faith as the Swami Vivekananda, is highly commended for his personal qualities and ability as a teacher by competent persons in England, where he has been teaching for some time under the auspices of Mr. E. T. Sturdy, of High View, Caversham Reading. The managers of the Greenacre School of Comparative Religion are deeply indebted to Mr. Sturdy for his kindness in giving the Swami Saradananda leave of absence to assist in the Greenacre work.[18]

Reverend William Norman Guthrie (1868-1944), a speaker at the Greenacre Conference in Maine in the summer of 1896, recalled:

> In the moonlight we sat, Swami Saradananda and we two friends, while our baby, a great pet of his, slept soundly, close wrapped in a warm shawl. Under a stunted pine he chanted for us—and enchanted us—and about midnight we rowed home.... That was the prelude to our friendship with Swami Paramananda.

The Reverend put together a short tribute to Lewis Janes after his passing away in 1902. He held the position of Episcopalian Rector at the prestigious St. Mark's-in-the-Bouwerie Church in New York City from 1911 until 1937. In addition, he taught modern languages and literature at the University of the South, Kenyon College, and at the University of Cincinnati. Swami Paramananda addressed Guthrie's Episcopal congregation in New York on more than one occasion in 1915, 1919-20, and 1922. The Reverend wanted Paramananda to open a branch Centre of his Vedanta Society in a building overlooking St. Mark's churchyard. Paramananda passed up the offer, one reason being there was already a Vedanta Society in the city of New York. After Paramananda's passing in 1940, Reverend Guthrie wrote in part:

> How fine and pure and humble at heart, how gentle, how highbred and noble he was, you know. Never did he go back from his vision of one human religion—uttering itself diversely in different ages and races, but to the same effect; and he most winsomely communicated his conviction, his hope, his benediction to all alike with the blended wealth of inspiration and holy experience. My wife and I feel we have lost a beautiful friend.[19]

Writing for *Outlook*, the American author Helen Stuart Campbell (1839-1918) gave her impression of Greenacre, revealing among other things:

> Personally, having deep affection for the Concord School and its memories, I went to Greenacre with some inward misgivings. But in camp and inn, in the big tent which served as auditorium under the great pine where the Swami Saradananda taught his morning class or held his sunset service—at every turn where people came together, one was at once conscious of a peculiar sweet friendliness and open-mindedness. There are distinguishing traits in the character of the organizer [Sarah Farmer], and they are strong enough to have infused themselves into the life and spirit and all external expression of both at Greenacre.[20]

During her younger years Helen Campbell penned books for children (1862-70), and then switched to philanthropic volumes and articles on social reform. As an activists and university professor in the home economics movement, she was particularly interested in informing the general public about *The Problems of the Poor* (1882) and *Women Wage Earners* (1893). Her knowledge of home economics was used to improve the lives of poor working women in urban ghettos by stressing sanitation, diet, nutrition, health care and budget management.[21]

After departing from Greenacre, Saradananda went to Sharon, Massachusetts, where Sara Bull's daughter lived. During September 17-28, he spent some pleasant days at the Forest Hill Hotel with Sarah Farmer and Emma Thursby. The resort hotel was located in the White Mountains of New Hampshire near the small town of Lisbon. They also visited Crawford Notch on October 2. Six days later, on October 8th Vivekananda wrote to Sarah Waldo, "Of Saradananda, the blessing of the greatest Yogi of modern India is on him—and there is no danger."[22] That day Saradananda sent a letter to Mrs. Bull from Lisbon, c/o Mrs. Augustee Foster.[23]

During that time the Swami made a brief visit to New York. On October 21 they held an informal reunion in honour of Saradananda at the house of Mary Phillips in New York. There he became acquainted with Swamiji's old friends like Sarah Waldo, Emma Thursby and William Flagg. Lewis Janes wrote to Sara Bull:

> We shall be glad to have the Swami Saradananda with us over Sunday. Our quarters are a little cramped, the house is full, but I trust we can make him comfortable. The children, as well as Mrs. Janes and myself, will be delighted to see him.

The *New York Tribune* of October 24 announced Saradananda's upcoming speech at the Brooklyn Ethical Association saying that the audience will

> listen to Oriental wisdom from the lips of a true Sannyasin—one who is not permitted to handle either silver or gold, who can posses no property, not even a home, and who is devoted to the acquisition and teaching of spiritual truths. The Swami Saradananda is a young man, born to the Brahmin caste, but who has risen above all caste distinctions in taking the vows of a Sannyasin. He is not only a master of the intricacies of the Vedanta philosophy, but can express his thought in good English speech.

On Sunday evening October 25, according to the *Brooklyn Standard Union* and the *Brooklyn Eagle*, a lecture "was given at the Pouch Mansion [of the Brooklyn Ethical Association] ... to a large and appreciative audience by the Swami Saradananda of India upon 'The Ethical Ideals of the Hindus.'" The *Greenacre Voice* of the 29th mentioned, "Swami Saradananda, the man with the holy face and the atmosphere of peace, spoke in Brooklyn, N.Y." In another letter from Lewis Janes to Mrs. Bull, he wrote, "I like the Swami's lecture very much. It will be an admirable contribution to our series and I am sure will be appreciated both in Brooklyn and in Cambridge."[24]

From New York City Lewis Janes reported to Sara Bull:

> The Swami had a crowded house last night. The lecture was well received by those who heard it, but his voice was hardly equal to the room and audience. He has decided to remain until Friday and speak at our Members' Meeting Thursday evening [October 29]. He will also see our New York friends and I hope harmonize their troubles. We enjoyed the day with him greatly.[25]

Josephine MacLeod appeared at his Brooklyn lecture and wrote to Sara Bull on November 1 of her favourable impression of Saradananda:

> I was amazed at his grasp of English and much pleased with his presentation of Vedanta. I thought him a fine man, with the poise essential to represent Vivekananda anywhere. We had a charming evening together, and I can quite realize the Cambridge School will make a firm foothold for itself if such men represent the different points of view.[26]

On the 28th of October a large audience gathered to hear him on the occasion of the opening for the new season of the New York Vedanta Society. A New York student wrote to the *Brahmavadin* on December 19 of Saradananda's success as a public speaker:

> The Swami's reputation had preceded him, and among his hearers were those who had learned to love his gentle and devoted character at Greenacre.... He held the close attention of his audience to the end of his lecture, which was given without notes, and answered questions for an hour later before the people were willing to disperse.

The Swami was a guest of Sarah Waldo for a few days in New York City. The "Discourses on Jnana Yoga" are recorded notes taken down by her in longhand from Vivekananda's classes on jnana yoga in New York and Thousand Island Park. An editorial note in the *Complete Works*[27] states, "Swami Saradananda while in America (1896) copied them out from her notebook," indicating that he played a role in their being published.[28]

Saradananda remained in residence at Mrs. Sara Bull's spacious house in Cambridge, Massachusetts, during the last two months of the year. In his letters he often addressed her as "Granny", a grandmother that she was, and referred to himself as "the monk, your boy". She was born fifteen years before him. Sara Bull compared Swamiji to the brilliant scorching sun and Saradananda to the cool, refreshing moon.[29] In the first week of November he spoke on the "Ethics of the Vedanta" at the Home Congress held in Boston. There were four other speakers, viz. Dr. S. M. Crothers of Cambridge, Professor Joseph Le Conte, a well-known geologist from the University of California in Berkeley whom Vivekananda once tried to make contact with in 1900, Jehanghier D. Cola of Bombay, and the familiar Lewis Janes.[30]

On the 12th of November he lectured at the Procopeia Club in Boston. John P. Fox stayed at the Studio House with Saradananda while Sara Bull was away. In the latter part of December he wrote to her, "Swami's last lecture at the Procopeia was very good indeed, as Mr. Cola can tell you.... at the close a rising vote of thanks was carried, and many expressed the hope of having Swami address the club again." Jehanghier D. Cola of Bombay represented Zoroastrianism (the religion of the Parsees of Western India) at the Chicago Parliament of Religions in 1893 and spoke at Mrs. Bull's Cambridge Conferences on December 13.[31]

While Saradananda was staying with Mrs. Bull, he would have had the opportunity to meet the following guest speakers at the Cambridge Conferences: Joseph Le Conte (November 8, 1896), Lewis Janes (November 15), Josiah Royce, the illustrious Harvard philosopher (November 22), Reverend William Alger (December 6), the Transcendentalist Charles Malloy (December 9), J. D. Cola of Bombay (December 13), and Reverend Charles Everett, dean of the Harvard Divinity School and admirer of Vivekananda (December 20).[32] At the Conferences, on the 29th of November he spoke on "Ethical Ideas of the Hindus". John Fox sent a letter on December 5 to Sara Bull which read, "Swami [Saradananda] will tell you of his Thursday's [December 3] class to which Prof. [William] James, Prof. Schilling, and Dr. [William Wallace] Curry [1824-1921] of the [Harvard] Divinity School came. Prof. James asked many and all the questions." Vivekananda's younger brother, Mahendranath Datta, the author of *Swami Vivekananda in London* (in Bengali), tells us:

> In her [Sara Bull's] house was held a small Conference of Religions, to which many important people were invited. The famous philosopher Prof. [William] James and many other notables came to meet Swami Saradananda. They respected him highly and he had plenty of influence. Seeing his steady mindedness, gentleness and politeness, everyone accepted and became fond of him. In one or two letters written to Sturdy and Fox at this time, there is written: "Though he has not the brilliance of Vivekananda, he is a sadhu (of the three qualities mentioned above)." Later: "Everyone is especially fond of him."[33]

At the December 15 meeting of the Metaphysical Club in Boston, Saradananda read a paper on "Doubt to Belief", showing how the Vedanta philosophy reconciles religion and science. A report of the speech appeared in the *Journal of Practical Metaphysics* of Boston and in the *Brahmavadin* of March 27, 1897. Concerning either this lecture or an address he gave at the Metaphysical Club in March, the *Journal of Practical Metaphysics* stated, "The paper read there by Saradananda is very able and lucid and is best suited to meet the intellectual requirements of the Western people. There is a great deal of truth in what he says."[34]

A newspaper report of December 1896 summed things up to some extent, telling its readers in part:

The Swami Saradananda has interested many in the Vedanta philosophy since coming to this country, presenting the truths of that oldest philosophy and religion in the world in a clear and interesting way. Besides the Procopeia and Greenacre, he has spoken twice before the Brooklyn Ethical Association, twice at the recent Home Congress, at Hingham and Waltham, before the Boston Metaphysical Club, and at the Cambridge conferences.

Whether or not the Vedanta affords a final solution to man's problems about his present life and destiny, it surely presents fundamental truths of the nature of the universe with remarkable clearness, force and simplicity. India's great past and future part in man's progress has been but little appreciated by the Western world. But now heathen India is not only giving us her vital truths, but is showing us deeper meanings in Christianity. The Vedanta in its catholicity shames our narrow sectarianism; it shows all modes of life and worship are of value and all lead in the end to the same goal—union with God or the Absolute. .

Hindu ethics have been much misunderstood in the West. Our standards of morality are so different from those of India that the opportunity to learn the Hindu ideas from a well-informed native is very welcome. The Swami Saradananda lectured on this subject at the Brooklyn Ethical Association and the Cambridge conferences, and repeats his lecture at the invitation of the Free Religious Association at the South Congregational Church, Newbury Street, on Sunday evening, at eight o'clock.[35]

The Year 1897

In the first week of 1897, Saradananda went to New York City accompanied by John Fox. There he could carry on the Vedanta work in an organized manner, speaking five or six times per week. According to the Bulletin of the New York Vedanta Society, Saradananda spoke there from January 6 until March 4, 1897, and during the following May. He slept in a little room on the third floor with a big window facing the street, while Miss Mary Phillips took care of his meals. Mr. Walton, the owner of the house, gave him the use of the hall on the ground floor without charge. Sara Bull sent him financial support for his personal use. At the New York Centre, Saradananda delivered lectures on Sunday mornings. In addition, according to the *Brahmavadin* of March 13, 1897, "Class instruction is given on Mondays and Saturdays in the morning, and on Mondays, Wednesdays, and Fridays in the evenings in the various Yogas." In New York he made contact with Josephine MacLeod and her sister Betty Leggett, Lewis Janes, William Flagg, Emma Thursby, Mary Phillips, and Florence Adams among others.[36]

He delivered his first Sunday discourse in the New Century Hall located at 509 Fifth-Ave. The *New York Tribune* of January 11, 1897 (p. 10) devoted a fair amount of space to paraphrasing the content of his lecture. The article concludes by writing:

> The Swami Saradananda is about twenty-eight years old, a sannyasin, or teacher, who renounces all property and accepts no pay. He has the classic features characteristic of his countrymen, is above medium height, with fine shoulders and chest. He speaks English well.

After interviewing the Swami, a reporter for the *New York Sun* characterized Saradananda as a "social success" and described his introspective appearance in this interesting and revealing way:

> He is of about medium height, his shoulders are broad and his chest is deep. His head is massive and well set upon his shoulders. His features are regular and refined. His face is smooth shaven.
>
> His eyes are the most peculiar feature of his appearance. They are set very deep in his head and the pupils are cloudy. Something seems to be the matter with his left eye. It looks as if it were trying to look in behind itself all the time. His hair is black and silky. His hands are large and powerful looking. He dresses in gray, the coat buttoned up like an Eton jacket close to the neck.[37]

He also took part in outside speaking engagements, addressing the Circle of Divine Ministry in New York City on January 24, 1897. This group was affiliated with Divine Science, which was an outgrowth of Christian Science.[38]

At an unknown date, Saradananda was the guest of Francis Leggett at his Ridgely Manor country estate where he became a good friend of Josephine MacLeod. Each morning she "would ask the swami, 'Did you sleep well?' It so happened that one Sunday while Saradananda was lecturing, Miss MacLeod fell asleep. Then, while shaking hands after the lecture, he asked, 'Did you sleep well?' Both laughed heartily."[39]

In the winter of 1897, a very distinguished group of individuals sent a letter to Vivekananda in India. The group included five members associated with Harvard University. It was comprised of Lewis Janes, Professor William James, John Henry Wright, Professor Josiah Royce, J. E. Lough, Arthur Lovejoy, Rachel Taylor, Sara Bull and John Fox. Among other complimentary statements, they wrote:

> We believe such expositions as have been given by yourself [Swami Vivekananda] and your co-labourer, the Swami Saradananda, have more than a more [mere?] speculative interest and utility—that they are of great ethical value in cementing the ties of friendship and brotherhood between distant peoples, and in helping us to realize that solidarity of human relationships, and interests which have been affirmed by all the great religions of the world.[40]

One woman told Saradananda that she was being bothered by all kinds of psychic experiences in her home. He told her, "Please train your mind firmly to think thoughts that are wholesome, good, and beneficial. By invigorating thoughts alone these occult phenomena and psychic experiences can be averted." He advised her that she should every day practise self-control, read inspiring books, and meditate on the Divine Spirit. Following his advice she became a transformed woman.[41]

Saradananda returned to the Cambridge Conferences, and on March 10, 1897 his subject was the "Social Conditions and Needs of Modern India". He gave classes at the Cambridge Conferences during the month of April, and in May he spoke on the "Vedanta Philosophy". During this time he would have had the opportunity to meet the following guest speakers there: Z. Sidney Sampson, president of the Brooklyn Ethical Association (March 7), Harvard theologian Crawford Toy (March 21), Anagarika Dharmapala, a Buddhist leader from Ceylon (April 4), Harvard Sanskritist Charles Lanman (April 7), the Harvard philosopher Josiah Royce (April 18), and others.[42]

Lewis Janes tells us that Edmund Burke Delabarre (1863-1945) invited Saradananda to be a guest speaker at the Philosophical Club at Brown University in Providence, Rhode Island, sometime during the 1896-97 school year, and in addition was his host while he was in the city. Professor Delabarre taught at Brown University for forty years during 1892-1932, except for a year when he directed William James' psychology lab at Harvard University. He invented the first long-tape kymograph to record muscular movement and made the first recording of eye-movements using kymograph tape. During that same school year, Saradananda spoke at the State Normal School for women located at Framingham, Massachusetts. A Normal School offers a two-year course after graduating from High School for those planning to become a teacher.[43]

In June 1897 Saradananda met D. Evans Caswell in Melrose, Massachusetts. Caswell, a magnetic healer by profession, had formerly entertained Vivekananda in Melrose when he gave a speech there on September 22 and October 1, 1894.[44]

Between July 3 and 12, 1897, "Swami Saradananda of India" gave an address at the Profile House located at Franconia Mountains in New Hampshire. The speech was given before the Appalachian Mountain Club, which was composed of cultivated and scholarly members. Herschel Parker was a member, and later Abhedananda joined the group.[45] Saradananda spoke at the Convention of the Free Religious Association in Boston along with Lewis Janes, Sarah Farmer, Jehanghier D. Cola, Anagarika Dharmapala, Reverend Kenneth Guthrie, and others. His address on "The Sympathy of Religions" appeared in the *Journal of Practical Metaphysics* (Boston) and *Brahmavadin*. Beautiful photographs of Saradananda at Greenacre, Cambridge, and at the Free Religious Association Convention appear in the fourth volume of Burke's research work.[46]

Because of his immense popularity and his friendship with Lewis Janes, Saradananda was invited back for a return visit to Greenacre near Eliot, Maine. The Conference ran from July 1 until September 2. The Swami offered ten classes during this period on Monday and Wednesday mornings at 11:00 a.m. He also gave four lectures on the literature of India quoting many passages from the Upanishads. Other speakers on the roster that had some connection with the Vedanta Swamis included Charles E. Fay, Kate Tannant Woods, Lewis Janes, Sara Bull, Horatio Dresser, Paul Carus, and Rabbi Charles Fleischer.[47] The *Boston Evening Transcript* of July 26 published a report nearly fifteen-hundred words in length on his speech with the following introduction:

> On Wednesday [July 21] morning, under the pines, to a most attentive audience the Swami Saradananda gave his first lecture in the course on "Ideals in Literature". His subject was the "Poetry of the Vedas". What follows is a brief condensation of his most delightful and finely worded paper.[48]

In a second article of about the same length, the *Boston Evening Transcript* of August 2, 1897 paraphrases two of his speeches. There it is mentioned:

> The School of Literature was closed this week by four consecutive lectures on the Literature of India by the Swami Saradananda. Two lectures of his were especially interesting, the one concerning the Modern Indian Drama, and another the Ancient Indian Drama, Kalidasa's Sakuntala being treated in detail. His most characteristic lecture was, however, on the "Indian Epics", marked by that true sympathetic insight which his deep acquaintance with Hindu literature permits him to so well express.... The Swami then in his beautiful and expressive words proceeded to show how these mighty epics are valuable as expositions of that true art which gains its inspiration through faithful depiction of nature, and nonetheless are impregnated with moral and religious sentiment of the highest rank. They are the fountainheads from which hundreds of works of art have gained their inspiration; they have held up to the people of India lofty visions of strength and virtue to be their stay throughout the ages. Well may the seeker after knowledge approach with reverence the fields of the epics of India, for the ground which he treads is holy ground.... As the second in his course of lectures on the Vedanta, the Swami Saradananda spoke on the "Evolution and Purpose of the Cosmos" from the point of view both of Sankhya and Vedanta philosophers.[49]

The Prospectus of the Monsalvat School for the Comparative Study of Religion at Greenacre read, "August 2–September 2, 1897. Special course on the Vedanta philosophy, Sankhya and Yoga philosophy of India." Concerning Saradananda, it said, "His ability and attainments as a teacher have been abundantly established by his work in Cambridge, New York & Boston during the past winter, and at the first session of the Monsalvat School." The School was led by Lewis Janes assisted by Saradananda, Dharmapala of Ceylon, Jehanghier Cola of Bombay, Virchand Gandhi of Bombay, and Reverend F. Huberty James, professor at the Imperial University of Peking, China, who held a favourable view of Taoism and Confucianism and was martyred in China in 1900.[50]

In a résumé of the Swami's talk, the *Boston Evening Transcript* of August 14 mentioned the following, which gives us some idea of the content of his speeches:

> The Swami Saradananda delivered on Wednesday an address, perhaps his finest effort hitherto, on the Zuana [Jnana] Yoga: that culture of knowledge by which the individual self may realize its unity with the infinite self, the ocean of bliss and light.... from the divine standpoint the eternal love is playing with itself, now appearing as many and now as one, but though we cannot understand this, we may become it, by the exercise of that highest inner-consciousness which is in each ray of the Divine, and which may become transcendent by careful spiritual exercise.[51]

The January 1898 edition of the *Prabuddha Bharata* carried an article from the London based *The Theosophic Review*. Annie Besant (1847-1933) [q.v.], the English leader of the Theosophical Movement, had lectured at Greenacre on September 1, 1897. During the course of the article in an ecumenical spirit, she stressed:

> The work set on foot by Swami Vivekananda in America, England and India is progressing steadily. In America, Swami Saradananda is winning both respect and affection; we met him at Greenacre [in 1897], the peaceful resort of men and women of all faiths, and enjoyed a pleasant interchange of thought; at once learned and modest, he recommends his teachings by his life. In India various centres are being started, and Swami Shivananda has gone to Ceylon, to teach the Hindu community in that island. All who work for the revival of spirituality in India must be regarded as fellow-labourers by the students of the "Divine Wisdom", and we heartily wish God-speed to all the efforts made in this direction by the disciples of Paramahamsa Ramakrishna.[52]

We do not have precise dates for the following event. A woman referring to herself as "The Suburban Girl" (c. b. 1875) was interviewed by the *New York Times* in 1903. She lived in New York's most attractive suburb, and suggested that the study of Hindu philosophy be part of the programme for the women's club she belonged to. She added:

> When I was at school in Boston, I belonged to a club for the study of the "New Thought". The members were all literary folks, and we used to entertain all sorts of celebrities. One evening we entertained the "Swami Saradananda", who was visiting the city. Oh! He was a swell Hindu. In his long red gown and his yellow turban he was a picture. We girls just stood

around and worshipped. He had such dark soulful eyes, you know ... The Swami was a vegetarian.

In 1903, one of Suburban Girl's friends was reluctant to study Hindu philosophy; but, says the Suburban Girl, "I showed her the Swami's [Saradananda] photograph and she changed her mind instantly."[53]

German born Rabbi Charles Fleischer (1871-1942) and Ralph Waldo Trine also spoke at the "New Thought" gathering in Boston along with the Swami. Rabbi Fleischer was in charge of the Temple Israel in Boston from 1894 to 1911. He then organized and became the leader of the Sunday Commons in Boston, a lecture series featuring outstanding speakers on contemporary topics from 1911 until 1922. In addition, he edited two magazines, *Democracy* and the *N. Y. American*. The Rabbi appeared along with Saradananda at the Greenacre Conference of August 1897, and with Abhedananda and others at the annual meeting of the Free Religious Association held at the Boston Museum on May 31, 1901. Rabbi Fleischer attended the seventy-five member Appalachian Mountain Club meetings, as did Abhedananda and Lewis Janes. The ten-day event was held in early July 1899 in North Woodstock, New Hampshire. Many years later on January 22, 1933, Charles Fleischer was a guest speaker in a celebration held for Vivekananda at the Vedanta Society of New York. At that time he told the audience, "He would never forget Swami Vivekananda as a man who had completely broken down the walls of narrow sectarianism." Fleischer "asked that the teachers of the East use the simplest terms to expound their great and rational principles of spirituality to the West."[54]

Swami Abhedananda travelled from England to the United States, arriving there on August 6, 1897 to take charge of the New York Centre. On September 27 Saradananda came from Boston to New York City to meet Abhedananda, his brother disciple. He accepted Saradananda's advice that to be successful in his work, he should set an example by being a strict vegetarian and a teetotaller. Abhedananda wrote in his diary:

> This was the first time I met him after he had left India nearly two years ago. I spent the whole day with him talking on different subjects and especially on the work he was doing in America. It was a great delight to me to meet my beloved Gurubhai after such a long time in a foreign country.... Swami Saradananda nursed me with the greatest brotherly love that I have ever heard of, for four months at the Alambazar Math when I had

seven operations on my foot ... many other incidents of our spiritual lives together in India became vivid in my memory when I met Swami Saradananda in New York. It was a day of unbounded joy and peace which I can never forget.[55]

In a letter dated October 4 addressed to Sara Bull, Saradananda wrote, "I went to see Felix Adler's school or, rather, the Ethical Society for the working men, and am invited to speak to the children some Monday while I am here. I am delighted to see the manual work department of the school." Adler's (1851-1933) Ethical Culture School in New York City emphasized manual training for its students. On the 12th he wrote to Sara Bull, "I am now looking into all sorts of schools and improved methods of training, so that when I go over to India, I might help a little in that direction. Tomorrow we go to see one of the best electrical factories and the day after, the Pratt Institute in Brooklyn."[56]

A Bulletin issued by the New York Vedanta Society in March 1897 stated that Swami Saradananda will return to New York at the beginning of October to teach and lecture until January 1898. On October 4 he wrote to Sara Bull:

> I have decided now once & for all to have nothing to do with the N.Y. work, but always to be their personal friend and I am doing it every day. I will always hold the attitude of an elder brother or father towards them, though they have perfectly misunderstood me.

While in New York, Saradananda had a falling out with some members of the Vedanta Society, who apparently believed he was under the control of Sara Bull. They thought when Saradananda arrived in the United States, he would come directly to the New York Centre and not spend nearly two months at Greenacre. It was the idea of Mary Phillips, Sarah Waldo, and others that he should be centred in New York, which had no Swami at that time, and spend far less time in Cambridge and the surrounding area.[57] Saradananda, like Vivekananda before him, and Abhedananda after him, did not want to permanently confine himself to a small group of devotees. Consequently, to spread the message of Vedanta, Saradananda spoke at many elite Religious Conferences in a number of cities, making contact with many interested people. These Swamis did immense good in correcting the gross misunderstandings many Western people had concerning India and the Hindu religion. They were able to take the ancient truths found in the sacred scriptures and present them in a way that was understandable to the modern mind. The exalted character of these Swamis made a strong impression on the people who heard them speak and conversed with them in private conversations.

After leaving New York City in early October, Saradananda went to the house of Mr. and Mrs. Wheeler in Montclair, New Jersey. Swami Atulananda tells us that during Saradananda's stay at the Wheeler's residence in Montclair,

> The swami often spoke about Sri Ramakrishna, and one day he produced his Master's photograph and showed it to the lady of the house [Mrs. Wheeler]. "Oh, Swami," she exclaimed, "it is the same face!" "What do you mean?" asked Swami Saradananda. And then she told him that long ago in her youth, before she was married, she had had a vision of a Hindu whose face was the same that she now saw in the photograph. "It was Sri Ramakrishna," she said, "but I did not know it until now. I was so impressed and charmed by the vision at that time that I remembered the face very distinctly. I have been going about here and there ever since I had the vision—whenever I heard that a Hindu had come to America—but I was always disappointed not to find the same face. At last I see that it was Ramakrishna."[58]

While in Montclair, Saradananda met Reverend Amory Howe Bradford (1846-1911) [q.v.], the minister of the local Congregational Church. He was a distinguished theologian who authored many religious books. Saradananda wrote about Bradford to Sara Bull on October 12, "He was very much interested too and said how many points of agreement Christianity and Vedanta have. He spoke from the pulpit last Sunday that the Christians ought to learn and study any system of philosophy, which is broad, and especially the Indian." In an article in the theological *Auburn Seminary Review* (1900), Bradford expressed the view that:

> It is but fair that a people should be judged by its highest and best thought. All the religious sects in India and all the schools of Indian philosophy culminate in the Vedanta. The teaching of the Vedanta has been preached in this country during the last few years with rare skill and intel-

ligence by some of its accredited teachers.... Swami Saradananda whom I believe to be a reverent searcher for truth, and a good man.

Chapter XVIII of this book mentions that Bradford, the associate editor of the popular Protestant journal *Outlook*, invited Abhedananda to his office for an interview the following year.[59]

On October 11, Abhedananda, along with Miss Waldo, came to see Saradananda at Mrs. Wheeler's residence located at 121 Gates Avenue in Montclair. After moving to Montclair in the beginning of October, Saradananda held classes on the premises. On the 13th Saradananda spoke on "Concentration" at Mrs. Wheeler's house. Abhedananda commented, "This was the first time I heard Swami Saradananda's speech. I was impressed by his method of delivery. He had a good voice and was eloquent." A "New York Friend" sent a correspondence dated October 29 that appeared in the *Brahmavadin* of December 16, 1897 (pp. 292-93). Referring to Saradananda's discourses at Montclair, the message stated:

> He recently spent a month in Montclair, visiting at the residence of a friend who is a staunch supporter of Vedanta. His host and hostess threw open their large parlour for lectures, three times a week, freely inviting all interested in the subject of the Vedanta to come and listen to Swami Saradananda. Large numbers availed themselves to the offer and attended the lectures, becoming more and more favourably impressed with each succeeding one they heard, until, at the close of the Swami's visit, they begged that the teaching might be continued.

Abhedananda accepted Saradananda's request to journey from New York and give at least two lectures a month at their residence. On the 13th Mrs. Wheeler took the two Swamis to the Ampere Electrical Works in East Orange, New Jersey. It is possible, but not clear, if Saradananda met the famous inventor Thomas Alva Edison there, but Abhedananda did.* On October 14 Saradananda left Montclair to return to Sara Bull's residence in Cambridge.[60]

Reverend Hiram Washington Thomas, an admirer and friend of Vivekananda, was president of the non-sectarian Christian "Liberal Congress of Religion". This organization held a five-day conference in Nashville,

* See Chapter XV.

Tennessee. On October 22, 1897 Saradananda presented an address at the meeting in Nashville as a member of the "Conference on Comparative Religions". Lewis Janes presided, and Jehanghier D. Cola, Virchand Gandhi of Bombay, and Paul Carus also spoke there.[61]

There is a good chance that Jehanghier D. Cola, a Parsee from Bombay, met Swamiji at Ridgely Manor in April 1895. On the 16th of April he told Mary Phillips in New York City about Swamiji's illness. Apparently Lewis Janes gave his support to J. D. Cola, because between November 1896 and October 1897 Cola spoke at the same locations that Janes had provided for Swami Saradananda to lecture at: the Home Congress, Cambridge Conferences and Free Religious Association in the Boston-Cambridge area, the Monsalvat School at Greenacre, and the Liberal Congress of Religion in Nashville, Tennessee. In early 1897, with the backing of Julia Ward Howe and Sara Bull, Cola got up a committee of influential Bostonians to take steps toward starting a relief fund for India.[62]

Granville Stanley Hall (1844-1924) [q.v.], a famous educational and adolescent psychologist, was the president of Clark University in Worcester, Massachusetts. At one time he met Vivekananda, and he later invited both Saradananda and Abhedananda to speak at his notable University that had only graduate students. Saradananda came to Worcester on October 27 and again in mid-November, and it might have been at that time that he addressed the students at the University.[63]

The *Worcester Daily Spy* gave a brief account of a lecture by Saradananda that appeared later in *The Theosophist* located in Madras. It stated:

> The Hindu does not come to this country to convert, because the essence of his religion is that every religion is true. He believes that there is a universal religion underlying the particular religions, a centre in which all races meet, a sun which illuminates all, a God who manifests himself equally to all. Believing this helps us to understand our own religion better, for if one religion stands on revelations, the others do, too; if one is false others are false. Why should statements in one scripture be true and those in another false? If God incarnated Himself in Christ, why should he not incarnate Himself to other races? If others besides Christ have purity and the same power as he of displaying spirituality, we must believe that they were all inspired by God.... To harmonize the tolerance which comes from this view of life and religion with the intensity which comes from devotion to one's own particular religion is not so difficult, if we can believe [that]

the different religions are adapted to different times, temperaments, and races, so many manifestations of the one universal religion.

The Swami is doing good work in America.[64]

Saradananda came back to Cambridge in mid-October and remained there most of the time with Sara Bull until January 1898. During that time the guest speakers for the Sunday Cambridge Conferences included, among others, Prince Peter Kropotkin of Russia who later met Swami Vivekananda (November 7), Professor Edward Cummings of Harvard (November 14), and Colonel Thomas Higginson (December 26). Saradananda also wrote an article for a quarterly New Thought magazine called *Immortality*. Annie Besant, Franz Hartmann, Swami Abhayananda and others also submitted articles to this periodical. On November 7 Saradananda made a one-day visit to Sharon, Massachusetts, to visit Sara's daughter Olea Vaughan. When he went to the train station to return to Cambridge, a spiritual mood came over him and he spent the whole night sitting there. He wrote:

> There was not a single man there in the depot and the moon and the pines were so pleasant and the silence was so charming that I decided not to return but to spend the time in sitting down and enjoying the whole thing.

Swami Saradananda submitted an article on "The Theory and Practice of Vedanta" to the journal *Mind* in December 1897. Concerning the essay, the reviewer for the magazine wrote:

> Perhaps the most significant feature of this teacher's contribution is that which suggests the charitable and tolerant attitude of the Vedanta toward other religions. It contains a lesson that we of the West should heed. It shows that the philosophy of the Vedantist is eminently constructive; whereas the sectarian religionists of our time and country are often not only mutually destructive, but immersed in a common antagonism toward the faiths of other lands.

In early January 1898, Saradananda and Sara Bull visited Josephine MacLeod and the Leggetts in New York. Saradananda and Bull dined with Abhedananda at the Murry Hill Hotel in New York.[65]

Swami Saradananda Leaves for India

After being in the United States for about a year and a half, on January 12, 1898, at the request of Swami Vivekananda, Saradananda sailed for India. Saradananda was recalled back to India for the important assignment of helping to organize the Ramakrishna Mission at Belur. Also, it was necessary for Saradananda to interview those people who possessed invaluable knowledge of the life events of Sri Ramakrishna. For example, Hriday Mukhopadhyay (1840-99), a devoted attendant of the Master for over twenty-five years, was nearing the end of his life on earth. In a brief note, the *New York Times* (and other newspapers) conveyed this information:

> Swami Saradananda, an Indian priest of the Vedanta philosophy, sailed on the Teutonic today. He was accompanied by Mrs. Ole Bull, widow of the violinist, and a Boston woman [Josephine MacLeod] whose name could not be learned. They go to India to help the priest in his work there.[66]

On the last day of January, "A New York Friend" wrote to the *Brahmavadin*:

> We all deplore his loss and feel that the work in this country can ill afford to spare him, but it seems that Swami Vivekananda and India need him more, so we are somewhat consoled by the thought that our loss is their gain.... Numbers of Swami Saradananda's friends gathered around him the day before he sailed, to bid him good-bye and wish him a safe and pleasant journey and every success in his work for India. He won much sincere affection from those who knew him here, by his earnest, unselfish character, and he did much good work in America, the effect of which we trust will be lasting in broadening our ideas as to religion and philosophy.[67]

The party stopped off in London where they met Edward Sturdy and the Galsworthys, and then moved on to Paris, Rome, Naples, and Brindisi. When Saradananda visited Paris, he heard Madame Calve singing in the adjoining hotel. Saradananda had previously met Madame Calve in Boston during the summer of 1897. In Rome he revisited St. Peter's Basilica and saw the Sistine Chapel, the Coliseum, and the Vatican library and Sculpture Gallery.[68]

Later Lewis Janes, a loyal supporter of the cause, expressed his high estimate of the Swami in the *Brahmavadin* of June 16, 1898:

> The many friends of the Swami Saradananda in Cambridge and vicinity cannot permit him to return to India without expressing through your columns their hearty appreciation of the excellent educational work which he accomplished in this country, and the fine accompaniment of personal character and influence which greatly strengthened the effect of the work wherever it was conducted. On every hand, the friends of Swami express a sense of personal loss in his departure, and hope that he may some time return to America where his work is so heartily appreciated.
>
> ....The Swami's exposition of the principles of the Advaita doctrine, in just comparison with other views which are held in India, was admirably lucid and clear. His replies to questions were always ready and satisfactory. His great fairness of mind and soundness of judgment enabled him to present the doctrine in a manner which at once convinced all of his sincerity and earnestness, while it disarmed that factious opposition which is sometimes stirred up by a more dogmatic and assertive manner.

Janes also mentioned that Saradananda spoke publicly in Boston, Waltham and Worcester, Massachusetts, and addressed the students at Clark University in Worcester and at Brown University in Providence, Rhode Island. He frequently addressed the Psychomath Club in Waltham, where Abhedananda also spoke.[69] In summary, during his stay in America, Saradananda lectured or gave classes in the following American locations and probably more: Greenacre, Maine; Cambridge and Framingham, Massachusetts; Franconia Mountains, New Hampshire; Montclair, New Jersey; Brooklyn and New York, New York; and Nashville, Tennessee.*

After Swami Abhedananda attended the Greenacre Conference in 1898, he wrote well of his brother disciple in the journal *Mind*:

> In 1896, his [Swami Vivekananda's] successor, Swami Saradananda came to Greenacre and taught Vedanta for two successive seasons. By his charming manners and unselfish love for humanity he succeeded in making a deep impression, as to the practical results of Vedanta teachings, upon the

* See Appendix I for the dates and locations of Saradananda's residences in the West.

minds of almost all who met him personally or heard his discourses under the "Swami's Pine" in the woods.[70]

In April 1899 in Worcester, Massachusetts, Abhedananda met Satish Chandra Chakravarti, a younger brother of Saradananda. He became a medical student and brahmacharin at Tufts College in Medford, Massachusetts. Satish is pictured along with Abhedananda, Virchand Gandhi and Lewis Janes in a short book on the history of Greenacre by Anna Ingersoll. On October 24, 1899, Chakravarti spoke before nearly a thousand people, mostly women, at the International Metaphysical League in Boston along with the president Charles Brodie Patterson, Sarah Farmer, Ursula Gestefeld and others. They emphasized spiritual living and pure health, and that we are a soul possessing a body not vice versa.[71]

Always ready to defend the faith, Lewis Janes wrote a letter to the editor of the journal *Outlook* on October 27, 1900, showing the errors in their article "Indian Famine Notes". He pointed out that the funds supplied by the Government of India for famine relief "was all raised by taxation in India", that the Ramakrishna Mission is taking an active part in famine relief and that

> The director of the relief work in Calcutta, I may add, is the Swami Saradananda, also well known in America. Some of these men have risked their lives in the care of cholera patients as well as in labouring for the famine suffers. The Swami Saradananda is only now recovering from a serious illness incurred in the prosecution of his work.[72]

The following year in 1901, Saradananda wrote a eulogy concerning the passing away of Lewis Janes:

> Even now all the dear days that I had the good fortune to pass with the Doctor are crowding in my memory, and I can hardly express my feelings. I had all hopes of seeing his fatherly face and meeting the warmth of his hand and heart once more; but alas! he is gone and America has lost one more charm for me. It is ever a mystery why such useful lives are cut away in their prime, when they have hardly done half the good that they would do were they allowed to remain! But none has as yet found a solution to it. All that we can do is to resign—resign ourselves to the inevitable—resign, believing there is a purpose, all good, underneath it all![73]

When the famous French opera singer Madam Emma Calve (1858-1942) [q.v.] visited Belur Math with an interpreter on December 2, 1910, Saradananda escorted her around the premise. She mentioned, "Swamiji used to repeat a nice chant which starts, 'Lead us from darkness to light.' Would you kindly repeat the whole chant, if you know it? I am anxious to hear it." With his sonorous voice he chanted the Sanskrit verses and this brought back sublime memories of Swamiji to her.*[74]

Saradananda first serialized in part his monumental Bengali biography *Sri Ramakrishna Lilaprasanga* in the *Udbodhan* journal in 1909, and then brought it out in book form between 1911 and 1919. It is the most detailed account of the life of Sri Ramakrishna, particularly during the time before the events of the *Gospel* took place. The task of researching these events going back to the birth of Ramakrishna's father in 1775, many of which were previously unrecorded, was staggering. It was translated into English in its totality by Swami Jagadananda with the title *Sri Ramakrishna, the Great Master* in 1952, and soon had an important impact on the growth of the Ramakrishna-Vedanta movement in the West. A more recent translation *Sri Ramakrishna and His Divine Play* (2003) is by Swami Chetanananda.[75]

In Dhaka and at the Town Hall in Calcutta, the first governor of Bengal, Sir Thomas David Gibson Carmichael (1859 -1926), publicly praised the Ramakrishna Mission's work. Later, on December 11, 1916, Carmichael expressed distrust and suspicion concerning the Mission in his Durbar speech made at the Government House, Calcutta. On the advice of Holy Mother, Saradananda met with the governor with the help of Josephine MacLeod and clarified the Mission's position, submitting a memorandum to him in January. Becoming aware of the facts of the matter, Carmichael wrote back to the Mission on March 26:

> I know the character of the Mission's work is entirely non-political, and I have heard nothing but good of its work of social service for the people.... I have full sympathy with the real aim of the true Ramakrishna Mission and it was this abuse of the name of the Mission that I wish to prevent. I hope the words I have used will help the Mission to guard against the illegitimate use of its name by unscrupulous people.

* See Chapter IX for more details on her visit.

Thus the Mission was saved from the ill will of the British government.[76] Scottish born Thomas Carmichael became the governor of Madras (1911-12) and the first governor of Bengal during 1912-17. As an able administrator he was faced with many overriding problems that brought about his critical nature, which included accelerated revolutionary activities, a Muslim-Hindu separation, slumps in the jute market, price rises due to repeated failures of winter crops, and the First World War.[77]

In 1917 Lord Ronaldshay (aka Lawrence Zetland, 1876-1961) [q.v.], the new governor of Bengal, stated:

> The whole life of India is built up on an atmosphere of religion; and this makes it all the more necessary that we should try to understand something of the spirit of Indian religious thought by recognizing that the religious practices of the country are characterized by much symbolism and are consequently open to much misunderstanding.... I am quite sure that if once a man begins the study of religions of India he will very soon find himself absorbed in an intellectual life—a life in which religion and philosophy go hand in hand more harmoniously than anywhere else I know—transcending in interests that of any other country of which I have knowledge.[78]

In 1919 Lord Ronaldshay came to look over Belur Math during the public celebration of Sri Ramakrishna's birthday. It was Saradananda who received him with due respect. He informed the governor about the Mission's spiritual and secular activities of feeding the poor without caste distinctions. The two of them standing before the portrait of Sri Ramakrishna in the shrine, Saradananda explained that the monastics came to the Temple to meditate three times daily, and that the Master's influence was the foundation of all their public works and the chief source of their personal dedication. Ronaldshay was so impressed by what he saw that he wrote highly of Ramakrishna in his book *The Heart of Aryavarta* in 1925.*[79]

Saradananda continued to inspire the Swamis that came to the United States. In 1923, at a meeting of the Trustees of the Math, the Swamis Shivananda, Saradananda, Subodhananda, and Shuddhananda decided to send a young Swami Prabhavananda (1893-1976) to America, who later recalled:

---

* See Chapter II for more details.

After the meeting I went back to Calcutta with Swami Saradananda in the same boat. Then we went to the Udbodhan; I was walking behind him. Right at the door of the Udbodhan, he turned to me and said, quoting a Bengali saying, "So you are going to cross the seven oceans and the thirteen rivers." "Yes Maharaj," I answered, "you are sending me. But I feel nervous. What do I know that I can teach or preach?" Swami Saradananda replied in English, and his words are still ringing in my ears. "That is none of your business! We shall see to that!" And they have seen to it.

In that same year, Saradananda gave spiritual initiation to Sarah and Rebecca Fox, two school teachers from Northern California, on a small boat on the Ganga in Varanasi. From him they received the Sanskrit names Premika and Radhika and remained in India for some time.[80]

In India Saradananda told Swami Aseshananda and other monastics:

The Master chooses his own men and women. We are mere instruments in his hands. It is a privilege to work under his banner. In America he already prepared the ground for me; I was not alone. He brought to me men and women of exalted character who helped me in our work and bore the great love for our Master.[81]

Before Swami Akhilananda (1894-1962), a disciple of Swami Brahmananda, left for America in 1926, Saradananda told him, "I have been to America. Learn from my experience. Some people will praise you to the skies and glorify you. Others will throw mud on you. Take both equally."[82]

Following Saradananda's mahasamadhi on August 19, 1927, Swami Atulananda wrote to Ida Ansell:

All the monks assembled in the swami's room, surrounded his bed, and began to chant in chorus "Hari Om Ramakrishna", and watched the great soul pass away. Solemnity was in the atmosphere as if the whole universe was in the peace of meditation. Everything was calm and quiet, not a sound was heard except the chanting of the monks: "Hari Om Ramakrishna."... The great swami has passed away, but he will ever remain in our hearts. May we all follow in his footsteps and become like him. May he come to us with his loving, sweet words when we are distressed. May his extraordinary calmness come to us in our troubles.[83]

When Romain Rolland (1866-1944) [q.v.] wrote *The Life of Ramakrishna* and quoted from the 1920 edition of *Sri Ramakrishna, the Great Master*, he mentioned:

> Saradananda, who died in 1927, was on terms of intimacy with Ramakrishna and likewise possessed one of the loftiest religious and philosophical minds in India. His biography, unfortunately unfinished, is at once the most interesting and the most reliable.... Saradananda is an authority both as a philosopher and as an historian. His books are rich in metaphysical sketches, which place the spiritual appearance of Ramakrishna exactly in its place in the rich procession of Hindu thought.[84]

When Saradananda visited America, Sister Devamata (1867-1942) [q.v.] was studying at the Sorbonne in Paris. In 1932, she discussed his popularity in America:

> I returned to New York in time to catch the afterglow of his lingering presence. Everyone spoke of him with a tenderness of feeling that told of the great love he had awakened in their hearts. Even today I meet those who express for him a depth of affection that takes no account of years. He left a trailing spiritual influence which is still felt by those who knew or heard him. He was not a brilliant speaker in English, but his words carried weight because they sprang from a radiating holy life.[85]

At one time Devamata had spent a lot of time in Holy Mother's quarters, and Saradananda would ask her, "What Holy Mother had said and done through the day?" About the Swami she recalled:

> I saw at once why he had called forth so much love wherever he went in the West. He seemed to possess an exalted gentleness, a graciousness and courtesy which made direct appeal. His was the highest breeding of all,—the breeding, not merely of manner or of culture, but of spirit. It was the outgrowth of Divine, rather than of human, relations.... With all his gentleness, there was something royal in his step and in the way he held himself. Both revealed a nobility of spirit which bore witness to the fineness of his early training and to the openness of his heart to Sri Ramakrishna's influence.[86]

> [Saradananda] was one of the mainstays of the Order. He possessed exceptional gifts of mind and soul. When I knew him in Calcutta I was impressed constantly by his gentle dignity and loving-kindness.[87]

After being in India from 1907 through 1909, Devamata came back to the U.S. She continued to receive letters from Saradananda and other Swamis of the Ramakrishna Order. With the passing of Brahmananda and Turiyananda in 1922, Saradananda became more indrawn. He said to the monastics, "Mother and Maharaj [Brahmananda] have left. Now you take the responsibility and get involved in the activities of the Order. I no longer have any enthusiasm or inclination to work."[88] From her correspondences with the Swami, Devamata concluded:

> I could discern from what was written how gradually he was drawing away from the outer world into his inmost being. As the days went by, fewer and fewer were the hours given to earthly tasks; more and more were the hours devoted to super-earthly communion, until his life became unbroken meditation and he was gone.[89]

In the West Swami Aseshananda (1899-1996), who for many years headed the Vedanta Society of Portland, Oregon, from 1955 until his passing, in 1982 came out with *Glimpses of a Great Soul: A Portrait of Swami Saradananda.* Aseshananda, a direct disciple of Sri Sarada Devi, served Saradananda as a secretary and confidant for seven years (1921-27) before the Swami's mahasamadhi. The biography covers the life, teachings and letters of Saradananda along with many spiritual insights and some reminiscences. Hideo Hashimoto, a Methodist minister and a Japanese professor of religion at Lewis and Clark College in Portland, Oregon, wrote an evaluation of the biography comparing Saradananda to a Zen master:

> This book provides us with glimpses into the life of a great soul [Swami Saradananda] who helped to nurture a small band of devoted followers of a Bengal mystic, Sri Ramakrishna, into a worldwide religious-philosophical movement which has an extraordinary impact on the thought of the twentieth century.... Swami Saradananda, "holy man, writer, editor, nurse, lecturer, administrator," was a direct disciple of Sri Ramakrishna, a man full of vitality, compassion, humour, and organizational skill.... *Glimpses* is full of spiritual insight reached by the author, Swami Aseshananda, through

his contact with the great leaders of the Vedanta movement, especially his guru, the Holy Mother, and his mentor, Swami Saradananda. This is like a story of a Zen master narrated by his intimate disciple, a next best thing to sitting at the feet of the master.[90]

For a list of dates and locations of Swami Saradananda's residences in the West, see Appendix I. For a selected list of the literature about Saradananda, see Appendices V and VI.

ENDNOTES

1 Aseshananda, p. 19; Chetanananda, p. 324.

2 Burke, IV, p. 559.

3 Aseshananda, p. 19.

4 Chetanananda, p. 324; Swami Saradananda, who researched and wrote the definitive biography *Sri Ramakrishna, the Great Master*, has been identified with the apostle Simon Peter. The oldest Christian Gospel in the New Testament was written by Mark, who did not belong to Jesus' inner circle of twelve intimate disciples. *The Gospel of Mark* was based on the preaching of Simon Peter according to Bishop Papias (c. 70-160), said to be a disciple of John by the early Fathers of the Church and by most modern Christian theologians. Mark acted as Peter's interpreter and faithfully recorded his teachings. Louis Hartman, tr., *Encyclopedic Dictionary of the Bible* (New York, McGraw-Hill Book Company, 1963), pp. 1450-51, 1817.

5 Aseshananda, pp. 19-20; Horner, pp. 67-73; Basu, pp. 101, 243, 492.

6 Burke, IV, p. 315.

7 Burke, IV, p. 312; *DAB* (1932), IX, pp. 606-07; *NCAB* (1904), pp. 114.

8 Burke, IV, pp. 314-15.

9 Prabuddhaprana2, pp. 197-98.

10 Saradananda, pp. 938-39; Aseshananda, p. 20; Anna Josephine Ingersoll, *Greenacre on the Piscataqua* (1900), pp. 16-17; *Outlook* (Oct. 3, 1896), p. 625; Basu, pp. 496-97.

11 *Boston Evening Transcript* (July 8, 1896), p. 6; also in Cameron, pp. 18, 71; slightly altered in *Brahmavadin* (Sept. 12, 1896), p. 11; Basu, p. 497.

12 Basu, p. 498; *Brahmavadin* (Sept. 12, 1896), p. 11.

13 Basu, pp. 498-99; *Brahmavadin* (Sept. 26, 1896).

14 Basu, pp. 496-97; *Brahmavadin* (Aug. 29, 1896).

15 *CW*, VIII:381-82.

16 *Boston Evening Transcript* (Sept. 3, 1896), p. 6; also in Cameron pp. 18, 77-78.
17 Basu, p. 118; Prabuddhaprana2, pp. 209-10.
18 Chaudhuri2, p. 601.
19 *MOTE* (March 1919), p. 72; (July-Aug. 1940), pp. 147-48, 179; (April-June 1944), pp. 114-17; Levinsky (1984), pp. 129-30, 258, 289; *WWWA* (1963), II, p. 226.
20 *Outlook* (Oct. 3, 1896), p. 625.
21 *WWWA*, IV, pp. 150-51; *ANB*, IV, pp. 278-79; Helen Campbell. Web: ocp.hul.harvard.edu/ww/people_campbell.htm.
22 *CW*, VI:377.
23 Burke, IV, pp. 329-30; Prabuddhaprana2, p. 217; "An Unpublished Letter of Swami Saradananda", *VK* (May 2005), p. 183.
24 Nelson, p. 95; Basu, pp. 501-02; Prabuddhaprana2, pp. 217-18, 221.
25 Prabuddhaprana2, p. 219.
26 Prabuddhaprana2, p. 219.
27 *CW*, VIII:3-35.
28 Basu, pp. 501-02; *Brahmavadin* (Dec. 5, 1896), p. 76; (Dec. 19, 1896), pp. 94-95; Burke, III, pp. 41, 100-01; IV, pp. 338-39.
29 Burke, V, p. 45; Prabuddhaprana2, p. 7.
30 *Harper's Bazaar* (Nov. 14, 1896), p. 951 on APS.
31 *Boston Daily Globe* (Nov. 13, 1896), p. 4 on PQHN; Nelson, pp. 97-98; Prabuddhaprana2, p. 187.
32 "The Cambridge Conferences", *Outlook* (Aug. 7, 1897), pp. 844-49 on APS; Prabuddhaprana2, pp. 189-90.
33 Datta, Pt. II, Sec. III; Prabuddhaprana2, p. 219.
34 *Brahmavadin* (March 27, 1897), p. 172; Sankari Basu, *Swami Vivekananda in Contemporary Indian News* (Gol Park, Calcutta: Ramakrishna Mission Institute of Culture, 1997), pp. 452-53; Prabuddhaprana2, p. 232.
35 Nelson, pp. 96-97.
36 Burke, IV, pp. 344-46; Prabuddhaprana2, pp. 236-38; *VK* (Mar. 2007), p. 116; (April 2007), p. 157.
37 The news story went out on the wire and appeared in the Omaha, Nebraska, *Morning World-Herald* (Feb. 1, 1897), p. 3.
38 *VK* (May 2007), p. 179; *New York Times* (April 13, 1907).
39 Chetanananda, p. 326.
40 Basu, pp. 176-77; *Brahmavadin* (Mar. 6, 1897).
41 Aseshananda, pp. 20-21.
42 *Outlook* (Aug. 7, 1897), pp. 844-49; Prabuddhaprana2, pp. 190-91.

43 Basu, p. 531 (591); Leonard Zusne, *Biographical Dictionary of Psychology* (Westport, CT: Greenwood Press, 1984), p. 94; *Annual Report* of Massachusetts Department of Education (1898), pp. 30-31 on GBS.

44 *Global Vedanta* (Summer 2009), pp. 6-8; *Melrose Reporter* (May 29, 1897); (June 19, 1897).

45 *Appalachia* (1898), pp. 400-01 on GBS.

46 *Brahmavadin* (Sept. 15, 1897), pp. 29-34; *Journal of Practical Metaphysics* (Aug. 1897); Burke, IV, opposite pp. 336-37.

47 Nelson, pp. 98-99; *Boston Evening Transcript* (July 1, 1897) p. 7; also in Cameron, pp. 79-80.

48 *Boston Evening Transcript* (July 26, 1897) p. 6; also in *Brahmavadin* (Oct. 1, 1897), pp. 76-79; and Cameron, pp. 18, 88-89.

49 *Boston Evening Transcript* (Aug. 2, 1897) p. 6; also in *Brahmavadin* (Oct. 15, 1897), pp. 125-27; and Cameron, pp. 18, 97-98.

50 Nelson, pp. 98-99; *Boston Evening Transcript* (July 1, 1897) p. 7; also in Cameron, pp. 32-33, 80, 162.

51 *Boston Evening Transcript* (Aug. 14, 1897), p. 13; also in Cameron, pp. 18 104.

52 Basu, p. 607; *PB* (Jan. 1898), pp. 186-88; Cameron, p. 80.

53 "Those Suburban Girls", *New York Times* (Feb. 1, 1903), p. SM10.

54 *Who's Who in American Jewry* (New York: The Jewish Biographical Bureau, 1928); *WWWA* (1963), II, p. 190; Ingersoll, pp. 17-18; *Boston Daily Globe* (July 9, 1899), p. 27; *New York Times* (June 1, 1901), p. 4; *Vedanta Darpana* (March 1933), pp. 15-16.

55 *CWSV*, X, pp. 10-12.

56 Prabuddhaprana2, pp. 249-50.

57 Prabuddhaprana2, pp. 194-95, 214-16, 252; Burke IV, pp. 397-98.

58 Atulananda, pp. 57-58.

59 Prabuddhaprana2, pp. 249-50; *The Auburn Seminary Review* (1900), pp. 32-33 on GBS.

60 *CWSA*, X, pp. 13-15; Burke IV, p. 397.

61 *Outlook* (Oct. 9, 1897), p. 387; *Chicago Daily Tribune* (Oct. 23, 1897), p. 16.

62 Burke, III, p. 78; *New York Times* (Feb. 1, 1897).

63 Basu, p. 531 (591); Prabuddhaprana2, pp. 250, 255.

64 *The Theosophist* (Jan. 1898), p. 256 on GBS.

65 Prabuddhaprana2, pp. 254, 256; *Outlook* (Nov. 13, 1897), pp. 681-82; *The Arena* (May 1899), p. XIV; *The Living Age* (Sept. 10, 1898).

66 *New York Times* (Jan. 13, 1898), p. 10; also in the *Boston Daily Globe* (Jan. 13, 1898), p. 9; and the *Cambridge Chronicle* (Jan. 15, 1898).

67 *Brahmavadin* (March 1, 1898), pp. 496-97.

68 Aseshananda, pp. 24-27; Prabuddhaprana2, pp. 257-58; *PB* (Jan. 1911), p. 20.

69 Basu, p. 531 (591); *Brahmavadin* (June 15, 1898); (June 1, 1899), p. 600.

70 *Mind* (1900), p. 34 on GBS; also in Basu, p. 541 (601); *PB* (Dec. 1899), p. 186; and (Dec. 1989), p. 520.

71 *Boston Daily Globe* (Oct. 25, 1899), p. 11; Burke, V, pp. 33, 66, 69; Anna Ingersoll, *Greenacre on the Piscataqua* (New York: Alliance Publishing Company, 1900) facing p. 12; *CWSA*, X, p. 92.

72 *Outlook* (Oct. 27, 1900), pp. 521-22.

73 *Lewis G. Janes* (Boston: J. H. West, 1902), pp. 184-85; Frank Parlato. Web: www.vivekananda.net/PDFBooks/HTML/LewisJanes.htm.

74 Aseshananda, pp. 57-58.

75 *Mission* (Nikhileswarananda), p. 745; Saradananda, p. 5.

76 *Mission* (Vimalatmananda), pp. 271-72; Chetanananda, p. 340; Gambhirananda, pp. 215-18.

77 Lord Carmichael. Web: www.boi-mela.com/banglapedia/ViewArticle.asp?TopicRef=1099; Riddick, p. 65.

78 *PB* (Feb-March 1917), p. 60.

79 Aseshananda, pp. 58-60.

80 Anandaprana, p. 76; *WWSV*, p. 195; Aseshananda, p. 95.

81 Aseshananda, pp. 23-24.

82 Swami Akhilananda, *Spiritual Practices* (Cape Cod, MA; Claude Stark, 1974), p. 6.

83 Atulananda, pp. 279-80.

84 Rolland, pp. 33-34, 299-300.

85 *PB* (Nov. 1932), p. 551.

86 *PB* (Nov. 1932), pp. 552-53.

87 Devamata, p. 259.

88 Chetanananda, p. 344.

89 *PB* (Nov. 1932), p. 553.

90 *Journal of the American Academy of Religion* (June 1983), pp. 321-22.

CHAPTER XV

SWAMI ABHEDANANDA: UP UNTIL 1906

When Sri Ramakrishna first met the future Swami Abhedananda (1866-1939) in the middle of 1884, he told him, "In previous birth you were a great Yogi. A small part of your sadhana remained to be completed. This is your last birth. Yes, I shall teach you yoga." Abhedananda later recalled, "A flood of purity and ineffable joy was then flowing through my mind." He returned to Ramakrishna's room:

> As I sat in the posture of yoga, Paramahansadeva asked me to take out my tongue. When I took out my tongue, he wrote a mula-mantra (bija-mantra) with his right middle finger on the tongue and stimulated power in me, and having attracted the power upwards by putting his hand on my chest, he asked me to meditate. I did so. In the course of meditation I lost sense-consciousness. Absorbed in deep meditation, I sat motionless like a log in samadhi and felt a strange bliss which I had never experienced before.[1]

In 1925, a devotee named Ganesh had a spiritual dream concerning the identity of Abhedananda. Abhedananda later wrote back to him, "Thakur used to tell me, 'When I see your eyes and eyebrows, I remember Sri Krishna.' (A part of the Divinity of Sri Krishna is incarnated in you.)." Swami Prabhavananda, who knew Abhedananda well during part of the 1921-23 period, later told his devotees, "Swami Abhedananda was with Lord Krishna" in a prior life. Long before he came to the West, he came to see Holy Mother at the house of Nilambar Babu in Belur and read the hymn "Prakritim", which he composed about her. "After listening to the hymn, Holy Mother blessed him, saying, 'May Saraswati, the goddess of learning, sit on your tongue.'" This prophecy was fulfilled in Abhedananda's remarkable oratorical skills as a spiritual teacher in the West.[2]

After Sri Ramakrishna's mahasamadhi, for ten years Abhedananda took up the itinerant life and travelled all over India. He met many admirable saints like Trailainga Swami, Swami Bhaskarananda at Benares, Pavhari Baba at Ghazipur, and many Vaishnava holy men at Vrindavan. Under the guidance of the great pundit Srimat Dhanaraj Giri at Rishikesh, he studied Advaita Vedanta. Dhanaraj Giri had a debate with him in Sanskrit and came to the conclusion that "His is a wisdom that is supernatural." He also learned the meaning of Patanjali's *Yoga Sutras* from Vedantavagish.[3]

At one time Swami Vivekananda came under attack from critics who claimed that he was not qualified to represent Hinduism in America.[4] Consequently, he wrote to his brother disciples in India, "Hold a public meeting in Calcutta approving of my activities in America and mentioning that I am accredited to represent Hinduism and send a letter of thanks to Dr. Barrows with a copy to me." Swami Abhedananda, along with Saradananda and Ramakrishnananda, worked hard in arranging a public meeting in the town hall of Calcutta to celebrate Vivekananda's activities in the West. Abhedananda visited many prominent citizens requesting them to attend the meeting, and helped to raise money for the event. Over four-thousand elite representatives of the various communities attended the meeting held at the Calcutta Town Hall on September 5, 1894. The gathering helped to bring about a wonderful response from the Indian people concerning Vivekananda's mission in America. Swamiji was highly appreciative of the great work that was done on his behalf, and to the public of Calcutta.[5]

In October 1895, Vivekananda sent a letter from Reading, England, to Abhedananda in India telling him:

> I shall this year leave again in November for America. So I require a man well-up in Sanskrit and English, particularly the latter language—either Shashi or you or Sarada. Now, if you have completely recovered, very well, you come; otherwise send Sharat [Saradananda]. The work is to teach the devotees I shall be leaving here, to make them study the Vedanta, to do a little translation work into English, and to deliver occasional lectures.[6]

Abhedananda sent a correspondence entitled "The Hindu Preacher" to the *Brahmavadin*, which appeared in the November 23, 1895 edition. In the message he stated:

> Moreover, it is now high time for us to send Hindu missionaries like Swami Vivekananda to distant lands for diffusing widely the highest doctrines of the Hindu religion, and for bringing men of all creeds under its benign influence. In Europe and America there must be earnest and sincere souls waiting to hear the sublime teachings of the Vedanta and accept the doctrine of Karma, of reincarnation and of the immortality of the soul. A great want of this age is a religious order of the Hindus, which, well-equipped with modern learning in science and in philosophy, possessing a knowledge of the world, and acquainted with the spirit of the times, will undertake the propagation of the Hindu religion in all countries and bring into existence the reign of peace and harmony in the midst of warring sects and religions.[7]

Soon after Saradananda left London for the United States in July 1896, Vivekananda sent Ramakrishnananda a cable at the Alambazar Math, Calcutta, stating, "Send Kali [Abhedananda] immediately to London to assist me in my work here. I am arranging the passage." The following month on the 12th Swamiji wrote from Switzerland to E. T. Sturdy:

> I had a letter from the Math stating that the other Swami is ready to start. He will, I am sure, be just the man you want. He is one of the best Sanskrit scholars we have ... and as I hear, he has improved his English much.[8]

Near the end of September, Abhedananda arrived in London to assist Vivekananda. He had a limited amount of formal Western education, little experience in public speaking, and felt reluctant to lecture. Swamiji told him, "Did I know anything about lecturing when I stood on the platform of the World's Parliament of Religions? Whatever I have achieved is all by the grace of the Master. Have faith in him and you will blossom as a fine preacher." Eric Hammond [q.v.], a journalist and poet, attended Abhedananda's first speech in the West entitled "An Introduction to the Philosophy of Panchadasi". It was given on October 27, 1896 at the Christo-Theosophical Society at Bloomsbury Square in London. Hammond reported Vivekananda's delightful reaction by observing:

> An overwhelming joy was noticeable in the Swami [Vivekananda] in his scholar's success. Joy compelled him to put at least some of itself

into words that rang with delight unalloyed. It was the joy of a spiritual father over the achievement of a well-beloved son, a successful and brilliant student. The Master was more than content to have effaced himself in order that his Brother's opportunity should be altogether unhindered. The whole impression had in it a glowing beauty indescribable. It was as though the Master thought and knew his thought to be true: "Even if I perish on this plane, my message will be sounded through these dear lips and the world will hear it."... He remarked that this was the first appearance of his dear Brother and pupil as an English-speaking lecturer before an English audience, and he pulsated with pleasure at the applause that followed the remark. His selflessness throughout the episode burnt itself into one's deepest memory.[9]

Vivekananda wrote to Alasinga Perumal, the editor of the *Brahmavadin*, "The new Swami delivered his maiden speech yesterday at a friendly society's meeting. It was good and I liked it; he has the making of a good speaker in him, I am sure."[10] After hearing the lecture Captain Sevier remarked, "Swami Abhedananda is a born preacher. Wherever he will go he will have success." In turn, Abhedananda completely accepted the religious and philosophical ideas of Swamiji and devoted his life to expanding upon them. He once told an audience in India, Vivekananda "achieved great success because he preached nothing but the Eternal Truth."[11]

On November 11 Josiah Goodwin wrote to Sara Bull:

> I am writing this while the two Swamis are having a big discussion in Bengali—12 midnight—which has already lasted over two hours on a sentence in the *Brihadaranyaka Upanishad* which you have often heard the Swami quote—"No man loves the wife for the wife's sake, but for the Self."[12]

Writing from London on the 27th of November, Abhedananda informed the *Brahmavadin* about Vivekananda, which was published on December 19, 1896:

> The spiritual light, which has been lit up in the minds of such of the English people as have attended his classes and heard his lectures, by his magnetic personality, his eloquence and his lucid explanations of the highest philosophy and religion of the Hindus, will, I hope, go on increasing after

> his departure. For there are many persons here who have really understood the Swami's teachings and who are so much interested in the Vedanta that they will carry on the work until the Swami comes back.

Vivekananda departed from London for India via Italy on December 15, leaving Abhedananda in charge of the British operation.

After spending over ten months in England, Abhedananda arrived penniless in the United States on August 6, 1897, as a guest of Mary Phillips. He was sent to America for the urgent purpose of taking over the New York Centre.* During the ensuing two years he met the following prominent supporters of Swamiji, most of whom are discussed in the chapters on Swami Vivekananda: Sara Bull, Sarah Farmer, William Flagg, Walter Goodyear, the treasurer of the New York Vedanta Society, and his wife, Egbert Guernsey, Charles Higgins, who regularly attended Abhedananda's public lectures, Colonel Thomas Higginson, Julia Ward Howe, William James, Lewis Janes, a close friend and helper of his, Leon Landsberg (Kripananda), Charles Lanman, Francis and Betty Leggett, Alice Mary Longfellow, Marie Louise (Abhayananda), Josephine MacLeod, Mary Phillips, Josiah Royce, Mrs. Arthur Smith, J. B. Street (Yogananda), Emma Thursby, Ralph Waldo Trine, and Sarah Waldo, a great helper. After Abhedananda arrived in New York City, Henry Van Haagen was often his companion and guide for the next couple of years. His first public lecture was held at Mott Memorial Hall in September.[13]

Many people are not aware of the deprivations and austerities that some of the early Swamis had to undergo. Abhedananda disclosed:

> I was determined to find ways and means for making a success of the Vedanta work in New York which was started by Swami Vivekananda. There were neither funds nor donations to carry on my work. I had to earn my living, pay the room-rent as well as for my meals in restaurants, the rent of the hall and meet my personal expenses and the expenses of weekly advertisements in various newspapers. I had no other source of income than the voluntary contributions taken in a basket after my classes and public lectures which were not enough to meet all these expenses. Therefore I tried to economize and sacrifice my personal comforts by accepting the invitations

* Appendix II gives a list of many of the city locations and years of Abhedananda's residences in the West over a twenty-five year period.

for my meals from the students of my classes. This was the *bhiksha-vritti* of the Hindu Sannyasins in India.[14]

On September 27, 1897, Swami Saradananda left Boston to visit Abhedananda in New York. In his *Diary* Abhedananda revealed:

> This was the first time I met him after he had left India nearly two years ago. I spent the whole day with him talking on different subjects and especially on the work he was doing in America. It was a great delight to me to meet my beloved Gurubhai after such a long time in a foreign country.... these and many other incidents of our spiritual lives together in India became vivid in my memory when I met Swami Saradananda in New York. It was a day of unbounded joy and peace which I can never forget.[15]

Abhedananda and Miss Sarah Waldo visited Saradananda at Mrs. Wheeler's home in Montclair, New Jersey, on October 11. A day or two later Mrs. Wheeler drove Abhedananda and Saradananda in a carriage to the Ampere Electrical Works. There Abhedananda conversed with the legendary inventor Thomas Alva Edison (1847-1931). Abhedananda related in his *Diary*:

> I met with Mr. Edison and had a talk with him on Hindu philosophy in which he was deeply interested.... He would sit up at his desk for hours deeply absorbed in concentration like a great Indian Yogi.... By his marvellous power of concentration he succeeded in becoming the world-renowned inventor of the most useful electrical machines which have benefited all the civilized nations of the earth.

The following year on July 11 they met again in East Orange, and Edison "was deeply interested in Hindu philosophy, especially in Vedanta".[16] Abhedananda recorded after his second visit:

> In scientific lines, Mr. Thomas Edison may be regarded as a real Yogi. However, when I met him, he was a little free, and as I hailed from India, he eagerly greeted me, and received me very cordially.... He talked with me very friendly and was very much glad to know that I came from India to preach the gospel of truth and Vedanta in that country. In low voice, he requested me to say something about India and also about the Vedantic

principles. I explained to him slowly some important problems of India and also about the Vedantic teachings. He listened to me with rapt attention and with reverential attitude, and was very pleased to learn. I stayed in his Laboratory for nearly two hours, and all the time the learned savant greeted me with joy and deep gratitude. When I was talking to him, I noticed all the time his bright and sweet look. True to say, I met no such a loving-hearted amiable man before.[17]

Once Edison went to a courthouse to pay his taxes. His mind was so absorbed in a scientific problem that when asked, he could not remember his own name no matter how hard he tried. His neighbour, seeing his embarrassment, reminded him that his name was Thomas Edison. Later he said, "At that time I could not recall my name even for a few seconds, even if my life depended on it."[18]

Thomas Alva Edison was the first person to become a member of the prestigious National Inventors Hall of Fame. His numerous innovations include the incandescent electric lamp, the phonograph, the carbon telephone transmitter, and the motion-picture projector. He created the world's first industrial research laboratory and many years later, for the benefit of the country, urged Congress to establish the first institution for military research. The Edison Electric Light Company formed in 1878 is the predecessor of the present General Electric Company.[19] As of 1878 Edison, a believer in reincarnation, became a member of the Theosophy Society for many years. He sent a cameraman to India and the Edison Company made eight silent movies about India (1902-12), including "Picturesque Darjeeling". During his last illness, when asked if he believed in survival after death, he answered, "The only survival I can conceive is to start a new earth cycle again."[20]

In its early years the Theosophical Movement attracted many eminent public figures. In addition to Thomas Edison, the list includes: psychologist Roberto Assagioli, Annie Besant, Emile Burnouf the Orientalist, G. N. Chakravarti, Mohini Chatterji, chemist and physicist Sir William Crookes, Buddhist leader Anagarika Dharmapala, General Abner Doubleday, at one time thought to be the inventor of baseball, astronomer Camille Flammarion, Kinza Hirai, Allan Octavian Hume who in 1885 became the "Father of the Indian National Congress", Charles Johnston, a translator of Indian scriptures, Wassily Kandinsky, the founder of Abstract Artistic Expressionism, Jiddu Krishnamurti, Maurice Maeterlinck, the 1911 Nobel Prize winner in literature,* abstract artist Piet Mondrian, Colonel Henry Olcott, author George Russell (A. E.), Rudolph Steiner, biologist Alfred Wallace, co-founder of the theory of evolution, Alexander "Mohammed" Webb, and the 1923 Nobel Prize winning poet and playwright William Butler Yeats.[21]

It was two Theosophists in England that first awakened a young Mahatma Gandhi's interest in Hinduism. They asked him to help them read the *Bhagavad Gita* in the original Sanskrit, along with Edwin Arnold's translation. He felt ashamed since he had never read the *Gita* in Sanskrit or Gujarati. Gandhi wrote, "I began reading the *Gita* with them.... The book struck me as one of priceless worth." They insisted he read Blavatsky's *Key to Theosophy*, and on so doing, states Gandhi, it "stimulated in me the desire to read books on Hinduism, and disabused me of the notion fostered by the missionaries that Hinduism was rife with superstitions."[22]

The Swami met Elmer Gates (1859-1923), an experimental psychologist, on December 12th at a luncheon as the guest of Josephine MacLeod and her sister Betty Leggett. In his *Diary* Abhedananda jotted down that Elmer Gates "was making psycho-physical experiments on various subjects to prove that the 'Mind' has controlling power over matter." They held a long conversation "on the powers of concentration and Raja Yoga in which he was deeply interested." At the Leggett home they met again and, "The Professor wanted to know some of the teachings of Raja Yoga and the effects of breathing exercises which I explained." Abhedananda visited Gates laboratory in Chevy Chase, Maryland. He "showed me his inventions and invited me to dine with him." Again, they met in Chevy Chase on May 22, 1898.[23]

Elmer Gates owned and ran the best-furnished private laboratory in the country. He sought to develop a system for augmenting human mental capacities and skills, which would bring about an increase in the structural elements of the brain cells. Gates placed emphasis on proper food intake. He believed that good, pleasant, and benevolent feelings produce healthy chemical substances in the body, and negative thoughts have the opposite effect. *The Relation and Development of the Mind and Brain* (1903) is his main published work. An attempt to revive his ideas was made in the 1971 New Thought publication *Elmer Gates and the Art of Mind-Using* by Donald Edson Gates.[24]

* His wife, a well-known opera singer, described herself as a "follower of the Vedanta Philosophy".

During 1897-98, the very active Swami lectured three times per week at Mott Memorial Hall and before the Twentieth Century Club, the Metaphysical Club, the Twilight Club of New York, and once in a week in Montclair, New Jersey, and held *Bhagavad Gita* classes in Brooklyn.[25]

1898 and After

On January 31, 1898, "A New York Friend" wrote out of respect for the Swami to the *Brahmavadin*:

> Swami Abhedananda has given us twelve lectures through the month of January, drawing large audiences and eliciting evidences of their steadily increasing understanding of, and interest in, the grand system of philosophy of which he is so gifted an exponent. He has acquired remarkable *savoir faire*, seeming to know intuitively what is best to say and what best to leave unsaid, and he clothes his teachings in simple and dignified language, expressing himself with great logical precision and clearness.... The Swami has met socially during the past month persons prominent in the world of art, science and religion, and in conversations with them has awakened their interest in the teachings of Vedanta.[26]

A grateful devotee from Montclair wrote in a letter that appeared in the *Brahmavadin*:

> The Swami Abhedananda's work here has been magnificent. He has held all the interest that the Swami Saradananda aroused and added to it. It would be impossible to tell how many will look back in after years to the teachings of the Swamis as a turning point in their lives.[27]

The following month a complimentary piece appeared in the *New York Tribune* of March 6 affirming that:

> The Swami Abhedananda is young, above medium height, sturdy, with the remarkable chest development of his fellow-teachers, from lifelong practice of breathing exercises, which are a part of their religious practices. His dark-hued face is finely chiselled, and with unusual intellectual strength shows the singular dignity, gentleness and repose of his people. His hands are no less individual and expressive of high character. He wears a turban of

Swami Abhedananda

> light orange colour and a simple robe of deep terra-cotta colour, the gown of the Sannyasins, the most ancient order of religious teachers which has existed in India since prehistoric times. His work is done without money consideration, and the lectures are free to all, his support depending upon voluntary gifts.
>
> As a speaker he is self-contained and attractive, and his lectures are clear, original explanations of philosophic subjects related to practical living. His command of English is as perfect as is his pronunciation, with rarely a slip in accent, which adds to the charm of a pleasing delivery.... To an occasional attendant, the growth of interest was unmistakable in steadily increasing audiences of intelligent persons, many of them members of orthodox churches, with a representation of well-known persons in public life.[28]

These statements were reprinted in the *Indian Mirror* on April 10 and, in a compact review along with a photograph of the Swami, in *The Critic* of March 19, a weekly review of literature and the arts. This review also delineates at what locations in the United States the Swami gave lectures and on what subjects.[29]

Abhedananda spoke at Mott Memorial Hall on "Sin and Sinners". The correspondent for the *New York Times* of March 21 (p. 10) observed:

> The lecture was closely listened to by an audience which filled the hall, and was followed by questions and answers. Swami Abhedananda has the advantage of a remarkably winning personality and the ability to make interesting abstract philosophic subjects relating to religious life. He wears the robe of an ancient order of religious teachers in India, a gown and sash of terra cotta colour and a turban of light orange colour.

On March 22 Abhedananda addressed the Vegetarian Society of New York on the subject "Why the Hindus are Vegetarians". Nearly four years earlier on May 1, 1894, Vivekananda spoke to the V[egetarian] Club at the St. Denis Hotel in New York on a similar subject. He mentioned that vegetarianism had its beginning in India.[30]

In the March 1898 number of *Intelligence* (later called *Metaphysical Magazine*) appears an article by Abhedananda titled "The Attributes of God, and Man's Relation to Them". In the frontispiece there is a full-page photograph of the Swami by H. J. Van Haagen and later this accolade:

> We present to our readers this month an exceedingly good likeness of the Swami Abhedananda, who brings to the Western world the good tidings of the Eastern teaching of true metaphysical principles. A more clear-cut type of the union of both heart and intellect is seldom seen in a human face, especially in this hard practical Western-world life.
>
> An essay by the Swami, which opens this number, shows this strength combined with simplicity in a marked way. His thought, while deep and true to the inexorable logic of reality, is yet so simple, so plain, so comprehensible, and so beautiful withal, that it carries no evidence of the "inexorable"—which seems to trouble the minds of some who have so strong a desire to be independent that the idea of logical exactness seems burdensome. The teachings of this article are plain metaphysical truth and well understood here by those who have studied Eastern lore ... Calmness is the first requisite of mental force. The Swami's valuable contribution verifies all of these thoughts.[31]

On May 16, the Swami met John Brady (1848-1918), the governor of Alaska. They held a discussion, and the governor invited him to come to Alaska during the summer months when the weather was warmer. Seven years later in 1905, Abhedananda and his friend Professor Herschel Parker of Columbia University came to Sitka, Alaska, where they were the guests of Governor Brady. The governor's daughter took them on a tour of some deserted homes of Native Americans and some other important sites. John Green Brady ran away from home at the age of eight, was taken care of by the government, and then worked on the farm of a philanthropist. After graduating from Union Seminary in New York, he went to Alaska to work as a missionary for the Presbyterian Church. Switching from religion to politics, he became one of four United States commissioners to Alaska and received appointment from U.S. President William McKinley to be the territorial governor of Alaska from 1897 until 1906. Brady probably did more than any person of his generation to inform the American public about the resources and needs of Alaska.[32]

Next, Abhedananda went to the White House and, on May 19, 1898, was introduced to William McKinley (1843-1901), the 25th President of the United States. At that time, the Spanish-American War was taking place. Abhedananda noted:

The President McKinley gave me a cordial reception and asked me several questions about the Vedanta philosophy on which I was lecturing in the city, and showed his interest in the political condition of the people of India under British rule. I was the first Hindu of India who was introduced to the President of the U.S.A.

William McKinley enlisted at seventeen years of age as a private in the Union army during the Civil War and rose to the rank of major. He served as a member of the United States Congress, governor of Ohio, and the president of the United States (1897-1901). Soon after his re-election, an anarchist shot McKinley at a public reception. Eight days later he passed away, his final words being, "It is God's way. His will, not ours, be done."[33]

Soon after Lewis Janes (1844-1901) [q.v.] met Abhedananda in Montclair, New Jersey, he invited him to speak at the Cambridge Conferences. Later in the month they got together again in Cambridge, and Janes asked the Swami to address the Free Religious Association of Boston. On the morning of May 27 the Swami lectured before the latter group and noted, "Col. [Thomas] Higginson was the president who introduced me to the audience as the accredited teacher from India, on whom had fallen the mantle of the illustrious Swami Vivekananda." Janes introduced him and said, "It gives me great pleasure to welcome our brother from India, Swami Abhedananda." The following day Janes took Abhedananda to Harvard and introduced him to the two world famous professors, William James and Josiah Royce.[34]

"A New York Friend" wrote in a June 16 edition of the *Brahmavadin*:

> Reverence does not find much place in our busy hustling life in America, but the devoted regard and reverential love of his students and hearers for Swami Abhedananda is sincere and unmistakable. The simplicity and purity of the Swami's life, his equanimity and gentleness, his unselfish and untiring efforts to help all who have wished to learn, have won for him and for Vedanta many sincere friends and students.

News about Abhedananda went over the wire throughout the country, and we find the following statement in the Oshkosh, Wisconsin, *Daily Northwestern* newspaper of August 1, 1898 (p. 7):

> The Swami Abhedananda is not only the most learned, but the most fascinating Hindoo who ever sought disciples on this side of the Atlantic. His

> personal beauty is undeniable, and the charm of his manner is recognized by men as well as women. He has great magnetism. These natural advantages, combined with his scholarly attainments, drew and held the largest class in the philosophy of the Vedas which New York has ever known... Add to his beauty of face his dignity and the deference and courtesy of the oriental and one may understand why he became a social fad in America last season.

Lewis Janes requested the Swami to give four classes at the Monsalvat (Mount of Peace) School for the Study of Comparative Religion held during August 1898 at Greenacre near Eliot, Maine. Abhedananda also spoke under a large tent before the general audience on "Science and Religion". He held morning classes on the *Gita* under the "Swami's Pine" where Vivekananda spoke four years before. His lecture on "The True Basis of Morality" was described by the *Boston Evening Transcript* as "an address of universal value". Other speakers included Lewis Janes, Cornell Professor Nathaniel Schmidt, and Rabbi Joseph Krauskopf of Philadelphia. Christian missionaries and teachers were encouraged to attend the meetings to gain more knowledge about non-Christian religions. Swamis Vivekananda, Saradananda, Paramananda, and Bodhananda also spoke at the Greenacre Conference on Comparative Religion.[35]

At Greenacre the Swami met Transcendalist Charles Malloy (1823-1914), the president of the Emerson Club of Boston, who "was a personal friend and disciple of Ralph Waldo Emerson, the greatest Vedantic philosopher in America...." The Swami stated:

> He asked me the meaning of Emerson's poem on *Brahm* ... He was surprised when I explained that this stanza was a free translation of two verses from the *Bhagavat Gita*. He said, "Now I understand the true source of Mr. Emerson's inspiration."

The two of them and Lewis Janes went to see Ralph Waldo Emerson's house. They found English translations of the *Law of Manu* (*Manu-Samhita*), *Vishnu Purana* and the Upanishads in Emerson's valuable library.[36] Charles Malloy, as a young man, worked as a cobbler and then came under the influence of Emerson. After the philosopher lent him a copy of his *Bhagavad Gita*, he was determined to copy the entire book longhand. His writings appear in the volume *A Study of Emerson's Major Poems*. Malloy wrote a series of monographs on Emerson's poems for *The Arena* in 1904, which were the most popular metaphysical papers submitted to the magazine that year. He served as a member of the Concord School of Philosophy and a founder of the Emerson-Browning Club in Waltham, Massachusetts, a city where Saradananda had lectured. Abhedananda and Malloy met again in Waltham in May 1899 when the Swami spoke before the Psychomath Society. Abhedananda and Charles Malloy drove from Waltham to Concord on the 9th of June 1899. They visited Walden Pond where Henry David Thoreau (1817-62) had lived the life of an Oriental ascetic for several years in a hut built by himself. In April of the following year, the Swami lectured on the "Motherhood of God" before the Psychomath Society, and Malloy made some complimentary remarks when the talk came to a close. In 1900 Abhedananda spoke at the Greenacre Lecture Course along with Charles Malloy and others.[37]

During his month-long stay at Greenacre in August 1898, the Swami met the veteran actor Joseph Jefferson (1829-1905) who addressed the subject of the "Possibility of Drama". Jefferson appeared in one of the two group photos of Vivekananda taken at Greenacre in 1894. He is standing in the back row to the right of Swamiji wearing a hat. A photograph of Jefferson, Sarah Farmer and Abhedananda at Greenacre appeared in the classy *Harper's Bazaar* magazine of 1899. Abhedananda was present at a comic play in New York featuring Joseph Jefferson, who gave a marvellous performance in spite of his deafness. Jefferson, who began his acting career at the age of four, is ranked as one of the four eminent American stage actors of the nineteenth century. During his seventy-year stage career, he excelled in the sentimentally comic role of Rip Van Winkle, a part he played in nine silent movie films. In 1893 he succeeded Edwin Booth as president of the Players' Club, marking him as the dean of American actors. Despite the fact that he had little formal education, he was in great demand as a lecturer. Joe Jefferson, a capable landscape painter and a talented writer, was known for his kindly, humorous and happy disposition.[38]

At Greenacre Swami Abhedananda met the noted American novelist William Dean Howells (1837-1920) who also lectured there. Dubbed the "Dean of American Letters", Howells received honorary doctorates from many universities, and was the first president of the American Academy of Arts and Letters. He produced a staggering volume and variety of influential literary works. Among novelists, Howells led the way toward realistic, morally oriented and politically committed fiction.[39]

On October 28, 1898, the Vedanta Society of New York that Vivekananda founded in 1894 was incorporated by Swami Abhedananda according to the laws of the State of New York, and Francis Leggett became its president. In April 1900 Abhedananda went one step further and amended the bylaws so that the Swami in charge of the Society would have control over its activities.[40]

Near the end of the year *The Criterion*, a New York magazine of literature, drama, music, and art, described Abhedananda's appearance this way:

> He wears the sweeping terra-cotta robes of his prehistoric order, with a turban of palest orange wound above his mystical eyes. The young man is built like a football player, with fine features, and his face though dark as a Moor's, is eloquent and spiritually beautiful.[41]

A brahmacharin from the New York Centre sent a letter to the *Brahmavadin* published on January 1, 1899, which states in part that Abhedananda explains Vedantic ideas

> with such clearness that even those who never heard of the Vedanta before and come for the first time to hear the Swami, feel quickly the grand, lofty and deep ideas and profound metaphysical thoughts which are hidden in every sentence of that wonderful work of Sri Shankaracharya. The secret lies in the Swami's method of teaching. The Swami expounds the teachings of the Vedanta and presents the Oriental ideals before the minds of the students through such expressions which are in perfect harmony with the concepts and ideals they already possess. Consequently, they seem quite attractive and easy to comprehend. After this explanation the Swami answers with great patience and kindness the many questions which the students ask freely. Then he teaches how to concentrate the mind on the Atman and how to meditate.[42]

For the benefit of those students who wanted to practise the teachings of Vedanta, Abhedananda held meditation and question and answer classes twice a week. He insisted that meditation and concentration are the only means to attain spiritual realization. "A New York Friend" tells us that in India people have been taught to meditate from earliest childhood. Compare that to the West, where people customarily live active, restless lives concentrating on external things. How difficult it is for them to learn the techniques of meditation. During the course of the 1899-1900 season, Abhedananda formed a yoga class open to members and non-members alike. He taught practical lessons in breathing exercises, concentration, meditation and self-control to earnest students who applied for instructions.[43]

In his *Diary* of January 1899, the Swami optimistically summarized his first seventeen months in the United States as a guest in people's homes:

> My hosts and hostesses never thought for a moment that I was a stranger and a foreigner of a different nationality, but they always treated me as a dear friend and regarded me as a spiritual master as well as a member of their own family. I could never forget the cordiality and kindness which I had received from those whom I had visited during my stay in different places. Knowing that I had no funds to support myself and that there was no one to help me financially, they kept me from starving by inviting me at their meals at noon and in the evening. Thus they gave me an opportunity to learn their mode of living as well as their manners, customs, etiquette and their likes and dislikes.[44]

Soon after seeking Holy Mother's advice in a letter of March 1899, Abhedananda received a message from her that contained in part this encouraging reply:

> I am also glad that your work there is going on very well. You are enlightening the mission of Thakur. I pray to Sri Thakur, and am also blessing, for the success of your work there. There is no doubt about it that he (Thakur) will help you in your work.[45]

She gave him permission to eat non-vegetarian food like fish.

On Easter Sunday, April 2, 1899, Abhedananda gave monastic vows to five brahmacharinis, and brahmacharya to Cornelius Heijblom, who received the Sanskrit name Gurudasa (later Swami Atulananda). In the summer of 1898 Heijblom had come to hear Abhedananda lecture at Mott Memorial Hall. After attending the powerful and logical lectures of Abhedananda, Heijblom remarked, "It was as though a sudden revelation had opened up. I knew all at once that this was Truth." Being a single man, he was able to practise the religion and to perform chores at Abhedananda's growing Centre.[46]

During April-May 1899, Abhedananda gave two lectures before the Cambridge Conferences. According to a newspaper account:

> The Swami Abhedananda of India, who is to speak at the Cambridge Conferences next Sunday, will receive a warm welcome from his many friends and admirers. The Swami returns with new honours, for both his lectures and his classes during the winter have been remarkably successful and have aroused much enthusiasm in New York. The Swami is a pupil and follower of Ramakrishna, the "real Mahatma" of whom he will speak next Sunday.[47]

Abhedananda's *Diary* in his *Complete Works* terminates on May 3, 1899. After this period, we have more limited information to work with in order to determine his contact with prominent Western personalities. Consequently, we have no information about many of his personal associations. The best original sources are the *Brahmavadin* and the *Vedanta Monthly Bulletin* put out by the New York Centre between April 1905 and 1909.[48]

In early May 1899, Abhedananda visited Melrose, Massachusetts, and met D. Evans Caswell, a magnetic healer who had hosted Vivekananda in the city when he gave two lectures between September 22 and October 1, 1894.[49] Travelling through the state, Abhedananda met his old friend Charles Malloy in Waltham, Massachusetts, in May 1899, when the Swami spoke before the Psychomath Society. While in Waltham, Abhedananda was the guest of Daniel O'Hara (1855-1912), who was largely responsible for raising the quality of American watch dials. The O'Hara Dial Co. made watch dials for all of the factories in the country, and sent dials to France, Germany and Japan. By 1898 serious competition reduced his sales markedly. The Swami also attended the Ministers' meeting in Fitchburg on May 22, 1899 where, according to the local newspaper, "this Hindoo priest contributed not a little additional interest to the meeting."[50]

Following a busy schedule, Abhedananda was a guest speaker along with the illustrious Julia Ward Howe and Kate Gannett Wells before the women's Submasters Club of Boston on May 26 at the Hotel Vendome. His speech was described by the newspaper as "an interesting address" delivered "in excellent English". Six days later he spoke at the meeting of the New England Cremation Society. A newspaper story in the *Boston Traveller* of June 2, 1899 reported, "Swami Abhedananda of India, a young man with an intelligent face and a command of the choicest English, spoke most interestingly of cremation in India, saying that it dated from prehistoric times."[51] A correspondent for *The Boston Evening Transcript* in 1899 made these appreciative statements concerning the Swami:

> The Swami Abhedananda is a young man of charming personality. He is a full-blooded Hindu, and has been away from India only three years. He speaks English fluently.... Swami Abhedananda is a man about thirty years old, perhaps, above the average height, with clear-cut features and a high forehead. He dresses in a flowing black gown, festooned tightly about the throat, and when he speaks in public he wears a graceful white turban. His English shows barely a sign of a foreign accent and his voice is soft and penetrating. He is a man who would attract attention anywhere.[52]

On the first day of July 1899, Abhedananda and Lewis Janes travelled to North Woodstock, New Hampshire, to take part in the ten-day meetings of the Appalachian Mountain Club. The seventy-five members were quartered in Deer Park and did a lot of hiking in the local mountains while the meetings were being conducted.[53] Abhedananda was one of the three-featured speakers, along with Reverend Benjamin F. Mills and Colonel Robert Ingersoll, the famous agnostic, at the Free Religious Association meetings held at the Hollis Street Theatre in Boston.[54]

Due to other speaking engagements in different cities, Abhedananda could give only three lectures during the last two weeks of August 1899 at the Greenacre Monsalvat (Mount of Peace) School for the Comparative Study of Religion. In the large assembly tent before the general audience, he discussed "Is Hinduism Pantheistic?" and "The Spiritual Influence of India in the West", and under the Swami's Pine his subject was "Reincarnation". "An American Brahmacharini" informs us that:

> This school is held under a tree which can shelter nearly 200 persons under its over-spreading branches. This is known as the Swami's Pine, named when Greenacre was founded in 1894 and the Swami Vivekananda taught there and consecrated it for use in the teaching of Vedanta. Only the Swamis ever teach under its protecting shelter.

At Greenacre, Charles Malloy offered four lectures on "The Bhagavad Gita and its Influence on the Thought of Ralph Waldo Emerson", and Virchand Gandhi of Bombay spoke five times on the religion, psychology and philosophy of the Jains. Other speakers included Lewis Janes, T. B. Pandian of India, Nathaniel Schmidt and Rabbi Joseph Silverman.[55]

In early September, Abhedananda received a telegram from Vivekananda asking him to join him at Ridgely Manor. "An American Brahmacharini" explains:

> The joy of this reunion of the brother Swamis after three years and more of separation by half the world must be imagined. For ten days the Swamis lived together in one of the cottages on the estate of their host, enjoying communion with each other, with loving friends and with nature.

During his stay at Ridgely he informed Vivekananda and Turiyananda of the progress of Vedanta in America, especially in New York where they had recently moved into their first permanent headquarters at 146 East Fifty-fifth Street. A couple of months later, while staying in New York as Dr. Egbert Guernsey's guest, Vivekananda conducted six or seven classes at the New York Centre during November 8-21. On the 8th when Vivekananda took charge of the meeting, "Swami Abhedananda introduced the Swami in words of love and reverence, as the founder of the present Vedanta work in New York, and the pioneer and prophet of Vedanta Philosophy in America." "On the 10th November a reception was tendered to the Swami, many old-time friends and students, as also others who had long desired to see the Swami, were happy for the privilege of greeting him."[56]

A letter to the *Brahmavadin* from "An American Brahmacharini" of September 1899 stated:

> In New York, the most difficult city in the United States in which to reach the spiritual nature of people, Swami Abhedananda has made a profound impression. Two years of patient, persistent, loving service has established Vedanta in a concentrated body of earnest students who are devoted to the continuance of the work. The outlook for extended work by Swami Abhedananda is most promising.

Four months later the Brahmacharini added, "The loving, grateful thought of many true friends and students follows Swami Abhedananda, who is steadily gaining in power as a teacher, and whose work, wherever he may be, is full of blessing."[57]

Miss Anna Josephine Ingersoll's (1852-1940) [q.v.] article "The Swamis in America" appeared in *The Arena* journal of October 1899. Photographs of Swamis Vivekananda, Abhedananda and Saradananda copyrighted by H. J. Van Haagen are part of the text. Concerning Abhedananda it mentions, "During the last season, he has given at Assembly Hall, in the Associated Charities Building, eighty lectures on the Vedanta philosophy to large and intelligent audiences." Her twenty-two-page booklet *Greenacre on the Piscataqua* issued in 1900 pictures Abhedananda with Lewis Janes and Virchand Gandhi (1864-1901), a contemporary of Vivekananda. In November 1893 Vivekananda mentioned, "A Christian lady from Poona, Miss Sorabji, and the Jain representative, Mr. Gandhi, are going to remain longer in the country and make lecture tours. I hope they will succeed."[58] A year later Vivekananda wrote to Diwanji about him:

> Now here is Virchand Gandhi, the Jain, whom you well knew in Bombay. This man never takes anything but pure vegetables even in this terribly cold climate, and tooth and nail tries to defend his countrymen and religion. The people of this country like him very well.[59]

Abhedananda added that Gandhi, the Jain representative at the 1893 Parliament of Religions, "was a great admirer of Vivekananda whom he met there". Gandhi delivered about 650 lectures in America, returning to the country in 1896 and 1899. He wrote many books on Jain philosophy and in the U.S. helped to establish the "International Society for the Education of Women in India". His statue presently stands at the Jain Temple in Chicago.[60] Other South Asian speakers who made a remarkable impression at the Parliament included A. Dharmapala, Pratap Mazumdar, Manilal Dvivedi, Jinanji Modi, Balwant Nagarkar, and G. N. Chakravarti.

Swami Abhedananda came out with *Three Lectures on Reincarnation* in 1898, and the following year a new and enlarged edition added two more lectures, which dealt with reincarnation in relation to heredity, evolution, resurrection and transmigration, each from a scientific standpoint. Concerning a section in this book, Frederick W. Mann M.D., the editor of the journal *Medical Age* from Detroit, in his "Editorial Notes—The Physiology of Reincarnation", made the informative statement that Abhedananda

> has been using the [August] Weismann [1834-1914] theory of heredity in support of the Vedanta doctrine of reincarnation. He maintains that the

notion of the continuity of the germ-plasm has come almost to the door of the doctrine of reincarnation. Weismann, in denying the inheritance of acquired characteristics, regards variations as a result of natural selection, the influence of which has reacted upon the germ-plasm. Vedanta teaches that the germ-plasm is a subtle reincarnating body containing potentially all the experiences, characters, and desires possessed by the individual in a previous form of life.[61]

Two additional affirmative evaluations of the work read as follows:

> In these discourses the Swami Abhedananda considers the questions of evolution and the resurrection in their bearing upon the ancient teaching of rebirth, the truth, logic and justice of which are rapidly permeating the best thought of the Western world. For the preservation of this doctrine, mankind is indebted to the literary storehouses of India, the racial and geographical source of much of the vital knowledge of Occidental peoples. Reincarnation is shown in the present volume to be a universal solvent of life's mysteries. It answers those questions of children that have staggered the wisest minds who seek to reconcile the law of evolution and the existence of an intelligent and just Creator, with the proposition that man has but a single lifetime in which to develop spiritual self-consciousness. It is commended to every thinker (*Mind*, February 1900).
>
> This is the work of a man of fine education and of fine intellect.... [Reincarnation] as expounded by Swami Abhedananda is very plausible, quite scientific, and far from uncomforting. The exposition contained in this little book is well worth reading by all students of metaphysics. There is not the slightest danger of its converting or perverting anyone to a new and strange religion. Reincarnation is not religion, it is science. Science was never known to hurt anybody but scientists (*Brooklyn Eagle*, December 13, 1907).[62]

In the *Brahmavadin*, "A Vedanta Student" drew attention to the Swami's practical and business sense:

> Swami Abhedananda has proved himself not only an able, efficient teacher, but has furthered the success of the work, as well, in every other way, by careful attention to its needs and to details. He is equal to every occasion that demands the vast judgment and consideration, advancing the

> interests of the work that it may be presented in the most helpful way to new students who are joining the classes at all times. Although unaccustomed to our Western business methods, he is yet able to decide the most weighty questions, that arise in the growth of the movement, as none of the members, unaided, could do, though many are prominent businessmen. Our gratitude and loyalty to Swami Abhedananda and all the Swamis for the helpful spirit of their teachings, will ever remain, unbounded, immeasurable.[63]

Swami Vivekananda did not get personally involved in the administration of the Vedanta Centres, and to some extent left Sara Bull (1850-1911) [q.v.] in charge of the American work. He concentrated more of his efforts on his lectures and writings. In April 1900, Abhedananda amended the bylaws of the New York Centre so that the Swami in charge would have control over its administrative activities. He and later Swami Trigunatita were interested in creating a more structured organization. Sara had a plan to centralize the American organization to coordinate the separate individual Vedanta groups under a single administration. This approach supposedly offered a check against stagnation and parochialism. Abhedananda opposed her plan and favoured local independence for each centre. In doing so, he antagonized Sara and her supporter Francis Leggett who soon resigned as president of the New York Vedanta Society. Sara thought that the young Abhedananda, whom she greatly underrated, lacked experience and training in organizational work. She sought Swamiji's support in the feud, but he remained neutral. However, he did tell Alice Hansbrough in California, "You people think the head of a society [Mr. Leggett, Mrs. Bull] can run things. You know, my boys can't work under those conditions." Due to Abhedananda's efforts, the future Swamis in the West of various temperaments and organizational philosophies were able to address their local needs, preserve their local autonomy, and manage their respective centres in the way that they saw fit. Consequently, a wide variety of reasonable approaches have been put into practice.[64]

Swami Abhedananda would occasionally depart on a lecture tour and do a wonderful job of addressing a wide variety of people. For example, in April 1900 he spoke in Lynn, Massachusetts, under the auspices of the Oxford Outlook Club, before the Psychomath Society in Waltham, at the Liberal Congress of Religion in Boston, and at the Cambridge Conferences under the inspiration of Lewis Janes. At the Oxford Outlook Club, before an audience of three-hundred women, he corrected many errors concerning their understanding of the position of women in Indian society.[65]

Lillian Montgomery [q.v.] attended Abhedananda's lectures in New York City in 1900. In a 1955-taped talk dealing primarily with her impression of Vivekananda, she revealed:

> I was really searching for something, and someone said they had heard a swami ... and that was Swami Abhedananda. I heard him several times and was very impressed because he was so different from us; he was very calm and poised and all that, and I was surprised that he knew so much about our literature and our sciences. I think I only heard him twice, when someone said another swami [Vivekananda] was coming. Abhedananda had been speaking in a hall, and they told us that this new swami would speak in a Vedanta House.[66]

Swami Vivekananda departed from New York en route to Paris on July 26, 1900. It was Swami Abhedananda's job to carry on the work established by Swami Vivekananda by creating interest in Vedanta in many locations in North America and Western Europe. This he did diligently through his books (still selling well), lectures and personal associations for the next twenty-one years. He continued his busy schedule by returning to Greenacre and lecturing along with Edward Everett Hale, Ralph Waldo Trine, Dr. Fillmore Moore, Charles Malloy, Nathaniel Schmidt, and others. He read Vivekananda's lecture on "My Master" at one of the sessions, which was enjoyed by all. The Maine Historical Society has preserved a sublime photograph taken at Greenacre, which can be viewed on the Internet. There is a coming together of three traditions, the Indian Vedantist Abhedananda, Transcendalist Charles Malloy, and New Thought representatives Ralph Waldo Trine and C. B. Patterson. On the 5th to 9th of August, he gave three lectures before audiences numbering 7,000 or more at the Indiana Association of Spiritualists in Chesterfield. After addressing the Appalachian Mountain Club of Boston in September, he spoke at the International Metaphysical League in the Madison Square Garden Concert Hall in New York City on the "Universality of Vedanta" in mid November. The four-day session "was a luminous success", featuring a number of prominent "New Thought" speakers. In the year 1900 he also addressed the audience at the New York State Conference of Religion.[67]

1901 and Later

"A New York Devotee" wrote to the *Prabuddha Bharata* in May 1901:

> Among the significant blessings ushered in with the dawn of the new century, is the evidence of a firmer foothold of the Vedanta philosophy in the lives of many Western students. We feel that is wholly due to Swami Abhedananda's persistence and untiring faithfulness, that so much has been accomplished.... how clearly every word reaches the most distinct part of the hall, with no apparent effort on the part of the speaker, a pleasing contrast to the excited manner employed by many of our pulpit orators, who resort to much noise and gesticulation in their effort to convince their hearers of certain truths. The Swami's power to hold their absorbed attention lies in the simplicity and directness with which he unfolds the Divine message.[68]

According to the *New York Times* report of June 1, 1901 (p. 4), Abhedananda spoke on the subject "Did Christ Teach a New Religion?" at the annual meeting of the Free Religious Association held at the Boston Museum on May 31st. Other speakers included Lewis Janes, Nathaniel Schmidt of Cornell University, Rabbi Joseph Silverman of Temple Emanu-El in New York, and Rabbi Charles Fleischer of Boston. On June 22 the Swami left New York City for the Pan American Exposition in Buffalo and then proceeded to Cleveland, Chicago, Yellowstone National Park, Seattle, Tacoma, and Portland, before he reached his destination of San Francisco in late July. In May 1900, Swamiji had written to Abhedananda, "I am trying my best to get one of you for a flying visit to this Coast—it is a great country for Vedanta."[69]

Laura Glenn mentioned:

> Once on his way, however, he met friends on all sides—those who had heard him lecture or had read his pamphlets, and who considered it a privilege to render him every service in their power. Invitations to talk and lecture were everywhere pressed upon him.[70]

A reception was held for him at the residence of Milburn Logan, the president of the Vedanta Society in San Francisco. Also attending the welcoming were vice-president Carl Petersen, secretary and treasurer Albert

Wollberg, and others. The *San Francisco Evening News* of August 1, 1901, expressed this appreciation:

> A pundit of unusual erudition and culture is with us in the person of the Swami Abhedananda, who arrived from New York last Monday, after a pleasant trip across the Continent. The Swami is reported to be a very wise man. He is reported to speak in epigrams, a sample of which is offered in the sentence, "Everything comes in time: exercise patience." It has been hinted that Swami Abhedananda has come preaching in the Occidental wilderness and that he intends to proselyte all who are awake to the light that dawns eternally in the East.[71]

In addition, the *San Francisco Chronicle* (p. 5) of the same day published a large size photograph of Abhedananda and told its readers:

> The Swami is a dignified intellectual looking East Indian. He has dark hair, eyes and complexion suggesting a handsomely chiselled piece of bronze. He speaks English fluently, and his thoughts as he gives them utterance, are so framed as to form an axiom. Sentence after sentence being epigrammatic.[72]

In a letter Turiyananda supplied Mrs. Alice Hansbrough with the information that Abhedananda remained at Shanti Ashrama for about a week. Fourteen students then occupied the retreat. Soon after he left Shanti Ashrama, the *San Jose Herald* of August 15, 1901 (p. 8) held an interview with the Swami. The newspaper correspondent describes him as:

> A very distinguished Hindu teacher, writer and philosopher, Swami Abhedananda, is a guest at Hotel Vendome for a few days.... Swami Abhedananda is a gentleman of most pleasing address, modest and simple in manners, speaking English perfectly, and expressing himself in the language of culture and education. He is familiar with the Bible, as also our best literature. He is the author of several works in English upon Hinduism.... The Swami says there are many students of Hindu philosophy in the United States, particularly in New York and San Francisco.[73]

The next day the *San Francisco Chronicle* (p. 7) wrote, "Swami Abhedananda is a gentleman of most pleasing address, modest and simple in manner, speaking English perfectly and expressing himself in the language of culture and education."

When the Swami lived in San Francisco, he stayed at the residence of Dr. Milburn Logan, a great admirer of Vivekananda. His house at 770 Oak Street served as the meeting place for the local Vedantists. Abhedananda gave a public lecture at Union Square Hall, 421 Post Street, on September the 1st on the subject "What is Vedanta?". By invitation, on the 6th Abhedananda publicly lectured as a guest of honour at the University of California in Berkeley.* Next, he made a trip to Los Angeles after visiting Yosemite and the Mariposa Big Trees. During his ten-day visit, he stayed as the guest of the Mead family (Alice Hansbrough, Carrie Wyckoff, and others) in their rented house in South Pasadena, which the Vedanta Society of Southern California now owns. Vivekananda lived there in January-February 1900, Turiyananda in July of the same year, probably in March-April of 1901 and again in January 1901, and Trigunatita in May 1903. At the residence of Dr. and Mrs. John Schmitz, he received a reception from the members of the Los Angeles Vedanta Society. At that time Abhedananda also made a visit to the city of San Diego. On his return journey to New York he stopped off in Salt Lake City, Denver, Colorado Springs, Pikes Peak, Chicago, Detroit, Toronto, Montreal, and Thousand Island Park before arriving on October 7th.[74]

A piece appeared in the *Salt Lake* (*City*) *Herald* of September 21, 1901 (p. 7) that read:

> Swami Abhedananda of Calcutta is at the Knutsford to make a few days' stay in Salt Lake City to study the Mormons and local conditions, and incidentally plant the seeds of his cult here. To do this he expects to arrange for a lecture or a series of lectures.... During a visit to the coast he encountered H. L. Culmer, and accepted an invitation from him to make a local visit. The Oriental will spend today in seeing the points of interest about the city under the guidance of Mr. Culmer.

A Mormon convert born in Kent, England, Henry L. A. Culmer (1854-1914) later settled in Salt Lake City. He became a well-known professional landscape painter and writer, and lecturer on art. At that time Culmer was president of the Utah Art Institute. When president of the United States

* See Chapter XVII.

Taft visited Utah in 1909, he was presented with one of Culmer's paintings as a souvenir of his visit. Two of his paintings can now be found at the Utah State Capitol building.[75]

A few days later Swami Abhedananda attracted the attention of the *Colorado Springs Gazette* of September 26, 1901, where the interviewer makes these comments:

> "Yes, yes, that is my name, Swami Abhedananda; you need not pronounce it. English tongues cannot master the liquid rhythm of Hindu consonants," and a smile as frank and innocent as a child's accompanied the remark, which was uttered in tones that were low, crisp and so melodious that the speaker could have made a transaction of cabbage and onions in the market-place sound as musical as chanted verse. Swami Abhedananda is a philosopher by profession, a lecturer by choice and a poet by nature. He is tall, berry brown through generations of basking in the tropical sun, and has hair and eyes of such inky blackness that there is nothing to compare them with. Moreover, he has the hauteur and pride of the aristocrat oriental which unconsciously makes one attribute to him a princely charm, would be termed unwarranted and ridiculous snobbishness. But Swami's soft, gentle voice, his cultured accent redeem him from such a base imputation.[76]

During these years, Swami Abhedananda was busy writing a number of books that are widely read today. *Three Lectures on Spiritual Unfoldment* (1901) covered the subjects of self-control, concentration and meditation, and God-consciousness. The journal *Mind* told their readers:

> This attractive little volume comprises three lectures on the Vedanta Philosophy. The discourses will be found vitally helpful even by those who know little and care less about the spiritual and ethical teachings of which the Swami is an able and popular exponent. As the Vedanta itself is largely a doctrine of universals and ultimates, so also is this book of common utility and significance among all races of believers. Its precepts are susceptible of application by any rational thinker, regardless of religious predilection and inherited prejudices. The principles set forth by this teacher are an excellent corrective of spiritual bias or narrowness, and as such the present work is to be commended. It has already awakened an interest in Oriental literature that augurs well for the cause of human brotherhood, and it merits a wide circulation among all who cherish advanced ideals.[77]

A steady supporter of the Vedanta movement was the journal *Mind: Science, Philosophy, Religion, Psychology, Metaphysics, Occultism* (1897-1906). Based in New York City and a leading exponent of New Thought, it was coedited by John Emery McLean (b. 1865) and Charles Brodie Patterson (1854-1917).

Abhedananda's audiences increased to 600, and so it was necessary to rent the Carnegie Lyceum to accommodate the overflowing crowd. Beginning in November 1901, he lectured there continuing on for twenty-six consecutive Sundays. A correspondent with the initials L. G. (most likely Laura Glenn, Sister Devamata) wrote to the *Prabuddha Bharata* of January 1902. The message said in part:

> Large audiences which gather each week in Carnegie Lyceum follow with rapt attention every word which the Swami utters; while the Society rooms on Tuesday evenings are filled to the doors with a public equally eager to hear him expound that portion of the Upanishads known to English speaking people through Edwin Arnold's translation as "The Secret of Death".
>
> He himself has come back to his winter's task with an unusually large store of force and vitality—thanks to a three month journey to the Pacific Coast, during which he was able for the first time to perceive how far his field of influence extends. At every turn, indeed, he met well-wishers and friends—those who had heard him lecture, or who had read his pamphlets, and who were more than anxious to render him any service within their power. Unable to resist their solicitations, he was occasionally prevailed upon to give a talk on Vedanta.[78]

When he spoke on Sri Ramakrishna, the *New York Sun* pointed out:

> On March 12 [1902] the Hindu preacher, Swami Abhedananda delivered a soul-stirring lecture before a distinguished gathering at the Vedanta Society's house. The occasion was the birthday celebration of his Master. The Swami said in the course of his lecture: "The saint of Dakshineswar, the greatest teacher the world has ever come to know, was the embodiment of Vedanta philosophy who realized with incomparable charm and power the splendid sympathy of the universal soul. In the teachings and life of Sri Ramakrishna one finds a unique thing scarcely to be found in the world. History has no record of such a saint who stood for the harmoniza-

tion of religions. We err not when we say he was the Messiah of spiritual democracy."[79]

News of Abhedananda's success reached the Vedanta Society in San Francisco. Under the heading of "New York Notes", the *Pacific Vedantin* for April 1902 commented, "Recent news from there assures that the 'Great Movement' was never more prosperous in New York than now. The best minds are taking a profound interest in it."[80]

During a two-month European tour beginning in August 1902, Abhedananda landed in Liverpool, England, and then went on to Glasgow, Scotland, and across the English Channel to Paris, France and Switzerland. He returned to New York in early October. During the summer recess which began on May 15, 1903, with two students he visited Italy, Switzerland, Germany, and Belgium before returning to New York on the 6th of October. Between June 28 and October 16, 1904, the Swami made a trip to Amsterdam, Holland, Austria (Alps), Munich, Germany, Paris and London. In Germany he was introduced to a high dignitary that might have been Kaiser Wilhelm (1859-1941), the emperor of the country. Being a skilled and adventurous mountain climber, with a rope and a guide he scaled some of the historic peaks of the Swiss Alps. Earlier, in 1902, he had joined the Appalachian Mountain Club in the United States, remaining a member for many years.[81]

How to Be a Yogi (1902) which, among other things, asked and answered the question "Was Christ a Yogi?", was well received by the public as indicated by the following evaluations in many areas of the country:

> The work is comparatively free from technical terms and will prove equally available to the student of Oriental thought and to the general reader as yet unfamiliar with this, one of the great philosophical systems of the world (*Washington Post*, November 17, 1902).
>
> The book is calculated to interest the student of Oriental thought and familiarize the unread with one of the greatest philosophical systems of the world (*Buffalo Courier*, November 23, 1902).
>
> This book is well worth a careful reading. Condensed, yet clear and concise, it fills one with the desire to emulate these Yogis in attaining spiritual perfection (*Unity*, Kansas City, December 1902).
>
> For Christians interested in foreign missions, this book is of moment, as showing the method of reasoning which they must be prepared to meet

if they are to influence the educated Hindu. To the Orientalist, and the philosopher also, the book is not without interest.... Swami Abhedananda preaches no mushroom creed and no Eurasian hybrid "theosophy". He aims to give us a compendious account of Yoga. Clearly and admirably he performs his task. In form the little book is excellent, and its English style is good (*New York Times Saturday Review of Books*, December 6, 1902).

The book has been kept comparatively free from technical and Sanskrit terms, so the work will prove easily understood even by those not already versed in the philosophy (*San Francisco Call*, December 21, 1902).

"How to be a Yogi" practically sums up the whole science of Vedanta Philosophy. The term Yogi is lucidly defined and a full analysis is given of the science of breathing and its bearing on the highest spiritual development. The methods and practices of Yoga are interestingly set forth, and not the least important teaching of the book is the assertion of how great a Yogi was Jesus of Nazareth (*The Bookseller, Newsdealer and Stationer*, January 15, 1903).

"How to be a Yogi" is a little volume that makes very interesting reading. The book contains the directions that must be followed in physical as well as in mental training by one who wishes to have full and perfect control of all his powers (*Chicago Record Herald*, February 28, 1903).

The Swami writes in a clear, direct manner. His chapter on Breath will elicit more than ordinary attention, as there is much in it that will prove helpful. The book makes a valuable addition to Vedanta Philosophy (*Mind*, June 1903).[82]

An evaluation of *Three lectures on Philosophy of Work* (1902) specified:

In this volume the Vedanta Society presents three lectures by the leader of the Hindu religious movement that is making much headway among philosophic minds throughout the United States. The book is an excellent antidote to the gospel of selfism now popular in many quarters, and a copy should be in the hands especially of every ambitious seeker after the loaves and fishes of material desire. It shows the folly of slavery to sense and the means of escape from the thralldom of egoism, while elucidating the Hindu concept of many things that are "race problems" because of individual ignorance of spiritual principles. These discourses merit a wide circulation among unprejudiced minds (*Mind*, February 1903).[83]

Abhedananda's speaking ability received the praise of the *New York Herald* of February 22, 1903:

> He is a strikingly handsome young man of great dignity, in absolute command of himself, and when he speaks in Carnegie Lyceum, it is as if a statue of some ancient Hindoo god has come to life to address the people. In a long robe, snugly and handsomely fitted to the form with tailor made perfection, fasted at the waste with a tasselled girdle, he stands before the audience, apparently enraptured, in absolute silence for a moment; then he begins a prayer in Hindoo, which he translates impressively, and proceeds with his discourse.[84]

On March 8, during a speech given at Carnegie Lyceum Hall, Abhedananda described his experiences with Vivekananda this way:

> I had the honour of living with this great Swami in India, in England, and in this country [United States]. I lived and travelled with this great spiritual brother of mine, saw him day after day and night after night and watched his character for nearly twenty years, and I stand here to assure you that I have not found another like him in these three continents and that no one can take the place of this wonderful personage. As a man, his character was pure and spotless; as a philosopher, he was the greatest of all Eastern and Western philosophers. In him I found the ideal *of Karma Yoga*, *Bhakti Yoga*, *Raja Yoga and Jnana Yoga*; he was like the living example of Vedanta in all its different branches.

Abhedananda used Swamiji's book on Raja Yoga as a text for all of his Raja Yoga classes.[85]

The *Divine Heritage of Man* (1903) brilliantly discusses God's existence, attributes, form and formlessness, Fatherhood and Motherhood, relation to the soul, incarnations, and Son, and the divine principle in man. From these and other book reviews, we can see that Swami Abhedananda reached a much larger audience than generally recognized in informing the public about the fundamental principles of the Vedanta philosophy. A very well received work, it stimulated these encouraging responses throughout the United States:

It is written in a plain and logical style, and cannot fail to interest all who are anxious for information concerning the philosophy of which the author is such an able exponent (*Pittsburgh Times*, June 1903).

There is no disposition on the part of the author to assail any of the Christian principles, but he simply presents his subject with calmness, not attempting to reconcile religion and science, for to him they are one (*Washington Post*, June 1903).

The student of religions will find much of value in the discourses, since they are full of historical information concerning the origin and growth of certain ideas and beliefs dominant in Christianity (*Denver Republican*, July 1903).

The Swami Abhedananda's writings are also companionable and readable.... The Philosophy of India, being the bringing together of the best thoughts and reasonings of the best men for the thousands of preceding years, had under consideration the self-same problems that are to-day vexing the souls of our philosophers. The Swami's book is therefore not so radical a departure from accepted thought as might at first be imagined.... It is not meant for babes, but rather will it give new lines of thought to the brightest intellects (*Boston Transcript*, August 1903).

His method of dealing with these fundamental questions is peculiarly free both from dogmatic assertion and from pure metaphysical speculation (*Chicago Inter-Ocean*, August 1903).

He bases his arguments, not on theological hypotheses, but on scientific facts (*Cleveland Plain Dealer*, August 1903).

This book is another notable contribution to Vedanta Philosophy. It is a clear exposition by Swami Abhedananda, who has done so much in New York to popularize Vedanta Philosophy. The book is full of good things from beginning to end, and will meet with a great deal of approval from those who do not accept the Hindu philosophy in toto. In one chapter, entitled "The Attributes of God", he shows plainly that it is ignorance that causes the great differences between people of varying religions.... We anticipate that the book will have a large sale and do much good in clearing up the many misconceptions concerning Vedanta Philosophy (*Mind*, August 1903, pp. 398-99).

A glance over a few of its pages would be sufficient to convince the reader of the necessity for him to restrain his pride, for he would find himself in the presence of an intellect of high order, more thoroughly acquainted with the philosophies and sciences of the Occidental world than most Europeans or Americans, re-enforced in addition by profound knowledge of the religious thought of the Hindoos, and armed with all the subtleties of the Oriental mind.... "Divine Heritage of Man" gives a rare insight into the religious views of educated Hindoos and in its argumentation furnishes an intellectual treat (*San Francisco Chronicle*, August 2, 1903).[86]

The Swami has such a mastery of English that it is always a pleasure to read what he has to say about the world-old problems of life and mind, of God and man, and as they present themselves to our Aryan forefathers and as they appear in the light of modern science. Perhaps the most interesting chapter is that on the Fatherhood and Motherhood of God (*Luzac's Oriental List*, 1903, pp. 248-49).

There is much in the religions of the East that appeals to the student of Truth, to the one who recognizes Truth wherever found, and the Vedanta Philosophy, in particular, contains many of the teachings which are embodied in what is known today as Practical Christianity, or, New Thought. The Swami Abhedananda presents this philosophy in a most pleasing and clearly understood manner, and this book—The Divine Heritage of Man—goes far to reconcile the prejudiced, orthodox Christian with what he has looked upon as a heathen religion. Beginning with a chapter on "The Existence of God", and closing with the chapters "Son of God" and "Divine Principle in Man", the attention of the reader is closely held, and he must admit that the book and its precepts are of common utility to all believers (*Unity*, 1903, p. 374).

1904 and After

During the Winter of 1903-04, Swami Abhedananda delivered twenty-two lectures in Carnegie Lyceum and in March and April on Sunday mornings spoke at the Society house. Gradual progress was being made in the work, but it did not come easily. Laura Glenn (later Sister Devamata) informed the *Prabuddha Bharata* in February 1904:

Few, however, beyond those who have watched the organization from the beginning can appreciate through what vicissitudes it has passed and what an inexhaustible store of determination, courage and perseverance it has needed to bring it to its present condition.... The churches so far recognize this that with few exceptions they have adopted a policy of compromise in order to hold their congregations and receive from them the required support. A religion, on the contrary, which, like Vedanta, attempts no compromise, but boldly preaches practical renunciation and non-attachment, must necessarily find a limited number of followers at the outset and these will inevitably be among the thinking class than among the rich. The Vedanta Society has therefore had to make its way slowly; but this very struggle has undoubtedly meant added vigour.[87]

Swami Nirmalananda, a disciple of Vivekananda who had been stationed at Mysore, was sent by the Belur Math to America. He worked as Abhedananda's assistant at the New York Centre from November 1903 until January 1905. According to Sister Shivani, he "was well liked by everyone". "I have met quite a few Swamis that are in America, but never had I the experience as I had with Swami Nirmalananda. In his presence I became speechless." Due to the popularity of Abhedananda's lectures in Brooklyn, a new centre was formed in the city and Nirmalananda was placed in charge on the 30th of January 1905. He conducted yoga classes there and held a weekly reception for about a year, leaving for India in January 1906. After returning to India, Nirmalananda stated, according to a second party, that, "He simply followed in the footsteps of his Guru, the late world-revered Swami Vivekananda during his stay at New York."[88] Having a capable assistant Swami made it possible for Abhedananda to lecture outside of the New York area. Through his speaking and travels, he was able to organize and spread the movement.[89] In future years, under his dynamic leadership, Abhedananda was instrumental in starting Vedanta Centres in Brooklyn, New York and Washington, D.C. (1905), Pittsburgh, Pennsylvania (1906), West Cornwall, Connecticut (1907), London, England (1908), Paris, France (1909), Los Angeles, California (1915 or 1916), Long Beach, California, sometime between 1915 and 1917, and San Francisco, California (1920). He also had some connections with the Sociedad Vedanta of Buenos Aires in Argentina. Between 1908 and 1911, one of his followers, Sister Avabamia, founded Vedanta Clubs in Sydney and other areas of Australia, and organized four in New Zealand.

The *New York Evening-Mail* favourably described Abhedananda in this manner:

He speaks English almost perfectly. Sometimes he departs a trifle from the strict idiom, but his language is always terse and expressive, never for a

> moment soaring into hyperbole. His "services", if they may be called that, are impressive….
>
> He is a particularly good-looking young man, of the dark-brown Bengali tint, and with full and expressive eyes. He is a man of really Oriental tact and grace, apparently with a knack for meeting people's natural curiosity about the most inconclusive and ambitious of all philosophies, without treading upon any one's theological corns. Beginning his lecture straightway after the invocation, he talks for a full hour extemporaneously or apparently so. At the close of the discourse he announces that he will answer questions concerning it … he does patiently and luminously answer. Then he calls upon the audience to rise, and deliver a benediction in Sanskrit, which also he translates into English.
>
> His discourses are extremely clever elucidation of the deepest Indian philosophy. They expound the ideas of reincarnation, of Karma or causation, and of Nirvana, or the attainment of the eternal God-consciousness—all with due and constant relation to Darwin and Herbert Spencer. Swami Abhedananda tells me that he thinks about one-quarter of the people who come to hear him really understand these ideas. So many would not follow him if it were not for his exceedingly clear way of putting things, and his unqualified adoption of the Western logic and terminology.[90]

On May 4, 1904, the Society moved to 62 East 71st Street. Nearly 300 people were accommodated in the spacious lecture hall. Consequently, Abhedananda began lecturing at the Vedanta Society rather than in rented halls, which meant less newspaper coverage and contact with the general public. The meditation room open to members and their friends was set apart allowing for an atmosphere of rest, silence and peace. Holding lectures in the Society House allowed the people who attended the lectures to gain personal insight into the real character and purpose of the Society. Their success brought more respect from the outside public concerning the importance of the Vedanta Society. Emily Cape [q.v.], the secretary for the New York Vedanta Society, adds:

> An altar, designated by the loving thought of our Blessed Swami Abhedananda, stands beneath a dome, and a few flowers are usually there placed by faithful hands. The picture of the Master, the Great soul, Ramakrishna, is living in this room; the American students have grown to love and reverence the Name of the Blessed Sri Ramakrishna.[91]

When Abhedananda attended the World's Fair in St. Louis, Missouri, in May 1904, he arranged for a display of Vedanta literature at the Book Fair. He also lectured at the Webster Groves Society. The next year he came back to St. Louis in October and gave an informal talk. In 1908 the *Vedanta Monthly Bulletin* mentions a centre (possibly meaning a study group) in St. Louis.[92]

Vedanta University opened in Washington, D.C. in the autumn of 1904 under the regent Albert S. Dulin, who also gave advertised public lectures at his Vedanta Society located at 1632 Nineteenth Street NW. The teachings of the school were based largely on the ideas of Vivekananda and Abhedananda. A long article in the *Washington Times* of December 18, 1904 displays good-sized photographs of Swamis Vivekananda and Abhedananda, and Albert Dulin. It tells us:

> The university which has been regularly incorporated under the laws, began its operation only a few short weeks ago. Already forty persons have registered, and are taking a course which teaches them the new philosophy.... Although Swami Vivekananda is no longer in this country, he has left behind an able teacher in the person of Swami Abhedananda. The Hindu sage has written many volumes on the subject of Vedanta and has lectured in most of the cities in the Union. Mr. Dulin expects him to come to Washington this winter to deliver lectures and to aid in the firm establishment of the cult here.[93]

For one year only the 1906 *Washington, D.C. Directory* lists a Vedanta University located at northwest corner of Connecticut and California Avenues NW.

In 1905 the Swami travelled to Toronto, and in late March and in April returned to Washington, D.C. to establish a new Vedanta Society affiliated with the New York Centre. Its location was in room 610 of the Corcoran Building. They formed a committee with Miss L. W. Browne as its secretary. In the nation's capital, on March 27, 1905 Abhedananda lectured at the Washington Club located at 1719 I Street at 8 o'clock on "The Science of Yoga and Its Practice". He soon revisited the city to deliver a series of talks on the *Bhagavad Gita* beginning from April 18. A long article appeared in *The Sunday Star* of Washington, D.C. quoting Abhedananda's explanation of the Vedanta philosophy and mentioning the newly formed Vedanta Society. The correspondent added:

He is apparently a man in the thirties, but with a face so calm and a bearing so well poised that it is difficult to judge his years.... He speaks excellent English so fluently as to leave no hint whatever of unfamiliarity with the vocabulary or the idioms of the tongue.[94]

A synopsis of *The Sayings of Ramakrishna* (1903), compiled by Swami Abhedananda, from *Luzac's Oriental List and Book Review* (1905) revealed:

Ramakrishna was a great Hindu saint of the nineteenth century who has already had an influence on the religious thought of America and England through the teachings of his disciples, Swami Vivekananda, Swami Abhedananda, and others. His Sayings are full of broad, practical, non-sectarian instructions concerning the spiritual life which cannot but give help and inspiration to the followers of all creeds. The present volume contains a larger number of Sayings than has yet appeared in any one English collection. For the first time also they have been classified into chapters and arranged in logical sequence under marginal headings, such as "All Creeds Paths to God", "Power of Mind and Thought", "Meditation", "Perseverance". As an exposition of the universal truths of Religion and their application to the daily life, this book takes its place among the great scriptures of the world.

About Abhedananda's volume *Self-Knowledge* (*Atma-Jnana*, 1905), *Luzac's Oriental List* in London acknowledged:

The Swami has addressed himself to the task of expounding in terms intelligible to the modern mind the chief ideas of Vedanta philosophy, especially as they occur in the Upanishads.... it must be acknowledged that he writes ably and persuasively, setting forth much of the Vedantic doctrine in a clear and attractive light, and doing good service in paving the way for a more general recognition by the West of some of the real merits of Indian thought.[95]

In the intellectual-cultural world outside of the area of religion, there was a growing awareness of the presence of the Vedanta Society in the West. As a sign of the respectability that the Society had earned, Emily Cape prepared a report on "The Vedanta Society" that occupied over one-third of a page in the 1905 and later editions of the *The World Almanac and Encyclopedia*. Among other things it stated that the purpose of the Society is

> to explain through logic and reason the spiritual laws that govern our lives; to show that the True Religion of the Soul is not antagonistic to, but in harmony with, philosophy and science; to establish that Universal Religion which underlies all the various sects and creeds of special religions; to propagate the principles taught by great seers of Truth and religious leaders of different countries and illustrated by their lives; and to help mankind in the practical applications of those principles in their spiritual, moral, intellectual and physical needs.

It also mentions a "correspondence class for non-resident members" conducted by the Society.

In 1905, Adelaide Louise Samson, the reporter for the New York based *Broadway Magazine*, made this observation:

> It is an interesting and curious phase of the many-sidedness of Manhattan that the asceticism and mysticism of the Hindus, that their spiritual teachers, the Swamis, should have secured a following so fundamentally strong that a brotherhood should be recognized, and that the Vedanta Society, on a solid financial basis, should be housed and equipped with lecture hall, meditation closet [room], classrooms and finally cloister-rooms for the priests.... The Sunday morning lectures have an average attendance of about five-hundred, drawn from varied ranks of life—the banker, the broker, the man of letters, the artisan, the woman of fashion, and the wage earner.[96]

Under Abhedananda's direction, the New York Centre published a large quantity of Vedantic literature, including most of his books. In 1901, Laura Glenn (the future Sister Devamata, 1867-1942) [q.v.] replaced Sarah Waldo as the manager of the Publishing Department for the Vedanta Society of New York. That year the Society published Vivekananda's *The Vedanta Philosophy* delivered at Harvard University. One of Laura's assignments was to edit Vivekananda's two-volumes on *Jnana Yoga* (1902) for publication.[97] The New York Vedanta Society initiated its own journal in April 1905 called the *Vedanta Monthly Bulletin*. In the first issue they described their intensions:

> The BULLETIN set out on its mission with a double purpose: to make known the universal message of Vedanta to those who have not yet heard it; and to draw the individual and scattered units of the work into closer union and cooperation. This must result in greater solidarity and fellowship, and add power and strength to the entire movement. We, therefore, earnestly appeal to all to further this new effort to spread the lofty truths of Vedanta.

Among other things, "each number contained a lecture by Swami Abhedananda or some other Swami, reports from the different branches of the Vedanta work in this country and in India, an account of all current events relating to the work, and notices of new books on Vedanta." According to Wendell Thomas, at its peak the *Vedanta Monthly Bulletin* had a circulation of over three-thousand, of which three-hundred were sent free to libraries and student organizations.[98]

Starting on June 29, 1905, Abhedananda made a long tour of North America with the accompaniment of his good friend Herschel Parker, a physics professor at Columbia University and a world-class mountain climber. Parker became the president of the New York Vedanta Society in 1900 following Francis Leggett, and held the position for about a decade. They travelled from Toronto to Fort William, Winnipeg, and Vancouver, Canada, and then went north to Sitka, Alaska (now part of the United States) to visit Governor John Brady, as earlier mentioned. At the urgent request of others, he gave a lecture on the lake steamer from Toronto and on the boat going to Alaska. At Lake Louise in Alberta, Western Canada, he devoted an entire evening answering the questions of about fifty people. He and Parker climbed some of the high peaks of the Canadian Rockies and then journeyed down the Pacific Coast to the Portland Fair for a few days. After this they visited Swami Trigunatita in San Francisco, and he was extremely gratified to learn that a plot of land had been purchased and they planned to build a Temple there. "In Los Angeles Swami Sachchidananda arranged a reception for Swami Abhedananda, who delivered a short address to the members. He was deeply impressed with their earnestness and general spirit of enthusiasm in the Society." Back in April, Abhedananda had scheduled a summer lecture on "Philosophy Vedanta" at the Venice Assembly near Los Angeles. They travelled to the Grand Canyon in Arizona, and on to Mexico City, meeting a number of devoted students of Vedanta who wanted him to establish a centre in Mexico, which he said was not possible, and then returned to New York City.[99] In 1904 a group of Swami Vivekananda's former students were hoping to initiate a Vedanta Society in Portland, Oregon, and in the following year in Vancouver, B.C., Canada, a number of Vedantists were holding weekly meetings also hoping to establish a Society.[100]

As an indication of the New York Vedanta Society's success in reaching the public, in the five years preceding October 1905, they sent out 39,836 books and pamphlets (often a single lecture) on Vedanta and received orders or inquiries from every state in the union. Swamis Vivekananda or Abhedananda authored the majority of books. Their publication department was delighted that they were receiving orders for Vedantic literature in small cities located in many Western European countries and in far-off places like Alaska, Hawaii, the Philippine Islands, Mexico and Puerto Rico. In this way, they were able to spread the message of Vedanta over a large geographical area.[101]

Abhedananda was a highly productive writer. Through his writings and lectures he became one of the early forces in effectively introducing Ramakrishna-Vedanta concepts to Americans and Europeans. Between 1899 and 1907 he published ten books, all of which are still in print, and several pamphlets of his lectures. Two of the ten were the *Sayings of Ramakrishna* (1903) and the *Gospel of Ramakrishna* (1907).* In 1905, he was also involved in other literary activities like writing on "The Ideals of a Hindu House-hold" for the prestigious family magazine *Good Housekeeping*, which has been in business for 125 years. It was written to counter the negative ideas held by many Americans on the subject of the Indian family, and his article was even discussed in faraway newspapers like the *Gainesville* (*Florida*) *Daily Sun*.[102]

Beginning in November 1905, Sir Ponnambalam Ramanathan (1851-1930), a Hindu philosopher, statesman and lawyer from Ceylon, was the guest of Mr. Dulin in Washington, D.C. Previously he spoke several times at the Greenacre Conferences of 1905 on "The Unity of Faith". Mr. Ramanathan, the solicitor-general of Ceylon, was also the guest of honour at Abhedananda's New York Centre the following January during the memorial services held for Vivekananda. There, as the final speaker, he praised Vivekananda's character and work and described his marvellous reception at Colombo after returning from America. Inspired by Vivekananda's journey to the West, Ramanathan came to the United States for ten months for the purpose of enlightening the intelligentsia in the United States. According to

---

* See Appendix V for the publication dates of the books that he produced.

the *New York Times*, his aim was "the unification of their religious views and the establishment of a reign of reason through the mutual understanding of the Orient and Occident." A warm friend Reverend Charles Cuthbert Hall, the president of Union Theological Seminary in New York, had been his guest in Colombo. Ceylon's first prime minister designated Ramanathan as "the greatest Ceylonese of all times", and Lord Salisbury described him as the most accomplished speaker in the British Empire.[103]

Many newspaper writers were amazed at the spiritual level of Sri Ramakrishna's disciples who became Swamis and came to the West. They had never seen anything like this before. In an undated newspaper report written around 1906, a correspondent for the *New York Tribune* wrote this glowing tribute:

> The Hindu Sannyasin, Swami Abhedananda, who is doing much good work in this and other Occidental countries for the past ten years, is now regarded as a much sought after person. His mission is peace, knowledge and truth. The Swami does not mix with politics. His set aim is to bring spiritual upliftment and regeneration to all humanity. A man of winning personality, he has free access to the social and domestic life of the American people who fondly call him "Prince Abhedananda". True, he has no princely kingdom, but a spiritual teacher of his stature is really a prince of men. It is his loving attitude to all and smiling countenance that have won for him an enviable position as a preacher. We also gather from similar accounts given by many other distinguished persons who had the privilege of coming in close contact with Swami Abhedananda that he was all humility and at the same time he was all strength. Whenever he talked to any body, he talked with fire and enthusiasm and he would lose himself entirely in his subject, forgetting everything else for the time being. He impressed everyone who heard him and all classes of people felt attracted towards him. Everyone regarded his company as precious. As a preacher Abhedananda had some higher qualifications—gifts or powers that he developed through a long period of self-discipline and mental control. There are innumerable instances that whenever anybody asked him any question, he would at once answer not from the intellect, but from within. In answering a question, he used to speak just a few words which could give so much satisfaction to the questioner. And how effective were his answers! None but a person highly trained and of concentrated mind can perform this miracle. Many students of Vedanta have admitted that Abhedananda, who possessed rare insight,

always used to keep his eyes on the questioner and his answers would come with flashes of illumination.[104]

Mrs. Emily Palmer Cape (1865-1953) [q.v.], who came from a Roman Catholic background, served as the secretary of the Vedanta Society of New York from 1904 until 1908. Sister Shivani, a personal friend of hers, relates, "Her keenly trained mind and her broad quick interest in the human problems of the members made her a dependable and able worker.... The Swami relied much upon her acumen and judgment." Emily Cape wrote an essay on "The Vedanta Philosophy" for the New Thought journal *Mind* in 1904, two articles for the *Prabuddha Bharata* in 1905 and 1906, and gave a short talk at the Vivekananda memorial service in 1906 and 1907. Emily read a farewell address from the members to the Swami before he sailed for India, which went as follows:

> For nine years, you have laboured tirelessly among us, enduring hardship, opposition, even enmity, yet pushing on your course undaunted and unchecked. When you came to New York, out of all those who had gathered so eagerly around Swami Vivekananda, you found scarcely a handful of earnest students. With these you began your labour. True to your Sannyasin spirit, in the heart of this commercial metropolis, asking aid of no one, and with the infinite wisdom, patience, courage and tenacity which have characterized your efforts at every step, you began to build, stone by stone, the solid structure of the Vedanta Society as it stands today. Only those who know the conditions of New York can appreciate how great have been the difficulties and how noble is your achievement.
>
> You are now returning to India bearing with you the fruits of many years' experience in this new and more vigorous country, and we believe that your visit will prove rich in results, both in India and for America. It is this alone that makes it possible for us to look forward with some degree of courage to the long months of separation which lie before us.
>
> You have been to us an ever wise and ever loving master and teacher. Many of us who came to you ill in body and mind are today strong in limb and full of new life. Others who crept into your presence bowed down with grief and despair, now walk with raised heads and joyful eyes. Not one has come to you in vain. Everywhere you have brought hope, gladness, strength and spiritual light. Never can we pay the mighty debt we owe to you, except in striving, day by day, nay hour by hour, to embody in our

> lives the lofty truths you have taught us, and to remain stanch and loyal to the work to which you have devoted your life. As you go forth to carry further your mission, we can but pray with our whole hearts to the Divine Mother and your own Divine Master, Shri Ramakrishna, that your journey may bring not only blessing to others, but to yourself a fresh store of peace, joy, strength and inspiration with which you may bear ever onward the banner of Vedanta in America and over the whole world.[105]

During the following year at the birthday celebration of Swami Vivekananda, Emily Cape said among other things:

> If the large-hearted, broad-minded, beautiful-souled man [Vivekananda] who brought the first fire of Vedanta to America were able to speak today to us, it would be one great theme he would flood our very inmost hearts with: Love, a cry of Divine Love; for no noble lasting work can ever be completed without the deep inspiring, sincere, self-forgetful Love.... Every heart in America who loved Vivekananda, who has watched the work of his brother workers, should rise with one great accord and, forgetting all minor differences and petty disagreements, rise with one magnificent force, and lay our hearts on the altar of Love.[106]

Emily Palmer Cape wrote the volume *Oriental Aphorisms* (1906), co-edited Lester Ward's posthumous six-volume *Glimpses of the Cosmos* that came out during 1913-18, and in 1922 brought out a biography of Lester Ward (1841-1913), a famous sociologist. Years before, Ward, a personal friend of hers, attended a series of lectures by Swami Vivekananda in New York City. Being an accomplished painter in oils and watercolours, she exhibited her work at the Milch Art Gallery and elsewhere.[107]

The Maharaja and the Maharani of Baroda also attended the farewell reception on May 14, 1906 in honour of the Swami. He came to the U.S. to study the country's industrial methods for the purpose of improving the standard of living of his own people in Baroda. Abhedananda had been the guest of the Maharaja fourteen years earlier when he lived the life of a wandering Sannyasin. The Maharaja

> spoke in high terms of praise of the work which Swami Abhedananda had accomplished in the United States, both in spreading the great teachings of Vedanta and in awakening a true sympathy and love for India. And he

pointed out that his noble achievement had but exemplified the meaning of his name—Abhedananda—which signifies, in Sanskrit, "bliss through Non-division or Unity".

Abhedananda left for India on May 16 and Swami Bodhananda (1871-1950), arriving fresh from India, took over the New York operation in his absence, with a reception being held on June 4, 1906. An initiated disciple of Holy Mother, Bodhananda got sannyasa from Vivekananda in 1898. While in Benares, Vivekananda told him, "I ask you to lead the life and work in your own natural way. Do not imitate others. Work in your own sincere way and success will be surely yours."[108] He later headed the Vedanta Society in Bangalore, and then was requested by Swami Brahmananda to proceed to America.[109]

ENDNOTES

1 Swami Abhedananda, *My Life Story* (Calcutta: Ramakrishna Vedanta Math, 1995), pp. 27-28.

2 Chetanananda, p. 458; *PB* (Dec. 1966), p. 520; *Epistles*, p. 93; Anandaprana, p. 148.

3 Radhakrishnan, p. 50; *PB* (Dec. 1966), p. 520; Chetanananda, p. 443.

4 *CW*, V:36.

5 Abhedananda (1995), pp. 177-81.

6 *CW*, VIII: 352-53.

7 Basu, p. 474; Ghosh, p. 22.

8 *CW*, VIII:386-87.

9 *Life*, II, pp. 135-36; Chetanananda, p. 463; "Preacher Chosen by Vivekananda", *Hindu* (Sept. 14, 2001). Web: www.hinduonnet.com/2001/09/14/stories/13141366.htm.

10 *CW*, V:119.

11 Burke, IV, pp. 387-88; Chetanananda, p. 463; Ghosh, p. 24.

12 Burke, IV, p. 386.

13 *CWSA*, X, pp. 3-96; *The Critic* (March 19, 1898) on GBS.

14 *CWSA*, X, p. 27.

15 *CWSA*, X, p. 10.

16 *CWSA*, X, pp. 13-14, 48.

17 Swami Abhedananda, *Thoughts on Yoga, Upanishad and Gita* (Calcutta: Ramakrishna Vedanta Math, 1970), pp. 78-79.

18 Dale Carnegie, *Little Known Facts about Well Known People* (New York: A. L. Burt, 1934), p. 236.

19 Thomas Alva Edison. Web: www.invent.org/hall_of_fame/50.html; *DAB* (1944), Sup. I.

20 Head, p. 290.

21 Bruce Campbell, *Ancient Wisdom Revisited* (Berkeley: University of California Press, 1980), pp. 81-82, 120, 147-73; Carl Jackson, *The Oriental Religions and American Thought* (London: Greenwood Press, 1981), pp. 157-77, 251-52.

22 Mahatma Gandhi, *An Autobiography* (Ahmedabad: Navajivan Publishing House, 1945), p. 60.

23 *CWSA*, X, pp. 17-18, 34-35, 37, 40.

24 *WWIA* (1916-17), p. 913; *NCAB* (1900), X, pp. 354-55; UCLC.

25 *The Critic* (March 19, 1898) on GBS.

26 *Brahmavadin* (March 1, 1898), pp. 497-98.

27 *Brahmavadin* (Feb. 16, 1898), p. 460; Basu, p. 206.

28 Basu, pp. 205-06; *New York Tribune*, Section II, p. 1; *The Critic* (March 19, 1898) on GBS.

29 Bagchi, pp. 288-89; "A Teacher of the Vedanta", *The Critic* (Mar. 19, 1898), p. 200. The article is unsigned, but a number of friends of Vedanta wrote articles for *The Critic*. They include: Abraham V. W. Jackson (Columbia University), Lucy Monroe and N. S. Shaler (Harvard University) who were Staff Contributors, and Nicholas Murray Butler (Columbia University), Edward Everett Hale, and Harriet Monroe were listed as "Occasional Contributors".

30 *New York Daily Tribune* (March 23, 1898), p. 14; *New York Times* (May 2, 1894), p. 5; *PB* (July 2005), p. 390; *CWSA*, X, p. 30.

31 *Intelligence* (March 1898), pp. 272-78, 339, 151 on GBS.

32 *CWSA*, X, pp. 38-39; Chetanananda, p. 471; *DAB* (1958), XI, p. 108.

33 *CWSA*, X, pp. 39-40; *DAB* (1961), VI, pp. 105-09. McKinley's death had a significant impact on American history, since he was followed by President Theodore Roosevelt, who made major changes in American foreign and domestic policies that have continued on to this day.

34 *CWSA*, X, pp. 36, 40-41; Shivani, p. 96.

35 *CWSA*, X, pp. 50-52; Bagchi, p. 307; Nivedita, II, p. 1247; *Brahmavadin* (Mar. 15, 1899), p. 396; *Outlook* (July 2, 1898), pp. 590-91; Basu, p. 541 (601); also in *PB* (Dec. 1899); (Dec. 1989), p. 520; *Mind* (1900), p. 34.

36 *CWSA*, X, pp. 51-52; *SACC*, p. 58.

37 *CWSA*, X, pp. 51-52; *Brahmavadin* (July 15, 1899), p. 690; (Jan. 1900), p. 168; (Aug. 1900), p. 686; UCLC.

38 *CWSA*, X, pp. 53, 63; *DAB* (1961), V, pp. 15-17; Mark Hawkins-Dady, ed. *International Dictionary of Theatre* (Chicago St. James Press, 1996), *Harper's Bazaar* (Aug. 26, 1899), p. 718; III; Nelson, p. 51; Internet Movie Database. Web: http://imdb.com/name/nm0420198.

39 *CWSA*, X, p. 54; *Brahmavadin* (Mar. 15, 1999), p. 397; *CA* (1992), vol. 134; *EWB*.

40 Burke, III, p. 382; VI, p. 257; *CWSA*, X, p. 67.

41 The article went out on the wire and appeared in the Columbus, Georgia *The Sunday Herald* (Jan. 1, 1899), p. 8.

42 *Brahmavadin* (Jan. 1, 1899), pp. 244-45; Shivani, p. 114.

43 *Brahmavadin* (Feb. 15, 1899), pp. 345-47; (Dec. 1900), p. 137.

44 *CWSA*, X, p. 75.

45 *Epistles*, p. 117.

46 "Swami Atulananda", *PB* (Oct. 1989), p. 429; Atulananda, p. 4; *CWSA*, X, p. 91.

47 Nelson, p. 109; *CWSA*, X, pp. 94-96.

48 Swami Prajanananananda, *The Philoosphical Ideas of Swami Abhedananda* (Calcutta: Ramakrishna Vedanta Math, 1971), p. 581 lists Abhedananda Diaries from 1899 to 1939 but they have never been published in English.

49 *Global Vedanta* (Summer 2009), pp. 6-8; *Melrose Reporter* (May 6, 1899).

50 *Brahmavadin* (July 15, 1899), p. 690; Daniel O'Hara. Web: www.antiquorum.com/vox/june_2002/poniz/poniz.htm; *Fitchburg Sentinel* (May 23, 1899), p. 6.

51 *LBD*, pp. 221-22; *Boston Daily Globe* (May 27, 1899), p. 8.

52 Bagchi, p. 285.

53 *Boston Daily Globe* (July 9, 1899), p. 27.

54 *San Francisco Chronicle* (July 30, 1899), p. 19.

55 *Brahmavadin* (Jan. 1900), pp. 171-72; *Outlook* (July 8, 1899), pp. 583-84; *Harper's Bazaar* (Aug. 26, 1899), p. 719; Basu, p. 541 (601); also in *PB* (Dec. 1899); (Dec. 1989), p. 520; Cameron, p. 114.

56 *Brahmavadin* (Jan. 1900), p. 172; (Feb. 1900), p. 304; Tathagatanandaı, p. 152; Hohner, pp. 90, 93-94.

57 *Brahmavadin* (Sept. 1899), p. 816; (Jan. 1900), p. 173; Burke, V, pp. 145-46.

58 *CW*, V:25.

59 Ibid., VIII:328-29.

60 *The Arena* (1899), pp. 429, 484 on APS; *CWSV*, X, p. 18; "Swami Vivekananda and Virchand Gandhi", *VK* (Oct. 1994), pp. 378-80.

61 Mann mistakenly attributes these specific ideas to Swami Vivekananda. *Medical Age* (Sept. 10, 1899), p. 662. For more on this subject see *Literary Digest* (July 8, 1899), pp. 47 ff. on GBS; or *Brahmavadin* (1899), pp. 724 ff. Swami Abhedananda, *Reincarnation* (Calcutta: Ramakrishna Vedanta, 1899, 1964), pp. 35-45.

62 These two evaluations are found in *GSW* (1911), p. 178 on GBS.

63 *Brahmavadin* (May 1900), p. 488.

64 Prabuddhaprana2, pp. 369-73; Burke VI, p. 257; Hansbrough's Reminiscences, *PB* (May 2007), pp. 343-44.

65 *Brahmavadin* (Aug. 1900), pp. 686-87; Satyananda, pp. 88-90; Shivani, p. 97.

66 Burke, VI, pp. 277-78.

67 *Brahmavadin* (Jan. 1901), p. 214; *Washington Post* (Nov. 19, 1900), p. 3; Bagchi, pp. 296-97; Maine Historical Society. Web: www.vintagemaineimages.com/bin/Detail?ln=16594; *Proceedings of the New York State Conference of Religion* (1900), p. 59 on GBS.

68 Shivani, p. 108.

69 *CW*, IX:139.

70 *Brahmavadin* (Dec. 1901), p. 115; Chetanananda, p. 470; Shivani, pp. 297-98.

71 Bagchi, pp. 297-98.

72 *PB* (Sept. 1901); Shivani, p. 109.

73 Shivani, pp. 110-11; *PB* (Oct. 1901); (May 1978), p. 212; *VK* (Jan. 2003), p. 4.

74 Chetanananda, p. 470; Shivani, pp. 111, 297-99; Stavig2, ch. 1; *Brahmavadin* (Jan. 1904), p. 46; Shivani, p. 299, wrote that he visited the Pan-American Exposition in Buffalo that lasted from May 1 to November 1 on his return trip from San Francisco; *San Francisco Call* (Aug. 31, 1901); (Sept. 1, 1901).

75 *New York Times* (Feb. 11, 1914), p. 11; *WWWA*, I, p. 283.

76 *SACC*, p. 20.

77 *SN* (1905), pp. 187 ff. on GBS; *Mind*, April 1902.

78 Shivani, p. 112; Chetanananda, p. 469; *SACC*, p. 79.

79 Bagchi, p. 304.

80 Shivani, p. 114.

81 Chetanananda, pp. 470-71; Shivani, pp. 225-26, 293-94; Tathagatananda1, p. 169; *PB* (Feb. 1903), pp. 35-36; (Feb. 1904), pp. 34-35: *Appalachian Mountain Club Register* (1908), p. 44 on GBS; *SACC*, pp. 92-93.

82 All six reviews are found in *GSW* (1911), p. 181 on GBS.

83 *GSW* (1911), p. 182 on GBS.

84 Sent to me by email from Professor Gerald Carney.

85 Tathagatananda1, pp. 138, 160-61; *Brahmavadin* (June 1903), pp. 329-30.

86 Seven of the first eight reviews are found in *GSW* (1911), p. 179 on GBS.

87 *PB* (Feb. 1904); also in (Feb. 2004), pp. 145-46; *SACC*, p. 77.

88 *PB* (July 1906), p. 138.

89 Shivani, pp. 121, 234; Gambhirananda pp. 117, 171, 177; Tathagatanandaı, p. 170; *Brahmavadin* (April 1905), p. 236.

90 *Brahmavadin* (April 1904), pp. 229-33 on GBS; Bagchi, pp. 290-91.

91 *Brahmavadin* (Jan. 1905), pp. 61-63; (April 1905), pp. 232-33; Chetanananda, p. 471.

92 Chetanananda, p. 471; *VMB* (1908), IV, p. 82 on GBS.

93 *Washington Times* (Dec. 18, 1904), Magazine Features p. 2 on CAM; *Washington Post* (July 2, 1904), p. 9 on PQHN.

94 *Brahmavadin* (May 2005), pp. 281-88; Shivani, p. 122; Tathagatanandaı, p. 170; *Washington Times* (Mar. 26, 1905), p. 6; *Washington Post* (Mar. 26, 1905), p. S7; *VMB* (May 1905), pp. 28-29; *The Philadelphia Inquirer* (Nov. 20, 1905), p. 4.

95 *Luzac's Oriental List* (July-Oct. 1905), p. 154.

96 *Brahmavadin* (June 1905), pp. 344-48.

97 Burke, III, pp. 463-64; Levinsky, pp. 94-95.

98 Tathagatanandaı, p. 165;*VMB* (May 1905), p. 1; Thomas, p. 115.

99 *VMB* (Nov. 1905), I, pp. 125-27; Shivani, pp. 123-24; Chetanananda, p. 471; *Los Angeles Herald* (Apr. 28, 1905), p. 3.

100 *VMB* (June 1905), p. 45; (Nov. 1905), pp. 126-27.

101 Tathagatanandaı, pp. 166-67; *VMB* (Oct. 1905), pp. 108-09; (Feb. 1906) p. 16; *PB* (March 1906), pp. 57-58.

102 *Good Housekeeping* (Sept. 1905), pp. 250-52; *Gainesville Daily Sun* (Nov. 19, 1905), p. 6 on CAM.

103 *PB* (Mar. 1906), p. 57; *New York Times* (July 23, 1905), p. 7; Tathagatanandaı, p. 162; *VMB* (Feb. 1906), pp. 146-47; Cameron, pp. 173-74; Sir Ponnambalam Ramanathan. Web: http://sangam.org/taraki/ articles/2006/04-13_ Ponnambalam_ Ramanathan.php?uid+1652.

104 Bagchi, p. 314.

105 Ghosh, pp. 36-38; Shivani, pp. 64-65, 129, 136-37, 148, 252; *VMB* (Feb. 1906), pp. 167-69; (March 1908), p. 207.

106 *VMB* (Feb. 1907), pp. 222-23; also in Tathagatanandaı, p. 163.

107 *WWWA* (1961-68), IV, p. 153; *New York Times* (Dec. 30, 1953), p. 23; UCLC.

108 *VK* (May 1924), p. 31.

109 *VMB* (June-July 1906), pp. 54-56, 72; Tathagatanandaı, pp. 174, 191; Gambhirananda pp. 117, 171, 177; *PB* (June 1950), p. 264; *VK* (May 1924), pp. 28-33; (July 1950), p. 120.

CHAPTER XVI

SWAMI ABHEDANANDA: AFTER 1906

WHILE RETURNING to India, Swami Abhedananda met his old friend Anagarika Dharmapala, the Buddhist representative at the 1893 Parliament of Religions from Ceylon. During the presentation of a speech given in Bangalore, Abhedananda optimistically stated, "The power that is working in the Ramakrishna Mission, is not human, but a divine power. It will take its course, no matter what obstacles are put in its way. It is bound to grow stronger and stronger." After a triumphant six-month tour of the country, having been accorded many warm receptions and delivering numerous lectures, Abhedananda left Bombay on November 10, 1906. From India he returned to the United States in December, accompanied by his new assistant Swami Paramananda (1884-1940). Being the youngest monastic disciple of Vivekananda, Paramananda joined the Order as a young man in 1900 and received initiation into sannyasa at the age of seventeen in 1902. He had an intimate association with Swami Ramakrishnananda from 1902 until 1906 while being stationed in Madras.[1] Years later, reflecting back on his early association with Swami Vivekananda, Paramananda recalled:

> I cannot begin to convey merely through words what my experience was with Swami Vivekananda. We imagine a great man as someone who we cannot approach. Swami Vivekananda, however, was the simplest of people. It would have amazed you! His interior was like a child, gentle and mellow, and that was the real Swami Vivekananda. A great, loving heart! Sometimes reading from his books, you do not get quite the picture. I have seen him weeping. I have seen this great soul weeping, when he thought no one saw him, for the suffering poor of India. His heart was heavy with sadness because there was so much suffering in humanity. It is this, not intellectuality, that makes people great.[2]

Over a year later after Paramananda conducted the birthday celebration of Vivekananda on January 25, 1908, one devotee wrote to the *Brahmavadin*:

> The Swami Paramananda is simple, and in his sorrow, saddened to feel he was no longer unknown and free, but a public man.... It is impossible in a report such as this to do justice to the simple dignity and feeling with which Swami Paramananda spoke.

Paramananda remained in New York for two years until the end of 1908. Accepting an invitation from Sara Bull, in January of 1909 he opened a Vedanta Centre in Boston, and in December in Washington, D.C. Being a highly successful Swami, he later founded the journal *Message of the East* in 1912, and established a new Vedanta Centre in La Crescenta near Los Angeles in 1923.[3] Upon Paramananda's passing away, his good friend and admirer Swami Nikhilananda of the Ramakrishna-Vivekananda Centre in the city of New York said this about him at his memorial service:

> It is a tremendous loss not only to his numerous devotees, disciples, and friends all over the United States, but to the Vedanta movement in this country as well. It is a very great personal loss to me. Since the very foundation of my work in New York he has never failed to stand by my side and give me encouragement in an arduous task.... among the teachers of the Ramakrishna Mission who came to this country after the passing away of Swami Vivekananda, he has been the most successful in disseminating the ideals of this ancient system of Hindu philosophy.... Above all, his sweet and gentle nature, his suave temperament, his dignified demeanour, and his unfailing courtesy have endeared him to all classes of people.... He was full of fun, merriment, and gaiety.[4]

Before Abhedananda left for India in 1906, a group of twenty Associate Members in Pittsburgh, Pennsylvania, formed themselves into a branch of the Vedanta Society of New York. One of Abhedananda's reasons for going to India was to acquire a new Swami for the expanding work. On January 23, 1907, Abhedananda accompanied Swami Bodhananda (1871-1950) to Pittsburgh, where he took charge of the newly formed Vedanta Society at 940 Beach Avenue, Allegheny, and later at the Century Building on Seventh Street, remaining there until 1912. Soon after lecturing to the students of Vedanta in Los Angeles two or three times per week from July through September 1912, Bodhananda, an exemplary sadhu, became the leader of the Vedanta Society of New York in October. There he faithfully discharged his duties until his passing away in 1950.[5] When Bodhananda visited California during the winter months of 1925-26 and 1926-27, Dorothy Mercer attended his lectures in San Francisco and later wrote:

> I do not know to this day why Swami Bodhananda made an impression on me. He was not as fatherly as Swami Trigunatita had been, nor had he the commanding presence of Swami Abhedananda, nor did he speak eloquently.... But I was uplifted for quite a period.[6]

In 1932 at a reception for Swami Nikhilananda, Dhan Gopal Mukherji (1890-1936), author of *The Face of Silence* (1926), a book about Sri Ramakrishna, "spoke of Swami Bodhananda as a man of spiritual realization, in great contrast to the merely intellectual guidance usually found in this country."[7] After spending a then record breaking forty-four years in the West, upon his passing away the *Prabuddha Bharata* paid him this tribute:

> Swami Bodhananda was a cherubic soul, gentle in spirit and full of the warmth of human kindness. He was a pleasing personality and a good speaker and inspired many men and women with the noble ideals of renunciation and spirituality.... The force of character behind his personality drew the love and respect of all those who had known him personally. His deep spiritual personality, his learning and intellectual attainments, and his rich inheritance of religious experience gained through the years of Sadhana and his intimate contact with Swamis Vivekananda and Brahmananda and the other direct disciples of Sri Ramakrishna eminently fitted him for the role of the great pioneer and spiritual teacher that he was. He will be missed by a large group of sincere students of Vedanta in America who are deeply indebted to him for rousing their spiritual consciousness through his spiritual guidance.[8]

During the winter of 1907, Abhedananda sent a letter to three-time U.S. presidential candidate William Jennings Bryan (1860-1925). It read as follows:

Dear Sir,

Last summer I was in India about the time when you were there and I wanted to meet you personally. Our mutual friend Dr. [John Harvey] Girdner gave me a letter of introduction which I herewith enclose. I met many Hindu gentlemen who saw you and heard you speak in Bombay, Allahabad, Calcutta and other places. Our friend Sister Nivedita spoke to me about your visit to her girls' school in Calcutta. I was very pleased to know your opinion through your splendid article published in the *New York Sun* of July 1st 1906. I have given similar expression in my lectures that were delivered before the Brooklyn Institute of Arts and Sciences last winter under the title of "India and Her People".

Those lectures are now published in a book form. I take the liberty of sending you a copy of it at the request of Dr. Girdner of New York, hoping that you will read it and that you will kindly let me know your opinion regarding my views.

I remain

Very sincerely yours
Swami Abhedananda of India.

Abhedananda heard Mr. Bryan's speech in Madison Square when the latter unsuccessfully campaigned for the presidency of the United States.[9]

William Jennings Bryan penned an article that criticized "British Rule in India", which appeared in the *New York Journal* of January 22, 1899.[10] In 1906 Bryan decided to go to India and check things out for himself. There he gave a series of speeches, which were immensely popular. At Allahabad he made an earnest appeal for free education for all classes of Indians, which won him the support of his Hindu audiences. Returning to the United States, Bryan published the pamphlet *British Rule in India* (1906). After Bryan met with leading English officials and educated Indians, saw the people in the cities and country, read statistics, speeches, reports and other literature, he favoured Indian independence. Sir Henry Cotton (1845-1915), the chief commissioner of Assam and a friend of Vivekananda, acknowledged, "My views coincide with those of Mr. Bryan."[11]

In 1896 William Jennings Bryan narrowly lost to William McKinley in his bid for the U.S. presidency. Four years later in 1900 and 1908, he was again a candidate for the U.S. presidency on the Democrat ticket, each time going down to defeat. Woodrow Wilson made him his secretary of state during the period 1913-15. After the sinking of the Lusitania, Bryan resigned his cabinet post because he wanted the country to remain neutral during the World War. In late 1915, when lecturing in Minneapolis, Minnesota, on his way to Los Angeles, Abhedananda told a reporter that he opposed Bryan's pacifism, and said if the United States took this course, it would find itself in the same position occupied by India today. The Swami also told the parable of the snake that was beaten up because it did not bite or hiss. As a Christian Biblical literalist, Bryan did not believe that evolution should be taught in public schools. He served as the attorney for the prosecution in the famous trial against John Scopes (1901-70), who taught the Darwinian theory of evolution in a Tennessee high school. Bryan, in decidedly bad health, won the case, but died five days later.[12]

The hard working Swami Abhedananda edited the *Spiritual Sayings of Ramakrishna* (1903) with the assistance of Sister Devamata. Four years later Abhedananda came out with the first English language translation of *The Gospel of Sri Ramakrishna*. In the Preface dated December 15, 1907, he informed his readers:

> At the request of Sri Ramakrishna's Sannyasin disciples, these notes were published in Calcutta during 1902-03 A.D., in Bengali, in two volumes, entitled the *Ramakrishna Kathamrita*. At that time 'M' wrote to me letters authorizing me to edit and publish the English translation of his notes, and sent me the manuscript in English which he himself translated, together with a true copy of a personal letter which Swami Vivekananda wrote to him.... At the request of 'M' I have edited and remodelled the larger portion of his English manuscript, while the remaining portions I have translated directly from the Bengali edition of his notes.... The completed work is now offered to the Western World with the sincere hope that the sublime teachings of Sri Ramakrishna may open the spiritual sight of seekers after Truth and bring peace and freedom to all souls struggling for realization.[13]

Concerning the translation, *Luzac's Oriental List* from London informed its readers:

> The name of Ramakrishna Paramahamsa is well known to English readers since the late Max Müller wrote his article "A Real Mahatman" in the "Nineteenth Century" of August 1896.... The little book is an interesting

record of a remarkable personality, whose singular devotional influence has not been limited to Bengal.[14]

The *New York Herald* came out with an extensive review of Abhedananda's translation of *The Gospel of Sri Ramakrishna*, along with a picture of the Panchavati where Sri Ramakrishna experienced Divine communion. The first half of the review contains a biography of Ramakrishna, and the second half presents extracts from the book. The *Gospel* was translated into Spanish by the Vedanta Society of Buenos Aires in Argentina (1912) and later edited by Ananda and published in Santiago, Chile (1923), where there was a small group of Vedanta devotees. A Russian version was published in St. Petersburg (1914) and later in Riga, Latvia (1931). It was also translated into the Portuguese (Brazil), Danish, Scandinavian and Czechoslovakian languages.* Today the 1907 version can be found in twenty-three and the 1947 edition in seventy-five Western universities and public libraries, and also on the Internet.[15]

In March 1907, Laura Glenn became Paramananda's first initiated disciple. She edited the instructive portions of his letters into the successful book *Path of Devotion* in 1907. She also edited Sarah Waldo's notes of Swamiji's Thousand Island Park classes with her permission and approval, and they were published as the *Inspired Talks* in 1908 by the Ramakrishna Mission, Mylapore, Madras.[16]

On March 2, 1907, Abhedananda bought a house for the Vedanta Society on West 80th Street. About that time, they also acquired a farmhouse property at Berkshire, Connecticut, to serve as an Ashrama for Vedanta devotees. Swami Paramananda took up residence at the Vedanta Ashrama in Berkshire from July 14 to early September 1907. There he held meditation classes, devoted time to reading aloud, and answered questions.[17]

The outstanding foreign war correspondent and journalist, James Creelman (1859-1915) [q.v.]† wrote an article in the October 1907 edition of *Pearson's Magazine*. It includes pictures of Ramakrishna, Vivekananda, whom he praises, Abhedananda, and the Dakshineswar temple gardens. It is likely Creelman got some of his information about Vedanta from Abhedananda and/or Paramananda. In the article he refers to the newly bought home of the Vedanta Society stating:

* See Appendix VII on "European Language Translations" for more details.

† See Chapters III and XIII.

> In the little chapel of the Vedanta Society in New York there is a brown wooden side-altar, with a photograph of Ramakrishna, standing in a trance, eyes and mouth open, hands twisted—and there are candles and flowers before the picture, and the soft-voiced Swamis will tell you that the saint of the temple of Kali, who lived in our own modern time, reached divinity through self-control and humility. On the same wall is a head of Christ.[18]

Swami Vivekananda spent some time in London in 1895-96 and 1899. Abhedananda lived in London part of the time in 1896-97, 1902, 1904, 1906-09, and 1915, totalling seventeen trips across the Atlantic. After departing for London on June 26, 1907, he left Paramananda in charge of the New York Vedanta Society. He returned to New York on September 6, and then left for London on January 29, 1908. There Abhedananda held several meetings with Sister Nivedita who discussed the difficulties she was facing with her school in India. In London he established a branch of the Vedanta Society at 22 Conduit Street. The *London Daily News* of February 14, 1908 wrote the following concerning his lecture at a crowded Caxton Hall, Westminster, with H. D. Harben presiding:

> The Swami is a handsome, well set-up man, with jet-black hair and eyes, and the dark face of a Hindu. He spoke in excellent English, and was listened to with profound attention. His lecture was given under the auspices of the newly formed English Vedanta Society, of which the secretary is Miss Bowles, 63 Clifton-Hill, N.W.

In London he delivered addresses at the University Settlement and at the Lyceum Club, an influential organization of distinguished women. Some of his lectures were translated into the French language.[19]

During the winter of 1908, the British composer of music Cyril Scott (1879-1970) [q.v.] came to see the Swami on many occasions. Mr. Scott wrote a book *Poems* and dedicated the poem "Dreams from the East" "To Swami Abhedananda, in admiration of himself and his works." Chapter XII discusses the significant influence of Swamiji's writings on *Raja Yoga* on Scott. At that time an editorial column in a *London Weekly* read:

> We recognize with joy and deep thankfulness to the one only source of Divine Truth, the many generous and noble indications of sincere and

> profound reverence for the sacred scriptures of which Swami Abhedananda's eloquent writings and speeches afford so many striking examples.[20]

In his 1920 book *The Adept of Galilee*, Scott devoted nine pages (6-14) to selections from Abhedananda's essay "Was Christ a Yogi?", which appeared in *How to Be a Yogi* (1902). Scott adds, "This lecture is clothed in straightforward and simple language particularly elucidating."[21]

According to a newspaper account, some wealthy and socially influential people were members of the Vedanta Society of New York. For example, Abhedananda's lectures in New York were attended by Katherine Gould (c. 1880-1930), the wife of Harold Gould (1871-1959), who was a son of the multi-millionaire financier Jay Gould (1836-92). Mrs. Gould was a good friend of "Buffalo Bill" Cody (1846-1917). Another prominent person was James Graham Phelps Stokes (1872-1960), a millionaire political socialist who, before the age of thirty, was president of the Nevada Central Railroad. He held joint membership in the Vedanta Society and the prestigious Grace Episcopal Church in the city of New York. A few years before his death he wrote *The One Lord of East and West* (1956) in conjunction with Swami Shivananda, the founder of the Divine Life Society. Also, Mrs. Robert A. Van Wyck, the wife of the first mayor of Greater New York with five boroughs (1898-1901), who is mentioned later, attended his lectures in New York and Paris. At one time Abhedananda revealed, "None of the members of your 'four hundred' [New York's upper echelon of society] has ever done anything for me or for the school. I have never asked them for money. They have never offered me any."[22]

Abhedananda came back to the United States on August 21, 1908, as a passenger on the Lusitania. While sailing to America, at the request of his fellow-passengers he spoke to about two-hundred voyagers on the subject of "India and Her People".[23]

Back in the summer 1905, Girindra Mukherji M. A., a young Indian agricultural student, represented the Vedanta religion at the Lewis and Clark Exposition in Portland, Oregon. He requested books and pamphlets from the New York Vedanta Society, which were sold at the exhibit, and a full set was requested by the Public Library of Portland.[24] While Abhedananda was in Europe, three years later Girindra Mukherji, a student at the University of California in Berkeley, wrote an article on "The Hindu in America" for the *Overland Monthly and Out West Magazine* of April 1908 praising Swamis Vivekananda (along with a picture) and Abhedananda. Mukerji mentioned:

> The most prominent achievement was made by the patience and energy of Swami Abhedananda, in New York. He has been in this country ten years, and has published many books on Hindu philosophy. For the first time in America, a systematic attempt at an intellectual appreciation of India began with this movement.

The Vedanta Society of New York sponsored a money-raising event at Duryea's Hall on December 27 to aid the victims of the Italian earthquake. Edwin Markham (1852-1940) recited his highly regarded poem "Lincoln, the Man of the People" during the proceedings. At least one of Markham's poems appeared in Abhedananda's *Vedanta Magazine*, which was reproduced in the *Prabuddha Bharata* of April 1909, followed by a second poem in August.[25] Markham began his career as a teacher, an elected county superintendent of schools and a school principal in Northern California. His life underwent a radical change with the publication of *The Man with the Hoe and Other Poems* (1899) and *Lincoln and Other Poems* (1901), which thrust him into international fame. The former poem, which makes an appeal for better treatment of the labouring class, has been translated into forty languages and might have earned a quarter of a million dollars in thirty-three years. Markham later enjoyed immense popularity as the "Dean of American Poets". Religiously he favoured the Swedenborgian religion, and had some association with the New Thought movement.[26]

Years later, after having a delightful talk with Edwin Markham in Boston in 1928, Paramahansa Yogananda (1893-1952) [q.v.] wrote, "Our souls met and we rejoiced at the expansion of our feelings and deep perceptions." "Mr. Markham impressed me as a divine child who, due to his simplicity and spiritual intuition, is a true singer of divine songs. His conception of Divine Womanhood is similar to that of our great Hindu poets." In 1933 Markham was a guest at Paramananda's Centre in Boston.[27]

At one time Sri Yukteshwar (1855-1936), the guru of Yogananda, had thought of making his organization, Sadhu Sabha (founded in 1903), part of the Ramakrishna Mission, but this was not possible because of incompatible approaches.[28] Yogananda, whose encounter with Mahendranath Gupta is discussed in the last chapter of this book, made contact with Luther Burbank (1849-1926), one of the world's greatest horticulturist and plant breeders.

Burbank was an early supporter of the practice of meditation and, in a letter dated December 22, 1924, disclosed:

> I have examined the Yogoda system of Swami Yogananda and, in my opinion, it is ideal for training and harmonizing man's physical, mental and spiritual natures.... Through the Yogoda system of physical, mental and spiritual unfoldment by simple and scientific methods of concentration and meditation, most of the complex problems of life may be solved, and peace and goodwill come upon earth.... I am glad to have this opportunity of heartily joining with the Swami in his appeal for international schools on the art of living, which, if established, will come as near to bringing the millennium as anything with which I am acquainted.[29]

Burbank is a member of the highly prestigious "National Inventers Hall of Fame." He developed more than 800 new strains and varieties of plants, including the Russet Burbank potato, the most widely cultivated potato in the world. His hybrid plants have been used around the globe to increase the food supply. He revealed, "I have often talked to my plants in order to create a vibration of love.... One person will plant a flower, attend it carefully, and it will wither. But under identical physical care, a second person may develop that same flower into a healthier thriving plant. The secret ... is love."[30]

Paramahansa Yogananda was officially received by the 30th president of the United States Calvin Coolidge (1872-1933), and is pictured with J. Balfour, the Second Secretary of the British Embassy. According to a report in the *Washington Herald* of January 25, 1927, he was "greeted with evident pleasure by Mr. Coolidge who told him he had been reading a great deal about him."[31] For twelve years, Elvis Presley (1935-77), the world famous singer, often consulted with Paramahansa Yogananda's successor, the President of Self Realization Fellowship, Daya Mata, who reminded him of his deceased mother.

In 1904 E. A. Kernwart (aka Ernst Arthur Weber, b. 1875) [q.v.], an outstanding Theosophist from Leipzig, Germany, translated Abhedananda's works into a 172-page volume titled *Flammen aus dem Orient* (*Flames from the Orient*). The following year the Vedanta Society in New York sold a volume of eight Abhedananda lectures, and another volume of Vivekananda's writings, both rendered into the German language by Kernwart. In 1908 Kernwart followed with a translation of Abhedananda's *Philosophy of Work* (1902) into the German language. In addition, Kernwart translated Thomas Á Kempis' *Imitation of Christ* (1903) and the *Uttaragita* (1907). An Orientalist named N. O. Einhorn brought Kernwart's these German language translations (plus one more) of Abhedananda's lecture pamphlets to Leo Tolstoy in Russia in 1909. Tolstoy liked one of these lectures so much that he personally rendered Abhedananda's twenty-page pamphlet "The Way to the Blessed Life" into Russian. This particular lecture had previously appeared in the *Brahmavadin* during May 1900. On the cover of the German edition (rendered back into English as "The Path to Beatitude"), Tolstoy wrote "excellent". He wanted to give some of Abhedananda's pamphlets to the publishing house "Posrednik" to be translated into Russian, but unfortunately he passed away before the task was accomplished. These Abhedananda pamphlets, translated into German by Kernwart, with Tolstoy's notes, have been preserved at Yasnaya Polyana where Tolstoy lived. The original English language versions that came out in 1900-02 are presently found in the New York Public Library. In 1909, Tolstoy looked over Abhedananda's English language 1903 book *The Divine Heritage of Man*. After reading it, Tolstoy recorded in his diary:

> Yesterday evening I read books about Hindu religion. One excellent book about the meaning of life—Atman. "Love the spirit which is in yourself; not yourself, but Atman, i.e., the unlimited spirit, and you will love everything, and you will live by the spirit, freely, beatifically." How happy I am that I begin to understand, experience, feel this not with my reason but with my entire soul.[32]

Through his writings and speeches Abhedananda did much to make Ramakrishna-Vedanta a respectable religion in the United States. In the higher culture of America, there was a growing awareness of the presence of the Swamis of the Ramakrishna Order. A short biography of Abhedananda appeared in *Who's Who in America* from 1908 to 1919. The reports point out, among other things, that he "organized the Vedanta Society of New York, of which he has since been the head; also established a Centre of Higher Thought and a School for the Comparative Study of Religions in West Cornwall, Conn.; [is a] leading exponent of Monistic Vedanta in America." They also list his writings and their publication date. Moreover, biographical paragraphs on Abhedananda appeared in America's number one religious encyclopaedia, the Protestant based *The New Schaff-Herzog Encyclopaedia of Religious Knowledge* (1908-12), *New International Encyclopaedia* (1914), *A*

Thousand Men of Mark Today (1917), the influential *Encyclopaedia Americana* (1918), *Who's Who in New York (City and State)* (1918), and the prestigious *Collier's New Encyclopaedia* (1921). It is possible he is mentioned in some earlier editions of these volumes, and is definitely present in later editions. Briefer mentions of Abhedananda are found in T. W. Herringshaw's *American Blue-Book of Biography* (1915) and in *The American Literary Yearbook* (1919), which states he is a member of "The National Geographic Society". Sizeable accounts of the Vedanta Society are found also in the United States Bureau of the Census, *Religious Bodies: 1906 and 1916*, and the *Yearbook of American Churches* (1918).*[33]

Mrs. Robert A. Van Wyck was the wife of the first mayor of Greater New York (1898-1901), after its five boroughs had been consolidated into a single city. Mayor Van Wyck (1849-1918) brought about the construction of the first subway railroad in Manhattan. He moved to Paris in 1906, and there, on June 13, 1908, Mrs. Van Wyck brought together a large audience at the hotel Continental to hear a lecture by Abhedananda. The large hall was filled primarily with fashionable American women. She had attended some of Abhedananda's lectures in New York and hoped he would open a similar Society in Paris. The Swami was scheduled to provide more lectures in Paris.[34] The following year Abhedananda arrived in Paris in the beginning of April 1909 and then departed for London on May 6. During that time he founded a Vedanta Society in Paris with eight members. On April 14 he presented a very interesting lecture on Vedanta Philosophy at the residence of Mrs. J. Branscombe Wood in Paris. The social event was attended by a number of prominent members of the cosmopolitan colony who showed attentive interest in his subject. They included two princes, two comtesse, and a Lady. He was entertained also by Mrs. Van Wyck and others. About these events in Paris, Mrs. J. Branscombe Wood wrote to the Vedanta Society of New York:

> The Swami's visit here has been very successful; he has made many friends and has left a deep impression upon all those who have had the privilege of meeting him and the benefit of his teaching. His magnetic personality, the great depth and breadth of knowledge as exemplified in his teachings and the earnest devotion to his work are all factors that go to make the sum total of a great mind.[35]

---

* See Chapter XVIII.

In response to newspaper comments, a letter entitled "Swamis do not Aid Revolutionists" appeared in the *New York Tribune* of January 31, 1909, sent to them by "One who Knows the Swamis", stating:

> Sir: A recent number of your esteemed journal gave space to a one and a half column article by an ex-attaché in which an effort is made to show that Americans are assisting the natives of India in their efforts toward freedom. Some of the statements may or may not be correct. But when the great teachers, the Swamis, who have come here to enlighten the minds of the western people as to the true meaning of religion, are included, it is necessary and right to say something in their defence.
>
> The Swami Abhedananda, who stands at the head of the Vedanta Society of America, is a man of rare power and unquestioned sincerity. He has worked quietly and modestly, doing much good in this and other Occidental countries for over twelve years. Before that time the Swami Vivekananda, an inspired and magnetic expounder of truth, was for a number of years among us.
>
> Both these gentlemen have worked without pay of any kind except as given by their students and friends for actual support, that they might continue to elevate our thoughts and bring us the light from the East.
>
> Their mission is peace, knowledge, truth. The philosophy of the ancient Vedic Scriptures, which so few seem to grasp, does not conflict in any way with Christianity or other religions and their ethics taught by western minds. If Americans would study the Vedanta teachings, they would reverence the Christ more, endeavour to live higher, purer lives and know the reasons why.
>
> The Swamis of India do not mix with politics, nor do they ask their students and friends to send ammunition to India, but their sole aim is to bring spiritual upliftment and regeneration to all humanity. They are not revolutionists, but they preach that the Kingdom of Heaven will be established on earth, not through fighting and revolution, but through peace, justice and good will. And if a hundred more should come, there would be hands stretched out to welcome and homes provided for them by their western friends.[36]

In 1961 Swami Ranganathananda (1908-2005), the future President of the Ramakrishna Order, visited the home of the sister of the artist Frank A. (aka Franz) Dvorak (1862-1927). His younger sister Helena was well over eighty years old at that time. From her and from other sources, the Swami learned that:

> Frank Dvorak and Helena were in Chicago during the Parliament of Religions of 1893. He had a ticket for the Parliament but could not attend it on the day Swami Vivekananda spoke due to a painting job on hand. He regretted this very much when a few years later he met Swami Abhedanandaji, another disciple of Sri Ramakrishna, in New York, and later in London, and learnt about Vivekananda and his great Master, Sri Ramakrishna. In the meantime he had painted Sri Ramakrishna from an experience of a vision, which painting he produced before Abhedanandaji when the latter showed him a photo of Sri Ramakrishna. Abhedanandaji took this painting to India. It is the best portrait of Sri Ramakrishna so far available and adorns many a publication of the Ramakrishna Mission. He later painted a similar portrait of Holy Mother.[37]

Helena Dvorak also showed Ranganathananda a photo frame with a print of Dvorak's painting of Holy Mother with the inscription in English, "With blessings and love of Srimati Sarada Devi to Mr. Frank Dvorak." Frank Dvorak formerly paid a visit to Abhedananda at the Society House in London on May 7, 1909. The previous month Abhedananda founded a Vedanta Society in Paris with eight members, and then left the city for London on May 6. In Paris, much interest was shown by American and English residents and he gave a series of lectures at the residence of Mrs. Branscombe Wood. Impressed by the majestic appearance of the Swami, Dvorak asked if he could draw a sketch of him, which he did. He said, "I feel myself extremely happy in drawing the sketch of such a majestic appearance as yours." After Abhedananda presented him with the available photos of Sri Ramakrishna, Dvorak made a bust portrait of Sri Ramakrishna that he presented to Saradananda. Abhedananda installed Dvorak's portraits of Ramakrishna and Holy Mother in the shrine of the Ramakrishna Vedanta Math in Calcutta, which can be viewed in Sister Shivani's book on Abhedananda (Facing pp. 44-45). It is not clear whether the well-known portrait of Ramakrishna was produced from a vision or was drawn at a later date. Dvorak made three fine oil paintings of Abhedananda, whom he considered to be his guru, in addition to a beautiful profile in pastel. Abhedananda said, "He was a gifted painter of rare talent." Rabindranath Tagore made visits to his art studio in 1921 and again in 1926.[38]

Frank Dvorak, a native of Prague, Bohemia, then a part of the Austro-Hungarian Empire, was a genre painter of considerable note in Europe. He was equally adept in the mediums of oil, watercolour and pastel. The well-travelled artist produced paintings in six countries covering two continents. He received his training at the Vienna Academy and at the Munich Academy, and spent the years 1888-90 in Paris. During the summer of 1894 and 1895, Dvorak was an instructor at the Detroit Art School in Michigan. He held exhibits at the Paris Salon in 1893, 1898, 1900, 1903-05, and at the Royal Academy Exhibition in London in 1909 and in 1911, where he submitted three paintings, all essentially religious in content: "Mystic Rose", "The Angel of the Birds", and "Guardian Angel". Dvorak remained in London until his passing away in 1927, where he often painted beautiful and elegant women, linked thematically with mysticism and religion. Some of his paintings can be viewed on the Internet.[39]

After Abhedananda returned to the U. S., according to an article that appeared in the *Atlanta Constitution* on June 6, 1909 entitled "Great Mahatma Will Visit City",

> Swami Abhedananda, the great Mahatma of India, that country of romance, mysticism and religion, has been invited to attend the Conclave of Truth, to be held in Atlanta in the Auditorium-Armoury, in September, immediately following the Chamber Civic Congress, and has signified his intention and willingness to accept the invitation. This disciple of the world's oldest religion is one on the most interesting figures in the east, and his visit to this city will be the occasion of bringing together many of the advanced thinkers of the United States.... Swami Abhedananda is at the head of the Vedanta Society at New York, and has a large following from the ranks of learned men and women of the United States. The philosophy of this disciple of Ramakrishna embodies much that is beautiful and all that is pure.

The *Atlanta Constitution* article added:

> During the World's Fair at Chicago several years ago, Swami Vivekananda was the most picturesque figure in the Congress of Religions held in that place. His yellow satin robe, yellow tall turban and beautiful face attracted notice from everyone who passed him or heard him explain the Yoga philosophy. It is said that when Swami Vivekananda returned to the banks of the Sacred Ganges, where he died, he had left more broken

hearts in America than any other man had ever done. This was done unwittingly, but Swami Vivekananda was physically more beautiful than most men, and mentally more fascinating than others who had expounded religion. Vivekananda was a teacher of Raja Yoga, which is the philosophy of concentration and meditation. He gave an impetus to the movement which has since become widespread in America.

The list of invited people included friends of Vedanta like Ella Wheeler Wilcox, Edwin Markham, James Hyslop, Professor William James, Charles Fillmore and many other prominent people. At this time we cannot be sure if Abhedananda attended this event, or waited for four additional years before his highly successful 1913 lecture tour of Atlanta, Georgia.[40]

At the Vedanta Ashrama in Connecticut, during the months of August and September 1909, Swami Abhedananda offered three lectures per week. A Brahmachari Satyananda wrote:

> The people of the neighbouring localities crowded the open pavilion in front of Mount Echo where the lectures were held. The clergyman in charge of the West Cornwall Congregational Church expressed his pleasure, after hearing one of the lectures, and said he was glad to know the swami had human respect for Christ. Swami answered that he had "more than human, nay divine respect for that God-Conscious Man."

In addition, E. M. Sekunna created a massive stonework at the Ashrama, with three inscriptions engraved in stone, "Om Tat Sat, Om" in the centre, and "Work is Worship" on both sides.[41]

Swami Abhedananda had a falling out with some of the leading members of the New York Vedanta Society. The major problem was his extended periods of absence from the Centre. In 1906 he left the Centre on a half-year trip to India. Attempting to spread the message to a wider audience, he spent several months in Europe in 1907, eight months in 1908 and another six in 1909. After Abhedananda established a Vedanta Society in London, he began working at two Centres an ocean apart. His departure from New York brought about a decline in membership and consequently in revenues. At the end of 1909, due to a lack of funds, the *Vedanta Magazine*, formerly named *Vedanta Monthly Bulletin*, ceased publication. After Paramananda left for Boston in December of 1908, for many months there was no resident Swami to run the New York Centre. Also Laura Glenn (Devamata), who was the key figure in the book catalogue and publishing and journal departments, left for India in 1907, and two years later followed Paramananda to Boston. A rift developed and consequently Swami Abhedananda departed from New York, never again to live in the Society building. In typical fashion, he left in a gentlemanly, positive, stoic and courageous manner, as far as we know, never uttering a harsh word concerning the matter against anyone. This move represented a new phase in his life.[42]

A curious advertisement appeared in the *New York Tribune* of October 2, 1910 announcing that "The Monk Tej Narayan, an American of the Order of Ramakrishna-Vivekananda (India)" was going to present a series of four lectures at the Carnegie Lyceum.

Swami Abhedananda at the Berkshire Ashrama

On May 5, 1910, Swami Abhedananda moved permanently to the 370-acre Berkshire Ashrama (Retreat) about a mile from the village of West Cornwall, Connecticut. Primarily with the proceeds he garnered from the sale of his books and public lectures, the Swami purchased the estate from the Vedanta Society of New York. The Vedanta Society had originally bought the property in 1907. A small group of loyal followers lived with Abhedananda at Berkshire, and received special training from him. They included Mary Hebard LePage (Shivani), Thomas LePage (Haridas), the manager of the Vedanta Ashrama, Elizabeth Ann Mayson (Bhavani), Miss Margaret Sinnett (Saraju) and John Wittine (Ramadas). The prospectus for the Berkshire Ashrama read in part:

> In this quiet and retired spot one may live a simple life of absolute peace and undisturbed harmony with nature, and study practical and spiritual philosophy as taught by the accredited teachers from India, whose works may be obtained from the library.[43]

Sister Shivani described it this way:

> The Connecticut Ashrama was a very beautiful acreage covering wooded hill and dale, an utterly ideal setting for a philosophical and religious retreat. There were several springs and a flowing stream watered the rolling pastures. Two large cottages, Peace Cottage and Lotus Cottage, and a few single cabins, ample barns and sheds.[44]

With the ashrama serving as his nucleus until the end of 1919, Abhedananda carried on extensive preaching work, lecturing in many cities of the United States and Western Europe. It is most unfortunate that we know little about the Swami's contact with eminent Westerners from the time he moved to the Berkshire Ashrama in 1910 until he left for India in 1921.[45] Based at the Ashrama, Abhedananda continued to give public lectures in the large cities. In the middle of 1911, the president of the Brooklyn Ethical Association invited Abhedananda to speak to his organization. Vivekananda and Saradananda spoke there previously when Lewis Janes was the president. The *Brooklyn Daily Eagle* reported, "He was frequently and heartily applauded. With him on the platform sat the president of the Association."[46]

At that time the Vedanta Society received some positive support from the popular press. Lauriston Ward (1882-1960) spent six months in India during the year 1911 as a correspondent for the *Boston Transcript* and the *New York Evening Post*. His area of specialization was the political situation in the Far East. In an article on "The Ethical Conquest of India", which appeared in the *Forum* of September 1911, Ward describes Sri Ramakrishna as "an inspired teacher, whose name the society now bears". He went on to say:

> From its earliest days, not many decades ago, the ideal of the [Vedanta] society has been in a large sense monastic, and its members have devoted themselves to a life of meditation, obedience and service to mankind. They profess a philosophical form of Hinduism and lay a great stress on the Sanskrit scriptures, but they admit none of the claims or restrictions of modern Hinduism and are more in sympathy with many phases of western thought than the Arya Samaj. In the practical sphere of charity they have shown great earnestness, often heroism, in their efforts to relieve distress in India, especially in recurring times of plague and famine.[47]

Lauriston Ward, a man of many talents, at the age of fifty-two received an archeology degree from Harvard. The University appointed him to be the curator of Asiatic Archeology at Harvard's Peabody Museum of Archeology and Ethnology. At the Boston Museum of Fine Arts he spoke on many subjects, including the prehistory of Asia and the art of India.[48]

In 1911 Abhedananda came out with *Great Saviours of the World*, his pluralistic comparative study of world religions. The volume features chapters on Krishna, Zoroaster, Lao-Tzu, Buddha, Christ, Mohammed and Ramakrishna. The *Washington Star* emphasized the author's religious tolerance mentioning, "These studies are scholarly and comprehensive reviews of historic facts.... The author's attitude is reverent toward all ... a good study fitted to open the heart and liberalize the mind." The Vedanta Society of New York also put out his *Human Affection and Divine Love* that year. Many of the lectures he gave in America up to 1921 were published in volumes that were compiled after 1939 by his Ramakrishna Vedanta Math in Calcutta.[49]

Swami Abhedananda accepted an offer to speak under the auspices of the "De Hart Equal Suffrage League" at Bergen Lyceum in Jersey City, New Jersey. The prospectus for the talk of December 6, 1912, read:

> Swami Abhedananda has an international reputation, having lectured in London, Paris, and for several years in New York. He is a graduate of the University of Calcutta, and has an excellent command of English, as well as a rarely dignified, attractive and picturesque personality. His lectures are both enjoyable and profitable to all who hear him, among the latter having been several Jersey City people included in our list of [thirty-four] patronesses. For the past year and a half Swami Abhedananda has been living in retirement, writing books and giving only class lectures. He is coming to the city especially for our lecture, and we feel that in bringing him here we are offering Jersey City an educational and intellectual treat.[50]

At that time Swami Brahmananda dispatched a friendly letter from Benares to Abhedananda dated 12th December, requesting that Abhedananda return to India. It read in part:

> Would it be too much to ask you again as I have done more than once before, to make up your mind to come back to India when you really mean to retire from your work there. Need I tell you how happy we all shall feel to have you amongst us once again, and what a joy it would be all round. Our Holy Mother I understand is eager to see you as she has not seen you for such a long time. You may live here in quiet if you like to enjoy rest after such a strenuous work as you have done for these long years. Nothing will be in your way of doing that and we shall try to do all to make you feel comfortable. Please do think over the matter seriously my dear Abhedananda and don't fail to comply with our request and to give into our heartfelt wishes.[51]

Abhedananda decided to remain in the West, and in February and March of the following year, the Swami travelled to the South. He spoke before large audiences in Fernandina, Florida, and delivered three lectures at the Methodist Church in Jacksonville, Florida. Everywhere he was warmly greeted by the best people of the community who gave him large receptions. A number of clergymen were interested in his lectures. After leaving Florida the Swami lectured throughout the State of Georgia, coming to Atlanta on the 1st of March. Upon his arrival to the city he was hailed as "Prince Abhedananda".[52]

Four years before, the Atlanta Psychological Society in the state of Georgia had five-hundred active members. A class with thirty members under the direction of Mrs. J. B. Chestney made an exhaustive study of Hindu philosophy, and had some knowledge of Ramakrishna, Vivekananda, and Abhedananda. In 1913 the Atlanta Psychological Society invited Abhedananda to give several talks in their city. He was featured in ten different articles that appeared in the *Atlanta Constitution*. One headline read, "Hindu Philosophy Unfolded by 'Missionary' from India; Atlantans Stand to Listen", under which there was a photo of him of over sixteen square inches. The report went on to say in part:

> The Carnegie library fairly swarmed with Atlanta people who wanted to be taught the philosophy of India. The fame of Swami Abhedananda who is the leader of the Vedanta cult in America with headquarters in New York had preceded him. Thus, it happened that the Atlanta Psychological Society which brought the philosopher to Atlanta could not entertain all the guests of the procession and dozens were turned away. Besides the lecture room, the entire basement of the Carnegie library was filled with people who stood up in the hall and stairways and heard the lecture through the door.

Swami Abhedananda told his audience things like, "Our souls are but reflections of God", "We are all part of one great universal soul", "The common aim of all religions is to discover truth", "Salvation simply means the attainment of perfection", "What you will be tomorrow, you are making and moulding now", and "Perfection of the heart comes through knowledge, not through ignorance or faith".[53]

Mrs. Rose M. Ashby, the president of the Atlanta Psychological Society, described three of Abhedananda's speeches this way for *The New Thought News* of March 25:

> The subject was "The Relation of Soul to God". It was treated in a masterly way both from a scientific and a metaphysical standpoint, satisfying both mind and heart, proving conclusively that all science leads to God, and showing the presence and immanence of God in and through and above all things, "a God at hand and not far off". After hearing this lecture, one felt that the relation of Soul to God is very close—very real and present—and that through the unifying principle of Love the Soul realizes union with God and has Divine Communion....
>
> The Ethical Society also invited the Swami to lecture before them and a large crowd of Atlanta's representative people gathered at the Auditorium to hear him lecture on "India's Contribution to the World's Ethics".
>
> His final lecture in Atlanta was on the very interesting subject, "Reincarnation", and the overflow audience that greeted him at Cable Hall, Sunday afternoon, March 9th, showed interest in this subject. The questions and answers pertaining to this great subject, Reincarnation, were a feature of this lecture. Having been cradled in the thought and being in his own element, the Swami answered scientifically and metaphysically all the intricate questions propounded to him on the subject. This meeting was one of great interest and worth and provoked much thought.[54]

In Atlanta Abhedananda also spoke daily to full houses at the Unitarian and Universalist Churches.* The *Atlanta Constitution* of March 9 wrote, "Probably the most noted teacher of his faith and head of the Vedanta School of Philosophy, Swami Abhedananda has delivered addresses before the foremost universities of this country, besides lecturing throughout England and his own home land."[55]

During April 1913, Abhedananda was the only Asian to receive a cordial invitation to present an address at the National New Thought Alliance Conference held in Detroit, Michigan. The list of invited participants to this event included friends of Vedanta like Charles Fillmore, Orison Swett Marden, Edwin Markham, Annie Rix Militz, Reverend Benjamin Fay Mills, Reverend R. Heber Newton, Ralph Waldo Trine, and Ella Wheeler Wilcox. Abhedananda conducted a series of eight lectures there from June 15 to 22.[56]

The Berkshire Ashrama in Connecticut was open all year round to receive students and friends. Concerning the Swami's life at the Ashrama, a student at the Vedanta Ashrama wrote to the *Prabuddha Bharata*:

---

* See Chapter XVIII.

The life of Swami Abhedananda is very simple; he works in the fields as do the Trappist Monks of Catholicism; and in the course of it he directs the men who are employed in the fields. In the evenings he conducts classes, and gives very interesting and helpful thoughts to the students and friends.[57]

Abhedananda wrote in his *Diary*, "The Ashrama looks like Fairyland." His view was confirmed by a woman guest who remained at the Vedanta Ashrama in the Berkshire Hills of Connecticut for three months with a dozen or more devotees during the summer of 1913. In a seven-column newspaper story that went out on the wire appearing in the Madison *Wisconsin State Journal*, she wrote:

> There is not, however, a trace of Oriental colouring visible to the casual observer.... The followers of this Hindu religion who have pitched their tents in the secluded valley in Connecticut.... There was absolutely nothing conventional or monastic in the atmosphere or surroundings.... I looked in vain for some outward visible sign of the Eastern monastery I hoped to find and discovered not a trace.... The spirit of the place is purely democratic and no distinction is made when it comes to work, or at any other time.... I was convinced that I had fallen in with the oddest, most delightfully queer and dearest people I had ever dreamed of.... I spent three months of happiness in this place.... They take their religion seriously but not sadly and believe that health and happiness rather than anemia and melancholy are the natural effects of the spiritual life. Every day had its interest and surprises at this place. I lingered on, loath to leave this charmed spot.

In the course of the article, she gives us some insight into Abhedananda's nature, describing him as:

> The spiritual teacher in charge of the place... a tall and imposing figure, looking the picture of poise.... Swami sat at the head of the table, made jokes and was as merry as a boy.... After a long walk, I returned to the ashrama and found every one hard at work. The Swami armed with a huge watering can was deeply absorbed in watering the flowers and vegetable garden.... At the long table where the Hindu Swami presided with marked suavity and grace.... The magnificent Hindu Swami.[58]

A newspaper article of February 1914 revealed that at the Vedanta Ashrama Society of West Cornwall, Abhedananda delivered lectures open to the public on ethics and spiritual philosophy. Occupants of the farm most often numbered three to twenty supporters. During the summer he sometimes erected tents and small portable cottages for devotees from New York and Boston. Most of the time the Swami lived on the farm. As expected, his neighbours described him as "a cultured, educated man of East India birth and blood". "His reputation in Cornwall is good in most parts and indeterminate in several quarters. The best people in the town pay him a high tribute in the matter of education and conversational qualities and charm." The property was worth about $10,000 (equivalent to $213,600 in 2008). During the months of February through May, he returned to New York City to present a series of lectures at Carnegie Chapter Hall and at the Lillian George Studio, followed by a summer course of lectures and classes at his Berkshire retreat.[59]

Swami Abhedananda made his final trip to Europe in 1915. He went to the booking office planning to buy a ticket from London to New York on the S.S. Lusitania. He recalled:

> A mysterious thing happened. I was about to buy the ticket, but immediately I heard a clear voice forbidding me to buy it. I was dumbfounded.... again I went to the counter and the same thing happened. Then I decided to return to the apartment without buying any ticket. However, I planned to buy the ticket the following day. The next morning I saw in the newspaper in big letters "S.S. Lusitania Is No More." I was overwhelmed. Tears rolled down my cheeks. I then realized that the Master had saved my life.

On May 7, 1915, a German submarine destroyed the British vessel and 1,198 passengers lost their life. This was only four months after the passing away of Trigunatita.[60]

With the advent of the First World War, the Swami spent more time on the West Coast of the United States. During the year 1900 when Vivekananda came to New York in June, he asked Abhedananda to go to California and told him, "California is the place where Vedanta will grow." Abhedananda later added, "The people there are sympathetic and open." He came to Southern California in December 1914 in response to an invitation from some of his former students, who had relocated from Brooklyn, New York, to Long Beach near Los Angeles. Abhedananda delivered a comprehensive course of nine public lectures at the I.O.O.F Hall on Broadway and American Avenue during January-February 1915. In Los Angeles he also established a Vedanta Library. In a letter to Carrie Wyckoff (Sister Lalita), Josephine MacLeod mentioned that Roxie Blodgett (d. 1915) informed her about Abhedananda's visit to Los Angeles.[61]

After Trigunatita's mahasamadhi on January 10, 1915, Abhedananda journeyed north from Los Angeles to San Francisco. At that time Swami Prakashananda (1874-1927) from Northern California introduced him at the podium of the Hindu Temple and told the audience:

> Ladies and gentleman: I deem it a pride and privilege to introduce to you Swami Abhedananda, who is one of those Swamis who have been called forth into existence by the Divine touch of Sri Ramakrishna, whose picture you see in this auditorium. All these eighteen years he has been in different parts of the United States and Europe lecturing and holding classes on Vedanta philosophy and higher ethics, illuminating the hearts and souls of many people. He knocked at the gates of big centres of civilization and everywhere people responded to the broad, scientific and illuminating messages of Vedanta philosophy. His recent lectures and classes in Long Beach and especially at Los Angeles have created such a widespread and considerable interest that people there want him to come back (because he goes away to New York) and he would respond to the call. He thinks California would be a great centre in the future, which would radiate this broad and universal teaching of Vedanta philosophy. Without further waste of time, I take pleasure in presenting to you our esteemed Swami.[62]

During the eulogy Abhedananda told the devotees, "I am standing on Swami Trigunatita's platform. He gave his life for this Temple. The blood of a Martyr is the seed of a Church and this Temple will stand." Hailed as "one of the greatest Vedantists in America", during March 1915, requested by Prakashananda, he spoke before a standing-room-only crowd at the Hindu Temple in San Francisco, and at the Pacific Vedanta Centre. If Abhedananda wished to do so, it was possible for him to become the leader of the San Francisco Centre, which did not have a director for nearly a year. Returning to the East, he established a Vedanta Library at 721 West 23rd Street in New York City. He offered classes there on Sundays, Wednesdays and Fridays. In December his speech in Minneapolis, Minnesota, roused great interest.[63]

After Trigunatita's passing away, the Los Angeles area was no longer under the unofficial jurisdiction of the San Francisco Centre. On January 30, 1916, members of the Vedanta Society of Los Angeles gathered to honour the blessed memory of Swami Vivekananda. Abhedananda, the founder of the Centre, was accompanied by five devotees who spoke of their acquaintance with Swamiji, one who had attended the Parliament of Religions in 1893.[64]

In a letter of 18 April 1916 from Swami Turiyananda in India to Dhira (Mrs. Bertha Petersen) in Northern California, Turiyananda had written:

> I hear that Swami Abhedananda intends building a temple for our Lord somewhere in America very shortly. I have not been informed of the place he would erect the Temple on. It would indeed be so nice if he can really do that. He has asked S. Premananda at the Belur Math to try to send a few very intelligent and young Sannyasins from the Math to help him found a Training School in his Ashrama at Connecticut.[65]

Monks were not dispatched from Belur Math, and subsequently Abhedananda devoted more time to the Southern California operation. Abhedananda lectured in Los Angeles for at least four consecutive winters from 1914-15 to 1917-18. According to the *Los Angeles Times*, his lecture locations in Los Angeles included: I.O.O.F. Hall, Ebell Club House, Coulter Building, Symphony Hall, and the Vedanta Library at 721 W. 23rd Street. During this period, Alice Hansbrough (Shanti), who spent months with Vivekananda in Northern and Southern California, was an intimate and faithful devotee of his. By January 1917 or earlier he organized a Vedanta Society in the city of Long Beach, along with the previously formed Vedanta Society of Los Angeles which resided in the Coulter Building located at 213 South Broadway/Hill Street in the downtown area. Members of the Vedanta Society of Los Angeles wrote to the *Prabuddha Bharata* on February 16, 1917:

> When it was learned that Swami Abhedananda was willing to establish permanent headquarters here, Swami Vivekananda's old students and friends, as well as many new, rejoiced in the opportunity for the study and practice of pure Vedanta under a competent guide.[66]

During World War I the Los Angeles *Evening Express* in 1917 made an interesting comment, "The Swami has received many letters from soldiers in the trenches since the beginning of the war, regarding his teachings and the lectures which he has given in different parts of the world." During a period of several years between 1915 and 1921, at times on the same day Abhedananda and Paramananda would offer talks to separate groups of Vedantists in Los Angeles, and they would have adjoining advertisements in the *Los Angeles Times*.[67]

On February the 1st, 1917, Abhedananda conducted a wonderful birthday service in the memory of Vivekananda in Los Angeles:

> [He] spoke very sweetly and lovingly of his spiritual brother whose life and work meant so much to both East and West. He told of their boyhood life together, how they had studied and chanted together, travelled together and together sat at the feet of their great Master Bhagavan Sri Ramakrishna and of how the inspiration of that wonderful life had fitted them for their own life work. Several speakers followed, students who had met Vivekananda here and in other parts of the United States. Abhedananda closed the service with meditation upon the character of Vivekananda; upon his great power of self-sacrifice, always sacrificing himself to the utmost for the help of others—upon his chastity and his purity which gave him his great power and upon his great love for humanity, which made humanity pause and listen to his message. After the closing meditation the offered fruits and flowers were passed among the audience.[68]

In the fall of 1918, he held a series of classes on the "Vedanta Philosophy" in New York City. Abhedananda sent a letter to his brother disciple Swami Brahmananda, the head of the Ramakrishna order in India in November. There he revealed his inner secret, "It is longtime that I have been left alone in this country. I have a strong desire to return to the Motherland and to see you.... I have done enough of preaching, I am now tired of this."[69]

A year later, near the end of 1919, Abhedananda sold his ashrama in West Cornwall, Connecticut, along with all of the furnishings. Sister Shivani relates:

> Tears fill my eyes and throat. He had worked so consistently, so tirelessly, so selflessly to make that wilderness productive, then beautiful. It fulfilled the fondest dream,—the utmost measure,—"and we were not ready"—not sufficient or strong to hold him here, this man from India.[70]

After a farewell reception given to him by Bodhananda and the New York devotees on December 15, 1919, receiving Brahmananda's approval he intended to return to India. Arriving in San Francisco on December 21, many old students of Trigunatita urged him to remain in the city. He then decided to stay there rather than to proceed on to India. An advertisement in the *San Francisco Chronicle* of January 2, 1920 lists four classes a week by Abhedananda on "Practical Psychology" at the Phelan Building. He later spoke at Scottish Rite Hall in San Francisco. Abhedananda also worked with Prakashananda for a while, and then opened a new ashrama in San Francisco that operated independently of the Vedanta Society of San Francisco. The wife of an orthodox San Francisco clergyman exclaimed, "The teachings of the Swami are revelations of a higher Christianity." Albert Wollberg honoured and loved Abhedananda, and spoke in detail of the time back in 1901 when he and his wife had entertained him in San Jose, California. Mr. Wollberg referred to Abhedananda as "The last of the Great Ones". The Swami offered two lectures and an additional class each week. Dorothy F. Mercer (1901-62) [q.v.], who "was entirely absorbed by the Vedanta and Swami Abhedananda", attended his Northern California lectures beginning in the year 1918 and revealed:

> Swami Abhedananda was tall, handsome, austere, and of commanding presence. An eloquent, scholarly and well-organized lecturer, he addressed hundreds every week, including many eminent San Franciscans. Even a maternal aunt and her husband went to hear him, not because they were eminent nor because they felt any religious need, but because Swami Abhedananda was one of the finest lecturers in the Bay Area. In a social group he was quiet and reserved, taking each man's measure.[71]

A Miss Bessett (Sister Jaya) heard Abhedananda lecturing when she was first investigating the teachings of Vedanta. She responded, "I was amazed to find myself in the grip of a Presence. No other word can express my reaction."[72]

Along with a picture of the Swami, the *San Francisco Chronicle* of May 8, 1920 (p. 10) reported:

> At the urgent requests of his friends in San Francisco, Swami Abhedananda, head of the Vedanta philosophy in America, has recently come from New York City, where for many years he held large audiences spellbound

> by his lucid and eloquent discourses on abstruse subjects, and also by his magnetic personality... He has lectured in London and Paris, and also before the faculties of Berkeley, Cornell, Toronto, Harvard, Columbia and other universities of America.... The spiritual awakening in California and especially among the people of San Francisco has made such a great impression upon his mind.

At that time Ernest C. Brown [q.v.], an old-time devotee who goes back to the days of Vivekananda, wrote:

> It was my privilege to take Swami Abhedananda out to lunch occasionally, and I remember taking him to the Advertising Club where I used to take Swami Trigunatita, and how I was always impressed by his abstinence in food. When he finished, nothing could persuade him to take another mouthful. His dignified carriage, like that of his brother disciple Swami Vivekananda, invariably attracted attention and his serious air had a pleasing effect on all who met him. Although on the invitation of Swami Prakashananda, the Swami-in-Charge, he gave several lectures at the [San Francisco] Centre, he never participated in any way in the affairs of the Centre and made no effort to do so.[73]

Going back a decade, on December 15, 1908, at the Berkshire Ashrama in West Cornwall, Connecticut, Sister Shivani (Mrs. Mary Hebard LePage, b. 1879) [q.v.] received "spiritual transfusion" through initiation from Abhedananda. She states this transfusion brought about a transformation in her character and way of looking at life. Her husband Thomas LePage (Haridas) for some time served as the manager of the ashrama. Sister Bhavani (Miss Elizabeth Ann Mayson) resided there and left the ashrama only twice in twelve years. Until they settled in South Los Angeles as of December 1916, the LePages were close intimate disciples of Abhedananda. During the year 1917, Mary LePage attended some of Abhedananda's public presentations in Los Angeles. After the close of the ashrama in Connecticut in December 1919, Sister Bhavani came to live with them. In 1920 the family moved to rural Tujunga, a few miles west of La Crescenta near Los Angeles. Twice Walter Goldschmidt, a member of the Vedanta Society, brought Abhedananda to their home. According to Sister Shivani, during his second visit to their home during 1920-21, Abhedananda drew her aside into the garden and made this surprising prophetic (and possibly overstated by her) statement:

> I want to tell you, Mrs. LePage, do not forget. There will be a spiritual wave starting in Los Angeles & San Diego and extending as far as Seattle in the North and from this Coast it will inundate the world.[74]

In his popular text *Higher Psychical Development: Yoga Philosophy* (1920), Hereward Carrington (1880-1958) [q.v.] intelligently uses several long quotations from Abhedananda's "Does the Soul Exist after Death?" and "Spiritualism and Vedanta", and from Vivekananda's *Raja Yoga.* Carrington assisted James H. Hyslop at the American Society for Psychical Research (1905-08). Hyslop, a professor at Columbia University, was a co-speaker at the 1899 annual convention of the Free Religious Association along with Swami Abhedananda.[75]

A reorganization meeting of the Vedanta Society of Los Angeles was convened at the residence of Mrs. Harry Wilhelm at Signal Hill in Long Beach. Their goal was to establish an office, meeting place, and library in downtown Los Angeles for Abhedananda, who was then teaching in San Francisco. Abhedananda responded by relocating to Los Angeles in December of 1920. He offered a series of public lectures at Native Sons' Building on January 16 and at the Walker Auditorium Building at 730 S. Grand Avenue. He remained in Los Angeles most of the time for six months, though he did give a reading on Emerson's poem "Brahma" under the direction of Paul Elder at his gallery in San Francisco on March 26. Paul Elder (1872-1948) owned a classy Arts and Craft Bookshop in San Francisco, and during his lifetime published four-hundred books under his own name. In Los Angeles Abhedananda spoke before a capacity and appreciative audience in the Native Sons' Building on June 26, and then delivered his final lecture on the *Bhagavad Gita* the following day. As a representative of the congregation, Miss A. M. Whitman, the secretary of the Vedanta Society, "expressed how deeply all the students in Los Angeles would miss the Swami and his teachings."

Upon his return to San Francisco, Ernest C. Brown [q.v.], the president of the Vedanta Society, described

> the good pioneering work that had been done so splendidly by Swami Abhedananda during his stay in America for the past twenty-five years. He also emphasized the value of the prolific published works of the Swami which contain lucid and masterly interpretation of abstruse philosophical subjects in the light of the truths taught in Vedanta.[76]

Soon before his departure, Abhedananda revealed:

> The East and the West will unite—such is God's will. The signs of the times greatly encourage me, and my visit and prolonged stay in this country has clearly convinced me that it is possible to make the world our home, and to love all as brothers and sisters. God's spirit is working everywhere. Blessed is he who sees the work, and realizes the Divine Spirit.[77]

After devoting a quarter of a century to diligently and intelligently spreading the message of Vedanta in the West, Abhedananda departed for India never to return to the U.S.[78] This marked the end of an era (1893-1921), in which five of Sri Ramakrishna's direct monastic disciples devoted a total of forty-seven years to spreading his message to the West.

Soon after Abhedananda departed the country, Brian Brown (b. 1881) [q.v.], in his widely read anthology *The Wisdom of the Hindus* (1921), devoted seventeen pages to selections from Sri Ramakrishna drawn from Abhedananda's *The Gospel of Ramakrishna* and *The Sayings of Ramakrishna*. In addition, he presented a five-page section on the "Wisdom of Abhedananda" derived from two of his other works.[79]

Abhedananda Returns to India

On July 27, 1921 Abhedananda set sail from San Francisco across the Pacific Ocean to Honolulu, Hawaii (now part of the United States), to be an Indian delegate* at the multinational First Pan-Pacific Educational Conference held during August 11-24. The president of the conference was Wallace Farrington (1871-1933), the territorial governor of Hawaii. The honorary presidents were the president or prime minister of seven countries, including Warren G. Harding of the United States. Over eighty delegates represented sixteen countries mostly bordering the Pacific Ocean. In a large group photograph, he is pictured dressed in a white suit and shoes. According to an article in the *Honolulu Star-Bulletin* of August 3 titled "Hawaiians Closely Linked with Indians Asserts Hindu Sage", he offered several lectures during his three-week sojourn in Hawaii.[80]

Swami Abhedananda then travelled to Japan; Shanghai, Hong Kong and Canton in China; Manila in the Philippines; Singapore; Kuala-Lumpur,

---

* Along with K. Kunhi Kannan (b. 1884), M.A. from Mysore.

Seremban, and Klang in Malaysia; and Rangoon in Burma on October 18, delivering a series of lectures before returning to Calcutta. He then went to Belur Math, the headquarters of the Ramakrishna Order, where "he was heartily welcomed by the brotherhood". In one speech he stated:

> Bhagavan Sri Ramakrishna used to teach us that God is the simplest thing in the world. We cannot find him because we are complex. If you want to find him you will have to remove all the complexities of modern civilization and become as simple as a child.[81]

Upon his return to India, his biographer, Moni Bagchi, described him as:

> Abhedananda at 55 was magnificent to look at. Physically he presented an imposing figure—tall, straight, rosy completion, strong-built carriage and bright penetrating eyes, dark flowing hair, wide forehead and a face flushed with purity and serenity ... In person, he appeared to be distinguished and strong; in bearing, generous and gentle; in intellect, a giant.[82]

In 1922, inspired by Nicholas Notovitch's *Unknown Life of Christ*,* Abhedananda travelled from Kashmir to Tibet, crossing the Himalayas on foot in order to reach his destination—the Hemis Monastery, north of the city of Leh. In India he was able to fulfil his desire to establish a permanent religious organization with dedicated lifelong followers. The following year he established the "Ramakrishna Vedanta Society of Calcutta", which was loosely connected with the Ramakrishna Order. In 1924 he opened a branch of the Society at Darjeeling with the name "Ramakrishna Vedanta Ashrama". As Swami Gambhirananda wrote, "Swami Abhedananda himself maintained the best of friendly relations with the monks of the Belur Math and its branches, who, in their turn, paid him frequent visits. Besides, he continued to be a Trustee of the Math and therefore a member of the Governing Body of the Mission till the last day."[83]

Sometime during 1922-23 at Belur Math, Abhedananda made the acquaintance of a young Swami Prabhavananda (1893-1976), who later mentioned to his monastic devotees, "Swami Abhedananda was handsome, tall, and well-built. I saw him when he was old. He became fond of me. He used

* Leon Landsberg was a co-translator of its first English language edition.

to send for me at the Belur Math." Possibly Abhedananda intuitively realized that Prabhavananda would soon go to America and become a leading Swami in the West. And rightly so, he did leave for America in 1923.[84]

On September 21, 1925, as president, Abhedananda presided over the 81st Birthday Anniversary of Mrs. Mary E. Foster (1844-1930), celebrated at the Dharmarajika Vihara in Calcutta. He mentioned that, "Mrs. Foster is my personal friend and a student." The most generous financial benefactor of the Maha Bodhi Society founded by Anagarika Dharmapala was Mary Foster of Honolulu, Hawaii. She supplied the Society with a large portion of the funds needed to build an Industrial School in Sarnath in 1901, the Mausoleum at Sarnath in 1915, the Buddhist Dharmarajika Vihara in Calcutta in 1920, and other establishments.[85]

Cara French, a disciple of Trigunatita, was a devoted student of Abhedananda when he was in Northern California. Abhedananda invited her to India and she served as his personal secretary when she came to the country with Paramananda during the year 1926.[86]

Abhedananda met Mahatma Gandhi in 1926 at the Darjeeling Ashrama and, during a discussion, told the great Indian leader the following:

> You are doing the work started by Ramakrishna and Vivekananda in the lines of removing untouchability and in encouraging cottage industries. Therefore, I bring to you blessings. You know that though a high caste Brahmin by birth, Ramakrishna ... went to the door of a lowly sweeper and washed the dirt of his door with his flowing long hair which he had on his head. Thus he set an example of the removal of untouchability which is the highest religion of this age.[87]

Four years before this, Swami Shivananda also had paid a tribute to Gandhi:

> There is no doubt about it that Mahatma Gandhi is really endowed with great powers. It is also true that there has been a special manifestation in him of the Primal Energy, the Mother of the Universe.... The Mother of the Universe who was awakened by Sri Ramakrishna for the good of the world is obviously working in various ways through the instrumentality of different persons.[88]

As previously mentioned in Chapter XII, Lord Lytton II (1876–1947) [q.v.], the governor of Bengal, and his wife were friendly with Abhedananda and invited him to dinner. Following the Swamis request, during 1926 they also paid a visit to Abhedananda's Darjeeling Ashrama.[89]

The Russian artist Nicholas Roerich (1874-1947) [q.v.], who is discussed in Chapter II, immigrated to India, and on December 16, 1928, sent a letter to Abhedananda. In the correspondence he describes Abhedananda's

> book, full of the precious teachings and uplifting ideas. Verily in our house the Great Names of Sri Ramakrishna and Swami Vivekananda are highly venerated. The precious teaching of Sri Ramakrishna first attracted our thought to India, and everything concerning these Holy men is near to us, as well as you are—Their great successor.... For the adornment of your Ashrama in Calcutta, I will send you some coloured reproduction of my paintings as a sign of my sincere feelings.[90]

In 1930, Wendell Thomas (b. 1896), a student of Vedanta who admired Abhedananda's understanding of Western knowledge, made the following positive assessment:

> Rather than overpower by flashy oratory, he seeks to convince by sweet reasonableness and a vast array of new and picturesque facts.... Moreover, in his treatment of the doctrine of reincarnation, he is very theosophic and modern, rejecting the notion of the god-man-beast-plant wheel of life from which escape is desirable, and stressing the creative, evolutionary, purposeful aspects of the soul's cosmic peregrinations. Finally, his handling of the doctrine of "work" is quite Western. Like Ramanuja, combining the *Gita* rule of unselfish devotion with the early Vedic idea of purposeful work for reward, he takes the "duties and work of our daily life as a means to a higher end", and declares that "all good or unselfish work brings as their results peace, good health, prosperity and happiness in the end."

Thomas' *Hinduism Invades America* is the source of this quotation. In spite of the book's sensational title, the manuscript is neither an attack nor a defense of Hinduism. The work provides an interesting history of the Indian religious presence in America up to 1930. Thomas obtained much of the material for the chapter on "Vedanta Centres, the Ramaḳrishna Movement in America" from Bodhananda in New York.[91]

In the meantime, Sister Shivani [q.v.] and her husband Haridas LePage moved to a 279-acre property near Palmdale, California, in September 1923, which they referred to as "Abhedananda Acres". Sister Bhavani remained in their house until June 1926. Occasionally they would attend the services at Paramananda's La Crescenta Centre. Then Sister Bhavani and Shivani's eldest son, Kalidas (b. c. 1909), left to study under Abhedananda's direct supervision at his ashrama at Darjeeling in the Himalayas. Because of her ill health, after three years at Darjeeling, she and Kalidas returned to the LePage residence at Abhedananda Acres. Abhedananda's "Hymn to Sri Ramakrishna"* and to Sri Sarada Devi† were originally written in Sanskrit and then translated by him into English. They were printed for the first time by Kalidas LePage and his brother Lachan on a hand press at Abhedananda Acres. His celebrated Sanskrit hymn composed to Sri Sarada Devi, "Prakritim", is regularly sung at many Ramakrishna Centres throughout the world during the vesper service. Shivani also received a visit from Herschel Parker, the ex-president of the Vedanta Society of New York and for many years a travelling companion of Abhedananda. He told her, "These Swamis have all of the virtues and none of the vices of other men."[92]

The end of an era occurred on September 8, 1939, on the eighth day of World War II. Abhedananda, the last of Ramakrishna's monastic disciples, entered into mahasamadhi. What followed was a new era of internationalism, and a dissemination to a large number of people of the spiritual knowledge, ethical precepts, and meditative practices laid down by Ramakrishna and his disciples.

It is a great tragedy that Shivani's house at Abhedananda Acres burned to the ground in 1943 and, along with it, thirty-five years of detailed records, and also the first third of her perspective book on Abhedananda. This event forced Shivani to write the biographical work *An Apostle of Monism* (1947), later renamed *Swami Abhedananda in America*, largely from memory and inspiration. The biography gives an intimate and firsthand account of Abhedananda's eventful stay in the West by one of his most ardent disciples. It adds significantly to our knowledge of Abhedananda's activities in the United States. She expressed her appreciation for Swamis Ashokananda and Bodhananda for their encouragement of the undertaking.[93] In the biography she made this revealing statement:

---

* "Vishvasya Dhata Purushastwamadyo", *Prabuddha Bharata*, March 1932.
† "Prakritim", *Prabuddha Bharata*, March 1954.

> The Swami was gifted with a deep and resonate voice—mellow, rich and inclusive. His very tones were of encouragement and appeal. He was the most ordinate yet powerful speaker I have ever heard.... In the States we have had many public speakers. Some of them world-renowned; of these, it has been my privilege to hear two, the Hon. William Jennings, called the "silver tongued orator" who moved the multitudes, and Franklin Delano Roosevelt, "the man with the golden voice". The texture of Swami's voice was different from the voices of these great speakers. Some quality in the composition of tone one could not place; it commanded, never implored nor besought. He could be heard at the end of the largest hall, yet he never raised his voice.... The Swami rarely gestured—always master of himself, he used none of the histrionic effects so often practised by the best of speakers. The flow of that majestic thought held the listeners as in a trance by its clarity. I have heard him address an audience some times for an hour and a half during which time he never hesitated for a word, never repeated. He spoke without notes or script as though impelled by the Light of some dynamic power. He lectured as one endowed with a mind illumined. His logic convinced. There was nothing to refute. His learning amazed one by its purity.[94]

At a later time Sister Shivani expressed her admiration for Abhedananda:

> I believe his was the greatest mind of the Twentieth Century that came out of India and gave a great heart to the redemption of all mankind. His clear thought, his loving kindness, his spiritual immediacy and grip on eternals, established one to his own inner immortality at every meeting with this great and simple character. Words can never adequately explain the grandeur that was Abhedananda. To meet him was to find profundity.[95]

Swami Lokeswarananda (1909-98) described his first meeting as a youth with Abhedananda back in 1927:

> I consider it a great privilege that I was able to meet and talk to that great scholar-monk, Swami Abhedananda, a few times.... I sat gazing at his magnificent figure—everything so well proportioned, so handsome, so close to the picture I had formed in my mind of what a Yogi ought to look like after reading his book. It was his face that attracted me most. I could

not imagine anything more beautiful.... He spoke briefly with remarkable clarity and emphasis. It was his dignity and poise with which he spoke that, to me at least, lent special meaning to each word that he said.

Lokeswarananda added nine years later:

> [When he spoke without the use of a microphone] in the old Town Hall of Calcutta, in the year 1936 while the Birth centenary celebration of Sri Ramakrishna was being inaugurated.... I remember how effortlessly he spoke. Words flowed from his lips smooth, easy and distinct, his voice even, and every syllable audible to the last man in the big hall.... He stood erect, a commanding figure, who never seemed to raise his voice, never showed a trace of emotion, but his words fell in an even flow, each word a gem. And the audience gasped with joy as it listened and I will never forget the applause it gave him when he finished.[96]

In her book *The Lost Years of Jesus*, Elizabeth Claire Prophet (b. 1940) attempts to prove that Jesus Christ spent seventeen years (age 13-29) in the Orient, primarily in India, Ladakh and Tibet. Her work features a powerful full-page photograph of Swami Abhedananda. To support her theses, Prophet devotes several pages to giving a background sketch of Abhedananda and telling of his views on Nicholas Notovitch's *Unknown Life of Christ* after he visited the Hemis monastery in Tibet in 1922. She adds selections from Abhedananda's work *In Kashmir and Tibet* that originally was published in Bengali and later translated into English. Centred in Montana, she is the spiritual leader of the Church Universal and Triumphant that belongs to the Theosophical and Gnostic Christian traditions.[97]

A biographical account of over seven-hundred words has been written on Abhedananda in *Religious Leaders of America* (1999), and he is also discussed in *Contemporary Authors* (2004). These reference volumes are read by an educated audience of intellectuals and scholars outside of Vedanta circles. *Religious Leaders of America* by John Gordon Melton (b. 1942) contains a biographical sketch of Abhedananda with a list of his books and the year of publication, and writings about him. Among other things, it states, "Through his speaking and travels he organized and spread the movement, and through his writings and university lectures he became one of the early forces in effectively introducing Hinduism to Americans." This book is an excellent biographical guide describing over 1,000 founders and leaders of religious bodies, churches, and spiritual groups in North America. It also includes accurate biographies of Ramakrishna and Vivekananda, and over 80 pages are devoted to Hindu and Buddhist groups in the United States. Melton, a prodigious author of a variety of reference works on several areas of religion, is an ordained Methodist Minister. One of his books was titled *A Bibliography of Hinduism in America Prior to 1940*. As a strong advocate of religious freedom and pluralism, it is his lifelong intention to properly inform the public of the many religious traditions in America.[98]

Swami Tathagatananda, the head of the Vedanta Society of New York, originally founded by Swamis Vivekananda and Abhedananda, being a prolific writer, is well known for his excellent historical studies and charming writing style. His history book on *The Vedanta Society of New York: A Brief Survey* (2000) covers the inspiring life of its leaders from Swamis Vivekananda, Saradananda, Abhedananda, Bodhananda, and Pavitrananda to the author himself. The section on Abhedananda is exceptionally well written, adding new and intriguing material to our knowledge of the Swami. In the "Introduction", Marie Louise Burke described this historical study this way:

> Here in the pages of this book is a treasure of religious history which can inform and inspire everyone who cares about preserving the spiritual light that is given periodically to the world—most recently, and perhaps most powerfully and universally, by Sri Ramakrishna and his great apostle Swami Vivekananda.

For a list of dates and locations of Swami Abhedananda's presently known places of residences, see Appendix II. Concerning the literature on Abhedananda, see Appendix V for the publication dates of his writings, Appendix VI for a selected list of books about him, and Appendix VII for European language translations of his books up to 1930.

ENDNOTES

1 *PB* (Jan. 1907), p. 13; Gambhirananda pp. 117, 177-78; Tathagatananda1, pp. 174-75.

2 Nelson, p. 111.

3 *Brahmavadin* (March-April 1908), pp. 199, 202; J. Gordon Melton, *Biographical Dictionary of American Cult and Sect Leaders* (New York: Garland Publishing,

1986), pp. 215-16; Ananda Ashrama. Web: www.anandaashrama.org/about-leadership.htm.

4 *MOTE* (July-Sept. 1940), pp. 169-71.

5 *VMB* (July 1906), p. 72; (Feb. 1907), p. 225; *VM* (July-Aug. 1909), pp. 159-60; Tathagatananda1, pp. 174-75; Gambhirananda p. 178; *PB* (Oct. 1912), p. 200; (June 1950), p. 264; *VK* (July 1950), p. 120.

6 Yale, p. 88; Tathagatananda1, p. 198.

7 *Vedanta Darpana* (Dec. 1932), p. 15.

8 Tathagatananda, pp. 191, 195-98, 201-02, 207; *PB* (June 1950), p. 264; *VK* (July 1950), p. 120; *Vedanta Darpana* (Dec. 1932), p. 15; *Times* (Dec. 5, 1925), p. A2; (Dec. 19, 1925), p. A2; (Jan. 2, 1926), p. 6; (Jan. 30, 1926), p. A2.

9 *Epistles*, p. 57; Satyananda, p. 92.

10 William Jennings Bryan, *Bryan on Imperialism* (Chicago: Bentley & Co., 1900), p. 52.

11 William Jennings Bryan, *British Rule in India* (India: Indian National Party, 1915), pp. 4, 12; Sunderland, pp. 50-51, 142; *VMB* (May 1906), p. 34.

12 *RLOA* (1991), p. 71; *Voice of Freedom* (Feb. 1916), p. 200 on GBS.

13 Swami Abhedananda, *Ramakrishna Kathamrita and Ramakrishna* (Calcutta: Ramakrishna Vedanta Math, 1984), pp. 11-12.

14 Luzac's Oriental List (Jan-Feb. 1908) on GBS.

15 *VMB* (Mar. 1908), 204-05; Ramakrishna, p. 12: WorldCat.

16 Burke, III, pp. 132-33; Levinsky, pp. 95, 103-05; WorldCat.

17 Gambhirananda, pp. 176-77; *Brahmavadin* (Oct. 1907), p. 552.

18 "The Ramakrishna Movement in the West", *PB* (Jan. 1908), pp. 10-13; reprinted from *Pearson's Magazine* (Oct. 1907) on GBS.

19 *VMB* (March 1908), p. 199; Tathagatananda1, p. 180; Chetanananda, p. 474.

20 Bagchi, p. 359.

21 *VMB* (Jan. 1908), pp. 179-80; Bagchi, p. 351; *The Adept of Galilee*, pp. 6-15 on GBS.

22 *Los Angeles Times* (Sept. 4, 1910), p. I9; *Hamilton Evening Journal* (Ohio) (April 4, 1925), p. 15; *New York Times* (Dec. 25, 1930), p. 21; Jacob Dorn, ed., *Socialism and Christianity in Early 20th Century America* (Westport, CT: Greenwood Press, 1998), pp. 205, 216; John Woolverton, *Robert Gardiner* (London: University of Missouri, 2005), p. 82.

23 *VMB* (Aug-Sept. 1908), p. 71.

24 *VMB* (Oct. 1905), pp. 110-11.

25 Tathagatananda1, p. 180; *VM* (1909), IV, pp. 105 on GBS.

26 *DAB* (1958), XXII, Sup. II, pp. 428-30; *CA* (1998), vol. 160, pp. 237-39.

27 *MOTE* (Oct. 1933), p. 256; EAST–WEST, Nov-Dec. 1928, Vol. 3-6. Web: http://mysticalportal.net/3-6.html#ed1928.

28 Poor Richard, *Dwapara Yuga and Yogananda* (Noble New, 2007), p. 48 on GBS.

29 Paramahansa Yogananda, *Autobiography of a Yogi*, ch. 38. Web: www.ananda.org/inspiration/books/ay/38.htm.

30 Web: http://www.invent.org/Hall_Of_Fame/21.html; Martin Gardner, *Fads and Fallacies in the Name of Science* (New York: Dover, 1957), p. 312; *DAB* (1928-1936); *EWB*.

31 Kamath, pp. 140-41; Thomas, pp. 145-49; Jackson, pp. 131-32; *EWB*, XVI, pp. 462-63.

32 Shifman, pp. 40-41; Tathagatananda2, p. 530; *SK* (1905), p. 191; VirtualCat; Web: http://catnyp.nypl.org/search/a?SEARCH=abhedananda.

33 Many of these books can be found on GBS; *WWIA* (1908-09), p. 6; (1918-19), p. 39.

34 *Boston Globe* (June 14, 1908), p. 25; *VMB* (July 1908), IV, p. 37; *Paris Herald* (July 4, 1908); Web: http://en.wikipedia.org/wiki/ Robert_Anderson_Van_Wyck.

35 *VM* (July-Aug. 1909), IV, pp. 156-60; Bagchi, p. 356.

36 *New York Tribune* (Jan. 31, 1909), P. C5; *VM* (1909), IV, pp. 101-02 on GBS.

37 Bagchi, p. 420.

38 Bagchi, pp. 353, 356-57, 419-21; Tathagatananda1, pp. 178-79; Shivani, facing pp. 44-45; *New York Times* (April 25, 1909), p. C3.

39 Franz Dvorak. Web: http://www.kurteschonltd.com/frankz_dvorak.htm; Arthur Gibson, *Artists of Early Michigan* (Detroit: Wayne State University Press, 1975), pp. 95-96.

40 *Atlanta Constitution* (June 6, 1909), p. 5 on PQHN.

41 *VM* (Oct. 1909), pp. 173-74 on GBS.

42 Jackson, pp. 54-56; Tathagatananda1, p. 187.

43 *The Washington Post* (Feb. 18, 1912), pp. SM 1-2 on PQHN.

44 *SACC*, p. 8.

45 Gambhirananda, pp. 178-79; Tathagatananda1, pp. 175-76, 187; Shivani, pp. 175, 177.

46 Bagchi, pp. 366-67.

47 *Forum* (Sept. 1911), pp. 289ff.

48 *NCAB* (1965), vol. 48, pp. 554-55.

49 Yale, p. 91.

50 *SACC*, pp. 79-80.

51 *SACC*, pp. 27-28.
52 *PB* (April 1913), pp. 79-80.
53 *Atlanta Constitution* (March 3, 1913), p. 7.
54 *PB* (June 1913), pp. 117-18.
55 Shivani, pp. 234-35, 304; Chetanananda, p. 476; *Atlanta Constitution* (June 7, 1909), p. 6; (March 5, 1913), p. 17; (March 9, 1913), p. 46; (March 10, 1913), p. 8; *PB* (June 1913), pp. 117-18.
56 *Epistles*, pp. 58-59; *PB* (Aug. 1913), p. 159.
57 *PB* (Oct. 1912), p. 197.
58 Madison, *Wisconsin State Journal* (Oct. 1, 1913), p. 10.
59 *Hartford Courant* (Conn.) (Feb. 22, 1914), p. X2; *New York Tribune* (Feb. 21, 1914) p. 9; (May 9, 1914), p. 14 on PQHN; Cost of Living.
60 Chetanananda, p. 476.
61 Burke, VI, p. 225; *PB* (May 1917), p. 94; *Los Angeles Times* (Jan. 2, 1915), p. 17; *PB* (Feb-March 1915), p. 60; (July 1915), p. 140.
62 "Introduction by Swami Prakashananda", VSSC Archives.
63 Pravrajika Brahmaprana, "Ida Ansell: Flaming Upwards", *VK* (June 1991), p. 228; *PB* (July 1915), p. 140; (Dec. 1915), p. 240; (Feb-Mar. 1916), p. 60; Levinsky p. 202; Shivani, p. 240.
64 *Voice of Freedom* (Feb. 1916), p. 217.
65 *VK* (April 1989), p. 154.
66 "Vedanta Movement in Los Angeles", *PB* (May 1917), p. 94.
67 *PB* (Feb.-March 1916), p. 60; (May 1917), pp. 94, 99; Shivani, pp. 193, 216; *Los Angeles Times* (Jan. 2, 1915), p. 17; (March 21, 1915), p. IV1; (Jan. 13, 1917), p. II2; (Jan. 20, 1917), p. II2; (March 24, 1917), p. II2; (Jan. 12, 1918), p. II2; (March 30, 1918), p. II2.
68 *PB* (May 1917), p. 94.
69 Nelson, p. 110; *New York Times* (Sept. 14, 1918), p. 11.
70 Shivani, p. 180.
71 Yale, pp. 86-87; Shivani, pp. 216, 305; Tathagatananda1, p. 188; Chetanananda, pp. 476-77; *VK* (May 1926), p. 40; *PB* (Apr. 1920), p. 96; (Jan. 1921), p. 10; *San Francisco Chronicle* (Jan. 2, 1920); (Oct. 28, 1920), p. 16.
72 Shivani, p. 216.
73 "Vedanta in America", *VFEW* (Sept-Oct. 1959), p. 17.
74 Shivani, pp. 70, 153, 193-96; *Los Angeles Times* (March 7, 1920), p. V8; (Dec. 31, 1920). p. 112; (Jan. 1, 1921), p. I12; (Jan. 8, 1921), p. II2.
75 Hereward Carrington, *Higher Psychical Development: Yoga Philosophy* (San Bernardino, CA: Borgo Press, 1920), pp. Index; EOP.

76 *PB* (Sept. 1921), p. 216.

77 Bagchi, p. 376; Chetanananda, p. 477.

78 *Los Angeles Times* (March 7, 1920), p. V8; (Dec. 31, 1920). p. 112; (Jan. 1, 1921), p. I12; (Jan. 8, 1921), p. II2; *San Francisco Chronicle* (March 26, 1921), p. 16; Tathagatananda1, p. 188; Paul Elder. Web: www.paulelder.org.

79 *The Wisdom of the Hindus*, ed. Brian Brown (New York: Brentano's 1921), pp. v-vi, 273-75.

80 *Bulletin of the Pan-Pacific Union* (Oct. 1921), pp. 2-14; *First Pan-Pacific Educational Conference* (Honolulu: Pan-Pacific Union, 1921); *SACC*, p. 47.

81 *VK* (June 2002), p. 22.

82 Bagchi (1968) p. 381.

83 Gambhirananda, pp. 259-62; Radhakrishnan, p. 52; *PB* (Dec. 1921), p. 287.

84 Anandaprana, p. 72.

85 *SACC*, p. 89; The Maha Bodhi Centenary Volumes (98-99), pp. 42-44 on GBS.

86 Shivani, p. 216; Levinsky, p. 316.

87 Ghosh, pp. 58-59; Satyananda, p. 131.

88 Gambhirananda, pp. 268-69.

89 Ghosh, p. 59.

90 *Epistles*, pp. 53-54.

91 Thomas, pp. 111-12, 264. Swami Abhedananda is the only monastic disciple of Sri Ramakrishna of whom we have a record of his voice. It is of a short speech of his given in Bengali on the occasion of the birth centenary of Ramakrishna Paramahamsa in 1936. According to an article in *The Statesman* (Oct. 7, 2004), they used modern computer technology to restore another speech made by Swami Abhedananda in 1936. They said it was recorded by the Megaphone Company and preserved by Dr. Baidyanath Biswas, one of the Swami's disciples.

92 Shivani, pp. 66, 211-12, 219; Pravrajika Vivekaprana in Southern California informed me about the present singing of the "Prakritim".

93 Shivani, pp. x-xii, 221-22.

94 Shivani, pp. 36-37.

95 *SACC*, p. 4.

96 *SACC*, pp. 91-94

97 Elizabeth Claire Prophet, *The Lost Years of Jesus* (Livingston, MT: Summit University, 1986, 1988) on GBS; *RLOA*.

98 *RLOA* (1999); *CA* (1984), vol. 110; (2004), vol. 218.

CHAPTER XVII

SWAMI ABHEDANANDA: PROFESSORS

At the request of Swami Vivekananda, Swami Abhedananda journeyed to England, arriving there near the end of September 1896, around the time of his thirtieth birthday. Abhedananda reveals:

> When I was in London, Swami Vivekananda took me to meet Professor Max Müller and Professor Paul Deussen of Kiel University, who had translated sixty Upanishads into the German language and who was the author of the *Philosophy of the Upanishads*. I had a conversation with them in Sanskrit.... [Max Müller] was deeply interested in the life and teachings of Ramakrishna and said, "Ramakrishna was an original thinker, for he was never brought up within the precincts of any university and, therefore, his teachings were new and original." This remark created a deep impression upon my mind. Later on, he published the *Life and Sayings of Ramakrishna*.[1]

When Müller bade farewell to Vivekananda and Abhedananda, he said, "It is not everyday one meets with a disciple of Ramakrishna Paramahamsa." Abhedananda also met the famous Indian scientist Jagadish C. Bose, who at that time was demonstrating his apparatus for millimetre electromagnetic wave research at the Royal Institution, London.[2]

After coming to America in early August 1897, Abhedananda made contact with a number of professors, most of whom had never met or seen Vivekananda. At the Twentieth Century Club in Brooklyn, on October 25, 1897, the Swami met Fridtjof Nansen (1861-1930), the celebrated Norwegian explorer. Nansen discussed his Arctic adventures and the Swami "had the opportunity of speaking with him about Indian and Hindu philosophy of Vedanta, which he admired very much." With a crew of twelve, Nansen led an exploration in the North Pole region (1893-96). As a professor of zoology at the University of Christiania, he became a pioneer in the study of oceanography. The versatile Mr. Nansen was Norway's Ambassador to Great Britain (1906-08) and the League of Nations high commissioner for refugees (1921-30). For his relief works in aiding millions of prisoners of war, Soviet famine victims, Russian noncommunist refugees, Greek and Turkish refugees, and displaced persons, Nansen received the 1922 Nobel Peace Prize. Typically, he gave the prize money to international relief efforts and continued to work unceasingly for the benefit of Armenian refugees. After his death, in 1931 the Nansen International Office for Refugees cared mainly for anti-communist Russians, Armenians and, later, for Jewish refugees from Nazi Germany, and in 1938 it received the Nobel Prize for Peace.[3]

The Swami and Henry Van Haagen went to a lecture on "The Vedas" delivered by Professor A. V. Williams Jackson (1862-1937) of Columbia University at the Brooklyn Institute of Arts and Sciences on February 22, 1898. Abhedananda tells us:

> After the lecture I was introduced to him. He took a great interest in my Vedanta Mission in America and afterwards became an honorary member of our Vedanta Society of New York, and wanted to help me in my work. Later on he invited me to his Sanskrit classes at the Columbia University... I used to go to his classes and through him I became acquainted with other Professors and Faculty of the University.

The Swami returned to hear Jackson's lecture on March 1. They met again on November 17 through the introduction of Herschel Parker of the physics department at Columbia University. Professor Jackson came to Abhedananda's discussion on "Evolution and Reincarnation" in the Assembly Hall, "and became deeply interested in the subject". On March 24, 1899, Jackson invited him to lunch, and afterwards the Swami spoke on the Upanishads to his students and answered many of their questions. On another occasion, Abhedananda talked about the *Gita* to the professor's class at Columbia University. They spoke together at an Educational Conference and the Swami responded to a resolution made by Jackson concerning the rights and duties of an individual.[4]

Abraham Valentine Williams Jackson, originally an instructor in the Zend language at Columbia University, became a professor of Indo-Iranian languages (1895-1935). Twice he was the president of the prestigious American Oriental Society in 1915-16 and 1929-30 respectively. Jackson studied the Avestan, Sanskrit and Prakrit languages in Germany and made seven journeys to India and Persia (Iran) during 1901-11, 1918-19, and in 1926. In India he interacted with the Zoroastrian Parsis while studying their religious practices and customs. The American scholar, being a distinguished authority on the Zoroastrian religion and ancient Persian history, received honour from the Parsi community in India for his detailed studies and sympathetic interpretations. Jackson produced many texts dealing with the language of the Avesta, Zoroastrianism, and various aspects of the Persian culture. His Indian writings include the scholarly *An Avesta Grammar in Comparison with Sanskrit* (1892), a translation of Harsha's seventh century Sanskrit drama *Priyadarsika* (1923), and the editing of the nine volume *History of India* (1906-07). Romesh Chunder Dutt (1848-1909), the great Indian historian, wrote the first volume, and Jackson the final volume. Jackson served on the General Committee for the Ramakrishna Centenary held in Calcutta during March 1937, the final year of his life. According to his contemporaries, Jackson was courteous, obliging to a fault, and seldom made a harsh remark.[5]

Lewis Janes invited the Swami to speak before the Free Religious Association of Boston, which he did on May 27, 1898. The next day Janes took Abhedananda to Harvard University, where he attended a class given by the philosophers Josiah Royce (1855-1916) [q.v.] and William James (1842-1910) [q.v.]. Abhedananda found their talks to be "extremely interesting", especially James' refutation of the idea of Unity. On the 29th day of the month at the Cambridge Conferences held at Sara Bull's house, Abhedananda discussed the subject of "Unity in Variety". Professors William James, with his students sitting by his side, and Charles Lanman (1850-1941) [q.v.], the Harvard Sanskritist, were in attendance. In his discourse Abhedananda brought up James' arguments against "Unity" and logically refuted them. He said, "At the close of the meeting Prof. James shook hands with me and congratulated me for my lucid and logical discourses on the subject of Unity and invited me to come to lunch with him in his house next afternoon." A four-hour discussion ensued, with the Swami supporting the unity, and William James the plurality of the universe. Abhedananda tells us:

> Prof. Royce, Prof. Lanman, Prof. Shaler and Dr. Janes supported my arguments against Prof. James, who was at last convinced that the Vedantic point of Unity of Brahman, the ultimate Truth, was unassailable. Dr. Janes remarked to me after the discussion was over that he never heard such a learned and wonderful discussion before.

Next Dr. Janes and the Swami went to Professor Lanman's house. Charles Lanman made the confession that he did not understand Shankara's commentary on the *Vedanta Sutras*. Abhedananda told him, "You needed a Guru, preceptor, who would have given you the key to open the secret door of your *buddhi*, the faculty of understanding, to realize the spiritual oneness of Vedanta." Lanman responded, "You were lucky to find such a Guru." Abhedananda added, "From that day Prof. Lanman became a good friend to me and attended my lectures in Boston and later on became an honorary member of the Vedanta Society of New York."[6]

The following year on April 30, 1899, Abhedananda lectured on "Religious Ideas in Ancient India" at the Cambridge Conferences. William James, Charles Lanman, and other distinguished Harvard professors attended the talk. On May 7, at the Conferences Josiah Royce spoke profoundly on "Immortality", and Abhedananda followed on the same subject, before an eminent crowd of Harvard professors and Protestant ministers. On June 2 the Swami spoke before an audience of one-thousand people at the annual meeting of the Free Religious Association of America. "Immortality" was supported philosophically by Josiah Royce, from the standpoint of spiritualist research by J. H. Hyslop, scientifically by Lewis Janes, and Abhedananda delineated the Indian viewpoint. In Chapter VIII, covering Vivekananda and the professors, there are short biographies of the professors mentioned above with the exception of Nathaniel Shaler. In 1900, on April 22nd, at the Cambridge Conferences, Professors Lanman and Sidney Fay of Harvard listened to Abhedananda's lecture on "Ramakrishna, a Real Mahatman". Lanman spoke on the "Spirituality of the Hindus". Four days later the Swami was invited to dine with Lanman. "A Student of Vedanta" mentioned, Lanman "expressed great sympathy and interest in the Vedanta work which the Swamis are conducting in this country. Abhedananda has since made Lanman an honorary member of the Vedanta Society." A week later on the 29th, the Swami attended a lecture by Josiah Royce on the German philosopher Friedrich Nietzsche (1844-1900). Afterwards Abhedananda was requested to speak, and he gave a ten-minute talk contrasting Nietzsche's ideas with those of the principles of Vedanta.[7]

The philosopher Josiah Royce was no doubt influenced by Abhedananda's debate with William James on the unity vs. the plurality of the Infinite, and by Vivekananda's lecture on the "Vedanta Philosophy"[8] given before the Harvard Philosophical Club in March 1896. Consequently, in the first volume of Royce's classic work *The World and the Individual* (1899), he extensively discusses the idea of the "Unity of Being" as found in the *Chandogya Upanishad*.*[9]

Nathaniel Southgate Shaler (1841-1906), mentioned above as attending the informal Abhedananda-James debate, served for two years in the Union army as a captain, became a Harvard professor of paleontology and geology (1869-1904), and the dean of the Lawrence Scientific School (1891-1906). In addition to his university pursuits, Shaler worked as a geologist for the state of Kentucky, and the director of the Atlantic Coast Division of the United States Geological Survey. He excelled in writing both geological and historical texts, and romantic dramas. As a teacher, he had an excellent rapport with his students, being well liked and respected, and was a brilliant conversationalist with a keen sense of humour.[10]

A physics professor at Columbia University, Herschel Clifford Parker (b. 1867) invited Abhedananda to a field meeting of the Appalachian Mountain Club of Boston on July 1, 1898. In September they climbed the steep side of Mount Washington in the White Mountains of New Hampshire. They remained at the Summit House for the entire night enjoying the scenery and glorious sunrise. Abhedananda described Herschel Parker as "a good guide and a delightful companion". The two camped and travelled together for days and separated in Kingston, New York. Even more important, on November 17 Professor Parker took the Swami to Columbia University and introduced him to the university president Seth Low, and to the Sanskrit scholar A. V. Williams Jackson, whom he had earlier met. The Swami and Herschel Parker met again on a number of occasions. Francis Leggett became the first president of the Vedanta Society of New York on October 29, 1898, after it was incorporated under the laws of the State of New York. In the spring of 1900, Herschel Parker became the second president of the Society, succeeding Leggett. Parker probably met Turiyananda and Vivekananda, who stayed at the Centre for six weeks during the summer of 1900. As president of the Vedanta Society, Parker gave a speech at the 1902 memorial service for Vivekananda, explaining, "What it had meant to us and to the world to have known so profound a thinker and so great a spiritual leader, and how irretrievable must be his loss to all concerned in the uplifting of the human race." The Swami and Parker made a continental tour during the summer of 1905, travelling across the continent to Alaska, and then south to Mexico, before returning to the East.[11]

* See Chapter VIII for more details on Royce.

Herschel Clifford Parker held the position of instructor during 1891-1903, and then professor from 1903 in the physics department at Columbia University. After this he became a consulting and mining engineer. He was a fellow of the American Geographical Society and the Royal Asiatic Society of London. Parker wrote a book on electrical measurement, and in 1905 he became a co-discoverer of the helion filament, which was nearly four-times as brilliant as the light bulb made by the Edison Company. His inventions include the quartz tube incandescent electric light, the helioscope and also a motor torpedo. In addition, Herschel Parker, an expert professional mountaineer and explorer, was the group leader of several expeditions that first ascended the peak of many mountains in North America. He received a great deal of newspaper coverage in 1912 while ascending Mount McKinley in Alaska, the highest peak in North America,* but not quite making it to the summit. After 1930 he lived in the city of Los Angeles. At that time he went to see Sister Shivani at Abhedananda Acres, near Palmdale, California. Referring to Abhedananda, Parker explained to her, "The grand humanness of the Swami should never be forgotten nor overlooked," and, "These Swamis have all the virtues and none of the vices of other men."[12]

While hiking with Herschel Parker, the Swami met Professor Niles, the president of the Appalachian Mountain Club, which was composed of cultivated and scholarly members. The professor explained how the mountains were formed from the different strata of the rocks. In September 1898, at the Appalachian Mountain Club meeting, Niles introduced Abhedananda to the members and in turn he gave a speech on the grandeur, majesty and beautiful scenery of the Himalayan Range of Mountains. Abhedananda was invited back for a reception the following year on May 3rd, with President Niles being present for the occasion. William Harmon Niles (1838-1910), a professor at Massachusetts Institute of Technology (1871-1902), held the position of head of the department of geology for over twenty years. During those years he also taught geology and natural science at Boston University, Wellesley College, and at the Massachusetts State Teachers' Institute. In addition, he served as the president of the Boston Society of Natural History (1892-97), and a fellow of the American Academy of Arts and Sciences and other scientific organizations.[13]

On November 17, 1898 Herschel Parker introduced Abhedananda "to Dr. Seth Low, the president of the [Columbia] University, who," states

* Over 20,000 feet in height.

Abhedananda, "was very pleased to know my mission and the teachings of Vedanta philosophy on which I was delivering public lectures." Seth Low (1850-1916) became the mayor of Brooklyn, the third largest city in the United States, president of Columbia University (1890-1901), the second mayor of New York City, defeating the Tammany regime, chairman of the Board of Trustees at the African American Tuskegee Institute in Alabama (1907-16), actively working with Booker T. Washington (1856-1915), and president of the New York Chamber of Commerce. Among other things, as mayor of Brooklyn he introduced the merit system, and as mayor of New York he developed the civil service system. At Columbia, he led the critical move of the College from midtown to Morningside Heights, contributed a million-dollar gift to build a new library, established trust funds for study and research, and supported higher education for women.[14]

At religious conventions, Nathaniel Schmidt (1862-1939) of Cornell University and Abhedananda's paths often crossed. They both spoke at the Monsalvat (Mount of Peace) School for the Study of Comparative Religion held at Greenacre, Maine, during August in the years 1898, 1899 and 1900. Abhedananda heard him lecture on April 23, 1899 in the Cambridge-Boston area, and they might have had an exchange of ideas at that time. They both were guest speakers in November 1900 at the "State Conference of Religion" in New York City, and at the annual meeting of the Free Religious Association held at the Boston Museum on May 31, 1901. Professor Schmidt, who knew Lewis Janes at Greenacre, the Cambridge Conferences, and at the Free Religious Association, and was a good friend of his, submitted a tribute to him after his passing away. Schmidt worked as a professor of Semitic languages and Oriental (Middle Eastern) history at Cornell University (1888-1932). His wide range of interests include the writing of *Outlines of a History of India* (1902). In his *The Coming Religion* (1930), he outlined a religion of the future that would be ethical and scientific, without dogmas or creeds, and expressed a new type of fellowship and organization. In 1931 he became the president of the American Oriental Society.[15]

On the flap of the cover on many of Abhedananda's books, it tells us that he "became acquainted with" many prominent people like "Prof. Hyslop of Columbia". At the 1899 annual convention of the Free Religious Association of America, Josiah Royce, James Hyslop, Lewis Janes, and the Swami were the guest speakers, as reported in the *Boston Herald* of June 2. Abhedananda quotes Hyslop in his writings on *Life beyond Death*. James Hervey Hyslop (1854-1920) taught at Columbia University as a professor of logic and ethics

(1894-1902). His textbooks on philosophy were widely read. Hyslop broke away from the mainline intellectual community and became a dominant force in psychical research and spiritualism. He founded the American Institute for Scientific Research in 1904, which became part of the American Society for Psychical Research. In his book *Life after Death*, Hyslop discusses his ideas on scientific empirically based studies of human survival.[16]

Granville Stanley Hall (1844-1924) [q.v.], the president of Clark University in Worcester, Massachusetts, met Vivekananda, and later invited both Swamis Saradananda and Abhedananda to lecture to the students. G. S. Hall, one of the outstanding educational and child psychologists in the world, was widely admired for his modern views on pedagogy and school reform. On July 12, 1899, Abhedananda travelled to Clark University to attend a series of thirty lectures at the summer school for teachers. In this way he learned of the most recent findings in child psychology, physiology, mineralogy, anatomy, Western philosophy, anthropology, and biology from top-notch professors in the field. In addition, on the 23rd day of the month Abhedananda addressed the student body at Clark University on the "Philosophy of the Hindus", with Louis N. Wilson (1857-1937) making the introduction. For forty years Wilson managed the library at Clark University, and later came out with a biography of G. S. Hall. One hearer remarked, "I wish our ministers would give such sermons in our churches."[17]

The Twentieth Century

On April 26, 1900, Abhedananda gave a speech before the Liberal Congress of Religions in Boston on "The Religious Ideals of the Hindus". At the afternoon reception in Cambridge, many eminent scholars were present, including Charles William Eliot (1834-1926), the president of Harvard University. He asked Abhedananda many questions about educational conditions in India and the causes of famine.[18] Two years earlier, in March 1896, Eliot might have met Vivekananda when he spoke at Harvard. He owned a copy of Mohini Chatterji's (Chatterjee's) translation of the *Bhagavad Gita*. During his forty-year (1869-1909) administration as president of the school, he aided in transforming Harvard from a small college into a large university known internationally for its academic excellence. Under his leadership Harvard developed an "elective system" to give students a better choice in their selection of classes, emphasized graduate studies by establishing M.A., D.Sc. and Ph.D. degrees, placed emphasis on modern subjects like the natural sciences rather than the classical languages, and significantly raised the entrance requirements. Following Eliot's liberal policy, the Harvard Divinity School switched from a denominational to a non-sectarian institution of higher learning.[19]

At the reception of the Liberal Congress of Religions in Cambridge on April 26, Abhedananda also met Harvard Professors Charles Carroll Everett, the head of the Divinity School, David Lyon, and Sidney Fay, who had heard him lecture at the Cambridge Conferences. David Gordon Lyon (1852-1935), a devout Baptist, was a professor of divinity, and later of Hebrew and Oriental languages at Harvard University (1892-1922). He was the founder and first curator of the Harvard Semitic Museum, which included archeological findings from the Near East. Lyon served as president of the Society of Biblical Literature.[20] Sidney Fay (1876-1967) taught European history at Harvard from 1900 to 1902. He later taught at Dartmouth, Smith College, and again at Harvard, and was elected president of the American Historical Association in 1946. His widely read *Origins of the World War* (1922) attempted to prove that Germany was not the sole cause of the First World War, that each nation involved bore some responsibility for the outbreak of the war.[21]

In a letter, Professor A. V. Williams Jackson invited Abhedananda to represent India and Hinduism, and to give a speech at the Max Müller memorial on November 7, 1900 held at Columbia University. According to the *New York Times* report of the following day:

> President Seth Low presided, and there were between 400 and 500 men and women students and lovers of literature in the hall. In front of Dr. Low, on a desk, were placed copies of the sixty-four different published works of Prof. Müller. President Low said he was very glad Columbia was paying a tribute to a man to whom the world of literature owed so much. Prof. A. V. Williams Jackson of the Chair of Indo-Iranian Languages of Columbia then said that Prof. Müller's contributions to the study of Sanskrit had made him a mentor for all students.... The Swami Abhedananda of India said he was glad of the opportunity to express the gratitude of India and himself for the work of the great man now dead. In his researches into Hindu literature he went further than any of his predecessors. Prof. Nicholas Murray Butler of the Chair of Philosophy in Columbia said Max Müller was equally great as a philosopher and a philologist. In a generation rich in scholars, no one could be called greater than Müller.[22]

Swami Abhedananda also mentions that the Indians would remember Max Müller for his wonderful book on Sri Ramakrishna. Brief addresses were also given by Adolphe Cohn, Richard Gottheil, Thomas Price and Calvin Thomas of Columbia University; Lawrence McLouth and Ernest Sihler of New York University; and Gabriel Engelsman of the College of the City of New York. It is stated in *The Life of Swami Vivekananda* by His Eastern and Western Disciples that all ten of the scholars mentioned here "were in sympathy with the Swami's work, with the Vedanta philosophy, and with Indian culture in general."[23]

Among the participants mentioned above was Nicholas Murray Butler (1862-1947), who later became the longstanding president of Columbia University (1901-45), which, by 1911, was the largest university in the world; and of the Carnegie Endowment for International Peace (1925-45). Serving as an adviser to seven U.S. presidents, in 1931 he shared the Nobel Peace Prize with Jane Addams, a friend of Vivekananda. As an internationalist, he favoured armament limitations, an independent international judiciary formulating the principles of international law, an economic "United States of Europe", and knowledgeable public education concerning peace. A short presidential address given by Butler at Columbia University in 1944 on "Men or Machines?" appeared in the *Prabuddha Bharata* of July 1945.[24] Adolphe Cohn (1851-1930) was a professor and department chairman of Romance languages and literatures at Columbia University.[25] Richard James Horatio Gottheil (1862-1936), a professor of Rabbinical literature and Semitic languages at Columbia University, founded and became the first president of the Federation of American Zionists, president of the Society of Biblical Literature and Exegesis, and of the American Oriental Society.[26] Thomas Randolph Price (1839-1903), a student of Sanskrit and comparative grammar with Franz Bopp and Steinthal in Berlin, Germany, became a professor of English language and literature at Columbia University.[27] Calvin Thomas (1854-1919), who had taught Sanskrit, became a professor of Germanic languages and literatures at Columbia University. In addition, he was the cofounder and president of the Modern Language Association of America.[28] Lawrence McLouth (1863-1927) was a professor of Germanic languages and literatures at New York University,[29] and Ernest Gottlieb Sihler (1853-1942), a professor of Latin and a lecturer in the graduate school at New York University.[30] Gabriel Engelsman (1863-1905), a student of Sanskrit and Jewish philology, taught the Classics at the College of the City of New York.[31]

Swami Abhedananda stayed with Dr. Milburn H. Logan, a great admirer of Swami Vivekananda, in San Francisco during August 1901. The Swami, Logan and Dr. Ross went to hear George Howison (1834-1916) lecture. After the talk, Abhedananda conversed on Vedanta philosophy with the professor, who was very impressed with what he heard. Consequently, according to the *Prabuddha Bharata* of January 1902:

> Unable to resist their urgent solicitations, he was occasionally prevailed upon to give a talk on Vedanta; and at the invitation of Professor Howison, Professor of Philosophy in the University of California [at Berkeley], he [Abhedananda] delivered a lecture before the faculty and students of that institution.

Abhedananda was specially selected to give a one and a half hour talk on the "Vedanta Philosophy", addressing a scholarly group of four-hundred at the Philosophical Union on September 6, 1901. When his presentation came to an end, Professor Howison and the audience warmly congratulated him. After the speaking engagement, the Swami went to Los Angeles for ten days where he stayed in Lincoln Park (South Pasadena) as a guest of the three Mead sisters.[32] George Holmes Howison advocated the philosophy of "personal idealism" dependent on a community of minds in the universe, rather than absolute idealism, as he explains in *The Limits of Evolution and other Essays* (1901), and other philosophical works. Lectures presented every three years or from time to time by well-known thinkers at the Philosophical Union was a unique creation of Howison who served as its chairman. Abhedananda's speech before this group was preceded by that of Josiah Royce who provided the first lecture in 1895, followed three years later by William James' presentation on the "Principles of Pragmatism".[33]

Five months after reviewing Vivekananda's volume *Lectures on Jnana Yoga*, Professor Louis Gray (1875-1955) [q.v.] of Columbia University made an appraisal of Abhedananda's 1902 book *How to Be a Yogi* for the *New York Times* of December 6, 1902. Gray remarked:

> For Christians interested in foreign missions, this book is of moment, as showing the method of reasoning which they must be prepared to meet if they are to influence the educated Hindu. To the Orientalist and the philosopher, also, the book is not without interest. Of the six orthodox systems of Indian philosophy, the most interesting is the Vedanta.... He

> aims, he tells us, to give us a compendious account of yoga, summarizing the four books of his predecessor in this country, the late Swami Vivekananda. Clearly and admirably he performs his task. His introduction discusses the meaning of religion. He presents the same problem which confronted the sages of ancient India ... they meditated in the forests, and gave to mankind the beauty of the Upanishads..... In form the little book is excellent and its English style is good.

Gray's analysis goes into some detail explaining to the reader the Swami's views on the various yogas and Christ as a yogi. Gray might have written the unsigned evaluation of Abhedananda's *Divine Heritage of Man* first printed in 1903, which appeared in the *New York Times* of September 5, 1903. The article acknowledges, "His arguments, like those of his fellow-teachers, are subtle and clever.... his utterances upon Vedantism, like those of his predecessor, Swami Vivekananda, were always interesting."[34]

Hiram Corson (1828-1911) held the position of professor at Girard College, St. John's College, Annapolis, and the professor of English literature at Cornell University in New York State (1870-1903). His numerous literary productions deal with English men of letters like Robert Browning (1812-89) and William Shakespeare (1564-1616). Corson, an intimate friend of Walt Whitman (1819-92), zealously opposed slavery, criticized organized religion, and was an active spiritualist taking part in many séance.[35] He sent an undated very appreciative letter to Abhedananda indicating:

> I have read carefully all of your publications and some of them several times, and I do not remember that I came upon anything which I could not endorse intellectually or spiritually. But your two works, "How to be a Yogi" [1902] and "Divine Heritage of Man" [1903], have a special interest from me. The former being such a comprehensive exposition of the several branches of the science of Yoga. I have recommended it to several friends as the best introduction to the Vedanta philosophy.... The question "Was Christ a Yogi" is most satisfactorily answered in the affirmative in the concluding chapter, which clears up so much in regard to Jesus. It is a conclusion to which Christian "orthodoxy" must finally come, or it will cease to have any true vitality.... This is a golden chapter and worthy of all acceptation, while volume on "Divine Heritage of Man" is, throughout, a golden treasury of religious thought; the chapters on "What is an Incarnation of God" and "Son of God" are doubly refined gold ... The spread of

the Vedanta philosophy will do much to bring about a return to essential Christianity as distinguished from Churchianity. Your lecture on "Why a Hindu accepts Christ and rejects Churchianity", I value very much.[36]

At the annual meeting of the New York Vedanta Society on January 14, 1904, a letter from Professor Corson was read. He desired to become a member of the Society. Corson praised the publications of Vivekananda and Abhedananda as being the best modern works on philosophy and psychology, and made a request that the latter lecture before the faculty and students at Cornell University. Corson first consulted the president of Cornell University Jacob Gould Schurman (1854-1942), who later served as the United States Ambassador to Greece (1912-13), China (1921-25), and Germany (1925-29). He in turn referred the matter to Evander Bradley McGilvary (1864–1953), the professor of ethics at Cornell, who had been a Presbyterian missionary to Thailand for three years but left since he could not accept Biblical inerrancy. McGilvary, who later became the president of the American Philosophical Association in 1912-13, set up the arrangements for his lecture.[37] Abhedananda complied and Hiram Corson introduced him when he gave an address the following month on the 24th at a gathering attended by three-hundred students and professors at Cornell University. The leading journal of Ithaca praised the Swami:

> Those who heard the celebrated Swami Abhedananda lecture at Barnes Hall last evening on "The Vedanta Philosophy and Religion" were deeply impressed by the ability and appearance of the speaker.... The Swami surprised the audience by his marvellous command of English. It was the unanimous testimony of those who heard him that seldom had an American speaker at Cornell displayed such fluency and polish in using his native tongue as did this Hindoo preacher. He described the famous philosophy of the Brahmin cult with rare sympathy and power.[38]

After the lecture, a conference was held at the residence of Professor Corson where Abhedananda was a guest. In turn, Corson lectured as the guest speaker at the Vedanta Society on October 15, 1906, stressing, "The Vedanta idea that the flesh bars in the spirit and prevents its completest manifestation was seen to be a cardinal principle of [Robert] Browning, and again like Vedanta, Browning and [Walt] Whitman both taught that man must not rest in things finite but ever reach onward to things infinite."[39]

In early February 1905, Abhedananda spoke at the Historical Society in the Conservatory Music Hall at the University of Toronto in Canada before a distinguished audience on "The Religion of the Hindus". The listeners included several hundred of Toronto's most prominent citizens, professors and ministers. Three separate newspaper accounts came to the following conclusions:

> The lecturer propounded some deep thoughts which several gentlemen thought to dissipate easily by questions at the close of the lecture, but the Swami had a ready answer for every one of them. His clear voice, clever English and philosophical manner contrasted favourably with the husky indistinct questions of the theorists in this enlightened Canada. His lecture dealt with the theology and religion of the Hindus and dispelled the idea that their religion springs from ignorance. He has a full grasp of the principal religions and presents his ideas with remarkable clearness.
>
> A lecture of remarkable depth and interest was delivered by Swami Abhedananda of India at the Conservatory Music Hall last night. Swami Abhedananda is well known as the foremost exponent of Hindu Philosophy on this continent.
>
> Swami Abhedananda, whose lecture on Friday night filled the Conservatory Music Hall with an audience not to be easily matched for culture and broad thought, met with much attention during his visit of four days in Toronto.... his brilliant mind and ready expression always invested these gatherings of friends with special interest and significance.[40]

In addition, in Toronto Abhedananda met with the chancellor and provost of Trinity College, and the lieutenant governor held a reception for him. Furthermore, his lecture and erudite extemporaneous responses to questions brought a request to open a Vedanta Centre in the city. At Toronto University he met the elderly Goldwin Smith (1823-1910), whose friendship he valued. Goldwin Smith, a former professor of modern history at Oxford University in England, founded and published a periodical titled *Bystander*, where he advocated the freedom of educational institutions from religious restraints and many controversial ideas.[41] Lady Gay, a local columnist, who had heard the Swami lecture in New York, was very much impressed by his winning personality. After he left the city, she wrote, "Swami Abhedananda of India by his lectures has roused the interest of the American people to such an extent that he has become a part and parcel of our religious life." In another report that appeared in the *Brahmavadin*, Lady Gay expressed her gratitude:

> "Our Swami", as a Torontonian called him, has travelled with this brilliant intellect, this calm poise, this just insight and wide wisdom, through many countries, and has gathered with the sympathy which knowledge exacts the essence of their lives and the burden of their conditions. Our Swami is a vegetarian, an abstainer ... the real Swami is a cheerful, sweet-tempered, sympathetic and a profoundly wise man baffling to the people of material instinct ... Swami Abhedananda is a great teacher, and the lessons he teaches are needed to-day as they have never been needed before.

Concerning Abhedananda's preparation during his early monastic years, Lady Gay wrote:

> He knew a joy beyond description while for twelve years he wandered from mountain to plain as the seasons alternate in India, living on one scant meal in twenty-four hours, and walking shoeless and unshielded from the storm or cold some thirty miles a day, sleeping under the trees or in a cave and wakening to a bright joyous consciousness, with never an ache or pain in all that long slice out of a young man's life.[42]

A prominent Toronto citizen wrote this affirmative statement to the Swami, "I have spoken with many but have not heard one discordant note, and I feel that your visit with us is merely a promise of much that is to come."[43]

Swami Abhedananda introduced "My friend, Professor Edward Howard Griggs, in his lecture on the 'Philosophy of Plato' before the Vedanta Society of New York." On March 25, 1905, Griggs mentioned, "Plato's belief in the conquest of the senses as the only means of attaining true knowledge, was preeminently Oriental and non-Greek." Abhedananda added that Plato's metaphor of the man chained in the cave is an allegorical presentation of the Vedantic doctrine of maya. He also told of a Hindu philosopher who came to Athens and held a discussion with Socrates. Twelve of Abhedananda's lectures at the Brooklyn Institute of Arts and Sciences, mentioned in the next paragraph, were presented under the joint auspices of the department of philology and philosophy, and Professor Griggs was probably a supporting factor.[44] Edward Howard Griggs (1868-1951) began as a professor of ethics and education at Stanford University during the 1890s. Next, he resigned to become a popular public lecturer, sometimes offering over four-hundred discourses in a single year. At the Brooklyn Institute of Arts and Sciences, he served as president of the department of philosophy and chairman of the council. The noted humanist scholar wrote books like *The New Humanism* (1900) and the *Philosophy of Plato and its Relation to Modern Life* (1910). On national radio Griggs gave thirty-two broadcasts on the "Lives of Great Men", and thirteen on the "Torch of Progress" during 1938-40.[45]

Because of the success of Abhedananda's lectures in Brooklyn, he received an invitation from Franklin William Hooper (1851-1914), director of the Brooklyn Institute of Arts and Sciences, to give a series of lectures. There he presented six lectures on "India" (November 14-December 19, 1905) under the auspices of the department of political science; six on "Great Religious Teachers" (January 8-February 12, 1907), and six on "Religious Ideals in India" (November 13-December 18, 1907), both under the joint auspices of the departments of philology and philosophy; and six on "The Philosophy and Religion of the Vedas" (November 12-December 17, 1908), under the auspices of the department of philology. At the Institute Abhedananda was one of five members of the committee on Oriental languages and literatures in the department of philology (1906-07).[46] Four of the "Great Religious Teachers" discourses mentioned above became the original edition of *Great Saviours of the World* issued in 1911, and later additional lectures were added to the volume.[47]

A Unitarian and an educator, Franklin William Hooper showed his respect for the Vedanta Society of New York by becoming an honorary member in 1906. He had been a professor of chemistry and geology at Adelphi College in New York City, the director of the Brooklyn Institute of Arts and Sciences (1889-1914), president of the board of Antioch College (1902-06), and an officer on numerous civic and educational organizations. Due primarily to Franklin Hooper's reorganizing and dynamic expansion efforts, by 1903-04 the Brooklyn Institute had eight-thousand members, and he presented six-hundred lectures per year free to its members with a total attendance of half a million people annually.[48]

Abhedananda's six lectures on "India", each given at the Brooklyn Institute before three to four-hundred people during November-December 1905, commanded a considerable amount of attention. The Brooklyn newspapers

(*Eagle*, *Standard Mission*, *New York Times*, *Citizen* and *Daily Standard Union*) printed long excerpts from these lectures and told their readers:

> "unique lecture by a famous Hindoo", "a brilliant exposition of the Indian life and culture, and religion", "In these discourses, he challenged the so-called truthful Christian missionaries and their worthy adherents—the Indian converts, contradicted their scathing and sweeping remarks on the social and religious conditions of the Hindus and silenced the detractors by his clear and forceful replies. The Americans for the first time came to know the real conditions of India from a native of the soil who keenly felt the wrongs and sufferings of his own people and many had to revise their general impression on the subject." "He explained with clearness and intense interest the great and the minute differences of the sects in India." "Everybody present at the meeting appreciated it with thundering claps," and "unique and highly instructive and original."[49]

These six lectures on "India" given by Abhedananda comprise the first six of the seven chapters of his celebrated 1906 volume *India and Her People* (referring to India using the feminine term "Her"). The book was written to remove the many misunderstandings prevailing among foreign nations concerning the people of India. Citing unimpeachable American and Western European authorities, he explains the negative economic, educational, political, and social effects due to successive foreign invasions of India. In verification of his theses, ever since India became an independent country in 1947, the people of the country have been making steady improvements in their economy and educational system. Offering a balanced survey of the conditions, Abhedananda also praises the virtues of British rule, which included the blessings of modern scientific education and technology for the masses, a desire for social reform, lessening the rigidity of caste rules, and an increase in national and patriotic aspirations among the Indian people.[50] In the Introduction to *India and Her People*, Franklin W. Hooper emphasized:

> I am very glad to learn that the course of lectures, recently delivered before the Brooklyn Institute of Arts and Sciences by Swami Abhedananda, is to be published. These lectures constitute an exceedingly valuable description of the social, political, educational, and religious conditions of India. They contain precisely what the American wants to know about

India. Delivered, as they were, by a native of India, they were not coloured by foreign prejudices. I am impressed, by what I heard of the lectures, with the fact that in the hurry and bustle of our Western civilization we have a great deal to learn from the East.[51]

While in London in 1897, Abhedananda met Romesh Chunder Dutt (1848-1909), who presented him with some of the history books he had written, which he read with enthusiastic interest. In *India and Her People*, Abhedananda quotes R. C. Dutt and expresses his indebtedness to him "for numerous valuable facts and statistics collected by him through years of tireless research in England, and embodied in his historical works."[52] Abhedananda also cites the appreciative statements concerning ancient Indian thought made by the Europeans Friedrich Schlegel and Victor Cousin,* and by Edward Washburn Hopkins (1857-1932), professor of Sanskrit and comparative philology at Yale University (1895-1926). An outstanding American Indologist and author of many books on India, Hopkins, who was twice president of the distinguished American Oriental Society (1908-09 and 1922-23), wrote in *Religions of India*:

> Plato is full of Sankhyan thought, worked out by him, but taken from Pythagoras. Before the sixth century B.C. all the religious-philosophical ideas of Pythagoras are current in India. If there were but one or two of these cases, they might be set aside as accidental coincidences, but such coincidences are too numerous to be the result of chance.
>
> Platonism and Christian Gnosticism owe much to India. The Gnostic ideas in regard to a plurality of heavens and spiritual worlds go back directly to Hindu sources. Soul and light are one in the Sankhya system, before they became so in Greece, and when they appear united in Greece it is by means of the thought which is borrowed from India. The famous three qualities of the Sankhya reappear as the Gnostic "three classes".[53]

Additional reviews of *India and Her People* include:

> The Swami possesses the exceptional advantage of being able to look upon his own country almost from the standpoint of an outsider and to

* See Chapter XVIII.

handle his subject free from both foreign and native prejudice (*New York World*, August 4, 1906).

It is a valuable contribution to Western knowledge of India, containing precisely what the American wants to know about that region (*Washington Evening Star*, August 4, 1906).

It is impossible to quarrel with his book. He writes interestingly and he is a man with a mission (*The Sunday Oregonian*, August 26, 1906).

[This book] has more than usual interest as coming from one who knows the Occident and both knows and loves the Orient.... The book is decidedly interesting.... for the student, the book has two admirable qualities: breadth in scope and suggestiveness in material (*Bulletin of the American Geographical Society*, September 1906).

This volume, written in an attractive style and dealing with the life, philosophy and religion of India, should prove a useful addition to the literature of a fascinating and as yet largely unknown subject. It is designed for popular reading, the metaphysical portions being so handled that the reader runs little risk of getting beyond his depth (*Literary Digest*, February 16, 1907).[54]

The views set forth in this work by Swami Abhedananda ... are interesting, as being those of a native of India who has devoted much time and attention to the study of those questions which affect the government and general administration of the country. The author has selected a wide range of subjects for treatment, embracing the social, political, educational, and religious conditions as they now exist, and, speaking generally, has invariably exercised sound tact and judgment in discussing the many different questions embraced under those headings (*Journal of the Royal Colonial Institute*, London, England, April 1907).

John Harvey Girdner (1856-1933), a friend of Abhedananda, addressed the subject of "The Breathing Exercises from a Physicians Standpoint" at the New York Vedanta Society in March 1906. Two months later, he also spoke impromptu at the farewell reception for Abhedananda, before he left for India. The Swami remained in India for a half-year stay, returning to the United States in the month of December. A practicing physician and surgeon, Dr. Girdner taught anatomy at New York University, and surgery at the New York Post-Graduate Medical School and Hospital. Girdner served as one of the attending physicians of U.S. President James Garfield when he was fatally shot in 1881, often came to the White House during Grover

Cleveland's two administrations, and became a close friend of three-time U.S. presidential candidate William Jennings Bryan.[55]

1907 and After

On January 14, 1907, a celebration was held combining the thirteenth anniversary of the New York Vedanta Society with the birthday service for Swami Vivekananda. Stansbury Hagar (b. 1869), the vice-president of the New York Vedanta Society, gave a short speech "on the impression Swami Vivekananda made upon him when for the first time he heard him lecture before the Ethical Society of Brooklyn." Twenty-two years later in 1929, Hagar attended the birth anniversary of Swami Vivekananda along with Walter Goodyear, who also had known Vivekananda. In addition, Hagar gave speeches at the New York Vedanta Society under the leadership of Nikhilananda for the Durga Puja of 1934, and at the Vivekananda birthday celebration of 1935.[56]

Stansbury Hagar, a lawyer and a fellow of the American Association for the Advancement of Science, held the position of president of the Department of Ethnology at the Brooklyn Institute of Arts and Sciences. Bernhard R. Baumgard, an active supporter of Vivekananda in Los Angeles, was also for a time an affiliate of the science department at the Brooklyn Institute. Hagar was adopted by the Hopi Indians of Arizona, and wrote that the division of Cuzco, the Inca capital, into twelve wards corresponded to the houses of the zodiac. In 1917 he put forward a theory that there is a striking similarity between the zodiacs of Peru, the Yucatan, Mexico and certain Pueblo tribes of North America, and that their zodiac is of Asian origin. As late as 1937, he joined the Citizen's Committee supporting future U.S. presidential candidate Thomas Dewey for political office.[57]

On March 10, 1908, the Swami spoke on the "Relation of the Soul to God" at the illustrious King's College at the University of London, England. As an indication of his success as a public speaker, the *London Observer* stressed:

> Since the days of Swami Vivekananda we have not heard such brilliant exposition on such an important subject. The speaker, Swami Abhedananda, who is a brother-disciple of Swami Vivekananda and who is now at present leading the Vedanta movement in both the continents of Europe and America, is no less remarkable in appearance than he is intellectually. His

face is full of gentleness, dignity and repose, and shows his high mental and spiritual development. He has not come to this country as a missionary to win converts to any particular sect, nor does he intend to antagonize Christianity. The aim of his teachings is to help mankind apply the principles, propounded by all the great religious teachers, to its spiritual, intellectual and physical needs. The lecture the Swami delivered recently at King's College before a distinguished gathering impressed everyone. The scene was reminiscent of those days when his predecessor Swami Vivekananda spoke in the same fashion.[58]

In the same vein, another London newspaper concluded:

> The Swami Abhedananda is not only the most learned but the most fascinating Hindoo who ever graced the platforms of London. His magnetic personality and the charm of his manner are recognized by all. As an expounder of Hindoo philosophy to the West, he stands second only to Swami Vivekananda who visited this country about a decade ago.[59]

During the first half of 1909, Abhedananda paid a visit to the house of the famous evolutionist and Theosophist Alfred Russel Wallace (1823-1913) in London. There he saw slate-writings created by deceased people and photographs of departed spirits. The Swami became interested in the scientific study of spiritualism, which he discusses in *Life beyond Death*, where Wallace is quoted. After reading the *Mahabharata*, Wallace considered the Indian epic to be excellent and preferred it to Homer's *Iliad.* The naturalist Alfred Russel Wallace, independent of the renowned Charles Darwin (1809-82), developed a theory of biological evolution. Darwin spoke on Wallace's theory, along with his more detailed conclusions based on twenty years of research, before the Linnaean Society in London in 1858. Independently, both men came up with the ideas of survival of the fittest and natural selection. Earlier, Wallace had made important biological expeditions to the Amazon and Negro Rivers of South America (1848-1852) and to the Malay Archipelago (1854-1862). Wallace was also known for his investigations into spiritualistic phenomena. His scientific writings on the subject testify to his personal experiences of witnessing levitation, telekinesis, and materialization of séance. These studies and experiences helped him to overcome his original materialistic philosophical scepticism about after-life, but reduced his credibility among other scientists who even thought of him as a lunatic.[60]

Abhedananda's lectures at the Brooklyn Institute of Arts and Sciences (1905-08) on India created such a sensation that Italian born Attilio Piccirilli (1866/68-1945) was assigned "the task of creating the four monolithic sculptures representing the civilization of India for the eastern facade of the [Brooklyn] Museum." The subjects of the proposed Indian sculptures were Indian law, philosophy, literature and religion. Working primarily with stone and marble, Piccirilli and his brother Furio created some of the most important monumental sculpture of the time. Piccirilli's Indian Literature and Indian Law Giver facade of the Brooklyn Museum (1909)* is considered to be one of his principle works. During his lifetime he was awarded many contracts for sculpturing monuments and won several medals. The *Bulletin* of the Brooklyn Institute that made mention of the sculptures greatly praised the ancient intellectual culture and civilization of India as "the home of a great branch of the Indo-European stock".[61]

A two-week conference of eminent educators and statesmen from all parts of the world was convened during September of 1909 to celebrate the 20th anniversary celebration of Clark University in Worcester, Massachusetts. Abhedananda now returned to this institution, having spoken there in the past, ten years ago. The college president and noted educational psychologist G. Stanley Hall opened the ceremonies. On the 13th day of the month, Dr. Archibald Coolidge (1866-1928) of the Harvard University history department presided. He is best remembered for his 1908 classic *The United States as a World Power*, which was a prophetic reminder to Americans and foreign nations alike, that the United States no longer followed the policy of aloofness in world affairs. Because of his published work *India and Her People*, Abhedananda was specially selected to deliver the only address on the following subject. His topic was "English Rule in India—as India Sees It". Abhedananda's discourse was followed by an informal discussion on political, social, education and religious conditions in India.[62]

During the late May-June 1911 trial concerning Sara Bull's will, Miss Siri Swanander testified that Arthur W. Dow (1857-1922) of Columbia University attended the lectures of the Ramakrishna-Vedanta Swamis. Dow, who lectured at the Greenacre Conference, taught art at the Pratt Institute in Brooklyn (1895-1904), and then became a professor of fine arts at Columbia University. His most popular work *Composition: A Series of Exercises*

* Inspired by Abhedananda's lectures.

in Art Structure for the Use of Students and Teachers (1913) underwent at least thirteen editions.[63]

Abhedananda met the young Indian professor Benoy Kumar Sarkar (1887-1949) who was visiting America at that time. The professor expressed his appreciation of the Swami with the statement:

> If Vivekananda placed India on the spiritual map of the world, Abhedananda did no less in putting her on the cultural map of the world. It was he who finally established the cultural supremacy of India during his prolonged stay in America and this might very well be regarded as the final upshot of the whole Vedanta movement there. His signal contribution in this regard has never been fully assessed or understood. He was India's first cultural ambassador to America.[64]

Benoy Kumar Sarkar is remembered for his books *The Positive Background of Hindu Sociology* (1914-21) and *Creative India* (1937). In the latter volume he wrote highly of Ramakrishna, Vivekananda, and the social service activities of the Order. Sarkar was a prominent spokesman for Bengali literature, as well as an active internationalist, being a member of German, British, French, Italian, Swiss and American intellectual societies. He emphasized in positive terms:

> As a student of world-culture and the creations of a modern India, it is possible to call the attention of scholars to Vivekananda as one of the "world conquerors" of our times. More than two decades ago (1912-13), even when the Vivekananda movement was in its infancy, the present writer ventured to foresee [and publish in a 1913 article] that the moral and spiritual values in the transcendental experiences of Ramakrishna and the self-control, self-sacrifice and social service personified in the men and institutions of the Ramakrishna-Vivekananda *Gestalt* or socio-cultural complex were destined to constitute the living religion of our country, of our masses and classes, during the present century.... It is indeed possible to talk an entire encyclopedia about Vivekananda's message and activities.[65]

Benoy Sarkar also spoke at the Ramakrishna Centenary Parliament of Religions, which commenced on 1 March 1937 in Calcutta, stating, "The Ramakrishna Mission today is a world force. With its branches and sub-branches this Mission constitutes a new empire of the Indian people."[66]

As a young lady Dorothy Mercer (1901-62) attended Abhedananda's lectures between 1918 and 1920 in San Francisco, California. John Tatlock (1876-1948) was her professor of English literature at the University of California at Berkeley. She was astonished "to find that he had known Abhedananda at Harvard and respected his judgment." Three decades earlier Tatlock was a Ph.D. candidate at Harvard between 1897 and 1903, when he made contact with Abhedananda. Tatlock's Ph.D. dissertation was on Walt Whitman, and at that time Abhedananda wrote to him that Whitman "must have studied the *Bhagavad-Gita*, for in his *Leaves of Grass*, one finds the teachings of Vedanta.... The 'Song of Myself' is but an echo of the sayings of Krishna." Tatlock taught at the University of Michigan, Stanford, Harvard, and at Berkeley during 1929-46. In 1907 he published *The Development and Chronology of Chaucer's Works*, which, after two-thirds of a century, was still regarded as the most authoritative and comprehensive treatment of the Chaucer's chronology.[67]

In 1925, Swami Yogananda (later Paramahansa Yogananda, 1893-1952) made the request that his monastic disciple Swami Dhirananda (1895-1977) move from India to Los Angeles to become his assistant at the Mount Washington Centre. Having a helper provided Yogananda with the opportunity of travelling around the country. Dhirananda had a quarrel with Yogananda in 1929, and then went out on his own, becoming a popular self-supporting independent teacher in Los Angeles. By personal invitation, in 1931 Dhirananda spoke at the Ananda Ashrama of Paramananda during the celebration of the birthday of Vivekananda. The following year Dhirananda left Los Angeles in December, renounced the monastic life and married an American woman.[68]

Reverting to his original name Basu Kumar Bagchi, Dhirananda and his wife were frequent visitors at Mary LePage's (Sister Shivani's) residence at Abhedananda Acres near Los Angeles. Mr. and Mrs. Bagchi set sail for India in 1937, and in Calcutta, at the request of the LePage, they called on Abhedananda several times during the last two years of his life. Bagchi was asked to write the introduction to Shivani's *The Apostle of Monism* (1947).* He became an eminent professor of encephlamology at the Neuropsychiatric Institute of the University of Michigan. Dr. Bagchi performed pioneer research that helped identify cerebral tumors and detect epilepsy. Between

* Renamed *Swami Abhedananda in America*.

1957 and 1969 he travelled to India and did a great deal of pioneer work using medical machines to record the physiological effects of yogic practices.[69]

In the introduction to *Swami Abhedananda in America*, Bagchi discloses:

> Many years ago at a Boston restaurant an elderly gentleman came over and sat at my table and, introducing himself, started to talk. He was the President of the Tuberculosis Association of that section of the country. [He asked] "Did I know Swami Abhedananda? Isn't it sort of unfair that you people send such brilliant men from India compared to the men that we send to your country as missionaries? I used to hear him. He was very convincing." I have heard spontaneous tributes paid to Abhedananda by many I met in New York, Los Angeles, and other places.
>
> I met the Swami for the first time much later in India. He was at the head of the Ramakrishna Vedanta Society in Calcutta. Natural graciousness was his. He was pleased to receive the greetings from some of his disciples in America which I conveyed to him. He impressed me as a dominant personality, a man of great weight and inner strength.... His illness did not seem to burden his spirit down, there was no tone of depression—but spontaneity of reactions to the subjects of his interest. When I saw him later during the advanced stages of his illness, he had the same spontaneity. His disciples told me how the night before his passing he called them in and informed them of the imminence of the event and assigned to them the details of the work. When his body was taken down the streets of Calcutta, thousands of residents joined the procession to pay tribute to his memory.[70]

In 1968 Moni Bagchi (Bagchee) came out with the very readable *Swami Abhedananda: A Spiritual Biography*. The volume has significantly added to our knowledge of the subject, since it incorporated many interesting previously unknown facts drawn from the Swami's *Diary*, along with invaluable newspaper and journal cuttings carefully preserved by Abhedananda himself.

An expert in Sino-Indian cultural interactions, the Chinese professor and director Tan Yun-Shan (1898-83) at Visva-Bharati University wrote of his association with the Swami that began in 1934 at the Ramakrishna Ashrama located at Darjeeling:

> I do not know why at the very first sight of his I began to love and admire him very much. He was so gentle, so kind, so charming and so noble.

> I put quite a number of questions to him. He answered them one by one so adequately and patiently just like a father explains things to his child.... He did enlighten me so much that I can hardly express them in words. Two years have already elapsed since he left the world, yet the impression he gave me is still fresh in my mind. Oh! I am ever grateful to him![71]

The world famous philosopher Sarvepalli Radhakrishnan (1888-1975) wrote, "I met Swami Abhedananda on one or two occasions and have had some correspondence with him. I was deeply impressed by his love for Indian Culture and loyalty to the great ideals of spiritual life. His work in America was quite impressive."[72]

In a posthumous analysis, A. D. Litman (1923-92) [q.v.], a professor from the Soviet Union, made a thorough study of Abhedananda's teachings and in 1971 concluded:

> Trying to represent Vedanta in the most attractive form for modern man, Swami Abhedananda turned to the connection of religion and science, to demonstrate that the Vedanta, far from contradicting science, like other philosophical systems, is on the contrary, organically linked with it....
>
> A dedicated patriot, he devoted himself for many years far from his country to the introduction to the West of the ancient never-fading wisdom of his great people. Therefore, the Indian people pay a tribute of well-deserved respect and affection to their outstanding son on his centenary.[73]

In review, Abhedananda lectured at the Brooklyn Institute of Arts and Sciences and at King's College in London, and at the following North American universities: California at Berkeley, Clark, Columbia, Cornell, Harvard, Toronto in Canada, and at Yale.[74] He also spoke at the Episcopal Theological School in Cambridge, Massachusetts. Charles Higgins of the Brooklyn Ethical Society thought that Swami Vivekananda had lectured at Yale University, which has not been verified. In addition, Vivekananda spoke at Drake University in Des Moines, Iowa, Harvard University, Radcliffe College for women, Smith College for women, University of Chicago Chapel, and at American College for Girls in Turkey. Saradananda spoke at Brown and Clark University, and the State Normal School at Framingham, and Trigunatita at the University of California at Berkeley.[75]

Prominent New York State and Harvard professors who showed an interest in India and who Abhedananda made encouraging contacts with include the following:*

Brooklyn Institute of Arts and Sciences:

Franklin Hooper (Director, 1889-1914); Edward Griggs (Philosophy); Stansbury Hagar (Science).

College of the City of New York:

Gabriel Engelsman (Classic).

Columbia University:

Arthur Dow (Fine Arts); Adolphe Cohn, Richard Gottheil, Louis Gray, A. V. Williams Jackson, Thomas Price, Calvin Thomas (Language/ Literature); Nicholas Butler, James Hyslop (Philosophy); Herschel Parker (Physics); Nicholas Butler (1901-45), Seth Low (President, 1890-1901).

Cornell University:

Hiram Corson (English Literature); Nathaniel Schmidt (Languages and Oriental History).

Harvard University:

David Lyon (Divinity and Hebrew and Oriental Languages); Sidney Fay (History); Nathaniel Shaler (Paleontology and Geology); William James, Josiah Royce (Philosophy); Charles William Eliot (President, 1869-1909); Charles Lanman (Sanskrit).

New York University:

Lawrence McLouth, Ernest Sihler (Languages); Frank Ellinwood (Religion); John Girdner (Science).

Union Theological Seminary:

Charles Hall (President, 1897-1908); Frank Ellinwood (Religion) mentioned in Chapter XVIII.

ENDNOTES

1 Radhakrishnan, p. 51.

2 Bagchi, pp. 273-74; Chetanananda, p. 463; J. C. Bose. Web: www.tuc.nrao.edu/~demerson/bose/emerson_delhi.pdf.

---

* Additional contacts are quite likely.

3 *CWSA*, X, p. 15; *EWB*, XI, pp. 304-05; "Fridtjof Nansen." *Historic World Leaders* (Detroit: Gale Research, 1994) on the Internet through some libraries; Fridtjof Nansen. Web: http://almaz.com/nobel/peace/1922a.htm.

4 *CWSA*, X, pp. 24-25, 71, 88-89; *Brahmavadin* (June 1, 1899), p. 599; Satyananda, p. 86; Swami Abhedananda, *Ideal of Education* (Calcutta: Ramakrishna Vedanta Math, 1984), pp. 40-45.

5 *DAB* (1958), XI, Sup1-2, pp. 338-39; Centenary, I, p. 10; UCLC; Abraham Valentine Williams Jackson. Web: www.vohuman.org/Author/ Jackson,AbrahamVW.htm.

6 *CWSA*, X, pp. 36, 41-44; Satyananda, p. 81.

7 *Brahmavadin* (June 1, 1899), p. 600; (July 15, 1899), pp. 689-90; (Jan. 1900), pp. 165-66; (Aug. 1900), pp. 686-88; *CWSA*, X, p. 96; Shivani, p. 99. Sister Shivani mentions receiving a personal letter from Charles Lanman in the early 1930s. The professor inquired about the whereabouts of that "good man, Swami Abhedananda". (Shivani, pp. 62-63)

8 *CW*, I:357-65.

9 Josiah Royce, *The World and the Individual* (New York: Dover Publications, 1959).

10 *DAB* (1964), IX, pp. 17-19; *ANB* (1999), XIX, pp. 707-08.

11 *CWSA*, X, pp. 46, 58-61, 70-71, 73, 77, 79, 92; Shivani, pp. 106, 123-24, 291, 295; Basu, p. 595; Tathagatananda1, p. 144; *Brahmavadin* (Dec. 1, 1898), pp. 170-71; (Jan. 1903), p. 55. *CWSA*, X, pp. 58-59.

12 *NCAB* (1917), XIV, pp. 260-61; *WWIA* (1930-31), p. 1720; Shivani, pp. 219-20; *Los Angeles Times* (Mar. 30, 1913), p. VI16.

13 *CWSA*, X, pp. 59-61; *NCAB* (1904), XII, pp. 481-82; *WWIA* (1910-11), p. 1414; *Brahmavadin* (July 15, 1899), p. 689.

14 *CWSA*, X, pp. 70-71; *DAB* (1961), VI, pp. 449-50; *EWB* (1998), X, pp. 11-12; Seth Low. Web: http://c250.columbia.edu/ c250_celebrates/remarkable_columbians/seth_low.htm.

15 *CWSA,* X, p. 94; Satyananda, p. 80; *Outlook* (July 2, 1898), pp. 590-91; (July 8, 1899), pp. 583-84; *New York Times* (Nov. 22, 1900), p. 5; (June 1, 1901), p. 4; Janes (1902), pp. 160-63; *DNB* (1958), Sup. II; *WWWA*, I, pp. 1088-89.

16 *Brahmavadin* (Jan. 1900), pp. 165-66; *LBD*, pp. 217-21, 237; *NCAB* (1967), XXVI, pp. 54-55; *DAB* (1961), V, pp. 454-55; *Biographical Dictionary of Parapsychology* (New York: Helix Press, 1964), pp. 150-51.

17 *Brahmavadin* (Jan. 1900), pp. 169-70; Satyananda, p. 82; *WWWA*, I, p. 1363.

18 *Brahmavadin* (Aug. 1900), p. 687; Shivani, pp. 98-99; Satyananda, p. 90.

19 *DAB* (1931), VI, pp. 71-78.

20 *Brahmavadin* (Aug. 1900), p. 687; *DAB* (1944), Sup. 1; Harvard University Archives: Faculty Names. Web: http://hul.harvard.edu/huarc/faculty_names.shtml#L.

21 *Brahmavadin* (Aug. 1900), p. 687; *ANB*, VII, pp. 776-77; *DAB* (1966-70), Sup. VIII. On the flap of the cover of many of Swami Abhedananda's books, it mentions that the Swami "became acquainted with" many prominent people like Professor Fay. It is also likely that he met Charles Ernest Fay (1846-1931), the four-time president of the Appalachian Mountain Club, including the year 1905, and for over forty years the editor of their journal *Appalachia*. Professor Fay, an internationally known mountain climber, received honours from the Canadian government by having one of the peaks in the Canadian Rockies named after him. At Tufts College in Medford, Massachusetts, he held the position of professor of modern languages (1871-1928) and dean of the graduate school. Charles Fay wrote a tribute to his friend Lewis Janes whom he met at the Cambridge Conferences.

22 *New York Times* (Nov. 8, 1900), p. 14; *Epistles*, p. 57.

23 *New York Times* (Nov. 8, 1900), p. 14; *Life*, II, p. 532; Satyananda, p. 92; Columbia University Faculty 1858-1900. Web: beatl.barnard.columbia.edu/stand_columbia/faculty_to_1900.xls. There are a number of errors in the report from the New York Vedanta Society to the *Brahmavadin* (Jan. 1901), pp. 214-15, concerning the spelling of the names, and the university and departmental affiliations of the professors.

24 *DAB* (1974), Sup. IV, pp. 133-38; The Nobel Prize. Web: www.nobel.se/peace/laureates/1931/butler-bio.htm.

25 *WWWA* (1960), I, pp. 239-40; Jewish Encyclopedia. Web: www.jewishencyclopedia.com/view.jsp?artid=636&letter=C.

26 *DAB* (1958), XXII, Sup. II, pp. 251-52; UCLC.

27 *DAB* (1935), XV, pp. 219-20; *NCAB* (1904), XII, p. 248.

28 *DAB* (1964), IX, pp. 422-23; *NCAB* (1941), XXIX, pp. 57-58.

29 *WWWA* (1960), I, p. 820; UCLC.

30 *WWIA* (1960), I, p. 1125.

31 *New Era Illustrated Magazine* (1905) on GBS.

32 Swami Abhedananda, *The Vedanta Philosophy* (Calcutta: Ramakrishna Vedanta Math, 1983), pp. 2-3, 6, 9; Shivani, pp. 112, 297-98; Bagchi, pp. 307-08.

33 Abhedananda (1983), p. 3; *DAB* (1961), V, p. 311; *ANB*, XI, pp. 361-62.

34 *New York Times* (July 12, 1902), p. BR13; (Dec. 6, 1902), p. BR25; (Sept. 5, 1903), p. BR13.

35 *DAB* (1958), II, pp. 453-54.

36 *Epistles*, pp. 61-62.

37 *SACC*, p. 32; Web: en.wikipedia.org/wiki/Jacob_Gould_Schurman; Web: en.wikipedia.org/wiki/Evander_Bradley_McGilvary.

38 *Brahmavadin* (Feb. 1904), pp. 118-19; (April 1904), p. 235; Satyananda, p. 99; Ghosh, p. 26.

39 Tathagatananda1, pp. 169-70; *PB* (Mar. 1904), pp. 53-54; Shivani, pp. 131-32; *VMB* (Nov. 1906), p. 155.

40 *PB* (April 1905), p. 76; *Brahmavadin* (April 1905), pp. 234-36.

41 *AII*, p. 184; *CA*, 1st Revision, XLI-XLIV.

42 *Toronto "Saturday Night"* (Feb. 9, 1905); in *SACC*, pp. 16-18; *Brahmavadin* (Aug. 1905), pp. 460-61.

43 Tathagatananda1, p. 171; Bagchi, p. 312; *VMB* (April 1905), pp. 11-12; *PB* (April 1905), p. 76.

44 *IHP*, pp. 223-24; Shivani, pp. 121-22, 308; Tathagatananda1, pp. 165-66; *VMB* (May 1905), pp. 17, 27-28.

45 *WWIA* (1950-51), p. 1072; *NCAB* (1906), XIII, p. 66; UCLC.

46 Shivani, p. 308; *VMB* (May 1906), p. 31; Tathagatananda1, p. 174; Bagchi, p. 317.

47 *GSW*, p, vii.

48 *NCAB* (1906), XIII, pp. 46-47; *WWNY* (1914), pp. 363-64.

49 Bagchi, pp. 317-22.

50 *IHP*, pp. 3-5, 110, 247-50; Tathagatananda1, p. 173; Shivani, pp. 126, 307-08.

51 *IHP*, p. 7.

52 *IHP*, p. 5; Bagchi, pp. 316-17.

53 *IHP*, pp. 24-25; Londhe #423. Edward Washburn Hopkins; *DAB*, Sup. 1-2.

54 Five of the six evaluations are found in *GSW* (1911), p. 177 on GBS.

55 Shivani, pp. 125, 128; *VBM* (April 1906); *WWWA* (1963), II, p. 211; The Girdner Family. Web: www.tamu.edu/ccbn/dewitt/mckstorygird1.htm.

56 *VMB* (Feb. 1907), p. 223; Tathagatananda1, pp. 163, 200; *PB* (Jan. 1936), p. 52.

57 *WWNY* (1924), p. 552; *WWWA* (1973), V, p. 296; American Anthropologist 1917. Web: www.publicanthropology.org/Archive/Aa1917.htm; Realm of the Golden Wand. Web: www.geocities.com/ elchasqui_2/ZSitchinbook4f3.htm.

58 Bagchi, pp. 353-54.

59 Bagchi, p. 354.

60 Bagchi, p. 357, *EWB* (1998), XVI, pp. 69-70; "Alfred Russel Wallace", *World of Biology* (Detroit: Gale Group, 1999); B. Bissoondoyal, *India in French Literature* (London: Luzac, 1967), p. 63.

61 *VM* (1909), IV, pp. 97-98 on GBS; *WWWA* (1963), II, p. 424; Attilio Piccirilli. Web: http://www.bronze-gallery.com/sculptors/ artist.cfm?sculptorID=96; Web: en.wikipedia.org/wiki/Attilio_Piccirilli.

62 *Christian Science Monitor* (Sept. 3, 1909), p. 6; *DAB* (1928-36) (Coolidge).

63 *WWWA* (1962), I; *Boston Daily Globe* (June 16, 1911), p. 4; *Miami Herald* (Florida) (June 14, 1911), p. 8.

64 Bagchi, pp. 367-68.

65 Benoy Sarkar, *Creative India* (Lahore: Motilal Banarsi Dass, 1937), pp. i, 669.

66 Centenary, I, pp. 77-78.

67 Yale, p. 90; *DAB* (1974), Sup. IV.

68 *MOTE* (Feb. 1931), pp. 63-64 (Oct. 1931), p. 256; *Los Angeles Times* (July 31, 1931), p. A1; The Devotee's Son. Web: www.rickross.com/reference/selfreal/selfreal3.htm.

69 Shivani, pp. vii-viii, 4-7, 220; Web: www.rickross.com/reference/selfreal/selfreal3.htm.

70 Shivani, pp. 6-7.

71 *SACC*, p. 35.

72 *SACC*, p. 37.

73 *The Bases of Indian of Culture* (Calcutta: Ramakrishna Vedanta Math, 1971), p. 698.

74 Abhedananda (1968), p. 184; *The Statesman* (Sept. 11, 1906); in *SACC*, p. 76.

75 "Charles Higgins", *New York Times* (May 31, 1897), p. 4.

CHAPTER XVIII

SWAMI ABHEDANANDA: RELIGIOUS LEADERS

When Abhedananda came to London in 1896, he and Vivekananda dined with Reverend Hugh Reginald Haweis, a leading Anglican clergyman, Samuel Travers Thornton, the first Anglican Bishop of Ballarat in Australia, and some other prominent people of London. Abhedananda met Haweis, a premier supporter of Swamiji, again at the house of Miss Emmeline Souter. The Reverend attended Abhedananda's lectures in London and presented him with a letter of introduction.[1]

After coming to the United States in August 1897, Abhedananda later explained his mode of operation:

> It was necessary for me to become acquainted with the broadminded Ministers of churches, for they had tremendous influence upon the minds of the respectable and educated inhabitants of New York City. Without their help and recognition, my works had no chance to prosper and to make headway. My policy was to march along the line of least resistance and not to antagonize the sectarian leaders of Christian churches who had full control over the minds of the people in all secular and religious matters. If they were not friendly to me and if they advised their parishioners not to attend my classes and public lectures on Vedanta, then I could not get influential people in my audience. Therefore, I had to work hard to arouse the interest of the good people of the city and to persuade them to help me in making the Vedanta Society a powerful religious organization in a Christian country.

At that time there was no permanent house for the Vedanta Society. Abhedananda had to live and hold classes in rented houses and apartments, and deliver lectures in the larger halls in the city.[2]

Swami Abhedananda gave a lengthy interview on the subject "A Hindu View of Christ" that appeared in *New York Sun* newspaper on December 26, 1897. His statements on this subject also were reprinted in *The Literary Digest*, along with an attractive photograph of the Swami. According to one source he also gave this lecture at a Christian church in New York, "attended by a large number of clergymen belonging to all churches. The Swami advanced the theory that Christ was a yogi which surprised the audience."[3]

Abhedananda made contact with a number of eminent preachers who had no personal contact with Vivekananda. In January 1898 he dined with Reverend Richard Heber Newton (1840-1914) [q.v.], the liberal minded Episcopal Minister, and showed him the letter of introduction given to him by Hugh Haweis. Abhedananda informs us:

> Dr. Heber Newton was very kind and cordial to me. He was a great scholar and had a saintly character. He never met Swami Vivekananda, but he was interested in the universal principles of the Vedanta Philosophy. He met Rev. Pratap Chunder Mazumdar, the great leader of the Brahmo Samaj and admired his *Oriental Christ*....
>
> I spent the evening with him talking on various religious subjects, especially on the all-embracing teachings of Bhagavan Sri Ramakrishna. He became deeply impressed by my broad views and universal ideals. From that day he took great interest in my lectures and classes which he used to announce to his audiences after delivering his sermons on Sundays and asked them to attend my lectures, the printed notices of which he used to keep along with his church leaflets.... Mrs. Newton loved me like her own son, and used to come to my lectures. Later on, Dr. Heber Newton became an honorary member of the Vedanta Society of New York after I had it organized. He allowed his name to be printed on the circulars of the Vedanta Society. This removed the prejudices from the minds of the Church-going Christian community and gave a firm footing to my mission.
>
> He introduced me to his friends and other Ministers of other churches and invited me to speak before Religious Conferences of Christian Ministers which he had organized in New York City. In these Conferences I lectured with him many times from the same platform.[4]

Abhedananda met Pratap Mazumdar (1840-1905) [q.v.], the successor of Keshab Chandra Sen (1838–1884) as the leader of the Brahmo Samaj. Mazumdar stayed in America as a guest of Reverend Newton. Abhedananda and Mazumdar spent the night discussing the subject of the spiritual awakening in America. Partly through the influence of Newton, the Vedanta Society received the support of at least five other eminent New York City Episcopalian pastors, two of whom were Bishops from 1887 to 1919: Bishop David Hummel Greer, William Guthrie, David Parker Morgan, Bishop Henry Codman Potter, and William Rainsford. In 1906, the Episcopal Church was basically an upper class religion that represented only 2.7% of the religious population in the United States. In England, Vivekananda had the support of Anglican (Episcopal) Ministers Hugh Haweis, Canon Wilberforce and Samuel Thornton. This is an indication of a significant contact of a Ramakrishna-Vedanta Swamis with mainline Protestant Christianity in the West at that time.[5]

The Swami lived as a guest for a few days in September 1898 at Newton's summer home on Long Island, New York. Books on the *Vedas* and the *Puranas* were part of the Reverend's personal library. About this experience Abhedananda wrote:

> He was extremely sympathetic with the teachings of Vedanta philosophy which I represented. He treated me like a member of his own family while Mrs. Newton was kind and loving to me as she was to her own son. I was delighted to be their guest in their home where they looked after my meals and all my comforts. They wanted to help me in my Vedanta lectures in every possible way because my views were unsectarian and universal in their scope.[6]

According to a June 1, 1899 account given by Sister Nivedita, in a sermon delivered at his Episcopal Church in New York City,

> Dr. Newton said it had been his privilege to know some of the children of the East, and to entertain them in his home, and with deep feeling dwelt upon the visit of Swami Abhedananda in his country home last summer. Of a certain twilight hour during this visit of a week, Dr. Newton said, out of the midst of ordinary conversation, the Swami gently led our thoughts to the great Reality, and each of the little company was imbued with a sense of communion, a serene, ecstatic, sweet and tender converse with the eternal and infinite Presence.[7]

The following year, during April 24-29, at the Liberal Congress of Religions meeting held at the First Unitarian Church in Boston, Reverend

Newton spoke appreciatively of Hindu thinkers and spiritual leaders. After the lecture, Abhedananda told him, "You paid us a great tribute." "You deserve it", was the emphatic reply. On the 26th Abhedananda spoke to 800 listeners, who, after hearing the engrossing lecture, wanted to know more about "The Religious Ideas of the Hindus".[8]

After Lewis Janes passed away in 1902, Newton composed an accolade about him in connection with the work he did at Greenacre. He also wrote a wonderful tribute to Sri Ramakrishna that appears in Chapter III of this book.[9] R. Heber Newton, an advocate of New Thought, and sometime president of the International Metaphysical League, contributed an article to the journal *Mind* of September 1904. In July 1913, the Theosophical Publishing House in Adyar, Madras, reprinted the article in the pamphlet "The Influence of the East on Religion". In his manuscript Newton affirms:

> Those who heard the dark-skinned Hindu Mozoomdar speak and pray in our churches, or who have more lately heard Swami Vivekananda or Swami Abhedananda lecture, must feel, as in no other way they could have felt, that if our Western faith had ought to give them and their countrymen, as we all believe, they have somewhat to give us in return.... The words of Chunder Sen concerning the Hindu gift of Yoga, the faculty of apprehending and communing with the Divine Presence came to my mind; and I perceived how truly there was active in this race a spiritual sense which seems numbed and dormant in our Western peoples. At evening I turned, as he had asked me to do, to the Upanishads, "where," said he, "breathes the early and deep Hindu consciousness of God"—and I knew afresh what a revelation there may be to us, who have so much religion and so little living sense of God. As the Hindu spirit breathes in our spirits, we, too, shall find quickening in us this blessed sense of God. So was I brought to "the gate that looketh toward the East," and I beheld "the glory of the God of Israel coming from the way of the East."[10]

Swami Vivekananda's major religious supporter in England, Hugh Haweis became a friend of Heber Newton in New York City before 1895. Haweis describes Newton's serene nature this way:

> His countenance seems ever radiant with peace and even joyousness. He speaks with flowing ease and grace, is full of anecdote and wit, and a most fascinating companion. A deeper note is frequently struck, and his

spiritual sensibility, as it were, shines through and irradiates the common affairs and occasions of life.

Reverend Richard Heber Newton (1840-1914), a Protestant Episcopal clergyman, became an ordained Priest and the Rector of St. Paul's Church, Philadelphia, head of the All Souls' Church in New York City (1869-1902), and a resident preacher at Stanford University in 1902, where he enjoyed immense popularity. He came out with many books on a number of religious topics. Newton, a leading liberal theologian, might have been the most influential preacher in the Episcopal Church at that time. He took special interest in the modern critical and historical study of the *Bible*. In this area, his best and most popular book sold twenty-five thousand copies in the first year. Two attempts by church leaders, during 1891-92, were not successful in bringing him to trial for heresy. This strengthened the liberal position that there is a place in the Episcopalian Church for such critical views. During 1904-08, Newton became president of the annual International New Thought Conventions. He showed an interest in psychic research and spiritualism, a popular topic among some professors and religious leaders at that time.[11]

Abhedananda mentions in his *Diary*:

> In the evening of March 7th, 1898, I called on Rev. Dr. Rainsford, the noted liberal-minded Minister of the Episcopal denomination, and presented the letter of introduction which Rev. Mr. Haweis gave to me in London. I had a long talk with him on the ideals of the universal religion of Vedanta. He took great interest in my broad views and promised to help me in my mission. Mrs. Rainsford came to my classes several times and introduced me to their church-going Christian friends.

The following year they dined together and the Swami reported, "I had a very pleasant conversation with him and we exchanged our views on religious topics. He became quite interested in the teachings of the Universal Religion of Vedanta."[12]

Like Swamiji's friends Bishop John Keane, Lord Kelvin, Josephine Locke, Charles Higgins, and Sister Nivedita, Reverend William Stephen Rainsford (1850-1933), an Episcopal clergyman, was born in Ireland. After being a Priest in England, he became the assistant Rector at St. James' Cathedral, Toronto, Canada, and eventually the Rector of the St. George's Episcopal Church in New York City during 1883-1906. His personal magnetism and organizing ability brought the support of well-qualified assistants and of a congregation that included many wealthy businessmen like financier and philanthropist J. P. Morgan. St. George's daily services and numerous organizations, with its four-thousand communicants, became the largest and most active parish in the Episcopal Church. An exponent of the "Social Gospel", Rainsford developed the concept of the "institutional church", being both a house of worship and a social centre. His church included organizations for boys, girls and women, a trade school, a cadet battalion, a gymnasium and even a shooting range. Due to poor health, he resigned from the active ministry and left the Church in 1912. He led an expedition to East Africa for the American Museum of Natural History and came out with an autobiography.[13]

On March 21, 1898, Amory Bradford (1846-1911) [q.v.] invited Abhedananda for a private interview. The Swami wrote:

> [I] had a long discussion with him on the subject of original sin of the first man Adam as described in the Genesis of the Old Testament of the Christian Bible. I gave him the Vedantic viewpoint on that subject. The Editor of the "Outlook" was deeply impressed by what I said about the origin of sin.

Abhedananda's article in the March edition of the periodical *Intelligence* on "The Attributes of God, and Man's Relation to them" attempted to prove that the description of the attributes of God are similar for all of the major religions. Soon after the interview, in April the *Outlook*, a popular Protestant journal, came out with a two-page critique of his article. They contended that Vedanta is pantheistic, believing that God is the All, while Christians hold that God is in all and over all. A Vedantist may practise Christian virtues, but his belief system differs from that of a Christian. A year before this in October, Bradford had held an intellectual discussion with Swami Saradananda, whom he described as "reverent searcher for truth, and a good man".* Reverend Bradford no doubt admired and respected the Swamis, but judging from his writings, he supported the missionary efforts and did not care much for the Indian religion.[14]

Amory Howe Bradford, a Minister at a leading Congregational Church in Montclair, New Jersey (1870-1911), became the president of the American

---

* See Chapter XIV.

Institute of Christian Philosophy, an associate editor of the *Outlook* (1892-99), moderator of the National Council, which was the foremost position in the Congregational fellowship, and the president of the American Missionary Association. He came out with numerous books drawn from his sermons and addresses, with some extra material added. By maintaining what was of value in the earlier Christian orthodoxy and restating it in modern terms, he promoted a progressive orthodoxy. In *My Brother* (1910), Bradford took a strong pro-African American position.[15]

Abhedananda visited Washington, D.C. from May 9 to 25, 1898. Described by the *Washington Post* newspaper as "a man of fine personal presence, address, and culture", he lectured as the guest speaker at Dr. Alexander Kent's (1837-1908) [q.v.] non-denominational People's Church. With a large group present on May 15, he spoke on "The Religion of the Hindus" before an appreciative audience. Later at night, Senator William V. Allen of Nebraska addressed the congregation. Vivekananda gave a lecture at the same church in 1894, and Sister Devamata would speak at their new location in 1915 after Dr. Kent's passing. Abhedananda remained in the city for three weeks as a guest of a lawyer.[16] On the last day of May, the Swami made contact with Reverend Van Ness, the pastor of the Unitarian Church of Boston, and commented, "I had a very pleasant interview with him." Thomas Van Ness (1859-1931) became a pastor in Denver, San Francisco, and then at the Second Unitarian Church in Boston during 1893-1928. Besides publishing monographs on religion, he put together two books describing his visit with Leo Tolstoy in Russia.[17]

On June 26, 1898, the Swami conducted the Sunday Service from the pulpit of the Unity Church of Montclair and spoke on "The True Basis of Morality" to the congregation numbering over two-hundred. He states, "The Unitarian Minister of the Church introduced me to the audience." The presiding minister, the liberal-minded Reverend Arthur Hastings Grant, met the Swami again at the end of the year, and Abhedananda attended his New Year's day sermon. Concerning the talk, a letter to the friends of Abhedananda in Montclair, New Jersey, read in part:

> As trustee of Unity Church and as a private individual, I wish to express to Swami Abhedananda our sincere appreciation of his kindness in speaking to us, and the entire acceptability of what he said. A review of western thought by an eastern mind is interesting and stimulating; but of still deeper significance was the fact that he stood in our pulpit, read our

> Emerson and Theodore Parker, followed our hymns with appreciative eyes, and dismissed us with beautiful words of spiritual meaning from his own sacred books.
>
> All fitted together harmoniously with the underlying thought of his sermon, as though there was no East and West, only one human cry, one human aspiration. As he read with us, responsively, of the blessedness of the service of Love, time, race, customs and all differences seemed to fade away, and for a brief space, at least, we lived in the realization of the time, when all men shall be as brethren. We cannot fully express to the Swami our deep sense of our debt to him for his helpful words, and even more, for his unspoken message from our far-off Aryan brothers. To feel that our faces are turned the same way, toward the same goal, is enough.[18]

Friends of Swami Abhedananda included at least ten Unitarian Pastors: Robert Collyer, George Cutter, Austin Garver, Arthur Grant, W. F. Greenman, Minot Savage, Thomas Slicer, Jabez Sunderland, Thomas Van Ness, as well as Dr. Wright. Of the 34.2 million people in the United States professing a religion in 1906, only about one in five-hundred (0.2%) were Unitarians.[19]

Ralph Waldo Trine (1866-1958) [q.v.], the most popular writer of New Thought literature in America and author of *In Tune with the Infinite*, attended Abhedananda's lectures and classes at the Greenacre School for the Comparative Study of Religion. The Swami went with a party of friends on an excursion to Mt. Agamanticas on August 27, 1898, and Trine "spent the whole day talking on the sublime ideals of Vedanta and enjoyed the beautiful scenery of the mountains and surrounding country." On another occasion, at Greenacre, Abhedananda gave Trine a copy of his recently published book *Reincarnation* (1899). They are pictured together at Greenacre in a photo preserved by the Maine Historical Society. Abhedananda spoke on "Universality of Vedanta" from October 23-26, 1900 at the Second Annual Convention of the International Metaphysical League held at Madison Square Garden in New York City. Other friends of Vedanta who appeared on the programme were Trine, Sarah Farmer, Lewis Janes, Annie Rix Militz, and R. Heber Newton.[20]

In September, through R. Heber Newton's influence, Abhedananda made the acquaintance of Reverend Dr. Greer. The Swami stated, "He was very pleased to hear my interpretation of the Divine Incarnation of Jesus the Christ." Three years earlier, Greer sat at the President's Table along with Vivekananda and other dignitaries at the annual banquet of the Sorosis Woman's Club in New York City. David Hummel Greer (1844-1919), the Rector of the Grace Church in Providence, Rhode Island, and of the St. Bartholomew Church in New York City (1888-1904), became Bishop Coadjutor of the diocese, and the Episcopal Bishop of the diocese of New York (1908-19). He succeeded Bishop Potter (1887-1908), who was also favourable to the Vedantic Movement. Bishop Greer was friendly to all sects, sensitive to the needs of the poor, an eloquent extemporaneous preacher, and an able administrator.[21]

On October 23, 1898, Abhedananda attended a sermon given by Reverend Minot Savage. On another occasion, the Swami heard Pratap Mazumdar speak on "The Oriental Christ" in Savage's church. The poem "Where is God?" by Savage appeared in the December 1909 edition of the *Prabuddha Bharata*. Minot Judson Savage (1841-1918), originally a Congregational Minister, became a Unitarian clergyman and author, and an early member of the American Society for Psychical Research. Between 1896 and 1906, he served as the pastor of the Third Unitarian Church of Chicago, the Church of the Unity in Boston, and the Church of the Messiah (now the Community Church) in New York City.[22]

In 1898, Dutch born Cornelius J. Heijblom (the future Swami Atulananda, 1870-1966) [q.v.] heard Abhedananda present a lecture in Mott Memorial Hall in New York City. Concerning the presentation, he later wrote:

> The discourse was lucid, convincing, and impressive. There was not much flourish, nor much eloquence, and hardly any gesticulation. It was a straightforward, well-reasoned-out exposition of the Vedanta philosophy, delivered in a calm, dignified manner. He had his subject well in hand. And his voice was clear and sonorous. Young, tall, straight, good-looking, the swami had his appearance in his favour.... The swami answered all questions without the least hesitation. Then he came down from the platform and was immediately surrounded by a number of people anxious to meet him personally and to exchange a few words with him.[23]

Hearing the teachings of Abhedananda, Heijblom became attracted to the Vedanta philosophy. He later remarked, "It was as though a sudden revelation had opened up. I knew all at once that this was Truth." Under Abhedananda's instructions, he commenced with regular religious practices, and devoted his spare time to helping out at the New York Vedanta Centre. On Easter Sunday April 2, 1899, he and five other students received brahmacharya from Abhedananda. He acquired the name Gurudasa, which means "servant of the guru". He met Vivekananda briefly in 1899 and 1900 and, during that same year, travelled to California to live in the ashrama of Turiyananda. In 1923 at Belur Math, Gurudasa Maharaj was given his final vows of sannyasa, receiving the name Swami Atulananda. Though Shivananda was then the president of the Order, he stepped aside requesting Abhedananda to initiate Gurudasa into sannyasa. Atulananda remained in India the remainder of his long life, attaining the status of sainthood.[24] He describes Abhedananda this way:

> He gave himself heart and soul to his work, and he needed hours of solitude to prosecute his studies and to prepare his carefully thought-out lectures, free from outside disturbances. But one could always be assured of his ready assistance, his sympathy, and encouragement when one made it a point to approach him.... Swami Abhedananda, always strong and positive, followed his own counsel. He wanted to spread Vedanta, so he had to follow his own plan. And he flourished: he became a very fine speaker, enriched the Vedanta literature with a goodly number of his productions, was invited to other cities to lecture, and was loved, admired, and applauded wherever he went.[25]

On February 25, 1899 Abhedananda records, "I went to Bartlelts Second Hand Book Store where I met Rev. Dr. Slicer, a Unitarian Minister, with whom I had a nice talk on Vedanta." At the end of the following year, at a meeting of the New York Council of Jewish Women, Abhedananda and Slicer were co-speakers at Temple Israel along with Richard Gottheil of Columbia University. Thomas Roberts Slicer (1847-1916), originally a Methodist Minister, converted to the Unitarian faith serving in Providence, Rhode Island, Buffalo, New York, and at the All Souls Church in New York City (1897-1916). Besides authoring a number of texts on religion, Slicer acted as the chairman of the Council of the National Conference of Unitarian Churches, and the National Commission on Prison Labour, and a member of other civic reform organizations.[26]

Reverend A. Garver, a local Unitarian Minister, introduced the Swami who spoke on the "Religious Ideas of the Hindus in India" at the Day Building, Room 19 in Worcester, Massachusetts, on April 14, 1899. The lecture given before over one-hundred people "was highly appreciated". Austin Samuel Garver (1847-1918) began his career as a Congregational Minister and then converted to the Unitarian faith as a pastor in Hopedale, and of the Second Parish Church in Worcester, Massachusetts (1885-1910). He was a trustee of Clark University and wrote works on Edward Everett Hale and other subjects. On April 27, Abhedananda lectured to the students at the Episcopal Theological School in Cambridge before students who were preparing to become Ministers in churches. One student exclaimed, "We want some more missionaries like you." On May 22, W. F. Greenman, "a broad and liberal Unitarian" Minister from Fitchburg, Massachusetts,* invited the Swami to attend a meeting of Ministers in the area. While staying with Dr. Kate Stanton in Newport, Rhode Island, on June 20th Abhedananda gave an address on the "Religious Ideas of the Hindus". He was introduced by Reverend George W. Cutter of the Channing Memorial (Unitarian) Church. At the close of the talk, a Congregational Minister told him, "I do not know whether I have made you a better Hindu, but surely you have made me a better Christian."[27]

The Twentieth Century

Swami Abhedananda came out with an article in *The Arena* of February 1900, with the title "The Vedanta Philosophy II. The Correct Interpretation: A Reply". He wrote it in response to "An Interpretation of the Vedanta" by Horatio Dresser (1866-1954) [q.v.], an expert on New Thought, which appeared in *The Arena* of October 1899. Dresser was originally a supporter of the Ramakrishna-Vedanta Swamis, but later got the idea that the followers of New Thought were giving too much credit to the teachings from India. Dresser's critical manuscript was replete with misinterpretations and errors concerning the Vedanta philosophy, which Abhedananda wished to correct "for the benefit of the many American students of this philosophy". For example, when Dresser writes, for a Vedantist "there is no permanent value in finite experience", Abhedananda replies:

> On the contrary, the Vedanta teaches that every experience has a permanent value. Every stage of evolution is necessary for the progress of the individual soul. At every step of our finite experience, we are learning

* Later in Milwaukee, Wisconsin, 1907-19.

something and helping ourselves in unfolding the higher powers latent within us.

While Dresser defines maya as "illusion", Abhedananda explains:

> This term never means "illusion", in a sense that the word is ordinarily used, but means conditional, relative, or phenomenal existence. The world, according to Vedanta, is not unreal, but conditional in its existence—the name and form of the world being a constantly changeable phase of Reality.

Abhedananda then quotes Shankara's definition of maya. To support his overall position, the Swami uses excerpts from western authorities like Max Müller (1823-1900), and cites tributes concerning the quality of Indian philosophy written by the German Friedrich Schlegel (1772-1829) and the French philosophy professor at the Sorbonne and statesman Victor Cousin (1792-1867),[28] who wrote:

> When we read with attention the poetical and philosophical monuments of the East—above all, those of India, which are beginning to spread in Europe—we discover there many a truth, and truths so profound, and which make such a contrast with the meanness of the results at which European genius has sometimes stopped, that we are constrained to bend the knee before the philosophy of the East, and to see in this cradle of the human race the native land of the highest philosophy.[29]

Friedrich von Schlegel, one of the chief founders of the German Romantic Movement, who is best remembered for his writings in literary theory and cultural history, declared:

> The divine origin of man, as taught by Vedanta, is continually inculcated, to stimulate his efforts to return, to animate him in the struggle, and incite him to consider a reunion and reincorporation with Divinity as the one primary object of every action and reaction. Even the loftiest philosophy of the Europeans, the idealism of reason as it is set forth by the Greek philosophers, appears in comparison with the abundant light and vigour of Oriental idealism like a feeble Promethean spark in the full flood

of heavenly glory of the noonday sun, faltering and feeble and ever ready to be extinguished.[30]

In his two-volume *The African Abroad* (1913, p. 405), William Henry Ferris (1874-41) emphasized, "I have seen Swami Abhedananda, Mazumdar and Bepin (Bipin) Chandra Pal, the distinguished Hindoo philosophers, lecture." Abhedananda met Mazumdar and Pal in the year 1900 when they spoke in the United States. *The African Abroad* is presently a valuable component of the African American Studies programme. Ferris earned MA degrees at Yale and at Harvard and took courses in the Divinity School (1897-1900). He accepted the pastorate of a Congregational church in Wilmington, North Carolina, and the African Methodist Episcopal Zion Church in Lowell and Salem, Massachusetts. Later he became the literary editor of Marcus Garvey's Back-to-Africa *Negro World*, which had a circulation of two-hundred thousand.[31]

Abhedananda, Bipin Pal, Lewis Janes, Heber Newton, Professor Edward Cummings of Harvard University and others spoke at the Liberal Congress of Religion held at the First Unitarian Church. William Ferris might have heard their lectures at that time when he was a student at Harvard. Bepin Pal recorded in his *Memoirs*:

> The subject matter of his lecture was "The Religious Conception of the Hindus". The vast audience present gave a tremendous ovation to Swami Abhedananda as he rose to speak. A good orator, he was no doubt with a command on English. I was very much impressed in the way he presented his thesis which showed that he was an erudite scholar.[32]

Bepin Chandra Pal (1858-1932) was a prominent Indian political leader. In the Indian National Congress, he advocated extremist measures like "boycotting British manufactured goods, burning Western clothes made in the mills of Manchester and strikes and lock outs of British owned businesses and industrial concerns".[33] After visiting England, Pal, on February 15, 1898, wrote to the *Indian Mirror*:

> On coming here I see that he has exerted a marked influence everywhere. In many parts of England I have met with men who deeply regard and venerate Vivekananda.... I must say that Vivekananda has opened the eyes of a great many here and broadened their hearts. Owing to his teach-

ings, most people here now believe firmly that wonderful spiritual truths lie hidden in the ancient Hindu scriptures. Not only has he brought about this feeling, but he succeeded in establishing a golden relation between England and India.[34]

On the ship from England to the United States, Pal received a present of fruits from a fellow passenger. He stated, "She sent me her gift with a friendly greeting to a countryman of Swami Vivekananda from an American, who owed her spiritual illumination to him. This was the first direct evidence I had of Vivekananda's influence in America." At a lecture given by Professor Charles Lanman of Harvard in New York City, Pal also met another woman keenly interested in Indian studies who had attended Vivekananda's Vedanta classes. Pal astutely added:

> His wonderful success as a powerful orator and defender of the religion of his people had immediately a remarkable repercussion in India, lending new force and inspiration to the infant national consciousness among us.... [His lectures] took his American audiences by surprise. It offered a stupendous shock to their old conviction and prejudice. There was no hesitancy, no suspicion of apology, no attempt to explain away, not the least trace of any inferiority complex in this bold challenge to civilized conceit in Vivekananda's message of Hinduism, to the crowded galleries of the Parliament of Religions. Vivekananda did not assign any reason, did not argue his position, but delivered his message with soul-compelling directness and simplicity, like the ancient seers and sages of our own country or the prophets of the Old Testament as truths that could not possibly be contested or controverted.[35]

Concerning his meeting with Abhedananda in January 1900, Bepin Pal later recalled:

> I came to New York to meet personally Swami Abhedananda and to gather from him some information regarding his activities in America. I met him at the Headquarters of the New York Vedanta Society. I was cordially received by him and we talked for an hour or so. It seemed to me that the gospel of Vedanta would never have travelled outside India without the efforts of the two great Hindu preachers—Vivekananda and Abhedananda. I was also taken by surprise at the interest evinced by Abhedananda regard-

ing the political situation in India at that time. I had a long discussion with him about the future political changes in India.[36]

Shortly before his passing away in February 1932, Bipin Pal mentioned the following about Sri Ramakrishna on the occasion of Vivekananda's birthday anniversary held at Albert Hall in Calcutta:

> The Master was a great spiritual force. He was therefore inevitably a mystery to a generation possessed by the un-understood slogans of what is called rationalism, which really means lack of that imagination which is the soul of all spiritual life.... It was given to Vivekananda to interpret and present the soul of Paramahamsa Ramakrishna and the message of his life to this generation in such terms as would be comprehended by them...
>
> Ramakrishna Paramahamsa's God was not the God of logic or philosophy, but the God of direct, personal, inner experience. Ramakrishna believed in his God not on the authority of ancient scriptures or traditions, nor on the authority of any Guru, but on the testimony of his direct, personal experiences.... He was not a philosopher; he was not a Pandit, whether modern or ancient, he was not a logician; he was a simple seer. He believed in what he saw.
>
> Paramahamsa Ramakrishna saw into the innermost composition of Vivekananda's nature and spirit and recognized in him a fit instrument for delivering the message of his own life.[37]

From the 5th to 9th of August 1900, Abhedananda offered three lectures before audiences numbering 7,000 or more at the Indiana Association of Spiritualists in Chesterfield. The *Anderson Daily Bulletin* reported, "It was a record breaker—the biggest day ever known in Camp Chesterfield." His speech was hailed as "an able and scholarly presentation of the religion of the Orient". In a letter dated 14 August 1900, Turiyananda wrote to Alice Hansbrough, asking her, "Do you know anything about Swami Abhedananda? He is now in Anderson, Indiana. I have received a letter from him. He is very willing to come to California even for a short visit."[38]

An honorary member of the New York Vedanta Society, Reverend Newell Dwight Hillis (1858-1929) was the pastor of the Presbyterian Church of Peoria and then Evanston, Illinois. In 1899 he succeeded Lyman Abbott, being called to the prestigious Plymouth Congregational Church in Brooklyn. Hillis favoured America's early involvement in the First World War and helped to raise one-hundred million dollars for the Liberty Loan programme. As a highly influential liberal Protestant Minister and an eloquent speaker, he wrote more than twenty-five widely read books.[39]

According to Abhedananda's biographer Sister Shivani, Reverend Robert Collyer (1823-1912) showed interest in the Vedantic ideas. He came to the United States from England in his twenties after having only two years of formal education. This self-made man became the Unitarian pastor of the Unity Church in Chicago (1859-79) and the Church of the Messiah in New York City (1879-1903). Several of his sermons were put into book form.[40]

On December 13, 1900, Abhedananda was invited to speak before the Council of Jewish Women at Temple Israel in New York City. He pointed out the similarity between the festivals of the ancient Jews and those of the ancient Hindus, and between the laws of Moses and those of the Indian Manu. His remarks were highly appreciated by an attentive audience.[41]

Frank Field Ellinwood (1826-1908) put out a report on "Vedantism in America" for the magazine *Current Literature* in 1901. He mentioned:

> Three Hindus with a good knowledge of English have won some reputation among non-Christian Americans as lecturers on Hindu philosophy. The first to appear among us was Swami Vivekananda, who took part in the Chicago Parliament of Religions, and who, by the boldness of his attacks on Christianity and Christian missions in the winter following, attracted considerable attention.... he was succeeded in this country by Saradananda, a veritable Brahman.... The present stated lecturer before the Vedanta society is Abhedananda, a young Hindu of considerable ability.... These men claim to belong to an ancient order of monks known as Sannyasin, and to have been pupils of Ramakrishna, whom the late Professor Max Müller regarded as "a man of rare spiritual power".... and seem highly popular with their followers.[42]

Reverend Ellinwood, a Presbyterian clergyman in Rochester, New York, became a corresponding secretary for the Board of Foreign Missions, and professor of comparative religion at New York University (1887-1908). A pioneering study of comparative religion, Ellinwood's volume *Oriental Religions and Christianity* (1892) was composed of a series of lectures he presented at the Union Theological Seminary in New York. In the book coming from a decidedly pro-Christian standpoint, he discusses ancient Hinduism and compares the *Bhagavad Gita* with the New Testament, and Buddhism with Christianity.[43]

According to the *Prabuddha Bharata* of January 1902:

> Clergymen of such authority and prominence as Bishop Potter are not only recognizing its [the Vedanta Society of New York's] existence, but are citing long passages from its publications—such as the Swami Abhedananda's lecture on "Woman's Place in Hindu Religion"—in order to correct the false impressions which Christian Missionaries have circulated concerning India and its religious beliefs.[44]

In the Episcopal periodical *The Churchman* of November 9, 1901, Bishop Henry Codman Potter (1835-1908) quoted at length from Abhedananda's lecture on "Woman's Place in Hindu Religion", referring to the Swami as "the accomplished gentleman and a scholar". He openly condemned the false impressions that Christian missionaries were circulating concerning India. In 1902 he came out with the book *The East of To-day and To-morrow*. Two of his six chapters are devoted to "Impressions of India" and "India: Its People and its Religion". It includes two long quotations from Abhedananda's lecture on "Woman's Place in Hindu Religion". Mrs. Christina G. Kelley, the wife of the vice-president of the Union Trust Company, conducted "The Students' Meeting" at the New York Vedanta Society. She also served as the Secretary of the New York Centre. Concerning her booklet *For the Union of all who Love, in the Service of all who Suffer*, the *Vedanta Magazine* of January-February 1909 (p. 106) mentions, "Bishop Potter, who was so keenly interested in all things pertaining to India, inspired the author through his lectures along these lines. The late Bishop himself distributed many of the booklets among his fellow clergymen and friends."[45]

Bishop Potter served as the Rector of Grace Church in New York, as assistant Bishop, and as the Episcopal Bishop of the diocese of New York (1887-1908). Under his leadership, Grace Church became an "institutional church", with workingmen's clubs, day nurseries, kindergartens, etc. As the Episcopal Bishop, in two different years he did not allow presentments against R. Heber Newton for trial for heresy for having questioned the authority of the *Bible*. He worked as a leader in the moral reform movement and an arbitrator in labour disputes that brought about the election of Seth Low as the mayor of New York City in 1901.[46]

Thomas Edison

Elmer Gates

President William McKinley

William Jennings Bryan

Luther Burbank

James Creelman

Edwin Markham

Lauriston Ward

Nicholas Murray Butler

Charles William Eliot

John Harvey Girdner

George Howison

James Hervey Hyslop

Seth Low

David Gordon Lyon

Fridtjof Nansen

Nathaniel Shaler

Goldwin Smith

Alfred Russel Wallace

Robert Collyer

Bishop Henry Codman Potter

William S. Rainsford

D. T. Suzuki

Pir Hazrat Inayat Khan

Edith Allan (Viraja Devi), Bertha Petersen (Dhirananda) and Clara Pettee (Durga Devi)

Alfred Kroeber

J. Robert Oppenheimer

Swami Prabhavananda

Mayor James Rolph

Benjamin Ide Wheeler

Paul Brunton

Albert Einstein

Lady (Countess) Minto

Paramahansa Yogananda

Earlier, David Parker Morgan (1843-1915) served as an Anglican Minister in England, and as the metropolitan secretary of the British and Foreign Bible Society in London. He became the assistant Rector and Rector during 1887-1907 at the Episcopalian Church of the Heavenly Rest in New York City, after which, due to ill health, he resigned, and until his death was a Minister in Sharon, Connecticut. He held the position of president of the prominent New York Churchman's Association, and at one time Abhedananda was its guest of honour. On March 6, 1905, Reverend Morgan introduced the Swami's speech, after which Abhedananda received an invitation to give a talk at the Hotel Vendome before forty or so prominent clergymen in New York City. There Abhedananda was able to correct some of the misconceptions that the clergy held concerning the Indian religion. After the address on "The Relation of the Soul to God",

> one clergyman rose and said: "We have heard a profound exposition of the highest form of natural religion, but our religion of course is supernatural or revealed religion." To which the Swami [Abhedananda] replied in substance: "India is the home of all revealed religions. The idea of revelation came from there. As to the distinction between natural and supernatural religion, that is purely arbitrary, depending entirely upon one's conception of nature. If that conception be narrow, then everything beyond the limit of that circle is accounted supernatural."[47]

1906 and After

Rabbi Rudolph Grossman of the Rodolph Sholom Temple in New York City at Lexington Avenue and Sixty-third Street invited Abhedananda to speak on "Buddha and Buddhism". On January 15, 1906 he presented the address before the Young Men's and Women's Culture Society. The Rabbi concurred with the Swami that after an extensive study he found "no instance recorded of the persecution of the Jews by the people of India".[48]

On Sunday evening April 8, 1906, Abhedananda offered the Vedanta Society House to the Buddhist Association of America. Over two-hundred people were present for the event celebrating the birth of Buddha. Throughout the country the story appeared in many newspapers. A sermon was delivered on "The Essence of Mahayana Buddhism" by Soyen Shaku (1859-1919), the leader of the Zen Buddhists in Japan and the Buddhist representative to the 1893 Parliament of Religions in Chicago. Soyen Shaku had just had a private interview with president of the United States Theodore Roosevelt in Washington, D.C. Zen believes that enlightenment is attained through meditation, in contrast to other Japanese groups that believe that only repeating the name of Buddha is necessary. The famous Zen philosopher D. T. Suzuki (1870-1966) served as Soyen Shaku's translator during his 1905-06 journey to the West, and might have been present for the celebration. Suzuki once wrote, "The study of Japanese thought is the study of Indian thought."[49] He was an editor and writer for the Open Court Publishing Company, working with its owner Paul Carus during 1897-1909. When Suzuki came to the West during the 1950s and lectured at Columbia University, he created a great deal of interest in Zen Buddhism among front-ranking thinkers like Erich Fromm, Karen Horney, Harold Kelman, Thomas Merton, Paul Tillich, Alan Watts and others, some of whom travelled to Japan to get a better grasp of the religion.

In the two-volume United States Bureau of the Census, *Religious Bodies: 1906*, Vedanta membership drawn from returns of the individual church organizations was reported to be 200 in New York (half being male), 50 in Pittsburgh, 50 in San Francisco, and 40 in Los Angeles, totalling 340 members in four cities. The Vedanta Society section of nearly a full page written by Reverend Edwin Munsell Bliss (1848-1919) mentions that two of the church edifices have a seating capacity of six-hundred, and that the New York Vedanta Centre gives "lessons and instructions by correspondence" for people residing outside of the city. In the *Vedanta Monthly Bulletin* of 1908, there is mention of Vedanta groups (which they call centres) in Washington, D.C., St. Louis, Denver and Canada, largely due to Abhedananda's activities. In fact the Swami paid a visit and lectured to the students in Denver in the fall of 1908. The next Religious Census report that came out ten years later in 1916 indicated that about sixty percent of the Vedanta Society members in the United States are females.[50]

As an indication of the growing respectability that the movement had attained within the Christian community, concise biographies, with separate headings of Vivekananda and Abhedananda along with a listing of their books, and a report on the Vedanta Society, appeared in the Protestant based *The New Schaff-Herzog Encyclopaedia of Religious Knowledge* of 1908-12. Edwin Bliss edited the piece on the Vedanta Society. Formerly a missionary in Turkey, editor of *Encyclopaedia of Missions*, and lecturer on foreign missions in the Yale Divinity School, he became an expert on religious bodies in the United States working for the National Bureau of Census (1907-19). Bliss describes the Vedanta Society as:

> An organization which is the outcome of a series of lectures on Vedanta philosophy in New York in 1894 by Swami Vivekananda. It was first organized in 1898, and gradually became strong enough to have centres in other cities, Pittsburgh, San Francisco, and Los Angeles, besides various retreats. Without attempting to form a new sect or creed, the society aims to set forth the end of wisdom, how it is attained, and give to religion a scientific and philosophical basis. It publishes works on religious philosophy and furnishes lectures by various Vedantists.[51]

The thirteen-volume *The New Schaff-Herzog Encyclopaedia of Religious Knowledge* recognized Vedanta Society as a legitimate and respectable religion in American society. This highly prestigious encyclopaedia was prepared by more than six-hundred religious scholars and specialists under the supervision of Samuel Macauley Jackson (1851-1912), the Editor-in-Chief. He was a Presbyterian clergyman who served as professor of church history from 1895 up until his death in New York University.[52]

The official *Yearbook of American Churches* (1918), put out by the Federal Council of the Churches of Christ in America, included a report on the Vedanta Society centred in New York City, stating as their objective, "To explain through logic and reason the spiritual laws by which we are governed and to establish the universal religion which underlies all religions." Centres are listed as being in New York, Boston, Pittsburgh, San Francisco, Los Angeles, Washington, D.C., and a Peace Retreat in California. Their 1923 edition featured an expanded account of over 350 words on the Vedanta Society in its section on "Directory of Religious Bodies", taken verbatim from the Bureau of the Census, *Religious Bodies: 1916*.[53]

In January 1908 Reverend Charles Cuthbert Hall (1852-1908) met Abhedananda at a meeting concerning the welfare of India held at the New York Bar Association clubrooms. After returning from his second tour of India, Hall critically spoke before the Bar Association about the British rule in India.[54] G. B. Smith of the University of the Chicago Divinity School mentioned:

> Dr. Cuthbert Hall, who was at one time the Barrows lecturer to India, was a man himself of conservative theology, a very profoundly religious man,

> but with the spirit of a Modernist. When he came back from his lectures in India, he was constantly telling the people in the West that when you went to India you found people who made religion their first business. He was greatly impressed with the large place which religious experience had in the life of the devoted Indian people, and he said that the Christianity of the future is going to be enriched and enlarged from what we may learn from the Orient.[55]

The *Brahmavadin* praised both of Dr. Hall's series of lectures in India. In 1903 the journal stated that Cuthbert Hall

> has done the utmost that the accomplished eloquence of an orator, the finished excellencies of modern literary scholarship, and the almost convincing nature of recent scientific and philosophical methods can do, to present the religion of Christ in its most acceptable form to a learned Hindu audience.

Four years later the *Brahmavadin* added, "We appreciate, are glad and are grateful for the sympathetic attitude of the lecturer towards the eastern peoples and their religion." Charles Cuthbert Hall, the pastorate of the First Presbyterian Church of Brooklyn (1877-97), became the president of the faculty at the highly respected Union Theological Seminary in New York City (1897-1908). There he worked as a professor of pastoral theology and of homiletics. Through his personal charm and his gift for making friends, he exerted a positive influence on many people. As the Barrows Lecturer to India and Japan (1902-03), he summarized his experience in *Christian Belief Interpreted by Christian Experience* (1905). Against the advice of his friends, he made a second trip to India. There he contracted an illness from which he never recovered. Hall's 1906 Barrows Lecturer speeches are found in *Christ and the Eastern Soul* (1909).[56]

In his biography of Abhedananda, Moni Bagchi mentions a Dr. Wright, a Unitarian clergyman who was present, along with Cuthbert Hall and Jabez Sunderland, at the New York Bar Association meeting dealing with the welfare of India. They were very much impressed with the personality of Abhedananda. Possibly Bagchi is referring to James Edward Wright (1839-1914), the pastor of the Unitarian Church of the Messiah in Montpelier, Vermont (1869-1909).[57]

Abhedananda, in his book *India and Her People*, provides a long quotation from a speech by Reverend Jabez Sunderland (1842-1936) [q.v]. In 1908 Sunderland became intimately acquainted with Abhedananda, and he also met with Sister Nivedita in 1911 during her visit to the United States. Sunderland acknowledged that Abhedananda's statements on India inspired him to write his outstanding book of 1928, entitled, *India in Bondage, Her Right to Freedom and a Place among Nations*.[58]

Sister Avabamia (or Avavamia, May Elizabeth Stevenson) [q.v.], who provided a wonderful tribute to Vivekananda,* claimed to have given lectures on over three-thousand occasions, before gatherings in Europe, Canada and the United States.[59] She was a graduate of the Royal College of Sweden and lived in Seattle, Washington, in 1907. A nice picture of her can be found in the *Vedanta Monthly Bulletin*, which is on the Internet.[60] After making contact with Abhedananda and receiving instructions from him, in 1908 the elderly Sister Avabamia travelled to Sydney, Australia, and for six months conducted classes on meditation and breathing. Earlier, back in 1897, Swami Shivananda had sent a woman named Mrs. Elsie Picket (Haripriya) to Australia and New Zealand to teach Vedanta.† Avabamia then proceeded to New Zealand establishing Vedanta Centres and Reading Clubs in Auckland (President Mr. Povey, Secretary Mrs. I. Borrison), Christchurch (President Mr. F. Holmes, Secretary Mrs. W. Hyman), Dunedin, and Wellington (Secretary M. L. Fordham). After eleven months of travel, she returned to Sydney (President Mr. W. Millar, Secretary Mrs. Millar), and then, in 1910, to Melbourne and Adelaide, forming Vedanta Centres. While in Australia and New Zealand, she delivered over twelve-hundred addresses and attracted quite a bit of attention. In her organization, prizes were "given to the best speaker, most energetic worker, and the [Vedanta] society which recruited the largest membership."[61]

The Evening Star of Dunedin in New Zealand on March 20, 1909 published a letter from Mr. J. S. Warner. Among other things, the long letter states:

> In regards to the Vedanta movement, I enclose a general outline of Vedanta as expressed by Swami Abhedananda, the present head of the Vedanta movement in the Western world, successor to the late Swami

* See Chapter VI.

† See Chapter XXI for more details.

> Vivekananda ... We owe to the Swami a deep debt of gratitude for the light and wisdom he has brought to us and which he has bestowed on us unreservedly by his tireless preaching. When all is said and done, the fact yet remains that the influence of Vedanta on the West as a whole is tremendous and the movement that has made it possible is the crowning success of a religious teacher who has been working in this country for the last twelve years. The spiritual awakening that we notice today in the West is all due to the Vedanta movement which is spreading day by day and which is also attracting more and more adherents. This should be regarded as an eventful development of the western civilization.
>
> To spend a few hours at the Vedanta headquarters of New York or elsewhere is just to feel the warmth of the universal doctrines of Vedanta which alone can lead us to light and immortality.[62]

At that time, Mr. Warner, the manager of Avabamia's journal, *The Star of the East*, situated in Sydney, also published a three-page letter in the *Brahmavadin* of June 1909 explaining Abhedananda's conception of "What is Vedanta?".

The Fitzroy City Press of Melbourne on September 23, 1910 described Avabamia this way:

> The gifted lecturer delivered two lectures every Sunday in the Masonic Hall, and during the week held two meetings. Her work carried conviction of its absolute truthfulness, and her words of wisdom must have been the result of laborious thought. Though a student for 25 years, Sister Avabamia, with her native modesty, says, her knowledge is only "like a spoonful of water to the ocean". She has a fine personality; robed in her renunciation dress, she shows a force of character and a brilliant ability to combat the problems of life. She is sympathetic with the Hospital Retreat, Hardwar, India, and has been asked by the manager to get some assistance here.[63]

The *Daily Herald* of October 14, 1910 in Adelaide depicted Sister Avabamia as, "A lady of advanced years, and at the same time with a youthful face alight with enthusiasm, she was at once convincing as to her earnestness, and with a charm of manner that won the sympathy of her hearers, she placed before them her views upon philosophy and religion, which she held should be happily combined."[64]

The *Adelaide Advertiser* of November 26, 1910 stated, "Sister Avabamia, representative of Vedanta, delivered one of the most interesting lectures ... upon concentration of mind. The sister, who is a highly intellectual lady and possesses great gifts of expression was listened to by an appreciative audience."

During her farewell visit to New Zealand in 1911, *The Evening Star* of Dunedin commented:

> The fact that there were fully 250 persons at a reception and conversazione tendered by Sister Avabamia in the Victoria Hall last night proves that the local centre is not founded on sand.... A short, interesting address was also given by Sister Avabamia, who is a fascinating speaker, with a quaintness apart. She is very vivacious, yet earnest, and holds the attention of her hearers all the time.[65]

In the fall of 1911, Sister Avabamia went to Ceylon and India and established some new Vedanta Centres, which the Swamis at Belur Math did not recognize. Inspired by Vivekananda's educational ideas, she established two schools in Ceylon, which were eventually taken over by the Ramakrishna Mission. In 1912 she left India and broke away from the Ramakrishna Order. News of her activities for the years 1905-12 appear in the monthly journal she initiated, *The Star of the East*, later named the *Vedanta Universal Messenger*, published first in Sydney and then in Melbourne, Australia.[66]

The original edition of Abhedananda's ecumenical book *Great Saviours of the World* (1911) was derived from four discourses presented in January-February 1907 at the Brooklyn Institute. A revised 1957 edition added on a series of talks on "The Great Saviours of the World", each given before an audience of about five-hundred people in the fall of 1905 at the New York Vedanta Society. The book discusses Krishna, Zoroaster, Lao-Tzu, Buddha, Christ, Mohammed, and Ramakrishna, accompanied by the famous painting by Frank Dvorak.[67] The earlier edition received the following review in the *Indianapolis Star* newspaper:

> Students of comparative religion and persons only casually interested in the subject will find a great deal of information agreeably presented in "Great Saviours of the World" by Swami Abhedananda, an East-Indian philosopher and writer who has been doing much to popularize Oriental mysticism in America.... the work will be found to be interesting in that

> it sets forth in picturesque language the principal events in the lives of his heroes and gives a good and concise idea of their teachings.[68]

Swami Abhedananda met Orison Swett Marden (1850-1924), the president of the "League for the Larger Life", a New Thought organization in New York City. Walter Goodyear, the former treasurer of the Vedanta Society of New York, was one of its officers. Being the founder of the modern success movement in America, Orison Marden inspired many people with his philosophy of cheerful optimism and self-confidence. *Success Magazine*, of which he was the founder and editor, during its peak, sold nearly half a million copies per issue. Marden wrote about sixty-five motivational books and some of them became best sellers. Translations of his books appear in twenty-five languages, with overall sales of over three million. As an indication of his worldwide popularity, four of his volumes, viz. *The Conquest of Worry*, *Cheerfulness as a Life Power*, *Every Man a King*, and *The Miracle of Right Thought* were translated into the Hindi Language in 1983-84.[69] Frederico Climent Terrer in Barcelona, Spain, translated twenty-seven New Thought volumes of Orison Swett Marden during 1913-24. He also translated nine of Vivekananda's works into the Spanish language.* [70]

During March 1913, Abhedananda spoke at many locations in Atlanta, Georgia.† There he met Dr. Ellenwood, a Universalist, and Rabbi Mark. He spent some time with Mrs. Rose M. Ashby, the president of the Atlanta Psychological Society. Around 1932, she came to India visiting Kamarpukar, the land of the "Man-God", and Abhedananda at Darjeeling. Writing in *The New Thought News* of March 25, 1913, Rose Ashby [q.v.] indicated:

> At the Unitarian Church the Swami gave a course of eight lessons on "Spiritual Unfoldment". These class lectures were largely attended by interested and sincere seekers after spiritual truth. He emphasized so vividly the importance of controlling and subjugating the lower nature by the awakening and conscious activity of the Higher.... The two final lectures of this course on God-Consciousness were gems of Spiritual worth, and the Divine afflatus felt by all will always linger.
>
> The Unitarian and Universalist ministers invited the Swami to fill their pulpits, and a sermon given by the Swami on Sunday morning, March the

* See Appendix VII.

† See Chapter XVI.

> 9th, in the Unitarian Church on account of the Spiritual power behind it and the veritable Power of the Presence, will go down in the lives of those who heard it as an hour of inspiration and uplift....
>
> The Unity Club of the city, composed of the ministers of all churches, gave the Swami a reception in the parlours of the Piedmont Hotel, thus extending brotherly love and kindness and exemplifying the principle of Unity.
>
> In all the Swami's sojourn with us he was never iconoclastic. Never tearing down or taking away, but giving a wider and more accurate perspective of all we had, he was truly eclectic, giving not only the best in Hindu philosophy, but the best in all philosophies.
>
> While he is from the heart of the Orient and his messages distinctly Oriental in its pristine purity, yet his only propaganda is the propaganda of Truth, and he teaches that no people, place or thing have a monopoly in Truth, but all have Truth in the degree that we live the life and unfold the Spirit from within, and that the only freedom we have is in Spirit, and that Spirit leads us into all Truth....
>
> His coming and going has left a spirit of love, harmony and a greater feeling of Unity and Peace.[71]

Concerning one of his addresses, the *New Thought Journal* reported:

> The lecture of the day was on the relation of soul to God. He discussed so ably the relation of science to religion that the head and heart of all present were really at peace. It proved that all science can lead to God. God at hand and not God far off ... Swamiji's peculiarity is that he does not go against the belief of any man. He makes our dear beliefs more dear and more ingrained by a *broader explanation of them.*[72]

The *Atlanta Constitution* added, "The Swami is a teacher and lecturer of international reputation. He is an eminent scholar and philosopher and his lectures at the Unitarian church have charmed and delighted many."[73]

In July 1913, Abhedananda attended the two-day convention of the Connecticut State Spiritualist Association held at Unity Hall in Hartford. The audience filled every seat and sat on the gallery stairs. He was billed as "a teacher and lecturer of fame in the circles of New Thought". Abhedananda said things like, God's "mind is the cosmic mind, and ours are little parts of the cosmic mind".[74] In another newspaper report, it mentions that

Abhedananda delivered two lectures as the keynote speaker at the Annual Convention of the Connecticut State Spiritualist Association in Hartford on May 4, 1918. He told his audience that immediately after death the body is one-half to three-quarters of an ounce lighter, which represents the weight of the soul. This important finding indicates that the subtle body (and subtle matter) has gross physical characteristics such as weight. In a separate speech on "Spiritual Needs of Today", Abhedananda urged his hearers to buy Liberty Bonds for the war effort to the limit of their capacity without thought of the morrow.[75]

ENDNOTES

1 Burke, IV, pp. 386-87, 400; Tathagatananda1, p. 141.

2 *CWSA*, X, p. 27; Gambhirananda, p. 176.

3 Bagchi, pp. 285-87. The date he provides of Dec. 27, 1897 for the lecture is not supported by Abhedananda's *Diary* (*CWSA*, X, p. 18). This statement did not appear in *The Literary Digest* (Jan. 15, 1898), pp. 80-81.

4 *CWSA*, X, pp. 20-21.

5 Bagchi, p. 304; *Schaff*, XII, p. 90.

6 *CWSA*, X, pp. 56-57.

7 Basu, p. 539 (599); *Brahmavadin* (June 1, 1899), pp. 575-76.

8 *Brahmavadin* (Aug. 1899), p. 687.

9 *PB* (June 1906), pp. 115-17; *Lewis G. Janes: Philosopher, Patriot, Lover of Man* (Boston: James H. West, 1902), pp. 35-41.

10 The Influence of the East on Religion by R. Heber Newton. Web: www.theosophical.ca/InfluenceEast.htm.

11 *DAB* (1962), VII, pp. 474-75; *NCAB* (1967), III, p. 304; Hugh Haweis, *Travel and Talk* (New York: Dodd, Mead, 1896), I, p. 75.

12 *CWSA*, X, pp. 27, 84.

13 *DAB* (1958), XI, pp. 618-19; *ANB* (1999), XVIII, pp. 83-84.

14 *CWSA*, X, p. 29; *Outlook* (April 30, 1898), pp. 1059-60; (Dec. 15, 1898), pp. 1757-58; *The Independent* (Dec. 15, 1898), p. 1757.

15 *DAB* (1929), II, p. 552; *ANB* (1999), III, p. 352; UCLC.

16 *CWSA*, X, p. 38; *Washington Post* (May 14, 1898), p. 10; *The Message of the East* (1915), pp. 115-16; *Brahmavadin* (Aug. 1, 1898), p. 889.

17 *CWSA*, X, p. 45; *WWWA* (1962), I, p. 1271.

18 *Brahmavadin* (Aug. 15, 1898), pp. 923-24; *CWSA*, X, pp. 46, 74-75.

19 *Schaff*, XII, p. 90.

20 *CWSA*, X, pp. 51, 54; Tathagatananda1, pp. 151-52; Horatio Dresser, *A History of the New Thought Movement* (New York: Thomas Y. Crowell, 1919), pp. 196-98; Web: http://horatiodresser.wwwhubs.com/ahotntm9.htm.

21 *CWSA*, X, p. 57; *DAB* (1960), IV, pp. 593-94; *New York Times* (Jan. 25, 1895), p. 8.

22 *CWSA*, X, p. 64; *EOP*, II, p. 1455.

23 Atulananda, pp. 24-25.

24 Vidyatmananda12; *CWSA*, X, p. 91; Atulananda, pp. 339, 341.

25 Atulananda, pp. 28, 37.

26 *CWSA*, X, p. 84; *DAB* (1964), IX, p. 200; *NCAB* (1910), Sup. I, pp. 126-27.

27 *CWSA*, X, p. 93; *Brahmavadin* (June 1, 1899), p. 600; (July 15, 1899), p. 690; (Jan. 1900), pp. 168-69; *WWIA* (1962), I, p. 442; UCLC.

28 *The Arena* (Feb. 1900), pp. 218-24; Shivani, pp. 282-89.

29 *IHP*, pp. 11-12; Shivani, p. 289.

30 *IHP*, pp. 33-34; Shivani, pp. 288-89; *EWB*.

31 Frank Mather, ed., *Who's Who of the Colored Race* (Detroit: Gale Research Co., 1976), I, pp. 221-22; *Who's Who in Colored America* (Brooklyn: Thomas Yenser, 1940), p. 182; William Henry Ferris: The African Abroad. Web: www.cwo.com/~lucumi/ferris.html; Bagchi, pp. 303-04.

32 Bagchi, pp. 303-04.

33 Wikipedia Free Encyclopedia. Web: http://en.wikipedia.org/wiki/Bipin_Chandra_Pal.

34 Basu, pp. 255-56; Lokeswarananda, p. 42.

35 Bipin Pal, *Memories of My Life and Times* (Calcutta: Bipinchandra Pal Institute, 1973), pp. 584-86, 597-98.

36 Bagchi, p. 303.

37 Bepin Pal, "Ramakrishna and Vivekananda", *PB* (July 1932), pp. 323-25; Lokeswarananda, p. 42.

38 Bagchi, pp. 296-97; Gargi, "Early Days at Shanti Ashrama", *PB* (Oct. 1977), pp. 421-22.

39 Shivani, p. 100; *DAB* (1961), V, pp. 56-57; *RLOA*, pp. 204-05.

40 Shivani, p. 100; *DAB* (1958), II, pp. 310-11.

41 *Brahmavadin* (April 1901), p. 394.

42 *Current Literature* 31 (July-Dec. 1901), p. 102.

43 *WWIA* (1908-09), p. 573.

44 Shivani, p. 111.

45 *Brahmavadin* (Dec. 1901), p. 114; Tathagatananda1, pp. 278-79; *VMB* (April 1908), p. 6; *VM* (1909), IV, p. 106 on GBS.

46 *DAB* (1935), XV, pp. 127-29; *Encyclopedia Britannica* 1911. Web: http://1.1911 encyclopedia.org/P/PO/POTTER_HENRY_CODMAN.htm.

47 Shivani, pp. 118-19; Bagchi, p. 325; *VMB* (April 1905), pp. 7-8; *WWNY* (1909), p. 949; *NCAB* (1921), II, p. 503.

48 Shivani, p. 125.

49 *VMB* (May 1906), pp. 31-33; *New York Times* (Apr. 10, 1906), p. 15; *Atlanta Constitution* (April 10, 1906), p. 1; Londhe, #187. D. T. Suzuki.

50 Bureau of the Census, *Religious Bodies: 1906* (Washington: Government Printing Office, 1910), I, p. 405; II, pp. 7, 658-59; (1916), II, pp. 713-14; *VMB* (1908), IV, p. 82 on GBS; *VM* (1909), IV, pp. 118-19 on GBS.

51 *Schaff*, I, pp. 11-12; VII, p. 394; XII, pp. 90, 219-20; *DAB* (1964), I, p. 371; UCLC.

52 *DAB* (1928-36).

53 GBS.

54 Sunderland, pp. 47-48; Bagchi, p. 350.

55 J. V. Nash, "The Message and Influence of Vivekananda", *Open Court* 39 (1925), pp. 740-41.

56 *Brahmavadin* (Feb. 1903), pp. 84-89; (Feb. 1907), pp. 101-09; *DAB* (1960), IV, pp. 119-20; *ANB* (1999), IX, p. 851.

57 Bagchi, p. 350; Vermont Historical Society Library. Web: www.vermonthistory.org/arccat/findaid/unitaria.htm.

58 *IHP*, pp. 210-11; Bagchi, pp. 350-51; Tathagatananda1, p. 180.

59 Jackson, pp. 93-94.

60 *VMB* (1908), IV, p. 110.

61 *Brahmavadin* (Dec. 1910), p. 531; *Adelaide Advertiser* (Oct. 14, 1910), p. 6; Tathagatananda1, p. 177; *VM* (July-Aug. 1909), pp. 157-59; Satyananda, p. 116; *PB* (July 1909), pp. 135-36; *Voice of Freedom* (Oct. 1910), p. 155; UCLC.

62 Bagchi, pp. 357-59.

63 *PB* (Dec. 1910), p. 238.

64 *PB* (Dec. 1910), p. 238.

65 *Brahmavadin* (June 1911), pp. 291-92; (July 1911), p. 350.

66 Jackson (1994), p. 94; *PB* (Aug. 1911), p. 159; Mission, p. 475.

67 *GSW* (1957), pp. vii, ix-xii, opposite p. 307.

68 (May 26, 1912), p. 18.

69 *AII*, p. 10; Dresser (1919), pp. 243-44; *DAB* (1961), VI, pp. 278-79; Orison Swett Marden. Web: http://website.lineone.net/~cornerstone/marden.htm; UCLC.

70 Library of Congress. Type in "Climent Terrer"; or Web: www.loc.gov/cgi-bin/zgate?ACTION=INIT&FORM_HOST_PORT=/prod/www/data/z3950/locils2.html,z3950.loc.gov, 7090&CI=002820.

71 *PB* (June 1913), pp. 117-18; Satyananda, p. 133; Shivani, pp. 235-36, 239.

72 Satyananda, p. 111.

73 *Atlanta Constitution* (Mar. 9, 1913), p. 46; (Mar. 10, 1913), p. 8.

74 *Hartford Courant* (May 5, 1913), p. 12.

75 *Hartford Courant* (May 4, 1918), p. 15; (May 5, 1918), p. 21; (May 6, 1918), p. 16.

CHAPTER XIX

SWAMI TURIYANANDA

When Swami Vivekananda decided to come to the West for the second time, he asked Turiyananda to accompany him on his journey. Swami Turiyananda (1863-1922) was very reluctant to accept Vivekananda's invitation to go with him to America. He was a man of meditation and not of public speaking:

> When all arguments failed, Swami Vivekananda put his arms around his neck, and actually wept like a child as he uttered the words: "Dear Haribhai, can't you see I have been laying down my life, inch by inch, in fulfilling this mission of the Master, till I am on the verge of death! Can you merely be looking on and not come to my help by relieving me of part of my great burden?"

Swami Turiyananda gave in to his beloved Naren and accompanied him and his Irish disciple Sister Nivedita, arriving in England on July 31, 1899. After a sixteen-day sojourn in London and Wimbledon, Vivekananda and Turiyananda, along with Sister Christine and Mrs. Mary Funke, went to Glasgow, Scotland, and then embarked for America.[1]

Mary Funke [q.v.] describes their wonderful Atlantic Ocean voyage this way:

> These were ten never-to-be-forgotten days spent on the ocean. Reading and exposition of the *Gita* occupied every morning, also reciting and translating poems and stories from Sanskrit and chanting Vedic hymns. The sea was smooth and at night the moonlight was entrancing. Those were wonderful evenings; the Master paced up and down on the deck, a majestic figure in the moonlight, stopping now and then to speak to us of the beauties of Nature.... We reached New York all too soon, feeling that

we never could be grateful enough for those blessed, intimate ten days with the guru.

They landed in New York City on August 28 and quickly proceeded by train to Ridgely Manor, the charming estate of Francis Leggett near Stone Ridge, New York. In the course of their conversations, Turiyananda explained to Vivekananda that platform work did not fit his temperament. In response, Swamiji inspired him by saying, "Well, then don't trouble yourself about lecturing. You just live the life. Be an example to them. Let them see how men of renunciation live." At Ridgely, when asked why his mattress was on the floor, Turiyananda replied, "But, you see, I cannot bring myself to sleep on the same level with Swamiji—so I have put the mattress on the floor."[2]

"An American Brahmacharini" from New York City wrote to the *Brahmavadin* dated September 15, 1899:

> Swami Turiyananda is beloved by all who meet him and is heartily welcomed as a needed teacher. Happy and blest are we by their presence, and their more active work later on is sure to bring knowledge and enlightenment to many who are now longing and searching for understanding and wisdom. Swami Vivekananda is resting quietly in the home of loving friends, where Swami Turiyananda also is, together with Swami Abhedananda. Swami Turiyananda has endeared himself to all who have met him, and his work is opening out to him in hearty welcome from students of Vedanta eager for his teaching.

The Brahmacharini added four months later, "Swami Turiyananda is beloved and revered by all who meet him and his very silence and quiet presence is making loving friends and students for him wherever he becomes known."[3]

After two months at Ridgely Manor, on October 27 Turiyananda moved to the residence of Mr. and Mrs. Wheeler in Montclair, New Jersey, about twenty miles west of New York City. Saradananda began giving classes at the Wheeler residence in 1897, and Abhedananda later carried on the tradition. There the Swami got a closer view of American family life. He had a high regard for Mrs. Wheeler's spirituality and concluded, "She is so sattvic, firm, quiet; she always does the right thing at the right time without the least fuss." Her husband, a Christian Scientist, was sympathetic toward Vedanta.

Turiyananda gave classes in Montclair and conducted services for children on the weekends at the New York Vedanta Centre. He told the youngsters a number of stories from the epics of India and from the *Hitopadesha*, a collection of ethical tales and fables compiled in the 12th century A.D. by Narayana, based in part on the larger and older work called *Panchatantra*.[4]

When Swamiji went to California, he had to cancel his engagement at the Cambridge Conferences conducted by Lewis Janes. They chose Turiyananda to be his replacement and, on December 10, he read a paper on "Shankaracharya".* Some professors from Harvard and other scholarly men attending the conference praised his lecture. He then spent some time with a wealthy woman in Boston who gave support to his work there. An admirer of the Swami wrote to the *Brahmavadin*, "Whoever became acquainted with Swami Turiyananda was immediately made to respect him. Wherever the Swami went, he created a band of loving devotees and students by his serene nature and controlled speech." At one time Gurudasa asked him, "Swami, how is it possible always to speak of holy subjects? Don't you ever get exhausted?" His reply was:

> You see, I have lived this life from my youth; it has become part and parcel of me. And Mother keeps the supply filled up. Her store can never be exhausted. Whatever goes out, she at once fills up again.

From April to June 1900 Abhedananda was away on a lecture tour. As his replacement at the Vedanta Society of New York, Turiyananda gave lectures and held a series of classes on the *Bhagavad Gita* and other scriptures, translating and explaining the text. He preferred to speak before small groups rather than large audiences. Turiyananda told his followers, "Lectures are to reach the public, but the real work can be done only through close personal contact. Both are necessary."[5]

Brahmachari Gurudasa, who later became Swami Atulananda (1870-1966) [q.v.], witnessed these events and observed:

> "Fresh from India" was a fit term for Swami Turiyananda. The Indian atmosphere still seemed to hover about him, as he was far from being Americanized. He represented India as the old students pictured her—the land of simplicity, meditation, and spirituality. Gentle, cheerful, meditative, little

* Published in the *Vedanta Kesari*, 1993, pp. 169-74.

Swami Turiyananda

concerned about the things of the world, Swami Turiyananda made a deep impression on the minds of those who took Vedanta most seriously—not merely as a philosophy to satisfy the intellect alone, but also as a practical guidance in their spiritual life.... Swami Turiyananda's face was like that of a happy, intelligent, thoughtful youth—at times very much so. In fact, as later I observed, his expression of face was subject to moods, more markedly than I have ever noticed in any human face. Sometimes his face indicated tremendous strength and indomitable will power, and at other times remoteness, as if his mind were withdrawn from the external world. Sometimes he looked the picture of humility, and again his face would be like that of a child—innocence and purity written in every line.... he would suddenly begin to discuss a subject which was troubling and weighing on the mind of someone present. There was nothing to lead up to the subject, and the person in question would be surprised how the Swami happened to solve his doubt and difficulty without asking.... when the Swami and I went out for long walks together, he would do almost all the talking. And I was so happy just to listen to him. I would feel so inspired! He talked with fire and enthusiasm, and he would lose himself entirely in his subject, forgetting everything else for the time being. Swami Turiyananda impressed everyone who heard him, and all classes of people felt attracted towards him.[6]

Atulananda also offered these insights:

The Swami's religion was not Sunday or special-day religion. He was what he taught. His talks came in torrents, ever-new flows, fresh currents from an inexhaustible spring. There was no set time; we never knew when a new supply would be released. We therefore wanted to be with him at all times, that we might not miss a single outpour from that hidden source deep down in his own heart. For in him dwelled the Divine Mother, using his lips to teach, to call Her children.... To live with the Swami was a constant joy and inspiration, and an education too, for one was learning all the time. And we felt that spiritual help came through him.[7]

Swami Turiyananda would often chant in a very low voice, "Om, Om, Om, Hari Om", or "Hari Om, Tat Sat", even in a crowded streetcar, pronouncing the "m" sound till it gradually died away.

[This] was an outstanding feature with the Swami. Everyone remarked about it and seemed impressed by it. It was new to us. This chant was peculiar with Swami Turiyananda. He would keep it up for hours at a time. When he was talking, he would chant in between. After asking a question, he would chant while listening to the reply. Walking, sitting, talking, in public or alone—always that soft, melodious chant went on.... Sometimes the chant would come loud and strong. Again it would be deep like a strong vibration, and would rise and end in a soft high note—very sweet. The tune also varied. This chant was with the swami as long as he was in America.

At Frank Rhodehamel's residence he would chant in a deep rich voice in Sanskrit chapter after chapter of the *Gita*.[8]

When Swami Vivekananda left San Francisco for Chicago and New York, Atulananda wrote that he told the devotees:

> I have lectured to you on Vedanta, in Swami Turiyananda you will see Vedanta personified. He lives it every moment of his life. He is the ideal Hindu-monk, and he will help you all to live a pure and holy life.[9]

Frank Rhodehamel added that Swamiji informed the Northern California devotees, "I will send you another, greater than I, one who lives what I talk about. I will send you Swami Turiyananda."[10]

Miss Minnie C. Boock attended the lectures of Abhedananda in New York City. She met Vivekananda after he left Northern California, and between June 7 and July 25, 1900, temporarily moved into the Vedanta Society of New York located at 102 East 58th Street. Vivekananda and Minnie Boock understood that the Vedanta movement should have an Ashrama (retreat) for devotees, who temporarily or permanently wished to live an intense spiritual life. In response she offered the Swami her California homestead, which had been government land issued to her by United States President Benjamin Harrison (1833-1901) in 1892. Though the property was remote, being fifty miles from the nearest railway station and market, it met the need of an Ashrama. Swamiji then asked Turiyananda to establish an Ashrama in Northern California, and told him:[11]

> "It is the will of the Mother that you should take charge of the work there." Turiyananda responded, "Rather say it is your will. Certainly you have not heard the Mother communicate Her will to you in that way.

How can we hear the words of the Mother?" Swamiji answered with great emotion, "Yes, brother, the words of the Mother can be heard as clearly as we hear one another. It only requires a fine nerve to hear the words of the Mother."[12]

On July 3rd Vivekananda, along with Turiyananda and Minnie Boock, left for Detroit, Michigan.[13] Just before they parted company in Detroit, Turiyananda asked for advice concerning his future work. Swamiji told him, "Go and establish the Ashrama in California. Hoist the flag of Vedanta there. From this moment destroy even the memory of India. Above all, live the life, and Mother will see to the rest."[14] Accompanied by Minnie Boock, Turiyananda arrived at the small town of Alhambra near Los Angeles on Sunday, July 8, 1900. Before proceeding on to Northern California, the Swami and Miss Boock remained for a two-week sojourn in Southern California. Turiyananda previously had mailed an introductory letter to Alice Mead Hansbrough (later Shanti, 1864-1955) [q.v.] from Vivekananda dated July 3, which read, "The best thing would be to help him [Turiyananda] to start a centre for quiet and rest and meditation in the land near San Jose." They were first the guests of Mr. and Mrs. Thomas Lister, Miss Boock's sister and brother-in-law. Alice Hansbrough sent her nephew Ralph Wyckoff to meet Turiyananda and Minnie Boock and, within a short time, they were living with the three Mead sisters in South Pasadena at 309 Monterey Road.* Turiyananda probably occupied the same room Vivekananda had lived in five months earlier. There are two photographs of this group of Vedantists picnicking in Rubio Canyon in *Swami Vivekananda in the West: New Discoveries* (Vol. V). He was taken to see the surrounding towns, the orange groves, and the Pacific Ocean during his stay in Southern California.[15]

On July 25, 1900, Vivekananda wrote to Turiyananda:

> I received a letter from Mrs. Hansbrough telling me of your visit to her. They liked you immensely, and I am sure you have found in them genuine, pure, and absolutely unselfish friends.... Revive the clubs [Pasadena and the Los Angeles Vedanta Club] a bit, and ask Mrs. Hansbrough to collect the dues as they fall and send them to India.[16]

* This property is now owned by the Vedanta Society of Southern California.

In a correspondence to the *Prabuddha Bharata* of May 1917, some of the Los Angeles students and friends of Abhedananda recalled:

> In July of the same year [1900], Swami Turiyananda came here from New York. He met all the members here [the Los Angeles Vedanta Society], as well as those of the Pasadena branch of the Society, and although he remained but two weeks, he made an impression upon the lives of some, which will never leave them and all felt the spiritual power of the great soul.

At a later date at the Shanti Ashrama, Turiyananda bestowed upon Alice Hansbrough the name "Shanti", though she did not become his disciple. Through correspondence, Turiyananda maintained a deep and abiding friendship with Mrs. Hansbrough. He found her to be very sympathetic and he confided with her freely. She received over twenty informative letters from him, which kept her up on the events occurring in Northern California. In a letter dated April 16, 1902, Turiyananda wrote:

> I would not try to say anything about my feelings toward you my dear Shanti, as it never can be adequately expressed. Mother knows it and I believe you too understand a little. I owe my coming back to health (if I do come) this time entirely to your timely caution and maternal care.

The Swami also corresponded with Helen Mead and Mrs. Kelley of Los Angeles.[17] Similarly, Vivekananda and Saradananda were very grateful to the Western devotees, the former to many people, and the latter especially to Sara Bull and Lewis Janes, who aided them in their mission.

Swami Turiyananda Departs for Northern California

The local devotees wanted him to remain in Los Angeles, but Turiyananda and Minnie Boock went on to San Francisco along with one or two of his Southern California devotees. They left Los Angeles by ship and arrived in San Francisco on the 26th of July.[18] In regards to the purchase of the Shanti Ashrama, the *Los Angeles Times* (p. 18) of August 2, 1900 gives us the following information:

> A deed has been filed at San Jose by which Minnie C. Boock of the city of New York conveys to Swami Vivekananda, formerly of Calcutta, but now

> of New York, two lots near the northeastern boundary line of Santa Clara county, containing 159.89 acres, and a value according to the revenue stamp of $1500. The property which is in the foothills is conveyed in trust for the use and benefit of the Vedanta School of Philosophy, or for any purpose that may be best calculated, in the opinion of the trustee or his successors to disseminate the teachings of the school.[19]

Swamiji once indicated that the future missionaries would be of two types, "those who move like wildfire, spreading ... their news, and those who dug deep into the soil of one place, putting down their roots, and shedding fragrance on those in their shade."[20] Swamis Turiyananda and Trigunatita were primarily of the second type. Previously, when Vivekananda's lectures were concluded in the spring of 1900, an organization was formed with the name "Vedanta Class". The class numbered twenty-five members, with Dr. Mary Plumb of Oakland and then Mrs. Mary Wilmot serving as its president. When Turiyananda arrived in San Francisco on the 26th, he lectured there until August 3. Concerning the Shanti Ashrama, back on the 22nd, a newspaper article in the *San Francisco Call* mentioned, "Persons who desire to join the party for the summer will have to provide tents, stores and housekeeping utensils, to pay their own expenses and to assist in the support of the Swami." He then established a retreat named "Shanti Ashrama (Peace Retreat)". The first group at the Ashrama included about a dozen devotees, many being teachers and faith healers from the Home of Truth. Swami Vivekananda had previously made a great impression at the Home of Truth. From Turiyananda this group of enthusiastic students received their first experience in practical spiritual life. One of their initial assignments was to build a cabin twelve-by-sixteen feet in dimension to serve as a meditation centre and classroom. There were few rules for the community, since all ran smoothly bound by the Swami's spirituality and love. At the Ashrama, Minnie Boock received the Sanskrit name "Saravamsaha". Later in the year Turiyananda wrote to Alice Hansbrough, Miss Boock "has a very beautiful trait in her character. She is really a noble soul." She eventually moved to Los Angeles working as a dressmaker, living at 1416 Bond Street. In 1911, when Trigunatita intensively reorganized the Vedanta Society of Los Angeles, he chose Boock to be one of the eleven "Mothers-Fathers" of the church.[21]

Within a short time the Shanti Ashrama attracted the curiosity of the local inhabitants, who wondered what was going on there. Consequently, in late August Blanche Partington, representing the *San Francisco Chronicle*, visited the retreat and wrote a long seven-column article accompanied by photographs of the Swami and the guest chamber. The article tells us of Swami Turiyananda and twelve chelas sitting in a charmed circle:

> At one side, immobile as a bronze Buddha and in the immemorial position assumed by that of an ancient teacher of men, sat the Swami Turyananda [sic], and about him his disciples, all with closed eyes, and a look of rapt contemplation upon their quiet faces. Now and again the deep musical chant of a Sanskrit hymn, intoned in a rich, low voice, broke through the silence.... the picturesque and unusual figure of the leader. Swami Turyananda [sic] garbed in a robe of elusive gray, dark as is the wont of the children of the sun, with bright, dark eyes, a brow covered with the fine lines of thought, a mild and gracious mien, yet withal an indefinable air of absolute aristocracy. He was a singular figure at a good American campfire.... The gentle face of a teacher, calm, dark and strong.[22]

At the Ashrama, Turiyananda ran an intense spiritual retreat. He once made the statement, "I could palpably see how Mother was directing every single footfall of mine." Concerning Shanti Ashrama, Turiyananda wrote to Alice Hansbrough on September 29, 1900:

> We are getting along pretty well as far as spiritual teachings and practices are concerned. We leave the rest to the Mother. Let us do all that is in our power and then Mother knows what is best. If it is not Her will that this Ashrama should go on, then let it drop. Who cares for it?

As a result of the intimate personal attention that Turiyananda gave to his followers, he brought about a transformation in many people's life, producing a number of dedicated lifetime Vedantists. If a devotee desired to live a regimen of total retirement, the Swami set a limit of three days. Some renunciants tried fasting, some devoted the entire night to praying and meditating, some took long walks, and others underwent a vow of silence for twenty-four hours.[23]

A devotee once emphasized at the Shanti Ashrama, "How wonderful it is, Swami, that men and women of such different temperaments can live together peacefully." Turiyananda's reply was:

> That is because I rule by love. You are all tied to me by the string of love. How else is it possible? Don't you see how I trust everyone and leave everyone free? That I can do, because I know you all love me. There is no hitch anywhere—all goes on smoothly. But remember, it is all Mother's doing. I have nothing to do with it. She has given us that mutual love, that Her work may flourish. As long as we remain true to Her, there is no fear that anything will go wrong. But the moment we forget Her, there will be great danger. Therefore, I always ask you to think of Mother.[24]

On one occasion, while the Swami stayed at the Ashrama, he was bitten by a poisonous beetle. He gave the matter no thought until his hand began to swell up. The following day his entire arm was swollen. What to do, since the nearest doctor was fifty miles away and they had no automobile. Unexpectedly, that evening a gentleman from New York came to the Ashrama. He turned out to be a doctor who had walked on foot fifty miles until he came across the Ashrama. At once he made an incision with some disinfectants, explaining that any delay might have proven fatal. Atulananda concluded, "The Mother had sent this young doctor to save the Swami's life."[25]

Of the twenty-three months Turiyananda lived in California, he spent about fifteen months at the Shanti Ashrama (about 65% of the time). He stayed there on three different occasions for periods of less than six, four and one-quarter, and less than five months. The Swami lived at the Ashrama from August 3, 1900, until some time between January 24 and 27, 1901. Leaving Gurudasa (later Swami Atulananda) in charge of the Ashrama with seven other devotees, he then journeyed to the Bay area for a two-month period. Every morning at 10:00 a.m. he held meditation classes at the house of Dr. Milburn Logan at 770 Oak Street in San Francisco. On Tuesday evenings he spoke on *Raja Yoga*, and on Thursday, on the *Bhagavad Gita*. While in San Francisco the Swami once got angry with a female student who was nursing him. She got disturbed and he told her, "We scold those whom we love, and for their own good. We never utter a harsh word to people to whom we are indifferent. We try to improve those whom we love."

For seven weeks the Swami conducted classes also in East Oakland at the residence of Frank Rhodehamel (Satya-Nishtha) on Friday nights and Saturday mornings. He spoke also in Alameda at Mrs. Mary Magee's (Mira) residence. This was the only time that Turiyananda gave a continuous series of lectures in these three cities.[26] At Frank Rhodehamel's house he told his students, "It is not a matter of philosophy, or even the *Gita*. The thing to do is to know *Mother*. This is the whole of religion. Nothing else counts. Take all of your troubles to Mother. She will right all wrongs." Rhodehamel wrote in his memoirs, "Though [he] was not a lecturer in the popular sense of the word, he was a speaker of persuasive power, frequently rising to heights of impassionate utterance. He soon became known to a large circle of students, friends, and admirers." In 1918, Rhodehamel later affirmed:

> His presence converted my home into an Ashrama. Priceless were those long, intimate talks and counsellings with him, and attempts at meditation in the sanctity of his presence. We took many long morning and evening walks which, though tangibly through city streets, were in a finer and truer reality far from the locale of industrial life.[27]

One man in San Francisco told his wife he did not like her attending the Swami's lectures. Since the woman was not able to change her husband's attitude, the Swami told her, "I would like to see your husband." She warned him that her husband might act rudely toward him. Nevertheless, Turiyananda went to her house and shook the hand of her husband. Remarkably, this handshake removed his antagonism, he began to act like a devotee, and the problem was solved.[28]

In anticipation of Turiyananda's arrival, the *Los Angeles Times* of March 25, 1901 (p. 12) indicated:

> A distinguished Hindu monk, Swami Turiyananda is expected in this city in a few days to take the place at the head of local followers of the oriental faith, left vacant by the departure of Swami Vivekananda for India some time ago. ...the believers in the faith are looking forward to the arrival of the new leader with great expectations.

Turiyananda placed the San Francisco class in the hands of Miss Lucy Beckham, the director of the Alameda Home of Truth. Along with Mrs. Bertha Petersen (Dhira, d. 1916), on March 24, 1901 Turiyananda travelled by ship to Los Angeles. At that time Turiyananda initiated Carrie Wyckoff (later Sister Lalita)* and her sister Helen Mead at their residence in South

* Her house in Hollywood later became the residence of the Vedanta Society of Los Angeles, and a large portion of it is now the bookshop of the Vedanta Society of Southern California.

Pasadena. Turiyananda made the prophetic statement to Carrie Wyckoff, "You have work to do, but it will be quiet work." The *Los Angeles Times* tells us:

> Swami Turiyananda, a Hindu monk, and a dozen or more of the faithful, who minister to him, together with a little girl and a neighbour, made up the party which on Tuesday [April 2] climbed the hill at Lincoln Park, South Pasadena, for a meeting of meditation in the open air.

According to the *Los Angeles Times*, Turiyananda spoke at the Blanchard Building during April 10-12, where Swamiji previously had given lectures. He held free classes on Wednesday and Friday mornings and on Thursday evenings. Turiyananda probably stayed with the Mead family and/or Mrs. K. A. Kelly, who months later wanted him to travel to Arizona, but he decided to decline the offer. During part of his stay in Los Angeles, he was the guest of a woman who owned a large oil company. "She wanted to control Turiyananda and tried to curb his freedom. Turiyananda boldly said to the woman, 'Madam, you have helped me with a few dollars, but that does not mean I have sold my head to you.'" After his departure, the Vedanta Society in Los Angeles continued to meet at 130 1/2 S. Spring Street.[29]

Years later, Swami Prabhavananda often recalled:

> When Swami Turiyananda was going to Shanti Ashrama, he told Sister Lalita (Carrie Wyckoff): "If I have one man realizing God, I will be satisfied." When Sister Lalita asked, "Do you have such a man?" Swami Turiyananda answered, "Yes, one."*[30]

In her notes and letters, Mrs. Eloise Roorbach, an attendant at Shanti Ashrama, recorded:

> Swami Turiyananda was our only teacher while I was there. I could write for hours on his beautiful life and words. He had no one to help him but Gurudasa. He often spoke gratefully of his help. Turiyananda was sad because he did not have more advanced students. We all had childish minds, no real enthusiasts among us. We were interested, determined to

* "Meaning, Gurudasa" [the future Swami Atulananda], Swami Prabhavananda always added.

> understand and to be Vedantists. But it was all over our dumb heads. We will never forget the ideal, the daily talks, the complete change in our lives and purposes. But we did not get far. Too immature! Still, the most wonderful experiences of my life were my meetings with Swami Vivekananda, and that stay at the Ashrama. I am deeply grateful for them.[31]

On April the 25th, Turiyananda returned to Shanti Ashrama along with Alice Hansbrough and others, remaining there until early September. Before journeying to Los Angeles in August 1901, Swami Abhedananda came to the Shanti Ashrama to visit his brother disciple for about a week. Fourteen students were at the retreat at that time. A student later recalled:

> Swami Turiyananda was up and doing all the time. He never spared himself. He didn't think of his own health or comforts; he had only one object—to bring the eager students to the feet of the Divine Mother. He spoke always about "Mother". Sometimes the Swami would call out: "Think of the Mother, forget your worldly things."[32]

In early September 1901, due to bad health, for five weeks Turiyananda stayed at Donner Lake, a rustic area located in the High Sierra. In mid-October he moved to Carl and Bertha Petersen's residence in San Francisco. After giving a lecture at Dr. Milburn Logan's house, Turiyananda fell ill on October 18, and remained there bedridden for over two weeks. The Swami spent the remainder of the year living quietly with the Petersens. On the last day of the year, Turiyananda travelled to Pasadena, Los Angeles, and Catalina Island during the first week of 1902. At that time he lived quietly with the Mead family in South Pasadena for a surprisingly short time, and then returned to San Francisco and Shanti Ashrama where he stayed from January 8 until June 1, 1902. During the year 1902, the Vedanta Society of San Francisco published *The Pacific Vedantin* magazine under the direction of Milburn Logan. It was not authorized, contained some inaccuracies, and Turiyananda wanted it to be terminated.[33]

Swami Vivekananda wrote in a letter from Benares on February 14, 1902:

> My dear Mrs. Hansbrough, I am eternally indebted to you for what you did for me in the past, and infinitely more now for what you are doing for Turiyananda. A gloom came over the Math when news reached Calcutta

> of his severe illness. Now I hope he has recovered completely, and I will be so glad to get news from you.... It will be better for him to come over to India whenever he thinks fit.[34]

After nearly two years, Turiyananda decided to leave Northern California because of declining health and to return to India. He hoped to meet Swamiji in India and have his own health restored. At that time Turiyananda had a vision, which he later revealed to Gurudasa as follows:

> The Divine Mother had come to the Swami and had asked him to remain in the Ashrama. But he had refused. Then She told him that if he stayed, the work would grow rapidly, and many beautiful buildings would be erected. Still Turiyananda had refused. At last She showed him the place full of disciples. "Let me go to Swamiji first," he had said. And the Mother, with grave countenance, vanished from his sight.[35]

Before leaving the country, Turiyananda told Gurudasa:

> I leave you in full charge. I have told you everything. I have kept nothing hidden from you. I have told you the most secret thoughts of my mind. You have seen how I have lived. Now try to do the same. Depend on Mother for everything. Trust in Her, and She will guide you. One thing rembember—never boss anyone. Look upon all alike, treat all alike. No favourites. Hear all, and be just.[36]

Leaving Gurudasa in control of the Ashrama, on June 6, 1902 he left San Francisco for India to meet with Vivekananda. A large delegation was present to bid him farewell. As fate would have it, ten days before his ship reached Calcutta, Vivekananda entered mahasamadhi on 4 July 1902. Many years later Turiyananda told Prabhavananda that he "wanted to return to America, but the woman on whom he depended for sending the money was killed in an auto accident. Her name was Shraddha [Mrs. Agnes Stanley]." She had been among the first group of thirteen students to go to Shanti Ashrama with Turiyananda during August 3-13, 1900, and was associated with the San Francisco Vedanta Centre until at least late 1904.[37]

Over sixty letters written by Swami Turiyananda to Western devotees have been published: twenty-two letters to Alice Hansbrough (Shanti, 1900-02),[38] twelve to Ida Ansell (1900-19), seven to Frank Rhodehamel (1901-14), four to Josephine MacLeod (Tantine, 1902-20), three to Bertha Petersen (Dhira, 1916), one to Gurudasa (1901), one to Lewis Janes (1901), and one to Mrs. Olea Bull Vaughan (1900). There are ten other letters to Westerners where the recipient is not identified with certainty (1901-03). A good number were dispatched after the Swami returned to India.[39]

Later Tributes

For many years Turiyananda received praise from his Northern and Southern California students. In 1916 a "California Disciple" described him this way:

> Swami Turiyananda is the product of India's best culture, and he is at once a gentleman of the purest type and a Sannyasin of traditional and glorious India. Above all things else, he is a Sannyasin, and, like Vivekananda, his character is evidently the culmination of ages of spiritual culture. The transcendental art of meditation seems to be co-existent with his personality. To know him is to love him. It is as if, in the formative period of his character, he reached out for all the graces and succeeded in building it from their Sattvic qualities. Again, to think of him is an easy and happy method of meditation, so intimately is his personality associated in the mind with all that constitutes entire consecration to God.[40]

After returning to India, Turiyananda would offer strong spiritual support and encouragement to some of the young Swamis who were headed for America. For example, Swami Prabhavananda told his monastics:

> When I was twenty-two years old [1916], I stopped in Varanasi on my way to Mayavati in the Himalayas. There I fell ill with chicken pox mixed with smallpox.... I had a high fever. Every day Swami Turiyananda would come, sit on my bed, and put his hand on my forehead. After a few days, he said to me, "Abani, ask a boon of me." I said, "Maharaj, please do not come and sit on my bed anymore. You may fall sick." Hari Maharaj seemed disappointed and said, "Oh, why do you ask for a thing like that!" He continued to visit me every day... [Later] he put his hand on my back and said, "Abani, where is there no contagion? But through Mother's grace, a big rock floats on water; fire loses its power to burn; water loses its power to drench."[41]

Prabhavananda wanted Turiyananda to teach him how to properly study the *Bhagavad Gita*. He gave him the extraordinary advice: first concentrate on a single verse, meditate on its meaning, and then live the verse for an entire week before proceeding onto the next verse.[42]

After Brahmananda's mahasamadhi, Shivananda, the President of the Ramakrishna Order, planned to send Prabhavananda to Singapore. Fortunately, Turiyananda did not like the idea. Not long before his mahasamadhi he replied, "As long as they are sending you outside of India, why don't they send you to America?" Consequently, the plans were changed and this is what happened.[43] Prabhavananda related that the last time I saw him,

> Swami Turiyananda reminded me of the first time I had massaged his feet. He said, "I knew that first time that [sic] you had a power in you." He also told me that I belonged to them, and said many other nice things. When I protested, "Maharaj, I am not any of these things you say I am," he replied, "What do you know about yourself? I see not what you are, but what you are going to become."[44]

After his passing away, in July 1922 Josephine MacLeod wrote:

> My beloved Turiyananda has died; now there are none of that stock left! Fire, power and knowledge. He just filled me with courage the few minutes I talked to him at Benares, coming up here! It was worth coming to India for that half-hour. He seemed at the *Centre*, pouring forth his power. Nothing hesitating, unsure or insecure.[45]

Prabhavananda made a ten-day pilgrimage with Prakashananda to the Shanti Ashrama and wrote in a letter of June 6, 1924 to Siddheswarananda at the Madras Math saying:

> And the spiritual atmosphere! One could feel it tangibly. The spirit of Hari Maharaj [Turiyananda] is still vibrating. Hari Maharaj once said that the atmosphere of spirituality that he created would remain for at least a century. Oh, it was such a relief, you can imagine, after a stay in a crowded, luxurious city.[46]

In 1927, Swami Atulananda (1870-1966) [q.v.] mentioned his respectful feelings toward Turiyananda:

The question that really matters is, how far have I personally been able to appreciate the greatness of the Swami and the real worth of India; how have I been affected, how have I profited, what have I gained by coming in contact with a singularly great personality, a man of staunch character, of deep spiritual realization?… Personally I have had the blessings of his association for years, a close and intimate association, that gave me the opportunity of watching him and of learning from him day and night. To me, his *life* was the greatest lesson, for of Swami Turiyananda I can say with conviction that he walked with God. He was devoted to his ideal, the highest, the noblest ideal man can aspire to. His ideal was ever before him, it was his polestar of which he never lost sight. And surely that in itself is greatness…. he said over and over again, "Sri Ramakrishna has [held] you by the hand; he will never let you go." These words thrilled me through and through; but I told the Swami there must be some mistake about me. The sweet smile and words with which he reassured me then will never be forgotten. They were a benediction. And now I still hope and pray that these words are true for all of us who loved the Swami.[47]

Again in 1938 in *With the Swamis in America* Atulananda recalled:

I met and lived with those students again, many years after the Swami had returned to India, and without a single exception they all agreed that those few months with him in the Shanti Ashrama constituted the most important period in their lives. And that is the reason why the Shanti Ashrama has always remained so dear to those students…. Swami Turiyananda had given us the very best that India had to give—that priceless treasure that India has fostered for countless ages and that now once more she offers freely to all the world.[48]

In 1952, Ida Ansell (Ujjvala, 1877-1955) informed her readers:

One day I found him sitting all alone and laughing heartily. "What is funny?" I asked him, but he only shook his head and continued to laugh. Then I said, "I would give anything in the world if I could see what is in your mind." Swami became very sober in a moment and said, "You would see on the surface this and that—Turiyananda—but underneath you would see all Ramakrishna."[49]

Dorothy Mercer (1901-62) [q.v.], who personally knew Swamis Trigunatita and Abhedananda and later became an instructor of English at the City College of San Francisco, imparted the following information:

> Swami Turiyananda's method was almost exclusively personal. He delivered scarcely any lectures, but, taking a few students, he trained these intensively in the discipline of meditation. On leaving California he was asked if he had accomplished his mission. He answered: "Yes. I leave here one who is on the way to reaching illumination." Turiyananda believed that if he could help one human being to realize God in this life, he would not have lived in vain. His work in California and India was singularly productive, and by training many second-generation monks who are today teaching in the West as well as in his native land, Turiyananda proved himself one of Sri Ramakrishna's most fertile spiritual sons.[50]

Swami Ritajananda (1906-94), who obtained his initiation from Swami Shivananda, served as an assistant minister at the Vedanta Society of Southern California from 1959 to 1961, and then, as head of the Ramakrishna Ashrama near Paris, France, came out with Turiyananda's life history in 1963 entitled *Swami Turiyananda*. In vivid and graphic language, Ritajananda supplies a wealth of new authentic biographical material used in this study. During 1977-78, Sister Gargi did a masterful job in authoring eight articles on "Early Days at Shanti Ashrama". With meticulous detail, she covers the life events of Turiyananda in California, coming up with many new letters he sent to Western devotees, particularly Alice Hansbrough. Pravrajika Brahmaprana [q.v.], then of the Sarada Convent in Santa Barbara, edited Turiyananda's translation of Shankara's 580-verse *Vivekachudamani* (1992). This volume is based on a shorthand rendering taken by Ida Ansell, an American devotee who attended Turiyananda's classes in Northern California at the beginning of the century. This translation echoes the spiritual experiences and intuitive wisdom of Turiyananda. His presentation borders on commentary revealing an original interpretation of Shankara's scriptural classic.[51] In addition, with some assistance from her associates, Brahmaprana compiled and edited Atulananda's *With the Swamis in America and India* (1988). The volume includes Atulananda's original book dealing with the early days of the Vedanta Movement in America, particularly under Turiyananda. A succinct and informative biographical sketch of Atulananda has been added. Part III includes extracts from two-hundred and fifty letters written by Atulananda to Ida Ansell (Ujjvala) during a period of over half a century (1901-54). These letters are replete with the quality of pious wisdom that only a person of high spiritual attainment could produce.

The leader of the Vedanta Society of St. Louis, Swami Chetanananda translated and edited *Spiritual Treasures: Letters of Swami Turiyananda* (1992). This impressive collection of letters is simple in expression and rich in wisdom, compassion and common sense. Francis X. Clooney, S.J. [q.v.], a Catholic Jesuit Priest teaching at Harvard University Divinity School, made this statement regarding the book:

> Swami Chetanananda, already the author of numerous works, bringing to the modern reader the lives and teachings of the monastic and lay disciples of Sri Ramakrishna, performs a great service by collecting in this one volume the quintessence of the letters of Swami Turiyananda, many of them appearing in English for the first time. This is a volume to be read slowly and savoured reflectively; as an old monk once said: "Whenever you feel a dry spell, depression, or stagnation in the spiritual life, please read the letters of Swami Turiyananda; you will get a boost instantly. It is truly an important addition to the classic genre of spirituality, "the letters of the saints".

Reviewing the same book, Reverend Robert B. Dunbar of St. Helena's Episcopal Church in Beaufort, South Carolina, ascertained:

> This impressive collection of Swami Turiyananda's letters is an invaluable treasury of wisdom of a direct disciple of Sri Ramakrishna. Swami Turiyananda speaks simply and directly about the spiritual life and spells out the more technical aspects of Vedanta in clear and practical terms. His letters impart a genuine reliance on the Lord's grace. He shows us the supreme goal of life and teaches us not to be impatient. His calm and gentle voice has an important message for today.[52]

Concerning this work, Lance Nelson, of the department of theological and religious studies at the University of San Diego, stressed:

> Swami Turiyananda was without doubt one of the spiritual giants of twentieth century India. We are fortunate to have this masterfully translated edition of the letters of this great monastic teacher. They will appeal to both

the spiritual seeker and the more academically inclined student of Hindu spirituality. The former will find in these pages inspiration and practical instruction, especially for dealing with periods of spiritual dryness. The latter will gain previously unavailable insight into the Vedantic path and methods of spiritual direction. The words of the letters resonate with extraordinary power and compassion arising out of Turiyananda's profound God-experience, of which they are profound evidence.[53]

Professor Nelson delivered public lectures at four Vedanta Society of Southern California locations, and has made contributions to the *Vedanta Kesari* and *Prabuddha Bharata* on the Advaita Vedantist Madhusudana Saraswati. He edited *Purifying the Earthly Body of God: Religion and Ecology in Hindu India* (1998). This work relates Hindu views of the environment with corresponding theories of karma, caste, gender issues and contemporary ethics. His additional activities include being the president of the Society for Hindu-Christian Studies (1998-2000).[54]

The Sri Ramakrishna Math at Mylapore, Madras, offers an excellent English language DVD entitled "Swami Turiyananda—The Master Vedantist" that devotes a great deal of attention to his stay in the United States.*

ENDNOTES

1 *Disciples*, p. 216; *Life*, II, p. 480; Hohner, pp. 86-88.

2 *Life*, II, pp. 480-81; Ritajananda, p. 55; *WWSV*, p. 114; Hohner, pp. 87-88.

3 *Brahmavadin* (Sept. 15, 1899), p. 816; (Jan. 1900), pp. 172-73; Basu, p. 541 (601).

4 *Life*, II, p. 485; Ritajananda, p. 53; Hohner, p. 92; Web: en.wikipedia.org/wiki/Hitopadesha.

5 Ritajananda, pp. 50-52, 55-56; Atulananda, p. 45; Chetanananda, pp. 371-72; *Brahmavadin* (May 1900), p. 487.

6 Atulananda, pp. 37-39, 43, 45.

7 *Global Vedanta* (Summer 2009), p. 11.

8 Atulananda, pp. 41-42; F. Rhodehamel, "Swami Turiyananda as My Guest", *PB* (June 1923), pp. 223, 225.

* Web: www.sriramakrishnamath.org. For a selected list of books and articles about Turiyananda in the West, see Appendix VI.

9 Swami Atulananda, "Moments with Swami Turiyananda in America", *PB* (1927), p. 414.
10 *PB* (1918), p. 107.
11 Atulananda, p. 62; Burke, V, p. 283; VI, pp. 291-93.
12 *Life*, II, p. 534.
13 *CW*, IX:144-45.
14 Ritajananda, p. 58.
15 Burke, V, pp. opposite 200-pictures, 285; VI, pp. 293-94; Gargi, *PB* (Aug. 1977), pp. 329-30; Atulananda, p. 63.
16 *CW*, VIII:529.
17 Madhavaprana, *VK* (March 1993), p. 108; Gargi, *PB* (June 1978), p. 253; The letters from Turiyananda to Mrs. Hansbrough are in "Early Days at Shanti Ashrama", *PB* (1977-78); Stavig2, ch. 1.
18 Gargi, *PB* (Aug. 1977), p. 330.
19 Stavig2; *Los Angeles Times* (Aug. 3, 1900), p. 18 on PQHN.
20 Tathagatananda1, p. 290.
21 *Brahmavadin* (Jan. 1904), pp. 44-45; *Mission* (Vedananda), pp. 344-45; Gargi, *PB* (Oct. 1977), p. 423; Gargi, pp. 107, 113-14; *Los Angeles City Directory* (1912); *San Francisco Call* (July 22, 1900).
22 *San Francisco Chronicle* (Aug. 26, 1900), p. 32.
23 Gargi, *PB* (Nov. 1977), pp. 448-49; *VK* (Aug. 2004), p. 266; *Disciples*, p. 220; Ritajananda, p. 66.
24 Atulananda, pp. 69-70.
25 Atulananda, pp. 76-77.
26 Gargi, *PB* (1978), pp. 9-10; Atulananda, p. 159; Gargi, p. 79; *Brahmavadin* (Jan. 1904), pp. 45-46; Ritajananda, pp. 81, 87.
27 "Shanti Ashrama Days", *PB* (1918), p. 108; F. Rhodehamel, *PB* (June 1923), p. 225; Gargi, *PB* (Jan. 1978), p. 10; Ritajananda, p. 84.
28 Ritajananda, pp. 82-83.
29 Gargi, p. 79; Gargi, *PB* (Jan. 1978), p. 12; Atulananda, p. 262; Anandaprana, p. 93; Chetanananda, p. 372; *Los Angeles Times* (March 25, 1901), p. 12; (April 4, 1901), p. 11; (April 9, 1901), p. 16; (Sept. 29, 1901); Stavig2, ch. 1.
30 Atulananda, p. xxv.
31 Gargi, *PB* (Feb. 1978), p. 68.
32 *Global Vedanta* (Summer 2009), p. 5.
33 Gargi, *PB* (May 1978), pp. 212-13; (June 1978), pp. 250-53; Gargi, pp. 79-80; Burke, VI, p. 296; Atulananda, p. 159; Shivani, pp. 110-11.
34 *CW*, IX:179-80.

35 Swami Atulananda, *PB* (Jan. 1925), p. 2; Ritajananda, p. 89; Gargi, *PB* (June 1978), pp. 254-55.

36 Ritajananda, p. 90.

37 Anandaprana, p. 45; Atulananda, pp. 342-44; *VK* (April 1989), p, 152; (1990), p. 354.

38 Sister Gargi, "Early Days at Shanti Ashrama", *PB* (Aug. 1977 –June 1978).

39 Pravrajika Brahmaprana, "Unpublished Letters of Swami Turiyananda", *VK* (1989-6 articles); (1990), pp. 354-55, 384-85; Swami Chetanananda, tr., *Spiritual Treasures, Letters of Swami Turiyananda* (St. Louis: Vedanta Society of St. Louis, 1992), pp. 233-51.

40 "Vedanta in California: Memories", *PB* (Feb.-March 1916), p. 39.

41 Anandaprana, p. 39.

42 Anandaprana, p. 29.

43 Anandaprana, pp. 73-74.

44 Anandaprana, p. 74.

45 Prabuddhapranaı, p. 166.

46 Anandaprana, p. 87.

47 Atulananda, *PB* (1927), pp. 410, 412-14.

48 Atulananda, pp. 80, 83.

49 *VW* (Nov-Dec. 1952), p. 172; *PB* (1954), p. 282.

50 Mercer, p. 41.

51 Swami Turiyananda, tr. *Vivekacudamani of Sri Sankaracarya*, Pravrajika Brahmaprana, ed. (Mylapore: Sri Ramakrishna Math, 2001), pp. iii-vii.

52 Chetanananda (1992), back cover.

53 Chetanananda (1992), back cover.

54 "Lance E. Nelson." University of San Diego. http://home.sandiego.edu/~lnelson/cv.htm.

CHAPTER XX

SWAMI TRIGUNATITANANDA

To the best of our knowledge, Swamis Yogananda and Trigunatitananda (affectionately known as Swami Trigunatita) were the only two monastic disciples of Sri Ramakrishna who received initiation from Holy Mother. In 1897, the Ramakrishna Mission placed Trigunatita (1865-1915) in charge of famine relief work in the Dinajpur district of north Bengal. His actions were selfless and heroic and, as a result, he contracted malaria. Describing this period of his life, years later Ernest C. Brown (Sajjana, 1871-1960/61) [q.v.], a devotee of his from Northern California, wrote:

> Standing foremost in every act of relief and mercy was the Swami Trigunatita. He counted his life as nothing in the balance, in the joy of service. Whatever the danger or privation, he unhesitatingly obeyed the call, no matter where it led. In the famine areas his tender heart could not brook the thought that others would starve that he might eat, and often, giving away his allotted portion, he was reduced to one banana a day and some days not even that could be obtained. Contagious diseases and all the other ills that the flesh is heir to, held no terror for him, secure in the consciousness of his Master's presence and protection.[1]

After Yogananda's passing away in March 1899, Trigunatita took care of Holy Mother's physical needs. Swami Nikhilananda reported the following incident:

> One day Holy Mother was coming to Jayrambati in a bullock cart. It was past midnight. Sarada (Trigunatita) was walking in front of the carriage as a bodyguard, with a heavy stick on his shoulder. Suddenly he saw a wide breach in the road made by a flood. At once he realized that when the carriage came to it, it would either be overturned or receive a terrific

jolt, not only disturbing the Mother's sleep but hurting her physically. Immediately he laid his large body in the breach and asked the driver to drive the vehicle over him. The Mother awoke, took in the situation, and rebuked the disciple for his rashness.[2]

On August 20, 1902 Premananda wrote to Abhedananda that Trigunatita will be leaving for America and that "Swamiji had arranged this before his death." Turiyananda wrote to Mrs. Albert Wollberg (Prasuti) on the 10th of September:

> Swami Trigunatita will start for San Francisco next month. He is such a beautiful soul. He will be of great use to you all in matters Spiritual and I am sure you all will spare nothing to make him feel quite at home when there.

Probably advised by Turiyananda, in Ceylon, on November 11, 1902, Trigunatita wrote a letter to Alice Hansbrough [q.v.] in Los Angeles. It said in part:

> [I] have heard much of your goodness & kindness. It is therefore, mother, that I venture to intrude upon your time. Mother, I am going to serve you. Pray to God the Almighty that I may be really & practically, by His unbounded Grace, serviceable to you.

Then he explained to her that he would arrive in San Francisco, which he did on January 2, 1903.[3]

As soon as Swami Trigunatita came to San Francisco, he attracted newspaper attention. Beneath a picture of him in the *San Francisco Chronicle* of January 3 are the captions:

> Swami Trigunatita Distinguished Hindoo Savant
> COMES TO TEACH HINDOO PHILOSOPHY
> Famous Vedantic Monk on a Tour of the World

> Swami Trigunatita, a distinguished Hindoo savant, arrived in San Francisco yesterday on the America Maru, direct from the Rama Krishna [sic] monastery at Calcutta, India, to make a pilgrimage around the world that will occupy from three to five years time. He will remain in San Fran-

> cisco for some weeks teaching the philosophy of the Vedanta to followers of the cult in this city and will then resume his journey. For the present he is staying at the residence of Dr. M. H. Logan of 770 Oak Street, who is the president of the local society and at whose residence the local society holds its weekly meetings.
>
> Swami Trigunatita is a man of about 40 years of age and said to be a learned scholar and one of the most able of the teachers of Hindooism. He is of medium height, has intelligent features and speaks English perfectly. His costume yesterday was a long flowing robe of some rich brown material fastened at the waist with a richly embroidered sash. On his head he wore a high turban of yellow colour. He is most gracious in manner, an entertaining conversationalist and is quite ready to talk of his philosophy. He is a strict vegetarian....

The first portion of the article appeared in newspapers as far away as Atlanta, Georgia.[4] The *San Francisco Chronicle* of January 8 tells us in part:

> Swami Trigunatita, the Hindoo monk and savant, who has come to this city from Calcutta, India, to spread the doctrines of the great Hindoo saint, Ram Krishna Paramahamsa, was given a reception at the home of Dr. Milburn H. Logan, president of the Pacific Vedanta Society last night.... Swami Trigunatita is a highly educated man, a graduate of one of the best universities in India and the publisher of the Vedanta magazine at Calcutta. Although this is his first visit to America, he speaks English well. He expects to remain in the city three months and to spend five years in the United States before returning to India. On January 18th he will give the first of a series of four lectures and will speak on "A Message from Heaven".

Apparently, upon arrival Trigunatita was not certain if his stay in San Francisco would be temporary or permanent.

Representing the Vedanta Society, Ramakrishna Mission, on January 26 Trigunatita lectured on the *Gita* at Colton Hall in the Pioneer Building, and on February 1st on "Message from Heaven" at the Union Square Hall.[5] In March the Society rented a large house at 40 Steiner Street where the Swami could live and conduct lectures and classes on the *Gita*, Upanishads and other subjects. His audience of forty church members included many followers of Turiyananda like Carl and Bertha Petersen, Milburn Logan,

Ida Ansell, Cornelius Heijblom (Gurudasa), Cara French and other supporters.[6]

A leading expert on the subject, Sister Gargi tells us of Trigunatita's nature:

> The fact is, the Vedanta Society had come under the guidance of a force. Swami Trigunatita had many outstanding qualities; he was boundlessly loving, endlessly patient; his will was indomitable; his mind was brilliant; his work was totally dedicated to Sri Ramakrishna and Swami Vivekananda. He was at times eccentric—his way of life, his way of work, his mode of expression were all markedly his own and were now and then astonishing—but pervading and overriding the idiosyncrasies of his personality was the sheer *force* of his being. "That strong will, that energy that could not be broken by anything! That was Swami Trigunatita," Carl Petersen would say of him years later. There was none who did not feel the Swami's power, and few who did not benefit by it.[7]

Concerning the virtue of patience, the Swami proclaimed:

> When you crave blessings, or whatever you ask from the Divine Mother, or whatever you need in life, be prepared and willing to wait, for years if necessary. Learn how to wait. Let her will be done, even if you wait forever. Rest assured that Mother knows what is best for Her children.

The "object" of the Vedanta Society of San Francisco was stated as:

> To propagate the Hindu philosophy, as we have already some idea from the works of the renowned Swami Vivekananda of the Ramakrishna Mission, for the welfare of humanity; and particularly, to have its effects in our own practical lives in all probable ways and respects.

The fact that the word "Hindu" is used instead of "Vedanta" is an indication of the difference between the approach of Trigunatita and Abhedananda. It was his goal to create an atmosphere for serious minded students. In less than a year the Swami organized a weekly Sunday public lecture, Monday class on the *Gita*, Thursday meditation class, Sunday-Monday-Thursday question class, and a Wednesday-Friday Sanskrit class. In addition, he offered a one-month long yoga class at the Shanti Ashrama, and occasionally offered public lectures in outside locations.[8]

Some devotees in Los Angeles invited the Swami to their city hoping he would start a Vedanta Centre there. On March 10, 1903, Trigunatita wrote to Alice Hansbrough:

> Mother, I intended to stay with Mother Mrs. Kelly—when I shall go to Los Angeles. But if you are there at that time, then I must stay with you for a while at your house as well. Even if you are in Pasadena, still I shall go there to see you.

The Swami travelled alone to Los Angeles by train, staying at the house of the affluent Mrs. K. A. Kelly for about three weeks beginning early in May 1903. Next for about a month, Trigunatita resided at the house that Mrs. Kelly rented for him at 1434 Flower Street during May through June. Then on June 22 he moved to the residence of Dr. and Mrs. John Schmitz (3000 South Main Street), president of the Vedanta Society of Los Angeles, until the end of July. According to an old-time devotee Gertrude Topham, Kelly and Schmitz knew Vivekananda. Part of the time Trigunatita resided in a house rented by the Mead sisters and their father in South Pasadena,* where Vivekananda, Turiyananda and Abhedananda had previously stayed.[9]

In the area, Trigunatita gave thirteen public lectures to audiences of 250 to 300 people, first in the Burbank Theatre Building (548-550 Main Street in Burbank), and the rest in the large auditorium at Brent's Hall at 534 1/2 South Spring Street in downtown Los Angeles, and also taught classes. In the latter location, for one of his public lectures (on May 3rd), at least one-hundred people were turned away due to the full house. To Ida Ansell in San Francisco, the Swami wrote on May 6, 1903, "My lectures here are very successful. Very large audiences are being drawn. All is Mother's will & act." With the help of Alice Hansbrough, the Swami worked hard to bolster up the Los Angeles Vedanta Society. Within a week after his arrival, with the assistance of Mrs. Hansbrough he printed up a twelve-page circular. It listed the title of his Los Angeles Sunday addresses for May, June and July, the basic doctrines of Vedanta, a brief history of the Los Angeles Vedanta Society, the purpose of the Society, its method of activity, the duties and privileges of membership, the organization of the Society and current offic-

---

* Now it is the property of the Vedanta Society of Southern California.

ers, and a list of Vivekananda and Abhedananda publications that could be ordered from the Society's secretary Alice Hansbrough. Trigunatita wrote to Turiyananda on May 22:

> I have started a meditation class under the Oak tree in Pasadena, where Swamiji and you used to sit for meditation. There I conduct reading from *Gita*, meditation and lecture, etc. Here I arranged regular public lecture in addition to meditation class, *Gita* class and question-answer class. Besides, I make them practise meditation at home four times a day. Everyone is exceedingly satisfied.[10]

At that location on Monday and Thursday evenings, he held "a school for the study of Indian philosophy" commencing on June 29, 1903. Trigunatita sent a small two-and-one-half inch by three-and-a-half inch card to Carrie Wyckoff (later Sister Lalita). On the front was written, "Lalita a beloved lady-companion of God." And on the back was written, "With the best wishes of the Vedanta Society of the Ramakrishna Mission, Los Angeles. 23rd July 1903, Trigunatita." After nearly a three-month rewarding stay in Los Angeles, the Swami returned to San Francisco on July 25.[11]

A beautiful full-page photograph of Trigunatita appeared in the *San Francisco Call* of August 23, along with his essay on the "Philosophy of the Vedas". The newspaper reporter added:

> And of these things has the brown-faced, bright-eyed Swami come to speak. In the yellow gown and turban of his priesthood, with the soft speech and the subtle thinking of the Hindu, he is advancing again the old thoughts of the Vedas and the newer thoughts and newer wisdom of the modern Vedantism.[12]

In November the Swami carried on the tradition initiated by Turiyananda of living for a time at the Shanti Ashrama. Nearly every year for one month the Swami would bring male and female devotees with him to the Ashrama. As many as thirty-seven retreatants attended his daily classes. When Trigunatita took charge of the Shanti Ashrama beginning in 1903, he gave a full month's course of intensive spiritual training. A typical day ran from 5:30 a.m. to 10:00 p.m., consisting of meditation, scriptural classes, cooking, and various manual labour duties. Trigunatita was a highly energetic man with an iron will. Over the years, Shanti Ashrama became a fully equipped and functioning establishment. A permanent caretaker lived on the property, additional cabins were constructed, better wells were dug, a windmill was installed to pump water from the wells to a storage tank, a distribution system transported water to the dining cabin, bathing facilities, living quarters, and a vegetable garden was cultivated, at times six acres were under cultivation, cows were kept, and a barn was built for the horses, the carriage, and to be used as a storage area.[13]

Swami Trigunatita came back to Los Angeles to visit the Vedanta Society he had previously brought into being. For about two months (from April 3 to May 29, 1904) he spoke to interested audiences on Fridays and Sundays at the Camera Club Hall and in the Wright & Callender Building. While residing in the Southland, he vacationed at a resort on Catalina Island. Gertrude Topham took Trigunatita to the top of Mt. Lowe (where Vivekananda had been four years earlier) and they enjoyed dinner there. The Swami lived at least part of the time in a small bungalow with Alice Hansbrough and her sister Carrie Wyckoff who had since moved out of their two-storey rented residence in South Pasadena. In Los Angeles he met Mrs. Druscilla "Drusie" E. Steele, who later generously donated the large lump sum of $7,000 (equivalent to $176,000 in 2008) to release the mortgage held on the San Francisco Temple in 1905.[14]

The members of the Society in Northern California thought they might lose their "beloved teacher Swami Trigunatita". In response, the officers and members of the Vedanta Society of San Francisco sent a message to Swami Brahmananda, the then President of the Ramakrishna Mission, concerning Trigunatita. The letter of April 1904 read as follows:

> We, the students of the Vedanta Society of San Francisco, wish to make an appeal to you as regards our beloved teacher, Swami Trigunatita. We wish to let you and all the other Swamis of the Math know how very popular and beloved he is by one and all of his pupils here, and how unselfishly and untiringly he works for the cause of the Society.
>
> When Swami Trigunatita first landed in San Francisco, there were many obstacles in his way. But by his right and strong ambition and hard work, he has now been able to establish the Society on a firmer basis. We all feel that we could not have anyone else here who would do better and more satisfactory work than Swami Trigunatita does, and no one whom we could love and honour more. So we beg of you to request him to stay as long as possible. It will be of great benefit to us and to the cause here, as he discharges his duties as a real and dutiful minister in every respect.

His philosophical and spiritual lectures from the platform and esoteric lessons at private interviews and spiritual discipline—all are really infusing a new light to the minds and souls of the aspirants of this growing city. His plans and methods of organization even in a spiritual community are really powerful and beneficial to the people of this country.

Hoping to hear from you soon, we all remain,

Ever one with you in the Absolute[15]

The letter was signed by the officers and most of the membership. Swami Brahmananda wrote back:

The Math, Belur, Howrah

The 9th June, 1904

To
The President of the Vedanta Society
of San Francisco, California, U.S.A.

Dear Sir

It gives me great pleasure to reply to the words of appreciation coming from the students of the Vedanta Society of San Francisco for Swami Trigunatita and to know of the entire satisfaction and kindly feelings that they entertain towards their teacher who has made himself so very popular and beloved amongst them. On behalf of the Ramakrishna Mission let me request you to kindly convey our heartfelt thanks to them for the same.

Swami Trigunatita is by nature amiable, hardworking and a man of resolute determination, with a strong power of organization, who will command love and respect wherever he may be. We have great confidence in him and his work.

You seem to be afraid—out of your love towards Swami Trigunatita—lest we recall him from there to work in other fields. Please let me assure you that no other thought is farther from our minds than that. Let him continue his work of love and spread the grand and noble ideas of the Master amongst our brothers and sisters of the Pacific Coast who are eager aspirants after Truth.

With all love and best wishes

Yours ever one in the Absolute,
Brahmananda,
President, Ramakrishna Mission.[16]

Dr. John Schmitz, the president of the Vedanta Society of Los Angeles, offered $100, only under the condition that Swami Sachchidananda II be selected as the new head of the Centre. Schmitz was impressed with some of the things the Swami had written in India. Trigunatita did not like the idea, but reluctantly submitted, since Dr. Schmitz conditionally offered the funds. Vivekananda wrote a long essay "Modern India",[17] and a short one "Knowledge: Its Source and Acquirements"[18] in Bengali for the *Udbodhan*. Sachchidananda II translated these works into English for the September and December issues of the *Brahmavadin* in 1899, along with a report on "The Paris Congress of Religions" in 1901.[19] The *Los Angeles Times* of May 14, 1904 (p. 12) informs us:

> Swami Trigunatita, the Hindu minister, has sent for another Swami from India, who will assist in the conduct of the work in Los Angeles alone. Swami Sachchidananda is the name of the new assistant and he is spoken of as a brilliant scholar of the University of Calcutta, and a learned disciple of the renowned Swami Vivekananda. He is said to be efficient in the conduct of Esoteric teachings and platform work.

Sachchidananda II came to San Francisco and, after gaining some seasoning from Trigunatita, went on to Los Angeles, arriving there on the last day of 1904 to take charge of the organization there. He held his first public discourse on January 15 at the Vedanta Society located at 1947 Estrella Avenue on "Nature of the Soul". Vedanta Society Headquarters moved to 1124 Quincy Street by August 1906, Vedanta School to 527 East 33D Street by September 1907 through 1911, and Vedanta Home to 1624 Hyperion Avenue in January-February 1912.[20]

The *Vedanta Monthly Bulletin* published by the New York Centre reported in June 1905:

> In January of last year [1904] we received a letter from Portland, Oregon, announcing that a small group of Swami Vivekananda's former students, still full of the enthusiasm and devotion which he infused into all who came in contact with him, were starting a Vedanta Society in that city, "prepared," as one of their number stated, "to devote their lives to the work." Since that time they have held faithfully together, learning what they could from books and striving to realize the great teaching of their master. Now word comes to us that Swami Trigunatita, head of the Vedanta

Society in San Francisco, is to pay them a visit and give them the help and inspiration of his personal direction for a season.

Atulananda mentioned that Trigunatita's "field of action was extended even to the state of Oregon".[21]

On August 25, 1905, the cornerstone for the first Indian Temple in the Western world was laid at Webster and Filbert Streets in San Francisco. Concerning the future of the Temple, Trigunatita stated:

> I shall not live to enjoy, others will come later who will enjoy.... Believe me, believe me, if there is the least tinge of selfishness in building this Temple, it will fall, but if it is the Master's work, it will stand.

Sister Gargi tells us, "The Temple was, in fact, designed by Swami Trigunatita; Joseph A. Leonard, the architect-builder, put the Swami's ideas into blueprint form and, with astounding rapidity, the building came into being." Erik Davis adds the following:

> Working with a local architect, Trigunatita designed the temple himself. Giving an ecumenical spin to the eclecticism of Victorian architecture, Trigunatita wrote that his building "may be considered as a combination of a Hindu temple, a Christian church, a Mohammedan mosque, a Hindu math or monastery, and an American residence." The windows and balcony are Moorish in design, while the towers draw from the scattered sacred structures in India, including the Taj Mahal.[22]

Mr. Leonard said he learned more from the Swami than the Swami learned from him. The building is described today by experts outside of the Vedanta Society "as the most unusual building in San Francisco", "still a neighborhood landmark", and "one of the most striking buildings in the City". Trigunatita worked in collaboration with the very successful Joseph Argyle Leonard (1849-1929) to build the multi-domed Vedanta Temple. Born in Texas, Leonard, "a kindly, gentle man", came to California in 1883 "with nothing but a hammer and a saw". As a contractor, architect, realtor and financier, he established the San Francisco and Suburban Home Building Company. At the time of his death, his businesses were worth over five-million dollars.* Eulogized as a business genius, he designed and built hundreds of high quality homes, and developed several new residential neighbourhoods and parks† in San Francisco, Alameda, and Berkeley, California.[23]

1906 and After

The dedication occurred on the 7th of January 1906, and they held the first service eight days later. The two-storey building combines Hindu, Christian and Muslim Moorish architecture. Over the entrance to the Vedanta mission, the inscription reads, "May the Absolute Bless All". An estimated 150 people can be seated in the auditorium.[24] Trigunatita told a newspaper reporter:

> I was educated in Calcutta, and when I took holy orders, I was obliged to put away all secular things, and with it I put away my English, which I am now recovering. Up to a few years ago the Hindoos never preached their religion to other countries or peoples, and owing to this fact, we were misrepresented by the clergy of other nations and races. It was Ramakrishna who suggested the idea of missions, and it was followed. I was one of the missionaries selected.[25]

The story went out on the wire and appeared in many newspapers throughout the country.

That year, on August 2 Swami Prakashananda (1874-1927), a monastic disciple of Swami Vivekananda and the younger brother of Swami Shuddhananda (1872-1938), a future President of the Ramakrishna Order, came from India to become the assistant Swami. Bertha Petersen (Dhirananda) sent word to the *Prabuddha Bharata* in November 1906 of Prakashananda's arrival at the Centre. She wrote:

> You can see that the Swami Prakashananda is a great help to the Swami Trigunatita, who has been vigorously working almost single-handed, for the past four years, in the face of great difficulties, to further the cause of Vedanta in this country. We certainly have found the Swami Trigunatita

* Equivalent to sixty-two million dollars in 2008.

† Including Ingleside Terraces, Jordan Park, Leonardville, Richmond Heights, and Twin Peaks Tunnel.

> a capable earnest teacher, a ready worker, ever willing to help others, and to adjust himself to our Western ways. In consequence, he has been highly successful in accomplishing much good in a short time.[26]

He remained until May of 1914 when he opened his own Centre in San Francisco. For over seven years Prakashananda conducted lectures, classes, and retreats, wrote for the magazine *Voice of Freedom*, supervised the monastery, was a gracious friend to all the devotees, and did menial work like cleaning the auditorium in a spirit of true humility and service.[27]

Many years later Ernest C. Brown [q.v.], writing under the pseudonym of "His Western Disciples", mentioned:

> The young men came to deeply love Swami Prakashananda for his unfailing cheerfulness under all circumstances and for his spotless purity of mind. They found him to be a true representative of the Divine Mother, his gentle, loving disposition winning every heart. He entered into all their trials and problems and was one of them. Regardless of self, wholly devoted to the service of all, he assisted in the work of the Temple, giving one or more of the three lectures on Sundays and humbly doing all the duties, no matter how tedious or lowly.

Prakashananda conducted daily meditation classes in addition to his weekly classes on the *Gita* and Upanishads.[28]

On April 10, 1907, at the University of California in Berkeley, "The largest and most interested audience of the year" totalling thirty-five hundred people honoured Swamis Trigunatita and Prakashananda in a unique celebration held at the open-air Greek Theatre. Only once before did this type of celebration occur at Berkeley when Theodore Roosevelt, the president of the United States, came to the campus. "Valuable assistance was given by Swami Trigunatita and Swami Prakashananda of the Vedanta Society, San Francisco, in the details of a Hindu religious festival, which is an episode in the play." "As the Swamis entered the theatre, they being the guests of honour, the University students in a body immediately rose and saluted them in oriental fashion." "The Swamis wore the gorgeous oriental robes, turbans, and sashes of their sacred order. President Wheeler was in his full University regalia."[29]

Benjamin Ide Wheeler (1854-1927), the dynamic president of the University of California at Berkeley for a score of years from 1899 to 1919, prophetically told the large audience:

> Our coming together here this evening represents another step towards the union between the East and West, demonstrating the coming together of all humanity as brothers from the common Aryan stock.... We are just beginning to acknowledge the gratitude we owe to the East, and to appreciate the hitherto underestimated influence of India on Western civilization.... In India we find, through all its literature and philosophy, that deep striving and yearning after an almost inscrutable perfection, testifying to our common interest in the Great Infinite.[30]

Turning to the Swamis, he affirmed, "You, the leaders of your people, we welcome here to-night, as representatives of the oldest Indo-European culture, to California. May this be but the beginning of an acquaintance that will be beneficial to us all." President Wheeler also quoted from various Hindu scriptures. Trigunatita and Prakashananda each gave a short address, which "was honoured by a deep salaam on the part of the actors and choruses who were gathered on the stage." Trigunatita gave thanks to Wheeler, Ryder, Holme and the rest of the participants for the honour accorded to them, India and its ancient Sanskrit literature. Next, the actors performed the beautiful play "Mrichhakatika" (The Little Clay Cart), translated into English prose and verse by Arthur William Ryder (1877-1938), the head of the Sanskrit department at the University of California. Earlier, in 1905, working under the editorship of Charles Lanman, Ryder, an instructor in Sanskrit at Harvard University, translated the play for the distinguished Harvard Oriental Series. Professor Garnet Holme (1873-1929) directed the play performed by the University students. Noresh C. Chakravarti (who had some connection with the San Francisco Vedanta Society) recited the prologue in the original Sanskrit. The performance featured a live Indian elephant secured from the Chutes Zoo in San Francisco, and one-hundred students in oriental dress. A newspaper account added:

> The part of the priest in the brilliant festival reproduced in the last act will be taken by Swami Trigunatita, a learned Hindu scholar who is living in San Francisco. The Swami expresses great delight that the university is

Swami Trigunatitananda

> to present a genuine old Hindu comedy, and his advice about the costumes and stage management has been of great assistance to Director Holme.[31]

Benjamin Ide Wheeler was formerly a professor of Greek and comparative philology, and a student of Sanskrit. During his presidency, the student body and faculty increased fourfold at the University of California. Professor Garnet Holme, one of the best outdoor dramatists in the business, later in 1914 staged Arthur Ryder's translation of Kalidasa's *Shakuntula* at the Greek Theatre in Berkeley. Arthur Ryder, an adherent of the Sankhya philosophy and a friend of Trigunatita, was an outstanding translator of Sanskrit literature, which included the *Panchatantra* in 1925. He had been an undergraduate student at Harvard at the time Vivekananda spoke there during the 1894-97 period, and a student of Sanskrit under Charles Lanman. Ryder was so talented with the use of words that he translated the entire *Bhagavad Gita* as beautiful poetry in which every verse rhymes. For example, canto 3:21 is rendered as:

> The world forever imitates
> The action of its best;
> Whatever law of life he sets,
> Is followed by the rest.

And 6:45 is rendered as:

> So struggling onward, cleansed of sin,
> His powers in full control,
> Perfected after many births,
> He wins the highest goal.

In a critical correspondence to the *Prabuddha Bharata* of 1920, Dhan Gopal Mukherji related, "In America I have found three Sanskrit scholars who perceive the truth of our point of view and try to live their lives accordingly. Prof. Arthur Ryder, Prof. Walter Clark, and Paul Elmer More who know Sanskrit and our philosophy as a thing to be lived." A little before his passing away, Ryder was a member of the General Committee for the Ramakrishna Centenary held in Calcutta in March 1937. In describing Arthur Ryder, one Italian Sanskritist said, "Ten men like him would make a civilization."[32]

The nuclear scientist J. Robert Oppenheimer (1904-67) acquired a deeper knowledge of the *Bhagavad Gita* when, in 1933, he studied Sanskrit at Berkeley under his teacher Arthur Ryder. Thirty years later, in answer to the question posed by the *Christian Century*, "What books did most to shape your vocational attitude and your philosophy of life?", Oppenheimer listed the *Gita* and Bhartrihari's *Shatakatrayam* as two of the ten books. He was the director of the Manhattan Project organized to develop the first nuclear bomb. When in 1945 Oppenheimer witnessed the first atomic test explosion at the secret Los Alamos National Laboratory in New Mexico, a gigantic nuclear cloud mushroomed up to the stratosphere 7.5 miles in height and the shock wave was felt over one-hundred miles away. At that moment he recalled the lines from the Hindu scripture, the *Bhagavad-Gita*, "If the radiance of a thousand suns were to burst at once into the sky, that would be like the splendour of the mighty one. Now I am become Death, the destroyer of worlds [11:12, 32]."[33]

At times Swami Trigunatita spoke in outside lecture engagements. For example, he lectured, gave informal talks, or held classes for many years at the Shanti Ashrama, and in 1903 in Burbank and South Pasadena, and in 1903-04 and in 1911 in Los Angeles. He probably conducted classes for Vedanta students in Portland, Oregon, in 1905. That same year on March 26 he addressed the audience at Golden Gate Hall on "The Condition of Women in America", stating that women should be eligible to become the president of the country. During the year 1906, Trigunatita lectured upstairs in Hamilton Hall at the corner of 13th and Jefferson in Oakland, "where his lectures are much appreciated". When he went to Oakland, he took a streetcar to the Ferry Building, the ferry across the bay, and then another streetcar to his East Bay destination.[34] In October 1907, he spoke to a religious class at the University of California in Berkeley on Vedanta as a living religious force. On the 26th of the following month, he came back to the university to address the California Branch of the "American Folk Lore Society". His subject of the "Aryan Mythology of India" was presented to an audience of about three-hundred. The announcement for his upcoming lecture was written up by the secretary of the Society, Alfred Louis Kroeber (1876-1960), the dean of American anthropologists who taught at the University of California at Berkeley for over forty years. An authority on the culture of Native Americans, his huge textbook *Anthropology* (1923) was regarded as the most authorative work in the field.[35]

As previously mentioned in Chapter VII, Baba Premananda Bharati (1858-1914) [q.v.], a Bengali Vaishnava monastic who established a Church in Los Angeles, came to San Francisco in July 1907 on his way back to India. His companions were six American devotees, including Christina Albers and Rose Anthon who had heard Vivekananda speak. Bharati recalled:

> We were sandwiched between two Swamis and they pressed us into sweet jelly by the warmth of the reception! We had Hindoo dinners, a dozen courses cooked in right orthodox Hindoo style by the younger Swami himself—Swami Prakashananda, the young man who speaks so little but loves so much to serve one with all his ascetic heart and soul. He snatched away from me all the laurels I had gathered in Los Angeles as a first class Hindoo chef. But the daintiness of his dishes took away all pangs of their loss. And dear, old Trigunatita, was amiability itself. He wears still the heart of the rambler of the Holy Road, despite his American dress. His old-world goodwill, the merry twinkle of his eye are still twinkling in our memory.[36]

Ernest Brown also informs us that Trigunatita's

> aim was to induce Swami Brahmananda to come and take full charge of the work in America. His faith and reverence for Maharaj were very great and he believed that if he could be persuaded to come, the work in America would receive a tremendous impetus through the impelling force of his great spiritual power. In pursuance of this idea he added a third floor to serve as living quarters for Swami Brahmananda.[37]

Consequently, after they added a third floor and completed the addition of a roof and tower on April 5, 1908, they rededicated the Hindu Temple in San Francisco. Maharaj sent final word that he would not be able to leave the work in India. Rather than coming to the United States, Brahmananda did a wonderful job of training a number of Swamis that later came to America and became the founders and organizers of a number of new thriving centres.[38]

A photograph of the Trigunatita and the San Francisco Hindu Temple appeared in the *New-York Tribune*. Though the following description of the Temple is not fully accurate, it gives some idea of its symbology:

> Above the temple rise the towers and minarets, which are the most interesting part of the structure. All have their significance. The canopy over the mosaic and marble entrance to the auditorium represents the supposed thousand-petalled lotus of the brain. The tubular lights on the side of the canopy are roughly symbolic of Ida and Pingala, certain deities of the faith. The temple being the first in America, the appreciation of the sect has been shown by carrying the architectural art of the temple, the Sushumna—the main channel of spiritual illumination—up to an American eagle. Each of the towers is a copy of a distinctive part of some one of the great temples of India.[39]

According to a later account of the Temple:

> Its clusters of gourd-like domes, its tower of meditation, and its minarets invest it with the appearance of having been transplanted from sacred Benares. The architecture of the roof is a composite of details from the Taj Mahal at Agra, and Temple of Shiva at Bengal, and of the Temple Garden of Dakshineswar at Calcutta, where Paramahamsa Sri Ramakrishna, the great master of Swami Vivekananda, and other adepts once lived. A canopy over the mosaic and marble entrance to the auditorium is made to represent the thousand-petaled lotus in the brain.[40]

Trigunatita, who proved to be a dynamic innovator, organized and managed the first monastery of the Ramakrishna Mission (1908-15) and convent (1908-12) in the Western world. A few months after dedicating the Hindu Temple in San Francisco, the Swami decided to utilize the spacious third floor and tower rooms on the roof as a monastery. Initially the monastery had five male members and expanded to ten, including Ernest C. Brown, the future president of the Society. The monastics spent much of their time earning a living in the outside world. They were expected to rise early in the morning, meditate regularly, and to participate in all of the religious functions of the church. In addition to his other duties, the Swami cooked all of the meals for the monastery to maintain its purity. The cloister ran well until 1913, when the monastic membership began to decline, and they decided to close it down after the passing away of Trigunatita. On October 25, 1908, Trigunatita organized the first Vedanta convent in America. Several women wanted to form a separate religious community under the direction of the Swami. Their intention was to live in a separate facility for the purpose of devoting their lives to spiritual practices. Female renunciates performed all of their cooking and housekeeping activities in the spirit of worship and service to God. They devotedly followed the rules the Swami laid down concerning eating, hour of rising and general conduct. Most of the nuns held jobs on the outside in order to pay their expenses. After a few years, in 1912 the convent came to an end after a gallant effort.[41]

In November 1908 they framed and installed a beautiful picture of "Jesus Christ in His Yoga Posture" in the auditorium of the Hindu Temple:

> Dressed in a flowing white robe, his long hair pulled back behind slight shoulders, this holy man sits, half-lotus style, eyes cast down, in meditation. A halo rings his head, and his body is framed, St. Francis-like, by wild animals.

Jesus is in the wilderness,* surrounded by a rabbit, two doves, a tiger and a snake. Originally, Trigunatita found a photograph believed to be of Jesus when he visited a Tibetan monastery in 1895. According to the *New York Times* of December 13, 1895 (p. 4), "He has seen pictures of Christ in the monasteries, and says that Christ is regarded by the Lamas as an Indian god." Trigunatita brought the photograph from Tibet to the United States. He expressed the idea of a painting of Jesus to Mrs. Eugene Theodosia P. Oliver (1845-1932) who agreed. Her painting "Jesus Christ in His Yoga Posture" now adorns the north wall of the Temple auditorium. In her diary, on June 26, 1908 she writes, "I went to see Swami Trigunatita about the picture and showed him the sketch I had made. He approved it, suggesting some slight alterations." Born in England of parents both of whom were born in Ireland, she was a Catholic woman, who often came to see Trigunatita while remaining a devout Christian. Trigunatita bought the copyright and they sold prints of Oliver's painting at the Hindu temple.[42] On Christmas day he would hold a fifteen-hour service, all of the time standing and speaking of Jesus. Some devotees would remain in their seats, fasting, listening, and meditating during those fifteen hours. He often lectured and gave classes on such Christian subjects as the *Bible* and *The Imitation of Christ*.[43]

That the original picture is of Jesus is quite possible, since the Tibetans had many contacts with the Christians before the time of Nicholas Notovitch (b. 1858). To give one example, Kublai Khan (1216-94) established

* For forty days according to Mark I:13.

a network of monasteries with the Buddhist Pope residing in Tibet. The network extended to Mongolia, Russia, and as far west as Latvia, Estonia, and Lithuania (and possibly Poland). Buddhism continued on in these areas into the twentieth century, producing genuine holy men like the Most Venerable Karlis A. M. Tennisons (1873-1962), the Buddhist Sangharaja (Archbishop) of Latvia, Estonia, and Lithuania. Born into a Latvian family that professed Buddhism for many generations, for many years the monk Tennisons moved about by dogsled, preaching Buddhism north of the Arctic Circle to reindeer-breeders and herdsmen. Later he won three medals as a battlefield Buddhist chaplain in the Russian army during World War I.[44]

Swami Trigunatita came out with a new magazine, the monthly *Voice of Freedom* (April 1909-March 1916), for the many devotees who could not attend his lectures. This magazine held to high standards and ideals of truth. His goal was to harmoniously blend the thought of the East and West in the magazine. Before this, Trigunatita had established the biweekly *Udbodhan* periodical in 1899, acting as its editor and manager for four years. In 1909 the *Vedanta Monthly Bulletin* from the New York Centre ceased publication, so this was the only Western Vedanta publication in circulation at that time. The prospectus of the first edition read:

> This periodical is called *Voice of Freedom* because when Freedom is realized, its *voice* and power reign supreme everywhere, whether in heaven or on earth, or beyond; in every age, whether within the span of history, or before or after. The idea of freedom.[45]

In 1909 Trigunatita spoke to the Golden Gate branch of the Theosophical Society on universal religion, and before the Fellowship Society in San Francisco he discussed the future of India; in 1910, to the Socialist Party of San Francisco he spoke on "Every Man and Woman is a Born Socialist", and at the Town Hall in Livermore his subject was "Hindu Manners and Customs". In April he also took part in a nationwide religious crusade through lecturing to combat tuberculosis. The following year in 1911 he gave a lecture on "Jesus Christ from the Hindu Standpoint" at the Bethany Congregationalist Church, and also on four other occasions in Long Beach, California. Other outside engagements included addressing the audience at the Mesa Redondo Club on "Hindu and American Women", and at the Laurel Hall Club on an unknown date speaking about Hindu life and religion. In addition, he prepared an article advocating that Americans use inexpensive labour from India.[46]

At the end of his two-year tour (1910-12) through the United States, Indian born Pir Hazrat Inayat Khan (1882-1927), the founder of the Sufi Order in the West, came to San Francisco. He wrote:

> [This marked the beginning of] the work of my Message. It is here that I found my first *mureed* [student] Mrs. Ada Martin. I was welcomed by Swami Trigunatita and his collaborator Swami Paramananda, who requested me to speak on Indian music to their friends at the Hindu temple, and was presented with a gold medal and an address. I saw among the audience a soul who was drinking in all I said.

She "was immensely impressed by the Message". Khan stated, "[Two days later I met] Mrs. Ada Martin, the first *mureed*, on my arrival to the West; knowing that this soul will spread light and illumination to all those who will come in contact with her, I initiated her and named her Rabia."

Khan added, "Since her initiation she has entirely devoted her life to spiritual contemplation and the service of humanity." After his passing away, Murshid Ada Martin became the leader of his Sufi Order in the United States. They taught religious pluralism, meditation, to treat others with dignity, and to hear the sound of the divine in the world around them.[47]

Through special arrangement with Mahendranath Gupta (1854-1932), the recorder of the *Gospel of Sri Ramakrishna*, Trigunatita brought out a reprint of the two volume Madras edition in 1912.[48] A very favourable review of the book given in Chapter III appeared in the Home of Truth periodical *Master Mind Magazine* edited by Annie Rix Militz.

After being in charge of the Vedanta Headquarters and Home in Los Angeles for five years from January 1905 until January 1910, Sachchidananda II was asked by the Belur Math to return to India. He continued to advertise in the *Los Angeles Times* (up to February 1912) as a religious teacher living at the Vedanta Home. His Vedanta organization operated independently of the Vedanta Society formed by Trigunatita. Sachchidananda II returned to India in 1913 according to Wendell Thomas, and then separated himself from the Ramakrishna Order.[49]

On January 12, 1911, Trigunatita left San Francisco to make his third visit to the Southern California. He spoke on subjects such as "Self Reliance" at the Blanchard Music Hall in downtown Los Angeles where Vivekananda had formerly lectured. For over one month, he intensively reorganized the Vedanta Society in Los Angeles. It was to be run by eleven handpicked Mothers and Fathers of the church like Minnie Boock (Saravamsaha), Fredericka Greenstidel, Alice Hansbrough (Shanti), Gertrude Topham, and Carrie Wyckoff (Lalita). Trigunatita drew up a set of seventy-five "Rules and Regulations Governing Vedanta Centres". The Mothers and Fathers were to first practise these rules (which were moral principles) in their own lives before teaching them to others. For example, one of the rules was, "Do all religious works as WORKS OF LOVE, just for the sake of God and Truth." Another read, "If you wish to find fault with anyone, it would be better if you do so with yourself." Weekly classes would be held at each local Vedanta Centre to get more people interested in the teachings. Trigunatita sent spiritual lessons to Gertrude Topham in Los Angeles, most often on a monthly basis from January 15, 1909, until April 15, 1911. They reveal his method of guidance and training. His spiritual exercises required meditation, japa, scriptural study, and a great deal of self-analysis in order to overcome one's personal shortcomings. On February 19 the Swami went back to San Francisco. After Trigunatita left the city, the Mothers and Fathers met on a monthly basis at one of their homes reading, meditating, singing, praying and debating on religious topics.[50]

Later in the year from August 6 until the 22nd, Trigunatita returned to Southern California to see how the Mothers and Fathers were faring. He was accompanied by Bertha Petersen, Edith Allan and Mrs. Jewel. Though the organization eventually died out, in later years some of its Mothers like Gertrude Topham, Mrs. Wilhelm, Alice Hansbrough, and Carrie Wyckoff were responsible for bringing Prabhavananda to Los Angeles and offering him subsequent support. When Paramananda and Abhedananda visited Los Angeles, they also received valuable assistance from some of these Mothers and Fathers.[51]

At that time, Dr. M. Alexander Schutz, president of the twenty-two-day World's Spiritual Congress, sent an invitation to Trigunatita to deliver four addresses on Hinduism in Long Beach, California, during the week of August 9-16, 1911. The Swami's picture appeared in the programme, was listed first among the many speakers, and was referred to as, "One of the greatest exponents of the Hindoo Philosophy and Religion in the Western World." His last three lecture titles were: "Wonderful Discovery of the Great Mine of Wealth", "Great Mystery of the Universe Unveiled", and "The Attitude of Vedanta Towards all Religions".[52] His opening presentation was covered by the *Long Beach Daily Telegram* of August 10, reporting (in this culled out version):

> A large and appreciative audience greeted Swami Trigunatita at his first lecture at the World's Spiritual Congress. The announcement that a representative member of the Hindu race, Swami Trigunatita, the great sage and philosopher, would deliver his first lecture on "The Essential Doctrines of Hinduism", brought out a large audience, which expected to hear something of unusual interest, as the fame of the Swami had preceded him there, but no one realized that the lecture would be of such an intense and instructive nature, and at the close of it he was cheered continuously for several minutes until he was forced to come forward and deliver another brief address.[53]

During the course of his talk on "The Essential Doctrines of Hinduism", Trigunatita made the following statement:

> It [Hinduism] is a religion; but not a religion to be practised only at stated times, and only in the church or mosque or in the temple. It is a religion to be practised in all of our actions and thoughts, nay at every breath, in our own everyday life. It says that no religion is a religion, if it cannot be literally applied in practical life; and no life is a life, if it be not religious; and no life is religious, unless it bears usefulness to others.... The seer of the Truth will be full of peace and bliss; always well contented, and wishing all well. Such a person neither disturbs anyone in any shape or form, nor is disturbed in the least by anything. That person sees nothing else but the Truth and Truth alone all around, and is always merged in the Everlasting Ecstasy.... This great Energy being divine and economical in its nature, will never stop until it can make itself really immortal by entering into the Absolute, no matter how many births and deaths it may have to pass through. It is God-made Law. None can stop it. None can resist it. If it does not succeed in one life, through one body, it must cast off the worn out body and enter into a new one.[54]

The heroic William Hopkinson (1878-1914) was employed by the Vancouver (Canada) Immigration Department. In addition, he worked for the Calcutta police as an undercover agent disguised as a poor immigrant Sikh, who infiltrated and monitored East Indian political activities in British

Columbia. In 1911 Hopkinson established good relations with Trigunatita when he came to Northern California to investigate the Bengali revolutionary Taraknath Das (1884-1958), who later became a professor of political science at Columbia University and other American Universities.[55]

1912 and After

Many of the leading citizens of San Francisco and the surrounding cities attended the Swami's lectures and at times came to him for counsel. For example, James G. Rolph (1869-1934), the mayor of the city, became a personal friend who, after many years in 1927, remembered him "with great pleasure and interest". "Sunny Jim" Rolph, a tolerant, friendly, honest, cheerful man of innate kindliness and goodwill, was the popular long-term mayor of San Francisco from 1911 until 1930. During his incumbency, they expanded the civic centre, school construction, park development, and created a municipal street railway. In 1930 Rolph became the Republican governor of the state of California. Due to the worldwide depression, he had to face many serious problems of poverty relief, unemployment, and declining state revenues.[56]

In a six-column article on the Vedanta Society in the *San Francisco Chronicle* of July 19, 1914 titled "Where Holy Swamis Teach Serenity to Women of Smart Set", the correspondent presented a "sketch of the philosophies preached by the Swami" and had the insight to discern:

> Whether or not the neophyte believes that unalterable happiness can be assured by practising the teachings of the Swami, she cannot deny that the dusky priest himself appears to have attained an insouance [insouciance] that is benign. He is a living and very material evidence of good faith. He is a swarthy, squat person, with the head of an escetic [ascetic?] sage, and he speaks of the Hindoo Temple and of the gospel he preaches, with a conviction that radiates the faith within him. He lives his mission. He never loses his equanimity nor forgets his high state of serenity.... Swami Vivekananda has since died. He was considered among the most learned of the Hindoo yogis, and his books and sayings are quoted by his disciples here with deep reverence.... The briefest of talks with him, however, will help one to understand why men like Schopenhauer, Max Müller, Victor Cousins and Frederick Schlegel took such profound interest in the Vedanta.

During his later years, between November 17 and December 26, 1914 Trigunatita revealed to his prize student, Mrs. Bertha Petersen (Dhira or Dhirananda):

> I am, if you will believe me, literally speaking, just an assistant and a servant, not a boss or tyrant, nor a self-deluded person, but guided by God just as He guides me to serve His children, just as He wants me to do, sacrificing my own peace, comfort, pleasure, reputation and welfare.
>
> I would rather like to enter into a cave and practise further and higher yoga, which I know positively that I can do without any trouble. I have been sacrificing all that personal welfare just to serve like a slave His children, just as He wants me to do. I would not do my will, even if I have the power to do so. I follow Him and His will, as far as I can understand.
>
> People have not the power, nor can they be expected to have any now, to see into my life, into my heart, into my soul. They simply look into my angry eyes, and pay attention to my angry and hot words and harsh and unkind treatment. They think that I am unjust, worldly and sensual. It will take some people twenty years of the hardest practice in order to understand practically that it is for their own benefit, my best, noblest, kindest, highest and most unselfish motive to them.[57]

Trigunatita told a disciple in 1914:

> The thought would come that the Mother's work must go on, and I set my will to force the body to carry on. The body has become a mere shell and may go to pieces at any time. For three years now I have held the body together by sheer force of will.

In the Spring of 1914, a student told the Swami that his voice quivered during his lectures in San Francisco. In December, a month before his release from the physical body, he replied:

> I have tried my utmost to control it so that it would not be noticeable to the audience, but always now, just as I go onto the platform, my Divine Mother appears to me and fills me full of such feelings of love that it is sometimes difficult for me to articulate. When by great effort I bring the voice under control, the quiver remains, as the result of the effort to control,

together with the impossibility of entirely controlling these feelings, as they are growing stronger.[58]

Among other things, he had Bright's disease of the kidney, a faulty valve in his heart and chronic rheumatism. Two days after Christmas, on the Sunday afternoon of December 27, 1914, Trigunatita was giving an address on "The Divine Peace" at the Vedanta Society in San Francisco. An ex-member walked up the centre aisle to the rostrum. Striking the rostrum three times with a package, he set off a bomb that killed himself and severely injured the Swami. Soon after the event, the Swami said, "I do not harbour any ill-will against the man."[59] At the hospital, a nurse reported, "I have never seen such a calm, uncomplaining, and enduring patient in my life." As a result of the bombing on the afternoon of January 9, 1915, Trigunatita told a young disciple that he would leave the body the next day. At the University of California Hospital, he entered mahasamadhi on January 10, the birthday of Vivekananda according to the Indian lunar calendar. Many people in San Francisco, including Catholic, Protestant and Jewish leaders, came to pay their last respects. A year later Swami Prakashananda buried his ashes on the Hill of Realization, the highest point of the Shanti Ashrama, "beneath the northern point of the largest earthen triangle on which the sacred Dhuni ceremony had often been held."[60]

Referring to the apostles of Sri Ramakrishna, at Belur Math Swamiji said in 1902:

> Know each of those who are here to be of great spiritual power; because they remain shrivelled before me, do not think them to be ordinary souls. When they will go out, they will be the cause of the awakening of spirituality in people. Know them to be part of the spiritual body of Sri Ramakrishna, who was the embodiment of infinite religious ideas.[61]

The highly disciplined training programme of Turiyananda and Trigunatita produced a number of dedicated lifetime devotees. No Swami in the West expected as much out of his inner circle of disciples as did Trigunatita. A partial list of his notable followers, who were prominent for many years, would include: Gurudasa (Swami Atulananda), Ida Ansell (Ujjvala), Alice Hansbrough (Shanti), Milburn Logan (Sthitadhi), Frank Rhodehamel (Satya-Nishtha), Minnie Boock (Saravamsaha), Sarah (Premika) and Rebecca Fox (Radhika), Clinton (Nishkama) and Cara French (Sarala), Ernest

Brown (Sajjana), Clara Pettee (Durga Devi), Carl (Nirmala) and Bertha Petersen (Dhira or Dhirananda), Albert (Karmavira) and Mrs. C. Wollberg (Prasuti), Thomas and Edith Allan, and others who played an important role in the future growth of the Society. For example, Ernest Brown tells us, "On a number of occasions [Trigunatita] was nursed back to health by Dhirananda [Bertha Petersen]. Her devotion was unbounded—no sacrifice could be too great for a son of Ramakrishna. Later, because of her spiritual attainments and devotion to the cause, she came to be Swami's leading disciple." Trigunatita once wrote to Turiyananda, "For two things I must specially thank you. For having established the Shanti Ashrama and for giving me Dhira." In 1909 Swami Trigunatita performed, "What was said to have been the first Hindu wedding in the Western world." Alexander Petersen, the son of Carl and Bertha (Dhira) Petersen, was married to Miss Mattie Polk in the Hindu Temple at Filbert and Webster Street in San Francisco.[62]

The January 1916 edition of the *Voice of Freedom* reported:

> Notwithstanding the many vicissitudes through which the San Francisco Vedanta Society has lately passed, the Sunday meetings and weekly meditation classes were conducted even in the absence of a Swami by a few earnest and faithful students. Through the indefatigable efforts and unremitting zeal of Mr. and Mrs. Petersen and a few devoted souls, the case which has been pending in the Superior Court of the State of California for about a year has been won in favour of the Temple, and the Court has given the final decree by appointing three trustees—Messrs. C. F. Petersen, H. O. A. Bartl and T. J. Allan. Moreover, the local centres have now been united and consolidated into one big and broad Society under the religious leadership of Swami Prakashananda.

Dhira's husband, Mr. Carl Petersen, who was the president of the Vedanta Society for seven years and who knew Swami Trigunatita intimately, made this verbal testimonial on January 30, 1916, a year after the Swami's passing away:

> Friends, today we commemorate a man with the strongest of character, a man who did not know the meaning of the word "fail"—there was no such word in his dictionary—a man who was truthful to a degree, a man who was not afraid of anything or anybody, whose every act, however it may have appeared to our eyes, was done with a great purpose,—to teach his students.

We who lived with him and knew him best knew his purpose. A man who had the courage of his own convictions and carried them through in spite of any opposition that could be offered. That was Swami Trigunatita. Anyone who was under [the] Swami knew he had a kindly heart, an exceedingly kindly heart, but he treated us all differently, according to our state of development. The one he could treat harshly, and the other he could not. And those students who could not stand his harsh treatment, even they must admit that that great man left an impression upon them which will stay with them through the balance of their lives and possibly in future lives. He knew our true characters better than we knew them ourselves. Is it any wonder that a man with such terrific force as he possessed should make enemies? And why? Because we do not like to be told the truth. All people with positive characters make enemies, because they have the courage to tell the truth and we cannot stand it. One of our members received lessons from Swami which are inspired and will show the true character of the man when they are published. It was his desire that they should be published, and they will be in a short while when the manuscript is ready; and when you read that, you surely will know what a terrific force that man was amongst us and amongst all who came in contact with him. He had energy enough for fifty men and then enough left over for himself. He would work until twelve, one and two o'clock in the morning, and was up again at four, morning after morning, with that poor sick body of his. Never faltered for an instant. Through all his sickness, he never remained in bed. That strong will, that energy that could not be broken by anything! That was Swami Trigunatita. I personally consider it a great privilege that I was allowed to live in the same house with him for twelve years. I am a different man now. That is the truth. And the same can be said of hundreds of other people who came in contact with that terrific force, that strong character. We will never forget that force. That force will remain with us until we pass on like he did. Born the 30th of January, 1865; passed the 10th of January, 1915.[63]

In a 1924 article entitled "With the Swamis in America", which appeared in the *Vedanta Kesari*, Mrs. Edith Allan (Viraja Devi) informed her readers that:

Swami Turiyananda was succeeded by the beloved and energetic Swami Trigunatita. During his ministration, the Temple was built and all the permanent buildings were put up at the Ashrama. The Swami himself led

> a life of the greatest asceticism whether in the Temple or at the Ashrama, allowing himself little sleep and working continually. When at the Ashrama he did all the cooking for 37 people, gave three classes a day on the meditation platform and two *Gita* classes at meal times. His energy was untiring, nothing was too small to demand his attention. He was interested in all the little details and daily occurrences in the lives of his students. He was like a fond mother always looking out for the welfare of her children, training them in various ways as their nature required, now by strict discipline, now gently taking them by the hand and leading them into paths of peace and blessedness.... In the passing away of Swami Trigunatita, those of us who had been blessed by his teaching, by his unending patience, and his ever watchful care for us, felt we had sustained an irretrievable loss, yet we feel his presence with us and the work for which he gave his life is being ably carried on by the much beloved Swami Prakashananda.[64]

In 1928, Ernest C. Brown (Sajjana, 1871-1960/61) [q.v.], an old time devotee writing under the pseudonym of "His Western Disciples", wrote a series of twelve articles for the *Prabuddha Bharata* on "The Work of Swami Trigunatita in the West". In this revealing personal and historical study, he makes the following four evaluations of Trigunatita:

> Swami was a consistent example of regularity and punctuality. Always to bed later than the others, he was yet the first to rise. Needless to say, his life was under continuous scrutiny by some of the young men for purity of mind and any motives of worldliness. There were those who never questioned, but there were some doubters, or unwilling believers, and these were eventually satisfied, for all that they found in his character was the one consuming purpose to give his life for the salvation of others and that all of his understandings were only means to that end.... when Swami became convinced that it was right to do a thing, he acted immediately, regardless of consequences, for by nature he was absolutely fearless.... The life of Swami was one long sacrifice and those who were privileged to be in his presence found their doubts and troubles melt away like snow before the sun. He veritably emanated holiness, for he ever lived in the consciousness of the Divine Mother. His life was also an example of self-discipline. As stated, he was always the first to rise and every moment from rising to retiring was full of ceaseless activity.[65]

Swami Trigunatita firmly believed that America was destined to be a great spiritual land, second only to India.... the mission of the East was to spiritualize the West—that spiritual light had always come from the East in the past and would continue to do so in the future.[66]

In the Swami Trigunatita this spirit of humility welled up in full volume from the very depths of his being. He who was honoured by the great of his time, yet felt that he was inadequate to carry on his Mother's work and like a child he leaned constantly on Her who was at once the source and the inspiration of all his undertakings. To Her he gave full credit for all the success of the work, disclaiming the least merit for himself and accepted Her will as final in everything.[67]

Those who were of his time were too close to grasp the significance of a life in which every thought and act were regulated by the all-inclusive requirements of Sannyasa as laid down in the Hindu Scriptures. Like one of the heroic figures of Vedic history, his figure will loom larger and larger as time rolls on and the perceptions of his followers deepen and widen. Undeviatingly holding aloft the ideal of the realization of the Absolute as the goal of humanity, he lived the One, he taught the One, but he was also a great devotee.

As a character-builder, he knew the force of a living example. What disciple could question the validity of the teaching embodied in the life of asceticism lived daily before him? No demand on his time or energy was ever disregarded—no appeal however trifling was ignored. His mind was a deep well of wisdom unfathomable to the ordinary intellect and every day was a new revelation of the many sidedness of his unique individuality.

Like some high mountain torrent, the never failing waters of which press their course resistlessly to the sea, Swami Trigunatita never rested from his purpose; his energy to accomplish the thing he had set himself to do was tireless and tremendous. "Endure to the end" was the living maxim placed before all disciples. He used to say, "Some will understand the motives behind my actions in five years, some in ten years, some in fifteen, others never."[68]

The saintly Swami Atulananda described Trigunatita as:

Cheerful, loving, strong in carrying out his own ideas, with an abundance of energy, Swami Trigunatita at once set to work to create an atmosphere of his own. He was strongly in favour of organization ... The swami

> was exceedingly active, and this quality, combined with his loving and cheerful nature, drew the admiration of some men and women who became his staunch disciples.[69]
>
> He was a man of austere type. When he first came to San Francisco, once he fasted for three days, maybe to accumulate power to carry on the work. He was a strict disciplinarian. Once on Thakur's birthday he spent fifteen hours in Puja, from the morning at 6:00 a.m. until the evening at 9:00 p.m., and delivered three lectures, all without leaving the platform.... He was a very jolly type of man and very active too. He encouraged others also to follow a tight routine—meditation, study, work, and so on.[70]

For Ida Ansell (Ujjvala), "His lectures too were very different from those of both the other swamis, being very precisely analytical and logical rather than emotionally inspiring. With the member students he was exacting and strict, but also kind and loving."[71]

Swami Ashokananda (1893-1969) [q.v.] took the vow of Sannyasa in 1923 from Swami Shivananda, the second president of the Ramakrishna Order, and in 1932 became the revered and highly successful leader of the Vedanta Society of Northern California. Under his direction the Society expanded to Berkeley and Sacramento. In a 1947 lecture, he informed his listeners that Swami Trigunatita

> could live on a single banana for days and days. It would not make any difference to him. Or if he so wanted he could eat a huge meal without any harm to him. He could sleep a half hour a day, lying down on a bench.... Sometimes he would work with 104-degree of fever in his body. No one would know he had a fever and he would keep right on working for days.... Once on the occasion of the birthday of Christ and the birthday of the Master, Sri Ramakrishna, he came onto the platform at three o'clock in the morning and did not leave until nine-thirty at night. He would not tire. He worked prodigiously. Most of the things accomplished here and existing here today were due to him. He literally gave his life to the establishment of the Vedanta work here.[72]

Dorothy Frederica Mercer (1901-62) [q.v.] had the good fortune of being "born into Vedanta". As a little girl, Trigunatita held her on his lap and deeply impressed her. Once every week her family went to see Trigunatita at the Hindu Temple and, in return, he would occasionally visit them. Concerning the Swami she recounted:

> Swami Trigunatita was an impressive ascetic. He held services continuously for eighteen hours on Ramakrishna's Birthday and Christ's Birthday. He conducted a voluminous correspondence, lectured twice a week to the general public, gave courses in Sanskrit, meditation, and the Upanishads, saw his numerous students privately on an average of once every two weeks, and thereby reduced his sleeping time to an hour or so a night.[73]

Dorothy Mercer, an instructor of English at the City College of San Francisco, wrote her Ph.D. dissertation on Walt Whitman's *Leaves of Grass and the Bhagavad Gita* (1933), which was published on seventeen occasions in *Vedanta and the West* (1946-65) and which appeared in *What Vedanta Means to Me* (1961). Swami Vidyatmananda, a good friend of Dorothy, tells us that she underwent a total transformation when she visited India in 1958-59. After returning, she only spoke about the people and places she had known in India connected with Sri Ramakrishna and his Math and Mission. She often described the love expressed by many of the senior Swamis like Atulananda, whom she had known as a little girl in San Francisco, Madhavananda and Dayananda, who she had been acquainted with when they were in charge of the Vedanta Society of Northern California, Sankarananda, the President of the Ramakrishna Math and Mission, "lovable" Abhayananda, and "dear" Nirvanananda. Near the end of her life she told Prabhavananda:

> "I know I am going to die; and it is all right." She said that she was maintaining, every moment, the recollectedness of Sri Ramakrishna. She said: "I know that Swami Trigunatita is going to come for me." And this is how, six days later, it was.[74]

In 1997, Sister Gargi (Marie Louise Burke, 1912-2004) came out with the much-needed biography *Swami Trigunatita His Life and Work*. While Trigunatita was working in America, many of his religious activities were unknown to the Swamis and devotees in India. A large amount of the detailed biographical information appears in print in this volume for the first time. In amazing detail and with many photographs, Gargi tells the story of this dynamic, selfless and heroic monk who ran the San Francisco Centre with complete commitment, devotion and an indomitable will. Swami Bhaswatananda mentioned:

> Sister Gargi maintains in her latest work the same high standards her earlier six-volume magnum opus reflected with regard to accuracy of information. It is her belief that "devotees have long hankered for such visual reports." In her realistic account, every phase of the life and the work of Swami Trigunatita has been examined faithfully and reverentially but at the same time with intelligence and understanding. The character of Swami Trigunatita is portrayed as one of great sweetness and strength.

Swami Yuktatmananda described this "masterpiece" as a "detailed account of Swami Trigunatita's pioneering work in the West in nurturing the seeds of Vedanta with the Ramakrishna-Vivekananda Movement."[75] After reading the book about Trigunatita, Allen R. Freedman, a devotee and a professor of mathematics at Simon Fraser University in Canada, concluded:

> It is a wonderfully touching, detailed and intimate portrait which is difficult to put down once the reader picks it up. Starting with his birth in an aristocratic family of Bengal, it follows his fascinating life with all its adventures, outstanding accomplishments, trials, and tribulations.[76]

At the birthday celebration for the Master (undated), Trigunatita lectured on "The Life of Sri Ramakrishna". Trigunatita told his audience in part:

> Sri Ramakrishna preached, above all, the unity of religions, one unity of all religions. That idea was not only given by him, but also by the previous prophets, especially by Krishna, but he made it part of his practical life. He passed through every stage of the mind and every stage of the heart, of each and every person. He must be a universal person if he be a prophet. All prophets are universal, can embrace all, can love all, can be loved by all. Such is the characteristic of prophets. He realized the state of mind of every person, and he first learned the spiritual process of one religion, and when he became perfect in that religion, then he commenced the other, and one after another, until he finished all the religions of the world, even Christianity....

Sri Ramakrishna could discover many truths that ordinary persons cannot discern. He could understand the future, which is natural for all highly advanced persons, far from speaking of prophets who directly come down from heaven, and he therefore could prophesize events regarding the future of the world and regarding the future of certain people. He spoke about the future of Swami Vivekananda and of many other people. Whenever a person appeared before him, he could read that person's past, present and future, and not only that, he had many other psychic powers, but he very seldom used them. He said it was not he who worked; it was not he who talked; but God from within talked and worked. He denied his own separate existence and became united with God. He realized the unity between himself and God....

And how in one life is it possible to perform so many practices of so many religions? In several lives we cannot perform all the practices of one religion, which he did in a few years' time. Not only that, he was a prophet, was born with Divine powers, but he came to teach the world by his practical life, and did not make a show of his Divine power. He proved himself mortal and as human as we are. From the human plane he grew, and his practical life will be a lesson to the world. How could he learn all the practices of so many religions? Because he first performed all of the practices of one religion very sincerely and ardently; and by that he showed that only sincerity of life and purpose can give us the Light of Truth.... So, all other religions were quite clear and transparent to Him. Whatever religion he took up, he could finish all the practices of that religion in a very short time, sometimes in three days. Why? Because he knew everything beforehand. It was in some other form, in some other name. All religions lead to the same goal, to the same point. Every religion has some similarity with every other religion. So he had no difficulty in finding the unity of all religions, and he taught that to his disciples....

Many speak of his life, especially his disciples. Every year they speak on his life, but they cannot finish describing his life. The more they study his life, the more truth and strength they get out of it. His life is ever fresh, ever new. The more we speak, we find newer and newer things in his life. Not only that, persons who study his life get some power from that study.[77]

For a selected list of books and articles about Trigunatita in the West, see Appendix VI.

ENDNOTES

1 "The Work of Swami Trigunatita in the West", *PB* (Jan. 1928), p. 29; Gargi, pp. 45-46, 88 identifies Ernest C. Brown as "His Western Disciples"; Chetanananda, p. 487.

2 Nikhilananda, p. 264; Gargi, pp. 61-62.

3 Gargi, p. 68.

4 *San Francisco Chronicle* (Jan. 3, 1903), p. 9; *Atlanta Constitution* (Georgia) (Jan. 4, 1903), p. 2 on PQHN.

5 *San Francisco Call* (Jan. 25, 1903); (Feb. 1, 1903); (Feb. 14, 1903) on CAM.

6 *PB* (Feb. 1928), pp. 78-79; Chetanananda, pp. 487, 503-04; Gargi, pp. 65, 68, 71, 93; Burke, VI, p. 298.

7 Gargi, p. 96.

8 *Brahmavadin* (Jan. 1904), pp. 43, 48-49.

9 Gargi, pp. 99-107; Stavig2, ch. 1; "Notes of Gertrude Topham", VSSC Archives. According to the *Los Angeles City Directory* (1902-03, 1905) in 1902, a widowed lady named Mrs. Kate A. Kelly resided at 1027 Maple Avenue, and she was probably there in 1903. In 1905 she spent part of the year at 1839 Gramercy Place.

10 Gargi, pp. 104-05.

11 Gargi, pp. 103-105, 115; *Los Angeles Times* (May 4, 1903), p. 5; (June 28, 1903), p. A2; (July 12, 1903), p. A2 on PQHN; "A Card from Swami Trigunatita to Lalita" (July 23, 1903), VSSC Archives; "Notes of Gertrude Topham", VSSC Archives; "Letter from Tom (Allan?) to Ida Ansell" (Oct. 10, 1932), VSSC Archives.

12 *Brahmavadin* (Nov. 1903), pp. 681-82.

13 *Mission* (Vedananda), p. 346; Gargi, pp. 120-22; Chetanananda, p. 508; *Oakland Tribune* (May 31, 1912), p. 9.

14 Gargi, pp. 160, 169, 172; *Los Angeles Times* (April 3, 1904), p. C1; (April 23, 1904), p. A7; (May 29, 1904), p. C1; (May 9, 1913), p. II6; "Notes of Gertrude Topham", VSSC Archives; Stavig2, ch. 1.

15 Gargi, p. 159.

16 Gargi, p. 160.

17 *CW*, IV:438-80.

18 Ibid., IV:430-37.

19 Ibid., IV:423-29.

20 "Notes of Gertrude Topham", VSSC Archives; Gargi, p. 107; Stavig2, ch. 1; *Los Angeles Herald* (Jan. 14, 1905), p. 7; *Los Angeles Times* (Jan. 29, 1905), p. IV1; (Aug. 12, 1906), p. IV1; (Sept. 1, 1907), p. IV1; (Feb. 5, 1911), p. IV1; (Jan. 21, 1912), p. IV1.

21 *VMB* (June 1905), p. 45; Atulananda, p. 87.

22 *PB* (March 1928), p. 132; Gargi, pp. 171-72; Erik Davis, *The Visionary State* (Chronicle Books, 2006), p. 83 on GBS

23 Web: www.outsidelands.org/leonard.php; Web: http:// www.sfgate.com/cgi-bin/article.cgi?file=/chronicle/archive/2004/04/10/ hogva61ghp1.dtl; *San Francisco Chronicle* (April 10, 2004); Madhavaprana, p. 25.

24 *Public Opinion* (Feb. 10, 1906), p. 185 on GBS; *PB* (March 1928), pp. 132-33; Gargi, pp. 171, 175; Some references say the Cornerstone was laid on August 21, others on the 25th.

25 *Public Opinion* (Feb. 10, 1906), pp. 184-85 on GBS; *Kansas City Star* (Jan. 20, 1906), p. 5; *Washington (D.C.) Bee* (Feb. 3, 1906); *Adair County News* (Columbia, Kentucky) (Mar. 7, 1906), p. 8 on CAM.

26 *PB* (Nov. 1906), pp. 215-16.

27 Madhavaprana, pp. 29-30; *VK* (Sept. 1924), p. 174.

28 *PB* (April 1928), p. 165; Gargi, pp. 186-91; *Brahmavadin* (Nov. 1906), p. 702.

29 E. C. Brown, *PB* (Oct. 1907), p. 194; *Brahmavadin* (Sept. 1907), p. 496; *University of California Chronicle* (1907), pp. 270-71.

30 *PB* (Oct. 1907), p. 194; *Brahmavadin* (Sept. 1907), pp. 495-96.

31 *San Francisco Call* (Mar. 31, 1907), p. 34; *Brahmavadin* (Sept. 1907), pp. 495-98; *PB* (Oct. 1907), p. 194; *Overland Monthly and Out West Magazine* (June 1907).

32 *WWWA*, I, p. 1071; *PB* (Oct. 1920), pp. 237-38; Centenary, I, p. 10; Arthur Ryder, *The Bhagavad Gita* (Chicago: University of Chicago, 1929), pp. vii, 54.

33 Londhe, #25. J. Robert Oppenheimer; Web: indianajones.wikia.com/wiki/Robert_Oppenheimer.

34 Madhavaprana, p. 4.

35 Gargi, pp. 147, 192, 383; *San Francisco Call* (Mar. 27, 1905), p. 12; (May 20, 1906) p. 24; (July 29, 1906), p. 44; *PB* (Feb-Mar. 1907), p. 48; *Oakland Tribune* (Nov. 25, 1907), p. 11; *Journal of American Folklore* (Apr.-Sept. 1908), p. 249; *World of Sociology* (Detroit: Gale Group, 2001); *EWB*. Some of these speeches are discussed in other sections of this chapter.

36 "Email correspondence with Professor Gerald Carney" (June 9, 2005); *Light of India* (Jan. 1908), p. 22.

37 *PB* (March 1928), p. 133.

38 *PB* (April 1928), p. 161.

39 *New-York Tribune* (Feb. 20, 1910), p. 3.

40 *San Francisco Chronicle* (July 19, 1914), p. 8.

41 *PB* (April 1928), pp. 161-65; (May 1928), p. 227; Gargi, pp. 211, 222; *Disciples*, pp. 238-39, 242-43; Chetanananda, pp. 505-07; Jackson, p. 60.

42 Gargi, pp. 40-41, 206-07; VNN Vaishnava News. Web: www.vnn.org/usa/US0312/US22-8488.html; Ancestry.com. Web: search.ancestry.com/cgi-bin/sse.dll?gl=allgs&gsfn=Thedosia&gsln= Oliver&gss=seo&ghc=20.

43 Madhavaprana, pp. 12-13.

44 William Peiris, *The Western Contribution to Buddhism* (Delhi: Motilal Banarsidass, 1973), pp. 230-33.

45 Chetanananda, pp. 501-02, 507-08; *PB* (May 1928), p. 226.

46 Gargi, pp. 147, 192, 383; *San Francisco Call* (April 24, 1910), p. 52; (Aug. 17, 1910), p. 4 on CAM.

47 Edward Curtis, *The Columbia Sourcebook of Muslims in the United States* (New York: Columbia University, 2008), pp. 47-51 on GBS; *RLOA*.

48 *PB* (May 1928), p. 226.

49 Gargi, p. 107; Levinsky, p. 201; Thomas, pp. 103-04; *Los Angeles Times* (Jan. 29, 1905), p. IV1; (Feb. 5, 1911); (Feb. 4, 1912), p. IV1.

50 Gargi, pp. 107-08, 111, 113-14; *Los Angeles Times* (Feb. 5, 1911), p. IV1; (Feb. 12, 1911), p. II2; Stavig2, ch. 1; Pravrajika Brahmaprana, "Unpublished Correspondence of Swami Trigunatita", *VK* (Jan. 1993), pp. 23-26; (Feb. 1993), pp. 75-77; (March 1993), pp. 93-95; (April 1993), pp. 132-36.

51 Gargi, p. 114.

52 "Official Programme of the World's Spiritual Congress" (Aug. 1911), VSSC Archives; *Los Angeles Times* (Aug. 6, 1911), p. I10.

53 *PB* (Oct. 1911), p. 200; (Nov. 1911), p. 219; *Voice of Freedom* (Sept. 1911), p. 120; "Official Programme of the World's Spiritual Congress" (Aug. 1911), VSSC Archives.

54 Swami Trigunatita, *The Essential Doctrines of Hinduism* (San Francisco: Vedanta Society, 1911), pp. 2-3, 12-13, 15.

55 Richard Popplewell, *Intelligence and Imperial Defense* (London: Frank Cass, 1995), pp. 150-54; Web: www.canadafirst.net/our_heritage/ hopkinson/index.htm.

56 *PB* (Sept. 1928), p. 412; *DAB* (1958), Sup. I, pp. 638-39.

57 Gargi, pp. 242, 245; *VK* (July 1998), p. 279.

58 *PB* (Nov. 1928), pp. 525-26.

59 San Jose *Evening News* (Dec. 28, 1914), p. 1; *PB* (Nov. 1928), p. 525.

60 *PB* (Dec. 1928), pp. 565, 567; Chetanananda, pp. 510-12; Madhavaprana (2008), p. 19; *VK* (Sept. 1924), pp. 174-75; *San Francisco Chronicle* (Jan. 11, 1915), p. 4.

61 *CW*, VII:258.

62 Gargi, p. xi; *PB* (Aug. 1928), p. 359; *PB* (Feb-March 1917), p. 44; *San Francisco Chronicle* (Aug. 30, 1909), p. 5. See Gargi, pp. 224-25 for an example of the high

standards that Swami Trigunatita expected from the people who managed the Centre.

63 *Voice of Freedom* (Feb. 1916), pp. 215-17 on GBS.

64 *VK* (Sept. 1924), pp. 173-75; Madhavaprana, pp. 17-18.

65 *PB* (April 1928), pp. 163-64.

66 *PB* (Aug. 1928), p. 356.

67 *PB* (Sept. 1928), p. 411.

68 *PB* (Dec. 1928), p. 568.

69 Atulananda, p. 87.

70 Swami Atulananda, *Atman alone Abides* (Madras: Ramakrishna Math, 1978), pp. 170-71; Chetanananda, p. 506.

71 Atulananda, p. 180.

72 "A Lecture Given by Swami Ashokananda" (Jan. 26, 1947), VSSC Archives.

73 Mercer, p. 42.

74 Vidyatmananda12-3; Yale, pp. 82-90; Tathagatananda, pp. 197-98.

75 *PB* (Jan. 1998), p. 173; *VK* (July 1998), p. 279.

76 *Global Vedanta* (Winter 1997-98), p. 13.

77 Swami Trigunatita, "Birthday Celebration for Sri Ramakrishna", VSSC Archives.

CHAPTER XXI

SWAMI SHIVANANDA, HIS BROTHER SWAMIS, AND OTHERS

OVER THE YEARS, Swami Shivananda (1854-1934) had occasional associations with Western devotees. For example, as mentioned earlier in Chapter V, after meeting Edward T. Sturdy in Almora in the Himalayas in 1893, prior to Sturdy's association with Vivekananda, Shivananda held discussions with him on religious topics.[1] After leaving the West in 1897, Vivekananda greeted Shivananda and a brother disciple in South India. An 1897 group photograph at Gopal Lal Seal's house in Calcutta shows Shivananda and some other Swamis, along with Colston Turnbull, an American admirer of Vivekananda, and T. G. Harrison, an English Buddhist. At Swamiji's request, Shivananda travelled to Ceylon, where he remained for seven or eight months establishing the Vivekananda Society of Colombo. There Shivananda conducted classes on the *Bhagavad Gita* and *Raja Yoga* before educated Hindus and Europeans. For three months he trained Mrs. Elsie Picket, a Theosophist whom he named Haripriya, to lecture on religion. Earlier, in January 1897, she met Swami Vivekananda who

> promised to lecture the following evening (Saturday, the 16th), and on the following Monday. I was fortunate enough to hear him, as he lectured in English, though especially to his own fellow countrymen. He kindly made an appointment with me for the following morning, when I had one of the momentous conversations of my long and varied life. The Swami told me also that a brother Sannyasin [Shivananda] would come to Colombo for imparting certain yoga instructions.[2]

She delivered a lecture on "The Comparative Study of Religions", pointing out "that religions so far from uniting men, were almost fruitful elements of discord." In March 1898 she wrote to the *Brahmavadin*:

> The Swami Shivananda sent me forth with his authority to prepare the way for some teachers of the Vedanta that may feel induced to visit Australia and New Zealand. In obedience to his desire, I remained in Adelaide for some weeks and met earnest students evening after evening in the drawing-room of Miss Crooks, who spared no pains to make everyone who came, most welcome. Miss Crooks herself, and several others, became ardent students of Vedanta; arranged to subscribe to the *Brahmavadin* through their bookseller and to send for several of the Swami Vivekananda's works.[3]

She also met earnest students of Vedanta in Victoria, Sydney, Hobart in Tasmania, and Nelson in New Zealand. Haripriya conducted classes with the aid of the *Brahmavadin* and books by Vivekananda.[4]

About Shivananda, Haripriya wrote to the *Brahmavadin*:

> The Swami is eminently a Teacher, for his power of grasping an even obscurely expressed question or difficulty is such that he embodies in his replies a vast body of teaching covering the whole ground of the inquiry. You get hold of the whole principle which answers not only a particular question but all difficulties related to its nature are met ... This is all due to Swami Sivananda's most telling teaching power and unselfish and patient painstaking, and our prayers will ever call down on him a rich reward for what we all, who have come into this circle of influence, have obtained. So you see, Mr. Editor, that there is a vast work done by him, ...that his fellow-workers ought to know of, and that there are European students hungering and ready for the treasures of the East.[5]

In 1910 Shivananda spoke with Lady Minto, the wife of the Earl of Minto (1845-1914), the viceroy and governor-general of India (1905-10). The Earl had to deal with a rising tide of Indian nationalism, which he did by maintaining law and order and laying the foundations of the gradual extension of self-government in India. When Shivananda guided her around the Belur Math, his hospitality, intelligence and spiritual character made a strong impression on her. Shivananda tells us:

> Lady Minto had the idea that it was Swamiji (Vivekananda) who founded the Order. In the course of conversation, I explained to her that it was not Swamiji or any other disciple who was responsible for it; it was Sri Ramakrishna himself who initiated the Order during his last illness at

> Cossipore. At that time the Master took Swamiji aside and taught him how to organize and conduct the work, telling him the secrets of the monastic organization to be. That was the foundation of the Math. Lady Minto seemed to be much surprised at learning this from me.[6]

On March 2, 1910, the day before Lady Minto came to Belur Math, she and two others paid a visit to Sister Nivedita and her school. Lady Minto wrote that Nivedita "has a charming face, with a very intelligent expression, and we made friends." A few days later, at Nivedita's request, Lady Minto accompanied her to the Dakshineswar Temple, where Sri Ramakrishna had lived for many years. She toured the grounds and was taken to the Master's bedroom. The following year after Nivedita's passing away, Lady Minto wrote a letter of consolation to Christine, saying in part, "Sister Nivedita had a wonderful personality, and I look back to the few meetings I had with her with pleasure, and with real admiration for her enthusiasm and single-minded desire to assist others. The world is the poorer for her loss."[7] In 1912 Swami Shivananda met Betty Leggett, Alberta Sturges, and George Montagu (the future Earl of Sandwich) during their visit to India.

Most important, Shivananda, as President of the Ramakrishna Order (1922-34), revitalized the foreign mission by dispatching ten high-powered and well-trained Swamis to the United States. Vividishananda relates that Shivananda "always took keen interest in the activities of the Order abroad.... His joy knew no bounds if he chanced to hear about the expansion of the movement.... The Swami used to write to them, cheering and praying for them." With the backing of Saradananda, he provided a strong basis of support for the American operation by sending Swamis Raghavananda, Prabhavananda, Dayananda, Akhilananda, Madhavananda, Gnaneswarananda, Vividishananda, Devatmananda, Ashokananda, and Nikhilananda to the West. Many were disciples of Brahmananda, as was Vijayananda, who was sent to establish a Centre in Buenos Aires, Argentina. Before Nikhilananda came to the U.S. in 1931 to be Akhilananda's assistant, Shivananda slapped him on the back and encouraged him by making the statement, "Wherever you go, you will be victorious!" That same year, when Bodhananda initiated the monthly publication *Vedanta Darpana*, Shivananda sent a blessing that begins with, "I hail with joy the project of the Vedanta Society of New York of starting a magazine for the coming year. We are living in an age of growing unity and harmony."[8] Five of these Swamis each remained in the U.S. for thirty-six or more years. They came to a foreign land, some having been monastics for less than ten years. All the Swamis, except for Raghavananda, who managed the Philadelphia Satellite Centre while assisting in New York, took charge of a Vedanta Society in America within three years. In 1922 there were three Vedanta Centres in the U.S. located in New York, Boston and San Francisco. During the following period of intense growth, these powerful and charismatic leaders founded permanent new Centres in Portland, Oregon (1925), Providence, Rhode Island (1928), Hollywood, California (1929), Chicago, Illinois (1930), New York, New York Eastside (1933), Seattle, Washington (1938), Berkeley, California (1939), Boston, Massachusetts (1941), Santa Barbara, California (1947), Trabuco Canyon, California (1949), Sacramento, California (1949), Honolulu, Hawaii (1954), Vancouver, B.C. (1978), and other retreat locations.[9]

In Romain Rolland's 1927 biography of Sri Ramakrishna, he wrote in the Author's Preface:

> In writing these two books [on Sri Ramakrishna and Swami Vivekananda], I have had constant recourse to the advice of the Ramakrishna Mission, which has been kind enough to place all the requisite documents at my disposal. In particular I owe a great deal to the present venerable head of the Belur Math and Superior of the Order, Swami Shivananda, who has been good enough to give me his precious personal memories of the Master.

Rolland added:

> The present Abbot of the Order, Swami Shivananda, wrote to me: "Ramakrishna had the power to raise others to the greatest heights of consciousness by transmitting to them the energy of his own spirituality. He did it either by the power of his thought or by his touch. Many of us had the privilege of being taken to higher planes of spiritual consciousness according to our capacity. It was neither hypnotism, nor a condition of deep sleep. I myself had the privilege of attaining this high spiritual consciousness three times through his touch and by his will, I still live to bear direct witness to his tremendous spiritual power."[10]

In India, Shivananda also inspired other young monastics like Swami Prabhavananda who later came to America. At a memorial service for Shivananda held in 1934, Prabhavananda revealed:

I lived with him for quite a long time, because he used to be always with my Master, Swami Brahmananda, and Swami Turiyananda. These three Swamis lived together. So I had the opportunity, while living with my Master, to live with these two great souls. Every day Swami Shivananda would go into the shrine and meditate. There was such intense peace and joy and something my language fails to express, something emanating from his mind that would charge the whole atmosphere, that would charm all who came, such beauty, such divine peace. We would go and bow down and prostrate at his feet. To think of such great lives is of itself meditation.[11]

When Josephine MacLeod passed away in Los Angeles in 1949, she left a typed copy of the following letter, which is now the property of the Vedanta Archives of Southern California. This informative autobiographical letter tells of Shivananda's relationship with Sri Ramakrishna. Two women mentioned in the letter, Annapurna (Mrs. Anna Worcester) and Bhakti (Helen Rubel), supplied Swami Akhilananda with the necessary funds to start a new Centre in Providence, Rhode Island, in 1928.[12]

Ramakrishna Math
P.O. Belur Math
February 17, 1932
Dt. Howrah, India

My dear Annapurna (Mrs. Anna Worcester)

I am very glad to receive your letter of January 5, 1932. I have received the draft for Rupees Eight-hundred enclosed therein and the money will be spent as you like it. I received the photographs in time. They were all very beautiful and we all liked them very much. Through the grace of the Lord your work is going on all right and Swami Akhilananda is also lecturing in Washington, D.C. May the Lord bless him.

Yes, I am writing a short note regarding my personal life as I promised previously. I am keeping indifferent health so I may not tell you everything as I desire to. However, I shall try to narrate the central theme of my life, past and present.

I was born in a middle class Brahmin family of Bengal in a village. My father was a lawyer and a devout worshipper of the Divine Mother. He used to earn much. But he was most charitably disposed for which he was well known in the locality. He would spend all his earnings month after month without husbanding anything for the future, to help scores of poor neighbours with money, food and clothing. He believed in education; so more than thirty students lived in our house, my father bearing all their expenses, viz. school-fees, food and other incidental charges. So when my father died, the family became poor. My mother, whom I lost at an early age, was a very pious, hard-working and motherly lady. She alone would do all the work of the family, cooking, feeding, nursing and all. If any help were offered, she would reply—"Am I not the mother?" I feel myself even now fortunate that I got such parents.

From my early boyhood I had a deep longing to know God and to realise Him. That intensity grew with my age. Urged by it I would go to the Brahma Samaj and visit religious men who I thought would be able to throw light on the subject. I would also practise what they advised me. Family life had no charm for me even from my childhood. I had to give up my studies early on the death of my father due to straitened condition of the family. Myself being the only male child with two sisters, one of them still living, I had to come to Calcutta to seek a job, which I secured at a mercantile firm, Messrs. Mackinon Mackenzie & Co. But this made my heart very heavy and I would often weep in my prayers to God to free me forever from all these ties. Here, where I served for nearly two years, I heard the name of Sri Ramakrishna and came in contact with Him. The first interview took place in the house of the late Dr. Ramchandra Datta, one of the most intimate devotees of the Master. Thakur [Sri Ramakrishna] had been invited to his house that evening. It was a nice gathering. The place had been surcharged with spirituality. I was struck to find that the conversation turned on Samadhi that evening, just the thing I wanted to know. I was perfectly satisfied with what I saw and heard there. A few days after this I left for Dakshineswar Kali Temple, about eight miles north of Calcutta. I reached the place when it was almost dark. Being new to the place, it took me a few minutes to find His room. In the dim oil light, I saw Him seated cross-legged calmly on the wood cot with three or four others sitting silently on the floor in front of Him. As I approached, He asked me who I was. I told him my name and the place of my birth. On this He mentioned my father's name and asked me if I were his son. I replied in the affirmative. Then He watched me a little and asked me to come again, next morning. That was because I had told him in the course of the talk that I would spend the night in the village itself with an acquaintance of mine. Later on, I learnt that He knew my father well when he had to visit the temple to worship the Mother Kali in connection with his professional calls. When we parted, He asked me to send a little ice for His use. This was done by Ram Babu and Suresh Babu.

This short audience was enough for me. I felt a deep attachment and was drawn towards Him. As if I knew Him for a long time, my heart became full of joy. This was the more so because I saw in Him my tender loving mother waiting for me. So with the confidence, faith and certitude of a child I surrendered myself entirely under His care. I positively also became certain that at last I had found Him whom I was searching all these days. All my longings were satisfied and happiness reigned in its place.

Since then I look upon Him as my mother. By the by, I may tell you that since the death of my mother I looked upon my father also as my dear mother. That sense deepened when I came in contact with my Master, Sri Ramakrishna. He also treated me the very same way. He once asked me, "What do you take me to be?" I replied, "You are my Mother Divine." A sweet celestial loving smile played on His lips and our relations were re-established through a new testament.

After this momentous visit, my life with the family, [and] hours in the office seemed to be a heavy load on me. I would run to Him at all possible opportunities to meet Him either at Dakshineswar or at Calcutta where he would at times come to visit the Bhaktas and pious men of all religions and thoughts.

During my second or third visit to Dakshineswar, when I was serving Him, in an ecstatic mood He suddenly touched my chest. This magic touch took away all my consciousness. In that state I don't know how long I remained. To bring me back to consciousness He prayed, "Mother come down! Come down!" The result of the touch was that I realized that everything became revealed to me, that I was the Eternal Soul, free, and that Sri Ramakrishna was that Eternal Principle, the Ishwara [Lord], Who has come down in mercy in human form for the good of mankind and also that I was on earth to serve Him. This kindness He once again showered on me at Dakshineswar under the Banyan tree in Panchavati.

Notwithstanding this, He would not allow us to rest on our laurels but would constantly urge us, with infinite patience, to taste by our own efforts the fruits of His own realization. He watched our efforts and directed us with meticulous care to proceed on our own lines through paths suited to our own attitudes. Sincerity only counted with Him. Bigotry, orthodoxy had no place in His teaching and in His life. He would accept all of all denominations with equal tolerance, love and sympathy and spurred us all to reach the ultimate goal through paths of our own. To come in contact with Him was to become spiritual forever. To live with Him was to live in the Presence of God.

I had to marry later on—against my conviction. This I had to do to get one of my sisters married with one of the members of the family from which my wife came. I had to agree to it on account of our poor pecuniary condition. This, at first, disheartened me very much. I felt as if a link of Maya's chain had been forged for my bondage. So with a disconsolate mind, soon after the ceremony I ran up to Him and prayed to give me permission to forsake the world before I got enmeshed in it. But he replied with all sympathy, "No, my boy, not now. Do not get dispirited; this marriage will enhance your Vairagyam (absence of worldly desires) and make you more fit for the spiritual life." Actually it happened to be so. My wife, with whom I never slept for a night in the same bed, and whom I always treated kindly, died within a year. That year was to me a year of intense preparation. My determination to renounce the world deepened as I would pray often a whole night with tears in my eyes to free me and not to bind me down with the chains of the world. So at the death of my wife, relieved of all bondages, I ran straight up to Him to Dakshineswar and prayed to allow me to stay with Him. He kindly accepted me. Since then, for the next three years He was with us in the body, I lived almost continuously with Him.

At Dakshineswar I met Premananda, Brahmananda and Swamiji. They came there before me. Swamiji amongst us was loved and trusted most my Him. He left with him the command to organize and bring this Order up. About it I need not dilate. You know all from the books published.

After His passing away I travelled much throughout the length and breadth of India and endeavoured much to know Him in His different aspects. I liked the Himalayas very much and also passed a considerable period in South India and Ceylon. Benares I loved much as that is the city, the abode of Siva. All my endeavours have ended in realizing Him everywhere. Sri Ramakrishna is the centre from where all the radii have travelled towards the circumference. So I write to you that I have not realized but seen God, not in astral form but in this gross human form. And I declare it to you that Sri Ramakrishna is the fuller and more developed manifestations of Him, for the present, the highest possible manifestation of Him in human form. Follow Him in your own way, you will surely reach through

Swami Shivananda

Swami Brahmananda

Swami Premananda

Swami Yogananda

Swami Adbhutananda

Swami Ramakrishnananda

Swami Vijnanananda

Swami Atulananda

Mahendranath Gupta

His grace to that ultimate peace and blessedness. You are fortunate that you have come within His orbit so early. As such I am sure you will not have to be born again.

I am doing tolerably well, though my blood pressure is still very high. That doesn't matter. I depend entirely on Him. I sent you one letter in the first week of this month. I hope you have received it. May this find you well and happy. My blessings and best wishes to you, Bhakti [Helen Rubel] and Frances.[13] Let me know if this letter satisfies you.

Affectionately ever yours,

Shivananda

SWAMI BRAHMANANDA

During the 1907-09 period, Swami Brahmananda (1863-1922) came to visit Madras for a period of six months. Sister Devamata (then Laura Glenn) (1867-1942) [q.v.] recalled:

Having been in charge of the publication department of a leading Centre of the Order for a number of years, I had had long training in book-making, but a difference of opinion never rose between us that I did not find that he was right and I was wrong. A light burned within him that illumined whatever it shone upon. He had developed his basic instrument of knowledge and it gave him universal power of knowing.... When I went to the monastery later, I found the entire household playing the new game and I understood its purpose,—it was to enlarge the English vocabulary of the younger men. Swami Brahmananda himself never played, but he always watched and gave help to all the players impartially. Occasionally he suggested some impossible combination of letters and we would exclaim, "But Swamiji, there is no such word in the English language." "Oh yes there is," he would reply quietly. "Get the dictionary and you will see." Some one would look in the dictionary and unfailingly the word was there....

As he was eating, he remarked to me, "I have been very much blessed in coming to your house today, Sister." I answered quickly, "Swamiji, it is I who have been blessed in having you come." "You do not understand," he replied, "I have had a great blessing here this afternoon. As you were reading the *Bible*, Christ suddenly stood before the altar dressed in a long blue cloak. He talked to me for some time. It was a very blessed moment." There was no more thought of food. I poured water over his hands, then some sweet perfume, and with Swami Ramakrishnananda he went back to the monastery radiant with the joy of the vision.[14]

After Brahmananda left Madras, he wrote a letter referring to Laura Glenn as "My dear Sister", that said in part:

> The memory of the happy days we spent in Madras still lingers in my mind,—in fact I cannot remember those days with any feeling but that of intense joy which I experience now all the more vividly by contrast. May you be pleased to let me hear from you now and then.
>
> My best wishes and loving affection always attend you.
>
> I remain,
>
> Yours affectionately
>
> Brahmananda.[15]

Swami Prabhavananda told one of his devotees that a Westerner

> decided to go to Belur Math and see Maharaj. But when he came, Maharaj refused to see him. The man begged and begged—but no. Then one day as the man was in a boat on the Ganges, he saw Maharaj coming out on the veranda of his room at Belur Math, and he fell down dead on the spot! Yes. He got liberation the instant he saw Maharaj, and Maharaj knew what would happen, so he took the pains not to be seen by him. On the Belur grounds, it would have created a terrible situation, and Maharaj knew this.[16]

In 1944 Prabhavananda came out with the biography, *The Eternal Companion: Brahmananda: His Life and Teachings.* Sister Daya, a nun from the La Crescenta Vedanta Centre, indicated her appreciation of the volume in the following words:

> Occasionally there comes into the hands of the devotee a volume that conveys living light to the soul. Such is "The Eternal Companion". It is the record of the life and teachings of the great Swami Brahmananda, first President of the Ramakrishna Mission, always known and revered as the spiritual son of Sri Ramakrishna ... This is truly a precious collection, bringing into clear relief a very great and holy life. The teachings in the form of

intimate conversation with disciples are of inestimable value to all sincerely struggling on the path.[17]

Concerning *The Eternal Companion*, Helen Rubel wrote to Prabhavananda:

> You have put in so much direct speech and actual incidents with the words that the heart and mind are struck directly and forcefully. It must have been fun to write it, and to relive the old memories which are so precious, and which probably mean more to you as every year passes. It has set fire to the memories of the Swamis here [at the Belur Math] to inspire them to tell a story, or describe a scene there from their own experiences. It is great fun; and it is also a very strong inspiration. Whether the reader already knows about your Master or not when reading the book, still it seems as if the reading must produce a strong spiritualizing effect.[18]

Swami Nikhilananda met the world famous theoretical physicist Albert Einstein (1879-1955). Pravrajika Vrajaprana of the Santa Barbara Convent added these details:

> According to Swami Prabhavananda, Einstein had read *The Eternal Companion: The Life and Teachings of Swami Brahmananda* and was deeply impressed. Upon finishing the book, Einstein remarked, "Maharaj [Brahmananda] was right. Meditation is important. We know what goes on in the external world but we don't know what goes on here (pointing to his heart)."[19]

Albert Einstein liked the idea of emphasizing meditation because, he said, people would by nature do the external work. Along this line, Einstein referred to Mahatma Gandhi as

> a leader of his people, unsupported by outward authority; a politician whose success rests not upon craft nor mastery of technical devices, but simply on the convincing power of his personality; a victorious fighter who has always scorned the use of force; a man of wisdom and humility armed with resolve and inflexible consistency, who had devoted all of his strength to the uplifting of his people and the betterment of their lot; a man who has confronted the brutality of Europe with the dignity of the simple

> human beings and thus at all times risen superior.... Generations to come will scarcely believe that such a one as this ever in flesh and blood walked upon this earth.[20]

In addition, Einstein read other Indian scriptures and acknowledged, "When I read the *Bhagavad-Gita* and reflect about how God created this universe, everything else seems so superfluous."[21] Einstein is also well known for his many enlightening quotes such as, "Great spirits have always encountered opposition from mediocre minds. The mediocre mind is incapable of understanding the man who refuses to bow blindly to conventional prejudices and chooses instead to express his opinions courageously and honestly." How well this describes the negative noncreative critics of Ramakrishna and Vivekananda. Someone asked Einstein's wife if she understood his Theory of Relativity. She said, "No, but the important thing is that I understand him."[22]

The successful author Gerald Heard (1889-1971), who was responsible for the Vedanta Society of Southern California acquiring the property for the Trabuco Monastery, remarked, "When I read Brahmananda, I feel that finding God is obviously the only possible concern for a human life." Henry James Forman (1879-1966), in the Foreword to Prabhavananda's *The Sermon on the Mount according to Vedanta* (1963), expressed the view, "The writings of Swami Vivekananda, and that priceless little book by Swami Prabhavananda, *The Eternal Companion*, all are filled with teachings similar to those of the Sermon [on the Mount] and other parts of our Bible." Forman, a student of Nikhilananda, wrote many popular religious books including *The Story of Prophecy* (1936), which was translated into five languages. He edited Pavitrananda's translation of the "Letters of Swami Turiyananda". They appeared in twelve editions of *Vedanta and the West* (1959-62), and again in Chetanananda's *Spiritual Treasures: Letters of Swami Turiyananda* (1992).[23]

Christopher Isherwood (1904-86), the eminent British-American author, made this respectful comment:

> Brahmananda was tall and well built, with eyes that were sometimes deeply searching and sometimes apparently unseeing, as though they were regarding an altogether different reality. He inspired people by his silences quite as much as by his words. It is said that he could change the psychological atmosphere in a room, making the occupants feel talkative and gay and then inclining them to silent meditation, without himself saying anything.

For the most part, his teachings were very simply expressed. "Religion is the most practical thing. It doesn't matter whether one believes or not. It is like science. If one performs spiritual disciplines, the result is bound to come. Although one may be practising mechanically—if one persists, one will get everything in time.... And if you go one step towards God, God will come a hundred steps towards you.... Why did God create us? So that we may love him."[24]

Claude Alan Stark (1935-1980) [q.v.] in his biography of Sri Ramakrishna noted:

> During those days in the company of Sri Ramakrishna, "Rakhal would be constantly in communion with God," a way of life which prepared him for the work which was to come. "Rakhal has the wisdom and capacity to administer a vast kingdom," Sri Ramakrishna once said of him. Several decades later this statement proved literally true. Isherwood writes that "under his direction the Ramakrishna Math and Mission were shaped and Vivekananda's plan translated into action."[25]

Concerning *The Eternal Companion*, Swami Yogeshananda [q.v.] of the Trabuco Monastery in Southern California emphasized, "The book became a kind of second Bible for me and surely it has been so for many others. In his presentation of the life and teachings of Maharaj, Swami has subtly, almost seductively, enticed the skeptic or agnostic to admire the portrait of contemplation and to entertain the possibility of relating oneself to God, the Person."[26]

The Catholic Priest Francis X. Clooney, S.J. [q.v.] at Harvard University Divinity School wrote an essay on "Seeing God in a World of Many Religions: Swami Brahmananda's Teachings on the Chosen Deity" (2006). Concerning the idea of the "Chosen Deity", he explained:

> Swami Brahmananda's teachings have helped me to trace the development of the idea, and to see its specific relevance in the modern world, how it is very fruitful for us to realize that people think about, visualize, and relate to God in different ways which are really different meditation practices.

Clooney goes on to elucidate on what he has learned from Brahmananda's teachings on the "Chosen Deity" and how it relates to Christian spiritual practices. He authored works of comparative theology like *Hindu God, Christian God* (2001), undergoing the admirable task of demonstrating how the proper use of reason creates mutual understanding and helps to break down the boundaries between religions. Hindu and Christian thinkers have a great deal to say to each other, because they have been studying the same subject for millenniums.[27]

In reviewing Swami Bhaskarananda's (head of the Vedanta Society of Western Washington) translation of *Reminiscences of Swami Brahmananda*, Allen R. Freedman, a devotee and a professor of mathematics at Simon Fraser University in Western Canada, discerned:

> Like a real son, he seemed to have inherited many of the traits of his guru, Sri Ramakrishna. Some of his brother monks felt that he even resembled Sri Ramakrishna physically. More importantly, he resembled the master in having many deeply spiritual experiences, including *nirvikalpa samadhi*. But, in order to avoid creating an overwhelming sense of awe in those who came near him (which might have negative effects), Swami Brahmananda, like Sri Ramakrishna, would hide his spirituality in various ways.[28]

SWAMI PREMANANDA

Sister Devamata had frequent associations with Swami Premananda (1861-1918) in India, and later received letters from him. In his correspondence, he sent her advice like, "Be His, absolutely and forever. In body, mind, soul, be His. In that becoming, everything that religion means and is, will be realized. By becoming His only do you reach the goal of all human duties and responsibilities." Devamata tells us:

> He never exercised his authority. He scarcely seemed to possess any, yet he had a way of wrapping each heart around with such tender love and sweetness that it gave willing spontaneous obedience. He never asked anything of anyone and was reluctant to take the place of honour. When he rendered service, he did it almost stealthily, as if afraid someone might know of it. Once when he was nursing a sick man, the man, angry that he did not have certain food, kicked him on the chest and hurt him quite badly. Swami Premananda told no one and it was discovered later only by chance. My association with the Swami was frequent and full of rich blessings.... Every morning I went to see how he was doing and sit near him.

> Sometimes he would talk with burning fervour of his Master or of the joy of serving the Lord and His children; sometimes he would not speak at all; but always, whether silent or talking, there emanated from him a light and glow of spirit which impelled to fresh spiritual effort. His influence was too subtle to be analyzed and too powerful to be resisted. His name discloses the dominating trait of his character. *Prem* is a Sanskrit word signifying "supreme devotion", and *Prem* or supreme devotion coloured his life, his speech and his thought. It enveloped him like a garment.[29]

Premananda was considered as a candidate to succeed Trigunatita in San Francisco. In a letter dated September 3, 1915, Swami Atulananda sent the following comment to Mrs. Mary Magee (Mira) in Northern California:

> He is a fine man. You remember what he has done for me the first five years I was here. No other Swami would have done it. It was from an Indian standpoint especially most caring and loving, and he did things for me which carried with them a great deal of risk. It was through him that I have enjoyed privileges that no Westerner has enjoyed in India.... He loves to speak about the Lord and Swamiji, and he thinks much of worship.[30]

With absolute humility, Swami Premananda expressed his appreciation of the Western disciples who journeyed to India:

> Our "Mother"—I mean Mrs. Sevier—is an example of superb renunciation. Her husband too was of the same type. I remember Goodwin—Swamiji's Ganesha [mythical recorder of the *Mahabharata*]—and Nivedita. What an exquisite ideal of self-sacrifice they showed. To tell the truth, the day when I have to perform worship in the shrine, I offer flowers in their memory. I know, I am a humble servant of these disciples of Swamiji.[31]

In 1914 Swami Gnaneswarananda (1893-1937) met Swami Premananda in Dhaka. He later revealed, "At that time, I was a rebel, almost an anarchist, as could be expected in India in those days. That holy man did not impress me by talk or philosophy, but by the sheer power, the sheer mysticism of love." Soon after his meeting with Premananda, he withdrew his membership from a revolutionary party committed to the overthrow of British rule in India. Gnaneswarananda came to America in 1930 and founded the Vedanta Society in Chicago that is flourishing today.

In India Swami Premananda told Swami Prabhavananda and others:

> Miss [Josephine] MacLeod, an American devotee of Swami Vivekananda, will be leaving for England by boat at this terrible time [during the First World War], when we hear reports of ships being sunk by the enemy. I received a letter from her today, saying, "When I am going with the blessings of a brother disciple of Swamiji, not only I, but all the passengers of the boat will reach the destination safely." See what faith! Faith and devotion transform a man into a god, a saint, a free soul. This American devotee lived in our guesthouse at Belur Math for nearly four months. She is very good and large hearted....
>
> [Premananda told a woman devotee]: If you had met Miss MacLeod, you would have seen what faith, what devotion she had, People like her are born in every age to do the Lord's work. She is our very own.[32]

SWAMI YOGANANDA

Pravrajika Virajaprana [q.v.], a nun in Northern California, presented a beautiful talk entitled "Swami Yogananda: Holy Mother's Attendant". She vividly portrayed the great monk this way:

> By nature the swami was gentle, calm, taciturn, and extremely tenderhearted, generous and kind to everyone, especially anyone in need. One of his brother disciples remarked, "We never saw him becoming angry or using harsh words even when there was a good reason for it." Yet, oddly enough, he had a very critical outlook that spared neither Swami Vivekananda nor even Sri Ramakrishna himself. Like his guru, he was unusually intelligent with a sharp discriminating mind. Always austere in his personal habits, he was the embodiment of purity. He loved solitude and preferred only a few books—the *Gita*, Upanishads, and others.... After his passing away, she [Holy Mother] would say, "No one loved me like Yogin. Whenever he was given some money or even some trifling thing, he would say, 'I'll keep it for Mother's use, she may have some need for it.'"... Many of his brother disciples, as well as the next generation of monks, spoke of his saintly qualities and testified to the uplifting intensity of the swami's presence.... The swami was a source of great attraction; his sweet amiable nature naturally drew others to him. Feeling at ease with the swami, the young men mixed with him freely. In fact, many who came into contact with him were so

charmed that afterwards they joined the Ramakrishna Order and became dedicated monks. One young member of the monastery wrote with regard to him: "He was such a great saint that it fills one with awe to belong to the Order to which he belonged."[33]

SWAMI ADBHUTANANDA

Sister Devamata also lived for some time in Calcutta, where she was a good friend of Holy Mother and Saradananda, as previously discussed. On a number of occasions at Balaram Babu's house she spent some time with Swami Adbhutananda (Latu, d. 1920). Devamata observed:

> Christ said: "He is greatest among you, let him be your servant." By this measure of values, Latu Maharaj was among the greatest of Sri Ramakrishna's disciples, for he was a living embodiment of the spirit of service. He was always the servant. He began life as the servant of man; contact with Sri Ramakrishna made him the servant of God, and after the Master's passing, he became the servant of the servants of the Lord. Even his plain, thickset body seemed built for carrying loads and lifting burdens. He never tried to cast aside his humble duties or change his *Dharma*....
>
> Some time after, he went to Benares and the closing days of his life were spent there. In his nature there was a rare combination of child and man, of gentleness and heroism. When he was nearing his end, it became necessary to remove an infected piece of bone from his leg. He refused to take an anaesthetic and, as the surgeon cut and sawed the bone, Latu Maharaj lay perfectly still, smiling with heroic calmness. His face was lighted by the same bright smile when he passed out of this world.[34]

SWAMI RAMAKRISHNANANDA

During Laura Glenn's (Sister Devamata's) two-year stay in India (1907-09), she worked with Swami Ramakrishnananda (1863-1911) as his stenographer in Madras. Partly through her efforts, his first book was published, *The Soul of Man*, which marked the beginning of the Madras Math Publishing House. Her *Days in an Indian Monastery* that came out in 1927 includes a twenty-page tribute to Ramakrishnananda, where she wrote:

Swami Ramakrishnananda stands as a towering figure in my Indian life.... There was always a bigness and a majesty about him that impelled. He had a way of sweeping aside the belittling details of life and leaving large spaces for nobler thought and action. I recall one afternoon when he sat on my upper veranda for four hours talking to me of God and godly living. His face was alight, his whole being seemed to glow with the exalted joy of his thought. Suddenly he rose, strode down the narrow brick stairway and along the dusty road to the monastery gate. His step was so uplifted, his bearing so lofty that as I watched him approach the gate, quite spontaneously and involuntarily I felt surprise that he was not as tall as the monastery. He looked to me taller. With a few words he could make a universe crumble.... The Swami's researches grew more and more introspective as he proceeded. He spent long hours in profound thought and interior seeking.... A profound acquaintance with the Vedas by no means gave the full measure of the Swami's Scriptural learning. He was an untiring student of all of the great Scriptures. He knew the Bible from cover to cover and expounded it in a spirit and with an understanding which are rare even in Christian countries.... My whole being was stirred by the living reality of his words and as we drove home, I asked how he could make them so real and living. He sat silent for a moment, then he said quietly and simply: "My Master used to tell me that in a previous life Saradananda and I were Christ's disciples."

There was one particular Festival of the Divine Mother which tested his endurance in prayer to the utmost. It comes in the late autumn and calls for continuous worship during twenty-four hours. This long interval is usually divided among several celebrants, but Swami Ramakrishnananda would take his place before the altar at six o'clock in the morning of the festival and remain there until six the next morning without moving from his seat. It was regarded as little short of a miracle even by his brothers in the Order. ... One day I asked him how he was able to do it. He replied modestly: "Devotion can accomplish anything."... Swami Ramakrishnananda's devotion was not a surface emotion. It reached down to the deepest roots of his being. There seemed no limit to his surrender and his trust. [He said] "I do not need anyone to help me. I am all full of God. What need have I of any one else? If He sends people to help me, I am satisfied. If He does not send, I am satisfied. I know that whatever He sends is for my good and is the best thing for me."... He was always an imposing figure, but his features were plain, save when they were lighted by his smile, which transfigured them and lent them a rare spiritual beauty. I had involuntary proof of this. I was standing on my upper veranda one late afternoon watching a carriage come down Brodie's Road. A face appeared at the carriage window and I thought quickly, "What a marvellous smile," then I saw that it was Swami Ramakrishnananda.[35]

SWAMI VIJNANANANDA

After spending twelve years in the West, in 1935 Swami Prabhavananda [q.v.] returned to India for a visit. In November he informed Swami Vijnanananda

> that I hoped to see my aged mother in Vishnupur and wished to visit Jayrambati and Kamarpukur on the way. At once he said, "I have never seen those places. Will you take me with you?" I replied, "Certainly, Maharaj, it will be a great blessing for me."... Going to Kamarpukur and Jayrambati with a disciple of Sri Ramakrishna was a wonderful pilgrimage indeed. In both places, Swami Vijnanananda was absorbed in meditation, with eyes closed.... After we returned to Vishnupur, Swami Vijnanananda remarked, "Isn't Sister Lalita wonderful! We travelled in the same car for so many hours, and she never said a word. How quiet!"... I feel that I got the blessed opportunity to live in Swami Vijnanananda's holy company for about two weeks.

Vijnanananda gave Prabhavananda a gift of a 1935 book he translated into English entitled *Srimad Valmikiya Ramayanam*, which the latter brought back to America.

The handwritten inscription reads, "Presented to Swami Prabhavanandaji Maharaj, Hollywood, U.S.A., with my best love and good wishes, Swami Bijyanananda [Vijnanananda]—Ramakrishna Math, Allahabad, UP. 14 January 36."[36]

A longtime Vedanta devotee from Santa Barbara, California, Edith D. Tipple (Nalini) in 2005 compiled *What the Disciples Said about it*. The remarkable volume lists the teachings of twelve monastic disciples of Sri Ramakrishna (including the Swamis mentioned in this chapter) concerning all aspects of spiritual life. Over six-thousand pertinent teachings are recorded in this anthology, drawn from nearly thirty sources, with a number of them no longer in print. They are classified into over two-hundred topics (e.g., Brahman, devotion, faith, grace, guru, japam, karma, liberation, ritual, samadhi, worship, and many more), and in every case the book cites the original source for the quotation. The anthology provides an in-depth study of the thoughts of Ramakrishna's disciples, with an emphasis on the practical applications of specific spiritual practice. The essential meaning of several books is compiled into a single volume.[37]

MAHENDRANATH GUPTA

A young Paramahansa Yogananda (1893-1952) [q.v.] described his first meeting with Mahendranath Gupta (1854-1932), the recorder of the *Gospel of Sri Ramakrishna*. "Silently I had entered the room in awe. The angelic appearance of Master Mahasaya fairly dazzled me. His silky white beard and large lustrous eyes, he seemed an incarnation of purity." His residence at 50 Amherst Street had once been Yogananda's family home. They often travelled together to the temple of Kali at Dakshineswar. "His body, mind, speech, and actions were effortlessly harmonized with his soul's simplicity.... So deep was his sense of identity with Sri Ramakrishna that Master Mahasaya no longer considered his thoughts to be his own." When Mahasaya "gently slapped my chest over the heart", I felt "an inexpressible ecstasy".[38]

The popular writer Paul Brunton (1898-1981) met Mahendranath Gupta in Calcutta, not long before he passed away. Brunton described him thusly:

> A venerable patriarch has stepped from the pages of the *Bible*, and a figure from Mosaic times has turned into flesh. This man with bald head, long white beard, and white moustache, grave countenance, and largely reflective eyes; this man whose shoulders are slightly bent with the burden of nearly eighty years of mundane existence, can be none other than the Master Mahasaya.... His character, with its commingling of perfect faith in God and his nobility of conduct, is written in his appearance for all to see.... "Will you tell me something about your master Ramakrishna?"
>
> "Ah, now you raise a subject about which I love best to talk. It is nearly half a century since he left us, but his blessed memory can never leave me, always it remains fresh and fragrant in my heart. I was twenty-seven when I met him and was constantly in his society for the last five years of his life. The result was that I became a changed man; my whole attitude towards life was reversed. Such was the strange influence of the God-man, Rama-

> krishna. He threw a spiritual spell upon all who visited him. He literally charmed them, fascinated them. Even materialistic persons who came to scoff became dumb in his presence." ...
>
> I picture the Master Mahasaya among them as a venerable prophet speaking to his people. How noble and dignified the man looks! His goodness, honesty, virtue, piety and sincerity are transparent. He possesses that self-respect of a man who has lived a long life in utter obedience to the voice of conscience....
>
> Night after night I come, less to hear the pious utterances of the Master Mahasaya than to bask in the spiritual sunshine of his presence. The atmosphere around him is tender and beautiful, gentle and loving; he has found some inner bliss and the radiation of it seems palpable. Often I forget his words, but I cannot forget his benign personality. That which drew him again and again to Ramakrishna seems to draw me to the Master Mahasaya also, and I begin to understand how potent must have been the influence of the teacher when the pupil exercises such a fascination upon me. When our last evening comes, I forget the passage of time, as I sit happily at his side upon the divan. Hour after hour has flown by; our talk has had no interlude of silence.[39]

Originally, Paul Brunton travelled to India in a spiritual quest with an interest in miracle producing holy men, since he himself had some psychic powers. He soon developed an attraction for the deeper metaphysical aspects of yoga. In his spiritual travelogue *A Search in Secret India* (1934), he tells of living among yogis, mystics and gurus, seeking the one who would give him the peace and tranquility that comes with self-knowledge. His search ends at Arunachala in South India, where he had a powerful spiritual experience while sitting with Sri Ramana Maharshi (1879-1950). In 1934 he became one of the first Westerners to draw attention to Maharshi. Expressing his thoughts in layperson's terms, his popular books sold nearly two-million copies, greatly arousing interest in yoga, meditation and the teachings of the Indian gurus among the Western devotees of his generation. He expressed views like, "For Indian culture is fruitful in the domain of psychology, philosophy, and religion, so fruitful that there are few doctrines which appeared out of original Western sources that have not already been anticipated and developed in India."[40] During the years 1937-39, Paul Brunton and Sarvepalli Radhakrishnan were Vedantic pupils of Pandit V. Subrahmanya Iyer (1869-1949). Brunton wrote to Iyer, "[You have] unfolded to me the higher wisdom of your land, expounded its most ancient books and explained its most imperishable philosophy. I was indeed fortunate to have the privilege of your instruction."[41]

GIRISH CHANDRA GHOSH

In the *Prabuddha Bharata* of October 1936, Mrs. Gray Hallock wrote of her experiences with Girish Chandra Ghosh (1844-1912) in India that gives us some idea of the person he became after receiving the grace of Sri Ramakrishna:

> I had a sense of feeling at home with Girish at once. His smile was very winning, his English perfect, his voice capable of conveying many shades of feeling. It is twenty years and more since I last saw him, but the personality is sharp and clear to me as when I saw him often, reclining at one end of this upper room. Strength, physical, mental, and spiritual, was the keynote of the impression he made.... But here was one who had genius and fire, who was not half dead nor atrophied, one who had renounced the world, the flesh, and the devil, knowing their charm, and yet lived actively and beneficently in the midst of life; who used his genius for his time and his people, yet knew that fame is a bubble and laid his work at the feet of his God. A saint, this, who meditated and had realized God—yet had time and compassion enough to help the small troubles of his world, who went to Calcutta slums with righteous indignation and medicines, who scolded and annihilated evil, but loved the sinner and gave spiritual, mental, and physical comfort in a brotherly way. A saint, this, with a love of God that does not crowd out God's children, his heart set on God yet his brain, its servant, inspired to write great dramas and poems.... The Hindu friend of G.C.'s circle, who found it and often helped the secretary, wrote to me as follows:
>
> "Through his last illness the great soul, so far as I could glean, had only one theme—to meet the Beloved in His indwelling and everlasting glory, free from all relativity. His ideal being to have no desire of his own, giving himself up entirely to the will of God, he justified himself in having even this wish, by his impatience to realize Him apart from all form. His last audible words were these: 'Now that you have come, dispel all my illusions and let me go! Let me go!' For the period that I had the privilege to sit at his feet, I cannot but feel eternally grateful. I feel how great would have been my

ignorance without his enlightening and loving gifts from day to day. How now to fill the blank? I could sit beside him and keep silence and listen for a hundred lifetimes, and not think it enough!..."

What most impressed me in India was Girish Chandra Ghosh, the biggest soul I have met. It was he who taught me and helped me to realize that what happens to us matters little, but that our attitude towards what happens to us is of immense importance.[42]

ENDNOTES

1 Burke, III, pp. 216-17.

2 Nelson, New Zealand *Colonist* (Nov. 1, 1898), p. 2 on GNS.

3 *Brahmavadin* (Mar. 16, 1898), p. 534.

4 *Brahmavadin* (Nov. 16, 1897), p. 211; (April 16, 1898), pp. 611-12; (Dec. 15, 1898), pp. 185-91; Vividishananda, pp. 40-42; Basu, pp. 530 (590), 536-38 (596-98).

5 *Brahmavadin* (April 16, 1898), pp. 611-12.

6 Vividishananda, p. 54; *Mission* (Mumukshananda) p. 221; Bhattacharya, p. 594; Riddick, p. 117.

7 Anandaprana, pp. 227-31.

8 Tathagatananda1, pp. 202-03; *Vedanta Darpana* (Feb. 1931), pp. 2-3.

9 Stavig2, ch. III; Vividishananda, p. 158; *Mission* (Brahmaprana), p. 353.

10 Rolland, pp. ix, 216.

11 Swami Prabhavananda, "Memorial Service for Swami Shivananda" (Feb. 25, 1934), pp. 9-10, VSSC Archives.

12 Vedanta Society of Providence. Web: www.vedantaprov.org/ aboutus.htm. Brahmachari Jnana Chaitanya is the curator of the Vedanta Archives in Hollywood, California. An abbreviated version of about half of the letter appears in Vividishananda, pp. 163-66.

13 Is this Frances Leggett (1896-1977) the daughter of Francis and Betty Leggett, who inherited Ridgely Manor in 1931 and who wrote *Late and Soon*?

14 Devamata, pp. 156, 161.

15 Devamata, p. 162.

16 *Conversations and Reminiscences with Swami Prabhavananda* (Southern California Vedanta Society: Unpublished, 1991), II, p. 27.

17 *MOTE* (1944), p. 256.

18 "A Letter from Helen Rubel to Swami Prabhavananda" (Dec. 5, 1944), VSSC Archives.

19 *Mission* (Vrajaprana), p. 1126.

20 H. T. Muzumdar, *Mahatma Gandhi Peaceful Revolutionary* (New York: Scribner, 1953), p. 96.

21 Londhe, #58. Albert Einstein.

22 Dale Carnegie (1934), p. 4.

23 *The Sermon on the Mount* (New York: Mentor Book, 1963), p. vi.

24 Swami Chetanananda, *A Guide to Spiritual life: Spiritual Teachings of Swami Brahmananda* (St. Louis: Vedanta Society of St. Louis, 1988), inside cover.

25 Stark, p. 150.

26 *The Sermon on the Mount* (New York: Mentor Book, 1963), p. vi; Swami Yogeshananda, *Six Lighted Windows* (United States: Swami Yogeshananda, 1995), p. 99.

27 Mission (Clooney), pp. 977-89.

28 *Global Vedanta* (Spring 2007), p. 13.

29 Devamata, pp. 259-62.

30 Atulananda, p. 190.

31 *VFEW* (Jan-Feb. 1961), p. 67

32 Swami Prabhavananda, *Swami Premananda, Teachings and Reminiscences* (Hollywood: Vedanta Press, 1968), pp. 54, 56; Web: www.vedantasociety-chicago.org/gnaneshwarananda.htm

33 *PB* (March-April 2001), pp. 162-63, 208, 210-11.

34 *PB* (Oct. 1932), p. 506; Devamata, pp. 257-59.

35 Devamata, pp. 16-17, 20-22, 26, 29-30, 34; Levinsky, pp. 108, 139-40.

36 Anandaprana, pp. 99-102; Peter Shneidre discovered the volume by Vijnanananda in a storage area in 2005.

37 Stavig2, ch. IX.

38 Paramahansa Yogananda, *Autobiography of a Yogi* (Diamond Pocket Books, 1969), pp. 75-82 on GBS.

39 Paul Brunton, *A Search in Secret India* (New York: E. P. Dutton, 1934, 1939), pp. 181-85; transcribed in *PB* (Sept. 1934), pp. 442-46.

40 *EOP*; Brunton (1939), pp. 301-05; Londhe, #271. Paul Brunton; Paul Brunton Philosophic Foundation. Web: www.paulbrunton.org.

41 "Paul Brunton." Web: www.wisdomsgoldenrod.org/publications/ cahn/PBThesisPt1.doc; *VK* (Feb. 1950), pp. 476-78.

42 *PB* (Oct. 1936), pp. 651-57; Swami Chetanananda, *Girish Chandra Ghosh* (Vedanta Society of St. Louis, 2009), pp. 429-37.

APPENDIX I

SWAMI SARADANANDA'S RESIDENCES IN THE WEST: LOCATIONS AND YEARS

Maine-Greenacre: 1896-97
Massachusetts-Boston, Cambridge and Sharon: 1896-97
  Framingham, Melrose, and Worcester (Clark U): 1897
  Hingham and Waltham: 1896
New Hampshire-Crawford Notch and White Mountains near Lisbon: 1896
  Franconia Mountains: 1897
New Jersey-Montclair: 1897
  East Orange: 1897
New York-Brooklyn: 1896-97
  New York City: 1896-98
  Ridgely: 1896 or 1897
Rhode Island-Providence (Brown U): 1896 or 1897
Tennessee-Nashville: 1897

England-London: 1896, 1898
France-Paris: 1898
Italy-Brindisi and Naples: 1898
  Rome: 1896, 1898

APPENDIX II

SWAMI ABHEDANANDA'S RESIDENCES IN THE WEST: LOCATIONS AND YEARS

(The following list is not complete since the Swami did a great deal of travelling, and not all of it has been recorded in English language publications.)*

United States: 1897-1921

Arizona-Grand Canyon: 1905
California-Berkeley (University of California): 1901
    Long Beach: 1916-18 (Centre Established), 1920-21
    Los Angeles: 1901, 1905, 1914-18 (Centre Established), 1920-21
    Pasadena, San Diego, San Jose, and Shanti Ashrama: 1901
    San Francisco: 1901, 1905, 1915, 1918-21 (Centre Established)
Colorado-Colorado Springs and Pikes Peak: 1901
    Denver: 1901, 1908 (Study Group Established)
Connecticut-Hartford: 1913, 1918
    West Cornwall (Berkshire Ashrama): 1907-19 (Centre Established)
Florida-Fernandina and Jacksonville: 1913
Georgia-Atlanta and other locations: 1909?, 1913
Illinois-Chicago: 1901, 1908
Indiana-Anderson and Chesterfield: 1900
Maine-Eliot (Greenacre): 1898-1900
Massachusetts-Boston-Cambridge: 1898-1900
    Fitchburg, Melrose and Walden Pond: 1899
    Lynn and Waltham: 1899-1900
    Medford, Newton, and Salem: 1898

* A partial list of sources includes: Radhakrishnan, p. 52; Bagchi, pp. 309-10, 356, 366, 369-74; Chetanananda, pp. 468-76; Satyananda, pp. 80-111; Shivani, pp. 225, 297-99; Tathagatanandaı, pp. 168-69, 175, 178, 180; Abhedananda, p. 8.

Worcester (Clark U.): 1899, 1909
Michigan-Detroit: 1901, 1913
Minnesota-Minneapolis: 1915
Missouri-St. Louis: 1904-05 (Study Group Established)
New Hampshire-North Woodstock: 1899
White Mountains: 1898-99
New Jersey-Jersey City: 1912
Montclair: 1897-99
Orange: 1897-98
New York-Buffalo: 1898, 1901
Hudson: 1907
Ithaca (Cornel U.): 1904-05
Lily Dale and Niagara Falls: 1899
Long Island: 1898
New Paltz: 1897
New York City-Brooklyn: 1897-1911, 1914-15, 1918-19 (Centre Established at Brooklyn, 1905)
Saratoga: 1902
Stone Ridge (Ridgely Manor): 1898-99
Thousand Island Park: 1901
Ohio-Cleveland: 1901
Oregon-Portland: 1901, 1905
Pennsylvania-Philadelphia: 1897, 1902
Pittsburgh: 1907 (Centre Established)
Rhode Island-Newport: 1898-99
Utah-Salt Lake City: 1901
Virginia-Fredericksburg: 1897
Washington-Seattle and Tacoma: 1901
Washington, DC: 1897-98, 1905 (Centre Established)

Other Countries

Alaska-Sitka: 1905
Austria-Alps: 1904 Belgium: 1903
Burma-Rangoon: 1921
Canada-Fort Williams, Vancouver and Winnipeg: 1905
Montreal: 1901
Toronto: 1901, 1905

China-Canton and Shanghai: 1921
England-London: 1896-97, 1902, 1904, 1906-09 (Centre Established), 1915
France-Paris: 1902, 1904, 1908-09 (Centre Established)
Germany: 1903
Alps, Berlin, and Munich: 1904
Hawaii-Honolulu: 1921
Holland-Amsterdam: 1904
Hong Kong: 1921
India: 1866-96, 1906, 1921-39
Italy-Genoa and Rome: 1903
Japan: 1921 Malaysia-Kuala-Lumpur: 1921
Mexico-Mexico City: 1905
Philippians-Manila: 1921
Scotland-Edinburgh and Glasgow: 1902
Singapore: 1921
Switzerland: 1902-03
Tibet-Leh (Hemis Monastery): 1922

APPENDIX III

DATES AND LOCATIONS OF SWAMI VIVEKANANDA'S LECTURES AND CLASSES IN HIS COMPLETE WORKS*

I:3-4; 9/11/93; Chicago, IL
I:4-5; 9/15/93; Chicago, IL
I:6-20; 9/19/93; Chicago, IL
I:20; 9/20/93; Chicago, IL
I:21-23; 9/26/93; Chicago, IL
I:23-24; 9/27/93; Chicago, IL
I:27-35; 12/13/95; New York, NY
I:36-51; 12/13/95; New York, NY
I:52-62; 12/20/95; New York, NY
I:63-71; 12/20/95; New York, NY
I:72-80; 1/3/96; New York, NY
I:81-93; 1/3/96; New York, NY
I:94-107; 1/10/96; New York, NY
I:108-18; 1/10/96; New York, NY
I:125-46; 12/14/95; New York, NY
I:147-59; 12/21/95; New York, NY
I:160-65; 1/4/96; New York, NY
I:166-70; 1/11/96; New York, NY
I:171-78; 1/18/96; New York, NY
I:179-88; 1/25/96; New York, NY
I:189-94; 2/1/96; New York, NY
I:195-210; 12/14/95; New York, NY
I:210-15; 12/21/95; New York, NY
I:215-22; 1/4/96; New York, NY
I:222-31; 1/11/96; New York, NY
I:231-39; 1/18/96; New York, NY
I:239-50; 1/25/96; New York, NY
I:250-57; 2/1/96; New York, NY
I:257-304; 2/8, 15, 22/96; New York, NY
I:317-28; 3/8/95; Hartford, CT
I:329-32; 12/30/94; Brooklyn, NY
I:333-43; 6/17/00; New York, NY
I:344-56; 10/13, 14 or 28/96; London, Eng.
I:357-65; 3/25/96; Cambridge, MA
I:366-82; 11/18/96; London, Eng.
I:383-86; 10/6/96; Wimbledon, Eng.
I:387-92; 3/28/96; Boston, MA
I:393-404; 2/12/96; New York, NY
I:405-16; 12/18/95; New York, NY
I:417-29; Possibly 10/28/96; London, Eng.
I:430-36; 12/6/96; London, Eng.
I:437-45; 4/1/00; San Francisco, CA
I:446-58; 5/26/00; San Francisco, CA
I:459-66; 5/28/00; San Francisco, CA

* Stavig6, based primarily on the findings of Burke.

I:467-80; 5/29/00; San Francisco, CA
I:481-84; 3/25/00; San Francisco, CA
I:489-502; 3/23/00; San Francisco, CA
I:503-12; 3/29/00; San Francisco, CA
I:513-21; 4/5/00; San Francisco, CA

II:1-9; 1/4/00; Los Angeles, CA
II:10-23; 1/8/00; Los Angeles, CA
II:24-37; 12/29/99; Los Angeles, CA
II:38-53; 2/9/96; New York, NY
II:57-69; 6/7/96; London, Eng.
II:70-87; 6/21/96; London, Eng.
II:88-104; 10/15/96; London, Eng.
II:105-17; 10/20/96; London, Eng.
II:118-29; 10/22/96; London, Eng.
II:130-43; Possibly 10/21/96; London, Eng.
II:144-54; 10/27/96; London, Eng.
II:155-74; 10/29/96; London, Eng.
II:175-88; 11/3/96; London, Eng.
II:189-202; 11/5/96; London, Eng.
II:203-11; 1/19/96; New York, NY
II:212-25; 1/26/96; New York, NY
II:226-37; 1/17/96; Brooklyn, NY
II:238-53; 2/2/96; Brooklyn, NY
II:254-62; 1/8/96; New York, NY
II:263-88; 2/16/96; New York, NY
II:291-308; 11/10/96; London, Eng.
II:309-27; 11/12/96; London, Eng.
II:328-40; 11/17/96; London, Eng.
II:341-58; 11/19/96; London, Eng.
II:359-74; 1/28/00; Pasadena, CA
II:375-96; 1/12/96; New York, NY
II:397-405; 1/5/00; Los Angeles, CA
II:406-15; 1/22/96; New York, NY
II:416-22; 2/5/96; New York, NY
II:423-31; 1/15/96; New York, NY
II:432-41; 12/18/95; New York, NY
II:442-53; 1/8/96; New York, NY
II:454-62; 1/15/96; New York, NY
II:463-74; 3/27/00; San Francisco, CA

III:1-5; 1/5/96; New York, NY
III:6-18; 1/22/96; New York, NY
III:19-28; 1/29/96; New York, NY
III:70-76; 1/27/96; New York, NY
III:77-85; 2/3/96; New York, NY
III:85-93; 2/10/96; New York, NY
III:93-100; 2/17/96; New York, NY
III:511-37; 2/2/00; Pasadena, CA

IV:1-12; 12/16/95; New York
IV:12-21; 12/16/95; New York, NY
IV:21-33; 12/23/95; New York, NY
IV:33-40; 12/23/95; New York, NY
IV:40-51; 1/6/96; New York, NY
IV:51-60; 1/6/96; New York, NY
IV:63-77; 1/31/00; Pasadena, CA
IV:78-101; 2/1/00; Pasadena, CA
IV:111-14; Between 1/14 and 2/20/00; Southern CA
IV:115-19; Between 1/14 and 2/20/00; Southern CA
IV:120-34; 2/3/00; Pasadena, CA
IV:135-37; 3/19/94; Detroit, MI
IV:138-53; 1/7/00; Los Angeles, CA
IV:154-87; 2/23/96; New York,
IV:188-91; 12/30/94; Brooklyn,
IV:192-95; Between 7/2 and 7/18/96; London, Eng.
IV:196-97; 3/26/00; Oakland, CA
IV:198-202; Between 3/9 and 3/19/94; Detroit MI
IV:203-17; 1/5/96; New York, NY

IV:218-26; 3/16/00; San Francisco, CA
IV:227-37; 4/3/00; San Francisco, CA
IV:238-49; 4/18/00; Alameda, CA

V:277-79; 3/22, 24/96; Cambridge, MA
V:297-310; 3/25/96; Cambridge, MA
V:310-11; 3/28/96; Boston, MA

VI:3-17; 5/14/96; London, Eng.
VI:28-32; Possibly 3/13/00; San Francisco, CA
VI:33-36; 3/20/00; San Francisco, CA
VI:37-40; 4/16/00; Alameda, CA
VI:41-45; 12/11/95; New York, NY
VI:46-48; 2/28/00; Oakland, CA
VI:49-58; 4/9/00; San Francisco, CA
VI:59-69; 4/10/00; San Francisco, CA
VI:70-78; 4/12/00; San Francisco, CA
VI:93-94; 3/23/00; San Francisco, CA
VI:94-95; 3/27/00; San Francisco, CA
VI:95-97; Possibly 4/13/00; Alameda, CA
VI:101-02; 4/18/00; Alameda, CA
VI:102-03; 1/31/00; Pasadena, CA
VI:123-25; 3/16/00; San Francisco, CA
VI:125-27; 3/15-16/00; San Francisco, CA
VI:128-36; Between 6/16 and 7/16/96; London, Eng.
VI:137-45; Between 6/28 and 7/16/96; London, Eng.
VI:145-50; 6/24/00; New York, NY

VII:3-104; 6/19, daily 6/23 to 7/3, daily 7/5 to 7/21, daily 7/23 to 8/6/95; Thousand Island Park, NY
VII:414-17; 11/26/93; Minneapolis, MN
VII:417-20; 1/17/94; Memphis, TN
VII:421-23; 1/19/94; Memphis, TN
VII:423-26; 1/21/94; Memphis, TN
VII:427-28; 3/19/94; Detroit, MI
VII:428-35; 4/13/00; Alameda, CA

VIII:3-35; Possibly 1/28 to 6/1/95; New York, NY
VIII:53-72; 1/18/00; Pasadena, CA
VIII:73-91; 1/27/00; Pasadena, CA
VIII:92-105; 3/18/00; San Francisco, CA
VIII:106-21; 3/30/00; San Francisco, CA
VIII:122-41; 4/8/00; San Francisco, CA
VIII:220-24; 11/16/95; London, Eng.
VIII:225-30; 11/23/95; London, Eng.
VIII:244-49; 3/20/00; San Francisco, CA
VIII:250-51; 6/10/00; New York, NY
VIII:252-53; 6/24/00; New York, NY

APPENDIX IV

TWO OR MORE REPORTS OF THE SAME LECTURE OR CLASS IN THE COMPLETE WORKS OF SWAMI VIVEKANANDA*

Note: In the following cases the same lecture or class is discussed in two or more volumes of *The Complete Works of Swami Vivekananda*. "N" signifies a newspaper report. For example, "The Hindu Religion" (*CW*, I:329-32) delivered on 12/30/1894 at the Brooklyn Ethical Association appears to be discussed in a newspaper report as "The Hindu View of Life" (II:499-503), and as "Indian Religious Thought" (IV:188-91). Obviously, the data in this Appendix is not finalized and is subject to further investigation.

Volume: Pages; Date;

I:3-4; 9/11/93; and IX:429-30 (N)
I:20; 9/20/93; and IX:431-34 (N)
I:329-32; 12/30/94; and II:499-503 (N); and IV:188-91
I:344-56; 10/13, 14 or 28/96; and IX:521-22 (N)
I:357-65; 3/25/96; and IX:497-98 (part) (N)
I:446-58; 5/26/00; and IX:276-78
I:467-80; 5/29/00; and IX:278-81
I:481-84; 3/25/00; and IX:272-73
I:489-502; 3/23/00; and VI:93-94

II:463-74; 3/27/00; and VI:94-95
II:479-81; 3/20/94 (N); and IX:458-59 (N)
II:497-99; 10/28/94 (N); and IX:476-79 (N)
II:499-503; 12/30/94 (N); and I:329-32; and IV:188-91
II:515-17; 4/7/95 (N); and IX:481 (N)
III:1-5; 1/5/96; and IV:203-17

* Stavig6, based primarily on the findings of Burke.

III:481; 11/20/93 (N); and IX:436-37 (N)
III:482-84; 11/27/93 (N); and IX:437-38 (N)
III:492-95; 2/15/94 (N); and VIII:204-08 (N)
III:503-05; 2/20/94 (N); and VIII:201-03 (N)

IV:63-77; 1/31/00; and VI:102-03
IV:135-37; 3/19/94; and VII: 429-30 (Old edition 427-28) (N); and IX:456-58 (N)
IV:188-91; 12/30/94; and I:329-32; and II:499-503 (N)
IV:203-17; 1/5/96; and III:1-5
IV:218-26; 3/16/00; and VI:123-25
IV:238-49; 4/18/00; and VI:101-02

VI:33-36; 3/20/00; and VIII:244-49
VI:93-94; 3/23/00; and I:489-502
VI:94-95; 3/27/00; and II:463-74
VI:101-02; 4/18/00; and IV:238-49
VI:102-03; 1/31/00; and IV:63-77
VI:123-25; 3/16/00; and IV:218-26
VI:145-50; 6/24/00; and VIII:252-53

VII:429-30 (Old edition 427-28) (N); and IV:135-37 and IX:456-58 (N)

VIII:201-03; 2/20/94 (N); and III:503-05 (N)
VIII:204-08; 2/15/94 (N); and III:492-95 (N)
VIII:214-19; 3/11/94 (N); and IX:450-56 (N)
VIII:220-24; 11/16/95; and IX:518-19 (N)
VIII:231-34; 2/25/00; and IX:510-11 (N)
VIII:244-49; 3/20/00; and VI:33-36
VIII:252-53; 6/24/00; and VI:145-50

IX:272-73; 3/25/00; and I:481-84
IX:276-78; 5/26/00; and I:446-58
IX:278-81; 5/29/00; and I:467-80
IX:429-30; 9/11/93 (N); and I:3-4
IX:431-34; 9/20/93 (N); and I:20
IX:436-37; 11/20/93 (N); and III:481 (N)
IX:437-38; 11/27/93 (N); and III:482-84 (N)

IX:450-56; 3/10/94 (N); and VIII:214-19 (N)
IX:456-58; 3/19/94 (N); and IV:135-37; and VII:429-30 (Old edition 427-28) (N)
IX:458-59; 3/20/94 (N); and II:479-81(N)
IX:476-79; 10/28/94 (N); and II:497-99 (N)
IX:481; 4/7/95 (N); and II:515-17 (N)
IX:491-93 (N); and possibly IX:496-97 (part) (N)
IX:497-98 (part); 3/25/96 (N); and I:357-65
IX:510-11; 2/25/00 (N); and VIII:231-34
IX:518-19; 11/16/95 (N); and VIII:220-24
IX:521-22; Possibly 10/13, 14 or 28/96 (N); and I:344-56

APPENDIX V

PUBLICATION DATES FOR THE ENGLISH LANGUAGE WRITINGS AND TEACHINGS OF SRI RAMAKRISHNA, HOLY MOTHER, AND SWAMIS VIVEKANANDA, ABHEDANANDA AND SARADANANDA

(Note: Since this information was drawn from incomplete library sources, it is subject to some future additions.)

Sri Ramakrishna:

Girish Chandra Sen, *Ramakrishna's Life and Teachings* (1887); Friedrich Max Müller, *Ramakrishna His Life and Sayings* (1898); Swami Abhedananda, *The Sayings of Ramakrishna* (1903); *The Sayings of Sri Ramakrishna*, ed. Brahmavadin Office (1905); Mahendranath Gupta, *The Gospel of Ramakrishna*, tr. Swami Abhedananda (1907); Mahendranath Gupta, *The Gospel of Sri Ramakrishna*, tr. Brahmavadin Office (1907); Mahendranath Gupta, *The Gospel of Sri Ramakrishna*, ed. San Francisco Vedanta Society (a reprint of the Brahmavadin Office Madras edition, 1912); *Sri Ramakrishna's Teachings*, ed. Advaita Ashrama (1916); *The Gospel of Sri Ramakrishna*, tr. Swami Nikhilananda (1942); *Tales and Parables of Sri Ramakrishna*, ed. Sri Ramakrishna Math, Madras (1943); *Ramakrishna, Prophet of New India*, tr. Swami Nikhilananda (1948); Katharine Whitmarsh, *A Concordance to Swami Nikhilananda's translation of the Gospel of Sri Ramakrishna* (1985).

Books/Pamphlets of less than 40 pages: "Sayings of Sri Ramakrishna", *Brahmavadin* (1895 and after); Mahendranath Gupta, *The Gospel of Sri Ramakrishna* (1897).*

Holy Mother:

Swami Tapasyananda, *Sri Sarada Devi the Holy Mother* ("Conversations" translated by Swami Nikhilananda, 1939); Swami Suddhasatwananda, *Thus*

* UCLC; WorldCat; VirtualCat; *Mission* pp. 743-45, 773-74.

Spake the Holy Mother (1965); *Teachings of Sri Sarada Devi the Holy Mother* (1982); *The Gospel of the Holy Mother* (1984).*

Swami Vivekananda:

Addresses on the Vedanta Philosophy (1896); *Bhakti Yoga* (1896); *Karma Yoga* (1896); *Raja Yoga* (1896); *Vedanta Philosophy: Address Before the Graduate Philosophical Society of Harvard* (1896); *Vedanta Philosophy: Lectures Delivered in New York Winter of 1895-6* (1896); *Yoga Philosophy* (1896); *From Colombo to Almora* (1897); *Vedanta Philosophy: Lectures* (1897); *Yoga Sutras of Patanjali* (1897); *Lectures on Gnana Yoga* (1898); *Lectures by the Swami Vivekananda on Raja Yoga and Other Subjects* (1899); *My Master* (1901); *Vedanta Philosophy: Eight Lectures* (1901); *A Collection of his Speeches and Writings* (1902); *Jnana Yoga* (1902); *Complete Works of Swami Vivekananda* (4 vols., 1907; 5 vols., 1907-10; 6 vols., 1915-19; 7 vols. 1919-23; 8 vols., 1915-26; 9 vols., 1997); *Religion of Love* (1907); *Epistles* (1908, 2nd edition); *Inspired Talks* (1908); *Realisation and It's Methods* (1908); *Science and Philosophy of Religion: Sankhya Vedanta, and Other Systems* (1908); *A Study of Religion* (1908); *Thoughts on Vedanta* (1908); Sister Nivedita, *The Master As I Saw Him* (1910); Sister Nivedita, *Notes of some Wanderings with the Swami Vivekananda* (1913); *Index to the Complete Works* (1926); *Teachings of Swami Vivekananda*, ed. Advaita Ashrama (1948).

Books/Pamphlets/Articles of less than 40 pages: "The Ether", *New York Medical Times* (Feb. 1895); "Metaphysics in India: Reincarnation", *The Metaphysical Magazine* (March 1895); "Is the Soul Immortal?" *New York Morning Advertiser* (1895); "Song of the Sannyasin", *The Metaphysical Magazine* (July-Dec. 1895); "Vedanta Philosophy: Lecture on Bhakti Yoga" (1896); "The Atman" (1896); "The Cosmos" (1896); "The Ideal of a Universal Religion" (1896); "On Doctor Paul Deussen", *Brahmavadin* (1896); "On Professor Max Müller", *Brahmavadin* (1896); "The Real and the Apparent Man" (1896); "Vedanta Philosophy: Lectures on the Cosmos" (1896); "The Education that India Needs", Bharati (1897); "The Problem of Modern India and its Solution", *Udbodhan* (Jan. 14, 1899); "The Bengali Language", *Udbodhan*; "Knowledge its Source and Acquirement", *Udbodhan* (Feb. 12, 1899); "Modern India", *Udbodhan* (March 1899); "Memoirs of European Travel (Part 1)", *Udbodhan* (1899); "Christ the Messenger" (1900); "The Paris Congress of History of Religions", *Udbodhan* (1900), "Memoirs of European Travel (Part 2)", *Udbodhan* (1900); "Addresses of Swami Vivekananda at the Parliament

* UCLC; VirtualCat.

of Religions" (1901); "Vedanta and Sankhya" (1904); "The Sages of India" (1905); "Pavhari Baba" (1907); "Women of India" (1924).*

Swami Abhedananda:

Three Lectures on Reincarnation (1898); *Vedanta Philosophy: Three Lectures* (1899); *Three Lectures on Spiritual Unfoldment* (1901); *Vedanta Philosophy: [Fifteen] Lectures* (1901); *Three Lectures on Philosophy of Work* (1902); *How to Be a Yogi* (1902); *Divine Heritage of Man* (1903); *The Sayings of Ramakrishna*, ed. (1903); *Self-Knowledge (Atma-Jnana)* (1905); *India and Her People* (1906); *Lectures and Addresses in India* (1906); *Mystery of Death* (1906 class-lectures; pub. 1953); *Abhedananda in India* (1906 lectures and addresses; pub. 1968); Mahendranath Gupta, *Gospel of Ramakrishna*, tr. (1907); *Nine Lectures* (Parts 1 and 2, 1909); *Great Saviors of the World* (1911); *Human Affection and Divine Love* (1911); *Yoga: Its Theory and Practice* (1901-15 lectures; pub. 1967); *Bhagavad Gita the Divine Message* (2 vols., 1907 and later lectures.; 1969); *Doctrine of Karma* (lectures in America; 2nd edition 1944); *Life beyond Death* (lectures in America; pub. 1944); *Science of Psychic Phenomena* (lectures in America; pub. 1946); *True Psychology* (1920 lectures; pub. 1946); *Attitude of Vedanta Towards Religion* (lectures in America; pub. 1947); *Philosophy and Religion* (lectures in America; pub. 1951); *Yoga Psychology* (1920 lectures; pub. 1960); *Thoughts on Sankhya and Vedanta* (lectures in America; pub. 1967); *Religion Revelation and God* (1898-1921 lectures and articles; pub. 1968); *Universal Religion and Vedanta* (1903-22 lectures; pub. 1968); *Travels in Kashmir and Tibet* (Bengali, 1922); *Lectures of Swami Abhedananda at Jamshedpur* (1923); *Complete Works of Swami Abhedananda* (1924), *Thoughts on Yoga, Upanishad and Gita* (1924 lectures; pub. 1970); *Ideal of Education* (1906-25 lectures; pub. 1945); *Epistles* (1895-1935 letters; pub. 1970); *Path of Realization* (1939); *Songs Divine* (1944); *Spiritual Teachings of Swami Abhedananda* (1962); *A Study of Heliocentric Science* (1968); *Complete Works* (10 vols., 1967-70).†

Books/Pamphlets/Articles of less than 40 pages: "An Introduction to the Philosophy of the Panchadasi" (1896, 1948); "The Attributes of God, and Man's Relation to Them", *Intelligence* (Later called *Metaphysical Magazine*, March 1898); "The True Basis of Morality", *Mind* (May 1898); "Cosmic Evo-

---

* *Schaff*, XII, pp. 219-20; UCLC; VirtualCat; Swami Vivekananda. Web: www.vivekananda.net/Library.htm.

† WorldCat; WWIA (1918-19), p. 39; Beginning of Swami Abhedananda's individual books; Radhakrishnan, p. 62 gives dates that differ slightly from other sources and apparently are incorrect.

lution and its Purpose" (1899); "The Motherhood of God" (1899); "Women in Hindu Society" *The Arena* (Dec. 1899); "The Vedanta Philosophy—the Correct Interpretation" *The Arena* (Feb. 1900); "Does the Soul Exist after Death?" (1900); "Philosophy of Good and Evil" (1900); "The Scientific Basis of Religion" (1900); "The Way to the Blessed Life" (1900); "Why a Hindu is a Vegetarian" (1900); "Divine Communion" (1901); Religion of the Hindus (1901); "Who is the Saviour of Souls?" (1901); "Why a Hindu Accepts Christ and Rejects Churchianity" (1901); "Woman's Place in Hindu Religion" (1901); "Christian Science and Vedanta" (1902); "The Word and the Cross in Ancient India" (1902); "Swami Vivekananda and His Work" (1903, 1924); "Spiritualism and Vedanta" (1904); "Simple Living" (1905); "Religion of the Twentieth Century" (192? lecture; pub. 1936); "Presidential Address by Swami Abhedananda" (1937); "The Steps Towards Perfection" (1967).*

Swami Saradananda:

Friedrich Max Müller, *Ramakrishna His Life and Sayings* (1898). (Note: Much of the life, not the teachings, of Sri Ramakrishna was written by Saradananda in 1896, with possibly some alterations by Vivekananda and Müller.)†

Articles: "The Literary Beauties of the Vedas and Upanishads", *Journal of Practical Metaphysics* (Nov. 1897); "The Theory and Practice of Vedanta", *Mind* (Dec. 1897).

* New York Public Library. Web: http://catnyp.nypl.org/; WorldCat.

† Aseshananda, p. 20.

APPENDIX VI

A SELECTED LIST OF ENGLISH LANGUAGE BIOGRAPHICAL BOOKS AND ARTICLES ABOUT SRI RAMAKRISHNA, HOLY MOTHER, AND SWAMIS VIVEKANANDA, ABHEDANANDA, AND OTHERS

Sri Ramakrishna:

Protap Chunder Mozoomdar, "The Hindu Saint", *Theistic Quarterly Review* (Oct. 1879); Charles Henry Tawney, "A Modern Hindu Saint", *The Imperial and Asiatic Quarterly Review* (Jan. 1896); Friedrich Max Müller, "A Real Mahatman", *Nineteenth Century* (Aug. 1896); Friedrich Max Müller, *Ramakrishna His Life and Sayings* (1898); Swami Vivekananda, *My Master* (1901); Protap Majumdar, *Paramahamsa Ramakrishna* (1907); Swami Saradananda, *Sri Ramakrishna, the Great Master*, tr. (Sri Ramakrishna Math, Madras, 2 vols. 1920-21); *Life of Ramakrishna*, compiled from various authentic sources, ed. Swami Gambhirananda (1924); Dhan Gopal Mukerji, *The Face of Silence* (1926); Sister Devamata, *Sri Ramakrishna and His Disciples* (1928); Romain Rolland, *Prophets of the New India*, tr. Elizabeth F. Malcolm-Smith (1930); Sister Devamata, *Sri Ramakrishna and St. Francis of Assisi* (1935); *The Gospel of Sri Ramakrishna*, tr. Swami Nikhilananda (1942); Swami Saradananda, *Sri Ramakrishna The Great Master*, tr. Swami Jagadananda (1952); Christopher Isherwood, *Ramakrishna and His Disciples* (1965); Hal French, *The Swan's Wide Waters: Ramakrishna and Western Culture* (1974); Swami Satprakashananda, *Sri Ramakrishna's Life and Message in the Present Age* (1976); Advaita Ashrama, *Sri Ramakrishna the Great Prophet of Harmony* (1986); Swami Prabhananda, *First Meetings with Sri Ramakrishna* (1987); Richard Schiffman, *A Prophet for a New Age* (1989); Swami Chetanananda, *Ramakrishna as We Saw Him* (1990); Swamis Smarananananda and Chetanananda, *Ramakrishna: A Biography in Pictures* (1991); Swami Prabhananda, *More About Ramakrishna* (1993); Akshay Kumar Sen, *A Portrait of Sri Ramakrishna*, ed. A. Salm, S. Dhir, and P. K. De (1998); Hans Torwesten, *Ramakrishna and Christ* (1999); Swami Prabhananda, *Journey with Ramakrishna* (2001); Swami Saradananda, *Sri*

Ramakrishna and His Divine Play, tr. Swami Chetanananda (2003); Swami Chetanananda, *They Lived With God* (2004).*

Holy Mother:

Swami Pavitrananda, *A Short Life of the Holy Mother* (1942); *The Holy Mother Birth Centenary Souvenir* (1955); Swami Gambhirananda, *Holy Mother: Sri Sarada Devi* (1955); Swami Nikhilananda, *Holy Mother* (1962); Her Direct Disciples, *At Holy Mother's Feet* (1963); Nanda Mookerjee, *Sri Sarada Devi Consort of Sri Ramakrishna* (1978); Swami Saradeshananda, *The Mother As I Saw Her* (1982); *Sri Sarada Devi The Great Wonder* (1984); *Sri Sarada Devi: A Biography in Pictures* (1988); Br. Akshaya Chaitanya, *The Compassionate Mother: Sri Sarada Devi*, tr. Swami Tanmayananda, (2002); *Reminiscences of Sri Sarada Devi*, ed., Swami Purnatmananda (2004).

Swami Vivekananda:

Ramakrishna Mission Dacca, *A Short Account of the Life and Teachings of the Swami Vivekananda* (1904); His Eastern and Western Disciples, *The Life of Swami Vivekananda* (1912-18); Swami Abhedananda, *Swami Vivekananda and His Work* (1903 lecture; pub. 1924); Romain Rolland, *Prophets of the New India*, tr. Elizabeth F. Malcolm-Smith (1930); Swami Nikhilananda, *Swami Vivekananda A Biography* (1953); Marie Louise Burke, *Swami Vivekananda in the West* (6 vols., 1958-73); His Eastern and Western Disciples, *Reminiscences of Swami Vivekananda* (1961); R. C. Majumdar, *Swami Vivekananda An Historical Review* (1965); *Western Women in the Footsteps of Swami Vivekananda*, ed. Pravrajika Atmaprana (1995); Asim Chaudhuri, *Swami Vivekananda in Chicago* (2000); Asim Chaudhuri, *Swami Vivekananda in America* (2008).†

Swami Abhedananda:

The Disciples of Ramakrishna, ed. Swami Pavitrananda (1943); Sister Shivani, *An Apostle of Monism* (1947, later renamed *Swami Abhedananda in America*); Swami Satyananda, *Abhedananda The Messiah of Vedanta* (1967); Moni Bagchi, *Swami Abhedananda A Spiritual Biography* (1968); Swami Prajnanananda, *The Philosophical Ideas of Swami Abhedananda* (1971); Swami Tathagatananda, *The Vedanta Society of New York* (Ch. 4, 2000).

---

* UCLC; WorldCat; VirtualCat.

† *Schaff*, XII, pp. 219-20; UCLC; WorldCat; VirtualCat.

Swami Saradananda:

The Disciples of Ramakrishna, ed. Swami Pavitrananda (1943); Marie Louise Burke, *Swami Vivekananda in the West* (vol. 4, 1996); Swami Aseshananda, *Glimpses of a Great Soul* (1982); Swami Chetanananda, *God Lived With Them* (Ch. 8, 1997); Swami Tathagatananda, *The Vedanta Society of New York* (Ch. 3, 2000); Pravrajika Prabuddhaprana, *Saint Sara* (passim, 2002).

Swami Trigunatitananda:

His Western Disciples (Ernest Brown), "The Work of Swami Trigunatita in the West", *PB* (Jan-Dec. 1928); *The Disciples of Ramakrishna*, ed. Swami Pavitrananda (1943); Pravrajika Brahmaprana, "Unpublished Correspondence of Swami Trigunatita", *VK* (Jan-April 1993); Swami Chetanananda, *God Lived with Them* (Ch. 12, 1997); Sister Gargi, *Swami Trigunatita His Life and Work* (1997).

Swami Turiyananda:

"Shanti Ashrama", *PB* (Nov-Dec. 1900, Oct. 1910, May-July 1918, Dec. 1921, Dec. 1922, Jan., Nov. 1925, Oct. 1926, Apr. 1929); Swami Atulananda, *With the Swamis in America* (1938); *The Disciples of Ramakrishna*, ed. Swami Pavitrananda (1943); Swami Ritajananda, *Swami Turiyananda* (1963); Marie Louise Burke, *Swami Vivekananda in the West* (1958-73); Sister Gargi, "Early Days at Shanti Ashrama", *PB* (Aug. 1977-June 1978); Swami Atulananda, *With the Swamis in America and India*, ed. Pravrajika Brahmaprana (1988); Swami Chetanananda, *God Lived with Them* (Ch. 9, 1997).*

* UCLC; WorldCat; VirtualCat.

APPENDIX VII

EUROPEAN LANGUAGE TRANSLATIONS OF SRI RAMAKRISHNA, SWAMI VIVEKANANDA AND SWAMI ABHEDANANDA BOOKS UP TO 1930

Sri Ramakrishna:

S. von der Wiesen, *Die Wissenschaft Des Atmens Nach Den Lehren Des Heiligen Vedanta* (Germany-Leipzig: 1911); *The Gospel of Ramakrishna*, tr. Swami Abhedananda—*El Evangelio de Ramakrishna* (Argentina-Buenos Aires: 1912), published by the Vedanta Society of Buenos Aires; Max Müller, *Ramakrishna, His Life and Sayings—Shri Ramakrishna Paramagamza*, tr. Ivan Nazhivin (1874-1940) (Russia-Moscow: 1913); *The Gospel of Ramakrishna*, tr. Swami Abhedananda—*Provozviestie Ramakrishny* (Russia-St. Petersburg: 1914); Carl Vogl (b. 1866), *Sri Ramakrischna, der Letzte Indische Prophet* (Germany-Wein: 1921); *The Gospel of Ramakrishna*, tr. Swami Abhedananda—*Evangelio de Ramakrishna*, ed. Ananda (Chile-Santiago: 1923); Carl Vogl (b. 1866), *Sri Ramakrischna, ein Prophet des Neuerwachenden Indien* (Germany-Leipzig: 1927); Edmond de Cocq, *Sri Ramakrishna Paramahamsa* (France-Louvain: 1928); Romain Rolland, *La Vie de Ramakrishna* (France-Paris: 1929); Romain Rolland, *The Life of Ramakrishna—Das Leben des Ramakrishna*, tr. Paul Amann (1884-1958) (Germany-Leipzig: 1929); Romain Rolland, *The Life of Ramakrishna—Het leven van Ramakrishna*, tr. J. Dutric (Netherlands-Arnhem: 1929); Gualtherus Hendrik Mees (1903-55), *Een Hindoe Heilige der Negentiende Eeuw: De Boodschap Van Sri Ramakrishna* (Netherlands-Den Haag: 1929); Emma von Pelet, *Worte des Ramakrishna* (Germany-Leipzig: 1930); *The Gospel of Ramakrishna* by Swami Abhedananda—*Provozviestie Ramakrishny* (Latvia-Riga: 1931).*

Swami Vivekananda:

Karma Yoga—Karma Yoga, tr. Franz Hartmann (Germany-Leipzig: 1901, 1921); *Practical Vedanta—Praktischer Vedânta*, tr. E. A. Kernwart (aka Ernst A. Weber) (Germany-Leipzig: 1905); *Yoga Philosophy—Filosofiia ioga*, tr. Yakov

* WorldCat; VirtualCat.

A. K. Popov(a) (Russia-St. Petersburg: 1906); *Raja Yoga—Raja Yoga*, tr. W.S. (France-Paris: 1910); *Raja Yoga—Radjha-ioge*, tr. Yakov A. K. Popov(a) (Russia: 1911); *Ideals of a Universal Religion—Idealet För En Universell Religion*, tr. H. Holst (Sweden-Stockholm: 1911); *Karma Yoga—Karma-Jooga K*, tr. Ilmari Saari (Finland-Helsinki: 1912); *Mestarini*, tr. Vaino Valvanne (Finland-Helsinki: 1912); *Karma Yoga—Karma-Ioga* (Russia-Moscow: 1912, 1916; St. Petersburg: 1913); *Practical Vedanta—Prakticheskaia Vedanta* (Russia-Moscow: 1912); *Karma Yoga—Karma Yoga*, tr. Vedanta Society (Argentina-Buenos Aires: 1914); *Bhakti Yoga—Bhakti-Ioga*, tr. Yakov A. K. Popov(a) (Russia-St. Petersburg: 1914); *Jnana Yoga—Dznana-Ioga*, tr. Yakov A. K. Popov(a) (Russia-St. Petersburg: 1914); *Karma Yoga—Karma-Ioga* (Russia-St. Petersburg: 1914; Petrograd: 1916); *Karma Philosophy—Karma Yoga*, tr. Karel Weinfurter (1867-1942) (Czech.-Praha: 1920); *Vivekananda, Ein Lebensbild und 9 Vortrage* (Germany-Lauenburg: 1921); *Jnana Yoga—Jnana Yoga*, trs. M. Lopez Villamil and Ricardo Vivie (Argentina-Buenos Aires: 1922); *Raja Yoga—Aforismi Di Yoga*, tr. Giovanni Battista Penne (b. 1859) (Italy-Torino: 1922); *Jnana Yoga—Inana Yoga*, tr. Fritz Otto Rose (b. 1876) (Germany-Stuttgart: 1923); *Yoga Philosophy—Filosafia Yoga* (Spain-Barcelona: 1923); *Jnana Yoga—Jnana Yoga*, ed. Ananda (Chile-Santiago: 1924); *Karma Yoga—Karma Yoga*, ed. Ananda (Chile-Santiago: 1924); *Yoga Philosophy—Filosafia Yoga*, ed. Ananda (Chile-Santiago: 1924?); *Yoga Philosophy—Jogicka Filosofie*, tr. Karel Weinfurter (1867-1942) (Czech.-Praha: 1924?); *Raja Yoga—Radz a Joga*, tr. Karel Weinfurter (1867-1942) (Czech.-Praha: 1925); *My Master—Mon Maitre*, (France: 1925); *Karma Yoga—Starfsraekt* (Iceland-Reykjavik: 1926); Romain Rolland, *La Vie de Vivekananda* (France-Paris: 1930); Romain Rolland, *Life of Ramakrishna and Vivekananda—Der Gotter-Mensch Ramakrishna und Das Universale Evangelium des Vivekananda*, tr. Paul Amann (1884-1958) (Germany-Leipzig: 1930); *Karma Yoga—Karma-ioga* (Latvia-Riga: 1930); Romain Rolland, *The Life of Vivekananda—Het leven van Vivekananda*, tr. Titia Jelgersma (Netherlands-Arnhem: 1930); *Bhakti Yoga—Bhakti Yoga*, tr. Federico Climent Terrer (Spain-Barcelona: 1930?); *Theosophical Conferences—Conferencias Teosóficas*, tr. Federico Terrer (Spain-Barcelona: 1930?); *Epics of Ancient India—Epopeyas de la Antigua India*, tr. Federico Terrer (Spain-Barcelona: 1930?); *Jnana Yoga—Jnana Yoga*, tr. Federico Terrer (Spain-Barcelona: 1930?); *Miscellaneous Theosophy—Miscelanea Teosófica*, tr. Federico Terrer (Spain-Barcelona: 1930?); *Problems of Modern India—Los Problemas de la India Moderna*, tr. Federico Terrer (Spain-Barcelona: 1930?); *Practical Vedanta—Vedanta-Practica*, tr. Federico Terrer (Spain-Barcelona: 1930?); *Raja Yoga—Raja Yoga*, tr. Federico Terrer

(Spain-Barcelona: 1930?); *A Trip Through Europe—Un Viaje por Europa Selections*, tr. Federico Terrer (Spain-Barcelona: 1930?).

Books/Pamphlets under 50 pages in length: Germany-Leipzig: "Das Eine Ohne Ein Zweites" ("One Without a Second"); "Der Mensch und Seine Erscheinung" ("The Person and its Appearance"); "Die Religion der Erkentnis," "Du Bist Das" ("You are That"); "Gibt Es Einen Personlichen Gott?" ("Is There a Personal God?"); "Praktischer Vedanta" ("Practical Vedanta") all 1905; "Budoucnost Duchovniho C Love Ka," tr. Karel Weinfurter (1867-1942) (Czech.-Praha: 1919).*

Swami Abhedananda:

Philosophy of Work (Karma)—Philosophie des Wirkens, tr. E. A. Kernwart (aka Ernst A. Weber) (Germany-Leipzig: 1908); *The Gospel of Ramakrishna*, tr. Swami Abhedananda—*El Evangelio de Ramakrishna* (Argentina-Buenos Aires: 1912), published by the Vedanta Society of Buenos Aires; *The Gospel of Ramakrishna*, tr. Swami Abhedananda—*Provozviestie Ramakrishny* (Russia-St. Petersburg: 1914); *Self-Knowledge—Samopoznanie=Atma-Jnana*, tr. V. S. Lempitsk(aia)(oi) and P. N. Batiushkov(a) (Russia-Petrograd: 2nd. Edition, 1917); *How to Be a Yogi—Kak Sdielat'sia iogom* (Russia-Berlinie: 19??) Russians sometimes referred to him as Suami Abkhedanandy; *How to Be a Yogi—Jak byti Joginem* (Czech.-Praha: 1919); *The Gospel of Ramakrishna*, tr. *Swami Abhedananda—El Evangelio de Ramakrishna*, ed. Ananda (Chile-Santiago: 1923);† *The Power of the Mind: When One Is A Yogi—De Kracht Van Den Geest, of: Wanneer Is Men Een Yogi*, tr. A. Lafeber (Netherlands: 1928); *The Gospel of Ramakrishna* by Swami Abhedananda—*Provozviestie Ramakrishny* (Latvia-Riga: 1931).‡ Swami Prajnanananda alludes to a Brazilian Portuguese version of Swami Abhedananda's *The Gospel of Ramakrishna* coming out soon after 1915.

Books/Pamphlets under 50 pages in length: "The Way to the Blessed Life", "The Philosophy of Good and Evil", "Who is the Saviour of Soul?" "Why Does a Hindu accept Christ and Reject Churchianity", "Why a Hindu is a Vegetarian", "Divine Communion", "Religion of the Hindus", "Does the Soul Exist After Death?" all tr. E. A. Kernwart (Germany-Leipzig: 1905

---

* WorldCat; Soviet Union, p. 12; VirtualCat.

† WorldCat; VirtualCat.

‡ WorldCat; VirtualCat.

or earlier), "The Word and the Cross in Old India", tr. E. A. Kernwart (Germany-Leipzig: 1907).*

* *SN* (1905), p. 191; New York Public Library. Web: http://catnyp.nypl.org/search/a?SEARCH=abhedananda; VirtualCat.

BIBLIOGRAPHY

AII — Swami Abhedananda, *Abhedananda in India in 1906* (Calcutta: Ramakrishna Vedanta Math, 1968).

ANA — Access Newspaper Archives available at the Los Angeles Public Library and other libraries. The database includes full-text articles from many small-town 19th-20th century newspapers.

Anandaprana — Pravrajika Anandaprana, *Conversations with Swami Prabhavananda* (Santa Barbara: Unpublished Manuscript, 1987).

ANB — John Garraty and Mark Carnes, *American National Biography* (New York: Oxford University Press, 1999).

APS — American Periodical Series available online at many universities. The database includes full-text articles of 1,100 periodicals, many going back to the 19th century like *The Arena*, *The Critic*, *Current Literature*, and *Outlook*.

Aseshananda — Swami Aseshananda, *Glimpses of a Great Soul* (Hollywood: Vedanta Press, 1982).

Atmaprana — Pravrajika Atmaprana, *Sister Nivedita of Ramakrishna-Vivekananda* (Calcutta: Sister Nivedita Girls' School, 1961, 1999).

Atulananda — Swami Atulananda, *With the Swamis in America and India* ed. Pravrajika Brahmaprana (Calcutta: Advaita Ashrama, 1988).

Bagchi — Moni Bagchi, *Swami Abhedananda* (Calcutta: Ramakrishna Vedanta Math, 1968).

Basu — Sankari Basu and Sunil Ghosh, *Vivekananda in Indian Newspapers* (Calcutta: Bookland Private Ltd., 1969).

Beckerlegge — Gwilym Beckerlegge, *The Ramakrishna Mission* (New York: Oxford University Press, 2000).

Bhattacharya — Sachchidananda Bhattacharya, *A Dictionary of Indian History* (Calcutta; University of Calcutta, 1967).

BRMIC — *Bulletin of the Ramakrishna Mission Institute of Culture*. The years 1898-1907 (Vols. 4-12) are on GBS on the Internet.

Buckland — C. E. Buckland, *Dictionary of Indian Biography* (London: Swan Sonnenschein, 1906).

Burke — Marie Louise Burke, *Swami Vivekananda in the West: New Discoveries* (6 vols.; Calcutta: Advaita Ashrama, V1-2000, V2-3-1994, V4-1996, V5-1998, V6-1987).

CA — *Contemporary Authors* (Detroit: Gale Research).

CAM — Chronicling America available online at many universities. This expanding database includes full-text articles from many newspapers for the 1890-1910 period such as the *San Francisco Call* and many others.

Cameron — Kenneth Cameron, *Transcendalists in Transition: Greenacre Conferences* (Hartford: Transcendental Books, 1980).

Centenary: — *The Religions of the World* (Calcutta: The Ramakrishna Mission Institute of Culture, Calcutta, 1938, 1988).

Chaudhuri1: — Asim Chaudhuri, *Swami Vivekananda in Chicago* (Calcutta: Advaita Ashrama, 2000).

Chaudhuri2: — Asim Chaudhuri, *Swami Vivekananda in America* (Kolkata: Advaita Ashrama, 2008).

Chetanananda: — Swami Chetanananda, *God Lived With Them* (Saint Louis: Vedanta Society, 1997).

Conger: — Talk by Cornelia Conger at the Vedanta Society of Chicago, January 1971, preserved on a cassette.

Cost of Living: — Calculator (1913-2008). Web: www.aier.org/research/cost-of-living-calculator/; Calculator (1774-2007). Web: www.measuringworth.com/ppowerus/?redirurl=calculators/ppowerus/

CW: — *The Complete Works of Swami Vivekananda* (Calcutta: Advaita Ashrama, 1962).

CWSA : *Complete Works of Swami Abhedananda* (Calcutta: Ramakrishna Vedanta Math, 1970).

DAB: *Dictionary of American Biography* (New York: Charles Scribner's Sons). Available in book form or online at the Los Angeles Public Library and some other libraries through Gale Biography Resource Centre.

Datta: Mahendranath Datta, *Swami Vivekananda in London,* tr. Swami Yogeshananda (Calcutta: Mohendra Publishing Committee, 1937). Web: www.vedanta-atlanta.org/online-books/

Datta, B.: Bhupendranath Datta, *Swami Vivekananda Patriot-Prophet* (Calcutta: Nababharat, 1954).

Devamata: Sister Devamata, *Days in an Indian Monastery* (La Crescenta CA: Ananda Ashrama, 1927, 1975).

DHM: Swami Abhedananda, *Divine Heritage of Man: Enlarged Ed. 2* (New York: Vedanta Society, 1903).

Disciples: *The Disciples of Sri Ramakrishna* (Calcutta: Advaita Ashrama, 1955).

DNB: *The Dictionary of National Biography* (London: Oxford University Press).

EOAB: John Garraty ed., *Encyclopedia of American Biography* (New York: HarperCollins, 1996).

EOP: Leslie Shepard, ed., *Encyclopedia of Occultism and Parapsychology* (Detroit: Gale Group, 1991).

Epistles: Swami Abhedananda, *Epistles* (Calcutta: Ramakrishna Vedanta Math, 1970).

EWB: *Encyclopedia of World Biography* (Detroit: Gale, 1998). Available in book form, or online at the Los Angeles Public Library and some other libraries through Gale Biography Resource Centre.

Gambhirananda: Swami Gambhirananda, *History of the Ramakrishna Math and Mission* (Calcutta: Advaita Ashrama, 1957).

Gargi: Sister Gargi, *Swami Trigunatita His Life and Work* (San Francisco: Vedanta Society, 1997).

GBS: Google Book Search. Web: books.google.com. Using "Advanced Book Search" the year can be specified. Using the Find Command millions of books can be searched.

Ghanananda: Swami Ghanananda, ed., *Swami Vivekananda in East and West* (London: The Ramakrishna Vedanta Centre, 1968).

Ghosh: Ashutosh Ghosh, *Swami Abhedananda The Patriot Saint* (Calcutta: Ramakrishna Vedanta Math, 1967).

GNS: Google News Search. Web: news.google.com/archivesearch. Using the Find Command millions of historical newspapers can be searched.

GSW: Swami Abhedananda, *Great Saviours of the World* (New York: Vedanta Society, 1911) on GBS on the internet.

Head: Joseph Head, and S. L. Cranston, *Reincarnation* (New York: Julian Press, 1961).

Hohner: Terrance Hohner and Carolyn Kenny, *Chronology of Swami Vivekananda in the West* (Portland, OR: Prana Press, 2000).

IHP: Swami Abhedananda, *India and Her People* (Calcutta: Ramakrishna Vedanta Math, 1906, 1945).

Ingersoll: Anna Ingersoll, *Greenacre on the Piscataqua* (New York: Alliance Publishing, 1900).

Jackson: Carl Jackson, *Vedanta for the West* (Bloomington, IN: Indiana University Press, 1994).

JSTOR: JSTOR available online at many universities. The database includes full-text articles for many late 19th-20th century periodicals.

Jyotirmayananda: Swami Jyotirmayananda, *Vivekananda His Gospel of Man-making* (Chennai: Jyotirmayananda, 2000).

Kamath: M. V. Kamath, *The United States and India 1776-1976* (Washington D.C.: Embassy of India, 1976).

LBD: Swami Abhedananda, *Life Beyond Death* (Calcutta: Ramakrishna Vedanta Math, 1984).

Levinsky: Sara Ann Levinsky, *A Bridge of Dreams* (West Stockbridge, MA: Inner Traditions Lindisfarne Press, 1984).

Life: *The Life of Swami Vivekananda by His Easter and Western Disciples* (2 vols; Calcutta: Advaita Ashrama, V1-2004, V2-1998).

Lokeswarananda: Swami Lokeswarananda, ed., *World Thinkers on Ramakrishna-Vivekananda* (Calcutta: Ramakrishna Mission Institute of Culture, 1987).

Londhe: Sushama Londhe, *A Tribute to Hinduism* (New Delhi: Pragun, 2008); download from Web: www.hinduwisdom.info.

Madhavaprana: Pravrajika Madhavaprana, "Swami Trigunatita, a Saint of Our City", (Unpublished Manuscript, 2008), later published in *PB* (Jan. 2009); Web: www.vedanta.org/reading/monthly/artiles/2009/3.Swam_Trig.htm.

Mazumder: Amiya Mazumder and Swami Prajnanananda, ed., *The Bases of Indian Culture* (Calcutta: Ramakrishna Vedanta Math, 1971).

Mead: *The Encyclopedia of Religious Quotations*, Frank Mead, ed. (Westwood, NJ: Fleming H. Revell, 1965).

Mercer: Dorothy Mercer, "The Vedanta in California: The Swamis of the Ramakrishna Order", *The Pacific Spectator* (Winter 1956), pp. 38-46.

Mission: *The Story of the Ramakrishna Mission* (Calcutta: Advaita Ashrama, 2006).

Mookerjee: Nanda Mookerjee, ed., *Sri Ramakrishna in the Eyes of Brahma and Christian Admirers* (Calcutta: Firma KLM Private Ltd., 1976).

MOTE: *The Message of the East* (Swami Paramananda's Magazine).

NCAB: *National Cyclopaedia of American Biography* (New York: James T. White).

Nelson: Elva Nelson, *Vivekananda and His Swamis in Boston and Vicinity* (Boston: Ramakrishna Vedanta Society of Massachusetts, 1992).

Nikhilananda: Swami Nikhilananda, *Holy Mother* (New York: Ramakrishna-Vivekananda Centre, 1962).

Nivedita: Sankari Basu, ed., *Letters of Sister Nivedita*

(2 vols; Calcutta: Nababharat Publishers, 1982).

PB: *Prabuddha Bharata*.

PQHN: ProQuest Historical Newspapers available online at the University of Southern California and some other University libraries. The database includes full-text articles from the *Atlanta Constitution*, *Boston Globe*, *Chicago Tribune*, *Hartford Courant*, *Los Angeles Times*, *New York Times*, *Washington Post* and other newspapers back to the 19th century.

Prabuddhaprana1: Pravrajika Prabuddhaprana, *Tantine* (Calcutta, Sri Sarada Math, 1990).

Prabuddhaprana2: Pravrajika Prabuddhaprana, *Saint Sara* (Dakshineswar Sri Sarada Math, 2002).

Prugh: Linda Prugh, *Josephine MacLeod* (Chennai, India: Sri Ramakrishna Math, 1999).

Radhakrishnan: S. Radhakrishnan, ed., *Contemporary Indian Philosophy* (New York: Macmillan Co., 1936).

Ramakrishna: *Studies on Sri Ramakrishna* (Calcutta: The Ramakrishna Mission Institute of Culture, 1988).

Raucher: Alan Raucher, "American Anti-Imperialists and the Pro-India Movement, 1900-1932: *Pacific Historical Review* (1932), pp. 83-110.

Reminiscences: *Reminiscences of Swami Vivekananda* (Kolkata: Advaita Ashrama, 2004).

Riddick: John Riddick, *Who Was Who in British India* (London: Greenwood Press, 1998).

Riepe: Dale Riepe, *The Philosophy of India and Its Impact on American Thought* (Springfield, IL: Charles C Thomas, 1970).

Ritajanạnda: Swami Ritajananda, *Swami Turiyananda* (Mylapore: Sri Ramakrishna Math, 1963).

RLOA: J. Gordon Melton, *Religious Leaders of America* (Detroit: Gale Research Inc. 1991, 1999). Available in book form or online at the Los Angeles Public Library and some other libraries through Gale Biography Resource Centre.

Rolland: Romain Rolland, *Life of Sri Ramakrishna* (Calcutta:

Advaita Ashrama, 1960).

SACC: Ashutosh Ghosh, *Swami Abhedananda Centenary Celebration*, 1966-67 (Calcutta: Ramakrishna Vedanta Math, 1966).

Saha: Panchanan Saha, *Tagore and America* (Kolkata: Jay Sarkar, 2001).

Sarada Devi: *Sri Sarada Devi The Great Wonder* (New Delhi: Ramakrishna Mission, 1984).

Saradananda: Swami Saradananda, *Sri Ramakrishna and His Divine Play*, tr. Swami Chetanananda (St. Louis: Vedanta Society of St. Louis, 2003).

Satyananda: Swami Satyananda, *Abhedananda The Messiah of Vedanta* (Calcutta: Sree Ramakrishna Sevayatan, 1967).

Schaff: *The New Schaff-Herzog Encyclopedia of Religious Knowledge* (1908-12).

Shifman: Alexander Shifman, *Tolstoy and India* (New Delhi: Sahitya Akademi, 1969).

Shivani: Sister Shivani, *Swami Abhedananda in America* (Calcutta: Ramakrishna Vedanta Math, 1947, 1991).

SN: Swami Abhedananda, *Self-Knowledge: Atma Jnana* (New York: Vedanta Society, 1905) on GBS.

Soviet Union: *Swami Vivekananda Studies in Soviet Union*, tr. Harish Gupta (Calcutta: Ramakrishna Mission Institute of Culture, 1987).

Stache-Weiske: Agnes Stache-Weiske, *German Indologists* (New Delhi: Max Müller Bhavan, 1990).

Stark: Claude Alan Stark, *God of All* (Cape Cod, MA: Claude Stark, 1974).

Stavig1: G. Stavig, "Western Supporters of Ramakrishna-Vedanta not Mentioned in M. L. Burke's Swami Vivekananda in the West", *BRMIC*, LVI (Oct. 2005).

Stavig2: G. Stavig, *Ramakrishna-Vedanta in Southern California: 1899-2005* (Hollywood: Unpublished Manuscript, 2006).

Stavig3: G. Stavig, "India in Russian Thought",

BRMIC (Oct. 1999), pp. 476-81.

Stavig4: G. Stavig, "The Western Clergymen Who Appreciated Swami Vivekananda", *Bulletin of the Ramakrishna Mission Institute of Culture* (Sept. 2006), pp. 406-13.

Stavig5: G. Stavig, "A Chronological Listing of the Dates and Locations of Lectures and Classes in *The Complete Works of Swami Vivekananda*", (Hollywood: Unpublished Manuscript, 2005), 16p.

Stavig6: G. Stavig, "The Dates and Locations of Lectures and Classes in the *Complete Works of Swami Vivekananda*", (Hollywood: Unpublished Manuscript, 2005), 18p.

Stavig7: G. Stavig, "Historical Contacts Between Ancient India and Babylon," *Journal of Indian History* (Platinum Jubilee Volume) (2001), pp. 1-16.

Sunderland: Jabez Sunderland, *India in Bondage* (New York: Lewis Copeland, 1932).

Tathagatananda1: Swami Tathagatananda, *The Vedanta Society of New York* (New York: Vedanta Society of New York, 2000).

Tathagatananda2: Swami Tathagatananda, *Journey of the Upanishads to the West* (New York: Vedanta Society of New York, 2002).

Thomas: Wendell Thomas, *Hinduism Invades America* (New York: Beacon Press, 1930).

TLWG: Swami Chetanananda, *They Lived With God* (St. Louis: Vedanta Society of St. Louis, 1989).

UCLC: University of California Library Online Catalogue. Web: http://melvyl.cdlib.org:80/F/?func=file&file_name=find-b&local_base=cdl90.

VFEW: *Vedanta for East and West* (England); later called *Vedanta*.

Vidyatmananda: Swami Vidyatmananda, *Making of a Devotee*, Ch. 3, 6, 10-12. Web: http://theworld.com/~elayj/Chapter3.htm.

VirtualCat: World Library. Web: www.ubka.uni-karlsruhe.de/kvk/kvk/kvk_en.htm. WorldCat can be found in this database.

Vivekananda: R. K. Dasgupta, ed., *Swami Vivekananda A Hundred Years Since Chicago* (Belur: Ramakrishna Math and Mission 1994).

Vividishananda: Swami Vividishananda, *The Saga of a Great Soul* (formerly *A Man of God*) (Mylapore: Sri Ramakrishna Math, 1986).

VK: *Vedanta Kesari*.

VM: *Vedanta Magazine* (1909) on GBS.

VMB: *Vedanta Monthly Bulletin* (1905-08), about 90% on GBS on the Internet.

VSSC: Vedanta Society of Southern California.

VW: *Vedanta and the West*.

WOI: Bridget Travers, ed., *World of Invention* (Detroit: Gale Research Inc., 1994).

WorldCat: WorldCat on the Internet bought through a paid subscription.

WWIA: Albert Marquis, ed., *Who's Who in America* (Chicago: Marquis Who's Who).

WWIE: *Who's Who In England* (London: A & C Black).

WWNY : John Leonard, ed., *Who's Who in New York* (New York: R. Hamersly).

WWSV: *Western Women in the Footsteps of Swami Vivekananda* (New Delhi: Ramakrishna Sarada Mission, 1995).

WWWA: Albert Marquis, *Who Was Who in America* (Chicago: Marquis Who's Who).

Yale: John Yale, ed., *What Vedanta Means to Me* (London: Rider & Company, 1961).

INDEX